Private
Independent
Schools

Bunting and Lyon, Inc., 238 North Main Street, Wallingford, Connecticut 06492

The former Davis Homestead (photograph ca. 1860) has been home to Bunting and Lyon since 1965. The Davis family were cousins of Harriet Beecher Stowe, one of Connecticut's most famous authors and abolitionists.

Bunting and Lyon was founded in 1936 by James and Elizabeth Webster Lyon Bunting and was incorporated in 1962. The Blue Book was first published in 1943, and our counseling of parents seeking schools followed shortly thereafter as our work became recognized.

Wallingford is conveniently located in central Connecticut, between New Haven and Hartford. We welcome visitors here on weekdays between 9:00 A.M. and 5:00 P.M.

Private
Independent
Schools

2000
The Fifty-third Edition

Published and Distributed by
Bunting and Lyon, Inc.
238 North Main Street
Wallingford, Connecticut 06492
U.S.A.
Telephone: 1-203-269-3333
Fax: 1-203-269-5697
E-mail BandLBluBk@aol.com
Web Site www.buntingandlyon.com

Copyright 2000 by Bunting and Lyon, Inc.
238 North Main Street
Wallingford, Connecticut 06492
Telephone 1-203-269-3333
Fax 1-203-269-5697
Printed and Bound in U.S.A.

Library of Congress Catalog Card Number:
72-122324

International Standard Book Number:
0-913094-53-6

International Standard Series Number:
0079-5399

$100.00

Foreword

"Can you give me a list of the ten best private schools in America. . .," the conversation invariably begins. Almost on a weekly basis, parents call Bunting and Lyon from all over the country with this very question. It seems a natural one. Most Americans love lists and rankings of all sorts. We speak of the "Number One" football or baseball team, the Top Ten list of *New York Times* bestsellers, or a ranking of best restaurants in our town or county. When our editors respond to these callers, as they always do, that "There is no such creature, nor should there be," parents looking for schools don't always like the answer. This is because the lack of such a list makes life harder for them; parents and guardians must search themselves and their child and come up with criteria that make sense to and for their own individual, independent families.

What matters most to one parent can mean literally nothing to another. The criteria put forth in a 1999 article in *U.S. News & World Report,* "Outstanding American High Schools," used state test scores, the percentage of students taking SAT/ACT examinations, the number of Advanced Placement tests being taken, and the length of time a child stays in one school as their measures for the designation of "outstanding." For any parent of a child who's had a life-changing experience at school, these measures mean little.

Children in adolescence, even those from traditional two-parent families, can struggle tremendously in the teenage years. Academic performance may be the least of a parent's worries. The issues surrounding social, physical, and emotional growth are equally important, if not more important than academics during these formative years. The ability to develop caring and compassionate behavior, ethical decision-making skills, and just being provided a safe place to grow to maturity cannot be measured in any way except for the subjective feeling you get at a school where these are important. How does one measure performance at a school that may literally have saved a struggling child's life? The parents of that child wouldn't care if even one student ever took an AP class at the school.

A highly subjective and very important question in choosing an independent school is one we never see mentioned in print — "Does the school's philosophy mirror our family's or the one that our family aspires to? Once the child returns from school at the end of the day or the end of the year, will he or she still feel a level of comfort in our home? Will we still feel that our child fits in with the rest of the family?"

Bunting and Lyon cannot subscribe to the notion that a magazine that deals mainly with the business, politics, and technological growth of the world would have more expertise in choosing outstanding schools than the parents of a child, who have watched and nurtured that individual through every step of his or her early life. If we will take some time to live the examined life, we all know what holds value for our children and what we most want them to learn when they leave home each morning.

To be sure, many of the facts and statistics put forth by *U.S. News* and other organizations are important in decision-making. Parents are interested in school and class size, per pupil expenditure, safety, level of technology, teacher turnover, Advanced Placement numbers, test scores, college acceptance rates, and graduation rates. They should be considered when seeking independent school placement. But parents need also to consider that instinctual feeling one gets upon visiting schools. It's a little like falling in love, a little like buying your first house, and kind of like the silver screen star Clara Bow, who was known as the "It Girl." It's all right in front of you. You either like the feel of the school or you don't. Consider the strength of your feelings along with the list of numbers and percentages.

In the final paragraph of one of the stories about the outstanding high schools, "What about independents?," *U.S. News & World Report* chides the majority of private, independent schools that refused to be defined by scores, percentages, and other numbers. The writer advised that such schools should have provided materials and participated because "Learning about their strengths could help all schools become better." As a business operation that works hand-in-hand with private schools, Bunting and Lyon understands that most of the schools listed in this directory participate in continuing internal and external evaluations, often overseen by their toughest critics — the parents who are paying to send their children to the school.

So, by what do we measure a school? We are reminded by one of our staff of a quotation from Mark Twain, who said, "There are three kinds of lies:

lies, damn lies, and statistics." An excellent school can be one with a million-dollar-plus athletic facility or a small, blacktop playground. It can be one that is fully integrated with state-of-the-art technological tools or one that provides a tiny Mac Lab for word processing only. A really great school is one that, regardless of campus appearance or size of endowment, teaches its children and its staff that there is a place for every person to learn and to grow. Such is the nature of the American independent school. Now, how can anyone put a number rating on that?

PETER G. BUNTING, *Publisher*

&

THE EDITORS

Contents

Index of the Schools

The following Index of the Schools includes the names and locations of all the private schools described in our book. The schools have made this publication possible by subscribing for full Descriptive Articles and 12-Line Listings.

Schools that have subscribed for Descriptive Articles are identified with an asterisk. These articles will give you a broad, general feeling for private schools as a group as well as an objective, in-depth definition of individual schools, both day and boarding.

Index of the Schools

Asterisk indicates a Descriptive Article.

Index of the Schools

Index of the Schools

Index of the Schools

O

P

Index of the Schools

Index of the Schools

Index of the Schools

The Schools

Our Blue Book is composed of descriptions of private schools that meet our standards of acceptance. The schools described on the following pages represent educational facilities from Alabama to the Virgin Islands and range in grade level from Nursery to Grade 12 and Postgraduate.

For easy reference, the schools are organized alphabetically within their respective states, followed by programs in other countries and territories.

Each Descriptive Article is written as "fact without opinion," from which readers may draw their own conclusions about each school. Every article follows a set pattern, allowing for clear comparisons between one school and another.

If you become interested in any of these schools, we suggest that you contact the Director of Admission or the Head of the School and request a catalog, a viewbook, and an application. You may also access information on schools by using our Web Site **www.bunting andlyon.com**

ALABAMA

Advent Episcopal Day School

BIRMINGHAM

2019 Sixth Avenue North, Birmingham, AL 35203. 205-252-2535

ADVENT EPISCOPAL DAY SCHOOL in Birmingham, Alabama, enrolls boys and girls in Kindergarten through Grade 8. It is located in the historic heart of downtown Birmingham, a leading medical, educational, and industrial center of the South. Many students live within the city while others commute up to 60 miles from surrounding areas. The School's location permits easy access to the theater, concerts, festivals, and special observances; visits to the Museum of Art (the largest in the Southeast), The Civil Rights Institute, the civic center, and the seats of city and county government; access to Birmingham's main library; tours of major educational and research centers; and participation in the annual historical celebration for which the city and The Advent have received national recognition.

The School was established in 1950 as a kindergarten. According to its mission statement, developed and approved by faculty, staff, and trustees, the goals of The Advent are "to provide a superior education by incorporating an enhanced and accelerated program in a caring, Christian environment at an independent, equal-opportunity school."

In a big, rapidly changing world, The Advent seeks to provide the stability of a wholesome, caring, small-school environment where students can experience the total learning process in an atmosphere of enthusiasm. In the belief that education is a continuing adventure to be shared with students and family, faculty develop learning concepts from day to day, emphasizing basic skills and exploring the relationships among the various disciplines.

A nonprofit institution, Advent Episcopal Day School was the first elementary School in Birmingham and Jefferson County to be accredited by the Southern Association of Colleges and Schools. It holds membership in the National Association of Independent Schools, the Southern Association of Independent Schools, the Alabama Association of Indepen-

dent Schools, and the National Association of Episcopal Schools. School policies are established by a 15-member Board of Trustees approved by the Chapter of the Cathedral Church of the Advent. The Board, which meets twice yearly, is made up of parents, members of the Cathedral, and members of the community.

THE CAMPUS. In 1991, the School's first major capital funds campaign resulted in the construction of a new three-story, air-conditioned building that includes a fully equipped Upper School science lab and a Lower School science lab, a computer lab, an art room with darkroom and kiln, a multi-use music room, a 17,000-volume library, classrooms, a media room, and administrative offices. Also renovated and expanded was the 200-seat Neal Gymnasium, which contains courts for basketball and volleyball. Students have lunch in the newly renovated 200-seat dining hall. A new outdoor playground was completed in early 1994.

THE FACULTY. Una Battles, appointed Headmistress in 1969, is a graduate of the University of Alabama (B.S. 1961, M.A. 1964). Her previous experience includes service as a teacher in Alabama public schools. Mrs. Battles and her husband, Craig, have one son.

The full-time faculty number 23 women and 2 men. They hold 26 baccalaureate and 19 master's degrees, representing study at Auburn, Birmingham-Southern, Emory, Furman, Huntingdon College, Judson, Louisiana State, Millsaps, Mississippi College, Mississippi State, Samford, Spring Hill, Troy State, Vanderbilt, and the Universities of Alabama (Birmingham, Huntsville, Tuscaloosa), Houston Baptist, and Montevallo. Faculty benefits include tuition assistance for advanced study, long-term disability insurance, leaves of absence, cancer insurance, life insurance, and a retirement plan. Three part-time instructors teach art, Lower School science and literature/composition. First aid is available at the School, and a hospital is ten minutes away.

STUDENT BODY. In 1999–2000, the School enrolls 155 boys and 187 girls. They come from communities throughout the metro area.

ACADEMIC PROGRAM. The School is divided into three components: Kindergarten, Lower School (Grades 1–4), and Upper School (Grades 5–8). Grades are departmentalized beginning in fifth grade. All students attend weekly chapel services, and religion classes begin in Grade 5.

The school year, from late August to late May, includes Thanksgiving, Christmas, and spring recesses and observances of national holidays. Classes have an average enrollment of 17 and meet five days a week. The school day begins at 8:00 A.M. for all students. Kindergarten is dismissed at 11:50 A.M., and all other grades are dismissed at 3:00 P.M. except during the first two weeks of school when Grade 1 follows the Kindergarten schedule.

Kindergartners have three hours of classroom instruction, snack, and recess daily. The schedule for Grades 1–8 is divided into 30-minute modules to accommodate approximately four morning and four afternoon class periods of varying lengths.

For an additional charge, some teachers are available to tutor students who need extra help. Grades are issued every six weeks, with parent-teacher conferences scheduled at the end of the first grading period.

The Kindergarten program consists of reading, mathematics, science, social studies, penmanship, arts, music, and French. To enter the second year of Kindergarten, four-year-olds must take a standard readiness test and receive a teacher recommendation. All children entering the two Kindergartens and Grade 1 must meet the September 1 birthdate deadline.

Alabama

The basic curriculum for Grades 1–6 includes instruction in reading (with emphasis on phonics), language arts, vocabulary and composition (includes the study of great literature, followed by critical thinking and writing), penmanship, French, social studies, mathematics, and science. Students in Grades 1–4 also have regular library periods, with instruction in library skills. Practice in study skills, which begins in Grade 3, is designed to prepare students for independent work in the higher grades. The social studies program in Kindergarten–Grade 3 gives students an awareness of the social and physical world around them. Grade 4 studies Alabama History; Grade 5, Introduction to U.S. History; Grade 6, Ancient World History; Grade 7, World History 500–1789 A.D.; and Grade 8, U.S. History to 1877. Literature and composition are added to the Grade 5 curriculum, emphasizing the study of novels, short stories, poetry, and the play. Laboratory techniques are introduced in Grade 5 science.

Seventh graders study English grammar, vocabulary, and composition, including expository writing and literature; French; ancient history and geography; modern mathematics, emphasizing geometry and the algebra of points and lines; basic physical science; and religion. The curriculum for Grade 8 consists of English grammar and composition as well as literature, French, civics, algebra, science, and religion.

Regular art classes begin in Grade 3 and continue through Grade 8. All students participate in the music program, which aims toward musical literacy and appreciation as well as performance. The physical education program begins with directed play in Kindergarten and progresses to team games and dance activities for the older children. Sports included in the program are basketball, kickball, hockey, soccer, volleyball, and various types of relays.

In 1999, eighth graders entered Altamont, Indian Springs, John Carroll, and School of Fine Arts.

STUDENT ACTIVITIES. The Student Council, made up of representatives from Grades 5–8 elected by class, meets biweekly with faculty advisers to discuss matters of student concerns and to organize School-wide service projects for local charities. The Council also holds fund-raisers, sponsors the spring dance for Grades 7–8, and awards a scholarship for leadership to a graduating eighth grader. A Christmas Service Project is organized by the Student Council, as well as a party day. A-Day activities, which include skits, sack and relay races, and a student-faculty volleyball game, are organized by the Student Council.

Field trips are scheduled for all grades. Places visited have included a bakery, a dairy, the local fire station, the zoo, Huntsville's Constitution Hall Village, the Birmingham-Southern planetarium, Oak Mountain State Park, Red Mountain Museum, city hall, the courthouse, and Birmingham Museum of Art. In addition, Grades 4–8 take long trips each year to such places as the State Capitol, Huntsville's Space Museum, the Tennessee Aquarium in Chattanooga, William Faulkner's home in Oxford, Mississippi, Washington, D.C., and Atlanta's Cyclorama and SciTech.

Individual classes present plays and concerts periodically. For younger students, there are in-class birthday parties.

Traditional events for the school community are a parent/alumni Open House, Christmas dinner at The Summit, Southern Cultures Celebration, the May Festival, and a carol sing.

Activities include basketball, volleyball, golf, French Club, Math Team, Chess Club, and a student newspaper.

ADMISSION AND COSTS. Advent Episcopal Day School admits students in all grades on the basis of a standardized School-administered entrance examination, previous academic records, and recommendations from teachers and other adults. The School admits students without regard to race, creed, or national or ethnic origin. Students currently enrolled are given priority for registration until the middle of February. At that time, new students are considered with the following priorities: siblings of current students, alumni children, members of the Cathedral Church of the Advent, and the earliest applicants. If vacancies exist, students may be enrolled at midyear. There is a $25 testing fee and a $200 registration fee.

In 2000–01, tuition is $3015 for Kindergarten and $4950 for Grades 1–8. There is a 5 percent tuition reduction for members of the Cathedral Church of the Advent. The cost of books and milk is included in the tuition; a Student Activities Fee, payable three times a year and which varies with grade level, covers special events and materials such as novels, field trips, and seminars. The charge for before-school care is $8 per month or 50 cents per day; after-school care is $180 monthly or $7.50 per hour. A tuition insurance refund plan is offered.

Financial aid of approximately $60,000 is awarded annually on the basis of need and academic achievement.

Dean of Faculty: Mrs. Rosemary Ham
Alumni Secretary: Mrs. Lady Anne Buchanan
Director of Admissions: Mrs. Mary W. Hoffman
Director of Development: Mr. Craig Battles
Business Manager: Mr. C. W. Neeley, Jr.
Director of Athletics: Mr. John Brown

The Altamont School   BIRMINGHAM

4801 Altamont Road, Birmingham, AL 35222. 205-879-2006;
E-mail sstevens@altamontschool.org;
Web Site www.altamontschool.org

THE ALTAMONT SCHOOL in Birmingham, Alabama, is a coeducational, college preparatory day school enrolling girls and boys in Grades 5 through 12. The School is on the crest of Red Mountain in a secluded, residential neighborhood five minutes from downtown Birmingham (population 350,000). The city offers diverse cultural and educational resources, including those available at the University of Alabama at Birmingham, Birmingham-Southern College, and Samford University.

The School was established in 1975 through the merger of the Birmingham University School and the Brooke Hill School. Birmingham University School was founded as a proprietary school in 1922 by Capt. Basil M. Parks and was reorganized as a nonprofit institution in 1945. Brooke Hill School was founded by Mr. and Mrs. George Blackburn in 1940 as the College Preparatory School for Girls.

In an atmosphere of encouragement and opportunity, Altamont strives to foster the moral fiber, academic inquisitiveness, self-discipline, and the recognition of individual abilities and limitations necessary to achieve success and satisfaction. The program of traditional college preparatory academics is designed to instill a love for learning and to provide educational opportunities that will assure continuing access to greater knowledge. Through consistent, individualized contact, teachers encourage students to take full advantage of the intellectual, cultural, and athletic opportunities available at the School and in the community. The School demonstrates commitment to its college search program by sponsoring an annual tour of New England and southern colleges in alternating years. The Altamont Honor Code encourages students to take full responsibility for their personal and academic conduct.

A nonprofit institution, the School is governed by a self-perpetuating Board of Trustees that includes parents, patrons, alumni, and friends. The Board meets monthly during the school year. Many of the nearly 2000 graduates participate in the activities of the alumni association, which sponsors fundraising activities for scholarships and other causes.

The Altamont School is accredited by the Southern Association of Colleges and Schools. It holds membership in the National Association of Independent Schools, the Southern Association of Independent Schools, The College Board, and the National Association of Secondary School Principals.

THE CAMPUS. The School is located on a 28-acre tract that includes six tennis courts, a track, and a soccer field. The main school building houses 40 classrooms, two science wings, a Fine Arts Center, a Student Center, an art gallery and sculpture garden, a complete computer network and lab, a 20,000-volume library, and special studios for chorus, art, orchestra, dance, and speech. Two gymnasiums provide volleyball and basketball courts as well as gymnastics and weight rooms. A second campus includes soccer and baseball/softball fields and a gymnasium. The School-owned plant is valued at $12,497,270.

THE FACULTY. C. Martin Hames has been the Headmaster/College Counselor of The Altamont School since January 1, 1991. Before his appointment, he had served the School in various capacities since 1964 when he came to the Birmingham University School. He received a B.A. with Honors in History from Birmingham-Southern College in 1958. In 1971, he received an M.A. in History from Samford. In 1980, he received an M.S. in Educational Administration, also from Samford. Mr. Hames is a published biographer, poet, and expert in the visual arts. He is active in a number of civic, social, and arts organizations and is a well-known speaker.

The full-time faculty number 35, 18 women and 17 men. They hold 35 baccalaureate and 35 graduate degrees representing study at Auburn, Birmingham-Southern College, Cornell College, Duke, Harvard, Hollins, Louisiana State, Mary Baldwin College, Middle Tennessee State, Mount Holyoke College, Randolph-Macon Woman's College, Samford, Tulane, Vanderbilt, Washington and Lee, Yale, and the Universities of Alabama, Chicago, Montevallo, North Carolina, the South, South Alabama, and Virginia. Part-time instructors teach private piano, instrumental music, and voice.

Faculty benefits include health, disability, and dental insurance, a retirement plan, and Social Security. Paid and unpaid leaves of absence can be arranged. First aid is available on the campus and at three hospitals that are within three miles of the School.

STUDENT BODY. In 1999–2000, The Altamont School enrolled 364 students as follows: 33 in Grade 5, 42 in Grade 6, 46 in Grade 7, 53 in Grade 8, 53 in Grade 9, 36 in Grade 10, 55 in Grade 11, and 46 in Grade 12. Most of the students reside in Birmingham; the surrounding communities of Helena, Homewood, Hoover, Irondale, Jasper, Leeds, Mountain Brook, Pell City, Pinson, Tuscaloosa, and Vestavia are also represented.

ACADEMIC PROGRAM. The school year, from early September to late May, is divided into three terms with a Thanksgiving recess, Christmas and spring vacations, as well as several long weekends. A typical day, from 8:00 A.M. to 3:05 P.M., includes seven class periods.

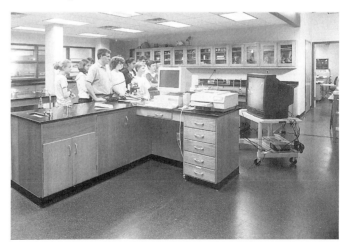

An average class enrolls 15 students. Five major departments conduct special-help sessions on the afternoon before assigned test days. The School provides faculty tutors, for which there is an extra charge, and can also recommend tutors in the community. Grades are issued and sent to parents every six weeks, with interim reports when a student receives a grade below 71.

The prescribed curriculum for Grades 5–8 includes English, foreign languages (French, Spanish, and Latin), social studies (geography for Grade 7, civics for Grade 8), mathematics (including algebra for Grade 8), science, and physical education. Electives include music, orchestra, art, drama, photography, creative writing, and computer mathematics.

To graduate, students in Grades 9–12 must complete four years of English, history (including American history), mathematics, and science (including at least two of the following: biology, chemistry, physics); three years of a foreign language; one year of speech; and one year of physical education and one year of health.

Among the required and elective courses offered are Grammar and Composition, Critical Introduction to Literature, American Literature, British Literature to 1798, Continental Fiction, History of the English Language, Survey of Twentieth Century Southern Literature, Writer's Workshop, Journalism, Fundamentals of Speech, America in the Twentieth Century; Introduction to French, Intermediate French, French Civilization, French History and Literature, Advanced French, Spanish Composition, Spanish Literature, Spanish History and Civilization, Elementary Latin, Intermediate Latin, Virgil's *Aeneid*, Cicero; Modern European Cultural History, American History, The History of Soviet Russia, Cultural Geography, History of England, Nineteenth Century European History; Algebra I–II, Geometry, Pre-Calculus, Calculus, Basic Programming and Computer Concepts, Math Team; Physical Science, Biology, Human Physiology, Chemistry, Physics, Astronomy; Basic Principles of Art, Advanced Principles of Art, Studio Painting, Ceramics, Printmaking, Arts and Crafts, Art History, Introductory Photography; Choral Club, Concert Choir, Orchestra, Piano, String Instruments, Wind Instruments, Music History; Typing; Health, Physical Education; and Drivers' Education. Altamont students who have demonstrated outstanding academic performance may study at the University of Alabama in Birmingham while completing requirements at Altamont. Courses that may be taken include those in math, science, the humanities, and social sciences. Credit for courses taken and passed at the University may be transferred to most accredited colleges or universities.

Graduates from the Class of 1999 are attending Auburn, Birmingham-Southern, Boston University, Brigham Young,

Brown, Georgetown, Harvard, Hollins, Middlebury, Stanford, Trinity (Connecticut), Tulane, Vanderbilt, Wellesley, and the Universities of Alabama, Colorado (Boulder), North Carolina (Chapel Hill), Notre Dame, Pennsylvania, Richmond, the South, and Virginia.

The extensive, six-week Altamont Summer Program offers courses for acceleration, academic enrichment, and reinforcement for boys and girls in Grades 3–12. In addition, there are camps for basketball, art, music, and drama as well as study-abroad opportunities.

STUDENT ACTIVITIES. The Altamont Student Government Association includes the student government officers, elected class representatives, and the presidents of the National Honor Society, the Junior Honor Society, and the senior class. Under the guidance of a faculty advisor, the student government helps plan student activities and assembly programs. The honor court of the student government considers violations of the Honor Code and presents findings and recommendations to the administration.

Qualified students are invited to join the National Honor Society and the Junior Honor Society. Student publications include *Lance* (the Upper School newspaper), *Dragon's Tooth* (the literary magazine), and *Altissimus* (the yearbook). Other extracurricular organizations include the Junior Classical League, Thespians, and the Art, French, Choral, Environmental, History, Key, Math, Music, Science, and Spanish clubs.

A member of the Alabama High School Athletic Association, Altamont competes with public and private schools in the region. The School fields boys' and girls' varsity teams in basketball, cross-country, soccer, tennis, and track and field. Boys also compete at the varsity level in baseball; girls participate in volleyball. Lower School teams are organized in baseball, basketball, cross-country, golf, soccer, and track and field. The entire student body is divided into Gold and White teams for challenge matches in athletic and academic activities, culminating in the award of the Team Cup.

Thursday assemblies offer programs of entertainment and enrichment. Throughout the year, the Altamont Fine Arts Center is host to art exhibitions, music recitals, dramatic productions, and lectures. Traditional events include Parent's Night, Feast of the Round Table, Homecoming, Spanish Week, Christmas Concert, Honor Society Lectures, Mardi Gras, Flower Day, Science Fair, French Week, Latin Week, Senior Film Series, The Roast Pig Feast, the Alumni Class Reunions, and May Day.

ADMISSION AND COSTS. Altamont seeks to enroll students who will benefit from a challenging college preparatory program. Candidates are admitted to all grades on the basis of their school records, Independent School Entrance Examination results, and personal interviews. Applications, for which there is a $50 fee, should be made in the fall preceding the year of desired enrollment.

In 2000–2001, tuition is $7992 for Grades 5–6, $9324 for Grade 7, $9492 for Grade 8, and $9960 for Grades 9–12. Extras include books (approximately $300), field trips, music lessons, and tutoring.

In 1999–2000, approximately 28 percent of the students received $288,515 in financial aid and scholarships. Students may contribute to their tuition by working as clerical, library, or laboratory assistants during the school year or as maintenance assistants during the summer. A tuition payment plan is available.

Associate Headmaster: James M. Wiygul
Dean of Students: Sarah Whiteside
Assistant Headmaster: Kim R. Crockard
Director of Admissions: James M. Wiygul
College Counselors: C. Martin Hames and Kim R. Crockard
Director of Development/Alumni Affairs: Ann Vrocher
Business Manager: Peggy Dupuy
Director of Athletics: Ralph D. Patton
Technology Coordinator: Casey Adams
Capital Campaign Coordinator: Christie Strauch

Bayside Academy   1967

P.O. Drawer 2590, Daphne, AL 36526. 334-626-2840;
*   Fax 334-626-2899*
Bayside East: 6900 Highway 59, Gulf Shores, AL 36542.
*   334-955-5211*

Founded by parents to enable both average and gifted students to reach their potential, Bayside is a college preparatory day school enrolling 499 boys and girls in Pre-kindergarten–Grade 12 in Daphne and Pre-kindergarten–Grade 6 at Bayside East. The traditional academic program includes Advanced Placement courses as well as computer, fine arts, and foreign language in all grades. Teams are fielded in eight sports; drama, publications, and service clubs are also offered. Tuition: $3965–$5940. Extras: $500. Financial Aid: $175,000. Arthur Edgar is Director of Admission; Thomas Johnson (Valdosta State University, M.E. 1972) was appointed Head in 1998. *Southern Association.*

The Donoho School   1963

2501 Henry Road, P.O. Box 2537, Anniston, AL 36202.
*   256-237-5477; Fax 256-237-6474; E-mail donoho@nti.net*

The Donoho School is a college preparatory day school enrolling 475 girls and boys in Pre-Kindergarten–Grade 12. The School's purpose is to provide a quality education for highly motivated and intelligent students. A challenging curriculum is offered in an atmosphere conducive to the development of good citizenship and religious principles. Tutorial help is available each day. Advanced Placement courses are available. Athletics, Student Council, community service, publications, clubs, and scouting are some of the activities. Tuition: $4205–$4900. Financial Aid: $100,000. Louise F. Marbut is Director of Admissions; George E. Gorey, Jr. (Jacksonville State University, B.S., M.S., M.Ed.), was appointed President in 1993. *Southern Association.*

Highlands School ⟩⟨   BIRMINGHAM

4901 Old Leeds Road, Birmingham, AL 35213. 205-956-9731;
*   E-mail ajohnstn@bellsouth.net*

Highlands school in Birmingham, Alabama, is a coeducational elementary school enrolling students in four-year-old Preschool through Grade 8. The School is located in the township of Mountain Brook, a residential suburb eight miles from downtown Birmingham (metropolitan population 500,000). Birmingham, Alabama's largest city, is an important educational and medical center. It is home to the University of Alabama at Birmingham, Samford University, Birmingham-Southern College, and Miles College, and supports a symphony orchestra, civic opera, several ballet and theater companies, and an art museum. Bus service is available to students in southern Jefferson and northern Shelby counties, but most families arrange their own transportation.

Highlands School was founded in 1958 as an outgrowth of The Bunny Hole, a nursery school established by Mrs. Evalina Brown Spencer. It opened with 60 students from four years of age through Grade 1, and a new class was added each year. From its rented quarters in a local church, Highlands moved to its present site in 1962. Mrs. Spencer, who also taught Kindergarten, served as the School's Director until 1967.

The motivating philosophy of the School is based on the belief that true education encompasses the student's mental, physical, social, and emotional growth. In a challenging, nurturing environment, faculty seek to affirm each child's self-worth and instill confidence and a genuine love of learning. The flexible curriculum is designed to meet a variety of individual needs and learning styles while providing a strong foundation in the traditional academic disciplines.

A nonprofit organization, Highlands is governed by a 15-member Board of Trustees and is accredited by the Southern Association of Colleges and Schools. It holds membership in the National Association of Independent Schools, the Southern Association of Independent Schools, and the Educational Records Bureau, among other professional affiliations. A Parents' Auxiliary lends support through special activities during the year.

THE CAMPUS. The spacious, wooded campus accommodates three classroom buildings; the Learning Center, containing offices, the Discovery Room, and a 16,000-volume library; and the Spencer Center, which features a 350-seat auditorium, a photography darkroom, and classrooms for French, art, media, and music. The gymnasium has a regulation basketball court, and there are playgrounds and a soccer field on the grounds.

THE FACULTY. J. Hugh Bland was named Head of Highlands in July 1995, becoming the School's fifth head. Mr. Bland has headed three elementary schools prior to coming to Birmingham. His administrative and policy degree was taken at George Peabody College at Vanderbilt University.

There are 30 full-time teachers and 5 part-time teachers. All instructional staff, including associates, are certified teachers.

STUDENT BODY. In 1999–2000, Highlands enrolls 296 students. There are two classes at each level from Preschool through eighth grade. Students come from Birmingham and surrounding towns and suburbs. There is a 15 percent minority population enrolled, encompassing African-Americans, Asian-Americans, and Latinos.

ACADEMIC PROGRAM. School begins in late August and ends the first week in June. Thanksgiving, winter, and spring holidays are scheduled, and national holidays are observed. Parent-teacher conferences are held twice a year for all grades. Parents of Preschool and Kindergarten students receive progress reports at these conferences, while reports on Grades 1–4 are mailed home. Faculty, with a 9:1 student-teacher ratio, are available to provide extra help after school.

Classes for Kindergarten through Grade 8 are held between 8:00 A.M. and 3:00 P.M. four days a week, with 2:00 P.M. dismissal on Friday. Extended-day care is available from 7:00 A.M. until 6:00 P.M.

Half-day Preschool classes enroll 15–16 students, with two

teachers in each. At this level, the development of social, emotional, motor, and intellectual skills is emphasized. Students are introduced to fundamental concepts in language, math, science, and social studies. The core curriculum is enriched by French, Spanish, music and art, physical education, dance and movement, and library skills.

In Grades 1–4, each class has a lead teacher and shares an associate teacher. As students progress through the Lower School, skills in reading, writing, and math are accelerated; more homework is assigned; and students change classrooms for some subjects in preparation for the Upper School.

In Grades 5 through 8, classes are departmentalized and taught by specialists in certain disciplines. All students take science, math, English, literature, social studies (American history, world history, civics, and geography), and French and/or Spanish. Science lessons are reinforced by lab activities and field trips to environmental camps.

Every classroom has computers, and keyboarding begins in Grade 4. Other enrichment courses include drama, art, and music classes with Orff instruction.

After leaving Highlands, students typically enroll in local public schools or independent schools including Altamont, Indian Springs, and John Carroll High School.

A summer program for Highlands students provides enrichment classes and all-day care.

STUDENT ACTIVITIES. Student leaders in Grades 7 and 8 serve on the Student Council, which coordinates social activities and community service projects, and serves as a liaison between students and the administration.

Among the extracurricular activities are the yearbook staff, scouting for boys and girls, and a variety of intramural athletic teams.

The Parents' Auxiliary sponsors a Halloween Fair and a Spring Fling, and occasional Sox Hops are held for Grades 5 through 8.

Traditional annual events include Parents' Night, the annual auction, drama presentations, math tournament, Grandparents/Special Friends Day, Book Fair, Dinner on the Grounds, and alumni reunions.

ADMISSION AND COSTS. Highlands seeks a diverse student body and welcomes children of good character who are motivated to learn and to benefit from the School's program. Students are admitted in all grades, depending on the availability of space. Preschool and Kindergarten applicants are screened by grade-level teachers to assess their readiness for the program. All other students are considered on the basis of a personal interview, recommendations, standardized test scores, and their previous school transcripts. Applications are accepted and processed year-round, with most candidates applying by February for the following year. New students are admitted during the year.

The 1999–2000 tuition ranges from $4830 to $6135, depending on grade. Financial aid based on need and merit is available. Highlands School subscribes to the School and Student Service for Financial Aid.

Director of Admissions: Annette N. Johnston

Indian Springs School   BIRMINGHAM

190 Woodward Drive, Indian Springs, AL 35124. 205-988-3350; Fax 205-988-3797; E-mail admissions@indiansprings.org; Web Site www.indiansprings.org

INDIAN SPRINGS SCHOOL in Birmingham, Alabama, is a coeducational college preparatory school enrolling 260 boarding and day students in Grades 8 through 12. Situated on the northern boundary of Oak Mountain State Park, Indian Springs is easily accessible from Interstate 65 and U.S. routes 31 and 280. The School's proximity to Birmingham, Alabama, 15 miles to the north, permits students to take advantage of the many educational and cultural resources found in the southeast's seventh-largest metropolitan area. The city is home to professional companies offering opera, ballet, symphony, and theater; an international "Festival of Arts"; and the Birmingham Zoo, Botanical Gardens, and Ruffner Mountain Nature Center. The faculty and facilities of the University of Alabama at Birmingham and Birmingham-Southern College are also available to students.

Indian Springs School was founded in 1952 through the bequest of Harvey G. Woodward, a Birmingham industrialist, to serve a diverse population of boys in Grades 9–12. Girls were accepted in 1975 and Grade 8 was added a year later.

The School's philosophy, reflecting the concept of "learning through living," fosters independence and responsibility within a rigorous academic program designed to educate the "whole person, not just for college but for life." The broad curriculum encourages experimentation and discovery with the goal of creating graduates who acquire "a hunger and thirst" for knowledge. Close student-faculty relationships promote mutual support that extends beyond the scope of academics.

Indian Springs is governed by a 15-member Board of Trustees, including several alumni. It is accredited by the Southern Association of Colleges and Schools and approved by the Alabama Department of Education. The School holds membership in the National Association of Independent Schools and the Council for Advancement and Support of Education, among others.

THE CAMPUS. Bordering 10,000 acres of state park in the scenic Cahaba River Valley, the 350-acre wooded campus, featuring oak, hickory, sweet gum, and pine trees, overlooks a spring-fed, freshwater lake that offers swimming, fishing, and canoeing.

Facilities include the administrative offices, 10 classrooms, 3 science laboratories, art studio, darkroom, computer workshop, 2 multipurpose assembly halls, and the recently enlarged and renovated 15,000-volume library. The dormitory circle contains rooms for 90 boarders, 4 faculty apartments, 2 faculty homes, and the infirmary; there are 20 additional faculty homes beyond the dorm area. Athletic facilities include three playing fields, a track, tennis courts, and a two-gymnasium field house. The new Town Hall, completed in the summer of 1998, houses a 300-seat theater for plays and town meetings and a 500-seat concert hall for choir performances and other musical events.

Indian Springs School is owned by a nonprofit trust and is valued at $12,000,000.

THE FACULTY. Douglas S. Jennings, appointed Director in 1987, earned his baccalaureate degree from Lafayette College and a master's degree from Teachers College, Columbia University.

There are 35 faculty members, 26 of whom hold advanced degrees, including 4 doctorates. Twenty-one teachers live on campus. The colleges and universities from which they graduated include Auburn, Birmingham-Southern, Brockport State, Columbia, Duke, Kenyon College, Lafayette, Livingston State, Manhattan School of Music, Middlebury, Oklahoma State, Peabody College, Presbyterian, Queens, Randolph-Macon Woman's College, St. John's, University College (Dublin), Vanderbilt, Western Michigan, and the Universities of Alabama, Florida, Georgia, Miami, Mississippi, Montevallo, North Carolina, Puget Sound, St. Thomas, the South, Virginia, and Western Ontario.

STUDENT BODY. In 1999–2000, Indian Springs enrolled 254 students, including 44 boarding boys, 22 boarding girls, 91 day boys, and 97 day girls. Enrollment was distributed as follows: Grade 8—35, Grade 9—58, Grade 10—57, Grade 11—59, and Grade 12—45. Most students come from Alabama; eight other states and seven foreign countries are represented. Minorities comprise 26 percent of the student body.

ACADEMIC PROGRAM. The school year, divided into trimesters, begins in late August and ends in early June, with major vacations at Thanksgiving, winter holidays, and in the spring. Classes, which are 45 minutes in length, are held from 8:00 A.M. to 3:19 P.M. and have an average of 15 students. The student-teacher ratio is 9:1.

The standard course load includes five academic subjects—English, history, math, foreign language, and science—and

physical education. To graduate, seniors must have successfully completed four years of English; three each of history, mathematics, and science; and two of a foreign language. New students accepted in the upper grades may have some requirements waived.

Among the yearlong and trimester courses are: English 8–11, Advanced Placement English, World Religions, Contemporary American Novel, Creative Writing Workshop, Expository Writing, Modern Irish Writers, Journalism, Philosophy, Psychology, Vocabulary Study; French I–V, Latin I–V, Spanish I–V; Social Studies (Grade 8), History (Grades 9–11), Advanced Placement European History, American Government, U.S. Military History, Economics; Psychology; Algebra I, Geometry, Algebra II & Trigonometry, Pre-Calculus, Calculus I–II, Discrete Math, Basic Computer, Advanced Computer, Advanced Placement Computer; Science (Grade 8), Biology (Grade 9), Advanced Placement Biology, Vertebrate Anatomy, Chemistry (Grade 10), Physics (Grade 11), Advanced Placement Physics; and Calligraphy, Ceramics, Weaving, Basic Design, Introduction to Architectural Design, Painting, Sculpture, Woodworking, Play Production, Music, Advanced Placement Music, Jazz, Music Ensemble Performance, and Recording Arts. Leadership seminars, independent study, work study, and volunteer community service are also available.

Indian Springs academic teams have ranked first in the state in Latin and Physics; the Latin team also placed third nationally. The Scholars' Bowls team ranked first nationally in computerized competition for schools of a comparable size. In the last four years, 51 Indian Springs students were National Merit semifinalists.

In 1999, all of the 53 seniors went on to college. They are attending such institutions as Auburn, Birmingham-Southern, Boston University, Colgate, Columbia University, Duke, Georgia Institute of Technology, Kenyon, Middlebury, Northwestern, Princeton, Stanford, Swarthmore, Trinity College (Ireland), Vanderbilt, Washington University, Wesleyan University, and the Universities of Alabama and Illinois.

STUDENT ACTIVITIES. School government is based on a constitution drafted by students for the overall government of the school community. A mayor and five commissioners, elected by students, oversee such aspects of school life as service, transportation, protection, recreation, and tutoring. A nine-member Student Judiciary conducts hearings and determines discipline on all but the most serious infractions of the School's regulations.

Music is an integral part of an Indian Springs education. The School's Concert Choir, including the Men's Glee Club, the Women's Choir, and the Chamber Choir, has toured Europe, sung in Austria with the Vienna Boys' Choir, and performed at Lincoln Center. Interest groups include French, Latin, Key, Amnesty International, Habitat for Humanity, and outdoor clubs, and the yearbook, newspaper, and literary magazine.

Other extracurricular activities include debate, Scholars' Bowl, varsity and interscholastic teams in soccer, baseball, softball, basketball, tennis, golf, cross-country, and volleyball. Other teams may be formed depending on student interest.

ADMISSION AND COSTS. Indian Springs welcomes students of good academic ability who are likely to succeed in the program and who will contribute to, and benefit from, a school-community life characterized by "responsible freedom and close interpersonal relationships." Application may be made beginning in September and continuing throughout the school year preceding entrance. Acceptance is based on academic records, recommendations from past schools, letters of reference, interviews, and the results of the Secondary School Admission Test. Applicants are usually notified of their status on or before March 10.

In 1999–2000, full boarding tuition is $18,500; five-day boarding is $15,500; day tuition, including lunch, is $10,200. Textbooks, private rooms, and other expenses are extra. Financial aid in the amount of $424,100 was awarded to 55 students on the basis of need.

Dean of Faculty: June Conerly
Dean of Students: John B. Lusco
Academic Dean: Bryn Roberts
Director of Admissions: Charles H. Ellis
Director of Development and Alumni Affairs: Marcy Jefferson
College Counselor: Betty Cortina Huck
Director of Finance: Drew Ann Long
Director of Athletics: Greg Van Horn

The Montgomery Academy 1959

3240 Vaughn Road, Montgomery, AL 36106-2725. 1-888-345-8210 or 334-272-8210; Fax 334-277-3240; E-mail kirk.r@mont-acad. pvt.k12.al.us; Web Site www.mont-acad.pvt.k12.al.us

This coeducational, college preparatory day school enrolls 890 students in Kindergarten–Grade 12. The curriculum features sequential, accredited courses in English, mathematics, science, social studies, foreign language; electives in fine arts and computer science; and 17 Advanced Placement courses. The program balances student activities, service opportunities, and boys' and girls' athletic teams. Admission is based on entrance tests, interview, and previous academic record. Tuition: $3960–$7200 (including lunch). Rhea C. Kirk is Director of Admissions; A. Emerson Johnson III (Hampden-Sydney, B.S.; University of North Carolina, M.Ed.) is Headmaster. *Southern Association.*

Randolph School 1959

1005 Drake Avenue, SE, Huntsville, AL 35802. 256-881-1701; Fax 256-881-1784; E-mail admiss@randolph.pvt.k12.al.us

Randolph is a coeducational, college preparatory day school that aims to develop independence, academic achievement, and good citizenship in its 750 students. The balanced curriculum, encompassing Kindergarten–Grade 12, integrates challenging studies in the arts, sciences, and humanities, including honors and Advanced Placement courses and numerous electives. College counseling begins in Grade 9, and Randolph students are consistently admitted to competitive institutions of higher learning. Activities include sports for boys and girls, National Honor Society, student government, music and drama productions, and various interest clubs. Tuition: $3550–$7100. Financial aid is available. Nancy Hodges is Dean of Admissions; Rick Keyser is Headmaster. *Southern Association.*

Saint James School 1955

6010 Vaughn Road, Montgomery, AL 36116. 334-277-8033; Fax 334-227-2542; E-mail asteineker@stj.pvt.k12.al.us; Web Site www.stj.pvt.k12.al.us

Montgomery's oldest and largest nonsectarian, college preparatory school, Saint James seeks to provide an educational program in which students can acquire the maturity, self-confidence, skills, and knowledge to become responsible, productive adults. The School's four divisions include 1300 girls and boys in Kindergarten 4–Grade 12 on two campuses. The curriculum emphasizes the liberal arts and sciences, with honors and Advanced Placement courses in the Upper School. After-school activities range from school government and interest clubs to drama, music, the arts, and interscholastic sports. Tuition: $3330–$5600. Aimee Steineker is Director of Admissions; John Bell (Huntingdon College, B.A.; Auburn, M.A.) was appointed Headmaster in 1997. *Southern Association.*

✗ St. Luke's Episcopal School 1961

980 Azalea Road, Mobile, AL 36693. 334-666-2991; Fax 334-666-2996; E-mail stlukesmob@aol.com; Web Site www.stlukesepiscopal.org

St. Luke's Episcopal School, founded in 1961 by parents of St. Luke's Parish, seeks to provide educational excellence within a Christian environment. Five hundred boys and girls in Pre-Kindergarten–Grade 8 are motivated to develop confidence and self-esteem through a traditional liberal arts program, enhanced by Spanish, computer science, and the arts. Musicals, band and chorus, publications, and a variety of sports and interest clubs are among the activities. Tuition: $2220–$4100. Extras: $250. Financial Aid: $45,405. Nancy G. Howell is Director of Admissions; John H. Wright, Jr. (University of the South, B.A. 1954; Harvard, Ed.M. 1966), was appointed Headmaster in 1996. *Southern Association.*

St. Paul's Episcopal School 1947

161 Dogwood Lane, Mobile, AL 36608. 334-342-6700; Fax 334-342-6700, Ext. 1140; Web Site www.stpauls.pvt.k12.al.us

St. Paul's Episcopal School enrolls 800 day boys and 700 day girls in Pre-Kindergarten–Grade 12. It seeks to prepare students to become sound, strong, moral citizens through a college preparatory program, which incorporates the tenets of the Christian faith as understood by the Episcopal church. The curriculum includes programs in art, music, drama, religion, community service, and computer science. Qualified students may take courses for college credit at Spring Hill College. Athletics, community service, various clubs, and social events are among the School's activities. Tuition: $2168–$5456. Julie L. Taylor is Director of Admissions; Robert H. Rutledge (Florida State University, M.S.) was appointed Headmaster in 1994. *Southern Association.*

Tuscaloosa Academy 1966

420 Rice Valley Road North, Tuscaloosa, AL 35406. 205-758-4462; Fax 205-758-4418; E-mail TAKnights@Tuscaloosaacademy.org; Web Site www.tuscaloosaacademy.org

Tuscaloosa Academy is a college preparatory day school enrolling 490 boys and girls in Montessori and traditional Pre-School–Grade 12. The Academy seeks to provide a supportive environment of intellectual freedom, to cultivate a love of learning, and to maximize each student's potential for academic achievement, character development, and readiness for life. Advanced Placement and English as a Second Language are offered. Classes are small, with a student-teacher ratio of 12:1. Among the activities are athletics, Odyssey of the Mind, student government, Key Club, and publications. Tuition: $4610–$5810. Financial Aid: $110,000. Mrs. Lane Parker is Director of Admission; William L. Campbell (Peabody College of Vanderbilt University, Ed.D. 1971) is Headmaster. *Southern Association.*

UMS–Wright Preparatory School 1893

65 North Mobile Street, Mobile, AL 36607. 334-470-9039; Fax 334-470-9050; E-mail comlys@zebra.net; Web Site www.ums-wright.org

In its 107th year of providing quality education, UMS–Wright Preparatory School enrolls 1275 day students in Pre-kindergarten–Grade 12. The curriculum is designed to give students the academic foundation they need to succeed in college. UMS–Wright emphasizes honor, responsibility, integrity, and self-discipline in an atmosphere of trust and support. Advanced Placement courses and programs in math, science, foreign language, computer science, and the arts are offered. Among the School's many activities are clubs, social events, community service, and state champion athletic programs. Tuition: $2960–$5370. Financial aid is available. Nan Lauten is Admissions Director; Tony W. Havard (University of Southern Mississippi, Ed.D. 1994) is Headmaster. *Southern Association.*

ARIZONA

All Saints' Episcopal Day School   1963

6300 North Central Avenue, Phoenix, AZ 85012. 602-274-4866;
Fax 602-274-0365; E-mail LBritton@allsaints.org

All Saints' Episcopal Day, enrolling 454 boys and girls in Kindergarten–Grade 8, seeks to develop each student's abilities in a supportive, nurturing environment through a curriculum that balances academic excellence, physical education, and spiritual awareness. Art, computers, drama/music, library, Spanish, and religious studies enrich the program. Activities include chorus, sports, instrumental music lessons, student council, junior honor society, publications, community service, and field trips. A competitive admissions process aims to identify academically talented students for the challenging program. Tuition: $7250. Financial Aid: $150,000. Lynn Britton is Director of Admissions; John Hyslop (McGill, B.A.; University of Michigan, M.A.) is Interim Head of School.

Green Fields Country Day School   1933

6000 North Camino de la Tierra, Tucson, AZ 85741.
520-297-2288; Fax 520-297-2072; E-mail gfadmit@flash.net;
Web Site www.greenfields.org

One of the oldest independent day schools in Arizona, Green Fields enrolls 230 boys and girls in Grades 4–12. The college preparatory curriculum has won regional and national awards in academics, fine arts, and student publications. Individual responsibility for school and community service is emphasized. Technology is integral to the program. Athletics are available for all ages. The campus includes a performing arts center, science labs, computer labs, a gym, and a library equipped with electronic data access systems, Internet access, and CD-ROM databases. Tuition: $9525. Books: $300. Financial Aid: $260,000. Carole Knapp is Admissions Director; Rick Belding (Princeton, B.S.E. 1969) is Head of School.

Phoenix Country Day School   1961

3901 East Stanford Drive, Paradise Valley, AZ 85253.
602-955-8200; Fax 602-955-1286; E-mail tsylvest@pcds.org;
Web Site pcds.org

Phoenix Country Day School, enrolling 700 boys and girls in Pre-Kindergarten through Grade 12, aims to provide a superior college preparatory program that will challenge and encourage students' curiosity and creativity. Basic skills developed in the early grades form the foundation for the liberal arts curriculum of the Middle and Upper schools. Advanced Placement courses are available in 15 subjects, and there are numerous electives such as International Relations and Studio Art. Publications, peer tutoring, sports, Student Senate, and interest clubs are offered as extracurricular activities. An academic summer session is available. Tuition: $7300–$12,600. Financial aid is available. Tom Sylvester is Director of Admissions; Galen Brewster is Head of the School.

St. Gregory College Preparatory School   1980

3231 North Craycroft Road, Tucson, AZ 85712. 520-327-6395;
Fax 520-327-8276

St. Gregory's, a nonsectarian, coeducational day school, seeks to offer a rigorous college preparatory program to 415 students in Grades 6–12. Advanced Placement is available in eight subjects, and with the exception of introductory courses, all other courses are honors level. A strong adviser and guidance system enables 100 percent of seniors to gain acceptance to a college of their choice. Each year, the entire school participates in a one-week Humanities term to explore a selected theme or subject in that field. Activities involve publications, studio arts, musical productions, Honor Committee, sports, and community service. Tuition: $8500–$9400. Financial Aid: $250,000. Debby R. Kennedy is Admissions Director; Donald Nickerson (Harvard, B.A., M.Ed.) is Headmaster. *North Central Association.*

St. Michael's Parish Day School   TUCSON

602 North Wilmot Road, Tucson, AZ 85711. 520-722-8478;
Fax 520-886-0851; Web Site www.stmichael.net

ST. MICHAEL'S PARISH DAY SCHOOL in Tucson, Arizona, is an Episcopal school enrolling boys and girls in Kindergarten–Grade 8. It is located on the east side of Tucson, the center of a metropolitan district of 1,000,000 and the home of the University of Arizona. The city is ringed by national and state parks and has many institutions that reflect the Native American, Hispanic, and European cultural streams contributing to its history. The School's location makes it easily accessible to most of the populace. A public bus line serves the School, and many come to the campus in car pools.

The School was established in 1958, five years after the formation of St. Michael and All Angels Parish. The Rev. John Clinton Fowler, first vicar of the parish, founded the School after observing that many children coming to Sunday School were lacking in academic skills. The School began with 34 students in Kindergarten and Grade 1, then expanded for five years until the elementary school was complete with eight grades.

St. Michael's focuses on the academic strength and traditional disciplines that Father Fowler summed up by saying, "We teach children to read, to write, to cipher, to sing, and to pray." Arts, languages, physical education, and religion enhance this program. St. Michael's seeks "to foster the intellectual, physical, ethical, and spiritual development of its students" in a traditional Episcopal setting. It strives to maintain a pluralistic community, drawing teachers and students from all social, economic, ethnic, and religious backgrounds. Religious instruction is given one day a week in Grades 4–8, and attendance at three weekly chapels and a weekly Eucharist is mandatory.

The School is a nonprofit organization as a subsidiary of the Vestry of the Parish and is entirely self-supporting, receiving no funding from the church. It is governed by a 15-member Board of Trustees, including some alumni. The board members, who serve three-year terms, are chosen by a nominating committee with approval by the Board and Vestry of the church. The School holds membership in the National Association of Episcopal Schools and the Southwest Association of Episcopal Schools.

THE CAMPUS. The School is situated on 3.3 acres that also encompass the church, its administrative offices, and parish hall. A public park adjacent to the property provides fields for athletics and recreation.

All of the buildings are designed in classic Southwestern style, using mud-adobe and timber construction. The academic facilities are arranged around courtyards and verandas in groups that accommodate Lower School (Kindergarten–Grade 3), Intermediate School (Grades 4–5), and Upper School (Grades 6–8). Special rooms for music and art and a multipurpose facility serving as an auditorium are common to all groups. Five new classrooms and a 28-station computer lab for Grades 6–8 were completed in December 1998. The new science discovery center, with special facilities for both primary and middle school science teaching, features an outdoor, hands-on wetlands area.

The plant is owned by the church and is valued at $3,900,000.

THE FACULTY. Patrick Brown, a graduate of Stanford University (B.A. 1980) and the University of Arizona (M.A. 1990), was appointed Head in 1994. A teacher of history and political science, Mr. Brown served St. Gregory College Preparatory School in Tucson for ten years as teacher, coach, Director of Athletics, and Dean of Students. He has been active in the community as Chair of the Lighthouse YMCA Board of Managers and was recently appointed to the Board of the Southwest Association of Episcopal Schools. He and his wife, Katy, have three sons, all of whom attend St. Michael's.

The full-time faculty consists of seven men and 18 women, with three part-time instructors also on staff. They hold 25 bachelor's degrees and 8 advanced degrees, including 2 doctorates, from such institutions as Georgetown, Macalester, Northern Arizona 2, Northwestern, Ohio State 2, Stanford, State University of New York (Brockport), Stephen Austin, and the Universities of Arizona 13, California, Colorado, Connecticut, Northern Colorado, Oregon, and Wisconsin 2. Faculty benefits include health insurance, retirement plans, and support for professional advancement. All teachers have training in basic first-aid and CPR. St. Joseph's Hospital is located less than 200 yards from the School.

STUDENT BODY. The School enrolls 154 boys and 168 girls in Kindergarten through Grade 8. They are distributed evenly through all levels with each grade having about 36 students, 18 to a section. All of the students come from the Tucson metropolitan area, most are Christian, and about 14 percent are Hispanic, African-American, and Asian-American. Some 60 students receive financial aid, which is awarded on the basis of need.

ACADEMIC PROGRAM. The academic year, divided into semesters, begins in late August and ends in late May. Vacations are scheduled for ten days at Christmas and one week at Easter. Classes are held five days a week between 8:00 A.M. and 3:10 P.M., with Kindergarten through Grade 3 being dismissed at 2:50 P.M. The normal class session for Grades 6–8 is 44 minutes, and the usual class size is 18. In the upper grades, students are expected to complete up to two hours of homework per night. Teachers provide extra help where it is needed, and supervised study halls are conducted by faculty after school. Contract tutoring services are also available. Grades are posted and sent to parents four times a year.

St. Michael's seeks to provide a rigorous academic experience and accommodates both competitive and cooperative modes of education. All students are instructed in the core subjects of language arts, social studies, mathematics, and science on a daily basis. Music, art, and physical education are offered at every level. Religious instruction is given one day a week in Grades 4–8, and Spanish is taught twice a week in Grades 4 and 5 and three times a week thereafter. Students in Grades 7 and 8 receive daily instruction in Latin. Technology is introduced formally to Grades 2–8 in a weekly computer-lab setting. All grades use technology through interdisciplinary studies.

The aim of the language arts curriculum is to develop students who can read, write, and speak thoughtfully and confidently. Grammar skills are taught at every level, and students are introduced to literature appropriate to their ages. They are encouraged to speak in the classroom and at school functions.

In social sciences, a broad view of the United States provides the early context, and students move into world cultures and history in Grades 4–6, and to U.S. history and government in Grades 7–8.

Age-appropriate mathematical skills are taught at each level, and advanced students can take a high school algebra course. In Grades 1–5, students undertake science units on life, physical and earth sciences, and health. They focus on physical science with lab units in Grade 7 and earth science with a similar approach in Grade 8.

Latin is required in Grades 7–8 to introduce ancient texts and to develop general language acquisition skills. Structured programs are offered for one to three days a week in music and art, Spanish, computers, and physical education. Religious instruction in the early grades focuses on the scriptures in that week's liturgy. In Grades 5–8, students examine the framework of Christian belief and study specific ethical issues.

A limited summer school program of remedial and enrichment courses is offered for St. Michael's students.

STUDENT ACTIVITIES. Students in Grades 6–8 elect officers and class representatives to a Student Council directed by a faculty member. The Council takes responsibilities for organizing certain social events and community service. In Grade 8, every student completes an eight-hour community service project.

Special-interest clubs are formed where student interests develop. Among the ongoing clubs are Chess, Creative Dance, and Karate.

Teams are formed in Grades 5–8 to compete in a 12-member independent league for private schools. St. Michael's fields interscholastic teams in soccer, basketball, flag football, and track for boys; and volleyball, soccer, basketball, softball, and track for girls.

The School calendar includes many special events organized for religious or academic enrichment or social purposes. Among the traditional events are St. Nicholas Day, a Lessons and Carols Advent Service, and Mardi Gras Pancake Luncheon. Spelling and Geography Bees and Declamation Day provide competitive academic experience. Musicians, storytellers, artists, and dancers visit classrooms, and field trips are frequently arranged to visit local museums and natural wonders. Eighth graders annually make a seven-day trip to Washington, D.C., to visit the sites of the national government.

The Friends of St. Michael's, a parents group, arranges a number of fund-raisers and events. Special events that include parents are Parents' Nights, Grandparents' Day, Fine Arts Night, and Family Science Day.

ADMISSION AND COSTS. St. Michael's Parish Day School seeks students of average and above-average ability who can manage the rigorous academic demands and accept the behavioral standards of the School. Most students are admitted in Kindergarten, but vacancies in the other grades are filled annually. Students in Grades 1–8 complete a two-hour evaluation that includes standardized tests. Kindergarten applicants have a half-hour readiness evaluation. Recommendations are required. Applications, with a $50 fee, should be made in February, and the School is fully subscribed by the end of March. The Headmaster serves as Director of Admissions.

Tuition for 1999–2000 is $3850, and the book fee is $150. A tuition insurance plan and three different payment plans are available. The School subscribes to the School Scholarship Service and awards approximately $120,000 in financial aid on the basis of need.

Assistant Head: Judi Breault
Director of Development: Virginia Healy
Business Manager: Judy Engstrand
Athletic Director: Shane Sherwood
Primary Coordinator: Barbara Faltico
Intermediate Coordinator: Jan Thompsen

Valley Lutheran High School   1981

525 West Colter Street, Phoenix, AZ 85013. 602-230-1600;
Fax 602-230-1602; E-mail valleyl@goodnet.com;
Web Site www.asd.com#68646

Valley Lutheran High, enrolling 118 day students, was founded by Lutheran churches to prepare young men and women for leadership in their school, their community, and their world. The arts and sciences are balanced with a distinctly Christian perspective through Bible studies in an environment influenced by the teachings of Jesus. Technology is integrated throughout the disciplines, and computer education and radio/television communication are offered. Seventy percent of students take part in music groups and the athletic program. Other activities include a foreign exchange program, peer ministry, and drama. Tuition: $4550. Financial Aid: $160,000. Rev. James L. Wiese (Concordia Seminary, B.A., M.Div.; Stanford, M.A.) is Executive Director.

Verde Valley School   SEDONA

3511 Verde Valley School Road, Sedona, AZ 86351. 520-284-2272;
Fax 520-284-0432; E-mail admissionvvs@sedona.net;
Web Site www.verdevalleyschool.org

VERDE VALLEY SCHOOL in Sedona, Arizona, is a coeducational boarding and day school enrolling students in Grades 9 through 12 and a postgraduate year. Sedona (population 15,000) is a resort community located in redrock country at an elevation of about 4200 feet. It is two hours north of Phoenix and an hour south of Flagstaff, and the campus is easily accessible by car via Interstate Highways 17 and 40.

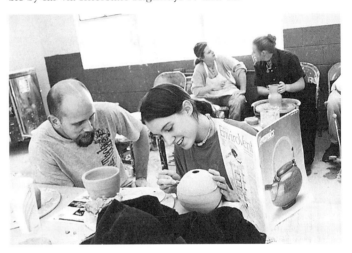

Hamilton and Barbara Warren founded Verde Valley School in 1948. Their goal was to create an educational setting in which young people from diverse backgrounds and life experiences could undertake challenging college preparatory work while gaining an understanding of other cultures, particularly those of the American Southwest and Mexico. Verde Valley aims to foster in students a deep commitment to social responsibility, world citizenship, harmonious relations among all races and ethnic groups, and an appreciation for their natural environment. The School's spectacular setting provides inspiration for artistic and musical expression and serves as a natural classroom for unique, field-based learning experiences, including anthropological and geological studies.

A nonprofit institution, Verde Valley School is governed by a ten-member Board of Trustees and is accredited by the Arizona Association of Independent Schools. It holds membership in the National Association of Independent Schools, National Association of College Admission Counseling, Western Boarding Schools Association, and A Better Chance, among other professional affiliations. More than 1200 graduates are represented by an active Alumni Association, and most continue to support the School's mission through fund-raising, recruitment, and other endeavors.

THE CAMPUS. Verde Valley's 167-acre campus, surrounded by national park and forest lands, features a natural 7000-seat amphitheater that is home to the annual Jazz on the Rocks Festival and the Jackson Browne concert for the benefit of the School's Native American Scholarship Fund. Most buildings are of white stucco, reflecting the region's Spanish influence. Academic facilities include ten classrooms; the Osgood-Morris Laboratories for the natural and physical sciences; a computer center; and studios for art, graphics, ceramics, sculpture, and photography. Brady Hall provides dance and theater facilities. Additional facilities include a nondenominational chapel, the 10,000-volume library with Internet access and multimedia technology, an art gallery, a 350-seat theater, and dance auditorium. Students reside in five dorms, while resident faculty, staff and their families occupy adjoining apartments and homes. A large dining room, a bookstore/student lounge, and a health center complete the physical plant.

On the grounds are tennis, volleyball, and basketball courts; a soccer field; riding stables and a riding ring; a ropes course; numerous trails for horseback riding, hiking, and biking; and thousand-foot-high formations for rock climbing.

THE FACULTY. The community at Verde Valley is such that there is little distinction between the roles of faculty and staff. All adults on campus actively participate in maintaining a safe, stimulating learning environment for students.

The Verde Valley School faculty is comprised of 18 instructors. All hold baccalaureate degrees and eight have earned advanced degrees, representing study at such colleges and universities as Amherst, Arizona State, Colorado, Columbia, Cornell, Duke, Harvard, Knox, Lock Haven, New Mexico, Northern Arizona, Oregon, Oxford, Rhode Island, University of the South, Vanderbilt, Vassar, Western State, Wyoming, and Yale.

The health center is staffed by a registered nurse, local health professionals are on call as needed, and hospital facilities are available in Sedona.

STUDENT BODY. In 1998–99, Verde Valley enrolled 72 boarding and 13 day students in Grades 9–12. They came from throughout the United States and from several countries around the world. Approximately 25 percent were students of color, with the largest group being Native Americans.

ACADEMIC PROGRAM. The school year extends from late August to the end of May and includes vacations at Thanksgiving, and in the winter and the spring. Each student is assigned an advisor who, as mentor and role model, maintains ongoing monitoring of the advisee's academic, social, and emotional growth while serving as a regular contact between home and school. Grades for achievement and effort are issued four times a year. Classes are small, with an average of 8 per class, and permit individualized attention from the teacher and full participation by the student in course discussions. The student:faculty ratio is 5:1.

Breakfast and dorm clean-up begin at 7:00 A.M. on a typical day, with classes from 8:00 A.M. to 2:30 P.M. Sports and work/jobs follow the last class. Dinner is at 5:45 P.M., and evening study hours begin at 7:30 P.M. Students must be in their dormitories by 10:00 P.M. on weeknights and by 11:00 P.M. on Friday and Saturday nights. Once a week, an all-school meeting is held for announcements, discussions of concerns and issues, and occasional presentations.

The college preparatory curriculum calls for four years of English and mathematics; three years each of science, history, and social studies; two years each of foreign language and fine arts; and one year of anthropology. English as a Second Language is available for international students.

In partial fulfillment of graduation requirements, all students undertake an 11-day Project Period in a field of their choice in January of each year. Students work outside the structure of a regular class day with a mentor on projects as diverse as jewelry making, language study, video production, and solar design. Students may also serve an internship in veterinary medicine, law, social work, and other professions.

Verde Valley students take a 16-day field trip each spring working and learning in other parts of the world. Field trips provide living experiences in Native American and Mexican villages, social service in large cities, and exploration of wilderness areas such as Baja California and the Grand Canyon.

Verde Valley offers The Shakespeare Sedona Institute for three weeks in July. Students 16 years of age and older are immersed in a curriculum that focuses on classical acting techniques and their practical application in performance. Renowned faculty from institutions such as Yale School of Drama and American Conservatory Theatre teach the participants, who may receive college credit for their work.

Professional college counseling services are available beginning in the freshman year but intensify in Grades 11 and 12, and 98 percent of Verde Valley students go on to further education. In the last five years, graduates have entered such colleges and universities as Amherst, Bard College, Brown, California Institute of the Arts, Carleton, Case Western Reserve, Colorado College, Hamilton, Hampshire, Haverford, Mount Holyoke, New York University, Northeastern, Oberlin, Pepperdine, Pitzer, Prescott College, Reed, Rice, St. John's (New Mexico), Sarah Lawrence, Stanford, Wellesley, Wesleyan, and the Universities of Alaska, California (Berkeley, Santa Barbara, Santa Cruz), Chicago, North Carolina, Northern Arizona, Oregon, Pacific, Southern California, and Utah.

STUDENT ACTIVITIES. The Verde Valley School community is democratic by design, and students have input and equal or majority representation on key School committees that deal with discipline, teacher hiring, admission decisions, health issues, field trips, and project periods. Adults and teenagers share caring, egalitarian relationships, and all members of the community are expected to interact with common sense and respect. In addition, all students participate in the work/job program, taking responsibility for maintenance of the grounds, service in the dining hall, and routine office work.

Clubs and other extracurricular activities are organized according to student interest. Among these are the school newspaper and the yearbook. The School also sponsors the appearance of outside guest speakers and artists.

Verde Valley's outstanding riding program enjoys wide participation, and students may use School-owned horses or bring their own to campus. Instruction is provided in Western and English riding techniques, and students can train for competition in area horse shows.

With the exception of competitive soccer, which is a Verde Valley mainstay, the athletic program is largely determined by student interest that varies from year to year. The School often fields teams in volleyball, basketball, and baseball. Aerobics, yoga, road and mountain biking, classical and modern dance, cross country running, martial arts, tennis, golf, rock climbing, and other pursuits are also offered.

Weekend trips take students hiking in the Grand Canyon, climbing in Joshua Tree National Park, river rafting, skiing and snowboarding, exploring Native American ruins, and visiting Sedona, Flagstaff, and Phoenix for cultural excursions, dining, and shopping.

ADMISSION AND COSTS. After submitting a preliminary application and fee of $45, candidates file a formal application consisting of official school transcripts, a recommendation from an English teacher and another teacher of the child's choosing, a peer recommendation, applicant and parent questionnaires, standardized test results, and any other relevant materials such as an art or writing portfolio. Applicants are strongly encouraged to visit the campus. Admission to the School is on a rolling basis, with decisions about financial aid and scholarships made in the spring prior to entry. Verde Valley does offer mid-year admission to a limited number of students.

In 1999–2000, boarding tuition is $22,500 and day tuition is $12,750, including required activities and travel. The School offers both need- and merit-based financial assistance to qualified applicants.

Interim Head of School: Anne Salzmann
Academic Dean: Judge Mason
Dean of Students: Kevin Warren
Director of Admissions: Aaron Thomas
Business Manager: Robert Klapproth

CALIFORNIA

All Saints' Episcopal Day School   1961

8060 Carmel Valley Road, Carmel, CA 93923. 831-624-9171;
Fax 831-624-3960; E-mail asds@asds.org

All Saints' Episcopal Day School, an integral part of the All Saints' parish program, enrolls 212 students in Pre-Kindergarten–Grade 8 and aims to provide high academic standards in a Christian environment. Mathematical and language skills are stressed, and the curriculum includes foreign languages (French, Latin, Spanish), social studies, science, music, art, and religious history. Students attend daily chapel services. An after-school enrichment program and a summer school providing academics for children and arts for children and adults are offered. Tuition: $7278–$9728. Financial Aid: $208,000. Jay Lentz (Maryville College, B.S.; Virginia Theological Seminary, M.Div.) is Head.

Archbishop Riordan High School   1949

175 Phelan Avenue, San Francisco, CA 94112. 415-586-8200;
Fax 415-587-1310; E-mail scottd@riordan.pvt.k12.ca.us;
Web Site www.riordan.pvt.k12.ca.us

Archbishop Riordan High School is an Archdiocesan, Roman Catholic high school for young men, conducted by the Society of Mary, the Marianists. Opened in 1949, the School is situated on an 11-acre site in San Francisco. Its student body of more than 700 young men is reflective of the cultural richness of the city. Archbishop Riordan High School engages its students in a process of education that promotes each student's personal growth and development in the intellectual, spiritual, social, and physical aspects of his life. The college preparatory program includes honors and Advanced Placement courses. Band, drama, video, and interscholastic sports are also offered. Tuition: $7325. Scott Donegan is Director of Admission; Fr. Timothy M. Kenney, SM, is Principal.

Army and Navy Academy   1910

Post Office Box 3000, Carlsbad, CA 92018-3000. 760-729-2385;
Admissions 888-76CADET; Fax 760-434-5948;
E-mail academy@adnc.com; Web Site www.army-navyacademy.com

Located on 16 oceanfront acres, Army and Navy Academy enrolls boys in Grades 7–12. The Academy offers a comprehensive program that prepares students for success. Ninety-five percent of graduates attend colleges and universities of their choice. Honors, Advanced Placement, and ESL courses are provided in a structured environment. Twelve sports programs develop teamwork and personal excellence, while the military program instills self-discipline and leadership skills. Parental involvement is encouraged. Assemblies and chapel services stress honorable character development and values. Boarding Tuition: $18,500; Day Tuition: $12,000. Col. Stephen Miller is President; Tom Bloomquist is Dean of Academics. *Western Association.*

The Athenian School   DANVILLE

2100 Mt. Diablo Scenic Boulevard, Danville, CA 94506-2002.
925-837-5375; Fax 925-855-9342; E-mail admission@athenian.org;
Web Site www.athenian.org

THE ATHENIAN SCHOOL in Danville, California, is a coeducational college preparatory school enrolling boarding students in Grades 9–12 and day students in Grades 6–12. Located 32 miles east of San Francisco, it offers both a rural campus and accessibility to the educational and cultural resources of the San Francisco Bay area. The Pacific Coast and the Sierra Nevada mountains are both within a few hours' drive.

Athenian was founded in 1965 by Dyke Brown, a graduate of Yale Law School and then Vice-President of the Ford Foundation. In accordance with his vision of the full development of each student, an Athenian education expands students' ability to think critically, solve problems, communicate effectively, and explore the world with imagination and resourcefulness. Athenian's rigorous academic programs and significant community activities are designed to prepare students for the rigors of college and lives of purpose and personal fulfillment.

The academic year in the Upper School is divided into three terms. Each term is devoted to the study of five to six subjects; some courses are yearlong and some are single-term seminars. Middle School students study six subjects, physical education, and an elective each term. In the Middle School, one day is devoted to interdisciplinary study each week.

A nonprofit institution, Athenian is governed by a Board of Trustees. Accredited by the Western Association of Schools and Colleges, Athenian holds membership in the National Association of Independent Schools, The Association of Boarding Schools, The California Association of Independent Schools, the Western Boarding Schools Association, The College Board, the National Association for College Admission Counseling, the Round Square Conference, A Better Chance, and the National Network of Complementary Schools.

THE CAMPUS. In September 1965, The Athenian School opened on a 119-acre site, previously a part of the Blackhawk Ranch. The facilities include science laboratories, a greenhouse, drama and music studios, a library housing 12,000 volumes, classrooms, Middle School buildings, the Fuller Commons Building, and the Kate and Dyke Brown Main Hall, which contains the kitchen, dining area, meeting and performance space, and administrative offices. A geodesic dome, constructed by students, serves as part of the arts center. There are 4 dormitories and 15 faculty homes, many of which are attached to classrooms. Other faculty members reside in apartments or townhouses attached to the dormitories.

Athletic facilities include playing fields for soccer and baseball, a gymnasium with two basketball courts, tennis courts, and a competition-size swimming pool.

THE FACULTY. Eleanor Dase, Head, graduated from the University of Michigan with a degree in mathematics and earned an M.A. from St. Mary's College. Since 1974, she has been a math teacher, the Director of College Counseling, and, from 1987 to 1992, the Assistant Head.

The faculty includes 50 men and women. They hold baccalaureate, master's, and doctoral degrees representing study at such institutions as Bates, Brown, Cornell, Georgetown, Harvard, Oberlin, Princeton, Smith, Stanford, Wellesley, Wesleyan, Williams, Yale, and the Universities of California and Michigan.

STUDENT BODY. Athenian enrolls 42 boarders and 364 day students as follows: 34 in Grade 6, 44 in Grade 7, 46 in Grade 8, 75 in Grade 9, 73 in Grade 10, 69 in Grade 11, and 65 in Grade 12. Students come from throughout the United States and from Australia, Brazil, Egypt, England, Germany, Hong Kong, Japan, Kazakhstan, Korea, the Republic of China, Russia, Taiwan, Thailand, Turkey, and Yugoslavia. Day students reside throughout the greater East Bay Area.

ACADEMIC PROGRAM. The school year begins in mid-August for Wilderness Experience participants and early September for others; it ends in mid-June. Long weekends occur within terms and regular vacations include Thanksgiving, winter, and spring breaks.

The daily schedule includes five academic periods ranging from 40 to 85 minutes each, followed by sports or drama. In addition, clubs, activities, school meetings, a performing arts period, and study time occupy a portion of each day. Each class meets four times per week, and class sizes average 15 students.

To receive the Athenian diploma, students must complete the equivalent of four years of English and three years of history, including American Studies (a course reflecting an integrated approach to American literature, history, and culture); three years of French or Spanish; Algebra I, Geometry, and Algebra II; three years of laboratory science; two and one-third years of fine arts, which includes one Arts & Society course (art history); and four years of physical education. Most students exceed these requirements. In addition, students must partici-

pate in community service each year and complete the Athenian Wilderness Experience.

Students also select a number of electives each year, many of which also fulfill requirements. Among these are Writing Workshops, Shakespeare, American Nature Writing, Latin American Fiction, African American Studies, *The Iliad* and *The Odyssey*, Women Writers, American Poets of the 20th Century, Japanese Literature; Art of Architecture, The Spanish Civil War, The Russian Revolution, Economics, Psychology; advanced language seminars; Advanced Physics, Honors Biology, Environmental Science, Paleontology; and 20th Century Music, and Jazz Ensemble. Advanced Placement courses are offered in Art History, Calculus AB, Calculus BC, English Literature, U.S. History, European History, Physics, French, and Spanish. In addition, students take Advanced Placement examinations in chemistry, biology, English Literature and Composition, French, Spanish, physics, Calculus AB, Calculus BC, Art History, and Studio Art. Honors courses are offered in all disciplines.

Students may arrange independent study in most fields. In addition, they may participate in Off-Campus Internships involving a seminar and field placement oriented toward community service and career exploration. The National Network of Complementary Schools program offers a short-term exchange of students between member schools of diverse strengths and resources across the country. In addition, international exchanges are possible for Athenian students through the Round Square Conference. On campus, Athenian's Program for International Students offers English as a Second Language and Introduction to American Culture.

In 1999, virtually 100 percent of Athenian graduates gained admission to four-year colleges or universities. Recent graduates attend a wide range of colleges and universities including the Ivy League, all University of California campuses, Georgetown, Harvard, Johns Hopkins, Oberlin, Pomona, Spelman, Tufts, United States Naval Academy, Williams, and the University of Chicago.

STUDENT ACTIVITIES. Faculty, staff, and students at The Athenian School participate in Town Meeting, which serves as a forum for addressing community issues. Student representatives participate in administrative and Trustee meetings. Students share responsibility for some school maintenance.

Athenian teams compete with other schools in the Bay Counties League of the North Coast Section of the California Interscholastic Federation. Teams for both boys and girls are organized in basketball, baseball, volleyball, soccer, tennis, swimming, and cross-country. The physical education program offers both team and individual sports and competitive games. Weekend activities for boarding and day students include skiing, hiking, biking, whale watching, and art and science field trips. Student-owned horses may be boarded near campus.

Enrichment opportunities, including studio work, are provided in all the fine arts, crafts, instrumental ensemble, chorus, speech, drama, dance, and theater. There are three major theatrical productions each year and small student-run productions. Students are encouraged to take advantage of the educational and cultural resources of the San Francisco Bay area through trips to museums, plays, operas, concerts, art exhibits, and sporting events, which are planned weekly. Traditional annual events for the school community are Tim Holm Day, a cultural theme week, a formal Christmas dinner, and Spring Fling.

ADMISSION AND COSTS. Athenian seeks students who will best profit from a warm, informal environment and who want a rigorous and diverse academic course of studies. The School has a nondiscriminatory admissions policy. Applications are evaluated on the basis of academic achievement, intellectual ability, character, motivation, creativity, and talents and interests. Candidates must submit a school transcript, two recommendations, an essay, and results of the Secondary School Admission Test (SSAT) or the Independent School Entrance Examination (ISEE). A visit to the campus and an interview are also required. Applications should be completed by January 20 for fall enrollment but will be considered later if openings remain. New students are admitted to Grades 6–12. There is a $40 application fee.

In 1999–2000, tuition, room, and board is $25,500 ($27,800 for international students); day tuition is $14,650 for Grades 9–12 and $11,025 for Grades 6–8. Expenses such as books, instrumental lessons, tutoring, and field trips are additional. Eligibility for financial aid is determined by the School and Student Service for Financial Aid and the Financial Aid Committee. In 1999–2000, 72 students receive financial aid in the amount of nearly $800,000.

Deans of Faculty: David Smock and Chris McCullough
Academic Dean: Dick Bradford
Dean of Students: Tom Swope
Alumni Coordinator: Barbara Goodson
Director of Admission: Christopher Beeson
Director of College Counseling: Jan Russell
Director of Finance: James Schloss
Director of Athletics: Ray Wilson
Middle School Coordinator: Marilyn Nachtman

Bentley School   1920

K–Grade 8: 1 Hiller Drive, Oakland, CA 94618. 510-843-2512; Fax 510-843-5162
Grades 9–12: 1000 Upper Happy Valley Road, Lafayette, CA 94549. 925-283-2101; Fax 925-299-0469

Bentley is a coeducational day school enrolling 450 students in Kindergarten–Grade 12. The K–8 program is located in the residential Hiller Highlands area of Oakland, while the high school division occupies a 12-acre campus in Lafayette. Bentley School provides a quality education for children with high potential.

The traditional academic curriculum is balanced by course work in art, music, drama, physical education, and foreign languages. A low student-teacher ratio is maintained at all grade levels. An after-school day care program for students up to Grade 8 is included in the tuition. Tuition: $11,300–$13,700. Financial Aid: $300,000. Pat Finlayson is Director of Admissions; Robert A. Munro (University of Aberdeen [Scotland], M.A. 1968) is Headmaster.

Berkeley Hall School   1911

16000 Mulholland Drive, Los Angeles, CA 90049. 310-476-6421; Fax 310-476-5748; E-mail admiss@berkeleyhall.org; Web Site www.berkeleyhall.org

Berkeley Hall School was founded to provide academic excellence in a moral and ethical environment. Encompassing Preschool–Grade 9, the School enrolls 230 girls and boys. The curriculum is centered around language arts, math, science, and social studies, with numerous opportunities to develop creativity in music, drama, dance, and other arts. Computer technology, field trips, and special cultural programs enrich and reinforce classroom instruction. Students take part in community service, sports, woodshop, photography, and other pursuits. Character education is a vital thread running through the program. Tuition: $8500–$11,600. Margaret Andrews is Director of Admission; Craig Barrows is Headmaster. *Western Association.*

The Bishop's School   1909

7607 La Jolla Boulevard, La Jolla, CA 92037-4799. 858-459-4021; Fax 858-459-3914; E-mail admissions@bishops. com; Web Site http://www.bishops.com

The Bishop's School is a college preparatory day school, affiliated with the Episcopal Church, enrolling 600 boys and girls in Grades 7–12. The 11-acre campus includes five tennis courts, 25-yard swimming pool, athletic field, gymnasium, library and resource center, five computer laboratories and 300 computers throughout the campus, and performing and visual arts facilities. More than half of the faculty hold advanced degrees. The average class size is 14. The curriculum includes Advanced Placement courses for college credit. Summer programs are scheduled. Tuition: $12,500. Extras: $750. Financial Aid: $800,000. Michael W. Teitelman (Albright, A.B. 1960; Brown, M.A.T. 1962) is Headmaster. *Western Association.*

The Branson School   1920

P.O. Box 887, Ross, CA 94957. 415-454-3612; Admissions 415-454-3636; Fax 415-454-4669; E-mail bridget_anderson@branson.org

The Branson School is a coeducational, college preparatory day school enrolling 320 students in Grades 9–12. The School strives for excellence in its curriculum, which balances the traditional and the innovative. The School offers Advanced Placement in all academic disciplines. Music and arts comprise a significant portion of the extracurricular activities, with community service and interscholastic sports being the other principal offerings. A summer program provides literature, math review, study skills, art, and computer science. Tuition: $15,500. Extras: $800. Financial Aid: $479,000. Richard P. Fitzgerald (University of Notre Dame, B.A. 1972; University of Virginia, M.A. 1973) was appointed Headmaster in 1988. *Western Association.*

California

Brentwood School LOS ANGELES

Grades 7–12: 100 South Barrington Place, Los Angeles, CA 90049.
310-476-9633; Fax 310-476-4087;
E-mail Keith-Sarkisian@bwscampus.com;
Web Site www.bwscampus.com
Kindergarten–Grade 6: 12001 Sunset Boulevard, Los Angeles, CA
90049. 310-471-1041; Fax 310-440-1989

BRENTWOOD SCHOOL in Los Angeles, California, is a college preparatory day school enrolling boys and girls in Kindergarten through Grade 12 on two campuses. Located within the limits of Los Angeles, the School makes use of the cultural resources of the area through field trips to museums, institutes, and natural wonders. Students at each grade level are involved in an extensive community service program. The School is easily accessible by car, and most students travel to and from the campus in car pools.

Brentwood has its origins in the Brentwood Military Academy, founded in 1902 by Miss Mary McDonnell, who acted as Director until 1920. A proprietary institution, the Academy was primarily a boarding school enrolling students of all ages. In 1972, the campus and buildings, constructed in 1930, were sold to the newly incorporated Brentwood School, which opened with coeducational classes in Grades 7–10. Grade 11 was added in the fall of 1973, the first class graduated from Grade 12 in 1975, and The Lower School opened in August 1995.

The School aims to prepare its students for success at the next higher academic level and to help them understand themselves and their roles in a complex world. It places strong emphasis on development of attitudes that foster a sense of excitement about learning and a striving to do the best that one can. The latest technology is incorporated into all aspects of school life.

Brentwood School is a nonprofit organization governed by a Board of 24 Trustees. It is accredited by the Western Association of Schools and Colleges and holds membership in the National Association of Independent Schools, The California Association of Independent Schools, the National Association of College Admissions Counselors, and A Better Chance.

THE CAMPUS. The eight-acre Middle/Upper School campus offers a suburban-type setting with mature trees and lawns and playing fields for football, soccer, baseball, and softball. A swimming pool and outdoor courts for volleyball and basketball are available. A 20-acre athletic complex adjacent to the School is under development.

The mission-style buildings are conveniently clustered and provide classrooms and special facilities for science, art, and theater. A $3,000,000 classroom/gymnasium complex (1984) provides space for gymnastics, volleyball, basketball, and physi-

cal education classes. A library, science, and performing arts complex was completed in 1990. The three-acre Lower School campus includes three classroom buildings, a large playing field, and a new multipurpose center.

THE FACULTY. Hunter M. Temple, a graduate of Colgate (A.B. 1959), Purdue (M.A.T. 1969), and Stanford (M.E.A. 1971, Ph.D. 1975), was appointed Headmaster in 1982. He previously served for six years as Headmaster of Western Reserve Academy in Ohio. He also taught at Punahou School in Honolulu and at the University of Hawaii, where he was Director of the Office of Economic Education.

There are 68 full-time teachers, 32 men and 36 women, and 8 part-time teachers in the Middle and Upper schools. They hold 76 baccalaureate degrees or the equivalent from a variety of colleges and universities in the United States and abroad. They also hold 40 advanced degrees, including 5 doctorates.

STUDENT BODY. In 1999–2000, Brentwood School enrolls 350 boys and 310 girls in Grades 7–12 and 300 students in Kindergarten–Grade 6. About 105 students enter Grade 7 each year, coming from some 30 public and private schools in the Greater Los Angeles area. New students also enter Grades 9–12, but in lesser numbers.

ACADEMIC PROGRAM. The academic year, divided into semesters, begins in September and extends to June, with ten-day vacations at Christmas and in the spring. Classes are held five days a week and are scheduled between 8:00 A.M. and 3:00 P.M., except on Fridays, when classes end at 1:35 P.M. Assemblies are held three days a week and adviser meetings twice. The average class has 11 to 20 students, and no class has more than 22. Faculty members are available for extra help or tutoring at no extra charge. An activity period is scheduled each Wednesday during a special period. Grades are sent to parents four times a year.

In the Lower School, there are two classes of 22 students at each grade level. In addition to the core curriculum, Lower School students meet with special teachers for art, music, and physical education; students in Grades 3–6 also meet with special teachers in science and Spanish. A reading specialist was added to the faculty in the current school year.

In the Middle School, students take English, Latin, Ancient World History, Mathematics, General and Physical Science, Physical Education, Art, Music, Word Processing, Human Development, and Computer Literacy. The English program emphasizes the mechanics of writing and introduces students to various forms of literature. Latin is a requirement for the first year of Middle School and may be continued for four more years in Grade 8 and in the Upper School. Other languages offered are French, Japanese, and Spanish.

In the Upper School, students must complete 23 units of credit in the major disciplines of English, history, mathematics, science, foreign language, and fine arts. The culmination of a student's academic experience at Brentwood is the senior seminar, a yearlong interdisciplinary course that offers students the opportunity to reflect on previous academic offerings. The four years of English cover study of composition and grammar, analysis of literature, American literature, and the writing of essays and a research paper. Foreign languages offered are French, Japanese, Spanish, Latin, and Greek. In history, students take American Civics, United States History, and Modern World History over the four years. In mathematics, the courses include Algebra, Geometry, Pre-Calculus, Calculus, and Multivariable Calculus. All students take a foundation course in Physical Science, an introductory course in Biology, and either Chemistry or Physics. They have the option of taking additional science courses, including Advanced Placement courses in biology, chemistry, physics, and environmental science. Studio Art and Performing Arts include workshop classes in drawing, painting, design, sculpture, ceramics, stained glass, acting, directing, dramatic productions, school orchestra, and choral work. In addition, a series of yearlong and semester-long elective courses are offered every year according to student and faculty interests. Advanced Placement courses are offered in English, Latin, French, Spanish, American history, government, calculus, computer science, economics, statistics, studio art, and environmental science. Once a year, in the fall term, all classes participate in a four-day retreat to such locations as Sequoia and Yosemite national parks, Big Bear, and the Colorado River.

Among the colleges accepting graduates of Brentwood School in recent years are Amherst, Bowdoin, Brown, Colby, Georgetown, Harvard, Howard, Kenyon, Morehouse College, Northwestern, Princeton, Stanford, Tufts, Washington University, Williams, Yale, and the Universities of Arizona, California (Berkeley, Los Angeles, San Diego, Santa Barbara, Santa Cruz), Colorado, Michigan, Pennsylvania, Southern California, Texas, Virginia, and Wisconsin.

STUDENT ACTIVITIES. In the spring, the students elect four senior Prefects. Each class elects a representative to the Dean's Council, which plans school activities, including dances, fundraising projects, and traditional observances. The Head Prefect and the President of each class sit on the School Senate with faculty and staff members. The Senate serves as a forum for discussion of school issues and for the exchange of ideas.

Among the extracurricular activities are the nationally award-winning newspaper, the yearbook, orchestra, choir, computer club, speech and debate, and an extensive community service program. Other groups are organized as interest arises and are scheduled during the activity period on Wednesday.

After-school activities for Lower School students feature interscholastic sports, musical theater, orchestra, tae kwon do, art, and community service.

Varsity teams compete in football, soccer, cross-country, basketball, volleyball, baseball, tennis, golf, and track for boys; and cross-country, basketball, volleyball, tennis, golf, soccer, track and field, and softball for girls. Middle School teams compete against other schools in flag football, cross-country, baseball, basketball, swimming, volleyball, soccer, softball, tennis, and track. All students play a team sport or take physical education classes.

In addition to regular dances, school activities include the Talent Show, fall play, and spring musical. Special occasions in which parents participate are Back-to-School Night, Homecoming, and the annual Parents' Association fund-raiser. There is a great deal of parent involvement through various committees.

ADMISSION AND COSTS. Brentwood School seeks students who have the ability to make the best of what the School offers and the energy and interest to contribute to the life of the School. Applicants are admitted primarily in Grade 7 but also in Grades 9–10 (and very rarely in Grades 11 or 12) on the basis of previous academic records, teacher recommendations, and potential for future achievement and growth. Independent School Entrance Examination results, a personal interview with both student and parent, and a $100 application fee are required. All applications must be completed by January 28 for fall entry.

Kindergarten applications are due in mid-October, and applications for Grade 6 are due in mid-January. Admissions decisions are mailed on March 24.

In 1999–2000, tuition ranges from $11,450 in the Lower School to $13,950, plus books, in the Upper School. The one-time, new-student fee is $1000. Hot lunches are extra. Tuition payment and tuition insurance refund plans are available. Brentwood School subscribes to the School Scholarship Service and awards $1,009,000 in scholarships in Grades 7–12 on the basis of admissions criteria and clearly demonstrated need.

Dean of Faculty: Martha Kermott
Dean of Students: Joanne Huchel
Alumni Relations: Nicole Heskin
Director of Admissions (Grades 7–12): Dave Velasquez
Director of Development: Mary Sidell
College Counselors: Trish Farber, Keith Sarkisian, Lolli Lucas, and Dave Velasquez
Business Manager: Don Winter
Director of Athletics: Pat Brown
Assistant Director (Kindergarten–Grade 6): Terrie Balak

Campbell Hall NORTH HOLLYWOOD

4533 Laurel Canyon Boulevard, North Hollywood, CA 91607; Mailing Address: P.O. Box 4036, North Hollywood, CA 91617-0036. 818-980-7280; E-mail admissions@campbellhall.org; Web Site www.campbell.pvt.k12.ca.us

CAMPBELL HALL in North Hollywood, California, is a day school enrolling boys and girls in Kindergarten through Grade 12. The campus is located in a residential neighborhood of a major Los Angeles suburb.

Campbell Hall was founded in 1944 by the Reverend Alexander K. Campbell, D.D., to provide solid academic training within the context of the Judeo-Christian religious heritage. Believing that "students are persons of both faith and reason," the school endeavors to stimulate each one "to nurture a quest for knowledge and to fit this knowledge into a meaningful pattern of faith for daily living."

A nonprofit institution, Campbell Hall is governed by a self-perpetuating Board of Directors. It is affiliated with the Episcopal church through the Diocese of Los Angeles. Daily chapel attendance is required for Elementary students, while

Junior High and High School students attend semiweekly services.

Campbell Hall is accredited by the Western Association of Schools and Colleges and The California Association of Independent Schools and holds membership in The Cum Laude Society, the National Association of Episcopal Schools, the National Association of Independent Schools, the Educational Records Bureau, The College Board, and the Commission on Schools of the Los Angeles Episcopal Diocese.

THE CAMPUS. A eucalyptus grove surrounds the 14-acre campus. At its hub stands The Academic Center and The Ahmanson Library, a three-story educational resource and teaching facility. The building encompasses 11 teaching spaces, three applications labs, an elementary science lab, a high school art studio, and a library with a 35,000-volume capacity. State-of-the-art technology is available for students and teachers throughout the facility, which also includes administrative offices. Other special facilities include the Fine Arts Building and the 22,000-square-foot Garver Gymnasium/Performing Arts/Classroom complex. A second gym, two athletic fields, three outdoor basketball courts, and tennis courts provide ample space for a variety of sports.

THE FACULTY. The Reverend Canon Thomas G. Clarke was appointed Headmaster of the school in 1972. A graduate of the University of Redlands (B.A. 1967) and Virginia Theological Seminary (M.Div. 1970), he formerly served the Church of the Epiphany in the District of Columbia.

The full-time faculty includes 54 women and 29 men, while 15 instructors teach on a part-time basis. They hold 92 baccalaureate degrees, 42 master's degrees, and 4 doctoral degrees representing study at such institutions as American University, Amherst, Art Center College, Baylor, Boston University, Bryn Mawr, California Institute of Technology, California Institute of the Arts, California Lutheran, California State, Calvin, Catholic University, Chapman, Claremont Graduate School, Colby, Columbia, Emmanuel, Florida Southern, Georgetown, Gonzaga, Gordon Barrington, Harvard, Holy Names, Humboldt, Hunter, Immaculate Heart College, Indiana University, King's College (England), Lawrence, Lehigh, Longwood, Loughborough College (England), Loyola Law School, National, Ohio State, Pepperdine, San Diego State, San Francisco State, School of American Ballet, Smith, Southwestern, Stanford, Swarthmore, Tufts, Tunghai (Taiwan), United States International, University at Albany, Ursinus, Washington and Lee, Wellesley, Wesleyan, Willamette, Yale, and the Universities of California, Connecticut, Delaware, Michigan, Minnesota, Montana, New Mexico, Pennsylvania, Puget Sound, Southern California, and Wisconsin.

The school infirmary, staffed by a registered nurse, is open daily.

STUDENT BODY. Campbell Hall enrolls approximately 800 students in Kindergarten through Grade 12.

ACADEMIC PROGRAM. The school year is divided into semesters at the secondary level and trimesters at the elementary level. The calendar includes Thanksgiving break, Christmas vacation, spring break, and observance of national holidays. The daily schedules vary with the grade level, with all Elementary School classes (Kindergarten–Grade 6) convening at 8:15 A.M. Kindergarten is dismissed at 2:00 P.M., Grades 1–2 at 2:30 P.M., Grades 3–4 at 2:45 P.M., and Grades 5–6 at 3:00 P.M. Junior High classes (Grades 7–12) are in session from 8:00 A.M. to 3:15 P.M., with several 7:15 A.M. (sunrise) classes and the schedule includes breaks for chapel, an activity period, nutrition, and lunch. On Fridays, all students are dismissed by 2:15 P.M.

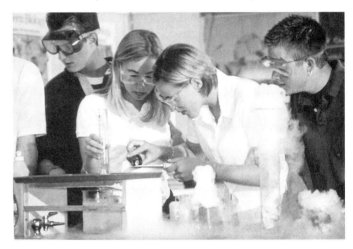

Classes meet five days a week. The student-faculty ratio is 25:1 in Kindergarten–Grade 8 and 19:1 in Grades 9–12. Academic grade reports as well as work habits and cooperation ratings are mailed home twice a semester/trimester, and a mid-period report is sent four weeks before the regular report if a student is doing below-average work. Tutoring sessions may be arranged at an additional charge.

The Elementary School program emphasizes thorough preparation in reading, mathematics, spelling, grammar, composition, literature, science, social studies, handwriting, and Spanish. Art, music, computer, library education, and physical education instruction are required. The Junior High curriculum requires seventh- and eighth-grade students to take five academic classes. Math honors is offered to qualified seventh graders. Spanish and math honors courses are offered for qualified eighth-graders. Qualified students in the eighth grade may elect to begin high-school-level courses. Seventh graders take minicourses in art, music, computers, theater, and study skills. Eighth graders are required to take two electives per year. They choose from offerings in art, music, study skills, stagecraft, film history, mock trials, yearbook, and music.

Students in Grades 7–12 study five academic solids each year plus elective courses. To graduate, High School students must complete 20 academic credits, including the following: English 4, foreign language 3, social science 3, mathematics 3, laboratory science 3, music history 1/2, art appreciation 1/2, and 3 additional credits to be chosen from social science, English, advanced mathematics, laboratory science, foreign language, or fine arts. Two years of physical education, a one-semester senior humanities course, and 50 hours of community service are also required.

The High School curriculum includes Modern World Literature and Composition, Ancient World Literature and Composition, American Literature and Composition, Senior English; Biology, Chemistry, Physics, Physiology; Ancient World History and Geography, Modern World History and Geography, United States History and Government; Ethics, Sociology, Economics; Algebra 1–2, Geometry, Pre-Calculus, Pre-Calculus Honors, Trigonometry, Trigonometry Honors, Calculus; French 1–4, Spanish 1–4, Japanese 1–3; Art History; and Music History. Typical electives include Astronomy, Ecology, Drawing, Sculpture, Printmaking, Chorus, Painting, Photography, Dance, Theater Arts, Programming and Multi-Media, Computer Applications, Yearbook, Physical Education, Weight Training, and Foundations of Visual Art. Tennis, volleyball, cross-country, eight-man tackle football, basketball, softball, baseball, soccer, and track teams are electives offered for C.I.F. competition.

Advanced Placement preparation is offered in 13 subjects. Qualified seniors participate in the UCLA Scholars Program.

Since 1996, Campbell Hall graduates have enrolled at such institutions as American University, Amherst, Barnard, Bentley, Boston University, Brandeis, Brown, Bucknell, California State, Carleton, Carnegie Mellon, Claremont McKenna, Colby, Colgate, Cornell, Dartmouth, Drew, Duke, Emory, Fordham, Georgetown, George Washington, Goucher, Hamilton, Johns Hopkins, Lake Forest, Lehigh, Massachusetts Institute of Technology, Morehouse, New York University, Northwestern, Pomona, Randolph-Macon, Rice, Rutgers, Saint Mary's, San Francisco Art Institute, Santa Clara, Skidmore, Smith, Southern Methodist, Stanford, Syracuse, Trinity, Tufts, Tulane, Vanderbilt, Vassar, Wake Forest, Wellesley, and the Universities of Arizona, California, Denver, Illinois, Massachusetts, Miami, Michigan, Northern Arizona, Northern Colorado, the Pacific, Pennsylvania, Redlands, San Diego, Southern California, Texas, Virginia, Washington, Western Ontario, and Wisconsin.

A six-week summer session offers preparatory and review as well as enrichment programs for students in Kindergarten–High School.

STUDENT ACTIVITIES. Campbell Hall has student governments at the Elementary and Secondary School. Elected and appointed representatives from each class serve on the Student Councils. Under the leadership of student body and class officers, students in Grades 2–12 assume responsibility for service and social activities.

Extracurricular organizations for Elementary School students include orchestra, chapel aides, teacher aides, math teams, dance, and cheerleaders. Organizations and clubs avail-able to Grades 7–12 include sound/video crew, honor societies, chapel aides, Junior Statesman, Amnesty International, math teams, Big/Little Sisters and Brothers, Teen Democrats and Republicans, Science, Student Council, Thespian Society, and language and service clubs.

Varsity and junior varsity teams are organized in several sports, and team competition is introduced in Grade 5. Girls take part in softball, track and field, volleyball, tennis, and basketball; the boys participate in football, track and field, volleyball, tennis, baseball, and basketball. High School students also compete in soccer and cross-country. Elementary Olympics and Junior High field days, held in the spring, engage the students in intramural-type competition.

School-sponsored field trips to programs at the Los Angeles Music Center, Los Angeles County Art Museum, Children's Museum, Norton Simon Museum, and similar sites are scheduled frequently. Attendance at some plays and concerts is required for High School students. Holiday parties are planned for all classes. Junior High students have evening dances as well as special club trips, theme days, and student productions. The High School calendar includes holiday parties, Homecoming, alumni reunions, informal dances, and two formal dinner dances. The outdoor education program provides a week's study of environmental encounters with California's geography for students in Grades 4–12: Grade 4—Sycamore Canyon, Grade 5—Camp Bloomfield, Grade 6—Camp Gilmore, Grade 7—Cedar Lake, Grade 8—Catalina, Grade 9—Joshua Tree, Grade 10—Colorado River, Grade 11—Camp Ramah, Ojai, and Grade 12—Camp JCA, Malibu.

ADMISSION AND COSTS. In evaluating an applicant, three important considerations are his or her academic potential, citizenship record, and participation in school activities. Campbell Hall seeks students from a variety of ethnic and religious backgrounds.

New students are admitted in Kindergarten–Grade 11 but rarely in Grade 12. Application should be made in the year prior to expected admission. All candidates must submit school transcripts and recommendations from two current academic teachers. A personal interview with the applicant and his or her parents is also required, as is admissions testing for each applicant.

In 1999–2000, tuition is $11,050 for Kindergarten–Grade 6 and $15,120 for Grades 7–12. There is an insurance fee for all grades and a one-time admissions charge of $500 for processing new families. Additional fees for books, supplies, and activities are approximately $500 for Kindergarten–Grade 6, $700 for Grades 7–12; a student-body fee of $45 for Grades 7 and 8 and $60 for Grades 9–12; and an environmental education fee ranging between $75 and $475 for Grades 4–12. All students wear uniforms. Tuition payment plans, loans, and financial aid are available. In 1999, 115 students received financial aid.

Director of Admissions: Alice Fleming
Director of Development: Rob Smith
Director of College Counseling: Vincent Garcia
Business Manager: Brandette Anderson
Directors of Athletics: Barbara Rodney (Girls) and Anthony Harris (Boys)

Carlthorp School   1939

438 San Vicente Boulevard, Santa Monica, CA 90402.
  310-451-1332; Fax 310-451-8559; E-mail carlthorp@earthlink.net; Web Site www.carlthorp.org

Founded by Ann Granstrom and Mercedes Thorp, Carlthorp is the city's oldest independent, nonsectarian day school. The School seeks to provide a traditional, structured approach to academics for 280 boys and girls in Kindergarten–Grade 6 with the goal of preparing them for challenging secondary schools.

The basic disciplines are presented at appropriate grade levels; Spanish is taught from Kindergarten onward. Chorus, intramural sports, art history, drama, ceramics, cooking, and chess are extracurricular activities. Tuition: $8350. Extras: $600. Financial Aid: $95,000. Dorothy Menzies (California Polytechnic [San Luis Obispo], B.S. 1967, M.Ed. 1968) was named Headmistress in 1983. *Western Association.*

Cathedral School for Boys   1957

1275 Sacramento Street, San Francisco, CA 94108. 415-771-6600; Fax 415-771-2547; E-mail dorow@csbsf.usa.com; Web Site http://www.csb.pvt.k12.ca.us

Located adjacent to Grace Cathedral (Episcopal), Cathedral School for Boys enrolls 244 day students in Kindergarten–Grade 8. The School offers a rich, challenging academic program for boys of all religious and ethnic backgrounds. Each child is encouraged to do his best, and the value of the individual and the development of mutual respect are emphasized. In Grade 3, students may audition for the Grace Cathedral Choir of Men and Boys. French, Latin, Mandarin, Spanish, music, art, drama, sports, science and computer labs, and extended care up to Grade 6 are offered. Environmental education and community service are part of the program. Tuition: $11,500–$11,750. Financial aid is available. Dorothy Sayward Wylie is Director of Admission; Michael Ferreboeuf is Canon Headmaster.

The Center for Early Education   1939

563 North Alfred Street, West Hollywood, CA 90048-2512. 323-651-0707; Fax 323-651-0860; Web Site www.cee-school.org

The Center for Early Education was founded by a group of parents who believed that children's emotional and social development were as important as their educational and academic growth. Enrolling 475 boys and girls in Preschool–Grade 6, The Center emphasizes a student body of different ethnic and socioeconomic backgrounds in a challenging, supportive setting. Team-taught curricular programs are designed to encourage students to become lifelong learners and to instill in them self-esteem, respect for each other, and commitment to the community beyond the school. Day-care, after-school, and summer programs are offered. Financial aid is available. Tuition: $4390–$11,735. Reveta Bowers is Head of School. *Western Association.*

Chadwick School   1935

26800 South Academy Drive, Palos Verdes Peninsula, CA 90274. 310-377-1543; Fax 310-377-0380; E-mail admissions@ chadwickk12.com

Chadwick School, enrolling 725 boys and girls from diverse cultural and economic backgrounds in Kindergarten–Grade 12, seeks to motivate students to pursue personal excellence in academic, athletic, and artistic endeavors. The liberal arts program emphasizes strong reading and writing skills across the disciplines. Field trips, Outdoor Education, an extensive community service program, and Upper School Advanced Placement courses enrich the core offerings. The diverse extracurricular opportunities include team sports, drama, yearbook, student government, Model U.N., and chorus. Tuition: $11,100–$13,775. Financial aid is available. Patricia G. Boig is Director of Admission; Frederick T. Hill is Headmaster. *Western Association.*

The Children's School   1972

2225 Torrey Pines Road, La Jolla, CA 92037. 619-454-0184; Fax 619-454-0186

The Children's School, enrolling 306 day boys and girls age 18 months–Grade 6, seeks to provide a success-oriented, academically challenging environment that inspires children to fulfill their potential. Using a developmental approach, faculty aim to nourish curiosity, creativity, and critical thinking through highly motivating instruction. The curriculum reflects an understanding of the physical, emotional, and intellectual growth of children. Physical education, the arts, and computer are integral to the program. A Summer School Program, an Extended Day Program, and after-school enrichment are offered. Tuition: $7300. Financial aid is available. Sarah Hillier is Admissions Director; Nancy Cohen (Sonoma State, M.A.) is Director. *Western Association.*

Chinese American International School   1981
中美國際學校

150 Oak Street, San Francisco, CA 94102. 415-865-6000; Fax 415-865-6089; Web Site www.cie-cais.org

Chinese American International School, enrolling 315 students in Pre-Kindergarten–Grade 8, provides academic programs through immersion in American and Chinese language and culture. Written and spoken fluency of English and Mandarin are emphasized through the mastery of skills in all major subjects. A background in the Chinese language is not required. Multicultural experiences, creative thinking, and developing confidence in interaction with all peoples of the world are major themes. Music, art, dance, sports, Chinese calligraphy, and a student exchange program with China are offered. Extended-care is available. Tuition and Fees: $9350–$10,300. Financial Aid: $336,000. Shirley Lee (California State [San Francisco], M.A. 1974) is Head of School.

Clairbourn School   1926

8400 Huntington Drive, San Gabriel, CA 91775. 626-286-3108; Fax 626-286-1528; E-mail admissions@clairbourn.org

Clairbourn School, an independent day school enrolling 420 boys and girls in Nursery–Grade 8, seeks to attain educational excellence in harmony with the teachings of Christian Science. Its basic elementary program is supplemented by the study of science, art, music, drama, and computers. Sports, Student Council, and scouting are scheduled after school. An academic summer program is also offered. Tuition: $5460–$8825. Financial Aid: $90,000. Janna Windsor is Director of Admissions; Robert W. Nafie (University of Minnesota, B.S. 1970; University of Wisconsin, M.A.; The Claremont Graduate School, Ph.D. 1988) was appointed Headmaster in 1979.

The College Preparatory School 1960

6100 Broadway, Oakland, CA 94618. 510-652-0111;
  Admissions 510-652-4364; Fax 510-652-4364; E-mail
  Lucia_Heldt@college-prep.org; Web Site www.college-prep.org

The College Preparatory School is a coeducational day school enrolling 338 students in Grades 9–12. The School strives to prepare students for productive, ethical lives in college and beyond through a challenging and stimulating education in an atmosphere of consideration, trust, and mutual responsibility. The rigorous academic program prepares students for Advanced Placement examinations in most subjects, and the student-teacher ratio is low. There are specialized facilities for music, art, dance, drama, and sports. Debate, class retreats, an intraterm program, and community service are integral features. Tuition: $14,750. Extras: $800. Financial Aid: $540,450. Lucia H. Heldt is Dean of Admissions; Murray Cohen (Johns Hopkins, Ph.D.) is Head of School. *Western Association.*

Convent of the Sacred Heart Elementary School 1887

2222 Broadway, San Francisco, CA 94115. 415-563-2900;
  Fax 415-929-6928; E-mail sacred.sf.ca.us;
  Web Site www.sacred.sf.ca.us

A Catholic, independent day school enrolling 324 girls in Kindergarten–Grade 8, Convent Elementary School, one of the Schools of the Sacred Heart, is part of a four-school complex including Stuart Hall for Boys, Stuart Hall High School, and Convent High School. The School seeks to prepare students for entrance into college preparatory high schools and to develop spiritual and social responsibility. Foreign languages, chorus, art, music, computer science, community service, and inter-scholastic sports are offered. A coeducational summer school program is also available. Tuition: $11,525–$11,725. Pamela

Thorp is Admissions Director; Financial aid is available. Pamela Hayes (Briarcliff College, B.A.; Manhattanville College, M.A.T.) is Head. *Western Association.*

Convent of the Sacred Heart High School 1887

2222 Broadway, San Francisco, CA 94115. 415-563-2900;
  Fax 415-292-3183; E-mail sacred.sf.ca.us; Web Site
  www.sacred.sf.ca.us

Convent of the Sacred Heart High School is part of a four-school complex including Convent Elementary School, Stuart Hall for Boys, and Stuart Hall High School. Named a National Exemplary School for a second time by the U.S. Department of Education, this Catholic, college preparatory day school enrolls 202 young women in Grades 9–12. Computer science, math, languages, science, art, music, sports, and community service are integral to the curriculum; 17 Advanced Placement courses are offered. Exchange programs with other Sacred Heart schools nationwide are available to qualified students. Tuition: $14,250. Financial aid is available. Anne Spyropoulos is Admissions Coordinator; Douglas Grant (University of San Francisco, B.S.) is Head. *Western Association.*

Cornelia Connelly School 1961

2323 West Broadway, Anaheim, CA 92804. 714-776-1717;
  Fax 714-776-2534; E-mail cornelia@exo.com

Established by the Society of the Holy Child Jesus, Cornelia Connelly is Orange County's only independent, college preparatory, Catholic high school for girls. An average class size of 18 enables students to excel in an academically challenging environment. Honors and Advanced Placement courses are available in all core subjects. Cocurricular activities include an award-winning theater arts program, varsity sports, and numerous clubs and organizations. Connelly emphasizes a holistic education that promotes self-esteem and social responsibility. In addition to rigorous academics, students are encouraged to participate in community service and faith-building activities. Tuition: $7300. Erica Lee is Director of Admissions; Sr. Francine Gunther, SHCJ, is Head of School. *Western Association.*

The Country School NORTH HOLLYWOOD

5243 Laurel Canyon Boulevard, North Hollywood, CA 91607.
  818-769-2473; Fax 818-769-2165; E-mail psinger924@aol

THE COUNTRY SCHOOL in North Hollywood, California, is a progressive, elementary day school enrolling boys and girls from 2.6 years of age through Grade 6. The School is situated in the east San Fernando Valley, about 15 minutes from downtown Los Angeles. Its location offers access to the cultural and recreational attractions of the city as well as to excellent beaches, mountains, and other natural resources.

The Country School was founded in 1948 by Rafe and Laura Ellis, educators with backgrounds in child psychology and early childhood development. Originally intended to serve preschoolers with special needs, the School soon redirected its focus to encompass a broader group. It moved to its present location in the early 1950s, and an elementary division was added in 1972.

Today, The Country School enrolls children of average to gifted ability in a developmentally appropriate program that emphasizes the needs of the individual student within an environment of balanced freedom and structure. Its mission to inspire in students a sense of competency and a lifelong love of learning is carried out by caring, nurturing teachers who provide the necessary learning tools, guidance, and support.

The Country School is guided by a 15-member Board of Trustees drawn from the parent body and from the city's academic and business communities. It is accredited by the California Association of Independent Schools and holds membership in such professional organizations as the National Association of Independent Schools, The Independent School Alliance for Minority Affairs, The Multicultural Alliance, and the Educational Records Bureau.

THE CAMPUS. The one-acre campus features two preschool buildings, a kindergarten building, a building for the elementary division, and a fifth housing administrative offices. There are also three play areas, one for the preschool and two for elementary school.

A capital development campaign will soon be under way for the expansion of the campus and facilities including the addition of a science laboratory, an art studio, and a multipurpose room as well as enlargement of the library and music rooms.

THE FACULTY. Paul M. Singer served as Head of School from 1979 to 1990 and returned to that position in February of 1994. A native of Pittsburgh, Pennsylvania, he earned a baccalaureate and two master's degrees from California State University Northridge and completed doctoral studies at the University of Southern California. Mr. Singer has extensive counseling and teaching experience and currently is an Adjunct Professor in the Department of Educational Leadership and Policy Studies at California State Northridge. He and his wife, Glenda, a first-grade teacher at The Country School, have two sons, both graduates of the School.

There are 25 full-time faculty on staff, 15 in the elementary division and 10 in the preschool. They have earned bachelor's and master's degrees from such colleges and universities as California Polytechnic, California State, Kalamazoo College, Pepperdine University, and the Universities of California (Los Angeles), Illinois, Iowa, and Missouri. Three part-time instructors teach music, computer, and art. Faculty benefits include health insurance and a retirement plan.

All staff members are trained in first aid and CPR.

STUDENT BODY. In 1998–99, The Country School enrolled 120 boys and 129 girls, from 2.6 years of age through Grade 6, as follows: 10 in the Beginner Program, 27 in the Junior Program, 34 in Pre-Kindergarten, 26 in Kindergarten, 22 in Grade 1, 27 in Grade 2, 29 in Grade 3, 24 in Grade 4, 22 in Grade 5, and 28 in Grade 6. Most students come from Beverly Hills,

Encino, Los Angeles, North Hollywood, Sherman Oaks, and Studio City. Approximately 20 percent are students of color, including African-Americans, Latinos, Asian-Americans, and Pacific Islanders. About 60 percent of the School's parents work in the entertainment industry, while the remaining are professionals and business owners.

ACADEMIC PROGRAM. The school year, from early September to early June, is divided into trimesters with 36 weeks of instruction. Vacations are scheduled at Thanksgiving, winter, and spring, and several religious and national holidays are observed. Evaluations are sent home twice a year in the preschool and three times in the elementary division. Class size varies between 12 and 30, according to age, with two teachers in every classroom. A one-hour study hall is offered after school, and teachers are available on an individual basis to tutor students not in their class. Outside tutoring can be arranged as needed.

Classes are held five days a week, from 8:30 A.M. to 2:50 P.M. in the elementary grades and from 9:00 A.M. to 2:00 P.M. in Pre-Kindergarten. On Fridays, dismissal is earlier. The three- or five-day Beginners program is conducted for three hours a day; the Junior Program operates for four hours daily, five days a week. Extended care before and after school is available.

At the preschool level, small classes and team teaching emphasize the development of social skills, self-esteem, and autonomy. Classroom instruction centers around language arts, dramatic play, art, concrete materials, manipulatives, and discovery to encourage students' curiosity and exploration. Children engage in outdoor play, science, music, puppetry, cooking, and group discussions as reinforcement of the learning experience.

In Kindergarten through Grade 6, the curriculum, which follows the mandated guidelines of the State of California, is based on mastery of basic skills that provide the foundation for strong academics. Team teaching and a low student-faculty ratio ensure that each child's unique readiness, potential, and learning style are accommodated. Language arts emphasize a love of reading, development of vocabulary, clarity of written expression, and an appreciation for literature. The math program emphasizes interactive learning, problem solving, and critical thinking. Enriching the core curriculum are activities such as music, physical education, science, art, and computer technology. Throughout the year, students compile portfolios of their work as a means of monitoring and reviewing individual progress.

Field trips, including an overnight excursion for Grades 5–6, are planned in all grades as an extension of classroom learning. As an example, first graders visit the zoo to record the environment of animals, while sixth graders gain an appreciation of the ancient Greek and Roman cultures through a tour of the Getty Museum.

The Country School collaborates with nearby Burbank

Boulevard Elementary, a public school, in a unique partnership designed to improve each school's resources and capabilities and promote multicultural harmony and understanding. Students from Burbank benefit from instruction from The Country School's technology teacher, while The Country School utilizes Burbank's auditorium for assemblies and performances. Children from both schools are involved in coordinate projects, such as music programs and visiting local nursing homes.

In a typical year, about 60 percent of graduating sixth graders enter independent secondary schools such as Brentwood, Buckley, Campbell Hall, Crossroads School for Arts & Science, Curtis, Harvard-Westlake, Marlborough, New Roads, Oakwood, Pacific Hills, and St. Michael's.

The Country School conducts a summer day camp for preschoolers featuring recreation and arts and crafts.

STUDENT ACTIVITIES. A Student Council consists of two elected representatives from each of Grades 2 through 6 and two appointed representatives from Grade 1. Members of the Council plan four special activities during the year.

After-school activities are offered ranging from tae kwon do and cooking to arts and crafts, magic, music lessons, and Shakespeare.

Students in Grades 5 and 6 may compete informally with other schools in girls' volleyball and basketball for boys and girls; interleague play is planned in the near future.

The School's most popular traditional event is the annual Variety Show in which 95 percent of the students participate. Other special activities include Back-to-School Potluck, Golf Tournament and Silent Auction, Country Fair, and the Elementary School Mini-Olympics.

ADMISSION AND COSTS. The Country School welcomes children of average to gifted ability with a wide range of interests and learning styles. It seeks diversity in its student body and does not discriminate on the basis of race, national origin, religious beliefs, or socioeconomic background. New students are admitted to the three preschool levels and Kindergarten and, in other grades, where vacancies exist. Admission is based on the parents' individual meeting with the Head of School or the Preschool Director. In addition, applicants to Kindergarten–Grade 6 spend a morning at the School for evaluation. Teacher recommendations are also required, beginning in Pre-Kindergarten. A $1000 reservation deposit is applicable to tuition.

In 1998–99, tuition ranged from $4785 for the three-day Beginner Program to $11,100 in Kindergarten–Grade 6. A one-time new family fee of $1000 is assessed in the elementary division. Other additional expenses include Kindergarten fee ($500), Parent/Support Organization and activity fee ($125), Grade 6 graduation fee ($500), and Building Fund fee ($500 per family). Extended care is offered at $8 per day or $4.50 per hour.

Crane School   1928

*1795 San Leandro Lane, Santa Barbara, CA 93108-9986.
  805-969-7732; Fax 805-969-3635;
  Web Site www.craneschool.org*

Crane School provides a traditional curriculum in which a thorough foundation in the fundamentals of English, mathematics, science, social studies, and Spanish is approached in an innovative manner. Visual arts, drama, music, athletics, and community service are essential parts of the program. Enrolling 228 day boys and girls in Kindergarten through Grade 8, Crane School seeks to provide a nurturing environment in which children may grow intellectually, realize personal creativity, develop self-assurance, and gain an appreciation of and respect for the diversity of the world around them. Tuition: $10,700–$11,700. Financial Aid: $347,000. Doris Cottam (Brigham Young University, M.S. 1988) was appointed Head of School in 1994.

Crossroads School for Arts & Sciences

SANTA MONICA

*Elementary Campus (Kindergarten–Grade 5): 1715 Olympic
  Boulevard, Santa Monica, CA 90404. 310-828-1196
Secondary Campus (Grades 6–12): 1714 21st Street, Santa Monica,
  CA 90404. 310-829-7391; Web Site www.xrds.org*

CROSSROADS SCHOOL is a college preparatory day school enrolling boys and girls in Kindergarten through Grade 12. Located in the beach community of Santa Monica, the School is housed on two campuses. Both campuses are situated near the Santa Monica Freeway, 20 minutes from downtown Los Angeles via cross-town buses, and offer students access to the cultural and educational opportunities of the entire metropolitan area.

Crossroads School was founded in 1971 by a group of educators and parents to provide a secondary education combining academic excellence with an imaginative curriculum. Housed in a local church the first year, Crossroads moved to a two-story structure on its present secondary campus site in 1972. In 1982, Crossroads School merged with St. Augustine-by-the-Sea School, allowing the School to provide K–12 education under one unifying philosophy. In 1997, the Elementary division moved to a new site within two blocks of the secondary campus. This site will house a gymnasium and playing field by 2000. The first senior class, totaling 19 members, graduated in 1976; the alumni now number 1838.

Crossroads strives to help each student develop a respect for learning, an awareness of the valuable traditions of the past, and a sense of social commitment and concern for the future of humanity. In addition, it aims to develop its students' aesthetic and imaginative faculties. To these ends, the School emphasizes a full academic curriculum, an extensive visual and performing arts program, environmental outdoor education, community service, human development, interaction between faculty and students, and parental involvement.

A nonprofit corporation, Crossroads is directed by a self-perpetuating Board of Trustees of up to 32 members, including parents and several educational consultants. The School is accredited by the Western Association of Schools and Colleges and holds membership in the National Association of Independent Schools, the California Association of Independent Schools, A Better Chance, The College Board, the Independent School Alliance for Minority Affairs, Network of Performing Arts Schools, and The Cum Laude Society. In 1984, the United States Department of Education named Crossroads as one of 60 Exemplary Independent Schools in America.

THE CAMPUS. Crossroads School's secondary campus occupies 17 properties in an industrial area two miles east of the Pacific Ocean. The Trives Administration Building houses offices, a photographic laboratory, a faculty lounge, and the Roth Gallery, a facility used for recitals and concerts that also contains a recording studio. The Upper School classroom building contains ten classrooms, a film-editing room, science laboratories, a language lab, a writing center, faculty and administrative offices, a counseling center, and a ceramics studio. The Stephen Morgan Middle School classroom building holds classrooms, science laboratories, a computer center, and administrative and faculty offices. The Upper School Administration Building provides administrative and faculty offices and a dance/gymnasium area. The Crossroads Theatre, which seats 150, is used for plays, musical performances, and assemblies. The 15,000-square-foot Peter Boxenbaum Memorial Arts Education Centre houses rehearsal and instruction space for music and dance, exhibit areas for visual arts, dressing rooms with showers and lockers, offices, a film-screening room, classrooms, and central gathering places. The Paul Cummins Library houses the school library, three special collections rooms, a computer center, a resource center, and three integrated math/science laboratory classrooms. The Keck Science Center features four science laboratories. Other facilities include a weight-training room, a drama scene shop, and a student lunch area. Several patios, two parking lots, and a basketball court complete the campus. The plant is valued at an estimated $20,000,000.

THE FACULTY. Roger Weaver, appointed Headmaster in 1993, received his B.A. in English from the University of California at Santa Barbara and a Master's in Education from the University of California at Los Angeles. Mr. Weaver is a founder of the Independent School Alliance for Minority Education and serves on the boards of the Ojai Foundation and School and the Eureka Communities Foundation. Paul Cummins, Headmaster

of 22 years, is now President of the School and Executive Director of the Crossroads Community Foundation, with special focus on community outreach and long-range planning.

The full-time faculty number 97, 52 men and 45 women. Fifty-three instructors teach part-time. Seventy-one faculty hold master's degrees; 4 hold doctorates. The School provides teachers with health, dental, and disability insurance; a retirement plan; and an allowance for professional development and summer study. A full-time nurse is available at the School, and Santa Monica Hospital is located approximately one mile away.

STUDENT BODY. In 1999–2000, Crossroads School enrolled 489 students in the Upper School, 354 in the Middle School, and 312 in the Elementary School. The students are from Southern California and ten foreign countries.

ACADEMIC PROGRAM. The school year, from early September to mid-June, is divided into semesters, with winter and spring vacations as well as several national and religious holidays.

There are two class homeroom sections for each elementary grade (Kindergarten–Grade 5). The integrated curriculum is based on social studies concepts outlined for the year. Nine specialist teachers in science, art, music, dance, drama, physical education, library media, Spanish, and technology work with the homeroom teachers to bring social studies concepts to life across many disciplines. In keeping with the philosophy, teachers at the Elementary School acknowledge and support different styles of learning, different levels of development, and different types of intelligence. Student evaluations are written three times yearly, and parent conferences are held twice yearly.

Middle School students (Grades 6–8) take courses in English, history, Latin (except Grade 6), mathematics, computer studies, Environmental Outdoor Education, Human Development, science, the arts (music, drama, visual arts), and physical education.

Upper School students (Grades 9–12) must take a minimum of four academic classes each semester. Students planning to apply to the more competitive colleges take five or six academic classes. The minimum graduation requirements are four years of English, three of mathematics, four of Human Development (including physical education), and two years each of history, foreign language, laboratory science, and art. Offerings include Classical Greek, Latin, Great Books, European and American film, Ethics, and many courses in the arts for nonmajors. Majors are available in music, drama, and visual art. These major programs admit students who undertake a demanding program of 10–15 hours weekly in their discipline in addition to fulfilling all graduation requirements. Upper School students may earn university credit in the following Advanced Placement courses: Art History, Biology, Calculus AB, Chemistry, English, French, Latin, Music Theory, Physics, Spanish, and Studio Art.

Honors courses are offered in Algebra, English, Geometry, Great Books, and U.S. History.

Because Crossroads believes deeply in holistic education that goes beyond the academic, the School requires that all students in Grades 6–12 participate in Human Development classes and the Community Service program. The School offers a Comprehensive Environmental Outdoor Education Program.

Of the 118 graduates in the Class of 1999, 117 went on to college. They are attending such colleges, conservatories, and universities as Amherst, Barnard, Boston University, Brown, Claremont McKenna, Columbia, Georgetown, Harvard, New York University, Northwestern, Occidental, Parsons, Pitzer, Reed, Rhode Island School of Design, Scripps, Skidmore, Smith, Stanford, Swarthmore, Tufts, Tulane, Vassar, Wesleyan, Wheaton, Yale, and the Universities of Arizona, California, Chicago, Colorado, Michigan, Oregon, Pennsylvania, and Southern California.

STUDENT ACTIVITIES. The elected Student Councils meet regularly and maintain close and open communications with the administration, staff, and faculty. The councils provide a forum for student concerns and discussion of school policy.

Varsity teams compete with nearby independent schools and those in the California Interscholastic Federation. Boys' teams are fielded in baseball, basketball, cross-country, soccer, track, tennis, and volleyball. Girls compete in basketball, cross-country, soccer, softball, tennis, and volleyball.

ADMISSION AND COSTS. Crossroads School—Secondary Campus seeks self-motivated students with a well-developed sense of responsibility. New students are admitted to the Middle School on the basis of previous transcripts, two academic recommendations, an administrative recommendation, results of the Independent School Entrance Examination (ISEE) in English and mathematics, and a personal interview. Upper School applicants must submit ISEE scores, transcripts, and academic recommendations; personal interviews are also required. Formal closing date for applications is December 31, but candidates for admission are urged to apply early in the fall for enrollment the following year. There is a $100 application fee.

In 1999–2000, tuition is $15,730 for Grades 6–12 and $13,246 for Kindergarten–Grade 5. Extras include $300 for various fees and art materials. In 1999–2000, members of the student body received $2,200,000 in financial aid, which is awarded on the basis of need. Tuition insurance is available.

Director of Upper School: Bob Riddle
Director of Middle School: Morgan Schwartz
Director of Elementary School: Joan Martin
Director of International Education: Jim Hahn
Dean of Faculty: Douglas C. Thompson
Director of Admissions: Gennifer Yoshimaru

Crystal Springs Uplands School   1952

400 Uplands Drive, Hillsborough, CA 94010. 650-342-4175;
  Fax 650-342-7623; E-mail jblak@CSUS.com

Crystal Springs Uplands School is a college preparatory day school enrolling 350 boys and girls in Grades 6–12. It seeks to maintain an atmosphere of "rigorous demand balanced by sensitive human support and trust" and cultivates the desire for lifelong learning. Its traditional curriculum is complemented by fine arts, competitive interscholastic sports, and Advanced Placement courses in all subjects. Student government, publications, drama, dance, and clubs are some of the activities. Tuition: $14,300. Financial Aid: $580,000. Richard A. Drew (Amherst, B.A. 1961; Stanford, M.A. 1966; Colorado School of Education, Ed.S. 1978) was appointed Headmaster in 1989. *Western Association.*

Curtis School   LOS ANGELES

15871 Mulholland Drive, Los Angeles, CA 90049. 310-476-1251;
  Web Site curtisschool.com

CURTIS SCHOOL in Los Angeles, California, is an independent day school enrolling boys and girls in Developmental Kindergarten through Grade 8. The campus is situated in suburban Los Angeles, adjacent to the San Diego Freeway and the top of the Sepulveda Pass. The School takes advantage of the opportunities afforded in the Los Angeles area for field trips to sites of historical, cultural, and environmental interest. Students travel to and from school on buses provided by an independent company or in car pools arranged by parents.

Curtis School was founded in 1925 as a proprietary school by Carl Curtis and was continued after a 1937 reorganization by his nephew, Carl F. Curtis. In 1964, the School was purchased by Willard E. Badham, who had been the athletic director for 18 years, and two partners. Over the next 10 years, enrollment grew from 100 to 400 under his leadership. The School was reorganized as a nonprofit corporation in 1975, and Mr. Badham continued as Headmaster. Curtis School moved to the Mulholland site in 1981.

Since its founding, the goal of Curtis School has been to provide sound academic training and to develop young people who are thoughtful, creative, and responsible citizens. A standard dress or uniform is worn in all grades. Morals and values are emphasized in daily teaching. Students also organize service projects to help the needy or handicapped. Because of the value the School places on a sound body, physical education and athletics are vital to the program, and all students engage in physical education daily.

Curtis School is governed by a self-perpetuating Board of 27 Trustees, which meets six times a year. The School is accredited by the Western Association of Colleges and Schools and holds membership in the National Association of Independent Schools and The California Association of Independent Schools, among other affiliations. The Parents' Association and the Alumni Association, which represents 2500 living graduates, assist the School in social, cultural, and fund-raising activities.

THE CAMPUS. The 27-acre campus, shaded by mature trees including many California redwoods, is located in the Santa Monica Mountains and is normally cooled by breezes off the ocean. Athletic fields and grassy malls surround low-rise, Spanish mission-style buildings with red tile roofs and functional design.

In addition to regular classroom buildings, the main features are the Ahmanson Building, a multipurpose structure housing the auditorium, and art, music, and science rooms; the library/administration facility; and the new Pavilion, a performing arts/gymnasium complex. The School library contains more than 14,000 volumes. In addition to fields for football, baseball, soccer, and track, other athletic facilities include an outdoor gymnastic pavilion, a 25-yard heated swimming pool, a volleyball court, three tennis courts, a handball/racquetball court, and three basketball courts.

The School-owned plant is valued at $20,000,000.

THE FACULTY. Stephen E. Switzer was appointed Headmaster of Curtis School in 1997. A graduate of Hanover College (B.A.) and Oberlin College (M.A.), he had previously headed Le Jardin Academy in Kailua, Hawaii; Episcopal Day School in Jackson, Tennessee; The Lotspeich School in Cincinnati, Ohio; and Community School in St. Louis, Missouri. Mr. Switzer is the past president of the Hawaii Association of Independent Schools and serves on the Board of Directors of the Council for Religion in Independent Schools. His wife, Patricia, was a teaching assistant in the Early Learning Center of Le Jardin Academy. She also taught science in summer school and was involved in the Upper School Outdoor Adventure Education Program. The Switzers are the parents of five children.

The faculty consists of 39 women and 12 men. They hold 51 baccalaureate and 19 advanced degrees, representing study at such institutions as Adelphi, Antioch, Asbury College, California State, Connecticut College, Columbia University, Claremont Graduate School, Illinois State, Immaculate Heart, International University, Linfield, Loyola Marymount, Miami University, Montclair State, Mount St. Mary's, New York University, Oregon College, Pepperdine, Pratt Institute, Princeton, Rhodes, San Diego State, State University of New York, Springfield College, Temple, Wake Forest, Wayne State, Westfield College, Wheaton, Williams, and the Universities of Alabama, California, Chicago, Colorado, Leister (England), North Carolina, Oklahoma, and Virginia.

Faculty benefits include health insurance, a retirement plan, Social Security, educational and personal development grants, and leaves of absence.

A health officer is on duty full-time at the School, and emergency facilities are available nearby at the UCLA Hospital.

STUDENT BODY. In 1998–99, Curtis School enrolled 270 day boys and 248 day girls in Pre-Kindergarten–Grade 8. The enrollments were distributed as follows: 20 in Developmental Kindergarten, 63 in Kindergarten, 63 in Grade 1, 62 in Grade 2, 63 in Grade 3, 63 in Grade 4, 67 in Grade 5, 66 in Grade 6, 32 in Grade 7, and 22 in Grade 8. Students represented Bel Air, Malibu, Marina del Rey, Pacific Palisades, Santa Monica, and other communities in the Los Angeles area.

ACADEMIC PROGRAM. Curtis School offers a well-balanced academic program, with necessary skills taught in lively and creative ways designed to teach students to read, write, speak, compute, and reason.

Most students enter Curtis in Developmental Kindergarten or Kindergarten. The Lower School (DK–Grade 3) aims to foster the natural curiosity and love of learning in young children. Reading is taught balancing elements of both phonics and whole language, and literature is a part of every classroom. The language arts curriculum stresses written and oral expression as well as the fundamental skills of grammar and spelling. The mathematics program also seeks a balance between conceptual understanding, problem solving, and the acquisition of basic skills. Social studies, a lab-based, hands-on science program, computers, and library round out the academic program.

The Middle School (Grades 4–8) focuses on the skills and attitudes needed for secondary school success. Writing, reasoning, and experiential and cooperative learning are emphasized. The English program continues to utilize literature with focus on comprehension and fluency. Writing remains at the core of the program, and students explore poetry and a variety of other genres. The formal written report is also a key part of the Middle School experience. The structure of language—grammar, syntax, and usage—increases in importance at these grade levels. Mathematics embraces a broad range of concepts and skills, incorporating the use of calculators and computers. The social studies and science programs become more project-oriented and are integrated with other subjects whenever possible. Students learn computer and technology skills appropriate to the age group. Many students go on to leading secondary schools at the conclusion of Grade 6.

Grades 7 and 8 form a bridge between elementary and secondary school for those students who would benefit from a small and structured environment. Each student has two periods of English per day with special emphasis placed on writing skills. Math, social studies, and a lab-based science program are also central to the academics. Additional tutorial periods are offered, and students act as "study buddies" for the younger children. Seventh and eighth graders participate in several outdoor experiences designed to build teamwork and raise self-esteem, and parents and children attend a drug awareness/healthy choice program in the fall. Teachers provide the support and attention needed to prepare students for secondary school, and most Curtis graduates matriculate to strong independent and parochial schools for Grade 9.

The arts form an essential part of the Curtis curriculum. Holiday and Spring Concerts are annual events, and drama performances, poetry recitals, and dramatic readings are organized on a regular basis by individual teachers or through the after-school Curtis Extension Program.

STUDENT ACTIVITIES. Representatives from Grades 4 through 8 are elected to the Student Council, which organizes school activities, assists at various functions, and acts as a liaison among students, faculty, and administration.

Students are chosen to be staff contributors to the *Curtis Chronicle,* a quarterly newspaper devoted to news and student literary works. Other students publish the yearbook. The Curtis Choraliers and other musical groups rehearse and perform on a regular basis.

Athletics are a major component of the Curtis program. Virtually every Curtis student has a sports class each day, and more than 90 percent of students in Grades 4–8 participate in the extensive interscholastic sports program, which emphasizes sportsmanship and fair play. Girls' team sports include volleyball, basketball, soccer, and track, while boys' teams compete in flag football, soccer, baseball, basketball, and track. Students in all age groups swim and learn water safety skills in the Curtis pool.

Field trips, many of them subject-related, are planned for all grades to take advantage of the cultural, historical, and community activities in the Los Angeles area. The Performing Tree, a community resource, presents a wide range of performing arts events for the entire School. Grades 5 and 6 take field trips to eastern cities, including Washington, D.C., during the spring break.

Special events on the school calendar include the Family Picnic, Curtis Fair, American Appreciation Day, Science Expo, Holiday Program, Spring Sing, and Dad's Day.

ADMISSION AND COSTS. The Curtis School seeks all-around students who will be good citizens. Students are accepted in all grades on the basis of entrance examinations and standardized test results, personal and teacher recommendations, and an interview at the School. Late applicants are sometimes accepted during the year if vacancies exist. A $100 fee is required with the application.

Tuition and fees are $11,400 for Kindergarten–Grade 6 and $13,100 for Grades 7–8. Uniforms, transportation, and field trip charges are extra. There is a one-time New Family Fee of $1000. Tuition insurance and payment plans are offered. The School awards $425,000 annually in financial aid on the basis of need.

Alumni Secretary: Mrs. Jan Valencia
Director of Admissions: Mrs. Mimi Petrie
Director of Development: Mr. Rick Wilson
Business Manager: Mrs. Beth Armstrong
Director of Athletics: Mr. David Pappin

Drew College Preparatory School   1908

2901 California Street, San Francisco, CA 94115. 415-346-4831

Educator John Drew founded this coeducational day school, which currently enrolls 185 students from diverse backgrounds in Grades 9–12. Situated in a residential area, Drew seeks to motivate young people to fulfill their individual potential through a challenging academic program. The curriculum focuses on the development of strong foundations in core disciplines, strengthened by honors and Advanced Placement courses and varied electives. English as a Second Language is available to a few qualified students. Students participate in school government, sports, music, the arts, Adventure Society, and community service. A summer program is offered. Tuition: $14,900. Financial Aid: $423,000. Elizabeth Tilden is Director of Admissions; Samuel M. Cuddeback III was appointed Headmaster in 1991.

Dunn School   1957

*P.O. Box 98, Los Olivos, CA 93441. 805-688-6471;
    Fax 805-686-2078; E-mail cadunnadmk@impresso.com*

Dunn is a coeducational, college preparatory school enrolling 110 boarders in Grades 9–12 and 87 day students in Grades 6–12. Honors and Advanced Placement courses are available. A Learning Skills Program offers additional assistance for a limited number of students with language difficulties. Extracurricular opportunities include sports, publications, clubs, and a weekend activities program. Boarding Tuition: $24,500; Day Tuition: $11,200; Learning Skills Program: $8800. Financial Aid: $250,000. James H. Matchin is Director of Admissions; James L. Munger is Headmaster. *Western Association.*

Flintridge Preparatory School   1933

*4543 Crown Avenue, La Cañada Flintridge, CA 91011.
    818-790-1178; Fax 818-952-6247*

Flintridge Preparatory School is a fully accredited, college preparatory day school enrolling 500 boys and girls in Grades 7–12. Located in the foothills above the Pasadena Rose Bowl, the School provides modern classroom and laboratory facilities and an athletic plant featuring a year-round Olympic swimming complex. A traditional curriculum is offered and a full program of interscholastic athletics and extracurricular activities is available. Tuition: $10,600–$11,200. Financial Aid: $445,000. Peter H. Bachmann (University of California, B.A.; University of Virginia, M.A.) was appointed Headmaster in 1991.

Foothill Country Day School   1954

*1035 West Harrison Avenue, Claremont, CA 91711. 909-626-5681;
    Fax 909-624-4251; Web Site www.foothillcds.org*

Foothill Country Day was founded by Howell and Betty Webb to provide an exciting environment in which children reach their full potential and develop character and values. The School enrolls 180 girls and boys in Kindergarten–Grade 8 and children ages 3–5 in a preschool program. The challenging curriculum emphasizes mastery of skills in core subjects, including Latin and Spanish, with enrichment in computer technology, library skills, drama, music, art, and physical education. Small classes and a structured program enable students to reach their educational goals. Each grade produces an annual play; students participate in community service, field trips, and daily chapel programs. After-school and summer programs are available. Tuition: $6595–$6895. Eleanor Pierson is Director of Admissions; Mark W. Lauria, Ph.D., is Headmaster.

The Hamlin School   1863

*2120 Broadway, San Francisco, CA 94115. 415-922-0300;
    Fax 415-674-5409; E-mail denezza@hamlin.org; Web Site
    www.hamlin.org*

The oldest nonsectarian day school for girls in the West, Hamlin enrolls 400 girls in Kindergarten–Grade 8. The School seeks to educate talented young women to meet the challenges of their times. It provides a balanced curriculum of humanities, science, mathematics, and fine arts in facilities that include the 11,000-volume Edward E. Hills Library, two science laboratories, a computer center, art studios, and a theater. Extended-day care and after-school activities are offered and intermural sports are scheduled after classes. Summer and vacation camps are available. Tuition: $11,785. Financial Aid: $467,000. Patricia DeNezza is Director of Admission; Coreen R. Hester (Stanford University, B.A., M.Ed.) is Head of the School.

California

Harbor Day School   1952

3443 Pacific View Drive, Corona del Mar, CA 92625.
949-640-1410; Fax 949-640-0908; E-mail sdupont@hds.
pvt.k12.ca.us

Harbor Day School, an elementary school enrolling 400 boys
and girls in Kindergarten–Grade 8, is located on a six-acre site
overlooking the Pacific. The School has a challenging academic
program and is committed to providing an environment conducive to the development of character and good citizenship.
Facilities include a library of more than 11,000 volumes, two
fully equipped science laboratories, three computer science laboratories, two art studios, a woodshop, a gymnasium, and athletic fields. Tuition: $9200. Financial aid is available. Mrs. Kris-
ten Rowe is Lower School Director; Sidney I. DuPont (Central
Connecticut State University, B.S. 1963, M.S. 1967; University
of Connecticut, Ph.D. 1976) is Headmaster. *Western Association.*

The Harker School   1893

Kindergarten–Grade 6: 4300 Bucknall Road, San Jose, CA 95130.
408-871-4600; Fax 408-871-4320
Grades 7–12: 500 Saratoga Avenue, San Jose, CA 95129.
408-249-2510; Fax 408-984-2325; Web Site www.harker.org

Founded in 1893, Harker offers a coeducational, independent
program for 1050 students in kindergarten through high
school. Covering 10-acre and 16-acre campuses, Harker blends
strong college preparatory academics with rich offerings in
technology, the arts, and athletics. New state-of-the-art
facilities, including a technology center, expanded library, and
athletic and performing arts centers, are planned. Full-day
activities are available for day students. Boarding for Grades 5
through 8, an internationally renowned summer camp, and
English as a Second Language programs are also offered.
Boarding Tuition: $26,000–$29,500; Day Tuition: $13,200–
$15,200. Howard E. Nichols (Stanford, B.A. 1963) is President.

Harvard-Westlake School   1989

Grades 7–9: 700 North Faring Road, Los Angeles, CA 90077.
310-274-7281; Fax 310-273-9560
Grades 10–12: 3700 Coldwater Canyon, North Hollywood, CA
91604. 818-980-6692; Fax 818-769-1743; Web Site http://www.
harvardwestlake.com

Harvard-Westlake is a college preparatory day school enrolling
1530 boys and girls in Grades 7–12. The School seeks able,
interested students who reflect the diversity of Greater Los
Angeles. It aims to provide an education that enables students
to appreciate and develop their spiritual, intellectual, and emotional gifts. Music, arts, and publications are offered; Advanced
Placement courses are available in all disciplines. Community

service and sports are extracurricular activities. There are student exchanges with Japanese and Russian schools and a summer program. Tuition: $14,450. Elizabeth Gregory is Director
of Admission; Thomas C. Hudnut (Princeton, A.B. 1969; Tufts,
A.M. 1970) is Headmaster. *Western Association.*

The Head-Royce School   1887

4315 Lincoln Avenue, Oakland, CA 94602. 510-531-1300;
Fax 510-530-8329; E-mail cland@hrs.pvt.k12.ca.us; Web Site
hrs.pvt.k12.ca.us

The Head-Royce School is an independent, coeducational day
school enrolling 735 students in Kindergarten–Grade 12. The
School offers a challenging program in the liberal arts and sci-
ences in a supportive environment. Honors and Advanced
Placement courses and accelerated programs at the University
of California and Mills College are available in the Upper
School. Tuition: $9800–$14,450. Financial Aid: $800,000. Crys-
tal Land is Director of Admission and Financial Aid; Paul D.
Chapman (Yale, B.A.; Stanford, M.A., Ph.D.) was appointed
Head of the School in 1984. *Western Association.*

Idyllwild Arts Academy   IDYLLWILD

P.O. Box 38, 52500 Temecula Road, Idyllwild, CA 92549-0038.
909-659-2171; E-mail behnke@pe.net;
Web Site www.idyllwildarts.org

IDYLLWILD ARTS ACADEMY in Idyllwild, California, is a boarding
and day school offering training in the preprofessional arts
and a college preparatory academic program in Grades 8
through 12 and a postgraduate year. Located in the San Jacinto
Mountains, the Academy is surrounded by more than 20,000
acres of protected forest and park land. The village of Idyllwild,
a community of 2500 year-round residents, is a center for
wilderness enthusiasts who make use of hundreds of miles of
hiking trails, boating and fishing opportunities in nearby lakes
and creeks, and cross-country ski trails. Idyllwild is about 100
miles from San Diego, 125 miles from Los Angeles, and 55
miles from Palm Springs.

Dr. Max and Beatrice Krone founded the Idyllwild Arts
Foundation in 1946. The school opened in 1950 as a summer
program for 100 students in that year. The summer program,
which reached an enrollment of more than 2000 children and
adults as it developed, was the core program for much of the
school's history, including 19 years during which it operated
under the auspices of the University of Southern California. In

1986, the year-round boarding Arts Academy was established with a full academic program in addition to pre-professional training in the performing and visual arts. Graduates meet University of California admission standards.

The Arts Academy seeks to prepare students for further education, for advanced arts studies, and for adult life as contributing, productive members of society. The Academy believes in a quality education that places demands on both faculty and students, who in turn must be committed to the good of the school community. Idyllwild Arts Academy is accredited by the Western Association of Schools and Colleges and is a member of the National Association of Independent Schools, California Association of Independent Schools, Network of Performing and Visual Arts Schools, Western Boarding Schools, and other professional organizations.

THE CAMPUS. The Academy is situated on 205 acres at an elevation of more than 5000 feet in the midst of a pine forest. Strawberry Creek flows through the campus, which also has playing fields, a swimming pool, and miles of riding and hiking trails.

The main buildings were constructed in the 1950s, 1960s, and 1980s and some have undergone recent renovation. These include: Rush Hall, an all-purpose building used for lectures, concerts, receptions, and assemblies; Idyllwild Arts Foundation Theatre, which seats 400 for concerts, dance, and theatrical performances; Bowman Arts Center, with administrative offices; Birchard Library and Studio; the Bella Lewitzky Studio and Fugl Studio for dance; a dining hall; science laboratories; Husch Hall, MacNeal Hall, Pierson Hall, and Oak and Manzanita chalets, all residential facilities; classrooms; and several other studio buildings for the various arts. The Holmes Amphitheatre and a number of dance platforms are available for outdoor rehearsal and performance. A new, state-of-the-art library will open in March 2000.

THE FACULTY. William M. Lowman, a graduate of the University of Redlands (A.B.), is Headmaster of the Arts Academy. A recipient of the Nevada Governor's Arts Award, Mr. Lowman founded the Nevada School for the Arts. He is a board member of the International NETWORK of Performing and Visual Arts Schools, the Committee on Boarding Schools, and serves as Executive Director of the Idyllwild Arts Foundation.

The full-time faculty, including administrators who teach, number 12 women and 15 men. All have distinguished themselves either as academic teachers or as professional artists by performance in music, dance, or theater in the United States and abroad, or by exhibition of their work in recognized galleries. They hold baccalaureate and graduate degrees from such institutions as Colby, Colgate, Massachusetts Institute of Technology, Middlebury, Northern Arizona, Oberlin, Wayne State, Scripps, Southern Methodist, Stanford, and the Universities of California (Los Angeles), Pennsylvania, and Southern California. Prominent performing artists are in residence at various

times during the academic year to conduct master classes and give performance examples.

STUDENT BODY. In 1999–2000, the Academy enrolled 132 boarding girls, 66 boarding boys, and 38 day students in Grades 8–12 and a postgraduate year. The enrollments are distributed as follows: 8 in Grade 8, 28 in Grade 9, 65 in Grade 10, 64 in Grade 11, and 77 in Grade 12. A majority of the students are from the Southwest; a total of 30 states and 13 foreign countries are represented.

ACADEMIC PROGRAM. The academic year, divided into semesters, begins in early September and ends in late May with vacations of three weeks at Christmas, two weeks in the spring, and extended weekends at Thanksgiving, Easter, and between terms. Classes are held Monday through Friday and on Saturday mornings beginning at 7:30 A.M. Academic classes are scheduled in the mornings and arts classes in the afternoons.

To graduate, students must complete 14 academic units in addition to their regular arts curriculum. The academic units must include: 4 units of English, 2 of foreign language, 3 of social studies, 3 of mathematics, 2 of sciences, 2 of physical education, and one semester of computer literacy.

In the arts program, students choose a major and plan individual schedules with faculty members and the Dean of the Arts. They choose among areas of study including music, dance, theater, technical theater, visual arts, and creative writing. For students wishing to explore all the arts, the interdisciplinary arts major can be pursued, provided the student has a 3.0 grade point average upon making application to the Arts Academy. Each program incorporates courses in four categories: theory, history, and fundamentals of the form; creation, production, presentation, or performance; specialized master classes and private instruction; and field trips to arts communities of Southern California to observe professionals at work.

Postgraduates engage in a one-year intensive program in the arts and are admitted with proof of graduation and a demonstration of talent through audition or portfolio.

Students are placed in arts courses according to levels of ability and experience and advance on the basis of performance. Among the regular courses offered are: Dance 1–3, Dance Ensemble, Ballet, Modern Dance, Pointe, Jazz, Men's Class, Pas de Deux, Dance Composition; Music Fundamentals, Introduction to Music Literature, Ear Training/Sight Singing, Music Theory, Music History, Voice Class, Chamber Music, Musical Ensembles, Class Piano, Piano Proficiency, Accompaniment, Repertoire Class; Voice and Diction, Technical Theatre, Drama History and Literature, Movement, Playwriting, Directing, Stage Design; Drawing and Painting, Art History, Ceramics, Sculpture, Printmaking, Design and Aesthetics, Photography, Computer Graphics Illustration; and Creative Writing courses in Fiction, Poetry, Short Stories, Literary Criticism, and Playwriting.

All of the 73 graduates in the Class of 1999 chose to continue their education. They matriculated at such colleges as Bard, Boston University, California Institute of the Arts, Carnegie Mellon, Chicago Art Institute, Columbia, Cornish School of the Arts, DePaul, Eastman School of Music, Hartt Conservatory, Johns Hopkins, Juilliard, New York University, Oberlin Conservatory, Rhode Island School of Design, Rice, San Francisco Art Institute, Smith, Stanford, State University of New York (Purchase), Wesleyan, Yale, and the Universities of California (Los Angeles, San Diego, Santa Cruz), Michigan (Ann Arbor), Nevada (Las Vegas), and Southern California.

Idyllwild Arts has a summer performing and visual arts program. The Summer Arts Program offers courses of weekend to two-weeks length for students of all ages. These include a Children's Arts Center, Creative Writing (youth and adults), Native American Arts, and comprehensive offerings in Jazz, Chamber Music, Dance, Theatre, Musical Theatre, and Visual Arts.

STUDENT ACTIVITIES. Students elect a student government, which, with the help of faculty advisers, organizes entertainment and other activities.

Clubs are organized around the arts majors, and there are clubs for hiking, bicycling, and rock climbing. Dances, concerts, and dramatic performances are scheduled on a regular basis.

On weekends, students enjoy the cultural attractions of the Los Angeles and San Diego areas—museums, theaters, art galleries, and concert halls. They also have access to many world-famous recreational areas including Disneyland, Knott's Berry Farm, Magic Mountain, Sea World, and the San Diego Zoo and Wild Animal Park.

ADMISSION AND COSTS. The Idyllwild Arts Academy seeks dedicated, motivated, and talented arts students. They are admitted in Grades 8–12 and a postgraduate year on the basis of academic transcripts, recommendations, a personal interview, and a demonstration of potential through audition or portfolio. Applications, with a fee of $35, can be made at any time and are accepted until quotas are filled in each major. Students can be admitted at midyear if space is available.

In 1999–2000, boarding tuition is $27,175; day tuition, $14,970. The Academy subscribes to the School Scholarship Service and awards approximately $1,800,000 in financial aid annually on the basis of talent and financial need. A tuition payment plan is available.

Dean of Academics: Sharon Adams
Dean of Arts: Nelms McKelvain
Dean of Students: Sean Owen
Dean of Admission: Anne Behnke
Director of Advancement (Development): Jill Burbidge
College Counselors: Don Put and Jill Jewell
Director of Athletics: Peyton Bray
Business Manager: Clyde Gibson

The John Thomas Dye School

LOS ANGELES

11414 Chalon Road, Los Angeles, CA 90049. 310-476-2811;
Fax 310-476-9176; E-mail rmichaud@jtdschool.com;
Web Site jtdschool.com

THE JOHN THOMAS DYE SCHOOL in Los Angeles, California, is an independent, coeducational day school enrolling approximately 325 students from Preschool through Grade 6. The campus occupies 11 hilltop acres in Bel Air overlooking Santa Monica, Palos Verdes, and the Pacific Ocean. The homelike and inviting campus provides a country environment in the midst of the Greater Los Angeles urban area. Students enjoy easy access to the city's parks, zoo, museums, libraries, and performing arts centers. They are within reach of nearby beaches, mountains, and national parks.

In 1929, founders Cathryn Robberts Dye and her husband, John Thomas Dye II, started the Brentwood Town and Country School in their home for their only son, John Thomas Dye III, and his friends. Known to their students as Aunty Cathryn and Uncle John, the Dyes sought to nurture children in a loving atmosphere.

The School's reputation for academic excellence, strong ethics, and its unique learning environment attracted many new students. By 1949, the School had outgrown its home. A new, larger facility called The Bel Air Town and Country School was built on the present site. In 1959, the School was renamed in honor of John Thomas Dye III, who was killed in action during World War II. Mr. and Mrs. Dye served as Headmaster and Headmistress until they retired in 1963.

The vision of the founders is being carried into the 21st century by a new generation of leadership. Building on the history and core strength of the School, the present Headmaster, Raymond R. Michaud, Jr., and his elected 21-member Board of Trustees, strive to prepare children for a rapidly changing world. The basics—reading, writing, mathematics, science, history, the arts, athletics, problem solving, self-esteem, social skills, and respect for individuality—are still at the heart of the program. Because technology skills and the ability to gather and process information are vital to today's children, the entire School is linked by a state-of-the-art computer network to the Internet and the Worldwide Web.

The John Thomas Dye School, a nonprofit corporation, is accredited by the Western Association of Schools and Colleges and the California Association of Independent Schools. It is a member of the National Association of Independent Schools. One hundred percent of the School's endowment fund is actively invested. There are 1200 living alumni, many of whom continue their relationship with the School through a variety of supportive activities, including Development.

THE CAMPUS. At the center of the campus is John Dye Hall, which houses administrative offices, an assembly hall, a music room, and computer and science labs. Classrooms are located in two identical wings extending east and west from the main building. The Lower School (Preschool, Prekindergarten, and Kindergarten) is located in a separate adjoining building. A multipurpose facility on the lower field furnishes a spacious gymnasium, an art studio, and a library with more than 8000 volumes. Also on the grounds are two large outdoor play areas for the younger children and an athletic field for the physical education and after-school sports program. The plant is owned by the School.

THE FACULTY. Raymond R. Michaud, Jr., has been affiliated with The John Thomas Dye School for 21 years and has been its Headmaster since 1980. He holds a bachelor's degree in History from the University of San Francisco, where he was also Assistant Director of Admissions. He received his M.A. in Educational Psychology from California Lutheran University and has held teaching and administrative positions at Harvard-Westlake School in Los Angeles.

All 42 men and women on the full-time faculty hold baccalaureates, and one-third have earned advanced degrees. Faculty benefits include medical/dental/vision plans, life insurance, a retirement and flexible spending plan, Social Security, and long-term disability. All faculty and staff are trained in first aid and CPR by the Red Cross, and medical emergencies are handled at the nearby UCLA Medical Center.

STUDENT BODY. Students come primarily from West Los Angeles, but also from many different areas of the city and its suburbs. They are about evenly divided between boys and girls. There are two classes each in Kindergarten through Grade 6 and one each in Preschool and Prekindergarten. One of the School's goals is to have its student body represent the cultural, economic, and ethnic diversity of the community.

ACADEMIC PROGRAM. The school year, from September to June, includes Thanksgiving, winter, and spring vacations and observances of several national and religious holidays. A typical day, including seven class periods, morning recess, and lunch, begins at 8:05 A.M. for all students. Preschool and Prekindergarten children have optional "Stay Days" on Tuesdays and Thursdays. All others finish at 3:10 P.M. Families may drop students off at school as early as 7:30 A.M. For an extra charge, an After-School Program lasting until 5:30 P.M. is also available.

Classes are small, with a 9:1 student-faculty ratio. Homework is part of the school program beginning in Kindergarten. Grades are sent to parents quarterly, and parent-teacher conferences are held at least twice a year. School-developed tests and Educational Records Bureau tests are conducted every spring to assess student progress.

The integrated curriculum focuses on the interrelationships among various disciplines. Problem solving and effective reading, writing, and oral communication skills are emphasized. Students are grouped heterogeneously to encourage them to learn from one another. In Preschool through fourth grade, classes are self-contained; fifth and sixth grades are departmentalized. Core subjects include reading, writing, and verbal skills; mathematics; social studies; and science. All students are taught by specialists in art, computers, library, music, and physical education.

After graduation, 100 percent of the Class of 1999 entered leading independent secondary schools in Los Angeles.

The John Thomas Dye School conducts a Summer School Program offering different learning opportunities in academic enrichment, sports, science, arts and crafts, and computers. Sessions are two, three, or five weeks in length. Summer School is open to students not enrolled in the regular year-long program on a space-available basis.

STUDENT ACTIVITIES. Boys and girls in Grades 4–6 may develop leadership and initiative by serving on the elected student government. Officers and two representatives from each of these grades are chosen by their peers. Assisted by a faculty advisor, the group plans student activities, including community outreach projects. In recent years, John Dye students have held Thanksgiving drives for the needy, adopted Head Start families, and, in 1998, raised monies through a Jump-a-Thon to benefit local nonprofit community organizations.

After-school athletics for Grades 4–6 include flag football, basketball, baseball, and track for boys. Girls compete in basketball, volleyball, soccer, and track. There are teams for every ability level, and everyone is encouraged to participate.

Students in Grades 4–6 also publish a school newspaper and a creative writing magazine. Older students mentor younger students; as an example, sixth graders act as Big Brothers and Sisters to first graders. Students may also serve on the Green Team, which takes responsibility for the school recycling program. Frequent informal student variety shows, called Music for Lunch Bunch, entertain the school community. The sixth-grade musical is an annual success.

Guest artists and lecturers visit the School; the Parents' Club plans field trips to enrich the classroom experience. The

Cultural Resource Project invites families to share their culture, traditions, and resources with the school community. The celebration of holidays and special events is a constant cycle in the life of the School. Back to School Night, Open House, Halloween, Thanksgiving, Hanukkah, Christmas, the Candle Lighting Ceremony, Grandparents' Day, the School Birthday, the fair, numerous festivals and feasts, and graduation provide lasting memories.

ADMISSION AND COSTS. John Thomas Dye welcomes bright, capable boys and girls who show promise of becoming strongly motivated, intellectually curious students capable of benefiting from the growth opportunities the School offers.

Acceptance of a candidate is based upon available space and upon an assessment of the child's readiness and academic ability. A study of his or her previous school record and of the results of School-administered testing helps determine readiness. Both standardized and teacher-developed tests are used. Children of alumni and siblings of current students are given priority once they have met the admissions requirements. Application, with a $75 fee, should be made one year prior to desired enrollment. The new Admissions cycle begins on August 1 and ends the third week in March, when notification of acceptance status is mailed out.

Tuition for the 1999–2000 school year is $11,200 for Preschool and Prekindergarten, $11,500 for Kindergarten–Grade 3, and $11,650 for Grades 4–6. Required uniforms are extra. A $1000 one-time New Student Fee helps support the School's Financial Aid Program, which awards funds based on financial need. In 1998-99, the School distributed $95,452 in financial aid and $28,280 in tuition remission for children of faculty and administrators.

Director of Admissions: Judy Hirsch
Director of Development: Lisa Handler
Business Manager: Robert E. Suppelsa

John Woolman School   1963

13075 Woolman Lane, Nevada City, CA 95959. 530-273-3183;
Fax 530-273-9028; E-mail jwsadmit@nccn.net; Web Site
www.pacific.net/~woolman

John Woolman School is a Quaker, coeducational college preparatory school enrolling 30 boarders and 10 day students in Grades 9–13. Dedicated to academic excellence in the context of human values such as community, service to others, nonviolence, and physical work, the School offers Advanced Placement classes and a "block schedule" for intensive, project-oriented learning. Daily work periods, music, sports, fine arts, a peer-helper program, and student committees comprise the cocurricular program. Boarding Tuition: $20,000; Day Tuition: $9000. Financial Aid: $200,000. Brian Fry is Director of Admissions; Elee Hadley is Principal. *Western Association.*

Laguna Blanca School   1933

4125 Paloma Drive, Santa Barbara, CA 93110. 805-687-2461;
Fax 805-682-2553; E-mail egrandi@lagunablanca.org;
Web Site www.lagunablanca.org

Situated on a 30-acre campus near the Pacific, Laguna Blanca is a college preparatory day school enrolling 330 boys and girls in Kindergarten–Grade 12. Committed to developing the intellectual, social, physical, artistic, and ethical lives of its students, Laguna emphasizes personal attention and traditional values and seeks to provide inspiring teachers and a comprehensive curriculum to a diverse student body. Advanced Placement courses in 18 subjects and 36 interscholastic sports teams enrich development. Field trips, music, drama, and an international exchange program are among the activities. Tuition: $9500–

$11,900. Financial Aid: $178,000. Eileen P. Grandi is Director of Admission; Stephen T. Repsher (Union College, B.A.; New York University, M.A.) is Headmaster. *Western Association.*

La Jolla Country Day School   1926

9490 Genesee Avenue, La Jolla, CA 92037. 858-453-3440;
Fax 858-453-8210; Web Site www.ljcds.pvt.k12.ca.us

La Jolla Country Day is a nonsectarian, nonprofit school providing a rigorous college preparatory curriculum through a liberal arts education. Country Day challenges each child to attain excellence in academic and extracurricular endeavors. The School seeks to instill values of respect, compassion, and citizenship; emphasizes community service; and fosters positive risk-taking and global awareness. The computer-networked, 24-acre campus includes state-of-the-art facilities: eight science labs, an observatory, three theaters, a double gymnasium, and a new Early Childhood Center. Financial aid, extended-day care, and transportation are available. Tuition: $5520–$11,600. Diane Mothander is Director of Admissions; John Neiswender (Furman, B.S.; University of South Carolina, M.A.T.) is Headmaster. *Western Association.*

Laurence 2000 School   1953

13639 Victory Boulevard, Valley Glen, CA 91401. 818-782-4001
or 323-873-4633; Fax 818-782-4004; E-mail office@
laurence2000.com; Web Site www.laurence2000.com

Enrolling 225 boys and girls in Kindergarten–Grade 6, Laurence 2000 provides an enriched environment that combines a comprehensive academic program with creative and experiential learning activities. Ability groupings in reading and math offer rewarding challenges and success. In addition to strong basic academics, the integrated curriculum includes character education, community service, and multicultural studies with an emphasis on brotherhood. Specialists teach science, art, physical education, Spanish, computers, library, and music/drama. The student-teacher ratio is 8:1 with an average of 16–20 per class. Graduates enter prestigious secondary schools. Extended-day and after-school programs are available. Tuition: $10,400. Lauren Wolke is Director of Admissions; Marvin and Lynn Jacobson are Directors. *Western Association.*

Lick-Wilmerding High School   1895

755 Ocean Avenue, San Francisco, CA 94112. 415-333-4021;
Fax 415-333-9443; Web Site www.lick.pvt.k12.ca.us

Formed by the merger of The Lick School (1895) and The Wilmerding School (1904), this coeducational, college preparatory day school enrolls 377 students in Grades 9–12. Offering an integrated curriculum in the liberal, technical, and performing arts, Lick-Wilmerding High School is dedicated to educating for both college and life. The School seeks to educate the hands and the heart as well as the head, and views itself as a private school with a public purpose. Its ethnic and economically diverse student body is committed to service "beyond the school yard." Tuition: $15,170. Tuition Assistance: $1,316,000. Marcia Bedford is Director of Admissions; Albert M. Adams II (Harvard, Ed.D.) is Headmaster. *Western Association.*

Live Oak School   1971

117 Diamond Street, San Francisco, CA 94114. 415-861-8840;
Fax 415-861-7153

Live Oak, a day school enrolling 190 boys and girls in Kindergarten–Grade 8, aims to provide an exemplary education in traditional disciplines while developing critical thinking skills, confidence, and responsibility and compassion toward others.

Located in the Castro district, the School enjoys strong neighborhood relationships in its urban setting. An Intergenerational Program, extended care, music, art, Spanish, and an extensive field trip program support the core curriculum. A summer program is available. Parents must work at least 60 hours per year at the School. Tuition: $7550–$8050. Financial Aid: $180,000. Theresa Crivello is Director of Admissions; Matt Allio (University of San Francisco, B.A. 1981; California State [Northridge], M.A. 1989) was named Director in 1994.

Loretto High School   1955

2360 El Camino Avenue, Sacramento, CA 95821-5689.
916-482-7793, Ext. 103; Fax 916-482-3621; E-mail
LorettoHS@aol.com; Web Site www.loretto.room.net

Loretto High School, a college preparatory day school enrolling 450 girls, is owned by the Institute of the Blessed Virgin Mary (Loretto Sisters). Loretto strives to develop the whole person—body, mind, and spirit—in an atmosphere of challenge, acceptance, and support. The college preparatory curriculum includes Honors and Advanced Placement courses, choir, visual arts, dance, drama, and competitive sports. National Merit Scholars graduated in 1995, 1996, 1998, and 1999. Student activities include speech and debate, science clubs, and social service. Tuition: $5775 plus $400 Registration. Financial aid is available. Mrs. Eileen Thomas is Director of Admission; Sr. Helen Timothy, IBVM (California State, B.A.; University of Notre Dame, M.S.), was appointed Principal in 1992. *Western Association.*

Marin Academy   1971

1600 Mission Avenue, San Rafael, CA 94901-1859.
415-453-4550; Admissions 415-453-2908; Fax 415-453-8905;
E-mail tkrackeler@ma.org; Web Site www.ma.org

Marin Academy is a college preparatory day school enrolling 385 students in Grades 9–12. The school asks students to think, question, and create as well as to accept the responsibilities posed by education in a democratic society. A demanding curriculum is complemented by extracurricular activities, a full interscholastic athletic program, a celebrated fine and performing arts program, and a weeklong minicourse program for exploration of special areas of interest. Advanced Placement courses are offered in all subjects. Community service and a unique outings/wilderness program are among the many activities. Tuition: $15,990. Financial Aid: $800,000. Tony Krackeler is Director of Admissions and Financial Aid; Bodie Brizendine (Towson State, B.A.; Johns Hopkins, M.A.L.S.) is Head of School.

Marin Country Day School   1956

5221 Paradise Drive, Corte Madera, CA 94925-2107.
415-927-5900; Fax 415-924-2224; Web Site www.mcds.org

Marin Country Day, founded by parents, enrolls 500 boys and girls in Kindergarten–Grade 8 on its 35-acre waterfront campus. The curriculum, with an interdisciplinary, hands-on orientation, includes English, foreign languages, math, physical science, and social science. The arts, athletics, and outdoor education are integral to the program. Dedicated faculty, a low student-teacher ratio, and varied enrichment and extracurricular activities are designed to instill confidence, a joy for learning, and support of the School's core values: respect, responsibility, and compassion. After-school care and a recreational summer program are offered. Tuition: $10,755–$12,850. Financial Aid: $665,000. Jeffrey Escabar is Admissions Director; Timothy W. Johnson (Lake Forest, B.A. 1971) is Head of School. *Western Association.*

Marlborough School   1889

250 South Rossmore Avenue, Los Angeles, CA 90004.
323-935-1147; Fax 323-933-0542; E-mail admissions@
marlborough.la.ca.us; Web Site http://www.marlborough.la.ca.us

The oldest independent school for girls in Southern California, Marlborough School enrolls 500 day students in Grades 7–12. The college preparatory curriculum is academically challenging and encourages students to discover their potential, to think critically, and to develop intellectual curiosity. Athletics, literary projects, fine arts productions, outdoor education experiences, and a computer science program enrich the curriculum. Marlborough School is committed to providing a learning environment where young women develop self-confidence, creativity, a sense of responsibility, and moral decisiveness. Tuition: $15,150. Financial Aid: $804,000. Jeanette Woo Chitjian is Director of Admissions; Barbara E. Wagner (Michigan State, B.M.; University of Colorado, M.M.E.) is Head of School. *Western Association.*

Marymount High School   1923

10643 Sunset Boulevard, Los Angeles, CA 90077. 310-472-1205;
Fax 310-476-0910; Web Site www.marymount-la.org

Founded by the Religious of the Sacred Heart of Mary, Marymount High School is a Catholic, college preparatory day school enrolling 375 girls in Grades 9–12. The School is committed to providing a quality education that is academically excellent, value oriented, and enriching in its cocurricular programs. Its primary goal is to develop in students a sense of worth and dignity; a creative, inquisitive mind; and an appreciation of the aesthetic. Sports, Christian Service Program, fine arts, a literary program, and a retreat week are among cocurricular activities. A summer school offers academic, remedial, and enrichment courses. Tuition: $10,485. Fees: $1395. Mrs. Sharon Stephens is Director of Admission; Dr. Mary Ellen Gozdecki is Head of School. *Western Association.*

Marymount of Santa Barbara   1938

2130 Mission Ridge Road, Santa Barbara, CA 93103.
805-569-1811; Fax 805-682-6892; E-mail mmtadmission@hot-
mail.com; Web Site www.Marymountsb.org

Founded by the Religious of the Sacred Heart of Mary, Marymount is an independent Catholic school enrolling 240 boys and girls of many faiths in Kindergarten–Grade 8. The school is committed to intellectual, moral, and physical excellence. Basic skills in English, language arts, the sciences, mathematics, and the arts are emphasized, and religion, computers, and Spanish are integral to the program. Activities include community service, field trips, and sports. After-school care is available and a recreational summer session is offered. Tuition: $8350–$10,195. Extras: $276–$718. Financial Aid: $130,000. Tina Merlo Messineo is Director of Admission; Dolores E. Pollock (University of California [Santa Barbara], Ph.D. 1991) was named Head of School in 1977. *Western Association.*

Mayfield Junior School   1931

405 South Euclid Avenue, Pasadena, CA 91101. 626-796-2774;
Fax 626-796-5753; E-mail Mayfield@mjs.org;
Web Site http://www.Mayfieldjs.org

Mayfield Junior School is a Catholic independent school founded by the Sisters of the Holy Child Jesus, enrolling 420 boys and girls as day students in Kindergarten through Grade 8. Its mission is to provide rich educational and cultural opportunities. The core curriculum, consisting of language arts, religion, mathematics, science, social studies, Spanish, computers, library, the arts, and physical education, is designed to promote a love of reading and a lifelong pursuit of knowledge. Classes enroll an average of 23 students, and the student-teacher ratio is 14:1. Intramural sports emphasize skills development, teamwork, and sportsmanship. Tuition: $7500; New Family Fee: $1000. Averyl Thielen is Director of Admissions; Stephanie D. Griffin, M.A., is Head of School. *Western Association.*

Menlo School   1915

50 Valparaiso Avenue, Atherton, CA 94027. 650-330-2000;
  Fax 650-330-2012; Web Site www.menloschool.org

Located 25 miles south of San Francisco, Menlo is a coeducational, college preparatory day school enrolling over 750 students in Grades 6–12. Its environment fosters self-reliance while striving to promote growth of mind, body, and spirit. The curriculum features Honors and Advanced Placement courses in all subjects, small class size, and individual attention that engages students in the life of the mind. More than 35 teams and sports provide opportunities for physical development. Visual arts, drama, music, dance, and extracurriculars, including community service, round out student growth. Tuition: $15,625. Financial Aid: $900,000. Glen Pritzker is Director of Admissions; Norman Colb (Brandeis, B.A. 1964; Harvard, M.A.T. 1965) is Head of School.

The Mirman School for Gifted Children   1962

16180 Mulholland Drive, Los Angeles, CA 90049. 310-476-2868;
  Fax 310-471-1532; Web Site http://www.mirman.org

One of the only schools in the country that is specifically dedicated to meeting the needs of highly gifted children (I.Q. 145 and above), The Mirman School enrolls 170 day boys and 185 day girls in Grades 1–9. It provides an educational setting where academically gifted children are encouraged to develop mentally, physically, socially, and emotionally. The School is located in the western part of the city, a short distance from the University of California. The campus includes two computer labs, two science labs, and a cocurricular program encompassing music, art, Spanish, Latin, sports, speech, choir, and orchestra. The School was founded by Dr. and Mrs. Norman J. Mirman. Tuition: $11,500–$12,100. Financial Aid: $195,000. Leslie Mirman Geffen is Director.

Mount Tamalpais School   MILL VALLEY

100 Harvard Avenue, Mill Valley, CA 94941. 415-383-9434

MOUNT TAMALPAIS SCHOOL in Mill Valley, California, is a coeducational day school enrolling children in Kindergarten through Grade 8. The suburban community of Mill Valley (population 13,000) is 12 miles north of San Francisco in Marin County. Students have access to the museums,

theater, opera, symphony, and ballet of the city as well as to the Pacific Ocean (6 miles from the campus) and Mount Tamalpais for hiking and nature study. Private bus service is available between the School and local communities; public bus stops are within walking distance of the campus.

Founder and Director Kathleen M. Mecca, Ph.D., established the School in 1976. From its original enrollment of 60 students in Kindergarten–Grade 6, the School has grown to an enrollment of 240 and has included the seventh and eighth grades since 1980.

Mount Tamalpais School seeks to provide students with a solid academic foundation and to foster a genuine enthusiasm for learning. The departmentalized, integrated curriculum for Grades 1–8 focuses on concepts and research skills and permits each teacher to use a variety of methods and materials to strengthen individual skills. In addition, small-group instruction maximizes the inherent potential of each child and fosters respect for each student's interests and abilities.

A nonprofit organization, Mount Tamalpais School is governed by a Board of Trustees that includes parents, past parents, and community members. The Parent Council holds social and fund-raising events and coordinates family volunteer assistance to the School. The School holds membership in the National Association of Independent Schools, the California Association of Independent Schools, the Educational Records Bureau, the Secondary School Admission Test Board, the Educational Testing Service, and the Western Association of Schools and Colleges.

THE CAMPUS. The ten-acre campus includes a large playing field and a playground with a variety of recreational structures. A one-and-one-half-acre cypress grove is used for nature study. The three school buildings, which total more than 30,000 square feet, provide classrooms, a computer lab, an art studio, a faculty workroom, administrative offices, and the Rappaport Library Learning Center, constructed in 1986. New construction, completed in the spring of 1995, includes a gymnasium-theater complex, tutorial rooms for individual instrumental instruction and learning assistance, two science laboratories, an art room, and a music room. The value of the School-owned plant is more than $5,000,000.

THE FACULTY. Kathleen M. Mecca, Ph.D., has been Director of the School since its founding in 1976. A native of New Jersey,

Dr. Mecca is a graduate of the University of California at Los Angeles (B.A. 1965, M.A. 1968, M.S.Ed. 1969), the University of California at Irvine (M.A. 1966), Stanford University (Ed.D. 1971), and the University of California at San Francisco (Ph.D. 1973). She has held teaching and administrative positions in public and private schools in California and has also worked as a reading specialist and child/adolescent psychologist. She was a mentor teacher and master teacher for the California State Department of Education. In addition, she has taught at the college and graduate levels.

The 30 full-time faculty hold baccalaureate and graduate degrees representing study at Bucknell, Dartmouth, Earlham, Harvard, Middlebury, Oberlin, Ohio State, Oregon State, Princeton, San Diego State, San Francisco State, Stanford, Wellesley, and the Universities of California, Michigan, Oregon, Pennsylvania, and Wisconsin. There are also 8 part-time instructors.

The School employs a full-time nurse, and first aid is available on campus at all times. Paramedics are within 5 minutes of the School, and a hospital emergency room is 15 minutes away by car.

STUDENT BODY. The School enrolls 240 boys and girls in Kindergarten–Grade 8. The students reside in communities throughout Marin County and San Francisco.

ACADEMIC PROGRAM. The school year, from late August to mid-June, is divided into trimesters and includes a Thanksgiving recess, winter and spring vacations, a mid-winter recess, and all legal holidays. The daily schedule for Kindergarten–Grade 8, from 8:15 A.M. to 3:15 P.M., includes morning and afternoon homeroom periods, eight 40- to 45-minute class periods, a 20-minute recess, and a 40-minute lunch period. After-school care is available to students for an additional hourly fee. On "minimum days," the schedule is adjusted to permit 12:15 dismissal for all students in order to allow time for parent-teacher conferences in the fall.

An average class, for which there are two teachers, enrolls 24–28 students. There is a supervised study hall every day from 3:30 to 4:30 P.M.; teachers are available to provide extra help during this hour.

Students in Grades 4–8 receive grades each trimester in addition to narrative evaluations, and students in Kindergarten–Grade 3 receive narrative evaluations using a check system. Written reports with teacher comments are sent to the parents of all students at the end of each trimester. The School encourages communication between parents and teachers, and conferences are scheduled at the end of the first trimester.

Throughout the year, parents are urged to consult with the homeroom teachers, who act as the child's counselors, to discuss general progress or concerns.

Homework, ranging from 30 minutes four times a week for the youngest children to more than an hour every day for students in Grades 6–8, is assigned to provide follow-up, reinforcement, and continuity.

The Kindergarten program is developmental and is designed to provide an introduction to the School's curriculum of departmentalized, experiential learning. Learning tasks offer opportunities for enjoyment and success as well as skill development. Students are placed according to developmental criteria that take into account each child's academic, social, and emotional maturation.

For Grades 1–8, the curriculum includes: Whole Language (reading, literature, language arts, grammar, spelling, and writing), World Language and Geography, Spanish, French, social studies, mathematics, computer science, science, study skills, music, chorus, drama, art, art history, health, physical education, ceramics, woodworking, dance, movement, and sewing. An Enrichment program during the regular school day for Grades 6–8 provides elective opportunities for students to increase their skills in creative writing, music, drama, computers, dance, fine arts, and video film making. For Grades 4–8, values and family life are also offered. Students in Grades 6–8 study Latin in addition to either French or Spanish as well as special classes in Shakespeare, Current Affairs, and Public Speaking.

Outdoor Education classes for Grades 4–8 complement the program of environmental study that begins in Kindergarten. Fourth and fifth graders spend three days at various California historic sites correlated with their social science curriculum. Sixth-grade students have a week at Point Reyes, followed by an all-day kayaking trip. Seventh graders spend a week near Lake Mead, camping and rafting along the Colorado River. The eighth graders spend a week at the Yosemite Institute in Yosemite National Park.

Mount Tamalpais graduates have entered leading independent secondary schools in California and throughout the United States and have been accepted at such colleges and universities as Arizona State, Brown, Cornell, Dartmouth, Dominican College, Georgetown, Ithaca, Lewis & Clark, Princeton, Reed, Smith College, Stanford, Williams, and the Universities of California, Colorado, Michigan, Oregon, Southern California, and Washington.

STUDENT ACTIVITIES. The Student Council is composed of two representatives each from Grades 3–8. With parent volunteers who help coordinate activities, the Council arranges spirit days, dances, and community service projects. Extracurricular activities include Computer, Brownies, Cub Scouts, and the Literary Magazine and Yearbook Committees. After-school classes in sewing, woodworking, chess, ceramics, art, dance, drama, voice, and instrumental music are available for a small fee.

Upper-grade students compete in basketball, soccer, volleyball, cross-country, and track and field with teams from other schools in San Francisco and Marin County. Soccer teams for Kindergarten–Grade 6 play in the Mill Valley Soccer League. Intramural sports include basketball, field hockey, gymnastics, lacrosse, and volleyball.

School spirit days are Halloween, Teddy Bear Day, Hat Day, Hawaiian Day, Olympic Day, Field Day, and Angel Island Day. Traditional events include Grandparents' Day, Founder's Day Picnic, and the Gala Spring Auction.

ADMISSION AND COSTS. Mount Tamalpais School seeks to enroll a diverse group of students who are responsible, willing to learn, and who can reach their full potential in a challenging academic environment. New students are admitted to all grades on the basis of very competitive enrollment criteria: three recommendations (including one from a current teacher), a school visit with an interview, standardized testing, a transcript of grades, and, for Grades 3–8, a writing sample. Parents are encouraged to observe classes in session before submitting an application for a student. Application must be made prior to January 31. The nonrefundable application fee is $75. The Director and an Admissions Committee handle admissions.

In 1999–2000, tuition is $11,150 for Kindergarten–Grade 8.

Mount Tamalpais School subscribes to the School Scholarship Service. The School offers financial assistance to approximately 15 percent of the students; in 1998–99, approximately $270,000 was awarded on the basis of need.

New Roads School

SANTA MONICA AND LOS ANGELES

Santa Monica Middle School: 1238 Lincoln Boulevard, Santa Monica, CA 90401. 310-587-2255; Fax 310-587-2258
La Cienega Middle School: 5753 Rodeo Drive, Los Angeles, CA 90016. 323-634-5560; Fax 323-634-5560
High School: 3131 Olympic Boulevard, Santa Monica, CA 90404. 310-828-5582; Fax 310-828-2582

Nᴇᴡ ʀᴏᴀᴅs sᴄʜᴏᴏʟ in Santa Monica and Los Angeles, California, is an independent educational community set on three campuses within Los Angeles County and currently serving 300 boys and girls in Grades 6 through 12. Los Angeles County (population 10,000,000) is a region rich in cultural and natural resources, and all three campuses enjoy easy access to beaches, canyons, recreation areas, and museums. Students travel to school via public bus and car pools.

New Roads School, the brainchild of Dr. Paul Cummins and the sister school to Crossroads School of Arts and Science, was established in 1995 by The New Visions Foundation as a model for education. To prepare young people for the challenges and opportunities they face, the School aims to promote personal, social, political, and moral understanding and to instill in students a respect for the humanity and ecology of the world in which they live. The demanding college preparatory curriculum not only emphasizes strong reading and writing skills, effective expression, and critical thinking, but seeks to go beyond ordinary "schooling" with a concern for the whole person.

A nonprofit, nondenominational institution, New Roads School is guided by a 25-member Board of Trustees. It holds membership in the Educational Records Bureau, The College Board, the Association for Curriculum Development, The Independent School Alliance for Minority Affairs, and the National Coalition of Educational Activists. New Roads is a candidate for accreditation by the Western Association of Schools and Colleges.

THE CAMPUSES. The Santa Monica Middle School is conducted in a 27,000-square-foot facility owned by the Santa Monica Boys and Girls Club. It provides six spacious classrooms, an art room, a large gymnasium, meeting rooms, and outdoor playing fields. New Roads students take part in many after-school activities on the site, which is located near the beach, community arts resources, and the local library. The La Cienega Middle School occupies a portion of the new, two-story Bahai Faith Center, which features eight teaching spaces including a science lab, seminar rooms, a large play area for physical education, and a small theater. The High School is located on the West Side of Los Angeles.

THE FACULTY. David Bryan, a native of Brooklyn, New York, was appointed founding Head of School in 1995. He is a graduate of the State University of New York where he earned a B.A. at Stony Brook and J.D. and Ph.D. degrees at Buffalo. Dr. Bryan also holds an M.S. in kinesiology from the University of California at Los Angeles. His professional experience encompasses teaching in both public and independent schools and universities, including Crossroads School for Arts and Science, where he also served as Dean of Human Development. Dr. Bryan is married to Lucia Vinograd, an artist and educator, and they have two teenage children.

In addition to the Head of School, there are 55 faculty who hold undergraduate and advanced degrees representing study at colleges and universities nationwide. Among these are Art Center for Design, Berklee College of Music, Boston University, Brown, California Institute of the Arts, California State (Long Beach, Los Angeles, Northridge), Columbia University, Dartmouth, Loyola, Mary Washington, Pepperdine, Santa Clara State University, Santa Monica College, Simmons, Stanford, Williams, Yale, and the Universities of California (Berkeley, Irvine, Los Angeles), Colorado, Pittsburgh, Southern California, Tulsa, and Wisconsin (Madison).

Faculty benefits include medical and dental plans, disability insurance, and a retirement program. Medical and first-aid services are offered on campus, and Saint John's Medical Center is available for emergencies.

STUDENT BODY. In 1999–2000, New Roads School will enroll 300 students in Grades 6 through 12, 170 boys and 130 girls. Students come from diverse racial, ethnic, and socioeconomic backgrounds that reflect the multicultural heritage of the Greater Los Angeles area. Half the students are Caucasian, while the other half is comprised of Latino (18 percent),

African-American (18 percent), Asian (12 percent), and Native American and others (2 percent).

ACADEMIC PROGRAM. The school year, divided into semesters, begins in early September and extends to mid-June, with Thanksgiving, winter, and spring breaks and days off for federal holidays. Grades are issued twice each semester, at eight weeks and at the end of the semester; marks are posted weekly for students who are experiencing difficulty. Classes, enrolling 15 to 20 students, are held five days a week from 8:00 A.M. to between 2:50 to 3:15 P.M., depending on the grade. Supervised study halls and writing and math labs are integrated into the daily schedule. Tutorials are available after school for students as needed.

New Roads offers an innovative, two-strand, college preparatory curriculum. The first strand emphasizes traditional mathematics, English, social studies, history, foreign language, and science, with numerous enrichment courses in the visual and performing arts. The second strand encompasses *The Workshop for Social, Economic, and Ecological Action,* in which students learn to apply their academic skills to solve such current issues as racism, sexism, population/overpopulation, stereotyping, and ecological regeneration and land use. They write journals and research papers, design and collaborate on community projects, and make oral presentations to their peers and the larger community.

The first seniors will graduate in the year 2000. To earn a New Roads diploma, students must complete four years of English; three years each of mathematics (through Algebra II), history/social science (including one year of American Studies), and laboratory science; and two of the same foreign language, the arts, and Psycho-Physical Education. Students must also take one course each year in human development and complete two Workshops.

Among the specific courses offered are American Studies, World History, World Civilizations 1–2; English 9–12; Math Fundamentals (Grade 6), Pre-Algebra, 8th Grade Mathematics, Algebra 1, Geometry, Algebra 2/Trigonometry, Pre-Calculus, Advanced Placement Calculus; Conceptual Physics, Biology, Chemistry, Physics; Spanish 1–5; Computers; and Drama, Dance, Visual Arts, Creative Writing, Comedy Writing & Performance, Music, and Storytelling.

New Roads conducts a six-week summer program of academics and the arts.

STUDENT ACTIVITIES. A faculty-supervised Student Council is responsible for planning and implementing activities, representing the School at conferences and other events, and serving as liaison between the student body and the administration. Organizations on campus are formed according to student interest and include Amnesty International, a theater/improv group, school dancers, and debate, games, and science clubs. Parents are encouraged to teach after-school courses in a field

of their expertise such as jewelry making, photography, computer building, and veterinary medicine.

New Roads athletes compete at the varsity and junior varsity level with other small independent schools in the region in cross-country, track and field, boys' basketball, and girls' softball and volleyball. Middle School students play these sports as well as flag football. Intramural teams are organized in floor hockey, indoor soccer, and Ultimate Frisbee.

Traditional events on the calendar include Back-to-School Night, All School Celebration Feast, Town Hall Meetings, the Midnite Special Reading, the talent show, and the All School Fund-Raiser, Kaleidoscope.

ADMISSION AND COSTS. New Roads welcomes students with grade-level skills who demonstrate a desire to become actively engaged in the School and greater community. Admission is offered based on the completed application, a student essay, previous academic transcripts, two teacher recommendations, an administrative evaluation, standardized test results, and an interview. The deadline for applying is early February, although late applicants may be considered if vacancies exist. The application fee is $80.

Tuition for all grades in 1999–2000 is $12,942. Books ($300–$500) and a one-time Family Fee ($500) are additional. Financial aid in the amount of $1,837,000 will be awarded to nearly 70 percent of the student body.

Head of School and Director, High School: David Bryan, Ph.D.
Director, La Cienega Middle School: Charletta Johnson, M.A.
Director, Santa Monica Middle School: Christine Elder
Business Manager: Adrienne McCandless

The Nueva School   1967

6565 Skyline Boulevard, Hillsborough, CA 94010. 650-348-2272; Fax 650-344-9302; E-mail rhunsic@nuevaschool.org; Web Site www.nuevaschool.org

The Nueva School was founded by Karen Stone-McCown to serve the academic needs of 300 gifted and talented children in Pre-Kindergarten through Grade 8. Nueva is a child-centered, progressive school that emphasizes integrated studies, creative arts, and social-emotional learning. Students help choose their programs and determine the pace at which they learn; teachers utilize materials, methodologies, and strategies based on the individual student's learning style. The program includes Menuhin Music Scholars, Japanese language study, and an eighth-grade trip to Japan. Extended care and a summer program are also offered. Tuition: $8500–$15,500. Financial Aid: $400,000. Rebecca Hunsicker is Admissions Director; Andrew Beyer was appointed Director in 1998. *Western Association.*

The Oaks School   1986

6817 Franklin Avenue, Hollywood, CA 90028. 323-850-3755;
Fax 323-850-3758; E-mail theoaksschool@netscape.net; Web Site
http://www.loop.com/~theoaks

The Oaks, a day school enrolling 144 boys and girls from Kindergarten through Grade 6, seeks to provide a loving, safe, mentally stimulating environment where students are "free to be themselves, explore the world around them, and learn to make sense of it." The preparatory curriculum is designed to develop children's full potential as seekers, learners, independent thinkers, and problem solvers. Student Council, an all-school campout, science fair, and a jogathon are among the activities. After-school enrichment programs are offered. Tuition: $8400. Financial aid is available. Chloe Eichenlaub (California State University) is Head of School. *Western Association.*

Oakwood School   NORTH HOLLYWOOD

Elementary School: 11230 Moorpark Street, North Hollywood, CA
91602-2599. 818-752-4444; Fax 818-752-4466
Secondary School: 11600 Magnolia Boulevard, North Hollywood, CA
91601-3098. 818-752-4400; Fax 818-766-1285;
Web Site www.oakwoodschool.org

Oakwood School in North Hollywood, California, is a coeducational, college preparatory day school enrolling 741 students from Kindergarten through Grade 12.

Oakwood was founded in 1951 as an elementary school by a group of parents who wanted their children's education to be more intellectually challenging, creative, and humane. From kindergarten through the senior year, Oakwood aims to create an environment that is authoritative without being authoritarian and demanding without being oppressive, where people of diverse backgrounds learn about their differences as well as their similarities, and where informality is balanced with intellectual rigor and seriousness of purpose combined with a great sense of play. Oakwood School's founders understood that character is nurtured in the context of rich relationships with caring adults, where students learn—and experience—how to argue, how to treat one another, what values to devote themselves to, what to hope for, and what commitments might be worth making in their lives.

A nonprofit institution, Oakwood is governed by a Board of Trustees composed of parents, alumni, and educators from the community. The School is accredited by the Western Association of Schools and Colleges and holds membership in the National Association of Independent Schools and the California Association of Independent Schools, among other professional organizations.

THE CAMPUS. The Elementary School includes 15 classrooms; a library/media center; specialized rooms for arts, music, and computer; a multipurpose hall, administrative offices; green spaces; and an adjacent athletic field. The Secondary School comprises multiple facilities including a specialized math and science building of 10 classrooms, five labs, lecture hall and meeting atrium; a new music, dance, and athletic center housing acoustically balanced studios and practice rooms for orchestra, choirs, and dance; and a 500-seat regulation gym complete with a separate weight-training facility, four team shower rooms, and staff offices with athletic fields nearby. Humanities, languages, and the arts are offered in 15 additional classrooms, plus an auditorium and theater arts facility, photography, video, sculpture, ceramic, computer, and journalism studios and labs as well as a 15,000-volume library with on-line connections to the University of California holdings. The School also has faculty and student lounges; administrative, business, and plant offices; subterranean parking; and green space/common areas.

THE FACULTY. James Alan Astman was appointed Headmaster in 1979. He is a graduate of the University of Rochester (B.A.); of Colgate Rochester Divinity School (M.A.); and of Claremont Graduate School (Ph.D.), where he also taught. The Elementary School Principal, Margo Alexandre Long, attended the University of California (B.A.), California State at Northridge (M.A.), and Claremont Graduate School (M.A.). R. Bruce Musgrave, the Principal of the Secondary School, is a graduate of Cornell University (B.A., M.A.T.).

In addition to Dr. Astman and the school principals, Oakwood's administrative organization includes a chief operating officer, chief financial officer, two directors of studies, and directors of admissions, development, community and public relations, operations, and support services. The Secondary School has middle and high school deans and a director of college counseling.

There are 80 faculty members, 25 in the Elementary School and 55 in the Secondary School. They hold degrees representing study at such colleges and universities as Amherst, Brown, California Institute of the Arts, Carnegie Mellon, Claremont, Columbia, Cornell, Dartmouth, Harvard-Radcliffe, Haverford, Northwestern, Occidental, Oxford (England), Pomona, Stanford, Swarthmore, Vassar, Wellesley, Yale, and the Universities of Arizona, California, Miami, Pennsylvania, and Rochester.

ACADEMIC PROGRAM. The 35-week academic year, from early September to mid-June, is divided into semesters. Recesses are scheduled at Thanksgiving, the winter holidays, and in the spring.

Elementary School class hours are 8:30 A.M. to 3:00 P.M. Monday through Thursday and 8:30 A.M. to 2:00 P.M. on Friday. Class sizes average 20 students per section, with two sections per grade. Including support teachers and teaching assistants, the student-teacher ratio is 10:1. Parent-teacher conferences are scheduled each fall and spring; additional conferences are held at the request of the parents or teachers. Parents receive written evaluations twice a year.

The daily curriculum includes a complete language reading/writing program, arithmetic (including elementary algebra and geometry), computer, science, and a multidisciplinary social studies/humanities program that encompasses history, geography, comparative cultures, the arts including instrumental music, and other academic studies.

Secondary School classes, with an average enrollment of 18, meet from 8:00 A.M. to 3:30 P.M. Monday through Thursday and 8:00 A.M. to 2:00 P.M. on Friday. Faculty are available for extra help, and tutorial assistance can be arranged. Written evaluations, including letter grades, are sent to parents four times a year.

The program for Grades 7–8 includes Humanities, French, Latin, Spanish, Pre-Algebra, Algebra, Life Science, Earth Science, Drama, Art, Music, Dance, Film/Video, Photography, Computer, Human Development, Physical Education, special studies, school service, and community service.

To graduate, students in Grades 9–12 must complete four years of English and mathematics and three years of one foreign language, social studies (including United States History), laboratory science, physical education, art, and community service.

The prescribed core academic program in Grades 9–10 includes math and science; foreign language; and a two-year chronological survey of Western civilization in English and social studies. Juniors select some, and seniors all of their academic and arts courses.

The Secondary School curriculum includes British and World Literature, American Literature, Shakespeare, Creative Writing, Nonfiction Literature, Modern American Literature, Science Fiction; French, Spanish, Latin; Ancient and Medieval History, Modern History, American History, Psychological Theory, U.S. Government, Film and Society: Hollywood, American Television, Social Philosophy, African-American Music and Society, Biblical Thought and Secular Society, Comparative Biography, African-American History in Los Angeles; Algebra I and II, Geometry, Trigonometry, Pre-Calculus, Calculus, Statistics; Computer, Web Technology and Development, Introduction to Programming; Biology, Marine Biology, Chemistry, Physics, Anatomy-Physiology, Physical Science; Drawing, Sculpture, Film/Video, Photography, Ceramics, Painting, Theatre Arts, Drama, Stage Craft, Play Production, Technical Theatre, Modern Dance, Chorus, Orchestra, Music History, Music Composi-

tion, and Music Theory. Advanced Placement courses are offered in American Government, American History, Biology, Calculus AB, Calculus BC, Chemistry, Computer Science AB, English Language, English Literature, French Language, Physics B, Physics C, Spanish Language, and Statistics. Independent study is encouraged, and seniors spend a significant portion of May acquiring extensive and concentrated experiences in a project of their choice.

A Special Studies Program of enrichment courses provides students in Grades 4–12 with opportunities for extended or specialized study in both traditional and nontraditional areas. In 1982, Oakwood began an Artists-in-Residence Program in affiliation with California Institute of the Arts. Oakwood students can study with graduate students from the arts college in dance, film and video, animation, theater, visual arts, and music.

Over the past five years, Oakwood graduates have enrolled in such colleges and universities as American, Bard, Barnard, Boston University, Brandeis, Brown, Carleton, Carnegie Mellon, Duke, Emerson, George Washington, Harvard, Haverford, Ithaca, Kenyon, Massachusetts Institute of Technology, New York University, Northwestern, Scripps, Skidmore, Stanford, Syracuse, Tufts, United States Military Academy, Vassar, Wesleyan, Yale, and the Universities of California, Colorado, Michigan, Oregon, Pennsylvania, Southern California, Texas, Virginia, and Wisconsin.

STUDENT ACTIVITIES. Students in the Secondary School participate in school governance through a Student Council, ad-hoc committees, and weekly grade meetings. Secondary School students also publish a yearbook, a nationally recognized art and literary magazine, and a school newspaper. Students in the Elementary School participate in frequent field trips designed to enrich the academic program. The sixth grade travels to Washington, D.C., in the spring. The Elementary School social studies programs culminate in dramatic and musical productions. Students in both schools participate in school and community service projects.

The Secondary School has varsity teams in soccer, cross-country, track and field, basketball, baseball, softball, and volleyball. Fencing and equestrian teams are also available. Elementary School sports include baseball, flag football, body movement, gymnastics, roller-skating, and track and field.

Students in the Secondary School present at least two plays and two concerts during the school year; the Elementary School holds a Winter Concert. Secondary School students participate in an Arts Festival, featuring student films, plays, music, art, and dance.

Social activities include dances, proms, faculty/student athletic events, and educational field trips. Each Secondary School class takes one extended trip per year to such places as Yosemite, Catalina Island, the Colorado River, Joshua Tree National Monument, and Big Bear Lake. Other annual events include an Open House, picnics, and alumni activities.

ADMISSION AND COSTS. Oakwood School seeks to admit a diverse group of highly motivated students of above-average intellectual ability. It is a school policy to accept students without regard to race, creed, or national or ethnic origin. For admission to the Elementary School, previous records and an interview are required. Entrance requirements for Grades 7–12 consist of the admissions tests (aptitude and verbal/mathematical achievement), personal interviews with teachers and a student, previous school records, and recommendations from teachers. For September enrollment, applications must be received by January 21 at the Elementary School and by February 1 at the Secondary School. If vacancies exist, students may be enrolled during the school year. There is an application fee of $100 for the Secondary School and $75 for the Elementary School.

Tuition for 1999–2000 is $11,850 for Kindergarten–Grade 6 and $14,550 for Grades 7–12. There is a one-time, new-student fee of $1250. Additional expenses include fees for books in the Secondary School. Tuition insurance and financial aid are available.

Headmaster: James Alan Astman, Ph.D.
Chief Operating Officer: Samuel H. Anker, Esq.
Chief Financial Officer: Elliot Spokane
Director of Support Services: Barbara Kornblau
High School Dean: Ellen Peters
Middle School Dean: Susan Schechtman
Director of Admissions: Sue Slotnick
Director of Development: Carol Kest
Director of Alumni Relations: Barbara Bickel
Director of College Counseling: Julie A. Taylor
Director of Community and Public Relations: Mikie Maloney
Director of Operations: Barbara Karsh
Director of Athletics: Eric Walter

Pacific Academy Preparatory School   1964

3065 Richmond Parkway, Richmond, CA 94806. 510-243-6400; Fax 510-243-6403; E-mail Admissions@PacificAcademy.com; Web Site www.PacificAcademy.com

Pacific Academy was founded by Faith Nomura to develop the mind, character, and body of each student through a challenging college preparatory curriculum that places equal emphasis on academics and values. The School currently enrolls 300 boys and girls in Pre-Kindergarten–Grade 9 on four campuses; a new grade will be added each year through 2002. Advanced Placement courses are offered, and computer technology, music, theater, and the visual arts are integral to the program. Class sizes average 18, with a student-teacher ratio of 12:1. Extended day care and a summer enrichment program are available. Tuition: $7600–$10,900. Jennifer Schicke is Director of Admission; Kiyoshi Nomura (Fukui University, B.S.; University of California [Berkeley], B.Arch.) is Administrator.

The Palm Valley School   1952

35-525 DaVall Drive, Rancho Mirage, CA 92270. 760-328-0861; Fax 760-770-4541; Web Site www.palmvalley.org

Palm Valley is a coeducational, college preparatory day school enrolling students in Pre-Kindergarten–Grade 12 on a 38-acre, state-of-the-art campus. A teaching and learning community, the School seeks to help children discover, develop, and apply their unique talents, both for their own satisfaction and for the good of society. Eagerness to learn, hard work, and willingness to participate are valued, as the School aims to inspire an understanding of the worth of achievement, a sense of joy and wonder, high ideals, an appreciation of the gifts of others, and hopeful confidence in the useful exercise of their own powers. Tuition: $7600–$11,600. Financial Aid: $300,000. O. Graham Hookey is Head of School.

The Pegasus School   1984

19692 Lexington Lane, Huntington Beach, CA 92646. 714-964-1224; Fax 714-962-6047; Web Site www.pegasus-school.net

The Pegasus School, a coeducational day school enrolling 500 students in Preschool–Grade 8, offers a strong, challenging academic curriculum, taught by fully certified faculty. Small classes are limited to 18 students, each with a teacher and a teacher's assistant. In Kindergarten–Grade 8, the program is enriched with technology, science, Spanish, music, and physical education. The 14-acre campus features a fully equipped state-of-the-art Technology Center, Lower and Middle School science labs, a 15,000-volume library, and a new 20,000-square-foot gymnasium/activities center. Camp Pegasus provides six weeks of summer enrichment. Tuition: $4600–$8400. Financial aid is available. Nancy Conklin is Admissions Director; Dr. Laura Katz Hathaway is Founder and Director.

The Phillips Brooks School   1978

2245 Avy Avenue, Menlo Park, CA 94025. 650-854-4545; Fax 650-854-6532

Phillips Brooks, a coeducational day school enrolling 244 students in Preschool–Grade 5, is committed to a tradition of academic excellence along with an emphasis on preparing each student to live a creative, humane, and compassionate life. Children are placed in self-contained classrooms for basic subjects, with specialist teachers for art, computer, French or Spanish, library skills, music, physical education, and science. Small classes and dedicated faculty permit individual attention. Chapel services are held weekly. The School values diversity and an understanding of world cultures. Extended Day care is available. Tuition: $5550–$9725. Financial Aid: $250,000. Beth Passi (University of Minnesota, B.A.; Michigan State, M.A.) is Head of School.

Polytechnic School   1907

1030 East California Boulevard, Pasadena, CA 91106. 626-792-2147; Fax 626-796-2249; Web Site www.polytechnic.org

Polytechnic enrolls 850 students in Prekindergarten–Grade 12 on a 15-acre campus with a state-of-the-art performing and fine arts center and professionally staffed libraries, computer rooms, and media centers. Students are encouraged to excel in academic, athletic, and artistic endeavors in an atmosphere that celebrates diversity and promotes community. The School emphasizes the skills needed for sound thinking and effective communication while fostering personal development, integrity, responsibility, and concern for others. Community service is integral to the curriculum; an extensive outdoor education program in Grades 6–12 enhances the Poly experience. Tuition: $8380–$12,740. Financial Aid: $1,026,328. Sally Jeanne Barnum is Director of Admissions; Sarah L. Levine, Ed.D., is Head of School. *Western Association.*

The Prentice School   1986

18341 Lassen Drive, Santa Ana, CA 92705-2012. 714-538-4511; Fax 714-538-5004; Web Site www.prentice.org

Prentice is an independent, nonprofit school for 228 students in Kindergarten–Grade 8. The state-certified School uses the Slingerland Approach to teach children with learning disabilities how to understand and use language. This teaching technique engages the auditory, visual, and kinesthetic learning pathways in integrated, simultaneous, multisensory instruction. Classes are small, and instructional assistants provide individualized help. The academic program is supplemented by classes in music, art, science, computers, and physical education. A clinical psychologist and two speech and language therapists are on staff. Many graduates attain honor role status at their high schools and colleges. Tuition: $9000–$11,500. Debra L. Jarvis is Executive Director. *Western Association.*

Presidio Hill School   1918

3839 Washington Street, San Francisco, CA 94118. 415-751-9318; Fax 415-751-9334; E-mail admissions@presidiohill.org; Web Site www.presidiohill.org

Enrolling 156 boys and girls in Kindergarten–Grade 8, this progressive program's enrollment policy reflects the cultural, economic, and racial diversity of the city. The average class size is 16, with one class per grade. Music and the arts are considered fundamental. Spanish is introduced in Kindergarten and continues through Grade 8. Physical education includes interscholastic sports in upper grades and creative movement and games in lower grades. Parent involvement is encouraged and considered essential. Tuition: $8585–$9210. Chelsea Russell is Admissions Director; Carey Davis (Princeton, A.B.; Harvard, Ed.M.) is Director.

Prospect Sierra   1997

2060 Tapscott Avenue and 960 Avis Drive, El Cerrito, CA 94530. 510-527-4714; Fax 510-527-3728

Prospect Sierra enrolls 515 boys and girls in Kindergarten through Grade 8 on distinct elementary and middle school campuses overlooking San Francisco Bay. The student body reflects the multifaceted diversity of the surrounding cities. The program is imaginative, joyous, and challenging. Science, foreign language, technology, middle school math, studio art, music, and physical education are taught by specialists. Extended-day programs include enrichment classes and interscholastic sports. Tuition: $9600–$10,150. Financial Aid: $560,000. Frederick W. Heinrich (Connecticut College, B.A.; University of Texas [Austin], M.A.) was appointed Head in 1990. *Western Association.*

PS #1 Elementary School   1971

1454 Euclid Street, Santa Monica, CA 90404-2713. 310-394-1313; Fax 310-395-1093

PS #1 Elementary School instills in children the joy of learning within a flexible, pluralistic setting that recognizes the individuality of each student. The School enrolls 165 boys and girls in ungraded, multiage classes encompassing Kindergarten–Grade 6. Two lead teachers in each classroom provide team teaching that enables students to learn according to their own style and ability level. The core curriculum emphasizes mastery of skills in language/arts, math, science, and social studies and integrates music, art, community projects, and environmental studies into the academic program. Diverse activities and an all-school, overnight camping trip enhance the children's experience in this unique school community. Extended care is available. Tuition: $11,250. Andrea Roth is Director of Admissions; Joel Pelcyger is Director.

Redwood Day School   1962

3245 Sheffield Avenue, Oakland, CA 94602. 510-534-0800; Fax 510-534-0806

Redwood Day School, enrolling 260 boys and girls in Junior Kindergarten–Grade 8, provides a challenging academic program in a creative and caring environment. The curriculum, including reading, writing, math, social studies, science, arts, languages, music, technology, and physical education, is enriched by a friendly and diverse community, interactive study, critical thinking, and cooperative lessons. Extended-care, enrichment, and interscholastic sports programs are available after school, and a summer program is offered. The 3.5-acre campus includes classrooms, a 10,000 volume library, gymnasium, auditorium, pool, and several outdoor play areas. Tuition: $9400–$10,400. Rick Clarke is Head of School.

Rolling Hills Preparatory School   1981

300A Paseo del Mar, Palos Verdes Estates, CA 90274. 310-791-1101; Fax 310-373-4931; Web Site www.rhp.pvt.k12.ca.us

Rolling Hills Prep School provides an educational environment conducive to the development of disciplined minds, sound character, healthy bodies, and creative spirits. Enrolling 224 boys and girls in Grades 6–12, the School features small classes, proven teaching methods, and up-to-date technology to carry out its traditional college preparatory program. Among the activities are outdoor education, community service, clubs, and athletics. English as a Second Language and a recreational summer program are optional. Tuition: $11,700–$13,700. Financial Aid: $285,000. Peter McCormack (York University, B.A. 1975; Exeter, P.G.C.E. 1976; Oxford, M.Sc. 1987) was appointed Head of School in 1993.

Sacramento Country Day School   1964

2636 Latham Drive, Sacramento, CA 95864. 916-481-8811; Fax 916-481-6016; E-mail alumni@scds.pvt.k12.ca.us; Web Site www.macnexus.org/scds/

Sacramento Country Day School is a coeducational, college preparatory school enrolling 500 students in Pre-Kindergarten–Grade 12. "The Mission of Sacramento Country Day is to provide a traditional, college preparatory education to students from a variety of backgrounds who possess both strong academic potential and respect for others and to develop in them the qualities of self-confidence, creativity, integrity, and responsibility." The student-teacher ratio is 10-1. Fine arts, technology, and educational field trips enrich the curriculum at all levels. Extended-day care and summer programs are available. Tuition: $4645–$9555. Financial aid is offered. Selden Edwards (Princeton, B.A.; Stanford, M.A.) is Headmaster. *Western Association.*

Sacred Heart Schools, Atherton   1898

150 Valparaiso Avenue, Atherton, CA 94027. 650-322-1866; Fax 650-322-7151; Web Site www.shschools.org

These fully accredited, Roman Catholic, coeducational day schools enroll 435 students in Grades 9–12 in Sacred Heart Preparatory and 550 students in Preschool–Grade 8 at St. Joseph's

School. Both schools on the 62-acre campus seek to develop academic excellence while fostering Christian values and social awareness. Programs include required religious studies, challenging curricula, and competitive athletic programs as well as a wide range of cocurricular activities and summer camps. The Prep offers Advanced Placement in 17 subjects and exchange programs with Sacred Heart schools worldwide. Tuition: $9700–$13,965. Financial aid is available. Carl Dos Remedios is High School Director of Admission; Richard A. Dioli is High School Principal; John O. Miller is Grade School Principal. *Western Association.*

St. James' Episcopal School   1967

625 South St. Andrew's Place, Los Angeles, CA 90005. 213-382-2315; Fax 213-382-2436; E-mail office@stjamesschool.net; Web Site www.stjamesschool.net

St. James' Episcopal School, a Blue Ribbon School of Excellence, enrolls 304 girls and boys from diverse faiths and cultures in Kindergarten–Grade 6. The academic program is designed to provide a strong foundation for further education and daily life. A comprehensive reading program forms the basis of the core curriculum, complemented by music, art, physical education, religion, Spanish, computer, and library. Worship and religion are integral to the program. Children take part in school choir, bell choir, scouting, and athletics, including tae kwon do. An extensive after-school program is available. Tuition: $8000. Financial Aid: $180,000. Andrew Taylor is Admissions Director; Janess W. Gardiner is Head of School. *Western Association.*

St. John's Episcopal School

RANCHO SANTA MARGARITA

30382 Via Con Dios, Rancho Santa Margarita, CA 92688. 949-858-5144; Fax 949-858-1403

ST. JOHN'S EPISCOPAL SCHOOL in Rancho Santa Margarita, California, is an independent, church-affiliated elementary school enrolling boys and girls in three-year-old Preschool through Grade 8. Located in Orange County about 40 miles southeast of Los Angeles, Rancho Santa Margarita (population 35,131) is a picturesque, Spanish-style town a short distance from the Santa Ana Mountains and vast expanses of national forest. Students come from Rancho Santa Margarita as well as Coto de Caza (Trabuco Canyon), Irvine, Laguna Hills, Mission Viejo, San Juan Capistrano, and other towns in Orange County.

St. John's Episcopal School was founded in 1988 by the Reverend Canon Ernest D. Sillers. From an initial enrollment of 250 children in Preschool–Grade 8, St. John's reached its current capacity of nearly 900 students by 1992, and, with generous support from private businesses and developers, the School's permanent facilities were completed by the end of the fifth year.

The mission of St. John's is to develop every student to his or her God-given potential, providing a challenging, age-appropriate academic program in a Christian atmosphere. All students, regardless of their faith heritage, attend chapel twice a week and take religion classes once a week. Faculty seek to instill a lifelong love of learning and to foster qualities of integrity, responsibility, and respect for others.

St. John's is a not-for-profit institution incorporated under the auspices of the Episcopal Diocese of Los Angeles. It is guided in its purpose by the Governing Body, consisting of members of the School and Bishop's committees. The self-perpetuating School Committee, which meets ten times a year, is responsible for the practical operation of the School. St. John's is accredited by the Western Association of Schools and Colleges, the California Association of Independent Schools, and

the National Association for the Education of Young Children. It holds membership in the National Association of Episcopal Schools and the Educational Records Bureau, among other organizations. The Alumni Relations program serves as a liaison between the School and its 420 graduates.

THE CAMPUS. Set on 5.8 acres, the campus accommodates play areas, an athletic field, and three school buildings. Hunsaker Hall (1989) contains 12 classrooms for the Preschool and Kindergarten, the library, and offices for the Lower and Upper Elementary principals, the chaplain, and the nurse. Sillers Hall (1991) houses the Middle School principal's office as well as 27 classrooms for Grades 1–8, two computer laboratories, an art studio, and a science lab. In addition to athletic and fitness facilities, the Gymnasium (1993) provides a drama/theater center with stage and sound panels and, on the upper level, offices for the Headmaster, Admissions, Development, Accounting, and Church. A Capital Campaign is underway to finance a chapel and academic enrichment center.

The plant is owned by the School and valued at $7,400,000.

THE FACULTY. James S. Lusby, Headmaster of the School, is a native of Atlanta, Georgia. After graduating from St. Paul's School in New Hampshire, Mr. Lusby earned a B.A. from Trinity College in Connecticut (1969) and an M.Ed. from Boston College in 1982. Prior to accepting his current position, he worked at independent schools in Massachusetts and California. He currently serves as a member of the Diocesan Commission on Schools for the Episcopal Diocese of Los Angeles.

There are 49 members of the St. John's faculty, 42 full-time and 7 part-time. All hold baccalaureate degrees and 7 hold advanced degrees representing study at Arizona State 2, Bowling Green State, California Polytechnic (San Luis Obispo), California State 11, Cleveland Art Institute, College of New Jersey, College of William and Mary 2, Columbus College 2, Eastern Montana, Florida State, Grand Canyon University, Lowell State College, McNeese State University, Northern Illinois, Ohio University, Stephen F. Austin State, Trenton State, Youngstown State, and the Universities of Bridgeport, California (Berkeley, Los Angeles), New Mexico, San Francisco, Southern California 2, Texas, and West Florida. Among the faculty benefits are Social Security, a retirement plan, and health, life, and disability insurance.

A registered nurse and nurse assistant are employed on a full-time basis, and Orange County Fire and Rescue are five minutes from the School.

STUDENT BODY. In 1998–99, St. John's Episcopal School enrolled 895 students, 420 girls and 475 boys, in three-year-old Preschool through Grade 8, as follows: 200 in Preschool, 88 in Kindergarten, 82 in Grade 1, 92 in Grade 2, 75 in Grade 3, 75 in Grade 4, 51 in Grade 5, 78 in Grade 6, 78 in Grade 7, and 75 in Grade 8. Reflecting the racial and religious diversity of the

Saddleback Valley, students include African-Americans, Asians, Caucasians, Hispanics, and Native Americans. Thirty-one percent are Roman Catholic, ten percent are Episcopalian, and the remainder come from other religious backgrounds, including several Christian denominations as well as the Jewish, Muslim, Hindu, and Buddhist faiths.

ACADEMIC PROGRAM. The school year is divided into trimesters, from early September to mid-June. Vacations are scheduled at Thanksgiving, Christmas, and Easter. Throughout the year, there are several long weekends and observances of religious and national holidays. Report cards are issued three times a year, with a midtrimester report in the first marking period and "as-needed" reports later in the term. Formal parent-teacher conferences are held in the fall and spring. Classes, which are held five days a week, have an average enrollment of 25 students in all grades except Kindergarten, where the average is 21 children. Full-time aides in each primary classroom lower the student-teacher ratio to between 10.5:1 and 15:1.

The school day begins at 8:25 A.M. with each grade level attending a 20-minute, age-appropriate chapel service twice a week. There are six 50-minute class periods plus mid-morning and lunch breaks; dismissal is at 3:05 P.M. for Grades 6–8 with Kindergarten through Grade 5 being dismissed at 2:45 P.M. Middle School (Grades 6–8) students attend a weekly study hall, during which they can do homework, prepare for tests, or receive extra help from a teacher. Faculty are also available for after-school tutorials when necessary for an additional fee.

The academic program emphasizes the building of strong skills and comprehension in basic disciplines. The Lower Elementary (Kindergarten–Grade 2) curriculum consists of language arts, math, history/social studies, and science. In the Upper Elementary level (Grades 3–5), subject matter in these areas becomes more complex. Religion, Spanish, computers, music, art, and physical education are also part of the K–5 curriculum. Students in Grades 6–8 are required to take Art, Acrylic Painting, Computer, Drama, English, History, Literary Magazine, Math, Music, Physical Education, Religion, Science, and Spanish.

Ninety percent of St. John's graduates elect to attend area college preparatory high schools such as Santa Margarita Catholic High School, Mater Dei Catholic High School, and St. Margaret's Episcopal High School.

St. John's provides four weeks of enrichment activities during the month of July for students entering Grades 1 through 8. An extended-care program is also offered year round for working parents.

STUDENT ACTIVITIES. Two student councils, consisting of officers and class representatives, are elected to represent the Upper Elementary and Middle School divisions, respectively. The Middle School Student Council organizes Spirit Days, dances, pep rallies, and other activities.

St. John's is a member of the Parochial Athletic League and competes against other independent schools in the region. Boys play flag football, basketball, and volleyball; girls' teams are organized in basketball, softball, and volleyball.

In addition to athletics, students may choose to take part in drama club, choir, band, cheerleading, and fly fishing club.

Enrichment activities are provided through the Orange County Performing Arts Center, which stages dramatic and musical performances throughout the year. There is also an eighth-grade American History trip to Washington, D.C., and Williamsburg, Virginia; a seventh-grade Marine Science trip to Catalina Island; and a sixth-grade Outdoor Science camp in the Saddleback Valley Mountains.

Special events on the school calendar include Fall Family Festival/Alumni Reunion, Grandparents' Day, Christmas Boutique, Jog-A-Thon, a spring dinner dance auction, and four Middle School dances.

ADMISSION AND COSTS. St. John's Episcopal seeks students from diverse racial, religious, and socioeconomic backgrounds who demonstrate the willingness and ability to participate successfully in the School's academic and extracurricular offerings. All candidates are evaluated by the Admissions Director or a grade-level principal or teacher. Application may be made at any time during the year. Placement is made as vacancies become available. Students are rarely accepted after February 1. After current students are re-enrolled, preference is given to siblings, then to members of St. John's Church. The application fee is $50.

In 1999–2000, tuition in the Preschool ranges from $2468 for two days per week to $5608 for a full week. In Kindergarten–Grade 8, tuition is $5908. Additional fees are charged for registration and required uniforms. The School, which is a member of the School and Student Service for Financial Aid, awards approximately $110,000 annually in assistance to families, based on demonstrated need. Tuition insurance is required, and tuition payment plans are offered.

Director of Admissions: Chris Connally
Director of Development: Gail Lusby
Finance Director: Dixie Auringer
Summer School Director: Caren McDonald

St. Joseph Notre Dame High School   1881

*1011 Chestnut Street, Alameda, CA 94501. 510-523-1526;
Fax 510-523-2181; E-mail SjndPilots@Connectinc.com;
Web Site www.sjnd.com*

Enrolling 560 students, this parish high school of St. Joseph Basilica was founded by the Sisters of Notre Dame and the Brothers of Mary to provide excellent, affordable Catholic education. St. Joseph Notre Dame's curriculum develops the whole person through the traditional liberal arts and sciences, four years of religious studies, Advanced Placement and college credit opportunities, the Christian Service Program, and liturgies. Students take part in sports, school government, National Honor Society, yearbook, newspaper, band, drama, and campus ministry. Tuition: $4800–$6000. Financial Aid: $245,000. Katherine Montserrat is Director of Admissions; Anthony V. Aiello (St. Mary's College, B.A.; San Francisco State University, M.A.Ed.) is Principal. *Western Association.*

St. Margaret's Episcopal School

SAN JUAN CAPISTRANO

31641 La Novia, San Juan Capistrano, CA 92675. 949-661-0108;
Fax 949-489-8042; E-mail jhaiding@smes.org;
Web Site www.smes.org

S**T. MARGARET'S EPISCOPAL SCHOOL** in San Juan Capistrano, California, is a college preparatory day school in the Episcopal tradition, serving boys and girls in Preschool through Grade 12. Located 60 miles south of Los Angeles, San Juan Capistrano (population 26,183) is in Orange County in the southwestern part of the state in a region of great natural beauty. The beaches of the Pacific Ocean are minutes away and the area abounds in national forests. Most students travel to and from the campus by car or bus.

St. Margaret's, named for Scotland's patron saint of education, was founded in 1979 through the efforts of Canon Ernest D. Sillers, an Episcopal priest, who persuaded the Bishop of the Diocese to acquire land on which a church and school could be built. The first 79 students attended classes in temporary buildings; the first permanent structures were begun in 1980, with additional facilities constructed over the next ten years.

The mission of the School centers on the development of each student's spiritual, emotional, physical, and academic growth and well-being. Students of all faiths are welcome, and the time-honored values of the Judeo-Christian philosophy form the basis of daily conduct. The School works in partner-

ship with parents and families to motivate and enable students to educate themselves independently and to "provide a broad educational exploration" in traditional disciplines. Multicultural diversity, acceptance of individual differences, and a strong sense of commitment to the community are among the goals the School seeks to promote.

St. Margaret's is governed by a 20-member Board of Trustees, chaired by the Bishop of the Episcopal Diocese of Los Angeles, that includes parents, clergy, and other friends of the School. An active Parent Teacher Fellowship organizes volunteers, develops programs for the entire school community, and assists in fund-raising efforts. The School is accredited by the Western Association of Schools and Colleges, the California Association of Independent Schools, and the National Association for the Education of Young Children. It holds membership in the National Association of Independent Schools, the National Association of Episcopal Schools, The Cum Laude Society, and the Council for Advancement and Support of Education, among other organizations.

THE CAMPUS. School facilities emphasize the Spanish-style architecture of the surrounding community and buildings are linked by a series of colonnaded walkways. There are separate buildings housing each of the divisions: Preschool, Lower School (Kindergarten–Grade 5), Middle School (Grades 6–8), and Upper School (Grades 9–12). In addition to classrooms, science, computer, and language laboratories; art and music areas; and a new state-of-the-art library, the School uses St. Margaret's Episcopal Church for daily chapel services. Athletic facilities include the gym and weight room, a football field, and other playing fields.

THE FACULTY. Markham B. Campaigne, appointed Headmaster of St. Margaret's Episcopal School in 1986, is a graduate of the United States Naval Academy (B.S. 1966) and the University of Missouri at Kansas City (M.A. 1974). He is married and the father of four children.

The 28 men and 73 women who comprise the faculty have earned baccalaureate and advanced degrees, including five doctorates, from such colleges and universities as Arizona State, Boston College, Boston University, California State, Chapman, Colgate, Florida Atlantic, George Mason, Harvard, James Madison, Louisiana State, Loyola University, Mary Baldwin, Occidental, Ohio Wesleyan, Oregon State, Pepperdine, Pomona, Princeton, Queen's University (Ireland), Regis, Scripps, Simon Fraser, Wellesley, Wesleyan College, and the Universities of Arizona, Calgary, California, Connecticut, Edinburgh, Houston, Minnesota, the Pacific, Redlands, St. Thomas Aquinas, San Francisco, the South, and Southern California.

Health services are administered by two registered nurses, and complete hospital facilities are located within a few miles of the School.

STUDENT BODY. In 1999–2000, St. Margaret's Episcopal School enrolled 1132 students in Preschool through Grade 12, distributed as follows: 121 in Preschool, 401 in the Lower School, 287 in the Middle School, and 327 in the Upper School. Representing a wide diversity of racial, religious, and ethnic backgrounds, they come from San Juan Capistrano and nearby towns.

ACADEMIC PROGRAM. The school year, divided into quarters, opens early in September and extends through the first week of June; there are recesses at Thanksgiving and Easter, a Christmas vacation, several long weekends, and observances of national holidays. Middle and Upper School report cards are mailed to parents every nine weeks, with deficiency reports sent at the five-week mark as needed. In the Lower School, reports are handed to parents following the first quarter parent/teacher conference and thereafter are sent home with the students.

School begins at 8:10 A.M. in the Lower and Middle schools and at 7:50 A.M. in the Upper School, with half-day Preschool ending at 11:30 A.M. and full day at 2:45 P.M. Monday through Friday. The Middle and Upper School rotating schedule consists of seven periods of 50 minutes, each meeting four days a week. In addition, there is a daily 30-minute tutorial time concluding at 3:30 P.M.

In the Early Childhood Development Center, St. Margaret's offers a developmental curriculum in which students are encouraged to build a positive self-image, learn moral values, and to increase their coordination and balance. Foundations are built for the basic disciplines through exploration of science and nature, families and culture, drama and art, language and numbers, and music and movement.

The Lower School curriculum emphasizes reading, language arts, and communications skills as the basis for a "strong, successful education." Beginning in Kindergarten, the program includes English, mathematics, science, social studies, art, music, and Spanish, and all students have computer instruction at least once a week. Field trips to the theater, museums, zoos and planetariums, and other places of interest enhance classroom instruction.

In the Middle School, the course of study is carefully structured to build on acquired skills and facilitate the transition to the Upper School. The core curriculum features English; mathematics through PreAlgebra or Algebra I; social studies, including United States History; Latin in Grades 6–7 and Latin, Japanese, French, or Spanish in Grade 8; science; physical education; and a choice of elective classes ranging from music, theater, and art to health, religion, and speech.

Nineteen academic credits are needed to graduate, including four years of English; three years each of mathematics, history, a foreign language, and physical education; two years of science; one and one-half years of religion; one year of fine arts; a half-year of computer science; and a service project.

Among the courses offered in the Upper School are English I–IV, Poetry and the Essay, Short Story and the Play, Philosophy of Literature, Journalism, Creative Writing, Public Speaking and Debate; Algebra I–II, Geometry, Precalculus, Calculus, Programming in Pascal, Computer Applications; Physical Science, Physics, Biology, Human Anatomy and Physiology, Environmental Science, Chemistry; Latin I–IV, French I–IV, Spanish I–IV, Japanese I–III; World Civilizations to 1500, World Civilizations Renaissance to Present, History of California, Current Affairs, American Government, Economics, United States History; Chorus, Studio Art I–III, Two-Dimensional Design, Art History II, Drama, Film Making, Humanities Through the Arts, Graphic Design; and Physical Education. There are Advanced Placement and honors courses in most disciplines.

All 56 seniors in the Class of 1999 were accepted at four-year colleges and universities, 3 by "early decision." They are currently attending such institutions as Bucknell, California Institute of Technology, Cambridge, Cornell, Emory, Georgetown University, Harvey Mudd, Haverford, Lehigh, Yale, and the Universities of California, Colorado, Miami, Michigan, Puget Sound, Redlands, Richmond, and Southern California.

STUDENT ACTIVITIES. Opportunities for leadership are available through the elected Middle School Student Council and, in the Upper School, the Associated Student Body, which sponsors major social and fund-raising events.

Lower School students are assigned to one of four "Houses," which engage in friendly competition in a variety of games and sports. In the Middle School, there are 12 boys' and girls' teams formed in volleyball, basketball, soccer, softball, and flag football. Students may also choose from activities such as pep band, the school newspaper, drama troupe, and special-interest clubs for lacrosse, computers, and mountaineering.

St. Margaret's Episcopal School is a member of the California Interscholastic Federation and fields varsity teams in cross-country, volleyball, soccer, basketball, softball, tennis, and track for girls; boys' teams are organized in cross-country, football, soccer, basketball, baseball, tennis, volleyball, golf, and track and field.

Students contribute art, poetry, and stories to the School's literary magazine and publish a yearbook. Qualified scholars may be invited to join the National Honor Society or The Cum Laude Society. Other groups available in the Upper School are International Club, chess, camping, Cultural Arts, Peer Counselors, and Safe Rides.

Special events are planned by the Associated Student Body throughout the year such as beach parties, class retreats, Spirit Week and Homecoming, special Christmas programs, drama productions, mixers, the winter formal, the prom, pep rallies, and a variety of assemblies.

ADMISSION AND COSTS. St. Margaret's Episcopal School seeks students with "inquisitive minds, lively spirits, and self-discipline" who possess sound character and demonstrate the ability to achieve success in the rigorous academic program. Admission is based on the applicant's past academic record, recommendations from teachers, and the results of the School's entrance exam. Special consideration is given to the brothers and sisters of current students, members of St. Margaret's Church, and other qualified Episcopal families.

In 1999–2000, tuition is $4165–$9775 in the Preschool, $9775 Lower School, $10,290 in the Middle School, and

$11,170 in the Upper School. Other expenses include book fees ($100–$300), school and gym uniforms ($250–$325), and field trips ($50–$250). Financial aid is awarded in the amount of $480,000, and there is a tuition refund plan.

Dean of Faculty: Lisa Merryman
Upper School Principal: Tim Quinn
Middle School Principal: David Boyle
Lower School Principal: Barbara Deubert
Preschool Director: Jody Prichard
Director of Admissions: Judy Haidinger
Director of Development/Alumni: Cindy Bobruk
Director of College Guidance: Mary Jane Greene
Business Manager: Richard Mortimer
Athletic Director: Brady Lock (Upper School)
Chaplain: The Reverend Lark Diaz

Saint Mark's School   1980

39 Trellis Drive, San Rafael, CA 94903. 415-472-8000;
  Admissions 415-472-8007; Fax 415-472-0722; E-mail
  elittle@marin.k12.ca.us; Web Site www.saintmarksschool.org

Saint Mark's is a nonsectarian day school enrolling 376 boys and girls in Kindergarten–Grade 8. It seeks to promote a love of learning in children of academic promise, to develop strong academic skills, and to instill fairness and self-confidence. Music, art, drama, computer, foreign languages, and physical education are required along with traditional subjects. Field trips, team sports, theater productions, the Headmaster's Reading Program, a national champion chess team, Computer Club, Science Fiction Club, after-school enrichment classes, and a summer program are among the activities. Tuition: $9275–$9750. Extras: $250–$375. Financial Aid: $301,000. Elizabeth H. Little is Director of Admissions; Damon H. Kerby (Kenyon, A.B. 1971; Stanford, M.A. 1999) was appointed Headmaster in 1987. *Western Association.*

St. Matthew's Episcopal Day School   1953

16 Baldwin Avenue, San Mateo, CA 94401. 650-342-5436;
  Fax 650-342-4019; E-mail handalianl@stmatthewsonline.org

St. Matthew's Episcopal Day School, enrolling 230 boys and girls in Pre-School–Grade 8, seeks to provide students with a challenging academic education while helping them to become compassionate members of the community. A rigorous, traditional course of study is enhanced by technology education, French, studio art, music, physical education, daily chapel, and field study programs in Grades 6–8. Students receive individual attention from a dedicated, supportive faculty. Class size is limited to 22 students, and a high degree of family participation in school activities is expected. Tuition: $5500–$9700. Financial Aid: $75,000. Linda Handalian is Admission Director; Mark C. Hale, M.Ed., is Head of School.

St. Matthew's Parish School   1949

1031 Bienveneda Avenue, Pacific Palisades, CA 90272.
  310-454-1350; Fax 310-573-7423; Web Site
  www.stmatthewsschool.com

Set near the ocean in a pastoral 33-acre campus, St. Matthew's is an Episcopal day school enrolling 320 boys and girls in Preschool–Grade 8. The School encourages each child's positive self-concept, sensitivity toward others, intellectual curiosity, and mastery of basic learning skills. In all grades, the curriculum includes laboratory science in two new science centers and computer science in five computer labs, plus art, music, drama, and foreign languages. A new sports/performing arts complex houses the drama, physical education, and interscholastic athletic programs. A summer program is offered. Tuition:

$6260–$11,935. Financial Aid: $70,000. A. Lee Quiring is Director of Admission; Les W. Frost (University of California [San Francisco], D.Phar. 1968) is Headmaster.

Saklan Valley School   1978

1678 School Street, Moraga, CA 94556. 925-376-7900; Admissions
  925-631-7802; Fax 925-376-1156; E-mail saklancasey@aol.com

Saklan Valley is a nonprofit, coeducational day school enrolling 150 students in Pre-Kindergarten–Grade 8. Rigorous academics are combined with interdisciplinary and experiential learning opportunities. Saklan has a strong focus on community and the development of respect, responsibility, and integrity among its students, faculty, and families. Saklan encourages students to be lifelong lovers of learning and conscientious citizens. As part of a nurturing community, all Saklan students and parents receive personal and individual attention. Financial aid is available. Tuition: $4300–$9500. Casey Malone is Director of Admissions; Jonathan Martin is Head of School. *Western Association.*

San Domenico School   SAN ANSELMO

1500 Butterfield Road, San Anselmo, CA 94960-1099.
  415-258-1990; Fax 415-258-9197;
  E-mail lleone@sandomenico.org

S AN DOMENICO SCHOOL in San Anselmo, California, is a Roman Catholic, college preparatory boarding and day school enrolling girls in Pre-Kindergarten–Grade 12 and day boys in Pre-Kindergarten–Grade 8. San Anselmo is a small community in Marin County, part of the Greater Bay Area, which thrives on abundant cultural, educational, and recreational assets including wilderness, museums, concert halls, and ski slopes. San Francisco is 20 miles to the south. Private buses provide daily service to the campus, and public transportation is also available.

The oldest independent school in California, San Domenico was founded in Monterey in 1850 by Sr. Mary Goemaere, O.P., a French Dominican nun. After moves to Benicia and San Rafael where it was known as the Dominican Convent School, it was established as San Domenico School in its present location in 1965. Boys have been admitted in the Primary and Middle schools since 1974.

San Domenico seeks to prepare students for college through contemporary and innovative academic training within the Dominican tradition of excellence and to prepare engaged, purposeful young women for the challenges of adult life. Small class size, the skill and willingness of teachers to directly engage individual students, and structuring small group interaction are integral to that style of learning. In the coeducational elementary grades, team teaching provides a flexible and creative approach to learning and problem solving. Students study different cultures and religions, including the Catholic tradition.

The School is a nonprofit organization under the direction of the Dominican Sisters and a Board of 25 Trustees. It is accredited by the Western Association of Schools and Colleges and is a member of the National Association of Independent Schools, the National Catholic Education Association, and several other professional organizations.

THE CAMPUS. The School occupies 626 acres of Canada de Herrera, a former Spanish land grant. The Pre-Kindergarten, Lower, Middle, and Upper schools each have their own facilities, administration buildings, and assembly halls.

The Upper School's main academic building is a two-story structure with 16 classrooms; a Macintosh computer laboratory; labs for biology, chemistry, and physics; and the college counseling office, bookstore, and student lounge. The library, built in recent years at a cost of $2,000,000, houses 22,000 volumes, 120 periodicals, computers, spaces for quiet study, and a counseling center. The Lower and Middle schools also have computer and science labs. Students in all grades have access to the Music Conservatory, which provides practice rooms, teaching studios, and pavilions for performances. Each school also houses its own art studio, which contains equipment for printmaking, pottery, and painting. All children make use of the gymnasium, Olympic-size swimming pool, softball and soccer fields, six tennis courts, and riding center with two barns and a covered arena. Upper School students live in three dormitories with kitchen and laundry facilities, computer and recreation centers, and faculty apartments.

THE FACULTY. Sr. M. Gervaise Valpey, O.P., was appointed Head of the School in 1989. She holds a B.A. degree in English from Dominican College and has engaged in further studies in administration and counseling at the Universities of San Francisco and Portland. Lauren Bedell is Assistant Head, John Bowermaster is Principal of the Upper School, Dr. Matthew Heersche is Principal of the Middle School, Carole Chase is Primary Principal, and Dorrie Chiarella is Early Education Coordinator.

The teaching faculty, some of whom live on campus, numbers 60 men and women. They hold degrees from institutions such as American Academy of Dramatic Arts, Colorado College, Dominican College, Fordham, Georgetown, Harvard, Haverford, Iowa State, Lewis and Clark, Pennsylvania State, St. Mary's, San Francisco State, Simmons, Sonoma State, Stanford, State University of New York (Albany), Syracuse, Wesleyan, and the Universities of Alberta, California (Berkeley, Santa Barbara, Santa Cruz), Chicago, Georgia, Michigan, Pennsylvania, Rochester, San Francisco, and Wisconsin. All faculty members have pursued additional studies beyond their degree programs. Faculty in the arts are also practicing professionals.

STUDENT BODY. In 1998–99, the School enrolled 510 students in Early Education–Grade 12, including 65 Upper School boarders. Day students come from within a 5-mile radius. Most boarders are from California, with others representing five states and ten foreign countries. About a third of the students are Catholic; 30 percent receive financial aid.

ACADEMIC PROGRAM. The academic year is divided into semesters and extends from late August to early June with

breaks at Thanksgiving, Christmas, and Easter. Classes are held five days a week between 8:10 A.M. and 3:30 P.M. The average class size is 12. Students work in the library or art studio or congregate in the student lounge during free periods. Most boarders have required two-hour evening study halls. Students in Grades 9 and 10 are expected to spend 30–40 minutes per subject on homework each night, with 45 minutes planned per subject for Grades 11 and 12. Teachers offer extra help, and tutoring services can be provided for a fee. Report cards are issued each quarter.

Lower and Middle School curricula consist of reading, writing and literature, spelling, grammar, handwriting, mathematics, religion, social science, health/science, safety, computers, art, music, French/Spanish, library skills, and physical education.

To graduate, a student must complete four years of English including American Literature; two of a modern foreign language; three of social studies; three of mathematics; one each of life science, physical science, visual fine arts, and History of Art and Music; four of religious studies; two of physcial education including Health; one term of computers; and completion of 100 hours of community service through the Service Learning program. The School strongly recommends three years of foreign language and science. All students take Freshman Foundations, in which the studies of literature, history, religion, arts, and writing are interrelated. Honors and Advanced Placement courses are offered in every subject.

The School maintains a special focus on the arts, helping students develop understanding and skills under the direction of professionals in music, drama, and fine arts. The Virtuoso Program in the Music Conservatory offers full scholarships to a select group of string instrumentalists preparing for careers in music.

Upper School course offerings include Literature and Composition 1–2, Writers of the American South, Twentieth Century British Literature, Slave Literature, Contemporary Fiction by Women Writers; English as a Second Language, French 1–5, Spanish 1–5, Japanese 1–2; World History and Religions, U.S. History and Government, International Relations; Introduction to Psychology; Math 1–3, an integrated program in Algebra, Geometry and Trigonometry, Precalculus, Calculus; Computer Skills, Graphic Design; Biology, Chemistry, Physics, Ecology and Environmental Biology; Art 1–3, Ceramics 1–3, Drawing/Painting 1–3, Printmaking, History of Art and Music; Drama 1–4, Dance 1–2; Hebrew and Christian Scriptures, Introduction to Philosophy, Religion and the Arts, History of the Christian Church; and Music Conservatory (private instrumental instruction), String Quartet, Orchestra da Camera, and San Domenico Singers. Noncredit electives are offered in Journalism, Riding, and Tennis.

Graduates of the Senior Class of 1998 attend Boston University, California State (Sonoma), Depauw, Hawaii Pacific, Instituto Tecnologico, Marymount Manhattan, Parsons School of Design, San Francisco Conservatory, Wellesley, Whitman, Willamette, and the Universities of California (Berkeley, Davis,

Irvine, Los Angeles), Chicago, Iberoamericano, Montana, Puget Sound, and San Francisco.

STUDENT ACTIVITIES. Students elect officers for each class and the Student Council, which meets weekly to organize student activities and discuss other issues.

Some ongoing activities are the newspaper, literary magazine, and yearbook; Gold Key Tour Guides, Drama, Early Education's Annual Candle Lighting Ceremony, the Lower and Middle Schools' Cultural Exchange Day, Environmental, Guitar, Photography, and Poetry clubs; International Association; and Girls' Athletic Association.

An outgrowth of the School's mission to reflect upon one's role in the global community, the ROSE Program helps students to engage in social service activities such as working for nonprofit organizations, visiting retirement homes, tutoring youngsters in lower grades, and implementing recycling and other environmental programs.

The Drama Department mounts five stage productions each year. The Conservatory features four string quartets and a quintet in residence who perform both at School and elsewhere by invitation. The Orchestra da Camera and San Domenico Chamber Singers also perform on campus and throughout the area.

Every student can play on a San Domenico team in interscholastic competition beginning in Middle School. The School is a member of the Bay Counties League and fields varsity and junior varsity teams in volleyball, badminton, cross-country, basketball, soccer, swimming, track and field, and water polo. The Physical Education program offers fitness opportunities such as hiking, dance, aerobics, karate, yoga, and swimming. The program also incorporates relevant adolescent health issues.

The Equestrian Center offers professional instruction for beginning to advanced riders, using School-owned or boarding horses.

The Student Council sponsors several dances each year. Other special events are Big and Little Sisters matching; Celebration of the Rings, a reception in which the seniors honor the juniors; Christmas Tableaux; Father and Daughter Day; and Mother and Daughter Day.

ADMISSION AND COSTS. San Domenico School seeks to enroll a diverse group of young people who are interested in enriching their lives and the world around them. In the Upper School, girls are admitted on the basis of previous academic performance, teacher recommendations, essays, SSAT scores, and personal interviews. New Upper School students are accepted primarily in Grades 9 and 10. For admission to elementary grades, the School seeks boys and girls who possess such qualities as curiosity, humor, and sensitivity to others. The application deadline is January 20 for fall admission. An application fee of $85 is required.

Tuition in Pre-Kindergarten–Grade 8 ranges from $6599 to $11,827; boarding tuition in Grades 9–12 is $26,528, and day

tuition, including hot lunch, is $16,132. Extras for international students range from $1500 to $2700. Fees for private music instruction, riding, and tennis are additional. Tuition payment plans and tuition insurance are available. The School provides financial aid on the basis of need.

Director of Admission: Elizabeth Clark Leone '70
Director of Development: Kathy Scollin
Director of Alumni Relations: Stephanie Bucknum Mason '69
College Counselor: Susan Lee
School Counselor: Dr. Nan Brenzel
Director of Finance: Lauren E. Bedell
Director of Athletics: Dave Geoffrion

San Francisco Day School   1979

350 Masonic Avenue, San Francisco, CA 94118. 415-931-2422; Fax 415-931-1753; E-mail cfenster@sfds.pvt.k12.ca.us; Web Site http://www.sfds.pvt.k12.ca.us

Founded by area parents, San Francisco Day School enrolls 400 boys and girls in Kindergarten–Grade 8. Emphasizing basic skills, critical thinking, creativity, and an understanding of diverse cultures, the School seeks to nurture each child's growth intellectually, culturally, and physically. An afternoon enrichment program offers sports, art, computer skills, science, games, drama, and cooking. Tuition: $11,210–$11,360. Financial aid is available. Jim Telander (University of Minnesota, B.S., M.A.) was appointed Head of School in 1991.

San Francisco University High School   1973

3065 Jackson Street, San Francisco, CA 94115. 415-447-3100; Fax 415-447-5801; Web Site www.sfuhs.org

San Francisco University High School is a coeducational, college preparatory school enrolling 390 students in Grades 9–12. Created to serve young men and women of above-average intellectual ability, the School encourages in its students a love of learning so that graduates may enjoy full, meaningful lives and the community may benefit from the development of creative, capable leaders. The college preparatory curriculum emphasizes the acquisition of essential academic skills. At the same time, the School is committed to the students' total emotional, moral, physical, and intellectual growth. Tuition: $16,175. Financial Aid: $868,000. Lorri Hamilton is Director of Admissions; Dr. Jeanne Amster was appointed Head in 1997. *Western Association.*

Santa Catalina School   MONTEREY

Mark Thomas Drive, Monterey, CA 93940-5291. 831-655-9312; Admissions 831-655-9356; E-mail admissions@santacatalina.org; Web Site www.santacatalina.org

SANTA CATALINA SCHOOL in Monterey, California, is dedicated to the education of young women. An all-girls' boarding and day school in the Catholic tradition, Santa Catalina was founded in 1850 by Soeur Mary Goemaere and established on its present site in 1950. The wooded campus, located on the Monterey Peninsula, is convenient to the educational opportunities of Stanford University, the University of California at Santa Cruz, and the San Francisco Bay Area.

The philosophy of Santa Catalina School is to integrate religious truth and values with life. The value of Christian service is emphasized through community involvement both on and off campus. The School seeks to prepare students to become lifelong learners and to choose their directions and contributions in life.

Strong science, computer science, and mathematics programs enable students to grasp the technological principles shaping modern civilization. Emphasis is also placed on communication skills, literature, and the humanities, including the fine and performing arts.

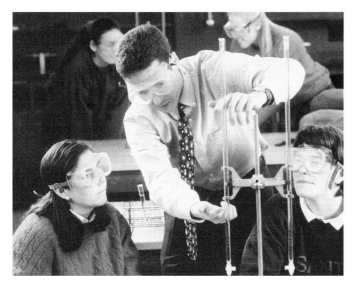

A nonprofit institution, the School is governed by a Board of Trustees. Through an annual giving fund, which helps with scholarships, faculty benefits, and capital improvements, the Board endeavors to implement the School's goal of "nurturing academic excellence, an outstanding faculty, and planned growth." Santa Catalina is accredited by the Western Association of Schools and Colleges and is a member of the National Association of Independent Schools, the California Association of Independent Schools, and the National Coalition of Girls' Schools, among other affiliations.

THE CAMPUS. The hacienda that served as the original school building is now encircled by classrooms, dormitories, and other facilities in a blend of traditional and contemporary Spanish-style architecture. The 36-acre campus, located one-half mile from Monterey's beaches, is graced by gardens, shaded walks, and California live oaks.

There are three classroom buildings, a gymnasium, a central library, a two-story science center, a performing arts center, and a music center and dance studio. Open seven days a week, the 33,000-volume Sister Mary Kieran Memorial Library is computerized for access to libraries and their materials worldwide. Art facilities include ceramics and general art studios, a kiln, a photography darkroom, and developing equipment. The Science Center contains chemistry, physics, and biology laboratories, a lecture amphitheater and projection room, and an observation deck equipped with a Questar telescope. The Sister Carlotta Performing Arts Center houses a 500-seat theater with professional lighting and sound equipment. The Mary L. Johnson Music Center provides soundproof practice rooms and a dance studio with a spring-loaded floor. A campus-wide computer network provides Internet access, which is utilized both in and out of the classroom. The Computer Center, Writing Center, and library and science laboratories are equipped with computer technology for student use.

The Bedford Athletic Complex incorporates a gymnasium, pool, tennis courts, and field areas. Health-care facilities include a health center and a nurse's office. Additional areas for student use are the Student Center and Snack Bar run by Senate members. All resident students attend church on Sunday in the Rosary Chapel, which is also available for optional weekday services and individual visits.

Residents live in three dormitories. Most resident students share double rooms, but single rooms are also available. Each dormitory contains living accommodations for resident faculty families.

THE FACULTY. Sister Carlotta O'Donnell has been Head of School for 36 years and holds A.B. and B.S. degrees from the College of Saint Catherine. There are 32 full-time faculty members and 10 part-time instructors. Ninety-one percent of the faculty hold advanced degrees. Representative colleges and universities of faculty members include Bombay University (India), Boston College, Bucknell, California State Polytechnic, Cornell, Dartmouth, Duke, Harvard, Hollins, Massachusetts Institute of Technology, Purdue, St. John's, Scripps, Stanford, Wellesley, Williams, and the Universities of California (Berkeley, San Diego, Santa Barbara), Chicago, Illinois, Montreal (Canada), New Hampshire, San Diego, the South, Texas, and Wisconsin.

STUDENT BODY. In 1999–2000, the Upper School enrolls 163 boarding students and 148 day students. Boarding students come from California, 12 other states, and 13 foreign countries.

ACADEMIC PROGRAM. The school year, which extends from early September to early June, includes a Thanksgiving recess, a Christmas vacation, a winter break, an Easter/spring vacation, and one open weekend each semester. Academic classes meet five days a week.

The basic curriculum for all Upper School students includes four years each of English and religious studies; three to four years each of history, mathematics, and foreign language; two to four years of science; and four years of an elective in the arts. Honors and Advanced Placement courses are available in every discipline. Fifth-year courses are open to qualified students in mathematics, science, history, and languages. Special-interest courses are also available.

The student-faculty ratio is 7:1. Students are placed according to individual ability levels, with an average of 12–15 students in a class. Individual assistance from faculty members is available to each girl as the need arises.

Each student has her own faculty advisor. These individuals assist and advise students in the development of their talents and potential. In addition to four grade reports per year, progress reports are sent with comments to parents. Individual college counseling begins in the junior year, at which time students begin regular appointments with the College Counselor. Annual visits to Santa Catalina by college representatives and the extensive individual college counseling program conducted by the Head of School and the College Counselor serve as significant aids in the application process.

The institutions in which Santa Catalina graduates are enrolled include Boston College, Brown, Carleton, Colby, Colgate, Connecticut College, Cornell, Dartmouth, Duke, Georgetown, Harvard, Johns Hopkins, Massachusetts Institute of Technology, Middlebury, Mount Holyoke, Northwestern, Princeton,

Santa Clara University, Scripps, Skidmore, Stanford, Trinity, Tufts, Tulane, Vanderbilt, Wellesley, Williams, Yale, and the Universities of California, Colorado, Michigan, Oregon, Pennsylvania, and Virginia.

The Santa Catalina Summer Camp, for girls entering Grades 3–9, consists of a full five-week session or two two-and-one-half-week sessions. A tennis clinic, musical theater workshop, riding, computer science, and marine biology are offered in addition to the arts and recreational activities.

STUDENT ACTIVITIES. Students publish the newspaper, yearbook, and school literary magazine. Activity groups at Santa Catalina include the Student Alumnae Organization, Junior Statesmen of America, Amnesty International, Rebel Shakespeare Company, Senior Prefects, Accents (student-run dance group), Schola, and ecco (student-run a cappella group). In addition, there are numerous community service opportunities. Girls tutor younger students and mentally handicapped adults as well as assist at a local convalescent home, the Salvation Army Day Care Center, the Boys and Girls Club, and a local hospital. Additionally, students participate in beach clean-ups, raise funds for food baskets, and sponsor underprivileged children through the School's Christian Children's Fund.

Concerts, dances, lectures, and movies are a part of campus life, and periodic assemblies in the Performing Arts Center provide the opportunity to enjoy guest musicians, vocalists, choral groups, and dance and drama workshops.

Santa Catalina teams compete interscholastically in cross-country, track and field, volleyball, basketball, tennis, golf, field hockey, lacrosse, softball, soccer, water polo, swimming, and diving. Every girl has the opportunity to become a member of a varsity or junior varsity team. Physical education courses also include riding, ballet, jazz, and aerobics. Through its membership in the United States Lawn Tennis Association, Santa Catalina hosts an annual Invitational Tennis Tournament that draws players from throughout the state.

Weekend activities are planned by the Director of Activities (a faculty member), the Activities Coordinator (a Student Senate officer), and class advisors. Traditional annual events include the Halloween Party, Fall Dance, many Christmas events, Winter Formal, Spirit Day, St. Patrick's Day Dance, Ring Dinner, Junior/Senior Prom, Parents' Weekend, Father-Daughter Weekend, Yearbook Dinner, and Class Night, held the evening before graduation.

Throughout the year, there are trips to the San Francisco Bay area for museum visits, plays, ballet, symphony orchestra concerts, sightseeing, and shopping. Other off-campus trips are taken to theme parks, ski resorts, and state and national parks for rafting, hiking, and camping. In addition, the Monterey Peninsula has many recreational and cultural opportunities.

ADMISSION AND COSTS. Santa Catalina School accepts students in all programs without regard to race, creed, color, disability, or national origin. Students are selected on the basis of scholastic achievement, strong personal qualifications, a personal interview, Secondary School Admission Test scores, and a written essay. The Upper School accepts students in Grades 9–11.

In 1999–2000, tuition is $25,100 for resident students and $14,100 for day students. Additional fees include $28 for accident insurance, a $500 bookstore deposit, $175 for resident students' local transportation, $100 for technology networking and supplies, and a $250 student activity fee. Financial aid, awarded on the basis of need as indicated by the School and Student Service for Financial Aid, is extended to 30 percent of the student body. A Merit Scholarship is offered to an outstanding freshman or entering sophomore for up to 20 percent of tuition. A low-interest loan program and several tuition payment plans are available.

Dean of Students: Susannah Pennell
Assistant Director of Upper School: Sr. Christine Price
Director of Alumnae Relations: Mary Dowson
Dean of Enrollment and Financial Aid: Meriwether Beatty
Director of Admission: Heather Willis Daly
Director of Advancement: Croom Beatty
College Counselor: William Peck
Treasurer: Sr. Jean Gilhuly
Director of Athletics: James Morton

The Seven Hills School   1962

975 North San Carlos Drive, Walnut Creek, CA 94598.
925-933-0666; Fax 925-933-6271;
E-mail suevl@sevenhills.pvt.k12.ca.us; Web Site
www.sevenhills.pvt.k12.ca.us

The Seven Hills School is a coeducational day school enrolling 350 students in Preschool–Grade 8. The School strives to provide a developmentally appropriate, integrated curriculum in a small-class setting. The program emphasizes the acquisition and application of academic skills in the liberal and fine arts, supplemented by French, Spanish, music, art, physical education, computers, and electives. Summer day camp, Middle School intramural sports, clubs, an Extended Day Program, bus service, and hot lunch are available. Tuition: $7250–$11,150. Financial Aid: $150,000. Susan A. VanLandingham is Director of Admission; William H. Miller (University of Notre Dame, B.A. 1970; University of San Francisco, M.A. 1980) was appointed Headmaster in 1992.

Sonoma Country Day School   1983

50 Mark West Springs Road, Santa Rosa, CA 95403. 707-524-2000;
Fax 707-573-4754; E-mail scds@scds.org; Web Site www.scds.org

Sonoma Country Day, enrolling 213 boys and girls in Kindergarten–Grade 8, is a classic preparatory school grounded in the old-fashioned, broad-based liberal arts and sciences. The program emphasizes a strong foundation in English, math, history, and science. The School offers a full drama, music, and art curriculum; second-language study in French, Latin, and Spanish; physical education at all levels; and team sports. Computer literacy is integrated throughout the program. An after-school program and summer school are available. Tuition: $9300–$10,500. Pat Marchand is Admissions Director; Philip C. Nix is Founding Headmaster. *Western Association.*

Stuart Hall for Boys 1956

2222 Broadway, San Francisco, CA 94115. 415-563-2900;
Fax 415-929-6928; E-mail sacred.sf.ca.us; Web Site sacred.sf.ca.us

A Catholic, independent day school enrolling 324 boys in Kindergarten–Grade 8, Stuart Hall for Boys, one of the Schools of the Sacred Heart, is part of a four-school complex including Stuart Hall High School, Convent Elementary School, and Convent High School. Stuart Hall seeks to prepare students for entrance into college preparatory high schools and to develop spiritual and social responsibility. Foreign languages, art, music, computer science, outdoor education, community service, and interscholastic sports are integral to the curriculum. A coeducational summer school program is also offered. Tuition: $11,525–$11,725. Financial aid is available. Pamela Thorp is Admissions Director; Gerald J. Grossman (Stonehill College, B.A.; University of Notre Dame, M.A.) is Head. *Western Association.*

Stuart Hall High School 2000

1715 Octavia Street, San Francisco, CA 94109. 415-563-2900;
Fax 415-292-3183; Web Site www.sacred.sf.ca.us

With the founding of Stuart Hall High School, the Network of Sacred Heart Schools completes its independent, Catholic, single-sex educational program in the city of San Francisco. The School will open in the fall of 2000 with an expected enrollment of 50 freshmen; an additional grade will be added in each of the next three years to serve a total of 200 young men in Grades 9–12. Stuart Hall High joins Convent of the Sacred Heart Elementary and High schools for girls and Stuart Hall for Boys at the elementary level in carrying on the Sacred Heart tradition of academic excellence within a values-oriented, college preparatory curriculum. Gordon Sharafinski (St. Mary's University, B.A.; University of St. Thomas, M.A.T.) is Head.

Town School for Boys 1939

2750 Jackson Street, San Francisco, CA 94115. 415-921-3747;
Fax 415-921-2968

Town School for Boys is an independent day school enrolling 400 students in Kindergarten–Grade 8. The academic program is complemented by a state-of-art science center, computer lab, classroom computers, and a media theater. A wide range of activities includes outdoor education, intramural sports, music, drama, publications, student government, special-interest clubs, and a strong commitment to community service. There is a coeducational summer program offering enrichment, academic, and athletic courses. Tuition: $10,800. Financial Aid: $350,000. Lynn McKannay is Director of Admission; W. Brewster Ely IV (Ithaca, B.A. 1970; Middlebury, M.A. 1975) was appointed Headmaster in 1989. *Western Association.*

Turningpoint School   BEL AIR

P.O. Box 49325, 1300 North Sepulveda Boulevard, Bel Air, CA
90049. 310-476-8585; Fax 310-476-0916;
E-mail ashelton@turningpointschool.org;
Web Site www.turningpointschool.org

TURNINGPOINT SCHOOL in Bel Air, California, is an independent, coeducational, elementary day school enrolling students in Primary (two years, ten months) to Grade 6. The School is located in the lovely residential area of Bel Air in Los Angeles (population 3,485,398), only minutes from the campus of the University of California at Los Angeles and major business and shopping centers. Its location permits students to enjoy the myriad of cultural and educational opportunities that abound in the City of Angels while benefiting from proximity to mountains, the Pacific Ocean, and wilderness areas. Most students commute via private car pools organized through the School community.

Turningpoint was founded as Montessori of West Los Angeles in 1970 by educators and business professionals who were strongly committed to the philosophy and principles advanced by Dr. Maria Montessori. In 1988, it was renamed to reflect the series of turning points that children and schools undergo as they flourish and mature.

Turningpoint's central philosophy is predicated on a basic understanding of, and respect for, each child as an individual, meeting the complex academic, emotional, social, and physical needs of multifaceted students. Within a warm, caring environment, students are challenged by rich experiences designed to inspire personal responsibility, good citizenship, leadership, and a lively appreciation of the joy of learning.

A nonprofit, nonsectarian institution, Turningpoint School is governed by a self-perpetuating Board of 17 Trustees who meet bimonthly. It is accredited by the Western Association of Schools and Colleges and the California Association of Independent Schools, holding membership in such professional organizations as the National Association of Independent Schools, the Educational Records Bureau, the Independent School Alliance for Minority Affairs, and the National Association of Principals of Schools for Girls. Turningpoint is also an affiliate of the American Montessori Society.

THE CAMPUS. Turningpoint currently leases a 3.5-acre campus in Bel Air abutting wooded mountains populated by deer and other wildlife. The four buildings together house 15 classrooms, a library, administrative offices, and a kitchen, with limited use of a large social hall, stage, and auditorium. There is an enclosed playground for the Primary Division and three grassy playing fields for older children.

In addition to classrooms, the planned new school will include a science laboratory, areas for expanded music and art instruction, and sports facilities.

THE FACULTY. Deborah Richman, who was appointed Head of School in 1988, earned her B.S.E. degree from Stephen F. Austin State University in 1970 and an M.Ed. degree from the University of Houston in 1975; in addition, she has completed postgraduate studies at New York University and Inter-American University. Prior to coming to Turningpoint, Ms. Richman held administrative positions at schools in Houston and was Head of The Baldwin School, a Pre-Kindergarten–Grade 12 college preparatory school in Puerto Rico.

The full-time teaching staff include 12 head teachers, 3 coteachers, 9 teacher interns, and 9 specialists. They hold 25 baccalaureate and 4 advanced degrees. Specialists teach art, music, science, Spanish, and athletics. Among the faculty benefits are a comprehensive health plan, a retirement plan, and tuition reduction for children.

At least half the staff is certified in infant and child CPR annually, and the UCLA trauma center is minutes from Turningpoint's campus.

STUDENT BODY. In 1999–2000, Turningpoint enrolled 233 girls and boys in Primary through Grade 6. They come from Bel Air, Brentwood, Beverly Hills, and other suburbs of the Los Angeles metropolitan region. The School adheres to a nondiscriminatory policy, and 10 percent of the children are students of color.

ACADEMIC PROGRAM. The academic year, from early September to the first week in June, is divided into semesters, with winter and spring vacations, a Thanksgiving recess, and observance of several national and religious holidays. Two full days of parent conferences are held each semester, during which teachers provide a detailed account of the students' academic progress as well as social, physical, and emotional development. Primary children do not receive written evaluations, but teachers in K-1 through Grade 4 share written reports with parents at the conferences. Letter grades are used beginning in Grade 5.

Each class is conducted by a head teacher and a coteacher or teacher intern. Classes, enrolling an average of 17 students, meet five days a week, from 8:30 A.M. to 3:00 P.M. for the Elementary level. In the Primary division, short-day classes are from 8:30 A.M. to 1:00 P.M.; full-day classes end at 2:30 P.M. Before- and after-school care is available from 7:30 A.M. to 6:00 P.M. at additional cost.

In the Primary division, Turningpoint seeks to create a unique environment, using Montessori and traditional learning practices and materials to encourage children to explore and advance their skills at a developmentally appropriate pace. Each child is exposed to all aspects of the subject matter, with repetition, extra time, and special attention provided as needed.

In self-contained classrooms, students in the Elementary division undertake a challenging, richly diverse academic program that emphasizes the mastery of basic skills in a sequential and interrelated format. Reading, language arts, mathematics, and social sciences form the core curriculum, with additional instruction in Spanish, science, music, art, and athletics provided by specialist teachers.

Turningpoint graduates are accepted to the middle schools of their choice. Alumni currently attend Berkeley Hall, Brentwood School, Buckley, Campbell Hall, Crossroads, Harvard-Westlake, Marlborough, Viewpoint, and Windward.

A seven-week recreational summer camp is conducted for Turningpoint students, with an array of activities including art, drama, sports, crafts, and special events.

STUDENT ACTIVITIES. After school, students may elect to take part in enrichment and extracurricular activities. These include classes in arts and crafts, cartooning, chess, choir, cooking, dance, French, karate, music, plant science, and sewing.

Turningpoint fields two volleyball teams that compete interscholastically in the School's annual tournament. Students in Grades 4–6 participate in an intramural league with other Westside schools including Brentwood, Calvary Christian, Carlthorp, Santa Monica Montessori, and Village School. Team sports include boys' and girls' basketball, volleyball, and track and field. Noncompetitive sports are available in baseball, basketball, fitness, hockey, lacrosse, soccer, track, and volleyball.

Special events are planned throughout the year such as individual birthday celebrations and parties for Halloween, Grandfriends' Day/Thanksgiving, Valentine's Day, and Spring Break. Other highlights on the school calendar are the Back-to-School Picnic, the Grade 5-6 sleep-away orientation/retreat, Grades 5-6 Washington, D.C., trip, Book Fair, Art Fair, Science Fair, Jog-a-thon, Week of the Young Child, Silent Auction/Dinner Dance, and end-of-the-year pizza party. For sixth graders, the culmination of their Turningpoint experience is the traditional class trip to Magic Mountain, followed by graduation luncheon, commencement, and a parent-sponsored graduation dinner.

ADMISSION AND COSTS. Turningpoint welcomes highly motivated youngsters from families who support the School's stated mission and policies. Candidates for the Elementary level must have academic preparation comparable to their peers and must demonstrate excellent conduct, reliability, and respect for themselves and others. Children are accepted in all grades beginning at the Primary level from age two years, ten months. The admissions process includes parent classroom observation, interviews with parent and child, previous transcripts, and School-administered testing. Families should apply in the fall of the year preceding desired enrollment. Decisions by the Admissions Committee are announced in the spring. The application fee is $50.

In 1999–2000, tuition is $10,140 for the short-day Primary program, $10,540 for full-day Primary, and $10,940 for Grades K-1 through 6. A discount of $300 is given to each sibling of an enrolled student, and a one-time entrance fee of $500 per child is required for each new student. Extras include study tours ($100 per year), milk and snacks ($100), and yearbook ($25).

Tuition payment plans are as follows: full payment in July or half payment in July and December.

Assistant Head of School: John Brumme
Primary Division Head: Patty Britton
Business Manager: Christine Turner
Athletic Director: Danny Porter
Administrative Assistant: Aria Shelton

The Urban School of San Francisco   1966

1563 Page Street, San Francisco, CA 94117. 415-626-2919;
   Fax 415-626-1125; E-mail jbeam@urban.pvt.k12.ca.us

This innovative, coeducational college preparatory school seeks to ignite a passion for learning and inspire its students to become self-motivated, enthusiastic participants in their education. With 250 students in Grades 9–12 and a faculty of 39, Urban combines a demanding academic program with an imaginative use of the city as an educational resource. The School sponsors many interscholastic athletic teams and provides numerous extracurricular opportunities. Through fieldwork, community service, and internships, students explore and contribute to the larger community. Tuition: $15,800. Financial Aid: $410,000. Jennifer Beams is Director of Admission; Mark Salkind (Yale, B.A. 1974) is Director. *Western Association.*

Viewpoint School   CALABASAS

23620 Mulholland Highway, Calabasas, CA 91302. 818-340-2901;
   Fax 818-591-1016; E-mail viewpt@aol.com;
   Web Site www.viewpoint.org

Viewpoint school in Calabasas, California, is a coeducational, college preparatory day school enrolling students in Lower School (Kindergarten–Grade 4), Middle School (Grades 5–8), and Upper School (Grades 9–12). The campus is located in Calabasas, about 25 miles from downtown Los Angeles. Students take trips to the city's museums, art galleries, and theaters.

The School was founded in nearby Encino in 1961 by a group of parents concerned about improving their children's education. Viewpoint moved to its present site in 1966.

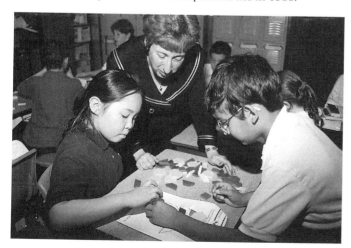

Viewpoint School maintains high academic standards in a nurturing environment; sequential development through the grades with a traditional, liberal arts curriculum; and the fostering of ethical values. Students learn to appreciate the unique contributions that each person adds to the School's diverse com-

munity. This blend allows students to experience a successful transition to college and to become responsible adults in today's global community.

The Viewpoint Educational Foundation is a nonprofit corporation governed by a self-perpetuating Board of Trustees, which meets monthly. The School is accredited by the California Association of Independent Schools and the Western Association of Schools and Colleges and is a member of the National Association of Independent Schools, Educational Records Bureau, Cum Laude Society, National Association of College Admissions Counselors, National Association of Secondary School Principals, National Association of Principals of Schools for Girls, and A Better Chance.

THE CAMPUS. Viewpoint School is situated on a rolling hillside campus of 25 acres with open spaces, scenic vistas, and large oak trees. Several athletic fields, two regulation-size swimming pools, the Rasmussen Family Pavilion for athletics, outdoor basketball courts, a weight-training facility, and playgrounds for the elementary grades are on the grounds.

The Behrens Building houses most of the Upper School's academic facilities. It provides classrooms, two science laboratories, two computer laboratories, the Prinn Library, and the School's administrative offices. The IBM computer labs are equipped with state-of-the-art technology, including CD-ROMs, laser printers, and scanners. The School's libraries contain approximately 25,000 volumes and offer CD-ROM access to Los Angeles County's library collection, the *Los Angeles Times* Network, and ProQuest magazine collection. Other buildings house art studios, music facilities, Lower and Middle School classrooms, separate science and computer laboratories for Lower and Middle School, physical education offices, and locker rooms. ECOLET is an outdoor natural science lab and classroom for field studies.

The plant, which is owned by the School, is valued at approximately $12,000,000.

THE FACULTY. Dr. Robert J. Dworkoski, appointed Headmaster in 1986, is a graduate of George Washington University (B.A. 1968), New York University (A.M. 1971), and Columbia University (M.A. 1972, Ph.D. 1979, European History). Prior to his appointment, Dr. Dworkoski taught history at Brooklyn College and was Department Chairman of Social Studies at Woodmere Academy in New York. From 1980 to 1986, Dr. Dworkoski was the Head of Upper School at the Harvard School in Los Angeles. A Fulbright Scholar in Europe in 1983 and the recipient of a grant from the National Endowment for the Humanities in 1993, Dr. Dworkoski has been active in the California Association of Independent Schools and the National Association of Independent Schools. He sits on the Boards of the Will Geer Theatricum Botanicum and the Gold Coast Performing Arts Association.

Viewpoint's faculty, selected for their academic expertise,

enthusiasm, and energy, consists of 69 full-time and 11 part-time teachers, including administrators with teaching responsibilities. They hold 84 baccalaureate and 46 advanced degrees, including six Ph.D.'s, from colleges and universities in the United States and abroad. Faculty members have received awards from the National Endowment for the Humanities, the Council for Basic Education, the National Science Foundation, and the Klingenstein Summer Institute.

STUDENT BODY. The 1999–2000 enrollment totals 680, with 220 students in Kindergarten–Grade 4, 215 in Grades 5–8, and 245 in Grades 9–12. Students come from the San Fernando and Conejo valleys, Malibu, and other neighboring communities and represent diverse backgrounds. Fifteen different languages are spoken in students' homes.

ACADEMIC PROGRAM. The academic year, divided into semesters, begins in early September and extends to early June. Block and traditional class schedules are used in the Middle and Upper Schools. The student-teacher ratio is 10:1 throughout the School. With classes of 10–22 students, teachers work closely with students both in and out of class to help them reach their full potential. The School sends grades to parents four times a year and provides four additional interim reports for parents of students with grades of C+ or less.

To graduate, an Upper School student must complete four years of English; three of mathematics; three of a single foreign language; three and one-half years of history, including United States History and American Government; three years of laboratory science; two semesters of the arts; the ninth-grade computer science integration project; one semester of speech; eight seasons of physical education; and 45 hours of community service along with two ninth-grade community service projects.

Viewpoint offers a traditional liberal arts core curriculum as well as honors and 18 Advanced Placement courses. In the spring of 1999, 89 students sat for 190 Advanced Placement examinations in 17 subject areas, with 92 percent of the exams receiving scores of 3 or above, and 76 percent receiving scores of 4 or 5. The elective courses include Contemporary Short Fiction, the Novel of Africa, Creative Writing, Modern Latin American History, Contemporary Politics, Humanities, Psychology, Computer Science (Animation, Programming, Artificial Intelligence, Robotics), Environmental Science, Oceanography, Speech, Drama, Chorus, Instrumental Music, Music Theory, Art History, Studio Art, Ceramics, Sculpture, Photography, and Film and Video.

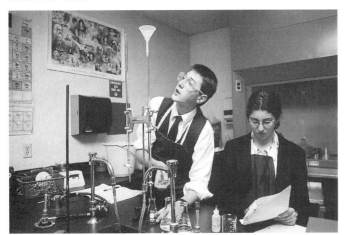

Recent graduates of Viewpoint are attending such colleges and universities as Amherst, Brandeis, Brown, Carnegie Mellon, Cornell, Dartmouth, Emory, George Washington, Harvard, Massachusetts Institute of Technology, Middlebury, New York University, Pepperdine, Stanford, Spelman, Tulane, Vanderbilt, Vassar, Wheaton, United States Air Force Academy, and the Universities of California, Colorado, Michigan, Pennsylvania, and Wisconsin.

Six-week summer programs, Camp Roadrunner (Kindergarten–Grade 4) and Camp Patriot (Grades 5–8), offer combined academic and camp activities. The School offers summer sports camps for basketball, volleyball, and football. An academic summer session is also offered to students in Grades 7–12.

STUDENT ACTIVITIES. Students in the Lower School elect classmates to the Student Action Committee for their student government. After-school classes are provided in chorus, dance, and martial arts, among others. The Middle and Upper Schools elect Student Councils, which work with the Assistant Division Directors on school service, student activities, charitable projects, and school spirit.

A wide variety of social and extracurricular activities includes the yearbook, newspaper, literary journal, speech and debate competitions, theatrical and musical productions, foreign language presentations, chess club, computer club, foreign language and community service honor societies, Amnesty International, Junior Statesmen, dances, domestic and international trips, and foreign exchange programs. Recently, the Upper School's String Ensemble traveled to Italy to perform and to tour sites of historical and musical interest. Another group lived with host families for two weeks in Valencia, Spain. Exchanges with other countries, including China, France, Japan, and Russia, have enabled students to make friends, learn about other cultures, and improve skills in foreign languages.

All students are required to participate in physical education, and 90 percent of Middle and Upper School students are involved in team sports. Upper School students compete interscholastically in cross-country, basketball, volleyball, baseball, softball, football, golf, soccer, tennis, equestrian events, and swimming.

Educational trips to the outdoors provide students in Grades 4–12 with additional learning opportunities. Fourth graders spend two days at the Orange County Marine Institute and participate in activities designed to enhance their study of California's history. Astrocamp, an environmental science program in Idyllwild, is the site of a three-day retreat for fifth graders. In late spring, sixth graders study the ecosystem of coastal California for three days. Seventh graders study marine biology on Catalina Island, and eighth graders spend a week hiking and exploring the natural history of the Yosemite region. To ease the transition from Middle to Upper School and to foster friendships, ninth graders spend three days in the early fall in the nearby mountains. Tenth graders work on group challenges and a ropes course, also in local mountain areas. Eleventh graders visit Sequoia National Park, while Catalina Island is the destination for the senior class for three days in the early fall.

Each spring, many students take the Voyage of Discovery, a nine-day tour of historic sites on the East Coast. Other trips include an East Coast tour of college campuses and excursions to Europe.

Family, alumni, and friends are invited to campus for special events such as Parents' Nights, Grandparents' Day, Great Pumpkin Day, French Fête, Homecoming, Open House, holiday programs, student performances, musical and theatrical productions, art exhibits, athletic events, and sports banquets.

ADMISSION AND COSTS. Viewpoint School seeks highly motivated, academically able students with diverse backgrounds, interests, and talents. The School admits students based on a review of entrance examinations, recommendations, transcripts from previous schools, and an interview for applicants for Grades 5–12. International students must demonstrate a strong command of English. Families should submit an application and a fee of $75 no later than February 1 for all grade levels for entrance the following fall. The School will consider later applications if openings are available.

Tuition for 1999–2000 is $10,950 for Kindergarten–Grade 4, $11,750 for Grades 5–6, and $12,650 for Grades 7–12. General fees are $400 for Kindergarten through Grade 6 and $350 for Grades 7 through 12. There is a one-time, new-family fee of

$500. Uniforms, purchased by the students, are required for Kindergarten–Grade 8. There is a dress code in the Upper School. Tuition payment and insurance plans are available. Viewpoint is committed to providing an education to qualified students, regardless of their families' ability to pay. To this end, financial aid is available in cases of demonstrated need. Kristin Dworkoski is the Director of Financial Aid.

Head of Upper School: Paul Rosenbaum
Head of Middle School: John O'Brien
Head of Lower School: Cathy Adelman
Associate Head for Academic Affairs: Margaret Bowles
Director of Admission: Kristin Dworkoski
Director of Development: Kathleen Mann
College Counselor: Sharon O'Callaghan
Business Manager: Paul Galvin
Director of Athletics: Patrick Moyal
Director of Summer Programs: Paul Rosenbaum

Village School   PACIFIC PALISADES

780 Swarthmore Avenue, Pacific Palisades, CA 90272-4355.
310-459-8411; Fax 310-459-3285;
E-mail bwilliams@village-school.com

VILLAGE SCHOOL in Pacific Palisades, California, is a coeducational elementary school enrolling children in Transitional Kindergarten through Grade 6. Overlooking the ocean, the beautiful suburban community of Pacific Palisades is only 10 miles from downtown Los Angeles. Students and faculty enjoy the clean air and secure environment of a small village while having access to the many educational, cultural, and recreational attractions of one of the nation's largest cities. Most students utilize the School's bus service or carpool with other families.

Village School was established in 1977 by a group of parents who sought to provide a nurturing, academically strong program within the atmosphere of a neighborhood school. Village has remained faithful to its founding mission, which aims to support and celebrate families who place a high priority on educational excellence. The broad, balanced curriculum is taught in small classes where each child is assured of receiving individual attention, nurturing, and challenge. The leadership of the current Head of School and a new campus and facilities have been important factors in the steady development and success of Village School.

A nonprofit, nondenominational institution, Village School is governed by a 13-member Board of Trustees. It is jointly accredited by the Western Association of Colleges and Schools and the California Association of Independent Schools. The Village School Parent Association provides essential support through fund-raising, volunteering in the classrooms, and planning special events.

THE CAMPUS. The School is housed in a large, three-story building designed in the style of a Spanish hacienda. It is constructed around a large central court that accommodates the playground, a covered lunch area, and a "village green." There are separate classroom areas for one section of Transitional Kindergarten and three sections of Kindergarten. Grades 1 through 6 are housed in two classrooms each. Additional facilities include a 6000-volume library, a visual arts studio, a large music studio, and a science room.

THE FACULTY. Nora Malone was named Head of School in July 1999, after serving two years as Village School's Assistant Head/Director of Admissions. A 20-year teaching veteran, Ms. Malone received both her Bachelor of Arts degree in English and her California teaching credential from California State University at Northridge. She is currently in that school's master's program for Educational Leadership and Policy Studies.

The full-time faculty includes 18 women and 5 men, all of whom have earned college degrees. Most have teaching credentials; many hold advanced degrees from colleges and universities in California and throughout the nation. Professional development is encouraged through workshops and in-service seminars. In addition to the teaching staff, several teaching assistants provide support in the classroom as well as outside supervision of the students. Faculty receive health insurance, a retirement plan, and additional benefits.

First aid is available on campus, and there are many emergency facilities within easy reach of the School.

STUDENT BODY. In 1999–2000, Village School enrolls 266 students, 129 girls and 137 boys, ages 4½ to 12 years. There are 10 students in Transitional Kindergarten, 37 in Kindergarten, 41 in Grade 1, 35 in Grade 2, 43 in Grade 3, 36 in Grade 4, 32 in Grade 5, and 32 in Grade 6. Students come from Brentwood, Los Angeles, Malibu, Pacific Palisades, Santa Monica, and other communities.

ACADEMIC PROGRAM. The school year, divided into trimesters, begins in early September and ends in early June, with vacation breaks at Thanksgiving, in the winter, and in the spring as well as the observance of several national holidays. Grades are issued three times a year, and parent-teacher conferences are held at the end of the first two trimesters. Classes, enrolling between 15 and 22 children, meet five days a week, from 8:20 A.M. to 3:00 P.M.

The Village School curriculum combines traditional and progressive approaches, with an emphasis on providing a strong foundation in basic reading, language, and mathematical skills. Spanish is introduced in Transitional Kindergarten and continues through all grade levels. Science, social studies, information technology, art, music, and physical education are also integral to the core program. At the same time, emphasis is given to the development of values, responsibility, and good citizenship as members of the school and larger community.

After graduation, a majority of sixth graders enter independent secondary schools in the area such as Brentwood, Crossroads School for Arts and Sciences, Harvard–Westlake, Marlborough, and Windward.

STUDENT ACTIVITIES. Children have the opportunity to serve their school and develop leadership qualities through membership on the Student Council, which consists of representatives from Kindergarten through Grade 6. The Council meets on alternate weeks.

The after-school enrichment program features activities such as journalism, yearbook, music, arts and crafts, science, and other areas of interest. Students stage two musical performances a year and take part in community service projects such as beach cleanup.

Village Viking teams compete in a sports league with four other schools. Athletes in Grades 4 through 6 play on teams in flag football, soccer, baseball, basketball, and volleyball. Students also receive training in track and field events.

Special events are the all-School social, Open House, School fund-raisers, and welcoming events for new families. Students who graduated in June are invited to return to the School for a day in the fall.

ADMISSION AND COSTS. Village School welcomes students of average to superior ability from all racial, ethnic, and religious backgrounds who demonstrate the potential to thrive in the School's nurturing environment and to benefit from its academic and extracurricular programs. Most students enter in the Transitional Kindergarten or Kindergarten levels, although admission is offered in any grade where vacancies exist. Students are accepted based on a school visit, recommendations, and the previous school record, as applicable. Application should be made a year in advance of the desired enrollment date. The deadline for submission of applications is December 31 for all grades. Occasionally, midyear enrollment is possible. The nonrefundable application fee is $100.

In 1999–2000, the tuition is $11,250, plus a one-time New Student Fee of $1000 and a Debt Reduction Fee of $750. Financial aid is awarded on the basis of need. A tuition payment plan is available.

Assistant Head of School: Barbara Ruth-Williams
Business Manager: RoseAnn Robbins

Villanova Preparatory School   OJAI

12096 Ventura Avenue, Ojai, CA 93023-3999. 805-646-1464; Fax 805-646-4430; Web Site www.villanovaprep.org

VILLANOVA PREPARATORY SCHOOL, in Ojai, California, is a coeducational, Catholic, college preparatory school enrolling boarding and day students in Grades 9 through 12. Situated outside the city of Ojai, a town of approximately 7000, Villanova is located 85 miles northwest of Los Angeles, 35 miles from Santa Barbara, and 12 miles from the Ventura beaches. The School's location permits students to take part in a wide range of outdoor activities as well as enjoy the diverse cultural, recreational, and educational resources of the area.

Villanova Preparatory School was founded in 1924 by priests of the Augustinian Order at the request of the Bishop of Los Angeles to meet the increased demand for a Catholic boarding and day school for boys in the Southern California region. In 1970, the School admitted girls as day students, and it became completely coeducational 17 years later when girls were accepted as boarders.

In addition to offering "rigorous college preparation," Villanova strives to foster in students a strong commitment to community life and to inspire them to act in accordance with the teachings of Christ.

The School is a nonprofit organization governed by a Board of Trustees that includes clergy, laypersons, and the Headmaster. It is accredited by the Western Association of Schools and Colleges and approved by the U.S. Department of Justice Immigration and Naturalization Service. Villanova holds membership in the National Catholic Educational Association, the Western Catholic Educational Association, and the Secondary School Admission Test Board.

THE CAMPUS. The Villanova Preparatory School's 127-acre campus, marked by California live oak trees and rolling hills, is located in the scenic Ojai Valley. Cantwell Hall, the boys' dormitory, accommodates 60 students, two clergy, and four male staff members. The School chapel, Keller Library, the dining room, and offices are also in Cantwell. Twenty-eight girls and two women staff members are housed in Glynn Hall. Academic facilities are centered in four buildings—Austin, Ingalls, and Yant halls and McGrath Science Building—which provide 17 classrooms, labs, a greenhouse, a computer science laboratory, an audiovisual center, and counseling offices. Clark Gymnasium was completed in the fall of 1990. Baseball, soccer, and softball fields, a swimming pool, and tennis courts complement the sports and extracurricular programs.

The facilities, which are owned by the Augustinian Order, are valued in excess of $5,000,000.

THE FACULTY. Andrew C. Smidt, Ed.D., appointed Headmaster in 1998, earned a baccalaureate degree from California State University at Northridge, a master's degree from Loyola University in Los Angeles, and a doctorate from the University of Southern California. Dr. Smidt has served as a high school teacher, school principal, director of personnel, deputy superintendent, and, for 16 years, as superintendent of a unified school system.

The faculty are comprised of 16 women and 13 men, including three Augustinian priests. They have earned 29 baccalaureate degrees, 10 master's degrees, and 3 doctorates.

A nurse is on duty at the School Monday through Friday, and nearby hospitals are available for medical emergencies.

STUDENT BODY. In 1999–2000, Villanova Preparatory enrolls 106 girls and 136 boys— 84 boarders and 158 day students—as follows: 61 in Grade 9, 73 in Grade 10, 52 in Grade 11, and 56 in Grade 12. Forty percent are members of the Roman Catholic faith. Most students come from California but Arizona, Hawaii, Nevada, Canada, Great Britain, Hong Kong, Indonesia, Japan, Korea, Mexico, People's Republic of China, Poland, Russia, Sri Lanka, Switzerland, Taiwan, and Thailand are also represented. Day students reside in Ojai and the towns of Camarillo, Carpinteria, Oxnard, Santa Barbara, Santa Paula, Somis, and Ventura.

ACADEMIC PROGRAM. The school year, divided into quarters, extends from late August to early June and includes vacations at Thanksgiving, Christmas, and Easter. The student-teacher ratio is 9:1. The average class size is 13. Numerical grades are issued quarterly, with 70 the lowest passing grade. Written progress reports are presented to parents at mid-quarter conferences.

The school day begins at 8:00 A.M. and ends at 2:25 P.M. on Monday, Wednesday, and Friday and 2:35 P.M. on Tuesday and Thursday. After school four days a week, extra help is offered for those needing it, and peer tutoring is available. At the end of the class day, boarders may receive additional help with their work or take part in athletics and extracurricular activities. Dinner is served at 6:00 P.M., followed by a short recreation period and supervised study from 7:00 to 10:00 P.M. The day ends with a brief chapel period and a light snack in the dining room.

"Lights out" is at 11:00 P.M. Students are required to conform to a dress code for school activities, maintain clean rooms, do their own laundry, and share serving duties at dinner.

To qualify for a Villanova diploma, students must carry six classes and earn 24 units of credit. Twenty-one units must be in the following required subjects: 4 each in English and religious studies; 3 each in foreign language, college preparatory mathematics, and laboratory science; 2½ in social science (including United States history and government); 1 in fine arts; and ½ in physical education. Most departments offer electives, and Advanced Placement courses are available in six disciplines.

Among the specific courses are Religion I–IV; English I–IV; French I–IV, Spanish I–IV, Latin I–IV; Algebra I–II, Geometry, Advanced Placement Calculus; Chemistry, Physical Science I–II, Biology, Physics; United States History, World History, Problems of Democracy/International Relations, Civics/Economics; Career Guidance/SAT Preparation; Drama, Art in Western Culture, Music in Western Culture; and Health and Physical Education.

A complete English-as-a-Second-Language program is offered. It is designed to develop skills in reading, writing, thinking, and listening, with the aim of preparing non-native speakers for success in American colleges and universities. Thirty-seven students are currently enrolled in the ESL program.

College guidance, provided by the college counselor and the assistant Headmaster, takes the form of career guidance, information, catalogs, and help in applying for financial aid and admission. In addition, representatives from a variety of schools visit the campus, and individual and group information sessions are held for parents and students at Villanova and in the Ventura County area.

The 52 graduates from the Class of 1999 were accepted at such colleges and universities as American University, Boston College, Boston University, Carnegie Mellon, Emory, Loyola Marymount, New York University, Pepperdine, Santa Clara University, Smith College, Thomas Aquinas College, Washington State University, and the Universities of Arizona, California (Berkeley, Davis, Irvine, Los Angeles, San Diego, San Francisco, Santa Barbara, Santa Cruz), Colorado (Boulder), Oregon, Southern California, and Washington.

STUDENT ACTIVITIES. Villanova's Associated Student Body Council serves as a link between the administration and faculty and plans special events such as orientation programs, pep rallies, and assemblies. Students may volunteer for community service with the local hospital and through fund drives and food banks for the needy. Villanova students also work with local senior citizens, assist disadvantaged children in Mexico, and are encouraged to participate in Red Cross blood drives.

Boys and girls are given equal opportunities in athletics, and teams are formed in soccer, volleyball, track, cross-country, tennis, basketball, baseball, softball, golf, water polo, and swimming. Villanova competes with other members of the California Interscholastic Federation (CIF); there are also intramural teams in volleyball, basketball, softball, and flag football.

On weekends, boarders may leave campus for shopping, surfing, hiking, back-packing, and other recreational activities. Mass is celebrated in the chapel or at the local parish on Sunday; non-Catholics are encouraged to attend services of their own faith and transportation is provided by the School, when necessary.

Traditionally, there are three formal dances, six informal mixers, and a number of other social events such as the Sports Barbecue, Beach Day, and Wildcat Day. Other activities include the Parents' Guild auction, the Christmas Luncheon, and the Alumni Barbecue.

ADMISSION AND COSTS. Villanova seeks academically talented, emotionally stable students who are capable of succeeding, both in the demanding curriculum and in the daily community life of the School. Acceptance is granted on the basis of High School Placement or Secondary School Admission tests, transcripts, previous records, and teacher recommendations. Applications, with a fee of $50 for day students and $100 for boarders, are accepted through the month of July.

In 1999–2000, tuition, room, and board is $20,500; day tuition is $5950. There is an additional $2000 charge for the ESL program. All students pay an inclusive fee of $200. Books are a separate expense, ranging between $250 and $475. Boarding students must provide a refundable deposit of $1000.

Some students are awarded tuition scholarships based on entrance test scores; other aid is given according to financial need in the form of tuition reduction or a family discount.

President: Rev. John P. Pejza, OSA
Dean of Students: Mr. Denver G. Compton
Director of Development: Ms. Jackie Martin
College Counselor: Mrs. Tanya Hanson
Business Manager: Mrs. Nancy D. Ventura
Director of Athletics: Mr. Jason Burt
Director of English as a Second Language Program:
  Mrs. Irene M. Snively

The Webb Schools   CLAREMONT

1175 West Baseline Road, Claremont, CA 91711. 909-626-3587;
  Admissions 909-482-5214; E-mail admissions@webb.org;
  Web Site www.webb.org

THE WEBB SCHOOLS in Claremont, California, comprise three institutions: Webb School of California, enrolling boarding and day boys in Grades 9 through 12; Vivian Webb School, a boarding and day school for girls in Grades 9 through 12; and the Raymond M. Alf Museum of Paleontology. Thirty-five miles east of Los Angeles, Claremont (population 37,000) is the home of the Claremont Colleges.

Webb School of California was founded by Thompson and Vivian Webb in 1922. It was operated as a proprietary institution until 1957, when they sold their interest to the Board of Trustees. Dr. Webb continued as Headmaster until 1962. Vivian Webb School, a coordinate institution for girls, was founded in 1981. The Raymond M. Alf Museum was built in 1968 and accredited in 1998 by the American Association of Museums.

The Webb Schools strive to foster "high academic, athletic, and moral standards" and to provide opportunities for leadership and creativity. Central to the philosophy is the Honor Code, which emphasizes honesty, trust, integrity, and "doing the right thing." The coordinate arrangement between the two schools is designed to permit full sharing of courses, activities, faculty, and the campus, while allowing boys and girls to assume separate leadership positions and create and maintain their own traditions. Each school has a director of student life and its own

student government and faculty advisory system. All students attend two nondenominational chapel service programs a week.

A nonprofit institution, The Webb Schools are governed by a 20-member Board of Trustees that meets four times a year. There are 2900 living alumni of The Webb Schools. The Webb Schools are accredited by the Western Association of Schools and Colleges. They hold membership in the National Association of Independent Schools, the Western Boarding Schools Association, and The College Board, among other educational associations.

THE CAMPUS. The 68-acre campus in the foothills of the San Gabriel Mountains has four athletic fields, six tennis courts, a quarter-mile track, and a swimming/diving pool.

Major academic facilities are: the Raymond M. Alf Museum of Paleontology building, which also houses science laboratories and classrooms; Seeley G. Mudd Mathematics Building, with an auditorium, classrooms, and a computer laboratory; the Art Studio complete with gallery to showcase student art; the Floyd E. Berry Computer Center; and the 20,000-volume W. Russell Fawcett Memorial Library.

Other campus buildings include the Vivian Webb Chapel, Price Dining Hall, Frederick R. Hooper Student Center, and the Les Perry Gymnasium. There are also ten dormitories and 37 faculty homes on campus.

The School-owned facilities are valued at $52,000,000.

THE FACULTY. Susan Nelson, who holds degrees from Wagner College (B.A. 1969) and New York University (M.A. 1971), was appointed Head of The Webb Schools in July 1991. Prior to her appointment, she served as Dean of Vivian Webb School from 1988 to 1991. Ms. Nelson also taught at Staten Island Academy in New York and served as Assistant Head there from 1983 to 1988. Patrick Collins (Amherst, B.A.; University of Massachusetts, M.Ed.) became Dean of Webb School of California in 1998; Jean Sanford Hill (Randolph-Macon Woman's College, B.A.; George Mason University, M.A.; George Washington University, J.D.) is Dean of Vivian Webb School.

There are 45 full-time and 2 part-time faculty and administrators. Thirty-eight teachers live on campus. Teachers and administrators hold baccalaureate, graduate, and professional degrees. Seventy-five percent of the faculty hold a master's degree or higher. Two or more degrees were earned at California State Polytechnic University, Claremont Graduate School, Georgetown, Harvard, Middlebury, Mount Holyoke, Princeton, Stanford, and the Universities of California (Berkeley), Delaware, North Carolina, Pennsylvania, and Southern California.

The campus health center is staffed 24 hours a day by two nurses, both of whom live on campus. There are three hospitals nearby.

STUDENT BODY. In 1999–2000, The Webb Schools enroll 124 boarding boys, 100 boarding girls, 64 day boys, and 56 day girls in Grades 9 through 12 as follows: 84 in Grade 9, 94 in Grade 10, 84 in Grade 11, and 82 in Grade 12. Boarders come from 12 states and eight foreign countries.

ACADEMIC PROGRAM. The school year, from early September to early June, is divided into semesters and includes a Thanksgiving recess; winter, midterm, and spring breaks; and several long weekends. Five days a week, the day begins with breakfast by 7:30 A.M., two 55-minute class periods, a midmorning chapel/assembly, two more classes before lunch, two afternoon classes, and an extra-help session. Classes meet four times a week on a seven-period, five-day rotating schedule. Sports practices and matches, dance and theater rehearsals, the museum internship program, and the Outdoor Adventure program activities are held between 3:30 P.M. and 5:30 P.M. Dinner is at 6:00 P.M., followed by quiet study. Dorm check-in is at 10:00 P.M. for freshmen and sophomores, 10:30 P.M. for juniors and seniors.

As coordinate institutions, Webb School of California and Vivian Webb School focus on the specific needs of boys and girls. Single-gender classes required in Algebra I, Geometry, freshman and sophomore English, freshman science, and world history are designed to maximize each gender's curricular needs, allowing for the creation of lesson plans and reading lists of particular interest to the students.

Classes have an average enrollment of 15. There are supervised study halls throughout the day and in the evening. Teachers are available to provide individual assistance during the extra-help sessions built into the daily schedule. Grades are posted and sent to parents four times a year. Faculty advisors also send quarterly letters outlining students' progress.

To graduate, students must complete a minimum of 18 credits, including four years of English; three and a half years of history; three years of science, math, and foreign language; one year of fine arts; and one semester of computer applications.

Full-year courses include The Craft of Composition, Introduction to Literature, American Literature; Modern European History, World History, Economics, American History; Integrated Science, Chemistry, Physics, Paleontology and Geological Processes, Museum Studies (both taught in conjunction with

The Raymond M. Alf Museum); Algebra I, Geometry, Algebra II, Functions/Statistics/Trigonometry, Pre-Calculus/Discrete Mathematics, and Calculus AB/BC; years 1–5 in French and Spanish; and String Sinfonia, Wind Sinfonia, Chamber Singers, VWS Chorus, and Webb Singers. Among the semester courses offered are Contemporary Literature, Justice in Literature, British Literature, World Literature, Women's Literature, American Government, National Independence to Globalism, International Relations, Probability and Statistics, Beginning Sculpture, Beginning Drawing, Art History, Drawing and Painting, Music History, Theory of Music, Theatre Arts Workshop, Advanced Art, and Speech Communication.

Eighteen Advanced Placement courses are available to qualified students. Advanced math and language students occasionally enroll in courses at the nearby Claremont Colleges. Seniors who qualify may design an advanced-level independent project under the supervision of a faculty member.

All 70 members of the Class of 1999 went on to college. Twenty-five percent of graduating seniors were admitted to Ivy League colleges. Other graduates are attending California Institute of Technology, Georgetown, Massachusetts Institute of Technology, Northwestern, Occidental College, Smith College, Stanford, Wellesley, Williams, and the University of California (Berkeley).

The Webb Schools Summer Studies program enrolls day students in Kindergarten–Grade 12. The five-week program offers enrichment courses in English, science, mathematics, computer science, foreign language, fine arts, and athletics.

STUDENT ACTIVITIES. Student councils at Webb and Vivian Webb identify and represent student needs to the administration, uphold the standards of each school, and coordinate activities programs. The Honor Committee at Webb School of California and the Honor Cabinet at Vivian Webb work to establish and maintain standards of attitude and behavior and participate in the disciplinary system. Dorm Councils at both schools ensure the smooth running of the dormitories.

Students publish a newspaper, yearbook, and literary magazine, and operate a radio station, KWEB. There are six music performance groups for which students may also receive credit. Other organizations include the Ski Club, International Club, Surf Club, Environmental Club, and Junior Statesmen of America.

The Webb Schools compete in the Prep League, which is part of the California Interscholastic Federation. Webb fields teams in baseball, basketball, cross country, football, soccer, swimming/diving, tennis, track and field, water polo, and wrestling. Vivian Webb teams compete in basketball, cross country, soccer, softball, swimming/diving, tennis, track, volleyball, and water polo. A supervised Outdoor Adventure program, museum internship program, Dance program, and comprehensive theater arts program featuring three full-length dramatic productions complement the athletic program.

Students take advantage of the Schools' location to enjoy the natural beauty and the wealth of cultural, educational, and recreational resources of the region. Skiing, hiking, and camping trips to the mountains and deserts; surfing and beach outings; and excursions to the colleges, museums, theaters, and galleries of the Los Angeles area enrich the academic and extracurricular program.

Traditional events for the school community include Parents' Day, Alumni Day, Women-in-Leadership speakers series, Men in the Arena speaker series, Vivian Webb Signing-in Ceremony, Vivian Webb Candlelight Service, Webb Candlelight Dinner, Webb Day, and senior trips to Grand Canyon and Yosemite.

ADMISSION AND COSTS. The Webb Schools seek well-rounded students who will bring a worthwhile sense of purpose and individual contributions to the community. New students are admitted to Grades 9–11 on the basis of the previous school record; recommendations from school heads, math and English teachers; and Secondary School Admission Test scores. Financial aid applications must be completed by February 15. All admission application materials must be received, and interviews and tests must be completed by February 1 to be considered for the first-round selection. Admission notifications are sent out in early March, but students may be admitted as long as vacancies exist. There is a $50 application fee for U.S. residents and a $100 fee for international students.

In 1999–2000, boarding tuition is $26,430; day tuition is $18,430. In 1999–2000, The Webb Schools offered more than $1,000,000 in financial aid on the basis of need. The Schools also provide financing options including loans and payment plans.

Head of Schools: Susan A. Nelson
Dean of Webb School of California: Patrick Collins
Dean of Vivian Webb School: Jean Sanford Hill
Director of Institutional Advancement: Taylor Stockdale
Director of Admission: Randy Roach
Director of College Guidance: Hector Martinez
Director of Finance and Operations: Janet Peddy
Director of Athletics: Mark Conroy
Director of the Raymond M. Alf Museum of Paleontology: Don Lofgren, Ph.D.

Westerly School of Long Beach   1993

2950 East 29th Street, Long Beach, CA 90806. 562-981-3151; Fax 562-981-3153

Westerly School of Long Beach was founded by interested parents to offer an enriched and comprehensive education for their children. Enrolling 180 boys and girls in Kindergarten through Grade 8, Westerly seeks to inspire a lifelong love of learning, intellectual curiosity, and creative thinking through a balanced program of academics and activities. The core curriculum emphasizes a strong foundation in language arts, reading, and mathematics with enrichment courses in Spanish, music, art, and physical education at every grade level. Publications, field trips, and Student Council are among the activities. Tuition: $9200. Carol I. Bernstein is Assistant Head; Raymond F. Bizjack (University of Notre Dame, B.A.; Universidad Catolica [Chile], M.A.) is Head of School.

Westridge School   1913

324 Madeline Drive, Pasadena, CA 91105. 626-799-1153; Fax 626-799-9236; E-mail hhopper@Westridge.Org.; Web Site www.westridge.org

Established in 1913, Westridge is a college preparatory day school enrolling 475 girls in Grades 4–12. Designed to promote independence and self-reliance in a cooperative and interdependent community, the School's rigorous academic program is enhanced by offerings in art, music, drama, and computer science. Extracurricular activities include clubs, sports, and student government. There is a community service requirement for all Upper School students. Tuition: $11,350–$11,850. Financial Aid: $556,875. Helen V. Hopper is Admissions Director; Fran Norris Scoble (Baylor University, B.A.; Vanderbilt University, M.A.) was appointed Head of School in 1990. *Western Association.*

Wildwood School   1971

12201 Washington Place, Los Angeles, CA 90066. 310-397-3134; Fax 310-397-5134; E-mail admission@wildwood.org; Web Site www.wildwood.org

Wildwood was founded by local educators and parents seeking a strong academic program in "a noncompetitive environment where children learn from each other as well as from their teachers." The spacious elementary campus provides a serene setting for Kindergarten–Grade 6; the new secondary campus, opening in 2000 with Grades 7–9, is designed to integrate opportunities for thoughtful learning and internships in the community. Curriculum is carefully integrated, emphasizing the major disciplines and the arts. Kindergarten–Grade 2 are multi-age-grouped, and after-school enrichment activities are offered. Elementary Tuition: $11,458; Entrance Fee: $1000. Hope Boyd (Pennsylvania State, B.S.; University of Missouri, M.A.) is Head.

Windrush School   1976

1800 Elm Street, El Cerrito, CA 94530. 510-970-7580; Fax 510-235-3554; E-mail windrush.org

Windrush, enrolling 246 students from diverse backgrounds in Kindergarten–Grade 8, is located on a 4-acre campus in the San Francisco/East Bay area. Built on a love of learning and accomplishment in a framework of academic excellence, the School is a partnership among children, families, and staff. Problem solving and cooperative learning are emphasized throughout the curriculum as students become proficient in various skills. Spanish is taught in all grades. Computer, physical education, music, art, drama, and community service enrich the curriculum. Tuition: $7800–$9050. Financial aid is available. Lynn Sargent De Jonghe (Harvard, B.A.; Simmons, M.A.; Cornell, Ph.D.) was named Director in 1998.

Windward School   1971

11350 Palms Boulevard, Los Angeles, CA 90066. 310-391-7127

Windward School, enrolling 420 boys and girls from diverse backgrounds in Grades 7–12, offers a well-rounded, challenging college preparatory curriculum designed to promote independent thinking, articulate communication skills, and an appreciation for learning. The program features Advanced Placement and honors courses and varied electives. The arts play an important role in developing students' imaginative and creative abilities through music, drama, dance, and other media. All students participate in community service projects; other enrichment activities include Student Council, athletics, overseas exchange programs, and a senior class trip to Europe. Tuition: $16,389. Sharon Pearline is Director of Admission; Thomas W. Gilder is Head of School. *Western Association.*

York School 1959

9501 York Road, Monterey, CA 93940. 831-372-7338; Fax 831-372-8055; Web Site www.york.org

A coeducational, Episcopal, college preparatory day school serving 217 students in Grades 8–12, York aims to foster excellence in a rigorous curriculum, which offers Advanced Placement in all disciplines. Strong sports and fine arts programs, individual and group activities, and computer and Internet technologies develop personal and intellectual skills and an appreciation for lifelong learning and service. York welcomes qualified students regardless of race, creed, national or ethnic origin, or economic background. Thirty-eight percent of the students receive financial aid. Tuition: $13,650. Financial Aid: $555,600. Joanne Doyle is Director of Admission; The Reverend Roger Bowen (The Citadel, B.A.; Virginia Theological Seminary, M.Div.) was appointed Head of School in 1994.

Woodside Priory School 1957

302 Portola Road, Portola Valley, CA 94028. 650-851-8221; Fax 650-851-2839; E-mail azappelli@woodsidepriory.com; Web Site www.woodsidepriory.com

Set on a 60-acre campus 5 miles from Stanford University, Woodside Priory School enrolls 250 boys and girls in Grades 6–12, including 40 boarding boys in Grades 9–12. As a Roman Catholic, Benedictine school, The Priory seeks to inspire a love of learning and an intellectual and spiritual quest that promotes the freedom of society and the individual. The college preparatory curriculum includes the arts, humanities, sciences, and theology. Electives and Advanced Placement courses are offered. The student-teacher ratio is 10:1. Sports, publications, and community outreach are among the activities. Boarding Tuition: $28,860; Day Tuition: $14,960. Financial aid is available. Al D. Zappelli is Director of Admissions; Timothy J. Molak (St. Mary's University, M.A.) is Headmaster. *Western Association.*

COLORADO

Alexander Dawson School 1970

10455 Dawson Drive, Lafayette, CO 80026. 303-665-6679; Fax 303-665-0757; E-mail kccassell@dawsonschool.org; Web Site http://www.dawsonschool.org

Alexander Dawson School enrolls 423 boys and girls in Kindergarten–Grade 12 in a competitive college preparatory program. The curriculum balances arts and humanities with science and technology, enriched by Advanced Placement and electives. Students take part in Town Council, publications, community service, clubs, and interscholastic athletics. Day Tuition: $7200–$11,400. Fees and Extras: $400. Financial aid is available. Keith E. Cassell is Director of Admissions; Andy Bryant (Millersville State College, B.S.; Duke University, M.A.) is Headmaster. *North Central Association.*

Aspen Country Day School 1969

3 Music School Road, Aspen, CO 81611. 970-925-1909; Fax 970-925-7074; E-mail info@aspencds.org

Aspen Country Day School is a coeducational preparatory school enrolling 150 day students in Pre-Kindergarten–Grade 9. The School aims to offer an academic program of distinction designed to enhance each student's intellectual, creative, and physical development in a nurturing family environment. The traditional curriculum is supplemented by an Outdoor Education program, and a wide variety of extracurricular offerings such as newspaper, yearbook, photography, music, art, dance, drama, soccer, hockey, and skiing. Tuition: $7500–$14,500. Financial Aid: $300,000. Gillian Baxter is Admission Director; John H. Suitor is Headmaster.

Colorado Academy 1900

3800 South Pierce Street, Denver, CO 80235. 303-986-1501; Fax 303-914-2589; E-mail claskey@mail.coloacad.org; Web Site http://www.coloacad.org

Colorado Academy is a coeducational day school enrolling 790 students in Preschool–Grade 12. Located on a 75-acre campus in southwest Denver, the Academy provides a 10:1 student/faculty ratio and a program emphasizing a well-rounded college preparatory program. Each division (Lower, Middle, and Upper) has its own principal, faculty, and facility. Fine arts and athletics are offered at all levels. Publications, sports, drama, community service, and clubs are among the activities. A summer recreational camp with computer instruction and sports is available. Tuition: $7220–$11,950. Financial Aid: $900,000. Catherine Laskey is Director of Admission; Christopher Babbs (Stanford, B.A.; University of Colorado, M.A.) is Headmaster.

Crested Butte Academy 1993

P.O. Box 1180, Crested Butte, CO 81224. 970-349-1805 or 888-633-0222; E-mail cba@crestedbutte.net; Web Site welcome.crestedbutte.net/cba

Crested Butte Academy is an independent, college preparatory, coeducational day and boarding school serving college-bound students in Grades 9 through 12. Focus is on the core academic subjects of English, history, science, math, and foreign language. World-class training and recreation are available for sports such as skiing, snowboarding, kayaking, mountain biking, rock climbing, and soccer. Students benefit from small classes and individualized attention. Dormitories have two students per room with private baths. Both Winter Tutorial and Full Year programs are available. Tuition: $13,000–$22,975. Laurie McCall is Director of Admission; David J. Rothman is Headmaster.

Foothills Academy 1985

4725 Miller Street, Wheat Ridge, CO 80033. 303-431-0920; Fax 303-431-9505; Web Site www.compusulting.com/foothills/index.html

Foothills Academy, a college preparatory school enrolling 200 boys and girls in Kindergarten–Grade 12, aims to address the intellectual, physical, social, and emotional development of each child. In a nurturing environment, dedicated teachers instill basic skills through traditional course work as well as integration and experiential learning opportunities. The Upper School program provides electives and the opportunity to earn college credit at the University of Colorado. All students contribute to the needs of the school community and the community at large through the Academy's service learning program. Outdoor education and athletics, and arts, history, and science field trips enhance the curriculum. Tuition: $6320–$7470. Mary L. Faddick is Head of School.

Fountain Valley School of Colorado 1930

6155 Fountain Valley School Road, Colorado Springs, CO 80911. 719-390-7035; Fax 719-390-7762; E-mail admis@fvs.edu; Web Site www.fvs.edu

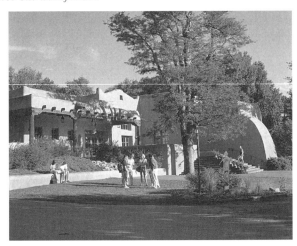

Fountain Valley, enrolling 225 boarding and day students from around the globe in Grades 9–12, offers a challenging program focused on academics, arts, and athletics. The college preparatory curriculum includes Advanced Placement and honors courses in every department, and the resources of the 1100-acre campus, rich in historical southwestern architecture, provide a variety of learning opportunities. Students develop leadership skills through the advising system and an environment distinguished by close peer and faculty relations. A campus-wide communication network and science building are among the state-of-the-art facilities on campus. Boarding Tuition: $24,200; Day Tuition: $13,750. Financial Aid: $926,500. Kilian Forgus is Director of Admission; John E. Creeden, Ph.D., is Headmaster.

Graland Country Day School 1927

30 Birch Street, Denver, CO 80220. 303-399-0390; Fax 303-388-2803; E-mail eharvey@graland.org; Web Site http://www.graland.org

Graland Country Day School, enrolling 630 students in Kindergarten–Grade 9, seeks to provide a firm foundation in academics, the arts, and athletics while enabling students to develop the moral and spiritual values that help them live healthy and productive lives. The balance between appropriately challenging academics and sensitivity to developmental issues is central to the School's mission. The comprehensive program includes offerings in art, music, drama, life skills, foreign languages, computers, and athletics. Summer courses are available. Tuition: $9370–$10,150. Extras: $100–$950. Financial Aid: $615,000. Mrs. Susan Bradford Hall is Admission Director; Alexander Harvey IV (Vanderbilt University, B.S.; Loyola University, M.A.) is Headmaster.

Kent Denver School   1922

4000 E. Quincy Avenue, Englewood, CO 80110. 303-770-7660; Fax 303-770-7137; E-mail KDS_Admissions@ceo.cudenver.edu; Web Site www.kentdenver.org

Kent Denver is a coeducational, college preparatory day school enrolling 618 students in Grades 6–12. The School seeks to provide a challenging liberal arts program that inspires imagination and confidence. The average class size is 15. The traditional middle school curriculum is complemented by an advisor system. Fourteen Advanced Placement courses are offered in the upper school. All students are involved in the arts, athletics, and community service, and may participate in clubs, panels, and publications. Summer courses and camps are available. Tuition: $12,100. Financial Aid: $825,000. Tony Featherston is Director of Admission; Todd R.W. Horn, Ed.D., was appointed Head of School in 1997.

The Lowell Whiteman School

STEAMBOAT SPRINGS

42605 Routt County Road 36, Steamboat Springs, CO 80487. 970-879-1350; Fax 970-879-0506; E-mail admissions@whiteman.edu; Web Site www.whiteman.edu

THE LOWELL WHITEMAN SCHOOL in Steamboat Springs, Colorado, is a coeducational, college preparatory boarding and day school enrolling students in Grades 9–12. Approximately one-half are day students. Steamboat Springs (summer population 7000; winter population 20,000) is 157 miles from Denver and 11 miles from the Continental Divide. Steamboat offers world-class skiing and competitive ski training facilities during the winter months; golf, fishing, white-water rafting, hiking, backpacking, horseback riding, mountain biking, and many other sports are available throughout the school year. Buses and commuter flights link Steamboat Springs and Denver. During ski season, there are direct flights to Steamboat from Chicago, Houston, Minneapolis, St. Louis, Newark, Dallas, Los Angeles, and Denver. The three-hour drive from Denver offers spectacular scenery.

Established in 1957, The Lowell Whiteman School evolved from a summer camp founded in 1946 by Lowell Whiteman. In keeping with the beliefs of the founder, the School has remained small and continues to offer a rigorous classroom education complemented by experiential education and a social climate that demands student responsibility and participation. The traditional academic curriculum accommodates students of average to outstanding abilities.

A nonprofit institution, The Lowell Whiteman School is governed by a self-perpetuating Board of Trustees that includes parents, past parents, alumni, and friends of the School. Whiteman is accredited by the Association of Colorado Independent Schools and by the Colorado State Board of Education. It holds membership in the National Association of Independent Schools, Rocky Mountain Boarding School Association, the

Western Association of Boarding Schools, and the National Association of College Admission Counselors.

THE CAMPUS. The 180-acre campus borders on 2,000,000 acres of wilderness with countless mountain lakes and streams. On the School property are a soccer field, a riding ring, and many riding trails.

The main classroom building, made of rough-cut pine timbers, houses nine classrooms, a new updated library, a darkroom, two computer labs, and administrative offices. Adjacent to the classroom building is the art studio. The girls' dormitory accommodates 25 students and has two apartments for dorm supervisors. There are two boys' dormitories with apartments for dorm supervisors. Also on campus are two faculty homes, two faculty cabins, eight faculty apartments, a tackhouse, an art building, storage sheds, and a maintenance shop. The gymnasium offers a basketball court, a billiard table, showers, a climbing wall, faculty offices, and a student lounge. New to the campus in 1997 were a 125-seat lecture hall/theater and two science labs.

The School-owned facilities are valued at $10,000,000.

THE FACULTY. Walt Daub was appointed Headmaster in May of 1998. He received his B.A. from Hamilton College and his M.A. from the University of Delaware. Prior to his appointment, Mr. Daub held various administrative positions and taught at Albuquerque Academy and Tower Hill School.

The faculty and staff number 32, 14 men and 18 women. Thirteen faculty members live on campus. They hold 25 baccalaureate and 13 graduate degrees representing study at American University, Colby, Colgate, Colorado State, Dartmouth, Duke, McGill (Canada), Middlebury, Pomona, Providence College, St. Mary's, San Diego State, State University of New York, Stevens, Vanderbilt, and the Universities of California (Santa Barbara), Colorado (Boulder), Denver, Miami, and North Carolina (Chapel Hill).

Faculty benefits include health and dental insurance and a retirement plan.

STUDENT BODY. In 1999–2000, the School enrolls 55 boarders and 42 day students as follows: 21 in Grade 9, 21 in Grade 10, 30 in Grade 11, and 25 in Grade 12. Boarding students represent 20 states and the U.S. Virgin Islands. International students come from Austria, Canada, England, Germany, and Mexico.

ACADEMIC PROGRAM. The school year, from late August to early June, is divided into four marking periods, each seven weeks long. Holidays and excursions include a six-day camping trip in October, a week-long Thanksgiving break, two weeks at Christmas, a spring break, and foreign travel in the spring.

A typical fall or spring weekday begins with breakfast at 7:30 A.M., followed by a modified block class schedule, lunch, afternoon activities from 3:00 to 5:00 P.M., dinner at 6:15, study hall from 7:15 to 9:15, an hour of free time, return to the dormitories at 10:15, and lights out by 11:00 P.M. In the winter, the class schedule ends earlier in the day in order to get competitive skiers to training by 12:15 P.M. and recreational skiers to the slopes by 1:30 P.M.

Classes enroll an average of eight students. All boarding students, except those with a high grade-point average, attend nightly faculty-supervised study halls. The average course requires 30–60 minutes of homework nightly. Regularly scheduled conference periods provide an opportunity for teachers to give students extra help when needed. Tutorials may be arranged for an additional fee. Grades are issued and sent to parents every marking period. In addition, parents receive deficiency and proficiency notices at the midpoint and teacher comments at the conclusion of each marking period. The School has academic awards (Dean's and Honors lists) for those achieving at a high level, and a formal academic probation for students whose work is unsatisfactory.

To graduate, students must complete four years of English, three each of history and mathematics, two each of a foreign language and science, and one year each of art and computer. A student must earn a minimum of 18 credits, at least 16 of which must be academic.

The courses offered are English 1–4, AP English, Film, Drama; French 1–4, Spanish 1–4; Geography, World History, United States History, 20th Century History; Algebra I, Geometry, Algebra II/Trigonometry, Pre-Calculus, AP Calculus; Computer, Computer Graphics, Computer Programming; Biology, AP Biology, Chemistry, Physics; and Art, and AP Art/Art History.

Recent Whiteman graduates are currently attending such colleges and universities as Boston College, Carleton, Colorado School of Mines, Colorado State, Cornell, Dartmouth, Fort Lewis, Harvard, Illinois Institute of Technology, Massachusetts Institute of Technology, Middlebury, Montana State, New England College, Oregon State, Reed, Stanford, and the Universities of California, Colorado, Denver, Texas, Utah, Vermont, and Wyoming.

STUDENT ACTIVITIES. The Student Council meets weekly to discuss matters of concern, plan activities, and raise funds for student projects. The Council acts to increase communication between students and administration. Community service projects are coordinated by the Council.

In the spring, five one-month overseas travel programs immerse Whiteman students and faculty in the firsthand study of other countries. Each group, consisting of approximately 11 students and two teachers, focuses on the history, language, and culture of the host country. In recent years, participants have sailed off the coast of New Zealand, dived on the Great Barrier Reef, trekked in the Himalayas of Nepal, witnessed the changes in Eastern Europe, and observed whirling dervishes in Turkey.

Skiing and snowboarding, either recreational or competi-

tive, are the primary winter activities for Whiteman students. Students range in ability from beginner to advanced, and most ski or snowboard three or five times a week.

The nationally recognized Steamboat Springs Winter Sports Club has a variety of ski programs; approximately 40 percent of Whiteman students are involved in competition. The Development Team offers an introduction to alpine racing, which requires at least two training sessions per week; coaching, for which there is a separate charge, is available four days a week. Nordic, freestyle, and snowboarding development programs are also offered.

The ability-class-level competitive ski program is for USSA-licensed racers. Students in this program begin dryland training in the fall and continue with snow training as soon as weather permits. They compete on all levels, from local to international Olympic events. Interested students must interview with the Steamboat Springs Winter Sports Club. Six current or former students competed in the 1998 Winter Olympics.

Other school activities include the yearbook, horseback riding, and photography, as well as dances, art shows, and musical performances throughout the year. In addition, there are frequent School-sponsored camping, hiking, and rafting trips. Traditional annual events include student-faculty softball, basketball, and soccer games, the Whiteman Olympics, and Commencement.

ADMISSION AND COSTS. The Lowell Whiteman School seeks to enroll students of average to above-average ability who have a high potential for academic achievement and who can contribute to and benefit from a unique community. New students are admitted to all grades on the basis of teacher recommendations, personal essays, academic transcripts, and a personal interview. The Secondary School Admission Test is recommended, but not required. Applications are considered on a rolling basis, and students are admitted as long as vacancies exist; however, July 30 is the outside date to ensure consideration for September enrollment. New students may be admitted at midyear if vacancies exist. There is a $30 application fee.

In 1999–2000, boarding tuition is $24,500; day tuition is $12,775. The cost of the foreign trip is approximately $3200–$3500. Books and miscellaneous expenses ordinarily total $400 to $700; students' personal allowances average $20 a week. Other expenses may include ski lift tickets and coaching ($1200–$1800) and riding ($375 for the fall program).

Financial aid is available for families who qualify through the School Scholarship Service.

Academic Dean: Joanne Z. Lasko
Dean of Students: Don Ciavola
Alumni Secretary: Joseph N. Roberts
Director of Admissions: Deb Smith
Director of Experiential Education: Margi Missling-Root

St. Anne's Episcopal School   1950

*2701 South York Street, Denver, CO 80210-6098. 303-756-9481;
Fax 303-756-5512; Web Site www.st-annes.org*

St. Anne's seeks to guide children toward personal development and fosters social responsibility and involvement. The School instills a genuine love of learning through a broad, challenging academic program in a supportive, nurturing environment. Committed to Judeo-Christian values, St. Anne's is a family school that embraces students of varied talents, abilities, and backgrounds. The 400 students in Preschool–Grade 8 are taught language arts, literature, math, computer, science, fine arts, and foreign language at all levels. Summer programs and extended day are available. Tuition: $5713–$9264. Financial Aid: $336,100. Rose Kelly is Director of Admission; Ramsay C. Stabler (Williams, B.A. 1977; Columbia, M.A. 1985) was appointed Headmaster in 1994.

St. Mary's Academy   1864

*4545 South University Boulevard, Englewood, CO 80110-6099.
303-762-8300; Fax 303-783-6201; Web Site www.smanet.org*

St. Mary's enrolls 775 students, with coeducation in Kindergarten–Grade 8 and all girls in Grades 9–12. This U.S. Department of Education Recognized School of Excellence was founded by the Sisters of Loretto to provide a values-based education that fosters creativity, imagination, and academic excellence. The curriculum places equal emphasis on religious studies, core subjects, foreign language, and the fine arts. Advanced Placement in seven subjects and a counseling program are key factors in college preparation. Students take part in liturgies, sports, six honor societies, publications, school government, drama, music, community service, and clubs. Extended-day care is offered through Grade 8. Tuition: $7315. Financial Aid: $360,000. Linda Ticer is Admissions Director; Judith Baenen is President.

Theodor Herzl Jewish Day School   1975

*2450 South Wabash Street, Denver, CO 80231. 303-755-1846;
Fax 303-755-3614*

Theodor Herzl Jewish Day School, serving 300 boys and girls in Kindergarten–Grade 6, seeks to provide an egalitarian, integrated, quality secular and Judaic education. The School offers a pluralistic approach to Judaism and teaches respect for the diversity of Jewish observance and religious values within a caring, supportive community. The study of Hebrew is incorporated into the curriculum, which emphasizes a strong foundation in language arts, math, science, and social studies. Before- and after-school programs, featuring enrichment activities such as Russian, sign language, music, and art, are offered to interested families. Tuition: $6690. Financial Aid: $225,000. Andrea L. Watson is Director of Admissions; Dr. Lorry Getz is Principal.

CONNECTICUT

Avon Old Farms School   AVON

Avon, CT 06001. 860-404-4100; Admissions 800-464-2866;
   E-mail admissions@avonoldfarms.com;
   Web Site www.avonoldfarms.com

AVON OLD FARMS SCHOOL in Avon, Connecticut, is a college preparatory school enrolling boarding and day boys in Grades 9 through 12 and a postgraduate year. Situated on 900 acres of suburban woodlands, the School is located 12 miles west of Hartford, offering convenient access to many cultural and recreational activities. Avon is easily reached via Interstate Highways 91 and 84 and is 20 miles from Bradley International Airport.

Founded in 1927 by Mrs. Theodate Pope Riddle "to provide instruction and activities [tending] to develop honor, courage, and culture," the School seeks to prepare individuals to function productively and responsibly and to stimulate their desire for knowledge. Recognizing that students progress at varying rates both in and out of the classroom, the School emphasizes student-faculty relationships through its faculty-adviser program. It also stresses individual development and responsibility through athletics, extracurricular activities, and student government. Avon Old Farms is nonsectarian, but boys are required to attend nondenominational services three times weekly.

A nonprofit institution, Avon Old Farms School is administered by a self-perpetuating Board of 24 Directors. There are more than 5300 living graduates, many of whom assist the School by means of financial support and recruitment efforts. The School is accredited by the New England Association of Schools and Colleges and holds membership in the National Association of Independent Schools and the Connecticut Association of Independent Schools.

THE CAMPUS. Designed primarily by the School's founder, most of the campus buildings are constructed in a Tudor Cotswold style of red stone with oak beams, leaded windows, and slate roofs. Each of the four large structures comprising the Pope Quadrangle has classrooms, dormitory rooms, and apartments for faculty and their families. The Science Building, which houses two laboratories and the School radio station, is near the quadrangle. Clustered around the "Village Green" are the Headmaster's house and office, the Riddle Refectory, the Dean's offices, the hockey rink, and the gymnasium. At the entrance to the grounds are the chapel, the Estabrook Fine Arts Center, Brown House dormitory, faculty townhouses, and the

Ordway Gallery. At the opposite ends of the campus are Faculty Row, Brooks House, the Health Center, the Hawk's Nest (store and lounge), Jennings Dormitory, Jamerson Dormitory, and the Ferrier Pavilion.

The gymnasium includes a regulation basketball court, two practice courts, three newly renovated international-size squash courts, a wrestling room, a swimming pool with spectators' gallery, a rifle range, and shower and locker facilities. The School has eight outdoor tennis courts, two paddle tennis courts, and an enclosed, heated, ice-hockey rink with a professional-quality weight training facility. A pond for swimming, fishing, and skating; baseball, football, lacrosse, and soccer fields; and a cinder track are also on the grounds.

The Jack R. Aron Academic Center contains a 400-seat auditorium, a science center, and the Baxter Library, which houses 30,000 volumes, archival reference material, and a state-of-the-art media center. Fiberoptic cable throughout the campus supports both IBM and Macintosh platforms to 500 terminals. All access the Internet and E-mail. The grounds and plant are valued at more than $100,000,000.

THE FACULTY. Kenneth H. LaRocque, appointed Headmaster in 1998, is a graduate of Phillips Exeter Academy (1971), Harvard College (B.A. 1975), and Harvard University (M.A. 1981). Before assuming his present duties, Mr. LaRocque served Avon as Provost for five years and as Dean of Students for ten years. He also served in various capacities at The Rectory School and Charles River Academy.

There are 47 full-time teachers and administrators who teach, 34 men and 13 women. Thirty-nine live on campus, 27 with families. They hold 50 baccalaureate and 25 advanced degrees representing study at such institutions as Alderson-Broadus, Allegheny, Amherst, Andhra University (India), Annhurst, Boston College, Bowdoin, Cleveland Institute of Music, Colby, Colgate, College of William and Mary, Columbia, Connecticut College, Cornell, Dartmouth, Duke, Harvard, Hofstra, Ithaca, Kent State, Middlebury, Montclair State, Mysore University (India), Nazareth, Queens College, Rutgers, St. Joseph's College, St. Michael's, St. Olaf, Shivaji University (India), Springfield College, Stanford, State University of New York, Syracuse, Trinity, Utkal University (India), Vanderbilt, Wake Forest, Washington and Jefferson, Wesleyan, Worcester Polytechnic Institute, Yale, and the Universities of California (Berkeley), Colorado, Connecticut, Delhi (India), Hartford,

Maine, Massachusetts, Michigan, New Hampshire, New Mexico, Pennsylvania, and Washington. Teacher benefits include health insurance, retirement plans, and Social Security. Leaves of absence can be arranged, and the School provides funds to finance summer travel and study by faculty.

Three nurses staff the health center, which is open 24 hours a day. A physician is always on call, and the University of Connecticut Health Center is 12 minutes away.

STUDENT BODY. In 1999–2000, the School enrolls 289 boarding boys and 84 day students ages 13–19 in Grades 9–12 as follows: 58 in Grade 9, 96 in Grade 10, 123 in Grade 11, and 96 in Grade 12. Approximately one-third of the students come from Connecticut; 31 other states and 14 foreign countries are also represented.

ACADEMIC PROGRAM. The school year, from early September to early June, is divided into three terms with Thanksgiving, Christmas, and spring vacations and two long weekends. Marks and comments are sent to parents six times annually.

Classes meet five days a week in four 45-minute periods and one 65-minute period before and after lunch. Athletics are scheduled daily after the final academic period. Evening study hours are from 7:45 to 9:45 P.M. Monday through Thursday, 7:00 to 8:30 P.M. on Friday, and 8:30 to 9:30 P.M. on Sunday. On school nights, boys must be in their dormitories by 10:30 P.M., and "lights out" is at 10:30–11:00 P.M.

Faculty members are available for extra help during an enrichment hour, which takes place before the two-hour study hall. Saturday morning sessions are required for students whose academic progress is not satisfactory.

Graduation requirements are four years of English; two years each of a foreign language, social science, including United States History, and science; three years of mathematics; a fine arts course; a computer course; and at least three additional credits.

The curriculum includes English 1–4; French 1–4, Spanish 1–4, Latin 1–3; Ancient History, United States History, American Presidency, The Cold War, World History, Asian Studies, Economics, Introduction to Public Speaking; Algebra 1–2, Geometry, Probability, Advanced Mathematics, Precalculus, Calculus, Computer Programming, Computer Word Processing, Computer Applications; Biology, Chemistry, Project Physics, Geology, Environmental Science; Architecture, Art and Man, Design, Ceramics, Woodworking; Photography; and Chorale. Students in Grades 9 and 10 are given the Harvard-Milton study skills program. Advanced Placement courses are offered in studio art, biology, English, French language, Spanish literature, French literature, Spanish language, economics, physics, calculus, computer programming, and United States history.

Departmental honors courses are offered in English, foreign languages, history, mathematics, and science. Selected candidates may spend a postgraduate year attending an English secondary school under The English-Speaking Union program.

In 1999, the 118 members of the graduating class matriculated at 87 colleges and universities; 7 were admitted by "early decision." Two or more are attending Bentley, Boston College 4, Connecticut College 4, Elon, Emory 4, Gettysburg, Hamilton 3, Lynn University, Manhattan, Northeastern, Southern Methodist, Trinity College 5, Wheaton, Yale, and the Universities of Connecticut 6 and Denver 3.

STUDENT ACTIVITIES. Organized as the Village of Old Farms, the School has its own laws, post office, and bank. The ten-member Student Council, an elective body, appoints student "officials" who operate a government patterned after that of an old New England township. Under the supervision of the Headmaster and the Board of Directors, these "officials" are responsible for creating and enforcing school rules and regulations.

Extracurricular organizations include *Winged Beaver* (yearbook), *Avon Record* (newspaper), WAOF (radio station), and the Community Service, Paintball, Spirit, Mountain Biking, Art, Habitat for Humanity, Polar Bear, Social Activities, Photogra-

phy, Fellowship, History, Drama, Nimrod, International, and Computer clubs. Cultural and social enrichment programs are offered through the School's participation in the WALKS Foundation (consisting of Westminster, Avon, Loomis Chaffee, Kingswood-Oxford, and Suffield schools). The drama program is coordinated with Miss Porter's School.

Varsity teams compete with teams from other independent schools in baseball, basketball, cross-country, football, golf, hockey, lacrosse, riflery, skiing, soccer, squash, swimming, tennis, track, and wrestling. Noncompetitive sports include recreational skiing, golf, tennis, bicycling, hiking, camping, paddle tennis, and skating. Students may participate in the Theatre Arts program instead of a sports activity. All students take part in the school work program.

A variety of weekend activities is planned regularly. The School obtains tickets and provides transportation to concerts, movies, ski outings, and events at the Hartford Civic Center. Social exchanges, dances, and informal get-togethers are held with Miss Porter's, Westover, Ethel Walker, and five other girls' schools. Seniors are allowed four overnight leaves per term, juniors may take three, and underclassmen, two.

On Sundays, transportation to nearby girls' schools, restaurants, a golf course, and other "activity areas" is also available.

ADMISSION AND COSTS. Avon seeks students exhibiting "character, integrity, academic potential and achievement, and the ability to compete successfully in a full college preparatory course of study." The School has a policy of admitting "students of any race, color, or national or ethnic origin." Applications are accepted for Grades 9–12; however, admittance into Grades 11 and 12 is limited, since those classes are filled primarily through promotion of underclassmen. The selection of students is based on a personal interview with the student and his parents, academic and personal recommendations, and the results of the Secondary School Admission Test. Candidates for admission are urged to apply before February 15. If vacancies exist, students may be enrolled during the school year. There is a $40 application fee.

In 1999–2000, seven-day boarding tuition is $25,900; a limited number of local boys may be accepted as five-and-one-half-day boarders at the same cost. Tuition for day students is $17,400. Additional expenses include a health fee (boarding $175); a general fee for athletics, weekend entertainment, and dances (boarding $350); and fees for laboratory science or fine arts courses. Tuition insurance is included in the tuition cost. Financial assistance totaling $1,700,000 is awarded annually on the basis of need to 31 percent of the student body. Avon Old Farms subscribes to the School Scholarship Service.

Provost: John T. Gardner
Dean of Faculty: William G. Kron
Director of Admissions: James A. Cunningham II

Director of Alumni: Peter M. Evans
College Counselors: Arthur Custer and Susan Nentwig
Business Manager: Walter J. Ullram
Director of Athletics: Richard F. Garber, Jr.

Brunswick School 1902

100 Maher Avenue, Greenwich, CT 06830. 203-625-5800;
Admissions 203-625-5842; Fax 203-625-5889;
E-mail jharris@brunswick.org; Web Site www.brunswickschool.org

A college preparatory day school enrolling 704 boys in Pre-Kindergarten–Grade 12, Brunswick offers an integrated program of academics, community service, and sports. Advanced Placement and honors courses and computer programming are offered. All boys take a semester of art or acting, or a year of band or chorus. Grades 9–12 coordinate with Greenwich Academy, a nearby girls' school, with more than 80 percent of classes being coeducational. Other coordinated activities include community service, concerts, and drama. Tuition: $10,600–$17,000. Financial Aid: $1,150,500. Jeffry Harris is Director of Admission; Duncan Edwards III (Princeton, B.A.; Columbia, M.A.) was appointed Headmaster in 1988. *New England Association.*

Canterbury School NEW MILFORD

Aspetuck Avenue, New Milford, CT 06776. 860-210-3832;
E-mail admissions@canterbury.pvt.k12.ct.us;
Web Site www.canterbury.pvt.k12.ct.us

CANTERBURY SCHOOL in New Milford, Connecticut, is an independent Catholic boarding and day school enrolling boys and girls in a college preparatory program in Forms III–VI (Grades 9–12). Guided by lay Roman Catholics, Canterbury's community is comprised of students and teachers of many faiths and backgrounds. The School is located on a hilltop campus in the western Connecticut town of New Milford (population 25,000) with views of the Litchfield Hills. New Milford is 80 miles from New York City, and 45 miles from Hartford, and local bus and train service are available. The area is rich in natural beauty, with access to the Appalachian Trail, the Berkshire Mountains, and the Housatonic River for outdoor activities.

Canterbury School was founded in 1915 by Henry O. Havemeyer, Clarence H. Mackay, and Nelson Hume. Dr. Hume was honored by Pope Pius XI as a Knight of St. Gregory for his outstanding work in Catholic education. Originally a school for boys, Canterbury has been fully coeducational for more than 25 years. The School is named for the tenth-century English school established by Saint Dunstan, Archbishop of Canterbury.

The hallmark of a Canterbury education is the School's willingness to accept students as they are, support them where necessary, stretch them where appropriate, and inspire them to become moral leaders in a secular world. Canterbury's spiritual tradition informs all aspects of the program, including academics, the arts, athletics, and community service, which aims to inspire in students a commitment to lifelong volunteer service.

Canterbury School, a nonprofit corporation operating under the patronage of the Archbishop of Hartford, is guided by a self-perpetuating Board of Trustees. Many of the 3600 alumni participate in the life of the School by hosting gatherings to introduce prospective students and their parents to Canterbury. The School, which is chartered by the State of Connecticut, is accredited by the New England Association of Schools and Colleges and holds membership in the National Association of Independent Schools.

THE CAMPUS. The campus is a rich architectural mix of traditional and modern buildings, with the Chapel at the physical and spiritual heart of the School. Canterbury encompasses 150 acres of land, of which 22 acres compose the main campus. This includes six fields, three baseball diamonds, six tennis courts, a track, a swimming pool, the Draddy Arena, an enclosed hockey rink, and the Field House.

The Old Schoolhouse (1938) was completely renovated in 1998, in a $2,000,000 project that retained the integrity of the original architecture. It houses classrooms and seminar rooms. A new athletic facility (1999) houses five international squash courts, new locker rooms, and rooms for training, weight and fitness, wrestling, and aerobics and dance. Internet and voice mail access is available in all classrooms and in dormitory common areas.

The Robert Markey Steele Hall has a dining room, a student snack bar, a computer center, a library with study center, a 100-seat auditorium, and offices. The Nelson Hume Building houses classrooms, a 400-seat auditorium, a student lounge, and a music room. Student dormitories and faculty apartments are situated in Carter, Duffy, Sheehan, and Ingleside houses, Havemeyer and Carmody halls, and Hickory Hearth. The total endowment invested in plant and equipment is $17,000,000.

THE FACULTY. Thomas J. Sheehy III was appointed Headmaster in December 1989 and assumed duties in July 1990. He had previously served as Headmaster at Old Westbury School of the Holy Child in New York. Mr. Sheehy is a graduate of Bowdoin College (B.A. 1969) and Pennsylvania State University (M.A. 1976). His concentrations were American History and Classics, respectively, and he teaches history and interdisciplinary courses at Canterbury. Mr. Sheehy and his wife, Betsy, live on campus with one of their four children.

The faculty hold 69 baccalaureate and 45 advanced degrees representing study at Assumption, Berklee College of Music, Boston University, Bowdoin, Colby, Colgate, College of the Holy Cross, Columbia, Cornell, Fairfield, Georgetown, Gettysburg, Goddard, Hamilton, Harvard, John Carroll, Lehigh, Marist, Middlebury, Montana State, Northwestern, Oberlin College Conservatory of Music, Oxford, Pennsylvania State, Princeton, Providence, Rensselaer, Rhode Island College, Rutgers, Sacred Heart, St. Joseph, Southern Connecticut, State University of

New York (Brockport), Texas Tech, Ursinus, Washington and Jefferson, Wesleyan, Wheelock, Williams, Yale, and the Universities of Rhode Island, North Carolina, Virginia, and West Virginia. Forty-six faculty members live on campus, 30 with their families.

A resident chaplain is on staff, and two registered nurses supervise the Health Center. A local doctor is on call with facilities available at nearby New Milford Hospital.

STUDENT BODY. In 1999–2000, there are 196 boarding students and 140 day students—214 boys and 122 girls—enrolled as follows: 65 in Form III, 67 in Form IV, 99 in Form V, and 105 in Form VI.

Approximately two-thirds of the students are from Connecticut, New Jersey, and New York; the remainder come from 16 other states and 11 foreign countries.

ACADEMIC PROGRAM. The school year, from September to June, consists of two semesters and extended vacations at Thanksgiving, Christmas, and in March. The academic year is divided into six-week marking periods, for which students and parents receive grade reports. Parents also receive detailed grade reports and comments at the end of each semester.

Classes are held six days a week, with morning classes only on Wednesday and Saturdays. Average class size is 12 students.

Faculty members are available for individual assistance throughout the day and the evening study hours. In Forms III and IV, students are required to attend supervised study halls during the school day unless they maintain a prescribed average. Boarders study in their rooms or the library from 7:30 until 9:30 P.M. Older students are eligible for late-night privileges.

The curriculum consists of a variety of full- and half-year courses. Yearlong courses are offered in such areas as English; Latin, French, Spanish; European History, American History, Economics; Algebra 1–Algebra 2, Geometry, Pre-Calculus, Calculus; Biology, Biotechnology, Chemistry, Physics; and Studio Art. Sample semester courses include Biology of the Brain, Anthropology, Vietnam War, Oceanography, Irish History and Literature, Introduction to Multimedia, Jazz Theory/Improvisation, Architectural Drawing, The Holocaust, Theatre Workshop, and Film. Theology courses concentrate on ethics, human relationships, the Old and New Testaments, and comparative religions. Advanced Placement classes in 15 subjects are available for qualified students.

Canterbury's English as a Second Language Program is offered to 15 international students who wish to pursue study at the School but who need improvement in English skills. The program goal is to mainstream students into the regular curriculum and to prepare them to qualify for a Canterbury diploma.

Qualified seniors may undertake independent study projects of their own choice in the spring semester.

All 105 seniors in the Class of 1999 went to college. They are attending such institutions as Boston College, Boston University, Colby, Colgate, College of the Holy Cross, Cornell, Denison, Fairfield, Fordham, Gettysburg, Hobart & William Smith, Middlebury, Northwestern, Providence, Roanoke, St. Michael's, Syracuse, Trinity, United States Military Academy, and the Universities of Denver and Vermont.

STUDENT ACTIVITIES. All students participate in the athletic programs, with three teams fielded in most sports to accommodate players of varying sizes, ages, and abilities; nontraditional options are available for Form VI students. Boys' teams are organized in football, soccer, cross-country, swimming, water polo, squash, wrestling, ice hockey, basketball, lacrosse, baseball, golf, tennis, and track. Girls compete in basketball, cross-country, field hockey, ice hockey, lacrosse, swimming, soccer, softball, squash, track, tennis, and volleyball. Form VI boys and girls may choose from beginning karate, SCUBA, ballroom dancing, weight training, and aerobics.

Other activities include Student Government, Dramatic Club, the monthly newspaper (*The Tabard*), the yearbook (*Cantuarian*), the literary magazine (*Carillon*), and the debate team. Interest clubs are formed for Canterbury Choir and Madrigals, the environment and recycling, the outdoors, photography, astronomy, chess and backgammon.

The Canterbury League, the community service club, supports the School's outreach missions. There are many opportunities to serve, including working at a soup kitchen and walking for CROP or the March of Dimes. Students participate in Urban Plunge, a church-sponsored public service project headquartered in Bridgeport, Connecticut. Each summer, a group of students and teachers assists pilgrims visiting the shrine at Lourdes, France.

The Student Activities Committee plans movies, dances, and field trips. Recent events include a white-water rafting trip, paintball games, ski trips, and a visit to the Six Flags Great Adventure Park. On-campus events include a concert series, dramatic productions, Homecoming, and Alumni Day. With permission, boarding students may walk into New Milford to shop or dine out.

ADMISSION AND COSTS. Canterbury seeks students who can compete academically at the college preparatory level, and who will contribute their talents to the school community. Applicants must submit Secondary School Admission Test scores, a transcript and reference from their current school, and letters of recommendation. In almost all cases, a personal interview is required. New students are accepted in all forms, with a limited number entering Form VI as postgraduates. Candidates are advised to apply early, and there is a $35 application fee.

In 1999–2000, tuition is $26,400 for boarding students and $17,900 for day students. Tuition insurance and a tuition payment plan are available. Approximately $2,000,000 in financial aid is awarded annually to 49 percent of the student body. Awards are based solely on need.

Dean of the School: Jean-Paul Mandler
Director of Student Affairs: Margie F. Jenkins
Director of the Annual Fund: Stephen F. Abbott
Director of Admissions: Patrick M. Finn
Director of Development and Finance: Bryan V. Kiefer
Director of College Counseling: Catherine Pietraszek
Director of Athletics: David Wilson

Cheshire Academy   CHESHIRE

10 Main Street, Cheshire, CT 06410. 203-272-5396;
E-mail admission@cheshacad.pvt.k12.ct.us;
Web Site www.cheshireacademy.org

CHESHIRE ACADEMY in Cheshire, Connecticut, is a coeducational college preparatory school enrolling day students in Kindergarten–Grade 5 and Grades 6–12 and a postgraduate year. Boarding students are enrolled in Grade 9–Postgraduate. Located near the center of town (population 25,000), the Academy is less than half an hour by car from the educational, cultural, and athletic opportunities of New Haven and Hartford; it is approximately two hours from New York or Boston and an easy drive from the Berkshire Mountains and Long Island Sound.

Founded as a coeducational community school in 1794, the Academy emphasizes faculty dedication, a challenging curriculum, and the opportunity to work and play in a familial atmosphere. Its mission is to help each student achieve his or her highest potential and become a confident, responsible, and successful member of the world community.

Cheshire Academy is a nonprofit institution governed by a self-perpetuating Board of 15 Trustees. The approximately 6000 living graduates are encouraged to take an active role in shaping and preserving the Academy. The school is accredited by the New England Association of Schools and Colleges and holds membership in the National Association of Independent Schools, among other affiliations.

THE CAMPUS. The 100-acre campus includes woodlands, a pond, eight playing fields, a quarter-mile track, and ten new hard-court tennis courts. Additional athletic facilities are housed in the Arthur N. Sheriff Field House, which contains a six-lane swimming pool, two basketball courts, a fitness center, locker rooms, history classrooms, offices, art studios, and the Black Box Theater.

Administrative offices are located in Bowden Hall (1796), the original school building. Adjoining Bowden is Bronson Hall, which contains offices, a meeting room, and a music studio. Woodbury Hall (1976) provides Learning Center, English, and foreign language classrooms. Hurley Hall (1940) houses the Morris Sweetkind Library, the Michael J. Vanacore College Center, the academic offices, and a girls' dormitory. Girls also reside in Horton Hall (1946). Walters and Skilton houses are faculty and senior/postgraduate house/dorms for boys. Additional living quarters for boys are located in Von der Porten Hall (1959), which also contains the Student Health Center. The John J. White '38 Science and Technology Center opened in 1998. Beardsley House provides classrooms for the Middle School. The new Lower School building opened in the fall of 1997. Meals are served in the Gideon Welles Dining Commons. Student lounges, meeting rooms, music practice rooms, the snack bar–solarium, and the bookstore are located in the Charles Harwood, Jr., Student Center (1988).

The school-owned plant is valued at $15,000,000.

THE FACULTY. Dr. Gerald A. Larson was named Headmaster of Cheshire Academy in July 1999. He is a graduate of the University of New Hampshire (B.S.), New Hampshire College (M.B.A.), and Boston University (Ed.D.). Before assuming his present position, he served for 14 years at Tabor Academy in Marion, Massachusetts, where he was an administrator, teacher, and coach. He has also taught on the college level at Boston University and Bridgewater State College. Dr. Larson and his wife, Cheryl, are the parents of a four-year-old son.

There are 63 full-time teachers and administrators, 43 women and 20 men. Thirty-five faculty members live on campus, 15 with their families. Faculty hold 59 baccalaureate and 26 master's degrees from such colleges as Bates, Boston College, Boston University, Colby, Colorado College, Columbia, Connecticut College, Cornell, Georgetown, George Washington, Hartwick, Middlebury, Mount Holyoke, New York University, Princeton, Providence, Skidmore, Tufts, Villanova, Williams, Yale, and the Universities of Connecticut, Massachusetts, and Michigan.

The five-bed Student Health Center is staffed by two nurses and two local physicians. A number of hospitals are located nearby.

STUDENT BODY. In 1999–2000, the Academy's Upper School enrolls 98 boarding boys, 44 boarding girls, 63 day boys, and 29 day girls as follows: 39 in Grade 9, 53 in Grade 10, 67 in Grade 11, 59 in Grade 12, and 16 in a postgraduate year. Boarding students represent 18 states, Puerto Rico, and 24 foreign countries. The Middle School enrolls 42 day students in Grades 6–8; the Lower School enrolls 53 day students in Kindergarten–Grade 5.

ACADEMIC PROGRAM. The school year, from mid-September to early June, is divided into three terms and includes a Thanksgiving holiday and Christmas and spring vacations. Classes, enrolling an average of ten students, are held on Monday through Friday plus two Saturdays a year. Faculty-supervised study halls are scheduled for all boarders on Sunday through Thursday evenings. In addition, the Learning Center is available for students who would benefit from learning strategies to improve their reading comprehension, study skills, writing, organization, computer study skills, vocabulary, and mathematics. Grades are sent to parents six times during the school year. All students participate in the Academy's College Guidance Program.

To graduate, Upper School (Grade 9–Postgraduate) students must earn at least 18 credits as follows: 4 in English, 1 in reading (Grade 9 only), 2 in foreign language, 3 in social studies (including 1 in United States History), 3 in mathematics, 2 in science, 1 in fine arts, and 3 in electives. Among the specific courses are English Levels I–IV, African-American Studies, History and Literature of the 1920's, Hispanic Cultural Studies, Pre-College Composition, Women's Literature, Shakespeare, Creative Writing; French 1–4, Spanish 1–4; United States History, World Civilizations, Modern World History, Russian History, Chinese History, Psychology, Introduction to Economics, American Government; Algebra 1–2, Algebra 2/Trigonometry, Geometry, Calculus, Computer Programming; Biology, Chemistry, Physics, Human Anatomy and Physiology, Ecology, Microbiology, Plant Physiology; and Survey of Art, Art Studio 1–2, Pottery and Sculpture, Printmaking, Photography, Music Appreciation, and Instrumental Instruction. Honors sections and Advanced Placement instruction are available in most disciplines. English as a Second Language is available for international students.

The postgraduate program features special English, reading, writing, and study skills sections as well as SAT preparation and Advanced Placement and honors-level courses. The postgraduate program enables students to become better equipped to succeed in college.

In 1999, all 63 graduates entered college. They are attending such institutions as Art Institute of Seattle, Babson, Bard, Brandeis, Denison, George Washington University, Hamilton College, Hartwick College, Johns Hopkins, Northeastern, Rhode Island School of Design, Sarah Lawrence, Tufts, United States Naval Academy, and the University of Connecticut.

Cheshire Academy offers a six-week academic and recreational summer program, including English as a Second Language, for approximately 130 boarding and day boys and girls in Grades 5–12.

The Middle School (Grades 6–8) curriculum stresses the fundamentals and includes courses in language arts, English, reading, Spanish, French, history, the social sciences, adolescent issues, mathematics, science, computer programming, art, music, and physical education.

In the Lower School (Kindergarten–Grade 5), small classes and a low student-teacher ratio allow for experiential learning with an emphasis on hands-on activities. The curriculum's literature-based focus incorporates a combined whole-language and phonetic approach. Spanish is introduced in Grade 1. Twice weekly music classes, based on the Kodaly and Orff theory, and weekly swimming lessons and physical education are also included. Computers are available in each classroom, and students visit the library weekly.

STUDENT ACTIVITIES. The Student Council, composed of class officers and elected student representatives, provides a forum for student decision-making. Council members also organize and support activities designed to build school spirit. The Board of Programmers provides a variety of social, cultural, and physical services to the school.

Other activities include the student newspaper, yearbook, a literary magazine, the Drama Club, the International Club, and Campus Guides. All students participate in community service and in the after-school activity program.

Varsity sports include football, soccer, cross-country, swimming, basketball, wrestling, tennis, lacrosse, baseball, golf, track, volleyball, and softball. For two consecutive years, 1997 and

1998, the boys' tennis team won the NEPSAC championship, and the boys' varsity soccer team won the CISAC championship. Middle School teams are fielded in baseball, basketball, volleyball, and soccer. Skiing, weight lifting, aerobics, and dance are offered on a noncompetitive basis. Students are encouraged to work with faculty members in organizing such activities as dances and class trips.

Traditional school events include Parents' Weekend, Mountain Day, Homecoming, Winter Carnival/Olympics, Headmaster's Day, Junior-Senior Prom, Alumni Reunion, and Spring Fling.

ADMISSION AND COSTS. Cheshire Academy seeks to enroll boys and girls, ages 5–19, who are interested in fulfilling their potential and who are committed to making a difference for the better, both in themselves and in the community around them. Candidates are admitted to all grades on the basis of a completed application form, personal essays, two faculty recommendations, prior academic record, a parental statement, a personal interview, and standardized test scores. Applications should be submitted in the fall preceding the year of desired admission, although late applications will be considered. Students may also be admitted at midyear, space permitting. There is a nonrefundable $50 application fee ($100 for international students).

In 1999–2000, comprehensive day tuition is $16,600 for the Upper School, $13,650 for the Middle School, and $10,460 for the Lower School; boarding tuition is $25,950. Personal expenses vary from $500 for Middle School day students to $1000 for Upper School boarding students.

In 1999–2000, approximately $700,000 in financial aid was awarded on the basis of need to 33 percent of the student body. A tuition payment plan is available. Cheshire Academy subscribes to the School and Student Service for Financial Aid.

Dean of Faculty: Mrs. Karen Smith
Director of Studies: Ms. Virginia Terzis
Dean of Student Affairs: Mr. Bevan Dupre
Alumni Director: Mrs. Barbara Dupre
Dean of Admission: Mr. Mark Werden
College Counselor: Mr. David Suter
Business Manager: Mrs. Patricia Willis
Director of Athletics: Mr. Bill Casson

Choate Rosemary Hall   WALLINGFORD

333 Christian Street, Wallingford, CT 06492. 203-697-2000;
Admissions 203-697-2239; Fax 203-697-2629;
E-mail admissions@choate.edu; Web Site www.choate.edu

CHOATE ROSEMARY HALL in Wallingford, Connecticut, is a coeducational, boarding and day, college preparatory school enrolling students in Grades 9–12 and a postgraduate year. Wallingford (population 41,000) is located off Interstate 91, 15 miles north of New Haven. New York and Boston are about two hours away; Bradley International Airport is 45 miles to the north.

Rosemary Hall (1890) was founded by Mary Atwater Choate and The Choate School (1896) by her husband, Judge William Gardner Choate, on the same site. Rosemary Hall moved from Wallingford to Greenwich in 1900 and returned to the Wallingford campus in 1971 as a coordinate school, completing the merger to coeducation in 1974.

Choate Rosemary Hall provides a rigorous academic curriculum and emphasizes the formation of character. The school encourages students to think critically and communicate clearly, understand various methods of intellectual inquiry, and develop global perspectives. Community service is mandatory.

Choate Rosemary Hall is a nonprofit corporation governed by a self-perpetuating Board of Trustees. The school is accredited by the New England Association of Schools and Colleges and holds membership in the National Association of Independent Schools, among other associations.

THE CAMPUS. The school is situated on 400 acres in a residential setting. More than 116 houses, dormitories, and classroom buildings are on campus, along with 13 athletic fields, 23 tennis courts, and a running track.

The Science Center (1989), designed by I.M. Pei, houses classrooms and laboratories, conservatory, and auditorium. The Paul Mellon Arts Center (1972), also designed by Pei, houses two theaters, a recital hall, art galleries, studios, practice rooms, and a music production studio. The Paul Mellon Humanities Center contains the English, History and Social Sciences, and Psychology, Philosophy and Religion departments and a computer center. The Andrew Mellon Library houses 56,000 volumes, including several special collections. A Language Learning Center with a 32-station laboratory is located in Steele Hall. Students can access the campus computer network from dormitory rooms. The Albert Schweitzer Institute for the Humanities, in residence at Choate Rosemary Hall, is dedicated to advancing the Nobel Peace Laureate's philosophy of "Reverence for Life" through programs of education and action.

The Johnson Athletic Center includes basketball courts, squash courts, weight rooms, wrestling room, rifle range, and a suspended $^1/_{10}$-mile indoor track. Other athletic buildings are the 25-meter Larry Hart Swimming Pool, Remsen Arena and Hockey Rink, Macquire Gym with climbing wall, Torrence Hunt Tennis Center, and Sylvester Boat House.

THE FACULTY. Edward J. Shanahan, a graduate of St. Joseph's College (B.A. 1965), Fordham University (M.A. 1968), and the University of Wisconsin (Ph.D. 1982), was appointed Headmaster in 1991. Dr. Shanahan was Dean of the College at Dartmouth for eight years and was previously Dean of Students at Wesleyan University. Dr. Shanahan is the father of three children, including two graduates of Choate Rosemary Hall.

Seventy-one men and 46 women, including 32 administrators, comprise the faculty. Most reside on campus and act as advisers to students who live with them. They hold 139 bachelor's degrees and 99 advanced degrees, including 6 doctorates, from such institutions as Allegheny 2, Amherst 2, Boston College 2, Boston University 2, Bowdoin 3, Brown 4, Bryn Mawr, College of the Holy Cross 2, Columbia 5, Cornell 2, Dartmouth 6, Duke, Hamilton, Harvard 5, Johns Hopkins, Kenyon, Madras (India), Michigan State, Middlebury 17, Mount Holyoke, New York University, Oberlin 2, Ohio University, Oxford (England), Princeton 4, Sarah Lawrence, Smith, Southern Connecticut 6, Springfield 2, Stanford, State University of New York 5, Trinity 5, Wesleyan 15, Williams 6, Yale 11, and the Universities of California 2, Chicago 2, Massachusetts, Michigan 2, New Hampshire, North Carolina, Paris (France), and Wisconsin.

A full-time physician and staff nurses provide round-the-clock medical care in the Pratt Health Center. Full-service hospitals are nearby.

STUDENT BODY. In 1999–2000, the school enrolled 608 boarders and 220 day students in Forms 3–6 (Grades 9–12). The male-female ratio is approximately 50:50. Students come from 40 states and 37 foreign countries and about 29 percent receive financial aid.

ACADEMIC PROGRAM. The academic year, divided into trimesters, begins in early September and ends in early June, with vacations at Christmas and in the spring. Classes are held five days a week and on 8 Saturdays. They are scheduled in seven 50-minute periods between 8:00 A.M. and 2:50 P.M. on four days; on Wednesdays and Saturdays, classes are held in four 50-minute periods and the academic day ends at 12:30 P.M. On academic nights, study hours are 7:30 to 9:00 P.M. and 9:45 to 10:30 P.M. Reports are sent to parents three times a year; progress reports for students on academic warning are sent at midterm.

To graduate from Choate Rosemary Hall, a four-year student must complete 12 terms of English; third-year level in a foreign language; one year each of U.S. History and World History; Algebra I & II and Geometry, in a total of 14 quantitative courses; one year each of physical science and biological science; one term each of psychology, philosophy, and religion; and three terms of arts, including two areas of the arts.

Course offerings include Composition and Literature, American Studies, British Studies, Etymology, Contemporary American Fiction, Public Speaking, Modernism; French 1–5, French Civilization, German 1 and 4, Beginning Italian, Japanese 1–4, Latin 1–4, Russian 1 and 4, Mandarin Chinese 1–4, Spanish 1–5, Spanish-American Studies; World History, British History, The Middle East, U.S. History, American Political Institutions, Modern Japan, Tsarist Russia, The Disintegration of China, Soviet Russia and Beyond, Law and Social Change, Colonial History of Africa, Macroeconomics, Microeconomics; Algebra 1–2, Geometry, Trigonometry, Probability, Statistics, Calculus 1–3, Multivariable Calculus, Linear Algebra, Data Structures and Algorithms; Physics, Astronomy, Electronics, Modern Physics, Astrophysics, Chemistry, Environmental Science, Organic Chemistry, Inorganic Chemistry, Biology, Marine Biology, Cell Biology; Adolescent Psychology, Child Development, Judaism, Christianity and Islam, Hinduism, Buddhism and Taoism, Moral Reasoning; Printmaking, Photography, Drawing, Oil Painting, Sculpture, Ceramics, Weaving, Art History, Acting, Directing, World Music, History of Jazz, Bach and his Contemporaries, Music Production, Theory/Harmony, and Dance. Honors and Advanced Placement courses are offered in most areas. Term-abroad programs are provided in eight countries. Seniors may undertake an independent study project under faculty direction.

Virtually all graduates go on to higher education. The most popular college choices for the Class of 1999 include 12 graduates each to Brown and the University of Pennsylvania, 10 to Yale, 9 to Boston College, 7 to Georgetown, 6 each to Boston University and Cornell, and 5 each to Bowdoin, Bucknell, Carnegie Mellon, Emory, George Washington, and New York University.

Summer programs include the Writing Project, the John F. Kennedy Institute of Government, English Language Institute, the Portfolio Project, Connecticut Scholars Program (a public/private collaboration), and programs for students of middle school age including FOCUS, CONNECT, and the Young Writers Workshop.

STUDENT ACTIVITIES. The Student Council provides a forum for student views. Students are also elected to the Judicial Committee, which aids the Dean of Students in cases of school rule violations.

Activities include the yearbook, newspaper, literary magazine, sports weekly, and campus radio station; language clubs, math team, tutoring society; and computer, science, and theater clubs. Community service programs allow students to volunteer locally. Choral groups, student orchestra, string ensembles, and the jazz ensemble provide performance opportunities. Six student theater productions are staged each year. Interest groups include Amnesty International, Students for a Free Tibet, Gold Key, International Club, and Film Club, among others.

All students participate in athletics, and the school fields varsity and junior varsity teams to compete in football, cross-country, field hockey, soccer, water polo, basketball, ice hockey, squash, swimming, volleyball, wrestling, archery, baseball, softball, crew, golf, lacrosse, tennis, track, and riflery. Intramural and noncompetitive sports include basketball, cycling, swimming, rock climbing, skiing, volleyball, tennis, weight training, dance, and others.

Theater productions, films, concerts, and dances are offered on campus, while field trips take students to museums and theaters in New York, Boston, and New Haven. Special events include Parents and Reunion weekends and programs sponsored by the Spears Endowment for Spiritual and Moral Education.

ADMISSION AND COSTS. Choate Rosemary Hall seeks to enroll students from diverse ethnic and social backgrounds who have the potential to do well with the school's resources. Applicants are admitted in all grades on the basis of previous academic performance and their ability to contribute to the community. Transcripts, standardized test results, and letters of recommendation are required along with a personal interview. The application fee is $50.

Boarding tuition for 1999–2000 is $25,400; day tuition is $18,635. Tuition insurance is included in the tuition; payment plans are available. Choate Rosemary Hall subscribes to the School Scholarship Service and offers financial aid amounting to about $4,000,000 annually. The Icahn Scholars Program, an initiative made possible by the Icahn Charitable Foundation of New York City, identifies bright, motivated, and talented middle schoolers from disadvantaged backgrounds and provides them with a fully funded Choate Rosemary Hall education.

Assistant Headmaster and Dean of Faculty: G. Edmondson Maddox
Dean of Academic Affairs: Donald W. Firke
Dean of Students: Elinor S. Abbe
Director of Admission: William W. Dennett, '64
Director of Development and Alumni Affairs: Catherine L. Spinelli
Director of College Counseling: Terence Giffen
Business Manager: John Burditt '70
Director of Athletics: Ned Gallagher

Cold Spring School   1982

263 Chapel Street, New Haven, CT 06513. 203-787-1584;
Fax 203-787-9444; E-mail admissions@coldspringschool.com;
Web Site www.coldspringschool.com

Cold Spring School, a day school encompassing Kindergarten–Grade 6, enrolls 94 boys and girls in a richly diverse urban neighborhood adjacent to city park and riverfront. Small, multiage classrooms, each with a master teacher and an associate teacher, are designed to foster the intellectual, social, and creative needs of students and provide them with a strong sense of community. The project-based curriculum, enriched by art, music, Spanish, and physical education, develops strong academic skills, a positive self-image, and the sense of civic responsibility. Tuition: $10,780. Financial aid is available. Nancy McDonald is Director of Admissions; Jeff Jonathan (Middlebury College, B.A.; Columbia University, M.A.) is Head of School.

Convent of the Sacred Heart 1848

1177 King Street, Greenwich, CT 06831. 203-531-6500;
Fax 203-531-5206; E-mail pamela_mckenna@cshgreenwich.org;
Web Site www.cshgreenwich.org

One of 200 Sacred Heart schools worldwide, this Catholic, college preparatory day school enrolls 570 girls in Preschool–Grade 12. Commitment to each girl's intellectual, spiritual, and physical well-being guides the program, which provides rigorous academics, leadership opportunities, and diverse athletic activities. Advanced Placement courses, fine arts, and overseas travel/study are available. Girls take part in Student Council, Model UN, music groups, publications, and community service programs. Tuition: $8000–$17,100. Financial aid is available. Pamela R. McKenna is Director of Admission; Sr. Joan Magnetti, RSCJ (Manhattanville, B.A. 1965; Union Theological Seminary, M.A. 1972), is Headmistress. *New England Association*.

The Country School 1955

341 Opening Hill Road, Madison, CT 06443. 203-421-3113;
Fax 203-421-4390

The Country School, a day school enrolling 255 boys and girls in PreKindergarten–Grade 8, balances strong academics with a rich program of visual arts, music, and physical education. Traditional courses are enriched by a computer program and foreign language instruction including French from Pre-Kindergarten and Latin and Spanish from Grade 6. Small classes and a student-faculty ratio of 9:1 allow each student to receive individual attention in a nurturing environment. Optional programs include before- and after-care, music instruction, and a summer session. Tuition: $7260–$11,650. Financial aid is available. Janice Crampton is Director of Admissions; Steven J. Danenberg (Columbia, B.A. 1965; M.A. 1969) was appointed Head in 1998.

Eagle Hill-Southport 1985

214 Main Street, Southport, CT 06490. 203-254-2044;
Fax 203-255-4052

Eagle Hill-Southport is an ungraded, private day school for boys and girls with learning disabilities. Approximately 85 students, ages 6–16, are enrolled. Using tutorials and small group classes, the school seeks to prepare students for traditional schools through a linguistically based language arts curriculum, adapted to each student's needs. An afternoon activities program provides soccer, cross-country, basketball, baseball, softball, art, and computers. A summer session offers skill enrichment for students who have experienced academic difficulties. Tuition: $26,900. Financial Aid: $95,000. Carolyn Lavender is Director of Education; Leonard Tavormina (Boston University, B.A. 1969; Fairfield University, M.A. 1980) was appointed Headmaster in 1985.

Fairfield College Preparatory School 1942

North Benson Road, Fairfield, CT 06430. 203-254-4200;
Admissions 203-254-4210; Fax 203-254-4108; E-mail
mstepsis@fair1.fairfield.edu; Web Site www.prep.fairfield.edu

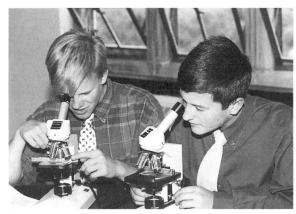

Founded by the Society of Jesus to provide a college preparatory day school for Catholic and non-Catholic boys, the School enrolls 800 boys in Grades 9–12. Through a rigorous academic curriculum, which includes theology courses and a program of retreats and community service activities, the School seeks to prepare leaders for the future. An interscholastic sports program and 40 nonsport activities are offered. Noncredit courses and enrichment courses for credit are available in the summer. Tuition: $8160. Financial Aid: $600,000. Mark A. Stepsis is Director of Admissions and Financial Aid; The Reverend Michael G. Boughton, SJ (Boston College, B.A. 1970, M.A. 1973; Weston School of Theology, M.Div. 1979), is President. *New England Association*.

Fairfield Country Day School 1936

2970 Bronson Road, Fairfield, CT 06430. 203-259-2723;
Fax 203-259-3249; E-mail vitalo@fcds.pvt.k12.ct.us;
Web Site www.country-day.org

Fairfield Country Day is a preparatory school enrolling 250 boys in Kindergarten–Grade 9. With the view that giving a boy "a good solid academic grounding and a sense of himself by the time he leaves ninth grade is the most important job there is," the School emphasizes the mastery of basic skills and expects students to show courtesy, truthfulness, sportsmanship, and consideration of others. A daily sports program is required for all; an outdoor hockey rink was completed in 1990. A variety of extracurricular opportunities is offered, including music, arts, drama, and public speaking. Tuition: $14,500–$16,500. Financial aid is available. Richard E. McGrath is Director of Admissions; Robert D. Vitalo (New York University, B.S.; Columbia, M.A.) was appointed Headmaster in 1992.

The Foote School 1916

50 Loomis Place, New Haven, CT 06511. 203-777-3464; Fax 203-
777-2809; Web Site www.foote.school.org

The Foote School, enrolling 470 day boys and girls in Kindergarten–Grade 9, seeks to provide educational excellence in a child-centered environment by a grounding in basic skills with emphasis on the aesthetic and intellectual development of each student. Foote is committed to a multicultural curriculum, designed to foster an appreciation of human differences. A computer literacy program begins in Grade 1, French or Spanish in Grade 4, Latin in Grade 7, and activities, sports, and community service in the upper grades. A summer program is available for ages 3–15. Tuition: $11,310–$12,500. Financial Aid:

$600,000. Laura O. Altshul is Director of Admissions; Jean G. Lamont (Middlebury, B.A. 1966; Columbia Teachers College, M.A. 1992) was appointed Head of School in 1992.

Greens Farms Academy 1925

35 Beachside Avenue, Greens Farms, CT 06436. 203-256-0717;
Admissions 203-256-7514; Fax 203-256-7501;
E-mail admissions@GFAcademy.org; Web Site www.GFAcademy.org

Greens Farms Academy, a coeducational, college preparatory day school enrolling 542 students in Kindergarten–Grade 12, aims to provide a solid academic training and wide extracurricular opportunities in a supportive environment that emphasizes personal and social values. In the Upper School, Advanced Placement courses are available in all major disciplines. Strong programs in the arts and computer applications are offered at all levels. Located between Fairfield and Westport, the school is accessible from many communities in the area. Summer programs are available. Tuition: $15,700–$17,400. Financial Aid: $637,000. Jennifer Galambos is Director of Admission; Peter T. Esty (Amherst, B.A.; Harvard, M.A.T.) was appointed Head of School in 1998. *New England Association.*

Greenwich Academy 1826

200 North Maple Avenue, Greenwich, CT 06830. 203-625-8900;
Fax 203-869-6580; E-mail nancyhoffman@greenwichacademy.org;
Web Site www.greenwichacademy.org

Greenwich Academy, enrolling 730 girls in Pre-Kindergarten–Grade 12, emphasizes rigorous academics, active community service, and extensive programs in athletics and the arts. Lower School encourages a love of learning and mastery of basics. Middle School develops skills of literary analysis, creative writing and research methods, and an understanding of math, world history, current events, and scientific principles. Upper School, coordinated with Brunswick School for boys, offers numerous required and elective courses, including Honors and Advanced Placement in most disciplines. The use of laptop computers is required in all classes in Grades 7–12. Tuition: $14,900–$17,100. Financial Aid: $841,163. Nancy E. Hoffman is Director of Admission; Patsy G. Howard (Smith, B.A. 1966; Teachers College, Columbia, M.A. 1967) was named Headmistress in 1988. *New England Association.*

The Greenwich Country Day School 1926

P.O. Box 623, Old Church Road, Greenwich, CT 06836-0623.
203-863-5600; Fax 203-622-6046

Enrolling 800 girls and boys in Nursery–Grade 9, The Greenwich Country Day School provides qualified students with opportunities for academic development, intellectual growth, and artistic and athletic appreciation. The traditional academic

program is supplemented by computer education and foreign language beginning in Kindergarten, art, instrumental music, chorus, and physical education that includes 14 interscholastic sports for Grades 7 through 9. Grades 7–9 are a lap top environment. The student-teacher ratio is 7:1. Tuition: $10,350–$16,300. Financial Aid: $1,200,000. Kirby Williams is Director of Admission; Douglas J. Lyons (Villanova, B.A. 1973; University of Pennsylvania, M.Ed. 1978, Ed.D. 1983) was appointed Headmaster in 1992.

The Gunnery 1850

Washington, CT 06793. 860-868-7334; Fax 860-868-1614;
E-mail admissions@gunnery.org; Web Site www.gunnery.org

In 1850, educator Frederick Gunn founded The Gunnery to promote academic rigor, strengthen character, and cultivate scholarship, integrity, social responsibility, and physical fitness. In a structured learning environment, students receive the support and attention needed to reach their full potential. Enrolling 255 young women and men in Grades 9–12, of whom 190 are boarders, The Gunnery offers a demanding college preparatory curriculum that includes many electives and offerings in the arts and computer technology. Activities range from community service and student government offices to drama, publications, and teams in 14 sports. Boarding Tuition: $26,000; Day Tuition: $18,700. Financial Aid: $1,100,000. Thomas E. Schenck is Director of Admission; Susan G. Graham is Head of School.

Hamden Hall Country Day School

HAMDEN

1108 Whitney Avenue, Hamden, CT 06517. 203-865-6158;
Fax 203-776-5852

Hamden Hall Country Day School in Hamden, Connecticut, is a coeducational college preparatory school enrolling 585 students in Pre-Kindergarten–Grade 12. Hamden (population 52,434) is situated in south-central Connecticut, 3 miles north of New Haven and Yale University. Hamden Hall is reached via Interstate 91 and the Merritt Parkway.

Hamden Hall was founded in 1912 as a day school for boys by Dr. John P. Cushing, its first Headmaster. Coeducation was introduced in 1927 and, within seven years, the School was expanded to encompass Grades 9–12.

The mission of Hamden Hall is to provide a challenging education that will foster academic excellence while formulating students' character, values system, and sense of independence. Dedicated faculty, all well-qualified in their areas of specialization, serve as role models and mentors in the classroom, on the playing field, and in other areas of school life. With an 8:1

student-teacher ratio, the School aims to offer a nurturing environment in which young people can reach their full potential intellectually, physically, and socially.

A nonprofit institution, Hamden Hall is governed by an 18-member Board of Trustees. It is accredited by the New England Association of Schools and Colleges and holds membership in the National Association of Independent Schools and the Connecticut Association of Independent Schools.

THE CAMPUS. Hamden Hall is set on 12 acres overlooking Lake Whitney. The Dolven Admissions Center contains administrative and college counseling offices and a large art studio. In front of Dolven is a colorful display of the flags of 35 nations, which represent the nationalities and ethnic backgrounds of the School's diverse student body. The three-story Joseph and Esther Schiavone Science Center houses classrooms, state-of-the-art facilities for science and the arts, Middle and Upper School computer labs, and the dining room. The Taylor Fine Arts Center features a fully equipped theater, music studios, and practice rooms. The Taylor Gymnasium includes basketball, wrestling, and weight-training facilities. Classrooms for the primary grades (Pre-Kindergarten–Grade 3) are located in the Ethyle R. Alpert Building, while the upper Elementary (Grades 4–6) and Middle School (Grades 7–8) and Upper School (Grades 9–12) are housed in Whitson Hall. The Ellen and Charles Swain Library, which has separate library facilities for the Lower and Middle/Upper schools, houses a collection of more than 25,000 volumes, 60 periodicals, and extensive reference resources. Swain is linked electronically to computer networks via the Internet.

The campus has an athletic field, a challenging ropes course, and a play area for younger children. Additional sports facilities are located 1.5 miles north of the campus, and students use tennis, squash, golf, and swimming facilities at Yale University and other local colleges.

The physical plant is valued at approximately $8,400,000.

THE FACULTY. James R. Maggart was appointed Headmaster in 1991. He holds a B.A. degree from the University of California, an M.A.T. from Brown University, and an M.B.A. from the Stanford Graduate School of Business. Prior to assuming his current position, Mr. Maggart headed independent schools in Istanbul, Turkey, and Houston, Texas.

The faculty include 13 administrators and 72 teachers.

They have earned 84 baccalaureate and 63 advanced degrees, including 3 doctorates, representing study at such institutions as Adelphi, Albertus Magnus, Amherst, Bates, Beirut College for Women, Boston University, Bowdoin, Brandeis, Brigham Young, Brown, Bryant, California College of Arts and Crafts, Clark, Colby, College of Mount St. Vincent, College of William and Mary, Colorado State, Columbia, Connecticut College, Dartmouth, Fairfield, Franklin and Marshall, Georgetown, Glassboro State, Hamilton, Howard, Illinois Wesleyan, Indiana University, Kings College (England), Knox, Lesley, Malone College, Miami University, Middlebury, New York University, Northeastern, Northern Michigan, Oberlin, Oxford University, Pennsylvania State, Pepperdine, Quinnipiac, Rensselaer, Rutgers, Sacred Heart, St. Lawrence, Sarah Lawrence, Seton Hall, Simmons, Skidmore, Southern Connecticut State, Springfield, Stanford, Syracuse, Temple, Thiel, Vanderbilt, Vassar, Wells, Wesleyan, Wheelock, Williams, Yale, and the Universities of Bridgeport, California, Connecticut, Dayton, Delaware, Guelph (Canada), Illinois, London, Louisville, Miami, Pennsylvania, Rhode Island, Rouen (France), Vermont, Virginia, and Wisconsin.

The staff also includes two librarians, a reading consultant, two computer resource specialists, a consulting psychologist, and an athletic trainer. Emergency medical services are available at nearby hospitals.

STUDENT BODY. In 1999–2000, Hamden Hall enrolls 585 boys and girls, including 247 in the Upper School. They come from diverse racial, ethnic, and religious backgrounds and represent 25 towns within a 30-mile radius of the School.

ACADEMIC PROGRAM. The school year, from early September to early June, is divided into two semesters, with Thanksgiving, winter, and spring recesses and observances of several national and religious holidays. Parent-teacher conferences are held in November and April, or more often if needed. Written progress reports are issued four times a year, with interim reports sent home in the middle of each marking period.

Classes, enrolling an average of 13 students, are held five days a week from 8:10 A.M. to 3:00 P.M. Periods are 45 minutes long, and extra-help sessions are incorporated into the schedule.

The Lower School curriculum emphasizes reading and writing, comprehension, and critical thinking as well as the mastery of problem-solving and computational skills in mathematics. The introduction of laboratory sciences enables children to observe, experiment, research, and discuss scientific theories and concepts. Understanding other cultures from a global perspective is the focus of the social studies program, which utilizes regular field trips, guest lecturers, and group projects to reinforce classroom instruction. Specialists teach music, fine arts, computer activities, and physical education. Latin is taught in Grades 5 and 6. An Extended-Day program provides after-school enrichment for students in Pre-Kindergarten–Grade 6.

The Middle School program is specially structured for students making the transition from childhood to adolescence. The curriculum builds on the skills acquired in the early grades, combined with new challenges and techniques designed to maximize learning. English classes emphasize classical authors while providing students with opportunities to produce their own creative and expository essays. In mathematics, basic computational skills lead to the mastery of problem solving and a preview of algebraic concepts. Life science and physical science studies offer an overview of scientific vocabulary, concepts, and methods of investigation. French, Spanish, or Latin and participation in studio arts, music, and theater are required. Beginning in Grade 7, students work with a faculty advisor who meets with them regularly.

Students in the Upper School carry five courses each semester. To graduate, they must complete 19 credits as follows: four years of English; two and one-half years of history, including U.S. History; through the third level of a foreign language; mathematics through the junior year, including Geometry and Algebra II; two years of science, including Biology and a physical science; one year of fine arts; and four years of physical education, including participation in fall sports and winter or spring sports. Students must also demonstrate proficiency in computers.

Among the required and elective courses in the Upper School are English 9–12, British Fiction, Creative Writing, Modern American Fiction, Literature of the Holocaust, American Literature, Shakespeare, Modern Poetry; African American History, History of the Modern World, Biblical History, Constitutional Law, U.S. History, Vietnam; Meteorology and Oceanography, Geology, Astronomy, Zoology, Anatomy and Physiology, Physics, Electronics, Chemistry; Latin I–III, Accelerated Italian, Spanish I–V, French I–V; Algebra I–II, Trigonometry, Pre-Calculus, Calculus AB/BC; and Introduction to Computers. Advanced Placement and honors courses are offered in most major disciplines. With the approval of the Director of Studies, students may undertake independent study projects.

In 1999, graduating seniors entered such colleges and universities as American University, Bentley, Boston College, Boston University, Brandeis, Brown, Bryant, Colby, Cornell, Duquesne, George Washington, Harvard/Radcliffe, Kenyon, Lehigh, Mary Washington, Morgan State, Sarah Lawrence, Skidmore, Swarthmore, Tulane, Union, United States Coast Guard Academy, Virginia Tech, Wesleyan, Wheaton, Williams,

Yale, and the Universities of Colorado, Connecticut, Massachusetts, Rochester, and Vermont.

Hamden Hall conducts a six-week summer program of academics, arts, and sports.

STUDENT ACTIVITIES. Hamden Hall participates in The Princeton Peer Leadership Program, through which selected seniors undertake training to help their fellow students solve problems, seek alternatives, and improve communications on social and ethical issues. An elected Student Government provides further opportunities to develop leadership qualities and share responsibility for the quality of life at the School.

Middle and Upper School students publish their own literary magazines and newspapers, and the Upper School issues the yearbook, *Perennial Pine.* Among the groups organized to meet diverse interests are Thespians, debate clubs, tour guides, peer tutoring, environmental and ski clubs, and Academic Decathlon. Students are active in the School's community service program through the Jewish Home for the Aged and inner-city tutoring.

Interscholastic teams are formed in football, soccer, wrestling, basketball, baseball, lacrosse, and tennis for boys; and field hockey, soccer, basketball, lacrosse, tennis, and softball for girls. Golf and cross-country squads are coeducational.

ADMISSION AND COSTS. Hamden Hall seeks motivated students who are academically strong and eager to participate fully in the life of the School. Acceptance is based on the candidate's potential, previous record, math and English teacher recommendations, and the results of standardized testing. A campus tour and personal interview are recommended.

In 1999–2000, tuition, including lunch, ranges from $9250 in Pre-Kindergarten to $15,240 in Grades 7–12. Hamden Hall awards financial aid to approximately 30 percent of its student body, based on need.

Head of Lower School: Mark R. Cunningham
Head of Middle/Upper School: Robert H. Schroeder
Director of Admission: Janet B. Izzo
Business Manager: Robert J. Izzo
Director of Development: Susie L. Black
Director of College Counseling: Frederick B. Richter, Jr.
Director of Athletics: Bernard J. Kohler

Hopkins School   NEW HAVEN

986 Forest Road, New Haven, CT 06515. 203-397-1001;
Fax 203-389-2249; E-mail hilltopper@hopkins.edu;
Web Site www.hopkins.edu

HOPKINS SCHOOL, in New Haven, Connecticut, is a coeducational, college preparatory day school enrolling students in Grades 7 through 12. Situated on a hill on the western edge of New Haven (population 135,000), the campus offers a country setting with access to all that Yale University and the city offer, including museums, historical sites, professional sports teams, theaters, orchestras, and dance companies.

Founded in 1660 with a bequest from Edward Hopkins, a former governor of Connecticut Colony, Hopkins Grammar School began as a one-room schoolhouse on the New Haven Green, seeking to fulfill its benefactor's goal of "the breeding up of hopeful youths." Then a boys' school, Hopkins moved to the present site in 1925. The Day School, founded in 1938, and Prospect Hill School, founded in 1930, were prominent girls' schools that merged in 1960. Cooperative ventures between Hopkins Grammar and Day Prospect Hill led to the 1972 merger that formed the school known today as Hopkins.

In an atmosphere of trust, encouragement, and mutual

support, Hopkins strives to foster knowledge tempered by ethical judgment, consideration for others, and aesthetic sensibility. The School offers a comprehensive college preparatory curriculum that seeks to prepare students for admission to competitive colleges while also instilling curiosity, love of learning, and the sense that education should help students serve generously for the greater good.

MALONE SCIENCE CENTER

A nonprofit organization, Hopkins is governed by a self-perpetuating Committee of Trustees, which includes parents and alumni, that meets bimonthly. Productive endowment totals approximately $20,000,000. The Alumni Association, representing approximately 6000 living alumni, is involved in fund-raising and social events; the *Views from the Hill* is published twice yearly. Hopkins is accredited by the New England Association of Schools and Colleges and the Connecticut Association of Independent Schools. It also holds membership in the National Association of Independent Schools and the Educational Records Bureau.

THE CAMPUS. The 108-acre campus offers 5 athletic fields, 11 tennis courts, and an outdoor adventure course. Baldwin Hall provides classrooms, a technology laboratory, and offices; there are also classrooms in Hopkins House as well as the admissions, business, and college counseling offices. The Day Prospect Hill Building houses seventh- and eighth-grade classrooms, while Lovell Hall offers an auditorium, dining room, and more classrooms. The Sherk Learning Center houses the library, gallery, and student lounge. Also on campus are the Alumni House and the Athletic Center with basketball courts, wrestling room, trainer's room, lockers, and swimming pool. The Head of School's residence adjoins the campus. The 25,000-square-foot Malone Science Center opened in October 1999. This state-of-the-art facility houses ten laboratories, a student-faculty project room, prep rooms, and an electron microscope. The School-owned facilities are valued at $18,000,000.

THE FACULTY. Head of School John Beall was appointed in 1999. A graduate of Miami University of Ohio, he has earned master's degrees at Cornell University and Columbia University and a doctorate in 1997 from Teachers College, Columbia. Before coming to Hopkins, Dr. Beall taught at Greenhill School and St. Mark's School, both in Texas; at King's School, Canterbury, in England; and at Collegiate School in New York City. He was awarded a Joseph Klingenstein Fellowship at Columbia for 1994–95.

The full-time faculty number 93—50 women and 43 men. There are also 8 part-time teachers and a full-time consulting psychologist. All hold undergraduate degrees; more than two-thirds have advanced degrees. Representative colleges and universities include Bowdoin, Colgate, Columbia, Cornell, Dartmouth, Georgetown, Harvard, Kenyon, Middlebury, Princeton,

St. Lawrence, Wellesley, Williams, Yale, and the University of Michigan.

First aid is available on campus; emergency facilities are nearby.

STUDENT BODY. In 1999–2000, the School enrolled 633 students as follows: 79 in Grade 7, 76 in Grade 8, 128 in Grade 9, 116 in Grade 10, 121 in Grade 11, and 113 in Grade 12. Many Hopkins parents are affiliated with Yale as faculty or administrators.

ACADEMIC PROGRAM. The school year, from early September to early June, is divided into two semesters and includes a Thanksgiving recess, Christmas vacation, midwinter recess, spring vacation, and observances of Rosh Hashanah, Yom Kippur, Martin Luther King's Birthday, Good Friday, and Memorial Day. A typical day for Grades 7–12 is divided into ten periods, two of which are dedicated to athletics, from 8:18 A.M. to 3:22 P.M. The schedule is adjusted to permit early dismissal on Wednesday, which accommodates athletic contests and club activities.

Average class size is 14 students. There are supervised study halls for Grades 7–10; juniors and seniors may study in the library, gallery, or student lounge during free periods. Grades and comments are sent to parents four times a year; interim reports may be issued for students experiencing academic difficulties. Parent-teacher conferences are held once a year.

The prescribed curriculum for Grades 7 and 8 consists of English, Latin, History, Pre-Algebra (Grade 7), Elementary Algebra (Grade 8), Life Science (Grade 7), physical science (Grade 8), and art, drama, music, and woodworking. French or Spanish may be elected as a second language.

To graduate, students in Grades 9–12 must earn four credits of English, three of a foreign language, two of history (including United States history), three of mathematics, two credits of lab science, and one credit of arts.

Among the full-year and semester courses offered are selected English courses such as The Writing Semester, Heroic Figures in Literature, Dante, Faces of New York, Love in Shakespeare's Plays, The Rise of Humanism–Shakespeare and the Renaissance, About Poetry, Great Novels, Creative Writing, Modern Literature, From Stratford to Hollywood, Russian Literature, Comic Vision, Literature, and Psychology and the Bible. Other courses include French 1–6, Chinese, Italian 1–2, Latin 1–5, Spanish 1–5; The Ancient World, World Citizenship, Modern European History, British History, United States History, Afro-American History, Europe in the Twentieth Century, Global Environmental Issues, Russia and the Soviet Union, The Holocaust and the Individual, Twentieth Century Democracy, Native American History, World Geography; Algebra, Accelerated Algebra, Geometry, Accelerated Geometry, Advanced Algebra, Functions, Statistics and Trigonometry, Pre-calculus, Calculus AB, Calculus BC, Multivariable Calculus, AP Computer Science, Fractals and Chaos, Linear Algebra; Biology, Biology: Form and Function, Chemistry, Experimental Chemistry, Physics, Conceptual Physics, Contemporary Issues in Biology, Astronomy; and Studio Art 1–2, Photography 1–2, Pottery, History of Film, Fiber Arts, Classical Ensemble, Jazz/Rock Ensemble, Concert Choir, Mixed Chorus, Public Speaking, Music Theory, Performance Workshop, Video Production, and Acting.

Advanced Placement and honors-level courses are offered in French, Latin, Spanish, United States History, Calculus, Probability and Statistics, Psychology, Biology, Computer Science, Chemistry, Physics, History of Art, and Studio Art.

Colleges attended by Hopkins graduates in the past four years include Boston College 11, Brown 13, Cornell 12, Dartmouth 9, Georgetown 13, George Washington 9, Hamilton 7, Harvard 15, Smith 10, Tufts 9, Wesleyan 14, Williams 7, Yale 27, and the Universities of Connecticut 9 and Pennsylvania 14.

The Hopkins Summer School offers two concurrent six-week programs, one academic, the other sports, for boys and girls in Grades 3–12 from late June to early August.

STUDENT ACTIVITIES. The Student Council, composed of elected representatives from Grades 9–12 and the President, elected by Grades 8–12, organizes school service and recreational activities. Council representatives and other students serve on faculty committees devoted to the examination of various school issues.

Students publish a newspaper (*The Razor*), literary magazine (*The Day Star*), and a yearbook (*Per Annos*). Among the many other organizations and activities available are a Debate Team, Varsity and Junior Varsity Math teams, the Concert Choir, Model UN and Stock Market clubs, the Hopkins Drama Association, SURE (Students United for Racial Equality). Numerous community service opportunities are available, including Summerbridge New Haven, a tutoring and mentoring program.

Hopkins teams compete with those of public and independent schools in Connecticut, Massachusetts, and New York. Boys' teams are organized in baseball, basketball, cross-country, football, golf, lacrosse, soccer, swimming, tennis, track, fencing, water polo, and wrestling. Girls compete in basketball, cross-

country, lacrosse, field hockey, golf, soccer, softball, swimming, tennis, track, fencing, water polo, and volleyball. Intramural competition is available in soccer, basketball, and tennis. Junior School teams include baseball, basketball, field hockey, lacrosse, football, soccer, swimming, tennis, and wrestling.

The entire Hopkins community avails itself of the Adam Kreiger Challenge Course, an outdoor experiential educational program.

Dances and drama productions are held throughout the year. Traditional events for the school community include Pumpkin Bowl, Homecoming, Reunion Weekend, Arts Fest, and various functions sponsored by the Student Council and the Parent Council.

ADMISSION AND COSTS. Hopkins seeks to enroll a diverse group of students who are eager to learn and willing to work hard. New students are admitted to all grades, although most often to Grades 7 and 9, on the basis of an application, a personal interview, standardized testing, a writing sample, the transcript from the applicant's previous school, and two teacher references. Application should be made in the fall; the application deadline is February 1. There is a $40 application fee.

In 1999–2000, tuition is $16,200. Tuition covers all costs except books ($300–$650), an activities fee ($250), student accident insurance, and trip and store charges. In 1999–2000, Hopkins awarded $1,324,700 in financial aid to 110 students. The financial-aid package may include a work plan through which students can earn up to $1400 during the summer and school year. There are three tuition payment plans and tuition insurance is available.

Assistant Head of School: William E. Powers
Director of Studies: Rosemary Benedict
Alumni President: Brian S. Smith '70
Director of Admissions: Dana L. Blanchard '63
Director of Development and Alumni Affairs: Marian Kling Halsey '68
College Counselors: Susan Moriarty Paton and A. H. Napier
Business Officer: William W. Bakke '60
Director of Athletics: Thomas A. Parr, Jr.
Director of Diversity: Angela Wardlaw '84
Director of Community Service: David Harpin

The Hotchkiss School   LAKEVILLE

Lakeville, CT 06039. 860-435-2591;
  E-mail admissions@mail.hotchkissschool.org;
  Web Site www.hotchkiss-school.org

THE HOTCHKISS SCHOOL in Lakeville, Connecticut, is a coeducational, college preparatory boarding and day school enrolling students in Grades 9 through 12 and a postgraduate year. Lakeville is a village in the Township of Salisbury, a community of 3700 people in the rolling hills of the Berkshires. The scenic region is popular for camping, fishing, boating, and hunting. The School schedules field trips to New York City, two hours and fifteen minutes away. Train and bus service to major cities is available from towns in the Lakeville area.

The School was founded in 1891, with an endowment from Mrs. Maria Harrison Bissell Hotchkiss, to prepare young men for Yale University. It developed under the leadership of Headmasters Huber Gray Buehler (1904–1924), George Van Santvoord (1926–1955), and A. William Olsen, Jr. (1960–1981), under whose direction the School initiated coeducation.

In a small-school community with a large-school diversity, Hotchkiss strives to develop in students a lifelong love of learning, responsible citizenship, and personal integrity. The School community is based on trust, mutual respect, and compassion, and all members are accountable for upholding these values. In and out of the classroom, all members of the community are expected to subject their views and actions to critical examination and to accept responsibility for them. Hotchkiss is committed to mastery of learning skills, development of intellectual curiosity, excellence and creativity in all disciplines, and enthusiastic participation in athletics and other activities. Students are encouraged to develop clarity of thought, confidence and facility in expressing ideas, and artistic and aesthetic sensitivity. The School hopes that graduates will leave Hotchkiss with a commitment to environmental stewardship and service to others and with a greater understanding of themselves and their roles in a global society.

The Hotchkiss School is a nonprofit corporation governed by a 32-member Board of Trustees, 25 of whom are alumni. Five trustees are elected by the alumni and others by the Board. The School has an endowment of more than $200,000,000. The Alumni Association maintains contact with more than 8160 living alumni, many of whom provide substantial financial support and are active in admission and speakers' programs.

The School is accredited by the New England Association of Schools and Colleges and the Connecticut Association of Independent Schools. It holds membership in the National Association of Independent Schools, the National Association of Principals of Schools for Girls, and the Council for Advancement and Support of Education.

THE CAMPUS. The School is situated on 510 acres of hills and woodlands bordering on two lakes. Tall shade trees and carefully landscaped lawns complement the more than 80 buildings on campus. The principal academic structures and dormitories are grouped near the Main Building, which has wings housing the student center, chapel, auditorium, dining hall, two computer labs, and the 65,000-volume Edsel Ford Library.

A nine-hole golf course and five miles of ski trails surround the main campus. Athletic facilities include a 400-meter all-weather track, an indoor swimming pool, a gymnasium and basketball courts with seating for 400, one indoor artificial-ice rink, two paddle tennis courts, 20 all-weather and three indoor tennis courts, a lakefront and boathouse accommodating 14 #420 sailboats, an indoor exercise complex with two basketball courts with a Tartan all-purpose surface, and a total of 12 playing fields for baseball, football, soccer, lacrosse, and field hockey. The fitness center (1995) contains new exercise equipment including Keiser weight machines. The recently renovated Cullman Squash Courts provide five international-size courts.

The plant is owned by the School and is valued at $87,000,000.

THE FACULTY. Robert H. Mattoon, Jr., was appointed Headmaster in 1996, succeeding John R. Chandler, Jr. Mr. Mattoon (Dartmouth, B.A.; Tulane, M.A.; Yale, Ph.D.) had previously served as Associate Headmaster and Dean of Faculty at Deerfield Academy.

The Hotchkiss faculty consist of 111 full-time teachers and administrators who teach. Ninety faculty members live on campus. They hold 109 baccalaureate and 78 advanced degrees from such institutions as Harvard and Middlebury, 7 each; Wesleyan and Yale, 6 each; New York University 4; University of New Hampshire 3; and Brown and Dartmouth, 2 each. The School physician and consulting psychiatrist are considered faculty members.

Faculty benefits include health and retirement plans, an SRA program, and group life and disability insurance.

The School maintains a 24-hour infirmary staffed by a medical doctor, a psychiatrist, a director of health services, counselors, and resident nurses. Athletic trainers are available on campus. Hospital facilities are located in Sharon, about five miles away.

STUDENT BODY. In 1998–99, the School enrolled 281 boys and 224 girls as boarding students and 18 boys and 24 girls as day students as follows: Grade 9—88, Grade 10—158, Grade 11—143, Grade 12—151, and postgraduate—7. Students came from 33 states, the District of Columbia, and 21 foreign countries. Day students were from nearby communities in Connecticut, Massachusetts, and New York.

ACADEMIC PROGRAM. The academic year, divided into semesters, begins in early September and ends in early June. Vacations are scheduled for three weeks at Christmas and three weeks in the spring. Classes are held six days a week in eight 45-minute periods between 8:00 A.M. and 3:05 P.M., except on Wednesdays and Saturdays, when classes end at 12:05 P.M. The average class has 13 students. Ninth- and tenth-grade boarding students have "room study" from 7:30 to 9:30 P.M., and a supervised study hall is held for those who need it. Teachers provide extra help without charge and senior tutors are available to help others. Grades are sent to parents four times a year.

To graduate, a four-year student must complete 17 one-year courses, or the equivalent in semester courses, including 4 of English, 3 of one foreign language, 1 of American History, 3 of mathematics, and 1 of biology, chemistry, or physics. One year of fine arts is required for incoming ninth and tenth graders. Students normally take 5 courses. More than 200 courses are offered including the following: English 1–5, Shakespeare and the Bible, Creative Writing, Great Books; French 1–6, German 1–4, Greek 1–4, Latin 1–5, Spanish 1–5; American History, Modern Europe Since 1789, Tudor England, China and Japan, American Studies, Russian History, Europe in the 20th Century, Environmental Studies, American Government, Macro-Economics, Micro-Economics, Economics Seminar; Algebra 1–2, Geometry, Trigonometry, Analytic Geometry, Calculus, Finite Math, Beginning through Advanced Computer; Biology, Evolution, Limnology, Introductory Chemistry, Organic Chemistry, Physics, Geology; Music History and Appreciation, Music Theory, Chamber Choir, American Music, Keyboard Instruction, Instrumental and Voice Performance; Theatre Crafts, Beginning through Advanced Acting and Directing, Stage Management, Stage Craft, Light Design; Introductory and Advanced Photography; Beginning and Advanced Studio Art, History of Art, Architecture, Ceramics, Foundation Design; and Old Testament, New Testament, Introductory Philosophy, Ethics, Bio-Ethics, Comparative Religion, and Humanities. Advanced Placement courses are given in English, economics, all the foreign languages, history, mathematics, physics, chemistry, biology, history of art, studio art, and computer. With faculty approval, second-semester seniors may undertake independent study on or off campus. Qualified students may participate in a Year Abroad Program in France, China, or Spain; the Maine Coast Semester Program; the CITYterm Program; and a South African exchange program. They also may apply through the English-Speaking Union for a postgraduate year of study at an English boarding school.

Three or more graduates of the Class of 1999 are attending the following colleges and universities: Amherst 4, Bowdoin 4, Bucknell, Colby, Columbia, Cornell, Dartmouth 5, Davidson 4, Duke, Emory, Georgetown 9, Harvard 6, McGill 4, Middlebury 5, New York University 5, Princeton 7, St. Lawrence 4, Southern Methodist 5, Stanford 3, Union, Vanderbilt, Yale 5, and the Universities of Chicago and Virginia 5.

STUDENT ACTIVITIES. The Co-Presidents of the student body and representatives from each class and each dormitory serve with several faculty members on the Student-Faculty Council, which deals with a everyday concerns of students. Elected student representatives also serve with full voting rights on a joint faculty-student Discipline Committee. The Social Committee, a student board with a faculty adviser, plans social and recreational events. The Dramatic Association, with three faculty members and eight elected students, plans major theater productions. St. Luke's Society works for the improvement of the School and surrounding community and supports a tutoring program, help for the disabled, and a Big Brother/Big Sister program in local schools. All students are required to participate in an all-school service program for a portion of the year.

erary magazine), *Crosswinds* (a multicultural publication), Chorus, Chamber Choir, and clubs such as French, German, Amnesty International, Blue and White Society, Current Events, Black and Hispanic Association, Asian Society, Debate, Alternative Film Society, Association for Cultural Awareness, Outing, Photo, Press, Students for Environmental Awareness, and WKIS radio station.

The Hotchkiss School athletic teams compete against other private schools and some college junior varsity teams in football, soccer, cross-country, basketball, ice hockey, squash, swimming, wrestling, baseball, golf, lacrosse, sailing, water polo, track, field hockey, volleyball, and softball. Intramurals are organized in soccer, tennis, basketball, skiing, volleyball, golf, tennis, sailing, softball, squash, paddle tennis, cross-country, and wood squad.

Weekend entertainment always includes a movie, a dance, and an Outing Club trip. There are also trips to cultural events such as Broadway shows and museums in New York City and the surrounding area. Three major plays are staged each year. In addition, there are a number of student-directed plays and coffeehouses.

Traditional events on the school calendar are Parents Day, Alumni Reunions, Hotchkiss Now, Annual Alumni Association Dinner in New York, Spring Carnival, Senior Dance, and Alumni Weekend.

ADMISSION AND COSTS. The Hotchkiss School aims to attract students from among the most accomplished and promising young people of diverse backgrounds, experiences, and expectations. It seeks to enroll students of academic ability, intellectual curiosity, good will, and strong character who will be examples of integrity and decency to their peers.

Students are accepted for fall entry on the basis of academic record, teacher references, school report, standardized testing, an applicant project, and a personal interview. Applications, with a fee of $40, should be completed before January 15.

For 1999–2000, tuition is $24,850 for boarding students and $21,100 for day students.

Dean of Faculty: J. Sherman Barker, Jr.
Assistant Headmaster for Student Affairs: John C. Virden III
Dean of Students: Christina L. Cooper
Dean of Studies: Lisa Motter
Director of Alumni Relations: Philip M. McKnight
Dean of Admission & Financial Aid: Peter S. Philip
Director of Development: Stewart Saltonstall
Co-Directors of College Counseling: Betsy F. Beck and
  Craig C. Allen
Chief Financial Officer: John P. Tuky
Director of Athletics: George R. Delprete

Other student activities include *The Mischianza* (yearbook), the *Record* and the *Whipping Post* (newspapers), the *Review* (lit-

The Independent Day School 1961

115 Laurel Brook Road, P.O. Box 451, Middlefield, CT 06455.
  860-347-7235; Fax 860-347-8852

The Independent Day School, enrolling 225 boys and girls in three-year-old Beginners through Grade 8, seeks to offer a strong academic program that emphasizes the mastery of fundamental skills in the traditional liberal arts and sciences. Phonics-based reading coupled with whole language, language arts, science, history, and mathematics form the core curriculum, and students participate in studio arts, drama, music, computers, outdoor education, and physical education or sports. Field trips, Ski Club, interscholastic sports, and class plays are some of the extracurricular activities. After-school care and a summer enrichment program are available. Tuition: $4420–$11,815. Mary Lou Stewart is Director of Admission; Robert R. Coombs, Jr., was appointed Headmaster in 1995.

Kent School   KENT

Kent, CT 06757. 860-927-6000 or 800-538-5368;
Fax 860-927-6109; E-mail admissions@kent-school.edu;
Web Site www.kent-school.edu

KENT SCHOOL in Kent, Connecticut, is a coeducational college preparatory school enrolling boarding students and a limited number of day students in Forms III through VI (Grades 9–12). The School is located on the Housatonic River in the town of Kent about 80 miles north of New York City and 50 miles west of Hartford.

Kent School, which has been affiliated with the Episcopal Church since its inception, was established in 1906 by the Reverend Frederick Herbert Sill, a member of the monastic Order of the Holy Cross. Enrolled are students of other religious and nonreligious backgrounds as well.

The School is dedicated to enabling students to develop intellectually, physically, and spiritually. Further, it structures the academic program and daily life to foster self-reliance and a sense of caring as an ethical foundation for living in the world.

Kent is accredited by the New England Association of Schools and Colleges and is a member of the National Association of Episcopal Schools, the National Association of Independent Schools, and the Connecticut Association of Independent Schools.

THE CAMPUS. The campus consists of approximately 1200 acres of woods and farmland traversed by Macedonia Brook. There are 13 outdoor tennis courts, 7 multipurpose fields for soccer, field hockey, and lacrosse, 2 for baseball and football, the John Phillips Field for soccer and lacrosse, Sanford Field for baseball, and a field for varsity football games. Other facilities include the Brainard Squash Racquets Courts, Nadal Hockey Rink, the Kent School Riding Stables, and the Sill Boathouse. Kent crews train and compete on the Housatonic River.

Most buildings are of brick construction in the Georgian style. The Schoolhouse contains the 45,000-volume John Gray Park Library, classrooms, dormitory rooms, faculty apartments, department offices, an audiovisual center, and a technology center. The Gifford T. Foley '65 Hall houses classrooms and offices. Fairleigh S. Dickinson Science Center holds classrooms, labora-

tories, and offices. Students reside in the Hadley Case '29 Dormitory (which also houses the Dickinson Health Center), the Bruce Robinson Field '81 Building (which also contains the art studios), North Dormitory, Dining Hall Dormitory containing the Student Center and store, and Middle Dormitory, which also houses a student lounge. Faculty live in dormitory apartments and in other on- and off-campus housing.

St. Joseph's Chapel—a Norman-style structure of slate and stone—includes a cloister, a garden, and a tower with ten bells used for "change ringing." Magowan Field House contains a six-lane, 25-yard swimming pool, dressing rooms and showers, two basketball courts, and a weight-training room. The Frederick Herbert Sill Trophy Room is located in the Field House. The Indoor Tennis House provides four full-size lighted courts. Other facilities are the Administration Building, the Auditorium, and the Old Main Admissions Office.

THE FACULTY. The Reverend Richardson W. Schell, appointed Headmaster and Rector in 1981, is a graduate of Kent School, Harvard (A.B. 1973), and Yale (M.Div. 1976). Previously, he served as a parish priest in Chicago and as Chaplain of Kent School (1980–81).

On the faculty are 68 full-time teachers. The average length of teaching experience is 16 years, and 11 faculty members are graduates of Kent. Thirty-three faculty and administrators live on campus. The faculty hold 84 baccalaureate and 50 advanced degrees; 2 or more degrees were earned from Amherst, Bowdoin 4, Brown 3, Bucknell, Colby 4, Colgate, Columbia 4, Dartmouth 4, Harvard 6, Middlebury 11, Pennsylvania State, Princeton, Trinity 6, Wellesley 3, Yale, and the Universities of Connecticut 3, New Hampshire 4, North Carolina 3, Pennsylvania 4, Vermont 4, Virginia 3, and Wisconsin.

STUDENT BODY. In 1999–2000, Kent enrolls 276 boarding boys, 24 day boys, 231 boarding girls, and 25 day girls in Forms III–VI. They come from 38 states and 21 foreign countries. More than one-fourth are children or siblings of Kent graduates.

ACADEMIC PROGRAM. The school year, from early September to early June, includes Thanksgiving, Christmas, and spring vacations. The daily schedule includes classes before and after lunch, free periods that may be used for conferences or study, regularly scheduled meetings with faculty advisors, afternoon sports, and evening study.

The average class size is 13, and the student-faculty ratio is approximately 7:1. Development of independent study habits is emphasized, although students are assigned to supervised study halls when necessary.

To graduate, students must complete four years of English, three years of a foreign language, American History, mathematics through the 11th grade, two laboratory sciences, General

Studies, two terms of theology, and minor courses in art and music.

The curriculum includes yearlong courses in English; French, German, Spanish, Japanese, Latin, Greek; Classical Civilization, Modern European History, American History; Mathematics (Algebra through Calculus and Analytical Geometry); Biology 1–2, Chemistry 1–2, Physics 1–2, Environmental Science; and Art History, Studio Art Survey, and Harmony and Composition. Numerous one-term electives are also offered. Typical term topics are Astronomy, Meteorology, Ecology, Computer Programming, Asian Studies, Global Studies, History of Constitutional Law, Introduction to Attic Tragedy, Virgilian Epic, Religion and the Arts, Ethics, Design-Architecture, Painting-Color, Ceramics, Photography, Music Fundamentals, and Music History.

All Third Formers take General Studies, which integrates the teaching of study techniques into a course in cultural history. Any student needing individual attention may use the services of the Learning Center.

Advanced Placement is offered in English, French, German, Spanish, Latin, American history, economics, mathematics, statistics, biology, chemistry, environmental science, art, computer science, and physics. An Independent Study Program allows students to pursue a specific topic in depth, usually in the Fifth or Sixth Form.

In 1997, Kent installed new wiring infrastructure, allowing students to connect globally. Every student is able to plug into the School's Local Area Network (LAN) and a direct Internet connection from his or her own room. Students may obtain individual Internet accounts by completing an orientation course. Kent School participates in the Microsoft Schoolbook Program, providing an affordable opportunity for every student to be equipped with a laptop computer and software. Students also have telephones in each room.

In 1999, all 146 graduates entered college; 24 were admitted by "early action" or "early decision." Three or more are attending Boston University 8, Bucknell, Colgate, Connecticut College 5, Cornell 4, Hamilton 5, Hobart 4, Lehigh, Syracuse 4, Vanderbilt, and the University of Vermont 4.

STUDENT ACTIVITIES. Students are expected to take responsibilities in many areas of school life. Every student at Kent participates in the self-help program. Underform students, supervised by Sixth Formers and teachers, help to clean the School and ensure smooth daily operation. Student leaders also serve as dormitory prefects and members of the Student Council.

Boys and girls organize clubs for French, Spanish, German, photography, and art. Many students join Kent Krew, a school-spirit group. Students may participate in drama through the Kent School Players and in music with the Bell Ringers Guild, Kentones, Kentettes, Choir, Concert Band, Jazz Band, String Orchestra, and other ensembles. Private music lessons are available, and recitals are given. Student publications include *The*

Kent News, a literary magazine, *The Cauldron*, and the yearbook, *Kent*. Students work with faculty as disc jockeys at WKNT, the School FM radio station.

Individuals may select a faculty-sponsored Designed Extra-Curricular Activity (DECA). These long-term projects have been offered in journalism, creative writing, community service, music, art, photography, sports medicine, and bell ringing.

All physically fit students participate in interscholastic or intramural sports. Boys' teams are organized in football, soccer, riding, hockey, basketball, squash, swimming, lacrosse, cross-country, baseball, crew, golf, and tennis. Girls compete in field hockey, tennis, crew, cross-country, squash, swimming, basketball, lacrosse, softball, soccer, riding, golf, and ice hockey.

On weekends, Protestant students worship at Episcopal services. Roman Catholic students attend Mass, and Jewish students attend services at synagogue in a nearby town. The Performing Arts and Lecture Series provides a variety of enrichment opportunities, and frequent art exhibits are displayed.

ADMISSION AND COSTS. Boys and girls are accepted in the Third through Sixth Forms (Grades 9–12) on the basis of academic accomplishment, character, and promise. Each applicant must submit an academic transcript, references from two former teachers, a student application form, and the results of the Secondary School Admission Test. Candidates are asked to make an appointment for a campus visit and interview, if possible.

In 1999–2000, the cost of tuition, room, and board is $26,000, and the cost for day students is $19,750. Additional mandatory fees for all students amount to $600. Additional fees are charged for international students. Approximately $700 will be necessary for personal expenditures. A tuition payment plan and tuition insurance are available. Approximately $3,100,000 is awarded annually in need-based financial aid.

Headmaster & Rector: Richardson W. Schell '69
Deans of Students: James MacLeod, Erik Carlson,
   Cathe Mazza '76, and Bettina Cloutier
Alumni Director: Laura Eldridge
Academic Dean: M. Willard Lampe II
Director of Studies: Diana Yammin
Director of Admissions: Mark C. McWhinney '75
Director of Development: Edward W. Probert, Jr.
College Counselors: Carol Rand and L. Cyrus Theobald
Business Manager: Thomas L. Sides
Director of Athletics: Todd Marble

King & Low-Heywood Thomas School 1865

1450 Newfield Avenue, Stamford, CT 06905. 203-322-3496;
Fax 203-329-0291; Web Site www.klht.com

King & Low-Heywood Thomas, a college preparatory day school, is committed to preparing students for lives of achievement while emphasizing mutual respect and support, teamwork, community, and responsibility. Its goal is to provide an excellent academic, cultural, and athletic curriculum responsive to the individual needs and talents of 630 boys and girls in Beginners (age 3)–Grade 12. Located on 40 acres, the School draws from Fairfield and Westchester Counties. College counseling begins in Grade 9 and includes full-time professionals and an on-site, state-of-the-art database. Advanced Placement courses are offered. Activities include athletics, drama, chorus, clubs, and community service. Tuition: $9000–$16,250. Merit scholarships and financial aid are available. Barbara Hartley Smith (Newberry, B.S.; The Citadel, M.A.T.) is Head of School. *New England Association.*

Kingswood-Oxford School 1969

170 Kingswood Road, West Hartford, CT 06119.
860-233-9631; Fax 860-232-3843;
Web Site www.ko.pvt.k12.ct.us

Kingswood-Oxford is a coeducational, college preparatory day school enrolling 565 students in Grades 6–12. The School provides a challenging, supportive environment that nurtures relationships among young people, parents, and teachers. The traditional preliberal arts curriculum emphasizes the development of analytical skills, critical thinking, intellectual independence, and confidence. Student government, publications, volunteer opportunities, and various athletics and clubs complete the program. Tuition: $17,925. Activity Fee: $325. Financial Aid: $1,642,278. James J. Skiff is Director of Enrollment; Lee Levison (Amherst, B.A.; Trinity, M.A.; Harvard, M.A., Ed.D.) was named Head of School in 1992. *New England Association.*

The Long Ridge School 1938

478 Erskine Road, Stamford, CT 06903. 203-322-7693;
Fax 203-322-0406; E-mail mail@longridgeschool.org;
Web Site www.longridgeschool.org

The Long Ridge School is an independent, coeducational, day school with an enrollment of 150 boys and girls in Nursery–Grade 5. An afternoon program is available for two-year-olds. Offering "a child-centered education in a challenging, supportive atmosphere," the School seeks to nurture each student's academic, social, and emotional growth. Stressing an active learning process with increasing self-direction as the child grows older, the School feels that "a genuine caring and respect for children" is central to all activities. Tuition: $2500–$12,200. Extras: $450. Financial Aid: $65,000. Ms. Kris Bria (Carnegie Mellon, B.A.; Teachers College, Columbia, M.A.; Bank Street College, M.Ed.) was appointed Head in 1989.

The Loomis Chaffee School 1914

Windsor, CT 06095. 860-687-6000; Admissions 860-687-6400;
Fax 860-298-8756; E-mail admissions@loomis.org;
Web Site www.loomis.org

A coeducational, college preparatory boarding and day school enrolling 710 students in Grades 9–Postgraduate, Loomis Chaffee seeks to combine rigorous intellectual formation with sensitivity to the unique potential of each student. More than 200 courses are offered; off-campus internships and independent study options are available to upperclassmen. The 300-acre campus includes a 56,000-volume library, science center, a new school center, six international squash courts, and a 40-bed dormitory (1997). A summer session is offered. Boarding Tuition: $25,500; Day Tuition: $18,600. Financial Aid: $2,900,000. Thomas D. Southworth is Director of Admission; Russell H. Weigel (Bowdoin, B.A.; George Washington, M.A.; University of Colorado, Ph.D.) became Head of School in 1996. *New England Association.*

Marianapolis Preparatory School

Route 200, P.O. Box 368, Thompson, CT 06277. 860-923-9565;
Fax 860-923-3730; Web Site www.marianapolis.com

Marianapolis Preparatory School in Thompson, Connecticut, is a Roman Catholic boarding and day school enrolling young women and men in Grades 9 through 12 and a postgraduate year. The charming New England town of Thompson (population 8668) is situated in the rolling hills of northeastern Connecticut, 55 miles east of Hartford and about 30 miles from Worcester, Massachusetts, and Providence, Rhode Island.

Marianapolis Preparatory School traces its roots to an earlier institution, founded by the Marian Fathers in Chicago in 1927, that combined high school and junior college programs with a novitiate for young men with vocations. In 1931, it was relocated to the former Ream estate in Thompson where it was incorporated as Marianapolis College. The college program was discontinued during the Second World War, and the School adopted its present-day mission to educate young people for higher learning in the Catholic tradition of academic excellence.

The School is a nonprofit organization owned by the Congregation of Marians and governed by a Board of Trustees. Marianapolis is accredited by the New England Association of Schools and Colleges and holds membership in the Connecticut Association of Independent Schools and the National Catholic Education Association.

THE CAMPUS. Adjoining the Town Common in the center of Thompson, Marianapolis Preparatory School occupies a 300-acre rural campus that features woodlands and meadows, landscaped lawns, and a pond.

The Academic Complex provides classrooms, the library, and science and computer laboratories. Ream Commons houses an assembly hall, recreation areas, and the infirmary, while Blessed George Matulaitis Hall contains the administrative wing and a student lounge.

Students are housed in single-sex dormitories that are staffed around the clock by religious or lay prefects.

The gymnasium provides a double basketball court with seating for 350 spectators, a wrestling room, a large exercise room, athletic department offices, and locker rooms. Other facilities include tennis courts, a natural hockey rink, a cross-country course, a baseball diamond, and fields for football and soccer.

THE FACULTY. The Reverend Timothy John Roth, MIC, was appointed Headmaster in 1988. Father Roth holds a B.A. degree in philosophy from Catholic University of America, an

M.Div. degree from Sacred Heart School of Theology, and an M.A. from Assumption College. He is Vice-President of the Connecticut Association of Catholic Secondary School Principals and has been active with Worldwide Marriage Encounter for more than 25 years. In addition to his administrative responsibilities, Father Roth teaches moral theology at the School.

There are 31 teachers and administrators on staff, 11 women and 20 men. They hold baccalaureate and advanced degrees representing study at such colleges and universities as Annhurst College, Arizona State, Bowdoin, Bowling Green State, College of the Holy Cross, Eastern Connecticut State, Edinboro University, Fairfield, Fordham, Franciscan University, Furman, Marianapolis College, Marquette, Mount Holyoke, Ohio Wesleyan, Plymouth State, St. John Seminary, Salve Regina, Simmons, Southern Connecticut, Wagner, Wesleyan, Wheaton, Worcester State, and the Universities of Bridgeport, Connecticut, and Michigan.

STUDENT BODY. Marianapolis Prep enrolls 200 students, about evenly divided between girls and boys, in Grade 9 through a postgraduate year. Approximately 50 percent are residents who come from throughout the United States and several foreign countries. They represent a wide diversity of racial, ethnic, and religious backgrounds.

ACADEMIC PROGRAM. The school year, divided into quarters, runs from September to late May, with vacations at Thanksgiving, Christmas, and Easter and several long weekends. Each student has a faculty advisor who provides guidance in academic matters. Grades are mailed to parents and guardians at the close of each quarter, and exceptional academic performance is recognized on honors, high honors, and headmaster's lists. Students who are experiencing academic difficulty may get extra help from faculty at scheduled hours during the school day and on weekends. Classes are small, with an average of 12 students, to allow for individual attention.

A typical day includes seven 40-minute academic periods between 8:00 A.M. and 2:00 P.M. Monday through Friday, with lunch served in the dining hall for all students. Extra help and athletics begin after classes. Evening study hours are from 7:00 to 9:00 P.M. Students with a grade point average of 3.0 or higher have independent study; other students in good standing are granted room study privileges, while those in academic difficulty attend supervised study halls.

The college preparatory curriculum at Marianapolis is designed to challenge students, to equip them for success in further education and careers, and to instill a lifelong love of learning. Students carry an academic course load of 6 credits per year with each yearlong course earning a full credit.

To graduate, a student must complete 22 credits as follows: 4 in English; 3 each in mathematics, science, and theology; 2 in foreign language; and 1 each in U.S. history, world history, computer science, word processing, art/music, and health.

Among the specific courses are English I–IV, World Literature, Latin and Greek Roots, Research Methods, Literature of the Holocaust; three levels of French and Spanish, Elementary German; Algebra I–II, Advanced Mathematics, Geometry, Probability and Statistics, Calculus I: Techniques, Calculus I: Applications; Computer Science I–II; Introduction to Physical Science, Biology, Chemistry, Physics, Geology, Marine Biology, Environmental Science, Anatomy and Physiology; Hebrew Scriptures, Christian Scriptures, World Religions, Christian Morality, Church History, Life Choices, Sacrament; World History, United States History, American Government, Political Science, Psychology, Sociology; Art I–II, Painting, Three Dimensional Art/Printmaking, Drawing, General Music, Music: Ensemble, and Chorus and Folk Group.

Marianapolis Prep offers an extensive English as a Second Language program, which includes preparation for the Test of English as a Foreign Language and special courses in biology and United States history for international students. Upon arrival at the School, students are evaluated and assigned according to their level of proficiency. When their skills are determined to be adequate, they are mainstreamed to the standard academic program. The comprehensive goals of the ESL program require that students speak English at all times, in and out of the classroom and at all off-campus, School-related activities; failure to do so results in work assignments.

College counseling for students and their families begins in the junior year, and virtually all Marianapolis graduates go on to further education. Recent graduates have attended such colleges and universities as Alfred, Assumption, Babson, Bentley, Boston College, Bowdoin, Bryant, Clark, College of the Holy Cross, Davidson, Duke, Fairfield, George Washington University, Hamilton, Hampshire, Hofstra, Kansas City Art Institute, Manhattan College, Merrimack, Michigan State, Northeastern, Ohio State, Pennsylvania State, Providence, Rensselaer Polytechnic, St. Michael's, Salve Regina, Stonehill, Syracuse, Virginia Wesleyan, Worcester Polytechnic, and the Universities of Cincinnati, Illinois, Massachusetts, New Hampshire, Notre Dame, Rochester, and Vermont.

The School conducts an academic summer session for remediation, accelerated studies, and English as a Second Language.

STUDENT ACTIVITIES. Marianapolis Prep's broad program of extracurricular options is designed to encourage students to explore new interests and hone leadership skills. All students are required to become involved in an interscholastic sport or a club activity.

Marianapolis competes in the Quinebaug Valley Conference in 12 sports including soccer, cross-country, basketball, baseball, softball, tennis, golf, and track. The School also fields a girls' cheerleading squad and participates in a ski program at Wachusett Mountain.

Students publish a yearbook, engage in community service with the elderly, and take part in chorus, pep band, and writer's group. Among the organizations formed on campus are art, computer/computer games, medieval, simulation war games, spirit, Spanish, chess, and role-playing clubs.

The Senior Prom and Winter Semi-Formal are among the special events on the school calendar.

ADMISSION AND COSTS. Marianapolis Prep welcomes students of average and above-average ability and excellent character who seek a challenging college preparatory program. Admission is offered at any grade level to students of all faiths, races, and national or ethnic origins based on the completed application, recommendations from the English and Math departments, previous school records, character references, standardized test scores, and a personal interview. Decisions are rendered when the application file is complete.

In 1999–2000, boarding tuition is $16,425; day tuition is $6996. Financial aid totaling approximately $300,000 was distributed in 1998–99 based on need. In addition, a number of merit scholarships are awarded each year.

Dean of Students: Mrs. Karen Tata 860-923-9565
Director of Alumni(ae) Relations: Mrs. Lori Quintal Wong
   860-923-1992
Director of Admissions: Br. Donald Schaefer, MIC 860-923-1992
Dean of Admissions: Ms. Stephanie Baron 860-923-1992
College Placement Advisor: Mr. Thomas J.N. Juko 860-923-9565
Athletic Director: Mr. Eric Gustavson 860-923-9565

Marvelwood School   1957

*476 Skiff Mountain Road, Kent, CT 06757-3001. 800-440-9107
  or 860-927-0047; Fax 860-927-5325;
  E-mail marvelwood.school@snet.net;
  Web Site www.themarvelwoodschool.com*

Marvelwood, a coeducational boarding and day school enrolling 150 students in Grades 9–12, aims to provide an environment in which young people of varying abilities and learning needs can prepare for success in college and in life. In a nurturing, structured community, students who have not thrived academically in traditional settings are guided and motivated to reach and exceed their personal potential. A Skills Program, math tutoring, and English as a Second Language are offered. The curriculum is enhanced by activities such as interscholastic sports, drama, chorus, yearbook, clubs, and community service. Boarding Tuition: $26,000; Day Tuition: $15,500. Financial Aid: $500,000. W. Bradley Gottschalk is Director of Admissions and Financial Aid; Anne Scott is Head of School. *New England Association.*

The Master's School   1970

*Westledge Road, West Simsbury, CT 06092. 860-651-9361;
  Fax 860-651-9363*

The Master's School is an independent, nondenominational, coeducational day school for more than 475 children in Nursery–Grade 12. Dedicated to nurturing excellence through outstanding teaching and a strong extracurricular activities program, all offered within a Christian atmosphere, the School enrolls academically able and highly motivated students. The 200-acre mountaintop campus includes nine buildings, the latest a 7000-square-foot structure completed in 1998. Tuition: $7600–$9800. Financial Aid: $804,000. Tom Tindall is Assistant Headmaster for Admissions; Don W. Steele (Gordon College, B.A. 1966; University of Lowell, M.A. 1978) is Headmaster. *New England Association.*

The Mead School   1969

*1095 Riverbank Road, Stamford, CT 06903. 203-595-9500;
  Fax 203-595-0735; Web Site www.meadschool.com*

The Mead School is an alternative learning environment committed to the development of the whole child. Enrolling approximately 250 boys and girls as day students in Nursery–Grade 9, the School combines developmentally appropriate academic programs with equal emphasis on the expressive arts and personal development. Honest and affectionate relationships, individualized programs, and the development of autonomous learners are priorities. Special-interest activities are incorporated into the regular curriculum. A summer program is available for children, ages 2–15. Tuition: $4500–$16,000. Financial Aid: $250,000. Margaret Hiatt is Director of Admissions; Norman Baron (City College of New York, M.S. 1969) is Director.

Miss Porter's School   1843

*Main Street, Farmington, CT 06032. 860-409-3500; Admission
  860-409-3530; Fax 860-409-3531; E-mail Admissions@
  MissPorters.org; Web Site www.MissPorters.org*

Miss Porter's, a leader in preparing young women for competitive colleges, enrolls 300 resident and day girls in Grades 9–12. The School offers demanding academics, collaborative environment, and supportive community. The rigorous curriculum features Honors, Advanced Placement, and elective courses. A program for juniors and seniors includes special courses, on- and off-campus internships, and independent studies that explore traditional and nontraditional subjects. All graduates go on to college. Boarding Tuition: $25,500; Day Tuition: $18,600. Financial aid is available. Rebecca Ballard is

Director of Admission; M. Burch Tracy Ford (Boston University, B.A.; Simmons, M.S.W.; Harvard, Ed.M.) is Head. *New England Association*.

Mooreland Hill School   1930

166 Lincoln Road, Kensington, CT 06037-1198. 860-223-6428; Fax 860-223-3318; E-mail mhs@mooreland.org; Web Site www.mooreland.org

Mooreland Hill School, founded by parents as a day middle school, is dedicated to the development of the child through the challenges of a strong, traditional academic curriculum with extensive opportunities for social and physical growth. Enrolled are 100 boys and girls in Grades 5–9 who follow a full academic schedule enriched with programs in music, art, computer, foreign language, and Human Growth and Development. All students participate in interscholastic sports and a chore program. Extracurricular activities include drama, Discovery Days, chorus, instrumental ensemble, student publications, and chess and computer clubs. Tuition/Fees: $13,151. Financial Aid: $129,000. Cheryl C. Carlson is Director of Admission; Dane L. Peters was appointed Headmaster in 1991.

Notre Dame of West Haven   1946

24 Ricardo Street, West Haven, CT 06516-2499. 203-933-1673; Fax 203-933-2474; E-mail admissions@notredamehs.com; Web Site www.notredamehs.com

Founded and operated by the Brothers of Holy Cross, Notre Dame of West Haven is a Roman Catholic, college preparatory day school enrolling 670 young men in Grades 9–12. The school's mission is to assist parents in educating their sons, working to develop respect, dedication, and excellence in each student. The curriculum, which includes honors and Advanced Placement courses, accommodates a variety of learning abilities, and a 12:1 student-faculty ratio permits close, individualized attention. A strong athletic program, the fine arts, student government, publications, and interest clubs are among the activities. Tuition: $5775. Financial aid is available. Michael J. Zaffino is Director of Admissions; Br. James Branigan, CSC, is Headmaster. *New England Association*.

Pine Point School   1948

89 Barnes Road, Stonington, CT 06378. 860-535-0606; Fax 860-535-8033; E-mail admissn@connix.com; Web Site http://www.pinepoint.pvt.k12.ct.us

Pine Point, a coeducational day school on 25 wooded acres, enrolls 265 students in Preschool–Grade 9 from throughout Southeastern Connecticut and Rhode Island. It offers a strong, developmentally based curriculum with emphasis on hands-on

learning and the importance of each student's social, emotional, and physical growth. All students participate weekly in dance, music, art, and physical education. The program in Grades 6–9 has advisory, community service, team sports, state-of-the-art science and technology labs, and an oceanology program with a School-owned research vessel. A summer day camp is offered for ages 3–15. Tuition: $2860–$11,280. Financial Aid: $219,000. Julie Abbiati is Admission Director; Paul G. Geise is Head of School.

Pomfret School   POMFRET

Pomfret, CT 06258. 860-963-6100; Admissions 860-963-6120; Fax 860-963-2042; E-mail admission@griffin.pomfretschool.org; Web Site www.pomfretschool.org

Pomfret school in Pomfret, Connecticut, is a college preparatory boarding and day school enrolling boys and girls in Grades 9–Postgraduate. The School, a nonprofit organization governed by a Board of Trustees, is located in northeastern Connecticut, 35 miles from Providence, 40 miles from Hartford, and 65 miles from Boston. New York City is three hours away.

William C. Peck, former Headmaster of St. Mark's School, established Pomfret as a proprietary school for boys in 1894. His program included challenging scholarship, rigorous athletics, and a "sane application of religion to life." In 1994, Pomfret School celebrated its 100th anniversary.

Pomfret School continues to maintain a challenging learning environment where students from diverse racial, ethnic, and socioeconomic backgrounds prepare for college and responsible adulthood within the context of a trusting educational family. Academics is the keystone of the School's three-dimensional approach. The *Pomfret Experience* is rounded out by expansive programs in the arts and in athletics. Each student's progress is monitored by the Academic Dean and by an advisor; the latter meets with his or her advisee on a regular basis.

Pomfret School is accredited by the New England Association of Schools and Colleges and holds membership in the National Association of Independent Schools and other professional organizations.

THE CAMPUS. The School's 13 playing fields are located on 500 acres of rolling hills and woodlands. The principal school buildings are grouped in the middle of the campus. The School House contains foreign language and history classrooms and administrative offices as well as the newly relocated music center. It is flanked on one side by four brick dormitories, and on the other by Hard Auditorium, the center for dramatic and musical productions.

Nearby is the Monell Science Building (renovated 1996), with laboratories for biology, chemistry, environmental science, and physics as well as lecture rooms furnished with video equipment. The adjacent Centennial Building (1996) houses all mathematics and English classes as well as two- and three-dimensional art studios, metal and wood shops, and a 120-seat, state-of-the-art theater. A new dance studio was completed in 1998.

The du Pont Library completes the current academic buildings. Along with its 15,000 volumes and the new Technology Center, the library provides students with an On-Line system, including library network, card catalogue, *New York Times* 1990-present, and magazine index. CD-ROM disks are also available. Through the library director, students have access to both Interlibrary Loan Books and the Internet.

Other nearby buildings include the Main House, containing the dining hall, mail room, school store, and Health Center, which is staffed by three registered nurses. The School physician is at the Center in the mornings. Clark Memorial Chapel also occupies a central location on campus.

The athletic facilities consist of Lewis Gymnasium, which houses basketball and squash courts, a wrestling room, and the Nautilus fitness center, containing 16 Nautilus machines as well as rowing ergometers, lifecycles, a treadmill, and a Stairmaster. The Brown Hockey Rink and several outdoor tennis and volleyball courts are also located on campus. The Strong Field House and Student Center provides four indoor tennis courts. The student center has a lounge, recreation area, TV room, and snack bar.

Four converted homes, four large brick dormitories, and the recently renovated Pyne Hall serve as student residences. A fiberoptic "backbone" connects all Pomfret dormitory rooms, classrooms, faculty apartments, and offices, permitting computer and telephone networking throughout the campus as well as through the World Wide Web.

The physical plant, owned by the School, is valued at $28,000,000.

THE FACULTY. Bradford Hastings, a graduate of Pomfret School, Union College (B.A. 1972), and Harvard University (M.Ed. 1979), became Headmaster in July 1993. After graduating from college, Mr. Hastings taught history at Pomfret and served as Director of Athletics and Assistant Director of Admissions. Following graduate school, he became Dean of Students and Assistant Headmaster at Deerfield Academy.

The full-time teaching faculty includes 32 men and 19 women; all live on campus. They hold 51 baccalaureate and 28 advanced degrees, including 2 doctorates, from such colleges and universities as Boston College, Brown, Colby, Columbia, Cornell, Dartmouth, Harvard, Middlebury, Princeton, Rhode Island School of Design, Tufts, Union, Wesleyan, Williams, Yale, and the Universities of Pennsylvania and Virginia. Two part-time instructors teach drama and photography.

Faculty benefits include retirement and health insurance plans, a sabbatical/leave program, and grants for summer study and travel.

STUDENT BODY. In 1999–2000, the School enrolled 183 boys and 128 girls in Grade 9–Postgraduate, distributed as follows: Grade 9–47, Grade 10–95, Grade 11–79, and Grade 12 and Postgraduate–90. Seventy-six percent of the students are boarders; 11 percent are students of color; 12 percent are international students who represent 14 countries.

ACADEMIC PROGRAM. The academic year, divided into trimesters, begins in early September and ends in early June, with vacations scheduled for one week at Thanksgiving, two weeks at Christmas, and three weeks in March. Classes are scheduled six days a week in eight 50-minute periods from 8:00 A.M. to 3:15 P.M. Sports are scheduled in the afternoon from 3:45 to 5:45 P.M. The class day ends at 12:25 P.M. on Wednesdays and at 11:30 A.M. on alternate Saturdays. Classes are small, averaging 13 students. Evening study hours are 8:00 to 10:00 P.M. Sunday through Friday. Grades are sent to parents six times a year, and written comments from teachers and advisors are included four times a year.

To graduate, a student must complete the following: four years of English; three of foreign language; three and one-third of history; four of mathematics; three of laboratory science, including biology; one trimester of religion; and one trimester of Social Issues. Students must also demonstrate computer literacy and fulfill an art requirement of two trimester courses for each year they attend Pomfret.

Among the courses are English 1–4, Language and Power; French 1–6, Advanced Communication in French, Introduction to French Literature, Spanish 1–6, Introduction to Spanish Literature, Latin 1–4; World History, U.S. History to World War II, Latin America in the Twentieth Century, American Political Institutions, Civil War and Reconstruction, Economics, The Holocaust, African-American History, The Middle East, Political Theory, The Russian Revolutions; The Bible, Women of the Bible, World Religions, Religion and Society; Algebra, Geometry, Elementary Functions, Pre-Calculus, Calculus; General Biology, Anatomy and Physiology, Marine Mammals, Marine Biology. Environmental Science, Chemistry, Physics; Music Theory and Composition, Art History, Ceramics, Studio Painting, Sculpture, Visual Design, Theater Skills; and Advanced Computer Applications. Honors and Advanced Placement courses are available in all disciplines. Opportunities for independent study are provided to qualified seniors.

In 1999, graduates matriculated at such institutions as Brown, Colby, Duke, Harvard, Mount Holyoke, Rhode Island School of Design, Yale, and the University of Virginia.

STUDENT ACTIVITIES. The Director of Student Activities coordinates all student activities. Weekend events are varied and well attended. They often include movies, dances, seasonal outdoor activities, and trips to theaters, shopping malls, and nearby cities.

The student body is governed by the Student Council. Students elect a president and two representatives of each class to the School Council, which includes two faculty representatives. The Council provides an open forum for all members of the Pomfret community, and its recommendations are presented to the faculty and administration for action.

Students, along with a faculty advisor, produce the yearbook, newspaper, and literary magazines. Other student organizations include Math Team; Key Society, a service organization; Vestry, which plans chapel services; the Voice, a multicultural support group; Amnesty International; Chorus, Griff Tones, Contemporary Music Performance; Athletic Association Council; and the Astronomy, Diplomacy, Environmental, International, and Outing clubs. Student volunteers work in local schools, day care centers, and service organizations.

Pomfret teams compete against other schools throughout New England and in New England championship playoffs. Varsity teams are fielded in cross-country, football, soccer, basketball, ice hockey, squash, wrestling, baseball, crew, tennis, golf, and lacrosse for boys; and cross-country, field hockey, soccer, basketball, ice hockey, squash, softball, crew, tennis, golf, and lacrosse for girls. Aerobics are available on an intramural basis.

Parents Weekends are scheduled in both the fall and the spring, and Alumni Weekend takes place in early May.

ADMISSION AND COSTS. Pomfret School seeks students who demonstrate the character, ability, motivation, and preparation to succeed in its programs. Most students are admitted in Grades 9 and 10, and a small number in Grade 11 and as postgraduates, on the basis of past school performance, standardized test results, teacher recommendations, and personal interviews. Application should be made by February 1 for September admission. Decisions are made by March 10.

Pomfret School admits students of any race, color, creed, handicap, sexual orientation, or national origin to all the rights, privileges, programs, and activities generally accorded or made available to students at the School. The School does not discriminate on the basis of race, color, creed, handicap, gender, sexual orientation, age, or national origin in the administration of its educational policies, admission policies, financial aid, or other programs administered by the School.

Boarding tuition and fees for 1999–2000 were $27,200. Day tuition and fees were $16,500. Private music lessons and tutoring are extra. Pomfret subscribes to the School and Student Scholarship Service and awards $1,650,000 annually in financial aid on the basis of need. Tuition payment and insurance plans are available.

Headmaster: Bradford Hastings '68
Assistant Head: P. A. Mulcahy
Director of Admissions: Monique C. K. Wolanin '87
Director of College Counseling: J. Roderick Eaton
Acting Director of Alumni and Development: Nancy A. Gingras
Business Manager: Stephen F. Larrabee
Director of Athletics: Bruce E. Paro

The Rectory School   1920

528 Pomfret Street, Pomfret, CT 06258. 860-928-7759; Admissions 860-928-1328; Fax 860-928-4961; E-mail recadmit@neca.com; Web Site www.com/~librs/o1/rectory.htm

The Rectory School, a junior school for 122 boarding boys and 60 coeducational day students in Grades 5–9, fosters self-confidence and self-reliance by providing opportunities for success across a broad spectrum of academic, athletic, and artistic interests. The Individualized Instruction Program is designed to meet the needs of each student. Grades are sectioned from honors to remedial. Small classes and a structured environment help students to focus, feel supported, and perform to their potential. Graduates enter such schools as Pomfret, Hotchkiss,

Salisbury, and Suffield. Tuition: $10,300–$22,250. Financial Aid: $248,000. Stephen A. DiPaolo is Director of Admission; Thomas F. Army, Jr. (Wesleyan University, B.A., M.A.L.S.), was appointed Headmaster in 1990.

Renbrook School   1935

2865 Albany Avenue, West Hartford, CT 06117. 860-236-1661; Fax 860-231-8206

This day school for 571 girls and boys age 3–Grade 9 offers academic challenge in a warm, supportive environment. An outstanding faculty respects the needs of the individual student while creating a classroom atmosphere that promotes success for a variety of learning styles. Interdisciplinary units and hands-on projects are found at every level. A strong traditional curriculum is enriched by the arts, athletics, and state-of-the-art technology. Foreign languages, independent study, honors courses, and community service enhance the program. Extended-Day and After-School programs, vacation care, and Summer Adventure day camp are available. Tuition: $7500–$16,500. Financial Aid: $1,100,000. Jane C. Shipp (Rhodes College, B.A.; Brown, M.A.) is Headmistress.

Rumsey Hall School   WASHINGTON

Washington Depot, CT 06794. 860-868-0535; E-mail rhsadm@wtco.net; Web Site www.rumsey.pvt.k12.ct.us

Rumsey hall school in Washington, Connecticut, is a coeducational boarding and country day school for students in Kindergarten through Grade 9. The boarding program begins in Grade 5. Situated in the southern range of the Berkshire Hills, Washington (population 4000) is 42 miles west of Hartford and 80 miles northeast of New York City. The area, which offers wooded countryside and access to several ski areas, is the site of numerous other independent schools and colleges.

Founded by Mrs. Lillias Rumsey Sanford in Seneca Falls, New York, in 1900, the School moved to larger quarters in Cornwall, Connecticut, in 1907, and to the present campus in 1948. Mrs. Sanford has been succeeded as Director by John F. Schereschewsky, Sr. (1941–1969), John F. Schereschewsky, Jr. (1969–1977), Louis G. Magnoli (1969–1985), and Thomas W. Farmen, the present Headmaster.

Since its inception in 1900, Rumsey Hall School has retained its original philosophy: to help each child develop "to his or her maximum stature as an individual, as a member of a family, and as a contributing member of society." The School aims to provide the support, nurture and care that children need while presenting appropriate academic challenge and rigor. The basic curriculum is designed to teach students to read, write, and calculate proficiently and to establish the educational foundations that prepare them for success in secondary school and college. Rumsey Hall embraces the ideal of "honor through effort" and emphasizes effort more than grades as the criterion for achievement.

A nonprofit institution, Rumsey Hall School is directed by a 25-member Board of Trustees, which meets quarterly. The School holds membership in the National Association of Independent Schools, the Connecticut Association of Independent Schools, the Educational Testing Service, the Educational Records Bureau, and the Secondary School Admissions Test Board.

THE CAMPUS. The 70-acre campus on the Bantam River provides landscaped and wooded areas, five athletic fields, and two skating ponds. The John F. Schereschewsky Center contains indoor athletic facilities, including three tennis courts.

The School is housed in 25 buildings, most of which have been constructed since 1950. Five structures provide a total of 22 classrooms, including the new Satyavati science laboratory and a computer center. Other buildings house the recently expanded library, the study hall, and the new J. Seward Johnson Fine Arts Center.

Younger girls reside in Foothills Dormitory, which is located on a 12-acre tract two miles from the main campus. Hilltop Dormitory, which was constructed in 1970 on a site overlooking the Bantam and Shepaug rivers, houses older girls. Boys live in Hull House, White House, Fitch House, the Cottage, and New Dorm. All dormitories are supervised by resident faculty members.

THE FACULTY. Thomas W. Farmen, appointed Headmaster in 1985, is a graduate of New England College (B.A.) and Western Connecticut State University (M.S.A.). He has also served at Rumsey Hall as a teacher, Director of Athletics, and Director of Secondary School Placement.

There are 53 full-time teachers, 18 men and 35 women. Thirty-one, including 10 with families, reside on campus. They hold 50 baccalaureate and 15 master's degrees, representing study at such institutions as Allegheny, Bates, Bethany, Bowdoin, Brigham Young, Columbia, Connecticut College, Dartmouth, Lafayette College, Long Island University, Lynchburg, Middlebury, Muskingum, New England College, Northern Kentucky, St. Lawrence, Southern Connecticut State, Springfield, Syracuse, Trinity, Tulane, Wesleyan, Western Connecticut State, Wheaton, and the Universities of Connecticut, Michigan, and New Hampshire.

Two nurses staff the school infirmary, and a local doctor is on call. Emergency facilities are located in New Milford, ten miles distant.

STUDENT BODY. In 1999–2000, the School enrolls 284 students including 73 boarding boys, 35 boarding girls, 110 day boys, and 66 day girls in Kindergarten–Grade 9 as follows: 9 in Kindergarten, 10 in Grade 1, 12 in Grade 2, 12 in Grade 3, 13 in Grade 4, 26 in Grade 5, 25 in Grade 6, 47 in Grade 7, 67 in Grade 8, and 63 in Grade 9. In addition to Connecticut, resident students come from 27 other states and 11 foreign countries.

ACADEMIC PROGRAM. The school year, from September to early June, provides 32 weeks of instruction, a Thanksgiving recess, and extended vacations at Christmas and in the spring. Classes, which have an average enrollment of 13, meet six days a week for the upper school and five days a week for the lower school. The daily schedule, from 8:00 A.M. to 4:30 P.M., includes a school meeting each morning, eight 40-minute class periods, lunch, extra-help sessions, and athletics in the afternoon. A supervised study hall is conducted from 7:00 to 8:30 P.M. each evening. Clubs and activities meet each Monday.

All faculty members are available to provide special assistance during the afternoon extra-help period. Individualized language skills programs, administered by reading specialists, and English as a Second Language are offered at additional cost.

Students have appropriate homework assignments, to be completed during study halls. Class assignments for the week are issued on Monday and graded each day. Faculty members meet once a week to review the work of each student and prepare reports, based on homework and class quizzes, that are issued biweekly to parents and students. Faculty members also compile a weekly effort list of students who the instructors feel have put forth maximum effort during that period. Effort-list students are granted such privileges as optional study hall attendance, tennis or fishing before breakfast, and permission to read other than assigned books during study hall. Both art and music are required in all grades.

In 1999, the School's graduates entered such independent secondary schools as Andover, Choate Rosemary Hall, Deerfield, Exeter, The Gunnery, Kent School, Loomis Chaffee, Taft, and Westover.

Rumsey's five-week academic summer session enrolls approximately 70 boarding and day students in Grades 3–9. The program offers courses in English, elementary mathematics, algebra, computer science/keyboarding, and study skills. Classes are held five days a week.

STUDENT ACTIVITIES. Students in the Upper School may join such interest groups as community service, computer keyboarding, biking, fly fishing, school newspaper, chorus, and drama clubs. In the Lower School, students can be involved in the creation of an original opera, either composing, writing, designing, set building, lighting, or performing. Student government organizations exist for students of all ages.

Interscholastic teams for students are organized in football, soccer, hockey, skiing, wrestling, baseball, tennis, and crew for boys, and in field hockey, hockey, volleyball, skiing, softball, tennis, and crew for girls. The student body is divided into Red and Blue teams, with intramural competition culminating in a Red and Blue Track Meet on Memorial Day. An equestrian program and recreational sports such as sledding, skiing, trapshooting, sailing, hiking, mountain biking, and fishing are also available.

Although boarding students have free time on weekends, they also participate in organized on-campus activities. Off-campus trips and various activities are planned each weekend, and day students are welcome to attend. Rumsey's location allows students to enjoy numerous cultural and entertainment activities in New Haven, Hartford, Boston, and New York City. Traditional annual events for the school community include Parents' Days, the Holiday Carol Sing, a winter ski trip, Grandparents' Day, and Commencement.

ADMISSION AND COSTS. Rumsey Hall seeks to enroll students of good character and ability without regard to race, creed, or color. Students are admitted to Grades K–9 on the basis of an application form, a personal interview, recommendations from previous teachers, and an official school transcript.

In 1999–2000, tuition is $24,025 for boarding students and between $7280 and $11,805 for day students, depending on grade. A limited amount of financial aid is available. In 1998–99, students received $433,000 in financial aid.

Assistant Headmaster: Rick S. Spooner
Dean of Students: Robert McGrew
Director of Admissions: Matthew Hoeniger
Director of Development and Alumni: Nancy Van Deusen
Placement Director: Francis M. Ryan
Business Manager: Dorota Habib
Director of Athletics: Jay Przygocki
Lower School Coordinator: Jody Lampe
Coordinator of Girls' and Women's Issues: J. Whitney Ryan

Sacred Heart Academy of Stamford   1922

200 Strawberry Hill Avenue, Stamford, CT 06902. 203-323-3173; Fax 203-975-7804; E-mail sha200adm@aol.com; Web Site www.shastamford.org

Sacred Heart Academy, founded by the Sisters of St. Joseph, is a Roman Catholic college preparatory school enrolling 100 girls as day students in Grades 9–12. It strives to be a Christian community, where each person is respected and education in its fullest sense can take place. The sports program includes cross-country, volleyball, basketball, softball, and tennis. Advanced Placement and college preparatory courses are offered. Publications, sports, environmental and language clubs, and community service are among the extracurricular activities. Tuition: $6450. Dr. Dana Wilkie is Director of Admissions; Sr. Jeanne Paulella (Marywood College, M.A. 1974) was appointed Principal in 1993. *New England Association.*

St. Luke's School   NEW CANAAN

377 North Wilton Road, P.O. Box 1148, New Canaan, CT 06840. 203-966-5612; E-mail info@stlukes.new-canaan.ct.us; Web Site http://users.aol.com/slsinfo/index.html

S T. LUKE'S SCHOOL in New Canaan, Connecticut, is a nondenominational, college preparatory day school enrolling boys and girls in Grades 5 through 12. New Canaan (population 30,000) is a charming New England town situated 60 miles from Manhattan in southwestern Fairfield County. The

School is reached from either Route 15 (Merritt Parkway) or Interstate 95 via Route 123. Most students arrange private transportation, and optional van service is available through the School.

Founded in 1927 by Edward Blakely, St. Luke's was originally a small day and boarding school for boys. Its first location was on Ponus Ridge in New Canaan on property belonging to New York City's Grace Church. Ten years later, it was purchased by two educators, Dr. Joseph Kidd and his partner, William von Fabrice, who shaped and guided the School for 24 years. The School moved to its present campus and the enrollment expanded to more than 280 students; the first girls were admitted to the Class of 1973.

St. Luke's School is firmly committed to providing the essential components of excellence in education: a caring, dedicated faculty; a friendly, respectful environment; small classes that foster clear thinking and academic effort; discipline and traditional values; and personal attention and college placement counseling. The School welcomes students of diverse backgrounds and strives to provide a challenging liberal arts program that meets the needs of both high achievers and those of more modest abilities.

Since 1971, the School has been a nonprofit institution governed by a Board of Trustees, 23 in number. The parents' organization assists with activities in and out of the classroom, while the St. Luke's Alumni Association serves the School's approximately 2500 graduates through fund-raising, recruitment, and planning special events. St. Luke's is accredited by the New England Association of Colleges and Schools and holds membership in the National Association of Independent Schools, Connecticut Association of Independent Schools, Fairchester Association of Independent Schools, and the National Association of Secondary School Principals, among other professional organizations.

THE CAMPUS. Located in a lovely rural, residential area of New Canaan, St. Luke's is set on a 41-acre hilltop campus of woodlands and open fields. The three-story academic building houses classrooms, two computer laboratories, a computer writing lab, a 15,000-volume library, the cafeteria, two tutorial centers, and boys' and girls' locker rooms. The arts/science wing contains art studios, two music classrooms, three music practice rooms, a fully equipped darkroom, science labs, additional classrooms, and faculty offices. A new art and photography center, two gymnasiums, including a new facility for the Upper School, the Headmaster's home, an exercise/weight room, five playing fields, and new fields for girls' softball, lacrosse, and field hockey complete the physical plant, which is owned by the School and valued at approximately $7,000,000.

THE FACULTY. Richard M. Whitcomb joined the faculty of St. Luke's in 1961 and served as a history teacher, football coach, athletic director, director of admissions, and assistant headmaster before being appointed Headmaster in 1980. Mr. Whitcomb graduated from Vermont Academy, where he was elected to the school's Hall of Fame, and earned baccalaureate and master's degrees from the University of Bridgeport. He also holds an M.Ed. degree from Fairfield University. An active member of several community and educational organizations, Mr. Whitcomb was recently honored by the Urban League, the only independent school administrator to be so recognized. He and his wife, Barbara, who teaches at St. Luke's, are the parents of two grown children, both graduates of St. Luke's.

The 50 faculty members, 24 women and 26 men, hold 49 baccalaureate, 33 master's, and 4 doctoral degrees, representing study at such colleges and universities as Amherst, Boston University, Bucknell, Case Western Reserve, Colby, Cornell, Fairfield, Fordham, Georgetown, Hobart, Lycoming, Manhattanville, McGill (Canada), Middlebury, New York University, Oberlin, Ohio University, Radford, Randolph-Macon, St. Leo's College, Tufts, Wesleyan, Wheelock, Yale, and the Universities of Connecticut, Pennsylvania, and Texas. Benefits for faculty include a pension plan; medical, dental, and life insurance; and tuition reimbursement. A registered nurse is on duty during school hours, and medical facilities are available nearby.

STUDENT BODY. In 1999–2000, St. Luke's School enrolls 400 boys and girls, with 200 in the Middle School (Grades 5–8) and 200 in the Upper School (Grades 9–12). They come from a total of 23 towns in Fairfield, New Haven, and Westchester counties, and represent a wide diversity of racial, ethnic, religious, and socioeconomic backgrounds.

ACADEMIC PROGRAM. The school year is divided into semesters beginning in early September and ending in early June. The calendar includes a Thanksgiving recess, two-week vacations in the winter and spring, and observances of national holidays. A strong adviser system enables students to meet frequently with teachers, on an informal basis or upon prior arrangement, to discuss matters of social, academic, and personal concern. Four in-house tutors are available for additional instruction. The student-teacher ratio is 7:1, and the student-college adviser ratio is 6:1.

The School's fifth-grade curriculum is created and structured to connect directly into the curricula of the sixth and seventh grades in each major discipline. A whole-language approach, rather than simple memorization, is used to promote true learning. The highly personalized Middle School curriculum, which offers individual attention on a one-to-one basis, is structured to provide adolescents with a firm foundation in basic disciplines in preparation for the college preparatory program they will follow in the upper grades. Reading and writing excellence and mathematics and computer skills are emphasized, and a fine arts program is integral to the course work, with alternating art and music classes scheduled for one period per day.

A minimum of 20 credits is needed to graduate from the Upper School, although most students earn more. The credits must be distributed as follows: 4 in English; 3 each in mathematics, history, science, and foreign language; 1 each in art, music, or computer; and 2 in physical education and health. Students must carry five academic courses and physical education each semester and must complete 80 hours of community service over the four-year period.

Among the course offerings available in the Upper School are English Competence, Literary Forms, Survey of Literature, Creative Writing, Reading Film, Generational Voices, Communication and Language, African-American Voices; Algebra I–II, Geometry I–II, Pre-Calculus, Calculus, Probability and Statistics, Topics in Discrete Mathematics; Computer Science, Word Processing, Desktop Publishing; Human Biology, Biology, Chemistry, Physics, Biochemistry, Ecology, Forensic Science, Astronomy; Regional Studies, Western Civilization, U.S. History, Psychology, World War II, Civil War, Vietnam, Anthropology; Spanish I–IV, French I–IV; Studio Art, Drawing/Painting, Photography I–II; Band, Choir, Theory, Music Seminar/Independent Study; Journalism; and Health and Physical Education. Qualified students may take Advanced Placement or honors courses in six subjects. With the permission of the Assistant Headmaster, juniors and seniors may arrange for independent study under the sponsorship of an appropriate faculty member. Individual instrumental instruction may also be arranged.

Virtually all St. Luke's students continue their education in colleges and universities throughout the nation. Over the past five years, graduates have been accepted at such institutions as Assumption, Bentley, Boston University, Bowdoin, Brown, Clark, Colgate, Denison, Dickinson, Duquesne, Duke, Emory, Fordham, Georgetown, George Washington, Hampshire, Haverford, Hobart, Lafayette, Middlebury, Northeastern, Princeton, Salve Regina, Southern Methodist, Syracuse, Tufts, Wake Forest, Wheaton, Yale, and the Universities of Arizona, Colorado, Delaware, Maine, Massachusetts, New Hampshire, North Texas, Pennsylvania, Redlands, Vermont, and Virginia.

St. Luke's conducts a five-week academic summer program and a Back to School Enrichment Program for students in Grades 5–12.

STUDENT ACTIVITIES. All students are expected to take part in one or more of the many extracurricular offerings, which are organized to meet a wide range of interests and abilities. Students may assume responsibility and leadership roles on the elected Student Council and the Homecoming, Prom, and Hospitality committees. Crusader Productions stages Broadway hits such as *Camelot* and *Little Shop of Horrors*, and the band and chorus perform in school and at all-state competitions. Students publish *The Caduceus* (yearbook), *The Sentinel* (newspaper), *Krypteia* (Upper School literary magazine), and *The Hilltop* (Lower School literary magazine). Other activities include Model United Nations, Model Congress, Youth Leadership Conference, and the Environmental Club. Community service is an essential component of a St. Luke's education, and there is a wide choice of options for fulfilling graduation requirements.

Crusader teams compete in football, soccer, cross-country, basketball, hockey, fencing, baseball, lacrosse, and tennis for boys; and field hockey, cross-country, basketball, volleyball, lacrosse, fencing, and softball for girls.

The St. Luke's calendar features special annual events that are traditional to the School such as Homecoming, Winter Concert, Spring Concert, the Junior/Senior Prom, Scholarship Banquet, and Commencement.

ADMISSION AND COSTS. St. Luke's welcomes qualified students without regard to race, creed, color, or sex. The Director of Admissions interviews each candidate and his or her parents. Admission is based on the completed application with a $35 fee, previous school transcripts, two personal recommendations, the ISEE admissions test, and a campus visit. A $1500 registration fee, credited toward tuition, is due upon acceptance.

In 1999–2000, tuition fees range from $16,500 in Grade 5 to $17,160 in Grades 9–12. Extras include lunches, transportation, and miscellaneous art, photography, and athletic fees. A tuition payment plan is available. Each year, St. Luke's awards a significant portion of its budget to financial-aid applicants based on need.

Assistant Headmaster: Robert Cook
Director of Studies: Julia Gabriele
Dean of Students: Carl Moeller
Middle School Head: Gareth Fancher
Alumni President: Fran Peacock
Director of Admissions and Communications: Carol Pursley
Director of Advancement: Diana Pulman
Director of College Counseling: Tim Cantrick
Business Administrator: Judith Sherwood
Directors of Athletics: Camille DeMarco-Havens (Girls) and Emil N. Bucci (Boys)

St. Margaret's-McTernan School   1972

565 Chase Parkway, Waterbury, CT 06708-3394. 203-236-9500; Fax 203-236-9494; E-mail dgoodman@smmct.org; Web Site www.smmct.org

St. Margaret's-McTernan was formed by the merger of St. Margaret's (founded 1865) and McTernan School (1912). The independent, nonsectarian, college preparatory day school enrolls 436 boys and girls in Prekindergarten to Grade 12. The School seeks to promote intellectual growth, artistic creativity, physical development, self-discipline, and personal values. Art, music, drama, computers, physical education, and interscholastic athletics are an integral part of the program. A day camp and academic, enrichment, and sports programs are offered in the summer. Tuition: $8300–$14,950. Financial aid is available.

Douglas J. Goodman is Director of Admission; Margaret W. Field (University of Bridgeport) is Head of School. *New England Association.*

Saint Thomas More School   OAKDALE

45 Cottage Road, Oakdale, CT 06370. 860-859-1900; Admissions Telephone 860-823-3861; Fax 860-859-2989; Admissions Fax 860-823-3863

SAINT THOMAS MORE SCHOOL in Oakdale, Connecticut, is a Roman Catholic, college preparatory boarding school for boys encompassing Grades 8 through 12 and a postgraduate year. Its lakeside campus is located in a rural area of eastern Connecticut, about 25 miles from New London and 10 miles from Norwich. The School is easily accessible by car from Interstates 395 and 95.

Saint Thomas More School was founded in 1962 by the first Headmaster, James F. Hanrahan, Sr. A long-time teacher and coach at Fairfield College Preparatory School, he purchased the property that became the Saint Thomas More campus in 1957 and ran a summer camp program there for several years. His experience helped him to recognize that many boys who have ability are persistent underachievers because they lack skills and discipline and do not have a setting in which they are encouraged to devote full effort to their studies. The School was founded to help such boys develop intellectually, physically, morally, and socially.

The School is dedicated to the preparation of all students for college education. It maintains a rigorous academic program, gives particular attention to the development of study skills, and provides extra help and peer tutoring where necessary. Boys adhere to a dress code during the academic day. All students participate in athletics and are expected not only to improve their performance but to learn the values of sportsmanship and good conduct. A Counseling Center provides help for students who are trying to work through problems in their lives.

The School accepts students of all faiths. A priest is available to assist students in their spiritual development. Students are obliged to attend Sunday Mass and have the option of attending two weekday Masses.

Saint Thomas More School is incorporated as a nonprofit organization governed by a Board of 12 Trustees, including alumni and parents. Active alumni and parent organizations provide financial support through an annual fund.

THE CAMPUS. The School is situated on 100 wooded acres on the shore of Gardner Lake, the largest natural lake in eastern Connecticut. Numerous athletic fields and ample lawns enhance the campus aspect.

Facilities include an administration building, a new admissions building, a new chapel, dining hall, three classroom wings, and a library. The library has a technology center with Internet stations. A separate computer laboratory offers personal computers and is used by computer and other academic classes such as Mathematics and English. Three dormitories provide facilities for 190 boys, most in double rooms and some in singles. Faculty members are resident in apartments within each dormitory, and many faculty houses are located on campus.

Athletic fields are provided for football, baseball, track, soccer, and lacrosse. A fully equipped gymnasium and indoor swimming pool are also available. A boathouse is located on the 4000-foot lakefront.

THE FACULTY. James F. Hanrahan, Jr., a member of the Class of 1972 and son of the founder, was appointed Headmaster in 1997. Mr. Hanrahan is a graduate of Fairfield University (B.S. in Mathematics) and Boston College (M.Ed.). He has been a teacher of mathematics, physics, and computers at Saint Thomas More School since 1976 and has also been coach of various athletic teams. He served the School as Business Manager and Assistant Headmaster before his present appointment. Mr. Hanrahan lives on campus with his wife, Gina, and two daughters.

The full-time teaching faculty includes 21 men and 4 women, all of whom live on campus. They hold 25 bachelor's degrees and 9 advanced degrees from American University, Boston College, Canisius 2, Central Connecticut 3, Connecticut College, Curry, Duke, Fairfield 2, Hobart, Holy Apostles 3, Linfield, Lynchburg, Mary Washington, Providence 3, Sacred Heart, Seton Hall, Skidmore, Southern Connecticut, State University of New York (Stony Brook), Temple, Westminster Choir College 2, and the Universities of Connecticut 2, Oregon, and Rhode Island.

A school nurse is on duty five days a week. Medical personnel are on hand for all home athletic contests.

STUDENT BODY. In 1999–2000, the School enrolled 190 boarding students. They were distributed as follows: Grade 8—12, Grade 9—28, Grade 10—36, Grade 11—40, Grade 12—52,

and Postgraduate—22. Students come from Connecticut, 17 other states, and 11 foreign countries. International students make up about 15 percent of the enrollment.

ACADEMIC PROGRAM. The academic year, divided into quarters, begins in early September and ends in late May. Vacations are scheduled for three days at Thanksgiving, two weeks at Christmas, a one-week midwinter break in February, one week in March, and one week at Easter. Classes are held five days a week and are scheduled in seven periods of approximately 45 minutes each between 8:25 A.M. and 1:45 P.M. A typical class has 12 students. Teachers remain in their classrooms for another period to offer extra help at the end of each class day. There is no limit on their availability to provide help, and peer tutors may also assist. A supervised study hall is scheduled for all students from 7:30 to 9:30 P.M. Sunday through Thursday evenings. Students in academic difficulty may be required to remain on campus for weekends and to attend a supervised study hall for two hours. Report cards with numerical averages, letter grades for effort, and written comments from teachers are given to students by their advisors and are sent to parents four times a year. A College Placement Office helps students to take a systematic approach to choosing colleges.

To graduate from Saint Thomas More School, a student must complete four credits in English, two in one foreign language, one in U.S. History, three in mathematics, one in laboratory science, one in religion, and one in fine arts. Postgraduate certificates are issued for successful completion of all courses in which the student is enrolled. A postgraduate is expected to study three hours a day, five days a week, to prepare for a successful college career.

Instructors are expected to teach not only their subjects but the study skills needed to master them. They concentrate on developing better listening and note-taking skills, time and stress management, memory techniques, improved test performance, and overall study plans.

Among the courses offered are Language Arts, English 8–10, American Literature, British Literature, World Literature; English as a Second Language 1–3; Spanish 1–3; Introduction to U.S. History, Global Studies, World History, U.S. History, Presidential Politics, Ancient and Medieval History, Economics; Pre-Algebra, Algebra 1–2, Geometry, Pre-Calculus, Calculus, Postgraduate Math, Introduction to Computers, Programming in Pascal; Life Science, Earth Science, Biology, Environmental Science, Chemistry, Physics; Music Appreciation, Art Appreciation; and Morality, Mythology, Death and Dying, and Comparative Religions.

A six-week, coeducational summer academic camp offers make-up, enrichment, and review courses, including English as a Second Language, for students in Grades 7–12. The camp begins in late June.

In 1999, the School graduated 46 seniors and issued 18

postgraduate certificates to students now enrolled at Assumption, Babson, Belmont Abbey, Boston University, Coastal Carolina 2, College of New Jersey, Concordia, C.W. Post, Detroit, Eastern Connecticut 3, Emory, Endicott, Fort Hays State, Franklin Pierce 2, Glendale Junior College, Gonzaga, Hofstra, Instituto Technologico de Monterrey, Lafayette, Lindenwood, Maine Maritime, Massachusetts College, Massachusetts Maritime, Mitchell, Nazareth College, New Hampshire College 2, North Carolina State, Old Dominion, Quinnipiac, Ramapo, Rider, Sacred Heart, St. John's University, Saint Louis University, St. Michael's 2, Seton Hall, State University of New York 2, Stonehill, and the Universities of California (Berkeley), Cincinnati, Colorado 2, Connecticut 2, Detroit, Massachusetts 2, New Haven, Puerto Rico, the South, Tampa, and Texas.

STUDENT ACTIVITIES. Students elect class representatives to a nine-member Student Council. The Council works with a faculty advisor to improve student life by enhancing recreational facilities, organizing social events and activities, and raising funds for various causes.

Student clubs are organized according to interests. Among the ongoing organizations are the student newspaper and yearbook, Altar Boys, Community Service, Big Brother Program, and the Ski and Dining clubs.

Afternoon athletics, dedicated to the development of good sportsmanship, competitiveness, self-discipline, and confidence, is a tradition at Saint Thomas More School. All students participate on teams or in a program of physical fitness and skill development, and everyone can compete for places on interscholastic teams. The School is a member of the Southeastern New England Athletic Conference, a division of the New England Prep School Athletic Conference. Varsity teams are fielded in football, soccer, cross-country, crew, basketball (varsity, postgraduate, junior varsity, and freshman), ice hockey, baseball, lacrosse, tennis, and golf. Intramural sports include volleyball, touch football, weight training, basketball, fencing, swimming, Ultimate Frisbee, and soccer.

On weekends, trips are often organized for movies, athletic events, and theatrical performances. The School cosponsors dances with sister schools. Special events on the calendar include Parents Day and Open House, Christmas Party, Multicultural Day, Spelling Bee, Talent Show, Spring Spree, and Alumni Weekend.

ADMISSION AND COSTS. Saint Thomas More seeks students who have college potential and who will benefit from the structured programs the School offers. Students are accepted in all grades after review of academic records and results of standardized tests and a personal interview. Candidates for the senior and postgraduate years must submit SAT scores. International students should submit SLEP or TOEFL results and may be asked to take additional tests for placement. Because admissions decisions are rendered on a rolling basis starting in February, early application is very important. Applicants are notified within two weeks of receipt of all materials.

In 1999–2000, tuition, including room, board, books, athletic gear, and laundry, is $18,325. For international students, tuition is $21,325, which includes instruction in English as a Second Language. A limited number of grants are awarded on the basis of need.

Academic Dean: Jay K. Thornton
Director of Admissions: Todd A. Holt
Business Manager: Sean Hanrahan
Director of Athletics: Scott Ruggles

St. Thomas's Day School 1956

830 Whitney Avenue, New Haven, CT 06511. 203-776-2123; Fax 203-776-3467; E-mail stthomas@connix.com

St. Thomas's is an Episcopal day school serving 160 children in Junior Kindergarten–Grade 6. As a mission of St. Thomas's Church, the School strives to educate students of all backgrounds by cultivating intelligence while engaging heart and spirit. It fosters academic excellence through a challenging, integrated curriculum with attention to each child's potential and learning style. St. Thomas's is characterized by a strong sense of community, a genuine commitment to children, and active parent participation. Extended-day and summer programs are available. Tuition: $10,665. Financial Aid: $245,000. Fred Acquavita (Kansas State, B.S. 1968; Bank Street, M.S. 1981) was appointed School Head in 1981.

Salisbury School SALISBURY

Route 44, Salisbury, CT 06068. 860-435-5700; Fax 860-435-5750; E-mail cchandler@salisburyschool.org
Web Site www.salisburyschool.org

S ALISBURY SCHOOL in Salisbury, Connecticut, is a college preparatory boarding and day school enrolling boys in Forms III–VI (Grades 9–12). The village of Salisbury is located in the foothills of the Berkshire Mountains. The campus is one hour from Hartford, two hours from New York, and two and a half hours from Boston, giving students access to the cultural and recreational resources of those cities and permitting shared activities with other private secondary schools and colleges in the region.

The Reverend George Emerson Quaile, an Episcopal clergyman, founded Salisbury School in 1901. From its inception, the School has sought to imbue young men with the self-confidence necessary to develop their maximum potential intellectually, morally, and physically. Salisbury seeks to foster trust, service to others, and faith based on Judeo-Christian values while promoting respect and appreciation for all backgrounds and beliefs.

The School is guided by a 29-member Board of Trustees and is accredited by the New England Association of Colleges and Secondary Schools. It holds membership in the National Association of Independent Schools and the Connecticut Association of Independent Schools, among other organizations. The Alumni Association is active in fund-raising, recruitment, and other functions supportive of Salisbury's goals. The School's endowment is valued at approximately $21,500,000.

THE CAMPUS. Salisbury is situated on a 700-acre campus, bordered on the west by the Appalachian Trail and on the north by Twin Lakes. The Main Building (1901) houses the School's newly refurbished dining hall, the kitchen, bookstore, post office, and administrative and faculty offices. Academic facilities are centered in the new Wachtmeister Mathematics and Science

Building, opened in September 1999. Other facilities include the Rudd Reading Center, art studios, a photography laboratory, and the solar car garage. The Phinny Library contains 23,000 volumes, 120 periodicals, the language and audiovisual center, and the Foreign Language Department. The library also provides CD-ROM access to a wide range of reference materials in major library collections across the country and maintains a video collection that enhances the curriculum.

Residential facilities include nine dormitories, seven faculty houses, and the Headmaster's home. Salisbury School provides phone service, voice mail, a campus computer network, and Internet services to every student's room.

Among the School's athletic facilities are the newly renovated, Olympic-size Rudd Hockey Rink with an all-purpose playing surface that includes three indoor tennis courts. Other offerings include the Harvey Childs gymnasium, seven outdoor tennis courts, two heated platform tennis courts, a lake, the Kulukundis Boathouse, and miles of cross-country trails. New soccer, baseball, lacrosse, and football fields were completed for the current school year. Additionally, Salisbury maintains a fully equipped weight training room and a rehab center on campus.

THE FACULTY. Appointed in 1988, Richard T. Flood, Jr., the School's sixth Headmaster, attended Noble and Greenough School, Williams College (B.A.), and Brown University (M.A.). His 42 years in education include 21 years as teacher, coach, and administrator at Noble and Greenough, where a scholarship has been established in his name. Under his leadership, the School recently completed a $10,000,000 campaign and developed Salisbury's Long Range Plan. Mr. Flood resides on campus with his wife, Sally.

The Salisbury School faculty and administration consist of 60 members. Thirty-one members hold advanced degrees, including two doctorates. Colleges and universities represented by faculty members include Amherst, Bates, Boston University, Brown, Colby, Dartmouth, Dickinson, Hamilton, Ithaca, New York University, Northeastern, Pennsylvania State, Smith, Temple, Trinity, Tufts, Vassar, Wesleyan, Williams, Yale, and the Universities of Connecticut, Illinois, Iowa, North Carolina, Texas, and Vermont.

The Health Center is staffed by a resident registered nurse, available 24 hours a day, and a medical doctor, who holds office hours for students on campus four days per week. A full-time athletic trainer lives on campus.

STUDENT BODY. In 1999–2000, Salisbury School enrolled 257 boys, 95 percent of whom were boarders, distributed as follows: Form III—37, Form IV—69, Form V—77, and Form VI—74. The largest numbers came from New York 77 and Connecticut 70, with 26 other states and 14 nations represented.

ACADEMIC PROGRAM. The school year, divided into trimesters, extends from early September to early June, with a Thanksgiving recess and Christmas, midwinter, and spring breaks. Each student is assigned an advisor who guides him and maintains contact with his parents regarding all aspects of school life. Reports and written comments from teachers are sent home regularly, and grades are issued to the student every five weeks as a gauge of academic progress. In addition, the Headmaster issues written comments on each boy at least once a year, and the entire faculty reviews each student's overall record. Teachers and advisors are available for consultation whenever necessary. The student-teacher ratio is 6:1, with an average class enrolling 11 boys.

Students who need extra help in reading, spelling, time planning, and other academic areas may be tested and referred to the Rudd Reading Center for one-on-one tutoring. A fee is charged for this service.

Classes are held six days a week, with half days on Wednesday and Saturday. A typical schedule begins with breakfast from 6:45 to 7:30 A.M., followed by dorm cleanup and seven 45-minute periods. All students take part in sports from 3:00 to 5:00 P.M. After dinner, evening study is held from 7:30 to 9:30 P.M., and boys must be back in their dorms at 10:15 P.M.

To earn the Salisbury diploma, a student must take four years of English; three years of history, including U.S. History; three years of mathematics; three years of one foreign language or two years each of two languages; two years of laboratory science; two trimesters of art; and one year of theology. Students must pass all their courses in the senior year to graduate.

Among the courses offered are English, Journalism, Political Literature, Modern Drama; United States History, German History, Russian History, American Military History (Civil War); Algebra 1, Algebra 2 and Trigonometry, Geometry, Pre-Calculus, Probability and Statistics, Calculus, Accounting; French I–IV, Spanish I–IV, Latin; Physical Science, Earth Science, Chemistry, Biology, Physics, Environmental Science, Freshwater Ecology, Forestry; Photography, Drawing, Woodworking, Printmaking, Ceramics, Sculpture; and The Bible, Comparative Religion, Ethics, and Religion and Society. Honors or Advanced Placement courses in most disciplines are available to qualified students, and English as a Second Language is provided for international students. Additionally, there are opportunities to study in France or Spain through School Year Abroad or to enroll in a postgraduate year in the United Kingdom through The English-Speaking Union.

Students in Forms V and VI may undertake independent study projects in a chosen field, working under faculty supervision in lieu of a scheduled course. Sixth formers in good academic standing may, with faculty approval, explore career options off-campus for eight or ten weeks in the spring.

College counseling begins in the Fifth Form, and representatives from colleges and universities throughout the United States visit the campus regularly. Seventy percent of Salisbury's graduates are accepted to their first- or second-choice colleges, and, since 1991, two or more have enrolled in such institutions as Babson, Boston College, Boston University, Bowdoin, Brown, Clarkson, Colby, Colgate, College of Charleston, Connecticut College, Dartmouth, Dickinson, Duke, Emory, Georgetown, George Washington, Gettysburg, Hamilton, Hobart, Holy Cross, Lake Forest, Lehigh, Middlebury, Ohio Wesleyan, Providence, Rensselaer, Rhodes, St. Lawrence, Skidmore, Susquehanna, Syracuse, Trinity, Tufts, Tulane, United States Military Academy, United States Naval Academy, Union, Washington College, Williams, and the Universities of Chicago, Denver, Vermont, and Virginia.

The Salisbury Summer School of Reading and English enrolls 105 boys and girls, ages 13 to 18, in a six-week program of reading and writing.

STUDENT ACTIVITIES. Students may participate in a wide range of extracurricular activities designed to develop leadership skills as well as provide social interaction and physical well-being. The 14-member Student Council, elected from each of the four forms, works with the Headmaster and faculty in planning and implementing events and advising on disciplinary infractions. Students involved in the Vestry share in the planning and organization of chapel liturgies and spearhead the School's social outreach and community service projects.

Students publish a newspaper, a yearbook, and a literary magazine. Two singing groups, the Glee Club and the Triple Quartet, perform concerts at the School and elsewhere, while the Drama Club stages three plays each year. Other groups include The Cum Laude Society, the Key Society, and the Debating, International, Lumberjacks, Outing, and Ski clubs.

On weekends, students take part in a variety of recreational and social activities, including dances, concerts, movies, and trips to New York or Boston. Many events are held in conjunction with nearby girls' schools. Popular outdoor pursuits include hiking, skiing, canoeing, camping, rock climbing, and flyfishing.

Athletic competition is organized at the varsity, junior varsity, and third levels, and the School's 35 interscholastic teams compete in cross-country, football, soccer, skiing, basketball, hockey, tennis and platform tennis, squash, wrestling, baseball, crew, cycling, golf, kayaking, and lacrosse.

Special events on the calendar include Fall Pep Rally, Hilltop Day/Reunion, Parents Weekend, Christmas Service of Lessons and Carols, Sophomore Wilderness Challenge, Junior Retreat, College Weekend, Awards Ceremony, and Graduation Day on the Quadrangle.

ADMISSION AND COSTS. Salisbury seeks young men of good character who demonstrate the ability to succeed in a college preparatory program and to contribute to the life of the School. Acceptance is based on an interview, previous academic records, a writing sample, recommendations from current teachers, personal references, and the results of standardized tests. A nonrefundable $750 deposit is due upon registration.

Tuition in 1999–2000 is $18,500 for day students and $26,300 for boarders. Day students are assessed a general fee of $450, boarding students, $600. The technology fee is $75 for day students, $180 for boarders. Extra expenses for supplies, laundry, trips, and special tests may range from $800 to $1000. Salisbury belongs to the School and Student Service for Financial Aid and, in 1999, awarded approximately $1,300,000 to 31 percent of the student body. A tuition payment plan is offered.

Director of Admissions: Chisholm S. Chandler
Associate Director: Peter B. Gilbert
Assistant Directors of Admissions: Andrew B. Noel and Daniel J. Donato

The Taft School   1890

Watertown, CT 06795. 860-945-7777; Fax 860-945-7808; E-mail Admissions@Taft.pvt.k12.ct.us; Web Site www.Taft.pvt.k12.ct.us

Taft is an independent, coeducational, college preparatory school enrolling 446 boarding and 109 day students in Grade 9–Postgraduate. The School seeks to foster individual development through vigorous academic, athletic, and extracurricular programs, while providing "the finest of liberal arts education" through its 200-course curriculum. Advanced Placement courses are offered in every discipline. Over 40 clubs and organizations, a variety of sports, and summer enrichment courses are available. Day Tuition: $18,200; Boarding Tuition: $25,000. Financial Aid: $2,850,000. Frederick H. Wandelt III is Director of Admission; Lance R. Odden (Princeton, B.A. 1961; University of Wisconsin, M.A. 1967) was appointed Headmaster in 1972. *New England Association.*

Town Hill School   1938

204 Interlaken Road, Lakeville, CT 06039. 860-435-2855; Fax 860-435-8876

Town Hill School was founded in 1938 and enrolls 70 boys and girls in Pre-Kindergarten through Grade 4. The School seeks to instill a love of learning through a student-centered educational approach that also develops basic academic skills. Students are encouraged to be independent learners with children, teachers, and parents as partners in the educational process. A well-balanced curriculum is enhanced by art, music, Spanish, computer, and physical education. A priority is placed upon exciting a child's natural curiosity and encouraging responsible citizenship. The student-teacher ratio is 8:1. Tuition: $7200–$7900. Susan F. Eanes is Director of Admission/Development; William R. Osier (B.A., M.A.) was appointed Headmaster in 1998.

Watkinson School   1881

180 Bloomfield Avenue, Hartford, CT 06105. 860-236-5618; Fax 860-233-8295; Web Site www.watkinson.org

A member of the Coalition of Essential Schools, Watkinson, enrolling 245 day boys and girls in Grades 6–Postgraduate, offers college preparatory and specialized arts curricula. Special courses are available in Writing, Computers, and Learning Skills. A Transition-to-College Year for high school graduates who may take courses at the University of Hartford is available. Homestays for international students and summer courses are provided. A $4,500,000 Arts & Athletic Center and a Computer Center are among the facilities. Activities include sports, dance, and theater. Tuition: $17,575. Financial Aid: $1,120,000. John J. Crosson is Director of Admission and Financial Aid; John W. Bracker (Haverford, B.A. 1984; Harvard, M.Ed. 1992) is Headmaster. *New England Association.*

Westminster School   1888

995 Hopmeadow Street, P.O. Box 337, Simsbury, CT 06070.
860-408-3000; Admissions 860-408-3060; Fax 860-408-3001;
E-mail admit@westminster-school.com;
Web Site www.westminster-school.com

Westminster School is a college preparatory school enrolling 133 boarding boys, 53 day boys, 102 boarding girls, and 67 day girls in Grades 9–12. Confident in its identity and traditions, the School strives to develop in students a sense of responsibility—not only to the community, but to their own aptitudes, strengths, and opportunities. The balanced liberal arts curriculum includes more than 80 course offerings taught by a 72-member faculty. Students participate in athletics, music, theater, publications, chapel, and social services. Boarding Tuition: $26,200; Day Tuition: $18,700. Financial Aid: $1,650,000. Jon C. Deveaux is Director of Admissions; W. Graham Cole, Jr. (Williams College, B.A.; Columbia University, M.A.), was appointed Headmaster in 1993. *New England Association.*

Westover School   1909

Whittemore Road, P.O. Box 847, Middlebury, CT 06762.
203-758-2423; Fax 203-577-4588; E-mail admission@
westover.pvt.k12.ct.us; Web Site www.westover.pvt.k12.ct.us

Westover, enrolling 125 boarding and 65 day students, is an academically rigorous school dedicated to challenging young women in Grades 9–12 to participate in all aspects of academic, community, and athletic life. Students take advantage of numerous electives, 17 Advanced Placement courses, visual and performing arts, and outdoor activities. Women in Science and Engineering, a joint program with Rensselaer Polytechnic Institute, and joint programs for preprofessional musicians with the Manhattan School of Music and for dancers with the Hartford School of Ballet enhance the curriculum. Boarding Tuition: $23,500; Day Tuition: $15,700. Financial Aid: $1,400,000. Kristin W. Martinkovic is Director of Admission; Ann S. Pollina (New York University, M.A.) is Head of School. *New England Association.*

Whitby School   1958

969 Lake Avenue, Greenwich, CT 06831. 203-869-8464;
Fax 203-869-2215

As the oldest American Montessori school, Whitby is committed to providing an educational experience that encourages children to become confident, competent, and joyful learners for life. The School enrolls more than 340 day boys and girls, ages 18 months–14 years, in a program designed to foster self-discipline and active involvement in the learning process. In multiage classrooms with Montessori-trained teachers, students work individually or in small groups in a developmentally appropriate learning sequence. The core curriculum, including foreign language, is enhanced by music, art, and physical education. Tuition: $8100–$15,300. Deirdre Fennessy is Director of Admission; Brenda Mizel (University of Chicago, B.A. 1983) is Head of School.

Wightwood School   1971

56 Stony Creek Road, Branford, CT 06405. 203-481-0363;
Fax 203-488-3985; E-mail wtmccoy@yahoo.com

Enrolling 83 children in PreK–Grade 8, Wightwood aims to provide a challenging program in a learning environment that is responsive to individual needs while fostering intellectual curiosity, creativity, confidence, and social responsibility. The curriculum follows a thematic approach in which a single grade-appropriate topic integrates all the academic disciplines. Specialists teach art, music, physical education, Spanish, library and multicultural studies at all levels. Small classes encourage strong relationships among students, faculty, and parents. Extended-day services, a flexible PreKindergarten schedule, a full-day Kindergarten, and summer sessions are offered. Tuition: $4800–$10,800. Walter T. McCoy (University of New Orleans, B.A., M.A.) is Head of School.

The Williams School   1891

182 Mohegan Avenue, New London, CT 06320-4110.
860-443-5333; Fax 860-439-2796;
E-mail admissions@williamsschool.org

Founded by Harriet Peck Williams, The Williams School is a college preparatory day school enrolling 135 boys and 150 girls in Grades 7–12. The School's mission is to "foster the intellectual, moral, and aesthetic development of young men and women in preparation for a lifetime of learning and active participation in a changing society." The School is situated on the grounds of Connecticut College, and selected seniors may take college courses. Extracurricular activities include sports, drama, music, and community service. Tuition: $12,600. Extras: $400–$1000. Financial Aid: $425,000. Karen Wehr is Director of Admission; Charlotte Rea (Lake Erie College, B.A.; New York University, M.A.; Columbia University, M.Ed.) is Head of School. *New England Association.*

The Woodhall School   1982

Box 550, Harrison Lane, Bethlehem, CT 06751. 203-266-7788;
Fax 203-266-5896

Woodhall offers an individualized educational program for young men of average to superior ability who have not succeeded in traditional schools. The School enrolls 42 boarding and day students in a college preparatory or general curriculum that features small classes, one-on-one instruction, remediation, and English as a Second Language. Students take part in a Communications Program for Skills of Self-Expression with Accountability, sports, community service, clubs, and social and recreational activities with area schools. Boarding Tuition: $36,500; Day Tuition: $25,600. Sally Campbell Woodhall (University of Paris, B.es L. 1963, C.E.L.G. 1965; Fordham, M.A. 1967, M.A. 1969) was appointed Head of School in 1983. *New England Association.*

Wooster School   1926

Ridgebury Road, Danbury, CT 06810. 203-830-3900;
Fax 203-790-7147; E-mail admissions@woostersch.org;
Web Site http://www.woostersch.org

Set high on a 150-acre hillside campus, Wooster enrolls 405 day students in Kindergarten–Grade 12. Throughout its 72-year history, Wooster has been guided by four cardinal principles: Intellectual Excellence, Simplicity, Religion, and Hard Work. The college preparatory Upper School offers honors and Advanced Placement courses, a year-abroad program to France and Spain, and a strong emphasis on moral and ethical values, including community service. Racial, social, economic, and cultural diversity are central to the School's educational mission and values. Tuition: $9620–$15,670. Financial aid is available. Cordelia Manning is Director of Admission; John B. Cheeseman '57 (Princeton, A.B.; Western Connecticut State, M.S.) is Headmaster. *New England Association.*

DELAWARE

Archmere Academy   1932

P.O. Box 130, 3600 Philadelphia Pike, Claymont, DE 19703.
   302-798-6632/610-485-0373; Fax 302-798-7290;
   Web Site www.archmereacademy.com

This Roman Catholic, college preparatory day school enrolls approximately 480 boys and girls in Grades 9–12. Staffed by Norbertine priests and lay faculty, the Academy maintains a student-teacher ratio of 9:1. Curriculum requirements include math, science, foreign language, religion, history, and English; electives include music, art, computer, and speech. Advanced Placement courses cover 18 subjects. Computer, writing, and language labs; media and guidance centers; and a full range of sports and activities are offered. Tuition: $11,830. Extras: $250–$1300. Financial aid is available. Daniel E. Hickey is Director of Admissions; The Reverend Timothy F. Mullen, O.PRAEM. (Villanova University, M.A.), was appointed Headmaster in 1997. *Middle States Association.*

Centreville School   1974

6201 Kennett Pike, Centreville, DE 19807. 302-571-0230;
   Fax 302-571-0270; E-mail adminasst@centrevilleschool.org

Centreville School, enrolling 101 children ages 4–13, equips learning-disabled students of average or above-average intelligence with the tools they need to succeed. The School's small classes, committed teachers, and nurturing environment provide students the self-esteem and strategies they need in order to rise above their challenges. Centreville is the only school in the area with a reading specialist, two speech/language therapists, and an occupational therapist on staff to aid in each child's educational program. Students are placed in developmentally based, ungraded classrooms. Tuition: $14,200. Need-based financial aid is available. Paul Capodanno is Director of Admissions; Victoria C. Yatzus (University of Newcastle upon Tyne, B.S.; University of Delaware, M.Ed.) is Head of School. *Middle States Association.*

The Independence School   1978

1300 Paper Mill Road, Newark, DE 19711. 302-239-0330

This coeducational day school enrolling 722 students in PreSchool (age 3)–Grade 8 strives for academic excellence in a structured environment that reflects traditional Judeo-Christian values. The curriculum emphasizes basic skills and the arts. Foreign language study (German, French, Spanish) and computer education begin in Grade 1; Latin is offered in Grades 5–8. Activities include jazz and concert bands, 11 sports, yearbook, chorus, computer club, drama club, Science Olympiad, Math League, Math Counts, and Odyssey of the Mind. Twelve-month extended care is offered. Tuition: $7300. Michele Wingrave is Director of Admission; Kenneth M. Weinig (Manhattan College, B.A. 1965; Fordham, M.A. 1967; University of Delaware, Ed.D. 1994) was appointed Headmaster in 1978.

The Pilot School, Inc.   1957

100 Garden of Eden Road, Wilmington, DE 19803. 302-478-1740;
   Fax 302-478-1746; E-mail Pilotskool@aol.com

Pilot School, enrolling 150 boys and girls ages 5–14 in an 11-month program, was established to meet the needs of bright students with learning differences. Its goal is to provide them with the specific learning tools, individual attention, and guidance they need to realize their full potential and achieve academic and personal success. Pilot's ungraded, language-based curriculum emphasizes the mastery of reading, writing, spelling, listening, and speaking skills. Dedicated, qualified faculty are supported by specialized therapists, and computer technology and library resources are integral to the learning process. Music, art, and physical education enrich the core curriculum. Tuition: $14,554. Kathleen B. Craven is Director.

St. Andrew's School   MIDDLETOWN

350 Noxontown Road, Middletown, DE 19709. 302-378-9511;
   E-mail lzendt@standrews-de.org; Web Site www.standrews-de.org

ST. ANDREW'S SCHOOL in Middletown, Delaware, is a coeducational, college preparatory boarding school enrolling students in Grades 9 through 12. The campus is three miles southeast of Middletown in lower New Castle County, an area of rich farmland and historic associations. The Chesapeake and Delaware bays are nearby, and tidal streams, lakes, ponds, and woods are plentiful. Middletown is 25 miles south of Wilmington and within range of Washington, D.C., Baltimore, Philadelphia, and New York City, all of which are visited by classes for various cultural activities. Wilmington is served by air, rail, and interstate highway, and buses run to Middletown, which lies on U.S. Route 301.

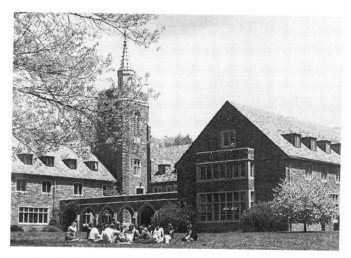

St. Andrew's School was founded in 1929 by A. Felix duPont. It was Mr. duPont's intention to establish a school of "a definitely Christian character," which would provide "an educational opportunity open to all, regardless of means." The first Headmaster, Reverend Walden Pell, set high standards of scholarship during his tenure, which ended in 1958. His successor, Robert Moss, broadened the curriculum, enlarged the student body, and introduced coeducation in 1973. Jonathan B. O'Brien, appointed as the School's third Headmaster in 1977, made many significant improvements to the campus facilities during his 20-year tenure.

St. Andrew's maintains a commitment to liberal education and strives to equip its students with the skills and understanding necessary to achieve their full potential. The School places an emphasis on community life, encourages close associations between students and faculty, and maintains an affiliation with the Episcopal church. Students are required to attend chapel services on Sunday mornings and Wednesday evenings.

St. Andrew's is accredited by the Middle States Association of Colleges and Schools and holds membership in the National Association of Independent Schools, among other associations.

THE CAMPUS. The School is situated on 2600 acres, flanked on three sides by bodies of water. Playing fields for football, soccer, field hockey, lacrosse, and baseball, a 3.1-mile cross-country course, 2 paddle tennis courts, 9 all-weather tennis courts, and boating facilities, including a 6-lane crew course, are on the campus.

Delaware

Founders' Hall, built in stages between 1929 and 1956, is a three-story building housing classrooms, computer labs, and the Irene duPont Library, which provides 30,000 volumes, 200 periodicals, an audiovisual center, and language laboratory. A 370-seat theater is part of Founders' Hall. The Amos Science Building (1967) offers science laboratories and classrooms, a lecture hall, photography darkroom, greenhouse, aquarium, astronomy deck, computer center, instrument and supply rooms, and a woodworking shop. An art gallery, music rooms, and a rehearsal hall are in a wing of Cameron Gymnasium; art studios are located in another building. The Edith Pell Student Center provides recreational facilities. Indoor athletic resources include two basketball courts, two wrestling rooms, five squash courts, a weight room, dance studio, rifle range, and a new six-lane swimming pool.

THE FACULTY. Daniel T. Roach, a graduate of The Nichols School, Williams College (B.A. 1979), and Middlebury College (M.A. 1984), was appointed the School's fourth Headmaster in 1997. He had formerly been a teacher, coach, and Assistant Headmaster at St. Andrew's School. His wife, Elizabeth Roach, teaches English. The Roaches live on campus with their three children.

The full-time faculty includes 35 men and 24 women; 54 faculty live on campus. They hold baccalaureate degrees from Amherst 3, Bard, Bates, Bowdoin 2, Brown 2, Colby 2, College of Wooster, Corpus Christi State, Dartmouth 3, Davidson, Duke 2, George Washington, Harvard, Haverford 4, Kenyon, Middlebury 2, Mount Holyoke, Oberlin, Peabody Conservatory, Pomona, Princeton 3, Purdue, Smith, Soochow University (Taiwan), State University of New York, Towson State, Trinity, Tufts, West Chester State, Williams 5, Yale 3, and the Universities of Delaware 2, Illinois, North Carolina, Orléans (France), Pennsylvania, the South, Tennessee, and Virginia. They also hold 46 advanced degrees, including 3 doctorates.

A registered nurse lives on campus and she or her assistant are available 24 hours a day. A school physician is on call, and two hospitals are within minutes of the campus.

STUDENT BODY. In 1999–2000, the School enrolls 142 boarding boys and 129 boarding girls as follows: 47 in Grade 9, 72 in Grade 10, 79 in Grade 11, and 73 in Grade 12. Students represent 26 states and ten foreign countries, with the largest groups from Delaware, Maryland, New Jersey, New York, Pennsylvania, and Virginia.

ACADEMIC PROGRAM. The academic year, divided into trimesters, begins in early September and ends in early June, with vacations of one week at Thanksgiving, two weeks at Christmas, and three weeks in the spring. Classes are held six days a week and are scheduled in 45-minute periods between 8:05 A.M. and 3:25 P.M., except on Tuesdays and Saturdays when the class day

is shortened. The average class has 11 students and meets nine times in a two-week cycle. Sports teams practice from 3:45 to 5:30 P.M. most days. Teachers are available for tutorial assistance and students have a quiet study period from 7:30 to 9:30 P.M. on school evenings. Grades are sent to parents three times a year along with teacher comments, and the student's adviser writes a review at the half-term in the fall and winter, and a complete review in June.

To graduate, a student must complete a minimum of 18 credits that include four in English, three in mathematics, two in foreign language, two in religious studies, two in history, and two in laboratory science. Students plan their programs each spring with their advisers.

Among the courses offered are English 1–4, covering grammar, composition, and literature up through the college freshman level; Public Speaking; French 1–5, French Civilization, Advanced Spoken French, Spanish 1–5, Hispanic Literature, Conversational Spanish, Advanced Spanish Composition, Chinese 1–2, Latin 1–5, Introductory Greek; United States History, Advanced American History, Western Civilization, Twentieth Century History, Early European and International Relations, History of East Asia; Algebra 1–2, Plane Geometry, Computer Programming, Pre-Calculus, Calculus AB and BC, Advanced Placement Statistics, Probability and Statistics, Finite Math, Topics in Mathematics; Biology 1–2, Chemistry 1–2, Physics 1–2, Advanced Placement Environmental Science, Art in Biology, Aquatic Biology, Astronomy, Human Anatomy, Computer Applications in Science, Optics, History of Science; Old and New Testaments, Health and Human Potential, Gender Issues in the 20th Century, Theology in Contemporary Film and Fiction, Introduction to World Religions, Religion in America; Introduction to Music, History of Music, Music Theory 1–2, Composition, Music Studio Seminar, Instrumental and Voice Lessons; and Studio Art, Materials and Techniques, Art History, Drawing, Printmaking, Pottery, Photography, and Studio Art Seminar. Honors and Advanced Placement courses are offered.

All 74 graduates of the Class of 1999 went on to college. They are attending Amherst, Boston University, Bowdoin, Brown, Carleton, Colby, Colorado College, Columbia, Connecticut College, Dartmouth, Davidson, Denison, Dickinson, Duke, Georgetown, George Washington, Georgia Institute of Technology, Hampshire, Harvard, Haverford, Kenyon, Massachusetts Institute of Technology, Middlebury, Mount Holyoke, New College, Oberlin, Princeton, Rice, Trinity, United States Naval Academy, and the Universities of Delaware, Rochester, South Carolina, Texas, Virginia, and Wisconsin.

STUDENT ACTIVITIES. Students share with faculty many responsibilities for the conduct of school life. Joint faculty-student committees deal with decorum, discipline, honor code, athletics, social activities, residential life, and vestry. Seniors also supervise the job program, which involves all students in cleaning, maintenance, and monitoring duties.

Other activities include the school newspaper, literary magazine, yearbook, band, choir, community service, Model United Nations, and clubs embracing such interests as astronomy, chamber music, chess, foreign languages, forestry, opera, outings, recycling, and sailing. Three dramatic productions are staged each year including a winter-term musical.

St. Andrew's is a member of the Delaware Independent School Conference and fields varsity teams in cross-country, football, soccer, basketball, squash, wrestling, baseball, crew, lacrosse, swimming, and tennis for boys, and cross-country, field hockey, volleyball, soccer, basketball, squash, crew, lacrosse, swimming, and tennis for girls. Aerobics is offered as a noncompetitive sport.

The concert choir and student chamber, jazz, rock, string, and folk ensembles give performances on campus, which are supplemented by visiting artists. Movies, dances, and shopping trips are scheduled routinely. Trips are also arranged to concerts, baseball games, museums, zoos, and theater.

Special events on the school calendar include Parents' Weekend, Christmas Carols Service, Sports Banquets, Arts Weekend, and Alumni Dinner.

ADMISSION AND COSTS. St. Andrew's School seeks students of good character whose past performance, enthusiasm, and willingness to contribute to the School's life give promise of success. Students are admitted in all grades but most enter in Grades 9 and 10. Acceptance is based on standardized test scores, a completed application, and a personal interview. Application, with a $35 fee, should be submitted by January 15.

In 1999–2000, tuition is $21,000; extras, including books, private music lessons, studio and lab materials, and personal expenses, should not exceed $800. St. Andrew's subscribes to the School and Student Service for Financial Aid and, in 1999–2000, awarded $1,500,000 to 40 percent of the student body based on need.

Assistant Headmaster for Residential Life: Peter J. Caldwell
Dean of Academics: Monica Matouk
Dean of Students: Harvey Zendt
Director of Admission: Louisa H. Zendt
Director of Development: Franchesa M. Profaci
College Counselor: Aimeclaire Roche
Business Manager: Michael C. Schuller
Director of Athletics, Boys: Robert M. Colburn
Director of Athletics, Girls: Gail A. LeBlanc

St. Mark's High School   1969

Pike Creek Road, Wilmington, DE 19808. 302-738-3300;
Fax 302-738-5132

St. Mark's High School is a Roman Catholic, diocesan day school enrolling 836 girls and 727 boys in Grades 9–12. The School aims to foster intellectual, spiritual, and social development according to each student's needs. The curriculum lists 300 courses on five ability levels, ranging from remedial to Advanced Placement. Extracurricular activities, including the Student Council, 47 boys' and girls' athletic teams, 19 clubs, 3 publications, drama, and music, are encouraged. Tuition: $5250. Financial Aid: $320,000. Mrs. Rachael Ali is Associate Principal. Mark J. Freund (Towson University, B.A.; Loyola College [Maryland], M.Ed.) was appointed Principal in 1998. *Middle States Association.*

Salesianum School   1903

1801 North Broom Street, Wilmington, DE 19802-3891.
302-654-2495; Fax 302-654-7767;
E-mail adm@salhs.pvt.k12.de.us; Web Site www.Salesianum.org

Founded by the Oblates of St. Francis de Sales, Salesianum provides college preparatory education to 1010 day boys of all faiths in Grades 9–12. The School develops the whole person based on the spirituality of St. Francis de Sales whose philosophy can be summarized in "Live Jesus." Courses are phased according to ability within a challenging curriculum with numerous Advanced Placement courses. Sports, the arts, publications, service groups, student government, and interest clubs are integral to the Salesianum experience. Tuition: $6280. Financial Aid: $550,000. Thomas B. Curran, OSFS (Georgetown, M.A.; Catholic University, J.D.; St. Joseph's, M.B.A.), is President; John J. Fisher, OSFS (De Sales School of Theology, M.Div.; Villanova, M.A.), is Principal. *Middle States Association.*

Sanford School   1930

6900 Lancaster Pike, Hockessin, DE 19707-0888. 302-239-5263;
Fax 302-239-5389; E-mail admissions@admin.sanfordschool.org;
Web Site www.sanfordschool.org

Sanford is an independent day school enrolling 344 boys and 319 girls in Junior Kindergarten–Grade 12. The college preparatory curriculum offers performing and studio arts, foreign languages, humanities, reading programs, literature, writing, history, mathematics, sciences, computer studies, and physical education, with Advanced Placement courses in 13 subjects. Sports include soccer, field hockey, cross-country, volleyball, basketball, wrestling, baseball, tennis, lacrosse, and golf. A summer program offers enrichment and review courses. Tuition: $8500–$13,275. Financial Aid: $740,000. Patricia A. McLaughlin is Director of Admissions; Douglas MacKelcan (Hobart, B.A. 1971; Wesleyan, M.A. 1979) was appointed Interim Head of School in 1998. *Middle States Association.*

The Tatnall School   1930

1501 Barley Mill Road, Wilmington, DE 19807. 302-998-2292;
Fax 302-998-7051; E-mail headmaster@tatnall.org;
Web Site www.tatnall.org

Tatnall, a college preparatory day school enrolling 680 boys and girls age 3–Grade 12, strives to provide the highest-level academic curriculum in a nurturing environment in which each student can grow in self-esteem and meet success. Art, music, drama, and athletics complement the academic program. Numerous Advanced Placement and college-credit courses are available. Students may take part in sports and more than 30 clubs and activities. A year-round Extended Day Program provides care up to 6:00 P.M. Summer programs are offered. Tuition: $5000–$13,260. Financial aid is available. Mario Ferrucci is Director of Enrollment and Financial Aid; Eric G. Ruoss (University of Virginia, Ph.D. 1992) is Headmaster. *Middle States Association.*

Tower Hill School   1919

2813 West 17th Street, Wilmington, DE 19806. 302-575-0550;
Fax 302-657-8373; E-mail thsadmit@towerhill.org;
Web Site www.towerhill.org

Tower Hill School is a college preparatory day school that enrolls approximately 700 boys and girls in Pre-Kindergarten–Grade 12. Stressing ethical, aesthetic, and physical as well as intellectual development, the School seeks to combine a strong and demanding academic program that is responsive to the needs of its students, with strong commitments to athletics and fine arts. Integrity and excellence are stressed in all undertakings. Athletics, publications, music, and drama are extracurricular activities, and summer programs are offered. Tuition: $6100–$13,780. Extras: $230–$1290. Financial Aid: $720,800. Timothy B. Golding (Haverford College, B.A.; Villanova, M.A.) was appointed Headmaster in 1986. *Middle States Association.*

Delaware

Ursuline Academy   1893

1106 Pennsylvania Avenue, Wilmington, DE 19806.
302-658-7158; Fax 302-658-4297; Web Site www.ursuline.org

Ursuline Academy is a private, Catholic, college preparatory day school for girls and boys age 3 through Grade 3 and for girls in Grades 4 through 12. Within the Ursuline tradition of education, students are challenged to strive for academic excellence, to embrace high standards of faith and morals, to practice self-discipline, and to serve society. Rigorous academic and artistic programs are complemented by clubs and comprehensive athletics. Grades 7–12 are part of the "Learning with Laptops" program. Extended-day and summer camp programs are available. Tuition: $4550–$8975. Financial Aid: $250,000. Marie Y. Smith is Director of Admission; Barbara C. Griffin (College of St. Elizabeth, B.A.; Fairleigh Dickinson, M.A.; Rutgers, M.Ed.) is President. *Middle States Association.*

Wilmington Friends School   1748

101 School Road, Alapocas, Wilmington, DE 19803.
302-576-2900; Admission 302-576-2930; Fax 302-576-2939;
E-mail admissions@friends.wilmington.de.us;
Web Site www.friends.wilmington.de.us

Wilmington Friends School, a Quaker, college preparatory, coeducational day school that recently celebrated its 250th anniversary, enrolls 708 students in Pre-Kindergarten–Grade 12. Friends' philosophy supports the complete intellectual development of each student by requiring independent thought, principled decision-making, and a rigorous approach to all academic, artistic, athletic, and extracurricular endeavors. Service is required in all divisions. Activities include athletics, cultural arts, and publications. After-school and summer camp programs are available. Tuition: $6875–$12,400. Financial Aid: $973,546. Pamela J. Jamison is Director of Admissions; Lisa A.H. Darling (George Fox College, B.A.; Princeton Theological Seminary, M.Div.; State University of New York, M.L.S.) is Head of School. *Middle States Association.*

DISTRICT OF COLUMBIA

Beauvoir, The National Cathedral Elementary School   WASHINGTON

3500 Woodley Road, NW, Washington, DC 20016. 202-537-6485; Web Site www.beauvoir@cathedral.org

BEAUVOIR, THE NATIONAL CATHEDRAL ELEMENTARY SCHOOL in Washington, D.C., is an Episcopal, elementary day school enrolling boys and girls from Pre-Kindergarten through Grade 3. Beauvoir is situated within the 60-acre Close of the Washington National Cathedral, a magnificent Gothic structure begun in 1907 that has been the focal point of numerous significant events throughout its history. Students and faculty make frequent use of the many cultural and educational resources of the nation's capital. There is limited bus service to the School; however, most families use car pools or make their own transportation arrangements.

The Protestant Episcopal Cathedral Foundation established Beauvoir in 1933 as the elementary division of National Cathedral School; in 1939, it was recognized as an independent institution.

The School aims to provide an educational environment that will foster a lifetime enthusiasm for learning and growth while nurturing the intellectual, emotional, spiritual, physical, aesthetic, and social development of each child. Faculty teach basic skills through a broad-based, integrated curriculum enriched by offerings in science, the arts, computer, physical education, and Spanish. Developing students' understanding of themselves in relation to the larger community and establishing a diverse faculty and student body are integral to the program. The School also supports a strong relationship among parents, students, and faculty as a means of implementing its guiding mission and philosophy.

Beauvoir is guided by a self-sustaining Governing Board and is accredited by the Middle States Association of Colleges and Schools and the Association of Independent Maryland Schools. It holds membership in the National Association of Independent Schools, the Mid-Atlantic Episcopal School Asso-

ciation, and the Association of Independent Schools of Greater Washington. Beauvoir parents, as members of the Beauvoir Parents Association, participate actively in all aspects of school life such as raising significant funds for scholarships and other needs, sponsoring book fairs, organizing community service projects, and supporting the educational programs in many ways.

THE CAMPUS. Beauvoir is located on the Close of the Cathedral of St. Peter and St. Paul, known familiarly as Washington National Cathedral, and shares the grounds with the National Cathedral School for girls and St. Albans School for boys. In addition to the completely renovated main academic building, which houses classrooms for each grade level, there is an interior courtyard, landscaped playground, and fields for outdoor play.

THE FACULTY. Paula J. Carreiro was appointed Head of School in 1992. She holds a B.S. degree from Northeastern Oklahoma State University and a master's degree from Oklahoma State University.

There are 52 faculty members, including 24 classroom instructors and 16 resource teachers as well as teaching associates and a school nurse. Approximately 80 percent of the faculty hold advanced degrees, with most others seeking such degrees or participating in courses. All faculty are trained and experienced in Early Childhood and Elementary Development and Curriculum.

STUDENT BODY. In 1999–2000, Beauvoir enrolled 383 boys and girls. Students come from throughout the Greater Washington metropolitan area and represent a wide diversity of ethnic, racial, and religious backgrounds. The Governing Board has a proactive Outreach Committee charged with increasing the diversity of the applicant pool.

ACADEMIC PROGRAM. The school year, from early September to early June, includes a Thanksgiving recess, vacations in the winter and spring, and observance of national holidays. The full-day program extends from 8:30 A.M. to 3:00 P.M. Monday through Thursday, with dismissal at 2:00 P.M. on Fridays. An Extended Day option until 6:00 P.M. provides activities, snacks, a rest period, and time reserved for homework and outdoor play.

Recognizing that there are individual learning styles and paces, the School evaluates each child's progress in terms of individual development based on his or her potential as well as on specific academic accomplishments. Parent conferences are held in the early fall, the late spring, and at other times as needed. Parents receive written reports twice a year. There are three classes in Pre-Kindergarten and four each in Kindergarten through Grade 3. Classes range in size from 18 to 21, with an overall student-teacher ratio of 10:1.

Following completion of Grade 3 at Beauvoir, students enter the fourth grade at other private and public schools including St. Albans and National Cathedral School.

Summer Program sessions for children ages four to nine are conducted on campus from mid-June through July. The Summer Adventure program includes art, music, drama, sports, movement, crafts, science, and swimming. Academic and Computer programs are available for students ages six to ten.

ADMISSION AND COSTS. Beauvoir seeks students, ages four to eight, of varying backgrounds, personalities, and talents, regardless of race, creed, color, or national or ethnic origin. Applicants for Pre-Kindergarten must be four years old by September 1 of the desired year of enrollment. Tours of the School are scheduled for prospective parents from October through the middle of January. Individual testing and school visits are required. Parents are notified of admissions decisions in mid-March.

In 1999–2000, tuition is $13,368. Financial aid in the amount of more than $500,000 was awarded to 59 children on the basis of demonstrated need.

Capitol Hill Day School   1968

210 South Carolina Avenue, SE, Washington, DC 20003.
202-547-2244; Fax 202-543-4597; E-mail admissions@chds.org

Located in a historic District of Columbia school building, Capitol Hill Day serves approximately 235 students in Pre-Kindergarten–Grade 8. The School offers a strong academic program in a creative environment. Faculty make use of the resources in the metropolitan area to augment the curriculum. The art program is integrated into other subjects—math, literature, science, and social studies. French and Spanish are introduced at the early-childhood level, followed by a choice of French or Spanish in Grade 1. The selected language is continued through Grade 8.

An after-school program and a summer camp are optional. Tuition: $10,500–$11,865. Financial Aid: $279,455. Mary Beth Moore is Admissions Director; Catherine Peterson (Smith, B.A.; Goucher, M.Ed.) was appointed Director in 1985.

Edmund Burke School   1968

2955 Upton Street, NW, Washington, DC 20008. 202-362-8882;
Fax 202-362-1914; E-mail firstname_lastname@eburke.org;
Web Site www.eburke.org

Edmund Burke School, a coeducational, college preparatory day school, serves 280 students in Grades 6–12. Located conveniently near the Van Ness Metro stop, the School offers a rigorous curriculum in an informal environment. The student-teacher ratio of 7:1 and the small classes allow individual attention. Edmund Burke has a complete sports program and encourages participation in drama, music, and the arts. Advanced Placement and independent study courses are available, and the Summer Programs feature academic courses, sports and arts programs, and a musical theater. Tuition: $14,700. Jean Marchildon is Director of Admissions; David Shapiro (Oberlin, B.A.; Columbia, M.A.; Baruch College, M.S.) is Head of School.

Georgetown Day School   1945

Lower/Middle School: 4530 MacArthur Boulevard, NW,
Washington, DC 20007. 202-333-7727;
Admissions 202-295-6210; Fax 202-295-6211
High School: 4200 Davenport Street, NW,
Washington, DC 20016. 202-966-2666;
Admissions 202-274-3210; Fax 202-274-3211;
E-mail info@gds.org; Web Site www.gds.org

Georgetown Day, a coeducational, college preparatory school enrolling 1020 students in Pre-K–Grade 12, honors the integrity and worth of each individual within a diverse school community. It is dedicated to providing a supportive atmosphere in which teachers challenge the abilities of its students and foster strength of character and concern for others. The High School offers 19 Advanced Placement courses. Each year, approximately 35 percent of seniors earn recognition in the National Merit and National Achievement Scholarship programs. Activities include athletics, the performing arts, publications, interest clubs, and required community service. Tuition: $14,257–$16,767. Extras: $400. Financial Aid: $1,600,000. Bruce Vinik is Director of Admissions; Peter M. Branch is Head of School.

Georgetown Visitation Preparatory School   1799

1524 35th Street, NW, Washington, DC 20007. 202-337-3350;
Fax 202-342-5733; E-mail
Name@visi.org; Web Site www.ee.cua/~georgvis

A Roman Catholic day school enrolling 435 girls in Grades 9–12, Georgetown Visitation Preparatory School seeks to provide a strong college preparatory curriculum; a Skills Development Program is open to a limited number of students. An 80-hour community service commitment is required before graduation. Activities include athletics, drama, chorus, instrumental music and orchestra, three publications, forensics, Model United Nations, and Christian Action Society. Tuition: $10,950. Financial aid is available. Laurie Clemente is Director of Admissions; Sr. Mary Berchmans Hannan, VHM (University of St. Thomas, M.A. 1977), was named President in 1989. Daniel M. Kerns (George Mason University of Law, J.D. 1980) was appointed Headmaster in 1989. *Middle States Association.*

Gonzaga College High School 1821

19 Eye Street, NW, Washington, DC 20001. 202-336-7101; Fax 202-336-7164; Web Site www.gonzaga.org

Following the challenge of St. Ignatius to educate "men for others," Gonzaga College High School, operated by the Society of Jesus, enrolls 871 young men in a rigorous college preparatory day program. The academic program requires completion of 25 graduation credits, including four years of religion, English, history, and math, and three years each of foreign language and science. Honors and Advanced Placement courses are offered, and some students may earn college credit at Georgetown University. Athletics, publications, Student Council, drama, and a TV station are among the activities. Tuition: $8450. Extras: $550. Financial Aid: $920,000. Joseph J. Ciancaglini (Columbia, Ed.D.) is Headmaster. *Middle States Association.*

The Kingsbury Day School 1984

1809 Phelps Place, NW, Washington, DC 20008. 202-232-1702

Founded as a division of The Kingsbury Center, this ungraded, coeducational day school enrolls 100 children, ages 5–13, with learning disabilities or developmental delays. The teaching of basic skills is integrated with social studies, science, art, music, dramatics, computer skills, and physical education. The emphasis is on diagnostic-prescriptive teaching, and the individualized curriculum permits students to proceed at their own pace. Individual psychotherapy and speech, language, and occupational therapy are also provided. A summer program to enhance learning skills is offered. Tuition and Fees: $17,450. Marlene S. Gustafson (University of Illinois, B.A.; George Washington University, M.A.) is Director.

The Lab School of Washington 1967

4759 Reservoir, NW, Washington, DC 20007. 202-965-6600; Fax 202-965-5106; Web Site www.labschool.org

This nonprofit day school enrolls 310 learning-disabled children ages 5–18 with average to superior intelligence. The individualized Lower School academic program is reinforced by skills taught in history clubs and in music, dance, drama, film making, art, and woodwork. Sciences, Humanities, Student Council, the yearbook, and team sports augment the Junior High and High School programs. Summer School includes remediation and an arts program. There is a postsecondary night school, a diagnostic and tutoring service, career counseling, college guidance, and a monthly lecture series for parents and professionals. Tuition: $17,400–$18,640. Sally L. Smith (Bennington, B.A.; New York University, M.A.) is Founder/Director.

Lowell School 1965

1640 Kalmia Road, NW, Washington, DC 20012. 202-577-2000; Fax 202-577-2001; Web Site www.lowellschool.org

Lowell School is a day school presently enrolling 225 boys and girls, age 3–Grade 5, from diverse backgrounds. In 2000–01, Lowell will serve 325 students up to Grade 6 on its new campus. The program reflects a progressive philosophy emphasizing the student's responsibility and expectation for attaining strong communication, collaborative, and academic skills. Within a nurturing environment, Lowell's stimulating thematic, integrated, project-oriented curriculum is enhanced by the arts, Spanish, physical education, field trips, and service learning. After School and summer programs are offered. Tuition: $7250–$11,575. Financial aid is available. Admissions Coordinators are Leslie Sinsay (Pre-Primary) and Michelle Belton (Primary); Abigail B. Wiebenson (Smith, B.A.; George Washington, M.Ed.) is Director.

Maret School 1911

3000 Cathedral Avenue, NW, Washington, DC 20008. 202-939-8800; Admissions 202-939-8814; Fax 202-939-8884; E-mail admissions@maret.org; Web Site www.maret.org

This coeducational, college preparatory day school, founded by educator Louise Maret, enrolls 600 students in Kindergarten–Grade 12. Located on the Woodley Estate, Maret uses the nation's capital as an extension of classroom instruction. Small classes, an advisor system, and a learning skills program provide strong student support. The humanities, math, science, computer studies, and foreign languages form the basis of the demanding curriculum. Advanced Placement and independent study opportunities are offered as well as summer study on campus or in Florida, Spain, or France. Tuition: $13,900–$16,510. Financial aid is available. Annie M. Farquhar is Admission Director; Marjo Talbott (Williams, B.A.; Harvard, M.Ed.) was named Head of School in 1994. *Middle States Association.*

National Cathedral School 1899

Mount St. Alban, Washington, DC 20016. 202-537-6300; Admissions 202-537-6374; Fax 202-537-2382; E-mail ncs.admissions@cathedral.org; Web Site http://www.ncs.cathedral.org

National Cathedral School is a college preparatory, Episcopal day school enrolling approximately 560 girls in Grades 4–12. The School aspires to excellence in education for girls, values the spiritual life of its students, and strongly supports a multi-cultural environment. A coordinate academic and social relationship is maintained with St. Albans School for boys. Extracurricular activities include sports, clubs, and the arts. Tuition: $16,750. Financial Aid: $1,000,000. Agnes Cochran Underwood (Connecticut College, B.A. 1963; Columbia, M.B.A. 1976) was appointed Headmistress in 1989. *Middle States Association.*

National Presbyterian School 1969

4121 Nebraska Avenue, NW, Washington, DC 20016. 202-537-7500; Fax 202-537-7568; E-mail school@natpresch.org; Web Site www.nps-dc.org/school

National Presbyterian School is a coeducational, elementary day school with 40 faculty and 233 students in Nursery–Grade 6. Its goal is to give each child a solid academic foundation in a nurturing environment that fosters intellectual, social, and personal growth within a Christian atmosphere. The traditional curriculum is enhanced by classes in science, French, art, music, handbells, religion, physical education, and drama. Technology is integrated into the core curriculum. After-school enrichment classes, summer camp, and extended day programs are offered. Tuition: $6202–$11,770. Financial aid is available. Stephanie Ward is Director of Admissions; Jay Roudebush (Occidental College, B.A.; American University, M.A.Ed.) was appointed Headmaster in 1997.

Rock Creek International School 1988

1550 Foxhall Road, NW, Washington, DC 20007. 202-965-8900; Fax 202-965-8973; E-mail sgalbraith@rcis.org

Rock Creek International School provides a dual-language immersion education to 180 children in Pre-Kindergarten through Grade 5. The School occupies a new campus at Foxhall and Q Streets, NW, featuring extensive fields and playgrounds. Rock Creek's two-track curriculum, in French/English and Spanish/English, implements the International Baccalaureate's Primary Years Programme, which emphasizes inquiry-based learning, transdisciplinary projects, and internationalism. Strong academic performance is achieved in a nurturing environment that fosters enjoyment in learning. Tuition: $13,995. Susan Galbraith is Director of Admission; J. Daniel Hollinger, Ph.D., is Founder and Head.

St. Albans School   WASHINGTON

Mount St. Alban, Washington, DC 20016. 202-537-6435; Fax 202-537-5613; E-mail dhardman@cathedral.org

ST. ALBANS SCHOOL in Washington, D.C., is an Episcopal, college preparatory school for day boys in Forms C through VI (Grades 4–12) and boarding boys in Forms III through VI (Grades 9–12). Its grounds form part of the Washington Cathedral Close, and its proximity to the Cathedral and its location in the nation's capital have had a significant influence on its history, purpose, and character.

In 1903, a bequest of Harriet Lane Johnston, President James Buchanan's niece, provided for the establishment of a boys' school and for a scholarship endowment to educate boys in the Cathedral Choir. The School opened in 1909 with 59 boys, including 12 choir boys; in the succeeding 90 years, its growth has been directed by Earl Lamont Gregg (1909–15), William Howell Church (1915–29), the Reverend Dr. Albert Hawley Lucas (1929–49), Canon Charles Martin (1949–77), the Reverend Mark Hill Mullin (1977–97); and John F. McCune (1997–99). Vance Wilson is the present Headmaster.

St. Albans is part of the Cathedral Foundation, which also includes National Cathedral School for Girls and Beauvoir, The National Cathedral Elementary School. Its Governing Board consists of 25 men and women representing parents, alumni, faculty, and the business and professional communities. The School is incorporated not-for-profit and operates without financial support from the church. It is accredited by the Middle States Association of Colleges and Schools and holds membership in the National Association of Independent Schools, the Educational Records Bureau, The College Board, the Council for Advancement and Support of Education, the National Association of Episcopal Schools, the Association of Independent Schools of Greater Washington, The Association

of Independent Maryland Schools, and the Washington, D.C., Language Consortium.

The purpose of the School is to help each student in his spiritual, academic, and physical development; to foster his individuality; and to encourage appreciation of his membership in the School, the church, and the community. Close association is maintained with the Cathedral and with the other institutions on the Close. Important school services are held in the Cathedral, where the choir boys and acolytes are traditionally St. Albans students. A number of classes and extracurricular activities are shared with girls from National Cathedral School.

THE CAMPUS. The school buildings occupy a part of the 59-acre Close, in the center of which rises the Cathedral. Outdoor facilities include athletic fields, a track, and 12 tennis courts.

The Lane-Johnston Building (1907) contains offices, classrooms, the refectory, dormitories, and faculty quarters. The Little Sanctuary, built earlier and subsequently enlarged, is used for chapel and for services for alumni, parents, and friends. In the Activities Building (1939) are team rooms, gymnasium, the Government Classroom, trophy room, wrestling room, weight-training room, and activities offices. The True–Lucas Building (renovated in 1997) contains Lower School classrooms, a library, a computer center, Upper School science laboratories and classrooms. Computers are used throughout the campus. The Lawrence Building (1963) houses an Amateur Athletic Union swimming pool. Other buildings, off the Close, include the Headmaster's House and five faculty homes.

Additional structures include the Ellison Library, the Trapier Theater, the Cafritz Refectory, expanded science facilities, the Charles Martin Gymnasium, and improved dormitory accommodations for boarders. The Steuart Building (1978) contains a student center and lounge, a bookstore, classrooms, art and music rooms, and the student exchange.

THE FACULTY. Vance Wilson, appointed Headmaster in July 1999, had previously served The Bryn Mawr School in Baltimore as Associate Head. A graduate of Yale University (B.A.) and the University of Virginia (M.A.), Mr. Wilson earned a diploma in Anglo-Irish literature from Trinity College, University of Dublin. A former adjunct professor of English at the University of Delaware, he taught English at Tower Hill School (Delaware) and at The Asheville School (North Carolina), where he served as Chairman of the English Department and writer-in-residence. Mr. Wilson had also taught English at The Lovett School (Georgia) and served as Head of the Upper School. He and his wife have two children.

There are 77 full-time faculty, 11 part-time faculty, 13 full-time coaches, 7 part-time coaches, 5 administrators, development office staff, a resident nurse, and school physicians on call. A Faculty Development Program affords travel and study assistance.

STUDENT BODY. In 1999–2000, the School enrolls 566 boys as follows: 40 in Grade 4, 44 in Grade 5, 47 in Grade 6, 65 in Grade 7, 66 in Grade 8, 76 in Grade 9, 76 in Grade 10, 76 in Grade 11, and 76 in Grade 12. Seventeen students are boarders.

ACADEMIC PROGRAM. The school year begins in September and ends in early June. The Upper School (Forms III–VI) schedule includes classes from 8:00 A.M. to 1:25 P.M., activities or chapel at 2:00 P.M., athletics at 3:30 P.M., and supervised study for boarders from 7:30 to 9:30 P.M. The Lower School (Forms C–II) schedule from 8:00 A.M. to 1:15 P.M. includes classes, a recess period, chapel, and lunch; supervised study followed by athletics concludes the day at 3:45 P.M.

There are 13 to 17 students in Lower School classes and an average of 15 in the Upper School; the ratio of students to full-time faculty is 15:1 in the Lower School and 10:1 in the Upper School. Homework for younger boys averages 90 minutes per evening; Upper School students are expected to spend at least an hour preparing for each class. Quarterly reports inform students and parents of academic progress.

Graduation requirements include four years of English, three and one-half years of a single foreign language, one and one-half years of history (including United States and Ancient history), four years of mathematics (through Precalculus), two years of laboratory science, and one semester each of fine arts, Bible, philosophy of religion, and ethics. A social service project of 60 hours is a graduation requirement.

A full range of courses, including Advanced Placement courses, is offered in the disciplines of art, computer science, drama, English, foreign languages (Ancient Greek, Latin, French, Spanish, Chinese, Japanese, German, and Russian), history, mathematics, music, religion, and science.

St. Albans attempts to take maximum advantage of its location in the nation's capital to broaden the educational experiences of its students, particularly the Fifth and Sixth Formers. Sixth Formers may, with faculty approval, undertake independent study. Some have been relieved of school obligations near the end of the Sixth Form year to work with a Washington community agency, business firm, or governmental department in the fields of medicine, religion, communications, arts, science, or research. Advanced Placement courses are available in all disciplines, and there is an Honors Program in mathematics that goes beyond the Advanced Placement level.

In the past five years, five or more St. Albans graduates have entered the following colleges and universities: Amherst 11, Bowdoin 15, Brown 13, College of William and Mary 6, Columbia 19, Cornell 8, Dartmouth 6, Davidson 5, Duke 10, Georgetown 11, Harvard 25, Haverford 5, Middlebury 6, Princeton 22, Stanford 12, Trinity (Connecticut) 9, Tufts 5, Vanderbilt 13, Yale 12, and the Universities of Pennsylvania 8 and Virginia 16.

A six-week summer school for boys and girls in Grades 7–12 offers review work and advanced study in most regular credit courses and special, noncredit courses such as English as a Second Language. In addition, there is a five-week basic skill program for students in Grades 2–5. There is a six-week, coeducational summer day camp, and various sports clinics are available in June and July.

STUDENT ACTIVITIES. The Upper School Student Council consists of student representatives elected by their peers. The Council, which has administrative and legislative duties, administers the Honor Code and works with the faculty toward common goals. Lower School leadership is provided by class officers and by eight prefects elected from Form II by the students of the Lower School.

The Upper and Lower schools each have Student Vestries that meet with the Chaplains to plan separate chapel services. On occasion, the two divisions meet together or with National Cathedral School for joint services in the Cathedral. Under the leadership of the Chaplains, the Vestries also plan social work programs designed to help St. Albans boys expand the role of the church in the community and develop their understanding

of segments of society with which they would not otherwise have contact.

Other extracurricular activities, many of which include representation from the National Cathedral School, are the Upper School Glee Club; Chamber Music Players; Lower School Choir; Madrigal Singers; Orchestra; Band; Service Club, whose members serve as hosts, ushers, pages, and guides; and the combined Upper School Drama Clubs of National Cathedral School and St. Albans. The Government Class is a political study group and debating organization. Publications include the yearbook, newspapers, and literary magazines.

All students are required to participate in physical education. At various age, weight, and grade levels, the School is represented in interscholastic competition in baseball, basketball, crew, cross-country, football, golf, ice hockey, lacrosse, soccer, swimming, tennis, track, and wrestling. Lower School competition is chiefly intramural in Forms C and B (Grades 4 and 5), with those students receiving training in coordination, running, and swimming. The option for interscholastic play begins in Form A (Grade 6).

The multifaceted Voyageur Program, offered to St. Albans and National Cathedral School students, is designed to give training in lifelong outdoor recreational activities as well as an understanding of the natural environment and its wise use. Daily, weekend, ten-day, and vacation activities teach sailing, camping, kayaking, rock climbing, and wilderness survival. Experienced Voyageur students serve as leaders of the Lower School outdoor programs.

Traditional events include a Lower School Field Day, an All-Sports Banquet, a Publication Banquet, a Student Art Exhibit, a Phi Beta Kappa Holiday, Prize Day Exercises, and a Lower School Science Fair.

ADMISSION AND COSTS. Candidates are accepted into Grades 4–11 on the basis of entrance tests, academic promise, previous record, and recommendations. The SSAT is required in Grades 9–11. Applications should be submitted by January 15, and the SSAT should be taken in either December or January. A campus visit and interview are required. Qualified applicants are admitted without regard to their race, creed, or national or ethnic origin.

Applicants for the 20-member National Cathedral Boys Choir (Grades 4–8) must meet the School's scholastic requirements as well as the Cathedral's music requirements. Each choir boy receives approximately a 40-percent scholarship.

The 1999–2000 fee for boarders' tuition, room, and board is $24,643; day tuition is $17,421 (including lunch). Books and incidental fees range from $250 to $450. A tuition payment plan and insurance are available. Currently, scholarship funds of $1,000,000 have been awarded to families who qualify on the basis of financial need only as measured by the School and Student Service for Financial Aid. Twenty-one percent of the students presently receive some financial aid.

St. Anselm's Abbey School WASHINGTON

*4501 South Dakota Avenue, NE, Washington, DC 20017.
202-269-2350; E-mail mainoffice@st-anselms.pvt.k12.dc.us;
Web Site www.ee.cua.edu/~stanselm*

ST. ANSELM'S ABBEY SCHOOL in Washington, D.C., is a Roman Catholic, college preparatory day school for boys in Forms A through VI (Grades 6–12). The School is accessible by city bus from all areas of Washington and its suburbs; Metro line subway trains link it with many areas by rail. Catholic University of America is within a few blocks of the School, and the resources of downtown Washington including the Capitol, the Library of Congress, the National Gallery of Art, and the Smithsonian Institution are approximately four miles away.

St. Anselm's was founded in 1942 by the Benedictine monks of St. Anselm's Abbey in order to offer high-quality, moderately priced college preparation to talented boys. The School, encompassing Grades 9–12, opened in a wing of the monastery with 20 students in Grade 9. In 1955, classes were moved to a new school building on the Abbey grounds and, with the addition of Grades 7 and 8, had grown to 107, with 20 students in Grade 7. Lay men and women joined the previously all-monastic faculty in 1968. In September 1990, Grade 6 (Form A) was added, and St. Anselm's was organized into Middle (Forms A–II) and Upper (Forms III–VI) schools.

The School strives to provide a "liberal education with maximum intellectual challenge" within a community of learning that reflects "the Rule of St. Benedict: peace and fraternity, respect for the value of work, self-discipline, and the development of personal talents for the service of others." While all students must take religion courses, attendance at school Masses is required for Roman Catholic students only.

The School is owned and operated by the Benedictine Foundation at Washington, D.C., a nonprofit religious and educational foundation. The Abbot and the Monastic Council of St. Anselm's Abbey serve as a board of trustees. A 20-member lay Board of Advisors, exercising many of the advisory functions of

a board of trustees, was established in 1978. There are more than 1000 living alumni.

St. Anselm's is accredited by the Middle States Association of Colleges and Schools; it holds membership in the National Association of Independent Schools, the National Catholic Education Association, the Association of Independent Schools of Greater Washington, the Association of Independent Maryland Schools, and The College Board.

THE CAMPUS. The School, the abbey church, and the monastery occupy 35 wooded acres, including flower gardens, overlooking a residential area in northeast Washington. The main school building (1955) contains ten classrooms, an auditorium, a music room, a student publications room, administrative and faculty offices, and a 9000-volume library with two reading rooms and a microfiche reader. The science wing, added to the main building in 1974, consists of biology, chemistry, and physics laboratories; an enclosed garden; and a greenhouse. In 1987, a new wing consisting of 4 classrooms, a computer room, a cafeteria, a student lounge, and faculty offices opened. The gymnasium (1945) has a basketball court, wrestling and gymnastics rooms, and a stage. Also included in the property are two baseball diamonds, two general athletic fields, and four new tennis courts.

THE FACULTY. The Reverend Dom Peter Weigand, OSB, was appointed Headmaster in 1992, having served as Second Master since 1976. Father Peter holds a master's degree in the teaching of science from the Catholic University of America.

There are 45 teaching positions, 10 of which are part-time. Ten faculty and staff members are monks who live at the Abbey on the school campus. Sixty-seven percent of the faculty and staff hold master's degrees, and of these, 11 percent hold doctorates. These represent study at American University, Boston University, Bucknell, Catholic University of America, College of New Rochelle, College of the Holy Cross, College of William and Mary, Cornell, Dominican College (Wisconsin), Drexel, Earlham, Fordham, Franklin and Marshall, George Mason, Georgetown, George Washington, Gettysburg, Iowa State, La Salle College, Lateran University (Italy), Loyola (Maryland), Lutheran Theological Seminary, Manhattan College, Messiah College, Michigan State, Ohio University, Randolph-Macon, St. Leo, St. Mary's (Maryland), Seton Hill, State University of New York (Buffalo), Trinity (Connecticut), Western Maryland College, William Smith, Yale, and the Universities of Chicago, Dayton, El Salvador, London, Maryland, Minnesota, Pennsylvania, Rochester, Scranton, Seville (Spain), Toronto, Wisconsin, and Zurich.

St. Anselm's offers faculty medical insurance, TIAA-CREF, and Social Security. A hospital is two blocks away.

STUDENT BODY. In 1999–2000, the School enrolls 248 boys as follows: 29 in Form A (Grade 6), 42 in Form I, 41 in Form II, 38 in Form III, 31 in Form IV, 35 in Form V, and 32 in Form VI. Sixty-five percent of the students are Roman Catholic, with the balance representing various other faiths. Twenty-nine percent are from the District of Columbia, 35 percent are from Montgomery County, 22 percent from Prince George's County, 13 percent from the Virginia suburbs, and 1 percent from other Maryland counties.

ACADEMIC PROGRAM. The school year, from early September to late May, consists of 34 weeks of instruction with a Thanksgiving recess and Christmas and spring vacations. The Middle School is on a trimester system; the Upper School year is divided into semesters. Classes meet five days a week, from 8:20 A.M. to 3:15 P.M., in a schedule that includes nine 40-minute class periods. Practices for interscholastic sports and drama rehearsals are held in the afternoon; debate meetings take place in the evening. Supervision is provided until 6:00 P.M. for students wishing to study in the library or use the computers.

The required course of study in the Middle School (Grades 6–8) includes three years of English Literature and Composition, three years of Religion, two years of Latin, one year of French or Spanish, three years of United States history, three years of science, three years of mathematics, three years of physical education, and one year each of art and music. All students receive computer instruction. They learn touch typewriting and word processing and to run application programs for courses. BASIC and PASCAL are offered.

The Upper School program (Grades 9–12) requires at least three years each of Latin and a modern language; four years each of English Literature and Composition, mathematics, and religion; three and one-half years of social studies; and three years each of science and fine arts. Seniors may fulfill some of these requirements for graduation through courses taken at the Catholic University of America as part of the ABBEY Program. Since 1974, St. Anselm's has conducted the ABBEY Program with Catholic University. Under this bridge program, St. Anselm's seniors matriculate as special students at Catholic University, normally taking one or two courses there. They receive college credit for these courses as well as for certain courses at St. Anselm's.

In 1999, all graduates entered college. They are attending Arizona State, Columbia, Dartmouth, Florida A&M, Hamilton, Manhattan College, McGill 2, Oberlin, St. John's University (Minnesota), St. Mary's College (Maryland), Skidmore, Swarthmore, Washington University (Missouri), Williams, Yale, and the Universities of Chicago, Maryland, Pennsylvania, Texas, and Virginia 3.

STUDENT ACTIVITIES. The Student Council consists of the student body president, two representatives from the senior class, and one representative elected from each of Forms A–V. The Council, which meets weekly with an advisor, serves as a liaison between students and the administration and organizes service projects, social events, and the school newspaper.

Extracurricular clubs and activities include the yearbook, news and literary magazines, drama, the Newman Forensic Society, Junior Classical League, St. Anselm's Saturdays, Math Counts, Abbey Singers, Knowledge Masters, and "It's Academic."

Interscholastic teams in baseball, basketball, cross-country, wrestling, soccer, and tennis compete with other independent schools in the metropolitan area, mainly with those in the Potomac Valley Athletic Conference, in which St. Anselm's holds membership. There is intramural competition in basketball, baseball, tennis, soccer, and wrestling.

Several dances each year, including a prom, are held with nearby girls' schools. The St. Anselm's Parents' Association helps to further the aims of the School by sponsoring community activities, such as the annual St. Anselm's Invitational Basketball Tournament, soccer and wrestling tournaments, the graduation reception, and dance classes.

ADMISSION AND COSTS. St. Anselm's seeks to enroll boys with "academic ability, self-motivated interest in learning, and

the potential for growth in self-discipline." Requirements for admission include previous school records, teacher recommendations, applicant essays, a personal interview, and St. Anselm's entrance examination. Application should be made by February 15, although it can be made until September if openings exist.

While most new students are accepted into Middle School and Form III, transfer students may be accepted in the higher forms if they have strong records in programs parallel to St. Anselm's. There is a $35 application fee, and a $500 registration fee (applicable toward tuition) is due upon acceptance.

In 1999–2000, tuition ranges from $10,400 to $11,150. Additional fees, ranging from $450 for the Middle School to $700 for Form VI, cover books, laboratory fees, field trips, gym uniforms, insurance, and other costs. Lunches and transportation are extra. Financial aid is offered on the basis of need, with all requests considered on an individual basis. Scholarships are reviewed annually, with renewal based on the student's continuing good scholarship and citizenship. Students may earn money by working in the school and monastic libraries or by performing clerical or maintenance work.

Secondmaster: Robert A. Loia
Upper School Master: Mark Fusco
Middle School Master: Robert A. Loia
Master of Students: Anthony Carnahan
Director of Admissions: Fr. Gabriel Myers, OSB
Director of Development: Monica Horton
Guidance Director: Sr. Patricia Scanlon, RJM
Business Manager: Matthew E. Seiler
Director of Athletics: Brian Murphy
Director of Summer School: Robert A. Loia

Sheridan School   1927

4400 36th Street, NW, Washington, DC 20008. 202-362-7900; Fax 202-244-9696

Sheridan School balances its city-based, academically challenging program for 216 boys and girls in Kindergarten–Grade 8 with a strong outdoor curriculum at a 130-acre mountain campus where students take overnight trips lasting one to five nights. Academic skills are taught in Grades 3–8 through immersion in a central subject. The diverse curriculum, comfortable size of the student body, and age range combine to build confidence and encourage risk taking. Extended day care, enrichment classes, vacation camps, and day and overnight summer programs are offered. Tuition: $12,700–$14,630.

Financial aid is available. Patricia E. Talbert Smith is Admissions Director; C. Randall Plummer (University of Missouri, B.S.; Boston University, M.Ed.) is Head of School.

St. Patrick's Episcopal Day School   1956

4700 Whitehaven Parkway, NW, Washington, DC 20007-1586.
  202-342-2805; Fax 202-342-7001;
  E-mail garner@stpatricks.washington.dc.us;
  Web Site www.stpatricks.washington.dc.us

Enrolling 442 boys and girls in Nursery–Grade 6, St. Patrick's Episcopal Day is committed to nurturing individual achievement within a stimulating program of study enriched by computer, art, music, video production, religion, physical education, and library skills. The modern facility features two fully equipped science labs, a spacious art studio, two music/rehearsal rooms, a computer/video production lab, and chapel, in addition to four playparks and a two-acre playing field. Numerous activities, extended day, and a summer camp are available. Tuition: $6975–$13,110. Extended Day: $2420. Financial Aid: $650,000. Jamie H. Garner is Director of Admission; Peter A. Barrett (Trinity, B.A.; Northwestern, M.A.T.) was appointed Head of School in 1994. *Middle States Association.*

Sidwell Friends School   1883

3825 Wisconsin Avenue, NW, Washington, DC 20016.
  202-537-8100; Fax 202-537-8138;
  Web Site http://www.sidwell.edu

Sidwell Friends School, founded by members of the Society of Friends, is a college preparatory day school enrolling approximately 1085 boys and girls in Prekindergarten–Grade 12. The School follows a Quaker philosophy, seeking the uniqueness of each individual and emphasizing spiritual and human values. In addition to traditional subjects, the curriculum includes music, art, dance, Chinese language and studies, and a School Year Abroad program. Athletics and 20 clubs are among the activities. Tuition: $14,180–$16,400. Financial Aid: $2,290,000. Diane R. Wilson is Assistant Head of School for Admissions; Bruce B. Stewart (Guilford College, A.B. 1961; University of North Carolina [Chapel Hill], M.Ed. 1962) was appointed Head of School in 1998. *Middle States Association.*

Washington Ethical High School   1964

7750 16th Street, NW, Washington, DC 20012. 202-829-0088;
  Fax 202-829-6669; E-mail wehs@aol.com;
  Web Site http://members.aol.com/wehs/wehs.html

Founded by Dr. Leon Eberhard to serve the needs of bright underachievers, this coeducational, college preparatory day school enrolls 40 students in Grades 9–12. It aims to present a challenging academic program emphasizing social justice and critical thinking. The curriculum includes English, social studies, mathematics, science, and a variety of electives taught to different learning styles. A community service project combines classroom learning with practical activity. Athletics, camping, rafting, and activity/learning trips in the city are among the extracurricular offerings. Tuition: $12,800. Financial Aid: $55,000. Elaine Mack is Admissions Counselor; David Mullen (University of Maryland, M.S.Ed.) was appointed Headmaster in 1991. *Middle States Association.*

Washington International School   1966

3100 Macomb Street, NW, Washington, DC 20008. 202-243-1800;
  Fax 202-243-1807; E-mail admissions@mail.wis.edu;
  Web Site www.wis.edu

Washington International is a college preparatory day school enrolling 770 boys and girls, representing more than 85 countries, in Pre-Kindergarten–Grade 12. Requirements in the Upper School include language and world literature in English and French or Spanish, world history and geography, mathematics, biology, chemistry, physics, fine and performing arts, and physical education. A bilingual curriculum is offered through Grade 8, while English is the primary language of instruction in the Upper School. The program culminates in the two-year International Baccalaureate. Tuition: $11,460–$15,400. Financial Aid: $800,000. Dorrie Fuchs is Director of Admission and Financial Aid; Anne-Marie Pierce (University of California [Berkeley], B.A. 1965; California State, M.A. 1973) is Head.

FLORIDA

Academy of the Holy Names   1881

Pre-K–Grade 4: 3319 South MacDill Avenue, Tampa, FL 33629.
813-839-5371; Fax 813-837-5710
Grades 5–12: 3319 Bayshore Boulevard, Tampa, FL 33629.
813-839-5371; Fax 813-839-1486;
E-mail webmaster@holynamestpa.org;
Web Site www.holynamestpa.org

This Roman Catholic day school was established by the Sisters of the Holy Names of Jesus and Mary to provide spiritual and academic enlightenment and to motivate young people to their best personal potential. The Academy enrolls more than 850 students in its coeducational elementary division (PK–Grade 8) and all-girls high school. It emphasizes a firm basis in learning skills as a foundation for the college preparatory curriculum of the upper school. Religious formation is integrated into the program through liturgies and values education. Students are involved in activities such as NFL, service organizations, publications, honor societies, athletics, and interest clubs. Tuition: $5270–$7230. Myra M. McLeod is Admission Director; Colleen K. Brady is President.

Admiral Farragut Academy

ST. PETERSBURG

501 Park Street North, St. Petersburg, FL 33710. 727-384-5500;
Fax 727-347-5160; E-mail admissions@farragut.org;
Web Site www.farragut.org

ADMIRAL FARRAGUT ACADEMY in St. Petersburg, Florida, is a coeducational college preparatory school enrolling boarding students in Grades 6–12 and day students in Kindergarten–Grade 12 and featuring a Naval Junior Reserve Officer Training Corps (NJROTC) program. The school is located in a bayfront residential area of St. Petersburg, 30 minutes from Tampa International Airport and 5 minutes from the Gulf beaches.

Admiral Farragut Academy was founded as a boys' school at Pine Beach, New Jersey, in 1933 under the leadership of Admiral S. S. Robison, USN (Ret.), a former Superintendent of the United States Naval Academy, and Brig. Gen. Cyrus S. Radford, USMC (Ret.). In 1945, when the school had reached a maximum enrollment, the Florida campus was established. Admiral Farragut Academy was declared an Honor Naval ROTC school by Act of Congress in 1946. As such, the Academy is authorized 17 nominations to the service academies. In January 1990, Farragut became coeducational, breaking a 56-year tradition of enrolling only males.

Admiral Farragut Academy is America's first school to develop a program of naval science approved by Congress and the Department of the Navy. The Academy is especially proud of its two astronaut graduates, Alan Shepard and Charles Duke. Shepard is well-known as the first American in space; both men walked on the moon in the 1970s.

Admiral Farragut Academy is accredited by the Southern Association of Colleges and Schools and the Florida Council of Independent Schools. It holds membership in the National Association of Independent Schools and other educational organizations. The nonprofit school is directed by a resident superintendent and a local Board of Trustees.

THE CAMPUS. Admiral Farragut Academy occupies a 55-acre campus with a yacht basin, tennis courts, two baseball diamonds, a football field, a quarter-mile asphalt track, and an out-

door heated swimming pool. The waterfront equipment consists of ten docks, a boathouse, several power boats, and a fleet of small craft.

Farragut Hall, a former resort hotel converted for school use, contains all cadet living quarters, the dining hall, the kitchen, lounges, a recreation room, a study hall, a barber shop, a tailor shop, the bookstore, the canteen, and administrative offices. The dormitory facilities (renovated 1997) have carpeting and air conditioning; each dorm room has its own bathroom. Female boarding students reside in a separate area of the dorm, staffed by resident female faculty members. Upper Division classes meet in the Duke Science Center and in the Russell Building, which has 17 classrooms and a large music room. Classes for the lower grades are held in the Michel Building and the Mills Science Center.

Other facilities include the Moyer Gymnasium, two field houses, an art building, a weight room, the DeSeta Chapel, the Parrott Memorial Library, the Farragut Museum, an indoor rifle range, the Ames Memorial Computer Center, the Rand Memorial Boathouse, and faculty apartments and living quarters.

THE FACULTY. Robert J. Fine, appointed Headmaster in 1998, is a graduate of Carroll College (B.S.) and National Louis University (M.Ed.). He previously served as Head of the Middle Division and as Assistant Headmaster.

On the faculty are 38 full-time teachers and administrators, 25 men and 13 women, plus 2 officers of the day. Seventeen faculty members live on the campus, including 3 with families. Faculty members have earned 38 baccalaureate, 21 master's, and 1 doctoral degrees from Auburn, Calvin College, Carroll College, Chaminade, Columbia College, East Stroudsburg, Florida Institute of Technology, Florida State, Hampden-Sydney, James Madison, Kennesaw State, Marshall, Miami (Ohio), Park College, Rutgers, Saint Louis University, Shepard, State University of New York, Villanova, West Chester State, Western Carolina, and the Universities of Alabama, California (Los Angeles), Florida, Georgia, Madrid (Spain), Missouri, South Carolina, South Florida, Toledo, and Washington.

The Naval Science Department staff consists of a Director and two Naval Science instructors, all of whom are retired Navy personnel.

A 14-bed infirmary with separate facilities for boys and girls is supervised by four registered nurses and a pediatrician.

STUDENT BODY. The Academy enrolls 189 boarding and 145 day students as follows: 25 in Kindergarten–Grade 2, 9 in Grade 5, 18 in Grade 6, 28 in Grade 7, 41 in Grade 8, 48 in Grade 9, 57 in Grade 10, 48 in Grade 11, and 60 in Grade 12. More than 18 states and 20 foreign countries are typically represented.

ACADEMIC PROGRAM. The school year runs from early September to late May and is divided into semesters. Thanksgiving, fall, winter, and spring breaks are scheduled. The school remains open during all breaks except winter and spring. Grade and deportment reports are sent to parents every six weeks. There is no "plebe period" nor do new students undergo any type of initiation. Weekend breaks normally begin at 3:00 P.M. on Friday and end by 9:30 P.M. on Sunday.

A typical day begins with reveille at 6:15 A.M., breakfast at 6:40 A.M., and the day's activities beginning at 7:30 A.M. Eight 45-minute academic periods run between 7:30 A.M. and 3:10 P.M., followed by an academic tutorial period. The afternoon athletic period begins at 4:00 P.M. Dinner is served at 6:00 P.M., followed by evening study hall from 7:30 to 9:30 P.M. Taps is at 10:30 P.M. Study hall and Taps are earlier in the Middle Division. Seven faculty members live in the boys' dormitory and supervise there. Two female faculty supervise the girls' dormitory. Normally, two or three cadets share living space.

The average class has 15 students. Evening study is required. Cadets whose grades are satisfactory may study in their dorm rooms, in the library, or in the multimedia computer lab; otherwise, they attend a faculty-supervised study hall. Cadets may obtain extra help in their classes during daily afternoon tutorials. Students select faculty advisors with whom they meet regularly.

The Middle Division structure allows for the completion of core academic classes by noon each day, leaving the afternoons free for tutorials, elective classes, outdoor activities, and off-campus trips. Middle Division cadets meet with advisors three times each week. Besides the core classes of math, science, social studies, and English, cadets may choose from a wide array of electives such as computers, journalism, foreign languages, drama, chorus, dance, art, public speaking, sign language, and health.

In order to satisfy Upper Division graduation requirements, students must complete 24 units as follows: English 4; foreign language 2; United States History 1, Social Studies 2; Algebra 2, Plane Geometry 1; Science 3, Computer Science 1, Naval Science (1 unit per year); Physical Education 2; Fine Arts 1; and electives 4.

The Upper Division curriculum offers English, SAT Preparation, Speech and Drama, Creative Writing, Journalism; French, Spanish, German; World History, United States History, Government, Economics, Psychology, Ethics; Engineering Drawing, Algebra 1–2, Analytic Geometry, Calculus, Trigonometry, Qualitative Analysis, Statistics; Physical Science, Biology, Anatomy and Physiology, Chemistry, Computer Science, Marine Science, Meteorology, Environmental Science, Aerodynamics, Naval Science, and Physics; Music, Music History, Art, Chorus; and Physical Education and Health. Dual-enrollment courses (a total of 80 semester hours) allow a student to earn college credit while simultaneously fulfilling high school graduation requirements. Offerings include English IV, U.S. History, Government and Economics, Spanish, Physics, Marine Science, Meteorology, Environmental Science, Oceanography, Calculus, Qualitative Analysis, Chemistry, and Computer Science. More than half of all juniors and seniors received college credit in 1999. All foreign students must have a basic knowledge of English. The Academy provides a class in English for Non-native Speakers, with enrollment limited to eight students.

The naval program revolves around the Junior Naval Reserve Officer Training Corps. Instruction, as prescribed by the Navy, is given in Navigation, Astronomy, Oceanography, Meteorology, Seamanship, Naval History, Communications, Infantry Drill, Boating, Sailing, and Riflery.

Four members of the Class of 1999 received appointments to service academies, and there were six Naval ROTC scholarship winners. Of the 57 graduates, 43 were accepted at the college of their first choice. The Class of 1999 earned in excess of $800,000 in college scholarships and tuition grants. They are matriculating at Auburn, Boston College, College of William and Mary, Embry-Riddle Aeronautical, Emory, Florida State, Lehigh, Massachusetts Institute of Technology, Ohio State, Old Dominion, Purdue, Rutgers, Stetson, Villanova, Worcester Polytechnic, and the Universities of Florida, Miami, North Carolina, and South Florida.

STUDENT ACTIVITIES. The cadet corps is organized as a battalion of five companies, one of which is the Middle Division in its entirety. Cadet officers, under adult supervision, are responsible for the performance of the battalion at formations, drills, parades, and ceremonies. Cadet officer authority is limited and closely supervised, especially in the dormitory, where resident faculty have primary responsibility for supervision.

School organizations include the Student Council, National Honor Society, Literary Society, Students Against Drunk Driving, Stage and Concert bands, and the Rifle, Flying, Monogram, Adventure, Key, Debate, Drama, Foreign Language, Model, Math, Art, Computer, Backgammon, Chess, Scuba, and Cotillion clubs.

Varsity and junior varsity teams compete in the Florida High School Activities Association in football, baseball, bowling, track, cross-country, swimming, diving, wrestling, basketball, golf, tennis, soccer, and riflery. Intramural competition, including major sports, swimming, volleyball, team handball, and sailing, is also scheduled in the Upper Division. Middle

Division soccer, basketball, baseball, cross-country, and track teams compete with local day schools. In 1999, Farragut's boys' athletic program was ranked first in Florida by the FHSAA.

Flight training provides a three-tier program, from flying orientation to accredited private pilot's license, for interested cadets. In 1998–99, more than 10 percent of the students were involved in this program.

Social events include entertainment programs, dances, beach parties, assemblies, concerts presented by the cadets, and special outings and parties for both Middle and Upper Division cadets. Weekend excursions include deep-sea fishing, professional sports events, theme parks, and area beaches. Cultural events include trips to museums, festivals, concerts, and plays. The Cotillion Club plans several formal dances each year. Campus facilities are open and staffed by faculty members every weekend.

The Middle Division program is distinct from the Upper Division's to avoid competition. Trips and activities are scheduled each weekend; special trips and extra privileges reward effort. Among the Academy's traditional events are Parents' Weekend, Homecoming, Awards Day, Grandparents' Day, and Open House.

ADMISSION AND COSTS. Cadets must be of good character, have the ability to do college preparatory work, and be able to participate in the physical activities of the Academy. The school has a policy of admitting qualified students of any race, creed, color, or national or ethnic origin. Candidates are accepted in all grades if openings exist and are encouraged to apply by May 1, although later applications are considered. Midyear enrollment is permitted. The Secondary School Admission Test is recommended but not required.

Tuition for 1999–2000 is $15,500 for boarding students and $7650 for day students; there is also a $150 application/registration fee. A Standard Outfitting Fee is required of all new cadets to cover uniforms, books, and miscellaneous matriculating expenses. The fee is $4000 for boarders and $2500 for day students. Elective spending, scuba lessons, and flight instruction are extra. Several tuition payment plans are offered. Financial aid is awarded annually on the basis of need and ability.

Director of Admissions: Lawrence J. Jensen
Assistant Headmaster: Edward L. Gilgenast
Head of the Middle School: William S. Ford
Dean of Students: David M. Graham
Director of Alumni: Roy H. Wheeler
Director of Development: JoAnne C. Linkner
College Counselor: Mark S. Hampton
Business Manager: E. William Monrose

The Benjamin School   1974

11000 Ellison Wilson Road, North Palm Beach, FL 33408.
  561-626-3747; Fax 561-626-8752;
  Web Site www.benjaminschool.com

Founded to meet the need for college preparatory education in the area, The Benjamin School is a coeducational day school enrolling 1088 students in Pre-Kindergarten–Grade 12. It aims to develop intellectual discipline, moral integrity, leadership, and resourcefulness in its students through a rigorous academic program and involvement in fine arts and athletics. Seniors undertake community projects for a two-week period in a vocation of their choice in order to gain experience in a particular field. Enrichment courses in mathematics and English are offered during the summer. Tuition: $5075–$8955. Financial aid is available. Rod L. Kehl (University of Nebraska, B.S.; University of Wisconsin, M.S.) is Headmaster.

Berkeley Preparatory School   TAMPA

4811 Kelly Road, Tampa, FL 33615. 813-885-1673;
  E-mail thomamar@berkeleyprep.org;
  Web Site www.berkeleyprep.org

BERKELEY PREPARATORY SCHOOL in Tampa, Florida, is a coeducational day school enrolling students in Pre-Kindergarten–Grade 12. The School's location allows convenient access for residents of the Tampa Bay and neighboring areas.

The Latin words *Disciplina, Diligentia,* and *Integritas* in the School's motto state the values underlying the rigorous college preparatory curriculum of Berkeley, founded in 1960 and opened for Grades 7–12 the next year. Kindergarten through Grade 6 were added in 1967 and Pre-kindergarten, in 1988. The School's purpose is to enable its students to achieve academic excellence in preparation for higher education and to instill in them a strong sense of morality, ethics, and social responsibility.

Incorporated as a nonprofit institution, Berkeley Preparatory School is directed by a Board of Trustees. The School is accredited by the Florida Council of Independent Schools and is a member of the National Association of Independent Schools, among other affiliations. In 1995, Berkeley was designated a Blue Ribbon School by the U.S. Department of Education.

THE CAMPUS. The 38-acre campus is located in the Town 'n' Country suburb of Tampa. It consists of classrooms, a Fine Arts Wing, a Science Wing, two libraries, computer laboratories, general convocation rooms, physical education fields, a Pre-Kindergarten Wing, a Kindergarten cottage, and administrative offices for Lower, Middle, and Upper divisions.

Berkeley Prep athletes participate in two gymnasiums, a junior olympic swimming pool, a wrestling/gymnastics room, a weight-lifting room, a rock-climbing wall, tennis courts, baseball and softball diamonds, and a stadium for football, track, and soccer.

The arts program is enhanced by a 634-seat performing arts center, which also includes a gallery for visual arts displays, a flex studio for dance recitals and small drama productions, dressing rooms, and an orchestra pit.

Present valuation of the School-owned campus is $12,000,000.

THE FACULTY. Joseph A. Merluzzi, appointed Headmaster in 1987, is a graduate of Western Connecticut State College and holds a master's degree in mathematics from Fairfield University. Prior to his appointment, Mr. Merluzzi served as Head of the Upper School, Assistant Headmaster, and Dean of the Upper School at Cranbrook-Kingswood School in Michigan.

There are 141 teachers and administrators. They hold 139

baccalaureate, 60 graduate, and 7 doctoral degrees from such colleges and universities as Agnes Scott, Amherst, Boston University, Florida State, Georgetown, Harvard, Heidelberg, Indiana University, James Madison, Marquette, Michigan State, Middlebury, Ohio State, Ohio University, Parsons School of Design, Pennsylvania State, State University of New York, Tulane, Vanderbilt, Wake Forest, West Virginia University, Williams, Yale, and the Universities of California, Florida, Illinois, Kansas, Kentucky, Missouri, New Brunswick, North Carolina, Oregon, Tampa, Vermont, and Wisconsin.

STUDENT BODY. In 1999–2000, the School enrolls 1170 students, 605 boys and 565 girls, in Pre-Kindergarten–Grade 12 as follows: 39 in Pre-Kindergarten, 61 in Kindergarten, 60 in Grade 1, 60 in Grade 2, 60 in Grade 3, 60 in Grade 4, 60 in Grade 5, 97 in Grade 6, 98 in Grade 7, 91 in Grade 8, 123 in Grade 9, 126 in Grade 10, 115 in Grade 11, and 120 in Grade 12.

ACADEMIC PROGRAM. The school year, from the end of August to the first week in June, includes Thanksgiving, Christmas, and spring vacations.

The average class size in the Middle and Upper divisions is 16–20. The day begins at 8:00 A.M. and ends at 3:15 P.M. An activity period and divisional convocations are scheduled into each class day. All Middle Division students, ninth graders, and other students who do not qualify for study hall exemptions attend supervised study halls when they do not have a scheduled class. Every class that meets five days a week for the year has one make-up period each week, and teachers are available for extra help during the activity period as well as at other times during the day. Grades are sent to parents four times a year.

In the Lower Division, students in Pre-Kindergarten through Grade 5 attend school from 8:00 A.M. to 3:10 P.M. Curricular emphasis is on the core subjects of reading and mathematics. Students receive a firm foundation in grammar and vocabulary development. Math skills are developed and used in problem-solving. Social studies and science curricula are designed to aid children in mastering the skills they need in a rapidly changing, technological society. An interdisciplinary approach is used in foreign language and social studies, and manipulatives are used extensively in both the science and mathematics programs. Music, art, drama, and physical educa-

tion are integral parts of the Lower Division curriculum. Each student also receives instruction in library skills and computers.

Academic requirements in the Middle Division (Grades 6–8) are English, English expression, mathematics, history, foreign language, science, computers, physical education, art, drama, and music. All students in Grade 7 and new eighth graders take Latin. Continuing students in Grade 8 have the option of Latin, French, or Spanish.

In the Upper Division (Grades 9–12), students take four or five credit courses each year in addition to the fine arts and physical education requirements. To graduate, students must complete a total of 22 credits. Specific requirements are 4 credits in English; 3 each in mathematics, history, science, and foreign language; 1 elective; one year of personal fitness/health and an additional year of physical education; one year of Microcomputers; and two years of fine arts. In addition, Berkeley students are required to take a course in public speaking and to complete 76 hours of community service. Advanced Placement courses are offered including English, Spanish, Latin, French, Modern European History, U.S. History, Calculus (AB and BC), Microcomputers, Biology, Chemistry, and Physics (B and C). Advanced topics seminar courses are also available in English: literature; English: writing; history; and science.

Traditionally, 100 percent of Berkeley graduates attend college. Members of the Class of 1999 were accepted at more than 110 colleges and universities throughout the United States and Canada; 90 percent were accepted at their first- or second-choice schools, including Boston University, Brown, College of William and Mary, Columbia, Duke, Emory, Georgetown, Johns Hopkins, New York University, Northwestern, Princeton, Stanford, Vanderbilt, Villanova, Washington and Lee, Yale, and the Universities of Florida, Miami, Michigan, North Carolina, and Pennsylvania. Scholarship offers totaling over $3,000,000 were made to 90 percent of the graduates. Twelve seniors were named National Merit Scholarship Semi-Finalists, seven were National Merit Commended Scholars, and two who scored 1600 on the SATs were named Presidential Scholars. In addition, 20 percent of the graduates have committed to pursue athletic competition at the collegiate level.

There is a six-week academic summer program for students in Pre-Kindergarten–Grade 12. Tuition ranges from $495 to $1025.

STUDENT ACTIVITIES. The Student Forum, is responsible for presenting student views to the Upper Division Director and the Headmaster for discussion, and for recommending new ideas to the administration. Other student leadership roles are given to 30 senior prefects who are selected each year by a faculty committee. The Student Guide organization assists the Director of Admissions in acquainting prospective families with Berkeley's campus and programs.

Students publish the *Fanfare*, the student newspaper; *Small Voices*, a literary magazine for Kindergarten–Grade 5; *Soundings*, a literary magazine for Grades 6–8; *Phoenix*, a literary magazine for Grades 9–12; and the *Buccaneer*, the student yearbook for Pre-Kindergarten–Grade 12. Qualified students may be invited to join The Cum Laude Society, the National Honor Society, or honor societies in French, Latin, Spanish, math, and drama. Opportunities are available for students to participate in the Latin Forum, and the Art, Photography, Social Services, Cheerleading, Drama, French, Mathematics, Music, Colloquium, Science and Environmental, Strategic Games, Amnesty International, Model United Nations, Latin, and Spanish clubs. Berkeley sponsors its own all-School philanthropy, Project Berkeley, which benefits a local food bank; students, faculty, administration, staff, and parents participate on a monthly basis. Varsity sports for boys are baseball, basketball, cross-country, diving, football, golf, soccer, swimming, tennis, weight lifting, wrestling, and track; sports for girls are basketball, cross-country, diving, soccer, softball, tennis, track, swimming, cheerleading, weight lifting, and volleyball. Berkeley competes in the Upper Division with schools of the Bay Conference and in the Middle and Lower divisions with schools in the Florida West Coast League or the Youth Sports League.

Seasonal sports award banquets, a homecoming football game, a spring field day, alumni day, grandparents' day, student retreats, Middle and Upper Division dances, and honors convocations are among the yearly events. The Berkeley Parents' Club and the Buccaneer Club hold fund-raising events for the School.

ADMISSION AND COSTS. Berkeley Preparatory School seeks students who are "able to compete in a college preparatory program" and who are "willing to accept a fairly structured program." The School has a policy of nondiscrimination regarding students on the basis of race, color, and national or ethnic origin or any other class protected by law.

The School uses the Secondary School Admission Test and its own testing program. Recommendations and transcripts from the previous school are required. Application should be made as early in the year as possible; most grades are on a wait-list basis by late spring. Students are enrolled during the school year if space is available. There is an application fee of $50.

Tuition is $7600 for Pre-Kindergarten–Grade 5, $9300 for Grades 6–8, and $10,500 for Grades 9–12. Books and uniforms are extra. Lower School students wear a uniform daily. Middle and Upper Division students must comply with the school dress code Monday through Thursday and must wear a uniform on Friday. A required tuition payment plan with five monthly payments is in effect. Scholarship funding and financial aid are available.

Director of Admissions: Mary Will Thomas
Director of Institutional Advancement: E.C. Smith
Upper Division Director: Betty-Bruce H. Hoover
Middle Division Director: Mark S. Heller
Lower Division Director: M. Joanne Moore
Business Manager: Charlie Simpson
Director of Development: Gwyn F. Schabacker
Dean of Students: Alfred E. Pisano, Jr.
College Counselor: Michael J. Kennedy
Director of Athletics: Bobby Reinhart

The Bolles School   JACKSONVILLE

7400 San Jose Boulevard, Jacksonville, FL 32217-3499.
 904-733-9292; Fax 904-739-9929; E-mail walkerd@bolles.org;
 Web Site www.bolles.org

T HE BOLLES SCHOOL in Jacksonville, Florida, is a coeducational, college preparatory school enrolling day students in Pre-Kindergarten–Grade 12 and boarding students in Grades 7–Postgraduate on five campuses: Upper School (Grades 9–12) on the San Jose Campus; Middle School (Grades

6–8) on the Bartram Campus; and three Lower Schools, Kindergarten–Grade 5 on the Whitehurst Campus in Jacksonville and in The Bolles School at St. Augustine and Pre-K–Grade 3 in The Bolles School at Ponte Vedra Beach. Boys' and girls' boarding programs are accommodated on the San Jose and Bartram campuses, respectively.

The Bolles School was founded in 1933 as a military boarding school by Col. Roger M. Painter and his wife, Agnes Cain Painter. In response to changing times, the School dropped the military programs in 1962 and adopted a comprehensive college preparatory program. Coeducation was instituted in 1971.

Bolles prepares students for the future by providing them with challenges that promote growth and development in academics, arts, activities, and athletics. Moral development is encouraged by an emphasis on respect for self and others, volunteerism, and personal responsibility.

A not-for-profit institution, The Bolles School is governed by a self-perpetuating Board of 29 Trustees. The Alumni Board and the Parent Association actively support the School and its programs through fund-raising, social events, and other endeavors. The School is accredited by the Southern Association of Colleges and Schools and holds membership in the National Association of Independent Schools and the Council for Religion in Independent Schools, among other affiliations.

THE CAMPUSES. The Upper School and the Whitehurst Campus Lower School occupy 52 acres on the St. Johns River. Five miles to the northeast, the Bartram Campus Middle School is set on 23 acres at 2264 Bartram Road. The Bolles School at St. Augustine is located on 10 wooded acres at 1533 Wildwood Drive in the southern part of St. Augustine. The Bolles School at Ponte Vedra Beach is set on 12 acres off A1A in St. Johns County.

On the San Jose Campus, Bolles Hall houses classrooms, boys' dormitory rooms, a dining room and kitchen, offices, and three meeting rooms. Other Upper School academic buildings are Clifford G. Schultz Hall, with 17 classrooms; the Michael Marco Science Center, housing three science labs; the Joan W. and Martin E. Stein Computer Laboratory; the Hirsig Life Science Center; Ulmer Hall, including 15 classrooms, a language lab, and two science labs; and a marine science classroom along the St. Johns River.

The 14,000-volume Swisher Library houses the Meadow Multimedia Center with a large-screen television, two satellite dishes, and computer labs. Other facilities include the 660-seat McGehee Auditorium; the Cindy & Jay Stein Fine Arts Center, providing the Independent Life Music Building and the Lucy B. Gooding Art Gallery; and the Lynch Theater. All academic buildings are air-conditioned.

Upper School athletic facilities include the Collins Stadium at the Donovan Baseball Field, Hodges Field, the Bent Tennis Complex, the Baker-Gate Petroleum Company Track Facility, and Skinner-Barco Stadium. The Davis Sports Complex includes the Huston Student Center, basketball and volleyball courts, the 25-yard Lobrano and 50-meter Uible swimming pools, and the Garces Aquatic Center. The Agnes Cain Gymnasium features a wrestling room and athletic offices.

Middle School academic facilities include the Curry-Hicks Computer and Science Center, the Murchison-Lane Hall for classrooms and administrative offices, Williams Building, the Art Barn, a marine science classroom along Pottsburg Creek, girls' dormitory rooms, a multipurpose auditorium for performances, and the Pratt Library.

Among the Middle School athletic facilities are a football and soccer field, Lane Courts, Pace Gym, Meninak Field including Collins Baseball Stadium, and a pool.

The Whitehurst Campus Lower School houses each grade separately in homelike classrooms set around a natural playground. The Bolles School at St. Augustine and at Ponte Vedra Beach are both modern, self-contained facilities.

THE FACULTY. Harry M. deMontmollin was appointed President and Chief Executive Officer of the School in 1976. A native of Palatka, Florida, Mr. deMontmollin is a graduate of Bolles, the University of Florida (B.S.), College of William and Mary (B.A.), and the University of North Florida (M.Ed.). He has served Bolles in various teaching and administrative capacities since 1964.

The Bolles School has 172 professional staff; 83 have earned master's degrees and 11 hold doctorates. The average teaching experience is 14 years.

STUDENT BODY. Bolles enrolls 1700 students, 100 of whom are boarders who represent 25 countries and 18 states.

ACADEMIC PROGRAM. The school year, from late August to late May, is divided into quarters with Thanksgiving, winter, and spring breaks. The daily schedule for the Upper School, from 8:00 A.M. to 3:45 P.M., includes seven 45-minute periods and "Zero Hour," a 30-minute period reserved for individual conferences and extra help. An average class enrolls 17 except for English classes, which average 15. Boarders have evening study in their rooms, with faculty available for extra help, and

supervised study halls are provided for students needing more structured assistance. Grades, with narrative reports from faculty advisors, are sent to parents twice each quarter.

The Middle School curriculum includes English, government, world cultures, world geography, United States history, general mathematics, pre-algebra, and science. All students take some form of music education, and may select from band, chorus, drama, dance, graphics, drawing and painting, ceramics and sculpture, computers, foreign language, and language arts on a rotating basis throughout the year. Each student has an advisor, and a full-time, on-campus guidance counselor assists with decision-making skills, peer relations, and alcohol and drug abuse awareness.

Upper School students must earn 22 credits for graduation, with a college-certifying grade of C minus or above. Specific requirements are four years of English; two of a single foreign language; three of social studies including United States History, World History, and American Government/Economics; three of mathematics through Algebra II; three of science including Biology and Chemistry; two years of physical education; one year of fine arts; one half-year of life management skills; and three and one-half years of additional electives.

Advanced Placement courses are offered in American history, biology, calculus AB and BC, statistics, chemistry, physics, American government and politics, comparative government and politics, computer science, English literature and English language, European history, French, Latin, Spanish, portfolio art, and art history.

Sequential courses in major areas are available in all college preparatory subjects, and honors courses are offered in each discipline as well.

The English Department offers strong literary analysis and composition experience at all levels. Electives include Literature of the Holocaust, Creative Writing, Introduction to Philosophy, Bible History, and Public Speaking.

The Science Department provides college-level laboratory courses in Introduction to Physics and Chemistry, Biology, Chemistry, and Physics. Human Anatomy, Marine Science, Environmental Science, Neurobiology Honors, and Life Skills are electives.

The Foreign Language Department offers sequential courses in Spanish, French, Latin, German, and Japanese.

The Mathematics Department requires Algebra I and II and Geometry. In addition, Pre-Calculus, Calculus, Algebra III, Probability and Statistics, Computer Applications, Programming in C++, Web Site Development, and Visual Basic are offered.

The Fine and Performing Arts Department offers academic courses in Dance, Theatre, Vocal, Instrumental Music, and the visual arts, including Foundations in Studio Art, Sculpture, Ceramics, Painting, Watercolor, Drawing, and Photography.

Physical Education or an approved alternative is required of all students for two years in Grades 9 through 12.

All students who attend Bolles are college-bound. Ninety-two percent of the Advanced Placement scores for 1999 were 3s or above. Within the Class of 1999, 12 were National Merit Semifinalists, 17 were National Merit Commended Scholars, 1 was a National Hispanic Scholar, and 1 was a National Achievement Semifinalist. Members of the Class of 1999 applied to a total of 176 colleges and are attending 66 different institutions.

STUDENT ACTIVITIES. The Student Council, including class representatives and the president of each class, meets weekly to organize extracurricular activities and to supervise the Honor Council.

Students publish a yearbook, a newspaper, and a literary magazine. The following extracurricular clubs are available: Art, Chess, Computer, Curie Society, Debate/Forensics, D-Fy-Ince, Dreams Come True, Ecology, Fellowship of Christian Athletes, French, Gamma Service Club, German, Interact Service Club, Japanese, Latin, League of International Students, Learning Place, Mu Alpha Theta, Outdoor Environmental, Perspective, Quiz Team, Royal Pointe, Students Against Drunk Driving, Senior Women, Spanish, Student Advocate Council, Video Production, Young Life, and Youth Against Cancer. The Thespian Club stages productions open to the general public. Private lessons are available with specialists in all musical disciplines. Community service opportunities are offered both on and off campus.

Bolles is a member of the Florida High School Activities Association. Boys' varsity and junior varsity teams compete in football, swimming, cross-country, basketball, soccer, wrestling, baseball, track, tennis, and crew. Varsity and junior varsity teams for girls are organized in volleyball, swimming, cross-country, basketball, soccer, softball, tennis, track, crew, and cheerleading. There are also boys' and girls' varsity teams in golf, sailing, and lacrosse. Middle School boys teams compete in football, basketball, soccer, baseball, wrestling, swimming, and track, while Middle School girls' teams are formed in basketball, volleyball, soccer, softball, swimming, track, and cheerleading.

ADMISSION AND COSTS. Bolles seeks to admit academically qualified students with qualities of leadership and creativity. Students are admitted on the basis of the Bolles entrance examination, academic transcripts, and two academic recommendations. Resident students may submit the results of the Secondary School Admission Test. Application should be made as early as possible after September 1 of the year prior to desired enrollment; midyear enrollment is possible if vacancies exist. There is a $45 application fee; a 10 percent deposit and a $500 facilities fee, nonrefundable but applicable toward tuition, are due upon acceptance.

In 1999–2000, day tuition is $4000–$6950 for Kindergarten–Grade 5, $8700 for Grades 6–8, and $9325 for Grades 9–12. Tuition is $18,500 for five-day boarders and $20,600 for seven-day boarders. A tuition payment plan is available. The Bolles School, which subscribes to the School and Student Service for Financial Aid, awards need-based financial aid.

Executive Vice President/Chief Operating Officer: Edward J. Stopyra
Senior Vice President/Operations-Student Services: F. William Borg
Senior Vice President/Elementary Education; Principal/The Bolles School at Ponte Vedra Beach: Frederick H. Scott
Vice President/Finance: Ruth M. Hartley
Vice President/Advancement: Marlene M. Spalten
Vice President/Admission Services: Douglas A. Walker
Director of Studies/Academic Dean: Charles V. Harmon

The Canterbury School   1964

8141 College Parkway, Fort Myers, FL 33919. 941-481-4323; Fax 941-481-8339; E-mail Mason_Goss@Canterbury.pvt.k12.fl.us; Web Site www.canterbury.pvt.k12.fl.us

The Canterbury School is a college preparatory day school enrolling 605 boys and girls in Pre-Kindergarten–Grade 12. It emphasizes rigorous academic standards but aims at the full development of individual students through competitive athletics, extracurricular activities, and personal as well as college counseling. Advanced Placement courses are available for qualified upper-level students, and elective options are available in all major academic disciplines, the arts, and computer science. Tuition: $6800–$9300. Financial Aid: $765,000. R. Mason Goss is Director of Admission; Jerry Zank (St. Olaf College, B.A.; University of Minnesota, M.A.) is Headmaster.

Canterbury School of Florida   1968

Hough Campus (PK–Grade 5): 1200 Snell Isle Boulevard, St. Petersburg, FL 33704. 727-823-5515; Fax 727-823-2317; Web Site www.canterbury-fla.com
Knowlton Campus (Grades 6–12): 901 58th Avenue NE, St. Petersburg, FL 33703. 727-525-1419; Fax 727-525-2545; Web Site www.canterbury-fla.com

Canterbury School of Florida enrolls 450 boys and girls in Pre-Kindergarten–Grade 12 in a college preparatory program. The School is committed to helping students discover their talents and abilities to aid in the development of high-level skills, values, confidence, and self-esteem. A student/teacher ratio of 9:1, combined with highly experienced faculty and Advanced Placement courses, provides students with many opportunities in college placement. Nearly all graduates attend four-year colleges. Affiliated with the Episcopal Church, Canterbury welcomes students of all faiths and backgrounds. Tuition: $5600–$6850. Financial aid is available. J. Russell Ball (Knowlton) and Janet Murray (Hough) are Directors; David H. Dike (University of Southwestern Louisiana, M.S.) is Headmaster.

Cardinal Mooney High School   1959

4171 Fruitville Road, Sarasota, FL 34232. 941-371-4917; Fax 941-371-6924; Web Site http://www.cmhs-sarasota.org

Enrolling 620 boys and girls in Grades 9–12, Cardinal Mooney High School, under the auspices of the Roman Catholic diocese of Venice, was founded to provide a "God-centered, comprehensive education" for area youth. The curriculum includes college preparatory and general courses. Honors and Advanced Placement are available. Extensive activities involve 90 percent of students. Tuition: $4300–$5150. Financial aid is available. Jane Barker is Guidance Director; Sr. Mary Lucia Haas, SND (Notre Dame College of Ohio, B.S. 1966; College of William and Mary, M.T.S. 1971), was appointed President in 1994. *Southern Association.*

Carrollton School of the Sacred Heart   1961

3747 Main Highway, Miami, FL 33133. 305-446-5673; Fax 305-529-6533; E-mail admissions@carrollton.org; Web Site www.carrollton.org

Carrollton, established by the Society of the Sacred Heart, is a Roman Catholic college preparatory school enrolling 640 girls as day students in Pre-Kindergarten–Grade 12. It aims to educate its students to a personal and active faith in God, respect for intellectual values, social consciousness, the building of community, and personal growth. A member of the Network of Sacred Heart Schools in 20 cities, all sharing the same traditions, the School conducts annual reviews of its programs and sets new directions accordingly. Tuition: $8575–$12,575. Financial Aid: $651,000. Ana Gloria Rivas-Vazquez is Associate Head for Institutional Advancement; Sr. Suzanne Cooke, RSCJ (Manhattanville, B.A.; University of Chicago, M.A.), is Headmistress.

Florida

Chaminade-Madonna College Preparatory 1960

500 Chaminade Drive, Hollywood, FL 33021. 954-989-5150;
Fax 954-983-4663; Web Site www.cmlions.com

Chaminade-Madonna College Preparatory is a coeducational day school enrolling 875 students from diverse cultural and religious backgrounds in Grades 9–12. Chaminade-Madonna, Catholic and Marianist in its identity, educates the heart and soul as well as the mind and body in a familylike community. The Einstein wing (1996) contains a state-of-the-art computer lab, and the media center houses 23 computer stations. Students participate in nearly 40 extracurricular activities, and a competitive athletic program boasts 29 teams. With 98 percent of graduates entering college each year, Chaminade-Madonna has been recognized as a Blue Ribbon School. Tuition: $4750–$5750. Financial Aid: $230,000. Br. John H. Campbell, SM, is President.

The Cushman School   MIAMI

592 North East 60th Street, Miami, FL 33137. 305-757-1966;
Fax 305-757-1632; E-mail admission@cushmanschool.org;
Web Site www.cushmanschool.org

THE CUSHMAN SCHOOL in Miami, Florida, is an independent, nondenominational school enrolling boys and girls as day students in three-year-old Nursery through Grade 8. The School is located on Biscayne Boulevard, approximately five miles from downtown Miami, and is easily accessible by car and major bus routes from all areas of Dade County. Miami (population 346,681) offers numerous attractions, and students and faculty take advantage of the enrichment opportunities provided by the Museum of Science, the Dade County Historical and Art museums, performing arts theaters, the Seaquarium, and Everglades National Park.

The present-day school was founded in 1924 by Laura Cushman, who conducted the first classes on the front porch of her home. Miss Cushman's goal was to develop children mentally, physically, and in character growth by providing a happy

learning environment in which students could reach their full potential.

The founder's philosophy remains central to the School, which promotes self-worth, responsibility, appreciation for the arts and literature, and respect for individual beliefs. In 1992, in recognition of its "demanding curriculum, extraordinary collegiality, and record of achievement and improvement," the U.S. Department of Education awarded Cushman a National School of Excellence Blue Ribbon.

A nonprofit institution, Cushman is governed by a 16-member Board of Trustees. Many of the 1500 living alumni assist the School through financial support, recruitment, and volunteerism. Cushman is accredited by the Florida Council of Independent Schools and the Florida Kindergarten Council; it holds membership in the National Association of Independent Schools, the Southern Association of Independent Schools, and the National Association for the Education of Young Children, among other professional organizations.

THE CAMPUS. Cushman's 5-acre campus is divided into three distinct areas. The Elementary School includes the main classroom/administration building, constructed in 1926 and designated a historic landmark by the City of Miami, housing Grades 2 through 6 as well as an art room, library, an outdoor patio and stage area, and a playground. A new portion of the campus houses the reinstated seventh and eighth grades. Across the street is the Primary School, which contains classrooms and offices for Preschool through Grade 1, a music room, science and computer labs, and two tree-shaded playgrounds.

The plant is owned by The Cushman School and is valued at approximately $4,000,000.

THE FACULTY. Headmistress Joan D. Lutton, Ed.D., has guided the School since 1981. A native of Jacksonville, Florida, she holds a baccalaureate degree from Rutgers University (1966), a master's degree from Barry College (1977), and a doctorate from the University of Florida at Gainesville (1982). Prior to assuming her current position, Dr. Lutton served as Assistant Principal at Cushman and held teaching posts in several independent and public schools in four states. She and her husband, Stephen, have three grown children.

The faculty, including two administrators who teach, have earned 35 baccalaureate and 12 advanced degrees, representing study at Auburn, Barry, Brown, Davidson, Emory, Florida State, Goldsmith's College, Lenoir-Rhyne, London University, Manchester College, Manhattanville, National-Louis, Northeastern, Ohio Wesleyan, Portland State, Southern Connecticut State, Stephen F. Austin State, Texas Women's, West Virginia Wesleyan, Winthrop, and the Universities of Colorado, Florida, Hertfordshire (England), Miami, Michigan, South Carolina, and Virginia. There are also three learning resource teachers who help students with special needs. Faculty benefits include Social Security, health insurance, a retirement plan, support for education and professional development, and sabbaticals and leaves of absence.

A registered nurse is on duty during school hours, and emergency medical facilities are available at nearby hospitals. The School also employs a guidance counselor.

STUDENT BODY. The Cushman School enrolls 380 boys and girls, distributed as follows: 16 in Nursery, 16 in a multiage class, 25 in Junior Kindergarten, 37 in Senior Kindergarten, 43 in Grade 1, 37 in Grade 2, 38 in Grade 3, 42 in Grade 4, 36 in Grade 5, 33 in Grade 6, 30 in Grade 7, and 27 in Grade 8. There are three Senior Kindergarten classes and two each in all other grades, beginning in Junior Kindergarten. Students come from ten communities within the Greater Miami metropolitan area and represent more than 30 nationalities; approximately 16 percent are Latino, 10 percent are African-American, and 8 percent are Asian-American.

ACADEMIC PROGRAM. The school year, divided into quarters, extends from early September to June with a Thanksgiving recess, Christmas vacation, a spring break, and observances of several national and religious holidays. Report cards are sent home quarterly; younger students receive written commentaries on their progress and achievements, while letter grades begin in Grade 4. The school day for the Primary and Elementary levels begins at 8:30 A.M. with the Salute to the Flag and ends at 3:05 P.M. The Middle School is in session from 7:50 A.M. to 3:10 P.M. Faculty-supervised study periods are provided within the daily schedule. Classes are small, enrolling an average of 17 students, and three learning resource specialists are available to help students with special academic or organizational needs. Parent-supervised playgrounds and extended day care are available after school.

The Pre-school division is comprised of four levels: Nursery, Multiage, Junior Kindergarten, and Senior Kindergarten. Nursery students must have reached their third birthday by December of the desired year of enrollment; Junior and Senior Kindergarten children must be four and five, respectively, by September of the year they enter.

At the Nursery and Multiage level, the program is designed to acclimate children socially to their new school environment. Junior and Senior Kindergarten focus on the development of motor skills, listening and communication techniques, and reading and math readiness to provide a firm foundation for the academic work of the first grade.

The child-centered curriculum encompasses all areas of reading, the related language arts, and mathematics with special enrichment classes in social studies, science, music (singing, folk dancing, introduction to musical instruments), art, conversational Spanish, computers, and library science. All students take part in physical education activities designed to promote teamwork, sportsmanship, and athletic skills. Classroom

instruction is enhanced by frequent field trips, monthly assemblies, and visiting guests.

The 6–8th grades are part of Anywhere, Anytime Learning, a laptop program in which all students work online on their own laptops for most of the day.

In 1996, Cushman instituted a Middle School program with the opening of a small seventh-grade class in a newly purchased building adjacent to the campus. Middle School students follow an integrated curriculum with some focus on life in South Florida through the study of Latin America, Spanish, and marine biology. Other subjects include mathematics, English, Latin, communications, study skills, art and art history, drama, speech, leadership, and physical education. "Character First," with an emphasis on community service and leadership, is the theme of the Middle School.

There were 64 graduates in the Classes of 1999. Among the schools they are currently attending are American Heritage, Carrollton School of the Sacred Heart, Cushman Middle School, Langley, Miami Country Day School, Ransom Everglades, St. Francis, and St. Timothy's of Maryland.

Cushman conducts four summer programs: Kindercamp, an eight-week half-day session for ages 3–6; Precamp, a two-week experience for ages 3–12; Spanish camp, a two-week morning program for ages 4–10; and the Learning Camp, a three-week academic session of two hours daily for students ages 7–12. Most participants are from Cushman, but students from other schools are welcome.

STUDENT ACTIVITIES. A Student Council for Grades 4 through 6 assists the School and community through service and fund-raising projects.

Cushman sponsors an after-school "Clubhouse" offering a variety of activities which may include chess, computers, cross-country, karate, piano, guitar, and geography.

Special events are scheduled throughout the year involving Cushman families such as a Halloween Fair and an annual family dinner-dance. Book Fair, Parents' Nights, Founder's Day, Grandparents' Day, Jog-a-Thon, Creativity Day, May Day Celebration, Fathers' Breakfast, the spring play, Awards Day, and Graduation are other highlights on the school calendar.

ADMISSION AND COSTS. The Cushman School seeks boys and girls from diverse racial and cultural backgrounds who are of average to superior ability and who show promise of benefiting from its programs and philosophy. Students are admitted to all grades as openings permit. Acceptance is based on an interview with student and parents and on previous academic transcripts. Application should be made, along with a $50 fee, by February for the following academic year. There is no closing date for applying.

In 1999–2000, tuition ranges from $6870 to $9150, depending on grade level. Other expenses include student insurance ($20), tuition insurance ($130–$170), books and supplies ($175–$210), and a registration/reenrollment fee ($50). Financial aid based on demonstrated need is awarded to 20 percent of the student body.

School Principal: Cheryl Rogers
Primary School Director: Beverly McCorquodale
Middle School Director: Shirley Davis
Director of Admissions: Barbara Sugarman
Director of Institutional Advancement: Eileen Immer
Business Manager: Ken Cebeck
Athletic Director: Larry Balseiro

Episcopal High School of Jacksonville   1966

4455 Atlantic Boulevard, Jacksonville, FL 32207.
904-396-5751; Fax 904-396-7209;
Web Site http://www.episcopal.high.jax.fl.us

Episcopal High School of Jacksonville is a coeducational day school serving approximately 800 students in Grades 6–12.

Episcopal takes pride in encouraging its students as they strive for excellence in academic, artistic, and athletic achievement, commitment to others, and moral leadership. The supportive teaching faculty, small class size, challenging college preparatory curriculum, and outstanding facilities combine to create a dynamic educational environment marked by high expectations, Christian nurture, and social diversity. Tuition: $8850–$9450. Financial aid is available. Peggy Fox is Admissions Director; Charles F. Zimmer is Headmaster. *Southern Association.*

Florida Air Academy   MELBOURNE

1950 South Academy Drive, Melbourne, FL 32901. 407-723-3211; E-mail rwilson@flair.com; Web Site www.flair.com

FLORIDA AIR ACADEMY in Melbourne, Florida, is a college preparatory boarding and day school for boys in Grades 7 through 12. Melbourne (population 65,000) is midway between Jacksonville and Miami on Route 192, about 50 miles east of Orlando. Nearby Melbourne International Airport and the Florida Institute of Technology cooperate with the Academy in its flight-training programs for cadets.

In 1961, Col. Jonathan Dwight founded Florida Air Academy to prepare "each cadet for college, for leadership, and for life in the twenty-first century." Florida Air Academy continues to operate under the leadership of the Dwight family. It is supervised by an eight-member Board of Directors, three of whom are actively involved in the operation of the school; the other directors meet periodically in an advisory capacity. The Academy is accredited by the Southern Association of Colleges and Schools and the Florida Council of Independent Schools; it is a member of the Southern Association of Independent Schools and the Association of Military Schools and Colleges of the United States, among other organizations.

THE CAMPUS. The school campus occupies more than 30 acres, including athletic fields, tennis courts, an outdoor basketball court, a swimming pool, a gymnasium, and a weight room. All interior living areas, classrooms, the dining room, the gymnasium, the library, and computer labs are fully air-conditioned. The Hall of Flags contains administrative offices, cadet living quarters, a student lounge, a Base Exchange, the dining hall, and the library. Dwight, Blatt, and Phelps halls contain administrative offices. Hart, Haerle, Adeline, and Donelson halls contain classrooms, the science laboratory, three computer labs, a language center, and laundry facilities. A school canteen is operated on campus. An Academy nurse is on duty in the infirmary.

THE FACULTY. LTC James Dwight, President and Headmaster of Florida Air Academy, is a graduate of Middlebury College (B.A.), Columbia University (M.A.), and the Florida Institute of Technology (M.S.).

In addition to Air Force personnel assigned to the JROTC program, the full-time faculty consists of 23 men and 12 women. Certified guidance counselors are available. The faculty members hold baccalaureate degrees, and more than half hold master's degrees. Representative faculty colleges are Columbia, Cornell, Florida Institute of Technology, Florida State, Georgia Institute of Technology, Indiana University, Marshall University, Princeton, Rollins, and the Universities of Arkansas, Central Florida, Florida, Kansas, Kentucky, Mississippi, South Carolina, Southern California, and South Florida.

STUDENT BODY. In 1999–2000, the Florida Air Academy student body included 325 boarding boys and 75 day boys, from 12 to 19 years of age. Approximately 50 percent of the boys are from Florida, and 20 percent come from 25 other states; the remainder are residents of United States territories or foreign countries.

ACADEMIC PROGRAM. The school year, from early September to early June, is divided into semesters. Leaves are scheduled at Thanksgiving, Christmas, and Easter. Cadets in good standing may take regular weekend leaves.

Classes, which meet five days per week, have an average of 15 students. A comprehensive honors curriculum, Advanced Placement, and dual enrollment provide an academic opportunity that is challenging and progressive. A typical daily schedule includes six class periods, activities, athletics, and a mandatory two-hour evening study hall. Four days per week, an afternoon period is scheduled, during which time faculty are available to offer academic assistance. This study time is supported by technology in three computer/language labs, which offer Internet and e-mail access, word processing, and other applications software. Internet and e-mail access as well as telephone service are available at each student's desk.

In Grades 7 and 8, the curriculum includes English, science, mathematics, history, physical education, and creative wheel (art, music, computers, and Aerospace Science).

To graduate, cadets must complete 26 credits, or the equivalent of 26 full-year courses, in Grades 9–12. Specific requirements are English 4, social studies 3, mathematics 4, science 3, foreign language 2, computer science 1, and physical education/health 1. In addition, cadets must take AFJROTC each year.

The Academy's college preparatory curriculum includes English 1–4, Journalism; Spanish 1–4; World History, United States History, American Government, Economics, World Geography, Psychology; Algebra 1–2, Geometry, Pre-Calculus, Calculus; Physical Science, Biology, Chemistry, Physics, Oceanography, Astronomy; College Board Preparation; Computer Graphics, Business Computer Applications, Electronic Publishing, Computer Programming; Art, Band, Music; and Driver Education.

Advanced Placement courses are offered in English, Spanish, Calculus, Biology, Chemistry, and Physics.

The AFJROTC Program consists of Aerospace Science courses covering such topics as aeronautics, space exploration, and leadership training. Flight training provides the ground training, simulator instruction, and aircraft experience needed to qualify for a Private Pilot Certificate. By special arrangement, advanced students may begin working toward a Commercial Pilot Certificate, Instrument Rating, or Multi-engine Rating.

In 1999, all 67 graduates were admitted to colleges such as United States service academies, College of William and Mary, Embry-Riddle Aeronautical University, Florida State University, Louisiana State, Loyola, Michigan State, Ohio State, Pennsylvania State, Purdue, Seton Hall University, and the Universities of Florida and Miami.

During the summer, Florida Air Academy conducts a six-week academic program. Cadets may earn credit for new or makeup courses. Tuition for the session is $2000 for day students and $4200 for boarding students. Flight training is available for boys in Grades 7–12. The summer flight training cost is $1000–$2500.

STUDENT ACTIVITIES. The AFJROTC Cadet Corps is organized as a Wing, with four Squadrons and a Headquarters Squadron. Under the supervision of the Commandant's staff and Aerospace Science Instructors, student officers govern the Corps through a military chain of command. A system of merits and promotions is used to reward excellence.

Typical activities are the Drum and Bugle Corps, National Champion Drill Team, National Honor Society, yearbook, newspaper, and Photography, Model Airplane, Surfing, Fishing, Military, and All-Sports clubs. All boys are encouraged to participate in athletics, and interscholastic competition is introduced in Grade 7. Students compete in soccer, football, tennis, golf, track, and cross-country, and Florida Air Academy earned the title of 3A State Champions in 1998 in basketball and baseball. Individual and intramural sports are also available.

The Activities Director schedules trips to Kennedy Space Center, Disney World, MGM, Epcot, Sea World, Universal Studios, and other points of interest. He also plans dances, barbecues, luaus, and pool parties as well as special events, such as Grad Night at Disney World, the Military Ball, and Homecoming Alumni activities. Senior High cadets in good standing may sign out for town leave on Friday and Saturday evenings. Transportation is arranged for those attending weekend worship services.

Traditional events are the senior trip, senior ring banquet and dance, the Military Ball, Homecoming for the Academy's parents and alumni, and dinner for graduates and their parents. Fall Open House and Spring Open House/International Festival provide opportunity for families to visit campus and talk with teachers in an atmosphere of celebration.

ADMISSION AND COSTS. Students are accepted in all grades on the basis of school records, character references, and a personal interview with a school official or alumnus. Applications are processed throughout the year, and late enrollment is permitted when vacancies exist. The $100 application fee is refunded if the candidate is not accepted.

Tuition for 1999–2000 is $17,200 for boarding boys and $5500 for day boys. Fees cover educational program, room and board, books, uniform use, laundry, linens, haircuts, dry cleaning, infirmary, and yearbook. Tuition payment plans are available.

Optional programs include Flight Program, Driver Education, Scuba, Tae Kwon Do, Computer Instruction, Tutorial Reading and Math, SAT Prep, and English as a Second Language. Academic financial assistance is available for students who qualify.

Commandant: LTC Steve Mayer
Alumni Director: Maj. Debra E. Landis
Director of Admission: LTC Raymond C. Wilson
College Counselors: LTC Reginald Bird and Ms. Deborah Dwight
Controller: LTC Barry Fredianelli
Director of Athletics: Mr. Don Kelbick

Gulf Stream School   1938

3600 Gulf Stream Road, Gulf Stream, FL 33483-7499. 561-276-5225; Fax 561-276-7115; E-mail agibb@gulf-streamschool.org; Web Site www.gulfstreamschool.org

Gulf Stream School, enrolling 225 day boys and girls in Nursery–Grade 8, is located near the ocean a mile north of Delray Beach. The School is committed to meeting the academic, creative, and physical needs of each student and to encourage success at each level. A close parent-school partnership creates a family atmosphere. A Montessori program is offered in Pre-Kindergarten; Grades 5–8 are departmentalized. The curriculum includes French, Latin, Spanish, art, music, and computer. Among the activities are publications, drama, choral group, bell choir, and sports. Winter-season students are accommodated. Summer programs are available. Tuition: $6325–$9950. Financial Aid: $97,000. Miss Anne G. Gibb is Headmistress.

Independent Day School   1968

12015 Orange Grove Drive, Tampa, FL 33618. 813-961-3087; Fax 813-963-0846; E-mail pbarfield@idsyes.com

Independent Day School emphasizes academic excellence, experiential learning, individual attention, and positive self-concepts for each student. Enrolling 400 boys and girls in Pre-Kindergarten–Grade 8, the School offers a precollege preparatory curriculum of language arts, math, science, social studies, Spanish, computer, music, art, library skills, and physical education. Activities include musical performances, art shows, a pond reclamation project, student book buddies, Student Council, athletics, and community service. Talented, dynamic teachers inspire students to love learning and set high goals. Tuition: $5700–$6200. Pam Barfield is Director of Advancement; Dr. Joyce Swarzman (Ohio State, B.A.; Columbia Teachers College, M.Ed., Ed.D.) is Headmaster.

Jacksonville Country Day School   1960

10063 Baymeadows Road, Jacksonville, FL 32256. 904-641-6644;
  Fax 904-641-1494; E-mail admiss@jcds.com;
  Web Site www.jcds.com

"Excellence in Education" was the founding principle that led to the establishment of Jacksonville Country Day School 40 years ago. Enrolling 500 students in Junior Kindergarten–Grade 6, the academic program emphasizes mastery of reading and language arts and a strong basis in mathematics, social studies, science, and the arts. Over 175 computers and a state-of-the-art science lab integrate technology into the curriculum. The music program features Orff instruments and chimes. The campus includes a 10,000-volume library, an art room with kiln, several athletic fields, and two swimming pools. An eight-week summer day camp is offered. Tuition: $4800–$5700. Extras: $300–$480. Sharon A. Keen is Director of Admissions; Geraldine Kelly (Loyola, B.S.; Columbia, M.A.) is Headmistress. *Southern Association.*

Lake Highland Preparatory School   1970

901 North Highland Avenue, Orlando, FL 32803. 407-206-1900;
  Fax 407-206-1933; Web Site http:\\www.lhps.org

Founded on "Christian principles and democratic ideals," Lake Highland Preparatory is a nondenominational, coeducational day school enrolling more than 1660 students in Pre-Kindergarten–Grade 12. The traditional liberal arts curriculum emphasizes developmental writing and hands-on learning activities in the Lower School, while the Upper School's structured program offers honors and Advanced Placement courses in all disciplines. Small classes, a comprehensive guidance program, and a varied spectrum of athletics, clubs, and interest groups are features of a Lake Highland education. Tuition: $6250–$8250. Financial aid is available. Dr. Betsy Folk is Admissions Director; J. Robert Mayfield (Auburn, Ed.D.) is President. *Southern Association.*

Julie Rohr Academy   1974

4466 Fruitville Road, Sarasota, FL 34232. 941-371-4979;
  Fax 941-378-5816; E-mail JRAcademy@aol.com;
  Web Site www.julierohracademy.com

Founded by Julie and Arthur Rohr to provide an academic private school for Sarasota County, the Julie Rohr Academy enrolls 110 boys and 135 girls as day students in Nursery–Grade 8. The school aims to provide a strong, individualized academic program geared to each student's rate of development. The curriculum emphasizes basic academics but also provides a performing arts program that seeks to teach poise, self-discipline, and expressiveness. Day-care services are available before and after school, and a recreational summer program is offered. Tuition: $3463–$4575. Extras: $260–$325. Cecilia R. Blankenship is Admissions Director; Julie Rohr McHugh (University of Miami, B.M. 1968, M.M. 1969) has been Principal since 1974.

Maclay School   1968

3737 North Meridian Road, Tallahassee, FL 32312.
  904-893-2138; Fax 904-893-7434; Web Site www.maclay.org

Maclay is a college preparatory day school enrolling 554 girls and 547 boys in Preschool–Grade 12. It seeks to teach the liberal arts creatively and to help students realize their full potential through self-discipline and persistence. Computer studies, creative writing, music, and drama complement the traditional curriculum. Sports, student government, honor societies, publications, theater, and service clubs are among the activities. A summer session offers remedial and enrichment courses. Tuition: $6450. Financial Aid: $300,000. William W. Jablon (Boston College, B.A. 1968; Florida State, M.A. 1972) was appointed President/Headmaster in 1976. *Southern Association.*

Miami Country Day School   1938

601 North East 107th Street, Miami, FL 33161-7199.
  305-759-2843; Fax 305-758-5107;
  E-mail admissions@mcds.pvt.k12.fl.us;
  Web Site http://www.miamicountryday.org

Miami Country Day, enrolling 950 boys and girls in Junior Kindergarten–Grade 12, offers a challenging college preparatory program within a learning environment characterized by Judeo-Christian values and respect for each individual within the school community. Named an Exemplary School by the U.S. Department of Education, its goal is to develop the whole child through a classical curriculum that includes the visual and performing arts, English as a Second Language, and Advanced Placement courses. Interscholastic varsity sports are among the activities offered to meet a variety of interests. A summer program is available. Tuition: $7840–$12,715. Financial Aid: $650,000. Adele Yermack is Director of Admission; Dr. John M. Knapp is Headmaster. *Southern Association.*

Montverde Academy   MONTVERDE

17235 Seventh Street, P.O. Box 560097, Montverde, FL 34756.
  407-469-2561; E-mail info@montverde.org;
  Web Site www.montverde.org

MONTVERDE ACADEMY in Montverde, Florida, is a coeducational school enrolling boarding and day students in Grades 7 through 12 and a postgraduate year. Montverde (population 1000) is 25 miles west of Orlando in central Florida's citrus belt. Among the area's attractions are Disney World and Epcot Center.

Founded in 1912 by Mr. and Mrs. H. P. Carpenter, the Academy was originally a country day and boarding school serving the surrounding county. In 1921, The Montverde School, as it was then known, began enrolling students from throughout the state. The school was renamed Montverde Academy in 1962.

The Academy seeks to provide an environment in which students can develop an intrinsic desire for learning and an abiding appreciation for "the higher values of life." Small classes encourage close interaction among students and between students and teachers, helping students to develop respect for and appreciation of each other and adults. Self-discipline and self-respect are encouraged as the Academy directs students toward the goal of becoming "responsible citizens of the community." Faculty members and administrators conduct a weekly nondenominational chapel service; attendance is required for all except Catholic students, who attend Mass at a local church.

A nonprofit institution, Montverde Academy is governed by a 13-member Board of Trustees. New board members, who may be recommended by the current board, alumni, or friends of the school, are elected annually. Montverde Academy is accredited by the Southern Association of Colleges and Schools. It holds membership in the Southern Association of Independent Schools.

THE CAMPUS. The 125-acre campus is situated between Lake Apopka and Lake Florence and is surrounded by groves of citrus trees. The Lake Florence waterfront is available for supervised swimming, sunning, boating, and waterskiing. An outdoor athletic facility features a six-lane, 440-yard asphalt running track; four tennis courts; a baseball diamond; and a soccer field. The Academy also has an outdoor swimming pool and an activities building.

Major school buildings, all renovated or newly constructed over the past several years, include the Duncan Student Center; Walter L. Stephens, Jr., Administration Building; McKenzie, which houses classrooms and the Academy's 20 new computer terminals; and Conrad Lehmann, another classroom building. The Fine Art Center includes a 446-seat theater and drama facility, a dance studio, and rooms for music, art, and photography. A 10,000-volume library/media center was completed in 1987. A science building consisting of chemistry and biology labs with lecture rooms was completed in 1992. Also on campus

are a weight-lifting room, a 60-foot bell tower, and the President's home and faculty living quarters.

Arnold Hall, a dormitory for boys in Grades 10–12, houses 65 boys and 2 houseparents; Carpenter Hall has a recreation room and rooms for 70 boys. Girls' dormitories are D.A.R. Hall, which houses 65 girls and several housemothers, and McCammack Hall, a two-story structure with a recreation room, offering rooms for 52 girls and 2 housemothers. All dormitories are air-conditioned. The dining hall accommodates 300 persons.

The Academy has an ongoing building program. A fitness center with state-of-the-art equipment opened in October 1997. The plant, which is owned by the Academy, is valued at $16,000,000.

THE FACULTY. Kasey C. Kesselring was appointed Headmaster of the Academy in 1999. A native of Maryland, Mr. Kesselring attended Saint James School. After earning his B.A. degree from Dickinson College, he returned to Saint James as a Latin and math teacher, coach, and dormitory master. In 1990, he became Director of College Counseling and later served the School as Assistant Director of Development. Prior to his appointment at Montverde Academy, Mr. Kesselring served The Webb School in Bell Buckle, Tennessee, as Dean of Students and Assistant Headmaster. While at Webb, he earned his M.Ed. in administration and supervision from Middle Tennessee State University.

The full-time faculty number 18, 12 men and 6 women. Seventeen faculty members and administrators live on campus, 10 with their families. The faculty hold 17 baccalaureate and 7 graduate degrees representing study at such institutions as Auburn, Barry, Dickinson, East Tennessee State, Florida Institute of Technology, Florida State, Georgia Southern, Jacksonville University, Misericordia, North Carolina State, Nova, Nova Scotia Teachers College, Piedmont, Rollins, Rutgers, Tusculum College, Valdosta State, and the Universities of Alabama, Central Florida, Florida, Massachusetts, Pittsburgh, and South Florida.

First aid is available on campus. Medical emergencies are handled at two hospitals, both within ten miles of the Academy.

STUDENT BODY. In 1999–2000, the Academy enrolls 100 boarding boys, 80 boarding girls, 12 day boys, and 8 day girls in Grades 7–12 and a postgraduate year. Most of the boarding students are from Florida, but eight other states and 30 foreign countries and territories are also represented.

ACADEMIC PROGRAM. The school year, from early September to late May, is divided into semesters and includes a Thanksgiving weekend recess, a three-week Christmas vacation, and a week-long spring vacation. Classes are held five days a week, with a half-day of classes on selected Saturdays throughout the year. A typical weekday, from 6:30 A.M. rising to 10:30 P.M. "lights out" for seniors, includes breakfast, seven 50-minute class periods, lunch, an activities period, and dinner.

There is a 90-minute supervised study period in the dormitories on weekday and Sunday evenings; students who need individual assistance meet with teachers during the 50-minute tutorial period after the close of regular classes each afternoon. The Academy offers English as a Second Language for students who need to master English before pursuing the regular curriculum. Grades are issued and sent to parents every six weeks.

All students in Grades 7–8 are required to take six courses each semester. The prescribed curriculum includes language arts, history, geography, mathematics, life or earth science, and physical education. Among the electives usually offered are developmental reading, speech, Spanish, art, music, and typing.

To graduate, students in the college preparatory program must complete four years of language arts, two of Spanish, three of social studies, three of mathematics, three of science, one of keyboarding/word processing, and two of physical education. Minimum requirements for students in the general program are four years of English, three each of social studies, mathematics, and science, and two of physical education.

Basic courses offered for students in Grades 9–12 include English 1–4, Language Arts 1–2; Spanish 1–4; Civics, World Geography, World History, American History, Government and Americanism vs. Communism; Pre-Algebra, General Math, Algebra 1–2, Geometry, Advanced Mathematics; Physical Science, Biology, Chemistry, Physics; and Keyboard/Word Processing. Electives, offered according to demand, may include Developmental Reading, Journalism, Family Life, Economics, Sociology, General Law, Current World Affairs, Computer Science, Art, Music, and Driver Education. English as a Second Language is available for international students.

In 1999, all of the 14 graduating seniors went on to college. They were accepted at such colleges and universities as American InterContinental University, Azusa Pacific, Barry, Boston College, Boston University, Drew, Duquesne, Embry-Riddle Aeronautical, Florida State, Georgia Southern, Georgia Southwestern State, Harvard/Radcliffe, Johnson & Wales, Marywood, Mercer University, Mount Holyoke, Rollins, St. Joseph's University, San Francisco State, Stetson, and the Universities of Alabama, Georgia, Hawaii, Illinois, Miami, San Francisco, South Florida, and Tampa.

The Montverde Academy Summer School offers courses for makeup, improvement, and enrichment. The six-week program enrolls day and boarding students in Grades 1–12.

STUDENT ACTIVITIES. The Student Council of Montverde Academy promotes cooperation throughout the school community, makes recommendations on matters of general concern, and carries out projects assigned by the administration. Composed of representatives from Grades 9–12 and one member of the administration, the Council also maintains an Honor Court that tries students for alleged rule violations and makes suggestions to the administration for final disposition of cases.

Student organizations and activities include the yearbook and the Discussion, Bike, Pep, Psychology, National Art Society, Fellowship, Computer, Music, Beta, Skating, Drama, and Fitness clubs. There are also opportunities for students to pursue special interests, such as dance, ceramics, and woodworking.

A member of the Florida High School Activities Association, Montverde Academy competes with public and independent schools in a number of sports. Boys' and girls' teams are organized in basketball, cross-country, tennis, and track. Boys also compete in soccer, and there are girls' softball and volleyball teams. Cycling, fishing, softball, swimming, and waterskiing are offered on a recreational basis.

With parental and school permission, students in good standing may leave the campus on designated weekends to visit home or another approved destination. The Academy provides transportation to and from the airport and bus and train stations in Orlando. For students who remain on campus, weekend activities include movies, interscholastic or intramural athletics, and trips to nearby shopping malls. Other trips scheduled throughout the year take students to Disney World, Epcot Center, Cypress Gardens, the John Young Planetarium, Sea World, and college football and basketball games.

Traditional events for the school community are the Halloween party and dance, Homecoming, the Christmas dance, Graduate Night at Disney World, annual barbecue, Honors Day, and the Baccalaureate Service and reception.

ADMISSION AND COSTS. Montverde Academy seeks to enroll young people who desire a quality education in a structured environment. New students are admitted to Grades 7–12 on the basis of the previous academic record and recommendations from the last school attended, character references, and a personal interview; an entrance examination is optional. Applications are accepted throughout the year, and students are enrolled as long as space is available. Because the Academy has a one-year residency requirement, seniors are not enrolled once the fall semester has begun. There is a $50 application fee.

In 1999–2000, boarding tuition is $13,350; day tuition is $5400. One-time additional fees are for books (approximately $600) and the Academy yearbook ($62). When applicable, fees are assessed for services and activities. Tuition payment plans are available.

Dean of Academics: Paul F. Ingrassia, Jr.
Dean of Students: Warren Delmolino
Director of Admission: Maureen C. Kesselring
College Counselor: James Marino
Business Manager: Jane Brewer
Director of Athletics: Dana Dodson

Oak Hall School   1970

8009 SW 14th Avenue, Gainesville, FL 32607. 352-332-3609; Fax 352-332-4975; E-mail oakhall@oakhall.pvt.k12.fl.us; Web Site http://oakhall.pvt.k12.fl.us

Oak Hall School is a coeducational, college preparatory day school enrolling approximately 385 students in Grades 6–12. The School aims to challenge college-bound students to reach the limits of their academic ability as they prepare for college and future responsibilities. A new Middle School facility opened in 1999; a state-of-the-art Media Center houses the School's computer lab. A full fine arts program is offered, and theater, community service, and athletics are principal cocurricular activities. Tuition: $6500. Alice Garwood is Director of Admissions; Richard H. Gehman (Princeton University, B.A. 1975; University of Massachusetts, M.Ed. 1980) was appointed Headmaster in 1993.

The Out-of-Door Academy   1924

PK–Grade 6: 444 Reid Street, Sarasota, FL 34242. 941-349-3223;
*   Fax 941-349-8133; E-mail hinckley@oda.edu;*
*   Web Site http://www.oda.edu*
Grades 7–12: 5950 Deer Drive, Sarasota, FL 34240. 941-349-3223;
*   Fax 941-907-1251*

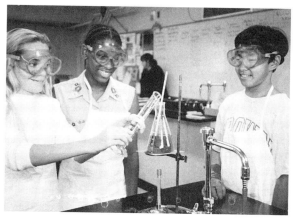

The Out-of-Door Academy is an independent, college preparatory day school enrolling 600 boys and girls from Sarasota and Manatee counties in Pre-Kindergarten–Grade 12. The school provides an environment conducive to the development of character, good citizenship, and a sense of personal responsibility. The traditional academic curriculum, which includes the opportunity to study foreign languages, is designed to prepare graduates for the most rigorous colleges and universities. Classes in music, fine arts, computers, physical education, and life skills are also offered. Summer day camp is available. Tuition: $7500–$8500. Financial Aid: $400,000. Scott Hinckley is Director of Admission; Dr. Michael A. Novello is Head of School.

Palmer Trinity School   1991

7900 SW 176th Street, Miami, FL 33157. 305-251-2230;
*   Admissions 305-251-9643; Fax 305-254-8812*

Palmer Trinity, a college preparatory, Episcopal day school for 500 students from diverse backgrounds in Grades 6–12, is com-

mitted to academic excellence and grounded in spiritual values. The average class size is 15, with a 9:1 student-faculty ratio. All students are encouraged to join any of the 33 sports teams and a wide variety of extracurricular activities. Palmer Trinity also offers an intensive English program for non-English-speaking students. In addition, students reinforce the School's support for the extended community through required service projects. Graduates are prepared to succeed at the university level and are inspired to make a positive contribution to a changing world. Tuition: $14,450. Extras: $1645. Financial aid is available. Laura C. Walker is Head of School. *Southern Association.*

Palm Beach Day School   1921

241 Seaview Avenue, Palm Beach, FL 33480. 561-655-1188;
*   Fax 561-655-5794; E-mail admissions@pbds.org;*
*   Web Site www.pbds.org*

Palm Beach Day School, enrolling 320 girls and boys in Kindergarten–Grade 9, aims to prepare students for college preparatory secondary schools. Basic skills are emphasized in the lower grades, along with computer, the arts, physical education, and foreign language. Laboratory science, biology, history, geography, algebra, plane and solid geometry, arts and activities, human growth and development, speech, and computer training are included in Grades 5–9. Sports, Student Council, publications, and library training are among the activities. Tuition: $8200–$12,000. Extras: $900. Financial Aid: $160,000. John L. Thompson (Trinity, A.B. 1958) was appointed Headmaster in 1988.

Pine Crest School at Boca Raton   1987

2700 St. Andrew's Boulevard, Boca Raton, FL 33434.
*   561-852-2800; Fax 561-852-2832;*
*   E-mail boca.admission@pinecrest.edu; Web Site www.pinecrest.edu*

Pine Crest School at Boca Raton is a coeducational, college preparatory school enrolling 860 day students in Pre-Primary (age 4)–Grade 8. The 20-acre campus has an 8-lane swimming pool, Student Activities Center, 750-seat theater, library/media center, fine arts center, and science laboratory classrooms. Afterschool Enrichment, Extended-Day Care, band and orchestra programs, and USS Swim teams are available. Academic summer school, tennis camp, fine arts camp, and a summer day camp are offered. Tuition: $9400–$10,600. Financial aid is available. Joyce R. Robinson is Admissions Director; DeHaven W. Fleming (University of Florida, B.S.Ed. 1965; College of Law, J.D. 1975) was appointed Headmaster in 1985.

PACE-Brantley Hall School   1972

3221 Sand Lake Road, Longwood, FL 32779-5898.
407-869-8882; Fax 407-869-8717;
E-mail PABHSchool@aol.com

PACE-Brantley Hall School was founded to meet the needs of students with diagnosed learning disabilities or attention-deficit disorders. Enrolling 200 boys and girls in Grades 1–12, the School offers a multisensory program, a 10:1 student-teacher ratio, and ungraded classes with the goal of teaching compensation skills while building confidence and self-esteem. Summer programs are available. Tuition: $8500. Additional Fees: $250. Limited need-based financial aid is available. Armando J. Sanchez (University of South Florida, B.A.; Florida Atlantic, M.Ed.) was named Executive Director in 1999.

Ransom Everglades School   1974

Upper School: 3575 Main Highway, Coconut Grove,
FL 33133. 305-460-8800; Fax 305-854-1846;
E-mail admission@ransomeverglades.org;
Web Site http://www.ransomeverglades.org
Middle School: 2045 South Bayshore Drive, Coconut Grove,
FL 33133. 305-250-6850

The Ransom School for Boys, formerly The Adirondack-Florida School, merged in 1974 with Everglades School for Girls to form Ransom Everglades School, enrolling 874 boys and girls in Grades 6–12. The School believes the pursuit of academic excellence should be complemented by a concern for each student's moral, physical, emotional, and aesthetic development. The curriculum encompasses visual and performing arts; activities include drama, sports, publications, and service groups. A summer academic program is offered. Tuition: $14,300. Financial Aid: $1,253,525. Elaine Mijalis is Director of Admission; Judith Chamberlain (George Washington University, B.A.; Catholic University, M.S.) is Head of School. *Southern Association.*

Riverside Presbyterian Day School   1948

830 Oak Street, Jacksonville, FL 32204. 904-353-5511;
Fax 904-634-1739; E-mail rlittell@rpds.com;
Web Site www.rpds.com

Riverside Presbyterian Day School, founded by the church bearing the same name, enrolls 492 boys and girls in Pre-Kindergarten–Grade 6. The School's primary goals are to "educate the mind, nurture the spirit, and foster the development of the whole child while affirming the teachings of the Christian faith." Art, music, Bible, computer, library, Spanish, physical education, and weekly chapel services enrich the basic program of reading, language arts, math, science, and social studies. Extended-day care is available on a year-round basis and includes creative activities and field trips. Tuition: $3780–$5840. Financial Aid: $71,500. Mary Lee Pappas is Admissions Director; Robert W. Littell (Colorado College, A.B.; Johns Hopkins, M.S.) is Headmaster. *Southern Association.*

Saint Andrew's School   BOCA RATON

3900 Jog Road, Boca Raton, FL 33434. 561-483-8900;
Fax 561-487-4655; E-mail admission@saint.andrews.pvt.k12.fl.us;
Web Site www.saint.andrews.pvt.k12.fl.us

SAINT ANDREW'S SCHOOL in Boca Raton, Florida, is a coeducational, college preparatory school enrolling boarding students in Grades 9–12 and day students in Grades 6–12. It is located in western Boca Raton (population 150,000), north of Glades Road. The city's beaches offer recreational facilities, while community resources, such as Florida Atlantic University, provide educational and cultural opportunities. Major roads, including Interstate 95 and the Florida Turnpike, connect Boca Raton with West Palm Beach, 25 miles north, and Miami, 50 miles south. The West Palm Beach, Fort Lauderdale, and Miami airports serve the region.

Saint Andrew's was founded in 1961 by the Episcopal School Foundation to prepare students for college. Originally a boys' school, Saint Andrew's has been coeducational since 1971. It is the School's goal to foster and encourage excellence in five areas: academics, mind, body, spirit, and stewardship.

Saint Andrew's School is a nonprofit corporation directed by a self-perpetuating Board of Trustees, which meets quarterly. The Board has 26 members; among them is the Bishop of the Diocese of Southeast Florida. The School endowment totals $3,600,000 and the campus is valued at $10,000,000. The School is accredited by the Florida Council of Independent Schools and holds membership in the National Association of Independent Schools, the National Association of Episcopal Schools, the National Association of College Admissions Counselors, the Secondary School Admission Test Board, The College Board, and the Educational Records Bureau.

THE CAMPUS. A central lake is situated on the 80-acre campus, which is landscaped with Florida pine and tropical shade trees. The outdoor facilities include ten tennis courts, a 25-meter swimming pool, and 18 acres of playing fields.

The fully air-conditioned school buildings are Bahamian colonial in architecture. Henderson Hall (1962) is a fully networked, 20,000-volume library. Rooks Memorial Science and Classroom Building (1963) houses laboratories and a new environmental science center. The Middle School complex contains six buildings totaling 32,000 square feet. In 1998, Saint Andrew's opened a Studio & Fine Arts Building. The Chapel of Saint Andrew the Apostle (1967) is the spiritual center of the School. The athletic buildings (1962) and gymnasium (1981) provide indoor athletic facilities. A classroom building with a computer center, computerized writing lab, and language and math classrooms and an administrative and faculty office building opened in September 1990.

Boarding students and faculty reside in two recently refurbished dormitories. Forty percent of the faculty live on campus. A student commons and activity center opened in the 1998–99 school year. The Infirmary (1963) contains six beds and a dispensary.

THE FACULTY. George E. Andrews II became Headmaster in July 1989. Reverend Andrews earned his baccalaureate degree from Trinity College in Hartford, Connecticut, and his Master of Divinity from Virginia Theological Seminary in Alexandria, Virginia. Before assuming his current responsibilities, he had been affiliated with University-Liggett, St. George's, and St. Paul's schools.

The faculty consist of 44 men and 68 women. They hold 54 graduate degrees, including 2 doctorates, from such institutions as Amherst, Brown, Clark, Columbia, Connecticut College, Dartmouth, Davidson, Dickinson, Facultad de Buenos Aires (Argentina), Florida Atlantic, Florida State, Franklin and Marshall, Georgetown, George Washington, Hamilton, Johns Hopkins, Lafayette, Middlebury, Muhlenberg, Pepperdine, Princeton, Rollins, Rutgers, St. Lawrence, Smith, Trinity, Virginia Theological, Wheaton, Yale, and the Universities of Alabama, Chicago, Connecticut, Florida, Illinois, Indiana, Maine, Maryland, Massachusetts, Michigan, North Carolina, Southern Maine, South Florida, Texas, and Wisconsin. Saint Andrew's provides health insurance, a retirement plan, and Social Security for teachers.

A registered nurse lives on campus; the Boca Raton Community Hospital is five minutes from campus.

STUDENT BODY. In 1999–2000, Saint Andrew's enrolled 105 boarders and 392 day students in the Upper School (Grades 9–12) and 241 day students in the Middle School (Grades 6–8). The distribution by grades is as follows: 80 in Grade 6, 81 in Grade 7, 80 in Grade 8, 117 in Grade 9, 133 in Grade 10, 149 in Grade 11, and 98 in Grade 12.

Day students reside in Boca Raton and nearby communities; boarding students come from 15 states and 28 foreign countries.

ACADEMIC PROGRAM. The school year, from late August to early June, is divided into semesters. Three long weekend recesses are scheduled in addition to Christmas and spring vacations. Classes, which meet five times weekly, have an average enrollment of 16 students. The typical daily schedule includes breakfast at 7:15 A.M., a daily advisor period at 7:50 A.M., eight academic periods between 8:00 A.M. and 3:15 P.M., and team practices from 3:30 P.M. to 5:30 P.M. Dormitory check-in is at 10:30 P.M.

Students are placed in supervised study halls during free periods if they are not meeting certain academic standards. Boarding students, except those doing honors work, also have supervised evening study. There are regularly scheduled extra-help sessions after school and in the evening. Tutoring may be

arranged at an additional charge. Grade reports are mailed to parents four times yearly; interim reports are sent each quarter by faculty.

In Grades 6, 7, and 8, the curriculum consists of English, Latin, foreign language, Geography, American History, Mathematics, Introduction to Computing, Environmental Science, Life Science, Earth Science, Music and Art Enrichment, and physical education.

To graduate, students must complete 20 credits in Grades 9–12; ½ credit is earned in each semester course. Course requirements are English 4, foreign language 3, history 3, mathematics 3, science 3, visual and performing arts 1½, theology 1, public speaking ½, and computer ½. Students must also perform community service.

A combination of year and semester courses is offered. Year courses include English 9–12; French 1–5, German 1–5, Latin 1–3, Spanish 1–5; Modern European Civilization, History of the United States, Politics and Economics, World History I–II; Algebra 1–2, Geometry, Precalculus, Calculus, Discrete Math & Statistics; Environmental Science, Biology, Chemistry, Physics, Anatomy and Physiology; and Introduction to Design, Drawing, Drafting, Graphic Arts, History of Art and Science, Stagecraft, vocal ensembles (Bonnies and Scotsmen, varsity singers, All-Americans), instrumental ensembles (beginning and advanced band), Music Appreciation, and Theater Appreciation. Eighteen Advanced Placement courses are offered including Computer Science and Studio Art. Typical semester courses include Expository Writing, Journalism, International Relations, Economics, Ethics, and Marine Science.

Typically, 100 percent of the School's graduates enter college. They attend such institutions as American, Auburn, Babson, Berklee College of Music, Boston University, Bowdoin, Brandeis, Brown, Carnegie-Mellon, Colgate, Cornell, Denison, Duke, Emory, Florida Atlantic, Florida Institute of Technology, Florida State, Franklin and Marshall, Furman, Georgetown, Gettysburg, Hamilton, Harvard, Middlebury, New York University, Northwestern, Princeton, Rhode Island School of Design, Trinity, Tufts, Tulane, Williams, Worcester Polytechnic Institute, Yale, and the Universities of Florida, Miami, New Hampshire, North Carolina, Notre Dame, Pennsylvania, and Vermont.

STUDENT ACTIVITIES. The Student Council and the Middle School Activities Council coordinate school activities. Other student organizations include the Key Club, Chess Club, Environmental Club, The Cum Laude Society, National Spanish Honor Society, foreign language clubs, an Outdoor Adventure Club, Model United Nations, Dramatics Club, Computer Club, newspaper staff, and yearbook staff. Students participate in the Scotsmen (boys' chorus), the Bonnies (girls' chorus), and the All-American Group (singers and dancers).

Saint Andrew's teams compete with private and public high schools in the area. Boys' varsity sports are football, baseball, soccer, lacrosse, basketball, swimming, tennis, golf, and cross-country. The girls' program includes swimming, tennis, volleyball, cross-country, lacrosse, basketball, soccer, golf, and softball.

Dances, concerts by student groups, and three or four plays are scheduled each year. Boarding students generally receive an unlimited number of weekend permissions, and special events are planned for those who remain on campus. Traditional annual events for the school community include New Family Welcoming Picnic, the Arts Festival, the Christmas Concert, the Spring Concert, Homecoming weekend, the Junior/Senior Prom, Commencement, and Alumni Day for more than 2000 Saint Andrew's graduates. The Parent's Association sponsors the Book Fair and the Parent-Faculty Dinner.

ADMISSION AND COSTS. Saint Andrew's seeks students with above-average "academic aptitudes, sound character, and a clear sense of right and wrong." It is school policy to accept applicants without regard to economic, social, racial, or denominational status. Candidates are evaluated on the basis of school transcripts, references, a personal interview, and results of the Secondary School Admission Test. New students are admitted in all classes, although few are accepted for Grade 12. Applications are received throughout the year. Fall application is encouraged, but later applications are considered if vacancies exist. There is a $50 application fee ($75 for international students).

Tuition for 1999–2000 is $24,000 for boarding students, $13,350 for Upper School day students, and $12,150 for Middle School students. Books and supplies (approximately $500) are extra. Parents who choose to use a tuition payment plan must purchase tuition insurance. Fees and tuition are subject to change by the Board of Trustees.

Saint Andrew's, which subscribes to the School and Student Service for Financial Aid, grants $800,000 in financial aid yearly to approximately 14 percent of the student body. Aid is awarded solely on the basis of need.

Associate Headmaster: Sidney A. Rowell
Head of Upper School: Ann-Marie Krejcarek
Director of Admissions: Bradford L. Reed
Director of External Affairs: Herb Soles
Director of College Guidance: A. J. Aucamp
Business Manager: Kathy Van Valkenburg
Director of Athletics: David Ahern

Saint Edward's School　　VERO BEACH

Middle/Upper Schools: 1895 Saint Edward's Drive, Vero Beach, FL 32963. 561-231-4136; E-mail info@steds.org;
Web Site www.steds.org;
Lower School: 2225 Club Drive, Vero Beach, FL 32963. 561-231-5357

SAINT EDWARD'S SCHOOL in Vero Beach, Florida, is a coeducational, college preparatory day school enrolling 880 students on two campuses, with a third campus, for Grades 6–8, opening in the fall of 2000. Vero Beach is a flourishing, upscale community on Florida's mid-Atlantic coast, known as the Treasure Coast. Vero Beach is equidistant from Melbourne to the north and Stuart to the south and is located in Indian River County, known for its pleasant climate, beautiful beaches, and abundant natural resources.

Saint Edward's was founded in 1965 to challenge and educate students of many faiths and cultures in a supportive, nurturing environment that promotes academic excellence, sound moral values, and high self-esteem within its Episcopal school tradition. Students adhere to an Honor Code designed to encourage responsible citizenship, ethical behavior, and an appreciation for diversity. Chapel services are attended by students on both campuses and led by the school chaplain, a

faculty member, an administrator, a community leader, and students.

A not-for-profit institution guided by a Board of 20 Trustees, Saint Edward's is accredited by the Florida Council of Independent Schools and holds membership in the National Association of Independent Schools, National Association of Episcopal Schools, Educational Records Bureau, Council for Religion in Independent Schools, and Council for Advancement and Support of Education.

THE CAMPUS. The Lower School campus was the original Riomar Country Club built in 1929, and was one of the first structures built on the barrier island. Bought by Saint Edward's in 1965, the six-acre site was renovated in 1988, preserving the Old Florida, Mediterranean-influenced architecture still evident today.

A pre-kindergarten and kindergarten complex, fine arts center, and two state-of-the-art computer labs were added in 1996.

The 27-acre Upper and Middle School campus was opened in 1972 and occupies a unique location along the Indian River. Currently, the School is expanding to include a separate Middle School, Fine Arts Building, a 750-seat Performing Arts Center, and an Administrative Services Building. The $18,000,000 "Celebrate Our Future" campaign will double the size of the current Upper School campus. A retrofit of Upper School classrooms will add state-of-the-art lab spaces and a foreign language multimedia center.

THE FACULTY. Diane B. Cooper, Saint Edward's fifth Head of School, earned an M.Ed. in English and Secondary Education from the University of North Texas and holds a doctorate in Private School Administration from the University of San Francisco.

The cornerstone of Saint Edward's is its 91-member, highly qualified faculty, most of whom hold advanced degrees. Their degrees represent colleges and universities such as Adelphi, Assumption, Babson, Ball State, Bates, Bowling Green State, Central Connecticut State, Central Michigan, Colgate, College of William and Mary, College of Wooster, Columbia, Cornell, Denison, East Carolina, East Stroudsburg State, Fairfield, Fairleigh Dickinson, Fitchburg State, Florida Atlantic, Florida Southern, Florida State, Harvard, LaSalle, Lehigh, Loyola (Chicago), Middlebury, New York University, Nova, Ohio State, Pennsylvania State, Quinnipiac College, Rollins, Southwest Texas State, Springfield College, State University of New York, Susquehanna, Syracuse, Temple, Tufts, Union, Wesleyan, West Chester State, Wilkes, Wittenberg, York College of Pennsylvania, and the Universities of Florida, Hartford, Iowa, London, Maryland, Massachusetts, Michigan, North Carolina, Pennsylvania, Pittsburgh, San Francisco, Scranton, South Florida, Texas, Vermont, Virginia, Washington, and Wisconsin.

The Richardson Wellness Center offers physical, emotional, and spiritual support programs and services, including student health education programs, faculty training programs, leadership workshops, and a student-led Spiritual Life Committee. A full-time guidance counselor, chaplain, and three registered nurses serve the School. Emergency medical service for both campuses is readily accessible.

STUDENT BODY. In 1999–2000, Saint Edward's enrolled the largest number of students in its history, including 473 in the Middle/Upper School. Students commute via car pool or by bus service arranged by the School from Vero Beach and the tri-county area. The student body represents a wide cross-section of racial, ethnic, religious, and socioeconomic backgrounds.

ACADEMIC PROGRAM. The 175-day school year, from early September to early June, is divided into four marking periods, with a Thanksgiving recess, vacations in December and in the spring, and observances of several national and school holidays. Teachers provide the individual attention each student needs in classrooms with a class size average of 17. All core courses are offered in regular college preparatory and honors tracks, with special accommodations for gifted, artistically talented, and musically talented students.

Students attend classes daily from 8:05 A.M. to 3:20 P.M. in the Lower School and from 8:05 A.M. to 3:25 P.M. in the Middle and Upper schools. All students are required to select six academic classes, and many concentrate their efforts in Advanced Placement courses.

The Lower School academic program provides a strong foundation in the traditional disciplines, beginning with reading and mathematics readiness in pre-kindergarten and building on mastery of those skills as students progress through the primary and intermediate grades. The schedule is departmentalized from Grade 4 on, with a major emphasis on language arts and math. The core academics are enhanced by mini courses in fine arts, music, computer science, ethics, and physical education.

To graduate, students must complete a minimum of 24 credits as follows: 4 each in English and mathematics; 3 each in foreign language, history/government, and science, including biology and chemistry; 2 in electives from the five major disciplines; and 1 in art, music, and religion. Saint Edward's does not provide class rank until graduation, and grades shown on transcripts are unweighted, although extra credit is awarded for Honors or Advanced Placement courses.

College guidance begins in the freshman year and continues throughout the entire application and admission process. Historically, 98 percent of Saint Edward's seniors attend their first or second college choice. Among the institutions where recent graduates have matriculated are American University, Amherst, Boston College, Boston University, Bowdoin, Catholic University, The Citadel, Clemson, Colgate, Columbia, Dartmouth, Duke, Georgetown, Georgia Institute of Technology, Harvard, Howard, Loyola, Massachusetts Institute of Technology, Northwestern, Princeton, Rhode Island School of Design, Rice, Southern Methodist, Stanford, Tufts, Tulane, Union, United States Military Academy, United States Naval Academy, Vanderbilt, Villanova, Washington and Lee, Wellesley, Worcester Polytechnic, Yale, and the Universities of California, Colorado, Florida, Kentucky, Miami, North Carolina, Richmond, South Carolina, Tampa, Texas, and Virginia.

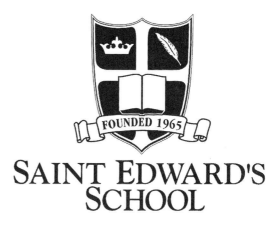

SAINT EDWARD'S SCHOOL

Saint Edward's offers extensive summer programs, including EXCEL, the Educational Center for Exceptional Learners, which enrolls academically gifted students in Grades 3–6 in a three-week session. A six-week program offers remediation and enrichment to approximately 200 students; a seven-week water-oriented summer camp program and various sports camps are also available.

STUDENT ACTIVITIES. A diverse extracurricular program engages students in leadership roles, special-interest clubs, and athletics.

More than 30 Class 2A interscholastic teams are organized in football, baseball, softball, lacrosse, golf, volleyball, soccer, cross-country, swimming, basketball, tennis, and cheerleading.

As members of a greater community, students are encouraged to become active volunteers on and off campus. Two of the most successful student outreach programs are the Pals in Partnership for special-needs children and the Care to Share program for the elderly.

Among the special events on the school calendar are the annual Fun Fun Run, Poetry Readings, Living Museum, Science Fair, annual speech presentations, fall drama, spring musical, Lagoon Days, Saint Edward's Day, Christmas Concert, Homecoming Weekend, and the Lower School class plays.

ADMISSION AND COSTS. Saint Edward's welcomes students who are good citizens with a desire for a first-rate education. Acceptance is based on standardized test results, current transcripts, evaluations by the student's mathematics and English teachers, recommendations from the principal or guidance counselor, writing samples, and a personal interview. For first-round consideration, applications are due by February 1. Subsequent applications will be considered on a space-available basis. Applications are acted on by the Admission Committee on April 1 of the year of intended enrollment. The nonrefundable application fee is $50.

For 1999–2000, tuition ranges from $4400 in Pre-Kindergarten and Kindergarten to $10,250 in Grades 9–12. Uniforms are additional, and tuition insurance is required. Annually, the School awards approximately $350,000 to students who have demonstrated financial need and academic ability.

Associate Head of School/Head of Upper School: Bruce R. Wachter
Head of Middle School: Christopher Angell
Head of Lower School: Robert T. Bond
Director of Admission: Jerry K. Jones
Dean of Students/Upper School: Linda Colontrelle

Dean of Students/Lower School: Jeffrey R. Lamscha
Academic Dean: Kristine Alber
Director of College Placement & Testing: Morris "Darby"
  Gibbons III
Athletic Director: Rosemary Hinton

St. Johns Country Day School   1953

*3100 Doctor's Lake Drive, Orange Park, FL 32073. 904-264-9572;
  Fax 904-264-0375; E-mail steve_russey@stjohnscds.com*

St. Johns, enrolling 750 students in Pre-Kindergarten–Grade 12, furnishes an environment that encourages academic excellence at all levels. A challenging college preparatory curriculum, athletics, and fine arts prepare students for selective colleges. Advanced Placement and honors classes, extracurricular, and summer academic and camp programs are available. Computer, foreign language, and science labs; a swimming pool complex; a fine arts center; and a Grades 6–8 educational center on the 26-acre rural campus address the varied needs of St. Johns students. Tuition: $3440–$7470. Financial Aid: $296,000. Jim Edwards is Director of Admissions; Stephen F. Russey (Bowdoin, B.A. 1963; University of Rhode Island, M.A. 1970) was appointed Headmaster in 1976. *Southern Association.*

St. Mark's Episcopal Day School   1970

*4114 Oxford Avenue, Jacksonville, FL 32210. 904-388-2632;
  Fax 904-387-5647; E-mail smeds@stmarksdayschool.org*

Enrolling 393 students in Pre-Kindergarten (age 3)–Grade 6, St. Mark's is a parish school that seeks to provide the highest degree of preparation for secondary education. The curriculum includes art, music, computers, Spanish, physical education, library, and Christian education and is enriched by special events and after-school opportunities. The School emphasizes independent study skills and is committed to discovering each student's talents. Small classes and a student-teacher ratio of 10:1 allow each child to receive individual attention while encouraging academic preparation. Extended-day and full summer programs are available. Tuition: $2230–$5760. Financial Aid: $86,000. Susan Kwartler is Director of Admissions; Nancy Wood was appointed Headmistress in 1989.

St. Mark's Episcopal School   1959

*1750 East Oakland Park Boulevard, Fort Lauderdale, FL 33334;
  954-563-4508; Fax 954-563-0504*

St. Mark's enrolls 624 day boys and girls in Pre-Kindergarten 3–Grade 8. The academic program is designed to provide excellence in education and a "unique learning environment within a solid Christian tradition." Beginning in Pre-Kindergarten 4, the School's enrichment program includes religion, Spanish, computers, art, music, library, and physical education. After-school activities include coed varsity sports, art, music, dance, karate, and scouts. This challenging preparatory program enables graduates to enroll in leading independent high schools. A state-of-the-art educational building for Grades 4–8 opened in 1995. Tuition: $3775–$6769. Financial aid is available. Mrs. Patti Dinger is Admission Director; James R. Colee, Ed.D., is Headmaster.

St. Mary's Episcopal Day School   1953

*2101 South Hubert Street, Tampa, FL 33629-5648. 813-258-5508;
  Fax 813-258-5603; E-mail stmarys@smeds.org*

Founded by parents who wanted a church-affiliated school with a strong academic program, St. Mary's enrolls 434 girls and boys in Pre-Kindergarten–Grade 8. Early grades emphasize basic skills, including computer use and Spanish, leading to advanced levels in writing, algebra, and lab sciences by Grade 8. All grades take physical education. Grade 6 takes Latin; Grades 7–8 take Latin or Spanish. Religion, computer science, music, and art are taught. Activities include competitive athletics, choir, publications, community service, student council, and drama. Before- and after-school care are offered. Tuition: $3950–$5800. Financial aid is available. Liz Smith is Director of Admissions; Scott D. Laird (West Chester, B.S. 1978; Florida Atlantic, M.Ed. 1987, M.A. 1993) is Headmaster.

Saint Michael's Independent School   1969

*1300 East Tenth Street, Stuart, FL 34996. 561-283-1222;
  Fax 561-220-9149; Web Site www.stmikesschool.org*

St. Michael's, a coeducational day school enrolling 340 students in Early Learning–Grade 8, provides a challenging yet nurturing environment that promotes academic excellence, sound moral values, and the development of the whole child. Classroom studies include a traditional core curriculum as well as music, art, computer sciences, and Spanish for all students. The physical education program is an important part of St. Michael's program and spirit. Organized and competitive sports include basketball, soccer, volleyball, softball, and lacrosse. Tuition: $3510–$7210. Financial Aid: $100,000. Candace Alcorta is Director of Admission; Raymond S. Roy (Spring Hill College, B.S. 1964; Florida Atlantic University, M.Ed. 1967) is Headmaster.

Saint Paul's School   1968

*1600 St. Paul's Drive, Clearwater, FL 33764. 727-536-2756;
  Fax 727-531-2276; Web Site www.st.pauls.edu*

Saint Paul's, enrolling 440 boys and girls in Preschool–Grade 8, is affiliated with the Episcopal church and celebrates the rich diversity of its school community. Its mission is to provide an excellent education in a nurturing environment, laying the foundation for successful academic progress, and to create a desire for lifelong learning. Intellectual, spiritual, and physical development are stressed through a challenging curriculum, hands-on science, fine arts, interscholastic athletics, foreign languages, a state-of-the-art technology center, summer programs, extracurriculars, and community service. A Child Development Program is also available. Tuition: $4000–$8450. Financial Aid: $200,000. Stephen D. McConnell is Director of Admissions; Douglas C. Eveleth is Head of School.

St. Thomas Episcopal Parish School 1953

*5692 North Kendall Drive, Coral Gables, FL 33156. 305-665-4851;
Fax 305-669-9449; E-mail VDouberley@stepsmia.org;
Web Site www.stepsmia.org*

St. Thomas, enrolling 431 students in Preschool–Grade 6, aims to provide an atmosphere that is both challenging and affirming. The academic program is concerned with the whole child, caters to the increasing demands of the information age, and is devoted to providing a solid foundation for future learning. Class sizes are small. The curriculum is enriched by special teachers in Spanish, dance, art, music, physical education, science, drama, library, and computers. An extended-day program features enrichment activities and sports; summer programs are also offered. Tuition: $5500–$7400. Financial aid is available. Valerie Douberley is Admissions Director; Murray E. Lopdell Lawrence (Victoria University of Wellington, B.A.; Wellington Teachers College, Dip.Tchg.) is Head of School.

San Jose Episcopal Day School 1954

*7423 San Jose Boulevard, Jacksonville, FL 32217. 904-733-0352;
Admissions 904-733-0355; Fax 904-733-2582; E-mail
sjepisch@mediaone.net; Web Site http://www.ccse.net/~sjepisch*

Founded in 1954, San Jose Episcopal Day School enrolls over 400 students in Pre-Kindergarten–Grade 6. Expansion plans include growth potential to 470 students by the year 2000. San Jose emphasizes academic achievement in helping to develop children's full potential for rich and productive lives in a Christian environment. The curriculum highlights language arts, mathematics, social studies, and science. Religion and chapel services are offered weekly. Spanish, computer, music, art, and physical education are included. Sports, school patrol, Student Council, Environmental Club, chorus, and library aides are among the activities. Tuition: $3700–$4900. Financial aid is available. Rebecca A. Faiella is Director of Admissions; Susan E. Currie (Bradley University, B.S.; Case Western, M.S.L.S.) is Principal.

Seacrest Country Day School 1983

*7100 Davis Boulevard, Naples, FL 34104. 941-793-1986;
Fax 941-793-1460; E-mail seacrest@seacrest.org;
Web Site www.seacrest.org*

Seacrest Country Day, enrolling 370 boys and girls from three-year-old Pre-Kindergarten–Grade 8, seeks to combine the "best of tradition with the latest research, technology, and learning models." The multisensory, interdisciplinary curriculum corresponds to the developmental levels of children, encouraging academic excellence and creative expression in all areas. Computers, global education, foreign language, the arts, and physical education enrich the core program. Before- and after-school care and summer sessions are offered. Tuition: $7800–$8700. Financial Aid: $290,000. Caroline Randall is Director of Admission; Lynne Powell (Trenton State, B.A.; Plymouth State, M.A.; Nova University, Ed.D.) was appointed Director in 1993.

Shorecrest Preparatory School 1923

*5101 First Street NE, St. Petersburg, FL 33703-3309.
727-522-2111; Fax 727-527-4191;
Web Site http://www.shorecrest.org*

Shorecrest Prep, Florida's oldest independent day school, enrolls 840 boys and girls in Early Childhood–Grade 12. A strong college preparatory program, providing close faculty support and small classes, is enhanced by the arts, foreign languages, laboratory sciences, and state-of-the-art computer facilities. The Upper Division offers a full range of Advanced Placement courses and individualized college counseling. The School encourages participation in athletic competition, extracurricular activities, visual and performing arts, and community service. Transportation and extended care are available.Tuition: $5875–$9200. Extras: $400. Financial Aid: $240,000. Diana N. Craig is Director of Admissions; Mary H. Booker (Nova, M.Ed. 1979) was named Head of School in 1989. *Southern Association.*

Sweetwater Episcopal Academy 1974

*251 East Lake Brantley Drive, Longwood, FL 32779.
407-862-1882; Fax 407-788-1714;
Web Site www.sea-kindzone.org*

Sweetwater Episcopal Academy, situated on Lake Brantley, enrolls approximately 250 children in Pre-K–Grade 5. Sweetwater offers a learning and loving environment that teaches respect and responsibility. The challenging academic program provides a strong foundation in English grammar, reading, math, social studies, and science. Current trends are investigated and implemented, including a virtual education classroom connected to a web site. All classrooms are networked and have Internet access. Specialists enhance the curriculum with library, music, physical education, computer, Spanish, religion, and art. After-school enrichment, an on-campus swimming pool, and canoeing are available. Tuition: $5075-$5425. Carol Mackoul is Head of School.

Tampa Preparatory School 1973

*625 North Boulevard, Tampa, FL 33606. 813-251-8481;
Fax 813-254-2106; E-mail admissions@tampaprep.usf.edu;
Web Site www.tampaprep.usf.edu*

Founded at the University of Tampa by parents and University trustees, Tampa Prep enrolls 510 day students in Grades 6–12. Designed for students of average to gifted ability, the School combines an accelerated academic program and strong athletics with training in the arts. Seventeen Advanced Placement courses are offered. A full range of athletics, National Honor Society, publications, drama, forensics, community service, and interest clubs are among the activities. A summer program offers academics, creative writing, and several enrichment courses. Tuition: $8775–$9390. Financial Aid: $470,000. Andrew C. Hill is Director of Admissions; D. Gordon MacLeod (University of York, B.A.; Brown, Sc.M.) was appointed Head in 1998.

Trinity Preparatory School   1968

5700 Trinity Prep Lane, Winter Park, FL 32792.
  407-671-4140; Fax 407-671-6935;
  E-mail inquire@trinityprep.org; Web Site www.trinityprep.org

An Episcopal school enrolling 780 day students in Grades 6–12, Trinity seeks to provide the finest educational experience, guided by outstanding professionals in a safe, caring, challenging environment. It aims to develop lifelong learners who are prepared for college, socially responsible, and able to succeed in a changing society. Trinity fosters spiritual growth while respecting cultural and religious diversity. The program offers 22 Advanced Placement courses, 35 sports teams, fine arts, and many activities and clubs. Tuition: $8980. Financial aid is available. Ethel S. Danhof is Director of Admissions; Craig S. Maughan (Washington University, B.A.; University of North Carolina [Chapel Hill], M.S.P.H.; University of Kansas, M.B.A.) is Headmaster.

University School of Nova Southeastern University   FORT LAUDERDALE

3301 College Avenue, Sonken Building, Fort Lauderdale, FL 33314.
  954-262-4400; Admission 954-262-4416;
  E-mail kelrick@nsu.nova.edu;
  Web Site www.nova.edu/cwis/univ-school

UNIVERSITY SCHOOL OF NOVA SOUTHEASTERN UNIVERSITY in Fort Lauderdale, Florida, is a college preparatory day school enrolling boys and girls in Pre-Kindergarten through Grade 12. The main campus is located in the Davie section of Fort Lauderdale, a city of 200,000 on the Atlantic coast, 15 miles north of Miami. A second facility for Pre-Kindergarten through Grade 8 is on the branch campus in Coral Springs, 3251 NW 101 Avenue (Telephone 954-752-3020), 15 miles north of the main campus. School bus service is available throughout Broward and North Dade counties.

Founded in 1971, the School aims to help each student reach maximum potential through its academic, social, and athletic programs. Its curriculum emphasizes acquisition and development of basic and higher-level skills with opportunities to use them creatively. Students are involved in the planning and implementation of their education.

University School is a nonprofit organization governed by the administrative team and advised by a Board, including the Headmaster, parents of students, and one alumni representative. The Board meets monthly.

University School is accredited by the Southern Association of Colleges and Schools, the Florida Council of Independent Schools, and the Association of Independent Schools of Florida. It holds membership in the National Association of Independent Schools, the National Association of Laboratory Schools, the Educational Records Bureau, and Brown University's Coalition of Essential Schools.

THE CAMPUS. The School is situated on a 17-acre corner of the 232-acre main campus of Nova Southeastern University and has three swimming pools, four tennis courts, and baseball and soccer fields on the grounds. An Upper School building provides 25 classrooms for Grades 6–12, 8 laboratories, a media/audiovisual center, a new fine arts wing, and administrative offices. A 23,000-square-foot sports center opened in 1997.

The Lower School facility on the main campus was dedicated in 1975. A single-story contemporary building houses Pre-Kindergarten–Grade 5 along with administrative offices. Sixteen classrooms, two science areas, a combination gymnasium-cafeteria-auditorium, and a media and technology center are included in the building. Arts, language, and keyboarding labs were opened in 1998.

The Coral Springs campus accommodates students in Pre-Kindergarten–Grade 8 in three buildings on 10 acres in the city. Two Lower School buildings and one Middle School building provide 40,000 square feet of space for classrooms, a library, cafeteria, gymnasium, two computer labs, and offices.

The plant, valued at $17,000,000, is owned by Nova Southeastern University.

THE FACULTY. Dr. Jerome S. Chermak, a graduate of State University of New York at Binghamton (B.A. 1969, M.A.T. 1971) and Boston University (Ed.D. 1981), was appointed Headmaster in 1999. His career includes positions in administration and teaching at the secondary, undergraduate, and graduate levels. He is a past president and director emeritus of the Association of Independent Schools of Florida and an adjunct professor of education at Nova Southeastern University. Dr. Elizabeth C. Brennan serves as Associate Head of School.

The full-time faculty, including administrators who teach, total 158 women and 26 men. They hold baccalaureate and advanced degrees from the following institutions: Adelphi, American Conservatory of Music, Boston University, City University of New York, Colby, Cornell, Duke, Florida Atlantic, Florida State, Harvard, Hofstra, Kent State, Lesley, McGill (Canada), Middlebury, Nova Southeastern University, St. Joseph's (Pennsylvania), State University of New York, United States Naval Academy, Wheaton, Yale, and the Universities of Edinburgh (Scotland), Florida, Hartford, Miami, Pennsylvania, Pittsburgh, Virginia, and Wisconsin. The faculty is supplemented by aides from the teacher preparation program at Nova Southeastern University.

Faculty benefits include health insurance; tuition reduction for children; free tuition at Nova Southeastern University; a retirement plan; Social Security; and arrangements for leaves of absence.

Nurses are on duty at each campus during regular school hours; a hospital is five minutes away.

STUDENT BODY. In 1999–2000, the School enrolled 1935 boys and girls as day students in Pre-Kindergarten–Grade 12, distributed as follows: Pre-Kindergarten—75, Kindergarten—149, Grade 1—150, Grade 2—152, Grade 3—162, Grade 4—172, Grade 5—140, Grade 6—151, Grade 7—154, Grade 8—141, Grade 9—122, Grade 10—128, Grade 11—126, and Grade 12—113. Students come from Broward, Dade, and Palm Beach counties.

ACADEMIC PROGRAM. The academic year, divided into trimesters, begins in September and ends in June, with vacations of approximately one and one-half weeks in December, one week in February, and one week in the spring. Classes are held five days a week between 8:15 A.M. and 3:00 P.M. In the Early Childhood and Lower schools, the scheduling is flexible; Upper School students have 47-minute periods with some double blocks. The average class has approximately 22 students. Tutorial sessions for students in need of help are held twice weekly after school hours. Special tutoring can be arranged at extra cost. Remedial help in reading and mathematics and a program for minor learning disabilities are available. Grades are sent to parents three times a year, and two individual parent-teacher conferences are scheduled annually in the Early Childhood and Lower schools.

The Early Childhood (Pre-Kindergarten–Kindergarten) employs small-group and individual experiences to develop language facility, problem-solving and concept ability, motor skills, creative expression, and social competence. In the Lower School (Grades 1–5), emphasis is placed on basic academic skills in reading, language, writing, and mathematics along with foreign language, social studies, science, art, music, and physical education. In the Middle School (Grades 6–8), students take a core program of language arts, mathematics, social studies, and science, and have electives in French, Spanish, art, band, performing arts, word processing, debate, newspaper, and intramural sports. Computer science is included in all programs.

To graduate from the Upper School, students must earn 24 credits, including the following: English 4, social studies 4, foreign language 3, mathematics 4, science 4, physical education 1, fine arts 1, health ²/₃, computer science ²/₃, expository writing ¹/₃, public speaking ¹/₃, and 1 elective. Courses are offered on average, honors, and Advanced Placement levels. Among the courses offered are Public Speaking, Journalism, Publications, English; French 1–AP, Spanish 1–AP; American History, European History, Psychology; Algebra I–II, Geometry, Pre-Calculus, Calculus; Anatomy/Physiology, Physical Science, Biology, Ecology/Marine Biology, Chemistry, Physics; Computer Liter-

acy, Computer Science I–II; Ethics; Drama, Art Appreciation, Painting and Drawing; Physical Education; and SAT Preparation. Students may take courses at Nova Southeastern University and do independent projects with the University's oceanographic, law school, and business programs. Some students earn a full year of college credit before graduating from the Upper School.

All 95 graduating seniors in 1999 enrolled in colleges and universities including Amherst, Brandeis, Carnegie Mellon, Duke, Emory, George Washington, Harvard, New York University, Northwestern, Tufts, Tulane, Vassar, Washington University, Wesleyan, and the Universities of Florida, Michigan, and Pennsylvania. These included 2 National Merit Winners, 8 National Merit Commended students, and 2 National Hispanic Scholars.

A summer camp program, Camp Nova, is scheduled in three three-week sessions and enrolls public and private school students in Pre-Kindergarten–Grade 9. Remedial reading and mathematics, learning development programs, science, computers, ballet, karate, crafts, and recreational activities are offered. In addition, summer institutes for ages 12–18 are offered in instrumental music, theater, and speech and debate.

STUDENT ACTIVITIES. Students elect representatives from each grade to the student government, which allows student participation in dealing with school matters such as dress and conduct codes and organizing projects and activities. Community service provides opportunities for students (Grades 9–12) to develop leadership skills and become involved in projects that benefit local cities and towns. Cultural arts activities are offered after classes for elementary students.

The University School fields varsity teams that compete against other independent schools in soccer, cross-country, swimming, baseball, basketball, wrestling, tennis, golf, and track and field for boys, and volleyball, swimming, basketball, soccer, cross-country, softball, tennis, golf, and track and field for girls. Intramural competition is organized in all sports.

Forensic and drama activities are regularly scheduled at the School. Activities include field trips within Florida and to other areas of the United States and Europe; theater trips; and book, art, and science fairs. A new-parent reception, the annual open house, and Grandparents' Day are special events.

ADMISSION AND COSTS. The University School seeks students of average to gifted ability who can work independently and accept responsibility. Students are accepted in all grades on the basis of an entrance test, achievement tests, previous records, recommendations, and a personal interview. Applications, with a fee of $100, may be made at any time, since students are accepted on a rolling basis, space permitting, during the academic year.

Tuition ranges from $7410 for Pre-Kindergarten to $9560 for Grades 10–12. Books for Grades 6–12 are extra. Limited financial aid is available.

Florida

Director of Admission: Mrs. Kiki Kelrick
Director of Lower School: Dr. Elizabeth C. Brennan
Director of Middle/Upper School: Mr. Bill De Salvo
Director of Coral Springs Campus: Dr. Jeanne Korn

Coordinator of Development: Mrs. Hillary Gurman
College Counselor: Dr. Cy Gruber
Business Manager: Mr. Dennis Fanning
Director of Athletics: Mr. Fred Malan

GEORGIA

Athens Academy   1966

P.O. Box 6548, 1281 Spartan Lane, Athens, GA 30604.
706-549-9225; Fax 706-354-3775; E-mail academy@
athensacademy.org; Web Site http://www.athensacademy.org

Athens Academy is a college preparatory day school enrolling 396 girls and 400 boys in Pre-Kindergarten–Grade 12. The Academy seeks to provide a challenging curriculum and an educational environment that contributes to the development of successful, happy young people. The coordinated curriculum offers a firm base of academic skills and opportunities for pursuit of special interests. A full program of athletics and activities complements the academic program and the school strives to involve all students according to their interests. Tuition: $3890–$8150. Financial Aid: $350,000. Stuart Todd is Director of Admissions; J. Robert Chambers (University of Georgia, B.S., M.A.) was appointed Headmaster in 1983. *Southern Association*.

Augusta Preparatory Day School   1960

285 Flowing Wells Road, Martinez, GA 30907. 706-863-1906;
Fax 706-863-6198; E-mail apds@mindspring.com;
Web Site www.apds.com

Augusta Preparatory Day School is a nonsectarian college preparatory school with an enrollment of 515 boys and girls in Pre-School–Grade 12. Augusta Prep provides a traditional education program that teaches students "how to think, not what to think." The School considers the development of self-esteem and commitment to the welfare of others the foundation for intellectual, personal, and social growth. Honors and Advanced Placement courses are offered. Activities include athletic and academic teams, publications, and service organizations. Tuition: $3600–$7440. Susan B. Byus is Director of Admissions; Jack R. Hall (Davidson, B.A. 1976; Georgia State, M.S. 1988; Columbia University, M.A. 1992) is Head of School. *Southern Association*.

The Bedford School   1985

2619 Dodson Drive, East Point, GA 30344. 404-669-2083;
Fax 404-669-4037

The Bedford School was founded by Miss Betsy Box to serve the educational needs of 60–80 learning-different boys and girls in Grades 1–9. The purpose of the program is to provide the intervention and specific remediation that enable youngsters to overcome their academic weaknesses and maximize their full potential for return to traditional schools. Classes, which enroll between 8 and 12 students, are formed according to ability and skill level rather than age and encompass traditional courses in English, math, science, and social studies. A daily activity period offers enrichment in the arts, computers, foreign language, and other areas. The School operates a residential summer camp for ages 7–16 who benefit from academic reinforcement year round. Tuition: $9995–$10,295. Betsy Box is Director.

Brenau Academy   GAINESVILLE

One Centennial Circle, Gainesville, GA 30501. 770-534-6140;
E-mail enroll@lib.brenau.edu; Web Site www.brenau.edu/academy

BRENAU ACADEMY in Gainesville, Georgia, is a college preparatory boarding school for girls in Grades 9 through 12. Gainesville/Hall County (population 100,000) is situated at the base of the Blue Ridge Mountains, 50 miles northeast of Atlanta. This versatile locale offers both opportunities to hike, camp, water ski, snow ski, sail, and swim in the outdoors and to enjoy the resources of a large city such as concerts, theatres, restaurants, and sports events.

Brenau Academy seeks to offer a unique education to a small number of select young women through the connection between the Academy and Brenau Women's College (1878). For over 70 years, Brenau Academy has educated students in the security and comfort of an appropriate high school setting, while affording them the additional facilities and programs of a women's college campus. The entire Brenau community commits to helping each young woman develop her full potential through encouragement, challenge, and support.

A nonprofit institution, Brenau is governed by a self-perpetuating Board of Trustees, which meets twice a year. Brenau Academy is accredited by the Southern Association of Colleges and Schools and is approved by the Georgia Department of Education. It holds membership in the Southern Association of Independent Schools, Georgia Independent Schools Association, National Association of Independent Schools, and The Association of Boarding Schools.

THE CAMPUS. The 52-acre campus, which is convenient to the Atlanta airport, includes an outdoor amphitheater, an athletic field, and a six-court tennis center. Indoor athletic facilities are housed in the gymnasium and in the natatorium, which offers an Olympic-size swimming pool, a sauna, a steam bath, a weight and exercise room, and ballet studios.

The Academy classrooms, library, post office, Campus Shop, tea room, auditorium, recreation room, administrative offices, laundry, kitchenette, and dormitories are in one central location. Dormitory life is supervised by adult house directors. Students' rooms have personal phones and voice mail for easy parent communication. Other facilities available for Academy student use include a cafeteria, science laboratories, state-of-the-art microcomputer laboratories, language laboratories, an 80,000-volume library, a Victorian fine arts auditorium, and a Visual Arts Center. Campus security is managed by off-duty police officers.

The combined facilities are valued at more than $28,000,000.

THE FACULTY. Frank M. Booth is the Headmaster of the Academy, having previously been associated with Athens Academy (Georgia) and Kentucky Military Institute. A native of West Virginia, Dr. Booth graduated from Hampden-Sydney (B.A. 1966) and has received master's degrees from Marshall University (M.A. 1971) and the University of Georgia (M.Ed. 1977) and a doctorate from the University of Georgia (1985).

There are ten teachers, two of whom also teach in the college; four house directors; and six administrators and support staff members. Most full-time instructors hold master's degrees; 40 percent hold doctorates. Brenau faculty and staff members have degrees from Brenau, Butler, Eastern New Mexico, East Texas State, Florida State, Georgia State, Indiana State, Lehigh, Louisiana State, Marymount (New York), North Georgia College, Nova, Transylvania, and the Universities of Georgia, Kentucky, Maine, Notre Dame, South Carolina, and Texas. Part-time teachers offer instruction in music, drama, dance, art, and physical education.

The Academy Health Center is staffed by a nurse; a Gainesville pediatric group conducts rounds at the infirmary. Emergency services are available at two Gainesville hospitals, one of which is adjacent to the Brenau campus.

STUDENT BODY. In 1999–2000, Brenau Academy enrolls 73 boarding and 7 day students, ages 13 to 18. The students come from Alabama, Florida, Georgia, Illinois, Kentucky, Michigan, Minnesota, New Hampshire, New Jersey, New York, North Carolina, South Carolina, Tennessee, Texas, Austria, the Bahamas, China, Germany, Japan, Korea, Nigeria, Saudi Arabia, and Spain.

ACADEMIC PROGRAM. The school year, from late August to late May, is divided into semesters with a Thanksgiving recess, a two-week Christmas vacation, and a one-week spring vacation. The daily schedule begins at 8:00 A.M. and concludes at 8:00 P.M. Boarding students must be back on campus by 6:30 P.M., in their own dormitories by 10:00 P.M., and in their own rooms with "lights out" by 11:00 P.M.

Classes are held five days a week. An average class enrolls 12 students, and the overall student-faculty ratio is 8:1. There is a dorm study, supervised by housemothers, from 7:45 to 9:30 P.M. preceding each school day.

Teachers are available to provide extra help during daily free periods and from 3:00 to 4:00 P.M. Ongoing tutorial programs may be arranged. In addition, there are Study-Skills and College-Choice seminars focusing on the development of sound study habits. Courses in SAT Preparation and computer competency are requirements. Grades are sent to parents and students every four weeks. For good students with diagnosed learning differences, the Learning Center, modeled after the Brenau College Learning Center, provides appropriate support.

To graduate, students must complete four years of English, three of social studies, two of mathematics, two of science, two of physical education, and one of Performing Arts as well as six elective credits.

Brenau places special emphasis on mastery of the English language. Every student is expected to earn more than one credit in English each year; among the courses offered are English 1–4 and Advanced English. Courses in other academic areas include French, Spanish; United States History, American Government, Economics, World History; Algebra, Geometry, Trigonometry/Analysis; Biology, Chemistry, Anatomy and Physiology, Physical Science; Music, Drama, Publications, Dance, Art;

and Physical Education. Advanced students may take honors courses in certain disciplines. Qualified students may earn dual credit for courses in most departments of Brenau University. An intensive program in English as a Second Language is available.

In 1998, all of the 19 graduates went on to college. About 1 of 5 graduating seniors has elected to attend Brenau University, although the Academy encourages students to seek whichever college is most suitable. Past college selections include Agnes Scott, College of Charleston, Converse, Eckerd, Emory, Furman, Florida State, Gardner–Webb, Georgia Southern, Meredith, Middle Tennessee, St. Mary's, Tulane, Vanderbilt, Young Harris, and the Universities of Alabama, Central Florida, Mississippi, the South, South Carolina, and Tennessee.

STUDENT ACTIVITIES. The Brenau Academy student government consists of two branches: the Honor Court and the Headmaster's Council. Girls are encouraged to participate in many extracurricular activities and organizations. They may choose from among *The Chattahall* (the Brenau yearbook), *The Metamorphosis* (the literary magazine of the Academy), and the Key Club, Environmental Club, and Beta Club. The school has its own TV studio and radio station and encourages students' hands-on experiences. Students participate in such activities as chorus, dance, drama, and art.

Brenau Academy teams compete with those of other public and private schools in tennis and volleyball. For students who plan to play collegiate tennis or beyond, the school offers a college preparatory tennis program, which enables girls to train and practice with members of the nationally ranked, All-American, Brenau Women's College tennis team. There is also a competitive intramural program. Among the recreational sports available are basketball, billiards, bowling, diving, hiking, jogging, snow skiing, softball, table tennis, touch football, and volleyball. Girls from Brenau sometimes serve as cheerleaders for Riverside Military Academy, a nearby boys' school.

Class-related outings are regularly made to points of interest in Atlanta, including the Fernbank Science Center, The High Museum, the Atlanta Civic Center, and the Alliance Theatre. Brenau arranges School-sponsored activities including movies; hiking and skiing trips; visits to local attractions, such as Lake Lanier, Calaway Gardens, Six Flags, Stone Mountain, the Atlanta Braves, and the Biltmore House; and eating out. On some Sundays, there are optional chaperoned trips to Riverside Military Academy for the weekly parade and chapel service. With parental permission, and according to school regulations, students may go on dates on Friday and Saturday nights. Some students go home for a weekend or, with parental permission, visit the homes of other Brenau students. Three closed weekends with many activities build bonding and school spirit.

Concerts, plays, and lectures are offered at the Academy and College. Former Attorney General Griffin Bell, Dan Rather, Roberta Peters, Jane Fonda, Steve Allen, William Warfield, the Augusta Opera, the Atlanta Symphony, the Atlanta Ballet, the Vienna Boys Choir, the Atlanta Boys Choir, Chuck Mangione, and the Ramsey Lewis Trio have appeared at Brenau. Recent campus art exhibits include Jasper Johns, Robert Rauschenberg, and Roy Lichtenstein. Traditional events include Halloween Carnival, the Christmas Dance, Dress-Up Days, "Monotony Breakers," Parents' Weekend, the Senior Banquet, the Senior Trip, the Dean's trip, and international travel opportunities.

ADMISSION AND COSTS. Brenau Academy seeks to enroll college-bound students from a wide range of academic abilities. Brenau does not require a certain grade point average or test score for entrance but carefully considers student potential. Girls are admitted to all grades on the basis of a completed application, three letters of recommendation, previous school records, and an interview with the Dean; a medical examination is required for enrollment. An interview with the Dean is generally required. Early application is encouraged, but applications are accepted for any school year through January. There is a $25 application fee.

In 1999–2000, tuition is $16,400 for boarding students and $7100 for day students. Extras include books and supplies ($400), driver education ($150), graduation/ring fees ($300), and private music lessons. A tuition payment plan is available. In 1999, $70,000 in financial aid was awarded, based solely on need.

Assistant Dean: Charles Burel
Director of Alumni Affairs: Debbi Thompson
Director of Admission: Jan Ewing
Vice President for Institutional Advancement: David Gines
College Counselor: Anita Langley
Business Manager: Dick Childers
Director of Athletics: Becky Whitton

Brookstone School   1951

440 Bradley Park Drive, Columbus, GA 31904-2989.
706-324-1392; Fax 706-571-0178; E-mail admissions@
brookstone.ga.net; Web Site www.brookstone.ga.net

Brookstone School is a coeducational, college preparatory day school with an enrollment of 887 in Four-Year-Kindergarten–Grade 12. The School aspires to help its students become self-motivated, prepared for future education, and able to be responsible citizens. Basic skills are emphasized in the Lower School. Art, music, drama, and computer training are offered in all grades. Advanced Placement courses are given in all Upper School disciplines. A full range of sports and extracurricular activities is conducted. Tuition: $4195–$7545. Financial Aid: $339,585. Becky Littlejohn is Director of Admissions; Robert A. Newton (Guilford College, A.B. 1958; University of North Carolina [Greensboro], M.Ed. 1966) is Headmaster. *Southern Association.*

Brookwood School   1970

301 Cardinal Ridge Road, Thomasville, GA 31792.
912-226-8070; Fax 912-227-0326;
Web Site www.brookwoodschool.org

Brookwood is a college preparatory day school enrolling 460 boys and girls in Pre-Kindergarten–Grade 12. The School seeks to create a total educational environment so each student may develop mentally, physically, and spiritually while growing into responsible citizenship. A traditional course of study is supplemented by electives, including computer study and Advanced Placement courses. There are activities in publications, clubs, sports, and drama. A summer program is offered. Tuition: $1750–$4750. Financial Aid: $95,000. William Baird Hudgins, Jr. (Rollins, B.A.; North Georgia College, M.Ed.; University of Georgia, Ed.D.) was appointed Headmaster in 1996. *Southern Association.*

Darlington School   ROME

1014 Cave Spring Road, Rome, GA 30161. 706-235-6051,
800-368-4437; E-mail admission@darlington.rome.ga.us;
Web Site www.darlington.rome.ga.us

DARLINGTON SCHOOL in Rome, Georgia, is a coeducational college preparatory school enrolling boarders in Grades 9–12 and a Postgraduate program and day students in Pre-Kindergarten through Grade 12. Rome, a community of 84,000 in the foothills of the Lookout Mountain Range 65 miles from both Atlanta and Chattanooga, Tennessee, is home to Berry, Floyd, and Shorter colleges.

The School was founded in 1905 by John Paul and Alice Allgood Cooper and was named for Joseph James Darlington, a teacher who had influenced Mr. Cooper. Mr. Darlington's pupils were determined to perpetuate his beliefs in academic excellence, diligent effort, and the development of character dedicated to the service of God and community. Those ideals remained prominent through many changes in the School, including the addition of a boarding division in 1923 and the establishment of coeducation and an elementary division in 1973.

Darlington's mission is to prepare students for college and for life by helping them develop intellectually, spiritually, socially, and physically. Most faculty live on campus, and further adult support is provided by "Rome parents," local families who volunteer to serve as away-from-home parents for boarders. The School fosters Christian values but is nonsectarian. Weekly chapel services are held, and boarding students attend the churches of their choice in Rome on Sunday mornings as well as Sunday vespers at the School.

Darlington School is a nonprofit organization governed by a self-perpetuating Board of 36 Trustees. A Board of Visitors provides counsel and support to the Trustees. Darlington is accredited by the Southern Association of Colleges and Schools and holds membership in the National Association of Independent Schools, among other professional organizations.

THE CAMPUS. The School covers more than 400 acres including woodlands and a small lake. The Upper School (Grades 9–12) buildings, grouped around the lake, are all wired for Internet access and house nearly 300 computers. All dormitory rooms have T1 Internet access, and most classrooms are equipped with Gateway Destinations, computers with large-screen monitors for multimedia presentations. Five computer labs contain computers for student use, including the Student Publications Laboratory, a high-tech design center used for teaching graphic design, web authoring, and desktop publishing as well as the production of student publications.

Major campus facilities include the Darlington Library, a two-story, fully automated facility with a capacity for 40,000 volumes; the Kawamura Science Center, with classrooms and laboratory facilities; Porter Hall, containing classrooms and the dining hall; Sydenham Hall, with administrative offices and the post office; Zelle Fine Arts and Student Center, which houses art, drama, and music studios, and a Nautilus weight room; Memorial Chapel; Wilcox Hall, a boys' dormitory with study hall, faculty offices, and school store; and South Hall, another boys' dormitory providing math and foreign language classrooms, and computer laboratories. Persons and Trippeer halls are girls' dormitories. The President occupies an 1832 house overlooking the lake, and 52 faculty residences are also located on campus.

Athletic facilities include a new stadium for football and track, a new soccer field complex, baseball and lacrosse fields, a football practice field, a cross-country course, a 12-court tennis complex, a gymnasium, and an indoor swimming pool. A $16,000,000, 85,000-square-foot athletic center is scheduled to open in August 2001.

THE FACULTY. David V. Hicks became Darlington's sixth President in August 1999, succeeding James P. McCallic, who served the School in that position for 20 years. Mr. Hicks graduated magna cum laude from Princeton University in 1970 and received a master's in philosophy, politics, and economics from Oxford University in 1972. He is a Rhodes Scholar and former head of three independent schools in Mississippi, Texas, and New Hampshire. His 1981 *Norms & Nobility: A Treatise on Education* won an Outstanding Book Award from the American Library Association in 1982. Mr. Hicks is also author of numerous articles, reviews, homilies, and essays, including "The Strange Fate of the American Boarding School," published in *The American Scholar* in 1996.

Of the 77 teachers and administrators in the Upper School, 60 live on campus. All hold baccalaureate degrees and more than half have advanced degrees. They have earned degrees from Bucknell, Colgate, Dartmouth, Davidson, Duke, Emory, Middlebury, Rhodes, Rutgers, Vanderbilt, Wake Forest, and the Universities of Georgia, North Carolina, and Virginia.

STUDENT BODY. In the 1999–2000 school year, Darlington's Upper School enrolled 185 boarding students from 15 states and 14 countries and 254 day students from ten counties in Georgia and two in Alabama. There were also 437 day students in Pre-Kindergarten–Grade 8.

ACADEMIC PROGRAM. The academic year, divided into three 12-week trimesters, begins in late August and ends in early June, with vacations of 10 days at Thanksgiving, 16 days at Christmas, and 9 in the spring. Classes, held 5 days a week, are scheduled in eight 45-minute rotating periods between 8:10 A.M. and 3:20 P.M. A one-hour period for athletics, fitness, fine arts, and other activities follows the class day. The schedule allows students to maintain five or more academic subjects, electives, and extracurricular activities through the day. The average class size is 13. Extra help is offered every morning in classroom sessions before school. Resident students have a supervised study hall of two and a half hours each evening. During that time, those in good academic standing may study in their rooms. Students on academic probation report to a formal study hall. Parents receive grades every 4 weeks and comments from every teacher at least once a trimester.

To graduate from the Upper School, a student must complete 21 credits including four years of English, two of a single foreign language, three of social studies, four of mathematics, three of science, one of fine arts, three of electives, and two of physical education.

Darlington offers a wide range of courses. English 1–4 covers grammar, composition, literary criticism, and American, British, and world literature. Language Department offerings include French 1–5, German 1–4, Latin 1–5, and Spanish 1–5. The History Department offers full-year courses in Ancient World History, Modern World History, Modern European History, American History, and Government/Economics, and electives in Military History and World Cultures. Math Department courses include Algebra 1–3, Geometry, Pre-Calculus, Calculus, and Computer. Courses in the Science Department consist of Biology, Environmental Science, Chemistry, and Physics. The Fine Arts Department offers Art 1–3, Graphic Design 1–3, Humanities, Drama 1–2, Cinema, Communications, Creative Writing, Desktop Publishing, Introduction to Journalism, Photojournalism, Video Production 1–2, Web Authoring, Yearbook Production, Chorale, Concert Choir, Instrumental Music, Music Appreciation, and Wind Ensemble. Additional courses include Physical Education, Health, Lifetime Fitness, Keyboarding, Word Processing, and Computer Application. Honors courses are available in most subjects; Advanced Placement courses are offered in 16 subjects: English, Math (AB or BC), Computer, Chemistry, Biology, Physics, French, Spanish, German, Latin, American History, European History, Government, Economics, Humanities (Art History), and Studio Art.

Virtually all Darlington graduates go to college and are systematically counseled from the start of their junior year. The 123 graduates in the Class of 1999 were accepted at 134 colleges and are attending 65 in 22 states and Canada. Among them are Boston University, Bowdoin, Davidson, Emory, Georgia Institute of Technology, Middlebury, New York University, Rhodes College, Vanderbilt, and the Universities of Alabama, California (Santa Barbara), Georgia, Illinois, Mississippi, North Carolina, the South, and Virginia.

A six-week summer session, conducted by members of the regular faculty, offers review and enrichment courses in which students can earn up to $1\frac{1}{2}$ credits. A full range of fine arts, athletics, and outdoor activities is provided in the afternoons and on weekends.

STUDENT ACTIVITIES. Students elect representatives to the Student Council, Honor Council, and "Y" Cabinet, which have major responsibilities for maintaining the quality of student life. The Student Council fosters school spirit and community service, organizes activities, and represents student views to the administration. The Honor Council administers the Honor System and deals with violations of the code. The "Y" Cabinet plans vespers services, leads devotionals, and finds opportunities for student social service.

Honor societies include the Cum Laude Society, National Honor Society, Quill and Scroll, and Mu Alpha Theta. Academic organizations consist of the Science, French, German, Latin, and Spanish clubs.

Activities in the Fine Arts include Darlington Players (which stages three drama productions each year), Set Crew, Literary and Scholar Bowl teams, Newspaper, Yearbook, Literary Magazine, Video, Photography, Choral Program, Instrumental Music, and Jazz Ensemble.

Other student organizations include the International Club, IMPACT (a diversity awareness group), Community Service, Environmental Awareness Club, Amnesty International, Fellowship of Christian Athletes, and Varsity "D" Club (an athletic club).

Varsity competition in the Georgia High School Association is offered in baseball, basketball, cross-country, football, golf, lacrosse, soccer, swimming and diving, tennis, track, and wrestling for boys. Varsity sports for girls include basketball, cheerleading, cross-country, golf, lacrosse, soccer, softball, swimming and diving, tennis, track, and volleyball. There are also junior varsity and freshman teams in many sports. Lifetime Fitness offers students not participating in a competitive sport a variety of noncompetitive activities such as aerobics, baseball, basketball, kayaking, lacrosse, martial arts, running, soccer, swimming, tennis, and weight-lifting.

Every weekend, activities are offered on campus, including movies, games, tournaments, dances, cookouts, and talent shows. Among the off-campus activities are excursions to Atlanta and Chattanooga shopping malls, amusement parks,

athletic contests, and cultural events. Phoenix Quest provides outdoor adventure in backpacking, canoeing, kayaking, mountain biking, rafting, rock climbing, and spelunking. Other activities are scheduled over vacations, from skiing trips to Colorado or Austria to hiking ventures in the Rockies or Appalachians to travel in Belize or England.

An active Parents Association sponsors dances, picnics, the Spring Festival, the Fine Arts Festival, Faculty Appreciation Week, the Junior-Senior Prom, and other events.

ADMISSION AND COSTS. Darlington seeks students of good character who have the ability and desire to make the most of the School's strengths. Most Upper School students are admitted in Grades 9 and 10, but applicants can be accepted for any grade. SSAT scores, previous transcripts, teacher recommendations, and a personal interview on campus are required. A decision is rendered within a month of completion of the admission procedure.

In 1999–2000, boarding tuition is $22,775; day tuition is $8850. Books are extra. Darlington subscribes to the School Scholarship Service and awards more than $1,000,000 annually in financial aid to 17 percent of its students on the basis of need (33 percent of boarding students receive financial aid). A number of payment plans, including a loan program, are available.

President: David V. Hicks
Headmaster: C. David Rhodes III
Vice President for Finance: Robert O. Rogers
Vice President for Development: Mollie Avery
Academic Dean: Sally D. Rudert
Dean of Studies and College Guidance: Samuel G. Moss III '63
Dean of Students: W. Gordon Neville, Jr., '55
Director of Admission: Lisa B. Schlenk
Director of Communications: William A. Bugg III
Director of Athletics: Jerry P. Sharp

Episcopal Day School   1944

2248 Walton Way, Augusta, GA 30904. 706-733-1192;
Fax 706-733-1388; Web Site http://www.usca.sc.edu/633/eds.html

Established by the Church of the Good Shepherd, Episcopal Day School enrolls 473 boys and girls in Three-year-old Pre-School–Grade 8. The School aims to provide an enriched and expanded education within a nurturing environment and to give full recognition to the differences in interests and abilities among its students. In addition to the standard curriculum, the School provides specialists in art, Spanish, Latin, music, physical education, computer education, research and study skills, and religious education. Students attend weekly chapel services. After-school care is available. Tuition: $1700–$5300. Jane Houston is Director of Admission; James C. Price (Kenyon, A.B. 1971; State University of New York [Albany], M.A. 1986) is the Headmaster. *Southern Association.*

Frederica Academy   1969

200 Hamilton Road, St. Simons Island, GA 31522. 912-638-9981;
Fax 912-638-1442; Web Site www.coastalgeorgia/fredericaacademy

Frederica Academy is a college preparatory day school enrolling 157 boys and 172 girls in Pre-Kindergarten–Grade 12. Founded by a group of parents who wished to combine a rigorous preparatory curriculum and a varied activities program, the school strives to help each student become an independent and resourceful adult. Computer skills and Spanish are introduced in the Lower School, Latin in Middle School, and Advanced Placement courses in Upper School. Tuition: $5150–$7400. Financial Aid: $229,000. Mrs. Jeris Wright is Director of Admission; Michael E. Collins (Castleton State, B.Se.; University of Arizona, M.Ed.) was appointed Headmaster in 1999. *Southern Association.*

The Galloway School 1969

215 West Wieuca Road, NW, Atlanta, GA 30342. 404-252-8389;
Fax 404-252-7770; Web Site www.gallowayschool.org

Founded by Headmaster Emeritus Elliott Galloway, this coeducational day school enrolls 729 students in Preschool through Grade 12. The student-teacher ratio is 10:1. The goals of the Galloway philosophy are to develop in each student a value for learning as a lifelong process, to encourage engaged and active learning, and to teach all members of the Galloway community to respect the dignity of the individual. Extracurricular activities range from student government and service clubs to interscholastic sports and a variety of interest groups. Galloway also conducts a Center for the Arts for children and adults. Tuition: $2215–$9755. Angela Griffin is Director of Admission; Linda Martinson (Stanford University, Ph.D.) is Headmaster. *Southern Association.*

George Walton Academy 1969

#1 Bulldog Drive, Monroe, GA 30655. 770-267-7578;
Fax 770-267-4023; E-mail cstancil@gwa.com

George Walton Academy, a college preparatory day school enrolling 890 students in Pre-Kindergarten–Grade 12, seeks to encourage young people to strive for excellence in everything they undertake. It offers a traditional curriculum enhanced by Spanish, Latin, French, fine arts, computer, and physical education. Advanced Placement and honor courses are offered in the Upper School. Students participate in a full range of varsity sports and extracurricular activities. Located 45 miles east of Atlanta, the school aims to provide a safe, drug- and alcohol-free environment. Extended-day care and summer sports camps are available. Tuition: $4060-$4600. William M. Nicholson (Georgia Southern, B.S.; University of Georgia, M.Ed., Ed.S.) is Headmaster. *Southern Association.*

The Heritage School 1970

2093 Highway 29 North, Newnan, GA 30263. 770-253-9898;
Fax 770-253-4850; E-mail mdoughty@heritagehawks.org;
Web Site www.heritagehawks.org

The Heritage School is a college preparatory day school enrolling 340 students in three-year-old Pre-Kindergarten through Grade 12. The School strives to maintain high academic and personal standards, challenging each student to achieve full potential in an environment of trust and encouragement. Advanced Placement courses are available. Sports, drama, and music are among the activities. A summer program offers remedial and enrichment activities and sports camps. Tuition: $4000–$7900. Financial aid is available. Martine C. Doughty is Director of Admissions; Thomas P. Hudgins, Jr. (Washington and Lee, B.A.; Old Dominion University, M.S.), was appointed Headmaster in 1998. *Southern Association.*

Holy Innocents' Episcopal School

ATLANTA

805 Mt. Vernon Highway, N.W., Atlanta, GA 30327. 404-255-4026;
Fax 404-250-0815; E-mail barbara.cartmill@hies.org;
Web Site www.hies.org

Holy innocents' episcopal school in Atlanta, Georgia, is a church-related day school enrolling boys and girls in Pre-School–Grade 12. Situated in the suburban Sandy Springs section of Atlanta, the School is easily accessible from all parts of the metropolitan area.

The School was founded in 1959 by parishioners of Holy Innocents' Episcopal Church to provide children with an enriching educational program in a Christian environment. The School opened with an enrollment of 70 students in Pre-School through Grade 1 and has grown today to 1300 students, age three through Grade 12. In 1998, Holy Innocents' was honored as a National Blue Ribbon School of Excellence.

In an atmosphere of warmth and acceptance, Holy Innocents' seeks to provide a superior program that encourages intellectual, social, spiritual, and physical growth. The School emphasizes learning as a lifelong process and strives to accommodate the individual learning styles of students. The religious program provides knowledge of Christian teaching while fostering respect for and understanding of other beliefs. All students participate in community service.

A nonprofit corporation, the School is governed by a 21-member Board of Trustees that meets monthly. Board members are elected by the rector, warden, and vestry of the church. The rector is chairman of the Board, and the Vice-Chairman is the Chair of the Executive Committee. The Parents' Association sponsors activities that help to enrich the academic program and improve the physical facilities.

Holy Innocents' Episcopal School is accredited by the Southern Association of Colleges and Schools. It holds membership in the National Association of Independent Schools and the Southern Association of Independent Schools, among other professional affiliations.

THE CAMPUS. The 34-acre wooded campus includes play areas, athletic fields, and a track. Principal facilities are the three Lower School buildings, renovated in 1998, which house Pre-first through Grade 5 and include computer and language labs, resource center, and a library; a Fine Arts Center (1988), with art classrooms, kiln room, darkroom, practice rooms, and a 356-seat auditorium; and the Parish Hall, which is the dining hall for the Lower School.

The Middle and Upper schools, completed by 1991, include a fully automated library, science laboratories, classrooms, a computer lab, kitchen, and dining hall. A second gymnasium (1992) contains basketball courts, a fitness center, classrooms for physical education, offices, and a student lounge. In 1996, the offices of Admission, Business, Development, and Communications moved into housing on property adjacent to the west end of the Campus. The Pre-School facility (1998) for three-year-olds, Pre-Kindergarten, and Kindergarten classes includes art and music rooms, a library, and an activity room. A state-of-the-art Upper School wing (1999) provides classrooms, administrative offices, and a student commons.

THE FACULTY. Dr. Susan R. Groesbeck was appointed Headmaster in 1996. She is an alumna of Skidmore College (B.A. 1972), where she was a member of Phi Beta Kappa. She also earned her master's and doctoral degrees from the University of Rochester and is certified in secondary teaching, building-level administration, and school district administration.

The full-time faculty, including eight administrators who teach, number 133. They hold 133 baccalaureate, 69 master's, and 5 doctoral degrees, representing study at 75 colleges and universities. Two or more degrees were earned at Emory, Florida State, Georgia State, Jacksonville University, Louisiana State, Oglethorpe, Vanderbilt, Wesleyan, William and Mary, and the Universities of Alabama, Georgia, Michigan, North Carolina, North Florida, the South, South Carolina, Tennessee, and Texas. Faculty benefits include health and disability insurance, retirement plans, Social Security, professional development, continuing education, and leaves of absence and sabbaticals.

Two nurses are on duty during school hours to provide first aid; emergency facilities are within a seven-minute drive of the campus. Four chaplains, all ordained ministers, are on staff as well as four counselors and two college placement counselors.

STUDENT BODY. In 1999–2000, Holy Innocents' enrolls 1271 students as follows: 32 in three-year-old Pre-School, 64 in Pre-Kindergarten, 72 in Kindergarten, 16 in Pre-First, 84 in Grade 1, 92 in Grade 2, 87 in Grade 3, 93 in Grade 4, 92 in Grade 5, 100 in Grade 6, 90 in Grade 7, 98 in Grade 8, 86 in Grade 9, 87 in Grade 10, 81 in Grade 11, and 90 in Grade 12. The students, 30 percent of whom are Episcopalian and 53 percent of whom represent other denominations, are from Atlanta and surrounding communities. The student-teacher ratio averages 9:1.

ACADEMIC PROGRAM. The school year, from late August to early June, includes vacations for Thanksgiving, Christmas, spring break, and Easter. A typical day for Grades 1 through 12 begins at 8:10 A.M. and ends at 3:00 P.M. Pre-School classes are in session from 8:30 A.M. to noon. Kindergarten and Pre-First are dismissed at 2:45 P.M. For a separate fee, working parents may enroll children from Pre-Kindergarten to Grade 12 in the School's extended-day program, which provides activities through 6:00 P.M.

Typical class sizes are 16 in Pre-School, 22 in Lower School, 22 in Middle School, and 19 in Upper School. There is an extra-help session four afternoons a week. In addition, students in the Middle and Upper schools can arrange tutoring sessions during the day according to teacher availability. Grades are issued and sent to parents three times a year, with parent-teacher conferences midway through each quarter. Conferences can also be scheduled at other times as necessary. A teacher advisory program offers one-on-one support for each student.

Through a curriculum that offers a strong foundation in basic skills and a wide range of creative and physical activities, the Pre-School (three-year-olds through Kindergarten) program is designed to be flexible and challenging while also fostering a sense of pleasure in academic success. Teachers help children to develop a positive self-image and to contribute productively to group activities. A transitional three-day week for

three-year-olds is offered until after Christmas, when all threes attend five days a week.

The Lower School (Pre-First through Grade 5) curriculum builds on that of the Pre-School, continuing to emphasize group participation while also encouraging self-discipline, intellectual independence, initiative, and responsibility. Throughout the Lower School, classrooms are flexible in design and furnishings to allow for cooperative teaching and group projects. Students receive regular instruction in language arts, social studies, mathematics, science, computer education, art, music, drama, and physical education. Spanish is taught in Grades 2–5.

The Middle School (Grades 6 through 8) course of study accommodates a variety of developmental needs, abilities, and differences in learning styles. English and history classes use primary source materials in addition to textbooks, and teachers emphasize good writing across the curriculum. Specific course offerings are English (including creative writing), French, Latin, Spanish, social studies (covering Western and non-Western civilizations, American history, and Georgia history), mathematics, pre-algebra, Algebra I, computer, science (including biology, natural science, and physical science), fine arts, the Bible, ethics, and health and physical education.

To graduate, students in the Upper School must complete four years of English; three each of mathematics and a foreign language; two each of history (including United States history), science, and religion; one year of fine arts and physical education; and two years of electives, one of which must be a science or history course. A variety of electives is available as well as honors and Advanced Placement courses.

In the summer, Holy Innocents' sponsors a three-week enrichment program for pre-schoolers, a reinforcement program for students entering Pre-First–Grade 8, and a two-week "brush-up" course for rising second through rising ninth graders.

STUDENT ACTIVITIES. The Middle and Upper School Student Councils, composed of elected representatives, sponsor community service activities and social events.

All students can take advantage of extracurricular opportunities. A Peer Counseling program is active. There is a strong program of retreats for students in all grades, from age 3 through Grade 12. A service project is also part of every student's yearly experience.

Day trips to points of interest throughout the Atlanta area

complement the academic program for all grades. In addition, there are occasional longer excursions, such as the eighth-grade trip to Washington, D.C., or New York City as well as opportunities to travel abroad.

There is competition in baseball, basketball, cross-country, soccer, tennis, swimming, golf, wrestling, and track and field for boys; and basketball, cross-country, soccer, softball, volleyball, tennis, swimming, golf, and track and field for girls. Holy Innocents' teams compete in Region 6A of the Georgia High School Association. The girls' basketball team won the state title in 1998. All students can take part in intramural sports.

ADMISSION AND COSTS. Holy Innocents' welcomes students of average to superior ability who want an excellent education within a Christian environment. New students are admitted to all grades, space permitting, on the basis of School-administered or standardized testing (depending on grade level); the previous academic record; recommendations from two teachers and a principal; and a personal interview. Application should be made by February 15 for possible fall admission, though late applications are accepted and students may enroll at midyear if space exists. There is a $65 application fee.

In 1999–2000, tuition ranged from $5961 for the five-day three-year-old program to $10,372 for the Upper School. Additional costs include uniforms ($225–$300), lunch ($475), and books for Middle and Upper School students ($295–$455, depending upon the grade).

In the 1998–99 school year, Holy Innocents' awarded $261,265 in financial aid to 42 students on the basis of need. Tuition refund insurance is available.

Assistant Headmaster/Head Chaplain: The Reverend John Merchant
Upper School Principal: Rich Webb
Middle School Principal: David Nelson
Lower School Principal: Dorothy Sullivan
Pre-School Principal: Janella Brand
Curriculum Director: Dr. Judith Hiles
Director of Development and Communications: Chris Pomar
Business Office Manager: Jim Griffin
Plant Operations Director: Gary Norris
Admissions Director: Barbara Cartmill
Upper School Chaplain: The Reverend Dr. Halley Willcox
Athletic Director: Emory "Buster" Brown
Fine Arts Director: Michael Bryant
Mentorship: Asha Sethi

LaGrange Academy   1970

1501 Vernon Street, LaGrange, GA 30240. 706-882-8097; Fax 706-882-8097

LaGrange Academy is a college preparatory day school enrolling 260 boys and girls in Kindergarten 5–Grade 12. It seeks to prepare its students to be independent and resourceful by providing them with a rigorous curriculum and a varied activities program. Fundamental skills, foreign languages, and computer science are introduced in the Lower and Middle Schools. Advanced Placement and college courses are available to qualified juniors and seniors. Field experiences and tours, athletics, drama, publications, Student Council, and activity and service clubs are also offered. Tuition: $3670–$5600. Financial aid is available. Martha Ann Todd (Emory, B.A. 1977; Columbus College, M.Ed. 1993) was appointed Head of School in 1992.

The Lovett School   1926

4075 Paces Ferry Road, NW, Atlanta, GA 30327. 404-262-3032; Fax 404-261-1967; E-mail fdraper@lovett.org; Web Site www.lovett.org

Lovett is a college preparatory school enrolling 1482 boys and girls in four-year-old Kindergarten–Grade 12. The curriculum includes honors and Advanced Placement courses and a Learning Lab, with academic and study skills support. Orchestra, band, voice, music, art, and drama are available in all divisions. Religion courses are offered, and chapel is held weekly for all students. A full athletic program fields varsity teams in 16 sports. Activities range from literary and honor societies to language and service clubs. A summer program is available. Tuition: $6170–$11,645. Financial Aid: $1,000,000. James P. Hendrix, Jr. (Davidson, A.B. 1963; Louisiana State, M.A. 1968, Ph.D. 1973), was appointed Headmaster in 1991. *Southern Association.*

Marist School   ATLANTA

3790 Ashford-Dunwoody Road, NE, Atlanta, GA 30319-1899. 770-457-7201; Fax 770-457-8402; E-mail marist@marist.com; Web Site www.marist.com

MARIST SCHOOL in Atlanta, Georgia, is a Roman Catholic, coeducational, college preparatory day school for students in Grades 7 through 12.

Founded in 1901 in downtown Atlanta by Bishop John E. Gunn of the Society of Mary, Marist School moved to its present campus in 1962 to accommodate its growing enrollment.

Marist offers a curriculum that cultivates the pursuit of academic, moral, physical, personal, and civic excellence and leadership. The School is guided by the educational mission and moral teaching of the Catholic Church. While the majority of the student body is Roman Catholic, the School maintains an atmosphere of acceptance and hospitality, admitting qualified students of any race, creed, or national origin.

Marist is owned by the Society of Mary (Marists) and is governed by a Board of Members and a Board of Trustees. Daily management of the School is by the Leadership Team composed of the School President, Headmaster, and Campus Pastor. The School has approximately 5500 living graduates and an active Alumni Association.

Marist School is accredited by the Southern Association of Colleges and Schools. It holds membership in the National Association of Independent Schools, the Atlanta Area Association of Independent Schools, Georgia Independent Schools Association, the Southern Association of Independent Schools, and the National Catholic Educational Association.

THE CAMPUS. The 57-acre campus is located in the Perimeter Center area ten miles north of downtown Atlanta. The main academic buildings contain 40 classrooms, 8 science laboratories, and a number of faculty offices. Two other buildings, completed in 1992, house a fine arts facility, a library, three computer laboratories, a dance studio, choral room, and instrumental music room. An elevator gives disabled persons access to all areas. Athletic facilities include Kuhrt Gymnasium, Cody Laird Gymnasium, Hughes Spalding Memorial Stadium, a baseball complex, tennis courts, a cross-country track, and soccer and softball fields. The performing arts are centered in Woodruff Auditorium. The Whitehead Cafeteria, Esmond Brady Chapel, and Marist Community Rectory complete the campus.

Marist has initiated a capital campaign to construct a student assembly center seating 2000, an aquatic center, alumni/development offices, renovations to Kuhrt Gymnasium and six science classrooms/labs, and endowment for tuition assistance, faculty development, and plant maintenance.

THE FACULTY. The Reverend James L. Hartnett, S.M., was appointed President in 1989. Father Hartnett graduated from Marist College (B.A.), and holds advanced degrees from The Catholic University of America (M.A.) and Duquesne University (M.A.). The Reverend Joel M. Konzen, S.M. (St. Meinrad, B.A.; Notre Dame School of Theology, M.Div.; Catholic University, M.A., M.A.Ed.), is Principal. The Reverend Ron Nikodem, S.M., Chaplain since 1996, holds a B.A. degree from Case Western Reserve University, a master's in education from Kent State, and an M.Div. degree from The Catholic University of America.

There are 82 full-time teachers, four librarians, five guidance counselors, and two campus ministers. An additional 12 administrators complete the staff. Eighty percent of administrators, faculty, and staff hold advanced degrees.

STUDENT BODY. In 1999–2000, Marist School enrolls 517 boys and 508 girls in Grades 7–12 as follows: 129 in Grade 7, 128 in Grade 8, 201 in Grade 9, 192 in Grade 10, 187 in Grade 11, and 188 in Grade 12.

ACADEMIC PROGRAM. The school year, from late August to early June, is divided into three terms. The calendar includes Thanksgiving, Christmas, Easter, and spring breaks. Parents receive progress reports at midterm and grade reports at the end of each term.

Each class meets four times per week on a rotating schedule, and an average class enrolls 19 students. The daily schedule, from 8:15 A.M. to 2:55 P.M., is divided into six 55-minute academic periods, lunch, and a brief homeroom. A tutorial period for individual assistance is held at the end of each day until 3:30 P.M. One period each week is reserved for extracurricular activities or tutoring. The library, the computer center, and a supervised study hall are available throughout the school day.

In Grades 7 and 8, the curriculum consists of English, Health, Languages, Social Studies, Mathematics, Science, Physical Education, and Religion. All new students must complete keyboarding and computer applications courses. Music is required of all students in Grades 7–8. Electives include drama/speech and art. The study of Spanish, French, Latin, or German begins in Grade 8.

To graduate, students must accumulate 360 quarter-hours of credit in Grades 9–12. (Five quarter-hours are earned for each term course.) Specific requirements are English and mathematics 60, social studies and science 45, religion 40, foreign language 30, physical education 15, computer science 10, and fine arts 5.

In Grades 9–12, the curriculum is a combination of term and yearlong courses. The following year courses are offered: English; French 1–5, German 1–5, Latin 1–4, Spanish 1–4; World History, American History; Algebra I and II, Geometry, Precalculus, Calculus; and Science 9, Biology, Chemistry, and Physics.

Many term courses are available. Among them are Drama, Creative Writing, Faith & Literature, Journalism; Biblical Archaeology, Women's Studies in Religion, World Religions, Peace and Justice; Ceramics, Humanities, Dance; Visual BASIC, Programming in PASCAL, Programming in C++; Historical Geology, Mechanics, Electricity & Magnetism; and The Modern Middle East, Postwar America, International Decision Making, and History and the Holocaust.

Advanced Placement courses are offered in U.S. History, European History, English, Spanish, French, German, Latin, biology, chemistry, calculus (AB and BC), physics, art history, macroeconomics, U.S. government, statistics, music theory, and computer science. In 1999, students took 514 Advanced Placement tests, and 92 percent achieved a passing grade. The Senior Career Project enables each senior to acquire a brief period of full-time "on-the-job" experience by observation and/or participation.

In 1999, 100 percent of Marist's seniors graduated and are attending such institutions as Auburn, Boston College, Catholic University of America, Clemson, Cornell, Davidson, Duke, Emory, Florida State, Furman, Georgia Institute of Technology, Harvard, Loyola, Massachusetts Institute of Technology, Miami of Ohio, New York University, Princeton, Rhodes, St. Mary's, United States Military Academy, United States Naval Academy, Vanderbilt, Villanova, Wake Forest, Washington and Lee, and the Universities of Colorado, Georgia, Notre Dame, Pennsylvania, and Virginia.

STUDENT ACTIVITIES. Class representatives and elected officers form the Student Council, which organizes student activities and represents student interests within the community. Other student groups include the National Honor Society, Marching Band and Color Guard, Jazz Band, Science Club, Thespians, Junior Classical League, French, Spanish, German, Latin, and Mathematics honor societies, Fellowship of Christian Athletes, Academic Team, Debate Team, Mock Trial, and religious organizations such as Emmaus, Damascus, Genesis, Nazareth, the Breakfast Club, and Mary's Circle. Marist holds the first high school charter awarded by Habitat for Humanity.

Marist is a member of the Georgia High School Association and competes in athletics with public and private schools. Varsity teams are organized in football, baseball, basketball, cheerleading, wrestling, golf, tennis, soccer, cross-country, track, volleyball, softball, and swimming. Junior varsity programs in most sports provide developmental opportunities for nonvarsity athletes. Archery, hiking, canoeing, weight training, skiing, gymnastics, and other physical activities are taught by the Physical Education Department.

Among the traditional school events are Homecoming, St. Peter Chanel Day, Open House, College Night, Awards Convocation, and breakfasts and luncheons for parents' groups. Parents may belong to the Parents' Club, Booster Club, Music Association, Friends of Woodruff, Marist Families in Action, Parents' Prayer Group, Parents' Multicultural Support Group, and Marist Singles.

ADMISSION AND COSTS. Marist School accepts new students in Grades 7–11 on the basis of their academic records, recommendations from their schools, their responses to a questionnaire, an interview, and results of the Secondary School Admission Test. Grades 7 and 9 are considered the primary entry points. Only students moving to Atlanta from other areas are admitted to Grade 12. Application for fall 2000–01 enrollment should be made between November 1, 1999, and February 5, 2000. Candidates are notified of admissions decisions in early April. There is a $60 application fee and a charge for the standard entrance examination.

In 1999–2000, tuition is $8500. Marist granted approximately $675,000 in tuition assistance for 1999–2000. Marist subscribes to the School Scholarship Service.

Academic Dean: D. Kay Betts
Dean of Students: Michael Trapani
Director of Admissions: James G. Byrne
Director of Development: Nancy Peterman
Director of Guidance: Regina M. Huneke
Director of Finance and Operations: William F. Schmitz
Director of Athletics: Tommy Marshall
Director of Mission Implementation: Rev. Richmond Egan, S.M.
Centennial Coordinator/Archivist/Public Relations: Joanne A. Davis
Alumni Coordinator: Kelei Sabatino

Mount de Sales Academy 1871

*851 Orange Street, P.O. Box 6136, Macon, GA 31208-6136.
912-751-3240; Fax 912-751-3241; E-mail tmermann@
mds.macon.ga.us; Web Site www.mds.macon.ga.us*

Mount de Sales Academy, a nationally recognized School of Excellence, enrolls 600 young men and women in Grades 7–12. The college preparatory program is designed to impart Catholic values and a strong core of knowledge in the major arts and sciences. Operated by the Sisters of Mercy, Mount de Sales offers a curriculum that features honors and Advanced Placement opportunities and varied electives. Students of all faiths take religion courses, perform community service, and participate in spiritual activities such as prayer services. The cocurricular program includes honor societies, the arts, publications, debate, Student Council, and sports. Tuition: $4049–$4309. Sr. Mary Rosina, RSM, is President; Terrence G. Mermann is Principal. *Southern Association.*

Oak Mountain Academy 1962

*222 Cross Plains Road, Carrollton, GA 30116. 770-834-6651;
Fax 770-834-6785; E-mail v.hardin@oak-mountain-academy.org;
Web Site www.oak-mountain-academy.org*

Oak Mountain Academy was established by the Basic Values Foundation to provide a nondenominational Christian educa-

tion for boys and girls in Pre-Kindergarten–Grade 12. Enrolling 280 students, the school offers a traditional college preparatory program, including Advanced Placement courses and the arts. Qualified juniors and seniors may take classes at West Georgia College. Participation in extracurricular activities such as sports, music, drama, and debate is encouraged; there is also a three-day "Winterim" of study and travel. Tuition: $5900. Extras: $100. Financial Aid: $200,000. John B. Meehl (Pomona College, B.A. 1965; Stanford University, M.A. 1966) is Headmaster.

Pace Academy 1958

*966 West Paces Ferry Road, NW, Atlanta, GA 30327.
404-262-1345; Fax 404-264-9376; E-mail alee@paceacademy.org;
Web Site www.paceacademy.org*

Enrolling 825 boys and girls in Pre-First through Grade 12, Pace Academy is a college preparatory day school committed to academic excellence within a framework of Judeo-Christian values. The School seeks to provide gifted, superior, and above-average students with a strong foundation in liberal arts, math, science, and computer technology. A demanding curriculum includes honors and Advanced Placement courses as well as a wide variety of electives. Students also participate in community service, peer leadership, and overseas exchange programs. Hallmark cocurricular activities include athletics, drama, debate, art, and leadership programs. Tuition: $7595–$12,270. Financial Aid: $500,000. Michael A. Murphy is Headmaster. *Southern Association.*

Paideia School 1971

*1509 Ponce de Leon Avenue, Atlanta, GA 30307. 404-377-3491;
Fax 404-377-0032; Web Site www.paideiaschool.org*

Paideia School was founded by a group of parents to provide a progressive, individualized, and intellectually challenging education for their children. Enrolling 840 boys and girls age 3 through Grade 12, Paideia offers a college preparatory program based on the liberal arts and sciences, enriched by diverse personal, ethical, and social issues courses and a community service internship program. Student government, three publications, drama, instrumental and vocal groups, various interest clubs, and interscholastic sports for girls and boys are among the activities. Tuition: $5805–$10,308. Financial Aid: $425,000. Caroline Quillian Stubbs is Director of Admissions; Paul F. Bianchi (Harvard College, B.A. [Honors]; Harvard University, M.A.T.) has been Headmaster since 1971.

Rabun Gap-Nacoochee School

*339 Nacoochee Drive, Rabun Gap, GA 30568. 706-746-7467;
800-543-7467; E-mail admission@rabungap.pvt.k12.ga.us;
Web Site www.rabungap.pvt.k12.ga.us*

RABUN GAP-NACOOCHEE SCHOOL in Rabun Gap, Georgia, is a coeducational college preparatory school enrolling boarding and day students in Grades 6 through 12. Rabun Gap is an unincorporated area 2 miles south of the North Carolina border near the towns of Dillard, Mountain City, and Clayton in Rabun County where 150,000 acres of national park, part of the Appalachian Trail, Rabun Bald Mountain, and the Tallulah Gorge are located. Georgia's only ski resort, Sky Valley, is 6 miles away. The campus is less than two hours by car from Atlanta, Georgia; Greenville, South Carolina; and Asheville, North Carolina, all of which are served by major airlines.

Rabun Gap-Nacoochee School was formed by the merger in 1927 of Rabun Gap Industrial School, founded in 1905 to meet the needs of isolated mountain families, and the Nacoochee Institute, founded in 1903 by the Athens Presbytery churches to provide Christian education for children of the Nacoochee Valley. The School retains its affiliation with the Presbyterian Church (USA).

The Rabun Gap experience is characterized by small groups—classes, residence hall life, advisee groups, and work teams—and promotes intellectual growth, self-esteem, and the development of close relationships among peers, teachers, residential faculty, and staff. A committed and sensitive faculty seeks to offer students the opportunities that will maximize their academic performance and personal development.

The School is a nonprofit institution governed by a self-perpetuating Board of Trustees; one-half of the nominees must be approved by the Presbyterian Synod of South Atlantic.

The School is accredited by the Southern Association of Colleges and Schools and by the Georgia Accrediting Commission. It holds membership in the National Association of Independent Schools, the Southern Association of Independent Schools, and the Georgia Independent Schools Association.

THE CAMPUS. The 1300-acre campus has woodlands, trout streams, a 20-acre lake, pastures, crop lands, barns, stables, a riding arena, a cross-country course, and a ropes course.

In recent years, all campus buildings have undergone renovation, preserving the original Federal architecture. Hodgson Hall, the main upper school building, houses computer labs, library, chapel, classrooms, and various school offices. The Morris Brown Center houses the music suite, art studio, herbarium, and science laboratories. There are two double-story and four single-story residence halls. The gymnasium, the natato-rium, weight room, lighted tennis courts, soccer, baseball, and softball fields, and track are key to the School's athletic program. The dining hall functions as the site of many social occasions and features a full range of food services in a family atmosphere. The student center, Gap Grill and Games, comprises a snack bar and television and billiards rooms.

The physical plant is owned by the School and is valued in excess of $20,000,000.

THE FACULTY. Gregory D. Zeigler (Washington and Jefferson College, B.A.; University of Utah, M.Ed.) is Headmaster.

The teaching faculty consists of approximately 40 men and women, most of whom live on campus. More than half of the faculty have earned advanced degrees.

Benefits for faculty include medical, dental, and life insurance, a retirement plan, and generous support of professional development.

The student health center is staffed full-time by a nurse, and doctors and dentists are on call nearby. Two hospitals are within 6 miles of the campus.

STUDENT BODY. In 1998–99, the School enrolls 275 students, about evenly divided between boys and girls. Approximately 65 percent are boarders. The majority of students come from Georgia, Florida, and the Carolinas, but other states and several foreign countries are also represented.

ACADEMIC PROGRAM. The curriculum is designed to challenge students and to prepare them for their choice of colleges. Classes range in size from 4 to 17 students, with an average of 13 students per class. Grades are based on a 4.0 scale, and progress reports are sent to parents two times each term. The faculty advisor program ensures that students experience regular contact for both academic and personal support. In addition to regular college preparatory and honors courses, Advanced Placement options are offered.

The student work program encourages responsibility and cooperation while developing self-assurance. All students participate through a wide variety of experiences, including cleaning classrooms and dormitories, working in the dining hall and gymnasium, and maintaining the campus.

Graduation requirements are 4 units of English; 4 units of mathematics; 3 units of science; 3 units of history including Ancient World History, Modern World History, and U.S. History; 3 units of the same foreign language; 1 unit of Bible; 2 units of visual or performing arts; 1 unit of physical and health education; and 1 unit of computer technology/keyboarding. A senior research project is required of all seniors. Traditional elective courses include anatomy/physiology, botany/genetics, environmental science, pre-calculus, calculus, creative writing, journalism, computer programming, art, drama, music (beginning band, wind ensemble, chorus) and industrial technology (woodworking, metalworking, mechanical drawing, and computer-assisted drawing).

English as a Second Language (ESL) is a standard course offering during the school year. International students begin the ESL Program during the summer and make the adjustment to life at the School prior to the start of full classes.

In 1999, all 40 graduating seniors planned to attend college in the fall. Acceptances in recent years include Auburn, The Citadel, Clemson, Davidson, Duke, Furman, Mary Baldwin, Rhodes College, Tufts, Vanderbilt, Virginia Tech, Washington and Lee, Wofford, and the Universities of Colorado, Georgia, Kentucky, North Carolina, South Carolina, and Tennessee.

STUDENT ACTIVITIES. The typical student day includes academic periods followed by a work period and athletics. Chapel services are held on Thursday and Sunday mornings.

Weekends offer students a variety of on-campus and off-campus options such as dances, sports events, hiking, or camping. Trips to museums, concerts, amusement parks, movies, and professional sporting contests are often scheduled. The School also provides transportation once a month so that boarding students may attend the church of their choice on Sunday mornings. Students are given the opportunity for monthly weekend leaves to visit their homes or make college visits.

Interscholastic athletics include cross-country, soccer, golf, volleyball, swimming, alpine skiing, basketball, tennis, softball, baseball, and track and field.

Other student activities include the newspaper and yearbook, literary magazine, Beta Club, Art Guild, astronomy and service clubs, cheerleading, National Honor Society, and the outdoor program, which is open to all students interested in hiking, backpacking, canoeing, rafting, kayaking, climbing, skiing, and fishing. The School's Equestrian Program seeks to provide students with an overall knowledge of caring for their animals and equipment as well as individual riding skills. Limited space is available for students to board their own horses.

ADMISSION AND COSTS. Rabun Gap-Nacoochee School seeks motivated college-bound students of average to above-average ability who desire a well-rounded and stimulating middle and/or secondary school experience. Candidates are evaluated based on school records, the Independent School Entrance Examination, references, and an on-campus interview.

In 1998–99, boarding tuition is $17,500; day tuition is $6900. Books and school clothes as well as some activities involve additional expenses. Merit scholarships and need-based grants are available.

Headmaster: Gregory D. Zeigler
Assistant Headmaster for Academic Affairs: Robert Brigham
Assistant Headmaster for Student Affairs: Stan Darnell
Assistant Headmaster for Advancement: Patricia Boyd

Director of Admission: Charlie Breithaupt
College Counselor: Holly White
Assistant Dean for Student Affairs: Ken White
Director of Communications: Arthur Moore

St. Andrew's School   1947

*601 Penn Waller Road, P.O. Box 30639, Savannah,
    GA 31410-0639. 912-897-4941; Fax 912-897-4943;
    E-mail standrew@hargray.com*

St. Andrew's is a coeducational day school enrolling 460 students in Kindergarten 3–Grade 12. The School centers all goals and efforts on the comprehensive development of the student, provides a strong college preparatory education, and guides growth through an appreciation for aesthetic, cultural, and moral values. Advanced Placement and honors courses are offered in the Upper School as well as a number of athletic and cocurricular opportunities. Students are also involved in community service. Parent support of and involvement in the efforts of the School are essential. Tuition including books: $4250–$6250. Financial aid is available. E. C. Hubbard is Headmaster. *Southern Association.*

St. Martin's Episcopal School   1959

*3110-A Ashford Dunwoody Road, Atlanta, GA 30319.
    404-237-4260; Fax 404-237-9311; E-mail smes@
    stmartinschool.org; Web Site www.stmartinschool.org*

St. Martin's Episcopal School is a parish day school enrolling 545 boys and girls, age two through Grade 8. The School seeks to offer a quality academic program based on a traditional curriculum within a Christian environment. Basic instruction is supplemented by art, music, language, physical and health education, computer, and religion. Small class size and individualized instruction characterize the three divisions within the School—Early Childhood (age 2–Pre-First), Elementary (Grades 1–4), and Middle School (Grades 5–8). There is a variety of extracurricular activities. Tuition: $2170–$6620. Financial Aid: $50,000. Jan Swoope is Director of Admissions; Jane B. Harter is Interim Headmistress.

St. Pius X Catholic High School   1958

*2674 Johnson Road, NE, Atlanta, GA 30345. 404-636-4109;
    Fax 404-633-8387; Web Site spx.org*

Serving 1060 young people in the Diocese of Atlanta, St. Pius X seeks to instill in its students the Christian message of hope and the desire to develop their full intellectual, spiritual, and social potential in the service of others. The college preparatory curriculum is taught on three levels of challenge, with an Advanced Placement program honored by the College Board as among the most outstanding in the region. Students produce three publications and take part in National Honor Society, Campus Ministry, varsity and intramural sports, Debate Team, drama, chorus, band, and other activities. Tuition: $6075. Financial aid is available. Shawn Sullivan is Admission Director; Donald T. Sasso was appointed Principal in 1991. *Southern Association.*

The Savannah Country Day School   1955

*824 Stillwood Drive, Savannah, GA 31419. 912-925-8800;
    Fax 912-920-7800*

Named a Blue Ribbon National School of Excellence by the U.S. Department of Education, Savannah Country Day is a college preparatory school enrolling 473 boys and 510 girls in Prekindergarten–Grade 12. Its aim is to instill an enthusiasm for learning, an ability to think critically, and a deep sense of personal integrity. Students are grouped by ability in the Upper School, where Advanced Placement and honor courses are offered. The average class size in the Upper School is 15 and the student-teacher ratio is 10:1. Tuition: $4205–$9105. Financial Aid: $488,000. Donna M. Herbert is Director of Admissions; Paul M. Pressly (Princeton, B.A. 1964; Harvard, M.P.A. 1968; Oxford [England], Ph.D. 1971) was appointed President/Headmaster in 1983. *Southern Association.*

Stratford Academy   1960

6010 Peake Road, Macon, GA 31220-3903. 912-477-8073;
Fax 912-477-0299

Stratford Academy was founded by parents to provide a college preparatory education in an environment that inspires each individual to fulfill high academic and personal expectations. Stratford's learning community is currently comprised of more than 100 faculty and staff and approximately 900 boys and girls in Preschool–Grade 12. The liberal arts curriculum places equal emphasis on the acquisition of a wide spectrum of knowledge and the development of sound moral and ethical values. Community service is required in the Upper School; other activities include 34 sports teams, three student publications, interest clubs, and a summer program. Tuition: $3650–$6350. John Paul Gaddy is Director of Admissions and Publications; Edward England is Headmaster. *Southern Association.*

Trinity School   1951

3254 Northside Parkway, NW, Atlanta, GA 30327. 404-231-8100;
Fax 404-231-8111; E-mail admissions@trinityatl.org;
Web Site www.trinityatl.org

Trinity School is a nondenominational day school enrolling 485 children in Pre-school–Grade 6. Established by Trinity Presbyterian, the School operates in the Judeo-Christian tradition. The challenging, developmentally appropriate program includes an integrated curriculum and cooperative learning methods. The child-centered atmosphere nurtures each student's positive self-image. Spanish, art, music, technology, and physical and outdoor education are vital parts of the curriculum. Many of the School's well-qualified faculty members hold advanced degrees. There is a summer camp and an after-school enrichment program. Tuition: $3050-$9480. Financial aid is available. Debbie Lange is Director of Admissions; Linda Perry (University of North Carolina [Chapel Hill], B.A., M.A.) is Head of School. *Southern Association.*

Valwood School   1969

1903 Gornto Road, Valdosta, GA 31602. 912-242-8491;
Fax 912-245-7894; E-mail VWS@valwood.org;
Web Site www.valwood.org

Enrolling 370 boys and girls in Pre-Kindergarten–Grade 12, Valwood was founded by parents to provide a challenging, well-rounded education for their children. The School is committed to the intellectual, artistic, physical, spiritual, and moral development of its students through a college preparatory program that emphasizes critical thinking, problem solving, effective communication skills, and the application of computer technology throughout the learning process. Advanced Placement courses, music and the arts, and overseas travel/study enrich the core program. Students engage in drama, debate, cheerleading, a literary society, and athletics. Extended care is available. Tuition: $1800–$5520. Financial Aid: $80,000. Laura H. Elliott is Director of External Affairs; Scott A. Wilson is Headmaster.

The Walker School   1957

700 Cobb Parkway North, Marietta, GA 30062. 770-427-2689

The Walker School is a coeducational day school enrolling 840 students in Pre-Kindergarten–Grade 12. The School seeks to provide quality education through the efforts of a caring faculty with the ability to motivate children to achieve. The major emphasis is a traditional college preparatory academic program that includes computer technology. In addition, there are programs in the visual and performing arts, publications, and physical education. Extracurricular activities include sports, clubs, music, and drama. Tuition: $5570–$9420. Financial Aid: $350,000. Donald B. Robertson (William and Mary, B.S. 1968; Rider University, M.A. 1974) was named Headmaster in 1985. *Southern Association.*

Wesleyan School   1963

5405 Spalding Drive, Norcross, GA 30092. 770-448-7640;
Fax 770-448-3699

Believing that all children are uniquely gifted, Wesleyan School offers programs in Kindergarten–Grade 12 that challenge, nurture, and strengthen each child. It seeks to foster in the student a desire to learn and become a steward and responsible citizen of the local community and the world beyond. The School strives to create a community that exemplifies Christian values through a liberal arts education that includes required language and Bible studies. Enrolling 940 students with a maximum class size of 20, Wesleyan offers a full range of sports, arts, and activities. Strict adherence to an honor code, uniform requirements, and a regular Chapel program are integral parts of school life. Tuition: $8010–$9975. Zach Young (University of Virginia, B.A.; Harvard, Ed.M.) is Headmaster.

The Westminster Schools   1951

1424 West Paces Ferry Road, NW, Atlanta, GA 30327-2486.
404-355-8673; Fax 404-367-7894; Web Site www.westminster.net

A Christian, college preparatory day school for 1725 boys and girls of various ethnic, religious, and economic backgrounds, Westminster seeks to develop each student's potential for sound values, continuing education, and community service. The academic program includes Advanced Placement courses in 28 subjects. Extracurricular activities include athletics, fine arts, performing arts, and an experiential education program. Graduates have attended 297 colleges and universities in 40 states and 6 foreign countries. The 171-acre campus is valued at $70,000,000 and the endowment is $235,000,000. Tuition: $7735–$12,080. Financial Aid: $1,000,000. Jere Wells is Director of Admission; William Clarkson IV (A.B., M.Div., D.Min.) was appointed President in 1991. *Southern Association*.

Westminster Schools of Augusta   1972

3067 Wheeler Road, Augusta, GA 30909. 706-731-5260;
Fax 706-731-5274; E-mail Admissions@WSA.NET

The Westminster Schools of Augusta offer a college preparatory education in a Christian setting with small classes, caring faculty, and many service opportunities and activities in athletics and the arts. Enrolling 561 day boys and girls in Pre-Kindergarten–Grade 12, Westminster provides Honors and Advanced Placement courses, foreign language, music, art, and drama. Among the activities are athletics, chorale, drama, and debate. Bible courses and weekly chapel services enrich the program. Graduates have been accepted at competitive colleges and universities nationwide. Tuition: $2180–$5700. Financial Aid: $165,000. Peggy Roberts is Director of Admissions; John H. Lindsell (Wheaton, B.A.; Gordon-Conwell Theological Seminary, M.T.S.; Harvard, Ed.M., Ed.D.) was appointed Headmaster in 1994. *Southern Association*.

Woodward Academy   METRO-ATLANTA

P.O. Box 87190, College Park, GA 30337-0190. 404-765-8200;
Admissions 404-765-8262; Fax 404-765-8259;
E-mail waadm@mindspring.com;
Academy Web Site www.woodward.edu;
Admissions Web Site www.mindspring.com/~waadm/waadm.html

Woodward academy in College Park, Georgia, is a coeducational college preparatory school enrolling 2800 day students in Pre-Kindergarten through Grade 12. Woodward Academy is comprised of six divisions. The Primary School (Kindergarten–Grade 2), Lower School (Grades 3–6), Middle School (Grades 7–8), and Upper School (Grades 9–12) are located on the main campus in College Park, a suburban community seven miles south of downtown Atlanta, and convenient to the Hartsfield International Airport. The Busey Campus (Pre-Kindergarten–Grade 6) is located in nearby Riverdale, Clayton County, and Woodward North (Pre-Kindergarten–Grade 6), is located in North Fulton County along the Chattahoochee River.

Founded in 1900 as Georgia Military Academy by Col. John C. Woodward, the school was originally a secondary military academy for boys; an elementary division was subsequently added. In 1964, the Academy became coeducational, and in 1966, the Academy's charter was amended to discontinue the military program and to rename the school in honor of its founder. Colonel Woodward was succeeded by his son-in-law, Col. William R. Brewster, Sr.; Capt. William R. Brewster, Jr., served as President from 1961 until December 1978. Dr. Gary M. Jones was installed as Woodward's fourth President in January 1979 and retired in July of 1990. Mr. A. Thomas Jackson became the fifth President of the Academy in August of 1990.

The Academy is incorporated as a nonprofit institution under a self-perpetuating Governing Board comprised of alumni and patrons of the school. Woodward Academy's productive endowments are valued at more than $50,000,000. Woodward is accredited by the Southern Association of Colleges and Schools; it holds membership in the National Association of Independent Schools, the Southern Association of Independent Schools, the Mid-South Association of Independent Schools, the Georgia Independent Schools Association, and the Atlanta Area Association of Independent Schools. The 7000 living graduates are served by an Alumni Association.

THE CAMPUS. The 75-acre College Park campus contains 50 buildings, practice fields, a football stadium, and eight tennis courts. Carlos Hall contains the administrative and business offices. West Hall contains Upper School offices and the infirmary, with Upper School classrooms located in the adjacent Brewster Hall. The Thalia N. Carlos Science Center contains 23,000 square feet of modern laboratories and classrooms. The Colquitt Student Center houses a snack bar, student lockers, and a recreation area. The George C. Carlos Library houses 25,000 volumes and includes conference rooms, reading areas, and study carrels for both Middle and Upper School students. The 60,000-square-foot Richardson Fine Arts Center contains classrooms, offices, studios, a gallery, a 400-seat auditorium, and a closed-circuit television station. The Alumni Center houses the alumni and development offices. The Paget Gymnasium Complex contains five basketball courts, a weight room, wrestling loft, and physical education offices. Adjacent to the Paget Complex is the Kennedy Natatorium, housing an eight-lane Olympic-size pool. More than 6000 spectators can be seated in the concrete, lighted Colquitt Stadium. Upper School meals are served in Robert W. Woodruff Hall. The 800-seat Richard C.

Gresham Chapel also contains two classrooms. Middle School offices, classrooms, laboratories, and study areas are located in Brand and Tucker Halls. Lower School offices, classrooms, a 15,000-volume library, computer lab, gymnasium, and cafetorium are located in the new $10,000,000 Thomas Hall. The Primary School Building and two annexes provide separate academic and extracurricular facilities for Kindergarten–Grade 2. Rutland Hall houses the campus store.

The 30-acre Busey School campus features a central complex containing administrative offices, classrooms, a library, and a cafetorium. The grounds also include an athletic field, a science center housing laboratory and classroom facilities, and a Pre-School building that accommodates 60 students. The 36-acre Woodward North campus includes a facility containing administrative offices, a cafetorium, a library, adjacent athletic fields, and nature trails.

THE FACULTY. President of the Academy A. Thomas Jackson, a native of Virginia, is a graduate of Williams College (B.A.) and American University (M.A.). Mr. Don A. Woolf, appointed Headmaster in 1980, is a graduate of the University of Georgia (B.S., M.Ed.).

The full-time faculty include 350 instructors. A nonacademic staff of 148 provide support services. Faculty and staff hold more than 222 master's or higher educational degrees, including 6 doctorates. Two or more degrees were earned at Agnes Scott, Auburn, Brenau, Cleveland State, Emory, Georgia Institute of Technology, Georgia Southern, Georgia State, Jacksonville State, LaGrange, Louisiana State, Memphis State, Mercer, Miami of Ohio, Michigan State, Milligan, Millsaps, Notre Dame College, Oglethorpe, Ohio State, Peabody, Purdue, Shorter, Wake Forest, West Chester State, West Georgia, West Virginia, William and Mary, and the Universities of Alabama, Arkansas, Central Florida, Georgia, Mississippi, North Alabama, North Carolina, South Carolina, South Florida, and Tennessee.

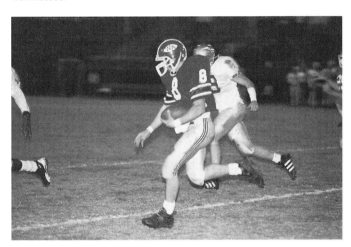

The Academy provides a salary schedule, supplements for extracurricular activities, merit pay, comprehensive major medical insurance, and a retirement program.

STUDENT BODY. Woodward Academy enrolls 2800 students, of whom 49 percent are boys and 51 percent girls. They come from communities throughout the metropolitan Atlanta area.

ACADEMIC PROGRAM. The academic year, from late August to early June, is divided into two semesters and includes Thanksgiving, Christmas, Spring, and Easter vacations. Classes begin at 8:30 A.M. and end at 3:15 P.M., depending on individual schedules.

A college preparatory curriculum is offered to all Upper School students; available electives include computer programming, television production, science fiction, astronomy, psychology, oceanography, satire, Shakespeare, and dance. Hon-

ors courses and Advanced Placement courses include English, European history, American history, mathematics, computer science, biology, chemistry, physics, French, German, Spanish, music, and art. Study abroad through the European Study Program is available for juniors and seniors. Report cards are mailed to parents at six-week intervals, and interim reports are sent to parents in cases of deficient or unsatisfactory work.

Middle School students are required to take Computer Science, Foreign Language, Study Skills, and Life Skills in addition to English, reading, mathematics, science, social studies, fine arts, and physical education. Honors and regular sections are offered in most departments; tutorials and study halls are available.

The Lower Schools offer a multilevel program of instruction. The upper elementary grades are departmentalized, and reading and mathematics receive primary emphasis along with computer science, social studies, science, art, music, drama, and physical education. The main campus Lower School offers a Student Transition Education Program. Tutorials, interim reports, and parent-teacher conferences chart a student's progress.

The 241 members of the Class of 1999 are attending such institutions as Auburn, Boston University, Brown, Colgate, Columbia, Cornell, Dartmouth, Davidson, Duke, Emory, Florida State, Georgetown, George Washington, Georgia Institute of Technology, Hampden-Sydney, Harvard, Johns Hopkins, Massachusetts Institute of Technology, Morehouse, New York University, Northwestern, Pepperdine, Princeton, Rhodes, Rollins, St. John's, Sewanee, Southern Methodist, Spelman, Stanford, Syracuse, Tulane, United States Naval Academy, Vanderbilt, Wake Forest, Yale, and the Universities of Alabama, Chicago, Colorado, Georgia, Miami, Michigan, Mississippi, North Carolina, Notre Dame, Pennsylvania, Southern California, Tennessee, and Virginia.

STUDENT ACTIVITIES. The Academy offers a wide variety of activities to students. Lower School activities include Cub Scouts, chorus, band, patrols, intramural sports, cultural programs, and educational trips. Middle School activities include a Student Government, class activities, a Camera Club, an Art Club, and Honor Council. Dances are held periodically. Upper School activities include Student Government, Honor Council, the National Honor Society, French and Spanish honor societies, debate, newspaper, yearbook, Camera Club, cheerleaders, flag corps, Art Club, choruses, Drama Club, band, a dance ensemble, ten service clubs, and the WATV crew. Upper School students are required to fulfill a 20-hour work contract during the year by working on campus. All Upper School students are involved in small group sessions through the Peer Leadership and Teacher Advisory programs. These programs assist students in dealing with peer pressure, academic stress, and other pertinent issues.

Interscholastic and intramural sports include football, baseball, basketball, soccer, swimming and diving, tennis, track, wrestling, cross-country, volleyball, fast-pitch softball, lacrosse, ultimate frisbee, and golf. Social activities include formal and informal dances and weekend outings.

Frequent assemblies provide a forum for various speakers and school groups.

ADMISSION AND COSTS. It is Woodward Academy's policy to admit students from a variety of racial, ethnic, and economic backgrounds who desire to attend the Academy and who provide evidence of good character, conduct, and academic achievement. Students must be able to participate in the physical education program. New students are accepted at all grade levels. An entrance examination, an interview, school records, teacher/principal evaluations, and evidence of extracurricular interests are required, especially for older students.

In 1999–2000, tuition is $5665–$10,395 for Pre-Kindergarten–Grade 6, $11,050 for Grades 7–8, and $11,200 for Grades 9–12. Additional charges for all students include textbooks ($300–$500) and uniforms (approximately $700). Additional fees may be levied for private lessons, private tutoring, developmental reading, the yearbook, and the diploma. An additional $6245 is required for students in the Transition Program to provide the small classes and individual tutoring such children require. Scholarship aid of $350,000 is awarded annually to approximately 10 percent of the students in the Middle and Upper schools.

Dean of Faculty: Mr. Don A. Woolf
Dean of Students: Mrs. Elaine T. Carroll
Alumni Director: Mr. Frank McKay
Dean of Admission: Mr. Russell L. Slider
Director of Development: Mr. John Anderson
College Counselor: Mrs. Missy Sanchez
Business Manager: Mr. James R. Chandler
Director of Athletics: Mr. Petty F. Ezell

HAWAII

Academy of the Pacific   1961

913 Alewa Drive, Honolulu, HI 96817. 808-595-6359;
Fax 808-595-4235; E-mail ddouthit@aop.net;
Web Site www.aop.net/

Academy of the Pacific was founded by concerned parents and educators to provide a supportive setting in which underachieving students receive personal instruction and individual scheduling. Serving 150 boys and girls in Grades 6–12, the school's goal is to enable students to face the challenges of today and the future. The curriculum emphasizes language arts, social studies, mathematics, computers, and health/science. Each student's education plan is tailored to maximize learning and allow development of unique abilities and learning styles. Electives, field trips, athletics, and guest lecturers enrich the program. Tuition: $8900. Dorothy B. Douthit (University of Texas, Ph.D.) is President/Head of School. *Western Association.*

ASSETS School   1955

One Ohana Nui Way, Honolulu, HI 96818. 808-423-1356;
Fax 808-422-1920; E-mail info@assets.pvt.k12.hi.us;
Web Site www.assets-school.net

ASSETS offers day programs for gifted, gifted-dyslexic, and dyslexic students in a supportive environment with small classes and individualized curricula to meet each child's special needs. Faculty are specially trained to provide acceleration, remediation, and enrichment. Developmental programs for dyslexic students who need structured language intervention use a multisensory approach. Elective and enrichment courses for all students are balanced between technology and the arts to encourage curiosity, self-expression, and acquisition of skills and concepts. Summer sessions include Science, Art, and Computer academies. Tuition: $9650–$11,950. Financial aid is available. Lou Salza (University of Massachusetts, B.A.; Harvard, Ed.M.) is Head of School. *Western Association.*

Hanahau'oli School   1918

1922 Makiki Street, Honolulu, HI 96822. 808-949-6461;
Fax 808-941-2216; E-mail rgpeters@hanahauoli.com;
Web Site www.hanahauoli.pvt.k12.hi.us.

A coeducational, nonsectarian elementary school enrolling 200 children in Junior Kindergarten–Grade 6, Hanahau'oli's philosophy of "learning by doing" informs its curriculum while creating an environment in which students share experiences and cooperate as a large family. The School seeks to foster a true love of learning through an integrated curriculum that teaches the "whole child" and respects the uniqueness of each individual. The development of basic skills and a strong foundation in traditional subjects, as well as foreign language and the fine and practical arts, are essential in opening up many avenues of communication and learning. Tuition: $9470. Robert G. Peters (University of Massachusetts, B.A., M.A., Ed.D.) is Headmaster.

Holy Nativity School   1949

5286 Kalanianaole Highway, Honolulu, HI 96821. 808-373-3232;
Fax 808-373-1284

An Episcopal day school enrolling 188 students in Pre-Kindergarten–Grade 6, Holy Nativity School provides a challenging academic program, which prepares students for independent secondary schools, in a caring, nurturing environment. Faculty and staff promote close communication between school and home and provide an atmosphere in which students gain an understanding and awareness of the principles of the Christian ethic. In addition to basic academic skills, special classes include Japanese language, music, art, religion, computer, Hawaiian studies, and physical education. A summer program offers various subjects in self-contained classrooms. Tuition: $6100–$6985. Financial aid is available. Mrs. Ella Browning is Admissions Director; Cynthia L. Hoddick (University of California [Berkeley], M.A.) is Head. *Western Association.*

Island School   1977

3-1875 Kaumuali'i Highway, Lihue, HI 96766. 808-246-0233;
Fax 808-245-6053; E-mail info@ischool.org;
Web Site www.ischool.org

Island School, Kaua'i's largest and oldest independent school, educates 225 students in Pre-Kindergarten–Grade 12. The curriculum is designed to meet the needs of students with average to above-average ability and to develop the academic, artistic, and athletic talents and interests of each individual. Specialists teach art, computer, drama, Hawaiian studies, music, physical education, and Spanish as part of the required curriculum. The High School's college preparatory program, enhanced by computer technology, meets the entrance requirements of selective colleges. Tuition: $4350–$6750. Financial Aid: $230,000. Paige Talvi is Admission Director; Robert Springer (Occidental College, B.A. 1959; University of the Americas [Mexico], M.A. 1966) is Headmaster. *Western Association.*

The Kamehameha Schools   1887

1887 Makuakane Street, Honolulu, HI 96817. 808-842-8211;
Fax 808-842-8411; Web Site www.ksbe.edu

Founded by Princess Bernice Pauahi Bishop, Kamehameha serves 3700 Native Hawaiians in Kindergarten–Grade 12 on three campuses: Maui, East Hawaii, and the largest, Kapalama, which accommodates 551 boarders in Grades 7–12. The curriculum is college preparatory. Extracurricular activities include athletics, academic and special-interest clubs, performing arts, and Hawaiian cultural events. Moral, spiritual, physical, and social development is emphasized. Off-campus preschools and summer programs are also offered. Boarding Tuition and Fees: $2547; Day Tuition and Fees: $935–$1292. Wayne Chang is Admissions Director; Michael J. Chun (University of Kansas, B.S. 1966, Ph.D. 1970; University of Hawaii, M.S. 1968) was appointed President in 1988. *Western Association.*

LA PIETRA—Hawaii School for Girls   1962

2933 Poni Moi Road, Honolulu, HI 96815. 808-922-2744;
Fax 808-923-4514; E-mail info@lapietra.edu;
Web Site www.lapietra.edu

LA PIETRA-Hawaii School for Girls, an independent day school enrolling 233 students in Grades 6–12, is committed to small enrollment, low pupil-teacher ratio, a broad college preparatory curriculum, and the values and advantages of an all-girls school. The Middle School emphasizes integrated learning. In the upper grades, expanded offerings in art and athletics complement the major disciplines. Extensive college counseling begins in Grade 9. Among the activities are technology club, hiking, peer leadership, and drama. Faculty are drawn from independent schools nationwide and locally. Tuition: $9100. Financial Aid: $450,000. Nancy D. White (University of Northern Colorado, B.S.) is Head of School. *Western Association.*

Mid-Pacific Institute   1864

2445 Kaala Street, Honolulu, HI 96822. 808-973-5000;
Admissions 808-973-5004; Fax 808-973-5099;
Web Site www.midpac.edu

Mid-Pacific offers a strong college preparatory curriculum to approximately 1050 students in Grades 6–12, with boarding available for Grades 9–12. Faculty are committed to providing an educational atmosphere in which each student can learn effectively. The curriculum is strengthened by technology, honors and Advanced Placement courses, the International Baccalaureate Program, a School of the Arts, English as a Second Language Program, and community service. Cocurricular offerings include a full range of sports and club activities. Day Tuition: $9585; Boarding & Tuition: $15,920; ESL: $988 per

class. Financial Aid: $720,760. Dorothy Crowell is Director of Admissions; Joe C. Rice (University of Washington, B.A. 1969; Central Washington University, M.A. 1982) is President. *Western Association.*

Maryknoll School   1927

1701 Wilder Avenue, Honolulu, HI 96822. 808-973-1888;
Admissions 808-973-1770; Fax 808-973-1799;
E-mail admissions@maryknollgs.com

The Maryknoll Society founded this Roman Catholic school to provide a college preparatory program that develops responsible individuals capable of making lasting contributions to society. Enrolling 1357 boys and girls in Pre-Kindergarten–Grade 12, Maryknoll offers a liberal arts curriculum enriched by a modified foreign language immersion program, student travel, Advanced Placement courses, and community service. Cocurricular activities include athletics, publications, performing arts, government, and various clubs. The high school is a member of the Coalition of Essential Schools. Tuition: $6600–$7500. Kathleen W. Shimabukuro is Director of Admission; Michael E. Baker (University of New England, B.A. 1962; University of Maine, M.A. 1970) is President. *Western Association.*

Punahou School   1841

1601 Punahou Street, Honolulu, HI 96822. 808-944-5711;
Admissions 808-944-5714; Fax 808-943-3602;
E-mail admission@punahou.edu

Founded by New England Christian missionaries, Punahou School is a college preparatory day school enrolling 3700 boys and girls in Kindergarten–Grade 12. Libraries, learning centers, and modern physical education facilities support faculty in their commitment to provide an environment that fosters intellectual, physical, spiritual, and social development. Numerous clubs and extracurricular activities offer students opportunities to become involved in campus and community life. Tuition: $9300–$9900. Financial Aid: $1,840,000. Curtis M. Hagen is Director of Admission and Financial Aid; James K. Scott (Stanford University, A.B. 1975; University of San Francisco, M.A. 1982; Harvard University, Ed.M. 1985, Ed.D. 1991) was named President in 1994. *Western Association.*

Sacred Hearts Academy   1909

3253 Waialae Avenue, Honolulu, HI 96816. 808-734-5058;
Fax 808-737-7867; E-mail kmuramoto@sacredhearts.org;
Web Site www.sacredhearts.org

This Roman Catholic day school offers a college preparatory program in an educational environment designed to develop personal self-confidence, independence, and Christian values. Enrolling 1025 girls from diverse backgrounds in Junior Kindergarten–Grade 12, Sacred Hearts' academic curriculum includes honors and Advanced Placement courses, required community service, and travel-study programs to Japan, Mexico, Europe, and Washington, D.C. Retreat programs encourage spiritual and moral development. All activities are integral to the overall program, and girls take part in drama, music groups, publications, and athletics. Tuition: $4562–$6200. Karen Muramoto is Director of Admissions; Betty White is Principal. *Western Association.*

St. Andrew's Priory School for Girls   1867

224 Queen Emma Square, Honolulu, HI 96813. 808-536-6102;
   Fax 808-538-1035; E-mail sawilson@priory.net;
   Web Site www.standrewsprioryschool.com

St. Andrew's Priory is an Episcopal day school enrolling 500 young women from many ethnic, cultural, and religious backgrounds in Kindergarten–Grade 12. It also has a coeducational preschool enrolling 150 children ages two to five. Following traditions set by its founder, Hawaii's Queen Emma, the School offers a well-balanced college preparatory education that is designed to prepare young women to meet the challenges and opportunities of college and adult life. Technology, athletics, and extensive visual and performing arts complement the curriculum. Tuition: $8125–$8400. Sue Ann Wilson is Admissions Director; J. Stevens Bean (Bowdoin College, B.A.; Brown, M.A.T.; Rutgers, Ed.D.) is Headmaster. *Western Association.*

Seabury Hall   1964

480 Olinda Road, Makawao, Maui, HI 96768. 808-572-7235;
   Fax 808-572-7196; E-mail seabury@maui.net

Seabury Hall is a coeducational, college preparatory day school enrolling 400 students in Grades 6–12. The curriculum includes the humanities, the fine and performing arts, foreign languages, computer studies, religion, and community service. English as a Second Language is offered, and students are involved in drama, a dance ensemble, publications, and sports as extracurricular activities. Tuition: $9975. Financial aid is available. Virginia Haines is Admissions Director; Daniel E. White (University of California [Riverside], B.A., Ph.D.; University of Washington, M.A.) is Headmaster. *Western Association.*

IDAHO

The Community School   1973

P.O. Box 2118, Sun Valley, ID 83353. 208-622-3955;
Fax 208-622-3962; Web Site http://www.communityschool.org

The Community School is a college preparatory day school enrolling 300 students in Pre-Kindergarten–Grade 12. Located in Sun Valley in the Sawtooth Mountains, the School integrates outdoor education with a rigorous academic program while striving to achieve a sense of community. Numerous activities include skiing, tennis, soccer, basketball, drama, and camping. The summer program provides academic courses and recreation. Tuition: $10,500–$12,400. Financial Aid: $400,000. Gina Cooley is Director of Admissions; Jon Maksik (University of Southern California, B.A. 1966; California State, M.A. 1970; University of California [Los Angeles], Ph.D. 1976) is Headmaster.

ILLINOIS

The Avery Coonley School

DOWNERS GROVE

1400 Maple Avenue, Downers Grove, IL 60515-4897.
  630-969-0800; Fax 630-969-0131;
  E-mail minicar@averycoonley.org; Web Site www.averycoonley.org

THE AVERY COONLEY SCHOOL in Downers Grove, Illinois, is an elementary day school enrolling bright and academically gifted boys and girls in Junior/Senior Kindergarten, Lower School (Grades 1–4), and Middle School (Grades 5–8). The School also offers a separate preschool program for three-year-olds. Downers Grove (population 47,883) is a suburban community approximately 20 miles southwest of Chicago off Interstate 55. Transportation is by private car and car pools, and a private transportation service is available to the local train station and contiguous communities.

The School was founded in 1906 in Riverside, Illinois, by Mrs. Avery Coonley, whose desire to offer an alternative to traditional public institutions was inspired by the educational philosophy of John Dewey and other progressive thinkers. The first classes were held in a cottage on Mrs. Coonley's estate, but as enthusiasm and enrollment increased, larger quarters were needed. In 1912, Mrs. Coonley opened Downers Grove's first kindergarten, a program that soon expanded to encompass a full elementary program. Further growth over the years led to the purchase by Mrs. Coonley of 11 wooded acres bordering Maple Grove Forest Preserve. In 1928, she commissioned a protégé of Frank Lloyd Wright to design the buildings and surroundings that today constitute the academic heart of The Avery Coonley School.

The challenging program consistently drew bright, highly motivated students and, during the 1960s, this emphasis was officially adopted by the Board of Trustees. In the belief that education is a lifelong process, The Avery Coonley School seeks to instill a sense of the joy and excitement of learning at an early age. Dedicated faculty and small classes encourage children to pursue a continuing quest for academic achievement, independent thought, and self-reliance. In affirmation of its goals and achievements, the U.S. Department of Education recognized The Avery Coonley School as an "Exemplary Elementary School."

A not-for-profit, nondenominational institution, the School is governed by an elected Board of Trustees, 15 to 21 in number, that sets policy and works for the betterment of students, faculty, and parents. There is an active Home and School Association, and the Office of Development keeps graduates abreast of current affairs through regular publications and communications. The Avery Coonley School is accredited by the Independent Schools Association of the Central States and holds membership in the National Association of Independent Schools, the Elementary Schools Heads Association, the Lake Michigan Association of Independent Schools, and the Council for Advancement and Support of Education.

THE CAMPUS. The 11-acre campus, featuring woodlands, lawns, and a pond, is dominated by the gracious main building, which houses classrooms, computer and science laboratories, an art and music wing, and administrative offices. Cloistered walkways connect the wings of the building, which is fronted by a reflecting pool. Outdoor facilities include athletic fields, picnic areas, an archery field, and a swimming pool.

A recently completed $3,500,000 capital campaign resulted in a major expansion program. The School has a new 2500-square-foot library/learning laboratory, a gymnasium and locker rooms, additional teaching areas, a Resource Center for Gifted Education, and a Performing Arts Center. In addition, most classrooms have undergone renovations.

THE FACULTY. J. Gaston Favreau, appointed Headmaster in 1991, earned his B.A. degree from Providence College in 1960 and a master's degree in Education from Boston University in 1972. He has also done graduate work in history at Harvard University and the University of Chicago. Prior to assuming his current position, Mr. Favreau served as Director of Kalamazoo Academy in Michigan and as Headmaster at The Overlake School in Redmond, Washington, and Ascension Academy in Alexandria, Virginia, among other administrative posts. He and his wife, Anne, have three grown children.

In addition to the Headmaster, there are 33 faculty members who hold baccalaureate and 18 master's degrees representing study at such colleges and universities as Augustana, Baylor, Concordia, DePaul, DePauw, George Williams, Hope, Illinois Institute of Technology, Illinois State, Indiana, Loyola, National-Louis, New York University, Northern Illinois, Northern Iowa, Northern State University of South Dakota, Northwestern, Oklahoma State, Quincy, Roosevelt, St. Xavier, Western Illinois, and the Universities of Chicago, Colorado, Denver, Detroit, Georgia, Illinois, Kansas, Michigan, and Wisconsin.

Several staff members are trained in first aid, and Good Samaritan Hospital is within a short distance of the campus.

STUDENT BODY. In 1999–2000, the School enrolls 362 girls and boys in three-year-old Early Childhood through Group 8. Students come from Downers Grove and 37 other communities in the Greater Chicago area and represent the cultural, racial, and religious diversity of the metropolitan region.

ACADEMIC PROGRAM. The school year, divided into trimesters, runs from September to June, with winter and spring vacations and observances of national holidays. Written reports for students in Grades 1–8 are shared with parents at the end of each trimester, and parent-teacher conferences are scheduled in October and April. For preschoolers, parent-teacher conferences are held twice a year, at which time written reports are shared. Exceptional academic achievement in groups 5, 6, 7, and 8 is recognized on the Honor Roll, and each month, faculty designate one child from each of the Lower and Middle schools as "Student of the Month," based on criteria of good citizenship, leadership, cooperation, and good sportsmanship.

Small classes, with a student-teacher ratio of 11:1, permit each child to receive a high level of individual attention, encouragement, and guidance, enabling him or her to reach full academic potential and proceed at an accelerated rate.

For its youngest students, the Early Childhood Program functions as a link between home and school. Guided play is used to develop the child's communications skills and build the important foundations for later learning in the basic disciplines. Activities such as story time aid in promoting listening skills, vocabulary expansion, and comprehension and memorization techniques. Hands-on experiences with a variety of manipulative materials help develop basic mathematics concepts. Throughout the program, there are numerous opportunities for gross-motor and fine-motor activities.

In the Junior and Senior Kindergartens, the multifaceted program introduces students to the fundamentals of reading, mathematics, science, and social studies through a series of age-appropriate presentations, discussions, and hands-on experiments. Daily music is an integral component of the curriculum, and time is set aside regularly for art. Students are encouraged to express themselves freely, often correlating their artwork with the language arts and other aspects of their studies. Physical education is scheduled daily.

In the Lower School, students are grouped by age in self-contained learning centers, and teachers provide ongoing diagnosis, evaluation, and encouragement to foster productive learning results.

Language arts focus on expanding the reading, writing, and speaking skills acquired earlier, with spelling, vocabulary, and basic grammar introduced as the child demonstrates readiness. As the student progresses, the breadth of knowledge evolves and expands to include various types of literature, including out-of-class reading assignments of carefully selected fiction, biographies, and works of Illinois authors. Mathematics lessons utilize written exercises as well as hands-on activities involving learning tools such as geo-boards, versa tiles, audiovisual materials, and computers. Instruction may be on a one-to-one, small-group, or large-group basis. Study of the social sciences begins with the theme of neighbors in Group 1 and progresses through the later stages of American history, including study of the history and geography of the state of Illinois. The French language is introduced in Junior Kindergarten. Art, music, health, computer skills, and physical education are all integral to the curriculum.

The departmentalized Middle School Program is designed to provide a smooth transition from elementary to secondary school. The traditional liberal arts subjects—English/language arts, French, mathematics, library skills, science, social studies, health, computer technology, music, art, drama, and physical education—are taught by teachers specialized in each discipline. Accelerated classes are offered in core subjects, and qualified eighth graders may receive advanced or honors placement in algebra, geometry, biology, English, and French. Homework assignments are "regular and considerable."

In 1999, Avery Coonley School graduates entered public and private high schools such as Benet Academy, Fenwick, Glenbard West High School, Hinsdale Central, Illinois Math & Science Academy, Naperville Central, Nazareth Academy, Phillips Academy, St. Charles, St. Paul's School (New Hamp-

shire), University of Chicago Lab School, and Waubansie Valley High School.

The School has a daily After-School Program until 6:00 P.M. and offers a summer program of academic and enrichment courses combined with recreational opportunities for students ages 4 (half-day only) through 13.

STUDENT ACTIVITIES. Leadership opportunities are offered through membership on the elected Student Council, which serves as a liaison with faculty and administration and plans events to build school spirit and community.

Among the elective activities are orchestra, chorus, ensemble, dramatic and musical productions, interscholastic and intramural athletic teams, and clubs relating to interests in science, math, social studies, spelling, French, chess, art, and literature.

Throughout the year, enrichment programs are carried out in the form of concerts, drama and opera study, assemblies, field trips, and major excursions to Pretty Lake Adventure Centre, Canada, France, and Washington, D.C. Parental involvement is encouraged at every level, and families are welcome to attend traditional special events such as curriculum nights, Fall Fest, Halloween parade, Grandparents' Day, Thanksgiving processional, science fairs, concerts, the annual auction, Spring Fair, and graduation.

ADMISSION AND COSTS. The Avery Coonley School seeks applicants who demonstrate excellent verbal proficiency, an early and deep interest in reading, intellectual curiosity, ingenuity, and creativity as well as above-average powers of concentration, abstraction, and synthesis. To apply, candidates must submit an application, a fee of $50, current school records, standardized intellectual aptitude and academic achievement test scores, and teacher recommendations. They also come for an on-campus visit and interview. The School administers psychological testing. The testing fee is $375.

In 1999–2000, tuition, including books, some field trips, and some basic supplies, is $3000 for Early Childhood, $6950 for Kindergarten, and $10,050 for Grades 1–8.

Baker Demonstration School 1918

2840 Sheridan Road, Evanston, IL 60201. 847-256-0615;
Fax 847-256-6542; E-mail ctyk@evan1.nl.edu;
Web Site www.ucls.uchicago.edu/cais

Baker Demonstration School, a laboratory school for the National-Louis University, formerly the National College of Education, enrolls 325 day boys and girls in Nursery–Grade 8. Its teachers, who are also on the faculty of National-Louis University, help students acquire essential skills, develop critical thinking and problem-solving abilities, and gain exposure to the arts. A wide range of learning experiences is available, including Spanish from Nursery School and Latin beginning in Grade 6. Activities include drama, Orff instruction in instruments, bell choir, sports, and swimming. Tuition: $4135–$9275. Charlotte Tyksinski is Associate Director/Admissions Director; Candace Scheidt is Director.

Bernard Zell Anshe Emet Day School   1946

3760 North Pine Grove, Chicago, IL 60613. 773-281-1858;
Fax 773-281-4709; E-mail ppopeil@ansheemet.org; Web Site
www.BZAEDS.org

Bernard Zell Anshe Emet Day School, enrolling 390 students in Nursery–Grade 8, is committed to excellence in education with an innovative curriculum that integrates general and Jewish studies. Jewish traditions and values serve as models for personal and moral development, as students are challenged to become responsible, creative learners. The Pritzker Science Lab offers hands-on experiences for all grade levels. Two networked, Internet-accessible labs prepare students for technological challenges in the 21st century. Faculty serve as writing mentors for middle-school students. After-school activities include chess, sports, dance, French, Spanish, and Junior Great Books. Tuition: $7500–$13,040. Financial Aid: $325,000. Pamela Popeil is Director of Admissions; Jane Herron is School Head.

Brehm Preparatory School   1982

1245 East Grand Avenue, Carbondale, IL 62901. 618-457-0371;
Fax 618-529-1248; Web Site www.brehm.org

Brehm is a coeducational boarding school for students with learning disabilities and attention deficit disorder. Approved by the State of Illinois, Brehm provides educational services for Grades 6–12 and a postsecondary program at the junior college level. Brehm's holistic focus addresses the academic, social, and emotional needs of students through strategy implementation in each area. Individualized programming and full support services develop academic and social skills required for success in college. Brehm has been a recipient of the Blue Ribbon Award of Excellence from the U.S. Department of Education. Boarding Tuition: $35,180. Donna Collins is Director of Admissions; Richard G. Collins, Ph.D. (Saint Louis University), is Executive Director. *North Central Association.*

The Chicago Academy for the Arts   1981

1010 West Chicago Avenue, Chicago, IL 60622. 312-421-0202:
Fax 312-421-3816; E-mail academy@mcs.net;
Web Site www.mcs.net/~academy

The Chicago Academy for the Arts is the area's only private high school specializing in a combined academic and intensive arts education in visual arts, music, dance, theater, writing/communication arts, and musical theater. Enrolling approximately 150 students, the Academy strives to prepare talented youth in Grades 9–12 for educated choices about continued study at universities and conservatories as well as the pursuit of professional careers in the visual and performing arts. Admission is by audition and academic testing. Most graduates enter four-year colleges or are recruited by major dance, theater, film, and recording companies. Tuition: $9750. Stephanie Strait is Director of Admission; Frank Mustari was appointed Headmaster in 1995.

Chicago City Day School   1981

541 West Hawthorne Place, Chicago, IL 60657. 773-327-0900;
Fax 773-327-6381

Founded in 1981 to provide high-quality education for city dwellers, the Chicago City Day School enrolls 265 boys and girls in Junior Kindergarten–Grade 8. Rigorous but nurturing education and the development of strong skills in reading, language arts, mathematics, and social studies are its aims. French, Spanish, science, art, music, drama, and physical education are offered at all levels; computer studies begin in Grade 1 and industrial arts in Grade 2. Sports, yearbook, and clubs are some of the activities. Tuition: $11,300–$12,700. Extras: $900–$1025. Galeta Kaar Clayton (Northwestern, B.A. 1961; Loyola, M.Ed. 1965; Erikson Institute, M.Ed. 1974) is the founding Headmistress.

Chicago Junior School   ELGIN

1600 Dundee Avenue, Elgin, IL 60120. 847-888-7910;
E-mail cjs@starnetinc.com; Web Site www.asgusa.com/cjs

CHICAGO JUNIOR SCHOOL in Elgin, Illinois, is a coeducational day and boarding school serving the Chicagoland area for more than 85 years. The boarding program offers the choice of a five-day or seven-day program to boys and girls in Grades 3 through 8. The day program includes an Early Education Department for children from age three through Grade 2. Located in a wooded setting on Illinois Route 25, the School is 3 miles from downtown Elgin (population 80,000). Interstate Highway 90 (the Northwest Tollway) is one-half block south and offers easy access to O'Hare International Airport, 25 miles away, and Chicago, 40 miles distant. Elgin city buses are available nearby, and the School provides transportation to the airport and interstate bus and train terminals.

The mission of the School is to educate the whole child through a values-based curriculum, conducted in a homelike environment, combining academic excellence with individual character development. Chicago Junior School was founded in 1913 by Morris Schwabacher, with the aid of V. P. Randall, to educate boys who would benefit from sound academic instruction and a homelike, country atmosphere. Today, Chicago Junior School seeks to provide the same homelike educational environment for boys and girls who have the ability to work at or above grade level.

Chicago Junior School is committed to developing both academic knowledge and high moral character in its students. A comprehensive character-development program based on specific qualities that are Biblically based is fostered through arts appreciation, environmental education, and social outreach activities. The academic program is oriented toward the student who will pursue a college preparatory course in secondary school. Small classes emphasize basic skills as well as provide numerous avenues for advanced enrichment and an overall context for discovering each individual's unique potential.

A nonprofit institution with a Christian Science heritage, Chicago Junior School is governed by 15 members of a self-perpetuating Board of Trustees. The School is accredited by the Independent Schools Association of the Central States.

THE CAMPUS. The 53-acre campus of rolling, wooded land includes a large playing field and 40 acres of hiking trails. In 1989, the State of Illinois designated 23 of these acres as a "Natural Heritage Landmark," which includes one of the State's only remaining white cedar forests as well as plant and animal life that has not changed since the presettlement 1800s. Facilities for indoor sports are the Katzenberger Indoor Swimming Pool and the Katzenberger Gymnasium. The Katzenberger complex also houses second- and sixth-grade classrooms and the Spanish Language office.

Hoxie House and Kilburn House contain classrooms for the Early Education Department and the Music Department. The Administration Building houses administrative offices, classrooms for Grades 3–8, library, computer lab, and ESL office. Cox, Westview, and Westview Garden dormitories accommodate 14 students each plus houseparents. Other facilities include the Dining Hall, which provides additional staff apartments; Molter, the Headmaster's House; Bates, housing art, environmental education, and after-school programs; and Allison for Grade 1 classrooms, both recently renovated. The School plant is valued at approximately $10,000,000.

THE FACULTY. William H. Haak, appointed Headmaster in 1992, is a graduate of Michigan State University, where he earned a B.A. in business administration and master's and doctoral degrees in K-12 school administration. He has served as a teacher, counselor, assistant principal for instruction, high school principal, and assistant superintendent.

The staff includes a director of admissions, a development administrator, an early education director, an academic head, a chief financial officer, assistant for student programs, and 28 faculty members. They hold baccalaureate and master's degrees representing the American Conservatory of Music, Bradley, Brigham Young, Colorado State, Culver-Stockton, Dartmouth, Eastern Illinois, Elmhurst College, Georgia State, Illinois State, Indiana University, Louisiana State, Miami University, Michigan

State, National College of Education, Northeastern Illinois, Northern Illinois, Principia, Regent University of Virginia, School of the Art Institute, St. Mary's, Trent Park College of Education, Western Illinois, Western Michigan, and the Universities of Illinois (Urbana), Nebraska, Tulsa, and Wisconsin. Faculty benefits include a service compensation plan, a pension plan, Social Security, on-campus housing, and a health-care plan.

Seven faculty teach specials, including Spanish, music, art, special reading, swimming, physical education, computer lab, and environmental education.

STUDENT BODY. In 1999–2000, Chicago Junior School enrolls approximately 235 students in Preschool–Grade 8, including 30 boarding boys and girls, and boys and girls in the Early Education Department. Students represent Florida, Georgia, Illinois, Michigan, New York, Texas, and Wisconsin as well as India, Japan, Korea, Mexico, and Taiwan. Day students come from a variety of Fox Valley communities including Elgin, St. Charles, Barrington, Algonquin, Schaumburg, and Sleepy Hollow.

ACADEMIC PROGRAM. The school year, from late August to early June, includes vacations at Thanksgiving, at Christmas, and in the spring. Early Education classes are 9:00–11:30 A.M. and noon–2:30 P.M. for Preschool and 9:00 A.M.–2:30 P.M. for Kindergarten. Extended care is available from 7:00 A.M. to 6:00 P.M. for all grades. For Grades 1–5, self-contained classes begin at 8:30 A.M. and are dismissed at 3:00 P.M. Grades 6–8 begin at 8:30 A.M. and end at 4:15 P.M.

Classes, with enrollment from 8 to 20, meet five days a week. Teachers are available for extra help. Houseparents supervise evening study for the boarding students. Grades are sent to parents four times a year; between report cards, written comments on student progress are issued. Parent-teacher conferences are scheduled in November but can take place at any time during the year.

The curriculum for the Early Education Department covers reading and mathematics readiness, motor development, science, and social studies concepts. Enrichment activities offer a comprehensive exposure to all the arts as well as personalized training in them; enrichment activities include Environmental Education, library, swimming, and physical education. Computer lab and Spanish begin in Kindergarten.

The curriculum for Grades 1–8 includes English, reading, mathematics, social studies, and science. A special curriculum required for all students includes art, music, computer lab, library, Spanish, physical education, swimming, and science/environmental education activities. English as a Second Language is offered for international students.

Graduates in the Classes of 1998 and 1999 entered Barrington High School, Culver Academy, Dundee-Crown High School, Lake Forest Academy, La Lumiere School, Morgan Park Academy, The Principia, University of Chicago Lab School, Wayland Academy, and Webb School (Tennessee) as well as

other public and private high schools in the Fox Valley and in the greater Chicagoland area.

STUDENT ACTIVITIES. A special activity program after the school day includes snacks, followed by swimming, arts and crafts, or supervised play suitable to the interest and needs of the age group. Quarterly electives for Middle School students include such subjects as batik, art in nature, softball, tennis, embroidery, and leadership training.

Students participate in a variety of field trips, attend the Elgin Symphony's children's concerts, and exhibit their art projects in area locations. All off-campus trips are supervised by staff members.

Chicago Junior School encourages children to spend weekends with their parents, but special activities are provided for students who remain on campus. Seven-day boarders are expected to attend a Sunday school of their choice. The School provides transportation to the Christian Science Sunday School and will help arrange any additional spiritual training. The weekend program includes many activities such as the use of the indoor pool and gym, ice-skating, museum visits (Chicago area), concerts, hiking expeditions, and selected films. Time is set aside for homework and study.

Traditional annual events include the Fall Parents Orientation Day, Grandparents Day, Fall Family Festival, Christmas/Holiday Sing, Spring Production, and Graduation.

ADMISSION AND COSTS. Chicago Junior School seeks the student who is performing at or above grade level and will accept children who can most benefit from its nurturing and caring atmosphere. Applicants are admitted in all grades on the basis of a personal interview, a campus visit, and previous school records. Final discretion on admissions decisions rests with the Admissions Committee. There is no closing date for applications, but candidates are urged to apply by January. Students may be enrolled throughout the school year, depending on availability.

For 2000–01, the five-day boarding tuition is $18,250 and seven-day boarding tuition is $21,300. Day tuition ranges from $1820 per year for Preschool and from $6400 to $8900 for Kindergarten–Grade 8. Comprehensive fees are $700 per year for Grades 1–8. A guaranteed tuition refund plan fee is required if tuition is paid on a deferred payment plan.

Financial aid is available to be awarded on an individual basis according to need.

Director of Admissions: Kathie Ann McNeil
Admissions Coordinator: Janell Orkfritz
Academic Head: Peter Mikulak
Director of Early Education: Mary Fran Doolin
Chief Financial Officer: Philip Calkins
Development Administrator: Angela Hicks
Assistant for Student Programs: Barbara Schmidt

Elgin Academy   1839

350 Park Street, Elgin, IL 60120. 847-695-0300; Admissions 847-695-0303; Fax 847-695-5017; E-mail ElginAcdmy@aol.com; Web Site http://members.aol.com/Elgin Acdmy

Elgin Academy is a college preparatory school enrolling 340 day boys and girls in Preschool–Grade 12. Foreign languages are introduced in elementary grades. Advanced Placement courses, independent study, and student exchange opportunities are available. Student government, dramatics, chorus, athletics, publications, and community service are among the activities. Tuition: $7450–$12,500. Financial Aid: $600,000. John R. Hopkins is Director of Admission; Susan J. Thompson (Indiana University of Pennsylvania, B.S. 1971; Pacific Oaks, M.A. 1985; Harvard, C.A.S. 1991) is Head of School. *North Central Association.*

Fenwick High School   1929

505 Washington Boulevard, Oak Park, IL 60302. 708-386-0127; Fax 708-386-3052

Founded by Dominican Fathers and Brothers, this coeducational, college preparatory day school enrolling 1100 students in Grades 9–12 has been designated an exemplary secondary school by the U.S. Department of Education. Fenwick emphasizes academic excellence and seeks to foster students' appreciation of their religious and cultural heritage in a Christian atmosphere. The program features three years of required theology, daily Mass, and activities including 24 varsity teams, music, publications, and clubs. Virtually all graduates enter college. A summer session is offered. Tuition: $6300. Maria A. Hill is Director of Admission; James J. Quaid (Benedictine, B.A.; Purdue, M.A.; Loyola, M.Ed.) is Principal; Fr. Richard LaPata, OP (Dominican House of Studies, B.A., M.A.), is President.

Francis W. Parker School   1901

330 West Webster Avenue, Chicago, IL 60614. 773-549-0172; Admissions 773-797-5101; Fax 773-549-4669; E-mail thomasr@iquest.net; Web Site www.fwparker.org

Francis W. Parker School, a college preparatory day school enrolling 878 boys and girls in Junior Kindergarten–Grade 12, aims to offer a superior education through its challenging and innovative programs and through its concern for the individual. Faculty guide students to think independently, to develop skills in making judgments, and to act responsibly on the basis of such learning. As a result of this philosophy, graduates are encouraged to become lifelong learners. Tuition: $10,480–$13,420. Financial Aid: $1,400,000. Thomas Rosenbluth is Director of Admission; Donald S. Monroe (Lake Forest, B.A. 1961; Northwestern, M.A.T. 1964; University of Illinois, Ed.D. 1969) was appointed Principal in 1995. *North Central Association.*

Hales Franciscan High School   1962

4930 South Cottage Grove Avenue, Chicago, IL 60615.
773-285-8400; Fax 773-285-7025

Hales Franciscan High is a Roman Catholic, college preparatory day school for boys that accepts students of all faiths. Enrolling 360 African-American young men, the historically Black School aims to inspire students "Unto Perfect Manhood" through a rigorous liberal arts curriculum formed by values upheld by Christian, Catholic, and Franciscan tradition. Religion courses, shared liturgies, retreats, and social outreach promote spiritual growth. Students participate in leadership programs, varsity sports, drama, academic competitions, honor societies, and a variety of special interest clubs. Tuition: $3500. Financial Aid: $250–$3500 (per student). Sean Stalling is Director of Recruitment and Admissions; Tim King is President. *North Central Association.*

Keith Country Day School   1916

1 Jacoby Place, Rockford, IL 61107. 815-399-8823;
Fax 815-399-2470; E-mail admissions@keith.lincon.org;
Web Site www.keith.lincon.org

Keith School offers a child-centered, college preparatory education for students age three–Grade 12. Faculty emphasize excellence in academics while fostering respect for the individual, integrity, creativity, and an appreciation for diversity. Through the Laptops for Learning program, all students and teachers in Grades 6–12 have laptop computers for use at school and home. The curriculum features French at all levels and Latin from Grade 7. Advanced Placement courses are offered in several subjects. The seminar program provides support for bright students with alternate learning styles. Summer sports camps are offered. Tuition: $3800–$8700. Extras: $200–$400. Financial Aid: $300,000. Kathy Scarpaci is Admissions Director; Roberta E. Ingrassia is Head of School.

Lake Forest Country Day School   1888

145 South Green Bay Road, Lake Forest, IL 60045. 847-234-2350;
Admissions Fax 847-234-8725; E-mail nicolec@lfcds.org
Web Site www.lfcds.lfc.edu (164.68.104.2)

Lake Forest Country Day School enrolls 425 boys and girls in Preschool (age 3) to Grade 9. Education in basic skills is stressed, along with a substantial program in interdisciplinary studies and the arts to help students develop the capacity to think independently, achieve their full potential, and interact effectively with others. Included are art, music, drama, computer, outdoor education, athletics, and community service programs. Summer offerings feature study skills, language arts, mathematics, and the arts, plus a computer and sports camp. Tuition: $5720–$13,750. Financial Aid: $226,000. Christine R. Nicoletta is Director of Admission; Kristi A. Kerins (Skidmore, B.A.; Virginia Commonwealth, M.Ed.) was appointed Head of School in 1998.

The Latin School of Chicago   1888

59 West North Boulevard, Chicago, IL 60610-1492. 312-573-4500;
Web Site www.latinschool.org

The Latin School, serving 1035 day students in Junior Kindergarten–Grade 12, emphasizes academic excellence in its college preparatory curriculum. Spanish begins in Kindergarten, French in Grade 3. Computer programming, a writing lab, and an arts cycle in Grades 6–8; an interdisciplinary humanities class in Grade 9 combining history, art, literature, and science; and a Math, Science, and Technology 2000 program help all grades develop important tools for understanding a complex world. The arts, athletics, individual attention, and community outreach prepare students for the challenges and choices of today's society. Tuition: $10,140–$14,640. Betsy Haugh is Director of Admissions; Frank J. Hogan (Loyola, B.S., M.Ed.; Chicago-Kent College of Law, J.D.) is Headmaster.

Loyola Academy   1909

1100 Laramie, Wilmette, IL 60091. 847-256-1100;
Fax 847-251-4031; Web Site www.goramblers.org

Loyola Academy is a Jesuit college preparatory school serving 2000 young women and men as day students in Grades 9–12. The school's aim is to develop the whole person fully and harmoniously. The curriculum is designed to meet the needs of gifted, highly motivated students as well as those who need structured, sequential learning techniques. Campus ministry, athletics, community service, drama, publications, and interest clubs engage students in after-school activities. Tuition: $6950. Financial aid is available. Rev. Theodore G. Munz, SJ (University of Detroit, B.A.; University of Chicago, M.B.A.; Jesuit School of Theology [Berkeley], M.Div., S.T.M.), was named President of the Academy in 1996. *North Central Association.*

Morgan Park Academy   1873

2153 West 111th Street, Chicago, IL 60643. 773-881-6700;
Fax 773-881-8409; Web Site www.mpacademy.org

Morgan Park Academy, situated in a historic, residential neighborhood, is a college preparatory day school enrolling 520 boys and girls in Preschool–Grade 12. Its mission is to prepare students, via a rigorous liberal arts program, to succeed in college and life by helping them to appreciate their own uniqueness as contributing members of a diverse community; develop intellectually, physically, creatively, emotionally, and socially; cultivate integrity and social responsibility; and make a positive difference in the world. Honors and Advanced Placement courses are offered. An arts program, athletics, and other activities enrich the curriculum. Tuition: $3500–$10,290. Financial Aid: $247,580. Sara Grassi is Admission Director; J. William Adams is Headmaster. *North Central Association.*

The North Shore Country Day School   1919

310 Green Bay Road, Winnetka, IL 60093-4094. 847-446-0674;
Fax 847-446-0675; E-mail info@nscds.pvt.k12.il.us; Web Site
http://www.nscds.pvt.k12.il.us

North Shore Country Day School, enrolling 430 boys and girls in Junior Kindergarten–Grade 12, provides a rigorous, college preparatory education within a supportive community. The School is committed to the highest quality of education, balanced with athletics and the arts, service to others, and cross-grade activities. North Shore Country Day also encourages its students to explore many extracurricular opportunities. To prepare students for the 21st century, the School has developed unique programs in languages, math, science, global consciousness, and technology. Tuition: $8228–$13,709. Financial aid is available. W. Thomas Doar III is Director of Admissions.

Quest Academy   1982

500 North Benton Street, Palatine, IL 60067. 847-202-8035;
Fax 847-202-8085; E-mail ccaadmin@starnetinc.com;
Web Site www.questacademy.org

Quest Academy, formerly Creative Children's Academy, is an independent day school for 275 gifted boys and girls in Preschool–Grade 8. The Academy's curriculum is based on a traditional liberal arts education with equal emphasis on the sciences, the humanities, and the arts. It has been designed specifically for gifted and talented children and reflects current research on the needs of able learners. Critical thinking and reasoning abilities, as well as character development, are taught and applied across content areas. Admission is based on transcripts, test scores, teacher report, parent statement, and a school visit. Tuition: $8950–$9450. Financial Aid: $200,000. Judy Jankowski is Admission Director; Marilyn Wallace is Head of School.

Roycemore School   1915

640 Lincoln Street, Evanston, IL 60201. 847-866-6055;
Fax 847-866-6545

Enrolling 230 day boys and girls in Junior Kindergarten–Grade 12, Roycemore aims to help each student discover his or her unique talents, to respond to individual learning styles, and to prepare for success in college. Faculty use various teaching methods to stimulate students' interest, creativity, concern for the broader community, and academic excellence. Advanced Placement courses are offered in all disciplines; qualified students may take courses at adjacent Northwestern University. A three-week interim program allows Upper School students to concentrate on an area of special interest. The arts, publications, and sports are among the activities. Summer programs are available. Tuition: $4175–$13,750. Financial Aid: $950,000. Joseph A. Becker is Headmaster.

Sacred Heart Schools   1876

6250 North Sheridan Road, Chicago, IL 60660-1799.
773-262-4446; Fax 773-262-6178; E-mail shschicag@aol.com;
Web Site www.shschicago.org

A Chicago landmark on Lake Michigan, Sacred Heart Schools enroll 400 day students. They are part of a Network of 150 Sacred Heart Schools in 32 countries. Kindergarten is coeducational; in Grades 1–8, girls attend The Academy and boys attend Hardey Prep. Computers and French begin in Grade 1. In addition to a rigorous academic curriculum, Sacred Heart Schools are dedicated to a values-based program concerned with the education of the whole child. An active faith, critical thinking, personal responsibility, a global vision, and concern for others embody a Sacred Heart education. Financial, ethnic, and religious diversity is promoted. Tuition: $8045–$8700. Financial Aid: $375,970. Judith Corrin is Director of Admissions; Sr. Susan Maxwell, RSCJ, is Director of Schools.

St. Ignatius College Prep   1870

1076 West Roosevelt Road, Chicago, IL 60608. 312-421-5900;
Fax 312-421-7124; Web Site www.ignatius.org

Founded in 1870 by members of the Society of Jesus to serve the "academically talented children of immigrants," St. Ignatius College Prep today offers a demanding college preparatory curriculum to 1300 day boys and girls in Grades 9–12. The school, located in the heart of the City of Chicago in facilities designated as a national historic landmark, enrolls a religiously, racially, and ethnically diverse student body drawn from the city and its suburbs. The core curriculum is enriched by Honors courses, electives, a complete athletic program, and 40 nonathletic clubs and activities. Tuition: $7180. Financial Aid: $1,050,000. Claire Molloy is Director of Admission and Recruiting; William Watts (Loyola [Chicago], Ph.D.) is Principal. *North Central Association.*

Summit School, Inc.   1968

333 West River Road, Elgin, IL 60123. 847-468-0490;
Fax 847-468-9392; E-mail Debbie@summitelgin.org;
Web Site www.msts.com/summitschool/

Summit School provides Early Learning and Elementary programs for children age 2 through Grade 8 as well as Parent/Infant programs for babies up to age 2. The School aims to provide a nurturing academic environment that combines learning with fun. Enthusiastic, well-qualified teachers focus on each child's talents and best interests. The enriched curriculum features mathematics, science, reading, social studies, foreign languages, art, music, physical education, and computers. Small classes enroll an average of 12–15 students. A full-day Kindergarten program and before- and after-school care are offered. Tuition: $1700–$6900. Scholarships are available. Debbie McCarthy is Admissions Coordinator. *North Central Association.*

The University of Chicago
Laboratory Schools   1896

1362 East 59th Street, Chicago, IL 60637. 773-702-9450;
   Fax 773-702-7455; E-mail lucinda@vertex.ucls.uchicago.edu;
   Web Site ucls.uchicago.edu

Founded by John Dewey to test his educational theories, The University of Chicago Laboratory Schools enroll 1650 students in a coeducational Nursery–Grade 12 program. The Schools offer a culturally and racially diverse community within which students actively engage in an academically rigorous, "hands-on" education. The program challenges each student to think independently by encouraging the individual's natural curiosity and cultivating his or her love of learning. The college preparatory program includes Advanced Placement courses in most disciplines. Many extracurricular activities and a summer program are available. Tuition: $6420–$12,675. Financial Aid: $600,000. Andrea Solow and Alice Haskell are Admissions Coordinators; Lucinda Lee Katz (University of Illinois, Ph.D.) is Director. *North Central Association*.

INDIANA

Canterbury School 1977

5601 Covington Road, Fort Wayne, IN 46804. 219-432-7776
3210 Smith Road, Fort Wayne, IN 46804. 219-436-0746;
 Fax 219-436-5137; Web Site www.canterburyschool.org

Canterbury School is an independent day school enrolling 855 boys and girls in Pre-Kindergarten–Grade 12. The philosophy of the School is to develop in students a love and appreciation for the challenges of learning, a sense of intellectual curiosity, and an understanding of the implications of Christian principles in our daily lives. The School provides a challenging educational program based on a strong college preparatory curriculum. Extracurricular activities include athletics, drama, music, clubs, and student publications. A summer enrichment program is available. Tuition: $7650–$7850. Financial Aid: $540,000. Jonathan Hancock (Oxford [England], B.A., M.A.; Harvard, Ed. M.) was appointed Headmaster in 1982.

Cathedral High School 1918

5225 East 56th Street, Indianapolis, IN 46226. 317-542-1481;
 Fax 317-543-5050; E-mail chslibl.Iquest.net; Web Site
 http:\\www.cathedral-irish.org

Cathedral High School is a Roman Catholic, college preparatory day school enrolling 1050 boys and girls in Grades 9–12. Seeking to maintain its "tradition of excellence and success" in academics and athletics, Cathedral is dedicated to Christian values and the total development of each student. Cathedral High School strives to provide a challenging environment that promotes self-esteem, personal responsibility, integrity, and self-discipline. Graduating seniors earned $5,200,000 in college scholarships. Tuition: $6250. Financial Aid: $900,000. Diane Szymanski is Director of Admission; Stephen J. Helmich is President; Rev. Patrick J. Kelly is Principal.

The Culver Academies CULVER

Culver, IN 46511. 219-842-7000; Admissions 219-842-7100;
 Fax 219-842-8066; E-mail pottsg@culver.org;
 Web Site www.culver.org

THE CULVER ACADEMIES in Culver, Indiana, offer a college preparatory curriculum within a boarding school environment for boys and girls in Grades 9–12 and a postgraduate year. The town of Culver (population 1600) is located in a rolling, rural portion of north-central Indiana, approximately 100 miles from Chicago.

Culver Military Academy was founded in 1894 by Henry Harrison Culver on Lake Maxinkuckee, with a classics scholar appointed as the first Headmaster. The Academy was owned and controlled by the Culver family until 1932, when it was incorporated as The Culver Educational Foundation. In 1971, Culver Girls Academy was founded and, with the Military Academy, is operated by the Foundation as a not-for-profit organization. The Foundation is directed by a Board of Trustees.

The goal of developing students intellectually, culturally, spiritually, and physically is met through discipline, competition, and acceptance of responsibility. In addition to providing academic preparation for college, Culver seeks to train students to become citizens who will fulfill roles necessary for the functioning of a democratic society. Culver also strives to instill an understanding of responsibility and commitment to something outside of oneself. Through academics, leadership development, and extracurricular activities, students are encouraged to utilize and enhance their skills and abilities in order to fulfill their potential.

The Academies are members of the Independent Schools Association of the Central States, the National Association of Independent Schools, Secondary School Admission Test Board, The College Board, and the Association of Military Colleges and Schools of the United States, among other affiliations. The Academies hold a Commission from the State of Indiana Department of Public Instruction and are accredited by the North Central Association of Colleges and Schools and the Independent Schools Association of the Central States.

THE CAMPUS. The Culver Academies occupy an 1800-acre campus bordering on Lake Maxinkuckee. Included are an airport with two runways, a parade ground, soccer fields, a nine-hole golf course, 15 tennis courts, an all-weather track, a baseball diamond, a football field, 11 intramural playing fields, outdoor riding rings, cross-country jumps, nature trails, bridle paths, and lakeshore walks. The 40-acre Elvera W. Beason Memorial Park, located on the Tippecanoe River, is also available for student recreational use.

Among the 38 stone and brick buildings are nine dormitories; the Administration Building; the Huffington Library with a capacity for 150,000 volumes, the latest educational technology, reading rooms, visual aids, reference rooms, study carrels, and an electronic information retrieval center; the Music and Art Building with 12 music studios and 4 art studios; the Chapel; and the Health Center.

The Gignilliat Memorial Quadrangle is the academic center of the campus. It includes four buildings—Eppley Hall of Science, Eppley Hall of Humanities, Huffington Library, and Gignilliat Memorial Hall—housing 53 classrooms and laboratories and two student computer centers. Eugene C. Eppley Auditorium includes two theaters used for assemblies and performances.

The Recreation Complex has two gymnasiums, two hockey rinks, a natatorium with a pool and diving tank, a Hall of Fame, a wellness center, a central locker building, and facilities for wrestling, fencing, gymnastics, weight training, basketball, indoor track, tennis, volleyball, racquetball, handball, squash, and paddleball. The Riding Hall and Stables contains a riding arena and an indoor polo field.

Other facilities include service buildings, 43 faculty residences, the Summer Naval School Headquarters, the Aviation Education Center, the Dining Hall and Student Center, and Beason Memorial Hall, a senior social center. The school plant is valued at $150,000,000.

THE FACULTY. John N. Buxton, formerly Vice Rector for Administration and member of the English faculty at St. Paul's School, was appointed Head of Schools in 1999. He is a graduate of Brown University (B.A. 1969) and a doctoral candidate at Boston University.

There are 74 full-time instructors and administrators who

teach, 49 men and 25 women; the faculty also include 12 teaching interns. Twenty faculty members, 4 with families, live on campus. All hold baccalaureate degrees and 83 percent hold graduate degrees. Two or more degrees were earned at Butler, Dartmouth, Davidson, Denison, Duke, Harvard, Heidelberg, Indiana University, Miami University, Northwestern, Ohio State, Purdue, Trinity, United States Military Academy, Wabash, Western Michigan, Williams, and the Universities of Cincinnati, Illinois, Iowa, Michigan, New Hampshire, North Carolina, Notre Dame, Valparaiso, Virginia, and Wisconsin. Three part-time instructors teach ballet, aviation, and driver education.

The Health Center staff includes two school physicians, a Director of Psychological Services, a Director of Culver Assistance Program, five registered nurses, and two licensed practical nurses.

STUDENT BODY. In 1999–2000, the schools enroll 640 boarding students, 402 boys and 238 girls, and 62 day students, 33 boys and 29 girls in Grades 9–12. There are 155 in Grade 9, 182 in Grade 10, 186 in Grade 11, 177 in Grade 12, and 2 postgraduates. Students represent 34 states, the District of Columbia, Puerto Rico, and 22 foreign countries.

ACADEMIC PROGRAM. The school year extends from early September to late May, with two-week vacations at Christmas and in the spring. Typical academic programs would include daily classes in English, foreign language, mathematics, history, laboratory science, and leadership training, along with semiweekly classes in physical education, and, for some students, modern dance, theater, music, or art.

Graduation requirements are four years of English, three years of one foreign language, three years of mathematics, one year of United States History with an additional year of history, three years of a laboratory science, and as many as five academic electives. In addition, physical education is required through one semester of Grade 11. A course in leadership is required for all students at each grade level.

The high school curriculum includes English; French 1–4, German 1–4, Latin 1–4, Spanish 1–4; Modern European History, United States History; Algebra 1–2, Geometry, Functions-Statistics-Trigonometry, Precalculus, Calculus, Advanced Mathematics; Biology, Chemistry, Computer Science, Physics; Music Theory and Composition, Modern Dance; and Leadership 1–4. One-semester electives are offered in such subjects as World Literature, American Literature, Speech, Shakespeare, Government, Russian History, Economics, Philosophy, Computer Programming, Astronomy and Geology, Art Appreciation, Studio Art, Photography, Ceramics, Driver Education, and Academic Skills.

Advanced Placement work is available in 13 subjects.

Classes have 20 or fewer students, and small tutoring groups are formed to help students in a particular subject. The schools maintain an inventory of microcomputers. Most students work in their rooms with nightly faculty supervision or in the library. The Academic Skills and Writing Centers are available to students who want to upgrade themselves in reading, writing, study skills, and word processing.

Ninety-six percent of the members of the Class of 1999 were accepted by at least one college or university on their first- or second-choice list. Their choices included Amherst, Bowdoin, Brown, Carnegie Mellon, Colby, Davidson, Harvard, Johns Hopkins, Massachusetts Institute of Technology, Miami of Ohio, Middlebury, Princeton, Rice, Stanford, United States Air Force Academy, Vanderbilt, Washington and Lee, Washington University, Wellesley, and the Universities of Michigan, North Carolina, Notre Dame, Pennsylvania, and Virginia.

More than 1400 students participate in Culver's five summer programs—Woodcraft Camp (boys and girls, 9–13 years of age); Summer Camp for Girls (13–17 years of age); and Naval Program, Horsemanship, and Aviation camps (all for boys, 13–17 years of age). In addition, more than 200 campers participate in Culver's 14 specialty camps.

STUDENT ACTIVITIES. Military Academy activities are organized around a traditional military structure. In addition to receiving Leadership instruction, each cadet is a member of the Infantry Battalion, the Band, the Artillery Battalion, or the Cavalry Squadron. Girls Academy activities are organized around dormitory programs and a Prefect Leadership structure, with the Girls Academy Council coordinating the various aspects of student life. All students help in a work program.

Among the numerous student interest groups are Art, Admissions, Bicycling, Chess, German, Lacrosse, Science, Scuba, Ski, Soccer, Photography, and Spanish clubs. Students may also participate in Dancevision, cheerleading, Lectors Guild, Culver Equestriennes, Lancers, Rough Riders, the Fellowship of Christian Athletes, and the Cordon Society, a religious organization. Students publish a newspaper, a literary magazine, and a yearbook. In addition to the Band, the Academies have a Chapel Choir, dance bands, and singing groups.

Girls' and boys' intramural, varsity, and junior varsity teams compete in many sports, including crew, football, horseback riding, tennis, cross-country, track, baseball, racquetball, diving, fencing, soccer, archery, badminton, basketball, handball, lacrosse, ice-skating, ice hockey, skiing, squash, swimming, wrestling, polo, volleyball, and golf. The lake is used for boating, shell rowing, and canoeing. Riding instruction is open to all girls, but only boys are eligible for the Black Horse Troop, the largest cavalry unit in the nation. Girls may participate in "Equestriennes," an honorary horsemanship program. A flight training program includes both ground school and flight time; students may earn private pilot licenses.

Social events are planned frequently. In addition, there are speakers and entertainers, concerts, plays, a weekly movie, and trips to performances and cultural events in nearby cities.

ADMISSION AND COSTS. Culver admits students who are capable of superior academic achievement in a competitive college preparatory, boarding school environment based on past academic performance, grades, teacher evaluations, Culver entrance examination results, results of other standardized tests, communication skills, and writing samples. Additionally, students who display the necessary academic ability must manifest mature, responsible, and self-disciplined behavior indicative of the ability to live independently in the Culver community.

Students are accepted in Grades 9–12 and occasionally for postgraduate study. Midyear enrollment is permitted if vacancies exist. Candidates are encouraged to register at least six months prior to the desired date of enrollment. There is a $30 application fee.

The 1999–2000 boarding fees at The Culver Academies total $21,150 for tuition, room and board, laundry, student activities and publications, various school fees, and routine medical services. Day student tuition is $15,000. A uniform is required of first-year students; the fee for boys' uniforms is $1495, the girls' wardrobe fee is $775. Additional expenses include riding ($3500), music instruction, Driver Training, Studio Art, and Aviation. Textbooks are approximately $250 per year, and incidental expenses vary with each student.

The Batten Scholarship Program, established in 1999, is a merit-based scholarship offered to six new ninth- and tenth-grade students selected for their superior record of academic achievement, personal character, and demonstrated leadership in extracurricular activities. A Batten Scholarship covers full tuition, room and board, books, uniforms, and other required fees. Batten Scholars participate in fully funded enrichment programs including a week-long service project and summer study program.

Scholarship aid amounting to approximately $4,800,000 in grants and $354,000 in student loans is awarded annually to more than 55 percent of the student body. Recipients are chosen on the basis of need as determined by the School Scholarship Service.

Principal and Dean of Faculty: Kathy J. Lintner
Dean of Students: Laura J. Weaser
Director of Alumni Relations: Alan H. Loehr
Director of Admissions: Larry A. Bess
Director of Development: Bruce L. Holaday
Director of College Advising: Dr. H. O'Neal Turner
Chief Financial Officer: Peter J. McCone
Director of Athletics: J. Allan Clark

Evansville Day School   1946

3400 North Green River Road, Evansville, IN 47715.
812-476-3039; Fax 812-476-4061; E-mail admission@eds.
evansville.net

Founded by parents, the Evansville Day School is a coeducational college preparatory school enrolling 340 students in Junior Pre-Kindergarten–Grade 12. The School provides a traditional curriculum stressing personal growth, academic excellence, and character education. The educational experience is enhanced by a wide range of learning and extracurricular activities including classes in fine arts and computer studies, and a variety of athletic teams. A personal development program and a caring faculty provide a positive learning atmosphere. A block schedule for Grades 8–12 includes numerous Advanced Placement courses. Tuition: $2805–$7585. Financial Aid: $250,000. Candace Brownlee is Director of Admission; Mary Jean Thielen is Head of the School.

Howe Military School   HOWE

P.O. Box 240B, Howe, IN 46746. 219-562-2131, Ext. 221;
E-mail admissions@howemilitary.com;
Web Site www.howemilitary.com

Howe military school in Howe, Indiana, is a military boarding school for boys and girls in Grades 5–12. Situated in the northernmost part of the state, the village of Howe (population 950) is midway between La Grange, Indiana, and Sturgis, Michigan. Accessible via the Indiana Toll Road (Interstate 80/90), the School is one hour from South Bend, Indiana; three hours from Chicago, Indianapolis, and Detroit; and five hours from Cincinnati.

The School was established in 1884 as the result of a bequest to the Episcopal church by the Honorable John Badlam Howe. The military program was instituted in 1895, and since 1920, the School has had a Junior ROTC unit sponsored by the Department of the Army. It is the only JROTC military institute in Michigan, Ohio, or Indiana. Howe has been designated an Honor Military School with Distinction by the Department of Defense.

Howe Military School seeks to provide a balanced education that affords opportunities for college preparation through the academic program, physical development through the athletic program, leadership and intelligent followership through the military program, and spiritual development through religious services and activities. Howe maintains its historic affiliation with the Episcopal church but admits students of all faiths. Cadets attend brief chapel services four times weekly and a service on Sunday.

A nonprofit institution, Howe is governed by a self-perpetuating Board of 20 Trustees, which meets quarterly. The Bishop of the Northern Indiana Episcopal Diocese heads the Board, whose members include the Superintendent, parents, and alumni. The Alumni Association, which represents the more than 3000 living graduates, elects 2 alumni board members. Howe is accredited by the North Central Association of Colleges and Schools and the State of Indiana. It holds membership in the National Association of Independent Schools, the Independent Schools Association of the Central States, and the Association of Military Colleges and Schools of the United States.

THE CAMPUS. The 150-acre campus includes landscaped lawns, parade grounds, two ponds, a 50-acre athletic complex, athletic fields, and six tennis courts. Indoor athletic facilities are located in the gymnasium, which provides a wrestling room, a basketball court, an indoor rifle range, a weight training room, and locker rooms. An indoor swimming pool adjacent to the gymnasium was resurfaced and updated in 1996.

High School academic classes meet in the Memorial Academic Building, which provides 20 classrooms, four science laboratories, and two new, state-of-the-art computer labs. The Junior High classes (Grades 5–8) meet in White Hall, which contains 7 classrooms, a science lab, a computer lab, and a gymnasium. The Grace Libey Library contains more than 14,000 volumes and three reference, multimedia computers. Internet access is available in the library and computer labs, with limited Internet access in high school cadets' dorm rooms.

Male cadets are housed in five barracks that also provide quarters for the Tactical Officers and their families. Female cadets are housed in their own barracks with an adult supervisor. Other school buildings are the Herrick Hall Administration Building, the Major Merritt Dining Hall, Bouton Auditorium, the Industrial Arts Building, St. James Chapel, All Saints Chapel, the 30-bed infirmary, the Quartermaster Store, and the Father Jennings Canteen and Recreation Center. Also on the campus are the Vicarage, the original Howe Mansion, which is on the National Registry of Historic Places, and several faculty residences.

THE FACULTY. CAPT William E. Sneath, USNR (RET), was elected Superintendent as of July 1, 1997. A graduate of Western Michigan University, CAPT Sneath retired from the U.S.

Navy, completing a 26-year career that began as a seaman recruit.

The full-time faculty consist of 20 men and 10 women. Six Tactical Officers and their families live in the barracks, while faculty members live on campus, in the village of Howe, or in surrounding communities. The faculty hold baccalaureate and advanced degrees from such institutions as Appalachian State, Ball State, Earlham, Eastern Illinois, Huntington, Grand Valley State, Illinois College, Indiana University, Kent State, Manchester College, Ohio University, Purdue, Saint Louis University, Syracuse, United States Military Academy, Western Michigan, and the Universities of Akron, Guadalajara (Mexico), Iowa, London, North Carolina, South Dakota, South Florida, Toledo, Virginia, and Wales.

A retired army officer and two noncommissioned officers conduct the JROTC program. The campus infirmary is open 24 hours with a daily check by a local physician. The infirmary is staffed and administered by Vencor Hospital in La Grange, Indiana.

CADET CORPS. In 1998–99, the School enrolled 204 boarding students, 164 boys and 40 girls. Approximately 85 percent of the cadets come from Illinois, Indiana, Michigan, and Ohio.

The Corps of Cadets is governed by the rules and regulations of the School. The Corps is expected to live up to the Cadet Code of Honor: "I will not lie, steal, or cheat, nor tolerate among us anyone who does." The School motto is "Faith and Honor."

ACADEMIC PROGRAM. The school year, from late August to late May, is divided into semesters with Thanksgiving, Christmas, and spring vacations. Classes, which have an average size of 10–12, meet five days a week. A typical day begins with First Call at 6:00 A.M. Three class periods are conducted in the morning and three in the afternoon, with a daily homework/study period beginning at 7:30 P.M. An athletic period is held from 3:30 to 5:30 P.M. Chapel is conducted at 6:15 P.M. three days a week, with Sunday services at 11:00 A.M. Taps is at 10:00 P.M. for high school cadets, 9:30 P.M. for junior high, and 11:00 P.M. for seniors.

Cadets may receive extra help from 3:00 to 3:30 P.M. daily. To encourage academic growth, each student is assigned a Potential Achievement Rate. The cadet is expected to attain and maintain this goal, which is revised periodically to reflect changes in performance. Marks are sent to parents every six weeks.

To graduate, cadets must complete 21 academic units, including 4 of English; 3½ of social studies, including United States History, Economics, and Government; 3 of mathematics, including Algebra I and II and Geometry; 3 of science; 2 of the same foreign language; 1 of computer science; ½ of health; 2½ of electives; 1 of physical education; and 1 JROTC class each year.

The curriculum includes full-year courses in English 1–4, Speech, Journalism; Spanish, French, German; Biology, Chemistry; Physics; Pre-Algebra, Algebra I, Geometry, Algebra II, Trigonometry and Calculus; United States History, World History; Christian Ethics; Accounting; Woods; and Physical Education. Semester courses are offered in Biochemistry; Data Processing, Computer Science; Geography, Economics, Sociology, United States Government; and Computer Literacy, Multimedia Computing, Graphics, Mechanical Drawing, Architectural Drafting, and Power Technology.

Computers are required in every high school barracks room for every student. A fiber-optics network links each cadet's room with every teacher in the high school, providing an electronic tutor for each high school cadet.

Military training for the younger students consists of drill, "the manual of arms, the school of the soldier, and other instruction contributing to the precision and poise of the individual and the esprit de corps of the group." High School courses cover a variety of topics, such as drill, weapons safety, marksmanship, land navigation, and military history.

There were 28 graduates in the Class of 1999. They are attending such colleges and universities as Central Michigan, The Citadel, Howard University, Indiana University, Johnson & Wales, Kent State, Kettering College of Medicine, Lake Superior State, Michigan State, New Mexico Military Institute, Ohio Northern, Ohio State, Purdue, St. Mary's College, Virginia Military Academy, and the Universities of Chicago, Illinois, Michigan, Minnesota, and Wisconsin.

Howe Summer Camp, enrolling boys ages 8–16, offers such sports as swimming, S.C.U.B.A., canoeing, air riflery, softball, soccer, sailing, golf, tennis, archery, and basketball. Younger campers take review classes in English and mathematics; high school campers must take one academic class for credit. Courses include English and algebra. The summer program offers a three-week session ($1425) and a six-week session ($2625). High school campers must enroll for six weeks.

CADET ACTIVITIES. The Sword and Shield, which consists of cadet-commissioned officers and cadet leaders, acts as a liaison between the corps and the administration. The Cadet Corps is organized as a military unit.

Cadets may join the staff of the school newspaper or the yearbook. They may also participate in Howe's chapter of the National Forensic League or the National Thespians. Qualified cadets are elected to The Cum Laude Society and Alpha Delta Tau. Musical groups include the marching band, the concert band, and the chapel choir. Other cadet organizations are the History, Radio, and Varsity Letter clubs and many additional groups. Cadets of all ages may receive acolyte training and participate regularly in chapel services, along with ushers or choir members. Other religious instruction is available.

Varsity teams in baseball, softball, basketball, cross-country, volleyball, golf, riflery, soccer, tennis, track, swimming, and wrestling compete with those of other independent and public high schools. There are intramural teams in volleyball, basketball, softball, swimming, and touch football; cadets may also play tennis on a noncompetitive basis. Field trips are arranged to such places as Greenfield Village, Kalamazoo Air Museum, Henry Ford Museum, Cedar Point, the Football Hall of Fame, and Chicago museums.

Cadets have free time on Friday evening, Saturday afternoon and evening, and Sunday afternoon, plus for a half-hour each evening and for brief periods during the school day. There is one "Open Weekend" scheduled each semester. Additional weekends may be earned. Social activities include movies, occasional professional entertainment, several informal and three formal dances each year, roller-skating parties, and bowling parties. Among the traditional annual events are a Family Picnic, Founders' Day, Winter Family Weekend, Alumni Weekend, and Mother's Day Weekend.

ADMISSION AND COSTS. Howe seeks young men and women of good character with the ability to do college preparatory work. Cadets are accepted in Grades 5–12 on the basis of test results, school records, teacher references, and a physical examination. Admission tests are administered at Howe; if candidates cannot take the tests at the School, they may arrange to do so under supervision at a more convenient location, or they may substitute the Secondary School Admission Test. There is a $100 application fee.

The 1999–2000 charge for tuition, room, board, uniforms, books, academic fees, school supplies, laundry, haircuts, entertainment fees, and incidentals totaled $18,300 plus a $550 computer fee for high school students. Medical, dental, transportation expenses, and a spending allowance are not included in this total. There are additional fees for music instruction and driver training. A delayed payment plan is available.

In 1998–99, $387,000 in scholarships was awarded to 82 cadets on the basis of need. Parents of prospective students desiring tuition assistance should contact the Director of Admission when applying for admission.

Headmaster: Mr. Carter Lohr
Junior High Principal: Mr. Duane Van Orden
Dean of Students: James Malerich
Alumni Coordinator: Ray Stuckey
Director of Admission: Brent Smith, Ph.D.
Director of Development: Ray Stuckey
College Counselor: Carol Keagle
Business Manager: Brenn Arklie
Director of Athletics: Leanne De Felice

Le Mans Academy   ROLLING PRAIRIE

5901 North 500 East, P.O. Box 7, Rolling Prairie, IN 46371-0007.
800-777-BOYS and 219-778-2521; Fax 219-778-4801;
E-mail LMASpartan@aol.com; Web Site www.lemansacademy.org

L E MANS ACADEMY in Rolling Prairie, Indiana, specializes in the academic and social development of middle-school-aged boys in Grades 5–9. Rolling Prairie (population 1100) is a rural farming community 20 miles west of South Bend, Indiana, home of the University of Notre Dame, and 75 miles east of Chicago. Amtrak trains serve South Bend and connect with Chicago, Detroit, and Cleveland; commuter plane service is also available to nearby airports. The school, which is easily accessible by car via the Indiana Toll road, arranges transportation to and from South Bend and Chicago for major vacations and long weekends.

Founded in 1955 by the Brothers of Holy Cross, the same congregation that established the University of Notre Dame, the school was originally called Sacred Heart Military Academy and was located in Watertown, Wisconsin.

In an environment that emphasizes strong Christian values and ideals, Le Mans seeks to guide each boy in becoming a committed, active, and creative contributor to society. Specifically, the school strives to help each boy to develop academically, spiritually, physically, and socially through a program that integrates the lessons of the classroom with those of community life. Students receive assistance in developing study skills and habits, organizational skills, and time-management strategies. The military component of the program builds self-esteem and confidence in each boy. All students, regardless of their faith, are required to attend weekly religious services and to take part in religious instruction that emphasizes Christian principles. Through the structured program, boys are encouraged to develop leadership skills and strength of character.

A not-for-profit association, Le Mans Academy is owned by the Brothers of Holy Cross and governed by a 13-member Board of Trustees that includes members of the Congregation, parents, alumni, and other friends of the school.

Le Mans Academy is accredited by the Department of Education of the State of Indiana and the Independent Schools Association of the Central States. It holds membership in the Indiana Non-Public Education Association, Midwest Boarding Schools, National Catholic Education Association, Association of Catholic Boarding Schools, Boys Schools: An International Coalition, The Association of Boarding Schools, and the Secondary School Admission Test Board.

THE CAMPUS. The 90-acre campus is adjacent to Silver Lake and surrounded by more than 600 acres of woods, fields, and farmland. Recreational facilities include a baseball field, two soccer fields, outdoor basketball and tennis courts, an indoor rifle range, sand volleyball courts, a large television room, and a multipurpose recreation center featuring an oversized gymnasium and a large student union. The main school buildings include the Residential Building, the Academic Building and Gymnasium; and the Elizabeth S. Warren Center for Achievement, which includes the Andre Science Center, the library and media center, and the computer center. The facilities, owned by the Brothers of Holy Cross, are valued at $5,200,000.

THE FACULTY. Br. William Dygert, CSC, President, has had extensive experience in educational administration. He holds an M.Ed. in Administration from Loyola University, an M.A.T. in English from Indiana University, and a master's in Christian

Spirituality from Creighton University. Mr. Steven Cash, the Headmaster, was formerly the Head of Florida Air Academy (Melbourne, Florida) for nine years. He holds a B.A. and an M.A. from California State University at Sonoma.

The faculty include three men and eight women. They have earned undergraduate degrees at Illinois Benedictine, Indiana University, Purdue, and Western Michigan University. Their advanced degrees were awarded at Indiana University, Notre Dame, and Purdue.

First aid is provided by a school nurse. A local doctor is on call. Medical emergencies are handled by hospitals in the nearby cities of South Bend, La Porte, or Michigan City.

STUDENT BODY. In 1998–99, the school enrolled 108 boarding boys as follows: 21 in Grades 5 and 6, 37 in Grade 7, 37 in Grade 8, and 13 in Grade 9.

ACADEMIC PROGRAM. The school year, from late August to late May, is divided into semesters and includes a summer English as a Second Language session for foreign students, a Thanksgiving recess, Christmas and Easter vacations, and two long weekend breaks per year.

An average class enrolls 13 students. There is close student-faculty contact in the classroom, in after-class tutorials and study periods, and in the dormitories, which are supervised by live-in teacher-interns. Faculty members supervise required evening study halls in the academic building.

The prescribed curriculum for Grades 5, 6, and 7 includes English, World Geography (Grades 5 and 6), World Cultures (Grade 7), computer science, mathematics, science, health, theology, and art. For Grades 8 and 9, the basic program includes English, pre-algebra (Grade 8), algebra (Grade 9), United States history and government (Grade 8), World History (Grade 9), French, General Science (Grade 8), Biology (Grade 9), theology, art, and computer science. Electives include choir, drum corps, and journalism. All students are required to take Physical Education.

Upon completion of the eighth grade, all students receive a diploma. Some students continue at Le Mans for Grade 9, while others transfer to another boarding school or return to an independent day or public high school near home. In 1999, 37 boys graduated from the Academy. Assistance is offered by the Academy in placing boys in other schools.

Le Mans Academy operates a summer orientation program for all foreign students enrolled for the regular school year. The curriculum includes English pronunciation, vocabulary, reading, phonics, and writing. There are also sports activities and field trips to local attractions. The fee for the two-week program is $1500.

STUDENT ACTIVITIES. The corps of cadets is organized into four platoons of 25 boys each. Platoon members live and work together, competing with the other platoons for awards in aca-

demics, service, and athletics. Through the corps of cadets, students are encouraged to develop leadership skills and advance through the ranks. Promotions are made on the basis of academic achievement, conduct, athletic participation, and a general concern for personal development.

Among the perennial clubs and activities are the Knights of the Altar (Mass servers), Drum Corps, Exhibition Drill Team, and Craft Shop. Other activities can be organized depending on student interest.

Varsity and junior varsity teams are organized in basketball and soccer; there are also varsity track and wrestling teams. Le Mans teams compete with those of local independent, religious, and public schools in South Bend, La Porte, and Michigan City. Intramural sports include basketball, bowling, cross-country, flag football, golf, rollerblade hockey, soccer, and softball. There are also opportunities for recreational handball, hiking, skiing, and tennis.

Two weekends a month, students are free to return home or, with parental permission, to visit the home of a friend. For those students who remain on campus on open weekends, activities include athletic matches, hiking, and games in the student union. There are also excursions for roller-skating, swimming, sports at Notre Dame, and drama at a local theater, as well as trips to museums and other cultural and athletic attractions in Chicago. On "closed weekends," all students remain on campus and take part in special activities, which usually include leadership workshops and character education courses.

Traditional annual events include Parents' Day, Family Weekend, Academic Day, and parent-teacher conferences.

ADMISSION AND COSTS. Le Mans Academy seeks to enroll boys of average to above-average ability who may be performing at less than their potential. To apply, candidates should submit the completed application form, a transcript of grades, two Le Mans Academy recommendation forms, results of a physical examination, and a nonrefundable application fee of $200. Application should be made in the spring or summer for fall admission, although applications are accepted at any time and students are admitted throughout the school year.

In 1999–2000, boarding tuition is $14,960. Foreign students should contact the school for their cost schedule. Additional expenses include uniforms ($716 to purchase, $100 to rent), texts and workbooks ($295), laundry ($510), personal account ($150), medical fee ($175), and graduation fee for eighth graders ($180). The school offers a need-based financial aid program; awards are made at the discretion of the Financial Aid Council.

President: Br. William Dygert, CSC
Headmaster: Mr. Steven Cash
Residential Director: Br. Shaun Gray, CSC
Academic Director: Dr. Paul McFann
Director of Admissions: Mr. John Novick, Jr.
Business Manager: Br. Paul Kelly, CSC
Athletics/Activities Director: Mr. Christopher Torrijas

Marian Heights Academy FERDINAND

812 East 10th Street, Ferdinand, IN 47532. 812-367-1431 or 800-467-4MHA; Fax 812-367-2121; E-mail academy@thedome.org; Web Site http://www.thedome.org/mha

MARIAN HEIGHTS ACADEMY in Ferdinand, Indiana, is a Benedictine, Roman Catholic, college preparatory boarding and day school enrolling girls in Grades 9 through 12. Founded in 1870, the school is owned and operated by the Sisters of St. Benedict, who are members of the oldest religious order in the Catholic Church. Ferdinand, a rural community of 2500, is located in the southwestern portion of the state, a mile north of Interstate 64, midway between Louisville, Kentucky, and Evansville, Indiana.

Committed to academic excellence in an intercultural community, Marian Heights strives to encourage its students to think creatively and independently. A high school "steeped in rich traditions and filled with future promise," the Academy calls its students to scholastic achievement, to personal responsibility, and to participation in character-building activities.

In its role as a Catholic-affiliated school for girls, Marian Heights emphasizes the dignity and equality of women, educating them for leadership and their right to participate without discrimination in a democratic society.

Administration of the school is guided by the Marian Heights Academy Board, consisting of 19 members who provide counsel and support on matters of policy. Active alumnae and a parent group promote the school and assist in fundraising and planning activities. The Academy is accredited by the North Central Association of Colleges and Schools, the Independent Schools Association of the Central States, and the Indiana Department of Education, having been distinguished by the latter with a First-Class Commission. The school is also a member of the National Catholic Educational Association, the Midwest Boarding Schools, the National Coalition of Girls' Schools, the Secondary School Admission Test Board, the National Association of Independent Schools, the Indiana Boarding Schools, the Indiana Non-Public Education Association, and the Catholic Boarding Schools Association.

THE CAMPUS. Marian Heights Academy shares a wooded, 190-acre campus with the monastery of the Benedictine Sisters and Kordes Enrichment Center, an ecumenical retreat and educational center. The monastery's domed church is considered one of the finest examples of Romanesque architecture in the country. Academic facilities include the classroom building, the library containing more than 30,000 volumes, science department, and an art studio. Residential life is centered in Madonna Hall, a modern, five-story building that contains single- and double-occupancy rooms for boarders as well as a large dining hall, a library, recreation room, cinema, lounges, kitchenettes, laundry rooms, study rooms, and suites for proctors.

Among the athletic facilities are the Marian Heights Gymnasium, a softball diamond, an outdoor swimming pool, four outdoor lighted tennis courts, a fitness center, and a fitness trail.

THE FACULTY. The Marian Heights Academy faculty consists of 19 full-time and 14 part-time teachers, 24 of whom have earned advanced degrees and 15 of whom live on or adjacent to the campus. They hold degrees from such universities as Ball State, Brescia College, Creighton, DePauw, Fontbonne College, George Peabody, Hanover College, Indiana State, Indiana University, Langston, Marian College, Mount St. Scholastica, Purdue, St. Benedict College, St. Francis College, Saint Louis University, St. Mary's College, St. Meinrad, Vanderbilt, Western Kentucky, Western Michigan, and the Universities of Evansville, North Carolina, Northern Iowa, Notre Dame, and Southern Indiana.

A registered nurse is available at all times; hospital facilities are located within a 15-minute drive of the campus.

STUDENT BODY. In 1999–2000, Marian Heights Academy enrolled 118 boarding and day girls, distributed as follows: Grade 9—20, Grade 10—34, Grade 11—26, and Grade 12—38. They represented 18 states, eight foreign countries, and a variety of religious, ethnic, racial, and socioeconomic backgrounds.

ACADEMIC PROGRAM. The school year, divided into semesters, begins in mid-August and extends through late May with vacations at Thanksgiving, Christmas, and Easter, and a four-day weekend in October and February. Block scheduling of classes is incorporated to allow for more in-depth teaching and individual attention in and out of the classroom. Students can take up to eight classes per semester. Progress reports from teachers are sent to parents at the midway point of each quarter; report cards are mailed to parents and distributed to students every nine weeks. Parent-teacher conferences are held twice a year, or more often upon request; the student-teacher ratio is low. Supervised study periods are conducted to help develop even more diligent study habits on an independent basis.

A typical school day begins with breakfast from 6:50 to 7:50 A.M., followed by newsbreak at 7:55 A.M., morning classes, lunch, and afternoon classes, and ends with homeroom from 3:30 to 3:45 P.M. Meetings, sports, and extracurricular activities take place from 4:00 to 6:00 P.M. After dinner on Sunday through Thursday, girls study from 7:00 until 9:00 P.M. Quiet hours begin at 9:45 or 10 P.M. with "lights out" at 10:30 or 11:30 P.M., depending on grade level.

Religious exercises are optional except on weekends when students must fulfill their Sunday church obligation by attending services on Saturday evening or on Sunday. Students are also required to attend services on holy days of obligation.

To graduate, a student must earn a minimum of 48 semester credits. Students must have 1 credit in religion for every semester in attendance at the Academy. Other credit requirements include 8 in English; 6 each in mathematics, science, and social studies; 4 each in foreign language and fine arts; and 1 each in chorus, health, physical education, and keyboarding.

The following semester and year-long courses are offered: English I-IV, Advanced Placement English, Literature and Language, Journalism; French I-IV, German I-IV, Spanish I-IV, Advanced Placement Spanish; Pre-Algebra, Algebra I-II, Pre-Calculus, Calculus, Advanced Placement Calculus, Discrete Math/Statistics, Geometry, Biology, Biology II/Advanced, Advanced Placement Biology, Health I, Chemistry, Chemistry II/Advanced, Physics, Physics II/Advanced; Psychology, United States History, Advanced Placement U.S. History, World History, U.S. Government, Economics, Advanced Placement Government, Sociology; Accounting, Computer Applications, Keyboard/Computer Science, Advanced Computers; Religion & Scripture I-IV; Art I-IV; Choir, Applied Music I-IV, Music Appreciation, Music Harmony/Music Theory, Dramatic Arts; Physical Education I-II; and Driver Education. Leadership training and team building are integrated throughout various disciplines of the curriculum.

International students enrolled in the English as a Second Language program take advantage of a full-immersion curriculum designed to develop proficiency and confidence in the use of English. Required courses include American Culture, Music, Religion, Computers, Audio-Visual, Performing Arts, and Applied Music, with elective courses offered in Art, French, Math, and Physical Education.

The 26 graduates in the Class of 1999 are attending Brown, Carleton, Chicago Institute of Art, Louisiana Tech, Marshall, Michigan State, Rend Lake College, Rockhurst, Western Michigan, and the Universities of Colorado, Evansville, Port-

land, and Southern Indiana as well as colleges and universities in Mexico.

STUDENT ACTIVITIES. The Marian Heights Student Council, formed to promote leadership, good citizenship, and school spirit, serves as a liaison between the student body and administration and seeks to enhance the local community through service projects. A Student Activities Committee plans and implements a variety of events both on and off campus.

Community volunteer opportunities enable girls to earn service hours through assistance to elementary school students, a nursing home, a soup kitchen, Habitat for Humanity, and other groups.

Opportunities for journalistic experience are provided by two student-produced publications: *Pax* (yearbook) and *Stella Maris* (school newspaper). Qualified students may be inducted into the National Honor Society, which promotes character, scholarship, leadership, and service and conducts a peer tutoring program on campus.

Other special groups include Melodettes, Playing Highlanders, Forensics Team, Dramatics, Church Choir, and Peer Ministry.

The Academy is a member of the Indiana High School Athletic Association and competes with area schools in cross-country, soccer, basketball, softball, tennis, and volleyball.

A variety of weekend events is planned such as dances, concerts, plays, movies, shopping trips, rollerblading, roller- or ice-skating, camping, white-water rafting, and skiing. Trips are planned throughout the year during vacations and long weekends. Trips planned for the 1999–2000 school year are: Niagara Falls, Boston, New York City, and Washington, D.C., over Thanksgiving break; New Orleans in February; and London, Paris, and Madrid over the spring break. Also available on campus are opportunities for bicycling, swimming, hiking, tennis, ice-skating, sledding, and dance lessons. Annual Halloween, Thanksgiving, Christmas, and Valentine dinners for staff and students are organized by the individual classes.

ADMISSION AND COSTS. Marian Heights Academy seeks girls from diverse religious and racial backgrounds, regardless of financial means, who possess average to above-average ability, good character, and the motivation to enable them to succeed in a rigorous college preparatory program. The school also offers a separate curriculum for international students who wish to learn English as a Second Language. Students applying for admission to the college preparatory program must take the Secondary School Admission Test. Those who enter the ESL curriculum take an English Proficiency Test, administered upon their arrival at the school.

Admission is based on previous school records, SSAT test results, teacher recommendations, school references, and interviews. Applicants from the United States must also visit the campus and participate in personal interviews. While visiting the campus for the personal interviews, prospective students may spend the night in the dormitory and attend classes with current students.

In 1999–2000, tuition was $15,500 for seven-day boarders and $13,850 for five-day boarders; day-student tuition was $4480. United States citizens may be eligible for financial aid based on academic accomplishment and economic need. Last year, the Academy awarded $240,640 in merit scholarships and financial aid. A tuition payment plan is available.

Head of School: Sr. Mary Austin Blank, President
Dean of Academic Affairs: Sr. Therese Dueñas, Principal
Dean of Student Affairs: Sr. Betty Drewes
Alumnae Director: Sr. Mary Philip Berger
Director of Admissions: Ms. Cindy Schipp
Director of Development: Sr. Rose Mary Rexing
College Counselor: Ms. Karen Mundy
Business Manager: Ms. Andrea Egloff
Director of Athletics: Ms. Patty Schlacter
Activities Directors: Ms. Juanita Mauer and Sr. Jean Marie Ballard

The Orchard School   1922

615 West 64th Street, Indianapolis, IN 46260. 317-251-9253; Fax 317-254-8454; E-mail dan_vorenberg@orchard.org; Web Site www.orchard.org

Orchard, a nonsectarian, coeducational, progressive school, enrolls 585 students in Preschool–Grade 8. The curriculum integrates learning through language arts, social studies, math, music, drama, science, Spanish, French, physical education, technology, and outdoor education. Core values, problem solving, critical thinking, field trips, components of the "Responsive Classroom," and service learning are integral to the social and academic curriculum. Learning support, speech-language therapy, assessment and evaluation, and school counseling are available. Extended-day care is offered. Tuition: $5377–$8005. Financial Aid: $566,175. Kristen Hein is Admissions Director; Daniel Vorenberg (Lake Forest, B.A.; Lesley College/Shady Hill School Joint Masters Program, M.Ed.) is Head of School.

Park Tudor School   INDIANAPOLIS

7200 North College Avenue, P.O. Box 40488, Indianapolis, IN 46240-0488. 317-415-2700; E-mail info@parktudor.pvt.k12.in.us; Web Site www.parktudor.pvt.k12.in.us

Park TUDOR SCHOOL in Indianapolis, Indiana, is a college preparatory day school for boys and girls in three-year-old Kindergarten through Grade 12. The School is located on the north side of Indianapolis, a city of nearly one million and the capital of the state. The city's cultural features include a symphony, opera and ballet companies, a symphonic choir, repertory theater groups, several museums (including the world's largest children's museum), five colleges, and a theological seminary. It is the home of professional football and basketball teams. A public bus line runs within half a block of the campus.

Park Tudor was established in 1970 by the merger of the Tudor Hall School for girls, founded in 1902, and Park School, founded as the Brooks School for Boys in 1914. The School seeks to prepare its students for a productive and satisfying experience in college and encourages them "to be curious about the world outside themselves." The School is a nonsectarian, nonprofit institution governed by a self-perpetuating Board of Directors; the 23 Directors, including parents and alumni, meet nine times a year. Many of the 3500 living alumni help in student recruitment and provide financial support through their Alumni Association's scholarship fund.

Park Tudor is commissioned by the Indiana Department of Public Instruction and is accredited by the Independent Schools Association of the Central States. The School also holds membership in the National Association of Independent Schools, The College Board, and the Educational Records Bureau as well as the Council for Advancement and Support of Education, The National Association of Principals of Schools for Girls, and the Indiana Non-Public Education Association.

THE CAMPUS. The School is located on a 55-acre campus, a gift to the School by the late Eli Lilly and the late Josiah K. Lilly. The buildings have earned design, planning, and craftsmanship awards from the Indianapolis Chapter of the American Institute of Architects and the city's Metropolitan Development Commission. The Hilbert Early Education Center (1997) houses classes for three-year-old Kindergarten and the Junior and Senior Kindergartens. The Lower School (1967) includes a 12,000-volume library, classrooms, offices, and computer and science laboratories. The Upper School Building (1970) has classrooms, computer and science laboratories, offices, a lecture hall, and a 17,000-volume library. The Ruth Lilly Science Center (1989) houses four laboratories, a computer laboratory, and a science resource center. The Middle School Building (1988) has eleven classrooms, a library, and a computer laboratory. The Frederic M. Ayres, Jr., Auditorium and Fine Arts Building (1976) has classrooms; music rehearsal rooms and studios; a music library; studios for art, ceramics, and ballet; and a 425-seat auditorium. Three gymnasiums (1967, 1970, 1992) contain a 750-seat varsity gym, fitness deck, suspended running track, clothing and accessory shop, and a snack bar. Also on campus are several playing fields and eight outdoor tennis courts. The Allen Whitehill Clowes Commons (1967) provides dining and reception facilities. Foster Hall (1927) is used for meetings and special events. The Headmaster's home is located on the campus.

The School-owned plant is currently valued at approximately $27,000,000.

THE FACULTY. Bruce W. Galbraith was appointed Headmaster in 1987. He holds a B.Mus. and an M.A. from the University of Michigan. Administrators include Thomas E. Black, Jr. (Wabash, A.B.; Purdue, M.S.), Associate Headmaster; Bradley E. Lyman (Hanover College, B.A.; Armstrong State, M.A.), Assistant Headmaster and Academic Dean; James Leffler (Butler University, B.S., M.S.), Director of the Upper School (Grades 9–12); Deborah M. Dominguez (Purdue University, B.A.), Director of the Hilbert Early Education Center (3K–SK); William H. Main, Jr. (Ball State, B.S., M.S.), Director of the Lower School (Grades 1–5); J. Michael Ayres (Butler University, B.A., M.S.), Director of the Middle School (Grades 6–8); and a director of student services, a director of college and career guidance, and a director of athletics.

The faculty of 129 include 85 women and 44 men; 110 are full-time and 19 are part-time. Some administrators teach part-time. They hold 129 baccalaureate, 68 master's, and 7 doctoral degrees from 68 institutions. Representative faculty colleges include Ball State, Bowdoin, Butler, Dartmouth, DePauw, Hanover, Indiana, Kent State, Lake Forest, Marian, Middlebury, New York University, Ohio State, Oxford University (England), Princeton, Purdue, Rutgers, Syracuse, Texas Christian, Valparaiso, Vanderbilt, Wabash, and the Universities of Colorado, Kansas, Michigan, North Carolina, Oklahoma, Paris (France), Toronto (Canada), and Wisconsin.

Faculty benefits include health insurance, long-term disability insurance, a retirement plan, Social Security, and subsidies for improvement of teaching skills. Leaves of absence can be arranged.

STUDENT BODY. In 1999–2000, the School enrolls 909 students, ages 3–18, divided among the Hilbert Early Education Center, Lower School (Grades 1–5), Middle School (Grades 6–8), and Upper School (Grades 9–12). Students come from throughout the metropolitan area with the largest numbers coming from Indianapolis, Carmel, Noblesville, and Zionsville. The School has a minority student enrollment of approximately 16 percent.

ACADEMIC PROGRAM. The academic year is divided into semesters and extends from August to early June. Two-week vacations are scheduled in the winter and in the spring. Classes are held five days a week. Schedules vary, but generally include nine periods from 8:00 A.M. to 3:00 P.M. The student-faculty ratio is 9:1. Supervised study periods are part of the daily schedule in the Lower and Middle schools. Upper School study halls are required for students who have academic deficiencies or who require supervision in free periods. Advanced students are used as tutors on an informal basis, and the School has a Director of Learning Services. Grades are sent to parents and presented to students, in conference with their advisers, at the end of each quarter. Midquarter warnings are sent when necessary.

Lower School students take a program of reading, language arts, social studies, mathematics, science, music and creative arts, physical education, and computer education. Spanish is completely integrated into the Lower School curriculum. The Middle School requires English, geography, United States history, mathematics, science, etymology, computers, and physical education. French, Latin, German, Spanish, music, art, drama, and algebra are offered as electives.

Upper School students must earn a minimum of 40 credits. At least 32 of these must be earned in the five departments of English, Mathematics, Foreign Language, Science, and Social Studies. Students must also take one year each of Speech and Fine Arts as well as three semesters of Physical Education and one of Health. Among the courses offered are English 1–4, Advanced Placement English, Creative Writing; French 1–5, Latin 1–5, Spanish 1–5, German 1–5, Japanese 1–5; World History, Modern European History, American History, Western Civilization, Non-Western Civilizations, Canadian Studies, Economics, Government, Sociology, Humanities; Algebra 1–2, Geometry, Calculus 1–2, Statistics; Advanced Biology, Advanced Chemistry, Physics, Physiology, Environmental Science; Studio Art, Advanced Art, Art History, Instrumental Music, Music History and Theory, Advanced Drama, Theater History, Film History; Computer Science; and Physical Education. There are more than 20 Advanced Placement courses.

Members of the Class of 1999 entered such colleges and universities as DePauw, Duke, Georgetown, Harvard, Indiana University, Miami of Ohio, Northwestern, Princeton, Purdue, Stanford, Vanderbilt, Vassar, and the University of Michigan.

A summer program provides enrichment, remedial, and credit courses for public and private school students from Kindergarten to Grade 12. Tuition is between $50 and $500, depending on the length of the course. The School also hosts one-week soccer, softball, and basketball camps.

STUDENT ACTIVITIES. Students in Grades 1–5 elect repre-

sentatives to a Lower School Council, which meets to plan assemblies and offer advice. Similar councils are elected by the Middle and Upper schools. A school dress code is in effect in the Middle and Upper schools; a school uniform is worn by Lower School students.

Among the organized activity groups in Grades 9–12 are Amnesty International, Brain Game, Chess Club, Multicultural Club, Model United Nations, Service Club, Speech & Debate, Student Council, Varsity Club, Thespians, and the student publications, *Chronicle* (yearbook), *Artisan* (literary magazine), and *Tribune* (newspaper). The art studio is open to all students for extracurricular projects during the school day.

Park Tudor varsity teams compete in the Indiana High School Athletic Association and against other private and public schools in the area. Boys' teams are fielded in baseball, basketball, crew, cross-country, football, golf, hockey, lacrosse, soccer, swimming, tennis, track, volleyball, and wrestling. Girls' teams compete in basketball, crew, cross-country, lacrosse, soccer, volleyball, tennis, track, golf, swimming, and softball.

Classes and clubs plan and sponsor social functions throughout the year. Special events on the school calendar include Homecoming, Parents' Night, Mom's Day, Dad's Day, and Alumni Reunion. The School's Mothers' Association sponsors Applefest, a fall festival, provides volunteer service throughout the school, and organizes car pools. The Fathers' Association also is active in planning activities.

ADMISSION AND COSTS. Park Tudor seeks the average and above-average student who plans to pursue college work. Students are accepted in all grades on the basis of ability, motivation, and potential for success in college as shown through standardized test results and written recommendations from former teachers and counselors. Application, with a fee of $50, should be made in October or November of the year preceding entry. Acceptances are made on a rolling basis while vacancies exist, and some students may be accepted in midyear.

Tuition is $6330 for half-day Kindergarten and $10,550–$11,200 for all other grades. Lunch is $540 for K–5 and $580 for Grades 6–12 for the year. Other extras total $200–$450. Tuition can be paid in annual, semester, or quarterly installments. A tuition refund plan is available. The School offers scholarship grants on the basis of need. About one student in five receives financial aid; in 1999, the average grant was one-half of the tuition. Park Tudor subscribes to the School and Student Service for Financial Aid.

Director of Communications: Lisa A. Hendrickson
Director of Admission: Mary Beth Marchiony
Director of Development and Alumni Relations: Suzanne Maxwell
College Counselor: Edith S. Enright
Chief Financial Officer/Associate Head of Operations: Maria L. Kimsey
Director of Athletics: Brad Lennon

Saint Richard's School 1960

*3243 North Meridian Street, Indianapolis, IN 46208-4677.
317-926-0425; Fax 317-921-3367; E-mail jfadely@
strichards.k12.in.us; Web Site www.inct.net/~strscl*

Founded on the model of a British parish day school, Saint Richard's combines the academic and behavioral expectations of a European school with an American liberal arts curriculum. Its population is diverse, and moral and religious development are blended into the academic program. Enrolling 378 students in Transitional Kindergarten–Grade 8, the School emphasizes the development of sound study skills within a structured, caring atmosphere. French begins in Transitional Kindergarten, and the arts and physical education are integral to the program. Extended care is available. Tuition: $7100. Extras: $400. Financial Aid: $285,000. Dr. James P. Fadely is Director of Admission and Financial Aid; David J. Peerless (Bristol University [England], Ed.B.; Northeastern, Ed.M.) is Headmaster.

The Stanley Clark School 1958

*3123 Miami, South Bend, IN 46614-2098. 219-291-4200;
Fax 219-299-4170; E-mail r.douglass@scs.tcpbbs.net*

This independent preparatory school, nationally recognized as an exemplary private elementary school in 1986, enrolls 199 boys and 207 girls as day students in Preschool–Grade 8. The goal is a relaxed, productive atmosphere for serious study. In addition to traditional academics, there are courses in dramatics, computers, foreign language, and optional minicourses. Activities include chorus, newspaper and yearbook, athletics, and band. There is an optional all-day Preschool and Kindergarten and an extended-day program. Tuition: $1860–$7865. Financial Aid: $277,252. Nanci B. Sanders is Director of Admissions; Robert G. Douglass (University of Bridgeport, B.A., M.A.) was appointed Headmaster in 1988.

Sycamore School   INDIANAPOLIS

*1750 West 64th Street, Indianapolis, IN 46260. 317-253-5288;
Fax 317-479-3359*

SYCAMORE SCHOOL in Indianapolis, Indiana, is a coeducational day school for academically gifted children in Preschool through Grade 8. It is located in the northwest quadrant of the state's capital and largest city (population 797,159), permitting access to historic, educational, and cultural resources, including a symphony orchestra, opera and repertory companies, museums, professional sports teams, and seven institutions of higher learning. Students travel to school via private car pools.

Sycamore School was founded by concerned parents and educators to meet the unique educational needs of gifted children. Through an enthusiastic partnership involving families, educators, and community leaders, a building was leased and refurbished to accommodate the 110 students who enrolled in the fall of 1985. Sycamore quickly outgrew its quarters and, in 1989, leased a larger facility where it continues to operate, with 412 students and more than 70 staff members. In July 1996, the building was purchased by the School, and significantly expanded and renovated in 1999 with capital campaign funds.

The mission of Sycamore School is to meet the special intellectual, social, and emotional needs of gifted, high-functioning students through a differentiated curriculum offering greater complexity, more depth, and a faster learning pace than traditional schools. Sycamore aims to provide an open, enriched environment characterized by stimulating peer and faculty interaction. It offers opportunities to discover and explore, and it encourages responsible, productive lives. In addition to its

commitment to the education of high-achieving students, Sycamore School has been a leader, program model, and action lab site for other schools and associations in the field of gifted education.

Sycamore is governed by a 19-member Board of Directors. The Sycamore School Association, comprised mainly of parents of current students, provides support for many fund-raising, recruiting, and social activities throughout the year, including operation of the bookstore and publication of a quarterly newsletter. The School is accredited by and holds membership in the Independent Schools Association of the Central States. It is also a member of the National Association of Gifted Children, the Indiana Association for the Gifted, and the Educational Records Bureau.

THE CAMPUS. Sycamore School is set on a 16-acre campus in a residential neighborhood of Indianapolis. All of the academic facilities—classrooms, laboratories, music and art studios, gymnasium/auditorium, and the library—are centered in a 76,358-square-foot building. The grounds also contain athletic fields and play areas for the younger children.

THE FACULTY. Nyle Kardatzke was appointed Headmaster in 1993. He earned a B.S. degree in 1962 from Anderson University and holds master's and doctoral degrees from the University of California at Los Angeles. Previously, Dr. Kardatzke had been an economics professor at Marquette University and served as Headmaster of Brookfield Academy in Wisconsin and Wichita Collegiate School in Kansas. He and his wife are the parents of three school- and college-age children.

In addition to the Head of School, the administration consists of the Business Manager, Heads of the Middle and Lower schools, Early Childhood Coordinator, Director of Admissions, and Director of Development.

The faculty includes 51 full-time and 7 part-time teachers, plus 19 other staff. All teaching staff hold baccalaureates, 24 hold master's degrees, and 1 has earned a doctorate. All classroom instructors are either endorsed in gifted education or are candidates for endorsement, and most teachers have had successful teaching experience in other schools as well as at Sycamore. Faculty have graduated from colleges and universities nationwide, the majority being from Indiana and the Midwest. Among the representative institutions are Columbia, DePauw, Indiana University, Purdue, and the Universities of California (Los Angeles), Michigan, and Notre Dame. Nonteaching personnel include a Director of Special Projects, a technology coordinator, a school counselor, and a librarian.

STUDENT BODY. In 1999–2000, Sycamore enrolls 412 students as follows: 113 in Early Childhood (EC-1–Kindergarten), 153 in the Lower School (Grades 1–4), and 146 in the Middle School (Grades 5–8). They come from the metropolitan region and nearby areas and reflect a variety of racial, ethnic, and socioeconomic backgrounds.

ACADEMIC PROGRAM. The school year is divided into four grading periods, beginning in late August and concluding with graduation the first week in June. Vacations are scheduled at Thanksgiving, in the winter, and in the spring, and there are observances of national holidays.

The school day for students in Kindergarten to Grade 8 runs from 8:15 A.M. to 3:15 P.M. Monday through Thursday, with dismissal at 2:15 P.M. on Friday. Depending on age, Preschool children are enrolled in two, three, or five half-days a week in morning or afternoon sessions. An Extended Day program is available for half-day Early Childhood students for the opposite half of their school day. Before- and after-school care is available for Kindergarten–Grade 8 students.

The Early Childhood division at Sycamore enrolls boys and girls from just under 3 years old through Kindergarten. For these young children, the program provides a positive introduction to school life through carefully selected activities appropriate to their age. Group interaction encourages gross- and fine-motor coordination and the development of problem solving and critical thinking skills. As they progress, students explore multidisciplinary thematic units integrating language arts and basic math concepts. In Kindergarten, children receive reading instruction utilizing both phonics and whole-language approaches. Math instruction includes the use of manipulatives and computation, while social studies and science units based on broad concepts challenge children's creative and critical thinking abilities. Special classes in art appreciation, music, computers, Spanish, and physical education are integral to the curriculum at all grade levels. Teaching assistants in every classroom work individually with students and accompany them to their special classes.

In the Lower School (Grades 1–4), Sycamore seeks to provide an environment in which students will be free to reach their highest potential academically while developing leadership skills, social awareness, and self-knowledge. The curriculum centers on the mastery of basic skills in language arts, humanities, mathematics, and science. Teachers employ techniques specifically designed to challenge and stimulate gifted learners, from brainstorming, logical reasoning, and puzzles to simulations and debate exercises. Enrichment activities are provided through field trips, presentations from resource persons and mentors within the community, and hands-on investigation and research of actual problems.

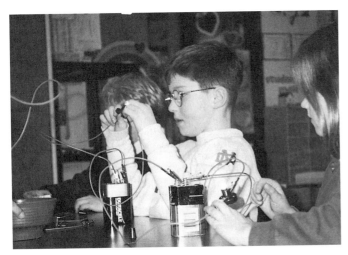

In the Middle School (Grades 5–8), the program builds on the foundation and experiences of the earlier grades to challenge gifted adolescents with increasingly complex subject matter. The core curriculum and special classes are interrelated to help students gain a broad understanding of their world. Course work is designed to sharpen existing skills in communi-

cations, critical thinking, reasoning, ethics, and finding new and alternate ways to solve problems. A flex-time program allows Middle School students to explore topics and activities of special interest. In February, as an extension of classroom learning, eighth graders take a week to gain insights into future career possibilities by "shadowing" professionals in such fields as medicine, law, science and health, engineering, radio, photography, the theater, and the environment.

Sycamore students enter competitive independent and public secondary schools. Among the schools at which graduates are currently enrolled are Brebeuf Jesuit Preparatory School, Carmel High School, Cathedral High School, Deerfield Academy, the Lawrence Township Schools, North Central High School, Park Tudor School, and Phillips Exeter Academy.

The School operates a summer program offering a series of educational, band, sports, and recreational day camps.

STUDENT ACTIVITIES. Many of the School's extracurricular activities revolve around its mission to educate gifted learners. Sycamore students are frequent participants in competitions such as Midwest Talent Search, Indiana State History Day contest, International Mathematics Olympiad, MathCounts, Knowledge Masters, National Geography Bee, and other academic challenges.

Sycamore musicians play in the School's symphonic and concert bands and in the string ensemble. Many sing in the choir, and some of these students also perform in the Indianapolis Children's Choir, Indianapolis Symphony Orchestra, and the New World Youth Symphony Orchestra. Students publish a yearbook under faculty supervision.

Educational trips regularly take students to Chicago, Amish Country, the Great Smoky Mountains, the Florida Keys, San Antonio, and Washington, D.C.

Students in Grades 5 through 8 compete with other independent schools in boys' and girls' basketball, girls' volleyball, and coed tennis, track and field, and soccer.

Students at most levels volunteer in community service projects.

Among the special events on the school calendar are Back-to-School nights, Creative Arts Festival, Lower and Middle School concerts, Grandparents' Day, Bookfair, Golf Outing, Carnival, All School Picnic, Auction for Advancement, a Middle School theatrical production, and Graduation.

ADMISSION AND COSTS. Sycamore School welcomes students from all racial, ethnic, and economic backgrounds. Children entering the half-day Preschool are assessed on the basis of their vocabulary, acute memory, alertness, curiosity, and concern for their environment as well as evidence of their social and emotional development. Formal cognitive and language assessment is done on site. Candidates in Kindergarten–Grade 8 should display superior intelligence, scholastic achievement, and age-appropriate development and behavior. Admission is based on multiple criteria including parent and teacher recommendations, intelligence testing, and a classroom visit. Lower and Middle School students must submit recent report cards demonstrating superior academic performance and must have standardized achievement test total battery scores at or above the 95th percentile.

In 1999–2000, tuition ranges from $2575 in Early Childhood-1 to $7200 in Grades 5–6 and $7350 in Grades 7–8. Financial assistance is available based on guidelines set by the School and Student Service of Princeton, New Jersey.

Head of School: Dr. Nyle Kardatzke
Head of Middle School: Michael Thompson
Head of Lower School: Diane Borgmann
Early Childhood Coordinator: Nancy Farrar
Special Programs Director: Carla Bennett
Director of Admissions: Dr. Susan Karpicke
Admissions Assistant: Libby Garrison
Director of Development: Marion Slipher
Development Assistant: Jill Stewart
Business Manager: Dianne Ridings
Athletic Director: Amy Smith

IOWA

St. Katharine's St. Mark's School   1884

1821 Sunset Drive, Bettendorf, IA 52722-6045. 319-359-1366;
Fax 319-359-7576; E-mail admissions@mail.st-kath-st-mark.pvt.
k12.ia.us; Web Site http://www.st-kath-st-mark.pvt.k12.ia.us/

Set on a bluff overlooking the Mississippi River, this caring and diverse day school enrolls approximately 235 boys and girls in Preschool–Grade 12. St. Katharine's St. Mark's, named a Blue Ribbon School by the U.S. Department of Education, offers intellectual, physical, and cultural opportunities designed to develop positive values, leadership, and academic excellence. Student Council, National Honor Society, community service, dramatic and musical productions, yearbook, art club, academic fair, and athletics, including crew, soccer, and basketball, are among the activities offered. Enrichment courses and ESL are offered in the summer. Tuition: $4032–$7205. Financial Aid: $310,000. Suzanne M. Johnson is Admissions Director; David B. Stephens is Headmaster.

KANSAS

St. John's Military School   1887

Box 827, End of North Santa Fe, Salina, KS 67402-0827.
913-823-7231; Fax 913-823-7236; E-mail Moniqueb@sjms.org;
Web Site http://www.sjms.org

Founded by the Episcopal Bishop of Kansas, St. John's Military School is a boarding school enrolling 200 boys in Grades 7–12. The School strives to provide each cadet with an understanding of the role of God in his life, an awareness of his potential, an appreciation of discipline, and the instruction and encouragement necessary for academic growth. High School ROTC and religion courses are required for all students. Sports, Chapel Council, forensics, service organizations, and interest clubs are among the activities. Tuition: $15,410. Extras: $2000 plus uniforms. Financial Aid: $80,000. Capt. E. A. McAlexander (United States Naval Academy, B.S. 1965; George Washington University, M.S.A. 1974) was appointed President in 1993. *North Central Association.*

Topeka Collegiate School   1979

2200 SW Eveningside Drive, Topeka, KS 66614. 785-228-0490;
Fax 785-228-0504; Admissions E-mail phuff@topekacollegiate.org;
Web Site www.ksnews.com/tcschool

Topeka Collegiate is a precollege preparatory school serving more than 280 girls and boys in Pre-Kindergarten–Grade 8. The challenging curriculum is taught by dedicated professionals who provide individual attention in small classes. The lower division emphasizes mastery of basic skills and the application of good study habits in anticipation of the more complex subject matter in the Middle School. The core curriculum at both levels consists of language arts, math, science, social studies, computer, and foreign language, enriched by art, music, and physical education; extra support is available to students with developmental reading disorders. Field trips and after-school activities are available. Tuition: $4390–$5390. Paula Huff is Admissions Director; Michael B. Roberts, Ed.D., is Head of School.

Wichita Collegiate School   1963

9115 East Thirteenth Street, Wichita, KS 67206. 316-634-0433;
Fax 316-634-0598 (Main Campus) or 316-634-0273
(Upper School); E-mail wcsadmit@feist.com; Web Site
http://www.collegiate.wichita.ks.us

Wichita Collegiate School is a college preparatory day school enrolling 930 boys and girls in Preschool–Grade 12. Faculty dedication, parental involvement, a culturally literate curriculum, and the teaching of values characterize the objectives of the School. The School complements traditional subjects with full programs in music, art, drama, and athletics. The Upper School provides Advanced Placement courses in 17 disciplines in addition to a vigorous varsity sports program, publications, and academic bowl competitions. Tuition: $1610–$8158. Financial Aid: $450,000. Susie Steed is Director of Admission; Dr. John W. Cooper is Headmaster.

KENTUCKY

Kentucky Country Day School   1972

4100 Springdale Road, Louisville, KY 40241. 502-423-0440

Louisville Country Day School for boys (founded 1950) and Kentucky Home School for girls (1863) merged to form Kentucky Country Day. The School enrolls 372 boys and 351 girls in Kindergarten–Grade 12. The college preparatory curriculum emphasizes excellence in academics, athletics, and the arts. The School aims to provide an atmosphere that stimulates learning and encourages personal growth. Students participate in team sports, publications, drama, and chorus. A summer day camp for ages 6–12 offers a recreation program. Tuition: $7450–$9625, including lunch. Extras: $100–$400. Financial Aid: $600,000. Ms. Kathleen Ary is Director of Admissions; Robert Blair is Headmaster.

Lexington Catholic High School   1951

2250 Clays Mill Road, Lexington, KY 40503-1797. 606-277-7183; Fax 606-278-4596; Web Site www.lexingtoncatholic.com

Lexington Catholic High School serves 860 Catholic students and students of other faith traditions by providing a high-quality secondary education that emphasizes the spiritual ideals and moral values of the Gospel. Lexington Catholic accomplishes this mission by offering a full academic, athletic, and cocurricular program in an intimate setting that provides each student a wide variety of ways to participate, to be challenged, and to excel. The curriculum emphasizes college preparation, including Advanced Placement and honors courses. Tuition: $3810 (Catholic)–$5100 (non-Catholic). Robert Bueter, SJ, is President; Mrs. Sally Stevens is Principal. *Southern Association.*

The Lexington School   LEXINGTON

1050 Lane Allen Road, Lexington, KY 40504. 606-278-0501; Web Site www.thelexingtonschool.org

THE LEXINGTON SCHOOL in Lexington, Kentucky, is a coeducational day school enrolling students in Montessori or traditional preschool classes and in Grades 1–9. Located in the heart of Kentucky's celebrated Bluegrass Country, the Lexington-Fayette metropolitan area (population 318,000) is served by a local airport and is accessible by car via interstate highways 64 and 75. Lexington, which is known for its many thoroughbred horse farms, also boasts a wealth of historic, cultural, and educational resources including the University of Kentucky and Transylvania University.

The Lexington School was founded in 1959 by Josephine Abercrombie and other interested members of the community who were committed to offering a quality independent education to local children. It opened with 5 teachers and 65 students and has expanded its facilities steadily to accommodate its present enrollment of over 500 students and a 64-member faculty.

The School's philosophy sets high standards of achievement in scholastics, athletics, and the fine and performing arts while instilling moral values, social responsibility, and respect for others. Through an academic curriculum that will prepare them for challenging high schools, students are encouraged to "learn to learn" with the expectation that the skills acquired at The Lexington School will lead to a lifetime love of learning.

The Lexington School is a nonprofit organization governed by a self-perpetuating Board of 24 Trustees, all of whom are parents, past parents, or alumni, that meets five times a year. More than 800 alumni assist the School through fundraising and support of events throughout the year. Parents, particularly the Parents' Association, play an active role in the school and in the planning and implementation of special events. The Lexington School is accredited by the Independent Schools Association of the Central States and holds membership in the National Association of Independent Schools, the Council for Advancement and Support of Education, the Educational Records Bureau, and the Kentucky Association of Independent Schools.

THE CAMPUS. Situated on an 18-acre campus in the southwestern suburbs, The Lexington School's original classroom building (1959) has been expanded three times to provide more spacious facilities, including two gymnasiums, a fine arts wing, a darkroom, computer laboratories, a theater, and a library of more than 15,000 volumes. There are also two soccer fields, two playgrounds, and an outdoor basketball court.

The property, which is owned by the School, is valued at more than $3,000,000.

THE FACULTY. John D. Fixx was named Headmaster in 1998. A native of Greenwich, Connecticut, Mr. Fixx holds an undergraduate degree in English from Wesleyan University and a Master of Business Administration degree from the University of Connecticut. Before coming to The Lexington School, Mr. Fixx taught sixth-grade English and was Assistant Headmaster and Director of the Upper School at The Country School in Madison, Connecticut. He has served as Director of Admissions, teacher, coach, and advisor at Westminster School in Simsbury, Connecticut; Bancroft School in Worcester, Massachusetts; and Hoosac School in Hoosick, New York. The past president of the Northeastern Boarding Schools Admissions Association, Mr. Fixx has sat on the Steering Committee of the Connecticut Association of Independent Schools' Commission on School Advancement, is a former member of the Public Relations Committee of the Secondary School Admission Test Board, and a Founding Convener of the Round Table.

There are 56 women and 8 men on the full-time faculty. They have earned baccalaureate and advanced degrees from colleges and universities in the United States and Canada including Baylor, Boston College, Centre College, Colgate, East Tennessee, Georgetown, Iowa State, Lander College, Louisiana State, Macalester, Michigan State, Middlebury, State University of New York, Transylvania, Western Kentucky, William and Mary, Xavier, and the Universities of Arkansas, Georgia, Illinois, Kentucky, Louisville, North Dakota, West Virginia, and Wisconsin. Faculty benefits include Social Security, health and retirement plans, and tuition remission.

STUDENT BODY. In 1999–2000, The Lexington School enrolled 509 students, 245 girls and 264 boys, in Preschool through Grade

9. They come from Lexington and surrounding counties and represent a variety of ethnic and socioeconomic backgrounds.

ACADEMIC PROGRAM. The school year, divided into quarters, begins in late summer and ends in early June with a Thanksgiving recess and Christmas, midwinter, and spring vacations. Classes, with an average of 16 students, are conducted on a six-day rotating schedule from 8:15 A.M. to 3:15 P.M. After-school supervision is available until 6:00 P.M. Grades are sent to parents twice a year, and conferences with faculty are regularly scheduled.

The Preschool programs include a Montessori classroom for children ages three to five, a three-year-old KinderKlasse, a four-year-old Pre-Kindergarten, and a Kindergarten for five-year-olds, each staffed by two teachers. Grades 1–3 are traditional, self-contained classrooms; Grades 4–5 are team-taught. The aim of the Lower School program is to stimulate each child's cognitive, social, emotional, physical, and creative development to the maximum. Instruction in science, music, art, computer literacy, library skills, and physical education is provided by special teachers.

In the Montessori class, sequentially ordered material introduces children to basic concepts in mathematics, language, science, and social studies.

The Pre-Kindergarten program, designed to foster self-esteem and a love of learning, is conducted in an action-oriented environment in which students work and play, either individually or in small, teacher-directed groups.

Readiness skills in mathematics and language are emphasized in the Kindergarten curriculum, and students have opportunities to develop fine- and gross-motor skills and to explore various artistic media. The daily routine also features discussion and free play.

Students in Grades 1–3 begin to explore the tools and techniques of reading, writing, spelling, and mathematics, and in Grade 3, use these skills in increasingly formal communication, problem-solving, research, and creative projects. Music, art, computers, science, library, and physical education are taught by special teachers outside the regular classroom. Foreign language is introduced in Preschool.

Because Grades 4–5 are team-taught, the schedule can accommodate interdisciplinary blocks of instruction in language arts and social studies as well as in science and mathematics. Music, art, library science, and computers are included in the curriculum, and, beginning in Grade 4, students elect the formal study of either French or Spanish.

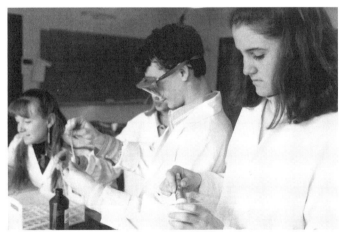

The Middle School (Grades 6–8) program consists of English, history, French or Spanish, mathematics, science, fine arts, and physical education and health. Mathematics classes are achievement-sectioned; all classes are small in size.

The computer lab is used to enhance all areas of the curriculum. A language arts writing lab helps strengthen students' grammar and composition skills.

The Grade 9 Freshman Experience is an accelerated academic program. While students share many of the facilities and routines of the Middle School, the program is designed to prepare them for the rigors of high school. Small class size, supportive relationships with teachers, and opportunities to hone leadership skills and increase a sense of personal responsibility for success are hallmarks of the program.

The majority of ninth-grade graduates enroll in Fayette County schools while approximately one-fourth enter independent boarding schools such as Andover, Deerfield, Episcopal High School, Exeter, Groton, Hotchkiss, McCallie, Miss Porter's, St. Paul's, Salisbury, Taft, Westminster, and Woodberry Forest.

Camp Curiosity is a two-week summer program for children ages 4–6 offering educational and recreational activities.

STUDENT ACTIVITIES. The Student Council plans and implements activities such as the Carnival, dances, a spring prom, and bake sales. Extracurricular groups, varying according to student interest, have included band, chorus, yearbook, newspaper, Spanish Club, Chess Club, Speech Team, and a string ensemble.

Traditional events are scheduled throughout the year for specific grades, including field trips to local points of interest for lower grades, a one-week program of outdoor physical and environmental education for sixth, seventh, and eighth grades, and a signature trip out west for Grade 9. Other special events are language festivals, the Community Service Program, and the Fine Arts programs. Interscholastic sports include soccer, basketball, volleyball, and tennis.

ADMISSION AND COSTS. The Lexington School welcomes students from a variety of backgrounds who can benefit from a rigorous scholastic program and who will contribute to the School's academic vitality. New students are accepted to all grades based on testing, teacher recommendations, and previous school transcripts. Application, accompanied by a $75 fee, may be made at any time, and students are accepted throughout the year if there are vacancies.

In 1999–2000, tuition, including lunch, books, and other expenses, ranges from $4900 in Pre-Kindergarten to $9040 in Grade 9. Financial aid of nearly $300,000 was awarded to 56 students on the basis of need. Tuition insurance and a monthly payment plan are offered. The Lexington School subscribes to the School and Student Service for Financial Aid.

Director of Admissions: Chip Audett
Boarding School Counselor: Jack Brost
Business Manager: Robert Thompson
Director of Athletics: Tom Parlanti

Louisville Collegiate School   1915

2427 Glenmary Avenue, Louisville, KY 40204. 502-451-5330;
   Admissions 502-479-0340; Fax 502-454-8549;
   E-mail admission@www.loucol.com; Web Site www.loucol.com

Louisville Collegiate School is a coeducational, college preparatory day school enrolling students in Kindergarten–Grade 12. The School strives to develop in all students an awareness of their potential, a respect for their peers, and a sense of responsibility to their community. Sophisticated technology is a major component in Collegiate's curriculum, which is also enhanced by an interim of special study in late winter and a summer program of enrichment and academic options. Activities include athletics, clubs, drama, student government, and publications. Tuition: $5550–$10,400. Financial Aid: $613,555. Barbara B. Groves (Oberlin, A.B.; Portland State University, M.S.T.) was appointed Head of School in 1998.

Millersburg Military Academy   1893

1122 Main Street, P.O. Box 278, Millersburg, KY 40348.
   606-484-3352; Fax 606-484-3342; E-mail kymilsch@aol.com

Founded to provide quality education for young men, Kentucky's only military school today enrolls 113 males as boarders and 15 males and 3 females as day students in Grades 7–12. Millersburg Military Academy, located in the heart of Bluegrass Country, offers a college preparatory curriculum combined with military training and discipline designed to prepare each cadet for the duties of citizenship and the responsibilities of life. Drill team, rifle teams, and varsity athletics are primary extracurricular activities. A summer session offers academics and leadership skills. Boarding Tuition: $11,290; Day Tuition: $6050. Patrick Baker is Director of Admissions; Roy W. Berwick (University of Nebraska, B.A.; Jacksonville State, M.A.; Creighton University, J.D.) was appointed President in 1998. *Southern Association.*

Shedd Academy   1974

401 South 7th Street, P.O. Box 493, Mayfield, KY 42066.
   502-247-8007; Fax 502-247-0637; E-mail shedd@apex.net;
   Web Site sheddacademy.org

Shedd Academy was developed by concerned parents and professionals to assist boys and girls with attention deficit, dyslexia, and other learning disabilities. The school enrolls 12 day students and 24 boarders in Grades 1–12. Its mission is to prepare these young people for college and the future through motivation, a highly personalized curriculum, counseling, development of learning skills, tutorial assistance, and the formulation of educational and career objectives. Classes average one teacher per every five students. A summer program offers remediation as well as courses for credit. Boarding Tuition: $16,350; Day Tuition: $10,250. Financial Aid: $30,000. Mrs. Debbie Craven is Admissions Director; Paul L. Thompson, Ed.D., is Executive Director.

University Heights Academy   1973

1300 Academy Drive, Hopkinsville, KY 42240-2654. 270-886-
   0254; E-mail uha~ky.org

University Heights Academy is a coeducational, college preparatory day school enrolling a diverse student body of 370 members in three-year Pre-School–Grade 12. In a stimulating intellectual environment, the school aims to inspire high ideals and academic standards of excellence in readiness for leadership in today's society. Small classes and a 10:1 student-faculty ratio permit individual attention and support. The curriculum emphasizes the liberal arts and sciences, complemented by hands-on technology, special programs, and field trips. Grades 9–12 enjoy an off-campus week of outdoor school. Among the activities are publications, clubs, and athletics. Tuition: $3145. Financial aid is available. Linda Ledford is Head of School.

LOUISIANA

Academy of the Sacred Heart 1887

*4521 St. Charles Avenue, New Orleans, LA 70115. 504-891-1943;
Fax 504-891-9939; E-mail dkilleen@ashrosary.org;
Web Site www.ashrosary.org*

A Catholic, college preparatory day school, Academy of the Sacred Heart enrolls 800 girls in Nursery–Grade 12. The Religious of the Sacred Heart guide the school, which aims to educate students to faith, intellectual vigor, and social awareness within a Christian community that is concerned for the personal growth of each member. While emphasizing strong academics, including Advanced Placement courses, the Academy offers athletics and cocurricular activities as well as exchange opportunities in the United States and abroad. Community service is required in the junior year. Tuition: $3750–$7000. Financial aid is available. Diane Killeen is Director of Admission; Sr. Shirley Miller (Duchesne, B.A.; St. Thomas, M.R.E.; University of Notre Dame, M.S.) is Headmistress.

Episcopal High School 1964

*3200 Woodland Ridge Boulevard, Baton Rouge, LA 70816.
225-753-3180; Fax 225-756-0507; E-mail hillr@ehsbr.org*

Episcopal High is a college preparatory day school enrolling 1020 boys and girls in Kindergarten–Grade 12. The rigorous academic program, along with a wide range of athletics, music, art, and drama, prepares students for entrance to selective colleges nationwide. The presence of the Episcopal Church encourages students to face issues of faith and social responsibility. Literature-based reading programs, writing across the curriculum, international studies, and computer-assisted instruction are major themes in the curriculum. Tuition: $5500–$8500. Financial Aid: $700,000. Ruth Hill is Director of Admission and Financial Aid; the Reverend Paul B. Hancock (Bristol University [England], M.A. 1972) was appointed Headmaster in 1983.

The Episcopal School of Acadiana 1979

*P.O. Box 380, Cade, LA 70519. 318-365-1416; Fax 318-367-9841;
E-mail esacadiana.com; Web Site www.esacadiana.org*

The Episcopal School of Acadiana, enrolling 400 day boys and girls in Grades 6 through 12, provides an "open, free, unconfin-

ing learning environment" designed to foster independence and responsibility within a Christian setting. The college preparatory curriculum is flexible and individualized to encourage the highest potential compatible with each student's abilities and interests. Advanced Placement and honors courses, independent study, and overseas travel enrich the program. Team sports for boys and girls, wilderness survival, and drama are among the activities. Tuition: $7300. Mary Buie Skelton is Director of Admissions; Hiram J. Goza (Vanderbilt University, B.A. 1975; University of Virginia, M.Ed. 1978) is Headmaster.

Isidore Newman School 1903

*1903 Jefferson Avenue, New Orleans, LA 70115-5699.
504-899-5641; Fax 504-896-8597; Web Site
www.Newman.K12.LA.US*

Philanthropist Isidore Newman founded this college preparatory school enrolling boys and girls in Pre-Kindergarten–Grade 12. In a challenging academic program, students gain knowledge in the humanities, sciences, and fine arts as they demonstrate mastery of material, meet high academic standards, and grow in conceptual understanding. In addition to foreign language, computer, and human development, Advanced Placement and independent study are offered across the curriculum. Athletics, publications, debate, community service, and student clubs are available. Newman also provides extended-day care, after-school activities, and a summer session. Tuition: $6540–$10,340. Financial Aid: $1,029,207. Merry P. Sorrells is Admission Director; Scott McLeod is Headmaster.

The Louise S. McGehee School 1912

*2343 Prytania Street, New Orleans, LA 70130. 504-561-1224;
Fax 504-525-7910; E-mail gate@mcgehee.k12.la.us; Web Site
www.mcgehee.k12.la.us*

Louise Schaumburg McGehee founded this independent, college preparatory day school in 1912, believing young women had a right to the challenge of learning in an atmosphere of intellectual and creative stimulation. Enrolled are 365 girls in Pre-Kindergarten–Grade 12. The School seeks to develop in its students the habit of considering themselves initiators and achievers. Extracurricular activities include athletics, drama club, choir, ensemble, spirit club, language clubs, and a community service club. Tuition: $4400–$9400. Financial aid is available. Pamela K. Schott is Director of Admission; Eileen Friel Powers (Marymount Manhattan College, B.S.; University of Massachusetts, M.A.T.) was appointed Headmistress in 1998. *Southern Association.*

Metairie Park Country Day School 1929

300 Park Road, Metairie, LA 70005. 504-837-5204; Fax 504-837-0015; E-mail admissions@mpcds.com; Web Site www.mpcds.com

Metairie Park Country Day School offers a unique learning environment that challenges students to fully develop their own talents. The nonsectarian, coeducational School enrolls 735 students in Kindergarten–Grade 12. All graduates pursue college degrees. The 14-acre campus in a quiet, safe residential neighborhood is accessible from all parts of the city. Honors and Advanced Placement courses are offered in all Upper School disciplines. The fine arts are emphasized at all age levels. The technology program includes a campus-wide network. Successful athletic teams involve 90 percent of Middle School and 75 percent Upper School students. Tuition: $8270–$10,245. Financial Aid: $600,000. Dr. David Drinkwater is Headmaster. *Southern Association.*

Ridgewood Preparatory School 1948

201 Pasadena Avenue, Metairie, LA 70001-4899. 504-835-2545; Fax 504-837-1864; E-mail RPS502JUNO.COM; Web Site WWW.RIDGEWOODPREP.COM

Ridgewood Preparatory School is a day school enrolling 527 boys and girls in Pre-Kindergarten–Grade 12. Its aim is to prepare students for college and life through development of intellectual skills, awareness of the world and its beauties, participation in society, and preparation for a vocation. Beginning in Pre-Kindergarten, the School provides a traditional curriculum including art, music, and physical education. Student government, service and activity clubs, publications, band, and interscholastic sports are among the activities. A summer program in instrumental music is offered. Tuition: $2940—$4620. Thomas Rouprich is Director of Admissions; M. J. Montgomery, Jr. (Loyola, B.S. 1959, M.Ed. 1962), was appointed Headmaster in 1972. *Southern Association.*

St. Andrew's Episcopal School 1957

8012 Oak Street, New Orleans, LA 70118. 504-861-3743; Fax 504-861-3973; E-mail office@standrews.k12.la.us

St. Andrew's Episcopal School, founded by the Reverend Ralph Kimball and the Vestry of St. Andrew's Episcopal Church, enrolls 80 day boys and 80 day girls in Pre-Kindergarten–Grade 6. The School aims to teach the fundamental skills necessary for academic success in a challenging and supportive atmosphere. Spanish, music, fine arts, computers, athletics, and library science are included in the curriculum. Students attend chapel programs three times a week. Publications, advisory council, dramatics, intramurals, and service programs are among the activities. Tuition: $4552–$5546. Financial aid is available. Gary J. Mannina (Tulane University, B.A., M.A.) was appointed Headmaster in 1986.

St. Martin's Episcopal School 1947

5309 Airline Drive, Metairie, LA 70003. 504-736-9917; Fax 504-733-2339

A diocesan-sponsored, coeducational day school enrolling 825 students in Prekindergarten–Grade 12, St. Martin's Episcopal School provides a challenging college preparatory education focused on developing the whole person within the context of a Christian, family environment. The Upper School offers 22 honors and Advanced Placement courses; community service is required. Performing and visual arts, computer literacy, and developmental and college counseling are integral to the program. Activities include student government, publications, and championship sports teams involving 70 percent of the student body. Tuition: $4700–$9650. Margaret Beacham Schuber is Director of Admission; Leo P. Dressel is President and Head of School.

Saint Paul's Episcopal School 1961

6249 Canal Boulevard, New Orleans, LA 70124. 504-486-0566; Fax 504-482-6893

This Blue Ribbon School of Excellence is a learning community comprised of 27 full-time faculty and 245 children from many faith backgrounds enrolled as day students in Kindergarten–Grade 8. The School, which was founded as an outreach of St. Paul's Episcopal Church, aims to offer an excellent education imbued with Christian values. The academic program emphasizes the liberal arts and sciences integrated with computer technology and religious instruction. Small classes, with a 9:1 student-teacher ratio, ensure individual attention to each child. Youngsters take part in Student Council, Panther Pride Choir, Chess Club, and athletics. Tuition: $6355–$6795. Pat Hemenway is Admission Director; Charles J. Hemenway is Head of School.

Southfield School 1934

1100 Southfield Road, Shreveport, LA 71106. 318-868-5375; Fax 318-868-0890; E-mail ccoburn@southfield-school.org; Web Site www.southfield-school.org

Southfield was founded by a group of local residents to provide the finest educational opportunity possible for the children of Shreveport. The preparatory day school serves 404 boys and girls in Preschool through Grade 8. The liberal arts curriculum challenges students' intellects and curiosity through coursework that emphasizes reading, writing, and language skills. The intelligent application of technology underscores every component of the program, and all students have access to state-of-the-art, computer-assisted instruction. Extended care is offered. Tuition: $1670–$5550. Financial aid is available. Clare Coburn is Admissions Director; Jeffrey Stokes (State University of New York, B.A.; University of North Carolina, M.A.T.) is Headmaster. *Southern Association.*

Trinity Episcopal School 1916

1315 Jackson Avenue, New Orleans, LA 70130. 504-525-8661; Fax 504-523-4837

This independent day school of Trinity Episcopal Church enrolls 200 boys and 200 girls in Pre-Kindergarten–Grade 8. Dedicated to the academic, emotional, social, and spiritual growth of its students, the School strives to develop individual learners and thinkers who are responsible for their lifelong learning. To achieve this end, high academic standards are maintained. The curriculum emphasizes strong basic skills that are augmented and expanded upon each year. Computer education, foreign languages, fine arts, and athletics are integral to the curriculum. An afternoon enrichment program for Kindergartners and extended care are offered. Tuition: $4450–$8700. Financial Aid: $259,000. Julian P. Bull (Dartmouth, A.B. 1982; Boston College, M.A. 1988) was appointed Headmaster in 1994.

MAINE

Bridgton Academy   1808

P.O. Box 292, North Bridgton, ME 04057. 207-647-3322;
   Fax 207-647-8513; E-mail admit@mail.bacad.bridgton.me.us;
   Web Site www.bacad.bridgton.me.us/banet

Bridgton Academy is the only college preparatory school in the nation exclusively devoted to a one-year postgraduate program for young men. The school is committed to helping 175 boarding and day students develop the academic skills, study skills, self-discipline, and self-confidence to succeed in college and beyond. Students with the potential, motivation, character, and commitment to benefit from and contribute to the program are welcome. Both the student's academic program and college counseling are individualized and monitored closely. School government, athletics, publications, and clubs are among the activities. Room, Board, and Tuition: $24,000; Day Tuition: $9000. Financial Aid: $800,000. Lisa M. Antell is Director of Admission and Financial Aid; Randall M. Greason was appointed Headmaster in 1997. *New England Association.*

Fryeburg Academy   FRYEBURG

Fryeburg, ME 04037-1329. 877-935-2001; Fax 207-935-4292;
   E-mail admissions@fryeburgacademy.org;
   Web Site www.fryeburgacademy.org

Fryeburg academy in Fryeburg, Maine, is a boarding and day school enrolling boys and girls in Grades 9 through 12 and a postgraduate year. Recognizing that young people of varying aptitudes, interests, and abilities must be prepared to meet the challenges of a complex world, Fryeburg offers both college preparatory and business/pre-vocational curricula. Students have the opportunity to study and explore both areas. While most are preparing for college, others may choose programs leading to work in specialized schools and institutes.

Since 1792, the Academy has served as a day school for youths from Fryeburg and nearby towns, while at the same time admitting boarding students from other states and foreign countries. The founders of the Academy were 15 leading citizens of the area, each of whom helped to underwrite the construction of the first building. The Charter of Incorporation, issued by the Commonwealth of Massachusetts, was signed by Samuel Phillips and John Hancock. Daniel Webster served as Headmaster in 1802–03.

Fryeburg Academy is incorporated not-for-profit and is supervised by the Headmaster for a self-perpetuating Board of Trustees consisting of 11 regular and 6 emeritus members. Included in the corporate assets are a physical plant valued at $9,500,000 plus approximately $4,700,000 in productive endowments. The school is accredited by the New England Association of Schools and Colleges and holds membership in the National Association of Independent Schools, The College Board, and the Maine Association of Independent Schools, among other affiliations.

THE CAMPUS. Located in the Eastern Slopes region of the White Mountains, Fryeburg is a rural community (population 3500) surrounded by lakes, streams, and mountains. The resort area of North Conway, New Hampshire, is 10 miles west; Portland, Maine, is 50 miles southeast; and Boston is 160 miles southeast.

The brick and frame buildings on campus represent several periods of construction. The main building is a large brick structure with administrative offices and two classroom wings, including a computer lab, and a library. A wing containing a dining hall/student union was added in 1984. The Eastman Science Building (1996) houses six modern laboratory classrooms. Students live in brick dormitories constructed between 1961 and 1969 and remodeled in 1998; each dormitory is supervised by resident faculty members. Gibson Recreational Center contains the main gymnasium, in addition to another building that houses a weight and exercise room. Other units include the infirmary, the industrial arts building, the music studio, the foreign language building, and a number of faculty homes and apartments.

Converse Fields, which occupy much of the central portion of the 25-acre campus, were rebuilt and substantially enlarged in 1962. A new baseball field was finished in June 1987. There are also football, soccer, and hockey fields; tennis courts; and a quarter-mile asphalt-and-rubber track. Within walking distance is a cross-country skiing course and a recreational hockey rink. Daily access is provided to four mountains for recreational/competitive downhill skiing and snowboarding.

THE FACULTY. Daniel G. Lee, Jr., who became Headmaster in 1993, is a graduate of Yale College and holds a masters degree from Wesleyan University. Prior to his appointment at Fryeburg Academy, Mr. Lee was Headmaster of Miss Hall's School from 1984 to 1992. Previously, he served as Director of Development at The Taft School and Director of Admissions at Trinity-Pawling School. He lives on the Academy campus with his wife, Susan, and son, Daniel.

The faculty consist of 51 instructors and administrators, 30 men and 21 women. Twenty-three faculty members live on campus, 9 with their families. The faculty hold baccalaureate and graduate degrees from such institutions as Ball State, Berea, Boston College, Bowdoin, Bucknell, Clarion University, Colby, Cornell, Drew University, Hamilton, Hobart, Husson, Massachusetts Institute of Technology, Rhode Island School of Design, Southern Connecticut State University, Thomas Jefferson, Western Illinois, Wheaton, Yale, Yankton College, and the Universities of Delaware, Maine, Minnesota, Nebraska, and Southern Maine. The teachers have a retirement plan and a medical insurance plan.

The infirmary is staffed by a full-time registered nurse. Doctors, dentists, and other health professionals are available in Fryeburg.

STUDENT BODY. The enrollment consists of 54 boarding boys, 36 boarding girls, 262 day boys, and 250 day girls in Grades 9–12 and a postgraduate year.

In 1999–2000, boarding students come from Florida, Illinois, Maine, Massachusetts, New Hampshire, New Jersey, New York, Pennsylvania, Austria, Bermuda, Brazil, China, France, Germany, Japan, Korea, Latvia, Saudi Arabia, Spain, Taiwan, Tibet, the Ukraine, Venezuela, and West Africa.

ACADEMIC PROGRAM. The school year, from early September to early June, is divided into two terms. The schedule includes a Thanksgiving recess; vacations at Christmas and in February and April; and long weekends for Columbus Day, Presidents' Day, and Memorial Day. Classes meet five days a week beginning at 7:55 A.M. and ending at 2:34 P.M.

There are 17 students in an average academic class and the ratio of students to faculty is 16:1. Faculty members and administrators serve as special advisers to small groups of students, providing counseling on an individual basis whenever necessary. Homework is required for each class meeting. All students have study periods during the class day and the opportunity to receive extra help in the learning center; boarding students also have two-hour supervised study periods on Sunday through Thursday evenings. Grades are sent to parents every six weeks.

Each new student is tested in the fall to develop an appropriate academic program. The individual programming enables a student to pursue specific areas of study without eliminating other possible objectives. For example, a student interested in Industrial Arts may choose applicable courses and, at the same time, satisfy basic college entrance requirements.

Among the courses offered are English; French, Spanish, Latin, Introduction to Languages; United States History, European History, World Cultures, World Geography, Problems of Democracy, Economics, Psychology; Algebra 1–3, Geometry, Calculus; Chemistry, Physics, Anatomy, Horticulture, Marine Studies, Biology, Anatomy; Computer Studies; Industrial Arts; Accounting, Driver Education; and Physical Education. Accelerated programs are available in English, social studies, mathematics, and science. Advanced Placement courses are offered in English, United States History, and calculus. A Special Services/Reading Program, available at additional cost, includes tutoring as well as specialized instruction by certified staff.

In 1999, 73 percent of the graduating class went on to college. They entered such institutions as Bates, Bentley, Boston University, Bowdoin, Clark, Clarkson, Colby-Sawyer, Embry-Riddle, Fordham, Maine College of Art, New York University, Northeastern, Purdue, Rensselaer, Rochester Institute of Technology, Roger Williams, St. Joseph's, Syracuse, Worcester Polytechnic, and the Universities of Maine, New Hampshire, Southern Maine, and Tampa.

STUDENT ACTIVITIES. A Dormitory Council is elected by resident students, and an elected student government provides liaison between students and faculty, while most disciplinary responsibilities rest with a committee composed of students, faculty members, and administration officials.

Clubs and activities are organized around current student interests. Typical extracurricular activities are the National Honor Society, the yearbook, the newspaper, student government, chorus, and the Latin, French, Spanish, Recycling, Junior Rescue, SADD, Debating, Outing, and Photography clubs. Instruction in vocal or instrumental music may be arranged, and numerous dramatic productions are presented throughout the school year. The Outing Club organizes climbs in the Presidential Range of the White Mountains, canoe trips on the Saco River, and hikes in nearby hills; overnight outings include faculty participation. Fishing and recreational ice skating, swimming, and skiing are also offered in season.

All students are encouraged to participate in an afternoon activity or an intramural or interscholastic sport. Because of the Academy's location, winter sports are popular, particularly skiing. Baseball, football, basketball, wrestling, skiing, track, cross-country, soccer, field hockey, tennis, golf, and softball are offered as team sports. Interscholastic teams compete with both private and public area schools.

Throughout the year, there are dances, parties, and such special events as Homecoming, Parents' Weekend, and Winter Carnival. Free time is available each day and on weekends for students to participate in social activities, attend movies, ski, take short trips, or pursue individual interests. Students are free to leave campus on weekends with parental permission and the Dean's approval.

ADMISSION AND COSTS. Admission to Fryeburg is based upon an evaluation of the applicant's character and capacity to benefit from the school's educational program. A personal interview at the Academy is recommended. The school has a policy of admitting students of any race, color, nationality, or ethnic origin.

The annual charge for tuition, room, and board in 1999–2000 is $20,800; day tuition is $8250. Extras include the application fee ($35) and insurance. An amount of $15–$20 per week is recommended for personal spending. The fee for the Special Services/Reading Program is $3000 per year; there is an additional $1250 fee per semester in the English as a Second Language program.

Scholarship assistance is available based on need and student citizenship. In 1999, 38 students were awarded $495,000 in financial assistance.

Deans of Students: David Turner and James Thurston
Alumni Secretary: Carolee Foster
Director of Admissions: Alan D. Whittemore
Director of Development: Timothy Scott
College Counselor: Louis Gnerre
Business Manager: Joseph Burney
Director of Athletics: Charles Tryder

Gould Academy   1836

Church Street, P.O. Box 860, Bethel, ME 04217. 207-824-7700; Admissions 207-824-7777; Fax 207-824-2926; E-mail contact@gouldacademy.org; Web Site www.gouldacademy.org

A boarding school enrolling 235 boys and girls in Grades 9–Postgraduate, Gould challenges students with solid academic records to take an active role in their own education. Key elements of the curriculum are a strong English department with emphasis on writing, a diverse art program, supervised study, international exchanges, and Internet and networked software access from all classrooms and dorm rooms. English as a Second Language, Scholastic Support Services, and nationally recognized ski and snowboard programs are offered. Boarding Tuition: $25,900; Day Tuition: $15,850. Financial Aid: $900,000. William P. Clough III (Colby, B.A.; Middlebury, M.A.) was appointed Headmaster in 1983. *New England Association.*

Hebron Academy   HEBRON

Hebron, ME 04238. 207-966-2100 or 888-432-7664 [Toll-free in U.S.]; Fax 207-966-1111

Hebron academy in Hebron, Maine, is a coeducational, college preparatory boarding and day school dedicated to fostering academic excellence, integrity, and community. Hebron's campus accommodates three divisions: Lower School (Kindergarten–Grade 4), Middle School (Grades 5–8), and Upper School (Grades 9–12 and postgraduates). Students enjoy modern facilities for research and study as well as an incomparable setting for environmental study and outdoor activity. Hebron is 6 miles from the twin towns of Norway and South Paris and 16 miles from the larger cities of Auburn and Lewiston. The Academy is an hour's drive from Portland and three hours from Boston.

Chartered in 1804 to provide college preparation in liberal arts and sciences, Hebron is governed by a self-perpetuating Board of Trustees. Hebron Academy is accredited by the New England Association of Schools and Colleges and is a member of the National Association of Independent Schools, The College Board, The Secondary School Admission Test Board, and The Cum Laude Society.

THE CAMPUS. Hebron Academy's 1500-acre campus is surrounded by the hills, streams, woods, lakes, and mountains of western Maine. At its center, the Academy's buildings surround a spacious open area known as The Bowl, with faculty homes, the Chabourne Outdoor Center, and athletic fields and running trails spreading out beyond. The focus of academic life is Sturtevant Hall (1897), listed on the National Register of Historic Places, which accommodates classrooms and offices. Flanking Sturtevant Hall are Treat Science Hall, which houses classrooms, laboratories, technology center, observatory, and greenhouse; and Hupper Library, center for the 16,500-volume circulating collection, reference and periodical collections, archives, and art gallery. There are more than 28 classrooms on campus plus two lecture halls, five art studios, two darkrooms, a musical recital room and practice rooms, and an outdoor center and classroom.

Hebron's athletic facilities include Sargent Gymnasium with a swimming pool, two basketball courts, weight room and dance facility, Robinson ice arena, five playing fields, two diamonds, a recently completed $75,000 all-weather track, six tennis courts, running and Nordic ski trails, and an 800-acre Wilderness Tract.

Students are housed in double and single rooms in three dormitories. Junior and senior boys live in the central dormitory, Sturtevant Home, which also houses the Fine Arts Center, school dining services, and the health center. Freshman and sophomore boys reside across The Bowl in Atwood Dormitory.

All girls live in Halford Hall, which also houses the Leyden Student Center. All dormitories have common rooms and are supervised by resident faculty and student proctors.

THE FACULTY. Dr. Richard B. Davidson, appointed Headmaster in 1993, received an A.B. degree in English from Amherst College, an M.A. from Harvard University, and a Ph.D. from the University of Colorado. He has taught, coached, and done administrative work at Cushing Academy, Fountain Valley School, and Cincinnati Country Day School. He has taught English at the University of Colorado, Idaho State University, and Bates College. Since coming to Hebron in 1982, Dr. Davidson has served as Director of Admissions, Head of the English Department, and Director of Development before becoming Headmaster.

Hebron's faculty represents a diverse and talented resource combining long-tenured experience with the vigor of recent research and scholarship. Of the 24 women and 28 men on the faculty, 22 hold master's degrees and 2 hold Ph.D.'s. Forty live on campus, and 18 faculty members or couples reside on-corridor in the three dormitories.

Hebron's Health Center is staffed by three registered nurses; school physicians hold office hours twice weekly and are available in case of emergency. The Academy also retains a psychiatrist.

STUDENT BODY. In 1999–2000, Hebron enrolled 125 boarding and 90 day students. There were 33 in Grade 9, 50 in Grade 10, 66 in Grade 11, and 66 in Grade 12. In addition, there were 62 students in Hebron's all-day Middle School and 48 in Lower School. Students came from 15 states and ten countries.

ACADEMIC PROGRAM. Learning and teaching at Hebron are in the active voice. Students work in a variety of contexts to develop and understand the process of inquiry and investigation. The curriculum is organized within traditional academic departments; however, learning also becomes integrated in interdisciplinary electives emphasizing ethics, humanities, mathematics, and technology.

Graduates of Hebron Academy will have taken at least five classes each year and successfully completed 18 credits including four years of English; three of mathematics; two years of the same foreign language; two years of laboratory science, including two years of Biology; two years of history, including United States History; and, for four-year students, one year of fine arts and one term of computer studies. Advanced Placement courses are available in six subject areas as well as honors sections of English, mathematics, and history. Over 20 electives include Human Anatomy and Physiology, Environmental Science, World Religions, International Relations, and Photography. English as a Second Language and a program for youngsters with mild learning disabilities serve 20 students each.

The academic day is organized by a rotating schedule of six periods of 45–60 minutes. Students are grouped by ability and interest in sections ranging from 4 to 18; the student-faculty ratio is 8:1. The academic year is divided into trimesters with major exams in the fall and spring. Advisors provide grade and progress reports for parents seven times each year, once after two weeks of school and again at the midpoint and close of each trimester.

Study hall is held between 8:00 and 10:00 P.M., Sunday through Thursday. Hupper Library and the Computer Center are available each weekday from 8:00 A.M. to 4:00 P.M. and from 6:30 to 10:00 P.M.

Throughout a student's experience but especially during the junior and senior years, two college counselors ensure that each individual receives the attention needed to move confidently through the admissions process and gain acceptance to a college or university appropriate for his or her particular needs, goals, and talents. Over 75 college representatives visit the Hebron campus each year, and students regularly attend college fairs.

In 1999, the middle 50 percent of SAT scores ranged from 460 to 600 Verbal and from 500 to 620 Math.

Of 71 graduates in 1999, 69 are presently attending college, 1 returned overseas, and 1 selected a postgraduate program. Among the colleges and universities currently attended by 2 or more Hebron graduates are Bates, Cornell, Dartmouth, Middlebury, St. Anselm's, and the Universities of Denver, Maine, and Vermont.

STUDENT ACTIVITIES. Students supplement their academic and athletic experiences with a rich mix of social, service, cultural, and physical activities. Student Council, proctors, Green Key guides, Young Women's Group, and Diversity Committee all shape the life of the community.

Students produce the *Spectator* (yearbook), *Etchings* (art and literary magazine), and the *Stanley Steamer* (newspaper). The drama group, community orchestra and chorus, Heebeejeebees a capella group, Midnight Transpositions jazz band, and the String Ensemble perform throughout the year, and some members are selected to Maine All-State orchestra and chorus.

Swimmers in the lifeguard program become mentors for children in community swimming. Hockey players teach local youngsters to skate. The Community Service Group volunteers in food pantries, foundations, and convalescent homes. The Outing Club maintains a local hiking trail and offers hiking, canoeing, white-water kayaking, snowshoeing, and rock climbing trips throughout the year.

On weekends, students may participate in special activities in the Leyden Center or travel to Auburn, Portland, or Boston for dining, movies, fairs, and malls. Winter Carnival and Casino Night is a midwinter extravaganza of games, a dance, and intramural competition. Senior Prom is held in late April, and seniors conclude the year with an overnight rafting trip in northern Maine.

All students participate in athletics at some level for two seasons of the year. Hebron fields 28 varsity and junior varsity teams in 14 interscholastic sports and seven activities. Varsity boys' and girls' team sports include soccer, cross-country running, basketball, Nordic and alpine skiing, ice hockey, swimming, lacrosse, tennis, and track and field. Additional sports for boys are football and baseball; for girls, field hockey and softball. Noncompetitive, coeducational activities include outdoor skills and physical conditioning. Hebron teams participate in the Maine Independent School League and the New England Prep School Athletic Conference. Individual athletes also compete in Junior Olympic running, swimming, and skiing.

ADMISSION AND COSTS. Hebron seeks students of strong character and the motivation to acquire good preparation for college. Candidates are selected based upon academic records, interviews, recommendations, and test scores. New boarding and day students are admitted in all four classes, and postgraduates are readily assimilated into the senior class. Postgraduate candidates are expected to have had a college preparatory program throughout high school. The Secondary School Admission Test is requested for ninth- and tenth-grade applicants. A campus visit is strongly encouraged for all applicants. A $1000 nonrefundable deposit is required of all students upon enrollment to reserve a place in the class. Inquiries, visits, interviews, and applications are welcome at any time throughout the year; however, most students apply for fall admission during the late fall or winter of the prior school year. Applications received after April 10 are considered as long as there are vacancies.

Tuition, room, and board in 1999–2000 were $22,400. Day tuition was $12,250. Transportation, books, music lessons, College Entrance Examination Board testing, and weekend activities are additional. More than 50 percent of students received need-based financial aid totaling more than $1,000,000 in 1997–98. Hebron Academy reaffirms its long-standing policy of nondiscriminatory admission regardless of race, color, national or ethnic origin, religion, sex, marital or parental status, or handicap.

Director of Admissions: William Wallace, Jr.
Assistant Headmaster/Dean of Students/Upper School Director: Jack Leyden
Assistant Headmaster for Advancement: Paul Domingue
Dean of Faculty: Elizabeth Found
Director of Studies: Silver Moore-Leamon

Director of College Counseling: Matthew McDonough '88
Director of International Program: Beverly Leyden
Director of Athletics: Leslie Guenther

Kents Hill School   1824

P.O. Box 257, Route 17, Kents Hill, ME 04349-0257.
   207-685-4914; Fax 207-685-9529;
   E-mail khsadmit@kentshill.pvt.k12.me.us

Since its founding by a Revolutionary War veteran 175 years ago, Kents Hill has sought to develop intellectual growth and moral character in young people. The School enrolls 200 boarding and day students in Grade 9–Postgraduate in a college preparatory program that features Advanced Placement courses, support for students with mild learning disabilities, and English as a Second Language. The curriculum is enhanced by outdoor education, the arts, and athletics including competitive skiing and snowboarding for boys and girls. Community service, Student Council, and clubs are among the activities. Boarding Tuition: $25,400; Day Tuition: $14,800. Matthew R. Crane is Director of Admissions; Rist Bonnefond (Cornell, B.A.) is Headmaster. *New England Association.*

North Yarmouth Academy   1814

148 Main Street, Yarmouth, ME 04096. 207-846-9051; Admissions 207-846-2382; Fax 207-846-2372; E-mail lbreen@nya.org; Web Site www.nya.org

North Yarmouth Academy, a college preparatory day school enrolling 260 boys and girls in Grades 6–12, aims to provide a rigorous liberal arts program that will develop each student's creativity, self-esteem, and academic potential. The core curriculum is strengthened by an advisor system, small classes, extra help and tutoring, and Advanced Placement courses in all major disciplines. A two-week social service project is required for graduation. Wilderness experiences challenge students to their personal best; publications, school government, varsity sports, and a variety of activities are also offered. Tuition: $13,050. Financial aid is available. Lynne M. Breen is Director of Admission; Robert P. Henderson (Dartmouth, B.A., M.A.L.S.) is Headmaster. *New England Association.*

MARYLAND

Academy of the Holy Cross   1868

4920 Strathmore Avenue, Kensington, MD 20895-1299.
  301-942-2100; Fax 301-929-6440; E-mail ahc@wdn.com

This college preparatory high school, a Blue Ribbon School of Excellence, was founded to provide a Catholic education for young women. Owned and operated by the Sisters of the Holy Cross, the Academy offers its 415 students a challenging curriculum of the liberal arts and sciences combined with opportunities for spiritual growth through religious studies, community prayer, and Christian service. Honors and Advanced Placement courses and internships enhance the program. Girls participate in a wide range of activities including publications, speech and debate team, Model U.N., drama and musical productions, and interscholastic teams in 11 sports. Tuition: $8625. Extras: $600. Mrs. Leslie Pike is Director of Recruitment; Sr. Katherine Kase, CSC, is Principal. *Middle States Association.*

The Barrie School   1932

13500 Layhill Road, Silver Spring, MD 20906-3299.
  301-871-6200; Fax 301-871-6706; E-mail admissions@barrie.org;
  Web Site www.barrie.org

Set on a 45-acre wooded campus, The Barrie School serves 500 boys and girls in Preschool–Grade 12. Lower School is Montessori; Middle and Upper schools are college preparatory. Barrie seeks to foster self-confident thinkers, creative problem solvers, and lifelong learners who value and respect themselves, others, and their natural environment. The program includes Advanced Placement, technology education, and community service and career/political internships. Field trips and foreign travel enrich the curriculum. Students participate in athletics, outdoor pursuits, music, publications, community service, drama, and the arts. Extended care and a summer program are offered. Tuition: $6790–$13,280. Julie A. Calloway is Director of Admission; Charles F. Szumilas is Head of School.

The Boys' Latin School of Maryland   1844

822 West Lake Avenue, Baltimore, MD 21210. 410-377-5192;
  Fax 410-433-2571; Web Site www.boyslatinmd.com

The Boys' Latin School of Maryland, enrolling 595 students in Kindergarten–Grade 12, provides a challenging and supportive academic program that fosters independence, responsibility, and personal growth. The curriculum includes English, history, foreign languages, math, science, computers, the arts, and physical education. Small classes in a friendly atmosphere enable students to achieve their best. Activities include athletics, publications, clubs, and community service. Tuition: $10,410–$12,970. Financial Aid: $660,000. James Currie, Jr., and Kathleen Berger are Directors of Admissions; M. Mercer Neale III (Hampden-Sydney, B.S.; Towson State, M.E.; Johns Hopkins, M.L.A.; University of Maryland, Ed.D.) is Headmaster. *Middle States Association.*

The Bryn Mawr School   1885

109 West Melrose Avenue, Baltimore, MD 21210. 410-323-8800;
  Fax 410-377-8963

Founded by five pioneering young women who believed in a challenging college preparatory education for girls, Bryn Mawr School enrolls 783 day girls in Kindergarten–Grade 12 and 177 girls and boys in a preschool and day care. Coordinate classes with Roland Park Country School for girls and Gilman School for boys are available in Grades 9–12. French begins in Kindergarten and computers in preschool. Activities include 44 teams in 15 sports, Dance Company, choral groups, art, drama, service clubs, and community service. The School enjoys an excellent college placement record. Tuition: $12,200–$13,560. Financial Aid: $1,065,918. Karyn Bysshe Vella is Interim Director of Admission; Rebecca MacMillan Fox (Bryn Mawr, A.B., M.A., Ph.D.) is Head of School. *Middle States Association.*

The Bullis School   1930

10601 Falls Road, Potomac, MD 20854. 301-983-5724;
  Fax 301-299-9050; E-mail info@bullis.org;
  Web Site www.bullis.org

The Bullis School is a coeducational, college preparatory day school enrolling 585 students in Grades 3–12. Bullis features a caring, challenging community in which a strong academic curriculum is balanced with athletics and fine arts. Bullis faculty are committed to providing personal attention in a diverse, structured environment in which the average class size is 14. The 82-acre campus features extensive academic and athletic facilities including the new Marriott Family Library and Technology Center. A broad array of Advanced Placement courses is offered. Tuition: $12,670–$15,360. Financial Aid: $575,000. Nancy J. Spencer is Director of Admission and Financial Aid; Richard K. Jung (Stanford, Ed.D. 1983) is Headmaster. *Middle States Association.*

The Calverton School   1967

300 Calverton School Road, Huntingtown, MD 20639.
  410-535-0216, 301-855-1922; Fax 410-535-6934;
  Web Site www.calverton.pvt.k12.md.us

The Calverton School is a coeducational, college preparatory day school enrolling 349 students in Pre-Kindergarten–Grade 12. The School's goals are to stimulate the desire to learn and to equip students with the skills essential to learning, to help students achieve their maximum potential, and to encourage them to develop strong moral values in preparation for the responsibilities of later life. Extracurricular activities include athletics, publications, drama, community service projects, and clubs at all levels. A Summer Activities Program is available. Tuition: $5070–$10,560. Financial Aid: $250,000. Eugene Chaney is Director of Marketing and Admissions; Elizabeth Bratton (University of Pittsburgh, M.Ed., Ed.D.) was appointed Director in 1987.

Calvert School   1897

105 Tuscany Road, Baltimore, MD 21210. 410-243-6054;
  Fax 410-366-0674; Web Site http://www.calvertschool.org

Calvert School enrolls 380 day students in Pre-Kindergarten–Grade 6. The School aims to develop solid fundamental skills, including the ability to read with comprehension, to write with style and discipline, and to use mathematical principles. Calvert has developed and tested a Home Instruction Program for Kindergarten–Grade 8, which allows parents who are inexperienced as teachers to choose a home-schooling experience for children who might benefit from that alternative. The regular curriculum includes French, computer, astronomy, art, and music. Tuition: $6100–$12,200. Financial Aid: $472,250. Deborah D. Frey is Admissions Director; Merrill Hall (Louisiana State, B.A. 1967, M.Ed. 1970; Johns Hopkins, M.L.A. 1990) was appointed Headmaster in 1983.

Charles E. Smith Jewish Day School   1965

Lower School: 1901 East Jefferson Street, Rockville, MD 20852.
   301-881-1400; Fax 301-984-7834
Upper School: 11710 Hunters Lane, Rockville, MD 20852.
   301-881-1404; Fax 301-881-6453; E-mail cesjds@cesjds.org;
   Web Site www.cesjds.org

This coeducational college preparatory school, enrolling 1275 students in Kindergarten–Grade 12, offers secular and Jewish studies to young people of varied Jewish religious and family backgrounds and seeks to integrate a sense of values in daily endeavors. A senior semester in Israel is a special feature of the rigorous academic program. Activities includes sports, social action and community service, drama, and clubs. Tuition: $9170 (K–6); $10,880 (Grades 7–11); $5440 (Grade 12 single semester). Financial aid is available. Susan Cohen is Director of Admissions; Dr. Geraldine Nussbaum is Lower School Principal; Rabbi Reuven Greenvald is Upper School Principal. *Middle States Association.*

The Chelsea School   1976

711 Pershing Drive, Silver Spring, MD 20910. 301-585-1430;
   Fax 301-585-5865

The Chelsea School, enrolling 110 boys and girls in Grades 5–12, offers a college preparatory program for dyslexic students of average to superior ability. The School specializes in remediation through the use of highly individualized, appropriate, multisensory teaching techniques in the areas of spoken and written expression, reading, and math, including Orton-Gillingham instruction. Counseling and related services are offered as needed. The structured curriculum is balanced by extensive offerings in the arts, extracurricular activities, community service, and athletics. A summer program is provided. Tuition: $23,332. Financial aid is available. Kara Figueredo is Director of Admission; Timothy Hall (Bates, B.A.; Boston University, M.B.A.) is President; Sylvia Jones (Spelman, B.A.; Howard, M.S.) is Academic Head of School.

Chesapeake Academy   1980

1185 Baltimore-Annapolis Boulevard, Arnold, MD 21012.
   410-647-9612; Fax 410-647-6088;
   Web Site www.chesapeakeacademy.com

Chesapeake Academy, an independent day school serving 290 children age 3–Grade 5, offers an individualized, multisensory approach to academics designed to develop students to their fullest potential. A creative, energetic faculty encourages delight in learning as a lifelong process through a challenging curriculum. The school believes in developing the whole child. Art, music, physical education, Spanish, computer, and library enhance the traditional curriculum. Before- and after-school care are available. Tuition: $2120–$8000. Mrs. Nancy Sabold is Admissions Director; Mrs. Jane C. Pehlke is Headmistress.

Connelly School of the Holy Child   1961

9029 Bradley Boulevard, Potomac, MD 20854. 301-365-0955;
   Fax 301-365-0981; E-mail BMurray@holychild.org

Connelly School of the Holy Child is a Catholic day school enrolling 420 young women in Grades 6–12. A member of a network of Holy Child schools founded over 150 years ago in England, it offers a rigorous college preparatory program in a nurturing environment. Honors and Advanced Placement courses are provided in most subjects. Athletics, Campus Ministry, community service, publications, art and drama, field trips to Washington, D.C., and travel abroad supplement classroom experiences. The School has been recognized as outstanding by the United States Department of Education. Tuition: $9800–

$10,875. Financial aid is available. Mrs. Maureen Appel (Rosemont, B.A.; Long Island University, M.S.) is Headmistress. *Middle States Association.*

The Country School   1934

716 Goldsborough Street, Easton, MD 21601. 410-822-1935;
   Fax 410-822-1971; Web Site www.countryschool.org

The Country School, a coeducational school enrolling 300 students in Kindergarten–Grade 8, offers a challenging program in a nurturing environment with small classes, individual attention, and outstanding teachers as its hallmarks. A traditional and structured yet creative and child-centered curriculum serves a range of diverse students within a family school context. The School creates an atmosphere of academic excellence designed to educate the whole child. It seeks to imbue students with a love of learning and provides sound preparation for secondary education. Activities include sports, fine and performing arts, community service, physical education, and life skills instruction. Tuition: $7650. Financial Aid: $207,500. Neil Mufson is Headmaster.

Friends Community School   1986

4601 Calvert Road, College Park, MD 20740. 301-699-6086

Founded by the Adelphi Friends Meeting, this Quaker day school enrolls 138 children in developmental Kindergarten–Grade 6. Friends Community School aims to provide a nurturing, values-based education that creates lifelong learners committed to "courageous risk-taking and joyous peacemaking." Students benefit from multiaged classrooms where they can learn to be both leaders and followers. The core curriculum centers around language arts, math, science, and social studies, complemented by art, music, and foreign language. Meeting for Worship nurtures children's spirits as they join in weekly Quaker services. Field trips, extended care, and summer programs are available. Tuition: $6600. Tom Goss is Interim Head of School.

Friends School of Baltimore   1784

5114 North Charles Street, Baltimore, MD 21210. 410-649-3200;
   Fax 410-649-3213; Web Site www.friendsbalt.org

Friends School of Baltimore is a Quaker, college preparatory day school, located on 32 acres, enrolling 505 boys and 495 girls in Pre-Primary–Grade 12. Approximately 140 new students enroll each fall, the largest entry points being Kindergarten and Grades 1, 6, 7, and 9. Extracurricular activities include athletics, community service, Meeting for Worship, publications, vocal music, dramatics, and student government. A summer program includes academics, day camp, and sports. Tuition: $10,895–$12,895. Extras and Lunches: $300–$400. Financial Aid: $1,669,000. Grant L. Jacks III is Director of Admission; Jon M. Harris (Harvard College, B.A. 1976; Wesleyan University, M.A.L.S.) was appointed Head of School in 1998. *Middle States Association.*

Garrison Forest School   OWINGS MILLS

Owings Mills, MD 21117. 410-363-1500; E-mail Gfs-info@gfs.org;
   Web Site www.gfs.org

GARRISON FOREST SCHOOL in Owings Mills, Maryland, is a college preparatory boarding and day school for girls enrolling 620 students in Preschool through Grade 12. The Preschool is coeducational, and boarding girls are accepted beginning in the eighth grade. Located 12 miles northwest of

Baltimore in the Green Spring Valley, the School offers convenient access to the cultural and educational opportunities of both Baltimore and Washington, D.C.

Founded in 1910 by Mary Moncrieffe Livingston, the School was moved from its original location in Pikesville, Maryland, to its present site in 1912.

Garrison Forest is dedicated to providing a college preparatory education that will inspire its young women to approach life with intellectual awareness, enthusiasm, and spirit in a setting in which all are encouraged to seek excellence and to develop their special talents.

Garrison Forest, incorporated as a nonprofit institution, is governed by a Board of Trustees. It is accredited by the Middle States Association of Colleges and Schools and is affiliated with numerous educational organizations, including The National Association of Principals of Schools for Girls, National Coalition of Girls' Schools, The Association of Independent Maryland Schools, the National Association of Independent Schools, the Council for Advancement and Support of Education, and the Educational Records Bureau.

THE CAMPUS. The 100-acre campus includes pasture, woodland, lawns, riding fields, two indoor and outdoor riding rings, newly refurbished stables and playing fields, and all-weather tennis courts.

Academic facilities include the Preschool; the F. Elizabeth White Middle School; the Jean G. Marshall-Nancy J. Offutt Upper School Academic and Administration Building, which contains classrooms, laboratories, a bookstore, study areas, and offices; the Charles S. Garland Memorial Theater, with a seating capacity of 500; and the newly renovated and expanded Lower School. A Fine and Performing Arts Center houses art studios, photography labs, and a 100-seat recital hall as well as practice rooms, classrooms, and a tiered choral room. The Upper and Middle School library was opened in 1987, providing also a four-room computer center and a 100-seat lecture hall. Manor House contains the Business, Development, and Alumnae offices, the dining hall, and the student Activities Center. Students are housed with faculty in three dormitories: Shriver, Meadowood, and Senior House. The Whitridge Pavilion, additional faculty housing, the Headmaster's home, the Infirmary, and the chapel complete the plant. Garrison Forest has its own server, and network access is installed in all school buildings and in every dorm room.

THE FACULTY. Peter O'Neill, appointed Head of School in 1994, is a graduate of St. Michael's College in Vermont, with a master's degree in American Studies from Trinity College (Connecticut). In addition to many academic and administrative positions, Mr. O'Neill served for six years as Headmaster of Wooster School in Danbury, Connecticut, and, most recently, was Interim Head at Whitby School in Greenwich, Connecticut.

There are 115 full-time faculty, 13 men and 102 women; 29 of the faculty members and administrators live on campus, including 8 faculty families. Sixty-two percent of the faculty hold advanced degrees from such colleges and universities as Columbia, Dartmouth, Dickinson, Duke, Goucher, Harvard, Hood College, Johns Hopkins, Loyola College, Maryland Institute of Art, Pennsylvania State, Princeton, Smith, the Sorbonne (France), Sweet Briar, United States Military Academy, Vanderbilt, Vassar, Washington University, and the Universities of Arizona, California, Chicago, Kansas, Maryland, Michigan, Missouri, Pennsylvania, Virginia, Wisconsin, and Wyoming. There are 14 part-time instructors.

The staff includes the Dean of Students, the Head of the Upper School, three residents in each dormitory, a college counselor and a guidance counselor, a licensed school psychologist, three admissions officers, a student activities director, a business manager, and four registered nurses. Physician specialists are on call.

STUDENT BODY. In 1999–2000, Garrison Forest enrolls 620 students as follows: 282 in the Preschool and Lower School; 129 in the Middle School (Grades 6–8); and 78 boarding and 131 day students in the Upper School (Grades 9–12). Students represent 21 states, the District of Columbia, and ten countries.

ACADEMIC PROGRAM. The 32-week academic year, from early September to early June, is divided into semesters and includes a week at Thanksgiving, a midwinter break, and two two-week vacations in the winter and in the spring. Academic classes meet five days a week until 3:45 P.M., and afternoons are devoted to extracurricular activities, sports, conferences, and study. Electives in computer, art, drama, and music are scheduled throughout the day.

The Lower School program is traditional in its primary goal of solid achievement in reading, writing, spelling, mathematics, social studies, and science. Emphasis is placed on building a firm foundation of basic skills in these areas. The academic program is enriched by regular instruction in computer, art, music, dance, and physical education.

In the Middle School, the emphasis is on a thorough mastery of reading, grammar, spelling, and arithmetic. Students are required to take courses in English, history, geography, algebra, science, and Latin; they elect French or Spanish. They also complete a series of Life Skills courses. A variety of extracurricular activities—in addition to art, music, dance, computer, and sports—is available to Middle School students. Field trips are an integral part of the program.

The 21½ units required for the Upper School diploma are as follows: English 4, foreign language 3, history 2½ (including United States History), mathematics 3, laboratory science 3, decision making ½, arts 1½ (including ½ unit in Basic Design), physical education 2, and at least 2 additional units, ½ of which must be in a multicultural course. A minimum of 5 units must be completed each year, and the School recommends that 5½ units be taken in Grades 9, 10, and 11.

The program of the Upper School offers a rigorous college preparatory curriculum that focuses on the core subjects of English, science, history, mathematics, and foreign languages. Thirteen Advanced Placement courses are offered in nine disciplines. Average class size is 12 students, allowing close contact between students and teachers. Each girl has regular conferences with her adviser to discuss her academic program. All faculty members are available for extra help, and tutoring can be arranged at additional expense. Reports with grades and comments are sent to parents four times a year.

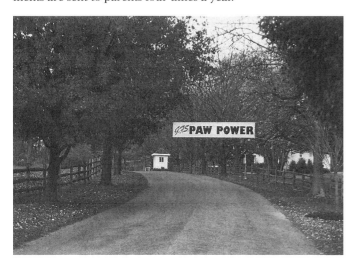

Courses offered in the Upper School are English, Creative Writing, Public Speaking; French 1–5, Latin 1–5, Spanish 1–5; World History, China in the 20th Century, United States History, America Since 1945, Black American Experience, Contemporary World Issues, American Mosaic, Major World Religions, Modern Latin America, Economics, Child Development; Algebra 1–2, Geometry, Algebra II/Trigonometry, Advanced Math, Pre-Calculus, Introduction to Calculus, Finite Math, Calculus; Introductory Programming, Topics in Programming, PASCAL Programming, Practical Computing, MAC World; Physical Science, Physics, Biology, Astronomy, Chemistry; Studio Arts and Crafts, Photography, Theater Arts, Art History; Music Appreciation, Applied Music; Dance, Advanced Dance; Decision Making; and Cardiopulmonary Resuscitation. Advanced Placement courses are offered in English, foreign languages, calculus, biology, computer, art history, studio art, and United States history. A three-week Independent Study Program for seniors is featured during the spring term.

All 51 members of the Class of 1999 are attending 36 colleges, including Bates, Boston College, Brown, Colby, Columbia, Cornell, Denison, Georgetown, Middlebury, Oberlin, Rice, Tulane, Wake Forest, and the Universities of Massachusetts, Richmond, Vermont, Virginia, and Wisconsin.

STUDENT ACTIVITIES. Upper School life is regulated by the Student Government Association. The major governing body of the Association is the Forum, composed of the president of the School, the day and boarding presidents of classes 9–12, two additional members from each Upper School class, and a recording secretary; three faculty representatives also attend Student Government meetings. There are also class and dormitory committees. The Service League offers both on-campus and community opportunities for volunteer work. Among other student groups are the Chapel Committee, Tour Guides, Black Student Union, the Activities Committee, G.R.E.E.N., Model UN, Cultural Awareness, Foreign Language, three class singing groups, and the Art, Computer, Drama, Student Advisers, Photography, Ski, and Riding clubs. There are three student publications.

Garrison Forest competes in all major sports with nearby schools. In addition, intramural teams, the Light Blues and the Dark Blues, challenge each other in academic, athletic, and extracurricular activities. Interscholastic sports include tennis, field hockey, cross-country, badminton, basketball, lacrosse, soccer, softball, and polo. Modern and jazz dance are also offered. Horseback riding is popular; experienced riders may play polo, hunt with the Green Spring Valley Hunt Club, participate in equestrian events with other schools, and compete in local and A-rated shows.

On weekends, the School arranges trips to Baltimore and Washington for concerts, plays, museum shows, and sports events. There are class parties, dramatic productions, dances and concerts with boys' schools, movies, lectures, canoeing, hiking, rafting, and skiing. The popular Host Family program fosters close friendships between resident and commuting students. Traditional annual events include Parents' Weekend, Open House, Fall Fest, Grandparents' Day, Alumnae Day, and Senior Entertainment.

ADMISSION AND COSTS. Garrison Forest does not discriminate on the basis of race, color, religion, or national origin. Admissions decisions are based on the applicant's previous school record, recommendations, and performance on standardized tests. An on-campus interview and the Secondary School Admission Test are required.

In 1999–2000, boarding tuition is $24,950. Tuition for day students ranges from $1870 to $13,650, plus optional transportation and lunch. Health insurance, tuition insurance, and a tuition payment plan are available. Garrison Forest subscribes to the School Scholarship Service and annually awards grants totaling approximately $980,000 on the basis of demonstrated family financial need. Low-interest loans are available to parents of Upper School students. Twenty-two percent of the students received financial aid in 1998–99.

Dean of Faculty: Joan Mudge
Dean of Students: Kristen P. Saunders
Alumnae Secretary: Alicia Matthai
Director of Admission: A. Randol Benedict
Director of Development: Kate Caldwell '71
College Counselor: Joan W. Mudge
Business Manager: William S. Hodgetts
Director of Athletics: Micul Ann Morse

Gibson Island Country School   1956

5191 Mountain Road, Pasadena, MD 21122. 410-255-5370; Fax 410-255-5590; Web Site www.gics.com

Gibson Island Country School is a coeducational, elementary day school enrolling about 100 students in Pre-Kindergarten–Grade 5. The School is dedicated to making each child's early academic experience challenging and joyful, and emphasizes hands-on, interdisciplinary learning. Basic curriculum is supplemented by specials such as French, waterfront science, physical education, and the fine arts. Using 18 networked computers, current technology is both taught and integrated into the curriculum. Activities include assemblies, sports, yearbook, community involvement, and relevant field trips. Tuition: $4600–$7650. Financial Aid: $60,000. Marie Hartman is Director of Admission; Carolyn W. Keenan (Brown, B.A.; Loyola, M.Ed.) is Head of School.

Gilman School   1897

5407 Roland Avenue, Baltimore, MD 21210. 410-323-3800; Fax 410-532-6513; E-mail admissions@gilman.edu; Web Site www.gilman.edu

The first country day school in the United States, Gilman is a college preparatory school enrolling 965 boys in Pre-First–Grade 12. The School aims to provide thorough academic instruction, to promote physical vigor, and to develop sound character. The Upper School curriculum, which includes electives, Advanced Placement courses, and a coordinate program with nearby girls' schools, is enriched by many diverse extracurricular activities. A summer session is offered. Tuition: $11,800–$12,660. Financial Aid: $1,350,000. Robert J. Demeule is Director of Admissions; Archibald R. Montgomery IV (University of Pennsylvania, B.A.; University of Texas, J.D.) became Headmaster in 1992.

Glenelg Country School   1954

12793 Folly Quarter Road, Glenelg, MD 21737-0190.
  410-531-7347; Fax 410-531-7363;
  E-mail glenelg.pvt.k12.md.us; Web Site www.glenelg.org

Glenelg Country School, enrolling 568 day students in Pre-K–Grade 12, emphasizes academic growth and the development of the whole child. The School balances rigorous academics, creative arts, interscholastic sports, community service, and social activities. The faculty provides personal attention in classes of 12–18 students. The Upper School features 14 Advanced Placement courses and a Director of College Placement. The School's 87 acres offer state-of-the-art classrooms, athletic fields, tennis courts, and a swimming pool. A summer program provides remediation and enrichment. Tuition: $6000–$12,600. Financial Aid: $550,000. Dr. Linda Resmini Handy is Director of Admission/Financial Aid; Ryland O. Chapman III is Headmaster.

Grace and Saint Peter's School   1805

707 Park Avenue, Baltimore, MD 21201. 410-539-1395;
  Fax 410-539-1306

A coeducational day school, Grace and St. Peter's School enrolls children from Preschool through Grade 5. Independent and affiliated with Grace and St. Peter's Church, it is the only school in downtown Baltimore accredited by the Association of Independent Maryland Schools. The School draws on the cultural resources of the Mount Vernon area as an integral part of the curriculum. Ties with city galleries, libraries, and museums are maintained. Art, music, Greek, Latin, dance, physical education, and karate are included in the program. Tuition: $6760–$7000. Financial Aid: $20,000. Mary Snead is Admissions Director; Sandra G. Shull (Miami University, B.S., M.Ed.; University of Baltimore, M.B.A.) is Head of the School.

Green Acres School   1934

11701 Danville Drive, Rockville, MD 20852. 301-881-4100;
  Fax 301-881-3319; E-mail GASNET@aol.com

Green Acres is a nondenominational, elementary/middle day school enrolling 320 boys and girls in Pre-Kindergarten–Grade 8. The School was founded by parents and teachers with the

aim of balancing the academic, social, emotional, physical, and creative development of students in an environment of intellectual rigor. The progressive curriculum is enriched by the creative arts, computer, physical education, outdoor education, and community service. Students may participate in a variety of after-school classes, including interscholastic sports for Grades 5–8. A recreational summer day camp is offered for ages 4–12. Tuition: $12,200. Marge Dimond is Director of Admission; Arnold S. Cohen (Dickinson, B.A. 1964; Ohio State, M.A. 1969, Ph.D. 1978) was named Head in 1993.

Gunston Day School   1998

P.O. Box 200, Centreville, MD 21617. 410-758-0620;
  Fax 410-758-0628 or 800-381-0077; E-mail gds@dmv.com;
  Web Site www.gunstondayschool.org

Gunston Day School, a college preparatory school enrolling 135 young men and women in Grades 9–12, offers a challenging core curriculum, including Honors and Advanced Placement classes, as well as a full range of cocurricular activities. Students may take part in 13 clubs, including Student Council and the National Honor Society, and to participate in athletics, both as individuals and as members of a team. Gunston's Bay Studies program focuses on the scientific, historical, and cultural dimensions of the Chesapeake Bay. Gunston Day School endeavors to inspire in its students a passion for learning, creative risk-taking, and fair play. Tuition: $11,490. Financial Aid: $160,000. Marc S. Buckley is Director of Admission; Peter A. Sturtevant, Jr. (Bowdoin, B.A.; Middlebury, M.A.), is Head of School. *Middle States Association.*

Harford Day School   1957

715 Moores Mill Road, Bel Air, MD 21014. 410-838-4848;
  Fax 410-836-5918; E-mail HDSLib@aol.com

Located 20 miles northeast of Baltimore, Harford Day School enrolls 340 boys and girls in Pre-Kindergarten–Grade 8. The School seeks to offer a program of challenging academics in a friendly, family atmosphere. The student-teacher ratio is 9:1. Fundamental skills, reasoning, independent thinking, and character building are emphasized, and frequent field trips to Baltimore, Washington, and Delaware enrich classroom learning. French, Spanish, Latin, computer skills, music, art, and athletics are offered at all levels. An Extended Day program is optional. Tuition: $6850–$7800. Financial Aid: $257,000. Donna Tower is Coordinator of Parent and Public Relations; Susan G. Harris (Bucknell University, B.S.) was appointed Head of the School in 1994.

The Holton-Arms School   1901

7303 River Road, Bethesda, MD 20817. 301-365-5300;
  Fax 301-365-6093; E-mail s_rodgers@holton-arms.edu;
  Web Site www.holton-arms.edu

Founded by Jessie Moon Holton and Carolyn Hough Arms in 1901, The Holton-Arms School is a college preparatory day school enrolling 661 girls in Grades 3–12. The School fosters a high standard of academic performance and a supportive environment where each student can develop to her fullest potential. Music and the arts complement traditional subjects, and Advanced Placement courses are available. Athletics, art, dance, drama, and publications are some of the activities. A summer program is offered. Tuition: $15,485–$15,860. Books: $500. Financial Aid: $1,004,750. Sharron Rodgers is Director of Admissions and Financial Aid; Diana Coulton Beebe (College of Wooster, B.A.; Boston University, M.A.; University of Tulsa, M.A.) is Head of School. *Middle States Association.*

The Heights School   1969

10400 Seven Locks Road, Potomac, MD 20854. 301-365-4300;
Fax 301-365-4303; Web Site www.heights.edu

The Heights School enrolls 400 day boys in Lower (Grades 3–5), Middle (Grades 6–8), and Upper (Grades 9–12) schools. The Lower and Middle schools are geared toward developmental needs while the Upper School liberal arts curriculum includes Latin, Greek, and Advanced Placement courses. Curriculum at all levels is complemented by a strong athletic and cocurricular program. The 50 faculty members, many of the Catholic prelature Opus Dei, cooperate with parents to help each boy realize his talents and capabilities. A summer day camp is offered for Grades 2–8. Tuition: $8150–$10,100. Financial Aid: $650,000. Kevin J. Davern is Director of Admissions; Richard B. McPherson (Harvard, A.B. 1978) is Headmaster.

Institute of Notre Dame   1847

901 Aisquith Street, Baltimore, MD 21202-5499. 410-522-7800;
Fax 410-522-7810

Institute of Notre Dame was founded by the School Sisters of Notre Dame to educate young women. Enrolling 431 girls in Grades 9–12, it seeks to motivate them to develop their full potential and to understand their relationship to the larger world. The school offers an Access Program for students who need to focus on basic academic skills, a traditional College Preparatory curriculum, and the Theresian Scholars Program, designed for above-average students. Religious studies are required, and the campus ministry program coordinates liturgies, retreats, and outreach projects. Gospel Choir, yearbook, dance, and sports are among the activities. Tuition: $5400. Sr. Mary Fitzgerald, SSND, is Principal.

The Ivymount School   1961

11614 Seven Locks Road, Rockville, MD 20854. 301-469-0223;
Fax 301-469-0778; E-mail lpender@ivymount.org;
Web Site www.america-tomorrow.com/ivymount/

Founded to serve children with special needs, Ivymount offers a therapeutic and academic environment that maximizes each student's intellectual, physical, and social potential. Ivymount enrolls 200 boys and girls from preschool age through 21 in a day program combining speech and language services, occupational and physical therapy, clinical social work, and adaptive physical education. Specialized teachers use innovative strategies and technology to implement Individualized Education Plans that emphasize written and spoken communication and visual motor skills. The expressive arts and a four-week summer program complement the educational and therapeutic programs. Tuition: $28,310. Stephanie de Sibour is Assistant Director for Admissions; Jan Wintrol is School Director.

Kent School   1967

6788 Wilkins Lane, P.O. Box 507, Chestertown, MD 21620.
410-778-4100; Fax 410-778-7357; Web Site www.kentschool.org

A day school enrolling 195 girls and boys in Pre-School–Grade 8, Kent seeks to foster intellectual, moral, and personal growth through a rigorous curriculum that engages students actively in their learning. Appreciation of the arts, use of language skills, critical thinking skills, and a strong sense of responsibility and involvement in the larger community are emphasized. Kent acknowledges the multiple talents of its students as it nurtures and celebrates each child's contribution to the School. Horizons is a summer program for youngsters who would, under other circumstances, be unable to attend Kent School. Tuition: $4575–$6875. Joan Flaherty is Admissions Director; Christopher J. Marblo (College of St. Rose, B.A.; New York University, M.A.) was appointed Headmaster in 1998.

The Key School   1958

534 Hillsmere Drive, Annapolis, MD 21403. 410-263-9231;
Fax 410-280-5516; Web Site keyschool.net

The Key School is a nonsectarian, college preparatory day school enrolling 660 boys and girls in Pre-Kindergarten–Grade 12. Recognized for academic excellence, the School encourages intellectual rigor, independence of thought, curiosity, creativity, and openness to differing ideas and perspectives. The curriculum includes music, art, and modern and classical languages, with electives in Non-Western Literature, Russian Studies, Dance, Estuarine Biology, and Music Theory. Theater, music groups, debate, and Model Congress are among the activities. Extensive field trips including outdoor education are integral to the program. Tuition: $6200–$12,500. Jessie D. Dunleavy is Director of Admission; Marcella M. Yedid (Indiana University, B.S.; Brown University, M.A.) is Head of School.

Loyola Blakefield High School   1852

P.O. Box 6819, Baltimore, MD 21285-6819. 410-823-0601;
Fax 410-823-0748; Web Site www.blakefield.loyola.edu

Loyola Blakefield, founded by the Society of Jesus, is a Roman Catholic, college preparatory day school enrolling 968 boys in Grades 6–12. Its aim is to graduate young men who are intellectually competent, open to growth, religious, loving, and committed to doing justice. Core requirements include 20 course units in English, mathematics, modern language, science, and social studies. Fine arts, computer programming, physical education, and religious studies are also required. Loyola Blakefield offers a variety of cocurricular activities. A coeducational summer session provides remedial and advancement courses. Tuition: $8035. Joseph McFadden is Director of Admissions; The Reverend John M. Dennis, S.J. (Jesuit School of Theology [Berkeley], M.Div.; Harvard, M.Ed.), is President. *Middle States Association.*

Landon School   1929

6101 Wilson Lane, Bethesda, MD 20817. 301-320-3200;
Fax 301-320-1133; Web Site www.landon.net

Landon School prepares talented boys for productive lives as accomplished, responsible, and caring men whose actions are guided by perseverance, teamwork, honor, and fair play. A college preparatory day school serving 635 boys in Grades 3–12, Landon is known for its rigorous academic program, with values and traditions to uphold and impart. With the help of a faculty advisor, students run an active community service program and administer their own Honor Code. Cross-registration and cooperation in dramas and musicals are available with a local girls' school. Tuition: $14,775–$16,075. Financial Aid: $1,000,000. Russell Gagarin is Admissions Director; Damon F. Bradley (Boston University, A.B.; Yale, M.Div.; Syracuse, M.Phil.) is Headmaster. *Middle States Association.*

Maryvale Preparatory School   1945

11300 Falls Road, Brooklandville, MD 21022. 410-560-3243;
Fax 410-561-1826; E-mail info@maryvale.com;
Web Site www.maryvale.com

Founded by the Sisters of Notre Dame de Namur, Maryvale is a college preparatory day school enrolling 310 girls in Grades 6–12. Maryvale challenges motivated, eager-to-learn students with a curriculum that emphasizes the liberal arts and sciences. Advanced Placement courses are offered in English, mathematics, science, and social studies. Honors courses offer an intensive study of course material. Enrichment includes athletic teams at three levels, Student Council, newspaper/yearbook, drama, and service and interest clubs. Tuition: $8800. Financial aid and scholarships are available. Monica Graham is Director of Admission; Sr. Shawn Marie Maguire, SND (Trinity, B.S. 1962; Temple, M.A. 1972; Loyola College, M.A. 1978), is Headmistress. *Middle States Association.*

Mater Dei School   1960

9600 Seven Locks Road, Bethesda, MD 20817. 301-365-2700;
Fax 301-365-2710

Mater Dei School, enrolling 223 boys in Grades 1–8, is a Catholic day school serving the Washington, D.C., area. The School strives to mix daily work with a sense of fun, perspective, and morality. Although the curriculum is broad, emphasis is placed on the basics, particularly religion, language arts, mathematics, social studies, science, and physical education. A one-week District of Columbia Cultural Program and a one-week Outdoor Environmental Camp are part of the curriculum in the upper grades. Tuition: $6975. Christopher S. Abell (Boston College, B.A. 1970; Georgetown, M.A. 1974; Catholic University, J.D. 1979) is President; Edward N. Williams (College of the Holy Cross, B.A. 1983; Harvard, M.Ed.) is Headmaster.

McDonogh School   1873

Owings Mills, MD 21117-0380. 410-363-0600;
Admissions 410-581-4720; Fax 410-581-4719;
E-mail admissions@mcdonogh.org; Web Site www.mcdonogh.org

McDonogh School enrolls 1254 boys and girls in Kindergarten–Grade 12, including 80 five-day boarding students in Grades 9–12. Emphasizing academic excellence, moral character, responsibility, and leadership, McDonogh "offers students the opportunities of a large school plus the advantages of a smaller one." Class size averages 15, and 17 Advanced Placement courses are offered. Upper School students choose from 24 interscholastic sports and 50 clubs and activities. The campus is set on 800 acres northwest of Baltimore. Bus transportation and lunches are included in tuition. Boarding Tuition: $18,320; Day Tuition: $11,800–$13,600. Financial Aid: $1,400,000. Amy Thompson is Director of Admission; W. Boulton Dixon (Princeton, A.B. 1965; Temple M.Ed. 1969) is Headmaster. *Middle States Association.*

The McLean School of Maryland   1954

8224 Lochinver Lane, Potomac, MD 20854. 301-299-8277;
Fax 301-299-1639; Web Site http://www.mcleanschool.org

Enrolling 390 students in Kindergarten–Grade 9, McLean serves students who thrive in a warm, supportive atmosphere and accommodates a variety of learning needs and styles. The college preparatory curriculum, which emphasizes the mastery of basic skills in the liberal arts and sciences, is structured to meet the needs of both traditional learners and those with mild learning differences. Students may be placed in classes according to their skill levels and academic strengths. All students engage in sports and electives in art, music, computer, drama, and publications. Grade 10 will be added in September 2000, with Grades 11 and 12 to follow in successive years. Tuition: $12,400–$15,200. Financial aid is available. Catherine A. Biern is Director of Admission; Darlene B. Pierro is Head of School.

Mercy High School   1960

1300 East Northern Parkway, Baltimore, MD 21239-1998.
410-433-8880; Fax 410-323-8816;
Web Site www.mercyhighschool.com

The Sisters of Mercy conduct this Catholic high school that serves 475 young women from diverse faith and ethnic backgrounds. Mercy's mission is to enable students to understand and respond to the challenges that face them according to Christian principles. Named an Exemplary Private School by the Department of Education, Mercy offers a college preparatory curriculum that includes a rigorous Honors Program, four years of religion, and electives in languages, math, science, creative writing, technology, and the arts. Involvement in Student Council, drama, athletics, and other activities provides opportunities for social and personal growth. Tuition: $5800. Ms. Jacqueline A. Stilling is Director of Admissions; Sr. Carol E. Wheeler is Principal. *Middle States Association.*

The Newport School   1930

11311 Newport Mill Road, Kensington, MD 20895.
  301-942-5247; Fax 301-949-2654

Located 8 miles from downtown Washington, D.C., this college preparatory day school enrolling 410 students in Nursery–Grade 12 is committed to academic excellence and individual growth. Small classes, personal attention, dedicated teachers, and a caring environment are the cornerstones of a Newport education. Students are given the opportunity to achieve their maximum intellectual, social, emotional, and physical development. The curriculum, emphasizing language arts, math, science, and the humanities, includes honors and Advanced Placement courses. Athletic, performing arts, and computer programs are among the offerings. A summer program is available. Tuition: $8500–$13,440. Financial aid is available. Marilyn Grossblatt is Director of Admission; Colin G. Stevens is Headmaster. *Middle States Association.*

Norbel School   1980

7310 Park Heights Avenue, Baltimore, MD 21208. 410-358-1233

Drs. Robert and Norma Campbell founded Norbel School to meet the needs of boys and girls with attention deficit disorder and other learning and language disabilities. Enrolling 100 children of average to gifted intellectual ability, age 3$\frac{1}{2}$–Grade 8, Norbel offers a 3:1 student-teacher ratio. The program emphasizes reading comprehension, phonic and visual recognition, and auditory and memory techniques as tools for developing strong skills in traditional disciplines. Speech communication, occupational therapy, and a Living Skills program strengthen the core curriculum. Art and music courses, field trips, and physical education enrich classroom instruction. Tuition: $9800–$14,800. Margaret R. Gold (University of Maryland, B.S.; Towson University, M.Ed.) is Director.

Norwood School   1952

8821 River Road, Bethesda, MD 20817. 301-365-2595;
  Fax 301-365-4912; Web Site www.norwood.pvt.12.md.us

Norwood, a coeducational day school for 480 students in Kindergarten–Grade 8, seeks to offer individual attention and superior instruction. The School's mission is to help each child grow intellectually, morally, physically, and socially. Norwood provides training in fundamental skills and logical and analytical thinking and encourages independence of mind and self-expression. The curriculum, emphasizing facility with spoken and written language and math, includes art, music, French, Spanish, Latin, science, social studies, technology, and physical education. Tuition: $12,700–$13,800. Financial Aid: $460,000. Dr. Armistead C. G. Webster is Director of Admissions; Richard T. Ewing, Jr., is Head of School.

Notre Dame Preparatory School   1873

815 Hampton Lane, Towson, MD 21286. 410-825-6202;
  Fax 410-832-2625 or 410-321-4809; E-mail develd@
  notredameprep.com; Web Site www.notredameprep.com

Notre Dame is a Roman Catholic, college preparatory day school enrolling 650 girls in Grades 6–12. Under the leadership of the School Sisters of Notre Dame, it seeks to foster the spiritual, moral, and intellectual growth of each student in a warm, supportive atmosphere. A broad and extensive curriculum includes academic subjects taught at four levels of challenge, allowing each student to work according to her ability and interest. Clubs and athletics, featuring 12 varsity sports, supplement the curriculum. Social service is an important component of school life. Tuition: $9000. Lillian Mihm is Director of Admissions; Sr. Christine Mulcahy, SSND (Salem State, B.S.; Villanova, M.S.), was appointed Headmistress in 1997. *Middle States Association.*

Oldfields School   GLENCOE

1500 Glencoe Road, Glencoe, MD 21152. 410-472-4800;
  Fax 410-472-6839; E-mail Admissions@Oldfields.pvt.k12.md.us;
  Web Site www.OldfieldsSchool.com

OLDFIELDS SCHOOL in Glencoe, Maryland, is a college preparatory boarding and day school for girls in Grades 8–12.

Oldfields was founded in 1867 by Mrs. John Sears McCulloch and has continued to reflect her desire to provide young women with the opportunity to make the most of their academic and personal potential. The mission of Oldfields is to provide a family like environment in which students can best develop intellectually, ethically, and socially by learning the values of self-discipline and self-respect.

Oldfields is governed by a self-perpetuating Board of Trustees made up of alumnae and parents of current and past students. Oldfields is accredited by the Middle States Association of Colleges and Schools and holds membership in the National Association of Independent Schools, The Association of Boarding Schools, the National Coalition of Girls' Schools, and the Association of Independent Maryland Schools.

THE CAMPUS. The 200-acre campus lies in rolling hills and woodlands, 25 miles north of Baltimore, with convenient access to the cultural and recreational activities available there, as well as in New York, Philadelphia, and Washington, D.C. Old House, the original school building, is more than 200 years old. New structures (1961–93) include Commons, which contains dining facilities, the school store, and rooms for social activities; a gymnasium; a dance studio; an academic building and fine arts facility; and eight dormitories. Plans are underway for an addition to the academic building that will include new science and library facilities.

THE FACULTY. Dr. Kathleen Jameson, appointed Head of Oldfields in 1997, holds a Bachelor of Arts degree in Music Education and a Master of Science degree in Education from Bucknell University. She received a doctorate in Educational Administration from Northern Arizona University.

There are 47 full-time and 11 part-time faculty members, of whom 10 are men. Twenty hold advanced degrees. Seventy-four percent of the full-time faculty live on campus and serve as dormitory parents in one of eight dormitories. Nurses have regular clinic hours in the health center and are on call 24 hours a day. Faculty are active members of the campus community, attending sporting events and art performances and participating in all areas of student life. In addition, each faculty member has a group of approximately five students for whom he or she acts as an advisor and as a contact for parents.

STUDENT BODY. Typically, Oldfields enrolls 145 boarding and 40 day students. The school size is limited to 185 girls in order to maintain its familylike atmosphere. Eighty percent of the students are boarders.

In 1989–99, the student body represented 23 states and 11 countries including Bermuda, Egypt, Germany, Japan, Korea, Mexico, and Saudi Arabia.

ACADEMIC PROGRAM. The school year is divided into semesters, with midyear and final exams given. Students carry at least five courses per semester. Grades and comprehensive comments from faculty members are sent home four times a year. The academic and social progress of each girl is reviewed at weekly faculty meetings. The average class enrolls 10–12 students, with a 4:1 student-teacher ratio. Extra help from teachers is available to students outside of class. Tutoring can also be arranged when necessary.

Oldfields is committed to providing each student with the college preparatory course of study most appropriate to her needs and interests. Each academic discipline offers courses on two tracks. Students in A track are challenged in their areas of strength, and students in B sections are supported in areas of weakness. The two-track system is flexible and allows a student to take classes in either track. Technology is integrated into the curriculum through the use of laptop computers, which are required of all students. All classrooms, the library, and other public spaces are wired for student use.

Nineteen credits are required for graduation. Students must take four years of English, three years of mathematics, two years of laboratory science, three years of a foreign language (including two of the same language), three years of history (including one year of U.S. history), the Freshmen Arts Program (for all four- and five-year students), one year of Fine Arts, and physical education each semester. In addition, students in Grades 8 and 9 are required to take classes in health and computer skills. Study skills are taught in the English classes. Qualified juniors and seniors may undertake an independent study in any academic discipline.

Students of exceptional ability are offered honors-level and Advanced Placement courses. In 1999–2000, Advanced Placement courses are available in studio art, U.S. history, European history, biology, calculus AB, English literature, English language, French, and Spanish.

Underclass students attend required study halls during their free periods in the morning. They also have room study, supervised by dormitory parents from 7:45 to 9:30 P.M., Monday through Thursday, and quiet hours on Sunday evenings. Juniors and seniors have freedom of study during these times. A teacher may recommend that an upper-class student be required to attend study hall.

During the two-week May Program, students may study abroad, participate in other off-campus experiences, or choose from on-campus programs offered in a wide array of academic and social disciplines. In 1998–99, students traveled to France and Costa Rica, completed community service projects in Appalachia and Baltimore, participated in outdoor experiences, and studied the history of musicals, riding, and Spanish cuisine on campus. Several juniors and seniors also created independent projects with the permission of the Director of Studies.

College counseling and aptitude testing begin in the fall of the junior year. The college counselor coordinates on-campus visits from more than 60 college representatives and plans college fair evenings. College testing is conducted on campus.

Oldfields School's commitment to academic diversity is reflected in the colleges students attend. Each year, graduates enroll in Ivy League institutions as well as large and small colleges nationwide. Notably, 63 percent of the class of 1999 entered their first-choice schools. Among the colleges and universities attended by recent graduates are Brown University, Carnegie Mellon, Denison, Hollins, James Madison University, Lafayette, Pepperdine, Randolph-Macon, Reed, Regent's College of London, Syracuse, and the Universities of Colorado and Vermont.

STUDENT ACTIVITIES. Participation in activities increases the feeling of community and offers each student avenues through which she can explore new interests or express her talents. The Student Council, made up of 11 elected students, helps to formulate and implement school policy. Selected seniors also help enforce the spirit and letter of the School's rules by serving as Resident Assistants in dormitories.

Campus co-curricular activities are organized and run by students. In recent years, students have contributed their time and enthusiasm to FOCUS, Black Awareness Club, Asian Club, Art Club, Environmental Awareness Club, and Tour Guides. Dubious Dozen and Images are a cappella choral groups that perform frequently for the Oldfields community. In addition, the school literary magazine, *Tidbit*, and yearbook, *Rarebit*, are produced entirely by students.

Competitive and non-competitive sports are offered at the interscholastic and intramural level. Field hockey, basketball, soccer, tennis, softball, volleyball, badminton, and lacrosse are played on the varsity and junior varsity levels. Third-squad intramurals are offered in many sports, depending on student interest. Varsity and junior varsity riding teams compete throughout the Middle Atlantic states. Dance (ballet, tap, jazz, and modern) and aerobics classes are also offered each afternoon. The traditional school spirit competition, Green and White, lasts throughout the year.

Lectures, workshops, concerts, and movies are presented on campus, along with trips to local and regional areas of interest. Plays, concerts, and dances with nearby boys' schools, as well as ski weekends and hiking trips, are scheduled regularly. All co-curricular events are chaperoned by faculty members. Theater excursions, museum trips, shopping, community service projects, sporting events, and restaurant trips supplement the weekend activities.

ADMISSION AND COSTS. The student body is comprised of young women with diverse talents and interests from various socioeconomic backgrounds. Oldfields welcomes girls of average to superior ability who are committed to making the most of their academic and personal potential. The two-track academic program can accommodate the motivated student of average ability as well as the gifted student.

Admission is based on the application, along with standardized test scores, a transcript, two teacher recommendations, and a personal interview on campus. Phone interviews are required when campus visits are not possible. International students must submit a written essay and results from TOEFL, or SLEP testing to determine English proficiency. A registration fee of $2000 for boarders and $1500 for day students, applicable toward tuition, is required with a signed entrance contract.

Tuition for 1999–2000 is $26,100 for boarders and $16,200 for day students. Additional expenses include textbooks, school supplies, activity fees, and laptop computer. Optional expenses include music, photography, and riding lessons.

Financial aid is available on the basis of need, and grants and loans are reviewed and awarded annually. Thirty-three students were awarded aid totaling $494,600 in 1998–99. All families applying for aid must complete the forms for the School and Student Service for Financial Aid and submit their last two tax returns. Oldfields School does not discriminate on the basis of race, color, or national or ethnic origin in the administration of its policies, admissions policies, loan programs, sports, or other school-administered programs.

Head of School: Dr. Kathleen Jameson
Assistant Head for Student Life: Susan Louis
Assistant Head for Advancement and Operations: Nancy Wolf
Director of Admission and Financial Aid: Kimberly Caldwell

Director of Studies and Technology: Laura Karey
Dean of Students: Dennie Hanley
Director of Alumnae Affairs: Kate Greeley
College Counselor: Anne Weeks
Business Manager: Kathleen Fernandez
Director of Athletics: Elizabeth Franks

The Park School   1912

Old Court Road, Brooklandville, MD 21022. 410-339-7070;
Fax 410-339-4125; Web Site www.park.pvt.k12.md.us

A college preparatory day school enrolling 885 boys and girls in Pre-Kindergarten–Grade 12, Park was founded in the belief that students who actively participate in their education develop a lifelong appreciation for learning. An academically challenging yet flexible curriculum provides a strong foundation in the basics and encourages critical thinking, self-reliance, and leadership. The program also integrates community service and activities into daily life at all levels. Park is located in a 100-acre wildlife sanctuary minutes from downtown Baltimore. Tuition: $11,930–$13,525. Financial aid is available. Dr. Wendy Owen is Admission Director; David E. Jackson (Williams, B.A.; Teachers College, Columbia, Ed.D.) was appointed Head of School in 1995. *Middle States Association.*

The Primary Day School   1944

7300 River Road, Bethesda, MD 20817. 301-365-4355;
Fax 301-469-8611

Established as a demonstration school for the Phonovisual Method, The Primary Day School enrolls approximately 174 boys and girls in Pre-Kindergarten–Grade 2. The School is dedicated to educational excellence and to meeting the needs of individual students. The traditional curriculum emphasizes fundamental skills, sound work habits, and the enjoyment of the arts. The Phonovisual Method, a phonetic system for young children, promotes success in reading, writing, and spelling. Weekly assemblies at which all students perform are an important means of developing poise and self-confidence. Tuition: $6300–$9300. Mrs. Louise Plumb (State University of New York at Oneonta, B.A.) was appointed Director in 1999.

Queen Anne School   1964

14111 Oak Grove Road, Upper Marlboro, MD 20774.
301-249-5000; Fax 301-249-3838; Web Site www.queenanne.org

A college preparatory, coeducational day school enrolling approximately 250 students in Grades 6–12, Queen Anne is located on 60 acres between Washington and Annapolis. Affiliated with St. Barnabas' Episcopal Church, the School offers a demanding, comprehensive program, including Advanced Placement courses, community outreach, and a biology of the Chesapeake Bay program. Fine arts, athletics, and other electives enhance the curriculum. Classes are small, and students are prepared to be critical thinkers and mature individuals. Tuition: $9500–$10,800. Need-based financial aid is available. Brenda B. Walker is Director of Admissions; J. Temple Blackwood (University of Hartford, B.S.; Washington College, M.A.) is Headmaster. *Middle States Association.*

Roland Park Country School   1901

5204 Roland Avenue, Baltimore, MD 21210. 410-323-5500;
Fax 410-323-2164; E-mail admissions@rpcs.pvt.k12.md.us;
Web Site http://www.rpcs.org

A college preparatory day school for 697 girls in Kindergarten–Grade 12, Roland Park offers comprehensive academic, arts, and athletic programs. The curriculum features Advanced Placement in all disciplines, BC Calculus, and seven languages including Russian and Chinese. Upper School coordination with Gilman School offers the option of coeducational classes. Superb facilities, strong school spirit and college placement, foreign exchanges, four honor societies, Model UN, student government, community service, senior internship, and interest clubs enhance the program. A summer camp is offered. Tuition: $12,000–$13,000. Financial Aid: $1,052,000. Cameron V. Noble is Director of Admissions; Jean Waller Brune (Middlebury, B.A.; Johns Hopkins, M.A.) is Head of School. *Middle States Association.*

Ruxton Country School   1913

11202 Garrison Forest Road, Owings Mills, MD 21117.
   410-356-9608; Fax 410-356-9690

Enrolling 225 day boys and girls in Kindergarten–Grade 8, Ruxton believes that small classes provide maximum learning opportunities. Skilled teachers accommodate varied learning styles. Strong academics are based on the liberal arts. Reading and math specialists are on staff in the Lower and Middle Schools. Core subjects are enhanced by art, music, drama, physical education, computers, and Spanish. Enrichment classes are offered in Grades 1–8. Tuition: $6300–$9925. Anne Breese is Director of Admission; Stephanie M. Fisher (Colorado College, B.A.; University of California [Berkeley], M.A.) was appointed Head in 1999.

St. Andrew's Episcopal School   POTOMAC

8804 Postoak Road, Potomac, MD 20854. 301-983-5200;
   Fax 301-983-4620; E-mail admissions@saes.org;
   Web Site www.saes.com

ST. ANDREW'S EPISCOPAL SCHOOL in Potomac, Maryland, is a college preparatory day school enrolling boys and girls in Grades 6 through 12. Situated in the suburb of Potomac, the School is in a residential neighborhood, only 10 miles from downtown Washington, D.C. Its convenient location enables students to take full advantage of the wealth of educational, cultural, and historical resources of the nation's capital. Students reach the campus via Metro trains, local buses, private car pools, and a School-sponsored shuttle bus service.

Founded in 1978, St. Andrew's was the first Episcopal, coeducational, secondary day school in the Washington metropolitan area. The first classes were held in the basement of the Pilgrim Lutheran Church, then moved to a public school in Cabin John, Maryland. The School was located in Bethesda, Maryland, from 1981 until the summer of 1998, when it moved to its permanent site in Potomac.

The School's mission is to nurture each student's intellectual development, personal integrity, and sense of self-worth within a cooperative environment that embodies the faith and perspective of the Episcopal church. Religious studies are required each year, and students must attend regular chapel services. A full-time chaplain is on staff.

St. Andrew's School is a nonprofit institution governed by a 21-member Board of Trustees, including a representative of the Bishop of Washington. It is accredited by the Middle States Association of Colleges and Schools and holds membership in the National Association of Independent Schools, the National Association of Episcopal Schools, and Council for Religion in Independent Schools, and other associations. The Parents Association promotes interest, support, and participation in the School and assists in communications, volunteerism, and planning special events. Many of the 948 alumni are involved in fund-raising, recruitment, public relations, and other supportive activities on behalf of the School.

THE CAMPUS. The beautiful new 19.2-acre campus features state-of-the-art classrooms, science and technology laboratories, a media center, and a theater/assembly hall.

THE FACULTY. James M. Cantwell was appointed Headmaster of St. Andrew's Episcopal School in 1989. He holds a baccalaureate degree from the University of Vermont, an M.A.T. from Antioch College, and M.Ed. and Ed.D. degrees from Columbia. A native of Syracuse, New York, Dr. Cantwell has served as Headmaster of the American International School in Dusseldorf, Germany, and The Harrisburg Academy in Pennsylvania. He also spent two years in Brazil as a Peace Corps volunteer. Dr. Cantwell and his wife, Andrea, have four children.

The full-time faculty and administrators who teach number 54, 24 men and 30 women. They have earned 53 baccalaureates and 34 advanced degrees, including a doctorate, representing study at such colleges and universities as American University, Bates, Boston University, Catholic University, College of William and Mary, Cornell, Denison, Dickinson, Duke, East Stroudsburg, Franklin and Marshall, George Mason University, Georgetown University, George Washington, Goucher, Hampton, Harvard, Howard, James Madison, Johns Hopkins, Kenyon, Lake Forest, Lock Haven, Middlebury, Northwestern, Oregon State, Pennsylvania State, Princeton, Rhodes, St. Lawrence, Swarthmore, Temple, Theological Seminary, Tufts, United States Naval Academy, Wesleyan, Williams, Wittenberg, Yale, and the Universities of Connecticut, Idaho, Maryland, Michigan, Missouri, North Carolina, Ottawa, Pittsburgh, Salamanca (Spain), Tennessee, and Virginia. Faculty benefits include health insurance, a retirement plan, and Social Security. Leaves of absence and sabbaticals are granted at the discretion of the Headmaster.

A full-time nurse is on duty during school hours, and complete hospital facilities are available approximately 6 miles from the School.

STUDENT BODY. In 1999–2000, St. Andrew's Episcopal School enrolls 450 day students, 236 boys and 214 girls, as follows: 45 in Grade 6, 69 in Grade 7, 58 in Grade 8, 77 in Grade 9, 67 in Grade 10, 70 in Grade 11, and 64 in Grade 12. They come from throughout the Greater Washington metropolitan area and represent a wide diversity of racial, ethnic, religious, and socioeconomic backgrounds. Seventy percent of the students are Christian; the remainder include Greek Orthodox, Hindu, Jewish, Muslim, and Quaker students.

ACADEMIC PROGRAM. The school calendar, which extends from early September to early June, is divided into 12-week trimesters, with Thanksgiving, Christmas, and spring vacations as well as observances of national holidays. Parents receive written evaluations of their child's progress in each course at the midway point and end of each trimester. Exceptional achievement is recognized on both the Academic and Effort Honor Rolls. All students are assigned a faculty advisor with whom they meet several times a week for guidance in academic and extracurricular matters. Teachers are available for extra help by appointment at specified times during the day. The School supports tutoring for students wishing additional academic assistance.

The school day begins at 8:25 A.M. with a morning meeting, followed by seven 40-minute class periods and a lunch break. Dismissal is at 3:05 P.M. in the Upper School and 3:25 P.M. in the Middle School. Students are assigned homework in all subjects, ranging from two to three hours nightly, depending on grade level.

St. Andrew's students generally carry five academic courses. To graduate, they must have completed the following requirements: four years each in English, history, and physical education; three years of science, including Biology, and mathematics, including Algebra I–II and Geometry; two years of foreign language; two trimesters yearly of fine arts; and one trimester each year of religion. In addition, students in Grades 9–11 must complete 20 hours per year of community service before entering their senior year. Twelfth graders take part in Senior Project during their final two weeks of school. This 60-hour program is coordinated by the School chaplain and involves students in providing service to day-care facilities, environmental agencies, and other volunteer activities.

Among the specific courses offered in the Upper School are English 9–12, Journalism, Creative Writing, French I–IV, Latin I–III, Spanish I–IV; Algebra I–III, Algebra II/Trigonometry, Geometry, Precalculus, Calculus; Survey of Computer Applications, Program Design and Analysis; United States History to 1900, America in the Twentieth Century World, Asia Since World War II, Ethnic Crisis and World Order, Comparative Political Economy, Latin America: Diversity, Dependency, and Democracy; Church History and Society, World Religions, The Bible, Religious Themes in Art and Literature, Modern Religious Expression; Biology, Molecular Biology Consortium, Chemistry I, Fundamentals of Organic & Biochemistry/Chemistry II, Earth Science, Physics I–II, Conceptual Physics; Video, Arts, Ceramics, Drawing, Design/Graphics, Painting, Photography; Improvisation, Production and Performance, Acting and Directing, Theater; and Band, Guitar, Jazz/Pop/Light Rock,

Songwriting, Traveling Chorus, Keyboard, Stage Band, and Orchestra. Advanced Placement courses are available in all major academic disciplines.

In 1999, all of the 57 graduating seniors entered college; 13 were admitted by "early decision." They are attending such institutions as Bates, Boston College, Bowdoin, Catholic University, Colby, College of Charleston, Dickinson, Drexel, East Carolina University, Emerson, Emory, Georgetown, Hampshire, Harvard, James Madison, Johnson and Wales, Kenyon, Lehigh, Manhattan School of Music, Mary Washington, Middlebury, St. Andrews University, St. Mary's, Salisbury State, Sarah Lawrence, Syracuse, Towson State, Trinity, Tufts, Williams, and the Universities of Maryland, the South, and Western Ontario.

STUDENT ACTIVITIES. Extracurricular activities at St. Andrew's Episcopal School are structured to provide leadership opportunities, encourage participation, and build a sense of community. Elections for the Student Government, consisting of the Upper School Student Council, the Middle School Committee, and officers from each class, take place in the spring. This group serves as the voice of the student body to the administration and plans a variety of special events throughout the year.

Students publish *Praeteritus* (yearbook), *Creaturae* and *The Little Critter* (literary magazines), and *The Mane News* (school newspaper). Other activities include Model United Nations, jazz band, stage crew, Tour Guides, dance and choral groups, musicals, Environmental Club, Film Club, drama, Diversity Club, Chapel Vestry, Equestrian Club, String Ensemble, and Leadership Weekend.

St. Andrew's is a member of both the Potomac Valley Athletic Conference (girls' teams) and the Mid Atlantic Conference (boys' teams). Teams are formed in cross-country, track, soccer, lacrosse, baseball, softball, basketball, tennis, golf, wrestling, and volleyball. Other activities include weight training, fitness classes, an Outdoor Program, and dance.

An active assembly program gives presentations on topics of interest to the entire student body. Dances for the Middle and Upper schools are planned regularly, and students take part in class lock-ins, activity days, and overnight and day field trips.

Among the special events on the school calendar are St. Andrew's Night, Homecoming, Fall Festival and Bulb Sale, Grandparents' Day, the Spring Musical, the Auction, alumni weekend, and the alumni Christmas gathering.

ADMISSION AND COSTS. St. Andrew's Episcopal School welcomes students of demonstrated scholastic ability and diverse backgrounds who possess "the enthusiasm and motivation to succeed in a multifaceted but traditional academic program." New students are accepted in Grades 6 through 12; under special circumstances, they may be admitted during the year if vacancies exist. Applications should be submitted by February 1 for fall entrance; later applications are reviewed as space is available. Admissions decisions are based on the student's transcripts, two teacher recommendations, the results of the Secondary School Admission Test, and an interview. The application fee is $50.

In 1999–2000, tuition is $15,200 for Grades 6–8 and $16,170 for Grades 9–12. Extra expenses include books ($400–$600) and transportation. Financial aid is available based on family need; a total of $418,000 in financial aid was granted for the 1999–2000 school year. St. Andrew's subscribes to the School and Student Service for Financial Aid. Tuition insurance and tuition payment plans are offered.

Upper School Head/Assistant Headmaster: John Holden
Middle School Head/Director of Counseling: James Lee
Dean of Students: Joanne Beach
Director of Admissions: Julie Jameson
Director of Development: Linda Kiser
Business Manager: Elliott F. Brumbaugh
Director of Athletics: Virginia Cobb

St. James' Academy 1821

3100 Monkton Road, Monkton, MD 21111. 410-771-4816; Admissions 410-329-3292; Web Site http://www.saintjames.org/ academy.html

Founded by the Vestry of St. James Church, this coeducational, Episcopal day school enrolls 360 students in Kindergarten–Grade 8. The Academy offers a program meeting the intellectual, social, emotional, and physical needs of each student in preparation not only for the demands of higher education but for living a creative, humane life worthy of a child of God and a contributing member of society. Each class has two teachers providing a curriculum that includes computer, French, Spanish, Latin, art, and music in all grades. Competitive sports and other activities are offered. Tuition: $5015–$8025. Extras: $275. Elizabeth Legenhausen (Catholic University, B.A.; Towson State, M.A.; Johns Hopkins, Ed.D.) was named Head in 1987.

Saint James School ST. JAMES

St. James, MD 21781. 301-733-9330; Fax 301-739-1310; E-mail admissions@stjames.edu; Web Site www.stjames.edu

SAINT JAMES SCHOOL in St. James, Maryland, is an Episcopal, college preparatory boarding and day school enrolling boys and girls in Grades 7–12. The campus lies 5 miles southwest of Hagerstown and approximately 65 miles from both Baltimore and Washington, D.C. The region offers many cultural and historic points of interest including the historic C&O Canal, Harpers Ferry, and Antietam and Gettysburg Battlefields. Faculty and students enjoy the cultural resources of the Baltimore–Washington metropolitan area on regular field trips. The campus is off Route 65 and is easily accessible by car. Washington County Airport, ten minutes away, is serviced by USAirways.

Saint James School was founded in 1842 by Bishop William Whittingham and is the oldest Episcopal boarding school founded on the English model in the United States. Originally a preparatory school and college, the School eliminated the college after the Civil War and began evolving toward its present shape. After admitting girls as day students for many years, a girls' residential program was started in 1991.

Saint James prides itself in providing its students with a family atmosphere. Simultaneously challenged and supported, Saint James students study a traditional core curriculum, which prepares them well for the rigors of college. Participation in sports at the interscholastic or intramural level is required of all in each term. An honor system calls for every student to take responsibility for the integrity of his or her own work. The

School maintains an affiliation with the Episcopal Diocese of Maryland, and students attend daily chapel services.

Saint James School is governed by a self-perpetuating Board of Trustees. It is accredited by the Middle States Association of Colleges and Schools and is a member of the National Association of Independent Schools, Association of Independent Maryland Schools, the Maryland Department of Education, the National Association of Episcopal Schools, and other educational organizations.

THE CAMPUS. Located in a rural setting, the Georgian-style campus of Saint James is situated on 400 acres of farmland containing a natural spring, fields, and streams. Seven athletic fields and six outdoor tennis courts are on the School grounds.

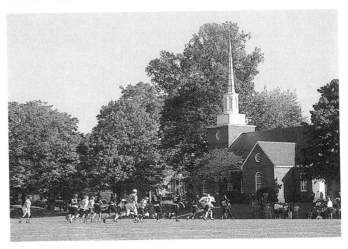

A tree-lined drive leads to the main circle of the campus. At the top, Claggett Hall (1926) contains the Headmaster's, Admission, and Business offices; the dining hall; and boys' dormitories. Kemp Hall (1851) houses the Detweiler Student Center (1997), the School bookstore, a snack bar, and administrative offices. Powell Hall (1965) is the main academic building with classrooms and the computer center. The Saint James Chapel (1964) provides for worship services. The Laidlaw Infirmary (renovated 1996) houses a full-time nurse and the School Chaplain.

Nearby is the Bowman-Byron Fine Arts Center, which has a full auditorium, art studios, and stagecraft and music rooms. The Alumni Hall Athletic Center (1986) has three squash courts; a wrestling room; weight, training, and locker room facilities; and a field house with three basketball courts that can be converted to tennis and volleyball courts. A new girls' locker room opened in 1999.

A new quadrangle on the east side of campus is comprised of the John E. Owens Library (1997), containing 12,000 volumes, with the School Archives, science laboratories, and classrooms located downstairs. Powell Hall, the Detweiler Student Center, and Coors Hall, the new girls' dormitory complete the quadrangle. Further to the east are Onderdonk Dormitory for younger boys, and Hershey Hall, another girls' dormitory. Faculty houses surround the perimeter of the campus.

Plans are under way for a campus technology network, and all students currently have Internet and E-mail access.

THE FACULTY. The Reverend Dr. D. Stuart Dunnan was appointed Headmaster in 1992. A graduate of St. Albans School and Harvard University (A.B., A.M.), he received a B.A. in Theology from Christ Church, Oxford and was awarded a certificate in Anglican Studies from General Theological Seminary in New York. At Oxford, he received his M.A. and completed his doctorate in philosophy. Father Dunnan was also a member of the faculty of Oxford University, where he served as Research Fellow and Chaplain at Lincoln College.

The faculty include 18 men and 12 women, who hold baccalaureate degrees from such institutions as Catholic University,

Colby, Colgate, College of the Holy Cross, Dickinson, Fordham, Franklin and Marshall, Georgetown, Gettysburg, Hamilton, Harvard, Haverford, Hobart, Kenyon, Lafayette, Long Island University, Shippensburg, Wesleyan, and the Universities of Maryland, New Hampshire, North Carolina, the Pacific, Richmond, and Toronto. They also hold 22 advanced degrees from Ball State, Duke, Fordham, Georgetown, Hood, Lehigh, Old Dominion, Oxford, Shippensburg, Simmons, Virginia Polytechnic, Wesleyan, and the Universities of Benin, Chicago, Connecticut, Maryland, North Carolina, and Virginia. Each faculty member acts as an advisor to 6–7 students, and most serve as athletic coaches.

STUDENT BODY. In 1999–2000, the School enrolled 211 boys and girls in Grades 7–12 (Forms I–VI). Day students come from Washington County and neighboring counties in Maryland, Virginia, West Virginia, and Pennsylvania. Most boarders are from Maryland, Pennsylvania, West Virginia, Virginia, and the District of Columbia, but nine other states are represented in the student body. Twenty-two international students come from 12 countries.

ACADEMIC PROGRAM. The academic year, divided into trimesters, begins in early September and extends to early June, with vacations of a week at Thanksgiving, two weeks at Christmas, and two weeks in March. Classes are held 5 days a week and are scheduled in 45-minute periods between 8:00 A.M. and 3:00 P.M. on Mondays, Tuesdays, Thursdays, and Fridays. On Wednesdays, classes end at 1:00 P.M. in order to accommodate athletic games. Extra help for students on academic probation, and others needing it, is regularly scheduled from 3:15 to 3:45 P.M. 3 days a week. An evening study period is required for all students, with those in good standing allowed to study in their rooms. Virtually all of the teachers live on campus; therefore, they are easily available to assist students who are having difficulty. Grades are sent to parents six times a year with comments four times a year.

The School provides English as a Second Language to prepare international students for standard English course work. Students are only admitted to this program if their English is of sufficient proficiency (intermediate level or higher) to allow them to be immediately mainstreamed into their other subjects.

Graduation requirements of Saint James School include 18 units of credit in their high school years, including 4 of English, 3 of foreign language, 3 of history, 3 of mathematics, 3 of laboratory science, and 2 electives.

A core program of English, foreign language (French, Spanish, or Latin), history, math, and science forms the basis for the academic curriculum in each form. Advanced Placement courses are offered in French, Latin, Spanish, U.S. History, European History, Biology, Chemistry, Calculus, and Physics. Electives include Political Economics, World Religions, Ethics,

Art History, Studio Art, Music Theory, Music History, and Computer Science.

All students attend college after graduating from Saint James. Recent graduating classes have matriculated at the following institutions: American University, Boston University, Bowdoin, Colgate, Connecticut College, Cornell, Dartmouth, Drew, Drexel, Duke, Georgetown, George Washington, Hobart, Johns Hopkins, Kenyon, Lehigh, Middlebury, Oberlin, Stanford, Virginia Polytechnic, Wake Forest, Washington and Lee, Wellesley, Wheaton, and the Universities of North Carolina, the South (Sewanee), Virginia, and West Virginia.

STUDENT ACTIVITIES. Ten seniors are elected to the Prefect Council, which preserves the traditions of the School and assists the faculty in the dormitories. The Honor Council, which upholds the Honor Code, and the Disciplinary Committee review instances of misconduct and recommend appropriate dispositions to the Headmaster.

Other organized activities are the *Bai Yuka* (yearbook), *The Jacobite* (newspaper), *Irving Society* (literary magazine), choir, Sacristan's Guild, lay readers, Historical Society, and clubs for music, chess, photography, drama, art, and skiing. A student tutoring group provides assistance to others needing academic help, and the Maroon Key Guides give campus tours to prospective students.

Saint James School offers a full athletic program, and every student participates in intramural or interscholastic sports each term. Varsity teams compete in field hockey, football, soccer, golf, cross-country, basketball, wrestling, squash, lacrosse, tennis, and baseball. Junior varsity teams are formed in most sports, and intramural sports include aerobics, skiing, and weight training.

Saint James is affiliated with 30 prep schools in the Baltimore–Washington area who host a variety of social events including mixers, dances, concerts, and theme parties as well as white-water rafting and outings to Kings Dominion, the Inner Harbor, and the Kennedy Center. Students attend symphony performances in the local area and attend dramatic productions and professional athletic events in Baltimore and Washington, accompanied by faculty. Field trips to historic sites, such as Gettysburg and Antietam, are also organized.

ADMISSION AND COSTS. Saint James seeks girls and boys of good character who have the curiosity and drive to make the most of their talents and who wish to participate fully in the life of the School. Students are admitted in Grades 7–11 on the basis of a completed application, Secondary School Admission Test or School and College Ability Test scores, transcript of previous academic work, English and math teacher recommendations, and a personal interview. Inquiries are welcome all year, and the application deadline is January 31. After this date, applications are welcome and considered on a space-available basis.

In 1999–2000, boarding tuition is $19,000; day tuition is $12,000. A nonrefundable 10 percent deposit is required by April 15th for new and returning students. Students enrolled in the English as a Second Language Program pay an additional fee of $3000. Financial-aid grants ranging from $1000 to $18,000 are awarded on the basis of need and total $635,000.

Academic Dean: Sandra Pollock
Director of Admissions: Win Sherman, '64
Admissions Associate: Britney A. Eyraud
Director of College Guidance: Patrick J. Gately
Business Manager: Richard Bettencourt
Director of Athletics: Christopher Baumann

St. John's Episcopal School   1961

3427 Olney-Laytonsville Road, Olney, MD 20832. 301-774-6804;
Fax 301-774-2375; E-mail sjschool@us.net

St. John's Episcopal School was established through the vision of the Reverend James Valliant, who sought to "send forth well-balanced, disciplined, courteous, self-reliant students generously equipped with academic knowledge." Enrolling 277 boys and girls in Kindergarten–Grade 8, the School specializes in educating students in the elementary and middle years through a curriculum designed to develop a strong foundation in reading, writing, and mathematics skills. Weekly chapel, active family involvement, and social outreach are integral to the program. Extended-day care and a summer program of academics and soccer are offered. Tuition: $7160. Financial aid is available. John Zurn was appointed Headmaster in 1989.

St. Paul's School   1849

P.O. Box 8100, Brooklandville, MD 21022-8100. 410-825-4400;
Admissions Fax 410-296-3145; E-mail admissions@
stpauls.pvt.k12.md.us; Web Site http://stpauls.pvt.k12.md.us

St. Paul's School is an Episcopal, college preparatory day school for boys and girls in Pre-First–Grade 4 and boys in Grades 5–12. Located on 64 acres, the School offers its 835 students honors and Advanced Placement courses, multilingual and computer experience in all grades, and a foreign exchange program. A chapel program, broad art and athletic programs, community service, and coordinate classes with the adjacent St. Paul's School for Girls complement the curriculum. The new 47,000-square-foot Athletic Center was completed in 1999. Tuition: $12,540. Financial Aid: $967,000. George L. Mitchell, Jr., '78, is Director of Admissions and Financial Aid; Robert W. Hallett (University of Pennsylvania, M.Ed.) was appointed Headmaster in 1985.

St. Paul's School for Girls   1959

Falls Road and Seminary Avenue, Brooklandville, MD 21022.
410-823-6323; Fax 410-828-7238;
E-mail info@spsfg.pvt.k12.md.us;
Web Site http://www.spsfg.pvt.k12.md.us

This Episcopal day school enrolling 351 girls in Grades 5–12 emphasizes traditional academic disciplines. The Middle School curriculum is designed to help students master skills necessary for academic growth and personal development; the college preparatory Upper School includes Advanced Placement and coordinated classes with St. Paul's School. St. Paul's School for Girls is concerned for the individual, not only academically but also with regard to her sense of personal and social responsibility. Sports, music, art, publications, student government, community service, and foreign travel enhance the program. Tuition: $13,025. Financial Aid: $465,000. Ann Oglesby is Director of Admission; Evelyn A. Flory (New York University, Ph.D.) is Headmistress.

St. Timothy's School   STEVENSON

8400 Greenspring Avenue, Stevenson, MD 21153. 410-486-7400;
Fax 410-486-1167; E-mail admis@sttimothysschool.com;
Web Site www.sttimothysschool.com

ST. TIMOTHY'S SCHOOL in Stevenson, Maryland, is a boarding and day school, affiliated with the Episcopal Church, enrolling young women in Forms Three through Six (Grades 9–12) and a postgraduate year. The School is located in a rural setting 15 minutes from downtown Baltimore and one hour north of Washington, D.C. It is easily reached by Interstate 95 and from the Baltimore-Washington International Airport. Students and faculty make excellent use of the rich cultural, historic, and recreational resources of the two cities and their environment as an extension of classroom learning.

St. Timothy's School was founded in 1882 by sisters Sally and Polly Carter, who shared a vision of a rigorous educational environment in which bright young women could stretch and expand their intellectual capabilities, without limitations, for their own enrichment and the betterment of their world. During the 1970s, St. Timothy's consolidated with Hannah More Academy, the first Episcopal school for girls in the country.

The School's mission is to provide the best possible preparation for higher education and life. Challenging academics are integrated with broad exposure to the arts and computer technology. St. Timothy's seeks to develop students' self-confidence in their own abilities as scholars, leaders, and citizens of the world. Girls live according to an Honor Code based on truth, trust, and kindness, which has been developed and administered by students throughout the years.

Governed by a 26-member Board of Trustees, St. Timothy's is accredited by the Middle States Association of Colleges and Schools and the Association of Independent Maryland Schools, and holds membership in the National Association of Independent Schools, the Association of Independent Maryland Schools, National Coalition of Girls' Schools, and the National Association of Episcopal Schools, among other organizations. Its $7,200,000 endowment is enriched by the $533,862 Annual Fund, which is supported by many of the School's approximately 2700 alumnae.

THE CAMPUS. St. Timothy's is situated in the countryside just 15 minutes from downtown Baltimore. Among the 22 buildings on the property is the Hannah More Arts Center, which houses a 350-seat theater, scenery and costume shops, a spacious dance studio, music practice rooms, and a gallery. The Art Barn holds facilities for two- and three-dimensional studies including design, photography, and ceramics. Fowler House, the academic building, has science and computer laboratories and the 22,000-volume Ella R. Watkins Library containing computerized catalog search capabilities. Each classroom is equipped with an on-line computer. Girls live two or three to a room in a stately 1930s mansion and a more contemporary residence, each containing living rooms, faculty apartments, study areas, and computer labs. A health center, chapel, bookstore, student bank, and the Irvine Natural Science Center, an independent nature education and conservation foundation, are also on campus.

Athletic facilities include basketball, paddle tennis, and eight all-weather tennis courts; an outdoor swimming pool; a gymnasium; and cross-country, hiking, and running trails. The School's extensive riding program, which involves students in interschool horse shows, is facilitated by indoor and outdoor riding rings, five fenced fields, and a 24-stall barn.

THE FACULTY. Deborah M. Cook, appointed Head of School in 1993, earned a B.S. degree from The College of New Jersey and a master's in educational administration from Rider University. Prior to coming to St. Timothy's, she was affiliated with The Pennington School where she served as Dean of the Middle School, Dean of Academic Affairs, Assistant Head of School, and Interim Head of School.

There are 29 full-time and 9 part-time members of the faculty and administration. Sixty percent have ten or more years' teaching experience. Sixty-three of the faculty and administration hold advanced degrees, and 72 percent live on campus. They have graduated from colleges and universities such as Amherst, Brown, Colby, Connecticut College, Drake University Law School, George Washington, Goucher, Johns Hopkins, Middlebury, Mount Holyoke, Princeton, Smith, Temple, Trinity, Tufts, Vanderbilt, Vassar, Williams, Yale, and the Universities of Bridgeport, Delaware, Maryland, Michigan, Pennsylvania, and Virginia.

STUDENT BODY. In 1999–2000, St. Timothy's enrolls 120 young women, 83 boarders and 37 day students, in Forms III through VI, as follows: 25 in Form III, 35 in Form IV, 35 in Form V, and 25 in Form VI. They come from 19 states and nine countries and represent a wide diversity of religious, ethnic, and racial heritages.

ACADEMIC PROGRAM. The academic curriculum at St. Timothy's School has the primary goal of giving students of above-average ability the strongest possible preparation for college and of developing critical and analytical thinking skills that will remain with them throughout their lives. Girls enrolled in the one-year English as a Foreign Language program are expected to become fully integrated into the regular academic program the following year.

Each girl has an adviser who keeps track of her academic progress and personal growth and maintains a liaison with her parents. With a 5:1 student-teacher ratio, classes average 9–12 girls, ensuring each student individual attention and encouraging full participation in the learning process.

The curriculum encompasses English Language and Literature, Mathematics, Classical and Foreign Languages, United States and World History, Physical and Natural Sciences, Comparative Religion, Dance, Drama, Music, Art History, and Studio Art. Honors and Advanced Placement courses are available in most disciplines, and in recent years, 70 percent of St. Timothy's students who have taken AP exams have scored 3 or higher.

To graduate, a student must earn a minimum of 18 academic credits and 1 athletic credit. Requirements include four years of English; three each of history, mathematics, and a foreign language; two years of laboratory science, including biology; and one year each of religion and art. One credit is awarded for four years of participation in athletics.

Among the specific courses offered are Advanced Composition and Literature, Introduction to Composition and Literature, Composition Writing, Old World/New World: African Literatures and Their Influences, The Search for Truth via Russian Literature, Essays; French I–IV, Spanish I–IV, Latin I–IV; Algebra I–II, Geometry, Pre-Calculus, Topics in Advanced Mathematics; Physical Science, Biology, Chemistry, Honors Chemistry, Physics; World History I–II, United States History, United States History Since 1945, Discovering the Asian-Pacific Rim; Comparative Religions; and Drama I–II, Art History, Art I–II, Photography I–II, and Modern Dance, Ballet, Jazz, and Tap. There are Advanced Placement courses in Biology, English, United States History, Calculus AB and BC, History of Art, Studio Art, Latin, Spanish, and French, and an Honors course in Chemistry.

Connections is an off-campus experiential program for ninth and tenth graders that integrates technology, research, and writing skills as students examine different aspects of the multifaceted environments of Baltimore, Annapolis, and Washington, D.C. Senior girls also undertake Independent Study Projects in the last three weeks of the spring term. These may include such varied programs as working in the corporate world, exploring a Brazilian rainforest, or volunteering at the National Gallery of Art.

College advising begins early and involves both the student and her parents. Each year, the School hosts many selective colleges and universities that give presentations about their programs and the admission process. One hundred percent of St. Timothy's girls attend college. In the last three years, graduates have been accepted at Bowdoin, Bucknell, Carleton, Colby, Cornell, Georgetown, Goucher, Haverford, Hollins, Johns Hopkins, Middlebury, Montana State, Oberlin, Sarah Lawrence, Skidmore, Spelman, Wesleyan, Williams, and the University of Virginia, among other institutions.

STUDENT ACTIVITIES. St. Timothy's provides a wide range of extracurricular opportunities that meet a variety of interests and abilities, involving students in leadership, community service, and social and athletic activities.

The riding program, headed by a professional horsewoman, is an integral component of the School's athletic offerings. Girls take part in competitive horse shows, fox hunting, combined training events, dressage, and trail and recreational riding. Varsity and junior varsity teams are formed in basketball, cross-country, field hockey, lacrosse, soccer, softball, and tennis; weight training, modern dance, ballet, jazz, tap, and a ropes course are also available.

On-campus organizations include Amnesty International, Choir, Bell Choir, two a cappella singing groups, Madrigals, literary magazine and yearbook, Dramat, Tour Guides, Student Chapel Committee, Current Events, Environmental Action, International Club, Riding, and Social Services Club.

St. Timothy's enjoys many time-honored traditions, among them the hard-fought Brownie-Spider basketball game that has been played just before Thanksgiving for over 100 years.

ADMISSION AND COSTS. The School welcomes girls who have high personal standards, leadership potential, and a good academic record. Candidates submit an application along with an essay. Acceptance is based on a personal interview; results of either the Secondary School Admissions Test (SSAT) or the Independent School Entrance Examination (ISEE); personal recommendations from the student's math and English teachers and principal or adviser; a parent's statement; the student's transcript; and the completed application. The application fee is $40.

In 1999–2000, boarding tuition is $26,900; day tuition is $16,100. Additional expenses include transportation, a $340 social activities fee, $400–$600 for books and academic supplies, and approximately $180 for the required school uniform. The optional Riding Program runs from $1000 to $1800 per year. Financial aid of more than $500,000 is awarded and distributed among more than one-third of the student body.

Head of School: Deborah M. Cook
Academic Dean: Deborah M. Cook
Dean of Students: Patricia Lindsay
Director of Admission: Sarah Morse
Director of Alumnae and Development: Meredith C. Boren
College Adviser: Sally E. Austin
Business Manager: Gordon J. Ringer, Jr.
Director of Athletics: Janet M. Powers

Sandy Spring Friends School

SANDY SPRING

Sandy Spring, MD 20860. 301-774-7455; E-mail apply@ssfs.org

Sᴀɴᴅʏ sᴘʀɪɴɢ ꜰʀɪᴇɴᴅs sᴄʜᴏᴏʟ in Sandy Spring, Maryland, enrolls day students in Pre-Kindergarten–Grade 12, while offering a boarding program for students in Grades 9–12. Established by Brook Moore in 1961 under the care of the Sandy Spring Monthly Meeting of Friends, the School provides a college preparatory liberal arts curriculum for students of varying ethnic, racial, economic, and religious backgrounds. The School is approximately 35 minutes from both Washington, D.C., and Baltimore.

As a Quaker school, Sandy Spring Friends shares the Quaker concern for the unique worth of the individual. Qualities of sensitivity, inventiveness, persistence, and humor are val-

ued along with intellectual traits. The School's goal is to help each student develop a sense of personal integrity and at the same time grow academically and learn to be a responsible member of the community. To accommodate individual academic needs, the School offers a diverse liberal arts curriculum with courses ranging from the basics to advanced independent study and seminars; athletics and fine arts courses are also an important part of the curriculum.

The School is approved by the Maryland State Board of Education, is accredited by the Association of Independent Maryland Schools, and holds membership in such organizations as the Friends Council on Education and the National Association of Independent Schools.

THE CAMPUS. The 140-acre campus includes woods, a stream, a pond, meadows, tennis courts, and athletic fields. The plant, valued at more than $9 million, includes a state-of-the-art science center, an expanded Lower School; a dormitory and classroom building; two administration and classroom buildings for the Middle and Upper schools; a performing arts building with a fine arts wing; a historic meeting house (1881); and faculty houses. Yarnall Hall, a $1,750,000 resource center, houses a 16,000-volume library, a gymnasium, an observatory, classrooms, and a conference room.

THE FACULTY. Kenneth W. Smith, appointed Head of School in 1996, is a graduate of Trinity University (B.S.), Princeton Theological Seminary (M.Div., Th.M.), and Southern Methodist University (D.Min.).

There are 65 full-time teachers and administrators who teach, 26 men and 39 women. Fourteen live on campus, 10 with their families. They hold 65 baccalaureate degrees and 31 degrees at the master's level or higher. Faculty degrees were earned at such institutions as American, Bank Street College, Brown, Bucknell, Catholic University, Colgate, Dartmouth, Earlham, Florida Southern, Frostburg University, George Washington University, Georgia State, Harvard, Haverford, Hood, Kenyon, Longwood, Manchester College, Middlebury, Mount Holyoke, New York University, Pennsylvania State, Pierce, Princeton, Princeton Theological Seminary, Sarah Lawrence, Smith, Southern Methodist, Stanford, Swarthmore, Tufts, Virginia Polytechnic Institute, Yale, and the Universities of Chicago, London, Maryland, Minnesota, Oregon, Pennsylvania, and Wisconsin.

STUDENT BODY. In 1999–2000, the School enrolls 491 students, 240 boys and 251 girls, as follows: 12 in Pre-Kindergarten, 26 in Kindergarten, 31 in Grade 1, 26 in Grade 2, 30 in Grade 3, 33 in Grade 4, 31 in Grade 5, 33 in Grade 6, 36 in Grade 7, 35 in Grade 8, 54 in Grade 9, 52 in Grade 10, 44 in Grade 11, and 48 in Grade 12. The boarding program enrolls 40 students from the Mid-Atlantic region as well as ten different countries.

ACADEMIC PROGRAM. The curriculum at Sandy Spring Friends School is intended to prepare students not only for entering college but also for being valuable citizens of the world. It stresses the challenge of Quaker values, academic excellence, and personal growth within a structured environment.

The school year, from early September to early June, includes Thanksgiving, Christmas, and spring vacations. A typical daily schedule includes six academic periods, jobs, lunch, an activities period, and sports. The school day is from 8:00 A.M. to 3:20 P.M. with sports and activities after school. Boarding students are required to attend dinner at 6:00 P.M. and study hall from 7:30 to 9:30 P.M. The average class size is 15 with a faculty-to-student ratio of 1:7.

The Lower School encourages exploration and creativity and fosters caring interaction with others. Basic skills in reading and mathematics are taught sequentially, and children are encouraged to apply these skills to other life contexts, to think analytically, and to evaluate in both verbal and quantitative areas.

The Middle School (Grades 5–8) offers a curriculum of English, general mathematics and algebra, social studies, science, foreign language, art, music, and sports. The program encourages the development of academic skills, preparing students for the Upper School curriculum. Enrichment activities include field trips, art and music programs, and science activities.

The required academic load for an Upper School student is six courses. To graduate, students must earn 24 credits, including English 4, foreign language 3, history 3 (including United States History), mathematics 3, science 3, electives 3, and fine arts 3. Additional noncredit requirements are participating in a physical activity each year and passing a semester course on Quakerism. Advanced Placement courses are available in English, History, Calculus, Statistics, Chemistry, French, and Spanish. Full-year courses are English; French, Spanish; History; Algebra, Geometry, Trigonometry, Functions, Analysis, Calculus, Computer Math; Biology, Chemistry, Physics, Astronomy, Geology, Advanced Science; Art, Orchestra, Chorus; Theater; Modern Dance; and Wood Shop.

The English as a Second Language Program is open to students in Grades 9–12. Currently, 29 students are enrolled.

"Intersession" week in the spring gives students an opportunity to participate in off-campus activities that supplement the standard curriculum. Projects have included trips to Kenya, Brazil, and throughout Europe; a theater improvisation workshop; inner-city service projects in the District of Columbia, Baltimore, and New York; and numerous outdoor exploration activities.

In 1999, 44 of the 46 graduates entered college. They are attending such institutions as Beloit, Bryn Mawr, Carnegie Mellon, Catholic University, Colgate, Duke, Earlham, Frostburg, Goucher, Guilford, Haverford, Hofstra, James Madison, Kenyon, Oberlin, Oglethorpe, Parsons School of Design, Philadelphia College of Textiles & Science, St. John's University (New York), St. Mary's College (Maryland), Swarthmore, and the Universities of Colorado (Boulder), Delaware, Maryland, and Massachusetts (Amherst).

STUDENT ACTIVITIES. A Town Meeting composed of students and faculty meets regularly to discuss issues of importance to the school community. Students present many dramatic productions and perform in dance recitals and choral concerts. Involvement in some aspect of the sports program is mandatory. Interscholastic teams in baseball, lacrosse, soccer, tennis, Frisbee, cross-country, volleyball, and basketball compete with other preparatory schools in the Baltimore-District of Columbia area. Students may also participate in a variety of intramural sports.

Student participation in Quaker study centers and conferences is encouraged, and a community service requirement is part of the curriculum. Frequent trips are made to Washington, D.C., or Baltimore for shopping, films, and cultural events.

ADMISSION AND COSTS. The School accepts students whose backgrounds represent diverse social, economic, religious, and cultural experiences. Students should apply before January 15 to be considered for the following fall. Candidates must submit application forms, a school transcript, and a photograph (optional). A personal interview and academic references are also required, and there is a $50 application fee.

In 1999–2000, tuition is $8750–$9650 in the Lower School, $10,275–$11,525 in the Middle School, and $12,625–$13,225 in the Upper School. Boarding tuition is $17,825 for five days and $21,625 for seven days. Several tuition payment plans are available. In 1999–2000, over $800,000 in financial assistance was awarded to 25 percent of the student body.

Head of the Upper School: Ellen Lawsky
Head of the Middle School: Nancy Preuss
Head of the Elementary School: Lynn Darman
Director of Advancement: Christina Warnick
Dean of Students: John Staehle
Director of Admissions: Victoria W. Garner
Director of Business and Finance: Carmen Johnson
College Counselor: Robert Hoch
Business Manager: Howard Zuses
Director of Athletics: Aaron Wright

Maryland

Severn School 1914

Water Street, Severna Park, MD 21146. 410-647-7700;
Fax 410-544-9451; E-mail admissions@severnschool.com;
Web Site http://www.severnschool.com

Located six miles from Annapolis, Severn School was founded in 1914 to provide academic preparation for the United States Naval Academy. Today Severn is a day school enrolling 550 boys and girls in Grades 6 through 12. The School strives to meet the needs of college-bound students while challenging them to realize personal excellence. The students are provided varied opportunities to demonstrate scholarship, leadership, citizenship, and sportsmanship both in and outside the classroom. Severn also offers a summer academic program and sports camps. Tuition: $12,855. Financial Aid: $500,000. Molly M. Green is Director of Admissions; William J. Creeden (University of Pennsylvania, B.S. 1968, M.S. 1972) was named Headmaster in 1993. *Middle States Association.*

Stone Ridge School of the Sacred Heart 1923

9101 Rockville Pike, Bethesda, MD 20814. 301-657-4322;
Fax 301-657-4393; E-mail admissions@stoneridge.org;
Web Site http://www.stoneridge.org

Stone Ridge, founded by the Society of the Sacred Heart, is a college preparatory school enrolling 774 girls in Junior Kindergarten–Grade 12 and 14 boys in Junior Kindergarten–Kindergarten. The School educates to a personal, active faith, respect for intellectual values, and social awareness. Activities include sports, publications, and drama. Extended-day and after-school study programs are offered. Stone Ridge received two U.S. Department of Education Blue Ribbon School Awards. Summer programs are offered. Tuition: $7725–$13,925. Financial aid is available. Christine Thornton is Director of Admission; Anne Dyer, RSCJ (Wheaton, B.A. 1959; Manhattanville, M.A. 1966; University of Notre Dame, M.S.A. 1979), became Headmistress in 1984. *Middle States Association.*

Thornton Friends School 1973

Upper School: 13925 New Hampshire Avenue, Silver Spring, MD
* 20904. 301-384-0320*
Middle School: 11612 New Hampshire Avenue, Silver Spring, MD
* 20904. 301-622-9033*
Upper School: 3830 Seminary Road, Alexandria, VA 22304.
* 703-461-8880*

Thornton Friends, committed to smallness, authenticity, and the values of Friends, enrolls about 50 students in each Upper School and 35 in the Middle School. Classes average 9 students, and a community-supported ambiance makes studying relevant and engaging. Over 90 percent of graduates enter the college of their choice. The School promotes core values of honesty, compassion, equality, trust, scholarship, self-discipline, nonviolence, and the dignity of work. A required community service program enriches all. Interscholastic sports include soccer, basketball, and softball. Tuition: $11,495–$12,795. Financial Aid: $160,380. Gail Miller (Alexandria High School), Norman Maynard (Silver Spring High School), and Jonathan Meisel (Silver Spring Middle School) are Principals; Michael W. DeHart (University of Maryland [College Park], B.A.; Catholic University, M.S.W.) is Headmaster.

Washington Episcopal School 1985

5600 Little Falls Parkway, Bethesda, MD 20816. 301-652-7878;
Fax 301-652-7255; E-mail kherman@w-e-s.org;
Web Site www.wes.pvt.k12.md.us

Washington Episcopal, a Blue Ribbon School of Excellence enrolling 300 girls and boys ages 3–Grade 8, is committed to fostering the intellectual, spiritual, physical, emotional, and social development of its students. The early grades emphasize the basic motor, auditory, and social skills, while the accelerated academic program for older students provides a strong foundation in the traditional academic disciplines. The resources of the nation's capital provide numerous enrichment activities. Religious education and chapel services are carried out according to Episcopal beliefs. An after-school program is offered. Tuition: $6100–$13,560. Financial aid is available. Mrs. Kathleen Herman is Admissions Director; Isabelle S. Schuessler is Head of School. *Middle States Association.*

West Nottingham Academy COLORA

Colora, MD 21917. 410-658-5556; E-mail admissions@wna.org;
Web Site www.wna.org

WEST NOTTINGHAM ACADEMY in Colora, Maryland, is a coeducational college preparatory school enrolling boarding students in Grades 9 through 12 and a postgraduate year and day students from Grade 6 through postgraduate. The Academy is situated in the farming country of northeastern Maryland, 3 miles from the town of Rising Sun (population 2000). It is 45 miles from Baltimore, Maryland; 35 miles from Wilmington, Delaware; and 55 miles from Philadelphia, Pennsylvania.

Celebrating its 256th anniversary of educating America's youth, West Nottingham Academy was founded in 1744 by Dr. Samuel Finley, pastor of the Nottingham Presbyterian Church. Dr. Finley, who later became President of Princeton University, desired to establish a school where young men in the area could prepare for the ministry and other professions. The school became known as a boarding school throughout a wider area circa 1800. First admitted as day students in 1900, girls were accepted as boarders in 1954.

The Academy offers a college preparatory curriculum in an intimate, familylike atmosphere. The school fosters considerable out-of-class interaction among teachers and students.

A nonprofit institution, the school is governed by a self-perpetuating Board of Trustees, which meets four times yearly.

210

There are approximately 1500 living alumni. West Nottingham Academy is accredited by the Middle States Association of Colleges and Schools and the Maryland State Department of Education. It holds membership in the National Association of Independent Schools, The Association of Independent Maryland Schools, and the Association of Delaware Valley Independent Schools.

THE CAMPUS. The 180-acre campus includes 20 acres of woodland; football, soccer, and hockey fields as well as newly reconditioned fields for soccer and field hockey; baseball and softball diamonds; and four tennis courts. Indoor athletic facilities are housed in Ware Field House (1964). The C. Herbert Foutz Center (1990) is the focal point of the Academy's master campus plan. It houses the Frank D. Brown Dining Room, the Hallock Student Union, and administrative offices.

Classes are held in Finley Hall (1961) with 11 classrooms, 3 laboratories, and a 9000-volume library. Magraw Hall, which was renovated and fully automated in 1999, provides classrooms, the library, a computer lab, and offices for admissions and department heads. East Dorm and West Dorm, both opened in 1998, house 22 boys and 22 girls, respectively. Other dormitories are Rush (1968), for boys and Rowland (1957) for girls. The oldest building on campus is Gayley Hall (circa 1700), which serves as the Head of School's residence and a center of campus life. Bechtel Hall (1900), Hilltop House (1945), and Log Cabin (1949) provide additional faculty housing. The school-owned plant is valued at $6,500,000.

THE FACULTY. Edward J. Baker, who earned his master's degree at Springfield College, was appointed Head of School in 1989. He is the recipient of the Robert Bell Crow Memorial Award for his contributions to independent school advancement programs and was named Outstanding Teacher of 1987 by the Council for Advancement and Support of Education. Prior to his appointment at West Nottingham, Mr. Baker was Director of Development and Alumni Relations at Brooks School in Andover, Massachusetts, and Director of Development at George School in Newtown, Pennsylvania.

There are 38 teaching faculty, 19 men and 19 women. Twenty-eight teachers and administrators live on campus, several with families. Faculty members hold baccalaureate and graduate degrees from Bryn Mawr, Colgate, Cornell, Emory, Georgetown, Gettysburg College, Guilford, Hollins, Johns Hopkins, Kenyon, Kutztown, Maryville, Millersville University, Muhlenberg, Murray State University, Pennsylvania State, St. Andrews (Scotland), St. Joseph's University, St. Mary's College, St. Michael's, Springfield, Towson State, Upper Iowa University, Washington College, West Virginia University, Williams, York College of Pennsylvania, and the Universities of Delaware, Denver, Maine, Pennsylvania, Pittsburgh, and Vermont. Faculty benefits include health insurance, a retirement plan, and Social Security.

A nurse is on campus during the week; the school physician resides three miles away. Hospital services are available in Havre de Grace, ten miles distant.

STUDENT BODY. In 1999–2000, the school enrolls 121 boarding and day boys and girls, ages 14–19, as follows: 22 in Grade 9, 32 in Grade 10, 43 in Grade 11, 23 in Grade 12, and 1 postgraduate. There are also 28 students in Grades 6–8. Boarding students come primarily from Maryland, Virginia, and Pennsylvania, with 10 other states and the District of Columbia also represented. International students come from Germany, Ghana, Japan, Korea, Nicaragua, Saudi Arabia, Taiwan, and Thailand.

ACADEMIC PROGRAM. The academic year, from September to early June, is divided into trimesters and includes a Thanksgiving recess as well as winter and spring vacations. Classes, which are 45 minutes in length, are held from 8:00 A.M. to 3:30 P.M. five days a week.

An average class has eight students; the student-teacher ratio is 5:1. Teachers are available for extra help during two daily "academic assistance" periods, which students may attend voluntarily or by faculty request. Boarding students have supervised study from 7:45 to 9:45 P.M. Sunday through Thursday. Parents are sent grades and comments six times yearly, with interim reports issued for students experiencing academic difficulty.

The Chesapeake Learning Center Program provides students of average to above-average intelligence who have specific learning difficulties with an opportunity to achieve academic success. Students follow a regular high school curriculum in an environment tailored to meet individual needs.

To graduate, students must complete a minimum of 19 academic units of credit including four years of English, three years each of mathematics and science, and two years of a foreign language. The school also requires three years of history, including United States History; a trimester of World Religions or Christian Ethics; and a trimester each in computers and art.

Courses offered are English Literature 1–4, English Composition 1–4; French 1–4, Latin 1–2, Spanish 1–4; World Geography, World History, United States History, American Government, Advanced Placement American History, European History, English History, Russian Studies, Ancient History, World War II, World Religions, Christian Ethics; Algebra 1–2, Geometry, Trigonometry, Calculus, Probability and Statistics, Computer Science; Physical Science, Environmental Science, Anatomy and Physiology, Biology, Chemistry, Physics; Drawing, Painting, Clay, Design, Sculpture, Survey of Western Art; and Health.

In 1999, all of the 32 seniors entered college. They are attending such colleges and universities as American University, Boston University, Carthage, Drexel, Georgetown, Ithaca, Johnson and Wales, Lafayette, Lynchburg, Muhlenberg, New York University, Pennsylvania State, Rensselaer Polytechnic, Springfield,

Ursinus, Western Maryland 4, and the Universities of Delaware 2, Massachusetts (Amherst) 2, Pittsburgh, and Wisconsin.

STUDENT ACTIVITIES. The Student Council provides a forum for matters of student concern. A Student Dormitory Council identifies problems in residential life and seeks solutions.

Club activity varies according to student interest, but all students are expected to take part in the activity program. It includes the yearbook, skiing, and the Computer, Library, Religion, Canteen, and Varsity clubs. Qualified students are invited to join the National Honor Society.

West Nottingham teams compete with those of other independent schools in Delaware, Maryland, and Pennsylvania. Interscholastic teams for boys include football, cross-country, soccer, basketball, wrestling, baseball, lacrosse, and tennis. Girls' interscholastic teams are field hockey, cross-country, basketball, soccer, softball, and tennis. Horseback riding is available for girls and boys. Students not on an interscholastic team choose from a wide variety of activities and clubs.

Periodic dances take place on campus and at neighboring schools. Weekend activities include outings to places and events of interest in Baltimore, Philadelphia, and the surrounding area. Traditional events and activities include Homecoming, Parents' Day, the Homecoming and Christmas dances, and the Senior Prom.

ADMISSION AND COSTS. West Nottingham seeks to enroll students who are capable of handling a college preparatory program successfully and who are committed to their own growth and involvement in the community. Applicants must submit a transcript of grades and three recommendations. The school accepts the results of the Secondary School Admission Test. Except in cases of extreme distance, a personal interview is also required.

Students are accepted in Grades 6 through 12 and post-graduate. Application should be made before June prior to fall enrollment, but applications are considered until classes are full. Midyear enrollment is possible if vacancies exist. There is an application fee of $50. An additional fee of $1200, applicable toward tuition and costs, is due upon acceptance.

In 1999–2000, boarding tuition is $23,460; day tuition ranges from $5100 in Grades 6–8 to $12,060 in the upper grades. Boarding tuition for the Chesapeake Learning Center is $28,700 and day tuition is $17,300. An estimated additional $1200 covers personal allowances, field trips, and testing fees. Financial aid of approximately $190,000 is granted annually on the basis of need. In 1999–2000, 30 students received financial aid. A tuition payment plan is available.

Dean of Faculty: Joseph C. Ray
Assistant Head of School: Dr. Sandra D. Wirth
Director of Admissions: Kenneth W. Michelsen
Director of Development: Vince Watchorn
Director of Studies: Victoria Londergen
Business Manager: Ronald Kupcinski
Director of Athletics: John Kampes

The Woods Academy   1975

6801 Greentree Road, Bethesda, MD 20817. 301-365-3080; Fax 301-469-6439; Web Site http://www.woodsacademy.org

A Catholic, coeducational day school enrolling students from many faiths and nationalities, The Woods Academy has celebrated the education of mind, body, and spirit for over two decades. A Woods education begins in Montessori Preschool and concludes as graduating eighth-graders choose from a wide range of selective secondary schools. The academic program is enhanced by daily French, Internet-assisted learning, Chicago Math, hands-on laboratory science, computer labs, and an 8000-volume library. Activities include student government, sports, publications, theater arts, and community service. Extended care and transportation are offered. Tuition: $5825–$8390. Financial Aid: $25,000. Barbara B. Snyder is Director of Admissions; Mary C. Worch (Trinity, B.A. 1987, M.A. 1991) is Head of School. *Middle States Association.*

MASSACHUSETTS

The Academy at Charlemont   1981

The Mohawk Trail, Charlemont, MA 01339. 413-339-4912;
Fax 413-339-4324; E-mail academy@charlemont.org;
Web Site www.charlemont.org

The Academy of Charlemont is a coeducational, college preparatory school enrolling 85 day and home-stay boarding students in Grades 7–12 and a postgraduate year. It is a closely knit community based on an honor code. The interdisciplinary curriculum is rigorous and challenging. Activities beyond the academic classroom include a full range of studio arts, choral and instrumental music, photography, performance and technical theater, computer studies, interscholastic and life sports, foreign exchanges, internships, and community service. Boarding Tuition: $19,250; Day Tuition: $10,250. Dianne Grinnell is Director of Admissions; Eric A. Grinnell is Headmaster. *New England Association.*

The Academy at Swift River

CUMMINGTON

151 South Street, Cummington, MA 01026. 800-258-1770;
Fax 413-634-5300; Web Site www.swiftriver.com;
E-mail bray@swiftriver.com

THE ACADEMY AT SWIFT RIVER in Cummington, Massachusetts, is a coeducational, year-round, college preparatory boarding school enrolling more than 85 students who have a history of social, academic, and familial problems. The Academy, founded in 1997, uses a broad range of experiential learning, wilderness, and emotional growth programs to help its students become well-rounded, motivated, and responsible individuals who show both character and confidence in meeting the challenges of life and school. Situated in the rolling Berkshire Hills, Swift River's hilltop campus is close to the cultural and educational resources of Northampton, Tanglewood, Jacob's Pillow Dance Festival, and Williamstown.

The Academy at Swift River's 14-month program consists of three major components: a 28-day Base Camp, followed by a 10-month stay on the Main Campus, and concluding with a four- to six-week service learning project in Costa Rica. The goal of the program is to facilitate the student's transition from being self-focused, to gradual adjustment to successful community living, and, ultimately, to providing service to others in need.

The Academy is owned by Aspen Youth Services, which operates a number of therapeutic programs throughout the United States. It is approved to grant a High School diploma and operates in accordance with Massachusetts General Education Law as a private school. Swift River's association with Aspen Youth Services provides access to a wide range of additional services including family participation in the National Parenting Support Program run exclusively for Aspen by Dr. James Jones, a California-based educational psychologist.

THE CAMPUS. Set on 626 acres of mixed forest, meadow, beaver ponds, and mountain streams, Swift River's campus was originally a working dairy farm; it was later used as both a YMCA camp and a ski resort before being purchased for use as a school. The Academy's construction of post-and-beam design throughout the living and academic areas includes boys' and girls' dormitories, administration and counseling offices, a dining room, a living room, and the Great Room, which is used for general meetings and as a recreation hall for the students, complete with fusbol, air hockey, Ping-Pong tables, and a widescreen TV and entertainment center. The Academic Building is a short walk from the Main Building.

Dormitory rooms are composed of large one- and two-story suites, each with their own bathrooms. Boys and girls are housed in separate wings, and students live four to six in a suite. The Academy's computer lab has nearly 20 Dell computer systems; limited Internet access for school projects is available with teacher supervision, and the system has fireblocks installed.

Three major building projects are underway at The Academy. Renovations to the Academic Building, which was previously used as a restaurant and lounge, include the installation of fully equipped science laboratories, relocation and enlargement of the current library, and enhancement of the space used for emotional growth seminars. Other building projects include the design of new counseling offices that will be more accessible to students throughout the day and refurbishing the dining room and administrative offices.

Swift River's 17 nature trails provide ample opportunity for hiking, walking, biking, skiing, and enjoying nature and the wildlife indigenous to the Berkshire Hills. The campus also has an outdoor swimming pool, outdoor skating rink, a fitness center, and tennis, basketball, and volleyball courts. A new indoor gymnasium is planned for the future. The medical office and infirmary are available to assist students around the clock, with a nurse dispensing student medications. Cooley-Dickinson Hospital is nearby for medical emergencies.

THE FACULTY. John T. Powers is Director of The Academy at Swift River, and Rudolph Bentz is Headmaster. Mr. Powers holds a bachelor's degree from Waynesburg College and a Master's in Special Education from William Paterson College. He has served in executive positions at a number of organizations, including the Rose F. Kennedy Center and The United Cerebral Palsy Association. Mr. Bentz holds an M.F.A. from the University of Massachusetts and is a doctoral candidate at Taft University, with nearly 20 years' experience working at therapeutic boarding schools in California and Georgia.

There are currently 70 staff members, including a consulting psychiatrist, counselors with master's degrees, teachers trained in their areas of instruction, expert wilderness coordinators and instructors, and various administrative and support staff.

STUDENT BODY. The Academy at Swift River enrolls more than 85 students in Grades 9–12, with a capacity of 90 boys and girls. Most students come from the northeast, with others attending from throughout the United States and abroad. Many are referred by educational consultants.

ACADEMIC PROGRAM. The first component of the 14-month program is the 28-day Base Camp experience, a multistage process using high-impact outdoor learning and the introduction of basic principles of healthy living. The strategy behind Base Camp is the elimination of external stimuli from students' lives, providing them the opportunity to focus on themselves and complete an honest personal evaluation. Although located on campus, the Base Camp is a separate and self-contained facility.

During the second phase, the 10-month Main Campus stay, students progress into daily academic classes and study halls, participate in focus groups, and complete an exhaustive four-part series of academic, family, social, and personal growth seminars. Participants in the seminars are given the following morning to rest, physically and emotionally. Students are challenged on a daily basis to raise their standards of academic and personal achievement, to receive positive peer/faculty reinforcement, and to identify and develop their true self as it relates to peers, family, and community.

The third and final phase involves students in a four- to six-week program of culturally diverse service learning projects in Costa Rica. Participants learn to overcome language barriers, understand social norms, and place greater value on others' needs while becoming fully immersed in a new environment. During the Costa Rican experience, students have daily academic studies including Rainforest Ecology, Central American and Costa Rican History, and intensive Spanish language instruction. The service learning project may involve cataloging plants and insects in an ongoing National Bio-diversity Research Project, a study of sustainable wood harvesting, and teaching English as a Second Language to local schoolchildren.

Throughout the three-step program, students learn to establish new patterns with their families through a series of visits, which are incremental in length to reintroduce the changing adolescent to his parents and siblings. Parents also maintain weekly telephone contact with their child's therapist and are encouraged to participate in Dr. Jones's National Parenting Support Program, which is available as a taped series with workbooks. Additionally, Academy staff assist parents with such activities as writing to and communicating with their children during their stay.

Students at Swift River begin their day at 7:15 A.M. with wake-up, dorm chores, and breakfast. There are four academic blocks in the morning and early afternoon, with a lunch break, followed by physical education, dorm time, dinner, recreation, free time, and lights out at 10:30 P.M.

Course offerings include English 9–12; Algebra I & II, Geometry, Pre-Calculus and Calculus; Biology, Chemistry, Physics, Health and Wellness; World and U.S. History, Geography, Government, Political Science; French and Spanish at all levels; and electives such as Human Ecology, Study Skills, and Nature Studies. Future offerings include Drama and Art. With its low staff-to-student ratio, Swift River limits enrollment to seven or eight students in each academic class. All students receive preparation for the Preliminary Scholastic Aptitude Tests and Scholastic Aptitude Tests and are expected and encouraged to take both examinations. Group therapy is scheduled on Tuesday and Thursday mornings in place of regular classes.

Students graduate in Peer Groups, according to the time

they began the program and their readiness to function in private and public high schools, colleges, and their families and communities. Administrators at The Academy suggest that families engage the services of professional consultants to help plan their children's future educational programs. Most graduates return to public or private high schools or attend a variety of public and private colleges and universities.

STUDENT ACTIVITIES. Activities at The Academy at Swift River are supervised and emotionally supportive in order to present children with age-appropriate demands and opportunities. Craft classes provide opportunities for students to make gifts for family and friends. Intramural sports include cross-country and downhill skiing, soccer, volleyball, ice skating, tennis, basketball, and swimming. A limited number of students participate in the local community in Alcoholics Anonymous and Narcotics Anonymous groups.

ADMISSION AND COSTS. The Academy at Swift River seeks average to exceptionally bright boys and girls, ages 13–18, who have a history of emotional and behavioral problems, low self-esteem, underachievement, and family conflicts. Students may have been diagnosed as having Oppositional Defiant Disorder, Substance Abuse, Attention Deficit Disorder, and Post-Traumatic Stress Disorder.

In 1999–2000, tuition is $4600 per month. There are no additional fees. Limited financial aid is available, and admission staff assist families with student loan programs. Students may enter The Academy at any time of the year and are generally enrolled with a Peer Group of 10 to 14 other students.

Director: John Powers
Headmaster: Rudolph Bentz
Director of Admissions: Brian A. Ray
Consulting Psychiatrist: Ralph Cohen, M.D.

Academy Hill School   1979

275 Maple Street, Springfield, MA 01105. 413-788-0800;
*   Fax 413-781-4806; E-mail academy@academyhill.org;*
*   Web Site www.academyhill.org*

Academy Hill was founded by parents and professionals to provide bright, curious, gifted children with a stimulating educational environment in which they can reach their full academic and personal potential. Seeking to build a foundation for a lifetime of learning, the School offers enriched and accelerated course work for 56 boys and girls in Kindergarten–Grade 6. Study in foreign language and the creative and visual arts begins in Kindergarten, and each child gains public speaking experience at the daily "Good Morning Program." Multiage enrichment clusters allow students to discover new interests with children from other grades. A 12:1 student-teacher ratio permits individual attention to every child. Tuition: $7900. Carolyn Price is Head of School.

The Advent School   1961

17 Brimmer Street, Boston, MA 02108. 617-742-0520;
*   Fax 617-723-2207*

The Advent School offers a child-centered education within an academic environment for 129 students in Kindergarten–Grade 6. The project-based curriculum integrates traditional disciplines complemented by courses in Spanish, computer, library, art, music, and physical education. Advent is a culturally diverse community that encourages a child's sense of self-worth and the development of reflective critical thinking. The School integrates Boston's cultural and historic resources into the educational program. An activities-based after-school program is available. Tuition: $10,700–$11,800. Financial Aid: $165,000.

Margo Lane is Director of Admission; Nancy Harris Frohlich (Beaver College, B.A.; Tufts University, M.Ed.) is Head of School.

Applewild School 1957

120 Prospect Street, Fitchburg, MA 01420. 978-342-6053;
Fax 978-345-5059; E-mail Admissions@Applewild.org;
Web Site http://www.Applewild.org

Enrolling 295 boys and girls in Kindergarten–Grade 9, Applewild is dedicated to academic excellence, the development of values, and the social, physical, and emotional well-being of each student. The liberal arts program is predicated on an understanding and knowledge of children, from early childhood through adolescence. The structured yet flexible program encourages growth and accomplishment through offerings in basic disciplines and the arts, music, and foreign language. Students take part in sports and physical activities, and there are numerous enrichment activities both in and out of the classroom. Extended-day care is offered for all grades. Tuition: $6545–$12,400. Financial aid is available. Cort Pomeroy is Director of Admission; Dr. William C. Marshall is Headmaster.

The Atrium School 1982

552 Main Street, Watertown, MA 02172. 617-923-4156

Enrolling 150 boys and girls in Preschool through Grade 6, The Atrium School offers an integrated curriculum designed to blend and balance the intellectual, social, and creative needs of its students. Daily conduct is based on the principle of respect for self, for others, and for the environment. Small classes, each with two teachers, enroll children of mixed ages, enabling students to develop a sense of community while learning from one another. The School encourages and celebrates diversity, and strong parental and family involvement in the educational process is essential to the program. The after-school program is open to all students. Tuition: $9450–$11,700. Ingrid W. Tucker is Director of Admissions; Richard Perry is Head of School.

Bancroft School 1900

110 Shore Drive, Worcester, MA 01605. 508-853-2640;
Fax 508-853-7824; E-mail admissio@bancroft.pvt.k12.ma.us;
Web Site bancroft.pvt.k12.ma.us

Bancroft School is a coeducational, college preparatory day school enrolling 591 students in Kindergarten–Grade 12. Attracting families from nearly 60 Worcester-area cities and towns, Bancroft's mission is to create a community of learners in which students develop "knowledge, wisdom, and virtue." Bancroft emphasizes academic excellence accompanied by a lively arts program, diverse activities, volunteer service, and interscholastic athletics. Tuition: $6300–$13,600. Financial Aid: $500,000. C. Robert Gielow is Director of Admission; Scott R. Reisinger was appointed Headmaster in 1999. *New England Association.*

Beaver Country Day School 1920

791 Hammond Street, Chestnut Hill, MA 02467. 617-734-6950;
Fax 617-566-6628; E-mail bcds@beavercds.com;
Web Site www.beavercds.com

Beaver Country Day School, just outside Boston, offers a balanced college preparatory curriculum in academics, arts, and athletics for Grades 6–12. The diversity of its student body and faculty, together with a mission that emphasizes innovation in learning and teaching, makes for a dynamic and challenging curriculum and community. With an average class size of 15, teachers provide attention and encouragement to all students.

Included on the 22-acre campus are a professional biotechnology lab, scanning electron microscope, three art studios, three gyms, and an open, spacious library. Tuition: $19,400. Aline Gery is Director of Admission and Financial Aid; Peter R. Hutton (St. Lawrence, B.A. 1974; Wesleyan, M.A. 1982), Head of School, was appointed in 1992. *New England Association.*

Belmont Day School 1927

55 Day School Lane, Belmont, MA 02478. 617-484-3078;
Fax 617-489-1942; E-mail www.belmontday.org

A few minutes from Boston, Belmont Day School offers a balance of strong academics and social competency skills to 186 children in Pre-Kindergarten through Grade 6. The challenging, nurturing environment supports the development of self-confidence, friendship, and mastery in an experientially based, individualized curriculum. The program emphasizes the joy of learning and integrates art, music, drama, French, technology, and physical education at all levels. After-school, extended-day, vacation camp, and summer camp programs are offered. Financial aid is available to qualified applicants. Tuition: $10,000–$13,300. Jan Saks is Director of Admissions; Lenesa Leana (Oberlin College, A.B.; University of Missouri, M.A.) is Head.

Belmont Hill School 1923

350 Prospect Street, Belmont, MA 02478-2662. 617-484-4410;
Fax 617-484-4829; E-mail admissions@belmont-hill.org

Belmont Hill School is a college preparatory day and five-day boarding school enrolling 422 boys in Grades 7–12. In its effort to develop "high ideals of moral character, trained intelligence, and physical sturdiness," the School seeks to combine a rigorous traditional curriculum with an outstanding art department and an expansive athletic program. Activities, many of which are coordinated with The Winsor School for Girls, include glee club, drama, debate, Student Council, and literary publications. A six-week, coeducational summer program is offered. Boarding Tuition: $23,080; Day Tuition: $19,180. Financial Aid: $1,111,000. Todd B. Bland is Director of Admission; Richard I. Melvoin (Harvard, A.B.; University of Michigan, M.A., Ph.D.) is Head of School. *New England Association.*

The Bement School 1925

Main Street, Deerfield, MA 01342. 413-774-7061;
Fax 413-774-7863; E-mail admit@bement.org;
Web Site www.bement.org

Bement, a junior boarding and day school, enrolls 240 boys and girls in Kindergarten–Grade 9. The curriculum is designed to motivate and challenge students with average to superior ability in classes averaging 12 in size. Math and foreign language teachers group upper school students by ability. English and history courses coordinate thematically, and the summer reading program highlights these themes. Daily participation in athletics and fine arts, advisor groups, and community service enrich the program. Mini-term, a three-week thematic focus, occurs in December. Boarding Tuition: $26,595; Day Tuition: $8885–$12,065; EFL: $500–$3000. Financial aid is available. Shelley Borror Jackson (Wheaton, B.A.; Ohio State, M.A.; University of Maine, C.A.S.) is Head.

Berkshire Country Day School 1946

P.O. Box 867, Route 183, Lenox, MA 01240. 413-637-0755;
Fax 413-637-8927; E-mail adm_bcd@berkshire.net;
Web Site http:/www.bcd.pvt.k12.ma.us

This educationally rigorous school enrolls 312 boys and girls in Beginner 3s–Grade 10. Its academic program offers small-group instruction, laboratory sciences, two languages by Grade 6, hands-on mathematics, and strong development of writing skills. Students at all levels receive instruction in art, music, shop, physical education, computer, and French. A full range of athletics and club activities includes soccer, lacrosse, alpine and downhill skiing, drama, chorus, and field trips. A summer academic program and Summer at BCD, a day camp for ages 3–10, are offered. Tuition: $4550–$12,900. Margaret D. Katz is Director of Admission; Robert R. Peterson (Williams, B.A.; Fairfield University, M.Ed.) was appointed Principal in 1994.

Berkshire School   SHEFFIELD

245 North Undermountain Road, Sheffield, MA 01257-9672.
413-229-8511; Admission 413-229-1003; Fax 413-229-1016;
E-mail enrollment@berkshireschool.org;
Web Site www.berkshireschool.org

BERKSHIRE SCHOOL in Sheffield, Massachusetts, is a coeducational, college preparatory school enrolling students in Grades 9–12 and a postgraduate year. The town of Sheffield (population 3000) lies in the Berkshire Hills in the southwestern corner of Massachusetts, about 10 miles from the borders of New York State and Connecticut. The region is noted for its natural beauty and provides an abundance of opportunities for vigorous outdoor activities.

Berkshire School was founded in 1907 by Seaver Burton Buck, a Harvard alumnus, and his wife, Anne. The School opened in the rented buildings of Glenny Farm with six boys and four masters. The first female students arrived on campus in the fall of 1969.

Berkshire School aims to provide students with the tools and skills needed to develop into mature, productive adults capable of achieving their best in college, in careers, and in all aspects of life. The academic and extracurricular programs are designed to guide and motivate each student intellectually, morally, physically, and spiritually.

Berkshire School, a nonprofit, nondenominational institution guided by a 27-member Board of Trustees, is accredited by the New England Association of Schools and Colleges and holds membership in numerous educational organizations including the National Association of Independent Schools. Many of the more than 4000 living alumni support the School through fund-raising, recruitment, and service on committees and advisory boards.

THE CAMPUS. The 500-acre campus, situated at the base of

Mount Everett, offers woodlands, landscaped lawns, playing fields, and hiking and riding trails.

Berkshire Hall, the primary academic facility, contains classrooms, science laboratories, a theater, and computer and writing centers with pentium processors and Apple Power PCs. The east wing was renovated in 1999. Memorial Hall houses administrative offices as well as classrooms, the performing arts studio, and Johnston Common Room. Adjoining Memorial Hall is Allen House, which contains the 430-seat Allen Theater, the School's radio station, the archives, and more administrative offices. The 45,000-volume Geier Library is fully computerized and provides additional classrooms and conference rooms. Other facilities include Bourne Field House, which furnishes ceramics studios, and the 18th-century Chase House.

Students reside in single and double rooms in dormitories located in ten school buildings throughout the campus. Each room has its own phone line and direct access to the Internet.

Among the athletic resources is the Rovensky Field House, providing three indoor tennis courts, concert facilities, and, in the winter, a newly renovated hockey arena. The Athletic Center furnishes full-size courts for basketball, volleyball, and tennis. A new addition to the athletic center includes 4 international squash courts and a fitness center. An all-weather track was completed in the summer of 1999.

The School-owned campus is valued at $70,000,000.

THE FACULTY. In 1996, Dr. Paul Christopher was unanimously elected Berkshire's 11th Head of School. A native of Wakefield, Massachusetts, he earned a B.S. in business administration from Norwich University and master's and doctoral degrees in philosophy from the University of Massachusetts. Dr. Christopher had previously taught English and philosophy at the United States Military Academy where he was Chair of the Philosophy Department and a leader in establishing ethical and moral issues as part of the curriculum. While a lieutenant colonel in the U.S. Army, he was infantry company commander of the 82nd Airborne Division and is the author of *The Ethics of War and Peace: An Introduction to Moral and Legal Issues.* Dr. Christopher and his wife, Elena, have a son and a daughter.

The full-time teaching faculty is comprised of 43 men and 21 women, 42 of whom live on campus, including 24 faculty families. In addition to baccalaureates, they hold 35 master's degrees and 3 doctorates representing study at such colleges and universities as Amherst, Antioch/New England, Bank Street College, Bowdoin, Colby, College of the Holy Cross, Columbia, Connecticut College, Dartmouth, Georgetown, Middlebury, New York University, Northeastern, Pennsylvania State, Princeton, Rensselaer Polytechnic, Rutgers, Springfield College, State University of New York, Trinity College, Tufts, Wesleyan, Wheaton, Yale, and the Universities of Connecticut, Hartford, Leeds, Massachusetts, Vermont, Virginia, and Washington. There are also 7 part-time teachers.

Berkshire retains the services of four pediatricians, a school nurse practitioner, four registered nurses, and two certified athletic trainers.

STUDENT BODY. In 1999–2000, Berkshire School enrolled 331 boarding and 54 day students in Forms III–VI (Grades 9–12) and a postgraduate year. They come from 30 states, the District of Columbia, and 24 foreign countries.

ACADEMIC PROGRAM. The school year is divided into semesters, from early September to late May, with vacations at Thanksgiving, in December, and March and two long weekends. Marks are posted and sent to parents at the midpoint and end of each semester. Each student is paired with a faculty advisor who provides guidance, monitors academic progress, and serves as a liaison with the family. Classes, with an average of 11 students, are held six days a week, with abbreviated schedules on Wednesday and Saturday. Boarding students have two hours of study hall nightly.

Students typically carry five courses per semester. To graduate, they must complete four years of English; three years each of one foreign language and mathematics, including Algebra I–II and Geometry; two years each of laboratory science and history, including American and European History; and one year of visual or performing arts. Third and Fourth Formers must participate in two competitive sports a year; upperformers, in one. Each term, all students take part in Pro Vita, a student-administered leadership and service program designed to promote moral maturity and personal responsibility. Students are also required to read one book of their choice per marking period.

Among the required and elective courses are English I–IV, College Writing; Chinese I–IV, French I–IV, Latin I–IV, Spanish I–IV; Ancient and Medieval History, European History, American History, American Government, Economics, Constitutional Law; Comparative Religion, Mythology and Religion, Introduction to Philosophy, Ethics; Biology, Chemistry, Physics, Human Genetics, Environmental Science; Algebra I–II, College Algebra and Trigonometry, Precalculus I–II, Calculus AB/BC; Computers and Data Processing I–II; 2-D Fundamentals, Drawing I–II, Ceramics I–III, Digital Art I–III, Photography I–III, Painting, Advanced Studio Art; and Introduction to Theater, Advanced Acting, Dance I–III, Music Synthesis I–III, Instrumental Ensemble I–III, and Chorus. Advanced Placement courses are offered in 18 subjects, and upperformers in good standing may undertake independent study projects with faculty guidance. English as a Second Language is taught at intermediate and advanced levels.

The Academic Support Program utilizes alternative learning techniques for students who need additional assistance due to different learning styles or minor learning disabilities. These methods include tutorials, structured study, and preteaching, in which students preview material in advance of classroom instruction.

The 115 graduates of the Class of 1999 were accepted at 160 colleges and universities. Among their choices were Amherst, Babson, Boston College, Boston University, Bowdoin, Brandeis, Bucknell, Carnegie Mellon, Clark, Colby, Colgate, Connecticut College, Cornell, Denison, Dickinson, George Washington University, Hobart, Johns Hopkins, Lafayette, Lehigh, Middlebury, Mount Holyoke, New York University, Northeastern, Rensselaer Polytechnic Institute, Rhode Island School of Design, Rochester Institute of Technology, St. Lawrence, St. Michael's, Smith, State University of New York, Tufts, Tulane, Union, United States Military Academy, Villanova, Washington University, and the Universities of Arizona, Chicago, Colorado, Connecticut, Denver, Maine, Massachusetts, Michigan, North Carolina, Vermont, and Wisconsin.

STUDENT ACTIVITIES. Four representatives from each class are elected by their peers to the student government, which provides a formal voice in school policy and in organizing activities to benefit the entire Berkshire community.

Students publish a newspaper, a yearbook, and a biannual literary magazine, operate the School's FM radio station, and stage several major productions each year. Concert and choral groups, bands, and small ensembles are among other performing opportunities on campus. Students may volunteer to undertake community service projects dealing with day care, senior citizen groups, homeless shelter, soup kitchen, and other social outreach activities.

Berkshire School competes in the Western New England Preparatory School Athletic Association. Twenty-six interscholastic teams in 18 sports include boys' and girls' regatta crew, cross-country running, soccer, basketball, ice hockey, alpine skiing, squash, golf, lacrosse, tennis, and track and field. Girls also play field hockey and softball, while boys' teams compete in football and baseball.

The Ritt Kellogg Mountain Program combines athletics and academics through seasonal Watch courses or the rigorous Wilderness Adventure, which involves participants in outdoor living experiences and activities such as rock and ice climbing, snowshoeing, cross-country skiing, and canoeing.

ADMISSION AND COSTS. Berkshire welcomes young people of good character and ability who demonstrate the potential to benefit from and contribute to the curricular and cocurricular opportunities offered at the School. Acceptance is based on previous school transcripts, a student essay, recommendations from math and English teachers, and results of standardized testing. A personal visit and interview are also required. Applications are accepted until February 15 for March 10 notification. After that date, admissions are on a rolling basis. The application fee is $50 for U.S. students and $100 for international candidates.

In 1999–2000, tuition is $25,900 for boarders and $18,200 for day students. Books and supplies ($500) and laundry and incidentals ($350) are additional. Financial aid and merit scholarships are awarded, and tuition insurance and payment plans are available.

Assistant Head of School for Enrollment: Phillip J. Jarvis
Assistant Head of School for Alumni & Development: Jeffrey S. Appel
Dean of Faculty: Arthur H. Charles
Dean of Students: Michael S. Dalton
Director of Alumni Relations: Susan Grabowski Clark
Director of College Counseling: Burgess N. Ayres
Chief Financial Officer: John E. Alden
Director of Athletics: Edward H. Hunt '61

Boston College High School   1863

150 Morrissey Boulevard, Boston, MA 02125-3391. 617-436-3900;
  Fax 617-282-7503; E-mail gill@bchigh.edu;
  Web Site www.bchigh.edu

Boston College High provides a challenging liberal arts program, grounded in the Jesuit tradition, for approximately 1200 college-bound young men from diverse backgrounds. The School strives to develop students who are open to growth, intellectually competent, loving, religious, and committed to justice. Taught by a Jesuit and lay faculty, the curriculum includes 17 honors and 21 Advanced Placement courses, five languages, and 35 electives. Varsity, club, and intramural teams in 21 sports and activities such as Student Council, publications, Model UN, National Honor Society, chorus, band, drama, and jazz/rock ensemble meet various interests and talents. Tuition: $6150. Financial aid is available. Richard D. Gill is Director of Admissions; Rev. Charles F. Kelley, S.J. (Fordham, M.Ed.), is President. *New England Association.*

Brimmer and May School   1939

69 Middlesex Road, Chestnut Hill, MA 02467. 617-566-7462;
  Admissions 617-738-8695

Brimmer and May, enrolling 375 students in Nursery–Grade 12, is celebrating its 120th year as a college preparatory day school. Located 3 miles west of Boston, the School uses the city's cultural and educational resources to expand classroom experiences. Strong academic programs, computer technology, creative arts, and physical education are emphasized at all levels. Middle and Upper School students participate in team sports. Community service is strongly encouraged. Extended-day care is available for Lower School students. Brimmer and May is a member of Brown University's Coalition of Essential Schools. Tuition: $9900–$18,900. Financial Aid: $610,000. Barbara Shoolman is Director of Admissions; Anne C. Reenstierna (Wheaton, B.A.; Lesley, M.Ed.) is Headmistress. *New England Association.*

Brooks School   1926

North Andover, MA 01845-1298. 978-686-6101;
  Fax 978-725-6298; Web Site brooks.pvt.k12.ma.us

Brooks is a college preparatory school enrolling 336 young men and women from around the world, nearly three-quarters of whom are boarders, in Grades 9–12. A dedicated faculty is at the core of the educational program, which encompasses the traditional liberal arts and sciences and a wide range of challenging electives. Enrichment opportunities include numerous field trips to Boston, independent study options, and overseas exchange programs. Students participate in 21 sports, publications, musical groups, drama, peer tutoring, Model UN, and special-interest clubs. Boarding Tuition: $25,820; Day Tuition: $18,610. Financial Aid: $1,313,581. Judith S. Beams is Director of Admissions; Lawrence W. Becker (Amherst, B.A.; Harvard, M.A.T.) is Headmaster. *New England Association.*

Brookwood School   1956

Brookwood Road, Manchester, MA 01944. 978-526-4500;
  Fax 978-526-9303; E-mail Admissions@Brookwood.edu;
  Web Site www.Brookwood.edu

Brookwood, a coeducational day school enrolling 372 students in Prekindergarten–Grade 8, stands on two foundation stones: a demanding program of academics, athletics, and arts and a

commitment to sociomoral and affective education designed to foster self-esteem, self-discipline, respect for others, and an appreciation of both competition and cooperation. Team sports, community service, student publications, field trips, multicultural assembly programs, and student government supplement the curriculum. There are before-school and after-school REACH programs. Tuition: $8000–$14,500. Financial Aid: $535,000. Barbara W. DiGiuseppe is Admissions Director; John C. Peterman (Wittenberg, B.A.; Loyola University [Chicago], M.Ed.) was appointed Headmaster in 1992.

Buckingham Browne & Nichols School   1974

80 Gerry's Landing Road, Cambridge, MA 02138. 617-547-6100;
  Fax 617-576-1139; E-mail admissions@bbns.org;
  Web Site www.bbns.org

Formed by the merger of The Buckingham School (1889) and The Browne & Nichols School (1883), this college preparatory day school enrolls 950 boys and girls in Beginners–Grade 12. The School, through its rigorous academic program, concern for the individual, and wide array of artistic, athletic, and leadership activities, aims to produce creative, independent thinkers who will act responsibly in the larger world in which they will live. Students in Grade 12 may spend the spring term off campus on a special-interest project. Tuition: $10,320–$20,250. Financial Aid: $2,100,000. Neville Lake is Director of Enrollment Management; Mary Newmann (Mount Holyoke, B.A.; Bank Street College of Education, M.A.; New York University, M.S.W.) was appointed Head of School in 1992. *New England Association.*

Buxton School   1928

Stone Hill Road, P.O. Box 646, Williamstown, MA 01267.
  413-458-3919; Fax 413-458-942 ;
  E-mail Office@buxton.williamstown.ma.us;
  Web Site www.buxton.williamstown.ma.us

Buxton is a coeducational, college preparatory school enrolling 94 boarding students in Grades 9 through 12. Founded to provide unique opportunities for intellectual, personal, and artistic growth, the School seeks to nurture creativity and independence within a small community setting. From its inception, Buxton has been an innovative school, one devoted to experimentation and change. The traditional core program is enhanced by courses and activities in art, music, and drama, among other areas. Work Program and the All-School Trip are of central importance. Comprehensive Fee: $25,500. Financial aid is available. Margo Cardner is Associate Director of Admissions; C. William Bennett (Williams College, B.A.) was appointed Director in 1983.

Cambridge Friends School   1961

5 Cadbury Road, Cambridge, MA 02140. 617-354-3880;
  Fax 617-876-1815

Cambridge Friends is a Quaker, coeducational day school serving 285 students in Pre-Kindergarten–Grade 8. Established by the Friends Meeting at Cambridge, it has a socioeconomically, racially, and culturally diverse student body and remains committed to fighting discrimination of every kind. School goals are to promote critical thinking skills and individualized cooperative learning; integrate the arts, sciences, and mathematics; and nurture the spiritual and intellectual growth of students. Tuition: $10,650–$12,950. Tuition Assistance: $685,000. Julia Turner Lowe is Admission Director; Wanda Speede-Franklin (Princeton, B.A.; Northwestern, M.A.) is Head of School.

Cape Cod Academy   1976

50 Osterville-West Barnstable Road, Osterville, MA 02655.
508-428-5400; Fax 508-428-0701; E-mail cca@ccacademy.pvt.
k12.ma.us; Web Site http://www.ccacademy.pvt.k12.ma.us

Cape Cod Academy, a coeducational college preparatory school serving 350 day students in Kindergarten–Grade 12, aims to offer a challenging education that emphasizes the liberal arts and sciences, underscored by the values of honesty, respect, and compassion. Small classes and a 9:1 student-teacher ratio provide daily opportunities for personal support and encouragement from faculty. Interscholastic athletics, drama, chorus, music, and outdoor club are among the activities. Facilities include a library, science and computer labs, eight tennis courts, and a 21,000-square-foot Student Activities Center with NCAA-size basketball court. Tuition: $10,000–$13,000. Financial aid is available. Judy E. Evans is Director of Admissions; Thomas M. Evans (Dartmouth, B.A.) is Headmaster. *New England Association.*

The Carroll School   1967

Baker Bridge Road, Lincoln, MA 01773. 781-259-8342;
Fax 781-259-8852; E-mail admissions@carrollschool.org

Encompassing Grades 1–12, The Carroll School provides college preparation for 235 bright boys and girls with language-based learning differences. Students are grouped according to ages and learning profiles rather than by specific grade levels. With only 6–8 children per class, qualified specialist instructors use proven teaching methods, specific strategies, and remedial support services to develop students' maximum potential and equip them for success in mainstream schools. Field trips, guest speakers, and diverse enrichment activities, including Bounders, Carroll's modified version of Outward Bound, enhance classroom instruction. Extended-day care and a summer program are offered. Tuition: $22,150. Dr. Laura S. Weiss is Director of Admissions; Sharon Lloyd Clark is Head. *New England Association.*

Chapel Hill–Chauncy Hall School

WALTHAM

785 Beaver Street, Waltham, MA 02452. 781-894-2644;
Web Site www.chapelhill-chauncyhall.org

CHAPEL HILL–CHAUNCY HALL SCHOOL in Waltham, Massachusetts, is a coeducational, college preparatory boarding and day school enrolling students in Grades 9 through 12 and a postgraduate year. Waltham (population 57,000) is a suburban community 10 miles west of Boston and 45 miles north of Providence, Rhode Island, just off Route 128. The home of Bentley College and Brandeis University, Waltham provides easy access to all that is offered in the Greater Boston area.

Incorporated in 1971, Chapel Hill–Chauncy Hall is the result of the merger of two older schools. Chapel Hill School was founded in 1860 as a girls' boarding school on the present campus. Chauncy Hall, a boys' day school, was founded in 1828.

Chapel Hill–Chauncy Hall embraces differences in learning style and culture in a small, supportive community. The School challenges young men and women to achieve their individual potential, experience academic success, and develop social and leadership skills. Chapel Hill–Chauncy Hall is "a school without labels" and provides "an education without limits."

A nonprofit organization, the School is governed by a self-perpetuating Board of 16 Trustees that includes parents and alumni. The Board meets four times a year. Approximately 3700 graduates are members of the Alumni Association, and there is an active Parents and Guardians Association. Chapel Hill–Chauncy Hall is accredited by the New England Association of Schools and Colleges. It holds membership in the National Association of Independent Schools, the Educational Records Bureau, the Association of Independent Schools of New England, and the Council for Advancement and Support of Education.

THE CAMPUS. The 37-acre campus, in a residential area adjacent to wooded conservation land, includes two playing fields, an outdoor swimming pool, and a pond. Among the 16 buildings are Wilkins Hall (1864), a brick classroom building with a state-of-the-art media center; Morgan Library, with 11,000 volumes, 75 periodicals, three daily newspapers, seven microcomputer terminals, microfiche files, and two study rooms; Peebles Hall, a Colonial house containing administrative offices; East Hall, the Head of School's residence; The Cottage, a small house where ninth-grade classes are held; Atwood House, housing English and computer facilities; and The Barn, the School's arts facility, containing a theater, music classrooms, a woodworking shop, and art, ceramics, dance, and photography studios. Boarding girls reside in South Hall and North Hall. North Hall also contains the Head of School's office, the infirmary, the dining room, the kitchen, and the School living room. Worcester 9/10 and Worcester 11/12 are the boys' dormitories. The residence halls each have three faculty apartments.

Machen Gymnasium (1981) contains a basketball and volleyball court, locker rooms, a student lounge and snack bar, and the college counseling office.

The School-owned plant is valued at approximately $7,000,000.

THE FACULTY. Donald H. Grace, a graduate of Harvard, was appointed Head of School in 1997.

In 1999, there are 37 full-time faculty—15 men and 22 women—as well as 3 part-time faculty. Twenty-two faculty members and their families live on campus. They hold undergraduate and advanced degrees from Bates, Boston College, Boston University, Brown, Clark, Colby, Connecticut College, Harvard, New England School of Photography, New York University, Northeastern, Princeton, Providence, Saint Joseph, St. Lawrence, Simmons, Swarthmore, Tufts, and the Universities of Connecticut, Massachusetts, Pennsylvania, Vermont, and Virginia. Faculty benefits include health insurance, a retirement plan, and Social Security.

Emergency facilities are available at the Waltham-Weston Medical Center.

STUDENT BODY. In 1999–2000, the School enrolls 38 boarding boys, 30 boarding girls, 56 day boys, and 44 day girls as follows: 36 in Grade 9, 43 in Grade 10, 50 in Grade 11, 38 in Grade 12, and 1 postgraduate. Boarders represent Massachusetts, three other states, Haiti, Hong Kong, Jamaica, Japan, Panama, Singapore, South Korea, Taiwan, and Thailand. Day students come from 48 area communities.

ACADEMIC PROGRAM. The school year, from early September to early June, is divided into trimesters with a one-week Thanksgiving recess, vacations of two weeks at Christmas and in the spring, and several long weekends. A typical day begins at 8:00 A.M. and contains six 50-minute class periods, lunch, two hours of athletics or activities, dinner, and two hours of study hall for boarding students. Also on the schedule each week are a conference with the advisor, two extra-help periods, an all-School assembly, and meeting blocks for clubs and organizations.

Classes in Grade 9 average between 8 and 12 students; in the other grades, the average enrollment is 12–15 students. Teachers are available to provide extra help. The Learning Center, open to all students, offers classes on topics such as writing, mathematics, research skills, and study skills. These classes, for which there is an extra charge, meet two to five times a week. Internal weekly progress reports are maintained; grades are issued and sent to parents quarterly.

The School offers a unique ninth-grade program that teaches study, organizational, and test-taking skills to help students in their transition to high school. The tenth-grade program extends the integrated approach to foundation skills begun in the ninth grade.

To graduate, students must complete four years of English, three of mathematics, and two each of science, social studies, fine arts, and a foreign language.

Courses include English 9–12, Writing, Boston Writers, Film and Society, Journalism Workshop; Spanish 1–5, English as a Second Language 1–2; World Cultures, United States History, American Political Behavior, Facing History, 20th Century Issues, Economics, Psychology, Geography, Law and Justice; Algebra 1–2, Geometry, Informal Geometry, Algebra II/Trigonometry, Probability & Statistics, Pre-Calculus, Calculus, Advanced Calculus, Math of Personal Finance; Biology, Advanced Biology, Practical Chemistry, Chemistry, Physical Science in the Environment, Environmental Science, Practical Physics, Physics; and Introduction to the Arts, Painting, Drawing, Materials and Techniques, Advanced Studio, Ceramics 1–2, Publications, Introduction to Photoshop, Photography 1–2, Performance Workshop, Advanced Theater Workshop, Dance Workshop, Instrumental Ensemble, Music Appreciation and Theory, and Chorus.

Independent study and Advanced Placement preparation are available in several areas. Qualified students may audit courses at local colleges. The International Student Advisor assists foreign students and their families.

In 1999, 97 percent of the graduates entered such institutions as American University, Bentley, Boston University, Clark, Drew, George Washington, Johnson and Wales, Morehouse, New England Conservatory of Music, Northeastern, Rochester Institute of Technology, Suffolk University, and the Universities of Massachusetts and Rhode Island.

STUDENT ACTIVITIES. Students participate on the Discipline Committee, Head's Council, and class committees, and as dormitory proctors, and student guides.

Students publish a yearbook and a newspaper. Extracurricular activities include art, dance, drama, photography, music, community service, yearbook, and woodworking. Weekend activities take advantage of the School's proximity to Boston and include cultural and sporting events, movies, and shopping trips as well as skiing and hiking.

Chapel Hill–Chauncy Hall competes in the Eastern Independent League with schools such as Bancroft, Beaver, Concord, and Pingree as well as nonleague schools. Boys' and girls' varsity teams are organized in soccer, cross-country, golf, basketball, and tennis. There are also girls' volleyball and softball, and boys' wrestling, lacrosse, and baseball teams. Students play recreational racquetball and tennis at a nearby racquet club.

Traditional events include Orientation, Parents and Guardians Weekend in October, a holiday program in December, Winter Carnival, and class reunions.

ADMISSION AND COSTS. The School seeks to admit college-bound students who want to improve their skills and share their talents. Students are admitted to all grades on the basis of the completed application, previous school records, teacher recommendations, an interview, a half-day visit (recommended), and results of educational testing. Applications are accepted as long as vacancies exist. There is a nonrefundable $45 application fee.

In 1999–2000, day tuition is $19,450; boarding tuition is $27,300. There are additional fees for the Learning Center and English as a Second Language program. Extras include books and tuition refund insurance.

In 1999–2000, the School awarded $375,000 in grants on the basis of need. Chapel Hill–Chauncy Hall subscribes to the School Scholarship Service in Princeton, New Jersey.

Assistant Head of School: William N. Lyons, Jr.
Dean of Academic Affairs: Thomas Roselli
Dean of Student Affairs: Diana Gleeson
Director of Admissions: Daniel I. Levine
Director of Development: Paul R. Amadio
College Counselor: Margaret Allen
Business Manager: Linda Myers
Director of Athletics: Nancy Sherwood

Charles River School   1911

56 Centre Street, Box 339, Dover, MA 02030. 508-785-0068;
Fax 508-785-8290; E-mail mearley@charlesriverschool.org

Charles River School, enrolling 197 day boys and girls in Pre-Kindergarten–Grade 8, is committed to a balance of academic, creative, physical, and social growth. The School challenges children to assume responsibility and be active learners and explorers. An interdisciplinary curriculum emphasizes critical thinking, writing, reading, and mathematics skills as well as science, social studies, class projects, computer, and foreign language and culture, art, music, and physical education. After School Sports and Extended Day programs are offered. Tuition: $8445–$12,410. Financial Aid: $233,000. Marion L. Earley is Director of Admissions; Catherine H. Gately (Boston University, B.A., M.Ed.) was appointed Head in 1993.

The Chestnut Hill School   1860

428 Hammond Street, Chestnut Hill, MA 02467. 617-566-4394;
Fax 617-738- 6602; E-mail admissions@tchs.org

The Chestnut Hill School is an independent, coeducational, elementary school located in a residential section of Newton, Massachusetts. The School encompasses a preschool program for three- and four-year-olds, an all-day kindergarten, and Grades 1 through 6. There are 180 children enrolled each year, with one class and two teachers at each grade level. Because of the comparatively small size and the favorable student-teacher ratio, Chestnut Hill is able to offer a rigorous academic program that embraces many perspectives and values the individual. Tuition: $9900–$14,000. Financial Aid: $350,000. Wendy W. Borosavage is Director of Admission; Susan C. Bryant (Wheelock College, B.S.; Harvard University, M.Ed.) is Head of School.

The Clark School for Creative Learning   1978

487 Locust Street, Danvers, MA 01923. 508-777-4699;
Fax 508-774-3088

The Clark School for Creative Learning is a pre-preparatory school for gifted and talented children, enrolling 55 day boys and girls in Kindergarten–Grade 8. The School seeks to encourage self-expression in academic and artistic endeavors. In a multiage learning environment, each student pursues an individualized program. Additionally, science, history, geography, philosophy, and Spanish are offered. Other activities include weekly swimming lessons, skiing, drama, puppetry, poetry, and field trips. Tuition: $9100. Sharon Clark (California College of Arts and Crafts, B.F.A. 1968; Wheelock, M.S.Ed. 1978) is Co-Founder and Director.

The Commonwealth School   BOSTON

151 Commonwealth Avenue, Boston, MA 02116. 617-266-7525;
Fax 617-266-5769; E-mail admissions@commschool.org

THE COMMONWEALTH SCHOOL in Boston, Massachusetts, is a day school enrolling boys and girls in Grades 9 through 12. The School is in the Back Bay area of Boston and is served by city and commuter buses and trains.

The School was founded in 1957 by Charles Merrill, who was Headmaster until his retirement in 1981. Commonwealth aims to give its students the ability to write forceful and effective English; a historical perspective on human nature and human affairs; well-grounded proficiency in mathematics, natural science, and computers; wide experience in literature and the art of reading; mastery of at least one foreign language; a rich field for creativity in the arts; and vigorous training in and enthusiasm for athletic endeavor. Through its community service requirement and its student job program, the School works to instill in its students the ideal of responsible action.

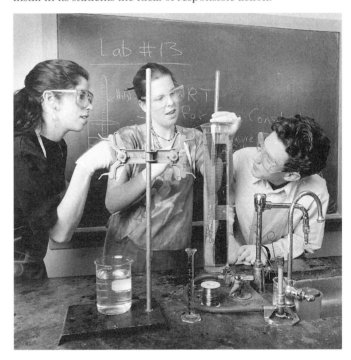

The School is a nonprofit organization whose 31-member Board of Trustees includes faculty and alumni/ae members and nonvoting student and faculty representatives. The endowment includes more than $5,000,000 in productive funds.

Commonwealth is accredited by the New England Association of Schools and Colleges and is a member of the National Association of Independent Schools and other organizations.

THE CAMPUS. Commonwealth's location in the heart of Boston, two blocks from the Boston Public Library and a short distance from the Museum of Fine Arts, encourages students to take advantage of the city's resources. Two adjoining 19th-century townhouses accommodate classrooms; library; laboratories; art, ceramics, and dance studios; a darkroom; lunchroom/gymnasium; student lounge; and offices. Nearby athletic facilities used by the School include squash courts at a local squash club, basketball courts at St. Leonard's Parish House, playing fields of the Metropolitan District Commission, and the Community Boating Club.

THE FACULTY. Judith Keenan, the School's Head, was appointed in May of 1990. She holds degrees from Swarthmore

College (B.A.) and Harvard University (A.M.) and was a Henry Fellow at Lady Margaret Hall, Oxford University. She has taught extensively in this country and abroad. She worked for nine years for Sen. Paul Sarbanes as his senior aide and adviser on major policy issues, and served as Executive Director of the Joint Economic Committee of the Congress.

There are 21 full-time teachers and administrators who teach, 11 men and 10 women. They hold 21 baccalaureate, 15 graduate degrees, and 7 doctorates from Barnard, Boston University, Brown, Federal Institute of Technology (Switzerland), Harvard-Radcliffe, Johns Hopkins, Massachusetts Institute of Technology, New York University, Oklahoma State, Pitzer, Reed College, Stanford, Swarthmore, Tufts, Williams, Yale, and the Universities of Cambridge (England), Kentucky, Michigan, Minnesota, Oxford (England), Paris (France), Toronto, and Virginia. There are also part-time instructors who teach history, literature, theater, ceramics, dance, jazz, music, and photography and printmaking.

Among the benefits for full-time faculty are health, disability, and life insurance; a retirement plan; sabbaticals; assistance with tuition at Commonwealth for faculty children; and partial reimbursement for study undertaken to improve professional skills.

There is always at least one faculty member at Commonwealth who is trained in first aid; several hospitals are nearby for more serious emergencies.

STUDENT BODY. In 1999–2000, Commonwealth enrolls 134 boys and girls as follows: 34 in Grade 9, 38 in Grade 10, 42 in Grade 11, and 20 in Grade 12. Most students come from Boston and surrounding communities. Those born abroad come from as far away as China, India, Russia, and Ukraine.

ACADEMIC PROGRAM. The school year runs from early September to early June. There are two-week vacations in December and March and several long weekends. The average class size is 11 students. Grades, teachers' comments, and advisers' letters are sent to parents three times per year; for freshmen and for students in academic difficulty, a fourth grading period is observed.

The school day, which begins at 8:30 A.M., is divided into seven or eight periods lasting 40–55 minutes. Full-credit courses meet four times a week and half-credit courses twice a week. On average, students carry five academic credits and two

art credits. Free periods are intended for study. A supervised study hall is held every Saturday morning for students with work outstanding. Tutorial help is available at no extra charge.

Students must complete a minimum of 16 credits for graduation, including four years of English, three of mathematics, two of science, three of foreign language, and two of history, one of which must be American history. Additional requirements each year include one course in the arts and participation in two of the three sports seasons. Freshmen and seniors also take half-credit courses with the Head in Current Events. Ninth-graders enroll in a City of Boston course for one semester. Community service is part of the tenth-grade curriculum.

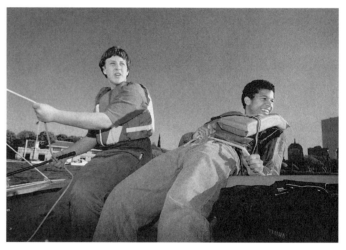

Once a week, the entire School meets for an assembly, often with public figures who come to speak to and take questions from the students. Each grade holds its own weekly meeting.

Among the full-credit courses offered are English 9–12; Ancient History, Medieval World History, United States History, Modern European History; French I–III, Latin I–IV, Spanish I–III, other languages on occasion; Biology I–II, Chemistry I–II, Physics I–II, Fundamentals of Physics, Fundamentals of Chemistry; and Algebra II, Geometry, Pre-Calculus, and two levels of Calculus.

Courses that receive half credit include Novel, African Literature, Southern Fiction, Poetry, Short Story, Fiction Writing, Literature of the Bible, Literature of Theatre; Film; Economics, City of Boston, Intellectual History, Afro American History, Art History, Birth of a Century, Latin American History, Ancient Philosophy, World Religions; Greek I–III, Latin V, Advanced French, Advanced Spanish; Biology III, Chemistry III, Space-time Physics, Chaotic Dynamical Systems, Combinatorics & Graph Theory, Probability and Statistics; Computers I–III; Music Theory I–III, Jazz Theory I–II, Conducting, Composition; and for art credit, Basic Drawing, Drawing and Painting, Life Drawing, Printmaking, Jazz Ensemble, Acting, Beginning and Advanced Dance, Ceramics, Photography, Chorus, Chorale, Orchestra, and Chamber Music.

Twice a year, the entire School adjourns to a camp in southern Maine for four days. Students and teachers take hikes, prepare meals for 150, make and launch hot-air balloons, perform skits, play games and sports, and hold activities and discussion sections on subjects ranging from mask-making to mushroom identification to foreign policy.

During Project Week, younger students have the chance to become involved in activities outside the scope of regular schoolwork. Students participate in projects ranging from hospital work to teaching to working in a senator's Washington office. In the spring, seniors engage in similar projects that last for a whole month.

Commonwealth participates in three-week exchange programs with schools in France and Spain. Financial aid is provided for all students demonstrating need.

All 33 graduates of the Class of 1999 were accepted to college. Graduates are attending such institutions as Barnard,

Boston College, Boston University, Brandeis, Brown, Carleton, Columbia, Duke, George Washington, Hampshire, Massachusetts Institute of Technology, McGill, Middlebury, Rensselaer, Rhode Island School of Design, Swarthmore, Vassar, and the Universities of Chicago and Massachusetts.

STUDENT ACTIVITIES. All students participate in the jobs program. Two nonvoting student representatives are elected to the Board of Trustees each year. Students tutor other students, give assemblies, publish the yearbook and literary magazine, and plan dances and ski weekends. They join the Mock Trial team, work for good causes, and take on a variety of responsibilities during the Maine weekends. Thursday afternoon ends with an all-School tea.

Commonwealth teams compete interscholastically in soccer, basketball, squash, sailing, fencing, and ultimate frisbee. All sports are open to all grades and to both boys and girls.

Traditional events include the Senior-Freshman Lunch, Ninth-Grade Cookout, New Parents' Evening, Parent-Teacher evenings for each grade, fall and spring Parents' Association meetings, Alumni/ae Reunions in various cities, November Open House, Beach Day, two choral concerts, dance and jazz concerts, two theater productions, and a spring art show.

ADMISSION AND COSTS. The Commonwealth School seeks boys and girls of character and intelligence, without regard to race, color, religion, or national or ethnic origin, who are willing to work hard for a good education. Applicants are asked to submit recommendations, transcripts, and Secondary School Admission Test scores. An interview with the applicant and parents and a full-day visit by the applicant are also required. Applications for fall admission must be completed by February 4. The School accepts new students later in the year if places remain.

In 1999–2000, tuition is $18,365, including lunches, with additional expenses of $450 for books, $225 for the two weekends in Maine, and a $500 activities fee. Scholarship aid of more than $590,000 was given in 1999–2000 to approximately one-third of the student body. Low-interest loans totaling $17,000 were also provided, and some student jobs are available. A Technology Grant Program is offered to students receiving financial aid to help in purchasing a computer. All grants are made on the basis of financial need.

Head of School: Judith Keenan
Director of Admissions: William Wharton
Director of Studies: Farhad Riahi
Acting Director of Student Life: James Milan
College Counselor: Brent Whelan
Consulting Psychologist: Kay Seligsohn
Director of Athletics: Martin Nastasia
Business Manager: Diane Morris
Director of Development and Parent Liaison: Patricia Sharaf
Development Officer and Alumni/ae Liaison: Laurence Geffin

Concord Academy 1922

166 Main Street, Concord, MA 01742. 978-369-6080;
Fax 978-369-3452; E-mail admissions@concordacademy.org;
Web Site www.concordacademy.org

Concord Academy is a college preparatory boarding and day school that emphasizes individuality, diversity, and quality among its faculty and student body. Enrolling 325 boys and girls in Grades 9–12, Concord offers a comprehensive and rigorous program within the framework of an intimate and creative environment. Set in a small, historic town near Cambridge and Boston, Concord Academy is a vibrant community enhanced by its culturally rich setting. Students participate actively in a broad range of athletic, artistic, and extracurricular opportunities. Boarding Tuition: $26,360; Day Tuition: $20,070.

Jennifer Hunter Cardillo is Director of Admissions; Thomas E. Wilcox (Colorado College, B.A.; Harvard University, M.Ed.) is Headmaster. *New England Association.*

Cotting School 1893

453 Concord Avenue, Lexington, MA 02421. 781-862-7323;
Fax 781-861-1179; Web Site http://www.cotting.org

Cotting, the nation's first day school for children with physical disabilities, offers comprehensive therapeutics and educational plans for students with moderate to severe physical and learning disabilities. Enrolling 115 students ages 3–22, Cotting is committed to preparing students for transition to traditional schools and for the workforce. Each student's unique strengths are evaluated and form the basis for his or her program, which integrates individualized academic curricula with appropriate physical, occupational, and communication therapy designed to help students reach realistic goals toward further schooling and careers. A new residential postgraduate component, which focuses on independent living and job skills, opened in January 2000. Bob Driscoll is Director of Admissions; Carl W. Mores, Ed.D., is President/CEO.

Dana Hall School WELLESLEY

45 Dana Road, Wellesley, MA 02482. 781-235-3010;
Fax 781-235-0577; E-mail admission@danahall.org;
Web Site www.danahall.org

Dana Hall School in Wellesley, Massachusetts, is a college preparatory boarding and day school enrolling girls in Grades 6–12. Wellesley (population 26,615) has a charming downtown area featuring ethnic restaurants, boutiques, and galleries and is easily accessible to Boston, 12 miles to the east.

The establishment of Dana Hall School was inspired by Henry F. Durant, the founder of Wellesley College, who thought that many of his students needed better preparation for higher education. Businessman Charles P. Dana donated a building that later served as the original site of Dana Hall School, which opened in 1881. Now in its 119th year, the School's purpose remains constant: to provide an excellent liberal arts program in a supportive, nurturing environment that empowers students to succeed in college and in life. The curriculum and activities are designed to meet the unique learning styles of young women, to instill a lifelong quest for knowledge, and to afford opportunities to develop leadership, creativity, and independence.

Dana Hall is a nonprofit, nondenominational institution governed by a 27-member Board of Trustees, 14 of whom are alumnae. The School is accredited by the New England Association of Schools and Colleges and holds membership in the National Association of Independent Schools, and The National Coalition of Girls' Schools, among other professional affiliations.

THE CAMPUS. Dana's 50-acre campus features landscaped lawns, gardens, wooded areas, and a pond that is the focal point of graduation exercises. Also on the grounds are three playing fields, five tennis courts, riding rings, and a stable for 43 horses. The Dorothy Dunning Mudd Gymnasium houses basketball and volleyball courts and a fitness center.

Students reside in seven dormitories supervised by house directors, house assistants, and student proctors.

The new Lucia Farrington Shipley Science Center and Dana Hall School Library, along with the recently refurbished Classroom Building, serve as the campus's academic center. The Shipley Science Center contains six labs, a separate room for project space, and a lecture room that seats 100. The Technology Department has over 50 computers, three scanners, three laser printers, and three color ink-jet printers divided among three computer rooms, which are accessible to all students. The Library seats 130 students at tables, carrels, and armchairs. There are also four group study rooms, a seminar room, and a media production room. The Library houses 20,000 volumes, 175 periodicals including four daily and two weekly newspapers, a pamphlet file, and the Dana Hall Archives. An automated system gives access to information through the Internet, on-line database searching, and CD-ROM technology. Fourteen computers are available for general use, and connections to the campus network enable laptop users to access a wide variety of applications. Bardwell Auditorium, the Dana School of Music, the Dana Hall Riding Center, Beveridge Hall, the Dining Center, the Health Center, and the Wayside Student Center complete the facilities.

THE FACULTY. Mrs. Blair Jenkins was appointed Head of School in 1993. She holds a B.A. degree from Wells College and an M.S. from Peabody College at Vanderbilt University. Mrs. Jenkins had formerly been Dean of Students, Director of the Upper School, and Associate Head at Dana Hall.

There are 54 faculty and administrators on staff. They hold 54 baccalaureate and 28 advanced degrees, including 4 doctorates, representing study at such colleges and universities as Amherst, Bates, Boston College, Boston University, Bowdoin, Brown, Colby, College of the Holy Cross, Colorado College, Cornell, Denison, Drew, Duke, Gettysburg, Goucher, Hamilton, Harvard, Ithaca, Johns Hopkins, Kenyon, Lake Forest, Marymount, Middlebury, New York University, Northwestern, Reed, Smith, Syracuse, Trinity, Tufts, Vanderbilt, Wellesley, Wesleyan, Wheaton, and the Universities of London, Massachusetts, Michigan, North Carolina, Pennsylvania, Virginia, and Wisconsin.

The Health Center is open five days a week, with a nurse practitioner on call on the weekends and psychologists available as needed. In-patient care and a fully equipped hospital are minutes from campus.

STUDENT BODY. In 1999–2000, Dana Hall School enrolled 396 young women including day students in all grades and boarding students in Grades 9–12. They came from 17 states and 16 countries. About 16 percent were students of color.

ACADEMIC PROGRAM. The school year, divided into trimesters from early September to early June, includes a Thanksgiving recess; longer vacations in December and March; and the observance of national holidays. Each student has a faculty advisor with whom she confers on a weekly basis. Midterm progress reports are written to students in academic difficulty, and term grades are given at the end of each trimester. The average class size is 12, with a student-teacher ratio of 7:1.

A typical academic day begins with either an all-school meeting or an advisor meeting at 8:00 A.M., followed by eight 42-minute class periods. Clubs and class meetings are held within that schedule. At the end of each day, there is a 45-minute conference period when students and faculty can meet with each other. Team practices take place in the late afternoon. Study halls are held during the day, and a two-hour evening study period is conducted for freshmen and sophomores Monday through Thursday. The Math and Writing Centers provide extra academic support from faculty and selected students, and tutoring can be arranged.

The Middle School (Grades 6–8) curriculum is designed to give the student a balance of English, mathematics, foreign language, science, and social studies, enhanced by visual and performing arts, physical education, and health education.

To earn a Dana Hall diploma, an Upper School student must complete 18 credits including the following: 4 credits in English, 3 credits in a single foreign language, 3 credits in mathematics, 2 in a laboratory science, 2½ in social science, and ½ each in the visual and performing arts. Physical education is required each year unless the student participates on an interscholastic team. Students must perform 20 hours of community service in their sophomore year to graduate.

Specific Upper School courses include Introduction to English, Literary Analysis, Introduction to Literature I–II, American Literature, Modern Drama: Beckett and Beyond; French I–V, Spanish I–V, Latin V, Classical Greek; Philosophy, History of Western Art; Algebra I–II, Geometry, Pre-Calculus, Calculus AB/BC, Finite Mathematics, Statistics; Computer Programming and Usage, Computer Pascal, Advanced Computer Topics; Biology, Chemistry, Physics; Western Civilization, Russian Studies, East Asian Studies: China and Japan, United States History, European Social History, Middle Eastern Studies, African Studies, Political Science, Economics; Acting I–IV, Ballet and Jazz Techniques, Modern Dance Fundamentals, Ballet II, Modern/Jazz II, Dance Theatre Workshop; Chorus, Chamber Singers, Chamber Music; Painting I–II, Drawing I–II, Studio Art, Ceramics/Sculpture, Architecture I, Design Fundamentals, Silkscreen Printing, Photography I–II, Independent Studio Art; and Physical Education. Honors and Advanced Placement courses are available in every department.

Qualified Dana students may take college-credit courses at Wellesley College. Study-abroad programs permit interested students to visit France or Spain; study for six weeks in Melbourne, Australia; or spend a semester in Colorado with the High Mountain Institute.

The Senior Project program provides a period of transition from Dana Hall to college, combining traditional coursework with independent study in a field of particular interest.

College counseling begins in Grade 11, and all Dana students go on to further education. Among the colleges and universities chosen by the Class of 1998 are Babson, Bates, Boston College, Carleton, Carnegie Mellon, Emerson, Harvard, Kenyon, Lehigh, New England Conservatory, St. Lawrence, Stanford, Tufts, Tulane, Union, Wellesley, Yale, and the Universities of California (Berkeley), Chicago, Massachusetts (Amherst), Pennsylvania, Rochester, San Francisco, and Virginia.

STUDENT ACTIVITIES. Leadership is developed through service as class officers, proctors, Blue Key (admissions guides), and the School Senate. The student-led Religious Life Advisory Board keeps the school community apprised of all upcoming religious holidays and observances. Other groups on campus include the International Student Club, Women of Color Club, and Student Activities Club. Students also publish an art and literary magazine, a newspaper, and a yearbook. Instrumental instruction is offered on campus at the Dana School of Music.

Dana Hall sponsors The Wannamaker Series, a program that brings noted authors, artists, and civic and corporate leaders to campus for lectures throughout the school year.

Dances, mixers, dramatic and musical productions, and other events are coordinated with Belmont Hill, Roxbury Latin, and St. Sebastian's, three nearby boys' schools. On weekends, boarding and day students are encouraged to participate in planned activities on and off campus such as ski trips and excursions to Boston for theater, sports, dining out, and shopping.

Athletic competition is organized at the interscholastic and intramural levels in basketball, cross-country, dance, fencing, field hockey, ice hockey, lacrosse, soccer, softball, tennis, and volleyball. Horseback riding and equestrian training are offered through the Riding Center.

Among the traditional annual events are Revels, Parents' Weekend, Alumnae Weekend, Step-Sing, Boston Harbor Cruise, Cabaret, Clambake, Spring Carnival, and Commencement.

ADMISSION AND COSTS. Dana Hall School seeks young women who demonstrate academic ability, intellectual curiosity, motivation, and good citizenship. Acceptance is offered on the basis of previous transcripts, teacher recommendations, and the results of standardized tests. A campus interview is recommended but not required. Decisions are announced on March 10. Late applications are considered if space permits.

In 1999–2000, day tuition and fees total $20,385 in all grades; boarding tuition and fees range from $27,500 for domestic students to $28,260 for international students. Nearly 22 percent of the student body received need-based financial aid totaling $1,400,000.

Dean of Students: Ann E. Selvitelli
Assistant Head: Nancy Rich
Director of Middle School: Joanna Anderson
President, Alumnae Association: Virginia Abbott '78
Director of Admission: Olive B. Long
Director of Development and Alumnae Relations: Joy Haywood Moore '77
Director of College Counseling: Helen Burke Montague
Business Manager: Thompson Greenlaw
Director of Athletics: Janet Sullivan

Dedham Country Day School   1904

90 Sandy Valley Road, Dedham, MA 02026. 781-329-0850; Fax 781-329-0551; E-mail charrison@dcd.pvt.k12.ma.us; Web Site www.channel1.com.dcd

Dedham Country Day School enrolls 225 boys and girls in Pre-Kindergarten–Grade 8. With close teacher-student rapport and an emphasis on excellence in traditional academics, the School seeks to develop independent thinking and personal responsibility. Art, music, drama, shop, and physical education, including team sports for upper grades, are offered at all levels. Spanish and Latin begin in Grade 6. Computer instruction is offered in all grades. Extended Day and summer camp are available. All-inclusive Fees: $10,125–$15,525. Financial Aid: $200,000. Carter Harrison is Director of Admissions; Sonia L. Valentine (Bicol University [Philippines], B.S. 1967; Fordham University, M.S. 1975) was appointed Head in 1996.

Deerfield Academy   DEERFIELD

Deerfield, MA 01342. 413-772-0241; Fax 413-772-1100; E-mail admission@deerfield.edu; Web Site www.deerfield.edu

Deerfield Academy in Deerfield, Massachusetts, is a coeducational, college preparatory school enrolling 599 boarding and day students in Grade 9–Postgraduate. Historic Deerfield (population 5400) is in the northwestern part of the state, 30 miles north of Springfield and 5 miles south of Greenfield. The scenic Pioneer Valley is home to five colleges and a wealth of cultural, intellectual, and recreational attractions. The school is accessible from Interstate 91, the Massachusetts Turnpike, and Bradley International Airport.

Deerfield Academy was founded in 1797 when Governor Samuel Adams signed a bill granting the charter for the school that was, according to its trustees, committed to the "instruction of youth and the promotion of piety, religion, and morality." Having recently celebrated its Bicentennial, Deerfield Academy has continually sought to provide a challenging curriculum taught by gifted faculty in an academic environment that demands excellence in all areas of endeavor. A wide range of extracurriculars and options for off-campus and overseas travel/study complement an academic program that is enriched by a diverse faculty and student body.

A nonprofit institution, Deerfield Academy is governed by a 28-member Board of Trustees. It is accredited by the New England Association of Schools and Colleges and holds membership in the National Association of Independent Schools and the Independent School Association of Massachusetts, among others. Many of the 10,000 living graduates of the Academy support the school through fund-raising and recruitment.

THE CAMPUS. Deerfield Academy is nestled in the heart of a small, 18th-century New England village. At the center of the 250-acre campus is the Frank L. Boyden Library, containing 70,000 books, periodicals, and audiovisual materials as well as the College Resource Room, the Archives, and a tutoring complex. The Helen C. Boyden Science Center houses the Peter C. Andrews Planetarium, the second largest in New England. The Science Center also provides 12,000 square feet of open lab space, the Technology Center, the Olin Science Resource Center, and 6 classrooms. Admission and other administrative offices are located in the Academy Building, along with 7 classrooms and a dance studio; the Arms Building and Kendall Classroom Building together contain an additional 37 classrooms, a 240-seat auditorium, and a language lab. The Dining Hall accommodates nearly 600 upstairs, with seating for 125 downstairs in the Parker Room. The Reed Center for the Arts contains two art galleries, art and architecture studios, a photography studio, music practice rooms, a radio station, a 650-seat auditorium, and a 175-seat black box theater. The Health Center furnishes inpatient space for 15, a nurses' station, and counseling offices. Students reside in 18 dormitories or houses, each with corridors of 12–14 students overseen by a faculty member and senior proctors. The Headmaster lives in The Manse.

Among the athletic facilities is the gymnasium complex, which contains the largest prep school natatorium in New England, featuring an 8-lane, 25-yard swimming pool with a separate diving well. The athletic complex also houses two basketball and eight squash courts, three international squash courts, a fitness center, student and athletic stores, ski rooms, and home and visitors' locker rooms. Sixty acres of athletic fields and a 6-lane, 400-meter, all-weather porous track are also on campus.

THE FACULTY. Dr. Eric Widmer was appointed Headmaster in July 1994. A member of Deerfield's Class of 1957, he earned a baccalaureate from Williams College and a doctorate in History and Far Eastern Languages from Harvard University. His wife, Dr. Meera Viswanathan, teaches History at the Academy. She is also an Associate Professor of Comparative Literature at Brown University.

In addition to Dr. Widmer, there are 115 faculty and administrators, 75 percent of whom hold advanced degrees. Among their representative colleges and universities are Amherst, Boston University, Bowdoin, Brown, Bryn Mawr, Carnegie Mellon, College of the Holy Cross, College of William and Mary, Connecticut College, Dartmouth, Denison, Dickinson, Duke, Emory, Georgetown, Harvard, John Carroll, Johns Hopkins, Juilliard, Manhattan, Middlebury, Mount Holyoke, New York University, Northwestern, Oberlin, Ohio University, Princeton, St. Olaf, Sarah Lawrence, Smith, Stanford, Temple, Trinity, Tufts, Wesleyan, Wheaton, Williams, Yale, and the Universities of British Columbia, Calgary, California, Chicago, Delaware, Hawaii, Massachusetts, Miami, Nantes, North Carolina, Oxford, Pennsylvania, Rhode Island, Rochester, Vermont, Washington, and Wisconsin.

The Health Center is staffed 24 hours a day by the school physician and registered nurses; complete medical facilities are available in Greenfield, 5 miles from campus.

STUDENT BODY. In 1999–2000, Deerfield Academy enrolled 513 boarders and 86 day students—286 girls and 313 boys. They came from 36 states, the District of Columbia, and 15 countries with the largest numbers from People's Republic of China 10, Canada 7, South Korea 6, and Thailand 4.

ACADEMIC PROGRAM. The school year, divided into three 11-week terms, extends from early September to the end of May. Each student has his or her own advisor who provides guidance and support in matters of academics, school life, and personal issues. Grades are sent to parents and students at the midpoint and end of each term, accompanied by comments and feedback from advisors and coaches.

Classes, ranging from 50 to 70 minutes each, are held five days a week. On a typical day, breakfast is served beginning at 7:00 A.M., followed by course work, athletics and other activities in the afternoon, and family-style dinner. Supervised study is held in the dorms between 8:00 and 10:00 P.M. with weeknight dorm sign-in ranging between 8:30 and 10:00 P.M., depending on grade.

Students carry five courses, each meeting four times a week on a rotating basis. To graduate, students must complete four years of English; three years of mathematics and one foreign language (or two years each of two languages); two years each of history and laboratory science; two terms of fine arts; and one term of philosophy or religion. Sophomores must complete a one-term course on health issues.

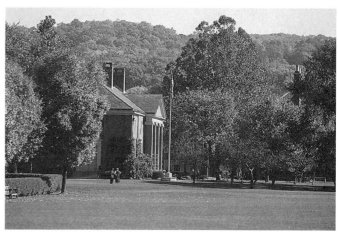

Specific courses include Computer Programming, Computer Programming in C++; English I–IV, Honors Literature, English as a Second Language; Introduction to Art, Introduction to Art History, Calligraphy, Raku Pottery, Ceramics, Photography, Drawing, Visual Design, Architecture, Advanced Architecture, Video, Topics in Contemporary Art; Introduction to Dance, Dance I–III, Advanced Tutorial in Dance; Chamber Singers, Academy Chorus, Concert Band, Chamber Music, Independent Study in Piano; Introduction to Performing Arts, History of the Theatre, Acting, Directing for Theatre, Advanced Tutorial in Acting; Western Civilizations, World Cultures, Asian Civilizations, United States History, American Studies, Honors United States History, 20th Century World History, History of the Civil Rights Era, Selected Topics in Asian History, Honors European History, Honors Economics; Latin I–V, Greek I–II, Chinese I–III, French I–VI, German I–V, Spanish I–IV; Algebra, Geometry, Honors Geometry, Functions, Statistics and Trigonometry, Precalculus, Accelerated Precalculus, Discrete Math, Advanced Calculus and Algebra; Ethics, Political Philosophy, Philosophy, Judeo-Christian Tradition, Religions of the World; Astronomy, Biology I–II, Chemistry, Accelerated Chemistry, Anatomy and Physiology, Physics I–II, Physical Geology, Environmental Science, and River, Valley, Rock: Environmental Science. There are 22 Advanced Placement courses as well as accelerated courses in all academic departments.

School Year Abroad provides language immersion studies in France, Spain, and China, including homestays with local families for the duration of the program. Depending on grade level, students may participate in similar travel-exchange options in Switzerland, Germany, Africa, and Japan. Maine Coast Semester and the Mountain School of Milton Academy also offer unique off-campus study opportunities.

During the spring term, seniors may undertake study and off-campus exploration in a field of particular interest. The Alternate Studies program allows qualified seniors to pursue a full program of prescribed and elected course work on a faculty-supervised project such as volunteer work in hospitals or schools, internships with various professionals, and art and media production.

In the last five years, 99 percent of graduates have entered accredited four-year colleges, with the largest numbers enrolled at Bowdoin College 34, Brown 38, Dartmouth 28, Georgetown 42, Harvard 28, Middlebury 33, Williams College 34, and Yale 30.

STUDENT ACTIVITIES. The Deerfield Council, comprised of

student officers elected by their classmates, serves as a conduit of information and opinion between the school community and the faculty and the Headmaster. Other leadership groups include the Diversity Task Force, peer support groups, and student tutors. Many students volunteer with Big Brothers/Big Sisters, day care centers, elementary schools, nursing homes, and a homeless shelter.

Students produce English and Spanish literary magazines, a yearbook, and a newspaper. Other organized interest groups include debate teams, WGAJ radio, tour guides, Black Student Coalition, Christian Fellowship, and clubs for foreign languages, the environment, politics, sailing, mountaineering, and investment.

Among the performing groups on campus are Concert Band, Jazz Ensemble, Academy Chorus, Madrigal Singers, boys' and girls' a cappella groups, and drama and dance troupes.

Both boys' and girls' teams compete in crew, cross-country, soccer, water polo, alpine skiing, basketball, hockey, squash, swimming, cycling, lacrosse, tennis, and track. Girls also play field hockey, volleyball, and softball, while boys compete in football, baseball, wrestling, and golf. Recreational and intramural pursuits such as lifesaving, aerobics, and dance are undertaken on a noncompetitive basis.

ADMISSION AND COSTS. Deerfield Academy welcomes academically able young people from diverse backgrounds who have character and a sense of responsibility toward themselves and others. Interested students are urged to visit the campus for a tour and interview or, if distance is a factor, to meet with one of Deerfield's regional admission representatives. Acceptance is based on classroom performance, two essays, school and teacher evaluations, the results of standardized testing, the previous school record, areas of contribution, and good citizenship. The application fee is $40 for students living in the United States and Canada and $75 for all others.

In 1999–2000, boarding tuition was $24,300 and day tuition was $18,600. Fees cover most expenses other than books and infirmary and health care. Financial aid in the amount of $3,695,000 was awarded to 33 percent of the students based on need.

Assistant Headmaster for Student Life: Pamela Bonanno
Assistant Headmaster and Director of College Advising: Martha C. Lyman
Assistant Headmaster for Alumni Affairs and Development: David G. Pond
Dean of Faculty: Richard A. Bonanno
Academic Dean: John Taylor
Dean of Admission and Financial Aid: Patricia L. Gimbel
Dean of Students: Stephen S. Murray
Assistant Treasurer and Business Manager: C. Michael Sheridan
Director of Athletics: Katherine Robertson

Derby Academy   1784

56 Burditt Avenue, Hingham, MA 02043. 781-749-0746;
Fax 781-740-2542; E-mail username@derby.hingham.ma.us

Founded in 1784 to provide equal education for girls and boys, Derby Academy enrolls 296 students in Prekindergarten–Grade 9. The school seeks to bring together motivated students, talented faculty, and a challenging program to provide a well-balanced education. The curriculum prepares students for the rigors of competitive secondary schools and allows them to develop individual strengths in the arts. A creative arts summer camp for ages 8–15, a summer academic program for Grades 2–12, and a variety of sports camps are offered. Tuition: $6650–$14,600 (all-inclusive). Financial Aid: $140,000. Jay K. Sadlon is Director of Admissions; Edward R. Foley (St. Michael's, B.A.; University of Vermont, M.Ed.) was appointed Headmaster in 1992.

Dexter School   1926

20 Newton Street, Brookline, MA 02445-7498. 617-522-5544

Dexter School, enrolling 370 day boys in Pre-Kindergarten–Grade 8, seeks to develop each student's mental and physical abilities and to help him form good social, moral, and spiritual attitudes and habits. Fundamental academic skills and traditional subjects are emphasized, including Latin in Grades 6–8, and are supplemented by classes in science, computer, art, shop, and music. All students participate in athletics using the gymnasium, indoor swimming pool, two indoor ice rinks, and four playing fields. A sister school, Southfield, enrolling 270 girls, was established in 1992 on the same 36-acre campus. Tuition: $11,760–$16,050. Financial Aid: $625,000. Endicott P. Saltonstall, Jr., is Director of Admissions; William F. Phinney (Harvard, A.B. 1950) was appointed Headmaster in 1964.

Eaglebrook School   DEERFIELD

Pine Nook Road, Deerfield, MA 01342. 413-774-7411;
E-mail /tlow@eaglebrook.org; Web Site www.eaglebrook.org

EAGLEBROOK SCHOOL in Deerfield, Massachusetts, is a boarding school for boys in Grades 6 through 9 that also enrolls day students and a small number of faculty daughters. The School is situated on Mount Pocumtuck, overlooking Historic Deerfield and the Connecticut River. Deerfield (population 8000) is the home of several other independent schools, and there are five colleges nearby. The town, located off Interstate 91, is 98 miles west of Boston and 180 miles northeast of New York City. Amtrak trains serve nearby Springfield, and Bradley International Airport is a 60-minute drive to the south.

The School was founded in 1922 by Howard B. Gibbs, who wished to establish an outstanding boarding school for young boys. C. Thurston Chase joined the faculty two years later and became Headmaster in 1928. He served until 1966 when he was succeeded by his son, O. Stuart Chase, the current Headmaster.

Within a small community, Eaglebrook strives to help each boy come into full and confident possession of his innate talents, to improve the skills needed for the challenges of secondary school, and to establish values that will allow him to be a person who acts with thoughtfulness and humanity. Eaglebrook seeks to make learning an adventure and encourages close student-faculty contact in the classroom and in the dormitories, where faculty members are in residence.

A nonprofit institution, Eaglebrook is operated by the Allen-Chase Foundation under the direction of a 37-member Board of Trustees. The self-perpetuating Board, which meets three times a year, includes parents and alumni. Many of the 3700 living graduates are active in school affairs.

Eaglebrook holds membership in the National Association

of Independent Schools, The Independent School Association of Massachusetts, and the Valley Independent School Association, among other associations.

THE CAMPUS. The 640-acre campus includes trails for skiing and hiking and a pond for nature study and recreation. The Learning Center, recently renovated and enlarged, houses classrooms, a newly computerized library, an audiovisual center, a computer center, and an assembly area. Flagler Science Building provides three laboratories, two classrooms, a project room, and a departmental office. Bryant Building houses a woodworking shop, music rooms, a publications office, and art studios (ceramics, stained glass, drafting, photography, drawing, and painting).

Six dormitories, built or renovated between 1957 and 1989, house the boarders and most of the faculty. Students and faculty take their meals together in Gibbs Dining Hall, which also contains the school store, a barber shop, the laundry room, a grist mill, and a bakery.

Also on campus are the Lodge (the oldest school building), which houses the Headmaster's and other administrative offices, and the Headmaster's home.

Athletic facilities include 9 playing fields, a newly constructed outdoor track, 10 tennis courts, 13 ski trails, and a snow-making facility. The sports center and connecting field house provide basketball courts, a wrestling room, squash courts, and a rifle range. The Schwab Family Pool, a six-lane facility, is available for competitive and recreational swimming. The Alfond Arena, an indoor hockey rink, opened in the winter of 1999.

The School-owned facilities, at replacement value, are worth more than $30,000,000.

THE FACULTY. O. Stuart Chase, appointed Headmaster in 1966, is a 1947 graduate of Eaglebrook. Mr. Chase also attended Phillips Exeter Academy (Class of 1950), Williams (B.A. 1954), and Columbia (M.A. 1963). The former Assistant Headmaster of New Canaan Country School, Mr. Chase has been chairman of the Elementary Schools Committee of the National Association of Independent Schools and a trustee of Historic Deerfield, Inc. He and his wife, Edmonia, have two adult children.

The full-time faculty, including administrators who teach, number 63—40 men and 23 women. Fifty faculty members, 23 with families, live on campus. They hold 53 undergraduate and 21 graduate degrees from such colleges and universities as American University, Amherst, Beloit, Brown, Colby, Columbia, Connecticut College, Cornell, Dartmouth, Harvard, Indiana University, Johns Hopkins, Macalester, Middlebury, Mount Holyoke, Oberlin, Princeton, Rutgers, St. Lawrence, Smith, Springfield, Temple, United States Naval Academy, Villanova, Washington State, Williams, Yale, and the Universities of Arizona, Colorado, Maryland, Massachusetts, New Hampshire,

New Mexico, North Carolina, Northern Illinois, Oslo, Rennes, Richmond, Salzburg, Southern Maine, and Vermont. There are also 6 part-time teachers.

Faculty benefits include health and life insurance, a retirement plan, Social Security, and financial assistance for graduate study. Leaves of absence and sabbaticals can be arranged.

The Allen-Chase Infirmary is staffed by nurses from 7:00 A.M. to 9:00 P.M.; a pediatrician holds daily office hours. At other times, the School uses the infirmary of Deerfield Academy or hospitals in nearby Greenfield.

STUDENT BODY. In 1999–2000, the School enrolls 180 boarding boys and 68 day students, including 4 girls who are faculty daughters, as follows: 27 in Grade 6, 49 in Grade 7, 95 in Grade 8, and 77 in Grade 9. The boys represent 27 states, 18 foreign countries, and a variety of cultural, ethnic, and religious backgrounds.

ACADEMIC PROGRAM. The school year, from mid-September to early June, is divided into quarters and includes a one-week Thanksgiving recess, a three-week Christmas vacation, a five-day Winter Carnival, and a four-week spring vacation. A typical weekday includes rising at 6:50 A.M. with breakfast at 7:15; classes, assembly, and lunch from 8:20 A.M. to 2:00 P.M.; study hall, athletics, tutorials, and activities from 2:00 P.M. to 5:00 P.M.; dinner at 6:00; study hall at 7:30 P.M.; and "lights out" between 9:15 and 10:00 P.M.

An average class enrolls 8–12 students. Grades are issued and sent to parents four times a year, accompanied by teachers' comments and a cover letter from the student's adviser. New students receive a progress report three weeks into the year. There are supervised study halls five days a week, and teachers are available to provide extra help as necessary. The School offers English as a Second Language, special instruction for a small number of students with mild language disabilities, and a course on organizational and study skills. Ongoing tutorials can be arranged for an additional charge.

The curriculum for Grade 6 consists of English, reading, an introduction to Latin, history, geography, mathematics, science, art, music, woodworking, and computer/word processing.

To graduate, students in Grades 7–9 must complete three years each of English and mathematics, two and one-half years of science, two years of a world language, two and one-half years of history and geography, one quarter of studio art, and one quarter of sex education.

Full-year and elective courses include English 1–3; French 1–3, Latin 1–3, Spanish 1–3; Civil War Era, Anthropology, Russian History and Society, Colonial History, Medieval History, English History, Contemporary American History, Greek and Roman History, Chinese History and Culture, Modern European History; Pre-Algebra, Algebra I, Geometry; Physical Science, Earth Science, Biology; Basic Electronics; Architecture, Pottery, Charcoal and Pastel, Painting, Printmaking; Band, Chorus, Instrumental Workshop; and Acting and American Film. Honors sections are offered in many subjects.

Among the schools graduates of the Class of 1999 are now attending are Avon Old Farms School, Berkshire, Cate, Brooks, Choate Rosemary Hall, Concord Academy, Deerfield Academy, Episcopal High School, Governor Dummer, Groton, Hotchkiss, Lawrenceville, Loomis Chaffee School, Middlesex, Millbrook, Milton, Northfield Mount Hermon, Peddie School, Pomfret, St. George's, St. Mark's, Salisbury, Suffield, Tabor, Taft, Western Reserve, Westminster, and Williston Northampton as well as various public schools.

STUDENT ACTIVITIES. The Student Council is composed of representatives from each form, dormitory, and the day students. Under the guidance of the Headmaster, the Council meets monthly to consider matters relating to all aspects of student life. Students are encouraged to demonstrate leadership on committees and through service activities such as conducting campus tours, waiting on tables, and assisting in the library.

Students publish a newspaper, a literary magazine, and a yearbook. Other activities include audiovisual photography, computers, musical groups, dramatic productions, woodworking, printing, and mechanical drawing.

Eaglebrook organizes varsity, junior varsity, and junior teams in baseball, basketball, cross-country, football, hockey, lacrosse, skiing, and soccer. Eaglebrook teams compete with those of other independent schools and local public schools. There is also instructional tennis, recreational cycling, and an outdoor program of hiking, trail work, and camping.

After the first month of school, boarding students may leave the campus on weekends if they have parental permission and if they have no academic or athletic commitments. Often, a boarding student will spend a weekend at the home of a day student. There are many weekend activities on campus—athletic contests, dances, films, concerts, and lectures—and day students are encouraged to take part. The School also organizes trips to historic sites, museums, and attractions in Boston. Attendance at the nondenominational vespers service on Sunday is required for all boarding students.

Traditional events include biweekly "Home Nights" (in which students have dinner with faculty advisers), Country Fair, the Christmas Candlelighting Ceremony, Winter Carnival, Reunion Weekend, Grandparents' Day, and athletic and academic awards banquets.

ADMISSION AND COSTS. New students are admitted in

Grades 6–8 and occasionally in Grade 9 on the basis of the completed application, the previous school record, teacher recommendations, and standardized testing. Application, for which there is a $35 fee, can be made at any time during the year prior to desired entrance. Applications are considered on a rolling basis, and midyear entrance is possible if vacancies exist.

In 1999–2000, boarding tuition is $26,675; day tuition is $16,675. Additional expenses are $600 for day students and $2000 for boarding students.

In 1998–99, Eaglebrook awarded $870,000 in financial aid to 27 percent of the student body. Tuition insurance and a tuition payment plan are offered. Eaglebrook subscribes to the School and Student Service for Financial Aid.

Dean of Faculty: Kirk R. Koenigsbauer
Dean of Students: Kirk R. Koenigsbauer
Director of Alumni: Andrew C. Chase
Alumni Secretary: Karen Kirkendall
Director of Admissions: Theodore J. Low
Director of Development: Andrew C. Chase
Business Manager: Richard C. Andriole
Director of Placement: Karl J. Koenigsbauer
Director of Athletics: Christopher M. Loftus

The Eliot Montessori School   1971

5 Auburn Street, South Natick, MA 01760. 508-655-7333;
Fax 508-655-3867; E-mail eliotadmissions@hotmail.com;
Web Site www.ultranet.com/eliot-ad

The Eliot Montessori School enrolls 90 boys and girls as day students in Grades Pre-1–8. Montessori philosophy is the foundation of the School's approach and program. Specially trained teachers discern and nurture each child's strengths and talents. Eliot's carefully prepared, child-centered environment and unique learning materials help students develop on many different levels. Through the Eliot Montessori School's integrated, rigorous, and diverse program curriculum, children develop the knowledge, self-confidence, and curiosity about learning that will last a lifetime. Tuition: $9500–$10,800. Polly Vernimen is Director of Admissions; Lucy Tannen (Cornell, M.S.; Brandeis M.S.) was appointed Head of School in 1996.

Fayerweather Street School   1967

74-R Fayerweather Street, Cambridge, MA 02138. 617-876-4746;
Fax 617-520-6700

Fayerweather Street School was founded by parents and educators to provide alternative schooling that would afford individualized education within a safe, supportive, stimulating environment. The School celebrates and promotes diversity in its student population, which includes 160 boys and girls in Kindergarten–Grade 8. Mixed-age classes enhance the curriculum and allow for a wider range of companions and learning partners. The curriculum is enriched by music, drama, library, woodshop, art, resource room, field trips, and a weekly School Meeting. An Afterschool Program is provided. Tuition: $10,400–$11,500. Financial aid is available. Andrea Myers is Director of Admissions; Susan Kluver (Simmons College, B.A.; Harvard University, M.Ed., Ed.D.) is Head of School.

Fay School   1866

Box 9106, 48 Main Street, Southborough, MA 01772-9106.
508-485-0100 or 800-933-2925; Fax 508-481-7872;
Web Site http://www.fayschool.org

Fay School enrolls 370 boys and girls from the United States and other countries, with day students in Grades 1–9 and boarders in Grade 6 upward. The college preparatory curriculum features classes with an average of 12 students, a flexible rotating schedule, and strong academic and personal support from faculty. Special programs address the needs of international students and those with different learning styles. The visual and performing arts are integral to the curriculum. Among the activities are Student Government, community outreach, clubs, and interscholastic sports. A summer program is optional. Boarding Tuition: $27,200; Day Tuition: $11,950–$16,300. Lois V. Poirot is Director of Admission; Stephen C. White is Headmaster.

The Fenn School   1929

516 Monument Street, Concord, MA 01742-1894. 978-369-5800; Fax 978-371-7520; Web Site www.fenn.org

The Fenn School is a day school enrolling 294 boys in Grades 4–9. It seeks to offer sound academic training in an intellectually stimulating atmosphere tempered with an understanding of the emotional needs of the early adolescent. Students develop basic skills at the fourth- and fifth-grade levels and enter a fully departmentalized program in Grade 6. French and Latin begin in Grade 6. The School has a long tradition of supporting its challenging academic program with extensive art courses and a competitive athletic program. Graduates are accepted at leading secondary schools nationwide. Tuition: $15,800–$17,250. Financial Aid: $345,000. Christopher Gorycki is Director of Admissions; Gerard J.G. Ward (Boston University, B.A.; Harvard, Ed.M.) was appointed Headmaster in 1993.

The Fessenden School   1903

250 Waltham Street, West Newton, MA 02465-1749. 617-630-2300; Fax 617-630-2303; E-mail admissions@Fessenden.org; Web Site www.fessenden.org

Fessenden, offering a traditional curriculum designed to be rigorous yet developmentally appropriate and supportive of each student's learning style, enrolls 350 day boys in K–9 and 106 five- and seven-day boarding boys in Grades 5–9. Homelike dorms are closely supervised by resident faculty and their families. The School offers strong athletics and arts programs for every age and ability level and a range of opportunities for students to develop leadership skills and exhibit their talents. Extended day and English as a Second Language programs are available. Boarding Tuition: $22,950–$28,550; Day Tuition: $11,925–$16,950. Financial Aid: $500,000. Caleb W. Thomson '79 is Director of Admissions; Frank M. Perrine (Lafayette, B.A.; New York University, M.A.) is Head of School.

The French-American International School of Boston   1962

45 Matignon Road, Cambridge, MA 02140. 617-499-1451; Fax 617-499-1454; E-mail ebcamb@mediaone.net

Ecole Bilingue, New England's first and only bilingual international school, enrolls 400 boys and girls in PreK–Grade 11 on two campuses; Grade 12 will be added in 2000. Each day, students complete a full French academic program, accredited by the French Ministry of Education, and a complete American program, accredited by the Association of Independent Schools in New England. English and French as second languages are offered. The high school program prepares students for the French Baccalaureate with the international and informatic options, as well as Advanced Placement and College Board examinations. Tuition: $8900–$9575. Financial Aid: $300,000. Joan Dimancescu (Hunter College, B.A.; Yale, M.A., M.Phil.; Columbia, M.A.) is Head of School.

Friends Academy   1810

1088 Tucker Road, North Dartmouth, MA 02747. 508-999-1356; Fax 508-997-0117; E-mail friends@ma.ultranet.com

Friends Academy was established by a group of New Bedford Quakers who shared a commitment to the importance of education and the value of the individual child. Today enrolling 300 day boys and girls in Preschool–Grade 8, the school emphasizes mastery of basic skills in the major disciplines. The college-oriented program is enriched by foreign languages, computers, library, art, music, and physical education. Students present two major drama productions each year, and the interscholastic program engages boys and girls in such sports as soccer, basketball, and lacrosse. Tuition: $3750–$11,500. Financial aid is available. Linda Kelsey is Director of Admissions; Claudia Daggett (University of Wisconsin, B.S.; National College of Education, M.S.Ed.) is Head of School.

Glen Urquhart School   1977

74 Hart Street, Beverly Farms, MA 01915. 978-927-1064; Fax 978-921-0060; E-mail glenurq@shore.net; Web Site www.gus.org

Glen Urquhart School, enrolling 200 boys and girls as day students in Kindergarten–Grade 8, stimulates "academic excellence, critical thinking skills, and artistic creativity" through a carefully sequenced, thematic curriculum. The cultural, physical, and human resources in the area are used extensively to complement the School's programs. Field trips, special events, and visiting artists are part of the program. Team sports are introduced in Grade 6. There are before- and after-school programs. A summer session provides a day camp, a special crafts/art program, and various sports. Tuition: $7175–$11,875. Financial aid is available. Leslie Marchesseault is Admissions Director; Raymond Nance (Texas Tech, B.A.; Southern Methodist, M.Th.) is Head.

Governor Dummer Academy   BYFIELD

Byfield, MA 01922. 978-465-1763; E-mail admissions@gda.org; Web Site www.gda.org

GOVERNOR DUMMER ACADEMY in Byfield, Massachusetts, is a college preparatory boarding and day school for boys and girls in Grades 9 through 12. The oldest independent boarding school in the United States, it was founded in 1763 under the will of Lt. Governor William Dummer of the Massachusetts Bay Colony. Female day students were admitted in 1971 for the first time since 1904; girls were accepted as boarders in 1973. Governor Dummer Academy is located in a country setting 5 miles from the city of Newburyport. It is 33 miles north of Boston via U.S. Route 1.

Governor Dummer Academy expects and promotes the individual's active commitment to integrity, learning, academic excellence, and the health of the community. Enriched by a unique tradition and beautiful surroundings, the school supports personal growth and achievement in academics, the arts, and athletics in a diverse community that values teamwork, service, and respect for others.

Governor Dummer Academy is incorporated not-for-profit and is directed by a self-perpetuating Board of 24 Trustees, which meets three times a year. The school is a member of the National Association of Independent Schools and The Independent School Association of Massachusetts; it is accredited by the New England Association of Schools and Colleges. There are approximately 5000 living graduates and an active alumni/ae group.

THE CAMPUS. The 350-acre campus, situated at the edge of an Atlantic salt marsh, continues to be shaped by evolutionary advances such as the state-of-the-art Carl A. Pescosolido Library (1997) and The Center for the Study of Mathematics and Science (1997). Along with the original Mansion House (1713) and the Frost Library (1957), these new buildings form the intellectual heart of the campus. Features include 45,000 volumes and computer workstations with Internet access. The creation of the Mathematics/Science Center reflects the interrelationship of the two departments in a closely integrated curriculum. The new construction contains 12 classrooms with computer connections at every mathematics desk, and conference space. Other academic facilities include Parsons Schoolhouse; the Wange-Goodhue Computer Center; Kaiser Visual Arts housing the Carl Youngman Gallery, a photography laboratory, and art and ceramic studios; and Thompson Performing Arts Center. There are nine dormitory facilities, The French Student Center, The Commons, Moseley Chapel, the Headmaster's residence, 12 faculty homes, and Phillips Building, which houses administrative offices, and the dining room.

The Carl A. Pescosolido, Jr., Field House contains an indoor track and tennis, volleyball, and basketball courts. Alumni Gymnasium offers a fitness center, training room, dance studio, wrestling room, and locker rooms. The Murphy-Frost Arena houses the ice hockey rink as well as indoor tennis courts. Six outdoor tennis courts and 12 playing fields, including the new Barbara F. Porter Field and Higgins Track (1998), complete the athletic facilities.

THE FACULTY. John Martin Doggett, Jr., appointed Headmaster in 1999, is a *cum laude* graduate of Williams College, with a bachelor's degree in American Civilization. He received his master's degree in history from New York University. Prior to his appointment, Mr. Doggett served as Associate Headmaster and Dean of Students at The Lawrenceville School in Lawrenceville, New Jersey. In his 25 years at Lawrenceville, he also served as history and economics teacher, housemaster, and coach.

There are 39 full-time teachers, 28 men and 11 women; 16 part-time instructors teach foreign languages, fine arts, and dance and provide tutoring. Forty faculty members live on campus with their families. The full-time faculty hold 53 baccalaureate and 39 advanced degrees, representing study at Allegheny, Amherst, Antioch, Bates, Boston College, Boston University, Bowdoin, Bucknell, Cambridge College, Carleton, Clarkson, Colgate, College of the Holy Cross, Dartmouth, Emerson, Florida State, Franklin and Marshall, Goddard, Gordon College, Harvard, Haverford, Hollins, Johns Hopkins, Mary Washington, Middlebury, New England Conservatory of Music, New York University, Northeastern, Oberlin, Princeton, Purdue, Roger Williams, St. Lawrence, Simmons, Southern Methodist University, State University of New York (Buffalo), Trenton State, Trinity, Tufts, Union, University College (Ireland), Vassar, Vermont Law School, Washington State, Wesleyan, Williams,

Wittenberg, Worcester Polytechnic Institute, Yale, and the Universities of Colorado, Connecticut, Iowa, Lowell, Maryland, Minnesota, New Hampshire, Pennsylvania, Rochester, Southern Maine, Vermont, and Virginia. Faculty benefits include group health insurance, a pension plan, and Social Security. Leaves of absence and sabbaticals may be granted under special circumstances.

A registered nurse resides in the eight-bed health center. The school physician is on call at all times.

STUDENT BODY. In 1999–2000, Governor Dummer Academy enrolls 133 boarding boys, 94 boarding girls, 60 day boys, and 79 day girls in Grades 9 through 12. There are 84 freshmen, 103 sophomores, 85 juniors, and 94 seniors. They originate from 12 states as well as Canada, Colombia, Germany, Hong Kong, Indonesia, Japan, Korea, Saudi Arabia, Taiwan, and Thailand.

ACADEMIC PROGRAM. The academic year, from early September to early June, includes 33 weeks of instruction and Thanksgiving, winter, and spring breaks. The daily academic schedule features 60- and 90-minute class periods, conflict-free time for musical performance groups, and some unscheduled time each day for students and faculty to prepare for classes, to meet for extra help, and for students to work together on group projects. The academic day begins at 7:45 A.M. and ends at 3:10 P.M. and includes time for faculty advisors and student advisees to meet as well as a convocation period for outside speakers or meetings of student organizations. These are in addition to three all-school meetings each week, one a nondenominational chapel service and one presided over by student body leaders.

An average class contains 13 students. Boarding students attend supervised dormitory study halls Sunday through Thursday evening. Grades are issued and sent to parents approximately every eight weeks; written comments accompany new students' grades for the first marking period and are sent with all grades at the end of each semester.

Students must successfully complete the following core courses in order to receive a Governor Dummer Academy diploma: four years of English, three years of mathematics, three years of a foreign language, two years of history, two years of science, one year of introductory fine arts, and a one-semester fine arts course. There is a community service requirement for graduation. Attendance at both on- and off-campus humanities events is also a requirement.

Among the full-credit course offerings are English 1–4; French 1–5, German 1–5, Latin 1–5, Spanish 1–5; Ancient History, African History, Economics, Modern European History, Russian Studies, United States History, Postwar America, Middle Eastern History, Chinese History, Psychology; Algebra 1–2, Geometry, Advanced Topics in Mathematics, Pre-Calculus, Calculus; Science, Biology, Ecology, Marine Science, Chemistry, Physics; and Accelerated Biology, Chemistry, and Physics. Half-credit courses are offered in Computer Science, Electricity 1–2, Art History, Photography, Studio Art, History of Music, Music Theory, Instrumental Music, Composition of Electronic Music, Probability and Statistics, and Theatre.

Students may sit for Advanced Placement Examinations in major disciplines. Independent Study is an option for one-half credit.

In 1999, 79 of 82 graduates entered college; 11 were accepted by "early decision" or "early action." Among the colleges they are attending are Amherst, Bates, Boston University, Bowdoin, Colgate, Cornell, Hartwick, Haverford, Mount Holyoke, Rhode Island School of Design, Stanford, Tufts, Wesleyan, and Williams.

STUDENT ACTIVITIES. Attending Governor Dummer Academy means becoming a member of a close-knit community of students and faculty members who share activities ranging from breakfast to evening study hall each day. The Academy community operates seven days per week and places a high priority on participation and achievement by all of its members. Boarding and day students learn to manage their time and plan weekdays and weekends to allow time for academics, extracurricular interests, and leisure activities.

After dinner each evening, there is an activity period in which many of the Academy's clubs and organizations hold regular meetings. The library and arts and computer facilities are all open during this time so that students may work or explore personal interests. An evening study hall, with quiet hours starting at 7:00 P.M., follows the activity period Sunday through Thursday. Students work at their desks in their dormitories under the supervision of dormitory parents and student proctors. Study and bed times are determined by grade level.

Clubs are formed in response to student interest. Current organizations include the Red Key (campus service organization), Model U.N., Harvard Model Congress, International Club, Social Committee, Chapel Committee, P.R.I.D.E., Jewish Fellowship; chorus, yearbook, newspaper, literary magazine; and art, drama, computer, debating, and photography clubs. There are several instrumental groups, including Chamber Ensemble and Jazz Band, under the direction of a full-time faculty member. The Director of Community Service supervises students as they pursue such activities as tutoring, Special Olympics, assisting in a convalescent home, and working with special-needs children.

The Academy is a member of the Independent School League (ISL). Interscholastic competition for boys is held in football, cross-country running, soccer, hockey, wrestling, basketball, track, lacrosse, tennis, and baseball. Girls compete in field hockey, basketball, soccer, softball, cross-country running, volleyball, hockey, lacrosse, tennis, and track, while coeducational teams have been formed in golf. Recreational golf, modern dance, tennis, skating, snowboarding, skiing, and an outdoor program are also available.

Boarding students receive weekend permissions according to their grade levels; there are five closed weekends each year. Social activities for students include concerts, coffeehouses, softball games, trips to professional sports events, movies, country fairs, and dances. Frequent trips to programs of interest in Boston are part of the Humanities program. Traditional annual events for parents and alumni/ae are Parents' Days in October, Reunion Weekend in June, Commencement, and alumni/ae gatherings in cities around the country.

ADMISSION AND COSTS. Governor Dummer Academy seeks highly motivated students who demonstrate ability, promise, and character, and who will gain from the Governor Dummer experience and contribute to it. Geographic, cultural, and economic diversity are desired along with extracurricular interests

and talents. The Admissions Committee takes into consideration school performance, test scores, recommendations, and extracurricular involvement. An on-campus interview is strongly suggested, but off-campus interviews may sometimes be arranged. Applications are due by February 1. There is a $35 application fee ($70 outside the United States). Governor Dummer Academy places a high value on diversity and does not discriminate on the basis of race, color, religion, or national or ethnic origin in admission or in the administration of school programs.

In 1999–2000, tuition is $26,500 for boarding students and $21,000 for day students. Extra costs average $2000. In 1999, $1,500,000 in need-based financial aid and loans was awarded to 30 percent of the student body. Governor Dummer Academy subscribes to the School Scholarship Service. Tuition payment and tuition refund plans are required.

Assistant Headmaster: Edward C. Young '73
Dean of Students: Lynda F. Bromley
Academic Dean: William F. Quigley, Jr.
Alumni Council President: Peter Butler '62
Director of Admissions: Gillian M. Lloyd
Director of Development: Patricia T. Peterman
College Counselor: Janet E. Adams-Wall
Chief Financial Officer: Richard R. Savage
Director of Afternoon Activities: Roberta S. McLain

Groton School   1884

P.O. Box 911, Groton, MA 01450-0991. 978-448-7510;
Fax 978-448-9623; E-mail admission_office@groton.org;
Web Site www.groton.org

Groton, a coeducational, college preparatory school affiliated with the Episcopal Church, enrolls 307 boarders and 37 day students from many religious, racial, and cultural backgrounds in Forms II–VI. Set on a 300-acre campus 40 miles from Boston, Groton offers a rigorous liberal arts program taught by a distinguished and dedicated faculty. Computer technology, modern and classical languages, Advanced Placement courses, the arts, and diverse electives round out the curriculum. Among the numerous activities are men's and women's sports, drama, music, community service, and leadership groups. Boarding Tuition: $27,000; Day Tuition: $20,250. Financial Aid: $1,745,000. John M. Niles is Director of Admission; William M. Polk '58 is Headmaster. *New England Association.*

Hillside School   MARLBOROUGH

Robin Hill Road, Marlborough, MA 01752-1099. 508-485-2824;
Fax 508-485-4420; Web Site www.ultranet.com/~hillsid-

HILLSIDE SCHOOL in Marlborough, Massachusetts, is an independent, nonsectarian school enrolling middle school boys as boarding and day students in Grades 5 through 9. The town of Marlborough (population 31,813) is 30 miles west of Boston and 17 miles east of Worcester. The rural, wooded areas surrounding the School provide opportunities for hiking, bicycling, canoeing, and other outdoor pursuits, while the nearby cities offer ample cultural, recreational, and historic attractions.

Hillside School was established in 1901 by sisters Charlotte Drinkwater, a social worker who founded the Boston YMCA, and Mary Drinkwater Warren, a teacher. Their purpose was to provide a home and school setting for needy and orphaned boys.

Hillside School offers a strong, fundamental education within a nurturing family environment. Caring, qualified faculty aim to instill core values of honesty, respect for others, responsibility, self-discipline, and hard work with the goal of developing each boy's academic strengths, civic and social awareness, and personal standards. Beginning in 1925, Hillside has been the recipient of generous assistance from the Daughters of the American Revolution, one of only six schools in the nation to be endowed by this organization.

A nonprofit institution since 1907, Hillside is guided by a 25-member, self-perpetuating Board of Trustees. It holds membership in the National Association of Independent Schools, the Independent School Association of Massachusetts, Secondary School Admission Test Board, The Junior Boarding School, and the Council for Advancement and Support of Education. The Hillside Parents Association is instrumental in organizing special events and financial support for the School.

THE CAMPUS. The Assabet River flows through the Hillside School's 260-acre wooded campus, which has its own spring-fed pond, a working farm, and 4 acres of athletic fields. The academic hub of the School is centered in Stevens Hall, which contains nine classrooms, a computer room, and the science laboratory. Linked to Stevens Hall are the Niles Memorial Library, the Whitehead Industrial Arts Building, and the Tracy gymnasium/auditorium. Drinkwater Hall houses the dining room and administrative, admissions, and business offices. Boys reside in three faculty-supervised dormitories: Williams for Grades 5–7, Whittemore for Grades 7–9, and the Farm Dorm for selected students in Grades 7–9 who choose to assist with the farm program.

The plant is owned by Hillside School and is valued at approximately $2,000,000.

THE FACULTY. David Z. Beecher was appointed Headmaster in 1998. An honors graduate of The Choate School, Mr. Beecher earned a B.A. degree in American Studies and Education from Lake Forest College, where he was named a Lila B. Frank Scholar. Prior to coming to Hillside, he served as Director of Admission & Financial Aid at Fay School and Wilbraham & Monson Academy, both in Massachusetts. Mr. Beecher also spent six years at Berkshire School as Dean of Students, teacher, dorm parent, coach, and member of the Admissions and Development departments. At Yale University, he served as Athletic Administrator and assistant men's varsity ice-hockey coach. Mr. Beecher and his wife, Carrie, have two daughters, Madeline and Haley.

In addition to Mr. Beecher, there are 20 faculty and administrators who teach, 9 women and 11 men. Faculty are chosen for their ability to motivate students through their teaching strategies and their commitment to helping young people reach their full potential. Faculty are involved in all aspects of the educational program. In addition to teaching, they are coaches, dorm parents, study hall supervisors, and advisors to the various clubs and campus groups.

A registered nurse staffs the Matthies Infirmary. Complete hospital facilities are available in Marlborough.

STUDENT BODY. In 1999–2000, Hillside School enrolls 90 boys as boarders and day students in Grades 5–9. The boys come from 11 states and two foreign countries.

ACADEMIC PROGRAM. The school year is divided into trimesters, beginning in September and concluding in early June, with vacations at Thanksgiving, Christmas, and in the spring. Grades are mailed to parents each trimester, and two parent-teacher conferences are scheduled each year.

All students take part in the tutorial program, with small groups working under the supervision of a teacher. This program is designed to remediate academic weaknesses and/or enrich the student's strengths. On Sunday through Thursday, boarding students attend evening study halls of 90 minutes to two hours, depending on grade.

Through the Hillside School Point System, students earn points in the areas of effort, organization, and respect for others. Points earned are averaged weekly and form the basis for establishing the student's allowance and privileges for that week. Ninth graders who maintain an A or B level status are exempted from the point system for as long as they exhibit good conduct and quality school work. Each student has a faculty advisor with whom he meets weekly to discuss his performance on the point system during the previous week. The school counselor is another resource person available to meet with each student to discuss social, emotional, and academic issues.

A typical school day begins at 6:30 A.M., with breakfast served for boarders at 7:30. Day students arrive on campus by 8:00 A.M. Classes are held five days a week, with nine 40-minute periods scheduled from 8:15 A.M. to 3:30 P.M., followed by athletic practices and the Outdoor Program. After dinner and evening study hall, students enjoy free time with open gym time, board games, an Open House with the Headmaster in his home, and other recreational activities. "Lights out" is between 9:00 and 10:00 P.M., depending on age.

Hillside School recognizes the importance of committed faculty, small classes, and a highly structured program as factors in developing the student's self-confidence, self-esteem, individual thinking, and decision-making ability. Students in Grades 5 and 6 learn in self-contained classrooms, with a core curriculum consisting of mathematics, language arts, social studies, and reading, and specialized instruction in art, science, and music.

In Grades 7–9, the curriculum includes English, history, science, math, studio art, wood shop, and French or Spanish. Music is offered in Grades 5 through 7.

Skills for Life program is required of all grades, with the goal of providing a forum for students to learn and discuss issues that confont society and themselves.

Excellence in academics, athletics, citizenship, and self-improvement is recognized by several awards and named scholarships. Among these are the E. Sherwin Kavanaugh Memorial Sportsmanship Award, Mentor of the Year, the Moody Robinson Award for excellence in English, the Dorothy Willard Award for improvement in math, and the Warren I. and Marion F. Higgins Award for outstanding contributions to the farm program by a returning student.

Among secondary school choices in the past were Blair Academy, Brewster Academy, Bronx School of Science and Math, Cambridge School of Weston, Eagle Hill, Forman, Marvelwood School, Millbrook School, New Hampton School, Peddie School, Pomfret, St. John's High School, Solebury School, Tilton, Trinity-Pawling, and Wilbraham & Monson Academy.

STUDENT ACTIVITIES. Extracurricular activities play an important role in the overall educational experience at Hillside. All students must take part in a sport or athletic activity in each trimester. Boys compete interscholastically in soccer, cross-country, basketball, wrestling, track and field, baseball, and lacrosse.

Boys who are selected to participate in the Farm Program live in their own dorm and take responsibility for rising early each morning to feed and water the animals.

The Outdoor Program features downhill skiing, hiking, canoeing, mountain biking, and sailing. On the weekends, students enjoy faculty-supervised activities including swimming, fishing, ice- and roller-skating, and sledding. The School also arranges off-campus trips throughout New England to high school and college sporting events, movies, museums, and bowling. Other organized groups include the school newspaper, the Drama Club, the yearbook, Mock Trial team, and Chess Society.

ADMISSION AND COSTS. Hillside School welcomes boys of average to above-average intelligence who will benefit from a supportive, structured environment. Many applicants have not worked up to their potential, either academically or socially. Candidates are admitted on the basis of past school transcripts, standardized test results, psychological/educational evaluations, and three character recommendations. The application fee is $25.

In 1999–2000, boarding tuition is $24,400 for five days and $27,300 for seven days; tuition for day students is $13,800. Extra expenses include the health fee ($15), the sports fee ($25), and an estimated spending allowance of $250 for day students and $450 for boarders. Approximately one-third of the student body receives financial aid.

Dean of Faculty: Richard Myer
Dean of Students: Patrick Slattery
Associate Dean of Students and Faculty: Kathleen Dolan
Director of Admission: Brian A. Campion, Jr.
School Counselor: Jeri Baily
Business Manager: David Wood
Director of Athletics: Rex Osae

The John Dewey Academy

GREAT BARRINGTON

*Searles Castle, 389 Main Street, Great Barrington, MA 01230.
413-528-9800; Fax 413-528-5662*

THE JOHN DEWEY ACADEMY in Great Barrington, Massachusetts, was founded by Dr. Thomas Edward Bratter in 1985. Accredited by the New England Association of Schools and Colleges and the National Independent Private Schools Association, the Academy is a year-round college preparatory, therapeutic school for gifted, self-destructive, angry adolescents who need a safe, supportive, and structured residential environment.

The Academy has three educational and psychotherapeutic goals. The first, intellectual growth, is promoted by teaching written and verbal communications skills. Nurturing the individual's psychological, moral, and spiritual integrity is the second goal. The third is to convince a college of quality to admit the student. Graduation from a competitive college provides closure to a painful past and maximizes future educational, professional, social, and personal goals.

The six psychotherapeutic guiding principles include teaching responsibility for attitudes and acts; developing a positive self-concept and a proactive philosophy of life; taking control of one's life; learning to trust and to be trustworthy, to respect and to be respected, to help others and to be helped, and to love and to become lovable; to gain self-respect through reasonable, responsible, and realistic decision-making; and to contribute to the betterment of society.

John Dewey students possess great academic potential, often not revealed in either standardized testing or previous performance. Most are artistically and intellectually gifted students whose needs have not been satisfied and who have lashed out at environments they see as hostile and sterile. Such students need answers to their existential concerns in order to thrive in a learning environment. These young people often wonder who they are, how they should live, where they are going, and what they believe.

THE CAMPUS. The Academy is situated on a 90-acre campus. Constructed in 1888 by the widow of railroad magnate Mark Hopkins, the 40-room Searles Castle is listed in the National Registry of Historical Landmarks. The Carriage House is used for additional housing and classroom facilities.

THE FACULTY. Dr. Thomas Edward Bratter, founder and President, earned his B.A. from Columbia College (1961) and Ed.D. (1970) in counseling psychology from Teachers College, Columbia University. Before founding John Dewey, Dr. Bratter developed and directed six community-based treatment programs for drug-dependent adolescents. He has authored four books and 150 articles. Dr. Bratter is married to Carole Jaffe Bratter, who is Vice President and Business Manager of the Academy.

The nine full-time and four part-time faculty members hold undergraduate degrees from Bates, Columbia, Middlebury, St. John's (Maryland), School of Visual Arts, Simon's Rock of Bard College, Tulane, Vassar, and the Universities of Michigan and Wisconsin. They hold master's degrees from Antioch, New School for Social Research, Oxford University, Smith, State University of New York, Teachers College Columbia University 4, Vassar, and Washington University. Doctorates were earned at Ca Foscari (Italy), New York University, Shakespeare Institute (University of Birmingham [England]), Stanford, State University of New York, and Teachers College Columbia University. Three were elected to Phi Beta Kappa; one is a Rhodes Scholar.

Community-based medical personnel attend to student health needs. Fairview Hospital's emergency services are nearby.

STUDENT BODY. In 1998–99, the Academy enrolled 21 students, 13 males and 8 females, ages 16 to 20. There were 7 sophomores, 8 juniors, 5 seniors, and 1 postgraduate. They came from California, Connecticut, Florida, Illinois, Kentucky, New Jersey, New York, Pennsylvania, South Dakota, Virginia, Canada, and Great Britain.

THERAPEUTIC AND ACADEMIC PROGRAM. The school remains in session year-round, and students visit home, on the average, twice a year. Classes vary in size from one to a maximum of ten students, with individualized instruction. Students have a minimum of three hours of student-monitored study hall daily.

The environment at John Dewey Academy is stressful and uncompromising. Escalating demands for academic achievement and moral integrity are at the center of the school's program. Students accept responsibility for personal behavior and regain self-respect by making positive choices.

Approximately 20 percent of a student's time is devoted to therapeutics, which nurtures psychological, moral, social, and spiritual growth. The adolescent develops a stable personal identity and learns how to form positive interpersonal relationships.

While there are opportunities for individual and family

counseling, group therapy is central to the program, with at least four such groups conducted each week. Nightly self-help groups meet without adult supervisors to relate to and identify with peers who suggest constructive and creative ways to change.

There are ten parent and family group experiences each year. Parent, intergenerational, and separate mother and father sessions are conducted. When there are sufficient siblings, a brother-sister's group meets.

The Academy offers a comprehensive academic curriculum including American Literature, Shakespeare, Composition, Advanced Composition, Literature of the Theater, Mythology, Literary Themes, Renaissance Literature, The Epic, The Novel, Literary Genres; French, Spanish, Italian, Latin, Greek, Russian; U.S. History, History of Western Civilization, European Affairs, World Affairs, Government, Philosophy, Anthropology, Economics; Algebra 1–2, Geometry, Trigonometry, Calculus, Advanced Calculus, Linear Algebra, Statistics; Biology, Chemistry, Physics, Life Sciences, Astronomy, Botany, Sociology, Psychology; and Studio Art, Art History, Drama, Film, Creative Writing, and Aerobics/Dance. Independent study may be pursued, and advanced students can take classes at Amherst, Rensselaer Polytechnic Institute, Williams, Union, and/or Smith colleges. Special summer classes make use of local cultural activities such as theater, music, and dance.

All graduates attend college. Alumni attend: Antioch, Babson, Bates, Berkshire Community, Boston College, Brandeis, Brown, Bucknell, Bryn Mawr, Carleton, Clark, College of the Holy Cross, Columbia College, Columbia University, Connecticut, Cornell, Emerson, Georgetown, George Washington, Hamilton, Hobart, Kalamazoo, Kenyon, Manhattanville, Mary Washington, New York University, Northwestern, Oberlin, Ohio Wesleyan, Pepperdine, Rollins, St. John's, Sarah Lawrence, Scripps, Skidmore, State University of New York (Binghamton, Purchase), Syracuse University School of Visual and Performing Arts, Trinity, Tufts, Union, Vassar, Wellesley, Williams, and the Universities of California (Los Angeles), Chicago, Hartford, Massachusetts, Michigan, Oregon, Rochester, and Tampa. More than 75 percent of the graduates complete college, and about one-fourth make the Dean's List at their respective colleges and universities.

STUDENT ACTIVITIES. Students participate in decisions that affect everyday life. Student department heads of the academic, business, kitchen, library, and maintenance teams meet weekly with the Dean of Students to solve problems. Students work on these five teams, and a number help in community events and volunteer for internships in congressional offices, town government, daycare centers, and public schools.

ADMISSION AND COSTS. Unlike other college preparatory schools that rely on standardized testing, prior academic achievement, and letters of recommendation, The John Dewey Academy admits students on the basis of a four-hour, on-campus interview conducted by a member of the clinical staff. A positive attitude about recognizing mistakes and wanting to improve are important criteria for admission. Since enrollment is voluntary, the student agrees to complete the two-year program. Before being admitted, each candidate completes a one-month orientation/probation. When the prospective student wants to enroll and is endorsed by the faculty, he or she requests a peer vote; a majority vote determines admission. Only those who can be helped to help themselves using a confrontational psychotherapeutic approach should apply.

Tuition for the 52-week residential program is $54,000. A $2000 student expense account to cover college visits, field trips, books, prescriptions, and other incidentals and a $4500 security deposit are additional. Work-study and academic scholarships are offered. Though the Academy is essentially educational and not a licensed residential treatment center, some insurance companies pay the tuition when convinced the individual needs prolonged, safe, structured, and secure treatment. Funding from school districts is sometimes available when families can prove failure to educate.

Codirectors of Admission: Drs. Thomas Edward Bratter and Kenneth Steiner

Lawrence Academy   1793

Powder House Road, Box 992, Groton, MA 01450. 978-448-6535; Fax 978-448-9208; E-mail admiss@lacademy.edu

Lawrence Academy offers a coeducational boarding and day program for 350 students from 19 countries and 20 states in a rigorous yet innovative college preparatory curriculum. Students are encouraged to assume leadership roles and value individual differences. Computers and the arts are integral to the program. Winterim, a two-week adventure term, promotes experiential learning. Daily advisor contact, internet access, English as a Second Language, and state-of-the-art music recording studio, Sony language lab, athletic complex with skating rink, and a new arts center enhance the program. Boarding Tuition: $26,350; Day Tuition: $19,375. Financial Aid: $1,500,000. Christopher G. Overbye is Director of Admission; Steven L. Hahn has been Headmaster since 1984. *New England Association.*

Lexington Montessori School   1963

130 Pleasant Street, Lexington, MA 02421. 781-862-8571; Fax 781-674-0079

The Lexington Montessori School enrolls 215 boys and girls ages 18 months–12 years in an ungraded program that seeks to nurture the child's natural enthusiasm for learning while attending to her need for security, order, and relationships with children and adults from diverse backgrounds. Along with its Montessori curriculum, the School offers foreign language, music, art, and physical education. It is centrally located off Route 2 on a 3.4-acre campus with three buildings, a playground, and playing fields. The preschool and elementary summer programs offer a variety of enrichment activities. Tuition: $7300–$11,600. Nancy S. Hartman is Director of Admission; Mrs. Jana P. Porter (Simmons College of Social Work, M.S.W.) is Head of School.

Lexington Christian Academy   1946

48 Bartlett Avenue, Lexington, MA 02420. 781-862-7850; Fax 781-863-8503; E-mail info@lexchristian.org; Web Site www.lexchristian.org

Founded by leaders of Boston's business and professional community, Lexington Christian Academy is an independent, college preparatory day school enrolling 310 boys and girls in Grades 6–12. A curriculum that integrates faith and learning in every subject includes courses in creative writing, music theory and composition, computer, and Christian studies. Drama, music, athletics, and a summer day camp are available. The Academy conducts formal exchange programs with the Republic of Armenia, Japan, and Australia. Tuition: $8800–$10,200. Financial Aid: $434,000. Jill C. Schuhmacher is Director of Admissions; J. Barry Koops (Calvin College, A.B.; University of Michigan, M.A., Ph.D.) was appointed Headmaster in 1990. *New England Association.*

Linden Hill School   NORTHFIELD

154 South Mountain Road, Northfield, MA 01360. 413-498-2906 or 888-254-6336 [Toll-free Admissions]; Fax 413-498-2908; E-mail admissions@lindenhs.org; Web Site lindenhs.org

LINDEN HILL SCHOOL in Northfield, Massachusetts, is a junior, ungraded boarding school for boys between the ages of 9 and 16 with dyslexia or related language-based learning differences. The School also provides a traditional Grade 9 program. The town of Northfield (population 2467), in the Pioneer Valley east of the Berkshires, is accessible via Interstate Highway 91; interstate buses serve the nearby town of Greenfield, and major airlines serve Bradley International Airport in Windsor Locks, Connecticut. The School's location offers opportunities for skiing, skating, biking, and other outdoor activities.

The School was founded in 1961 to provide a family atmosphere in which the Orton/Gillingham phonics approach could be implemented for the remediation of dyslexic boys. The original dairy farm estate was renovated to provide a country setting for approximately 40 students.

Today, through a multisensory approach based on a synthesis of the methods of Dr. Samuel T. Orton and Anna Gillingham, Linden Hill helps boys of inquisitive mind and good intellect strengthen areas of weakness by establishing a sound language foundation. Each student receives daily remedial language instruction tailored to meet his needs. The School also endeavors to awaken creative and athletic talents through extracurricular offerings.

A nonprofit institution, Linden Hill School is governed by a 14-member self-perpetuating Board of Trustees, including alumni, which meets three times annually. Linden Hill is accredited by the New England Association of Schools and Colleges. It holds membership in the National Association of Independent Schools, The Independent School Association of Massachusetts, and the Pioneer Valley Independent Schools Association.

THE CAMPUS. The heavily wooded, 300-acre campus overlooks the Connecticut River. It includes a soccer field, an apple orchard, a maple-sugar house, and cross-country running and skiing trails.

The main school building is the former Bennett farmhouse (circa 1835), which provides offices, common rooms, a kitchen and dining room, accommodations for two faculty members, and a small dormitory. Haskell Hall contains classrooms, a science laboratory and greenhouse, an art room, the library, computer center, a study hall/conference room, and a gallery/student lounge. The dormitory (1971) provides students' living quarters, two dormitory masters' apartments, a common room, and a workshop. A multiuse gymnasium facility opened in 1998. White Cottage (1999) is a freshman dorm adjoining a new student center. There are also faculty homes, a faculty duplex, and several small buildings. The School-owned plant is valued in excess of $1,500,000.

THE FACULTY. Michael P. Holland was appointed Headmaster in 1998. A graduate of Niagara University, he has been a member of Linden Hill's Board of Trustees since 1997. Prior to his appointment, Mr. Holland was Founding Director of The Gow School Summer Programs and also served as Assistant Headmaster at Gow. He is a member of the International Dyslexia Association, Children and Adults with Attention Deficit Disorder, Learning Disabilities Association, and the American Camping Association.

There are 12 full-time faculty members, eight men and four women. Eight faculty members live on campus, four with their families. They hold baccalaureate and master's degrees from such institutions as Boston College, Keene State, Lesley College, Marymount, Smith, Springfield, and the Universities of Massachusetts, Montana, and the South.

The support staff include a pediatrician, a registered nurse, and a psychologist. All are available on a 24-hour basis.

STUDENT BODY. Linden Hill enrolls boys between the ages of 9 and 16. They represent many states and foreign countries.

ACADEMIC PROGRAM. The school year, from early September to late May, includes a Thanksgiving recess, Christmas and spring vacations, and optional long weekends. Classes are held five days a week. The daily schedule, from 7:00 A.M. rising, includes six academic periods, morning jobs, meals, athletics, an all-School meeting emphasizing pragmatics, and structured free time. All boys have the opportunity to attend area religious services each week.

The ratio of students to faculty is about 3:1. Classes range in size from a 2:1 ratio in Orton-Gillingham language-training sessions to a maximum of seven students. Each student has a 30-minute supervised free reading session and a 75-minute evening study hall each academic day. The structured reading period fosters independent reading for pleasure, and the evening study hall is a time for supervised preparation for classes. These two language skill sessions are an integral part of the boarding school program at Linden Hill School. Faculty members can provide individual assistance during both of these periods and at other times by arrangement. Narrative reports and grades are sent to parents six times yearly.

Individual tests are administered at the beginning of each year. Standardized tests are administered to all students twice yearly.

At the appropriate time, Linden Hill assists, in concert with educational advisors from the Independent Educational Consultants Association, each boy in the selection of a secondary school. In the past, students have gone on to attend such schools as Brewster Academy, Cardigan Mountain, Eagle Hill, Forman, Gow, The Gunnery, Kents Hill, Kildonan, Landmark, Proctor, St. Andrew's, South Kent, and Vermont Academy. Some students return to their home schools if the programs are appropriate to their needs.

STUDENT ACTIVITIES. Linden Hill teams compete with those of other schools in the Pioneer Valley in soccer, downhill and cross-country skiing, softball, wrestling, tennis, and basketball. Wednesdays during the winter are devoted entirely to skiing. Hockey, ice-skating, gymnastics, bicycling, table tennis, tennis, touch football, volleyball, and track and field are coached on a recreational basis. These programs promote good motor-coordination skills as well as helping to build self-confidence. Movies and concerts are provided at the School. The students also attend area cultural events in Greenfield and at Deerfield Academy and Northfield Mount Hermon School. Weekend activities include trips to nearby towns for movies, fairs and other community events, river races, and roller-blading. Linden Hill also has fishing and paddle boating on site. Students have the option of participating in Middle School Night at the local YMCA. A Boy Scout troop meets on campus each Sunday.

ADMISSION AND COSTS. Linden Hill School enrolls bright, inquisitive, language-disabled or dyslexic boys who have become frustrated at their own shortcomings and frequent failures. Boys are admitted on the basis of previous academic records, teacher comments, academic evaluations, and a personal interview. Linden Hill has a policy of nondiscrimination on the basis of race, color, or national or ethnic origin. Applications are accepted throughout the year, and midyear enrollment is possible if vacancies exist. There is a $50 application fee. A deposit, applicable toward tuition, is due upon acceptance.

In 1999–2000, tuition, room, board, and fees total $32,900. Extras, including laundry, haircuts, other personal items, and additional clothing, amount to approximately $750. Under the provisions of Public Law 94-142, boys may be eligible for state funding of the cost of a Linden Hill School education. In addition, the cost of attending the School may qualify as a medical expense.

The Meadowbrook School of Weston   1923

10 Farm Road, Weston, MA 02493. 781-894-1193;
Fax 781-894-0557; E-mail ADMISSIONS@Meadowbrook-
MA.org; Web Site www.Meadowbrook-MA.org

The Meadowbrook School of Weston, a nationally recognized School of Excellence, enrolls 192 boys and girls in Nursery–Grade 6. It seeks to help students to achieve excellence in academics and to develop honesty, courtesy, and respect for others. The curriculum emphasizes basic skills. French, art, music, ceramics, and computer studies are offered at all levels. A modified Outward Bound program, field trips, drama, glee club, and an athletic program are among the activities. An Extended Day program and summer camp are available. Tuition: $10,525–$15,560. Financial Aid: $190,000. Barbara T. Vincent is Director of Admissions; Stephen T. Hinds (Miami University, B.S. 1972; Boston University, M.Ed. 1978) was appointed Headmaster in 1986.

The MacDuffie School   1890

One Ames Hill Drive, Springfield, MA 01105.
413-734-4971; Fax 413-734-6693;
E-mail headsoffice@macduffie.com; Web Site www.macduffie.com

MacDuffie prepares students for college and develops their individuality within a supportive, diverse community. The School enrolls 190 day students in Grades 6–12 and 20 Ames Hill international boarding students in Grade 8–postgraduate who live with families in an on-campus homestay program. The curriculum offers Advanced Placement and Honors courses, an extensive arts program, and three levels of English as a Second Language. Activities include athletics, music, theater, publications, and clubs. College placements in 1999 include George Washington, New York University, Tufts, Washington University, and Wellesley. Boarding Tuition: $24,500; Day Tuition: $12,200–$12,600. Financial aid is available. Susan M. Clayton is Director of Admissions; Kathryn P. Gibson (Vassar, B.A.; Columbia, M.A.) is Head of School. *New England Association.*

Milton Academy   1798

170 Centre Street, Milton, MA 02186. 617-898-1798;
Fax 617-898-1701; E-mail admissions@milton.edu;
Web Site www.milton.edu

Milton Academy, now in its third century of educating young people, enrolls 974 boys and girls in Kindergarten–Grade 12, with nearly 300 boarders in Grades 9–12. The rigorous college preparatory curriculum includes honors and Advanced Placement courses, semester-long programs on a Vermont farm or in Boston, and opportunities for overseas study and travel in England and Japan. Students may choose from six languages and a diverse array of electives. The visual and performing arts, community service, interest clubs, and sports are popular activities. Boarding Tuition: $26,000; Day Tuition: $19,850. Financial Aid: $3,200,000. Geoffrey Theobald is Director of Admission; Robin A. Robertson, Ph.D., is Head of School. *New England Association.*

Milton Academy Lower School   1807

170 Centre Street, Milton, MA 02186. 617-898-2509

The Lower School at Milton Academy, a coeducational day school for Kindergarten–Grade 6, serves 200 children from the Boston metropolitan area. The program provides a challenging curriculum with high academic standards; developmental considerations shape decisions about curriculum and the school day. It is a community that respects the diverse strengths and differences of individual children. A Home Reading Program, electives, and an After School Program are also offered as enrichment. Tuition: $11,000–$15,700. Financial aid is available. Colin E. Gibney is Director of Admissions; Amy Sullivan (Skidmore, B.A.; Tufts, M.A.) was appointed Principal in 1999.

Miss Hall's School   PITTSFIELD

492 Holmes Road, Pittsfield, MA 01201. 413-499-1300;
Fax 413-448-2994; E-mail info@misshalls.org;
Web Site www.misshalls.org

Mᴵss ʜᴀʟʟ's sᴄʜᴏᴏʟ in Pittsfield, Massachusetts, is a college preparatory boarding and day school enrolling girls in Grades 9–12. The School's location in the Berkshires gives students exposure to a variety of cultural opportunities and adventures including exploration of the Hancock Shaker Village, Norman Rockwell Museum, and the Clark Art Institute. The area also offers activities for a wide variety of interests such as skiing, horseback riding, camping, and hiking on the

Appalachian Trail. Pittsfield is two and one-half hours from Boston and three hours from New York. Bus transportation is available in Pittsfield, and the Albany and Bradley International airports are approximately one hour away.

Founded in 1898 by Mira Hinsdale Hall, Miss Hall's is a successor to the first girls' boarding school in Massachusetts. The entire community focuses on the education and growth of girls, and the School's commitment to maintaining a small-school environment enables students to prosper from individual attention and a personal touch.

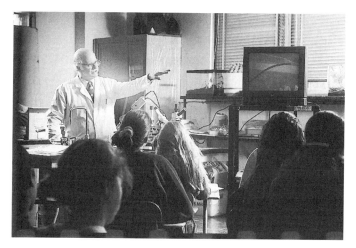

A nonprofit institution, Miss Hall's is governed by a 24-member Board of Trustees, 14 of whom are alumnae of the School. Accredited by the New England Association of Schools and Colleges, Miss Hall's holds membership in the National Association of Independent Schools, the National Coalition of Girls' Schools, the Secondary School Admission Test Board, the Independent School Association of Massachusetts, National Association for Foreign Student Affairs, The Cum Laude Society, and the Council for Advancement and Support of Education.

THE CAMPUS. Located in the Berkshires and bordered by the Housatonic River, the campus includes the Georgian-style main building (1923) with dormitory rooms and faculty apartments; The Mira H. Hall Memorial Library (1948), which includes a computer center; The Schoolhouse (1958) with classrooms, laboratories, practice rooms, and choral rehearsal space; The Jessie P. Quick Ski Chalet; The Ara West Grinnell teaching greenhouse (1972); the Elizabeth M. Fitch Center (1973), used as an auditorium; and the Witherspoon Hall (1983) and Groves Hall (1986) dormitories. Capital expansion is providing for renovation of the athletic center and construction of a new library/technology center, arts center, and student center.

Athletic facilities include an athletic center with basketball and volleyball courts. There are also eight all-weather outdoor tennis courts, cross-country ski trails, and playing fields for soccer, field hockey, lacrosse, and softball.

THE FACULTY. Ms. Jean K. Norris was appointed Head of School in 1996. She is a graduate of Pittsburg State University (B.M.Ed.) and Temple University (M.M.). She previously served as Director of Admissions and Financial Aid and then Assistant Head for Enrollment at The Madeira School. The mother of two daughters, Ms. Norris has 20 years of experience as a teacher and administrator of all-girls schools. She is currently a Trustee of the National Coalition of Girls' Schools. Ms. Jennifer Chandler is the Assistant Head of School.

There are 45 full-time and 8 part-time faculty and administrators. They hold 47 baccalaureate and 20 master's degrees from Berklee College of Music, Boston University, Bryn Mawr, Carleton, Catholic University (Ecuador), Coe, Colgate, College of the Holy Cross, College of William and Mary, College of Wooster, Columbia, Cornell, Earlham, Fairleigh Dickinson, Gar-

land College, Georgetown, Harvard, Hood, Johns Hopkins, Lycee de Jeunes Filles de Bordeaux (France), Middlebury, Mount Holyoke, New England Conservatory, New York University, Northwestern, Pennsylvania State, Princeton, Purdue, Russell Sage, Rutgers, St. Lawrence, St. Michael's, St. Olaf, Southern Methodist, State University of New York (Albany), Temple, Trinity, Ursinus, Wells College, Wesleyan, Westfield State, Wheaton, Williams, and the Universities of Maine, Massachusetts, Minnesota, Oklahoma, Paris, the South, and Vermont.

STUDENT BODY. In 1999–2000, the School enrolls 130 girls in Grades 9–12. The diversified student body originates from 20 states, with the largest numbers from Connecticut, Massachusetts, and New York. Eleven foreign countries are also represented.

The health center is staffed by four registered nurses. The Berkshire Medical Center hospital is less than 4 miles away.

ACADEMIC PROGRAM. The school year, divided into three terms, begins in early September and ends in early June. There are vacations at Thanksgiving, December Holiday time, and in the spring, and long weekends in the fall and winter. An average class has 8 girls, and full-credit courses meet five times a week. Grades are sent home six times a year along with detailed written comments from teachers. Each girl has an advisor who oversees her progress and serves as a liaison between the family and the School.

Minimum graduation requirements for a Miss Hall's diploma are four years of English; three years of history, including United States History; three years of a foreign language; three years of mathematics; three years of science, two of which must be a laboratory science; and one to five additional credits in electives.

Courses offered include English 9–12, AP English, and spring senior electives in International Literature, British Literature, and Creative Writing. Other courses include Algebra I and II, Geometry, Pre-Calculus, and AP Calculus (AB); French I through AP French Literature and AP French Language, Spanish I through AP Spanish Literature and AP Spanish Language, Latin 1–4, English as a Second Language 1–3; Introductory Physical Science, Biology, Chemistry, Physics, Conceptual Physics, Anatomy/Physiology; World Cultures, European History, Contemporary World History, U.S. History, American Politics and Government, Women's Studies, Psychology, Non-Western Cultures, Religion and Philosophy, AP United States History, AP European History; Introductory Studio Art, Advanced Drawing, Advanced Painting, AP Studio Art, Introduction to Photography, Advanced Photography, Drama 9, Advanced Drama, Dance and Choreography, History of Music, and Practical Music. Students also participate in Horizons, a yearlong community service/internship program that enables girls to experience the world of work and service in area professional offices, cultural centers, businesses, social service agencies, and the Berkshire Medical Center. Seniors design their own internship program in such areas as architecture, radiological medicine, computer graphics, professional dance, veterinary medicine, and the law, among other possibilities.

Colleges and universities attended by Miss Hall's graduates over the last four years include Boston University, Colby, Columbia University, Cornell, Dickinson, George Washington, Kenyon, Lake Forest, Macalester, Mount Holyoke, Muhlenberg, Northeastern, Oberlin, Rhode Island School of Design, St. Lawrence, Smith, Vassar, Wellesley, Wheaton, Yale, and the Universities of Massachusetts, New Hampshire, Southern California, and Vermont.

STUDENT ACTIVITIES. Students at Miss Hall's play a significant role in the operation of the School, and every girl contributes time to the work program. The Student Council, with representatives from each class, provides an open forum for students to bring recommendations pertinent to school life to the attention of the Head of School. The Judicial Committee, elected by students and faculty, handles minor rule infractions; the Student-Faculty Advisory Committee, appointed by the Head of School, hears disciplinary matters of a more serious nature. The Social Committee organizes social events and weekend activities. Students publish a newspaper *(Hallways)*, the yearbook *(The Hallmark)*, and a literary magazine *(Sol)*. There are two theatrical productions each year and opportunities for participation in vocal and instrumental music ensembles.

Miss Hall's athletic teams compete against other independent schools in alpine ski racing, basketball, field hockey, lacrosse, riding, soccer, softball, tennis, and volleyball. Noncompetitive physical alternatives include modern dance, aerobics, cross-country and alpine skiing, snowboarding, Nautilus, and riding. The Wilderness Program offers instruction and participation in rock climbing, backpacking, orienteering, caving, cross-country skiing, snowshoeing, and camping.

Traditional events include Blue-Gold Days, Music and Dance Nights, Thanksgiving Banquet, Parents' Weekend, Founder's Day, and the International Holiday Banquet.

ADMISSION AND COSTS. Miss Hall's seeks students of sound character and academic ability who can bring a diversity of talents, interests, and experiences to the School. Applicants must submit a school transcript; recommendations from their English and math teachers and the guidance counselor; results of standardized testing; and a writing sample. A personal interview is required, and there is a $35 application fee ($50 fee for international students). Applications should be submitted by late winter for September admission. Notification is sent out in early March. An applicant may apply under the Early Decision Program if Miss Hall's is her first-choice school.

In 1999–2000, boarding tuition is $25,500, and day tuition is $14,900. Textbooks average $375. A tuition protection plan is strongly recommended.

Endowed scholarships and other financial assistance are available to encourage economic and geographic diversity in the student body. In 1999–2000, financial aid awards totaled $636,000. Applications for financial assistance should be made by mail through the School and Student Service for Financial Aid in Princeton, New Jersey.

Director of Admission: Elaine Cooper
Director of Development: Janis Martinson
Director of Annual Giving & Alumnae Affairs: Dallas C. Briney
Director of Business and Finance: Andrea Nix
Director of Residential Life: Sarah Virden
Director of College Counseling: Sarah McFarland

Montrose School   1979

45 East Central Street, Natick, MA 01760. 508-650-6925;
Fax 508-650-6926

Parents and educators founded Montrose School to provide a challenging academic program integrated with the Christian values that develop sound character and prepare students for life. Enrolling 113 day girls in Grades 6–12, the School offers a classical liberal arts curriculum, including selected Advanced Placement courses, options in Spanish and French, and Catholic theology courses. Computer science and the fine arts are also offered. Cocurricular activities include newspaper, yearbook, drama, chorus, speech team, Student Council, the National Honor Society, athletics, and other clubs. Tuition: $7000–$7200. Financial aid is available. Ellen M. Cavanagh (Syracuse University, B.M.Ed.; Boston College, M.Ed.) is Head.

Nashoba Brooks School   1980

200 Strawberry Hill Road, Concord, MA 01742. 978-369-4591;
Fax 978-287-6038; Web Site www.nbsc.org

Nashoba Country Day School (founded 1958) and The Brooks School of Concord (1928) merged in 1980 as an elementary day school. Enrolled are 149 boys and girls in Preschool–Grade 3 and 146 girls in Grades 4–8. The School strives to recognize each student's contributions to the community, whether they be academic, artistic, dramatic, or athletic. Art, music, physical education, French, and Latin are included in the curriculum. Tutoring may be arranged; a summer program is offered. Tuition: $8925–$14,975. Deanne Benson is Director of Admission; E. Kay Cowan (Manhattanville College, M.A.) is Head of School.

Newman Preparatory School   1945

245 Marlborough Street, Boston, MA 02116. 617-267-4530;
Fax 617-267-7070; E-mail admissions@newmanprep.org;
Web Site www.newmanprep.org

This coeducational day school, named after Catholic Cardinal John Henry Newman, enrolls 260 students in a college preparatory, liberal arts-oriented curriculum. An intensive English as a Second Language program enrolls 25 international students. The School features a semester-based curriculum enabling students to concentrate their studies in three or four areas at a time. Activities include competition with other independent schools in soccer, basketball, softball, baseball, crew, and sailing. Colleges accepting recent graduates include Babson, Boston University, Drew, Fairfield, Holy Cross, Skidmore, Tufts, and Wheaton. Tuition: $4000–$7500. Karen Briggs is Admissions Officer; J. Harry Lynch (Holy Cross, B.A.; Northeastern, M.B.A.) is President and Headmaster. *New England Association.*

Newton Country Day School of the Sacred Heart 1880

785 Centre Street, Newton, MA 02458. 617-244-4246; Fax 617-965-5313; E-mail crumpler@ncdsnet.net

Newton Country Day School is an independent, college preparatory, girls' day school enrolling 280 students in Grades 5–12. The school offers a rigorous curriculum, which includes a full honors and Advanced Placement program. In keeping with the Sacred Heart tradition, the School educates to five goals: a personal and active faith in God, respect for intellectual values, social awareness, community building and service, and personal growth. Exchange programs with other Sacred Heart schools worldwide are available. Tuition: $17,900. Financial Aid: $850,000. Mary Delaney is Admissions Director; Sr. Barbara Rogers (Manhattanville, B.A. 1974; Yale, M.B.A. 1988) was appointed Headmistress in 1989. *New England Association.*

Noble and Greenough School 1866

10 Campus Drive, Dedham, MA 02026-4099. 781-326-3700; Fax 781-329-1329; Web Site www.nobles.edu

Noble and Greenough is a college preparatory school enrolling 489 boys and girls as day students, and 31 boys and girls as five-day boarders in Grades 7–12. It aims to provide a rigorous program to stretch academic abilities and foster curiosity, involvement, self-reliance, honesty, and a commitment to others. Intellectual skills and the use of language and technology in effective communication are emphasized. All students participate in an afternoon program including athletics, performing arts, or community service. Boarding Tuition: $24,600; Day Tuition: $19,400. Financial Aid: $1,500,000. Steven Inzer and Linda Woodard are Co-Directors of Admission; Richard H. Baker (Harvard, A.B. 1962; University of California [Berkeley], M.A. 1967) was appointed Headmaster in 1987. *New England Association.*

Notre Dame Academy 1951

425 Salisbury Street, Worcester, MA 01609-1299. 508-757-6200; Fax 508-757-7200; Web Site www.nda.mec.edu

This college preparatory day school was founded by the Sisters of Notre Dame de Namur to prepare young women for higher education and Christian leadership. Enrolling 320 girls in Grades 9–12, Notre Dame Academy aspires to high academic and moral standards and encourages its students to make responsible decisions and to serve others. The curriculum includes advanced courses as well as career and college seminars, and technology is integrated throughout all disciplines. Juniors and seniors take part in community service in conjunction with theology classes. Girls are involved in Student Council, sports, Model UN, music ensembles, drama, peer leadership, and publications. Tuition: $6150. Mary C. Lazar is Director of Admissions; Ann E. Morrison, SND, is Principal. *New England Association.*

Northfield Mount Hermon School 1879

Northfield, MA 01360. 413-498-3000; Admissions 413-498-3227; Fax 413-498-3152; E-mail admission@nmh.northfield.ma.us; Web Site http://www.nmh.northfield.ma.us

A coeducational college preparatory school, Northfield Mount Hermon enrolls over 900 boarders and 200 day students in Grades 9–12 and Postgraduate. Innovative educational programs, a diverse student body and staff, individual attention, study abroad, sports opportunities, and values education are hallmarks of the Northfield Mount Hermon experience. The School provides academic focus by having a three-term year where students take only two major courses each term. Laptop computers are used in classes, and the average class size is 13. College counseling, 65 sports teams, and a variety of clubs and organizations round out the program. Pamela J. Safford is Director of Admission; Richard Mueller (College of William and Mary, A.B.) is Head of the School. *New England Association.*

The Park School 1888

171 Goddard Avenue, Brookline, MA 02445. 617-277-2456; Fax 617-232-1261; Web Site www.parkschool.org

Park is a coeducational day school serving a diverse student body from the Boston metropolitan area. Located on a 24-acre wooded campus, Park enrolls 500 students in Nursery–Grade IX. Small classes, rigorous academics, and close contact with parents are emphasized. Three sections of 15–18 children at each grade level ensure individual attention. Music, art, and drama are integral to the program. Activities include interscholastic sports and community service. New facilities for science, math, physical education, and the After School Program opened in 1998. Park offers a summer arts camp and soccer camps. Tuition: $10,000–$16,500. Financial Aid: $800,000. Caroline Hoppin is Director of Admission; Jerrold I. Katz (Harvard, Ed.D.) was appointed Headmaster in 1993.

Phillips Academy 1778

180 Main Street, Andover, MA 01810-4161. 978-749-4050; E-mail admissions@andover.edu; Web Site www.andover.edu

The nation's oldest incorporated boarding school, Phillips Academy offers a rigorous college preparatory education in an environment marked by a deep sense of continuity and community tradition. Approximately 1080 students from the United States and 31 countries pursue academic excellence through a curriculum that includes 290 courses in 18 academic departments. The program is enhanced by honors and Advanced Placement classes, overseas travel/study, an active community service program, and involvement in more than 65 clubs and 60 athletic offerings. Boarding Tuition: $24,500; Day Tuition: $18,900. Financial Aid: $7,135,000. Jane F. Fried is Dean of Admission; Barbara Landis Chase (Brown, A.B.; Johns Hopkins, M.L.A.) is Head of School. *New England Association.*

The Pike School 1926

Sunset Rock Road, Andover, MA 01810. 978-475-1197; Fax 978-475-3014; E-mail info@pike.pvt.k12.ma.us; Web Site http://www.pike.pvt.k12.ma.us/pike.html

Pike enrolls 424 boys and girls in Pre-Kindergarten–Grade 9 on a 36-acre campus. The lower (PreK–Grade 2), middle (Grades 3–5), and upper (Grades 6–9) schools offer a coordinated program that emphasizes fundamental skills in the basic disciplines. Outdoor education, which stresses environmental issues, begins in Grade 5; foreign language instruction, in Grade 6. Physical education and visual and performing arts are integral to the program at all levels. Graduates attend a variety of secondary schools, including leading independent schools. Tuition: $7500–$12,600. Financial Aid: $155,000. Ann E. Smith is Director of Admissions; John M. Waters (Middlebury, B.A. 1974; Trinity, M.A. 1988) is Head of School.

Pingree School 1960

537 Highland Street, South Hamilton, MA 01982. 978-468-4415; Fax 978-468-3758; E-mail pinginfo@pingree.org; Web Site HTTP://www.pingree.org

Pingree School is a college preparatory day school enrolling 250 boys and girls in Grades 9–12. Emphasizing close relationships between students and teachers, the School seeks to develop intellectual, physical, and personal potentials. A 105-acre countryside campus, with a 10,000-volume library, a field house, an ice hockey rink, and an arts center with space for ceramics, photography, electronic music, an art studio, and a 400-seat theater, provides the setting for a comprehensive athletic program and wide-ranging extracurriculars. Summer courses and a summer camp are available. Tuition: $18,100. Financial Aid: $600,000. Stuart B. Titus is Director of Admission; Christopher M. Teare (Amherst, B.A. 1980; Columbia, M.S. 1985; St. John's College, M.A. 1990) was appointed Head of School in 1998. *New England Association.*

The Rashi School 1986

400 High Street, Dedham, MA 02026. 781-329-1313; Admissions 781-329-9430, Ext. 24; Fax 781-329-6314; Admissions 781-329-0542; Web Site www.rashi.org

This Boston Area Reform Jewish day school enrolling 250 students from throughout the region in Kindergarten–Grade 8 aims to provide an educational setting based on a strong, fully integrated curriculum of secular and Jewish studies that mirrors contemporary American Jewish life. Specialists teach Hebrew as a modern language. The curriculum also includes math, science, language arts, reading, writing, social studies, geography, Spanish, Jewish Studies, music, physical education, and art. There is also an optional after-school program. Tuition: $9950. Financial aid is available. Anne C. Puchkoff is Admissions Director; Jennifer Miller (Witwatersrand [South Africa], B.A. 1974; Johannesburg College of Education, H.Ed. 1975; Providence College, M.A. 1991) is Head.

The Rivers School 1915

333 Winter Street, Weston, MA 02493-1040. 781-235-9300; Fax 781-239-3614; Web Site www.rivers.org

A college preparatory day school enrolling 349 boys and girls in Grades 7–12, Rivers challenges its students with high academic standards, while also emphasizing personal development in a community atmosphere. In addition to meeting academic requirements, students must give time to athletics, the arts, activities, and community service. Focus on the individual is augmented by the 1:8 faculty-student ratio and an average class size of 16. Merit-based community scholarships are available. Tuition: $19,400. Financial Aid: $1,074,000. Thomas P. Olverson was appointed Head of School in 1997. *New England Association.*

Riverview School 1957

551 Route 6A, East Sandwich, MA 02537. 508-888-0489; Fax 508-888-1315

Riverview is a coeducational boarding school on Cape Cod that specializes in educating learning-disabled adolescents whose IQ is between 70 and 100. The School's primary goal is to enable them to reach their full potential in a structured, supportive environment. Students receive remedial and compensatory services combined with academic and vocational skills designed to equip them for meaningful and productive lives. Students are assigned according to ability levels to academic teams, each of which has several instructors and one advisor. Ongoing evaluation, individual attention, and independent drill and reinforcement aid students in the realization of their goals. Tuition: $46,810. Janet M. Lavoie is Director of Admission; Richard Lavoie is President. *New England Association.*

The Roxbury Latin School 1645

101 St. Theresa Avenue, West Roxbury, MA 02132-3496. 617-325-4920; Fax 617-325-3585

The Roxbury Latin School, the oldest school in continuous existence in North America, enrolls 285 day boys in Grades 7–12. This college preparatory school strives to develop intellectual excellence and personal values in a diverse socioeconomic community where every boy has the opportunity to occupy a leadership role. About one-third of the boys are on scholarships. An increasingly flexible curriculum includes programs in art, music, dramatics, and independent study. A variety of extracurricular activities is available. Tuition: $11,600. Financial Aid: $713,286. Michael C. Obel-Omia is Director of Admission; The Reverend F. Washington Jarvis (Harvard, A.B. 1961; Cambridge, M.A. 1963; Episcopal Theological School, M.Div. 1964; Bowdoin, L.H.D. 1998) is Headmaster. *New England Association.*

St. John's Preparatory School   1907

72 Spring Street, Danvers, MA 01923-1595. 978-774-1050;
Fax 978-774-5069; Web Site www.stjohnsprep.org

St. John's Preparatory School was founded by the Brothers of The Congregation of St. Francis Xavier to prepare young men for college and for life. The School enrolls 1000 day students in Grades 9–12. Courses include Religion, English, Science, Mathematics, Foreign Languages, Social Studies, Computer Science, and Physical Education. Electives include Music, Art, Drama, and Independent Study. Athletics, debate, publications, and Student Council are among the School's activities. Tuition and Fees: $8250. Financial Aid: $800,000. Brian J. Flatley is Director of Admissions; Br. William P. Drinan, CFX (Catholic University, B.A. 1954, M.T.S. 1965; Jesuit School of Theology [Berkeley], C.T.S. 1985), was appointed Headmaster in 1989. *New England Association.*

St. Sebastian's School   1941

1191 Greendale Avenue, Needham, MA 02192. 781-449-5200;
Fax 781-449-5630

St. Sebastian's School is a Roman Catholic, college preparatory school enrolling 338 boys in Grades 7–12. The School has a structured academic curriculum, with carefully sequenced courses in English, mathematics, classical and modern foreign languages, science, and social studies. Courses are taught on standard, honors, and Advanced Placement levels. The extracurricular program features 9 interscholastic sports and 18 nonathletic clubs. Tuition: $18,250. Financial Aid: $816,500. William L. Burke III (Middlebury College, B.A.; Boston College, M.A.) is Headmaster. *New England Association.*

School Year Abroad   1964

Phillips Academy, Andover, MA 01810. 978-725-6828;
Fax 978-725-6833; E-mail mail@sya.org; Web Site www.sya.org

School Year Abroad offers students entering Grades 11–12 a year of study and travel while immersing themselves in the language and culture of a foreign country. It provides a rigorous, nine-month academic program in France and Spain and both a four- and a nine-month session in China. Students live with host families and study a traditional college preparatory program taught in French, Spanish, or Mandarin. English and math are taught by American faculty, students are assigned college counselors, and all standardized testing is available. Academic credits earned are applied toward the diploma offered in the student's American school. Tuition: $24,000. Financial aid is available.

Shady Hill School   1915

178 Coolidge Hill, Cambridge, MA 02138. 617-868-1260;
Fax 617-868-0387; Web Site www.shs.org

Professor and Mrs. William Ernest Hocking founded Shady Hill to offer a more liberal and imaginative alternative to the public education of the times. Situated in a quiet residential area, the School enrolls 480 boys and girls in four-year-old Pre-Kindergarten–Grade 8. The curriculum is designed to instill a zest for learning "within a rigorous intellectual and physical setting." Mastery of basic skills in the humanities, arts, and sciences and the interrelationship among the disciplines are emphasized. Music, art, woodworking, and drama are a regular part of the curriculum. An Afterschool Program is optional. Tuition: $8900–$12,970. Financial aid is available. Kim Buell is Director of Admission; Bruce A. Shaw (Macalester, B.A. 1967; Antioch, M.A.T. 1973) was named Director in 1994.

Shore Country Day School   1936

545 Cabot Street, Beverly, MA 01915. 978-927-1700;
Fax 978-927-1822; E-mail Lcarey@shore.pvt.k12.ma.us;
Web Site http://www.shore.pvt.k12.ma.us

Founded by the 1936 merger of two schools, Shore Country Day enrolls 440 boys and girls in Readiness for Kindergarten–Grade 9. Within its challenging curriculum, the School encourages each student's positive self-image, respect for others, intellectual curiosity, and development of fundamental learning skills. Shore's traditional program includes laboratory and computer sciences, art, music, drama, and sports. Each age level is supplemented by appropriate activities, field trips, speakers, and presentations. Tuition: $10,130–$13,820. Extras: $375–$1070. Financial Aid: $610,000. Lilia N. Carey is Director of Admissions; Lawrence A. Griffin (Florida Atlantic University, B.A. 1975; Dartmouth, M.A.L.S. 1980) was appointed Headmaster in 1987.

Southfield School   1992

10 Newton Street, Brookline, MA 02445-7498. 617-522-6980

Southfield is a day school for 270 girls from Pre-school through Grade 8. Established in 1992 as a sister school to Dexter and located on the Dexter campus, it emphasizes the same traditional academic subjects, including Latin in Grades 6–8, and moral and spiritual attitudes as its counterpart. Southfield has its own classroom complex and shares the Dexter administration as well as the buildings, fields, two indoor rinks, and indoor pool. All students participate in a full program of athletics in addition to classes in laboratory science, computer, art, music, and shop. Tuition: $11,760–$16,050. Financial Aid: $475,000. Jacalyn Wright is Director of Admissions; William F. Phinney (Harvard, A.B. 1950) was appointed Head in 1992.

Smith College Campus School 1926

Gill Hall, Prospect Street, Northampton, MA 01063. 413-585-3270;
Fax 413-585-3285; Web Site www.smith.edu/edu

Smith College Campus School is a coeducational, laboratory day school enrolling approximately 335 children, ages 3 to 12. It serves as a resource for undergraduate and graduate teacher education programs and for other departments at Smith and area colleges. The facilities of Smith College are available to the School and make possible a variety of enriched programs. An Infant-Toddler Program and an Extended Day Program for Preschool and Kindergarten children are available. Tuition: $4715–$6000. Financial Aid: $180,000. Maureen Litwin is Admissions Director; Cathy Hofer Reid (Hamline University, B.A. 1971; Utah State, M.S. 1972; University of Connecticut, Ph.D. 1981) was appointed Principal in 1996.

Stoneleigh-Burnham School

GREENFIELD

Greenfield, MA 01301. 413-774-2711; Fax 413-772-2602;
E-mail admissions@sbschool.org; Web Site www.sbschool.org

STONELEIGH-BURNHAM SCHOOL in Greenfield, Massachusetts, is a college preparatory boarding and day school enrolling girls in Grades 9 through 12 and a postgraduate year. The School is 40 miles from Springfield and 100 miles from Boston. Students have access to cultural events in the five-college area, and the ski areas of both Vermont and New Hampshire are nearby. Chartered buses transport students to and from Bradley International Airport and to Amtrak at vacation times. Shuttle buses run to neighboring schools and areas on weekends.

Stoneleigh-Burnham was formed in 1968 by the merger of the Mary A. Burnham School, founded in Northampton in 1877, and the Stoneleigh-Prospect Hill School, established in 1869. The School continues its 129-year tradition of encouraging girls to develop their interests to the best of their abilities, to enjoy the challenge and rewards of learning, and to gain self-confidence and independence.

The School is a nonprofit corporation directed by a 27-member Board of Trustees composed of alumnae, parents, and friends. There is an active Alumnae Association. Accredited by the New England Association of Schools and Colleges, Stoneleigh-Burnham holds membership in the National Association of Independent Schools, the National Coalition of Girls' Schools, and The Independent School Association of Massachusetts.

THE CAMPUS. The School occupies more than 100 wooded acres. The Main Building, with the addition of Mary Burnham Hall, houses classrooms, the mathematics and technology center, the library, a greenhouse, the infirmary, several student lounges and common rooms, and dining facilities. A newly constructed science center for chemistry, biology, and physical science houses laboratories, lecture and discussion space, and a reading resource room. There are faculty apartments and student rooms on the second floor as well as in Ferdon House (1984). Bonnie's House is used as a student center. Emerson Hall has a gymnasium, a dance studio, and an auditorium. The Student Arts Center contains teaching and studio facilities for drawing, painting, ceramics, photography, weaving, and other arts.

Included on the campus are five tennis courts, a paddle tennis court, an outdoor swimming pool, three playing fields, and cross-country ski trails. The School's state-of-the-art riding facilities include stables for 60 horses, two indoor riding arenas, two outdoor riding rings, the McDonald Jumper Derby course, a cross-country riding course, and a hunt course.

THE FACULTY. Head of School Raymond A. Nelson, appointed in 1998, is a graduate of Williams College (B.A. 1954) and Harvard University (S.T.B. 1957). He succeeds Patrick M. Collins, who headed the School for three years. Prior to assuming his position at Stoneleigh-Burnham, Mr. Nelson was Head of School at the Saddle River Day School in Saddle River, New Jersey.

There are 49 faculty and administrators, 12 men and 37 women. They hold 49 baccalaureate and 31 advanced degrees from such institutions as Amherst, Assumption, Boston University, Brown, Colgate, Columbia, Connecticut College, Dickinson, Harvard, Juilliard, Middlebury, Northwestern, Providence, St. Lawrence, Smith, Springfield, Wesleyan, Wheaton, Williams, and the University of Massachusetts.

The School physician, a gynecological nurse practitioner, an orthopedic/sports physician, and three registered nurses staff the infirmary. Hospital facilities are located in Greenfield.

STUDENT BODY. In 1999–2000, the School enrolls 190 girls in Grades 9–12 and a postgraduate year, 121 boarders and 69 day students. There are 45 students in Grade 9, 50 in Grade 10, 50 in Grade 11, and 45 in Grade 12. Students represent 24 states and 14 foreign countries.

ACADEMIC PROGRAM. The school year, divided into trimesters, begins in early September and ends in early June. There are vacations at Thanksgiving, and in the winter and spring. Stoneleigh-Burnham's tracking system is designed to place each girl in classes most commensurate with her scholastic ability, and each discipline offers college preparatory, honors, and Advanced Placement courses. The Academic Skills Program provides a support system for students who need additional academic help; classes in reading, writing, mathematics, and organizational skills are offered. Students are assigned faculty advisers who monitor academic progress and assist with problems relating to general life at school. The student-faculty ratio is approximately 9:1. Evening study hall, held from 8:00 to 9:30 P.M. five nights a week, and one 40-minute study hall during the day five days a week are required of all students. Grades are issued every two weeks to students and mailed to parents along with written teachers' comments at the end of each trimester.

To graduate, students must earn a minimum of 18 credits

in Grades 9 through 12, including four years of English; two years of foreign language; three of mathematics; two of laboratory science; two of social studies, including one of United States History; two trimesters each year in the arts; one trimester of computer literacy; one trimester of health; and four years of physical education.

English courses for students in Grades 9–12 focus on vocabulary, grammar, writing, and literature, with a mandatory poetry class in Grade 10. Honors classes are available in all grades, and Advanced Placement courses are offered in all disciplines. A variety of English electives, including Comparative Literature and Issues in Children's Literature, is available to seniors. Among the full-term and elective courses offered are French, Spanish, Latin; Basic Algebra–Algebra II, Geometry, Calculus, Computer Literacy; World Cultures, European History, American History, African-American History, Political Science, Philosophy, Law, Women in History, Current World Issues; Physical Science, Biology, Chemistry, Physics, Equine Studies, Health, Ecology, Marine Biology, Anatomy and Physiology, Psychology; Drawing I–II, Painting, Design and Color, Watercolor and Gouache Painting, Computer Art, Advanced Placement Studio Art, Art History, Desktop Publishing, Digital Illustration, Photography I–III, Papier Maché Sculpture, Ceramics I–III, Weaving I–II; and Music Theory, Music History, Chorus, Octet, Advanced Acting III, Technical Theater, and Directing I. Private music lessons are available, there is an instrumental ensemble group, and instruction is offered in ballet, jazz, and modern dance at all levels. Theater classes are taught on a trimester basis. Advanced Placement courses are available in studio art.

English as a Second Language provides help in basic English skills at three levels, and an oral communications course prepares students for taking the Test of English as a Foreign Language examinations.

Graduates from the last three years are attending such colleges and universities as: Bates, Boston University, Bucknell, Colgate, Cornell, Dickinson, Georgetown, Lehigh, Lynchburg, Massachusetts Institute of Technology, Middlebury, Mount Holyoke, Providence, Reed, Rhode Island School of Design, Skidmore, Smith, Southern Methodist University, Syracuse, Trinity, Union, Vanderbilt, Wheaton, William Smith, and the Universities of California (Berkeley), New Hampshire, Vermont, and Virginia.

STUDENT ACTIVITIES. The Student Council is divided into two areas. The Proposal Committee considers proposals sub-

mitted by students and forwards them to the Headmaster. The Judicial Committee reviews rule violations. All girls participate in the daily work program, and many volunteer time to a variety of community organizations. Students may participate in social activities, which are offered each weekend.

Clubs and activities are offered for a variety of interests, including the Literary Society, Peer Tutors, Peer Counselors, Blue Key Guides, Debate Society, Student Activities Committee, CARE, Diplomats, and the Art, Dance, Drama, Chorus, Riding, Community Service, French, and Spanish clubs. Students publish a newspaper, yearbook, and literary magazine.

Stoneleigh-Burnham athletes compete in the Western New England Prep School Association. Teams are organized at the varsity and junior varsity levels in soccer, field hockey, skiing, cross-country, basketball, volleyball, softball, lacrosse, and tennis.

The Stoneleigh-Burnham Riding Program is one of the most extensive in the country. Competitive riders are instructed in dressage and combined training and equitation on hunters and jumpers. The School hosts numerous horse events each year for Stoneleigh-Burnham riders and the outside community.

Stoneleigh-Burnham offers two three-week sessions of the Bonnie Castle Summer Riding Camp for girls ages 10 to 15 beginning in early July. Residential camps in volleyball, softball, debate, and dance are also held on campus for girls.

ADMISSION AND COSTS. Stoneleigh-Burnham seeks bright, motivated girls who will contribute positively to the School community. Students are accepted into Grades 9–12 and a postgraduate year. Candidates must submit a transcript with subjects and marks to date, standardized test scores, a personal reference, references from the candidate's school counselor and English and math teachers, and the parent-guardian and student questionnaires. The application fee for 1999–2000 is $35; the application deadline is February 15.

In 1999–2000, tuition for boarding students is $24,500 and $15,500 for day students. There are additional fees for the horseback riding programs.

Financial aid is available on the basis of need as determined by the School Scholarship Service. In 1999, approximately $900,000 was awarded to 90 students. There is an Honor Scholarship Program, and the Alumnae Association funds a scholarship to be awarded each year to the daughter of an alumna.

Director of Academics: Ms. Martha Griswold
Dean of Students: Mrs. Lisa Bailey
Director of Admissions: Mrs. Carolyn J. Smith
Director of Development and Alumnae Relations: Ms. Sue R. Higgins
College Counselors: Mr. Tommus S. Iampietro and
   Mrs. Andrea Patt
Business Manager: Mr. John Burns
Director of Athletics: Alison MacDonald

Tabor Academy   MARION

Marion, MA 02738. 508-748-2000; Fax 508-748-0353;
E-mail admissions@tabor.pvt.k12.ma.us;
Web Site www.taboracademy.org.

Tabor academy in Marion, Massachusetts, is a college preparatory boarding and day school enrolling boys and
girls in Grades 9–12. Located in Marion, a community of
4500 on the western shore of Buzzards Bay across from Cape
Cod, the campus is 55 miles south of Boston and 40 miles east
of Providence, Rhode Island.

The Academy was founded in 1876 by Mrs. Elizabeth
Taber who wished to create a school "to serve the youth of the
area and of the nation" and who named it for Mount Tabor, a
peak in the Holy Land. Tabor's location on Buzzards Bay provides an outstanding resource for naval sciences, oceanography,
sailing, and crew. It is the only high school in the country maintaining a 92-foot Tall Ship, *The Tabor Boy*, as well as a fleet of
more than 70 small sailing vessels and crew shells. Also, Tabor is
one of two Naval Honor Schools in the United States, allowing
the school to nominate graduates to all service academies.

Tabor Academy seeks to provide a rigorous academic program leading to an understanding of fundamental ideas in all
academic disciplines and an appreciation of the goals, purposes,
and directions of a healthy and moral life. Active involvement in
community activities and the opportunity to participate in competitive athletics, drama, music, and the visual arts are part of
every student's program.

The Academy, a nonprofit institution, is governed by a self-
perpetuating Board of Trustees. An active alumni association
represents more than 7700 living graduates.

Tabor Academy is accredited by the New England Association of Schools and Colleges and is a member of the National
Association of Independent Schools, The Association of Independent Schools of New England, and A Better Chance. It also
participates in the John Motley Morehead Foundation and the
English-Speaking Union exchange.

THE CAMPUS. The wooded, 80-acre campus stretches along a
half-mile frontage of Sippican Harbor on Buzzards Bay. About
25 acres are used as playing fields for football, soccer, field
hockey, lacrosse, softball, and baseball. There is an all-weather
track, 11 tennis courts, Stone Gymnasium with basketball and
squash courts, and the wrestling room. The newest building on
campus is the Fish Health and Athletic Center featuring an
indoor ice rink, field house, squash courts, a fitness center,
health center, locker rooms, and a snack bar. The waterfront
provides moorings for the Academy's fleet.

Academic facilities are grouped near the center of the campus. The Academic Center houses 42 classrooms, an observa-

tory, lecture halls, and laboratories for biology, chemistry, and
physics. Hayden Library has 22,000 volumes, 2 computer classrooms, a photo lab, and offices for student publications. Brait-
mayer Art Center provides art studios, and the Fireman Center
for the Performing Arts houses a 650-seat theater with orchestra
pit, sound studio, dance studio, soundproof practice rooms, and
other features. A smaller theater is located in Lyndon South. An
oceanology laboratory is located on the waterfront. Students
take their meals in Johnson Dining Hall overlooking the harbor
and are housed in residential units with a faculty-student ratio
of 9:1. School gatherings are conducted three times a week.

The plant is owned by the school and is valued at approximately $20,000,000.

THE FACULTY. Jay S. Stroud, a graduate of Carleton College
(B.A. 1966), Dartmouth College (M.A. 1980), and Columbia
University (M.Ed. 1982), was appointed Headmaster in 1988.
Mr. Stroud had earlier been Assistant Headmaster and Dean of
the Faculty at Holderness School where he was a member of the
faculty for 17 years. He has also been Resident Director of the
Johns Hopkins Center for the Advancement of Academically
Talented Youth.

Fifty-one men and 32 women comprise the teaching faculty.
They hold 83 baccalaureate degrees and 42 advanced degrees,
including 3 doctorates. Their undergraduate degrees were
earned at such institutions as Amherst, Bates, Boston University,
Bowdoin, Brown, Cambridge (England), Carleton, Colby, Col-
gate, College of the Holy Cross, Cornell, Dartmouth, Florida
Institute of Technology, Georgetown, Gettysburg, Hamilton,
Harvard, Haverford, Hobart, Johns Hopkins, Massachusetts
College of Art, Middlebury, Ohio Wesleyan, Smith, Tufts, United
States Naval Academy, Wake Forest, Williams, Yale, and the Uni-
versities of Massachusetts, Michigan, New Hampshire, Notre
Dame, Vermont, Virginia, Washington, and Wyoming.

Four nurses, a physician, and a director staff the Health
Center. Tobey Hospital in Wareham is five miles away.

STUDENT BODY. In 1998–99, the school enrolled 280 boys
and 195 girls, including 135 day students, in Grades 9–12.
Thirteen percent are international students, representing 25
countries.

ACADEMIC PROGRAM. The academic year, divided into
semesters, begins in early September and ends in early June
with vacations scheduled for 18 days at Christmas and 20 days
in the spring. Grades are sent to parents six times a year. Classes
are held five days a week from 8:00 A.M. to 2:35 P.M. Approximately every other Saturday throughout the year is devoted to
school programs including classes, awareness days, testing days,
parents' weekends, and other activities. Teachers are available in
their offices for half an hour before the start of classes and also
by appointment to provide extra help. English as a Second Language is offered.

Students typically take five major subjects for the full year.
Some elective courses are offered on a half-year basis. To graduate, students must complete a minimum of 17½ credits including 4 in English, 2 in foreign language, 2 in history or social sciences including 1 in United States history, 3 in mathematics, 2
in laboratory sciences including 1 in Biology, ½ in fine or performing arts, and 4 in electives.

More than 70 courses are offered. Among them are
English 1–4, Twentieth Century Poetry, African-American Literature, Creative Writing, Speech and Debate; French 1–4, German
1–4, Spanish 1–4, Russian 1–3, Latin 1–5, Greek 1–3, Greek and
Roman History; Modern European History, United States His-
tory, Economics, Modern Russian History, History of China &
Japan, American Government, America in Vietnam, History of
the Civil Rights Movement, Law and Society, Women of the
World; Algebra 1–2, Geometry, Elementary Functions, Precalcu-
lus, Statistics, Calculus, Advanced Calculus, Vector Calculus;
Introductory Ecology, Biology, Chemistry, Physics, Astronomy,
Meteorology, Introduction to Oceanography, Advanced Oceanol-
ogy, Environmental Studies, Geology, Physiology; Seamanship,
Piloting, Celestial Navigation, Maritime History, Marine Architec-

ture, Lifeboatmanship, *Tabor Boy* (sail-training on the schooner); Computer Competency, Art, Art History, Photography, Ceramics 1–3; and Music 1–2, Chamber Ensembles, Chorus, Madrigal Singers, Jazz Bands, Wind Ensemble, Acting 1–2, Advanced Acting/Directing Seminar, and Lighting Design and Stagecraft. Honors courses and 17 Advanced Placement courses are offered.

Ninety-nine percent of Tabor Academy graduates in the Class of 1999 went on to college. They enrolled at such colleges as Babson, Barnard, Boston University, Bowdoin, Brown, Colby, Colgate, Columbia, Connecticut College, Cornell, Denison, Franklin and Marshall, Gettysburg, Lafayette, Mount Holyoke, New York University, Oberlin, Rensselaer Polytechnic Institute, Rollins, St. Lawrence, Skidmore, Smith, Trinity, Tufts, Union, Vassar, and the Universities of Chicago, Colorado, Maine, Montana, New Hampshire, Oregon, Pennsylvania, Vermont, and Virginia.

The Tabor Academy Summer Program offers six- and four-week camping sessions for boys and girls ages 9–15. Academic enrichment courses, which can earn credit, are optional, and a full program of recreational, art, drama, and sports programs, featuring sailing and other water activities, is offered.

STUDENT ACTIVITIES. Students elect class representatives and a president to the Student Council, which serves as a forum for students on campus issues. Students also serve on the Activities and Disciplinary committees.

A variety of interest groups are organized into clubs. Some currently active are Bell and Madrigal choirs, Cum Laude Society, Speech and Debate, Peer Listening, Community Service, Tour Guides, Drama, dance, newspaper, literary magazine, yearbook, radio station, Stock, International Students, mountain biking, jazz band, and language clubs.

Tabor is a member of the New England Preparatory School Athletic Council and fields varsity teams against other prep and public schools in football, soccer, cross-country, sailing, basketball, hockey, wrestling, squash, baseball, track, lacrosse, tennis, golf, and crew for boys; and soccer, crew, cross-country, ice hockey, squash, basketball, lacrosse, sailing, field hockey, softball, and tennis for girls. While many students participate in three sports, there is a wide variety of afternoon activities, including art, music, and drama, from which they may choose. Some students choose at some point to crew on *The Tabor Boy*, which cruises the New England shoreline on weekends and takes longer voyages during vacation periods. Newly enrolled students are invited to participate in one of seven "Summer Orientation at Sea" cruises. The program brings 14 new students together with Tabor's oceanography instructor, faculty chaperones, and the captain and student crew of the vessel.

The Student Activities Committee plans weekend entertainments including dances, films, and excursions. Athletic contests and musical and dramatic performances by Tabor groups or visitors are among the regularly scheduled events.

ADMISSION AND COSTS. Tabor Academy seeks students of good character who have demonstrated the ability and the desire to profit from a challenging preparation for college. Candidates are admitted on the basis of a personal interview, Secondary School Admission Test results, official transcripts, and teacher recommendations. Applications, with a fee of $35, should be submitted by January 31 for fall entry.

Boarding tuition for 1999–2000 is $25,900; day tuition is $17,600. New students are charged an enrollment fee of $350, of which $100 is deposited against final billings. Books are extra. Need-based financial aid is offered, and about $1,750,000 is awarded to approximately 38 percent of the student body.

Dean of Faculty: Richard E. Roller
Dean of Students: Jay Houck
Director of Studies: Joseph Doggett
Director of Admissions: Andrew L. McCain
Director of Alumni and Development: Christopher R. Latham
Director of College Counseling: Richard E. Roller
Business Manager: Paul C. White
Director of Athletics: Richard C. Muther

Tenacre Country Day School   1910

78 Benvenue Street, Wellesley, MA 02482. 781-235-2282;
Fax 781-237-7057

Tenacre Country Day School enrolls 185 students in Pre-Kindergarten–Grade 6. A well-rounded program focuses on basic skills, math, language arts, social studies, science, music, art, computer, and physical education. Good citizenship and character development are also emphasized. Small classes, talented teachers, a nurturing yet challenging environment, a diverse population, and attention to the needs of each child prepare students for highly competitive secondary schools. An After School Program is open to all grades. Summer day and sports camps enroll boys and girls ages 4–12. Tuition: $9770–$14,480. Financial aid and limited transportation are available. Ms. Sam R. Reece is Acting Director of Admissions; Christian B. Elliot (Princeton, A.B. 1974) was appointed Head of School in 1995.

Thayer Academy   1877

745 Washington Street, Braintree, MA 02184. 781-843-3580;
Fax 781-380-8785; E-mail admissions@thayer.org
Web Site http://www.thayer.org

Thayer is a coeducational day school enrolling 660 students in Grades 6–12. Located 13 miles south of Boston, it is accessible via the MBTA and minutes from routes 128, 93, and 3. Thayer offers a rigorous and challenging college preparatory education to students from diverse social, ethnic, economic, and academic backgrounds. The Academy seeks to equip students with the skills, knowledge, and experience to realize their potential in college and beyond. It is the school's belief that students will find academic success when given opportunities for individual achievement and self-expression. Tuition: $17,900. Financial Aid: $1,800,000. Jonathan White is Director of Admission; Eric M. Swain (Pomona College) was appointed Headmaster in 1995. *New England Association.*

The Tower School   1912

75 West Shore Drive, Marblehead, MA 01945. 781-631-5800;
Fax 781-631-2292; E-mail Tower@towerschool.org;
Web Site www.towerschool.org

A Blue Ribbon School, Tower is a day school enrolling 310 boys and girls in Pre-Kindergarten–Grade 9. The School is committed to the cognitive and emotional development of its students. High academic standards are sought within an atmosphere of trust and cooperation among students, teachers, and parents. Tower expects its graduates to be intellectually and socially competent, self-reliant, and respectful of the views and dignity of others. Sports, publications, and clubs are among the activities. Arts and day camp summer programs are available. Tuition: $6880–$12,730. Financial Aid: $285,000. Hope Crosier is Director of Admission; James K. Bonney (Ohio Wesleyan, B.A. 1968; Boston University, M.Ed. 1970; Harvard, D.Ed. 1983) was appointed Headmaster in 1985.

Valley View School   1970

Oakham Road, P.O. Box 338, North Brookfield, MA 01535.
508-867-6505; Fax 508-867-3300; E-mail valview@aol.com

A clinical psychologist founded this residential school to help boys ages 11–16 who function below their academic and social potential. Typically, Valley View School enrolls 54 students who may demonstrate attention deficit disorder, depression, oppositional behavior, or other nonpsychotic syndromes that interfere with their adjustment to the world around them. Valley View's structured, 12-month program offers intensive remediation and a broad range of success-oriented experiences such as athletics and drama designed to motivate learning and promote the boy's self-esteem and confidence in himself. Travel in the United States and abroad affords special challenge and enrichment. Most students are mainstreamed after two or three years. Tuition: $43,500. Philip G. Spiva, Ph.D., is Founding Director.

Wilbraham & Monson Academy

WILBRAHAM

Wilbraham, MA 01095. 413-596-6811;
  E-mail admissmail@wma.pvt.k12.ma.us;
  Web Site wma.pvt.k12.ma.us

WILBRAHAM & MONSON ACADEMY in Wilbraham, Massachusetts, is a coeducational college preparatory school for boarding and day students in Grades 6 through 12 and a postgraduate year. Boarding begins in Grade 9. The Academy is located in the center of the town of Wilbraham, in south central Massachusetts. The town, incorporated in 1763, is essentially rural in character, though many residents commute to nearby Springfield and to Hartford, Connecticut.

Wilbraham Academy was founded in New Hampshire in 1817 by Methodists and moved to Wilbraham in 1824. It was known as Wesleyan Academy until 1912, when it terminated its association with the Methodist church. In 1971, Wilbraham merged with nearby Monson Academy, which had been established in 1804.

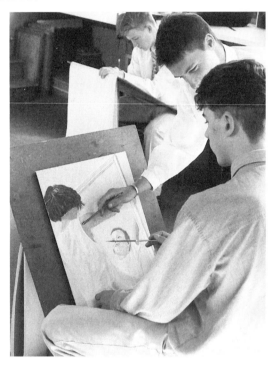

Wilbraham & Monson Academy is a nonprofit organization and is operated by the members of the Board of Trustees. The annual operating budget of the Academy is $7,000,000; its endowment is currently valued at $2,800,000.

THE CAMPUS. The campus occupies 300 acres, which was once rich farmland and wooded hillsides. The acreage extends to the western slope of Wilbraham Mountain. Beyond the central green, where most buildings are located, are woodlands, meadows, and two hillside ponds. There are 9 all-weather tennis courts, 12 large playing fields, and a quarter-mile cinder track. The Greenhalgh Athletic Building contains 3 basketball courts, a weight-training room, and a 25-yard pool.

Major academic buildings include Chamberlin Hall, the

Blake Middle School Center, which was extensively renovated and expanded in 1997; Old Academy (1824, rebuilt 1969), which houses classrooms for English and foreign language studies; Binney Fine Arts Center (renovated 1991) houses the art and music departments; Fisk Hall contains the theatre (renovated 1992) and classrooms for mathematics and social studies; Mattern Hall (1971), the science and computer center; and the Benjamin Gill Library. Rich Hall houses administrative offices and dormitory rooms for boys, Lak dining hall, the Campus Center (school snack shop), the bookstore, post office, and games lounges. Smith Hall (1896) and Wallace-Blake Hall (1976) provide accommodations for students and faculty members. Other facilities include additional housing for faculty and students, the Alumni Memorial Chapel, and a health services building.

THE FACULTY. Richard C. Malley was appointed Head of School in July of 1989. A graduate of Kenyon College (A.B. 1968), he also studied at Lehigh University. Mr. Malley came to Wilbraham & Monson Academy after 21 years at Blair Academy in New Jersey, where he taught history and served as Director of Studies and Assistant Headmaster.

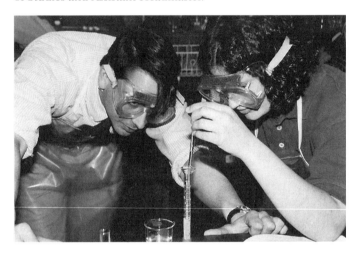

There are 53 full-time teachers and administrators who teach on the faculty, 33 men and 23 women. Of these, 42 live at the school, including 15 with families. All hold baccalaureate degrees, 2 have doctorates, and 29 have graduate degrees from such institutions as American International College, Fordham, Harvard, Lehigh, Middlebury, Rensselaer Polytechnic, Springfield, Trinity College, Worcester Polytechnic, and the University of Michigan.

Three registered nurses staff the health services department. The school physician is a quarter-mile from the campus, and several hospitals are within 20 minutes.

STUDENT BODY. Wilbraham & Monson Academy enrolls 137 day boys, 84 boarding boys, 82 day girls, and 57 boarding girls in Grades 6–12 and a postgraduate year.

In 1999–2000, boarding students come from 18 states and 19 foreign countries including Germany, Japan, Mexico, Nigeria, Saudi Arabia, Thailand, and Venezuela. Day students reside in nearby Massachusetts and Connecticut towns.

ACADEMIC PROGRAM. The 33-week school year, from early September to early June, is divided into trimesters. There are vacations at Thanksgiving, Christmas, and in the spring. Eight 40-minute class periods meet from 7:50 A.M. to 3:00 P.M. Monday through Friday, with the exception of Wednesday, which is a half-day. An extra-help period is built into the daily schedule, and each course includes an expanded 70-minute period every week or on alternate weeks, depending on the course.

The average class size at the Academy is 12–16 students. Students are required to observe supervised evening study hours in their rooms. An evening study period with faculty tutors is offered to all students and required for new students and students who are experiencing difficulty. Extra help from classroom teachers is available at no extra charge, and arrangements for tutorial support can be made for an additional charge. Evaluations, consisting of teacher comments and ratings, are issued and sent to parents six times a year. The ratio of students to faculty is 8:1.

The Middle School, which enrolls students in Grades 6 through 8, emphasizes basic skills, and children are encouraged to work with materials to understand concepts better. Among the subjects they study are English, social studies, environmental science, mathematics, computers, the visual arts, music, and athletics. Foreign language instruction in Latin, French, and Spanish is available in Grades 6 through 8.

The Academy requires 54 credits for graduation. Each full-year course is worth 3 credits. Departmental requirements include four years of English, three years of mathematics (Algebra I, Algebra II, Geometry), two years of a foreign language, two to three years of laboratory science, two to three years of history, and, for students in Grade 9, five trimesters in the fine and performing arts.

The program of studies includes a wide range of courses, which may meet for one trimester or a full year. Among those offered are Honors English at all levels; French, Spanish, Latin; Modern European History; Biology, Chemistry, Physics; Algebra, Geometry, Computer Science, Calculus; and Art and Design, Sculpture, Photography, Advanced Study in Art, and a repertory theatre company. Advanced Placement courses are offered in English, Latin, French, Spanish, European History, American History, mathematics, and sciences. A comprehensive program in English as a Foreign Language is available for international students. A mainstreamed Academic Service Program provides support for students with learning differences.

The 73 graduates in the Class of 1999 were admitted to a variety of four-year colleges and universities. They are attending such institutions as American University, Boston College, Bryant, Johns Hopkins, Pennsylvania State, Rensselaer Polytechnic, Roger Williams, Vassar, and the Universities of Massachusetts, New Hampshire, and Vermont.

STUDENT ACTIVITIES. Academy organizations include *The Bell* (newspaper), *The Hill* (yearbook), the *Rubicon* (literary magazine), Academy Singers, Academy Repertory Company, Academy Players (drama), Student Senate, and environmental organizations.

The Academy has boys' interscholastic teams at various levels in football, soccer, cross-country, basketball, hockey, wrestling, baseball, golf, lacrosse, and tennis. Girls compete in cross-country, soccer, volleyball, basketball, lacrosse, tennis, and softball, while coeducational teams are formed in riflery, track, swimming, skiing, water polo, modern dance, and an outdoor program.

Trips to concerts, plays, museums, and lectures are frequently organized to take advantage of the cultural offerings available on the college campuses in the Amherst-Springfield-Hartford area. Special weekends are planned for alumni, parents, and friends; there are also regional alumni gatherings and frequent Parents' Association activities.

ADMISSION AND COSTS. The Academy seeks students who are preparing for entrance to a college program and who wish to take advantage of the opportunities the school offers. Wilbraham & Monson does not discriminate against any person in admission, employment, or otherwise because of race, color, national origin, disability, sex, or age in violation of existing state or federal laws or regulations.

The completed application form, appropriate transcripts, Secondary School Admission Test results, test records, recommendations, and a $50 application fee are required. A visit to the school is also required whenever possible. Postgraduates should take the Scholastic Aptitude Test. Students with diagnosed learning disabilities who are applying for the Academic Services program are required to take a WISC-III test prior to their interview. Application should be made early in the school year, although some students are accepted after the school year has begun if space is available.

The boarding fee is $25,200; day tuition ranges from $13,150 to $15,300. Allowances and transportation to and from the school must be individually arranged. A tuition payment plan is available. Scholarship aid of $1,100,000 is granted to approximately 34 percent of the student body on the basis of need; other factors are the Academy's desire for diversity and the student's ability to make a "positive contribution to the life of the school community." Wilbraham & Monson subscribes to the School and Student Service for Financial Aid.

Assistant Head: Karen O'Meara Pullen
Dean of Students: Paul Jette
Dean of Studies: Rebecca Bouchard
Alumni Director: Brian Easler
Director of Admission: Brinley M. Hall
Admission Associates: Deborah Barnes Hardaker and
Peter S. Wagoner
Director of Development: Thomas H. Barclay
Director of College Counseling: Michael Thompson
Business Manager: Karen White
Director of Athletics: Skip Jarocki
Director of International Program: Anthony Carey

The Williston Northampton School   1841

Easthampton, MA 01027. 413-529-3000;
Admissions 413-529-3241; Fax 413-527-9494;
E-mail admissions@williston.com; Web Site http://www.williston.com

Formed by the 1971 merger of Williston Academy and Northampton School for Girls, The Williston Northampton School is a coeducational college preparatory school enrolling

260 boarders and 180 day students in Grades 9–12 and a post-graduate year, and 90 day students in Grades 7–8. The School aims "to build independence and to encourage individual growth through a balanced, rigorous curriculum and a supportive environment." The new 40,000-square-foot Reed Campus Center enhances student life and opportunities in the arts. Boarding Tuition: $26,200; Day Tuition: $17,900. Financial Aid: $2,500,000. Ann C. Pickrell is Director of Admission; Brian Wright (Occidental, B.A.; Princeton, M.P.A., M.A., Ph.D.) is Headmaster. *New England Association.*

The Winchendon School   WINCHENDON

172 Ash Street, Winchendon, MA 01475. 978-297-1223; E-mail winchendon@admissions.org; Web Site www.winchendon.org

THE WINCHENDON SCHOOL in Winchendon, Massachusetts, is a college preparatory boarding and day school enrolling boys and girls in Grades 8 through 12 and a postgraduate year. The School is located in the town of Winchendon (population 7500), in north central Massachusetts, 65 miles from Boston, 35 miles from Worcester, and 20 miles from Keene, New Hampshire. Bus service to surrounding cities is available from a bus station within walking distance of the campus.

The Winchendon School was founded by Lloyd Harvey Hatch in 1926 in Dexter, Maine, "to create a structured and traditional atmosphere for 'good' underachievers." After a period in Newport, Rhode Island, the School was moved in 1961 to its present location. Girls were first admitted in 1973.

The Winchendon philosophy is that most young people can succeed when surrounded by an atmosphere of caring attention to their individual needs. To that end, the School seeks to offer academic programs that are closely tailored to each student's strengths and weaknesses, in a traditional environment designed to encourage moral and spiritual growth. Small classes, a personalized approach, and flexible guidance and support systems are intended to stimulate an interest in

learning and to teach students that they themselves are "the most valuable contributors to their own education."

The School is a nonprofit institution governed by a self-perpetuating 17-member Board of Trustees, which meets at least three times per year. At present, the Board includes several of Winchendon's 1600 alumni.

The Winchendon School is accredited by the New England Association of Schools and Colleges and is affiliated with the National Association of Independent Schools.

THE CAMPUS. Winchendon's 236 acres include such outdoor facilities as a swimming pool; tennis courts; an 18-hole golf course; cross-country ski trails; and baseball, lacrosse, and soccer fields. Three academic buildings (1966) house science laboratories, a 20,000-volume library, and classrooms specially designed for the School's small classes. Ford Hall (1888) contains administrative offices, classrooms, a dormitory, the infirmary, and the dining hall. Other facilities include an art building, a performing arts building, seven dormitories, a gymnasium (1990), a student union, faculty residences, a golf pro shop with locker rooms, and the Headmaster's residence, Homewood (1921).

The plant, which is valued at $9,000,000, is owned by the School.

THE FACULTY. J. William LaBelle was appointed Headmaster in 1988. A native of Massachusetts, Mr. LaBelle attended the University of Massachusetts (B.S. 1958; M.S. 1968) and Massachusetts State College (M.Ed. 1967). After receiving his baccalaureate degree, he taught science at Trinity-Pawling School, where he also coached soccer, wrestling, and lacrosse and served as a dormitory master and Director of Athletics. For the 15 years immediately preceding his appointment at Winchendon, he was Associate Headmaster and Dean of the Academy at Wilbraham & Monson Academy. Mr. LaBelle's wife, Marilyn Peach LaBelle, is the Academic Dean.

There are 27 full-time faculty and administrators who teach, 20 men and 7 women. Of these, 24 live at the School, 8 with their families. Faculty members hold baccalaureate and advanced degrees from Allegheny 2, Amherst, Bates 2, Boston College, Boston University, Colby 3, Colgate, College of the Holy Cross, Connecticut College, Creighton, Dartmouth, Hamilton, Massachusetts College of Liberal Arts, Middlebury, Smith, Yale, and the Universities of California (Berkeley), Connecticut, Iowa, Massachusetts 4, Miami, New Hampshire, Pennsylvania, Rhode Island, and Virginia. Faculty benefits include insurance and retirement plans and financial assistance with further education.

The school infirmary is staffed by a full-time nurse, and other staff members are certified in first aid and sports training. A school physician is on call; hospitals and emergency rooms are nearby.

STUDENT BODY. In 1998–99, Winchendon enrolled 170 boarding students, 120 boys and 50 girls; 5 boys and 3 girls were admitted as day students. Enrollment was distributed as follows: Grade 8–5, Grade 9–25, Grade 10–39, Grade 11–44, Grade 12–50, and Postgraduate–15. Boarding students came primarily from New England, with 30 other states and 18 foreign countries also represented.

ACADEMIC PROGRAM. The school year runs from early September until late May, with vacations at Thanksgiving and Christmas and in early spring. Classes are held five days a week from 7:50 A.M. to 12:40 P.M. and are followed by a two-hour sports period and a conference period. A typical weekday for boarders begins at 7:00 A.M. and includes, in addition to classes, recreation, meals, a clean-up period, school meeting, evening study period, and lights-out at 10:30 P.M. Twice weekly, the usual cafeteria dinner is replaced by a "sit-down" meal for faculty and students.

The Winchendon approach to education is based on highly personalized attention to each student. Classes have an average of six students, and the student/faculty ratio is approximately 5:1. Following extensive testing in September, an academic schedule is created for each student, based on test scores, previous grades, and teacher recommendations. Placement in courses is determined by students' needs rather than their grade level; most students take five courses per term. Faculty-supervised study halls are held in the evening, with an additional conference period scheduled daily to allow for individual consultation between teachers and students. To help students monitor their progress, grade slips are issued daily in all classes and are reviewed with dorm parents during the evening study period. Parents are also sent grades and comments once a week by their child's academic advisor.

Winchendon offers remediation in mathematics, writing, and reading to help students with specific learning disabilities. To graduate, students must successfully complete four years of English, four of mathematics, three of social science (including United States History), and two years of science. The study of a foreign language is encouraged, but not required. Among the required and elective courses offered are English I–IV, English as a Foreign Language; Latin I–III, French I–IV, Spanish I–IV; Political Science, Psychology, Economics; Algebra II, Trigonometry, Calculus; Physics, Advanced Biology, Chemistry; Music Appreciation; Art History, Graphic Arts, Photography; and Computer Programming, Word Processing, and Typing.

Winchendon offers English as a Second Language, focusing on reading, writing, and oral communications at beginning, intermediate, and advanced levels. Courses in other disciplines and preparation for the Test of English as a Foreign Language are designed to help international students strengthen academic skills and assist in their adjustment to American life and customs.

The members of the Class of 1999 were accepted at the following colleges and universities: Assumption, Bentley, Boston College, Bradford, Canisius, Clark, Connecticut College, Elmira, Gettysburg, Hartwick, Harvard, Hofstra, Manhattan, Merrimack, Northeastern, Norwich, St. Anselm, St. Lawrence, Salve Regina, Seton Hall, Siena, Temple, United States Military Academy, Wentworth, Wheaton, and the Universities of Maine, Maryland, Massachusetts, New Hampshire, Notre Dame, and Pittsburgh.

The School offers a six-week summer program for boys and girls in Grades 8 through 12, with remedial, make-up, and enrichment courses. The program also includes recreational sports and field trips for relaxation and enrichment. The director is Elliot C. Harvey.

STUDENT ACTIVITIES. The Winchendon Student Council, with representatives from each class, plans student activities and special events, as does the Student Activities Committee. Students also sit on the Judiciary Board, which advises the Headmaster on major disciplinary cases.

Because Winchendon believes that a carefully crafted athletic program can complement and enhance students' growth in other areas, participation in athletic activities is required for each season. Varsity sports include boys' and girls' soccer, basketball, and lacrosse; boys' ice hockey, wrestling, and baseball; and coeducational golf, tennis, cross-country running, and alpine skiing. Both boys and girls participate in intramural and recreational sports.

Students publish a yearbook (*Vestigia*), newspaper (*Progress*), and literary magazine (*Impressions*), and may join special-interest groups such as the Photography and Outing clubs. There are performing arts activities in instrumental and choral music, theater, and dance. School-sponsored weekend trips to Boston and Worcester allow students access to the cultural and recreational resources there; closer to home, the School's location in the foothills of the Monadnock Mountains provides excellent nearby skiing and ice-skating. Other local entertainment includes movies, bowling, and activities at colleges in the area. With parental permission, students may spend the weekend off campus.

ADMISSION AND COSTS. Winchendon welcomes students who have the potential to do successful college work, despite previous academic weakness. Admission is made to all grade levels, based on a recent Wechsler test, a transcript, teacher recommendations, and a personal interview on campus. Applications are accepted throughout the year on a rolling basis; the application fee is $50.

In 1999–2000, boarding tuition is $25,595 and day tuition is $15,645. Additional expenses include a fixed fee of $2000 to cover such items as laundry, bedding and linen, athletic supplies and services, arts and crafts materials, and textbooks. There is an extra fee for Driver Education.

Financial aid is offered according to need as determined by the School Scholarship Service. In 1998–99, 25 percent of the student body received financial aid.

Dean of the School: Marilyn P. LaBelle
Dean of Faculty: David A. Stone
Dean of Students: Elliot C. Harvey
Director of Admissions: Daniel J. Driscoll
Director of Development: C. Jackson Blair
Director of Counseling: Pamela S. Blair
Director of College Counseling: David A. Stone
Director of Athletics: Daniel P. Chrieten

The Winsor School   1886

Pilgrim Road, Boston, MA 02215. 617-735-9500;
*   Fax 617-739-5519; E-mail admissions@winsor.edu;*
*   Web Site www.winsor.edu*

Founded by Mary Pickard Winsor, The Winsor School is a college preparatory day school enrolling 420 girls in Grades 5–12. The School offers an academically challenging curriculum, features small classes, uses the cultural resources of Boston for field trips, and shares some activities with nearby boys' schools. Physical education and fine arts are integral parts of the program. A science wing contains seven laboratories, preparation rooms, and a computer center. Students in Grade 11 can participate in the Mountain School Program in Vermont for a semester. Tuition: $19,100. Financial Aid: $1,000,000. Jane Frank Siewers is Admission Director; Carolyn McClintock Peter (Wellesley, A.B. 1964; Brown, M.A.T. 1976) was appointed Director in 1988. *New England Association.*

Worcester Academy   WORCESTER

81 Providence Street, Worcester, MA 01604. 508-754-5302;
*   Fax 508-752-2382; E-mail admission@worcesteracademy.org;*
*   Web Site www.worcesteracademy.org*

WORCESTER ACADEMY in Worcester, Massachusetts, is a college preparatory day and boarding school enrolling boys and girls in Grades 6–12 and a postgraduate year. New England's second-largest city, Worcester (population 170,000) is home to ten colleges, a nationally known civic center, and many museums, theaters, concert halls, and shopping malls. Students are involved in city affairs through required community service. Boston and Springfield are about an hour away, and ski areas are within close proximity. The school is easily accessible by train and bus.

Founded in 1834 by local citizens under the leadership of Isaac Davis, Worcester Academy was originally coeducational, but became an all-boys school in 1882 and then returned to coeducation in 1974. It has occupied its present site since 1869.

The Academy seeks to prepare able and motivated students for college and later life through intensive engagement in academics, athletics, and the arts. It relies on a firm grounding in inquiry, honesty, hard work, and respect for others and strives to foster independence in students as they advance in age and learning. This approach prepares students to become responsible citizens in a global society of increased technological complexity.

Worcester Academy is organized as a nonprofit corporation governed by a self-perpetuating Board of Trustees who

meet three times a year. About 5300 living alumni provide financial and other support for its programs.

The Academy is accredited by the New England Association of Schools and Colleges and holds membership in the National Association of Independent Schools, the Association of Independent Schools of New England, and other professional organizations.

THE CAMPUS. The Academy is situated on a 12-acre campus on Union Hill and has athletic fields on another 11-acre tract, Gaskill Field, a few blocks away.

Six major buildings are listed in the National Register of Historic Places. Walker Hall (1890) houses administrative offices, classrooms, the Nelson Wheeler Library, the Rader Art Gallery, the Ackerman Media Center, and the Andes Performing Arts Center, used for theater classes and performances. Kingsley Hall (1897) holds classrooms, science laboratories, the Center for Academic Support, the Middle School lounge, a computer room, and the audiovisual room. The Megaron (1905) is a large room used for social events and as a student lounge; its basement contains the art studios. The recently renovated and updated Lewis J. Warner Memorial Theatre (1932) houses the music department and is used for plays, movies, and assemblies.

The Kellner Student Center (1991) contains the school store, mail room, and recreation rooms. Adams Hall (1893) holds the dining hall and kitchen. Dexter, Davol, and Heydon Halls are dormitories with faculty apartments. Stoddard Hall houses music practice rooms, the infirmary, and a weight-training room. Abercrombie House (1897) is the Headmaster's home.

Daniels Gymnasium (1915, expanded 1986) holds two basketball courts, a swimming pool, a weight-training room, a wrestling room, an indoor track, and support facilities. Gaskill Field, completely renovated in 1994, includes a six-lane, all-weather track; tennis courts; playing fields for football, soccer, baseball, and softball; and the Michael L. Gould Field House.

THE FACULTY. Dexter Morse, former Head of the Upper School at Phoenix Country Day School, was appointed Headmaster in 1997. He is a graduate of Phillips Academy, Bowdoin College (A.B. 1962), and the University of Vermont (M.Ed. 1967).

The full-time faculty, including administrators who teach, is comprised of 33 men and 22 women, who hold 55 baccalaureate degrees and 34 advanced degrees, including a doctorate, 2 law degrees, and a master's of divinity, from such institutions as Babson, Bates, Berklee School of Music, Boston College, Boston University, Bowdoin, Brigham Young, Brown, Clark, Colby, College of the Holy Cross, Dartmouth, Elmira, Harvard, Massachusetts College of Art, Middlebury, Princeton, Regis, St. Lawrence, Springfield, Syracuse, Texas Christian, Trinity, Tufts, Wesleyan, Wheaton, Worcester Polytechnic Institute, Union, Yale, and the Universities of Chicago, Cincinnati, Maine, Maryland, Massachusetts, Michigan, New Hampshire, Pennsylvania, Toronto, and Vermont. Twenty-one faculty live on campus.

A resident nurse staffs the infirmary, a physician is on call, and a city hospital is two blocks from the campus.

STUDENT BODY. In 1999–2000, Worcester Academy enrolled 459 students, including 94 five- and seven-day boarders and 365 day students in Grades 6–12 and a postgraduate year. There are 24 in Grade 6, 58 in Grade 7, 46 in Grade 8, 65 in Grade 9, 81 in Grade 10, 77 in Grade 11, 75 in Grade 12, and 34 postgraduates. Boarding students come from 12 states, China, England, France, Germany, Hong Kong, Indonesia, Japan, Korea, Spain, Taiwan, Thailand, Turkey, and Ukraine; day students are from Worcester and its suburbs. About 40 percent of the students receive some form of financial aid.

ACADEMIC PROGRAM. The academic year, divided into semesters, begins in early September and ends in early June, with vacations of two weeks at Christmas and in March. Classes, with an average size of 12 students per class, are held five days a week and are scheduled in seven 42-minute sessions between 7:45 A.M. and 3:00 P.M. Extra-help sessions, study halls, activity periods, and assemblies are scheduled into the regular school day. Resident students have a two-hour study period each evening. Grades, with written comments from teachers, are sent to parents four times a year.

In the Middle School (Grades 6–8), students earn 5 credits per year from a curriculum that includes English; French, Spanish, or Latin; History; Mathematics; Science; Music, Art, Drama; Study Skills; and Health. To graduate from the Upper School, a student must complete 18 credits including four years of English; two of foreign language; two of history, including U.S. History; four of mathematics; two of science, including biology; one and one-half of studio art/music/drama; and at least one elective, in addition to satisfying physical education and community service requirements.

Postgraduate students can earn a Worcester Academy Diploma or a Diploma of Postgraduate Study, which entails a demanding college preparatory curriculum as well as skill development and SAT preparation.

Among the courses offered in the Upper School are English 1–4; English as a Foreign Language; French 1–5, Latin 1–5, Spanish 1–5; Western Civilization 1–2, U.S. History, European History, Soviet History, The Holocaust, American Govern-

ment, Constitutional Law, History and the Media, U.S.-China Relations, World History; Algebra 1–2, Geometry, Pre-Calculus, Calculus; Earth Science, Biology 1–2, Chemistry 1–2, Physics 1–2, Conceptual Physics, Global Science; Studio Art 1–2, Drawing, Printmaking, Three-Dimensional Design, Photography, Understanding Art; Instrumental Ensemble, Academy Singers, Academy Chorus, Music Theory, Jazz Combo; Acting 1–3, Theater Experience, Directing, Stagecraft, Theater Internship; and Health and Human Development. Opportunities for independent study, honors sections, and Advanced Placement study in 12 subjects are available.

Of the 97 seniors who graduated in 1999, 96 went on immediately to higher education while one international student returned to his native country to seek university admission. The graduates are enrolled at 70 different colleges including Boston College, Brandeis, Carnegie Mellon, Colgate, Emory, Harvard 2, Middlebury, Rensselaer, Smith, Trinity 6, Tufts, Wesleyan 2, Williams 2, Worcester Polytechnic 2, and the Universities of Michigan 3 and Pennsylvania.

STUDENT ACTIVITIES. There are many opportunities for student leadership. The Board of Monitors oversees all school activities and provides assistance and service to faculty and other students.

Other activities include the newspaper, literary magazine, yearbook, International Student Association, Ambassadors, math teams, and drama, foreign language, history, law, international relations, debate, outing, photography, science, and varsity clubs. Middle School students have their own newspaper, yearbook, and athletic teams and stage their own school play.

All students participate in organized athletics or physical education classes. Boys' varsity teams in football, basketball, and baseball compete against Class A prep school schools of New England and college junior varsity teams; other boys' and girls' teams compete against independent and public schools of comparable size. Other varsity sports for boys are cross-country, soccer, skiing, swimming, tennis, track, and wrestling. Girls compete in softball, basketball, volleyball, cross-country, soccer, skiing, swimming, tennis, and track. Golf is coeducational. Intramurals include basketball, softball, volleyball, tennis, and water polo.

Weekend dances with students from other schools, pool tournaments, and shopping and ski trips enhance campus life.

Parents and/or alumni are invited to attend special events such as Homecoming, Winter Carnival Weekend, Parents Weekend, Grandparents' Day, Musical "Pops" Night, Alumni Day, and an annual golf tournament.

ADMISSION AND COSTS. Worcester Academy seeks students of diverse abilities, interests, and backgrounds who are willing to extend themselves to meet the challenges of a college preparatory program. Students are accepted on evaluation of a completed application, with a $40 fee, two essays, recommendations from English and math teachers, a complete transcript of grades, and a personal interview. SSAT exams are required for students entering Grades 6 through 11; SAT I or ACT results are required for Grade 12 and postgraduate applications. No tests are required for international students. Priority consideration is given to applications completed by February 10.

Tuition for 1999–2000 is as follows: Middle School, $12,600; Upper School day students, $13,800; five-day boarding, $20,650; and seven-day boarding, $24,500. International students pay an additional $2000 for health insurance, activities, and services. Several tuition payment plans are offered, and tuition refund insurance is required. The Academy awards approximately $1,700,000 annually on the basis of need.

Assistant Headmaster: Joel B. Strogoff
Director of Middle School: Judith B. Evans
Dean of Students: George Whittemore
Director of Admission: Jonathan G. Baker
Director of Development: Kathleen Damon
College Counselor: Jonathan G. Baker
Business Manager: William Toomey
Director of Athletics: Patrick Smith

MICHIGAN

Cranbrook Schools   BLOOMFIELD HILLS

1221 North Woodward Avenue, Bloomfield Hills, MI 48303-0801.
248-645-3000; Admissions 248-645-3610;
E-mail cranbrook@cc.cranbrook.edu; Web Site www.cranbrook.org

CRANBROOK SCHOOLS in Bloomfield Hills, Michigan, comprise three divisions on four adjoining campuses. Brookside Lower School is coeducational, serving day students in Pre-kindergarten through fifth grade. The Middle School (Grades 6–8), also enrolling day students, provides single-sex education on separate campuses, with girls on the Kingswood campus and boys on the Vaughan campus. The Upper School (Grades 9–12) accommodates boarding and day students, with boys' dormitories at Cranbrook and girls' dorms at Kingswood. Bloomfield Hills (population 4000) is a residential community about 25 minutes northwest of Detroit.

George Gough and Ellen Scripps Booth began the Cranbrook Educational Community in the early 1920s with Brookside, an independent, coeducational elementary school. Eliel Saarinen, the renowned Finnish architect, was commissioned to design the Cranbrook School for boys (1927) and the Kingswood School for girls (1931). After operating independently for more than a half century, the two schools merged in 1985.

From the earliest grades through senior year, Cranbrook Schools seek to offer a broad and rigorous curriculum in the liberal arts. Humanities, the sciences, fine and performing arts, a challenging athletic program, and a wide range of activities are integrated into a demanding college preparatory program designed to develop each student's unique talents and strengths to the fullest. Moral, intellectual, and physical development and social responsibility are emphasized so that students will be inspired to contribute positively to the world as young adults.

Cranbrook Schools are governed by a 21-member Board of Trustees. The nonprofit institution is accredited by the Independent Schools Association of the Central States and holds membership in numerous professional organizations.

THE CAMPUS. The beautiful 315-acre campus of the Cranbrook Educational Community has been called one of the masterpieces of American architecture. In 1989, it was designated a National Historic Landmark, an honor accorded only two other

independent schools in the United States. Sharing the grounds with the Schools are the Cranbrook Academy of Art and Museum (1932) and the Cranbrook Institute of Science (1930), both considered preeminent in their fields. Cranbrook House, the home of the founders, is surrounded by 40 acres of gardens, lawns, and woodlands.

In 1996, Brookside created an additional wing to the Lower School and began the Vlasic Early Childhood Center. Lerchen Hall, the Schools' performing arts center underwent a $1 million renovation in 1993. Other buildings include St. Dunstan's Playhouse, the Greek Theatre, an Italian-style boathouse, a greenhouse, and Thornlea, the former home of the founders' son.

Athletic facilities include a football stadium, a newly renovated, 12-month, enclosed ice arena, two gymnasiums, 15 outdoor tennis courts, a new sport and fitness center, training rooms, an eight-lane indoor pool, and playing fields for baseball, soccer, and other sports.

Boarding girls live in a three-story dormitory wing on the Kingswood campus, and boarding boys are housed in six dorms on the Cranbrook campus.

The total school plant is valued at more than $100,000,000.

THE FACULTY. The faculty include 108 women and 71 men, 70 of whom live on campus. They hold baccalaureate and advanced degrees, including 104 master's and 15 doctoral degrees, representing study at such colleges and universities as Brown, Bucknell, Carnegie Mellon, Columbia, Cranbrook Academy of Art, Dartmouth, Denison, DePauw, Dickinson, Gallaudet, Hamilton, Harvard, Lafayette, Miami University, Middlebury, Oakland University, Oberlin, Ohio State, Princeton, Stanford, Syracuse, Temple, Trinity, Vanderbilt, Wayne State, Wesleyan, Xavier, and the Universities of Angers (France), Bridgeport, California (Los Angeles, Santa Barbara), Detroit, Illinois, Michigan, Minnesota, Nebraska, Vermont, and Wisconsin.

Registered nurses staff the Health Centers, a doctor visits the campus twice weekly, and hospital facilities are readily accessible. The Schools also employ the services of five consulting psychologists, two full-time counselors, and an athletic trainer.

STUDENT BODY. In 1999–2000, Cranbrook Schools enrolled 1575 students as follows: 506 in the Lower School, 324 in the Middle School, and 745 in the Upper School, 253 of whom were boarders. They came from 20 states and 17 foreign countries and reflected a diversity of races, ethnic origins, and religious beliefs.

ACADEMIC PROGRAM. The school year, from September to June, is divided into semesters, with Thanksgiving recess, winter and spring vacations, and observances of national holidays.

The program at Brookside has been carefully developed to introduce children to academic skills in a positive learning environment. Traditionally, Brookside has been a school with a strong commitment from parents, faculty, and administration. The teachers' careful and thoughtful instruction takes place in a nurturing way with special attention tailored to each child's specific needs and style of learning. The focus is on strong academics and a balance of the fine arts in a liberal arts education. Homework is introduced gradually and varies according to grade level. Students participate in art, music, drama, science, Spanish, computers, visual studies, health, physical education, and library classes with specialists. Grades 4 and 5 have a departmental system with one teacher for reading and language arts, another for mathematics and social studies, and specialists for all the additional classes.

The single-sex program on separate campuses in the middle schools accommodates the specific physical, emotional, and learning differences between boys and girls in the adolescent years. The Middle School schedule is divided into trimesters. The core curriculum consists of English, mathematics, science, and social science with particular emphasis on the basics of writing and math. In addition, students participate in fine and performing arts, foreign language, computers, and physical education. Grade 6 has a week of outdoor education programs, and Grades 7 and 8 travel to such places as Boston, Toronto, West Virginia, and Washington, D.C.

Students in Grades 6–8 participate in interscholastic athletics that promote teamwork rather than competition. The Middle School schedule also incorporates time for photography, publications, games, and other pursuits.

Recognized nationwide for academic excellence, Cranbrook Kingswood Upper School has been named an Exemplary School by the U.S. Department of Education. The curriculum is college preparatory, offering a broad selection of courses in English, math, science, history and social science, foreign language, religion, computer science, and the performing and fine arts. To graduate, students must earn a minimum of 4 credits in

English, 3 in mathematics, 2 each in foreign language and history/social science, 2 in science, and 1 each in religion and fine/performing arts. They must also satisfy a computer requirement by taking Computer Applications or passing prescribed diagnostic tests. Most students carry at least five courses each semester.

Advanced Placement and/or honors-level courses are available in the following departments: English, History, Science, Mathematics, Foreign Language, and Computer Science. Among the semester and yearlong courses offered in the Upper School are English 9, Expository Writing, Western Literary Traditions, Shakespeare, Satire, Current Literature, Literature and Film, Modern Voices of Doubt, Writing Workshop; Algebra I–II, Geometry, Pre-Calculus, Introductory Calculus, Calculus AB, Advanced Calculus; Latin I–II, Cicero & Ovid, Vergil, French I–V, Spanish I–IV, German I–IV; Earth Science, Measurement and Analysis, Biology, Chemistry, Physics, Anatomy and Physiology, Astronomy, Environmental Science, Geology, Genetics, Botany; Patterns in Civilization, United States History, American Studies, Russia and Eastern Europe, Principles of Psychology, Great Decisions, Economics, Model UN, Great Books; History of Religion, Western Religions, Ethics, World Religions; Concert Choir, Madrigals, The MasterSingers, Concert Band, Symphony Band, Orchestra, Dance I–IV, Acting and Theatre, Speech; Basic Design, Drawing, Painting, Photography, Drawing Studio, Ceramics Studio, Sculpture, Weaving/Fibers, Metalsmithing/Creative Jewelry; and Computer Applications and Computer Science.

Sophomores go on a Wilderness Expedition, a two-week backpacking trip in Tennessee's Great Smoky Mountains.

Qualified seniors can explore career interests or acquire technical proficiency in a field of interest through the three-week Senior May Project.

Ninety-nine percent of the 189 members of the Class of 1999 have enrolled in college. The choices include Amherst, Art Institute of Chicago, Boston University, Brown, Carnegie Mellon, Clark, Colby, Colorado College, Columbia, Cornell, Denison, Duke, Emory, Indiana University, Johns Hopkins, Massachusetts Institute of Technology, McGill, Michigan State, New York University, Northwestern, Oberlin, Ohio State, Princeton, Rhode Island School of Design, Spelman, Tulane, Vassar, Wake Forest, Washington University, Wellesley, Williams, Yale, and the Universities of Chicago, Colorado, Michigan, Notre Dame, Pennsylvania, Vermont, and Wisconsin.

STUDENT ACTIVITIES. Student Council is a coalition of Upper School students, faculty, and administrators formed to review school policies and plan special events. Dorm councils and the Dining Hall Committee work to improve student life; Cabinet organizes community outreach projects; and the All Campus Activities Committee organizes events for boarders and day students.

Upper School students publish *Brook/Woodwinds* (yearbook), *Crane-Clarion* (newspaper), and *Gallimaufry* (literary arts magazine). Other interest groups include African American Awareness Association, Amnesty International, Asian American Cultural Society, Ergasterion (drama support group), Forensics, Gold Key, Jazz Band, Varsity, SADD, World, French, Spanish, German, and Latin clubs.

Seventy athletic teams (varsity, junior varsity, freshman) are formed, including soccer, tennis, track, cross-country, football, basketball, skiing, golf, wrestling, hockey, swimming, lacrosse, and baseball for boys; and field hockey, soccer, basketball, volleyball, swimming, cross-country, softball, tennis, lacrosse, ice hockey, skiing, golf, and track for girls. Biking, ice-skating, bowling, dance, martial arts, and strength and fitness are also available.

Special traditions are observed each year such as Convocation, the White Gifts Assembly, Parent's Weekend, Christmas Pageant, Junior Ring Ceremony, and Commencement.

ADMISSION AND COSTS. Cranbrook Schools welcome students of sound academic ability, character, motivation, and, for those entering Middle and Upper school, participation in extra-curricular activities.

In 1999–2000, tuition for day students ranges from $6660 for half-day Prekindergarten to $16,100 for Grades 9–12. Boarding tuition is $22,980. Financial aid is available based on need, and tuition payment and tuition refund plans are offered.

Director of Schools: Arlyce Seibert
Head of the Lower School: Brian Schiller
Head of the Girls Middle School: Rebecca Dickinson
Head of the Boys Middle School: Larry Ivens
Head of the Upper School: George Swope
Director of Administrative Services: Matt Berg
Director of Athletics: Jeff Vennell
Director of Admissions: D. Scott Looney

Detroit Country Day School

BEVERLY HILLS

22305 West 13 Mile Road, Beverly Hills, MI 48025. 248-646-7717; Fax 248-646-2458; Web Site www.dcds.edu

DETROIT COUNTRY DAY SCHOOL in Beverly Hills, Michigan, is a college preparatory day school for boys and girls in Preschool through Grade 12. The Lower, Junior, Middle, and Upper schools are located on four campuses. Preschool, Junior Kindergarten, Kindergarten, Grades 1 and 2 are on the Maple Road Campus at 3003 West Maple Road (Telephone 248-433-1050); Grades 3–5 are on the Village Campus at 3600 Bradway Boulevard (Telephone 248-647-2522); Grades 6–8 are on the Hillview Campus at 22400 Hillview Lane (Telephone 248-646-7985); and Grades 9–12 are on the 13 Mile Campus at 22305 West 13 Mile Road (Telephone 248-646-7717). Beverly Hills is a suburban area 5 miles from Detroit's northern boundary.

In 1914, F. Alden Shaw founded Detroit Country Day School as an all-boys' school located in the city. Girls were admitted to the Lower School in 1941 and the School became fully coeducational in 1972. As enrollment expanded, the School was moved several times before 1957, when the 13 Mile Campus was acquired. In 1975, the Village Campus was purchased, in 1986, the Maple Road Campus was added, and in 1991, the Hillview Campus opened on property adjoining the 13 Mile Campus. In 1999, a 750-seat performing arts center and new science wing opened on the 13 Mile Campus. Detroit Country Day School's mission is "to provide a superior college preparatory, liberal arts educational opportunity to young people of cultural and intellectual diversity. Within a supportive setting, the School promotes the academic, artistic, moral, character, leadership, and physical development of all students."

A nonprofit institution, Detroit Country Day School is directed by a 15-member self-perpetuating Board of Trustees, which includes parents. The School holds membership in the National Association of Independent Schools, among other professional affiliations.

THE CAMPUS. The 13 Mile Campus and the Hillview Campus are located on an 80-acre site within three miles of the 10-acre Maple Road Campus and the 3-acre Village Campus.

On the 13 Mile Campus, the main building contains administrative offices, a performing arts center, classrooms, language and science laboratories, art studios, music and computer rooms, a library, two gymnasiums, and facilities for weight and fitness training. The adjacent Learning Center provides a multipurpose area for assemblies, classrooms, and kitchen facilities. Ten all-weather tennis courts, an outdoor swimming pool, an all-weather track, and athletic fields complete this campus.

On the Hillview Campus is a newly completed three-story building, which houses 20 classrooms, 5 science laboratories, art and music studios, computer rooms, a library, a dining room, and offices.

The Village Campus features a Tudor-style building containing classrooms, a science laboratory, a library, an art room, a music-dance studio, offices, a gymnasium, and kitchen facilities.

On the Maple Road Campus, a one-story building houses classrooms, a library, a gymnasium, and art, speech, French, science, music, and activities rooms. There are also offices, a clinic, and kitchen facilities.

THE FACULTY. Gerald T. Hansen (B.A. Northern Michigan, M.A. Rutgers) is Headmaster and Glen P. Shilling (B.A. Albion, M.Div. Harvard, J.D. University of Detroit) is Assistant Headmaster.

The Directors are Bradley M. Gilman (B.A. Dartmouth, M.A. Occidental) for the Upper School, Cynthia Goldberg (B.A. Central Michigan University, M.A. Michigan State) for the Middle School, Joseph D'Angelo (B.S. University of Detroit, M.A. Wayne State) for the Junior School, and Ruth Rebold (B.A. Michigan State, M.A.T. Oakland University) for the Lower School.

There are 179 full-time faculty members and administrators who teach and 5 part-time teachers, 53 men and 131 women. They hold 104 master's and 12 doctoral degrees from 85 colleges and universities. Among the schools attended are Albion, Amherst, Dartmouth, Drake, Georgetown, Harvard, Kalamazoo, Princeton, Rutgers, and the Universities of Michigan and Notre Dame.

There are three full-time registered nurses. The School is

located three miles from a hospital, and first-aid equipment is available on campus.

STUDENT BODY. In 1999–2000, Detroit Country Day School enrolled 1504 students, 668 girls and 836 boys. There are 290 students in Lower School (Preschool–Grade 2), 239 in Junior School (Grades 3–5), 371 in Middle School (Grades 6–8), and 604 in Upper School (Grades 9–12).

The students, 3 to 18 years of age, reside in 55 nearby communities. A Cottage Boarding program enables a limited number of students to live on campus with faculty families.

ACADEMIC PROGRAM. The school year runs from early September to mid-June. The calendar includes Thanksgiving, winter, midwinter, and spring vacations.

The average class size is 15 pupils. Students have opportunities to take both art and music classes every year. The Middle and Upper schools operate on a rotating schedule. Class periods are scheduled from 8:00 A.M. to 2:50 P.M. for the Middle School and 3:20 P.M. for the Upper School, followed by athletics for Grades 7–12. Grades 6–8 have several weekly assemblies and daily activity periods. Grades 9–12 have weekly assemblies and activities. Grades 11 and 12 may use the commons room at their discretion.

A new computer-based learning program, one of only a few in the nation, requires all Middle and Upper School students and faculty to have laptop computers for class exercises, homework, tests, research, and other functions. Some 1200 notebook computers are networked to provide Internet resources and improve communication among students, faculty, and parents.

Grade reports are sent to parents every ten weeks in the Middle School and every eight weeks in the Upper School. Marks are posted quarterly in the Upper School and three times a year in the Middle School. All teachers participate in an adviser-advisee program and are available to give tutorial assistance.

The Lower and Junior schools foster early academic development and values through a broad-based, integrated, stimulating curriculum that includes basic instruction in language arts, math, social studies, science, French, the arts, movement education, and computer science. A PM program of enrichment activities is also held after school. The faculty are dedicated to meeting the needs of the whole child and developing character through exposure to time-honored values.

The Middle School curriculum offers basic subjects, supplemented with enrichment courses for qualified students. Among the courses are English, Writing, French, Spanish, Latin, German, History, Geography, Mathematics, Pre-Algebra, Algebra, Geometry, Computers, General Science, Chemistry, C.A.R.E. Program related to adolescent growth and development, Art, Music, and Physical Education. Interdisciplinary classes are also offered.

To graduate, students must complete requirements in three categories: academic, athletic, and activities. Academic credit requirements include English 4, foreign language 3, history 3, mathematics 3, science 2, and fine and performing arts 1. Students must also complete courses in Speech and Health Education. Additional requirements include sports and fitness and skill- and service-oriented activities.

Flexible scheduling allows Upper School students to take more than one class in a particular area of concentration. Among the yearlong courses are French, German, Latin, Spanish; World History, Contemporary World History, American Studies, European History; Geometry, AB and BC Calculus, College Algebra; Advanced Biology, Advanced Physics, Advanced Chemistry; Comparative World Literature, Theory of Knowledge; and Advanced Harmony and Composition. Advanced Placement study is available in English, foreign languages (including Latin), history, mathematics, computer sciences, and other sciences. Interdisciplinary courses are offered in mathematics and physics.

Typical semester electives are Shakespeare, The Tragic Hero, Modern Themes in Literature, The American Novel; American Legal History, The Supreme Court and Civil Rights; Microbiology, Ecology, Human Genetics, Bioethics, Zoology, Environmental Science; and Painting and Drawing, Ceramics, and Photography.

Honors courses are available at all levels. The Advanced Placement Program is designed for students who are progressing at a rapid pace in a particular subject. Qualified students are offered the opportunity to enroll in the demanding International Baccalaureate program. Graduates of this two-year liberal arts curriculum are eligible for admission to universities throughout the world or for sophomore standing in most American colleges and universities.

Detroit Country Day School and the local business and professional community cooperate in the Senior Project. Students in Grade 12 spend four weeks as observers and interns in such fields as architecture, advertising, medicine, law, and banking.

In 1999, all 142 of the graduating seniors entered college. They are attending such institutions as Albion, Colgate, Columbia, Cornell, Dartmouth, Georgetown, Harvard, Johns Hopkins, Massachusetts Institute of Technology, Michigan State, Northwestern, Princeton, Rensselaer, Yale, and the Universities of Michigan and Pennsylvania.

During the summer, Detroit Country Day School conducts both academic and recreational programs. The five-week academic program offers Enrichment and Tutorial classes for students in Kindergarten–Grade 12, a writing workshop, an Advanced Math and Science Academy, and a five-week Study Skills course for students in Grades 6–9. The Day Camp and tennis, soccer, baseball, lacrosse, field hockey, basketball, and other sports camps provide recreational activities.

STUDENT ACTIVITIES. Participation in activities is required for graduation. Directed by students, with help from faculty advisers, these include the yearbook, literary magazine, and newspaper; the Student Government; the drama, photography, art, community service, computer, debate, and foreign language clubs; Contemporary Issues; the Model United Nations; Quiz Bowl; Academic Games; and others.

Detroit Country Day School athletic teams compete with area public and private schools. Teams are formed in soccer, lacrosse, football, cross-country, basketball, hockey, wrestling, baseball, tennis, track, field hockey, volleyball, skiing, swimming, softball, cheerleading, and golf. Strength and conditioning is offered as an alternative to competitive sports.

Throughout the year, there are assemblies, dances, dramatic productions, concerts, lectures, films, and field trips. Extended trips include Space Camp in Huntsville, Alabama (Grade 5), and Washington, D.C. (Grade 8). Traditional events for the school community include Auction, Scholar/Athlete Dinner, Homecoming, Parents' Night, athletic banquets, an ice cream social, and the Alumni-Varsity Basketball and Ice Hockey games.

ADMISSION AND COSTS. Detroit Country Day School seeks

students who show evidence of "ability, ambition, achievement, character, and discipline." The School has a policy of socioeconomic diversification, enrolling students "without regard for race, creed, or ethnic origin." Admission is highly competitive and is based on previous school records, entrance examinations, recommendations, and an interview. The entrance examinations, which are given by appointment only, consist of the Educational Records Bureau Assessment tests and the Otis Lennon aptitude and intelligence test. New students are accepted for all grades. There is a $50 application and testing fee.

Tuition ranges from $10,530 for all-day Pre-Kindergarten to $16,130 for the Upper School. This basic fee covers lunches, athletic uniforms, tutoring and study skills, and reading evaluations. Among the additional expenses are books, laptop computers, transportation, personal athletic equipment, field trips, and school uniforms. Tuition payment plans and tuition insurance are available. Detroit Country Day, which subscribes to the Tuition Aid Data Services, awarded financial aid to 189 boys and girls in 1999–2000. Financial aid is given on the basis of financial need, citizenship, prior academic performance, and leadership.

Deans of Students: Jackqueline Coleman, Joe Hansen, and Betsy
　　Moss (Upper School); Stan Chodun, Judy Leybourn, and
　　Lisa Zimmerman (Middle School)
Alumni Director: Terri Ross Morawski
Director of Admission: Jorge D. Prosperi
Director of Development: Scott C. Bertschy
College Counselor: Anne Sandoval
Director of Athletics: Dan MacLean

Eton Academy   1980

*1755 Melton, Birmingham, MI 48009. 248-642-1150;
　Fax 248-642-3670; E-mail eton@aol.com*

Eton Academy provides a supportive educational environment for students of average or above-average ability who have dyslexia or other learning disabilities. It enrolls 140 day boys and 50 day girls in Grades 1–12 and seeks to develop their academic skills, to instill confidence in their ability to learn, and to prepare them for productive lives. Considerable individual instruction, career counseling, and computerized instruction are integral to the program. Publications, sports, arts and crafts, dances, and other recreation are among the activities. Tuition: $12,725–$14,300. Financial Aid: $150,000. Mrs. Sharon Morey is Director of Admissions; Mary Bramson Van der Tuin (Wellesley, B.A. 1961; Michigan State University, M.A. 1992) is Headmistress. *North Central Association.*

Everest Academy   CLARKSTON

*5935 Clarkston Road, Clarkston, MI 48348. 248-620-3390;
　Fax 248-620-3942*

Everest academy in Clarkston, Michigan, is a Roman Catholic elementary and middle school conducted by the Legionaries of Christ, enrolling boys and girls as day students in Preschool through Grade 8 and boys as boarders in Grades 6 through 8. The village of Clarkston is located at the head of several small lakes surrounded by a chain of tree-covered hills, and the school is 1.5 miles from Interstate 75. The region enjoys the quiet charm and pastoral beauty of the rural countryside while providing accessibility to the cultural and educational resources of Detroit and Flint, both within an hour's drive. Pine Knob Music Theater, 5 minutes from the

school, attracts more than a million visitors each summer. The area also provides skiing and water sports, popular recreational activities for students.

Set on a 90-acre campus, Everest Academy is the only Catholic school for miles in a developing northern area of Oakland County. The school opened in September 1992 with 20 students, now enrolls 430, and continues to grow.

The school's name reflects its motto, "Always Higher," which refers to its pursuit of high academic and spiritual ideals. Everest Academy operates under the guidance of the Legionaries of Christ, a religious order founded in 1941. The Legion of Christ presently directs more than 100 educational institutions, including primary and secondary schools, universities, and postgraduate institutes. As educators, the primary objective of the Legion of Christ is to develop in each child a sense of justice, sincerity, honesty, teamwork, and loyalty that will form the basis of his or her ethical and religious conduct. Academic standards demand the best effort from students. Instruction in the Catholic faith is provided.

THE CAMPUS. The spacious Everest Academy campus features the original school building, which contains classrooms, a chapel, language and computer laboratories, and administrative offices. In 1996, to accommodate its steady enrollment increase, the Academy added 52,000 square feet of space that includes a boys' dormitory, a dining room, a gymnasium, a stage, an indoor swimming pool, and a kitchen designed to serve 900 people. Plans call for the construction of a high school by the year 2002 with a capacity for 500 students.

THE FACULTY. Richard W. Cross is Director of the Boys School, and Jenny Sysko is the Director of the Girls and Elementary Schools. There are approximately 45 teachers and administrators on staff, including two priests who serve as chaplains.

STUDENT BODY. In 1999–2000, Everest Academy is coeducational in Preschool through Grade 3, with an enrollment of 322 children. Grades 4 through 8 are separated by gender, with 47 girls in one division and 61 boys in the other.

ACADEMIC PROGRAM. The school year, divided into nine-week quarters, begins in late August and extends to early June.

Progress reports and grades are sent to parents after quarterly examinations. A low student-teacher ratio ensures that each child receives individualized attention, and teachers are available for scheduled conferences each afternoon until 3:30 P.M. Homework is assigned daily and varies according to subject and grade level. All students wear uniforms and adhere to a dress code. After-school care is available.

Classes are held five days a week from 8:35 A.M. to 3:10 P.M., with a typical day consisting of seven 40-minute periods and a lunch break. Daily Mass is celebrated, and students are welcome to attend on a voluntary basis.

The core curriculum includes mathematics, English, science, social studies, and Spanish. Course work in the lower grades is designed to provide children with a strong foundation in math concepts and phonics, spelling, and writing. As they progress, students undertake more challenging assignments that build on the skills acquired in the earlier grades. The curriculum is enriched throughout by computer studies, art, music, and physical education. Religion is taught at all levels.

International students in Grades 6–8, who constitute less than 10 percent of the total enrollment, are thoroughly immersed in their English-speaking environment and participate fully in the regular academic and extracurricular programs of the Academy. Tutorial programs and individual tutoring can be arranged as needed.

STUDENT ACTIVITIES. Everest Academy's extracurricular program includes after-school sports such as street hockey, basketball, track, soccer, volleyball, swimming, and flag football. Students may also take part in tennis, ski, and soccer clinics according to season. Everest considers sports an important element in the formation of character since athletes are expected always to do their best, display teamwork, respect the authority of the coaches and officials, and obey the rules.

Other activities include the Christmas show, various plays and talent shows, academic competitions, and field trips to museums, historic sites, and the aquarium as well as organized outings for hiking, fishing, boating, horseback riding, skating, and skiing.

During the Christmas vacation, Academy students from overseas make a ten-day trip to Rome where they attend Christmas Eve Mass in St. Peter's and take part in an audience with the Pope. During the Easter holiday, they make a one-week trip to Washington, D.C., and New York City.

Other activities on the school calendar are the Back to School Reception, annual auction fund-raiser, Christmas Program, Spring Luncheon/Children's Fashion Show, the May Crowning, Field Days and Olympics, and the Awards Ceremony and end-of-year picnic.

ADMISSION AND COSTS. Everest Academy welcomes students of average or above-average ability who have the character and willingness to take full advantage of the school's academic, cultural, human, and religious offerings. The Academy does not discriminate on the basis of race, color, or national and ethnic origin in the administration of its admission policies. Admissions decisions are based on an interview, entrance testing, and past records of academics and behavior. A fee of $50 covers the application process and testing, with a $250 registration fee due following notification of acceptance. The Everest Academy "Adopt-a-Family" program aids incoming families in adjusting to the new school environment.

In 1999–2000, day tuition ranged from $2000 in the Preschool to $3950 in Kindergarten–Grade 8. Boarding tuition information is available upon request. Reductions are given for families with more than two students enrolled.

Headmaster: Richard W. Cross
Dean of Academics: Paul Flynn
Business Manager: John Lutz
Chaplains: Fr. Lorenzo Gomez, LC, and Fr. Juan Guerra, LC
Administrator: Br. Donald Kaufman, LC

Gibson School   1972

12925 Fenton Avenue, Redford, MI 48239. 313-537-8688; Fax 313-537-0233; E-mail GIBSON@AGIS.NET; Web Site www.gibsonschool.org

Gibson School, enrolling students ages 4–13, is a coeducational day school for intellectually gifted children. A Child Development Center serves children ages 2½ to 5. The School strives to challenge students to their potential, nourish their desire to learn, and encourage them to be self-confident individuals. A core curriculum (language arts, mathematics, science, and social studies), tailored to meet individual student needs, is enriched by classes in art, computer science, Spanish, library science, music, and physical education. Financial aid and latchkey programs are available. Tuition: $7400. Carol Green is Admissions Director; Suzanne M. Young serves as Director.

Greenhills School   1968

850 Greenhills Drive, Ann Arbor, MI 48105. 734-769-4010;
 Fax 734-769-5029; E-mail admission@greenhillsschool.org;
 Web Site www.greenhillsschool.org

Greenhills School is a college preparatory day school enrolling 240 boys and 268 girls in Grades 6–12. Founded by several families to broaden educational opportunities in the Ann Arbor area, the School offers a challenging, traditional liberal arts program and emphasizes creative expression as well as the development of critical thinking and communication skills. Activities include forensics, publications, athletics, and numerous interest clubs. Summer programs include a writing camp and a tennis camp. Tuition: $10,910. Financial Aid: $363,300. Melvin Rhoden is Director of Admission; John Anthony Paulus II (Stanford, B.A. 1972; Boston University, M.Ed. 1979) was appointed Head of School in 1993.

The Grosse Pointe Academy

GROSSE POINTE FARMS

171 Lake Shore Road, Grosse Pointe Farms, MI 48236.
 313-886-1221; Fax 313-886-4615

THE GROSSE POINTE ACADEMY in Grosse Pointe Farms, Michigan, is an independent day school enrolling boys and girls in a Montessori Early School (ages 2½–5) and Grades 1 through 8. Grosse Pointe Farms is a suburb located six miles northeast of downtown Detroit and is the central community of the five Grosse Pointes. The school makes extensive use of the museums and other cultural resources of Detroit. The Academy operates its own bus service for students, which enables the school to serve families from the Detroit metropolitan area.

The Grosse Pointe Academy was founded as the Academy of the Sacred Heart in 1885. It was operated by the Religious of the Sacred Heart as a day and boarding primary, middle, and upper school for girls. The Academy's coeducational Montes-

sori Early School was built in 1887. In 1969, the school was reincorporated under the original charter as The Grosse Pointe Academy and ownership was transferred to the Academy Board of Trustees. In September of that year, The Grosse Pointe Academy opened as an independent, coeducational day school with 270 students from metropolitan Detroit enrolled in Pre-Kindergarten through Grade 8.

The Grosse Pointe Academy holds that learning is a continuous and highly personalized process extending throughout life and requires a strong intellectual, moral, and physical foundation. Moral values and Montessori principles, emphasizing attention to individual needs, govern the Early School and are sustained throughout the grades. Ecumenical in outlook and Catholic in tradition, the Academy has Christian Life classes for students in Grades 1–8. Several times a year, the entire school meets for ecumenical religious services.

The Academy is a nonprofit organization governed by a self-perpetuating Board of 25 Trustees, which meets eight times a year. There are approximately 808 living alumnae of the Academy of the Sacred Heart and 994 alumni of The Grosse Pointe Academy. The Academy, through its Parent Coordinating Council, operates an active parent volunteer program. Parents, alumni, and friends assist the school financially through Annual Giving and "Action Auction," a yearly fund-raiser involving the entire community.

The Grosse Pointe Academy is a member of the Independent Schools Association of the Central States, the National Association of Independent Schools, the Association of Independent Michigan Schools, the American Montessori Society, and the Educational Records Bureau.

THE CAMPUS. The Academy is situated on a 20-acre campus overlooking Lake St. Clair. The historic facilities, which include a half-mile double row of maples known as the Nun's Walk, appear in local, state, and national registers of historic sites. Four tennis courts, a baseball diamond, a playground, and fields for lacrosse, field hockey, and soccer are located on campus.

The Lakeshore Building, completed in 1885 as the Academy and Convent of the Sacred Heart, now houses business, alumni, and development offices. It is also used for meetings and social functions. The Montessori Early School (circa 1887) has spacious classrooms. An additional classroom and a new gymnasium were added in 1987. The Academy's Main School Building (circa 1929) houses classrooms, a library, a cafeteria, an auditorium, and the school's original gymnasium. The Tracy Fieldhouse gymnasium/auditorium was dedicated in 1990. The Grosse Pointe Academy Chapel (circa 1899) is the site of many weddings and school religious services. Other buildings include the Head of School's residence (circa 1937) and the caretaker's home, known as the Moran House (circa 1855). The school-owned plant is valued at more than $10,000,000.

THE FACULTY. Thomas G. Lengel (Yale University, B.A. 1981; Rutgers University, M.A. 1990) is the Academy's fourth Head of School. He is the former Head of Stuart Hall School for Boys in San Francisco, California. At Delbarton School in Morristown, New Jersey, Mr. Lengel served as Director of Admissions and Financial Aid, taught United States History, and coached junior varsity hockey and Middle School lacrosse. He has been trustee and secretary of Project Discover, a year-round enrichment program for San Francisco inner-city youth in Grades 3–6. Mr. Lengel and his wife, Disty Reeves Lengel, have three sons.

The full-time faculty consist of 7 men and 33 women. They hold 45 baccalaureate degrees from Albion, Baldwin-Wallace, Barat College, Central Michigan, College of St. Catherine, Denison, Eastern Michigan 5, Georgia State, Gettysburg, Kalamazoo, Marygrove 3, Mercy, Miami University, Michigan State, Nazareth, Northern Illinois, Northwestern, Saginaw Valley, St. Mary's College, St. Mary's of Notre Dame, Wayne State 5, Western Michigan, and the Universities of Akron, Dayton, Denver, Detroit, Indiana, Maryland, and Michigan 2. They hold 13 advanced degrees from Boston College, Eastern Michigan, Marygrove, Middlebury College, Wayne State, and the University of Detroit.

Faculty benefits include health and dental insurance, life insurance, long-term disability, a retirement plan, and Social Security. Leaves of absence are granted on approval of the Board of Trustees.

A school nurse is on duty at the Academy and three hospitals are located nearby.

STUDENT BODY. In 1999–2000, the Academy enrolled 210 boys and 212 girls in Early School through Grade 8. The enrollment was distributed as follows: Early School—117, Grade 1—33, Grade 2—40, Grade 3—38, Grade 4—34, Grade 5—27, Grade 6—44, Grade 7—44, and Grade 8—45. Students came from the Grosse Pointes and 32 metropolitan Detroit communities and reflected a wide range of socioeconomic backgrounds.

ACADEMIC PROGRAM. The academic year, divided into semesters, begins in early September and ends in mid-June. Vacations are scheduled at Christmas and in the spring. Classes are held five days a week between 8:30 A.M. and 3:20 P.M. In the Early School, students are taught on an individualized basis, using Montessori methods of education. No more than ten children are in the charge of each adult. Grades 1–3 are in self-contained classrooms and Grades 4 and 5 provide a transition to the fully departmentalized programs of Grades 6–8. The emphasis on individual attention is maintained throughout the Middle School years. Academy teachers pride themselves on enabling students to achieve in all areas and are available to assist students as necessary. Grades are sent to parents four times a year supplemented by regular conferences scheduled in October and February.

All students in Grades 1–5 take reading, language arts (including spelling, vocabulary, writing, grammar, and literature), French, social studies, mathematics, computers, science, religion, music, art, library/reference skills, and physical education. The emphasis is on mastery of basic skills. Both French and Spanish are offered beginning in Grade 6. Multitexts and teacher-designed programs for reinforcement and enrichment are used so that each student can progress at his or her level. Computers, videotapes, and video disks are employed. Electives in music, art, the social sciences, and science supplement the regular program. Instruction in environmental education is also offered. A formalized leadership program is a hallmark of the eighth-grade year.

Before- and After-School Care programs are available, at an extra charge, for children ages 3 to 12 on a daily or occasional basis.

Students graduating from The Grosse Pointe Academy enroll at private, parochial, and public high schools. In recent years, graduates have attended the Academy of the Sacred Heart, Andrews School, Cranbrook, DeLaSalle Collegiate, Detroit Country Day, Fay School, Grosse Pointe North, Grosse Pointe South, The Gunnery, Hotchkiss, The Hun School of Princeton, Kingswood, Lake Forest Academy, The Leelanau

School, Lutheran East, Marian High School, Mercy, Our Lady Star of the Sea, Pomfret, Portsmouth Abbey, Proctor, St. George's School, St. Mark's, University Liggett School, University of Detroit High School, Westover School, and Woodberry Forest.

Academy Adventures, a summer program for boys and girls ages 10 to 15, offers a variety of learning opportunities.

STUDENT ACTIVITIES. Two representatives from each Middle School group are elected to the Student Council, which chooses its own officers. The Council operates the bookstore and a number of extracurricular programs.

Students are involved in school activities through the yearbook, crafts, and cooking. After-school activities include band and piano and violin lessons. Grades 4–8 participate in volunteer services and fund-raising for organizations such as UNICEF and Focus HOPE. Grades 7 and 8 perform 20 hours of community service each year.

Middle School teams compete with other private schools in soccer, basketball, baseball, track, and tennis for boys; and tennis, basketball, volleyball, track, and softball for girls. Teams from Grades 4 and 5 play limited interscholastic schedules.

Intramural sports programs, which begin in first grade, include soccer, cross-country, basketball, softball, and track.

Special events include Back to School Picnic, Parents' Orientation Nights, Fall and Winter/Spring Sports Awards Assemblies, Alumni Reunions, Book Fair, Christmas Concert, Alumni Scholarship Benefit, Dads' Day, Grandparents' Day, Spring Musical, and the William Charles McMillan III Lecture Series.

ADMISSION AND COSTS. The Grosse Pointe Academy seeks academically strong and motivated students whose parents value the individual attention that accommodates the needs of their children. Students are admitted in all grades with available spaces on the basis of standardized tests, recommendations, and personal interviews. Applications, with a fee of $40, should be submitted before July 1. Students may be admitted during the school year under special conditions.

In 1999–2000, tuition for half-day Early School is $6500; for full-day Early School, $9400; the fees for Grades 1 through 8 range from $9900 to $11,700, depending on grade. Tuition insurance and payment plans are available. The Grosse Pointe Academy subscribes to the School and Student Service for Financial Aid and offers approximately $250,000 in financial aid annually to 13 percent of the students on the basis of need and academic standing.

Principal, Early School and Grades 1–3: Camille DeMario
Principal, Grades 4–8: Patricia Falk, Ed.D.
Director of Informational Technology: W. Scott Tily
Director of Admissions: Molly McDermott
Director of Development: Patricia D. Palm, C.F.R.E.
Director of Finance & Operations: Betty Boaz

Michigan

Interlochen Arts Academy   1962

P.O. Box 199, Interlochen, MI 49643-0199. 231-276-7200;
*   Admissions 231-276-7472; Fax 231-276-7464;*
*   E-mail admissions@interlochen.k12.mi.us;*
*   Web Site www.interlochen.org*

Dr. Joseph Maddy founded the Academy to enable talented young people to develop their creative abilities in a "wholesome community guided by an exemplary faculty of artists and educators." The coeducational school enrolls 425 boarding and day students in Grades 9–Postgraduate. The accelerated college preparatory curriculum includes preprofessional training in visual arts, creative writing, dance, theater arts, and music. Advanced Placement and English as a Second Language are available. A summer camp offers a fine arts program for Grades 3–12. Boarding Tuition: $23,650; Day Tuition: $13,950. Extras: $1250. Financial Aid: $2,750,000. Tom Bewley is Admissions Director; Tim Wade is Dean of Education.

Kalamazoo Academy   1979

4221 East Milham Road, Kalamazoo, MI 49002. 616-329-0116;
*   Fax 616-329-1850; Web Site www.remc12.k12.mi.us/Kalamazoo-*
*   Academy*

Kalamazoo Academy, founded by a group of families interested in providing quality education in the area, enrolls 250 day boys and girls in Pre-School–Grade 8. It aims to provide a supportive environment that emphasizes active learning, enhancement of self-esteem, and promotion of individual talents and community responsibility. French, Spanish, computers, music, art, and drama complement the traditional subjects. Students with learning differences are accommodated. Science fair, speech festival, Student Council, ski club, and sports are among the activities. Tuition: $4412–$5680. Financial aid is available. Sheila Bridenstine (Saint Louis University, A.B.) is Director.

Kingsbury School   1953

5000 Hosner Road, Oxford, MI 48370. 248-628-2571;
*   Fax 248-628-3612; E-mail Kingsburys@aol.com;*
*   Web Site www.kingsburyschool.org*

Founded by Carlton and Annette Higbie, the Kingsbury School is a day school enrolling 170 boys and girls in Junior Kindergarten–Grade 8. The School seeks to recognize individual needs and develop individual potential. In addition to core subjects, students are involved at every level in Spanish, music, environmental education, art, computers, and physical education.

Grades 6–8 are fully departmentalized. Competitive and recreational sports are available all year round. A summer program offers nature, sports, art, and computer courses. Tuition: $7800–$8800. Financial aid is available. Annette Mueller is Director of Admissions; Andrew K. Smith (Haverford, B.A. 1974; Harvard Graduate School of Education, Ed.M. 1982) was appointed Head of School in 1998.

Kensington Academy   1968

32605 Bellvine Trail, Beverly Hills, MI 48025.
*   248-647-8060; Fax 248-647-4239; E-mail dtloken@moa.net*

Founded by a group of Catholic parents, Kensington Academy is an independent, elementary day school enrolling 218 students in coeducational Pre-Kindergarten–Grade 8. Its goal is to help each student develop self-confidence and strong study habits to prepare for the challenges of high school. A broad exposure to art, music, drama, computers, and Spanish is provided. Physical education is offered in all grades, and interscholastic sports are organized in Grades 5–8. Tuition: $9900. Financial aid is available. Deborah Trojan is Director of Admission; Thomas J. Herbst (St. Joseph's College, B.S.; Michigan State, M.A.) was appointed Headmaster in 1983.

The Leelanau School   GLEN ARBOR

One Old Homestead Road, Glen Arbor, MI 49636. 231-334-5800;
*   Admissions 231-334-5820 or 800-LEELANAU;*
*   E-mail admissions@leelanau.org; Web Site www.leelanau.org*

THE LEELANAU SCHOOL in Glen Arbor, Michigan, is a nondenominational, college preparatory boarding and day school enrolling boys and girls in Grades 9 through 12. Leelanau, which means "land of delight," is located in the heart of Sleeping Bear Dunes National Lakeshore, 1½ miles north of Glen Arbor. The campus overlooks Lake Michigan's Sleeping Bear Bay, Manitou Island, and the Crystal River. Glen Arbor, a summer and winter resort community in cherry-growing country, is 30 miles from Traverse City, 260 miles from Detroit, and 340 miles from Chicago. Traverse City is served by three major airlines and a public bus service.

The School was founded in 1929 by William "Skipper" Beals and his wife, Cora, both teachers at The Principia in St. Louis, as an outgrowth of a boys' camp they had run for several years. A girls' school, Pinebrook, was established in 1940. The schools were incorporated in 1963 and merged to form The Leelanau School in 1969.

The mission of The Leelanau School is "to inspire, encourage, and support the discovery and fulfillment of individual potential" through a caring, familylike atmosphere, stimulating learning environment, and hands-on educational programs.

The School provides opportunities for well-rounded development—intellectually, morally, physically, socially, and spiritually. It seeks to set an example of high moral standards, cultivating self-discipline and engendering the ability to make right decisions based on Judeo-Christian values. Leelanau prepares high school students for success in college—and life—and fosters a sense of stewardship for the environment through the use of campus and area resources throughout the curriculum.

The Leelanau School is a nonprofit organization governed by a self-perpetuating Board of Trustees. There are 2700 living alumni. The School is certified by the State of Michigan, accredited by the Independent Schools Association of the Central States, and a member of the National Association of Independent Schools and the Association of Independent Michigan Schools, among other affiliations.

THE CAMPUS. The 50-acre campus includes a wildlife preserve, beaches, dunes, wetlands, a river, and a heavily wooded forest.

The main school building (1952, 1966) includes classrooms, a greenhouse, an auditorium, a 10,000-volume library/study area, and the administrative center. Kindel Dormitory for boys was dedicated in 1968, and Pinebrook, the girls' dormitory, was built in 1974. In 1987, the Karman Activities Center was added to the Student Center (1972), a complex that includes recreational facilities and a dining room as well as the School's business operations. A gymnasium was constructed in 1975, and, in 1976, the Lanphier family donated an observatory complete with a 14-inch telescope and classrooms. The Cora Mautz Beals Visual Art Center was completed in 1991. Athletic facilities include four outdoor tennis courts, a baseball diamond, a soccer field, and a track. Downhill and cross-country ski facilities are available nearby.

THE FACULTY. Timothy A. Daniel, a graduate of Deerfield Academy, Northwestern University (B.A.), and the University of Tulsa (M.A.), was appointed President and Head of School in 1997. Prior to his appointment at Leelanau, Mr. Daniel served as a teacher and administrator at three other independent secondary schools: Portsmouth Abbey School in Rhode Island, Memphis University School in Tennessee, and The Grand River Academy in Ohio.

There are 12 full-time teachers, seven men and five women, and two part-time teachers. The faculty and administration hold 20 baccalaureate, 9 master's degrees, and 1 Juris Doctorate from Adrian College, The College of Social Work (Denmark), DePaul, Eastern Michigan, Grand Valley, Hillsdale, Hope, Kalamazoo, Keller School of Management, Lesley, Michigan State, Nazareth, Northwestern, Ohio State, Ohio Wesleyan, Olivet, Saginaw Valley, Saint Mary's University, Western Michigan, West Virginia, and the Universities of Arizona, Hartford, Massachusetts, Michigan, Missouri, New Hampshire, Tulsa, Val-

paraiso, and Wisconsin. Faculty benefits include health and life insurance, a retirement plan, and funds for professional development through the Weatherwax Endowment.

The health center is supervised by a registered nurse. There is emergency medical service available in Glen Arbor and a hospital in Traverse City.

STUDENT BODY. In 1999–2000, Leelanau enrolls 39 boarding boys, 4 day boys, 26 boarding girls, and 2 day girls in Grades 9–12. Seven states and five foreign countries are currently represented in the student body.

ACADEMIC PROGRAM. The school year is divided into semesters and extends from early September to late May. There is a one-week break at the October midterm, one week at Thanksgiving and the February Midterm, and extended breaks at Christmas and in March. The school day begins with breakfast at 8:00 A.M. and concludes with "lights out" at 10:30 P.M. for underclassmen and 11:00 P.M. for seniors and honor students. An all-school assembly and quiet period meet on Monday through Friday mornings before the seven class periods begin. Classes, which average ten students, are 45 minutes in length. The School offers the Reading Development Program for students who experience difficulty in reading, spelling, and comprehension.

The School believes that each student must be effectively instructed in the uses of language, the fundamentals of mathematics, and the development of disciplined study habits. Students are normally required to take five courses a term. To earn a diploma, a student must take four years of English; three years of mathematics, science, and history; and two consecutive years of a foreign language. Other requirements include a choice of academic electives; two terms of fine arts; and term electives in health education, computer literacy, and Footsteps, an environmental studies course designed to teach technical proficiency in outdoor skills as well as the good judgment and leadership skills associated with them. Students must also complete the Senior Week program, a senior thesis, and 12 seasons of athletics and physical education, plus the School's work program. Advanced Placement courses are offered in English, science, and history.

Environmental education at Leelanau capitalizes on the School's location to enable each student to appreciate the environment and become a responsible steward of it. Footsteps involves students in outdoor educational experiences five days a week under faculty supervision. All students complete weekend or week-long camping trips, and, in addition, there is an Environmental Studies course in which several instructors team-teach about environmental issues from their unique perspectives, disciplines, and interests.

In 1999, 18 seniors graduated and were accepted to or are attending such institutions as Adrian, Alma, American University in Paris, Arizona State, Carthage, Davenport, Eastern Michigan, Eckerd, Ferris State, Flagler, Grand Valley State, Indiana University, Lake Superior State, Lesley, Maryville, Michigan State, Montclair State, Northeastern, Northland, Northwood, Ohio State, Olivet, Richmond, Roosevelt, Seton Hall, Stetson, Western Michigan, and the Universities of Arizona, Central Florida, Massachusetts, Michigan, New Orleans, Rochester, South Florida, Tampa, Toledo, and Wisconsin.

Two faculty and staff members anchor each of the School's Family Advisory Units. Approximately six students are assigned to each unit, which handles minor discipline and school and social issues, and plans group activities.

The Leelanau School operates a wide variety of summer enrichment programs for students and adults. Continuity of purpose between the School and the enrichment programs is reflected in seminars, conferences, and workshops in the fine arts, outdoor education and recreation, professional development, and personal growth. A Summer School program is offered for students in Grades 8–11.

STUDENT ACTIVITIES. The Student Council, consisting of a President, Vice-President, and Secretary/Treasurer, is elected each fall. Each grade elects two representatives to the Council. The Council meets regularly to discuss issues of concern to students and also plans and moderates the weekly Town Meeting, a gathering of the entire School community. In addition, the Council's President meets regularly with the Head of School. Students are involved in community service and the environmental/recycling group and may become campus tour guides.

Students publish a newspaper (*The Pinetree Press*), a yearbook (*The Signpost*), and a literary magazine. There are a number of special-interest groups and activities such as a camping group. Students usually remain on campus on weekends, and planned activities as well as informal recreational opportunities are available.

The School believes that athletics are an essential complement to its academic offerings, and students are required to participate in either interscholastic sports or physical education every term. Each term must be spent as a participant, manager, trainer, or statistician in an interscholastic sport. Leelanau is a member of the Cherryland Athletic Conference, a two-county association of independent and public schools. Varsity sports include basketball, volleyball, and softball for girls, and basketball and baseball for boys. Soccer, golf, and tennis are coeducational activities. Noncompetitive offerings normally include running, weight training, tennis, cycling, downhill and cross-country skiing, canoeing, and horsemanship.

ADMISSION AND COSTS. The Leelanau School enrolls college-bound students in Grades 9–12. Applicants are admitted to all grades, but primary entry is in Grades 9–10. Candidates must submit the School's application, a current transcript, results of standardized testing, and academic and personal recommenda-

tions. Admission is on a rolling basis with entry available in September and January. There is a $50 application fee.

In 1999–2000, the fee for tuition, room, and board is $21,400. Day tuition is $6000. Books and other supplies are approximately $300. Ski passes, special events, and trips are all at extra cost. Financial aid is awarded on both need and merit and totaled $225,000 in 1999–2000. Incentive rates are available for prepayment, and there is an extended-payment plan. Leelanau also subscribes to the PLEASE and CONSERN loan programs.

Head of School: Timothy A. Daniel
Director of Studies: Robert Karner
Director of Development: Phyllis L. Petty
College Counselor: Sandy Mitchell
Director of Athletics: Duane M. Petty

Marian High School   1959

*7225 Lahser Road, Bloomfield Hills, MI 48301. 248-644-1750;
Fax 248-644-6107; E-mail carolw@marian.pvt.k12.mi.us*

The Sisters of the Immaculate Heart of Mary founded this high school to foster in young women an appreciation of human diversity and to equip them for leadership roles in the global community. Enrolling 600 Catholic and non-Catholic students, Marian High provides a solid college preparatory program underscored by Christian principles in its academic and extracurricular offerings. Thirty honors and Advanced Placement courses are available, and all students take four years of theology. Girls enjoy numerous social, extracurricular, and athletic activities and participate in meaningful liturgies, retreats, and community service. Tuition: $5800. Financial aid is available. Carol Wiseman is Director of Admissions; Sr. Lenore M. Pochelski, IHM, is Principal. *North Central Association.*

Notre Dame Preparatory   1994

*1300 Giddings Road, Pontiac, MI 48340. 248-373-5300;
Fax 248-373-8024; E-mail ndp@ndprep.pvt.k12MI.US; Web Site
www.ndprep.pvt.k12.MI.US*

Notre Dame Preparatory is a Roman Catholic, college preparatory day school enrolling boys and girls in Grades 9–12. Founded by the Marist Fathers and Brothers, the school seeks to develop students as good citizens who respect the dignity of all individuals and who are well prepared for further study in terms of both learning and discipline. Nearly 100 courses are offered, including 14 Advanced Placement courses. A full range of activities, including athletics for girls and boys, is provided. Tuition: $4900. Financial Aid: $168,000. Rev. Leon M. Olszamowski, SM (Boston College, B.A. 1970; Catholic University, M.A. 1980; Ph.D. 1984), was appointed Principal in 1994.

The Roeper School   1941

2190 North Woodward Avenue, Bloomfield Hills, MI 48304.
248-203-7300; Fax 248-203-7350; Web Site www.roeper.org

The Roeper School is a college preparatory day school for gifted children enrolling approximately 640 students in Pre-Kindergarten–Grade 12. Founded by George and Annemarie Roeper, it seeks to "provide an environment that fosters intellectual stimulation, independence, breadth of view, and compassion." The Lower School is in Bloomfield Hills; the Middle/Upper School is in Birmingham. A basic curriculum is enhanced by a broad selection of classes and activities to meet the interests of students. Tuition: $9800–$13,700. Financial Aid: $500,000. Betsy Turner is Admissions Director; Ken Seward (Middlebury College, A.B.; Case Western Reserve University, M.A.) was appointed Head of School in 1998.

The Rudolf Steiner School of Ann Arbor   1980

2775 Newport Road, Ann Arbor, MI 48103. 734-995-4141;
Fax 734-995-4383

Inspired by the philosophy and methods of educator Rudolf Steiner, this coeducational day school is one of more than 700 Waldorf schools worldwide dedicated to the nurturing of the whole child, in body, mind, and spirit. The School enrolls 280 students in Kindergarten–Grade 12. The curriculum, which balances the sciences, the humanities, and the arts, is designed to correspond to children's ability to comprehend as they mature and unfold developmentally and intellectually. Among the courses are French, German, language arts, science, math, music, and art. Tuition: $6300–$7600. Financial aid is available. Daryl Honor is Faculty Chair; Becky Schmitt is Admissions Director.

St. Mary's Preparatory School

ORCHARD LAKE

3535 Indian Trail, Orchard Lake, MI 48324. 248-683-0532;
Fax 248-683-1740

S<small>T. MARY'S PREPARATORY SCHOOL</small> in Orchard Lake, Michigan, is a Roman Catholic college preparatory school enrolling boarding and day boys in Grades 9–12. The School is located in the community of Orchard Lake, an affluent suburban town between Detroit and Pontiac. It is accessible to Detroit Metropolitan Airport and can be reached by car via several major highways. Toledo, Ohio, is 80 miles to the southwest; Chicago is 200 miles distant. In addition to the cultural opportunities found in the Greater Detroit area, students make extensive use of the School's 125-acre campus and 1200-foot lakefront for a variety of athletic and recreational activities.

St. Mary's Preparatory was founded in 1885, along with St. Mary's College and SS. Cyril and Methodius Seminary, by Fr. Joseph Dabrowski, a Polish priest who wanted to establish a complete educational complex for the increasing number of immigrants interested in the priesthood. One hundred and fifteen years later, Father Dabrowski's dream has developed into a community of three distinct schools sharing the same campus.

The School's religious tradition is firmly rooted in the teachings of the Roman Catholic Church. All boys are required to attend Mass twice weekly, dressed in the school uniform, and to take four years of Theology for graduation credit. Students may also participate in retreats and community service.

The St. Mary's philosophy focuses on the individual student with the aim of developing his natural talents and fulfilling his potential in an atmosphere of "firm commitment to learning." It is the School's goal to produce young men who can "analyze contemporary problems and pursue social justice with spiritual insight." An average class size of 15, a student-teacher ratio of 10:1, and a strong emphasis on respect and the family facilitates attainment of these goals.

A nonprofit corporation, St. Mary's is governed by a 12-member Board of Trustees. The School's 2600 living alumni take an active role in recruitment and fund-raising activities. The productive endowment is approximately $2,000,000. St. Mary's Preparatory holds membership in the Independent Schools Association of the Central States, the Association of Independent Michigan Schools, and the Midwest Boarding Schools Association.

THE CAMPUS. St. Mary's Preparatory School occupies a scenic 125-acre campus on the shores of Orchard Lake. The oldest Preparatory building is the Academic Building (1889); St. Maximillian Kolbe Hall and St. Albertus Hall, the dormitory, were constructed in 1971. Other facilities include Alumni Memorial Library; "Galeria," the art gallery; Shrine Chapel of Our Lady of Orchard Lake; the Dining Commons (1966); and Dombrowski Fieldhouse, which contains the gymnasium and a television and recording studio. A new science center opened in 1999. There are athletic fields for track, football, baseball, lacrosse, soccer, and other sports events.

The campus and buildings, owned by the Board of Regents, are valued at $80,000,000.

THE FACULTY. James Glowacki, a 1985 graduate of St. Mary's, was named Headmaster in 1999. He earned baccalaureate and master's degrees from Wayne State University and served as head of the English Department before being appointed Headmaster.

The full-time faculty number 37, 24 men and 13 women. Seven faculty members reside on campus. They have earned 37 baccalaureate and 15 graduate degrees from Albion, Central Michigan, Columbia, Grand Valley State, Hamline, Indiana University, LaSalle, Marietta, Mercy College, Michigan State, Northern Colorado, Northern Michigan, Oakland University, Ohio State, Ohio University, Sacred Heart College, United States Coast Guard Academy, Wayne State, Western Michigan, William Smith, and the Universities of Detroit, Michigan, Missouri, Notre Dame, Paris, and Pennsylvania. Three part-time instructors teach Geography, Current Events, Japanese, and Polish.

An on-campus nurse handles minor medical problems; for more serious problems, there are two hospitals and a clinic in the area.

STUDENT BODY. In 1999–2000, St. Mary's enrolled 93 boarding boys and 314 day boys as follows: 103 freshmen, 103 sophomores, 100 juniors, and 101 seniors. Most students are from Michigan, but three other states and Canada, Germany, Japan, Korea, Mexico, Poland, Spain, and Taiwan are also represented. The majority are Roman Catholic and come from a variety of socioeconomic backgrounds.

ACADEMIC PROGRAM. The school year, extending from late August to the end of May, is divided into two semesters of three marking periods each. Vacations are scheduled at Thanksgiving, Christmas, and Easter, and there is a winter break in February. Students attend seven 45-minute class periods a day. Although no study periods are conducted during regular school hours, residents attend supervised study halls from 8:00 to 10:00 P.M. Sunday through Thursday. Extra help is available by request during or after school.

To earn a St. Mary's diploma, boys must complete 28 credits including 4 in Theology and English; 3 each in Mathematics, Science, Social Studies, and foreign language; 1 each in Speech, Art, and Physical Education; and 1/2 credit each in Business, Computer Science, and Word Processing. Specific courses are English 1–4, Poetry, Nobel Prize-Winning Authors, Science Fiction, Journalism; Theology 1–4; Algebra 1–2, Geometry, Trigonometry, Pre-Calculus, Calculus, Probability and Statistics; Biology 1–2, Chemistry, Physics, Physical Science, Earth Science, Zoology, Anatomy, Botany, Environmental Science; Spanish 1–4, French 1–4, Polish 1–4; Western Civilization, United States History, United States Government, Geography, Principles of Economics, Current Events, Speech, Debate, Drama, Common Law; Art 1–4; Accounting, General Business; Computer Science, Advanced Computer Science; and Physical Education. Advanced Physical Education, Twentieth Century Literature, Mythology, Creative Writing, and Drafting are offered as electives. Qualified juniors and seniors may take up to 11 college-credit hours per semester at St. Mary's College. English as a Second Language is also available.

A full-time guidance counselor aids students in selecting and applying to college, and the School arranges frequent visits from representatives of various colleges throughout the year. Of the 103 seniors in the Class of 1999, 102 are pursuing postsecondary education. Recent graduates have matriculated at Albion, Brown, Central Michigan, Columbia, Indiana University, Kettering, Loyola (Chicago, New Orleans), Michigan State, Ohio State, Princeton, Purdue, Syracuse, Wayne State, Western Michigan, Yale, and the Universities of California (Berkeley, Los Angeles), Miami, Michigan, Notre Dame, Pennsylvania, and Virginia.

STUDENT ACTIVITIES. The Student Council, consisting of three officers and representatives from each class, plans a variety of social activities and community service. The yearbook staff, debate team, forensics, Ski Club, Key Club, and other groups are active on campus and offer opportunities for leadership, self-expression, and fun.

St. Mary's competes with other private independent schools throughout the state. Varsity and junior varsity teams are organized in cross-country, football, rowing, and golf in the fall; basketball, hockey, skiing, bowling, and wrestling in the winter; and baseball, lacrosse, track, and rowing in the spring.

The intramural program includes soccer, flag football, softball, floor hockey, and one-on-one and two-on-two basketball.

During the year, a variety of social events is scheduled. In October, "Spirit Week," featuring competitions between classes, culminates in Homecoming Weekend and Dance. Other dances are coordinated with Catholic girls' schools in the area. Weekend ski trips and off-campus outings are also offered. The Moms and Dads Club plans activities for parents, including Autumnfest in September, parent get-togethers and guest speakers, and the Country Fair in May.

ADMISSION AND COSTS. St. Mary's Preparatory School, which adheres to a nondiscriminatory admissions policy, welcomes young men of average to superior ability who are willing and able to succeed in the "rigorous but highly rewarding" academic curriculum.

Admission requirements include application with a $30 fee; academic transcripts; recommendations from an English, mathematics, or science teacher and the principal or counselor at the student's current school; and the results of the High School Placement Test. Applicants are required to interview with either the Director of Admissions or the Headmaster. Interested applicants are also invited to spend a day visiting classes with a current student. A $500 registration fee, applicable to tuition, is required to secure a place following acceptance.

In 1999–2000, tuition, room, and board are $13,500 for seven-day boarders and $11,000 for five-day boarders; day tuition is $5900. The fee for international students is $17,500. Fees of approximately $500 cover testing, insurance, identification card, yearbook, and field trips. Other extras are books ($350), uniforms, and transportation. Need-based financial aid of about $150,000 is awarded annually.

Headmaster/Dean of Faculty: Mr. James Glowacki
Academic Dean: Mr. Leonard Karschnia
Dean of Students: Mr. Richard Rychcik
Dean of Resident Students: Mr. Patrick Tansill
Alumni Director: Rev. James Mazurek
Director of Admissions: Mr. Joseph Whalen
Chancellor/Director of Development: Rev. Msgr. Stanley Milewski
College Counselor: Mr. John Smith
Business Manager: Ms. Stephanie Whalen
Director of Athletics: Mr. George Porritt

University Liggett School   1969

1045 Cook Road, Grosse Pointe, MI 48236. 313-884-4444; Fax 313-884-1775; Web Site http://www.uls.pvt.k12.mi.us

University Liggett is a coeducational, college preparatory day school enrolling 800 students in Pre-Kindergarten–Grade 12. Established by the merger of Grosse Pointe University School (1899) and the Liggett School (1878), the School is located on 30 residential acres. Combining high expectations with individual assistance, University Liggett challenges students to reach the highest levels of their ability. The School's goals support growth of self-reliance, self-respect, concern for others, and commitment to community service. Strong programs in athletics and the creative arts supplement the curriculum. Honors and Advanced Placement courses are available. Sara Boisvert is Director of Admissions and Financial Aid; Matthew H. Hanly (Bowdoin, A.B.; Harvard, M.Ed.) is Headmaster.

MINNESOTA

The Blake School   1900

Northrop Campus (Upper School): 511 Kenwood Parkway, Minneapolis, MN 55403.
Blake Campus (Lower/Middle School): 110 Blake Road South, Hopkins, MN 55343.
Highcroft Campus (Lower School): 301 Peavey Lane, Wayzata, MN 55391.
Admissions 612-988-3420; Fax 612-988-3455;
Web Site http://www.blake.pvt.k12.mn.us

Blake is a coeducational, nonsectarian, college preparatory day school committed to "a tradition of academic excellence in a supportive environment" for 1240 students in Pre-Kindergarten–Grade 12. Educational leadership is realized in an experienced faculty, a challenging course of study, a sensitivity to learning styles, and community service programs. The School values diversity and global awareness. Advanced Placement courses are available in all academic areas. Summer programs are offered. Blake is a three-time recipient of the U.S. Department of Education School of Excellence award. Tuition: $6900–$13,600. Financial Aid: $2,128,000. Adaline Shinkle is Director of Admissions; John C. Gulla (Amherst, B.A.; Columbia Teachers College, M.A.) is Head of School.

Breck School   MINNEAPOLIS

123 Ottawa Avenue N., Minneapolis, MN 55422. 612-381-8100;
E-mail info@breckschool.org; Web Site www.breckschool.org

BRECK SCHOOL in Minneapolis, Minnesota, is a college preparatory day school enrolling boys and girls in Preschool through Grade 12. The School uses the cultural and educational resources of the Twin Cities metropolitan area (population 2,500,500) to offer a vigorous college preparatory

curriculum. It is the only school in Minnesota to have all divisions—Lower, Middle, and Upper—honored by the U.S. Department of Education. The Lower School received the "School of Excellence" award in 1987. The Middle and Upper schools received the "Blue Ribbon" award in 1993.

Named for a pioneer missionary, the Reverend James Lloyd Breck, the School was established in 1886 in Wilder, Minnesota, to provide children with a top-quality education under the auspices of the Episcopal church. In 1916, Breck moved to St. Paul; in 1956, a new facility was built on the Mississippi River in Minneapolis; and in 1981, the School relocated to the present 50-acre campus just west of downtown Minneapolis.

Breck strives to create a supportive and caring environment where the emphasis is on building self-worth. Friendship, respect, and mutual support among all members of the school community are stressed in an academic setting. Breck aims to be warm and friendly, academically rigorous but not driven, competitive but not compulsive, and structured but not rigid. Mastering basic skills is emphasized in the lower grades, enabling students to take advantage of increased options—such as independent study, internships, and Advanced Placement courses—in the upper grades. Students are encouraged to participate in sports, community service, and on-campus extracurricular activities. Chapel attendance and religion courses are required.

A nonprofit institution, Breck is affiliated with the Episcopal Diocese of Minnesota, and the Bishop is Chairman of the Board. The School is directed by a lay Board of Trustees, 24 in number, which meets monthly and includes parents, past parents, alumni, and friends of the School.

Breck is accredited by the Independent Schools Association of the Central States; it holds membership in such organizations as the National Association of Independent Schools, the Council for Spiritual and Ethical Education, the National Association of Episcopal Schools, and other professional organizations.

THE CAMPUS. Breck's campus, including two wildlife ponds, a stream, and woods, is located at the juncture of Glenwood Avenue and Highway 100, just north of Interstate Highway 394, a main artery linking Minneapolis and St. Paul. Two football fields, three soccer fields, three baseball fields, and seven tennis courts are on site.

The School houses 8 science laboratories, 3 gymnasiums, and a five-lane swimming pool. It also contains the Cargill Theatre (a 450-seat production theater with stage), 2 library/media centers, 2 band and orchestra rooms, 2 practice rooms, and many classrooms, interior courtyards, and commons areas. The Chapel of the Holy Spirit, seating 1300, is the focal point of the campus and the center of the School's spiritual life. In addition, Breck owns an ice arena for hockey and figure-skating programs.

THE FACULTY. Samuel A. Salas, Headmaster, is a graduate of the University of Chile (B.A.) and the University of Michigan (M.A. 1968, M.S. 1974). Prior to his appointment at Breck School, Mr. Salas served as Headmaster of The Cranbrook Schools. A native of Chile, Mr. Salas also teaches advanced Spanish at Breck School.

The faculty include 83 full-time and 21 part-time teachers recruited on a national basis. Faculty and staff hold 65 baccalaureate and 38 graduate degrees.

STUDENT BODY. In 1999–2000, the School enrolled 594 girls and 570 boys as follows: 443 in the Lower School (Preschool–Grade 4), 346 in the Middle School (Grades 5–8), and 375 in the Upper School (Grades 9–12). Students come from 61 communities; approximately 11 percent are Episcopalian. Students of color represent 19 percent of the student body.

ACADEMIC PROGRAM. The school year, from late August to early June, is divided into two semesters. The Middle and Upper schools are further divided into quarters, with a special May program in the Upper School. School vacations include Labor Day, Thanksgiving, Christmas, Presidents' Day, spring break, Good Friday, and Memorial Day. School convenes at 8:30 A.M.; students in the half-day Preschool and Kindergarten programs are dismissed at noon. For all other students, including full-day Preschool and Kindergarten students and afternoon-session Preschool students, the academic day concludes at 3:15 P.M.

Auxiliary services for students include two college placement counselors, a nurse, a health education counselor, an educational psychologist, consulting psychologists, mentors, and professional tutors.

The Preschool and Kindergarten programs introduce students to language arts, mathematics skills, science, creative arts, and physical education. Students attend chapel and take field trips to local businesses and museums. Lower School students study Chinese or Spanish beginning in Kindergarten.

The program in the Lower School (Grades 1–4) is designed to encourage basic skills, good study habits, and sound moral values. In addition to Chinese or Spanish, students have daily instruction in language arts, mathematics, science, social studies, and physical education as well as regularly scheduled classes in music, art, modern languages, and library skills. All classrooms have their own microcomputers for drill and enrichment activities. The Suzuki String Program offers instruction in violin, viola, and cello to students in Preschool–Grade 4. Parent volunteerism is strongly encouraged.

In the Middle School (Grades 5–8), the basic curriculum consists of English, modern language (Chinese, French, German, and Spanish), history, mathematics, science, and physical education, including Project Adventure. All grades have a social skills program, which includes religious study, health, and Skills

of Adolescence. Electives for all Middle School students are band, orchestra, drama, art, dance, and chorus.

To graduate, students must accumulate the following full-year credits in Grades 9–12: English 4, mathematics 3, foreign language 3, science 3, history (including United States History) 3, visual and performing arts 1, religious studies ½, physical education 1½, health science ½, and electives 3½.

The Upper School curriculum includes English, Senior English, Shakespeare, British Literature, Creative Writing, American Literature, Advanced Composition, Advanced Placement English; French 1–5, Advanced Placement French, German 1–5, Advanced Placement German, Spanish 1–4, Advanced Placement Spanish, Chinese 1–4; Medieval World History, United States History, Advanced Placement United States History, Modern World History, Political Ideologies, The Constitution, Comparative Government, Utopia, Economics, The Middle Ages and the Emerging World; Senior Ethics, Comparative Religions, Philosophy, Spiritual Questions; Computer Literacy, Algebra, Geometry, Advanced Algebra, Pre-Calculus, Honor Advanced Algebra, Advanced Placement Calculus AB and BC; Physical Science, Biology 1–3, Chemistry 1–3, Physics 1–2, Advanced Placement Biology, Advanced Placement Chemistry, Advanced Placement Physics; Theater/Drama, Speech, Studio Art, Ceramics, Printing, Drawing, Jazz Ensemble, String Ensemble, Chorus, Dance, Band; Student Service; and Physical Education.

Through the Upper School's Wednesday Program, all Upper School students and faculty perform community service at more than 20 different sites in the Twin Cities. Twenty hours of service to the School are also required for graduation.

During May, Upper School juniors and seniors may pursue a directed study in an academic or research area. Internships in the professions or business management may also be arranged. International study trips have included programs in China, France, Russia, Greece, Spain, Kenya, and Japan.

In 1999, all of the 88 graduates went on to college. They are attending 65 colleges and universities, with 2 or more attending Boston University 5, Dartmouth, Gustavus Adolphus College 4, Northwestern, St. Olaf 4, Stanford 3, United States Air Force Academy, Washington University 4, and the University of Wisconsin 6.

STUDENT ACTIVITIES. Middle and Upper School class presidents and vice-presidents serve on the Student Councils. Students may join the staffs of the yearbook, newspaper, and literary journal; other activities are the Mock Trial, Math League. Odyssey of the Mind, and Quiz Bowl teams; and the Computer, Chess, and Science clubs.

The after-school athletic program involves most students in Grades 7–12. There are interscholastic teams for boys in baseball, football, and wrestling; for girls in gymnastics, softball, and volleyball; and for boys and girls in basketball, tennis, swimming, cross-country running, golf, slalom and cross-country skiing, soccer, ice hockey, and track. Intramural programs (Grades 4–6) field coeducational teams in flag football, soccer, basketball, tennis, softball, skating, gymnastics, cross-country skiing, and track and field.

Separate dances are held each year for Grades 7–8 and Grades 9–12. In addition, there are overnight camping trips for Grades 6–12 and frequent field trips to The Guthrie Theater, the University of Minnesota, Orchestra Hall, the Minneapolis Art Institute, the Children's Theatre, the Science Museum, the Minnesota Zoological Gardens, and other places of interest. Traditional school events include Senior Weekend, Parents' Nights, athletic awards banquets, graduation festivities, Grandparents' Day, alumni class reunions, and evening parent coffees.

ADMISSION AND COSTS. In evaluating candidates, Breck looks for motivation, evidence of sound character, and strong academic achievement or potential. Academic transcripts, letters of reference, and a personal interview are required. The School also requires achievement testing.

In 1999–2000, tuition is $7995 for half-day Preschool, $11,250 for full-day Preschool, $8075 for half-day Kindergarten, and $11,250 for full-day Kindergarten. Tuition is $11,495 for Grades 1–12. Fees ($934–$1883) include the lunch program, student activities, and other items. In addition, transportation costs range from $650 to $1200.

In 1998–99, need-based scholarship aid was granted to 14 percent of the student body. Applicants for scholarship aid apply through the School Scholarship Service.

Academic Dean, Upper School: Stefan Anderson
Dean of Students, Upper School: Brett Bergene
Director, Upper School: Kevin Michael
Director, Middle School: Richard Lewis
Director, Lower School: Peg Bailey
Director of Admissions: Michael Weiszel
College Counselor: Melissa Soderberg
Business Manager: Wendy Engelman
Director of Athletics: John Thiel

Convent of the Visitation School   1873

2455 Visitation Drive, Mendota Heights, MN 55120-1696.
  651-683-1700; Fax 651-454-7144; E-mail adoffice@eta.k12.mn.us

Visitation enrolls 551 day students, with boys and girls in Preschool–Grade 6 and girls only in Grades 7–12. The School provides a challenging college preparatory program within a sound religious environment. The curriculum emphasizes the liberal arts and sciences, enhanced by theology, computers, and Advanced Placement courses in the Upper School. Seniors undertake a two-week service project, and all grades perform community service. Student government, clubs, and varied cocurricular activities are available. Students in Grades 7–12 collaborate with young men from Saint Thomas Academy, Visitation's brother school, in many areas. Tuition: $4072–$9890. Sr. Katherine Mullin, VHM, is Admissions Director; K. Michele Clarke is Principal.

Friends School of Minnesota   1988

1365 Englewood Avenue, St. Paul, MN 55104. 651-917-0636

Friends School, a Quaker school serving more than 130 boys and girls in Kindergarten–Grade 8, is grounded in the values and practices of the Religious Society of Friends, including justice, simplicity, equality, nonviolence, and silent reflection. Guided by the principles of progressive education, the School features small classes, Spanish, hands-on and project-based math and science, an emphasis on cooperative learning, and a multicultural curriculum. A nationally recognized conflict resolution program and a commitment to building a nurturing community enable students to thrive academically, socially, and emotionally. Tuition: $6100–$6900. Financial Aid: $130,000.

Jane Schallert is Admissions Coordinator; Mark Niedermier (St. John's [Annapolis], B.A.; New School for Social Research, M.A.) is Head of School.

Marshall School   1904

1215 Rice Lake Road, Duluth, MN 55811. 218-727-7266;
  Fax 218-727-1569; E-mail adoser@marshallschool.org;
  Web Site www.marshallschool.org

A coeducational, college preparatory day school with 556 students in Grades 5–12. Marshall is located on a 35-acre campus overlooking Lake Superior and downtown Duluth. In addition to Advanced Placement and honors courses, the core curriculum is enriched with innovative computer courses, ethical studies, and strong options in the performing arts and foreign language. Students also benefit from community service, outdoor education, and 22 athletic teams for boys and girls. Marshall is committed to preparing students for admission to highly competitive colleges and universities. Tuition: $5320–$5880. Financial aid is available. Amanda Doser is Director of Admissions; Marlene M. David (Wayne State University, B.S., M.S.; Johns Hopkins, M.L.A.) is Head of School.

Saint John's Preparatory School

COLLEGEVILLE

P.O. Box 4000, Collegeville, MN 56321-4000. 320-363-3315;
  Admissions 320-363-3321 or 800-525-PREP; Fax 320-363-3322;
  E-mail admitprep@csbsju.edu; Web Site www.csbsju.edu/sjprep

Saint John's Preparatory School in Collegeville, Minnesota, is a Benedictine college preparatory school enrolling boarding and day boys and girls in Grades 9–12 and postgraduate studies and day students in Grades 7–8. Collegeville is a small community 15 miles west of St. Cloud (population 50,000) and 90 miles northwest of the Minneapolis-St. Paul metropolitan area (combined population 2,500,000). Collegeville is home to Saint John's University for men, with which the School shares a campus, and nearby College of Saint Benedict for women. Students make extensive use of the University's educational and athletic facilities and plan frequent excursions to art galleries, theaters, concerts, and major league sports events in the Twin Cities region.

The Benedictine monks of Saint John's Abbey founded the School in 1857 to prepare young men for success in colleges, universities, and other institutions of higher learning. Girls were admitted in 1973 and now constitute approximately 45 percent of the student body.

In keeping with the 1500-year tradition of the Benedictine order, the School is dedicated to providing academic challenge and excellence as well as upholding high moral and ethical standards of conduct. Development of each student's social, spiritual, and physical growth is considered equal to scholastic achievement. Although it is rooted in the precepts and heritage of the Roman Catholic faith, the School welcomes students of all religions.

A nonprofit institution, Saint John's Preparatory School is governed by a 23-member Board of Regents. The Prep School is accredited by the Independent Schools Association of the Central States and holds membership in the National Association of Independent Schools, among other organizations. Active parent and alumni organizations support the School through fund-raising, recruitment, and other volunteer efforts.

THE CAMPUS. The campus housing Saint John's Preparatory School and Saint John's University comprises 2500 acres of woodlands and hills on Lake Sagatagan in central Minnesota. Resident boys live in a spacious, air-conditioned residence hall on the Prep campus, in carpeted rooms clustered in "villages" that open into common areas. Girls reside in their own residence hall on the grounds of the College of Saint Benedict, a liberal arts institution for young women located four miles away in St. Joseph, Minnesota. The School provides free transportation between the two campuses.

Resources shared by the Prep and the University include the Saint John's Main Auditorium, the Abbey Church, Alcuin Library, the Science Center, student dining hall and cafeteria, a snack bar, and the Warner Palaestra, containing an indoor track, tennis and raquetball courts, and an Olympic-size swimming pool. The College of Saint Benedict features a beautiful new recreation and dining center located next to the girls' residence hall. In 1999, Prep built the 7400-square-foot Weber Center, which houses a fine arts center, an area for private worship, and a student center. Plans are underway for a 10,000-square-foot science addition, scheduled for completion in the summer of 2000.

THE FACULTY. Fr. Gordon Tavis, OSB, was appointed President in July 1998. Father Gordon is a graduate of Saint John's University (B.A. 1954) and Massachusetts Institute of Technology (M.Mgt. 1972). Prior to his appointment at Saint John's Prep, he served for 17 years as treasurer of the Order of St. Benedict, Collegeville, Minnesota, and 20 years as a member of the Board of Regents. He also served 5 years as Prior of Saint John's Abbey and, for the past 3 years, was a member of the Prep School staff.

The 18 men and 7 women on the faculty hold baccalaureate and 19 master's degrees. Virtually all faculty are actively involved in school life outside the classroom, serving as mentors, coaches, and advisors to student groups.

A physician is available daily. The Health Center provides medical attention, and a pharmacy is located on campus. St. Cloud Hospital is 20 minutes away by car.

STUDENT BODY. In 1999–2000, Saint John's Prep enrolled 262 students, including 28 boarding girls, 49 boarding boys, 69 day boys, 69 day girls, in Grade 9–Postgraduate, and 5 students in Grade 9–PG participating in the Austrian study-abroad program. Forty-two students from the local area are enrolled in Grades 7–8. Boarding students came from 11 states and ten countries and represented a broad spectrum of racial, ethnic, and religious backgrounds.

ACADEMIC PROGRAM. The school year is divided into fall and spring semesters, beginning in late August and ending in late May. Thanksgiving, Christmas, and Easter recesses are scheduled, and most months have a long weekend. Grades are sent to parents four times a semester for purposes of ongoing assessment, but only final grades are recorded on the student's official transcript. Parents are encouraged to meet with their child's teachers at any time there is concern about schoolwork or other issues. In addition to having individual faculty advisors, students receive academic and personal support from a professional counselor and college tutors as needed. The average class has 15–18 students, and the student-teacher ratio is 10:1.

A typical class day, Monday through Friday, begins at 8:00 A.M., with eight 42-minute periods, a lunch break, and time scheduled for supervised study. Boarding students also have evening study hall.

To graduate from Saint John's Prep, students must complete 21 credits, though most earn more than the minimum. They are required to take the equivalent of four years each of English and social studies; three years each of mathematics, science, a foreign language, and theology; two years of physical education; two years of fine arts; and one year of health.

Specific required and elective course offerings include English 9–11, World Literature; Algebra I–II, Geometry, Functions/Statistics/Trigonometry, Pre-Calculus; German I–IV, Spanish I–IV; Biology, Chemistry, Engineering, Physics, Advanced Placement Environmental Science, Conceptual Physics; World History, United States History, World Affairs, Economics, Law and Government, Advanced Placement World History, Advanced Placement United States History; Theology 9–10, World Religions, The Christian Monastic Tradition, Community Service, Issues of Justice and Peace; Introduction to Theater, Acting I–II, Drawing, Design, Painting, Calligraphy, Beginning and Advanced Ceramics, Sculpture, Basic Photography; Band/Wind Ensemble, Choir, String Ensemble, Madrigals Singers; and Physical Education. Advanced or accelerated coursework is offered in all disciplines. Qualified students may take courses for credit at Saint John's University or the College of Saint Benedict. Independent study projects can be undertaken to address deficiencies in a particular subject or for in-depth examination of a field of special interest. Such projects require the advance approval of the sponsoring teacher, the department head, and the principal. In addition, instruction in vocal and instrumental music is offered.

International students may enroll in a comprehensive program in English as a Second Language, which features conversation, composition, cultural integration, and United States history.

The School offers a yearlong travel/study option at the 900-year-old Benedictine Abbey in Melk, Austria. This program features a full academic curriculum enriched by travel throughout Austria, England, Greece, and other countries on the Continent.

Traditionally, about 98 percent of Saint John's seniors go on to higher education. In recent years, graduates have entered such colleges and universities as Boston College, Carleton, College of Saint Benedict, Creighton, Georgetown, Harvard, Marquette, Massachusetts Institute of Technology, Princeton, Saint John's, Tulane, United States Military Academy, United States Naval Academy, Washington University, and the Universities of Minnesota and Notre Dame.

In the summer, the School conducts German Camp, Circus Camp, and Show Choir Camp as well as Summer Leadership Camps for students ages 10–15.

STUDENT ACTIVITIES. Saint John's provides a wide range of opportunities for student involvement after the school day. Student government, campus ministry, and peer ministry help develop leadership skills, while the National Honor Society recognizes high academic achievements. Students publish a yearbook and take part in speech and debate competitions, mock trials, band, chorus, and Spanish and German clubs. The drama group stages five productions annually.

Saint John's teams compete at intramural, club, junior varsity, and varsity levels in soccer, football, volleyball, cross-country, basketball, cross-country skiing, swimming, tennis, track, softball, hockey, baseball, and golf.

On weekends, there are many activities organized on and off campus. The School conducts a program of visiting artists and lecturers, and many trips are planned to movies, shopping malls, restaurants, and other places of interest, including many free concerts and activities at Saint John's University and the College of Saint Benedict.

ADMISSION AND COSTS. Saint John's Prep welcomes young men and women of good character, academic ability, and leadership potential who show promise of benefiting from, and contributing to, the life of the School community. Acceptance is based on a campus interview, the results of an entrance exam, a student essay, letters of recommendation, and the student's transcripts. Students may visit the campus during Discovery Days, held monthly from November through April, or individual appointments can be scheduled through the Admission Office. Upon acceptance, a deposit of $200 is required from day students and $500 from boarding students.

In 1999–2000, tuition is $7834 for day students and between $15,822 and $17,758 for residents. Tuition for students in Grades 7–8 is $4200. A five-day residency option is also available. An additional $2967 is assessed for international students. Approximately $370,000 in financial aid was awarded to 70 percent of the student body. Tuition payment plans are available.

Principal: Fr. Ian Dommer, OSB
Dean of Students: Matt Steinkamp
Director of Admission: Bryan Backes
Director of Development and Alumni Relations: Michael Mullin
College Counselor: Mary Jo Leighton
Business Manager: Jeana Koenig
Director of Athletics: Pete Cheeley

Shattuck-St. Mary's School   FARIBAULT

P.O. Box 218, 1000 Shumway Avenue, Faribault, MN 55021.
507-333-1500; Admissions 507-333-1618; Fax 507-333-1661;
E-mail admissions@ssm.pvt.k12.mn.us; Web Site www.s-sm.org

SHATTUCK-ST. MARY'S SCHOOL in Faribault, Minnesota, is a college preparatory boarding and day school enrolling boys and girls in Grades 6–12 and a postgraduate program. The School is located in Faribault (population 19,000), near the educational and recreational facilities of Carleton and St. Olaf colleges, and 45 minutes from the world-class offerings of metropolitan Minneapolis/St. Paul.

Shattuck-St. Mary's was opened by Dr. James Lloyd Breck in 1858, with 45 white and Native American mission school students and 6 divinity school students. By the early 1900s, Shattuck-St. Mary's had grown into four separate schools: Shattuck School for boys, St. Mary's Hall for girls, St. James School for younger boys, and the Seabury Theological Seminary. In 1933, Seabury merged with Western Theological Seminary and moved to Illinois. The remaining three schools merged and formed the present Shattuck-St. Mary's School in 1972.

The School's rigorous academic, arts, and athletic programs foster excellence, self-confidence, and well-roundedness, all in the context of strong Midwestern values. Shattuck-St. Mary's is affiliated with the Episcopal Church and strives to educate the whole person—mind, body, and spirit—in a caring Christian environment. All students attend chapel once a week and take a one-term course called "Introduction to the Bible" as juniors. Course work and presentations on ethics and values, plus a 20-hour-per-year community service requirement, help prepare students to become responsible, contributing members of society. The Middle School (Grades 6–8), with its own facility and faculty, addresses the developmental needs of 50 younger students in a small, intimate environment.

Shattuck-St. Mary's, a nonprofit corporation, is governed by a 20-member Board of Trustees. The endowment is valued at $13,000,000. There are more than 5000 alumni, many of whom are active in fund-raising and admissions. The School is accredited by the Independent Schools Association of the Central States and holds membership in the National Association of Independent Schools, the National Association of Episcopal Schools, and the National Association for College Admission Counseling, among other organizations.

THE CAMPUS. The 250-acre campus, with its collegiate Gothic buildings, has been designated a National Historic District. Athletic facilities on campus include an 18-hole golf course, a hockey arena, a baseball diamond, tennis courts, soccer and football fields, an outdoor track, two gymnasiums, and an indoor swimming pool. A 30-acre area of the campus is used for field biology and ecology studies.

Shumway Hall (1887) is the School's main academic and administrative building. Johnson Armory (1909) includes a gymnasium, a weight room and conditioning center, and the 25,000-volume Homer T. Hirst III Memorial Library. Dobbin Hall (1907) houses classrooms, a music center, the infirmary, and a swimming pool. The facilities of the renovated Kingham Science Hall include laboratories and a computer center. Other campus buildings include the Chapel of the Good Shepherd (1872), five dormitories, the Headmaster's residence, and faculty homes. The School-owned plant is valued at $31,000,000.

THE FACULTY. Gregory J. Kieffer, appointed Head of School in 1993, is a graduate of the United States Naval Academy (B.S. 1969) and the University of Washington (M.S. 1973). Prior to becoming the Head, Mr. Kieffer taught chemistry, chaired the science department, and served as Director of Studies at Shattuck-St. Mary's. He and his wife, Kathy, live on campus.

The full-time faculty number 50, 28 men and 22 women, nearly all of whom live on campus. The faculty hold 56 baccalaureate and 27 graduate degrees from such colleges and universities as Albion, Allegheny, Alma, Amherst, Bemidji State, Berklee, College of William and Mary, Colorado College, Colorado State, Columbia, Concordia, Duke, Eastern Kentucky, Florida State, Hamline, Harvard, Iowa State, Jamestown, Johns Hopkins, Kansas State, Luther, Oral Roberts, Purdue, Rensselaer Polytechnic, St. Benedict, St. Cloud State, St. John's, St. Olaf, St. Scholastica, St. Thomas, Syracuse, United States Naval Academy, Washington University, Wheaton, and the Universities of California, Manitoba, Maryland, Massachusetts, Minnesota, Notre Dame, Tennessee, Washington, and Wisconsin. Seven part-time faculty teach English, history, science, German, and Spanish.

The infirmary is staffed by registered nurses, and hospital and clinic facilities are less than a mile away.

STUDENT BODY. In 1999–2000, the School enrolls 133 boarding boys, 54 day boys, 86 boarding girls, and 22 day girls as follows: Grade 6—7, Grade 7—14, Grade 8—21, Grade 9—55, Grade 10—61, Grade 11—70, Grade 12—64, and Postgraduate—3. Boarding students come from Minnesota, Wisconsin, Illinois, Iowa, California, Washington, Texas, Michigan, and 21 other states; also, Canada, England, Germany, Hong Kong, Japan, Korea, Morocco, Russia, Saudi Arabia, and Taiwan.

ACADEMIC PROGRAM. The school year, which runs from late August to early June, is divided into three terms and includes vacations of one week in the fall and three weeks at Christmas and in the spring. Classes are held from 8:00 A.M. to 3:20 P.M. Monday through Friday, with a schedule of rotating class periods daily. Class sizes average 13 to 16 students.

An extra-help session, held each day after classes, allows students and teachers time to work together on an individual basis. Faculty-supervised study halls are held during the school day and for two hours each night. Study skills and tutoring are also available for an additional fee. Grades are sent to parents six times each year and are recorded at the end of each term, with final grades announced at the end of the year.

The Middle School (Grades 6–8) is a distinct yet integral part of the school community, with its own activities, dormitories, and athletic programs. The curriculum is designed to prepare students for the academic program in the Upper School. Graduation requirements for Upper School students include four years of English; three years of mathematics; three years of science, including one of physical science; three years of history; two consecutive levels of the same foreign language; two terms of physical education per year in Grades 9 and 10; and one term of fine arts per year of attendance. Students must also pass a computer competency course and complete 20 hours of community service per year.

Among the full-year and term courses offered are English I–IV (honors sections at the upper levels); French I–V, Spanish I–V, German I–IV, Latin I–IV; World Cultures, Modern European History, United States History, Economics, Medieval History, Introduction to the Bible, Ethics; Algebra I–II, Geometry, Trigonometry/Functions, Calculus, Computers; Physical Science, Biology, Chemistry, Physics; Chorus, Orchestra, Music Appreciation, String Ensemble, Music Composition, Music Theory; History of Art, Photo I–II, Drawing I–II, Painting I–II, Pottery I–II; Public Speaking, Introduction to the Theater, Directing; and Physical Education. Advanced Placement courses are offered in English, French, Spanish, United States History, European History, Calculus AB and BC, Computer Science, Biology, Chemistry, Physics, and Music Theory. Seniors and postgraduates may arrange for independent study projects.

Extensive courses in choral and instrumental music, drama, and dance, plus numerous opportunities to perform on campus and to tour domestically and abroad, make it possible for young artists to pursue preprofessional training within a college preparatory program. The School also offers English as a Second Language at three levels of proficiency and prepares students for the Test of English as a Foreign Language.

In 1999, 54 of 60 graduating seniors and postgraduates elected to enter college immediately, 4 by "early decision." They are attending such colleges and universities as Antioch, Barnard, Boston College, Canisius, Carroll, Columbia, Creighton, Emory and Henry, Florida Southern, Georgetown, Gustavus Adolphus, Hampshire, Ithaca, John Carroll, Massachusetts Institute of Technology, Michigan Tech, Minnesota State (Mankato), New York University, Niagara, Northwestern, Ohio State, Rhodes, St. Cloud State, St. John's, St. Mary's, Salve Regina, Texas Tech, Trinity (Connecticut), Westminster, Willamette, William Smith, and the Universities of Alaska, Chicago, Denver, Iowa, Miami, Rochester, St. Thomas, South Dakota, Southern Colorado, Texas, and Wisconsin. Two seniors elected to attend a postgraduate program, and 4 are playing junior hockey.

The School's four-week summer Discovery program and the English Language Institute offer academics and activities for American and international students in Grades 5–11. Other summer programs include one-week camps in music and soccer and four one-week camps in ice hockey.

STUDENT ACTIVITIES. The Student Council represents student interests and makes recommendations to the Headmaster and faculty.

Students publish a newspaper and a yearbook. The Dramatic Association produces three full-length plays and a one-act play each year, and participates in statewide drama competitions. Among the other student organizations are language clubs, Art Club, Student Vestry, Gold Key Club, Chess Club, and boys' and girls' drill teams.

The School fields interscholastic teams in soccer, basketball, hockey, fencing, tennis, golf, baseball, and track for boys. Girls' teams compete in tennis, volleyball, soccer, basketball, fencing, hockey, softball, golf, and track. There are also intramural programs in golf, tennis, archery, weight lifting, cycling, cross-country skiing, aerobics, and swimming.

Students enjoy activities ranging from canoeing and camping trips to dances, museum visits, and shopping. Movies, lectures, and concerts are all offered on campus. Weekends may be spent off campus, with appropriate permission. Among the traditional annual events at Shattuck-St. Mary's are Fall Family Weekend and Winter Carnival.

ADMISSION AND COSTS. The School seeks "students of good character who are qualified to pursue a demanding college preparatory program." New students are accepted in Grades 6–12 and the postgraduate program on the basis of previous school records, the results of standardized tests, and recommendations. Most students are accepted up to late July, with a very small number of midyear admissions. Applications, accompanied by a $30 fee, should be submitted as early as possible, and no later than the middle of July.

In 1999–2000, tuition is $21,100 for boarding students and $13,000 for day students. Approximately $1500 is required for students' personal expenses. About 50 percent of the student body receives financial aid, which is based on need. In 1999–2000, a total of $925,540 was distributed in grants. There are six academic merit scholarships awarded annually, each worth $7500 for every year the recipient attends. Eight performing arts scholarships worth $5000 each are awarded annually on the basis of an audition in dance, drama, or music. Low-interest loans are also available, as are tuition insurance and a tuition payment plan. Shattuck-St. Mary's subscribes to the School and Student Service for Financial Aid.

Director of the Upper School: John F. Nelson
Dean of Students (Upper School): Corbin P. Smith
Director of the Middle School: Margaret (Bobbi) S. Sumner
Director of Admissions: Phillip R. Trout
Director of Development: Peter H. Mansfield
Director of Annual Fund and Alumni Affairs: Sonja A. Johnson
College Counselors: D. Lynn Redmond and Phillip R. Trout
Director of Student Services: D. Lynn Redmond
Business Manager: Steven H. Stolp
Director of Athletics: John R. Sumner

MISSISSIPPI

All Saints' Episcopal School   VICKSBURG

Vicksburg, MS 39180. 601-636-5266, 800-748-9957;
E-mail allsaint@vicksburg.com;
Web Site www.vicksburg.com/~allsaint

ALL SAINTS' EPISCOPAL SCHOOL in Vicksburg, Mississippi, is a college preparatory boarding and day school for boys and girls in Grades 8 through 12. The School's 40-acre campus is located in historic Vicksburg, less than a mile from the business center of the city and two modern shopping centers. The site of a National Military Park and the headquarters for the Mississippi River Commission of the United States Corps of Engineers, Vicksburg (population 40,000) supports an active community theater as well as museums, concerts, and professional theater. Jackson, Mississippi, is 42 miles to the east; New Orleans, Memphis, Little Rock, and Mobile are all within a 200-mile radius of the School.

Founded in 1908 as a school for girls by the Right Reverend Theodore D. Bratton, D.D., All Saints' first admitted boys in 1971 and is now fully coeducational. The School is committed to a college preparatory program designed "to meet the educational needs of the gifted student, the average student, and the student with certain learning problems"; its goal is to help each student achieve continuous progress according to his or her needs and capabilities. The School also operates an Educational Assessment Center, the purpose of which is to discern a student's educational strengths and weaknesses, to design an educational program based upon this assessment and upon the determined goals of the student and his or her family, and to help the family find the proper school environment.

Although All Saints' considers that its primary responsibility is the promotion of its students' intellectual growth, as a church school, it "finds its basic purpose in the development of the individual as a truly mature person whose intellectual, emotional, and social growth has been accompanied by a corresponding spiritual and moral growth." All students participate in the Wednesday covenant program prior to a service of worship. Covenants include study of scripture, drama and liturgy, and media and life issues. Seniors also take a half-year religious studies course. All Saints' seeks students of every religious faith in the belief that such diversity adds to the educational experience.

The School is owned by the Episcopal Dioceses in Arkansas, Louisiana, and Mississippi; it is managed by a 20-member Board of Trustees, 17 of whom are elected by the Diocesan Councils and 3 of whom are elected by the Board. The Board, whose membership includes the Bishops in Arkansas, Louisiana, and Mississippi and an alumni representative, meets at least twice a year. The School is accredited by the Southern Association of Colleges and Schools. It holds membership in the Southern Association of Independent Schools, the National Association of Independent Schools, and the National Association of Episcopal Schools.

THE CAMPUS. Situated on landscaped hills, the campus buildings curve in an arc around a dell in which the Olympic-size swimming pool and recreational center are located. The main building, Green Hall (1908, renovated 1965), together with Allin Hall (1979), contain classrooms, the library, music and art studios, the dining hall, the Educational Assessment Center, and administrative offices. Other buildings include Johnson Hall (1979), a dormitory for boys; St. Mary's Hall, St. Catherine's Hall, and St. Anne's Hall, dormitories for girls (1965); All Saints' Chapel (1956); the Rectory (1956); the Gymnasium (1972); and several homes for staff members (1965). The physical plant is valued at $6,000,000.

THE FACULTY. The faculty consists of 26 full-time teachers and administrators who teach, 9 men and 18 women. Two faculty members and their families live on campus. The faculty hold 26 baccalaureate and 12 advanced degrees representing study at Arizona State, Birmingham-Southern, Boston University, College of Charleston, Columbia College, Davidson, Delta State, Florida State, Huntingdon, Louisiana State, Millsaps, Mississippi College, Mississippi State, Mississippi University for Women, Randolph-Macon, St. Mary's (Minnesota), Southern Illinois, State University of New York, Tulane, Vanderbilt, and the Universities of Mississippi, the South, Southern Mississippi, and Virginia. The faculty also include a librarian, a teacher of theater arts, and 5 teachers of physical education.

There are two nurses on duty in the infirmary, and a doctor is on call. Medical facilities in the community include the Parkview Medical Center and Vicksburg Columbia Medical Center.

STUDENT BODY. In 1998–99, All Saints' enrolls 75 boarding boys, 6 day boys, 81 boarding girls, and 2 day girls as follows: 11 in Grade 8, 33 in Grade 9, 39 in Grade 10, 53 in Grade 11, and 28 in Grade 12. They come from Alabama, Arkansas, California, Florida, Georgia, Idaho, Illinois, Kentucky, Louisiana, Mississippi, Missouri, New Jersey, Oklahoma, Tennessee, Texas, China, Japan, Korea, Saudi Arabia, Thailand, and Vietnam. Approximately 50 percent of the students are Episcopalians.

ACADEMIC PROGRAM. The school year, from September to May, includes vacations at Thanksgiving, at Christmas, and in the spring. Classes are held five and one-half days a week. The daily schedule, from 7:00 A.M. rising to 11:00 P.M. (midnight for older students) bedtime, includes seven one-hour class periods, a midmorning break, assembly, and time for sports, activities, and recreation. Classes meet until noon on Saturday. Students have a long weekend or a holiday each month.

The maximum class size is 15 students, with time for help sessions during the lunch periods. Work in the School's Academic Resource Center supplements the student's regular academic program with concentrated study in specific skills. Counselors monitor supervised study in dormitory rooms from 8:00 to 10:00 P.M. Sunday through Friday. Grades are posted and reported to parents four times a year.

Twenty-four credits are required for graduation. All Saints' students are expected to take all four core subjects—English, mathematics, science, and social studies—every year. Courses include English 8, English I–IV; History 8, Ancient & Medieval History, Geography, World History, U.S. History, Contemporary U.S. History, Government, Economics, Psychology, Sociology, Bible; General Math, Pre-algebra, Algebra I, Intermediate Algebra, Geometry, Algebra II, College Prep Math, Advanced Math, Calculus; Science 8, Physical Science, Biology I–II, Chemistry I–II, Physics, Environmental Science, Botany; Keyboarding, Computer Literacy, Advanced Computer Applications; Spanish I–II, French I–III, Latin I–II, English as a Second Language; and Drama, Studio Art, Ensemble, Music Enrichment, Poetry Writing, Personal Exploratory Writing, Screen Writing, and Film Making.

Typically, 100 percent of All Saints' students enter college after graduation. In 1999, the 35 graduates are attending Converse, Delta State, Hendrix, Louisiana State, Millsaps, Mississippi State, and the Universities of Alabama, Mississippi, Southern Mississippi, Tennessee, and Texas.

STUDENT ACTIVITIES. A comprehensive program of physical education, aerobics, and recreation is required of all students. It includes swimming, lifesaving, synchronized swimming, canoeing, cycling, basketball, volleyball, softball, tennis, archery, badminton, gymnastics, soccer, conditioning, jogging, weight lifting, camp counseling, climbing/rappelling, orienteering, and backpacking. Among the School-sponsored group activities are canoeing, camping, cycling, hiking, movies, dances, concerts, theater, ball games, and trips within the United States and abroad. Students are governed by an Achievement/Trust System in which privileges and freedom are determined by the student's productivity and behavior.

ADMISSION AND COSTS. Students are admitted to Grades 8–12 on the basis of School-administered ability and achievement tests and a personal interview. Candidates may be accepted during the school year if space is available.

Tuition for 1999–2000 is $16,250 for boarding students and $4500 for day students. Books, laundry, travel, and personal items are extra. All Saints' subscribes to the School Scholarship Service. In 1997–98, approximately $75,000 in scholarship aid, granted each year on the basis of need, was awarded to 28 students.

Interim Headmaster: Charles Craft
Academic Dean: Linda Hall
Dean of Students: The Reverend Charlene Miller
Director of Admissions: Patsy Hodges
Director of Development: Sarah Randall
School Psychometrist: DuAnn Beck
Business Manager: Dorothy McInnis
Physical Education/Recreation Director: Greg Head

St. Andrew's Episcopal School   1947

370 Old Agency Road, Ridgeland, MS 39157. 601-853-6000;
   Fax 601-853-6001; E-mail sa@gosaints.com;
   Web Site www.gosaints.com

St. Andrew's Episcopal is a coeducational day school enrolling 1110 students in Pre-Kindergarten–Grade 12. Along with a strong college preparatory curriculum, St. Andrew's offers a wide variety of sports, Speech and Debate, and the visual and performing arts. St. Andrew's, a member of the Cum Laude Society, offers 18 Advanced Placement courses and a Japanese exchange program for boys. Two-thirds of the student enrollment is non-Episcopalian; 14 percent are students of color. In addition to the academic requirements, upper school students must complete 100 school and community service hours prior to graduation. Tuition: $2970–$6715. Financial aid is available. Ellen M. Ford is Director of Admission; David E. Wood (Davidson, A.B.; Middle Tennessee State, M.A.) is Headmaster. *Southern Association.*

St. George's Episcopal Day School   1959

1040 West Second Street, Clarksdale, MS 38614. 662-624-4376;
   Fax 662-624-4314; E-mail office@stgeorgesds.edu;
   Web Site www.stgeorgesds.edu

This elementary school, founded as an educational ministry of St. George's Episcopal Church, enrolls 140 boys and girls in three-year-old Kindergarten through Grade 6. The mission of St. George's is to inspire students to live "intelligently, creatively, and humanely" according to Christian precepts. All students regardless of faith affiliation take part in regular chapel services and religion classes, and values education is an integral component of the program. Enhancing the core curriculum are special programs such as Drop Everything and Read, Book Buddies, and Writing and Loving It. Students participate in age-appropriate extracurricular activities, and before- and after-school care is available. Tuition: $1050–$3200. Susan Berryhill is Principal. *Southern Association.*

MISSOURI

Andrews Academy   1979

888 North Mason Road, St. Louis, MO 63141. 314-878-1883

Andrews Academy is a coeducational day school enrolling 250 students in Kindergarten–Grade 6. The philosophy of Andrews Academy is committed to the highest intellectual, physical, and social development of each child. The curriculum places emphasis on basic skills and individualized instruction. Computer instruction, Spanish, physical education, art, music, science laboratory, and library are offered at all levels. A summer camp, located on the Academy's 40-acre campus, offers numerous activities to approximately 300 campers. Extended-day care for working parents is offered at no extra fee. Tuition: $8880. Joseph C. Patterson (Washington University, B.S., M.Ed.) was appointed Headmaster in 1983.

The Barstow School   1884

11511 State Line Road, Kansas City, MO 64114. 816-942-3255;
Fax 816-942-3227; Web Site www.barstowschool.org

Barstow is a college preparatory day school enrolling 550 culturally diverse boys and girls in Preschool–Grade 12. Through both academics and extracurricular activities, Barstow challenges its students intellectually, emotionally, and physically. Within a supportive environment characterized by small classes and a strong sense of family, students undertake a liberal arts curriculum that features Advanced Placement classes and a rich variety of electives. Interscholastic athletics, student government, publications, instruction in the performing arts, special-interest clubs, and community service are among the after-school activities. Tuition: $6575–$10,800. Sherrie LeMoine is Director of Admissions; Charles H. Sachs (Colgate, B.A.; Middlebury, M.A.) is Head.

Chaminade College Preparatory School   1910

425 South Lindbergh Boulevard, St. Louis, MO 63131-2799.
314-993-4400; Fax 314-993-4403; E-mail email@chaminade.
st-louis.mo.us; Web Site www.chaminademo.com

Chaminade College Preparatory School was founded by the Society of Mary to educate young men of strong average to superior ability in Grades 7–12. Enrolling 40 boarding and 800 day students, Chaminade offers a challenging combination of academics, extracurricular opportunities, and athletics. The formation of faith and good character are encouraged through religious studies and shared liturgies in the Catholic tradition. All students perform community service. There are 17 Advanced Placement courses, and English as a Second Language is offered in the summer. Concert and jazz band and 15 varsity sports are among the activities. Boarding Tuition: $14,650–$15,600; Day Tuition: $7650. Financial Aid: $460,000. Matthew J. Saxer is Admission Director; Fr. Ralph A. Siefert, SM, is President.

Chesterfield Day School   1962

St. Albans Road, St. Albans, MO 63073. 636-458-6688;
Fax 636-458-6660; Web Site www.chesterfielddayschool.org
1100 White Road, Chesterfield, MO 63017. 314-469-6622;
Fax 314-469-7889

Chesterfield Day School enrolls 449 boys and girls in two suburban locations: Chesterfield (Toddler–Grade 6) and St. Albans (Preschool–Grade 8). In a caring, loving environment, Chesterfield promotes independence, cooperation, curiosity, and concern for others. The curriculum implements the Montessori methodology in the early years (18 months–Grade 1) and makes the transition to more traditional approaches in Grades 2–5. The School is striving toward the implementation of the Middle Years Programme (Grades 6–10) and the International Baccalaureate Diploma Programme (Grades 11–12) in preparation for formal authorization. Computers, German, art, music, library science, and physical education are taught at all levels. Tuition: $1675–$9000. Janet Lange and Chris Blair are Directors of Admission; Barbara Fulton, Ph.D., is Head.

Community School   1914

900 Lay Road, St. Louis, MO 63124. 314-991-0005;
Fax 314-991-1512; E-mail mail@communityschool.k12.mo.us
Web Site www.communityschool.k12.mo.us

Community School, located on a 16-acre campus in suburban St. Louis, is a coeducational day school enrolling 326 students in Nursery–Grade 6. The School aims to provide a setting in which each individual can develop and emerge with positive attitudes and values and strong academic achievement. Basic skills are emphasized; French is introduced in Grade 1; science, social studies, art, shop, band, drama, computer, and physical education are included in the curriculum. After-school care for all grades and a summer program for three- to five-year-olds are also offered. Tuition: $9450. Financial aid is available. Sheillah Rogers (Webster University, B.A. 1976; University of San Francisco, M.N.A. 1989) is Head of School.

Crossroads School   1974

500 DeBaliviere Place, St. Louis, MO 63112. 314-367-8085;
Fax 314-367-9711; E-mail admission@crossroads.st-louis.mo.us;
Web Site http://www.crossroads.st-louis.mo.us/

Located in the historical Central West End, Crossroads School enrolls 185 college-bound day students in Grades 7–12. The School enjoys a rich tradition of cultural diversity, which is reflected in its challenging, multicultural curriculum. Staff are committed to providing individual attention, team teaching, and a student-faculty ratio of 9:1. The curriculum offers English, science, history, math, foreign language, fine arts, and Advanced Placement opportunities. An internship and college-level class are required in the senior year. Activities include sports, student council, community service, yearbook, drama, journalism, and chess. Tuition: $10,200. Financial aid is available. Armond Lawson is Director of Admission; Billy Handmaker was named Head of School in 1996.

Forsyth School 1961

6235 Wydown Boulevard, St. Louis, MO 63105. 314-726-4542;
Fax 314-726-0112; E-mail afb@forsythonline.com;
Web Page www.forsythonline.com

Forsyth, a coeducational elementary school with 350 students Age 3–Grade 6, offers a challenging and engaging academic program, a commitment to diversity, 8:1 student-teacher ratio, team teaching, year-round programs, and before- and after-school classes and sports. Named a Blue Ribbon School by the U.S. Department of Education, Forsyth fosters a love of learning, self-confidence, and a sense of responsibility in a warm, supportive environment. In addition to classroom fundamentals, the School employs full-time specialists in science, art, music, French, Spanish, Latin, creative movement, physical education, outdoor education, and drama. Tuition: $8870. Rebecca Glenn (Washington University, Ph.D.) was appointed Head in 1986.

John Burroughs School 1923

755 South Price Road, St. Louis, MO 63124. 314-993-4040;
Fax 314-993-6458; E-mail wthomas@jburroughs.org;
Web Site www.jburroughs.org

John Burroughs School is a coeducational, college preparatory day school enrolling 586 students in Grades 7–12. The 40-acre campus includes a library, science and fine arts buildings, a sports and performing arts facility, and a newly renovated academic and administrative building. The School is committed to providing an educational experience that balances academics, arts, athletics, and activities. Taught by 105 full- and part-time faculty, students are provided with a firm foundation in the five basic disciplines: English, science, mathematics, social studies, and foreign languages. Tuition: $12,550. Financial Aid: $985,700. Keith E. Shahan (Amherst, B.A.; Harvard, M.A., Ed.D.) was appointed Headmaster in 1986.

Logos School 1970

9137 Old Bonhomme Road, St. Louis, MO 63132-4417.
314-997-7002; Fax 314-997-6848;
E-mail dthomas@logosschool.org; Web Site www.logosschool.org

Logos is an alternative, therapeutic day school enrolling 110 boys and girls in Grades 7–12 who have been unsuccessful in the traditional classroom. It specializes in serving adolescents who struggle with depression, ADD, AD/HD, learning disabilities, poor motivation, anxiety, and low self-esteem. The unique, 12-month program combines strong academics, weekly individual and group therapy, and weekly parent support meetings. With a 6:1 student-teacher ratio, Logos treats each student's learning style and needs individually, developing specific goals

in each class. Logos offers honors courses, sports, and a regionally recognized fine arts program. All teachers are certificated. Tuition: $15,600. Financial aid is available. Kathy Heimburger is Director of Admissions; David C. Thomas, Ph.D., is Director/CEO.

Mary Institute and Saint Louis Country Day School 1859

101 North Warson Road, St. Louis, MO 63124. 314-993-5100;
Fax 314-872-3257; E-mail jwinkeler@micds.org;
Web Site www.micds.pvt.k12.mo.us

Mary Institute and Saint Louis Country Day School, enrolling 1215 students in Junior Kindergarten–Grade 12, is a community where people strive to think critically, live virtuously and compassionately, and act responsibly. The college preparatory program is designed to foster academic excellence, leadership, and self-confidence. The curriculum includes English, history, science, math, foreign language, and the arts, with Advanced Placement in all disciplines. Student Council, publications, sports, and clubs are among the activities. A summer program is offered. Tuition: $10,300–$12,700. Financial Aid: $1,800,000. Patricia C. Shipley is Director of Admission; Matthew E. Gossage (Vanderbilt, B.A., M.A.T.; Harvard, M.Ed.) is Head of School.

The Metropolitan School 1967

7281 Sarah Street, St. Louis, MO 63143. 314-644-0850;
Fax 314-644-3363; E-mail info@metroschool.org

Metropolitan School is a state-approved, coeducational day school providing a special-educational program for adolescents who have learning disabilities, attention deficits, or other atypical learning styles. The School enrolls 70 students in Grades 5–12. A challenging academic curriculum with highly individualized instruction is provided by fully certified staff at a 9:1 student-teacher ratio. An outdoor challenge program, social skills curriculum, and indoor-outdoor summer experience are adjuncts to classroom instruction. Tuition: $13,100. Zachary McBee is Admissions Administrator; Rita M. Buckley is Executive Director; Judi Thomas is Head of Middle School; Jeff May is Head of Upper School. *North Central Association.*

Missouri Military Academy 1889

204 Grand Avenue, Mexico, MO 65265. 573-581-1776,
888-JOIN-MMA (Toll-free/USA); Fax 573-581-0081;
E-mail admissn@mma.mexico.mo.us;
Web Site www.mma-cadet.org

Missouri Military Academy provides a structured, college preparatory boarding program for boys from across the United States and abroad in Grade 4–Postgraduate. The Academy offers young men real-life experiences and leadership opportunities. Cadets are trained mentally, physically, spiritually, culturally, and socially and given leadership opportunities that result in experience advantages not normally gained until later in life. The academic program features supervised study and extra-help sessions. Eleven varsity sports, intramural athletics, and numerous extracurricular activities engage boys and their families in Academy life. Boarding Tuition/Fees: $20,200–$21,000. Financial aid is available. MAJ Roger J. Mick is Director of Admissions; COL Ronald J. Kelly is President.

The Pembroke Hill School   1910

400 West 51st Street, Kansas City, MO 64112. 816-936-1200;
Fax 816-936-1238; E-mail csullivan@pembrokehill.org;
Web Site www.pembrokehill.org

The Pembroke Hill School, formed by the 1984 merger of The Pembroke-Country Day School and The Sunset Hill School enrolls 1129 day boys and day girls in Early Years–Grade 12. Located on two campuses in close proximity, the School provides facilities to accommodate a broad academic program. Extended-day programs are available. The curriculum is enriched by Advanced Placement courses and fine and performing arts. Publications, student government, community service, and sports are available. Summer offerings include enrichment courses for ages 2¹/₂ to 18. Tuition: $4575–$10,875. Financial Aid: $1,200,000. Carolyn Sullivan is Admissions Director; Richard D. Hibschman (Ball State, B.S.; Northern Illinois, M.S.; Harvard, Ed.D.) is Headmaster.

Rockhurst High School   1910

Greenlease Memorial Campus, 9301 State Line Road,
Kansas City, MO 64114. 816-363-2036; Fax 816-363-3764;
E-mail jreichme@rockhursths.edu; Web Site www.rockhursths.edu

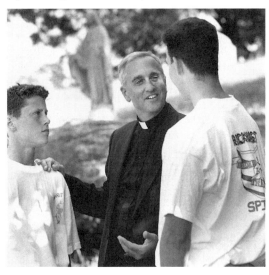

Rockhurst, a Roman Catholic, Jesuit college preparatory high school, enrolls 980 young men in Grades 9–12 from throughout the metropolitan Kansas City area. It provides a rigorous education in the Jesuit tradition of excellence. As "men for others," students and graduates are distinguished by their competence, conscience, and compassion. Advanced Placement and college-credit courses are available. Theology courses are required. Cocurricular, pastoral, and service opportunities complement academic requirements. The summer academy offers courses for returning students and incoming freshmen. Tuition and Fees: $6150. Financial Aid: $630,000. Jack Reichmeier is Director of Admission and Financial Aid; Rev. Thomas A. Pesci, SJ (Fordham University, P.D.), is President. *North Central Association.*

Rohan Woods School   1937

1515 Bennett Avenue, St. Louis, MO 63122. 314-821-6270;
Fax 314-821-6878; E-mail rohanwoods.org;
Web Site rohanwoods.org

Rohan Woods, a day school enrolling 145 boys and girls in Junior Kindergarten (ages 4–5)–Grade 6, offers an enriched traditional curriculum within a small-school setting with an 8:1 student-teacher ratio. It seeks to provide challenge within a supportive, nurturing environment where children can attain academic excellence. Reading, a "problem-solving" approach to math, creative writing, French, inquiry-based science, computer classes, and intramural sports are emphasized. After-school enrichment, extended care, after-school homework supervision, and vacation camps are offered. Tuition: $8650. Financial Aid: 10 percent of tuition. Julie Gaebe is Admissions Director; Robert P. Ciampoli (University of Missouri, B.A. 1970; Webster, M.A. 1980) is Headmaster.

Rossman School   1917

12660 Conway Road, St. Louis, MO 63141-8625. 314-434-5877;
Fax 314-434-1668; E-mail adm@rossmanschool.org;
Web Site www.rossmanschool.org

Rossman is an elementary day school featuring a challenging academic program for boys and girls in Junior Kindergarten (age four)–Grade 6. Seeking to maximize each child's potential, the School holds to a student/teacher ratio of 8:1. The curriculum focuses on the basics of mathematics and language arts and integrates computers, science, social studies, French, Latin, music, art, library, and physical education. A cultural enrichment program, field trips, and athletics supplement the curriculum. After school Enrichment and Extended Day are available. Tuition (including lunch): $10,185. Applications for financial aid are welcome. Katherine A. Betz (William Jewell, B.A.) is Head of School.

Saint Louis Priory School   1955

500 South Mason Road, St. Louis, MO 63141. 314-434-3690;
Admissions 314-434-7178; Fax 314-576-7088;
E-mail dguilliams@priory.org; Web Site www.priory.org

Saint Louis Priory School, enrolling 380 college-bound boys from many faiths in Grades 7–12, is operated by the Benedictine Monks of the Abbey of Saint Mary. In addition to providing academic challenge, the School seeks to impart a strong formation in the knowledge and practice of Catholicism. The curriculum includes Advanced Placement in most subjects, theology, and electives in language and the arts. At least 80 hours of community service and completion of the Senior Thesis are required for graduation. Student Council, athletics, publications, plays, and interest clubs are among the activities offered. Tuition: $9720. Financial aid is available. Dennis Guilliams is Admissions Director; Rev. Gregory Mohrman, OSB (University of Pennsylvania, B.A.; Saint John's, M.A., M.Div.; Middlebury, M.A.), is Headmaster.

St. Paul's Episcopal Day School   1963

4041 Main Street, Kansas City, MO 64111. 816-931-8614;
Fax 816-931-6860; E-mail stpaul@tfs.net

St. Paul's Episcopal Day School seeks to maintain a caring, loving environment in an academically challenging atmosphere. Founded to provide a program that included spiritual and character development, the School enrolls 460 boys and girls in Early Childhood–Grade 8. The curriculum emphasizes basic skills and traditional subjects enriched by foreign language, art, music, creative movement, and computer. Student Council, sports, yearbook, math and service clubs, and choir are among the activities. Academic enrichment courses and a day camp are offered in the summer. Tuition: $1235–$6165. Financial Aid: $100,000. Mary Dobbins is Admissions Director; Terry Bartow (University of Massachusetts, B.S. 1976; Cornell, M.S. 1980) is Head of School.

Thomas Jefferson School ST. LOUIS

4100 South Lindbergh Boulevard, St. Louis, MO 63127.
314-843-4151; E-mail admissions@tjs.org; Web Site www.tjs.org

THOMAS JEFFERSON SCHOOL in St. Louis, Missouri, is a boarding and day school for boys and girls in Grades 7 through 12 and a postgraduate year. The campus is located in the suburban community of Sunset Hills (population 5000), 15 miles from the center of St. Louis.

Thomas Jefferson School was founded in 1946 by three Harvard alumni—Robin McCoy, Graham Spring, and Charles E. Merrill, Jr. After 25 years as a school for boys, it became coeducational in 1971, and girls now make up about one-half of the student body. A college preparatory school, it seeks "to provide thorough academic training under conditions that help a student develop the habit of hard work and a sense of responsibility for his own affairs."

The School is a nonprofit institution controlled by a self-electing Board of Trustees, the majority of whom must be active teachers at the School. Every full-time teacher becomes a Trustee within three years of joining the faculty.

Thomas Jefferson School holds membership in the National Association of Independent Schools, the Educational Records Bureau, The Association of Boarding Schools, Midwest Boarding Schools, and the Independent Schools Association of the Central States.

THE CAMPUS. The school property, acquired in 1946, is a 20-acre former estate landscaped with lawns and many varieties of shade trees. The back part of the property includes an athletic field and track and five tennis courts.

The Main Building contains the Headmaster's office, the business office, teachers' offices, classrooms, computers, the library, the common room, and the dining room. Boarders live in the Gables—a two-story building that is part of the original estate—and in six student houses of modern construction and design (1960, 1994). Each house has four double rooms with private baths and outside entrances, providing quiet, privacy, and independence for the students. Every room has telephone and Internet access. A new academic building, Sayers Hall (1992), contains state-of-the-art science labs, several classrooms, and a reference library.

The gymnasium provides facilities for basketball and volleyball. The entire plant is valued at approximately $1,600,000.

THE FACULTY. Lawrence A. Morgan became the School's second Headmaster in the summer of 1980, succeeding Robin McCoy. Mr. Morgan was born in Norman, Oklahoma, attended Thomas Jefferson School and Harvard University (A.B. 1957), and holds master's degrees from Washington University and Webster College (St. Louis). He has taught at the School for 42 years and was Director of Admissions for 14 years.

In addition to the Headmaster, who also teaches, there are 11 full-time faculty members, five men and six women. Seven teachers live on campus. The faculty hold ten baccalaureate and six master's degrees representing study at Colgate, Columbia, Georgetown, Harvard, Johns Hopkins, Kenyon, St. John's, Swarthmore, Washington University, Webster, Wesleyan, and the Universities of Illinois and Missouri.

Two nearby hospitals and several doctors' offices are available as needed.

STUDENT BODY. In 1999–2000, Thomas Jefferson School enrolls 22 boarding boys, 22 day boys, 18 boarding girls, and 14 day girls, ages 12–18, as follows: 12 in Grade 7, 11 in Grade 8, 10 in Grade 9, 14 in Grade 10, 16 in Grade 11, and 11 in Grade 12. Boarding students come from Arkansas, Illinois, Indiana, Kansas, Kentucky, Michigan, Missouri, Oklahoma, China, Honduras, Hong Kong, Poland, South Korea, and Thailand. Day students reside in St. Louis and its suburbs.

ACADEMIC PROGRAM. The school year, from early September to early June, includes 32 weeks of classes, a Thanksgiving recess, a 4-week vacation at Christmas, and a 3$\frac{1}{2}$-week vacation in March.

Classes, which have an enrollment of 3 to 16, meet five days a week for Grades 7–11 and four days a week for Grade 12. The weekday schedule follows: 7:50–8:10 A.M., breakfast buffet; 8:30 A.M.–12:30 P.M., classes; 12:30 P.M., lunch; 1:20–5:30 P.M., labs, athletics, other activities, and independent studies; 5:45 P.M., dinner; and 6:15–bedtime, study and leisure. Day students are on campus from 8:30 A.M. to 5:00 P.M.

The boys and girls may study anywhere on campus they wish; there are study halls only for those in academic difficulty. Boarders in the 7th through 10th grades have bedtimes according to their age and academic status; juniors and seniors are expected to use good judgment in determining their bedtimes. On Saturdays and Sundays, a student in good standing is free to plan his or her own schedule.

Discipline is handled through a demerit system, and penalties generally involve work around the School on weekends, such as cleaning jobs and yard work. An effort is made to keep supervision of as many disciplinary chores as possible in the hands of the students.

The curriculum for Grades 7–8 includes English, Latin, Mathematics, Science, and Social Studies. Students in Grades 9–12 take four years of English, two years each of two foreign languages (including Greek), two years of history (including United States History), four years of mathematics, and at least two years of laboratory science. In addition, each student has a choice of one or two more laboratory sciences, a third year of one foreign language, or a third year of history. Among the courses offered are English; French, Greek, Italian; Ancient History, European History, United States History; Algebra, Geometry, Advanced Algebra and Trigonometry, Precalculus, AB and BC Calculus; and Biology, Chemistry, and Physics. English courses usually include Shakespeare, selections from the Bible, and other classics of English and world literature. There is a strong emphasis on grammar, spelling, and writing skills as well as daily discussion of reading. Supplementary English-as-a-Second-Language instruction is offered to international students.

All students take either four (Grades 10–12) or five (Grades 7–9) academic courses per year, plus a fine arts class, which meets once a week. Alternatives include drawing, photography, ceramics, music appreciation, and art history.

Qualified students take Advanced Placement Examinations in English, United States History, European History, French, Biology, Physics, Chemistry, and Calculus. Some students prepare independently for other Advanced Placement exams in Latin, Government, Computer Science, and other subjects. There are frequent quizzes in most courses, one-hour quarterly examinations, and longer midyear and final examinations. Reports are sent home quarterly. In addition, each student is given the Educational Records Bureau tests in the fall, and each junior and senior takes SAT I and II examinations.

Thomas Jefferson School graduates are currently studying at Bowdoin, Brown, Butler, Columbia, Davidson, Gettysburg, Grinnell, Haverford, Johns Hopkins, Knox, Lake Forest, Purdue, Reed, Saint Louis University, Stanford, Swarthmore,

Washington University, Wesleyan, Williams, and the Universities of Chicago, Illinois, Kansas, Missouri, and Pennsylvania.

STUDENT ACTIVITIES. An active Student Council casts a vote in faculty meetings on any decision affecting student life.

Athletics are both intramural and interscholastic. Participation is required three or four days each week, and the program includes tennis, soccer, and other alternatives in the fall; basketball, aerobics, volleyball, and ice skating in the winter; and tennis, softball, and other alternatives in the spring.

In its social life, the School leaves the initiative with the students. Dances are held from time to time, and boarders in good standing may get permission to leave the campus on Friday or Saturday nights. Other weekend activities include leisure or study time, informal athletics, and off-campus trips to places of interest.

Thomas Jefferson School encourages use of the cultural facilities in St. Louis by securing tickets and providing transportation to ballets, concerts, and plays and by organizing trips to the Art Museum, the Botanical Garden, the zoo, and downtown St. Louis. The entire student body attends the six annual play productions at the Repertory Theater of St. Louis. The School often plans and supervises trips to Europe during vacations, most frequently to Florence and London in the summer. In Europe, the students visit museums and go to the theater and have free time to explore and shop.

ADMISSION AND COSTS. Requirements for admission include a transcript of the applicant's previous school record, four entrance examinations requiring about two hours (an I.Q. test, a reading test, a spelling test, and a written composition), and an interview. The SSAT and the ISEE are accepted as an alternative to the School's own testing. "Natural ability, past performance, liveliness, ambition, and willingness to work hard" are important considerations in evaluating candidates. Thomas Jefferson School has a policy of admitting students "without regard to race, color, creed, or national or ethnic origin."

New students are accepted in all grades, and applications will be considered for a postgraduate year.

For 1999–2000, the annual fee is $22,000 for full-time boarding students, $21,000 for five-day boarders, and $13,200 for day students. Total yearly expenses for books, supplies, athletic clothes, and play and concert tickets (all available through the School bookstore) come to $1000 or more. Day students provide their own transportation. Financial aid totaling approximately $220,000 is awarded annually.

Alumni Secretary: Jane Pesek
Director of Admission: William C. Rowe
Director of Development: Jane Pesek
College Counselor: Lawrence A. Morgan
Business Manager: Lawrence A. Morgan
Director of Athletics: Boaz Roth

Visitation Academy of St. Louis County   1833

3020 North Ballas Road, St. Louis, MO 63131. 314-432-5353; Fax 314-432-7210; E-mail srmmgibson@visitation.com

Visitation Academy is a Roman Catholic, college preparatory day school enrolling 640 girls in Toddler–Grade 12 and 19 boys in Toddler and Montessori I programs. The Academy maintains a learning environment that encourages students to "Live † Jesus" and to develop to their full potential in all areas. Emphasis is placed on achieving self-identity as Christians and a positive self-image. Speech and the arts enrich the curriculum, which includes Advanced Placement courses. Montessori orientation, sports clinics, and enrichment courses are offered in the summer. Tuition: $4000–$7500. Financial aid is available. Sr. Margaret Mary Gibson is Director of Admissions; William M. Gallop (St. Joseph's University, B.S. 1959; Temple University, M.Ed. 1965) is Head of School. *North Central Association.*

Wentworth Military Academy and Junior College   LEXINGTON

1880 Washington Avenue, Lexington, MO 64067. 660-259-2221;
Fax 660-259-2677; E-mail admissions@wma1880.org;
Web Site www.wma1880.org

WENTWORTH MILITARY ACADEMY AND JUNIOR COLLEGE in Lexington, Missouri, is one of the nation's oldest military schools. Established in 1880 as a private secondary school, Wentworth today enrolls young men in Grades 6–12, young women in Grades 11–12, and both men and women in the Military Junior College. Wentworth prides itself on providing a structured educational environment for youths with potential.

The historic town of Lexington (population 5000), a Civil War battle site, lies on the bluffs of the Missouri River at the junction of U.S. Highways 24 and 13, about 40 miles east of Kansas City. Its location permits students to enjoy the cultural and recreational resources of the metropolitan area without the daily distractions of an urban location.

Both the Junior College and the High School divisions of the Academy are accredited by the North Central Association of Colleges and Secondary Schools and hold membership in the Association of Military Colleges and Schools of the United States. The Wentworth Parents' Association, Alumni Association, and Red Dragon Booster Club are active in fund-raising and other supportive efforts on behalf of the Academy.

THE CAMPUS. The 137-acre tree-shaded campus includes landscaped lawns, athletic and drill fields, tennis courts, and woodlands used for military exercises and outdoor recreation.

The academic heart of the school is the Sellers-Wikoff Scholastic Building, containing classrooms, computer laboratories, and the Sellers-Coombs Library, with approximately 17,000 volumes, more than 4000 microfilms of periodicals, and 170 magazines and newspapers. Groendyke Hall houses a new state-of-the-art computer lab, most college classrooms, rooms for special activities, and a spacious lounge containing the Hall of Honor. The 65,000-square-foot Wikoff Field House holds three basketball courts, a handball court, a six-lane indoor track, a wrestling room, a weight room, a pole vault and jumping pit, and an Olympic-size swimming pool. Other facilities include the Administration Building, Memorial Chapel, and the 16-bed Student Infirmary. Students reside in four barracks containing double rooms.

THE FACULTY. Col. Jerry E. Brown, USAF (Ret.), was named Superintendent of Wentworth Military Academy in December 1994. He earned a B.S. degree from Washburn University and an M.S. degree from the University of Southern California.

The teaching faculty include 20 men and 7 women who hold 34 baccalaureate, 20 master's, and 4 doctoral degrees.

The Student Infirmary, under the supervision of a registered nurse and staff, is available 24 hours a day. The Academy retains the services of local physicians, dentists, and psychologists, as needed, and excellent emergency facilities are available.

STUDENT BODY. The student body is representative of 31 states and five foreign countries. Most students board full time, but a day-student program is also available as well as a postgraduate program.

ACADEMIC PROGRAM. The school year, from late August to the middle of May, is divided into semesters, with winter and spring vacations. The academic program at Wentworth is predicated on the belief that students thrive best in a structured environment, with small classes and individual attention. Faculty employ traditional, proven methods of instruction and, through motivation and encouragement, seek to foster self-confidence, determination, and a lifelong love of learning. Exceptional effort and achievement are recognized through citation on the Dean's List, extra privileges, and the awarding of ribbons.

Most students carry six solid subjects per semester. To graduate, cadets must earn a minimum of 22 academic credits for a general diploma and a minimum of 24 credits for a college preparatory diploma. In the college preparatory curriculum, the following requirements must be fulfilled: 4 units of English; 3 units each in Math, Science, and Social Studies; 2 units each in foreign language, Physical Education, and Junior Reserve Officer Training Corps (JROTC); 1 unit each in Fine Arts and Practical Arts; $1/2$ unit each in Computer Science; and 3 electives. The general course of studies is similar, but only 3 units of English and 2 units of Science are required, with 7 electives and no foreign language requirements.

Among the specific courses offered in the High School are English I–IV, Speech, ACT/SAT English Preparation, Journalism, Library Aide; German I–II, Spanish I–IV; Geography, World History, American History, American Government, Economics, Psychology, Sociology; Pre-Algebra, Algebra I–II, Geometry, Trigonometry, Pre-Calculus, ACT/SAT Math Preparation, Consumer Math; Introduction to Computers, General Business, Elementary Accounting; General Science, Physical Science, Biology, Chemistry, Physics; JROTC I–IV; Music Appreciation, Band, Chorus, Art; and Physical Education and Health, Life Saving, and Water Safety.

The JROTC is taught by recently retired U.S. Army personnel. The course is designed to develop good citizenship, self-reliance, leadership, and responsiveness to constituted authority. Junior High cadets are members of the Wentworth Cadet Corps but are not formally enrolled in JROTC.

English as a Second Language is available for nonnative

speakers, and qualified students may earn advance college credits at Wentworth Junior College. Career counseling and college placement assistance are available through the school guidance counselor.

The Academy provides a reading support program taught by a specialist to improve the skills of students who are having difficulty in that area. Additionally, Wentworth also conducts a Summer School program offering academic review, enrichment, English as a Second Language, and a Living History Civil War Camp.

For Junior College students, Wentworth offers a well-rounded and carefully balanced two-year program with the same courses in Liberal Arts and Science that are available at leading universities.

All Military Junior College cadets participate in the Army Reserve Officer Training Corps (ROTC) program, which is conducted by active-duty Army personnel stationed at Wentworth for a three- or four-year tour of duty.

Junior College cadets enroll in one of two ROTC courses: Basic Course (Military Science I–II) without any military obligation, or the Advanced Course (Military Science III–IV), leading to a commission at graduation from Wentworth.

Wentworth Army ROTC offers two options for becoming an Army officer. Only a few other schools in the country offer either of these scholarship programs. One option is through the Early Commissioning Program, in which Junior College cadets may earn an appointment as a second lieutenant in just two years. The other option is the 2+2 program, which is designed for up to four years of college study and Army ROTC training, starting at Wentworth and continuing at a four-year college, with a scholarship to cover tuition at both. Through this program, a candidate may earn a bachelor's degree and officer's commission at the same time.

Another service opportunity is the Falcon Scholar Program. Wentworth is one of only five schools in the nation selected by the Falcon Foundation to partnership with the United States Air Force Academy. Falcon cadets attend Wentworth through a scholarship program to prepare for admission to the Air Force Academy.

STUDENT ACTIVITIES. In cooperation with the Battle of Lexington State Park and Museum, Wentworth has a Civil War Living History Program in which cadets "study by doing" etiquette, historic events, military life, and weaponry of the War Between the States. Included in the program are field trips and battle reenactments as far away as Gettysburg, Pennsylvania.

For cadets who are seriously considering careers in the military, the Ranger Platoon gives specialized training in military skills and tactics. The Academy also conducts an FAA-approved aviation flight-training program, taught by FAA-rated instructors. Cadets can earn Solo, Private Pilot, Instrument Rating, and Flight Instructor certificates.

The Wentworth Military Academy Band performs at many special on- and off-campus events and presents an annual concert. Beginning Band is designed for cadets who wish to learn a band instrument.

Cadets publish *Pass in Review*, the school yearbook.

Several clubs are formed to pursue various hobbies and interests, such as Boy Scouts, model building, chess, debate, bridge, and Alpha Phi Omega, a national service fraternity. Qualified students may be invited to join the National Honor Society.

Athletic teams are formed at several levels in the junior high, high school, and junior college, and every student at the Academy is encouraged to become proficient in one or more sports, choosing from football, soccer, cross-country, basketball, wrestling, swimming, golf, tennis, and track. Cadets may also engage in volleyball, weight lifting, and hiking.

Special events are scheduled throughout the year including Parents' Weekend, Homecoming, the Military Ball, and Graduation.

ADMISSION AND COSTS. Wentworth accepts students without regard to race, religion, or national or ethnic origin. Decisions are based on previous records, letters of reference, a physical examination, and, for junior college entrants, ACT or SAT test scores and proof of graduation from high school or a general equivalency diploma. The application fee is $100.

For the academic year of 2000-2001, Junior High/High School boarding tuition and associated fees are $18,081. Military Junior College fees are $18,975 for males and $19,217 for females. Financial aid, ROTC scholarships, and loans are available to eligible college students.

Dean of Admissions: Maj. Todd L. Kitchen, Sr.

Whitfield School   1952

175 South Mason Road, St. Louis, MO 63141. 314-434-5141; Fax 314-434-6193; E-mail alversc@whitfieldschool.org; Web Site www.whitfieldschool.org

Whitfield's intellectually focused curriculum emphasizes critical thinking, reading, and writing across the academic disciplines, in addition to offering challenging fine and performing arts experiences. With classes of 15 or fewer, the student-centered atmosphere allows for a "teacher as coach, student as worker" approach to education, resulting in confident, articulate graduates prepared for the rigors of college. The state-of-the-art computer network provides one workstation for every three students and connects a multimedia language lab, publications room, and more than 100 other workstations. Students at all levels may participate in any of ten extracurriculars and 15 sports. Tuition: $13,425. Financial aid is available. Cynthia Crum Alverson is Admission Director; Mary L. Burke, Ph.D., is Head of School.

MONTANA

Mission Mountain School   CONDON

*P.O. Box 980, Guest Ranch Road, Condon, MT 59826.
406-754-2580; Fax 406-754-2470*

MISSION MOUNTAIN SCHOOL in Condon, Montana, is a small, highly personalized boarding school for young women in crisis who need special programs of therapy, education, and recreation within a group setting. The School is located in northwestern Montana, 90 miles by car from airports in Missoula and Kalispell. An escort service to and from the School can be arranged. The region is home to the Bob Marshall Wilderness Area, the famed Mission Mountains, Big Mountain Ski Resort, and Glacier National Park, providing ample opportunity for girls to engage in a wide range of outdoor activities.

Mission Mountain School was founded in 1990 to provide troubled young women in crisis a setting in which they can heal and grow physically, socially, and morally and become environmentally conscious, self-actualized individuals capable of successful reentry into the family and community. The program is centered around quality counseling, education, and recreation within a supportive, familylike setting.

The typical Mission Mountain School student is verbally skilled and above average in intelligence. She may have been traumatized or troubled at home or at school. Symptoms may range from oppositional-defiant disorders, attention deficit disorders, and sexual abuse to chemical dependency and addictive-compulsive behaviors. Each girl's history is evaluated in order for the School's professional staff to implement the appropriate therapies needed to recover from past pain and regroup toward a healthy, positive future. Each girl also commits to undertake a personal education plan based on her interests and abilities that will help her achieve success in college and in the work force.

Mission Mountain School is operated by the Montana Educational Consulting and Programs, Inc. The School is a fully accredited member of the Pacific Northwest Association of Independent Schools.

THE CAMPUS. The program of Mission Mountain School is carried out on the 240-acre Double Diamond Ranch, a former guest ranch turned wildlife preserve in the heart of the Swan Valley. The location, abounding in rugged wilderness, forests, mountains, lakes, and rivers, discourages runaway attempts while offering a serene setting for contemplation, reflection, and renewal. Daily life is centered in a modern, ranch-style facility that contains classrooms, a computer room, a dining hall, and lodging. Each dorm room accommodates two to four girls. The main building also contains a weight room, sauna, hot tub, student lounge, and an audiovisual room. Retreats and family activities are held at Mission Mountain's large ski cabin in a setting some distance from the main campus.

THE FACULTY. John K. Mercer, M.S., is School Head. He has 18 years' experience in teaching and administering experiential education for adolescents and individuals with special needs. In addition to Mr. Mercer, there are 17 staff members, 4 men and 13 women, who provide academic instruction, counseling, therapeutic treatment, and other vital services. A licensed practical nurse administers and monitors prescription medications under the supervision of a consulting psychiatrist. All staff members are degreed, certified, and experienced in their fields.

STUDENT BODY. In 1999–2000, Mission Mountain School enrolls 32–36 young women, ages 13 through 18, in Grades 8–12. They have exhibited symptoms and behaviors that have prevented them from leading normal, healthy lives at home and in school. These may include poor academic performance, conflict with parents, chemical dependency, substance abuse, and eating disorders. The typical student has not suffered any irreconcilable traumatic events nor does she have a history of violent crime or psychotic illness. She may have experienced a painful and significant event such as a death in the family, separation or divorce, or physical or sexual abuse. Many students are referred to Mission Mountain School following diagnosis by an outside mental health professional.

THE PROGRAM. Mission Mountain School's program is designed to combine crisis management, intervention, and therapeutic treatment with a college preparatory curriculum within a secure, drug-free environment. The School operates 24 hours a day on a year-round basis. A staff-to-student ratio of 2:1 ensures that each girl receives ample attention and support as she begins the pathway to recovery.

The Mission Mountain School program is based on developing problem solving skills and does not require conformity or participation in a level system. Upon entrance to Mission Mountain, each student starts with her own Individual Recovery Plan. The plan outlines specific objectives targeted at resolving her unique issues, which, if not addressed, could become serious, lifelong character defects. The staff formulates the plan based on data obtained through the application, enrollment forms, and intake interview. It is reviewed regularly by the treatment coordinator and evaluated periodically by the student herself. The success of the plan, which is set within a specific time frame, is predicated on the student's acknowledgment and understanding of her problem and its impact on her quality of life. Each girl's Individual Recovery Plan includes participation in a minimum of 17 hours of group counseling each week and, when needed, regular attendance at 12-step programs on campus or in the community.

Integrated with the Individual Recovery Plan is the general treatment path, which challenges each girl to accept her issues without shame and to develop a strong sense of personal identity and self-esteem. Toward this end, students acquire daily life skills and the tools for resolving problems; they identify career and vocational interests while seeking to understand family dynamics and issues.

A typical day at Mission Mountain School begins at 7:00

A.M. and includes academic classes, counseling and therapy sessions, and chores three times a day. Time is also allocated for exercise and personal activities. Nutritious meals are served family style; special dietary needs can be met, and students with eating disorders plan their meals with the school nurse. "Lights out" is between 9:30 and 10:30 P.M.

Family and group counseling and retreats are also integrated into the program as vital components in reaching set goals. The family system treatment begins upon a student's admission to the School with the assignment of a family counselor who guides the family through the formulation of a treatment program and continues with frequent telephone follow-up. Extended family weekends are scheduled after the girl has been at the School for between four and six months. With their student, family members take part in the daily program including counseling sessions and recreation. Parents of Mission Mountain School students are expected to address and change their own problem behaviors and to confront dysfunction within themselves and their children. Intensive mother-daughter and father-daughter retreats involve two or three parents and their child in a program of recreational, experiential, and therapeutic activities.

Mission Mountain School's academic curriculum, based on high school programs and college entrance criteria nationwide, provides a solid foundation in the major disciplines. To earn a high school diploma, girls must complete 24 credits as follows: 4 each in English and electives; 3 each in math, sciences, and social studies; 2 each in expressive arts, psychology, and outdoor/physical recreation; and 1 in computer science. Among the courses offered are English I–IV; Spanish; Algebra I–II, Geometry, Functions/Statistics/Trigonometry; Geography, U.S. History, World History; Natural Science, Ecosystem Biology, Ecology, Environmental Science; Personal Computers; Explorations in Art; Social Psychology; Music I–II, Drama Therapy; Equestrian Skills I–II; and Health.

The time frame for each girl's treatment varies according to the individual, with the average length of stay approximately 22 to 26 months. Generally, during the first eight months, the student will identify her negative and self-defeating behaviors and express to the group and to her family her decision to give up those behaviors. During months 9–16, she will begin to demonstrate positive changes in her behavior by implementing problem-solving strategies and applying new dynamics in her life. In the final eight months, most girls will have begun to complete their journey toward a new identity through contribution to the well-being of others and the setting of goals consistent with the new identity. At this point, students are ready to reenter their family and community and to lead happy, productive lives. The School furnishes each departing student with a plan for continuing therapy as needed, and continues to follow her progress by telephone for up to three months.

STUDENT ACTIVITIES. Mission Mountain School's beautiful wilderness location is ideal for enjoying a wide range of outdoor activities. Girls can engage in hiking, mountain biking, trout fishing, camping, wildlife study, and field botany. Interaction with horses is a valuable tool for building compassionate and supportive relationships. Girls are encouraged to learn all aspects of equine care and handling; they develop basic equestrian skills and may progress from area to trail riding.

Depending on the season, a daily regimen of physical recreation may include basketball, volleyball, soccer, baseball, telemark and cross-country skiing, swimming, and aerobics and fitness exercise.

Celebrations of traditional holidays are planned, and girls are encouraged to practice their religious beliefs as they choose.

ADMISSION AND COSTS. Mission Mountain School welcomes gifted young women between the ages of 13 and 18 who are in crisis and who are willing to make the necessary changes in their behaviors through the therapeutic and academic programs of the School. Interested candidates should contact the Head of School to arrange an interview. A short profile of the student and her family situation is required, along with a statement of placement goals and financial resources. Admission is based on evaluations by medical and psychological professionals, previous transcripts, and the completed application.

In 1999–2000, the total cost of the program, including boarding fees, academic instruction, counseling, and therapy, is $4250 per month. A $1500 personal expense fund is also required. Clothing and equipment charges are approximately $4000 and include a Mac Powerbook laptop computer.

Registrar/Academic Supervisor: Colleen Harrington
Counseling Coordinator: Gary Kent
Outdoor Education Supervisor: Mike Finn
Nurse/Daily Life Skills Coordinator: Debra Finn

NEBRASKA

Brownell-Talbot 1863

*400 North Happy Hollow Boulevard, Omaha, NE 68132.
402-556-3772; Fax 402-553-2994; E-mail megathje@brownell.edu;
Web Site www.brownell.edu*

Nebraska's oldest secondary school, founded by Episcopal Bishop Joseph Talbot, Brownell-Talbot is an independent college preparatory day school enrolling 433 boys and girls in Pre-Kindergarten–Grade 12. The School is committed to developing each student's creative, intellectual, physical, spiritual, and social self. Athletics, fine arts, and chess are among the activities. The campus features a fine arts center, field house, high school library, university-level Internet access, and a six-lane indoor swimming pool. The School also sponsors summer camp sessions. Tuition: $1925–$9200. Financial Aid: $300,000. Melissa Gathje is Director of Admissions; Dianne Desler (University of Nebraska, B.S. 1969, M.S. 1971, Ed.S. 1981) was appointed Head in 1989.

NEVADA

The Meadows School 1984

*8601 Scholar Lane, Las Vegas, NV 89128. 702-254-1610;
Fax 702-254-2452; Web Site www.themeadowsschool.org*

Meadows, a nonsectarian, college preparatory, coeducational day school serving 760 students in Preschool–Grade 12 on a 40-acre campus, seeks to develop in its students a love for learning and to inspire each to seek knowledge independently while preparing for higher academic pursuits. The Spanish-immersion program begins in Kindergarten and is mandatory, along with computer; Latin is added in the Middle School. Twenty-five Advanced Placement and 27 Honors courses, 100 percent four-year college placement, competitive athletics in 18 varsity sports, and a full range of extracurricular programs are offered in a drug-free environment. Tuition: $6000–$11,400. Financial Aid: $600,000. Isabelle Holman is Lower School Director; Lorna Ramsey is Middle School Director; William H. Richardson (University of Nevada, M.Ed.) is Headmaster and Upper School Director. *Northwest Association.*

NEW HAMPSHIRE

Brewster Academy WOLFEBORO

*80 Academy Drive, Wolfeboro, NH 03894. 603-569-1600;
Admissions 603-569-7200; E-mail Admissions@Brewsternet.com*

BREWSTER ACADEMY in Wolfeboro, New Hampshire, is a coeducational, college preparatory boarding and day school with Grades 9 through 12 and a postgraduate year. Situated on Lake Winnipesaukee in the foothills of the White Mountains, the school's surroundings offer opportunities for many outdoor activities. Wolfeboro is 100 miles from Boston, 50 miles from Manchester and Portsmouth, and 38 miles from Concord. Bus service is available to and from Boston, and there are airports at nearby Manchester and Laconia.

The school was founded in 1820 by citizens who raised funds to erect a "building for higher education." It eventually served surrounding towns as a regional high school. In 1887, its name changed from Wolfeborough and Tuftonborough Academy to Brewster Free Academy in honor of John Brewster, who had endowed the school, and boarding students were admitted. In 1965, a regional public high school was established, and Brewster became a private secondary school.

The Brewster Academic Program seeks to provide a highly personalized, 21st-century education in a traditional boarding school environment, combining a quality education with contemporary practices in curriculum, teaching, and technology to prepare students for the compelling demands of life and work in the information age. BrewsterNet, a fiber-optic computer network, accesses educational resources from locations in the library, classrooms, and dormitories. All incoming students and their teachers are required to have a Macintosh Powerbook in order to maximize teaching and learning opportunities provided by the Academic Program.

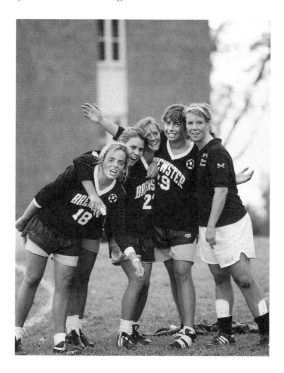

Brewster, a nonprofit corporation, is directed by the Headmaster for a self-perpetuating Board of Trustees, which includes representatives of the Parents' Association, the Alumni Association, and the John Brewster Estate. The school is accredited by the New England Association of Schools and Colleges; it is a member of the National Association of Independent Schools and the Independent Schools Association of Northern New England.

THE CAMPUS. Brewster's 75-acre campus encompasses a half-mile of Lake Winnipesaukee's southeastern shoreline, including beaches and docks. On campus are seven playing fields and a gymnasium with a regulation basketball court, the Kaywin Fitness Center, and the athletic trainer's room.

Faculty members live with students in 17 dormitories. In 1988, dining facilities were completed adjacent to the Spaulding-Emerson Student Center, built that year. The Academic Building (1903) contains the Wilson Center for Teaching and Learning, which includes classrooms, the Academic Support Center, Media Center, a recording studio, the Writing Program Center, student publications room, the Kenison Library, and offices. Also on campus are an expanded Art Center (1989); an infirmary; Admissions House; the Headmaster's residence; and a music center containing private practice rooms. Pinckney Boathouse houses crew, sailing, boat repair, and function facilities.

THE FACULTY. David M. Smith, who became Headmaster in 1974, is a graduate of St. Anselm College (B.A. 1966) and Villanova University (M.A. 1967). Prior to becoming Headmaster, Mr. Smith served Brewster as Acting Headmaster, Director of Admissions, Dean of Students, dorm master, teacher, Student Council moderator, and coach.

The Academy employs 80 teachers and administrators who teach, 41 men and 39 women. Forty-seven faculty members, 19 with their families, live on campus. Faculty members hold 72 baccalaureate and 38 graduate degrees representing study at such institutions as Amherst, Boston College, Boston University, Bowdoin, Brown, Clark, Clemson, Colby, Connecticut College, Cornell, Dartmouth, Duquesne, Harvard, Hollins, Johns Hopkins, Lafayette, Mount Holyoke, Pratt Institute, Simmons, Smith, Stanford, Syracuse, Trinity, Villanova, Wesleyan, William and Mary, Yale, and the Universities of Adelaide (Australia), Alaska, Berlin (Germany), California, Colorado, Denver, London, Maine, Massachusetts, New Hampshire, North Carolina, Toledo, Utah, Vermont, and Virginia.

One full-time and two part-time registered nurses staff the school infirmary. The area hospital is nearby.

STUDENT BODY. In 1999–2000, Brewster enrolled 196 boarding boys, 88 boarding girls, 36 day boys, and 27 day girls ages 14–18 as follows: 52 in Grade 9, 99 in Grade 10, 93 in Grade 11, 80 in Grade 12, and 23 postgraduates.

Day students reside in nearby cities and suburbs. Boarding students come from 40 states and 11 foreign countries.

ACADEMIC PROGRAM. Brewster's college preparatory curriculum is designed to meet students at their current level of performance and accelerate them in their mastery of content and skill. The school's goal is to ensure that a Brewster student graduates having thoroughly mastered those skills that predicate success in college.

Brewster's mission is to develop self-esteem, independence, and leadership by teaching students to "learn to learn" within a challenging curriculum. Winner of Macintosh's 1997 School of the Year Award for advancement and use of technology, Brewster offers students a highly innovative, state-of-the-art academic and community living program designed to challenge and support a diverse student body.

The trimester school year extends from early September to early June. There are two long weekend breaks—in October and February—and Thanksgiving, Christmas, and spring vacations. Classes are held six days per week and courses meet five times a week, supplemented by frequent individual student-instructor conferences. Classes are 50 minutes in length, with double periods for laboratories, and are limited to 10–12 students. Following afternoon athletics or activities, students may go to downtown Wolfeboro until the evening meal. Study hours begin at 8:00 P.M. in the dormitories and academic building.

All students in Grades 9–11 attend supervised study hall during the school day. All students participate in supervised evening study hall in the dormitories and academic building. Grades and comments are sent to parents five times a year. Each student is assigned to a faculty adviser. Advisers' comments are sent home after the first three weeks of the fall term.

To graduate, students must accumulate four units of credit for each year prior to entering Brewster and five units per year at Brewster. Specific requirements are English 4, social studies (including United States History) 3, mathematics (Algebra I and II and Geometry) 3, and science (including Biology) 3. Studying a foreign language through the second year is required and French and Spanish are offered through the fourth-year level.

Among the numerous full-year and semester courses are Writing the Essay, Studies in Modern Literature, Studies in World Literature; World History, European History, History of the Soviet Union, International Economics; Algebra, Geometry, Calculus, College Entrance Review Math; Beginning Computer Graphics, Advanced Computer Graphics; Chemistry, Physics; and Introduction to Art, Advanced Studies in Art, Pottery, Computer Graphics, Music Laboratory, Instrumental and Voice Instruction, and Music Theory and Harmonic Structure. Advanced Placement courses are offered in English, United States history, biology, and calculus. The Writing Program is integrated into all disciplines across the curriculum, for all grade levels. Special programs are offered in study skills and a postgraduate study in college skills and composition. During March vacation, one or more study trips go abroad; the most recent trips were to Russia, Europe, and Africa.

Selected seniors may elect a Senior Project during the spring term consisting of one month of off-campus work and study. Senior Projects have focused on oceanography, law, television, silversmithing, wilderness survival, and law enforcement and rehabilitation.

The Class of 1999 yielded a 100 percent acceptance rate among the following colleges and universities: American University, Bentley, Boston University, Colby, College of Wooster, Cornell, Franklin and Marshall, Gettysburg, Hobart, Lake Forest, Lehigh, Muhlenberg, and Wheaton.

STUDENT ACTIVITIES. Brewster's Leadership Program fosters student involvement in the operation of the school. Student proctors are trained to support the transition of new students, to serve as role models throughout the community, and are involved in dormitory government and in school discipline through a Student Judicial System. Students publish a school newspaper, a yearbook, and a literary magazine. Clubs include the Afro-Latino club, International Student club, Gold Key Society (tour guides), Interact, and the Environmental Awareness club. The Drama Program stages productions throughout the year. Students work in the community as hospital aides, elementary school tutors, clean-up crews for the town docks and lakeshore, and Big Brother/Big Sister volunteers.

Brewster students enroll in an afternoon commitment that affords them an opportunity to pursue activities of interest. All students commit to one season of interscholastic sports; they may choose to participate in the school's enrichment program during the other two seasons. The enrichment program provides choices in academic and athletic/fitness classes, which meet three days a week. Academic opportunities include drama, studio art, pottery, computer graphics, and Latin. Among the athletic activities are sailing, horseback riding, jogging, fitness and weight training, rock climbing, outdoor skills, and recreational tennis and golf.

Social activities include gatherings at the Student Center, dances, concerts, Winter Carnival, and off-campus trips to concerts, theaters, museums, the White Mountains, and sports events in Boston, Manchester, Hanover, Portland, and at the University of New Hampshire. Brewster requires both faculty and written parental permission for students to leave campus on weekends. Parents Weekends are in October and April; Alumni Weekend is in June.

ADMISSION AND COSTS. Brewster seeks candidates "who are committed to values emphasizing scholarship, fairness, responsibility, initiative, and leadership." Applicants are accepted on the basis of achievement records, test results, and recommendations; they are required to take the Secondary School Admission Test. A personal interview with the applicant is required. Students are accepted in Grades 9–12 and the postgraduate year, and late enrollment is permitted if vacancies exist.

Tuition for 1999–2000 is $26,400 for boarding students and $14,500 for day students; books, laundry, and personal supplies are extra. A tuition payment plan is available.

Brewster subscribes to the School and Student Service for Financial Aid. A limited number of scholarships are awarded on the basis of need, academic accomplishments, and potential for contributing to school life. In 1999–2000, students received $950,000 in financial aid.

Academic Deans: Marilyn Shea (Upper School) and Peter Hess (Lower School)
Dean of Students: Seth Ahlborn
Dean of Community Life: Byron Martin
Director of Admissions: Lynne Palmer
Director of College Placement: Shirley R. Richardson
Business Manager: Robert G. Simoneau
Director of Athletics: Douglas Algate

Cardigan Mountain School   1945

Canaan, NH 03741. 603-523-4321; Fax 603-523-3565;
  E-mail jdriscol@cardigan.org

On a 500-acre lakeside campus near Dartmouth, Cardigan provides small classes in which 200 boys in Grades 6–9 can develop skills, discipline, and self-confidence. Tracked classes allow students to learn alongside their academic peers. About 20 percent of the students are served by academic support programs. Interscholastic athletics are featured. Weekend activities are diverse at Cardigan where 90 percent of the students are boarders. Graduates enter such schools as Hotchkiss, Holderness, Lawrenceville, and St. Paul's. A coed summer program is offered for Grades 4–9. Boarding Tuition: $26,520. Financial Aid: $620,000. T. Jeff Driscoll is Director of Enrollment and Financial Aid; Dr. Cameron "Chip" Dewar (Bowdoin, B.A.; Boston University, M.Ed., Ed.D.) is Headmaster. *New England Association.*

The Derryfield School   1964

2108 North River Road, Manchester, NH 03104. 603-669-4524;
  Fax 603-625-9715; E-mail faculty@derryfield.com

The Derryfield School is a college preparatory day school enrolling 350 boys and girls in Grades 6–12. The School seeks to foster intellectual growth and is committed to the education of the whole person. Student participation in the fine arts and athletics is required. Community service, publications, student government, and other activities further enhance school life. Advanced Placement courses are available in American history, biology, calculus, English, French, Latin, and Spanish. Tuition: $13,500. Financial Aid: $550,000. Nancy S. Boettiger (University of Pennsylvania, B.A. 1964; Dominican College, M.A. 1971) was appointed Head in 1994. *New England Association.*

Dublin School   1935

Box 522, New Harrisville Road, Dublin, NH 03444-0522.
  603-563-8584; Fax 603-563-8671; E-mail
  admission@dublinschool.org

Dublin, a coeducational boarding and day school for Grades 9–12, promotes self-reliance and self-confidence in a small, structured community. Students achieve success through strong academics, arts, and athletic programs. Commitments to daily jobs, Saturday work gang, humanities, and community service are required. The Learning Skills and Evening Study Assistance programs assist students requiring academic support. English as a Second Language, independent study, and extracurriculars are available. The Whitney Gymnasium (1998) brings new life to the athletic program. Boarding Tuition: $26,500; Day Tuition: $15,900; Learning Skills: $5600; Evening Study Assistance: $1100 (semester). Financial Aid: $465,000. Marylou T. Marcus is Director of Admission; Christopher R. Horgan is Head of School. *New England Association.*

Hampstead Academy   1978

Mailing Address: P.O. Box 1208, Atkinson, NH 03811.
  603-362-5814
320 East Road, Hampstead, NH 03841. 603-329-4406;
  Fax 603-329-7124; E-mail LKutz@mediaone.net;
  Web Site www.hampsteadacademy.org

Hampstead Academy is a coeducational day school enrolling 252 students in Nursery–Grade 8 with facilities in Atkinson for Preschool and in Hampstead for Elementary and Junior High. Blending hands-on experience with a solid academic curriculum in liberal arts, fine arts, and sciences, Hampstead Academy uses eclectic teaching styles to "educate the whole child." Designed to engender a love of learning, this approach embraces such values as discipline, perseverance, character, and ethical behavior. A new "gymnatorium" enhances the sports, drama, and music programs. Students are actively involved in community service projects. Tuition: $6995–$7700. Financial aid is available. Lyn E. Kutzelman (Lesley College, M.Ed. 1984) is Head of School. *New England Association.*

Kimball Union Academy   1813

Meriden, NH 03770. 603-469-2000; Admissions 603-469-2100;
  Fax 603-469-2041; E-mail admissions@kua.org;
  Web Site www.kua.org

Founded in 1813, Kimball Union is a nondenominational, coeducational, college preparatory school enrolling 200 boarders and 90 day students in Grade 9–Postgraduate. Small classes, supervised study, and required participation in art and athletics are enriched by an environmental studies program designed around the school's 900-acre wilderness area and a new environmental science center. The Flickinger Arts Center and the Whittemore Athletic Center provide excellent facilities for extracurricular activities. A new dining hall opened in April 1999. Boarding Tuition: $25,600; Day Tuition: $15,600. Financial Aid: $1,175,000. Joe Williams is Director of Admissions; Timothy Knox (Dartmouth, B.A. 1961; Columbia, M.A. 1963) was appointed Headmaster in 1989. *New England Association.*

New Hampton School   1821

New Hampton, NH 03256. 603-744-5401; Fax 603-744-3433;
  Web Site http://www.newhampton.org

New Hampton School, enrolling 230 boarding and 80 day students in Grade 9–Postgraduate, emphasizes personal responsibility and respect for individuals as the foundations on which the unique strengths of each student are developed. Structure, extra help, and small classes are features of the college preparatory curriculum. The fine and performing arts, athletics, and community service programs challenge students to excel in all areas of their lives. The School's motto is "In a world that expects you to fit in, we teach you to stand out." Boarding Tuition: $26,200; Day Tuition: $14,500. Financial Aid: $1,450,000. Andrew Churchill is Dean of Admission; Dr. Jeffrey P. Beedy (University of Maine, B.A., M.Ed.; Harvard, Ed.D.) is Headmaster. *New England Association.*

Proctor Academy ANDOVER

P.O. Box 500, Andover, NH 03216. 603-735-6000;
Admissions 603-735-6212; Fax 603-735-6284;
E-mail admissions@gw.proctor.pvt.k12.nh.us;
Web Site www.admissions@proctornet.com

Proctor academy in Andover, New Hampshire, founded in 1848, is a coeducational, college preparatory boarding and day school enrolling a highly diverse student body. Located in Andover, a small New England village between Kearsarge and Ragged mountains, the 2000-acre campus provides the ideal setting for the school's unique experiential activities. Public bus service is available to and from Boston, and the school provides transportation to airports in Boston and Manchester at vacation time.

Proctor's humanistic approach to education prizes positive attitude and personal responsibility within a close community. The challenging curriculum includes extensive elective opportunities and is balanced by overt support services and clear structure. The school assumes that all Proctor students are capable of academic mastery. Accountability is great, while students are motivated through informal relationships with faculty to act as young adults.

Proctor Academy is accredited by the New England Association of Schools and Colleges and holds membership in the National Association of Independent Schools, the Secondary School Admission Test Board, and the Independent Schools Association of Northern New England. Governed by a 32-member Board of Trustees, Proctor has $18,000,000 in endowment, and the school plant is valued at $27,000,000. Total annual giving is $5,000,000.

THE CAMPUS. The campus spans a valley with a central village, open fields, private ski area, trout stream, and extensive woodlands on the south face of Ragged Mountain.

Academic facilities are clustered at the center of a village campus. The Fowler Learning Center (1994) includes the Faxon Computer Center, Lovejoy Library, and Harman Learning Skills Center. The library is fully automated on computer. The Computer Center networks more than 100 Macintosh computers with students' own computers in dorm rooms.

Shirley Hall houses science labs, history classrooms, and the math department. English and foreign language classes meet in Maxwell Savage Hall, and daily assemblies are held in Holland Auditorium. Additional facilities include music, arts, and ceramics studios; a machine shop; the Proctor Forge; the Maple Sugaring House; the Forestry Building; and a boatbuilding woodshop.

Athletic facilities include the Farrell Field House with basketball courts, an athletic cage, two indoor tennis courts, a Nautilus weight-training room, and locker rooms; an indoor hockey rink; 15 miles of cross-country ski trails; a downhill ski area with a 1500-foot T-bar, snow-making, lighting, and 15- and 30-meter ski jumps; six athletic fields; and eight tennis courts. Yarrow's Ski Lodge offers wood-heated warming rooms, a game room with snack bar, and a sundeck with a large grill.

Twenty small houses, built between 1792 and 1998, provide homelike dormitories that average 11 students. Students live in singles and doubles and enjoy much contact with dorm parents.

THE FACULTY. Steve Wilkins became Head of School in 1995. The former Director of the Jemicy School and the Carroll School, he is a graduate of Colgate University (B.A.) and Harvard University (Ed.M.) and was a Faculty Associate at Johns Hopkins University from 1991 to 1995. A noted lecturer on teaching methodologies, Mr. Wilkins is the author of "The Teacher's Guide to the Brain" and "Changing the Variables: Improving Classroom Instruction."

The faculty, consisting of 43 women and 36 men, hold 80 baccalaureate, 33 master's, and 4 doctoral degrees. Undergraduate colleges include Amherst, Bowdoin, Brigham Young, Colby, Colby-Sawyer, Colgate, Colorado, Dartmouth, Davidson, Dickinson, Duke, Elmira, Emmanuel, Gordon, Grinnell, Harvard, Hollins, Keene State, Lawrence, Michigan State, Middlebury, Nasson, Nichols, Northeastern, Providence, Rivier, Roanoke, Rutgers, St. Lawrence, St. Michael's, Skidmore, Southern Oregon, Springfield, Syracuse, Western State, Wheelock, and the Universities of Colorado, New Hampshire, Rhode Island, and Wisconsin.

STUDENT BODY. In 1999–2000, Proctor Academy enrolled 267 boarding and 68 day students in Grades 9–12. They represent 33 states, with the largest percentage of students coming from New Hampshire, Massachusetts, New York, California, Connecticut, and Pennsylvania.

ACADEMIC PROGRAM. The school year, divided into trimesters, begins in early September and ends in early June. There are vacations at Thanksgiving, Christmas, and in the spring, and long Bonus Weekends in the fall and winter. Classes, 55 minutes in length, meet Monday through Friday from 7:40 A.M. to 2:30 P.M. and most Saturdays from 9:00 to 10:30 A.M. The average class enrolls 12 students. A half-hour assembly is held each day to give faculty and students the opportunity to report on events and voice concerns. All students observe study hours from 8:00 to 10:00 P.M.

Proctor is structured to challenge and support college-bound students of diverse academic achievements and skills. Students are required to take four academic majors per trimester, but most take five to satisfy distribution requirements and strengthen college preparation. A full-year course is 3 credits. To graduate, a student must earn the following credits: English, 12; math, 9; science, 9; social science, 8 (including 3 in U.S. History); and foreign language, 6.

Learning Skills is an elective program for students of strong aptitude who benefit from regular tutorial support. Learning Lab provides instruction in organization, time management, and study skills.

Courses offered include Environmental Issues, Environmental Science, Environmental Applications; Introduction to Literature, American Literature, British Literature, Themes in Literature, Poetry, Crafting Fiction, Advanced Placement English; French 1–5, Spanish 1–5; Algebra I–II, Geometry, Problem Solving, Statistics, Trigonometry, Data Exploration, Probability, Math Design Theory, Earth Algebra, Precalculus, Calculus, Computer Programming I–II, Surveying; Biology, Chemistry, Physics, Forestry, Geology, Astronomy, Wildlife Science, Anatomy and Physiology; World Cultures, United States History, Asian History, Modern European History, Native American Studies, Middle East History, Vietnam War, Economics, Sociology, Psychology, and Modern Foreign Policy. Skill electives include Studio Art, Ceramics, Photography, Applied Music, Recording Techniques, Theory and Composition, Jazz/Rock Band, Steel Drum Band, Weaving, Drama; The Sampler Course (blacksmithing, metal turning, welding), Boatbuilding, Jewelrymaking, Woodshop, Life Skills; and Word Processing. Honors sections and Advanced Placement are available in all major academic courses.

Proctor incorporates experiential education programs across the curriculum. Faculty oversee language study programs in Aix-en-Provence, France, and Segovia, Spain. Students who choose to participate experience total immersion while living with a French or Spanish family for ten weeks and attending language-intensive classes. Each trimester, ten students may elect to participate in the Mountain Classroom Program. Living on a separate portion of campus for the first three weeks, they prepare for a western field trip that finds them living with the Hopi and Navajo, rock climbing in the Canyonlands, and rafting on the Colorado River. Ocean Classroom, offered during the fall term, is a full-credit, academic ocean voyage aboard the 130-foot *Spirit of Massachusetts.* Following two weeks of preparation ashore, 17 students and ten adults sail this classic schooner from the Gulf of Maine to the Caribbean Sea, with research stops at 16 Atlantic ports. Each term, two students study at the American School in Tangier, Morocco. Students electing Environmental Classroom live in Eco-dorm while studying Advanced Placement Environmental Science. These programs are offered at no additional cost and exemplify the school's commitment to experiential education.

Ninety-seven percent of the Class of 1999 were admitted to four-year colleges. They are attending Boston University, Bucknell, Carnegie Mellon, Clark, Colorado College, Dartmouth, Denison, DePaul, Dickinson, Emerson, Fairfield, George Washington, Guilford, Hobart & William Smith, Lynchburg, Macalester, Middlebury, New York University, Northeastern, Pitzer, Reed, Rochester Institute of Technology, Roanoke, St. Lawrence, Skidmore, Susquehanna, Trinity, and the Universities of Colorado, Denver, New Hampshire, Rhode Island, San Diego, and Vermont.

STUDENT ACTIVITIES. Many opportunities exist for students to demonstrate leadership abilities. The Student Council meets weekly to discuss and debate campus issues, and the Student School Leader is an active member at faculty meetings. There is also Student Council representation on the Honor Court and the Discipline Committee. Students volunteer for more than 30 community service projects and programs, either in the school or the surrounding community. The Proctor Fire Department, managed by students who assist the town's volunteers on an emergency basis, maintains the school's fire trucks and conducts campus fire drills. Additional campus activities include the Academy Theatre, WPRC radio, Jazz/Rock Ensemble, Proctor Environmental Action, Proctor Mountaineering, and Peer Counseling.

Proctor students are required to participate in at least one team sport each year. Teams are formed at the varsity, junior varsity, and reserve squad levels to compete against other members of the Lakes Region and other schools in New England. Girls participate in field hockey, soccer, cross-country, alpine and cross-country skiing, ice hockey, snowboarding, basketball, lacrosse, horseback riding, cycling, softball, and tennis. Boys' teams are formed in football, soccer, cross-country, alpine and cross-country skiing, ski jumping, ice hockey, snowboarding, wrestling, basketball, lacrosse, baseball, cycling, and tennis. Students use the school's extensive woodlands for camping, kayaking, rock climbing, and hiking.

Traditional annual events include new-student orientation, a five-day backpacking hike in the White Mountains, Head's Holiday, Earth Day, Parents' Weekends, and Senior Canoe Trip.

ADMISSION AND COSTS. Proctor offers admission to new students in Grades 9–12, with the majority entering in the 9th and 10th grades. A positive attitude toward work, self, and others is the highest priority in admission screening. An academic transcript, recommendations, and a personal interview are required, as are the results from a Secondary School Admission Test or the Independent School Entrance Examination. Aptitude testing is encouraged and may be requested by the Admission Committee.

Proctor adheres to the March 10 notification date, after which spaces are limited and admission is offered on a rolling basis. The application fee is $35.

In 1999–2000, boarding tuition is $26,400, and day tuition is $13,900. There is an additional charge for enrollment in

Learning Skills and Learning Lab programs. Tuition plans are available. Students applying for financial aid should submit applications through the School and Student Service for Financial Aid in Princeton, New Jersey. In 1999–2000, $1,300,000 in need-based scholarships was awarded.

Dean of Faculty: Karl Methven
Dean of Students: Anne Swayze
Director of Admission: Michele Koenig
Director of Studies: Bert Carvalho
Director of Diversity: Robert Dais
Director of Financial Aid: Michele Koenig
Director of Development: Jay Goulart
Director of Communications: Chuck Will
College Counselors: Timothy Norris, Michael Koenig, Kristen
    Nesbitt, and Ellen Yenawine
Athletic Director: Tom Eccleston
Business Manager: Donald Macdonald

St. Paul's School 1856

325 Pleasant Street, Concord, NH 03301-2591. 603-229-4700;
    Fax 603-229-4771; E-mail admissions@sps.edu;
    Web Site http://www.sps.edu

Set on a beautiful, 2000-acre campus, St. Paul's is a college preparatory boarding school in the Episcopal tradition enrolling 520 young men and women from diverse backgrounds in Grades 9–12. Within a dynamic learning community, students undertake a curriculum that emphasizes communication, critical thinking, and problem solving of important global issues. Science, the humanities, technology, modern and classical languages, and the arts form the core program. Students are involved in school government, interest clubs, academic competitions, drama, music groups, and athletics. Tuition: $24,000. Financial Aid: $2,900,000. Joanne S. Thorp is Director of Admissions; The Right Reverend Craig B. Anderson, Ph.D., is Rector. *New England Association.*

Tilton School TILTON

30 School Street, Tilton, NH 03276. 603-286-4342 or
    Admissions 603-286-1733; Fax 603-286-1705;
    E-mail jrand@tiltonschool.org

TILTON SCHOOL in Tilton, New Hampshire, is a college preparatory, boarding and day school enrolling boys and girls in Grades 9 through 12 and a Postgraduate year. The town of Tilton, a community of 4000, is located in the Lakes Region near the White Mountains, about 1 mile west of Interstate 93 and 20 miles north of the state capitol at Concord. Boston is 90 minutes away by car.

Tilton School was founded in 1845 by Methodist churchmen and operated under several names reflecting its various functions through a colorful history. It has been a coeducational boarding school, a boys' boarding school, a female college, a junior college, and a secondary school. Originally situated in Northfield, it relocated in 1869 after a fire destroyed parts of the original buildings. In 1939, Tilton became an independent school for boys and, in 1970, resumed coeducation.

The School seeks to provide an excellent preparation for college-bound students in an environment that supports personal integrity, a sense of community, and a spirit of intellectual and artistic creativity. The faculty sees learning as an active, student-centered project and encourages young men and women to learn by doing as well as by reading and listening.

Tilton School is incorporated as a nonprofit organization governed by a Board of 18 Trustees, half of them graduates of the School. About 4500 living alumni provide financial and other support.

Tilton is accredited by the New England Association of Schools and Colleges and holds membership in the National Association of Independent Schools and other organizations.

THE CAMPUS. Tilton School is situated on 140 acres with open fields, woodlands, trails, streams, and a pond. School property includes a football field, four all-purpose fields, an oval track, two baseball fields, a softball field, three outdoor tennis courts, an outdoor swimming pool, a 60-acre outdoor laboratory, the Constance S. Evans Outdoor Theater, and a 3-mile Nordic skiing and running trail.

Plimpton Hall houses the Computer Center, 12 classrooms, and three science labs; the Fred A. Smart Chapel provides a facility for all school meetings and additional classrooms on the lower level for foreign language and English as a Second Language instruction; and Pfeiffer Hall Dormitory has classrooms for Learning Center support. The Helen Grant Daly Creative Arts Center furnishes studios and equipment for ceramics, printmaking, painting and drawing, a photo lab, woodshop, and exhibition gallery. Hamilton Hall provides a 200-seat performance theater, a music classroom, studios, and a music lab.

The Lucian Hunt Library, with a collection of 17,000 volumes, 60 periodicals, and six daily newspapers, is located in the Tilton Mansion; additional materials are accessible by computer.

Networked PC and Macintosh computers in classrooms and labs have Internet access. Fiber-optic intranet networks provide links to student rooms for those who have their own computers.

The newly renovated Memorial Athletic and Recreation Center includes two basketball courts, two squash courts, fitness center, trainer's room, rock-climbing wall, and a wrestling and dance room. Renovations to the MacMorran Field House, completed in 1999, include a new hockey rink and multipurpose floor for tennis courts and recreation as well as new locker rooms, a warming room, and a pro shop.

THE FACULTY. James R. Clements, a graduate of the University of New Hampshire (B.A.) and Plymouth State College (M.B.A.), was appointed as the 25th Head of School of Tilton School in 1998. Mr. Clements is the former Head of School of Chapel Hill-Chauncy Hall School, where he also served as teacher, dorm parent, coach, Dean of Students, and Assistant Headmaster. He and his wife, Beverly, are the parents of two daughters, both enrolled at Tilton.

Eighteen men and 17 women make up the faculty, including administrators who teach. They hold a total of 35 bachelor's degrees and 17 master's degrees, including a Ph.D., from Antioch, Assumption, Babson, Bowdoin, Bucknell, Colby 3, Colgate, College of the Holy Cross, Dartmouth, Johns Hopkins, Kenyon, Middlebury 3, Mount Holyoke, National University of Ireland, Northwestern, Plymouth State 3, Princeton, St. Lawrence 3, Trinity College, Utica, Villanova, Williams, and the Universities of Illinois, Maine, Massachusetts, New Hampshire 2, Paris, Rhode Island, and Vermont 2.

A registered nurse is on duty daily in the School Health Center. School physicians conduct clinics twice a week.

STUDENT BODY. In 1998–99, the School enrolled 139 boys and 68 girls, including 150 boarders, in Grades 9–12 and a post-graduate year. Students came from New England and other regions in the United States. Twenty-six international students represented Bermuda, Canada, China, England, Germany, Indonesia, Japan, Korea, Saudi Arabia, Thailand, and Venezuela. More than a third of the students receive financial aid.

ACADEMIC PROGRAM. The academic year, divided into trimesters, begins in early September and extends to the end of May, with long vacations at Thanksgiving, December Holidays, and in the spring. Classes are held six days a week between 8:00 A.M. and 3:00 P.M., with short schedules on Wednesdays and Saturdays. Students spend free periods in study hall or working in the library. Teachers have two scheduled conference periods for students during the week and are routinely available for extra help. A supervised study period for boarders is held for two hours each evening from Sunday through Friday. Achievement and effort grades are reported to students and parents at the midpoint and end of each trimester.

Students with specific academic needs or mild to moderate learning differences can enroll in the Learning Center, which has a faculty of language and mathematics specialists. Classes are held during the academic day and are part of a student's curriculum.

To graduate from Tilton School, a student must complete a minimum of 18 credits, including 4 in English; 2 in one foreign language; 2 in history, including U.S. History; 3 of mathematics (through Advanced Algebra); 2 of science, including one laboratory course; one of Fine Arts; and one trimester of Health and Human Development. All students are evaluated on their computer literacy skills. The normal academic load is five courses. Students taking English as a Second Language (ESL) must complete one regular sequence of English trimester courses.

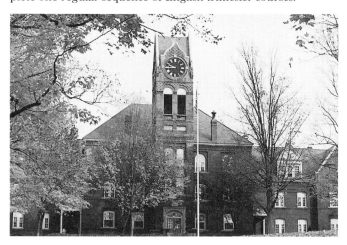

Among the courses offered are English 1–4, including grammar and composition, analytical reading and writing, and study of various genres, and one-term courses in Classic Comedy, Science Fiction, Creative Writing, Public Speaking, Voices of the South, Women in Literature; French 1–5, Spanish 1–5; Geography and Its World History 1–2, U.S. History, Global Studies, Economics, 20th Century European History; Introductory Algebra, Plane and Analytic Geometry, Advanced Algebra, Elementary Functions, Precalculus, Statistics, Calculus AB & BC; Introductory Biology, Physics, Chemistry, Biology, Geology; and Music, Visual Arts, Theater, Studio Art, Photography and Graphics, Printmaking, Painting 1–2, Ceramics 1–2, Fundamentals of Western Music, Chorus, Stage Band, and Music Theory and Composition. Advanced ESL is offered with courses in Writing, Literature, World History, and U.S. History. Honors sections are available in all academic subjects, and Advanced

Placement courses are offered in most. Independent study projects are available as a complement to the regular curriculum.

Of the 61 graduates in the Class of 1999, 2 elected to take the next year off, 3 to study abroad and 1 to play Junior Hockey. The others are enrolled at such schools as Assumption, Babson 4, Bentley, Berklee College of Music, Bowdoin, Champlain, Clarkson, Goucher, Hofstra, Keene State, Lewis & Clark, Lynchburg, Marietta, Massachusetts Institute of Technology, Merrimack, North Dakota State, Plymouth State, Providence, Rensselaer Polytechnic Institute, Roger Williams, Rollins 3, St. Michael's 4, Salisbury State 2, Salve Regina 3, School of the Museum of Fine Arts, Skidmore, Williams, Worcester Polytechnic Institute, Wright State, and the Universities of Denver, New Hampshire 2, and South Carolina.

STUDENT ACTIVITIES. Students take an active role in campus governance, electing officers of the Student Assembly, class presidents, and representatives to faculty-student committees handling academics, discipline, student life, and the Plus/5 program.

Through the Plus/5 program, students meet certain requirements each year in the following areas: Art and Culture, including performance in music, theater, campus publications, and workshops; Community Service, including volunteer work in homeless shelters, the veterans' home, the environment, and community projects; Leadership, including service in elective office, dormitory proctoring, athletic team captainships, and work program supervision; Outdoor Experience, such as hiking, climbing, canoeing, and camping; and Athletics, where each student takes part in interscholastic competition in two of the three seasons. Tilton competes in the New England Prep School Athletic Conference, including the Lakes Region League, and fields teams in baseball, basketball, football, ice hockey, lacrosse, soccer, tennis, and wrestling for boys; basketball, field hockey, ice hockey, lacrosse, soccer, softball, and tennis for girls; and coed teams in cross-country, cycling, golf, and skiing.

Some of the special events on the school calendar are Parents' Weekend in the fall, two theater productions in fall and winter and student-directed plays in the spring, Honors Dinner, Prize Night, and Alumni Weekend in June.

ADMISSION AND COSTS. Tilton School seeks to admit young men and women who are able and willing to share its commitment to academic excellence and community spirit. Students are admitted on the basis of a completed application form, academic transcripts, teacher and counselor recommendations, standardized test results, and a personal interview. A $50 fee is required with the application for international students and a $35 fee for all others.

Boarding tuition for 1999–2000 is $25,900; day tuition is $14,450. Enrollment in ESL or the Learning Center is extra.

Tuition payment plans and loan programs are available. Tilton subscribes to the School and Student Service for Financial Aid and awards more than $900,000 in scholarships each year based on need and merit.

Dean of the Faculty: Kendall P. Didsbury
Dean of Students: Jeannine McDonald

Director of Admissions: Jonathan C. Rand
Director of Communications: Tricia Martin
Director of Development: Joe Bucchino
Director of Alumni and Parent Affairs: Sandra M. Hollingsworth
Director of Residential Life: Richard Stewart
Controller: Richard V. Fabian, Jr.
Director of Athletics: Kenneth S. Hollingsworth

NEW JERSEY

Academy of Saint Elizabeth 1860

*P.O. Box 297, Convent Station, NJ 07961-0297. 973-290-5200;
Fax 973-290-5232; E-mail SEA1860@aol.com*

The Academy of Saint Elizabeth, under the direction of the Sisters of Charity, is a Catholic, college preparatory day school enrolling 250 girls in Grades 9–12. The school aims to develop the whole person through a rigorous curriculum and comprehensive activities. Honors and Advanced Placement courses and independent study projects are available. Student Council, campus ministry, publications, sports, forensics, and clubs are some of the activities. Tuition: $7500. Financial Aid: $70,000. Kathy Thomas is Director of Admissions; Sr. Patricia Mary McMullen (College of St. Elizabeth, B.A. 1947; Seton Hall University, M.A. 1955) was appointed Principal in 1986. *Middle States Association.*

Bishop Eustace Preparatory School 1954

*Route 70, Pennsauken, NJ 08109-4798. 856-662-2160;
Fax 856-665-2184; E-mail eustaceprep@msn.com*

Founded by the Pallottine Order, Bishop Eustace Prep is a coeducational day school enrolling 750 college-bound students in Grades 9–12. The faculty of religious and lay teachers emphasize commitment to education in the Catholic faith toward the goals of academic excellence and spiritual development. The curriculum features honors and Advanced Placement courses, and motivated students can earn dual college credits. Theology studies include required community service in Grades 11–12. Sports for boys and girls, publications, chorus, drama, Amnesty International, and interest clubs are among the activities. Tuition: $7250. Rev. John Biermann, SAC, is Principal. *Middle States Association.*

Blair Academy BLAIRSTOWN

*Blairstown, NJ 07825. 908-362-6121; Admissions 800-462-5247;
Fax 908-362-7975; E-mail admissions@blair.edu;
Web Site www.blair.edu*

BLAIR ACADEMY in Blairstown, New Jersey, is a coeducational college preparatory school enrolling boarding and day students in Grades 9–12 and a postgraduate year. Blairstown (population 4600) is located between Newton, New Jersey, and Stroudsburg, Pennsylvania, near the Delaware Water Gap. It is less than 90 minutes from midtown Manhattan and is easily accessible via Interstate Route 80. The area is served by buses from the New York Port Authority and commercial airports in Newark and Allentown/Bethlehem.

The Academy was founded in 1848 by local merchants and Presbyterian clergy led by John Insley Blair, a prosperous manufacturer, banker, and railroad developer. Originally intended as a day school, the education offered by the Academy attracted students from beyond the immediate area and, within two years, a boarding department was added. Founded as a coeducational institution, the Academy became exclusively male in 1915. Coeducation was reestablished in 1970.

Although associated with the Presbyterian Church since its inception, Blair's program of required weekly chapel and monthly vespers services is nondenominational and reflects a commitment to Judeo-Christian traditions. Students may also attend the services of area congregations.

A nonprofit corporation with a $39,000,000 endowment,

Blair is governed by a 28-member Board of Trustees that includes alumni, current and past parents, and Presbyterian clergy. There are active Alumni and Parents' associations. The Academy is accredited by the Middle States Association of Colleges and Schools and holds membership in the National Association of Independent Schools.

THE CAMPUS. Blair's 315 hilltop acres contain landscaped grounds, playing fields, 11 tennis courts, a nine-hole golf course, and a cross-country course. The Walker Gymnasium contains basketball courts, a running track, Olympic-size Wallace Pool, and wrestling and fitness rooms. In 1992, new construction added three international squash courts, a golf and tennis pro shop, conference room, and trophy area to the athletic complex. The Delaware Water Gap and the Appalachian Trail provide opportunities for both recreation and the development of outdoor skills. Skiing is available locally and in the nearby Pocono Mountains.

In 1992, a 55-acre portion of the campus containing 22 buildings was placed on the National Register of Historic Places. In October 1997, the Armstrong-Hipkins Center for the Arts was dedicated, beginning a new era of the arts at Blair Academy. The Arts Center includes two working theaters, an art gallery, a dance studio, and four music practice rooms. The newly renovated Timken Library, a state-of-the-art facility that includes classrooms and a computer center, opened in June 1998. A new girls' dormitory was completed for the 1999–00 academic year. Bogle Hall (1989), the Academy's math, science, and computer center, contains the Durland Computer Laboratory.

THE FACULTY. T. Chandler Hardwick III, a graduate of the University of North Carolina at Chapel Hill (B.A.) and Middlebury College (M.A.), was named the Academy's 15th Headmaster in 1989. Prior to his present appointment, he served as a member of the English Department, Dean of the Senior Class, and Director of the Summer School at The Taft School, Watertown, Connecticut. Mr. Hardwick and his wife, Monie, have three daughters.

The faculty consist of 63 teachers and administrators who teach, 33 men and 30 women. They hold 61 baccalaureate, 38 master's, and 2 doctoral degrees from such institutions as Amherst, Bates, Brown, Bryn Mawr, Carnegie Mellon, Colby, Colgate, College of the Holy Cross, Columbia, Cornell, Dartmouth, Davidson, Denison, Dickinson, Fordham, Franklin and Marshall, Georgetown, George Washington University, Hamilton, Harvard, Hobart, Kenyon, Lafayette, Lawrence, Lehigh, Middlebury, Northwestern, Oberlin, Princeton Theological Seminary, Rutgers, St. Lawrence, Smith, Syracuse, Temple, Trenton State, Trinity, Villanova, Wesleyan, Williams, Yale, and the Universities of Florida, Iowa, Maryland, Massachusetts, New Hampshire, North Carolina, Pennsylvania, Rhode Island, South Carolina, Vermont, and Wales.

STUDENT BODY. In 1999–2000, Blair enrolled 313 boarders and 99 day students as follows: 81 in Grade 9, 106 in Grade 10, 111 in Grade 11, 87 in Grade 12, and 27 in a postgraduate year. Academy students represented 21 states and 19 countries.

ACADEMIC PROGRAM. The school year, from early September to early June, is divided into three terms with Thanksgiving and winter-term recesses and Christmas and spring vacations. The average class contains 8 to 12 students and meets within a rotating schedule for four 55-minute sessions during a six-day week. The class day runs from 8:00 A.M. to 3:00 P.M. on Monday, Tuesday, Thursday, and Friday. On Wednesdays and Saturdays, interscholastic sports and special activities follow morning classes. Most students are permitted room study; for others, supervised study halls are held during the academic day and in the evening. Grading is on an unweighted 6.0 scale. There are two marking periods each term. Each student has a Faculty Adviser and Class Monitor who act as academic and personal advisers. The student-teacher ratio is 9:1.

Virtually all students carry five academic courses, each earning 1 unit per term. To graduate, a four-year student must successfully complete 12 units of English; 9 units of mathematics to include Algebra, Geometry, and Algebra II; 6 units of United States History and 3 units of World History; 6 units of laboratory science; 6 consecutive units of a modern or classical language through Level II; 4 units of fine and/or performing arts; and 1 unit each of religion and health. A student must also complete 3 units of Physical Activity each year.

Among the full-year and term-length courses offered are English 1–4 (including an elective program in English 4), Chinese 1–4, French 1–4/5, Latin 1–3/4, Spanish 1–4/5; World History, United States History, European History, Politics and Law, Economics, Asian History, Africa; Algebra 1–2, Geometry, Precalculus, Calculus; Computer Applications, Biology, Chemistry, Physics, Environmental Science; The Philosophy of Religion, New and Old Testament, The Psychology of Becoming, Morals and Ethics; Printmaking, Drawing, Painting, Ceramics, Jewelry, Photography, Art History; Mechanical Drawing, Architectural Drafting and Design; and Theater, Music History, Applied Music Instruction, Dance, Choral Music, and Technical Theater.

Advanced Placement courses are offered in English, French, Latin, Spanish, United States History, European History, Economics, Calculus (AB and BC), Computer Science, Government, Biology, Chemistry, Physics, Art History, and Studio Art. Special programs include Senior Projects and Aviation Career Development

In 1999, all 126 graduates entered college. Members of the Class of 1999 will be attending colleges and universities including Bates, Brown, Cornell, Dartmouth, Davidson, Duke, Georgetown, Harvard, Massachusetts Institute of Technology, Middlebury, Northwestern, Rutgers, Trinity, United States Military Academy, United States Naval Academy, Wellesley, Williams, and the Universities of North Carolina and Virginia.

STUDENT ACTIVITIES. Each class is represented by an elected council, which meets weekly during the school year. The School Council, consisting of representatives from each of the Class Councils, meet regularly with the Headmaster and Assistant Headmaster. Recommendations and suggestions are sent by the School Council to the Headmaster and other administrators. The Rules and Discipline Committee, a faculty-student group, hears disciplinary cases when expulsion from school is a possibility.

Student organizations and activities include the Blue and White Key, the Academy Players, the Academy Singers, *Between the Lines* (literary magazine), *The Blair Breeze* (newspaper), Earth-shine (environmental club), *ACTA* (yearbook), Film Society, "Doo-Wop," International Awareness Club, Math Team, Model UN, Multicultural Student Union, wind and jazz ensembles, the Admissions Committee, Community Service, and Library committees, and the Computer and Photography clubs. The Society of Skeptics is responsible for weekly programs that bring to campus speakers from a variety of fields who represent diverse viewpoints.

Interscholastic teams for boys are organized in baseball, basketball, football, lacrosse, soccer, squash, swimming, tennis, spring track, and wrestling. Girls compete in basketball, field hockey, lacrosse, soccer, softball, squash, swimming, tennis, and spring track. There are coed teams in crew, cross-country, golf, ice hockey, skiing, and winter track. Intramural sports activities include dance, golf, aerobics, swimming, volleyball, and weight training. The Outdoor Skills Program offers courses in basic outdoor skills, canoeing, and kayaking.

The Academy seeks to strike a balance between a sense of community and the need for students to get away from campus occasionally through a system of "closed" and "open" weekends. Organized weekend activities include sports events, outing club trips, dances, films, and musical and dramatic productions. Off-campus trips to New York City and other places of interest are also arranged frequently. Traditional annual events include Parents' Weekend, Peddie Day (a fall all-sports competition with The Peddie School), Christmas Vespers, Alumni Day, Baccalaureate, and Underclass Prize Day.

ADMISSION AND COSTS. Blair seeks students of diverse talents and backgrounds who feel that learning and growing are enjoyable and are determined to make the most of their secondary school years to prepare for college and life beyond the classroom. Students are admitted to all grades on the basis of a student questionnaire, a personal interview, academic and personal recommendations, transcripts of previous academic work, and results of standardized tests. There is a $50 application fee.

In 1999–2000, tuition for boarding students is $26,000; day tuition is $18,200. Financial assistance is awarded on the basis of demonstrated need and proven personal and academic merit.

Financial aid awards are competitive and must be renewed annually. Blair subscribes to the School Scholarship Service.

Dean of Academics: Selden D. Bacon, Jr.
Assistant Headmaster for Student Affairs: David T. Low
Dean of Admission: Barbara H. Haase
Assistant Headmaster for Finance and Development: Dennis W. Peachey '62
Dean of College Counseling: Lewis Stival
Business Manager: James Frick
Director of Athletics: James Stone

Chapin School   1931

4101 Princeton Pike, Princeton, NJ 08540. 609-924-2449;
  Fax 609-924-2364; Web Site 70067.2363@compuserve.com

Chapin is a coeducational day school enrolling 329 students in Pre-Kindergarten–Grade 8. Believing that self-esteem is a cornerstone of learning, Chapin seeks to challenge each student at his or her own level. Math and language arts classes in particular are taught in small classes; foreign language begins in Grade 2. The School is networked for direct access to the computer lab, school library, and local library system. Grades 6–8 undertake a research project that culminates in a Curriculum Fair. Graduates attend secondary schools such as George, Hill, Hun, Lawrenceville, Peddie, Pennington, and St. Andrew's. Tuition: $9500–$12,900. Barbara Pasteris is Director of Admission; Richard D. Johnson (Princeton, B.A. 1969; University of Virginia, M.Ed. 1973) is Headmaster. *Middle States Association.*

The Craig School   1980

15 Tower Hill Road, Mountain Lakes, NJ 07046. 973-334-4375;
  Fax 973-334-2861; Web Site www.craigschool.org

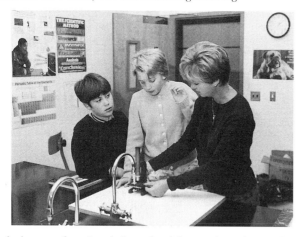

Craig is a coeducational day school for students in Grades 1–8 who have been underachievers in traditional settings because of learning difficulties. Its environment emphasizes development of academic and social skills in small learning groups where students can gain the confidence needed to return to mainstream classrooms. Orton–Gillingham-trained teachers provide individualized instruction. Computers are used throughout the curriculum as a word processing, research, and motivational tool. The physical education program includes weekly winter skiing. Positive behavior management and a mentor system reinforce self-esteem. A summer session is available. Tuition: $17,050. Janet M. Cozine (Rowan, B.A.; Montclair State, M.A., L.C.) is the Director.

Collegiate School   1896

Kent Court, Passaic Park, NJ 07055. 973-777-1714;
  Fax 973-777-3255

Collegiate School is a coeducational, college preparatory day school enrolling 175 students in Pre-Kindergarten–Grade 12. It aims to provide a traditional and classical academic program in a nurturing climate that will motivate students to think independently and to meet the future with industry and challenge. Collegiate School offers small classes and individual attention. Sports, clubs, and scholastic competitions are the principal extracurricular activities. Tuition: $5675–$6925. Angela C. Gibson (Barnard, A.B.; Columbia Teachers College, M.A.; Columbia University, M.A.) is the Headmaster. *Middle States Association.*

Delbarton School   1939

230 Mendham Road, Morristown, NJ 07960-5089. 973-538-3231;
  Fax 973-538-8836; Web Site www.delbarton.org

Founded by Benedictine monks, Delbarton School is a Roman Catholic, college preparatory day school enrolling 515 boys in Grades 7–12. The School places emphasis on academic achievement but seeks personal and social development in its students as well. A traditional, liberal arts curriculum emphasizes reading, writing, and critical thinking. Advanced Placement courses are offered in every subject. Sports, publications, drama, singing groups, and service groups are among the activities. Tuition: $14,640. Financial Aid: $450,000. Reverend Luke L. Travers, OSB (Columbia University, M.A.), was appointed Headmaster in 1999. *Middle States Association.*

Dwight-Englewood School   1889

315 East Palisade Avenue, Englewood, NJ 07631. 201-569-9500;
  Fax 201-568-9451; Web Site http://www.d-e.org

Dwight-Englewood, a college preparatory day school enrolling 1000 boys and girls in Preschool–Grade 12, seeks to develop students of integrity, tolerance, and service to others. The curriculum emphasizes the liberal arts and sciences, enriched by honors and Advanced Placement courses, independent study, a senior research program, and required community service. Students take part in such activities as seven publications, team sports for boys and girls, Mock Trial, Amnesty International, SADD, and special-interest clubs. Tuition: $6520–$16,427. Financial Aid: $1,100,000. Ralph E. Sloan (Harvard University, B.A., M.A., Ed.D.) was appointed Headmaster in 1998. *Middle States Association.*

The Elisabeth Morrow School   1930

435 Lydecker Street, Englewood, NJ 07631. 201-568-5566;
  Fax 201-816-9416; E-mail mail@elismorrowsch.com;
  Web Site www.elismorrowsch.com

A day school for 500 boys and girls in Nursery–Grade 6, The Elisabeth Morrow School pursues the highest educational standards in a supportive, creative environment. The program develops a positive self-image, the ability to function effectively with others, and the attitude that learning is a lifelong experience. In an atmosphere of intellectual challenge, the School seeks to meet the individual needs of its students through a comprehensive educational program and close contact between home and school. Summer, after-school, and child-care programs are offered. Stephen P. Jones (Trinity College, B.A. 1963; State University of New York, M.A. 1966) was appointed Head in 1989.

Far Brook School   SHORT HILLS

52 Great Hills Road, Short Hills, NJ 07078. 973-379-3442;
E-mail farbrook@farbrook.org; Web Site www.farbrook.org

FAR BROOK SCHOOL in Short Hills, New Jersey, is a coeducational day school enrolling students in Nursery through Grade 8. The School is approximately 2 miles from the center of Millburn Township (population 18,630), a suburban community 21 miles west of New York City. Classroom studies are supplemented with field trips to such places of interest as the Cloisters, the Metropolitan Museum of Art, the Museum of Natural History, and the Bronx Zoo. Bus and train services are available within 2 miles of the School.

Far Brook School was founded in 1948 on the former site of Buxton Country Day School by a group of parents who wanted to provide an "education of uncommon quality" for their children. The School was initially directed by Winifred Moore, the former Lower School Director of Buxton. Emphasizing the development of creative thinking, self-assurance, and initiative, Far Brook strives for "academic excellence through the integration of the liberal arts and sciences with the creative arts." Central to the School's philosophy is the expectation that children are capable of intellectual depth and of meeting rigorous standards of achievement. The School provides a "supportive and challenging environment, where concern for each individual's dignity and growth is paramount."

Incorporated as a nonprofit institution, the School is governed by a parent-elected Board of Trustees. The Board, which meets approximately eight times a year, is composed of up to 18 members, including a maximum of 6 nonparents. Parents play an important role at Far Brook, organizing annual parent activities, publishing a bimonthly "Bulletin," serving on subcommittees of the Board, and participating in fund raising. The Annual Fund, supported mainly by parents and some of the approximately 500 alumni and their families, raised $265,697 for 1998–99. The School completed its first Capital Campaign of $2,400,000 in May 1996 for new construction, renovation, and endowment. More recently, the Board of Trustees has identified additional capital improvements in renovation, technology, and endowment. Board members have committed more than $675,000, and others have pledged significantly as well toward meeting these needs. Far Brook School holds membership in the National Association of Independent Schools, the New Jersey Association of Independent Schools, the Educational Records Bureau, and the Council for Advancement and Support of Education and is accredited by The Middle States Association of Colleges and Schools Commission on Elementary Schools.

THE CAMPUS. Far Brook's seven-and-one-half-acre campus encompasses playing fields, woods, a pond and brook, and a pony paddock. The School's facilities include the Junior High Building; the Lower School Building, housing Nursery through Grade 2 as well as the woodshop and jewelry-making room; the Winifred S. Moore Hall for daily Morning Meetings of the entire school community as well as dance and drama classes and presentations, and containing a small kitchen and faculty room; the Small Barn; Moore Cottage, providing living quarters for the caretaker; the Gymnasium; and four new buildings financed through the Capital Campaign. These include the Ruth and Max Segal Family Library; a new building with classrooms for Grades 3–6 on the upper level and the School's computer laboratory and Middle School science laboratory on the lower level; a new administration building; and the Laurie Arts Center, which houses an expanded arts facility, vocal and orchestral rehearsal rooms, and individual lesson studios. An addition to the campus in the fall of 1993 was a new playground structure, designed by a faculty and Trustee committee, funded by Far Brook families, and built by parents.

The plant is owned by the School and is valued at $4,000,000.

THE FACULTY. Mary Wearn Wiener was appointed Director in 1979. A Phi Beta Kappa graduate of Agnes Scott College (B.A. 1964, magna cum laude), Mrs. Wiener served as a teacher of French at St. Anne's School and the Charlottesville City Schools of Virginia; as an editorial assistant in the children's department of Alfred A. Knopf, Inc.; and as a teacher at Far Brook for 13 years before becoming Director.

There are 28 full-time teachers, 5 men and 23 women. They hold baccalaureate and graduate degrees from Brooklyn College, California State, Carleton, City University of New York, Columbia, Dickinson, Elizabethtown, Fordham, Hamilton, Harvard, Haverford, Kean College of New Jersey, Loyola, Montclair State, Mount Holyoke, Northwestern, Ohio State, Rutgers, St. John's, State University of New York (Potsdam), Temple/Tyler School of Art, Vanderbilt, Yale, and the University of Pennsylvania. There are 6 part-time faculty for computer science, dance, and Lower School music as well as part-time assistants in the nursery and one kindergarten and a part-time remedial reading teacher. Faculty benefits include health, disability, and life insurance; a retirement plan; and Social Security.

For emergency situations, there are two nurses who share full-time coverage and several faculty members with first-aid and CPR training. St. Barnabas Hospital is approximately one mile from the School.

STUDENT BODY. In 1999–2000, Far Brook enrolls 105 boys and 115 girls as follows: 21 in Nursery, 28 in Kindergarten (two classes), 27 in Grade 1 (two classes), 22 in Grade 2, 23 in Grade 3, 20 in Grade 4, 20 in Grade 5, 19 in Grade 6, 20 in Grade 7, and 20 in Grade 8. Students represent 32 local communities as well as a variety of racial, religious, and economic backgrounds.

ACADEMIC PROGRAM. The academic year, from mid-September to mid-June, includes Thanksgiving, Christmas, winter, and spring vacations. The school day begins at 8:15 A.M. and ends at 3:00 P.M. on Monday through Thursday and at 2:00 P.M. on Friday. The school day begins with Morning Meeting at 8:25 A.M., when the students gather in the Hall to hear poetry, to see faculty and student presentations, and to sing the songs and rounds that have become an integral part of the Far Brook experience. Class size ranges from 13 to 23 students. Traditional grading begins in Grade 7. A part-time remedial reading teacher provides tutoring. Instruction in instrumental music is available.

Lower School (Nursery–Grade 3) children experience the security of belonging to a community whose life and work they find challenging and stimulating. Through an enriched sensory-motor and language experience, the curriculum stresses the development of sound basic skills and problem-solving processes. Children master skills sequentially in reading, writing, and computation, and develop facility in the scientific process. In Grades 2 and 3, study focuses on the interrelatedness of various disciplines through a core curriculum. The second grade focuses on Child and Universe; the third grade on Native Americans. Classroom studies include language arts, literature and writing, social studies, science, mathematics, and art. In addition, specialists work with children in art, music, drama, dance, library/research skills, woodworking, and physical education, which are available in all grades. Private instrumental lessons are offered as early as Kindergarten.

Beginning in Grade 4, classroom studies are centered around a history core curriculum. Each grade studies a civilization or historical period in depth, learning about its architecture, music, art, literature, scientific principles, agriculture, clothing, and everyday life. In Grade 4, students study Sumeria and Ancient Egypt; in Grade 5, Ancient Greece; and in Grade 6, Rome and the Middle Ages. Other Middle School studies include reading, creative writing, language arts; French; mathematics; laboratory science; minicourses in art, drama, computers, library, and woodworking; choir, orchestra; and team sports.

The primary focus of the Junior High School is to ready students for secondary school and college work. Core curriculum studies focus on the Renaissance in Grade 7 and on American History in Grade 8. Students study English, French, mathematics, laboratory life science, and laboratory physical science; also available are Algebra 1–2 and Geometry. All students take minicourses in art, computers, drama, library, and woodworking and are members of the School choir and sports teams. Many are also in the orchestra and special vocal groups. Each year, students and faculty members retreat to Vermont for a week of living and working together in a community.

Of the 33 graduates in 1998 and 1999, 19 entered the following schools: Delbarton, Montclair Kimberley 3, Morristown-Beard, Newark Academy 3, Phillips Academy, Pingry 9, and St. Benedict's Preparatory School. Fourteen entered area public high schools.

Lower School facilities are leased for a seven-week summer Mini-Camp for children three to six years of age. The Mini-Camp Director is Paula Levin, who serves as a Nursery teacher and as Pre-School Coordinator for Far Brook during the academic year.

STUDENT ACTIVITIES. Students with strong interests in particular fields or areas of study are given special opportunities to pursue these interests.

Interscholastic sports, beginning in Grade 5, include soccer and baseball for boys and field hockey and softball for girls. Touch football, basketball, volleyball, badminton, floor hockey, speedball, and coeducational softball are also included in the sports program. Complementing their study of Greece, Grade 5 students participate in a yearly "Greek Olympics," competing in the shot put, the discus throw, the broad jump, and running.

Traditional events include the Thanksgiving Processional, the Christmas Masque, the Class Plays, Pergolesi's *Stabat Mater,* and either Shakespeare's *The Tempest* or *A Midsummer Night's Dream* at graduation.

ADMISSION AND COSTS. Far Brook School is committed to a diversified student body. The School seeks students from varied economic, racial, and religious backgrounds who are "high average or above intellectually, serious about learning, motivated, and disciplined." Students are accepted in all grades except Grade 8 and at times when openings are available. Application may be made in the fall preceding the year of desired enrollment. A play-group screening for Nursery, both play-group and individual screenings for Kindergarten, and student visits for Grades 1–8 are required as part of the application process. Application and testing fees range from $30 to $90.

In 1999–2000, tuition ranges from $10,700 for full-day Nursery to $15,800 for Grade 8. Financial aid is awarded on the basis of need as well as the academic or social contribution a student makes to his or her class. The Edwin A. Finckel Scholarship for the Arts and the Mary Adams Scholarship for Math/Science each offer a minimum of $1000 per year to incoming seventh graders on the basis of merit. More aid is available based on need. The George Bartol Scholarship provides tuition and transportation to an economically disadvantaged student with academic promise. The Barbara Jordan Endowment provides partial tuition assistance for an economically disadvantaged student of color. In 1999–2000, 29 students received financial aid, including scholarships, totaling $261,295. Far Brook School subscribes to the School Scholarship Service.

Director of Admissions: Iris D. Leonard
Director of Development and Public Relations: Pat Lawler
Business Manager: Donna Chahalis
Director of Athletics: Nancy Muniz

Far Hills Country Day School   1929

P.O. Box 8, Far Hills, NJ 07931. 908-766-0622;
Fax 908-766-6705; E-mail admission@fhcds.k12.nj.us

Far Hills Country Day, serving 340 boys and girls in Pre-Kindergarten–Grade 8, is committed to strong academics based on a developmental philosophy recognizing multiple intelligences and is dedicated to developing well-rounded individuals with unique talents and strengths. A challenging, integrated curriculum emphasizes basic skills, written and oral communication, mathematical abilities, integrated technology and computer science, athletics, foreign language starting in Kindergarten, Latin in Grades 7–8, an Adventure program, interpersonal skills, studio art, music, and drama. Tuition: $6000–$13,100. Financial Aid: $178,446. Jayne Geiger Wyatt (Rutgers, B.A. 1971, M.Ed. 1989; Bank Street, M.S. 1975) is Head.

Gill St. Bernard's School   1900

St. Bernard's Road, Gladstone, NJ 07934. 908-234-1611;
Fax 908-719-8865; Web Site www.gsb.k12.nj.us

Gill St. Bernard's is a coeducational, college preparatory day school enrolling 542 students in Pre-School through Grade 12. The School's curriculum is designed to provide students with a strong academic program and the self-reliance and independence necessary for success in higher education. Teachers seek to challenge all students to superior achievement while considering the talents of individual students. High expectations, personal attention, and academic excellence define a Gill St. Bernard education. Tuition: $7000–$16,000. Financial Aid: $250,000. Joyce Miller is Admission Director; Christine G. Cox (Vassar, B.A. 1971; George Washington University, M.A. 1972; Harvard, C.A.S. 1986) was appointed Head of School in 1986. *Middle States Association.*

Hilltop Country Day School   1967

32 Lafayette Road, Sparta, NJ 07871. 973-729-5485;
Fax 973-729-9057; E-mail pohalloran@aol.com

Hilltop Country Day School enrolls approximately 190 students in Preschool through Grade 8. Hilltop provides its students with a family-oriented, academically challenging environment where children learn how to learn, discover the excitement of learning, develop good study habits, acquire a sensitivity and respect for the rights of others, and learn to accept responsibility and meet personal challenges. In the lower school, basic skills are emphasized, and standard subjects in both the lower and upper schools are enriched by the reading program, a writing workshop, music, the arts, physical education, and computer. Foreign language is introduced in Kindergarten. Tuition: $3000–$8140. Financial Aid: $50,000. P. David O'Halloran, Ph.D., is Headmaster.

The Hudson School   1978

506 Park Avenue, Hoboken, NJ 07030. 201-659-8335;
Fax 201-222-3669; E-mail hudson@hudsonet.com

Founded to provide challenging academic and arts programs for gifted and talented students, The Hudson School enrolls more than 160 urban students from diverse racial and cultural backgrounds in Grades 5–12. The college preparatory curriculum, which emphasizes the creative and performing arts, classical and modern languages, science, and math, is enriched by Advanced Placement and honors courses, retreats, field trips, and student exchanges abroad. Electives include chess, chorus, instrumental music instruction, dance, sports, theater, and community service. Tuition: $7250–$8500. Financial aid is available. Suellen Newman (Oberlin, B.A.; University of Chicago, M.Ed.) is Founding Director.

The Hun School of Princeton

176 Edgerstoune Road, Princeton, NJ 08540. 609-921-7600;
Fax 609-279-9398; E-mail admiss@hun.k12.nj.us;
Web Site http://www.hun.k12.nj.us

THE HUN SCHOOL OF PRINCETON in Princeton, New Jersey, is a coeducational, college preparatory school encompassing Grades 6–12 and a postgraduate program. Resident students are admitted from Grade 9 through postgraduate. Situated in central New Jersey, Princeton is home to 12,000 year-round residents and the 6500-member student body of Princeton University. The School is about 45 miles from both New York and Philadelphia. Students benefit from the many cultural, historic, and recreational opportunities available at the University and elsewhere in the region.

The Hun School of Princeton was founded as a boys' boarding school in 1914 by John Gale Hun, a member of the faculty at Princeton University who sought to provide a dynamic learning environment in which students were free to exchange ideas and share their understanding of the world. Girls were first welcomed as day students in 1971 and later as boarders in 1975.

The Hun School offers a challenging liberal arts curriculum that places equal emphasis on lasting values and academic achievement. Faculty are united in the common purpose of preparing students from widely diverse backgrounds for success in college and for full, productive citizenship in today's global community. School life is conducted according to an Honor Code that stresses integrity, kindness, respect, trust, and commitment.

Hun is a nonprofit, nonsectarian institution governed by a 25-member Board of Trustees, 9 of whom are alumni. The School is accredited by the Middle States Association of Colleges and Schools and holds membership in the National Association of Independent Schools, the New Jersey Association of Independent Schools, and numerous other professional organizations. Hun is aided in its mission by the Alumni Association, which represents the School's 3600 graduates, and the Parents' Association. Both groups are active in fund-raising, recruitment, and other supportive endeavors.

THE CAMPUS. Formerly a private estate, Hun's 45-acre campus is graced by wooded areas, open meadows, formal gardens, and a brook, with ample space to accommodate five athletic fields, a natural cross-country trail, and a 400-meter all-weather track.

Most Upper School classrooms are located in the Chesebro Academic Center, which contains the Michael Dingman Center for Science and Technology, the Perry K. Sellon Information Center, and the Mary Miller Sharp ceramics studio. Together these facilities include 28 classrooms, 6 science labs, a wet lab, aquarium, greenhouse, a 34,000-volume library with on-line and CD-ROM databases, and three 20-work-station computer labs. The Alexander K. Buck '49 Student Activity Center (SAC) provides Middle School classrooms as well as television and radio broadcast studios, a computer center, art and music studios, and the student bookstore. Adjacent to the SAC is a Nature Center used as an environmental resource laboratory that enables students to transform the campus into a wildlife sanctuary.

Russell Hall, at the heart of the campus, is a Tudor-style mansion that furnishes administrative offices, an infirmary, faculty apartments, and a boys' residence hall. Additional housing for boys is located in Poe Hall; girls reside across the quad in Carter Hall. Meals are served in the Dining Hall adjacent to Poe. An athletic center and gymnasium complete the School's facilities.

A $20,000,000 capital campaign currently underway will provide for 14 major projects to be completed over the next five years, including extensive new construction, renovations to existing buildings, and upgrading of athletic facilities.

THE FACULTY. James M. Byer, Ed.D., a graduate of Hun's Class of 1962 and a Hun faculty member and Dean of Students from 1966 to 1972, was appointed Headmaster in 1994. He earned a baccalaureate in economics from Marietta College (1966), a master's degree in guidance and counseling from Rider College (1970), and Ed.S. and Ed.D. degrees from Nova

University (1978, 1993). Previously, Dr. Byer held administrative and teaching posts at independent college preparatory schools in Florida.

More than half of Hun's 95 full-time faculty and administrators hold advanced degrees, with 5 holding doctorates.

Two registered nurses staff the infirmary during the day and are on call 24 hours. Complete medical services are within minutes of the campus.

STUDENT BODY. In 1999–2000, the Upper School enrolls 85 boarding boys, 180 day boys, 61 boarding girls, and 150 day girls, including 10 students in a postgraduate year. The Middle School enrolls 100 day students in Grades 6–8. Boarding students represent 16 states and 14 countries; day students live in Princeton and communities within a 20-mile radius of the School.

ACADEMIC PROGRAM. The school year, which is divided into semesters, includes 35 weeks of instruction, with a recess at Thanksgiving and winter and spring vacations. Grades are mailed to parents four times per year, and progress reports are issued three or more times a year. Each Hun student has a faculty advisor with whom he or she confers weekly. The student-faculty ratio is 14:1. Teachers are available for consultation at different times during the school day and daily after the last scheduled period.

A typical day for resident students begins with breakfast between 7:15 and 7:40 A.M. Classes are held between 8:00 A.M. and 2:33 P.M., followed by the consultation period. Athletics and extracurriculars are held after school, with dinner at 5:45 P.M., followed by study hall from 8:00 to 10:00 P.M. "Lights out" is at 11:00 P.M.

The Middle School (Grades 6–8) curriculum consists of English, French or Spanish, pre-algebra, algebra 1, science, social studies, computer instruction, health, and art/drama/music throughout the three years.

To graduate from the Upper School (Grades 9–12), students must earn at least 19½ credits, including the following: 4 in English; 3 each in history and mathematics; 2 each in science and a foreign language; and 1 in fine arts. Students must also contribute 10 hours of community service each year and satisfy a computer-literacy requirement.

Several programs are available to meet the learning needs of Hun's diverse student body. The International Student Program uses field trips and the study of United States history to introduce international students to American life; English as a Second Language is taught at four levels. The Academic Learning Skills Program, limited to an enrollment of 30, offers support to students with specific, diagnosed learning differences. Additionally, all students can benefit from the resources of the Writing Center, which is staffed by peer tutors who assist classmates in the preparation and refinement of written assignments.

Members of the Class of 1999 matriculated at 80 colleges and universities, with 2 or more entering Boston College, Boston University, Bucknell, Carnegie Mellon, Drexel, Harvard, Indiana University, Lafayette College, McGill (Canada), Mount Holyoke, Rollins, Rutgers, Tufts, Tulane, United States Naval Academy, Washington University, Whittier College, Villanova, and the University of Delaware.

The Hun School's summer session includes academic enrichment and credit courses, English as a Second Language, SAT preparation, and theater production.

STUDENT ACTIVITIES. Extracurricular activities at Hun are numerous and diverse. Among the leadership groups formed are the Student Council, Honor Council, and the Resident Life and Resident Judiciary committees. Middle School students publish their own yearbook *(The Yearling)* and newspaper *(The Attila)*; and Upper School students issue *The Mall* (newspaper) and *The Edgerstounian* (yearbook). All grades are welcome to contribute to the art and literary magazine, *The Hun Review.*

The School stages three dramatic productions annually, and students perform in music groups such as the chorus, pit and jazz bands, and an instrumental music ensemble.

Among the organizations on campus are the Model United Nations program, Mock Trial, Key Club (community service), Environmental Club, Speech and Debate Team, Philosophy Club, Outing Club, Art Club, Future Investors of America, Diversity Club, and The Janus Players.

More than 50 athletic teams compete interscholastically, with 10 seasonal sports available for the Middle School and 17 for the Upper School. Some of these sports are offered on a "no-cut" basis. Intramurals are also offered each season.

Resident students enjoy planned weekend activities both on and off campus, including movies, shopping excursions, and field trips to cultural and athletic events in Princeton, Philadelphia, and New York City.

ADMISSION AND COSTS. The Hun School seeks students who exhibit a willingness to work hard, a strength of purpose, and an excellent citizenship record. Admission is based on a personal interview, previous school performance, three academic recommendations, and the results of the Secondary School Admission Test. First-round admission decisions are made in early March. Applicants are urged to apply early in the year for the following fall. There is a $50 application fee.

In 1999–2000, tuition is $25,600 for residents and $17,100 for day students. The fee for the Academic Learning Skills program is $9860; the fee for English as a Second Language is $5380. A $700 deposit is due with the contract to secure a place. Other charges include $350–$550 for books and a $250 infirmary fee for resident students. Tuition insurance is required. Twenty-five percent of the students receive financial aid, and approximately $1,100,000 is awarded each year. The Donald-

son Scholarship awards full tuition to one entering ninth- or tenth-grade student. The remainder of financial aid is need-based.

Dean of Students: William E. Long
Middle School Head: Roberta J. King
Alumni Board President: Thomas J. Valeri, Jr. '72
Director of Admissions and Financial Aid: P. Terence Beach
Director of Institutional Advancement: Joseph Claffey '79
Director of Business and Finance: Richard L. Fleck
Director of College Counseling: Susan A. Mott
Director of Athletics/Physical Education: William H. Quirk, Jr.

Immaculate Conception High School   1925

33 Cottage Place, Montclair, NJ 07042. 973-744-7445;
Fax 973-744-3926

Immaculate Conception High offers a challenging academic program in a setting informed by Catholic values. Enrolling 260 young men and women from many cultural, religious, and ethnic backgrounds, the School provides a college preparatory curriculum that includes honors and advanced courses, computer technology, and four years of required religious studies. Immaculate consistently ranks as one of the top three Catholic schools statewide in science, and 98 percent of its graduates go on to college. Among the activities are Student Council, honor societies, drama, publications, a gospel choir, and athletic teams. Tuition: $4875. Willard L. Taylor, Jr., is Director of Admissions; Sr. Maureen Crowley is Principal.

Kent Place School   1894

42 Norwood Avenue, Summit, NJ 07902-0308. 908-273-0900;
Fax 908-273-3240; E-mail admission@kentplace.summit.nj.us;
Web Site www.kentplace.org

Founded in 1894, Kent Place School is New Jersey's largest nonsectarian, college preparatory day school for girls, enrolling over 600 students in Nursery–Grade 12. Kent Place is committed to an overall program of excellence that allows each girl to achieve her maximum academic, physical, and creative potential. Small classes taught by "inspired faculty," a state-of-the-art primary facility, and a strong college advising program are hallmarks of the School's high standards. Tuition: $4935–$16,118. Financial aid is available. Nancy Humick is Director of Admission and Financial Aid; Susan C. Bosland is Interim Head of School. *Middle States Association.*

The Montclair Kimberley Academy   1887

201 Valley Road, Montclair, NJ 07042. 973-746-9800;
Fax 973-509-4526; E-mail admissions@mka.pvt.k12.nj.us;
Web Site www.montclairkimberley.org

The Montclair Kimberley Academy is a coeducational, college preparatory day school enrolling 1035 students in Pre-Kindergarten through Grade 12. Located 15 miles west of New York City in the heart of Essex County, the Academy is recognized for its college placement record, ethics and character education, technology, fine and performing art offerings, and interscholastic athletics program. High academic standards are set within a caring, supportive community. Tuition: $10,400–$16,500. Financial Aid: $1,500,000. John D. Zurcher is Director of Admissions and Financial Aid; Dr. Peter R. Greer (University of New Hampshire, M.A.; Boston University, Ed.D.) is Headmaster. *Middle States Association.*

Moorestown Friends School   1785

*110 East Main Street, Moorestown, NJ 08057. 856-235-2900;
Fax 856-235-6684; E-mail mailadmissn.mfriends.org;
Web Site www.mfriends.org*

Moorestown Friends School operates under the care of the Moorestown Monthly Meeting of the Society of Friends. The college preparatory day school enrolls 625 girls and boys in Pre-School–Grade 12 and provides a challenging liberal arts education consistent with Quaker practice. Students participate in athletic, dramatic, and musical activities. Community service projects are encouraged. Tuition: $7175–$10,900. Financial Aid: $675,000. Alan R. Craig (Sir George Williams, B.A.; McGill, M.Ed.) was appointed Headmaster in 1990.

Mount Saint Mary Academy   1908

*1645 U.S. Highway 22 at Terrill Road, Watchung, NJ 07060.
908-757-0108; Fax 908-756-8085;
Web Page http://members.aol.com/msmalion*

Mount Saint Mary Academy, founded by the Sisters of Mercy, is a Roman Catholic, college preparatory day school enrolling 350 girls in Grades 9–12. The Academy stresses the importance of having a caring faculty work with small classes within an environment in which personal integrity and moral values are nourished. Honors classes, Project Acceleration in cooperation with Seton Hall University, and the Gifted/Talented Program are features of a traditional curriculum. Student government, clubs, drama, music, and varsity sports are among the activities. Tuition: $7800. Financial Aid: $70,000. Donna Venezia Toryak is Director of Admissions; Sr. M. Eloise Claire Kays, RSM (Georgian Court, B.S.; Rider College, M.A.), was appointed Directress in 1984. *Middle States Association.*

Newark Academy   LIVINGSTON

*91 South Orange Avenue, Livingston, NJ 07039. 973-992-7000;
Fax 973-992-8962; E-mail admission@newarka.edu.inter.net;
Web Site www.newarka.edu*

NEWARK ACADEMY in Livingston, New Jersey, is a coeducational, college preparatory day school enrolling 540 students in Grades 6–12. Livingston (population 28,000) is located in north central New Jersey, 11 miles west of Newark, 7 miles east of Morristown, and 40 minutes from New York.

The 13th-oldest day school in the country, Newark Academy was founded in 1774 in Newark by Alexander Macwhorter, a leading New Jersey cleric and advisor to George Washington. Closed during the Revolution, the school reopened in newly built quarters in 1792. In 1964, the Academy moved from Newark to Livingston; in 1971, it became fully coeducational.

In January 1991, the Academy was authorized as the only school in New Jersey to grant the International Baccalaureate Diploma, recognized worldwide as a standard of achievement and excellence. It is awarded following successful completion of a rigorous, comprehensive, two-year curriculum for students in Grades 11 and 12. The Diploma is accepted by universities around the globe and carries course credit and/or advanced standing at approximately 375 leading American colleges and universities.

Newark Academy offers a distinctive educational experience to young men and women of strong academic ability and sound character through a focused and traditional program of English, mathematics, science, languages, the arts, and humanities. The curriculum, which includes 20 Advanced Placement courses and independent study, also seeks to stimulate students' curiosity, develop creativity, and encourage a sense of service to society. Close student-faculty contact is encouraged, and stu-dents are urged to view education as a cooperative venture in which they can learn from one another.

A nonprofit organization, Newark Academy is governed by a 31-member Board of Trustees that includes alumni and parents. Parents and alumni also support the school, particularly through fund raising and recruitment.

Newark Academy is accredited by the Middle States Association of Colleges and Schools and approved by the New Jersey State Department of Education. It holds membership in the National Association of Independent Schools, the Educational Records Bureau, and other professional organizations.

THE CAMPUS. The 68-acre campus is bordered by the wooded upper reaches of the Passaic River. Among the outdoor facilities are two baseball diamonds, a softball field, an all-weather track, a field hockey area, two lacrosse and soccer fields, two football fields, four basketball half-courts, a cross-country course, and eight tennis courts.

The Academy building, a red-brick structure in the colonial style, has a 550-seat auditorium, a large stage workroom, 5 science laboratories, 40 classrooms, a language laboratory, and a 350-seat dining room. The 20,000-volume Hawkes Memorial Library houses a periodicals and microfilm collection. The 20,000-square-foot Elizabeth B. McGraw Arts Center houses studios for the fine and performing arts, classrooms, gallery, and "Black Box" theater. The Morris Interactive Learning Center offers state-of-the-art computer facilities.

Indoor athletic facilities include the Wrightson Memorial Gymnasium, Olympic-size swimming pool, and an exercise room. The Academy broke ground in October 1998 for the William E. and Carol G. Simon Family Field House, a 45,000-square-foot addition to existing athletic facilities.

The Academy-owned campus is valued at $6,500,000.

THE FACULTY. Elizabeth Penney Riegelman was appointed Head of School in 1997. She is a graduate of Albert Ludwigs Universitat (1973), Radcliffe College (A.B. 1974), Harvard University (M.Ed. 1978), and Columbia University (M.A. 1993). Ms. Riegelman previously served as Assistant Headmaster at The Peddie School in Hightstown, New Jersey.

The full-time faculty number 78, 37 men and 41 women, who hold 78 baccalaureate, 47 master's, and 6 doctoral degrees. Two or more degrees were earned at Brown, Columbia, Cornell, Fairleigh-Dickinson, Glassboro State, Hamilton, Kean College of New Jersey, Middlebury, Montclair State, New York University, Pennsylvania State, Rutgers, Syracuse, and the Universities of Rochester and Virginia. Faculty benefits include sabbaticals, reimbursement for advanced education, and medical and dental insurance. The Academy broke ground in October 1998 for the William E. and Carol G. Simon Family Field House, a 45,000-square-foot addition to existing athletic facilities.

A full-time nurse staffs the infirmary; a local physician is also on call.

STUDENT BODY. In 1999–2000, Newark Academy enrolled 547 students as follows: 32 in Grade 6, 53 in Grade 7, 60 in Grade 8, 110 in Grade 9, 94 in Grade 10, 98 in Grade 11, and 100 in Grade 12. Students represent 15 countries and 85 communities.

ACADEMIC PROGRAM. The school year, from early September to early June, includes a Thanksgiving recess, Christmas and spring vacations, and several long weekends. A typical day begins with Morning Meeting at 8:10 A.M. followed by classes from 8:30 A.M. to 2:40 P.M. Twice a week, the Morning Meeting features a program or performance planned by students or faculty.

A typical class enrolls 12 students. Teachers are available to provide extra help after school and during free periods. Each student is part of an advising group that meets regularly with a faculty counselor. Counselors also meet with parents and students in the fall. Each student has a lead counselor who assists with serious academic or personal problems and long-term academic planning. Grades are issued and sent to parents three times a year.

The program for the Middle School (Grades 6–8) consists of English, humanities, language, science, mathematics, arts, and physical education. Specific courses include English, French, Latin, Spanish, German, Social Studies, American Studies, World Cultures, Mathematics, Pre-algebra, Science, Ecology, Physical Science, Chorus, Band, Drama, Music, Dance, and Studio Art.

To graduate, students in the Upper School (Grades 9–12) must take five academic courses each term and complete 20 credits as follows: 4 in English; 3 each in a foreign language, humanities, science, and mathematics; 1 in the arts; 1/3 in computer science; and 2 2/3 in electives. In addition, students must take physical education and give ten hours to community service each year.

Full-year courses include English 1–4, Twentieth Century Studies; French 1–5, German 1–5, Latin 1–5, Spanish 1–5; The Ancient World, Western Heritage, The American Experience; Algebra 1–2, Geometry, Analysis, Pre-calculus, Calculus AB, Calculus BC; Computer Applications, Pascal Programming 1–2; and Introduction to Physical Science, Earth Science, Biology, Chemistry, Physics, and Geology. Among the term and elective courses are The Essay, Creative Writing, Public Speaking, Comedy; Music Arts, Economics, Understanding Art, Leadership in the Third World, Science and Society; Probability and Statistics, Linear Programming; Robotics, Animal Behavior, Field Biology; and Chorus, Band, Ensemble, two years of Acting Skills Beginning through Advanced, Ceramics 1–3, Architecture, Introduction to Sculpture, and Painting 1–2.

There are Advanced Placement or Honors sections in all of the major disciplines. Qualified students may arrange independent study or take courses at a nearby college. The International Baccalaureate Diploma is offered as a two-year program for 11th and 12th grades.

All 101 graduates of the Class of 1999 received acceptances from such colleges and universities as Boston University, Bucknell, Brown, Columbia, Cornell, Duke, Franklin and Marshall, Harvard, Lafayette, Princeton, Stanford, Vassar, Yale, and the Universities of Michigan, Pennsylvania, and Virginia.

Newark Academy offers an academic summer program for advanced credit, enrichment, skill development, and remediation. The Academy is also the site of a summer session, a day camp, and various sports camps.

STUDENT ACTIVITIES. The School Council is made up of student and faculty representatives. Academically qualified students are elected to The Cum Laude Society and may also be awarded departmental distinction or one of the Academy's many named awards for academic achievement.

Each year, there are more than 30 extracurricular clubs and activities offered. Students publish *The Minuteman* (newspaper), *Prisms* (literary magazine), *The Polymnian* (yearbook), *N.A. Today* (Middle School newsletter), and *Reflections* (Middle School literary magazine).

Students must take three terms in the Arts program, selecting from such offerings as drawing, photography, jazz band, dance, and choral singing. The school stages three theatrical productions, several music concerts, and informal evenings of group music, and hosts the Invitational Arts Festival.

Varsity and junior varsity teams compete in the Colonial Hills Conference, New Jersey State Interscholastic Athletic Association, and New Jersey Independent School Athletic Association. In the Upper School, boys' teams are organized in baseball, basketball, cross-country, fencing, football, golf, ice hockey, lacrosse, soccer, skiing, swimming and diving, tennis, track, and wrestling. Girls compete in basketball, cross-country, field hockey, golf, lacrosse, soccer, skiing, softball, swimming, tennis, track, and volleyball. Middle School teams are organized in many of these sports. In addition, there is a wide variety of intramural offerings.

There are frequent performances, dances, barbecues, sports nights, and speakers throughout the school year. Traditional annual events for the school community include Parents Day, Arts Festival, End-of-Year Slide Show, Homecoming, and the Senior-Parent-Faculty Dinner.

ADMISSION AND COSTS. Admission to Newark Academy is based on the previous school record, results of school-administered testing, teacher recommendations, and an interview with the Admission staff. Space permitting, new students are accepted in all grades.

In 1999–2000, tuition for Grades 6–8 is $16,150 and

$16,650 for Grades 9–12. This includes class fees. Additional expenses include a lunch program ($675) and books and supplies. A tuition payment plan is available to parents through an outside agency. Each year, Newark Academy offers more than $600,000 in need-based financial aid.

Upper School Principal: Richard Di Bianca
Middle School Principal: Joan Parlin
Dean of Faculty: Blackwood B. Parlin
Dean of Students: Pegeen Galvin-Scott
Director of Alumni Relations: Brooke Keller
Director of Admission: Frederick R. McGaughan
Assistant Head for Institutional Development: Sarah Sherman
Director of Counseling: Carol Spooner
College Counselor: Lauren Carr
Business Administrator: Sam Goldfischer
Director of Athletics: Stephen Griggs

Oak Knoll School of the Holy Child   1924

44 Blackburn Road, Summit, NJ 07901. 908-522-8100;
   Fax 908-277-1838

Oak Knoll School of the Holy Child is an independent, Catholic, college preparatory day school enrolling 519 students in Kindergarten–Grade 12. The Lower School, for boys and girls in Kindergarten–Grade 6, is departmentalized by subject area beginning in Grade 1. The Upper School, for girls in Grades 7–12, sends its graduates to selective colleges and universities. The curriculum of each division seeks to engage intellectual curiosity and challenge academic ability in a values-centered environment. Tuition: $13,270–$16,200. Financial Aid: $700,000. Mary A. Worboys is Director of Admissions; Bettina Hummerstone (Smith, B.A. 1961; State University of New York [Stony Brook], M.A. 1973) is Head of School. *Middle States Association.*

The Peck School   1893

247 South Street, Morristown, NJ 07960. 973-539-8660;
   Fax 973-539-6894

Enrolling 300 day students in Kindergarten–Grade 8, Peck seeks to educate the whole child through a challenging curriculum, a supportive environment, and a community that celebrates diverse talents, perspectives, and cultures. Basic skills in reading, writing, and mathematics are emphasized, and French, Latin, science, and social studies are offered. The School follows a comprehensive plan in integrating technology into each subject area. The physical education and sports program focuses on fitness and sportsmanship. Art, music, family life, and community service are vital to the program. Tuition: $11,550–$15,400. Patricia E. Dodge is Director of Admissions; David A. Frothingham (Stanford, B.A.; Middlebury, M.A.) was appointed Headmaster in 1997.

The Peddie School   1864

South Main Street, Hightstown, NJ 08520. 609-490-7500;
   Fax 609-490-0920; E-mail mgary@peddie.org;
   Web Site www.peddie.org

Set on 280 acres surrounding Peddie Lake, this nondenominational, college preparatory boarding and day school enrolls 518 students in Grade 8–Postgraduate, half of whom are supported by financial aid. Peddie provides a curriculum that combines rigorous academic traditions with dynamic innovations. Liberal arts subjects are complemented by Advanced Placement and honors courses. Each student receives a laptop computer as part of tuition. Activities include sports, the arts, publications, clubs, and community service. Boarding Tuition: $25,750; Day Tuition: $18,700. Financial Aid: $3,600,000. Michael Gary is Director of Admission; Thomas A. DeGray (Williams, B.A.; Bowdoin, M.A.) was appointed Head of School in 1989. *Middle States Association.*

The Pennington School   1838

112 West Delaware Avenue, Pennington, NJ 08534. 609-737-1838;
   Admissions 609-737-6128; Fax 609-730-1405;
   E-mail admiss@pennington.org

Pennington was founded by the United Methodist Church as part of its mission to provide education that develops students intellectually, physically, and spiritually. The coeducational School enrolls 400 day and boarding students in Grades 6–12 and prepares them for college through a curriculum notable for its sensitivity to how students learn. Its Center for Learning is designed for bright, learning-different students who need accommodations to fulfill their potential. English as a Second Language is available. Boarding Tuition: $25,650; Day Tuition: $17,000. Financial Aid: $700,000. Diane P. Monteleone is Director of Admission; Lyle D. Rigg (Miami University, B.A.; West Texas State, M.A.; Harvard, Ed.M.) was appointed Headmaster in 1998. *Middle States Association.*

The Pingry School   1861

Kindergarten–Grade 6: Country Day Drive, Short Hills, NJ 07078.
   973-379-4550; Fax 973-379-1861; Web Site www.pingry.k12.nj.us
Grades 7–12: Box 366, Martinsville Road, Martinsville, NJ 08836.
   908-647-5555; Fax 908-647-5035; Web Site www.pingry.k12.nj.us

The Pingry School is a college preparatory, country day school on two campuses of 226 acres, enrolling nearly 1000 boys and girls in Kindergarten–Grade 12. The School hopes to create an environment in which the student can be challenged and supported by enthusiastic and sensitive faculty members, leading to his or her complete mental, physical, social, and spiritual development. The School offers extracurricular opportunities including athletics, music, drama, art, and computers. A summer day camp and school are conducted. Tuition: $12,085–$16,325. Financial Aid: $851,146. John Hanly (Oxford [England], B.A., M.A.; Columbia, M.A.) has been Headmaster since 1987. *Middle States Association.*

Princeton Day School   1965

The Great Road, P.O. Box 75, Princeton, NJ 08542.
609-924-6700; Fax 609-924-8944;
Web Site http://www.pds.k12.nj.us

Princeton Day, a college preparatory school enrolling 875 students in Junior Kindergarten–Grade 12, aims to instill excitement about learning, confidence in creative thinking, and commitment to oneself and others. Small classes foster close interaction between enthusiastic faculty and students. The 92-acre campus includes a new Science Center; a planetarium and outdoor astronomy site; fully networked lower, middle, and upper school computer labs; an architectural drafting room; an art gallery; a theater, a skating rink, and a photo lab. More than 95 percent of the 1999 graduating class were admitted to highly competitive colleges. Tuition: $13,375–$17,450. Financial Aid: $1,200,000. Terry Breault is Admissions Director; Lila B. Lohr is Head of School. *Middle States Association.*

Princeton Montessori School   1968

487 Cherry Valley Road, Princeton, NJ 08540. 609-924-4594;
Fax 609-924-2216; E-mail pmonts@pmonts.edu;
Web Site www.pmonts.edu

Princeton Montessori School, enrolling 300 children from 6 weeks to Grade 8, provides Infant, Toddler, Primary, Elementary, and Middle School programs based on the philosophy of Dr. Maria Montessori. Children are encouraged to exercise "freedom within limits" and progress in a personalized curriculum that includes practical life experiences within a developmentally appropriate environment. Respect for others and the environment is emphasized. Activities include math, computer, French, sports, and the arts. Piano, Suzuki violin, and a summer

enrichment program are available. Tuition: $3125–$14,700. Financial Aid: $210,000. Marsha Stencel (Vanderbilt-Peabody, B.S. 1970; Wright State, M.S. 1972) is Director. *Middle States Association.*

Queen of Peace High School   1930

191 Rutherford Place, North Arlington, NJ 07031-6091.
201-998-8227; Fax 201-998-3040; Web Site www.qphs.org

Queen of Peace, twice named a Nationally Recognized School of Excellence by the U.S. Department of Education, is a parish school in the Newark Archdiocese enrolling 730 boys and girls from diverse religious and socioeconomic backgrounds. As a learning community, the School endeavors to lead students to success in their lives through a program based on Catholic values and sound academic principles. The curriculum features honors, average, and remedial courses to serve a broad range of abilities. Spiritual growth is fostered through theology, a campus ministry, retreats, and liturgies and prayer services. Students participate in publications, 25 clubs and organizations, and athletics. Tuition: $4000. Sr. Mary Elizabeth Farrell, SSJ, is Principal; Richard J. Ingraffia is Director of Admissions.

Ranney School   1960

235 Hope Road, Tinton Falls, NJ 07724. 732-542-4777;
Fax 732-544-1629; E-mail hrudisi@ranneyschool.com;
Web Site www.ranneyschool.com

Ranney School, enrolling 560 day students age 3–Grade 12, offers a college preparatory curriculum that nurtures intellectual inquiry, creative expression, and diversity. The School emphasizes basic and traditional learning skills, refined by the fine and performing arts, foreign languages, computer science, and athletic and extracurricular programs. Students are required to begin French or Spanish in Grade 2 and Latin in Grade 6. Small classes allow students to become fully involved in their learning. All Ranney graduates attend college, with the majority of students enrolling at the most prestigious universities. Tuition: $5800–$14,600. Lawrence S. Sykoff (University of San Diego, M.Ed., Ed.D.) was appointed Head of School in 1993. *Middle States Association.*

The Rugby School at Woodfield 1977

Belmar Boulevard & Woodfield Avenue, P.O. Box 1403, Wall,
NJ 07719. 732-681-6900 or 800-RUGBY-19;
Fax 732-681-9140; E-mail poppled@aol.com;
Web Site www.rugbyschool.org

Rugby's mission is to prepare emotionally challenged young people to become productive members of society. Enrolling 120 students in Grades 1–12, it provides appropriate clinical services and individualized education tailored to specific academic and career goals. Small, structured classes, specialized teachers and staff, and ongoing clinical therapies are integral to the program. Older students may combine course work with on-the-job training; a professional counselor guides students in the college admission process. Students enjoy art, music, drama, and horseback riding. Rugby's location minutes from the Atlantic Ocean and Indian ruins facilitates environmental and archaeological programs. Donald J. DeSanto is Executive Director; John H. Flammer is Principal.

The Rumson Country Day School

RUMSON

35 Bellevue Avenue, Rumson, NJ 07760. 732-842-0527;
Fax 732-758-6528

THE RUMSON COUNTRY DAY SCHOOL in Rumson, New Jersey, is a coeducational, elementary day school enrolling students in Nursery through Grade 8. Rumson (population 7000) is a residential community situated on the Atlantic Ocean in Monmouth County. It is about one hour south of New York City via car, bus, and rail, and a high-speed ferry transports passengers across the bay to the southern tip of Manhattan.

The Rumson Country Day School was established in 1926 by local parents who sought a challenging independent education for their children. It opened with 23 students and five teachers on a 2.5-acre site that featured a 19th-century church building. Since its founding, the School has periodically undergone major renovations and expansions to the facilities, and adjoining properties have been acquired. Today, Rumson Country Day enrolls 441 children, with triple sections in every class, on a 12-acre campus.

The School's mission over the years has remained constant: to provide students from all communities with a challenging academic experience in a supportive environment; to nourish academic excellence, individual and social responsibility, civic awareness, and leadership skills; and to inspire graduates to become lifelong learners, able to thrive, contribute, and excel in a demanding secondary school environment and in tomorrow's society.

The Rumson Country Day School is a nonsectarian, not-for-profit institution governed by a 19-member, self-perpetuat-ing Board of Trustees who meet six times a year. The School is accredited by the Middle States Association Commission on Elementary Schools and holds membership in the National Association of Independent Schools, the Council for Advancement and Support of Education, and other organizations.

THE CAMPUS. Located in a residential area, The Rumson Country Day School's spacious campus accommodates a baseball diamond, three playing fields, two playgrounds, and two gyms. The main school building houses Beginners (Kindergarten) through Grade 8. Students have the use of three libraries: The main library contains 12,000 volumes, 45 periodicals, and a comprehensive collection of audiovisual and resource materials; the Pre-School and Beginners libraries each hold 1000 volumes. Students and teachers have the use of 165 computers; 17 of these are in a new computer/multimedia center, and the other 148 are in classrooms. Two fully equipped science labs, arts and crafts studios, an observatory, a two-room music center with Orff instruments, and a 200-seat auditorium for student productions complete the academic facilities. Students and faculty share a hot lunch in two spacious dining rooms. The Pre-School is housed in a separate building that also provides the Headmaster's residence.

The plant is owned by the School and valued at $4,600,000.

THE FACULTY. Chad B. Small was appointed Headmaster in 1989. A graduate of Millbrook School in New York, he holds a B.A. from Ohio Wesleyan (1976), an M.Ed. from the University of Virginia (1979), and is currently enrolled in a doctoral program at Seton Hall University. Mr. Small has taught in public and private schools and, before assuming his present position, was Head of St. Richard's School in Indianapolis, Indiana. He and his wife, Susan, have three children, all of whom are current RCDS students or graduates.

There are 48 full-time faculty members, 10 men and 38 women, and 6 part-time teachers. The average teaching experience is 14 years, with an average of 10 years spent at the School. All hold baccalaureate degrees or the equivalent; additionally, they have earned 22 advanced degrees, including a doctorate, from such colleges and universities as Albright, Allentown, Bank Street College, Birmingham University (England), Brandeis, College of Saint Elizabeth, Drew, Fordham, George Washington, Kean College, Lehigh, McGill, Monmouth, New England Conservatory of Music, Northeastern, Occidental, Rutgers, St. Peter's College, State University of New York, Syracuse, Temple, and the Universities of Delaware, Kentucky, Maryland, Miami, Michigan, North Carolina, Oregon, Pennsylvania, and Richmond. Faculty benefits include Social Security, a retirement plan, health and life insurance, and unpaid leaves of absence.

A full-time registered nurse is on campus, and several faculty members are trained in first aid; the nearest hospital is five minutes away.

STUDENT BODY. The Rumson Country Day School enrolls 441 students, 219 boys and 222 girls, as follows: 28 in Nursery, 32 in Pre-Kindergarten, 45 in Beginners, 48 in Grade 1, 48 in Grade 2, 49 in Grade 3, 50 in Grade 4, 48 in Grade 5, 33 in Grade 6, 23 in Grade 7, and 37 in Grade 8. Students come from 30 communities within a 20-mile radius of the School; approximately five percent are students of color.

ACADEMIC PROGRAM. The school year, which is divided into trimesters, begins after Labor Day and extends to early June. The calendar includes a Thanksgiving recess, vacations in December and March, and the observances of several national and religious holidays. Classes are held five days a week on a rotating basis, beginning at 8:00 A.M. and ending between 3:15 and 3:30 P.M., depending on grade level. Half-day classes are held for Nursery (age 3), while Pre-Kindergarten (age 4) is offered on a half- or full-day basis. From the Pre-School level through Grade 5, students are grouped heterogeneously.

The Lower and Upper School schedules incorporate a midday extra-help period for students requiring additional support, and after-school and summer tutoring are available from some teachers at extra cost. Every Upper School student has a faculty advisor.

The core curriculum is centered on English literature and language arts, math, science, social studies/history, and Spanish or French. Art, shop, crafts, computer, health, and physical education are integrated into the weekly schedule. Students in Kindergarten–Grade 4 study French, with the choice of French or Spanish in Grades 5–8. An honors program is available for qualified Upper School students in English, math, and foreign languages. Latin is required for all students in Grades 7 and 8, and speed-reading instruction is offered in Grade 8. Students in all grades participate in community service as part of the curriculum.

On a typical day, Upper School students take three classes, then a 10-minute break, followed by three more classes, a conference or reading period, and lunch. There are three afternoon periods prior to dismissal.

The 28 graduates in the Class of 1998 entered a variety of public and independent schools including Christian Brothers Academy, Freehold Regional High School, Hotchkiss, Kent, Lawrenceville, Portsmouth Abbey, Ranney, Red Bank Catholic High, Rumson-Fair Haven Regional High, St. Andrew's, and St. George's.

STUDENT ACTIVITIES. The Rumson Country Day School offers extracurricular activities designed to provide leadership experiences as well as social, recreational, and enrichment opportunities. Upper School students elect officers and homeroom representatives to a Student Council that provides communication between the student body and the Administration and organizes social events.

Upper School students can choose from a variety of weekly minicourses and become involved in forensics, chorus, newspaper, and a Weekend Club. The Drama Club stages a musical, and individual grades present plays and concerts for schoolmates and families. There are also overnight class trips for Grades 5–8. Lower School activities include after-school games and crafts, Brownies, and Drama Club. After-school care is available on Monday through Thursday.

The athletics program, open to Grades 5–8, involves competition with other independent, parochial, and public schools. Boys compete in football, soccer, basketball, baseball, and lacrosse; girls' teams compete in soccer, field hockey, basketball, softball, and lacrosse.

Among the family events on the school calendar are a New Parent Party, Field Day, Halloween Potluck Supper, Holiday Alumni Brunch and Program, Homecoming, Grandparents' Day, Class Day, and Graduation.

ADMISSION AND COSTS. The Rumson Country Day School welcomes students from diverse racial, ethnic, and religious backgrounds who show evidence of good character and integrity and who are eager to participate fully in the School's academic and extracurricular offerings available. The application process for Beginners–Grade 8 includes on-site testing, teacher recommendations, and a classroom visit. Notification is sent in March. No testing is required for Pre-School; early application is recommended. The School's cut-off date is September 1. The application fee is $50 for Pre-School and $75 for Beginners–Grade 8.

In 1999–2000, tuition ranged from $3700 for four half-day Nursery (age 3) to $12,675 in Grades 6–8. Included in the tuition are all hot lunches, books, supplies, and lab fees. An activity fee of $50 in Pre-School and $100 in Beginners–Grade 8 covers field trips, athletic trips, minicourses, testing, and other incidentals. There are additional charges for the wilderness education trips in Grades 5–8. Two payment plans are available. In the current year, 27 students received $150,000 in need-based financial aid.

Headmaster/Upper School Head: Chad B. Small
Lower School Head: Jayne S. Carmody
Director of Admissions/Institutional Advancement: Suzanne R. Post
Dean of Studies: Lawrence R. Landman
Dean of Students: Beth Luzio
Director of Development: Diana N. Flippo
Business Manager: Linda M. Schottland

Rutgers Preparatory School   SOMERSET

1345 Easton Avenue, Somerset, NJ 08873. 732-545-5600;
Web Site www.rutgersprep.k12.nj.us

RUTGERS PREPARATORY SCHOOL in Somerset, New Jersey, is a coeducational day school for students in Pre-Kindergarten through Grade 12. Located in Somerset, the School enrolls students from a variety of geographic, economic, social, and ethnic backgrounds. The metropolitan area of Central New Jersey, nearby Rutgers University, and accessibility to New York City offer students additional educational and cultural experiences. The School provides bus and van service to 39 communities.

The oldest independent school in New Jersey, Rutgers Preparatory School was founded in 1766 under the same charter as Queens College, now Rutgers—The State University of New Jersey. In 1957, the School adopted its own charter and moved to its present Franklin Township site. In 1993, the Council for American Private Education and the U.S. Department of Education named Rutgers Preparatory a Blue Ribbon School.

The School values intellectual curiosity and personal integrity and emphasizes a strong academic program, creative problem solving, cooperation and group interaction, appreciation of culture and beauty, and healthy emotional and physical growth.

Rutgers Preparatory School is a nonprofit institution governed by a Board of Trustees. The active Parents' Association provides support through volunteer activities and fund-raising events. The School is accredited by the Middle States Association of Colleges and Secondary Schools and holds membership in the National Association of Independent Schools, among other organizations.

THE CAMPUS. The 35-acre campus is bounded by wooded areas and the Delaware and Raritan Canal. The 18th-century Elm Farm House, formerly the home of one of the School's founders, houses administrative offices. A campus-wide building program includes a new media and computer center, computer classrooms, and two physical education facilities. Seven additional buildings of pre-Revolutionary War and modern architecture lend themselves to age- and class-appropriate activities.

Athletic facilities include playing fields, the field house, and tennis courts.

THE FACULTY. Steven A. Loy, appointed Headmaster in 1992, is a graduate of Princeton University (B.A. 1974), Stanford University (M.A. 1976), and the University of California, Los Angeles (Ed.D. 1979). He was previously Headmaster of Dunn School and Assistant Headmaster of Brentwood School, and has had teaching experience in England, Scotland, and Denmark. Dr. Loy and his wife, Philomena, have three sons who attend the School.

There are 104 full-time faculty members, including administrators who teach. They hold 99 baccalaureate, 52 master's, and 3 doctoral degrees representing study at Bank Street College, Boston University, Carleton, Cornell, Emory, Harvard, Lehigh, McGill, Middlebury, Montclair State, Moore College of Art, New York University, Oberlin, Pace, Pennsylvania State, Princeton, Rutgers, Seton Hall, Stanford, Trinity College, Yale, and the Universities of Pennsylvania and Virginia.

There is a full-time nurse on duty, and St. Peter's Hospital is located nearby.

STUDENT BODY. In 1999–2000, Rutgers Preparatory School enrolled 672 students. There were 219 in the Lower School (Pre-Kindergarten–Grade 4), 179 in the Middle School (Grades 5–8), and 274 in the Upper School (Grades 9–12). Students came from 60 communities in Central New Jersey.

ACADEMIC PROGRAM. The school year, divided into semesters, begins in early September and ends in mid-June. There are vacations in the winter and spring. Parent conferences are held in the fall, and grades are sent home quarterly. The school day begins at 8:20 A.M. and ends at 3:05 P.M. Before- and after-school programs are available beginning at 7:30 A.M. and ending at 6:00 P.M.

Lower School students are taught in self-contained classrooms. The basic skills of reading, writing, science, social science, mathematics, and computers are emphasized, and foreign language study begins in Grade 1.

The Middle School curriculum is departmentalized. These students take courses in English, foreign language, mathematics, social studies, science, art, drama, music, library skills, computer skills, and health/physical education.

To graduate from the Upper School, students must earn 20 credits, including 4 in English; 3½ in mathematics, with Algebra I, Geometry, and Algebra II required; 2 in a foreign language; 2 in science; 3 in social studies, with Western Civilization and two United States history courses required; 1 in fine arts; and four years of physical education and health.

Advanced Placement courses are available in English, French, Spanish, Latin, computer science, European history, psychology, United States history, government, economics, calculus, biology, and chemistry. Independent study programs are possible on a semester basis with the approval of the student's adviser, the department involved, and the Principal. Select students in Grade 12 participate in an Interpersonal and Group Communication Theory course and hold small group discussions with students in Grade 9.

All of the graduates in the Class of 1999 are attending college. They are matriculating at such institutions as Boston College, Bryn Mawr, Carnegie Mellon, Cornell, Dartmouth, Davidson, George Washington, Harvard, Haverford, Lafayette, Middlebury, Muhlenberg, New York University, Rutgers, Stevens Institute, Syracuse, and the Universities of Pennsylvania and Virginia.

The Rutgers Preparatory School summer session offers advanced credit and review courses as well as a Summer Fun Program for ages 4 and 5 and an Ultimate Recreation Program for ages 6 to 14.

STUDENT ACTIVITIES. Each Middle School homeroom elects a representative to the Middle School Student Council. The Council is encouraged to assume responsibility for social activities in the Middle School. The Upper School Student Council, elected by the student body, discusses and acts on matters of student business, provides assembly time for club presentations, funds budget requests from clubs, and plans after-school social events. The Judiciary Board meets on cases involving rules infractions and makes recommendations to the administration. Senior prefects are elected to serve as role models to underclassmen.

Lower School students are introduced to a variety of clubs and community service projects and publish a newspaper, *40:32* (a literary magazine), and *Ye Dial* (a yearbook). All Lower School students participate in the Science Fair and a school-wide Writing Day. Scouting programs are offered after school. Music lessons are available in keyboard, strings, and wind instruments, and concerts are given in the winter and spring.

Middle School students publish *Flash* (a newsletter) and *Ye Dial* (the yearbook). They present dramatic and musical productions each year and participate in field days and the Outing Club as well as in some Upper School clubs.

Upper School activities include academic teams, Math League, Model Congress, Model United Nations, Forensic League, Maroon Stock Exchange, Amnesty International, SADD, and the Chess, Computer, French, Spanish, Outing, and Video clubs. There are dramatic and musical productions each year, and students publish *Argo* (a newspaper), *Excelsior* (the literary magazine), and *Ye Dial* (the yearbook). Middle and Upper School students also have the opportunity to study abroad or host visiting students through foreign exchange programs.

Interscholastic competition begins in Grade 7. Boys compete in soccer, wrestling, basketball, lacrosse, baseball, and tennis. Girls' teams are organized in soccer, tennis, basketball, volleyball, lacrosse, and softball. There are coeducational teams in cross-country, swimming, and golf.

Traditional annual events include the Writing Fair, Ethnic Pride Festival, winter and spring music concerts, Spring Family Picnic, Book Fair, Career Day, Foreign Language Tea, Upper School Honors Convocation, Senior Retreat, College Night, Sports Award Dinner, Creative Arts Dinner, and Commencement.

ADMISSION AND COSTS. Rutgers Preparatory School seeks students who are able to apply themselves to a rigorous academic program and are willing to make a commitment to the school community. Applicants are urged to apply early in the school year. A personal interview is required. After receipt of an application, the School will notify the candidate of testing procedures and request the release of school transcripts and teacher recommendations.

In 1999–2000, tuition is $7870 for half-day Pre-Kindergarten, $10,290 for full-day Pre-Kindergarten, $11,440 for Kindergarten, $13,100 for Grades 1–5, $14,070 for Grades 6–7, and $15,570 for Grades 8–12. A 10 percent deposit is due by March 15. Tuition payment plans are available.

Financial aid is available for applicants who demonstrate need and evidence of academic, social, and leadership promise.

In 1999–2000, up to 26 percent of the Upper School students and 14 percent of the Middle School students received financial aid.

Upper School Principal: Richard Karman
Middle School Principal: Joseph Stefani
Lower School Principal: Rose Ann Howarth
Co-Directors of Admission: Patria Sullivan, Janet Halpern, and Diane Glace
Director of Development: James Ackerman
College Counselor: Lloyd Peterson, Jr.
Athletic Director: Mary Coyle Klinger

Saddle River Day School   1957

147 Chestnut Ridge Road, Saddle River, NJ 07458. 201-327-4050; Fax 201-327-6161; E-mail and Web Site Saddleriverday.org

Enrolling 304 boys and girls in Kindergarten–Grade 12, Saddle River Day School is committed to providing a rich college preparatory curriculum that enables students to develop "both competence and conscience." Classes are small, with a student-teacher ratio of 7:1. The Lower Division emphasizes a strong foundation in basic academic skills in readiness for the challenges of the upper grades. Activities include drama, choir, Academic Decathlon, publications, and community and school service groups. A full, three-season athletic program is offered at three levels. A summer program is available. Tuition: $7994–$14,958. Donald G. Treue is Assistant Head; Timothy J. Saburn (St. Lawrence University, B.A.; Harvard University, Ed.M.) was appointed Headmaster in 1998. *Middle States Association.*

St. Benedict's Preparatory School   1868

520 Dr. Martin Luther King, Jr., Boulevard, Newark, NJ 07102. 973-643-4800; Fax 973-643-6922; E-mail graybee@sbp.org; Web Site www.sbp.org

St. Benedict's Preparatory School is a Roman Catholic, college preparatory day school enrolling 550 boys in Grades 7–12. Founded by monks of the Order of St. Benedict at Newark Abbey, the School aims for academic and personal excellence in a student body that reflects the racial and cultural diversity of the city. A rigorous curriculum is supplemented by special projects, elective programs, and short-term exchanges with other schools. A full athletic program, publications, drama, choir, and clubs are among the activities. A six-week summer session is mandatory. Tuition: $5200. Financial aid is available. The Reverend Mark Payne, OSB, is Director of Admissions; The Reverend Edwin D. Leahy, OSB (Seton Hall, A.B.; Woodstock College, M.Div.), was appointed Headmaster in 1972. *Middle States Association.*

St. Mary's Hall/Doane Academy   1837

350 West Delaware Avenue, Burlington, NJ 08016-2199. 609-386-3500; Fax 609-386-5878; E-mail bishopdoane@home.com; Web Site www.thehall.org

Situated on the banks of the Delaware River, St. Mary's Hall/Doane Academy is a coeducational, college preparatory day school. It is nonsectarian and enrolls 180 students in Kindergarten–Grade 12. The school's rigorous academic program is complemented by athletics and extracurricular activities that include art, music, drama, literary publications, and computers. The low student-faculty ratio and a strong sense of community encourage students to develop their full potential as individuals and as members of society. Tuition: $6300–$8300. Financial Aid: $100,000. Lisbeth S. Mosgrove is Director of Admissions; Donald M. Saunders (Carnegie Mellon University, M.A. 1973) was appointed Headmaster in 1997. *Middle States Association.*

Stuart Country Day School of the Sacred Heart   1963

1200 Stuart Road, Princeton, NJ 08540. 609-921-2330;
*   Fax 609-497-0784; E-mail admission@stuart.k12.nj.us;*
*   Web Site www.stuart.k12.nj.us*

Stuart Country Day, an independent, college preparatory day school, enrolls 538 students in Pre-School–Grade 12, with boys in Pre-School only. Students begin French and Spanish in Kindergarten and continue through Advanced Placement language and literature, with Latin beginning in Grade 8. Innovations in the math curriculum permit students to take two years of AP Calculus before graduation. Advanced students may take courses at Princeton University. As a member of the 200-year-old Network of Schools of the Sacred Heart, Stuart focuses on academic excellence and a commitment to service. Tuition: $4900–$16,800. Financial Aid: $749,400. Anne Pierpont is Director of Admission and Financial Aid; Frances de la Chapelle, RSCJ, is Headmistress. *Middle States Association.*

Villa Victoria Academy   1933

376 West Upper Ferry Road, Ewing, NJ 08628.
*   609-882-1700; Fax 609-882-8421; E-mail admissions@*
*   villavictoria.org; Web Site www.villavictoria.org*

Founded by the followers of Saint Lucy Filippini, Villa Victoria Academy is a Roman Catholic, college preparatory day school serving 140 boys and girls in Pre-Kindergarten through Grade 6 and 130 girls in Grades 7 through 12. Located on a beautiful 44-acre campus, the Academy emphasizes liberal and fine arts in a Christian environment that provides opportunities for spiritual growth as well as intellectual achievement. The traditional curriculum includes foreign languages, computers, and private art, music, and ballet lessons. Community outreach, athletics, honors courses, Advanced Placement, and after-school care are available. Tuition: $5800–$6350. Donna Higgins is Admissions Director; Sr. Lillian Harrington, MPF, is President. *Middle States Association.*

The Wilson School   1909

271 Boulevard, Mountain Lakes, NJ 07046. 973-334-0181;
*   Fax 973-334-1852*

The Wilson School, enrolling fewer than 100 boys and girls in Pre-Kindergarten–Grade 8, aims to provide an environment that develops independent, thoughtful, and confident learners. Grade-level teams encompass two-year chronological age spans,

and "allied" instructors teach French/Spanish, art, music, physical education, and swimming. A child-centered approach to learning employs thematic units in the lower grades and interdisciplinary units in the Middle School. Wilson encourages a strong home-school partnership to provide each child with support in reaching his or her level of potential. Extended-day, summer camp, and Summer Institute complete the program. Tuition: $10,350–$13,300. Debra Kelton is Assistant Head of School and Admission Director; Carolyn K. Borlo is Head of School. *Middle States Association.*

The Wardlaw-Hartridge School   1882

1295 Inman Avenue, Edison, NJ 08820. 908-754-1882;
*   Fax 908-754-9678; Web Site www.whschool.org*

Formed by the merger of two schools founded more than a century ago, The Wardlaw-Hartridge School is a coeducational, college preparatory day school enrolling 465 students in Pre-Kindergarten–Grade 12. It aims to provide a humanistic environment in which students can achieve intellectual growth, moral development, self-realization, and social commitment. Small classes, individual counseling, a variety of extracurricular activities, and a vigorous athletic program help each individual develop according to his or her potential. Tuition: $7275–$15,200. Gregory M. Wyatt is Admissions Director; Christopher B. Williamson (Williams College, B.A.; University of New Hampshire, M.A.) was appointed Head of School in 1994. *Middle States Association.*

The Winston School   1981

100 East Lane, Short Hills, NJ 07078. 973-379-4114;
*   Fax 973-379-3984; E-mail pbloom1@cybernex.net;*
*   Web Site http://winstonschool.org*

The Winston School was established to meet the needs of intellectually able boys and girls who were encountering problems in school due to learning difficulties. Enrolling 48 day students ages 6–14, the school seeks to provide students with the strategies needed to achieve academic success. Each student's program is individually designed based on the results of diagnostic testing. Classes, taught by certified specialists, are limited in size to eight to ensure personalized attention and support. The program includes art, music, physical education, computers, and occupational therapy. Tuition: $16,765–$20,280. Financial aid is available. Paula Lordy is Assistant to the Head; Pamela R. Bloom (George Washington, B.A.; Harvard, Ed.M.) was appointed Head of School in 1992. *Middle States Association.*

NEW MEXICO

Albuquerque Academy   1955

6400 Wyoming Boulevard, NE, Albuquerque, NM 87109.
505-828-3200; Admissions 505-828-3208; Fax 505-828-3128;
E-mail hudenko@aa.edu

Albuquerque Academy is a coeducational, college preparatory day school enrolling 1030 students in Grades 6–12. Emphasizing mastery of fundamentals and independent judgment, the Academy seeks the full academic, creative, moral, and physical development of each student. It offers a challenging curriculum with 16 Advanced Placement courses, requires participation in a wilderness experience, and provides exchange programs with schools in this country and abroad. Student Council, debate, sports, clubs, and publications are some of the activities. A six-week summer school and day camp are available. Tuition: $8550. Financial Aid: $2,600,000. Judy Hudenko is Director of Admission and Financial Aid; Timothy R. McIntire is Headmaster.

Albuquerque Country Day School

ALBUQUERQUE

5801 Carmel Avenue North East, Albuquerque, NM 87113.
505-797-2200; Web Site www.acds.k12.nm.us

Albuquerque country day school in Albuquerque, New Mexico, a nonprofit, nonsectarian, coeducational day school governed by a Board of Founding Trustees, was established in 1996 by a group of educators and parents who shared the common vision of a learning community that inspires high academic and personal expectations and a commitment to excellence. The School celebrates the individuality of each child and offers an educational program marked by small classes, personalized attention, and appropriate resources for each child. Its common principles, based on work by Theodore Sizer and the Coalition of Essential Schools, focus on helping young people develop the habit of using their minds well, helping students master essential skills and defined areas of knowledge, personalized teaching and learning, documenting teaching and learning based on student performance of real tasks, and engaging family members as vital participants in the school community.

Albuquerque Country Day School enrolls 67 students from PreKindergarten through seventh grade. During the 2000-01 school year, the enrollment will expand to include Grade 8. Classroom experiences are extended to incorporate the diverse historical, cultural, and natural resources of the area, supplemented by rich cultural and scientific centers of the region and easy access to museums, an aquarium, zoo, botanical gardens, and public libraries. A developmentally appropriate athletic program is directed by Ed Burch and his staff in the facilities of the Gold Cup Gym, a block from the School.

Albuquerque Country Day is a member of the National Association of Independent Schools in the First Five Year classification and is accredited by the North Central Association of Schools and Colleges. It is a charter member of the New Mexico Association of Independent Schools.

THE CAMPUS. The School's new campus, opened in 1998 in Northeast Albuquerque, occupies a one-acre site with contiguous land available for future expansion. It is immediately accessible to Interstate 25 in an area experiencing rapid residential and commercial growth. It is less than one hour from Santa Fe and just minutes from Placitas and Bernalillo. The campus houses two academic buildings, both constructed in the Northern New Mexico style. Primary grades hold classes in one building, while intermediate and middle school classes are held in the other. Large, grassy play areas and playground equipment are located on site.

THE FACULTY. Charles H. Como is the founding Headmaster of the School. Mr. Como, a graduate of the University of Massachusetts with a Bachelor of Arts degree in Music, holds an M.Ed. degree from Bridgewater State College and has done postgraduate study at Harvard Graduate School of Education, Lesley College, Brandeis University, Wright State University, and Boston University. He has headed two schools supported by the Department of State in Warsaw, Poland, and Athens, Greece, serving in the interim as a principal in the Lexington, Massachusetts, public schools and as a consultant to the Administration of Overseas Schools. During a four-year sabbatical, Mr. Como was a corporate executive in a large manufacturing firm in Dallas, Texas.

The staff is made up of 15 full- and part-time faculty members with diverse talents and interests. They hold degrees from Bridgewater State, College of Mount Saint Vincent, College of Santa Fe, Cornell, Lesley College Graduate School, Manhattan College, Oberlin, Oklahoma State, State College of Boston, Texas Woman's University, Virginia Polytechnic Institute, Yale University, and the Universities of Massachusetts, Michigan,

New Mexico, Northern Iowa, and Southern Illinois. The faculty participates in the Teachers Insurance Annuity Association and College Retirement Equities Foundation and has options for health insurance, a tuition remission program for their children, and other benefits.

STUDENT BODY. There are 67 students enrolled for the 1999–2000 calendar year. The student population is drawn from throughout the state of New Mexico and represents a diverse range of racial, ethnic, religious, and economic backgrounds. It is anticipated that the enrollment will grow to approximately 200 students by the year 2005.

ACADEMIC PROGRAM. The school year runs from late August and extends into late May. It is divided into quarters and honors all major national holidays. Classes, which are limited to 12 students, meet five days a week from 8:30 A.M. until 3:30 P.M. The PreKindergarten operates on a flexible schedule with three or five half-days or full days. The Kindergarten offers five half- or full days. After-school care is available for $3 an hour until 6:00 P.M.

STUDENT ACTIVITIES. Albuquerque Country Day participates in the University of New Mexico's Bosque Ecosystem Monitoring Program. The School has a Student Council, a newsletter that is published regularly under the direction of a faculty advisor, and a tennis program, and it is exploring other areas of interest to students.

ADMISSION AND COSTS. Albuquerque Country Day School admits students on the basis of an extensive personal interview and recommendations. Returning students and their siblings are given preference for enrolling, while new students are evaluated according to their merits and date of application.

Annual tuition is $6650. Fees for Pre-school and Kindergarten are as follows: $3600 for half-day Kindergarten, $6150 for full-time Pre-school, $3300 for five half-days in Pre-school, $3895 for three full days in Pre-school, and $2100 for three half-days in Pre-school. Fees include $50 for the application, $50 for testing when appropriate, and $50 for school supplies. A nonrefundable deposit of 10 percent of the annual tuition is due upon acceptance. The remaining obligation is due either in a single payment or in ten installments, beginning August 1.

Installment payments must be supplemented by tuition insurance, which is approximately 2.8 percent of the tuition. Incidental costs not exceeding $100 may be charged during the year. Financial aid is available.

Head of School: Charles H. Como
Director of Admissions: Judith L. Como
Director of Development: Kati Pinders Lambert

Brush Ranch School   SANTA FE

P.O. Box 2450, Santa Fe, NM 87504. 505-757-6114;
Fax: 505-757-6118

BRUSH RANCH SCHOOL in Santa Fe, New Mexico, is an ungraded boarding school for boys and girls, ages 10 through 18, who have been diagnosed with mild to moderate learning problems. Located on the Pecos River in the Sangre de Cristo Range of the Rocky Mountains, 11 miles north of Pecos on State Highway 63, the School is 37 miles northeast of Santa Fe and 90 miles north of Albuquerque. The nearest commercial airport is in Albuquerque; private planes fly to Santa Fe Airport.

Founded in 1970 by Mr. and Mrs. Newcomb Rice, Brush Ranch School is designed for boys and girls who are unable to function successfully in the normal classroom situation. The School maintains individual educational programs in a structured, active, and nurturing learning environment. Brush Ranch's goals are to increase achievement in the basic skill areas of reading, language arts, and mathematics; to develop independence in learning and social areas; and to increase self-esteem. The School prepares the student to enter society and cope successfully in academic, vocational, and social environments. More than 90 percent of recent graduates have attended two- or four-year colleges and universities.

The School is a nonprofit educational corporation and is governed by a Board of Directors. Brush Ranch is approved by the New Mexico State Department of Education and the North Central Association of Colleges and Schools. Brush Ranch belongs to the Orton Dyslexia Society, the Learning Disabilities Association, the Council for Exceptional Children, Children and Adults with Attention Deficit Disorders, the National Association of Private Schools for Exceptional Children, and the New Mexico Association of Non-Public Schools.

THE CAMPUS. The School is situated on 283 private acres entirely surrounded by the Santa Fe National Forest, offering unlimited areas for hiking, riding, and backpacking. The Pecos River, which flows through the property, provides excellent trout fishing; there are also two well-stocked ponds. Other facilities include four Laykold tennis courts, recreation center, athletic fields, ropes course, heated swimming pool, riding ring, and barns with 16 stalls and two tack rooms. Classrooms and living accommodations are of log construction and are completely modern.

THE FACULTY. Gary R. Emmons, a graduate of Southeast Missouri State University (B.A., B.S., M.A.), is the current Headmaster.

There are eight full-time teachers, a Dean of Academics, a Dean of Students, and five additional administrators. They hold graduate and undergraduate degrees from institutions around the world as well as certification in special education. The 18 residential adviser/instructors, who live in the cabins with the students, hold undergraduate degrees and teach elective, enrichment, and athletic classes.

STUDENT BODY. The student body is comprised of boys and girls from 10 through 18 years of age. There is an approximate 60:40 ratio of boys to girls. Students are enrolled without regard to race, creed, or national origin. The School enrolls students from all over the United States and several foreign countries.

ACADEMIC PROGRAM. The school year runs from early September until late May with vacations in the winter and spring. Each child has an individual educational plan designed to meet his or her specific educational needs. Classes, which have an average enrollment of eight students, meet five days a week. Schedules are adjusted to follow individual educational programs. Course work includes reading, mathematics, language arts, social studies, and science. Students use computers for word processing, research, and skill reinforcement. The elective programs include courses in computer awareness, ceramics, journalism, cooking, drama, art, carpentry, photography, landscaping and gardening, equine management, and career education. The students participate in daily outdoor athletic activities. Basketball, fishing, football, hiking, horseback riding, skating, skiing, soccer, softball, swimming, tennis, tobogganing, volleyball, weight lifting, and a ropes course are part of this program.

The Terra Nova is given at the beginning and end of each school year as one measure of academic growth. Parents are informed of the academic and social progress of their children through quarterly reports and parent conferences. After graduation, most of the students attend college or vocational schools.

STUDENT ACTIVITIES. The Alpine Leadership Program (ALPS) is a wilderness outdoor education program. Students work together on the high and low ropes, their two- and three-day backpacks into the wilderness, and their solving problems in expedition planning, orienteering, and map reading all contribute to developing students' confidence. Horse packing is also a part of ALPS.

Student government representatives are elected from each cabin. This leadership position develops self-esteem and empowers individuals as they find themselves making a difference. The student government plays an active role in coordinating many of the activities on campus. Students also oversee the honor code through the Honor Council.

Weekend life varies with wilderness trips, school social events, trips to Santa Fe for shopping and movies, campus work projects, Sunday devotional, and special off-campus excursions.

Leadership opportunities abound. Students may participate in any facet of the Work Incentive Program, including several community service projects. They may also apply for and serve on the Honor Council or be selected as a Prefect.

Santa Fe and the surrounding area offer unique and wonderful opportunities to broaden students' experiences at Brush Ranch. Excursions to the theater, musical events, art exhibits, museums, archeological sites, and professional sporting events are planned and attended by the students.

ADMISSION AND COSTS. Students who have been classified as having a specific educational need are accepted on the recommendation of a psychologist, educational diagnostician, guidance counselor, or, in some cases, a physician familiar with learning problems.

An educational evaluation and previous school records are required. The evaluation should include results of tests of intelligence, achievement, processing, and behavior. Records precede the candidate's visit to Brush Ranch School with his or her parents, which is a prerequisite for enrollment. Application may be made any time during the school year, although enrollment for the fall is generally completed during the summer months. There is a nonrefundable $50 application fee.

In 1999–2000, tuition is $28,900. Additional expenses include allowances ($150–$200 per month) and an optional fee (approximately $275) for the ski program at the beginning of the second semester.

Headmaster: Gary R. Emmons
Director of Admissions: Yvette Madrid

Desert Academy at Santa Fe 1994

242 Los Pinos Road, Santa Fe, NM 87505. 505-474-7800;
  Fax 505-474-0590

Desert Academy provides a fully accredited, college preparatory curriculum for Grades 7–12. Students have the opportunity of challenging themselves and individualizing their curriculum while benefiting from the support of small academic class sizes (15 maximum). A day school enrolling 130 students, Desert Academy offers electives in fine and performing arts, life skills, literary and media enrichment, and community service. In addition, Desert Academy has collaborated with Santa Fe Performing Arts, National Dance Institute, and Assistance Dogs of the West, providing students with exceptional enrichment experiences. Tuition: $9800. Financial aid is available. Peter Breslin and Marie White are Co-Heads of School.

Manzano Day School 1938

1801 Central Avenue NW, Albuquerque, NM 87104-1197.
  505-243-6659; Fax 505-243-4711;
  E-mail Admission/nr@mds.k12.nm.us;
  Web Site www.mds.k12.nm.us

Manzano Day School, a Blue Ribbon School of Excellence enrolling 405 children in pre-kindergarten–Grade 5, seeks to provide a strong basic curriculum in a nurturing environment. The student-teacher ratio is typically 9:1. Spanish, art, physical education, music, library, and technology studies supplement the regular curriculum. Students visit the School ranch, 80 miles distant in the Jemez Mountains, for two or three days at a time for nature and environmental studies. An after-school program and summer session are available. Tuition: $8450. Kay Pickett (Tulane University, M.A.Ed.) is Head of School.

The Menaul School ALBUQUERQUE

301 Menaul Boulevard, NE, Albuquerque, NM 87107.
  505-345-7727; Fax 505-344-2517

THE MENAUL SCHOOL in Albuquerque, New Mexico, is a coeducational boarding and day school affiliated with the Presbyterian Church (U.S.A.) and enrolling students in Grades 6 through 12. Albuquerque is the state's largest city (population 589,131) and a center of finance, industry, trade, and research in the fields of energy, space, and military defense. Albuquerque is about 60 miles southwest of Santa Fe near the Sandia Mountains, which provide excellent skiing opportunities and other recreational facilities. The University of New Mexico, Albuquerque's Little Theater, and three symphony orchestras are among the cultural attractions of the region.

Presbyterian missionaries founded the School in 1881 in concert with the United States government to educate Native New Mexicans. Today, The Menaul School, as one of eight racial ethnic schools affiliated with the Presbyterian Church (U.S.A.), enrolls a student body that is reflective of the diversity of northern New Mexico. Students, many of them Hispanic and Native American, come from throughout the state, from elsewhere in the U.S., and from several continents; approximately 50 percent are Roman Catholic.

The Menaul School's mission is to provide a "world-class" education in a caring, safe environment. As a "family within a school," students and faculty are linked by a common goal of developing intellectual competence along with the solid spiritual foundation they need to face the challenges of life in the 21st century. Learning how to think critically and make important value judgments share equal emphasis with the mastery of skills and concepts in academic disciplines.

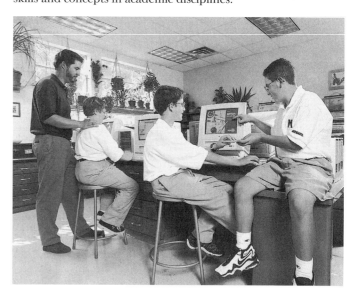

The Menaul School, which is accredited by the North Central Association of Colleges and Schools and by the New Mexico State Board of Education, is governed by a 14-member Board of Trustees. The Menaul Parents Association is instrumental in organizing social and fund-raising activities to support the School and its programs.

THE CAMPUS. The 50-acre campus, which is on the National Register of Historic Places, is modeled after that of a small college, with ten main buildings, many of historic and architectural significance. Separate dormitories for girls and boys accommodate boarding students in Grades 8–12. Academic facilities include state-of-the-art technology and fully equipped science and language labs. Two recent additions to the campus are Alumni Plaza, which features an expanded stage, canvas coverings, and a stair-stepped fountain, and Baez Plaza, made up of native plants, rock, and a fountain. There is a full gymnasium, plus a football field, track, tennis courts, a baseball diamond, and a girls' softball field.

THE FACULTY. Dr. James R. Garvin was appointed President of The Menaul School in 1996. He earned his baccalaureate degree from State University of New York and holds master's and doctoral degrees from the University of New Orleans. Dr. Garvin has written numerous scholarly books and articles and is the author of ten children's books. In addition to his administrative responsibilities, he teaches Religion and Creative Writing.

Dr. Garvin is supported by a faculty of 46 men and women, all of whom hold baccalaureate degrees. In addition, they have earned 31 master's degrees and 2 doctorates, representing study at colleges and universities in New Mexico and elsewhere in the nation.

STUDENT BODY. In 1998–99, The Menaul School enrolled 422 students in Grades 6–12. More than 100 students annually receive financial assistance.

ACADEMIC PROGRAM. The Menaul School seeks to provide a strong college preparatory curriculum within the context of Presbyterian teaching and tradition. The school year is divided into three terms: fall, spring, and E-term. Students carry seven courses per term. The regular class day starts at 8:00 A.M. and ends at 2:50 P.M. The daily schedule for boarding students includes designated study periods and time for chores before "lights out" at 11:00 P.M.

Beginning with the Class of 2000, students must earn 28.5 academic credits to graduate, including the following: 4.5 credits in social studies; 4 credits each in English and mathematics; 3 each in a lab science, modern language, and the visual and performing arts; 2 in religious studies; and 1 each in physical education and the work program. An additional 3 credits are awarded for successful completion of the required Enrichment Term.

E-Term, as it is known, is a period of in-depth study in a field of interest outside the regular curriculum. Students may select from a variety of opportunities in such areas as art and architecture, Web Site design, silversmithing, lifetime sports, creative writing, history and film, children's literature, and birding. Honor roll students have first choice of their selections, and students who are deficient in some academic areas may be asked to use this period to take remediation classes. Credit is awarded based on attendance, participation, and the final project.

In Grades 6–8, course work focuses on the development of a strong foundation of understanding in math, literature, geog-

raphy, history and social studies, science, computer technology, reading and writing, Spanish, and religion.

Among the specific courses available to high school students are Reading to Write, Drama and Novels, American Literature at a Glance, World Literature, Academic Writing; Pre-Algebra, Algebra I–II, Geometry, Pre-Calculus, Trigonometry; Biology, Biology II–Microbiology, Biology II–Anatomy and Physiology, Applied Chemistry, Chemistry, Physics; Native American Studies, Global Issues, U.S. History, Economics and the Markets, America's Wars, Ancient Cultures, Cultural Anthropology, Child Development, Adolescent Issues, Comparative Economics, Political Economics, The Constitution, Psychology; Spanish I–II, Advanced Spanish, French I–III, English as a Second Language; Life and Times of Christ, The Human Spirit and the Human Condition, Comparative World Religions and World Views, Catholic Tradition and Reform Theology, Morality and Social Issues, Literature of the Old Testament, Native American Traditions and Christian Thought; Computer I, Computer Graphics, Web Publishing and Maintenance; and Theatre Arts I–II, Theatre Production I–II, Advanced Acting, Beginning Band, Advanced Band, Beginning Strings, Advanced Strings, Guitar I & II, Concert Choir, Vocal Techniques I & II, Drawing I–II, Painting I–II, Printmaking I–III, Metal Sculpting, Southwest Arts and Crafts, Photography, and Native American Dance. Participation in the School's work program is required for Grades 8–12, and volunteerism in community outreach projects is encouraged.

Three times a week, all students are involved in chapel services that include Biblical readings, skits, stories, and "energizer" sessions designed to stimulate open discussion of issues relevant to teenagers.

Ninety-eight percent of the 48 seniors in the Class of 1998 chose to continue their education at the college level. Twenty-three graduates enrolled at the University of New Mexico, while others entered such institutions as Catholic University of America, Lewis and Clark, New Mexico Highlands, New Mexico State, Point Loma Nazarene, Regis, Rhodes, Wayland Baptist, and the Universities of Denver and Texas (Austin).

STUDENT ACTIVITIES. The Menaul School offers extracurricular activities intended to develop students mentally, physically, and socially and to provide opportunities for personal growth. The Student Council and Senate, consisting of class, club, and resident hall presidents and day student representatives, encourages teamwork for the betterment of the School community. Membership in National and Junior National Honor societies is open to students of good character and high academic achievement.

Clubs are formed in response to interest and may change according to students' needs. Some of these organizations include the Thespian Society, Junior Civitan, Tribe (Native American Club), Science People Inc., Band, Choir, and Chess Club. Students also publish *Sandstorm,* the School yearbook.

Interscholastic sports are played at varsity and junior varsity levels, and Panther teams compete in baseball, football, basketball, and track for boys; and in volleyball, basketball, track, soccer, tennis, and softball for girls. Girls may also try out for the varsity and junior varsity cheerleading squads. Golf and swimming teams are organized on a coeducational basis.

Throughout the year, the School sponsors many special events such as Science Fair, Homecoming, play productions, Science Olympiad, Mathcounts, and choral and band concerts.

ADMISSION AND COSTS. The Menaul School welcomes students from all racial, ethnic, and faith backgrounds who share its commitment to academic excellence and the formation of strong moral character.

For the 1999–2000 school year, tuition is $5576, which covers the use of textbooks. The fee for room and board is $8992. A nonrefundable $200 registration fee is required prior to enrollment. Other charges include a class fee for Grades 11–12 ($30–$50), activity fee ($200), and E-Term ($50). The initial application fee is $20. Other expenses may involve optional trips, travel to and from home for boarders, and sundry personal needs.

President: James Garvin, Ph.D.
Registrar: Sarah Fair
Director of Admissions: John B. Thayer
Director of Institutional Advancement: Michael L. Gaylor, Ed.D.
Chief Accounting Officer: Mike Stabler
Men's Athletic Director: Robert Martin, Ph.D.
Women's Athletic Director: Lisa Todd
Chaplain: Rev. Buddy Monahan

New Mexico Academy for Sciences and Mathematics   1998

7300 Old Santa Fe Trail, Santa Fe, NM 87505. 505-954-4000; Fax 505-986-9095

The New Mexico Academy for Sciences and Mathematics offers a complete college preparatory liberal arts curriculum with

emphasis on social sciences, applied sciences, and mathematics to 80 boys and girls in Grades 7–12. A new grade will be added each year through 2001. The Academy's mission is to give students the study skills to research and learn; to reach conclusions based on logic and evidence; to communicate well verbally and numerically; and to gain admission to their first-choice college. Participation in at least two extracurricular activities is recommended. Students may choose from more than 20 clubs and a range of sports, including horsemanship. Tuition: $10,000 plus fees. Financial aid is available. Fernando Multedo (Columbia, Ed.D. 1997) is President.

New Mexico Military Institute   1891

101 W. College Boulevard, Roswell, NM 88201-5376. 800-421-5376; Fax 505-624-8058; E-mail admissions@ yogi.nmmi.cc.nm.us; Web Site http://www.nmmi.cc.nm.us

New Mexico Military Institute, a coeducational boarding school, enrolls 400 boys and 120 girls in Grades 9–12 and junior college. The Institute receives support from the State of New Mexico enabling it to provide an affordable education for young men and women. Students follow a college preparatory curriculum with small classes and supervised study. The military training program offers a values-based educational environment. Many sports and extracurricular activities are offered in state-of-the-art facilities. Tuition, Room and Board, and Uniforms: $9000. Financial Aid: $500,000. LTC Peter C. Nacy is Director of Admissions; LTG Robert Beckel is Superintendent. *North Central Association.*

Rio Grande School   1978

715 Camino Cabra, Santa Fe, NM 87501. 505-983-1621; Fax 505-986-0012; E-mail rgstwo@rt66.com

Rio Grande is an independent coeducational day school enrolling approximately 120 students in Kindergarten–Grade 6. The School offers an integrated curriculum that includes traditional academics, fine and performing arts, and outdoor activities. Small classes and personalized attention for each student are features of the program. Class activities are enlivened by field trips to study local cultures, overnight stays, and wilderness experiences. An extended-day program is available as well as a summer program. Tuition: $9035. Extras: $215. Financial aid is available. Claire Romero is Director of Admission; Linda M. Harris (Columbia Teachers College, M.A.Ed.) was appointed Head of the School in 1995.

Sandia Preparatory School   1966

532 Osuna Road, NE, Albuquerque, NM 87113. 505-344-1671; Fax 505-345-2336; E-mail etomelloso@sandiaprep.org; Web Site www.sandiaprep.org

Founded by Mrs. Albert G. Simms II, Sandia Prep is a college preparatory day school enrolling 565 students in Grades 6–12. The joy of learning and living is at the center of its curriculum. Sandia Prep provides a well-balanced program. It supports the quest for human excellence by helping students discover their strengths and explore new horizons as they prepare for college. Sandia Prep has received awards for its effective advisory program, community outreach, drama program, and no-cut sports program. Tuition: $8600. Financial Aid: $602,000. Ester Tomelloso is Director of Admission; Richard L. Heath (Cornell, A.B. 1969; Colgate, M.A.T. 1972) is Headmaster.

Santa Fe Preparatory School   1961

1101 Camino de la Cruz Blanca, Santa Fe, NM 87501.
  505-982-1829; Fax 505-982-2897

Santa Fe Preparatory School is a coeducational day school enrolling 311 students in Grades 7–12. Prep students develop intellectual and life skills through a curriculum that emphasizes critical thinking and expression. This curriculum is enhanced by athletics, art, and community service opportunities. Prep's faculty demonstrate respect for scholarship, love of learning, and social consciousness, helping students acquire a broad understanding of the arts, the sciences, and the world. The School is a caring community that values diversity and has personal academic development at its center. Tuition: $10,300. Financial Aid: $265,000. Marta Miskolczy is Director of Admissions; James W. Leonard is Head of School.

NEW YORK

Abraham Lincoln School   1994

12 East 79th Street, New York, NY 10021. 212-744-7300;
   Fax 212-744-5876

Abraham Lincoln School enrolls 88 boys and girls in three-year-old Nursery–Grade 5, with Grade 6 scheduled to be added in Fall 1999 and Grades 7 and 8 to follow in subsequent years. The School seeks to provide an innovative educational experience designed to nurture and free children to lead harmonious, fulfilling lives. The curriculum is respectful of all religions and cultures, integrating classical Eastern thinking with traditional American learning. In addition to philosophy, Sanskrit, and the lessons found in nature, students from Kindergarten upward master fundamental skills in English, mathematics, and science. Art, music, and physical education complete the program. Tuition: $7000–$9500. Regina Flecha is Director of Admission; Howard Schott is Headmaster.

Academy of Mt. St. Ursula   1855

330 Bedford Park Boulevard, Bronx, NY 10458. 718-364-5353;
   Fax 718-584-1507; E-mail admissions@amsu.org;
   Web Site www.amsu.org

Founded by the Ursuline nuns in 1855, Academy of Mt. St. Ursula is a Roman Catholic, college preparatory day school enrolling 510 girls in Grades 9–12. The school aims to meet the needs of today's students in a context of unchanging spiritual and moral values. As part of the college preparatory program, the Academy has up-to-date technological resources. Advanced Placement courses are given in five subjects, and qualified seniors may take college credit courses. A wide range of activities is organized. Tuition: $3950. Extras: $400 fee. Sr. Barbara Calamari is Director of Admission; Sr. Mary Beth Read (Catholic University of America, B.A.; Fordham University, M.S.) was appointed Principal in 1992. *Middle States Association.*

The Academy of St. Joseph   1856

1725 Brentwood Road, Brentwood, NY 11717. 516-273-2406;
   Fax 516-231-4155; E-mail stjoseph@ix.netcom.com;
   Web Site http://home.earthlink.net/~stjoseph

The Academy of St. Joseph, a Roman Catholic college preparatory school, enrolls 135 boys and girls in Pre-Kindergarten–Grade 6 and 306 young women in Grades 7–12. Curriculum in the Lower School is child-centered, integrative, and holistic. Upper School features a liberal arts and science core and an introduction to computer and Internet research within an automated library. Activities range from publications, drama, and music groups to special-interest clubs, athletics, and community service. Tuition: $1950–$5150. Sr. M. Aquinata, CSJ, is Head of the Lower School; Sr. Valerie Scholl, CSJ (St. John's University, M.S.; Fordham, Cert.Admin.), is Directress; Sr. Joanne Forker, CSJ (Fordham, M.S.; Columbia, M.A.), is Principal. *Middle States Association.*

The Academy of the Holy Names   1884

1075 New Scotland Road, Albany, NY 12208. 518-489-2559;
   Fax 518-438-7368

This Blue Ribbon School of Excellence is committed to the education of young women in a stimulating, supportive environment guided by Catholic-Christian values. Set on a 64-acre campus, The Academy of the Holy Names enrolls 505 students, with boys and girls in Pre-Kindergarten and girls only in Kindergarten–Grade 12. Religion, computer literacy, foreign language, and library skills begin in Pre-Kindergarten. The Upper School curriculum offers Advanced Placement courses and opportunities for students to earn college credit through the State University of New York. Campus Ministry, community service, peer leadership, music, drama, interest clubs, and sports are among the activities. Tuition: $5200–$6200. Colleen Geary is Director of Admissions; Sr. Constance Casey, SNJM, is President.

Adelphi Academy   1863

8515 Ridge Boulevard, Brooklyn, NY 11209. 718-238-3308;
   Fax 718-238-2894

Adelphi Academy, Brooklyn's oldest coeducational institution and one of the nation's oldest, enrolls 200 students in Pre-Kindergarten–Grade 12. It offers a challenging college preparatory curriculum in a nurturing setting. The program is designed to enable young people to reach their full potential through a strong foundation in the liberal arts and sciences. Core subjects are complemented by topics in psychology, computer science, creative writing, and leadership. Community service is required for graduation. Student government, sports, music, art, and drama are also offered. Tuition: $5800–$12,800. Financial aid is available. R. Kenneth Pierce is Headmaster. *Middle States Association.*

Albany Academy for Girls   1814

140 Academy Road, Albany, NY 12208. 518-463-2201;
   Fax 518-463-5096; E-mail lewisj@albanyacademyforgirls.org;
   Web Site www.albanyacademyforgirls.org

Albany Academy for Girls enrolls 363 day students in a program developed to meet the needs of the whole child. The school has three divisions: Primary (PK–Grade 4), Middle (Grades 5–8), and Upper (Grades 9–12). Art, drama, music, dance, and foreign language are offered in all divisions. The computer technology department features more than 300 networked computers in labs and classrooms, all Internet accessible. The Upper School is college preparatory, and students enroll in selective colleges throughout the country. Cross-enrollment is available with the neighboring boys' school, The Albany Academy. Tuition: $7800–$12,995. Financial Aid: $360,000. Joan G. Lewis is Admissions Director; Caroline B. Mason (Denison, B.A.; Case Western Reserve, M.A.) is Headmistress.

The Allen-Stevenson School   1883

*132 East 78th Street, New York, NY 10021. 212-288-6710;
Fax 212-288-6802*

Founded in 1883 to teach young men "intelligent habits of study and to develop straightforward, manly characters," Allen-Stevenson enrolls 375 day boys in Kindergarten–Grade 9. The traditional curriculum prepares students for entrance to challenging secondary schools. Courses include French, Spanish, Latin, computers, shop, music, and art. Extracurricular activities include orchestra, Student Council, publications, and arts and drama groups. New facilities include a gymnasium, shop, art, and multipurpose room. Tuition: $18,900–$20,700. Financial Aid: $700,000. Ronnie R. Jankoff is Director of Admissions; David R. Trower (Brown University, B.A. 1968; Union Theological Seminary, M.Div. 1973) was appointed Headmaster in 1990.

The Anglo-American International School   1872

*291 Central Park West, New York, NY 10024. 212-724-2146;
Fax 212-724-2539; Web Site http://www.dwight.edu*

The Anglo-American International School formed a consortium with The Dwight School in 1993. The challenging college preparatory program, balancing the humanities, sciences, and fine arts, enrolls 400 students in Kindergarten–Grade 12. The full school follows the International Baccalaureate (IB) curriculum; students may also take IGCSE exams. The School has a strong international component and a coordinate program with Woodside Park School in London. State-of-the-art technology, French beginning in Kindergarten, and eight other languages are provided. Activities include publications, sports, and outdoor education. Tuition: $16,000–$18,500. Susan George (K–8) and Elizabeth Callaway (9–12) are Admissions Directors; Stephen H. Spahn is Chancellor; Dr. Joyce M. Robinson is Head. *Middle States Association.*

Bank Street School for Children   1915

*610 West 112th Street, New York, NY 10025. 212-875-4420;
Fax 212-875-4454*

Bank Street School for Children, enrolling 435 day boys and girls ages 3–13, is the demonstration school for the Bank Street College of Education. The School sees social, emotional, and intellectual growth as equally important and inseparable. Read-

ing and writing skills are developed in the core social studies and language arts program. Science and mathematics are presented as methods of inquiry with skill acquisition related to concepts. Curricular activities include social studies trips, creative arts, music, and physical education. After-school and summer recreational programs are available. Tuition: $12,810–$16,680. Financial Aid: $1,066,818. Betsy Hall is Coordinator of Admissions; Reuel Jordan (University of Dayton, B.A.; Bank Street College of Education, M.S.) is Dean.

The Berkeley Carroll School   BROOKLYN

*181 Lincoln Place, Brooklyn, NY 11217. 718-789-6060;
E-mail cweeks@berkeley-carroll.org; Web Site www.berkeleycarroll.org*

THE BERKELEY CARROLL SCHOOL in Brooklyn, New York, enrolls day boys and girls in Preschool–Grade 12. Located in the historic Park Slope section of Brooklyn, the resources of New York City are accessible to students and faculty. Bus and subway transportation is available from throughout the city.

The School was formed in 1982 by the merger of two neighboring schools—The Berkeley Institute, founded in 1886 as a college preparatory school for girls, and The Carroll Street School, founded in 1966 as an outgrowth of the Montessori School of Brooklyn. The Berkeley Carroll School strives for academic excellence and seeks to foster in its students intellectual curiosity, ethical values, social maturity and responsibility, leadership, and physical well-being.

A nonprofit institution, the School is governed by a 25-member Board of Trustees that meets ten times a year. There are approximately 1000 living alumni.

The Berkeley Carroll School holds a charter from the New York State Board of Regents and is accredited by the Middle States Association of Colleges and Schools. Membership is held in the National Association of Independent Schools and other associations.

THE CAMPUS. The School has three campuses within walking distance of one another. The Middle and Upper schools are located at Lincoln Place and the Elementary and Lower schools are located at two separate Carroll Street facilities. Lincoln Place consists of the Main Building, built in 1895 for The Berkeley Institute, with classrooms, a library, computer center, art labs, ceramics studio, science laboratories, music room, photography darkroom, cafeteria, student lounge, auditorium, theater, dance studio, and a gymnasium. An award-winning, five-story classroom building, connecting the main building and gymnasium, opened in 1992.

The 701 Carroll Street brick facility, housing the Elementary School, contains classrooms, a library, music studio, science laboratory, art room, and computer center.

The 712 Carroll Street campus, a brownstone residence built at the turn of the century, was purchased by the School and renovated in 1981 for use by the Lower School. The building has classrooms, a library, recreation room, music studio, and an outdoor playground. An adjacent gymnasium is rented for use by the Elementary and Lower schools. A new gymnasium with swimming pool is under construction.

All buildings are owned by the School and are valued at $8,000,000.

THE FACULTY. Bongsoon Zubay is Headmistress of The Berkeley Carroll School. Dr. Zubay received a combined B.A. and M.A. from the University of Minnesota, an M.Ed. from Columbia, a Montessori Diploma from Fairleigh Dickinson, and an Ed.D. from Teachers College of Columbia. She was a teacher at the Dalton School in New York City before being named Headmistress of The Carroll Street School in 1975. Dr. Zubay is married to Geoffrey Zubay and has one son.

The full-time faculty, including administrators who teach, number 99, 26 men and 73 women. They hold 99 baccalaureate, 68 master's, and 2 doctoral degrees representing study at such institutions as Amherst, Bank Street College, Barnard, Brown, Carleton, College of Mount Saint Vincent, Columbia, Connecticut College, Cornell, Fordham, Hamilton, Harvard, Johns Hopkins, Juilliard School, Kenyon, Liverpool Polytechnic (England), Mount Holyoke, New York University, Pratt Institute, Sarah Lawrence, State University of New York (Binghamton, Stony Brook), Vassar, Wellesley, Wesleyan, Yale, and the Universities of Birmingham (England), Chicago, London (England), Massachusetts, Miami, North Carolina, Pennsylvania, and Pittsburgh.

Faculty benefits include health insurance, retirement plans, and professional development. Leaves of absence can be arranged.

There is a full-time nurse on the staff and hospital facilities are located within ten blocks of the School.

STUDENT BODY. In 1999–2000, The Berkeley Carroll School enrolls 785 students in Preschool through Grade 12. There are 80 students in the Preschool, 57 in Kindergarten, 53 in Grade 1, 56 in Grade 2, 56 in Grade 3, 50 in Grade 4, 55 in Grade 5, 65 in Grade 6, 61 in Grade 7, 56 in Grade 8, 45 in Grade 9, 51 in Grade 10, 56 in Grade 11, and 44 in Grade 12. Students come from the immediate neighborhood and other areas of Brooklyn, Staten Island, Manhattan, Queens, and New Jersey.

ACADEMIC PROGRAM. The school year, divided into trimesters, begins in early September and ends in early June. There are vacations in December, February, and April. Evaluations and/or marks are sent to parents of Lower School students twice a year, Elementary, Middle, and Upper School students three times a year, and Upper School students four times a year. Classes are held Monday through Friday beginning at 8:35 A.M. for Lower School students, 8:30 A.M. for Elementary, and 8:10 A.M. for Middle and Upper School students. Classes end at 3:10 P.M. Class size averages 15 students. The Extended Day Early Bird and Afterschool programs offer educational opportunities for children before and after school hours.

The Early Learning Program in the Lower School (Preschool and Kindergarten) develops essential skills for elementary education. Language skills and self-expression are emphasized through classroom activities and weekly sessions with music, movement, and library specialists. Mathematics, science, and social studies are presented as learning activities.

The Elementary School (Grades 1–4) curriculum focuses on the fundamentals of reading, writing, mathematics, science, and social studies. There is an emphasis on library skills, physical education, music, and visual arts, and a specialist begins to establish computer literacy and proficiency.

The Middle School (Grades 5–8) uses an interdisciplinary approach and includes the study of literature, language arts, science, history, social sciences, mathematics, Spanish, and French. Classes are held in computer science, visual arts, theater, dance, and choral and instrumental music.

Upper School graduation requirements are a minimum of 20 academic units based on a normal course load of 5 units each year. These units must include 4 in English; 3 in a foreign language; 3 in history and social sciences, including 1 in American history; 3½ units in mathematics with the completion of Algebra I and II, Geometry, Trigonometry, and Statistics; 3 in laboratory science; 1 in applied arts and communications; and ½ in Introduction to the Arts. One semester of service and the completion of a senior year internship are also required. In addition, 4 units of physical education and ¼ unit of health are New York State requirements.

Upper School course offerings include Myths and Legends, Freshman Writing, Literature of the Journey, Transformations, Power Culture and Identity, Romanticism, Great Works of Literature, Humanities, Women Speaking to Men, Autobiography,

Society and Literature, Coming of Age, Murder Most Foul, Shakespeare, Creative Writing, Journalism, Poetry; French, Spanish; World History, Asian Studies, Economics, American History, European History, Democracy in America, American Social and Cultural History; Algebra 1–2, Algebra/Trigonometry, Geometry, Trigonometry, Probability and Statistics, Pre-Calculus, Calculus; Environmental Science, Biology, Chemistry, Physics, Marine Biology, Astronomy, Introduction to Engineering; Drawing, Graphic Design, Sculpture/Mixed Media, Photography, Photojournalism, Computer Arts, Video and Animation, Ceramics, Art History; Jazz Dance; Acting Workshop; and Choir, Chamber Ensemble, Jazz Ensemble, and Peer Leadership. Advanced Placement courses are offered in English, French, Spanish, United States History, European History, Calculus, Biology, Chemistry, Physics, Art History, and Studio Art. Advanced Placement courses are offered in every discipline. Sophomores in good standing may participate in the annual exchange programs in France and Spain.

The 47 students who graduated in 1999 are attending 34 colleges and universities nationwide. Two or more are enrolled at Columbia University, Goucher, Haverford, New York University, North Carolina School of the Arts, Skidmore 4, State University of New York, Temple, Tufts 4, Vassar, and Yale. Other representative schools include Boston University, Brooklyn College, Fordham, Georgetown, Princeton, Rensselaer, and the University of Chicago.

Summer opportunities at the School are the Creative Arts Program for boys and girls ages 8 to 14 and the Children's Day Camp for boys and girls ages 2¹/₂ to 8. An International Students Program, Adult Education Program, and a Toddler Program are also available.

STUDENT ACTIVITIES. Officers and class and homeroom representatives are elected to the Middle and Upper School Student Councils. The Councils work to build a strong community, plan social events and fund-raising activities, and address student concerns.

Extracurricular activities in the Lower, Elementary, and Middle schools revolve around the Afterschool Program, which includes music lessons and practice for concerts, preparation for drama productions, club activities, and after-school courses. Upper School students publish a student newspaper (*Blotter*), a literary magazine (*Reflections*), and a yearbook (*Lion*) and are also involved in drama, dance, and musical productions.

A member of the Athletic Conference of Independent Schools, the School's Upper and Middle School teams compete in volleyball, basketball, softball, soccer, basketball, baseball, cross-country, track, and judo. Intramural teams are organized beginning in Grade 5.

Traditional events include the Upper School Retreat, Thanksgiving Sharing Assembly, Holiday Choral Festival, Perspectives on Diversity Jazz Afternoon, Junior Class Variety Show, Performing and Visual Arts Month, and the Lower School Spring Festival.

ADMISSION AND COSTS. The Berkeley Carroll School seeks self-motivated, intellectually curious students who will benefit from the School's program. Students are accepted in all grades when vacancies exist. The application process should be completed by January 15 and requires two teacher recommendations, the previous school record, testing results, and a personal interview. There is a $30 application fee.

In 1999–2000, tuition ranges from $7000 for half-day Preschool to $16,250 for Grade 12. There is a $500 refundable bond deposit for new students.

Dean of Studies: Dr. Marvin Pollock
Alumni Director: Lenora A. Brennan
Directors of Admissions: Margaret Granados and Christopher Weeks
Director of Development: Dana A. Booth
College Counselor: Melanie Choukrane
Business Manager: Frank Bookhout
Director of Athletics: Walter Paller

The Birch Wathen Lenox School
NEW YORK

210 East 77th Street, New York, NY 10021. 212-861-0404;
E-mail admissions@bwl.org; Web Site www.bwl.org

THE BIRCH WATHEN LENOX SCHOOL in New York, New York, is a college preparatory day school for students in Kindergarten through Grade 12. The School was founded in 1991 by the consolidation of The Birch Wathen School (founded 1921) and The Lenox School (founded 1916).

The School seeks to provide a challenging academic curriculum with a balance among traditional education, student achievement, and social development. Birch Wathen Lenox implements its curricular commitments with small classes, a student-faculty ratio of 8:1, and an emphasis on individual attention to students.

The Birch Wathen Lenox School is a nonprofit corporation directed by a self-perpetuating Board of Trustees, which includes alumni and parents. An active Alumni Association represents more than 3600 living graduates. The School's program is accredited by the State University of New York and the Middle States Association of Colleges and Schools, and it is registered by the New York State Board of Regents. Birch Wathen Lenox is a member of the New York Guild of Independent Schools, the New York State Association of Independent Schools, the National Association of Independent Schools, the Association of College Admissions Counselors, The College Board, and the Educational Records Bureau.

THE CAMPUS. The entire School—Lower (Kindergarten–Grade 5), Middle (Grades 6–8), and Upper (Grades 9–12)—is housed in a traditional, spacious building on Manhattan's Upper East Side. Facilities include a gymnasium, library, computer center, science laboratories, auditorium, music and art studios, cafeteria, and a rooftop play area.

THE FACULTY. Frank J. Carnabuci, formerly Assistant Headmaster of The Dalton School, was appointed Headmaster in 1992. He holds a B.A. degree from Drew University and master's degrees in education from Columbia and Harvard.

There are 35 men and 42 women on the faculty. All faculty members hold baccalaureate degrees, 48 hold master's degrees, and 8 hold doctoral degrees. The staff include instructors of music and art, reading specialists, science and mathematics coordinators, a full-time nurse, a librarian, two computer specialists, college guidance counselor, and a school psychologist.

STUDENT BODY. The Birch Wathen Lenox School enrolls 400 boys and girls, 5 to 18 years of age, in Kindergarten–Grade 12.

The diverse student population is drawn from all parts of New York City.

ACADEMIC PROGRAM. The school year, from mid-September to mid-June, includes Thanksgiving recess, four religious and patriotic holidays, and two-and-one-half-week vacations at Christmas and in the spring. Classes meet on a five-day schedule. School begins at 8:30 A.M., with dismissal at 3:30 P.M. A typical school day includes five class periods, activity and athletics periods, lunch, and time for independent study and teacher conferences. Homework, assigned in all grades, ranges up to one hour per day in the Lower School and 20 to 30 minutes per subject per day in the Middle and Upper schools. There is standardized testing throughout the year in all three divisions.

The curriculum provides a program in English, composition, mathematics, science, and history. Foreign languages begin in Grade 4. Computer science, word processing, art, drama, speech, instrumental and vocal music, and woodworking are taught from Kindergarten through Grade 12. Advanced Placement course work is offered in all major curricular areas.

A full, extended-day after-school program is available for Lower and Middle School students. There is a comprehensive physical education program. The full interschool athletic sports program includes soccer, softball, volleyball, tennis, team handball, basketball, swimming, modern dance, and karate.

Birch Wathen Lenox graduates have enrolled at such colleges and universities as Brown, Colgate, Columbia, Cornell, Duke, Harvard, Northwestern, Princeton, Tufts, Yale, and the University of Pennsylvania.

STUDENT ACTIVITIES. The Student Forum, headed by an elected speaker, meets periodically and plans assembly programs. The Student Council, composed of a president and class representatives, brings questions to the attention of the Forum and has responsibility for the annual Student Activity Budget. There is also a Student-Faculty Judiciary Committee.

The traditional academic curriculum is complemented by extensive cocurricular activities such as the School newspaper, the literary journal, and the yearbook; the Community Services Program and the Model U.N.; chorus; and Business, Foreign Language, Photography, and Drama clubs.

ADMISSION AND COSTS. Birch Wathen Lenox has a policy of accepting students "without regard to race, creed, or nationality of applicants." Students are accepted in Kindergarten–Grade 12 on the basis of entrance examination results, previous school records, teacher recommendations, and an interview. Applicants may take either the Educational Records Bureau tests or the Secondary School Admission Test. Application should be made six to nine months in advance of entrance. Applications for Kindergarten and Grade 1 should be received no later than November 30. The application fee is $25.

In 1999–2000, tuition is $15,903 in Kindergarten, $16,970 in Grades 1–4, $17,243 in Grade 5, $18,043 in Grades 6–7, $18,577 in Grades 8–9, and $19,282 in Grades 10–12. Lunch is approximately $1000. A tuition payment plan is available. The Harrison W. Moore Merit Scholarship Award is presented annually in the Upper School, and scholarship aid is available at all grade levels based on need, ability, and character.

Director of Admissions: Nancy King
Director of Development: Alex Narasin
College Counselor: Curtis March
Business Manager: Ann Glickman
Director of Athletics: Todd DiVitorrio

The Brearley School   1884

610 East 83rd Street, New York, NY 10028. 212-744-8582;
Fax 212-472-8020; E-mail SBorbay@Brearley.ORG

Founded in 1884, The Brearley School is a college preparatory day school enrolling 659 girls in Kindergarten–Grade 12. Serving able students who reflect the diversity and vitality of New York City, its program is designed to challenge them intellectually and promote a sense of accomplishment and pride through academic achievement, experience in the arts, athletic activity, and the pleasure of helping other people. Community service is an integral part of the Middle and Upper School program. Tuition and fees: $17,250–$19,250. Financial Aid: $2,200,000. Priscilla Winn Barlow (University of Liverpool, B.Sc., Ph.D.) was appointed Head of the School in 1997.

The Brick Church School   1940

62 East 92nd Street, New York, NY 10128. 212-289-5683;
Fax 212-289-5372

Founded by and affiliated with The Brick Presbyterian Church, this coeducational day school offers a developmentally appropriate early childhood program for 124 children in Nursery–Kindergarten (ages 3–6). In an environment marked by warmth and mutual respect, students are introduced to the areas of literacy, mathematics, science, social studies, cooking, dramatic play, art, and music. Teachers, all of whom are certified in Early Childhood Education, use various activities and materials designed to inspire self-confidence, curiosity, and joy in learning and play. A weekly nondenominational chapel service involves the entire School. Tuition: $8850–$11,400. Holly Burke is Admissions Director; Lydia Spinelli (Tufts, B.A.; Teachers College, Columbia University, M.A., M.Ed., Ed.D.) is Director.

The Browning School 1888

52 East 62nd Street, New York, NY 10021. 212-838-6280;
Fax 212-355-5602; E-mail jcasey@browning.edu

The Browning School is a college preparatory day school enrolling 340 boys in Pre-Primary–Grade 12. It seeks to provide an education that emphasizes self-discipline, student participation, and the achievement of excellence. The curriculum focuses on basic skills with an enrichment program in Language Arts and Computer Science. Foreign languages are introduced in Grade 5. Advanced Placement courses and diverse electives are offered in the Upper School. Drama, clubs, publications, and sports are among the activities. Tuition: $15,526–$17,906. Financial aid is available. Jacqueline A. Casey is Director of Admissions; Stephen M. Clement III (Yale, B.A. 1966; Union Theological Seminary, M.Div. 1970; Harvard, M.Ed. 1975, Ed.D. 1977) is Headmaster.

Buckley Country Day School 1923

I. U. Willets Road, North Hills, Roslyn, NY 11576. 516-627-1910;
Fax 516-627-2141

Buckley Country Day School is an elementary school enrolling 169 boys and 158 girls in Nursery–Grade 8. The School's commitment to traditional education emphasizes scholastic achievement and personal growth. Buckley seeks to provide a balanced program in academics, the creative arts, physical education, and extracurricular activities. French begins in Kindergarten and Latin in Grade 6. All students participate in daily athletics. Tuition: $5300–$14,100. Financial Aid: $238,245. Thomas J. Reid (University of Pennsylvania, B.A. 1973; University of Connecticut, M.A. 1987) was appointed Headmaster in 1988.

The Buckley School 1913

113 East 73rd Street, New York, NY 10021. 212-535-8787;
Fax 212-535-4622; E-mail BRPWALSH@aol.com

The Buckley School is a day school enrolling 350 boys in Kindergarten–Grade 9. The School aims to teach boys basic skills, to develop respect for disciplined thought and action, to encourage sensitivity for the needs of others, and to nurture the joy of learning and the satisfaction of pursuing excellence. The traditional curriculum is supplemented by such courses as computers and woodworking and by frequent cultural field trips to museums, special exhibitions, and events in the city. Weekly "Showcase" assemblies provide the students an opportunity to perform, learn, and be entertained. Tuition: $16,500–$17,200 (plus fees). Financial Aid: $400,000. JoAnn Lynch is Admissions Director; Brian R. Walsh (Yale, B.A. 1957; Harvard, Ed.M. 1966) is Headmaster.

The Buffalo Seminary 1851

205 Bidwell Parkway, Buffalo, NY 14222-9904. 716-885-6780;
Fax 716-885-6785

The Buffalo Seminary is a college preparatory day school enrolling 137 girls in Grades 9–12. While the school has no religious affiliation, values are emphasized. The Seminary aims to develop scholarship, leadership, sportsmanship, and a commitment to service through a rigorous academic curriculum, studio and performing arts programs, and activities including athletics, honor societies, self-government, music, and drama. Advanced Placement and honors courses are available by invitation. Tuition: $9400. Financial aid is available. Marjorie E. Barney (Cornell, A.B.; Indiana University, M.Ed.) was appointed Head of School in 1995. *Middle States Association.*

The Caedmon School 1961

416 East 80th Street, New York, NY 10021. 212-879-2296;
Fax 212-879-0627; E-mail caedmon@liii.com

The Caedmon School, offering an ungraded program based on Montessori principles of self-education, enrolls 190 day boys and girls in the equivalent of Nursery–Grade 6. The School strives to provide academic excellence and personal attention for all students. The curriculum includes courses in French, computer science, art, music, dance, and physical education. Extracurricular activities are offered in an extended-day program. Tuition: $6900–$12,400. Financial Aid: $249,545. Carol Gose DeVine (Albertus Magnus College, B.A. 1970; American Montessori Society Certification, 1974; Columbia, M.A. 1980, Ed.M. 1983) is Head of the School.

The Cathedral School NEW YORK

1047 Amsterdam Avenue, New York, NY 10025-1702.
212-316-7500; Fax 212-316-7558;
E-mail ethurber@cathedralnyc.org; Web Site www.cathedralnyc.org

THE CATHEDRAL SCHOOL in New York City is an Episcopal day school enrolling boys and girls of all faiths in Kindergarten through Grade 8. The School is located on Manhattan's Upper West Side on the Close of the Cathedral of Saint John the Divine, the world's largest Gothic cathedral. Its proximity to the Cathedral, Columbia University, and the resources of New York City enables students and faculty to participate in educationally enriching experiences beyond the classroom. Students reach the School by public transportation, private van, or bus service.

The Right Reverend Henry Codman Potter, Episcopal Bishop of New York, founded The Cathedral School in 1901 as a boarding school for 40 choirboys. In 1964, Cathedral became a day school for boys of all faiths; coeducation was implemented in 1974.

Cathedral seeks to develop confident, open-minded young people who share a respect for different ideas, cultures, and religions and who accept responsibility as active citizens of their community and the world around them. It aims to offer a strong experience-based foundation of knowledge and skills, combining traditional and innovative teaching methods and state-of-the-art technology within a spiritually rich and nurturing environment.

A nonprofit institution, Cathedral is governed by the School Board. The School is accredited by the New York State Association of Independent Schools and holds membership in the National Association of Independent Schools and the National Association of Episcopal Schools, among other affiliations. An active Parents Association assists the School in numerous supportive capacities.

THE CAMPUS. Set on 13 countrylike acres, the Cathedral Close is graced with herb, bulb, and flower gardens, blossoming trees, and colorful peacocks that wander freely about the grounds. The historic stone building that houses the academic facilities contains 22 classrooms, a completely renovated Library/Technology Information Center, two science laboratories, a gymnasium, two art studios, a music room, a dining room, and a Common Room. Students also use the unique facilities of the Cathedral for chapel, music, art, physical education, and all school gatherings. Two playgrounds are on campus, and nearby Morningside Park provides additional athletic and play areas.

THE FACULTY. Phillip G. Foote was appointed Headmaster in 1995. Mr. Foote earned baccalaureate and master's degrees from the University of Texas at Austin. Before accepting his current position, he served as Headmaster at the Horace Mann School in New York City and, prior to that, was the Headmaster of Greenhill School in Dallas, Texas. He has held a Fulbright teaching grant and a Clark Foundation Scholarship and has taught in the Texas public schools and at the American Farm School in Greece. Mr. Foote and his wife, a practicing psychologist, have three children.

In addition to the Headmaster, there are 49 teachers, administrators, and learning specialists. They hold 49 baccalaureate and 31 advanced degrees representing study at such colleges and universities as Adelphi, American, Bank Street, Boston University, College of William and Mary, Columbia, Cooper Union, Fordham, Gettysburg, Harvard, Hofstra, Howard, Hunter, Middlebury, Mount Holyoke, New York University, Seton Hall, Rhode Island School of Design, Rice, Tufts, Virginia Theological Seminary, Wesleyan, Williams, Yale, and the Universities of Chicago, Louisville, Maryland, Massachusetts, North Carolina, Pennsylvania, Texas, Virginia, and Wisconsin.

STUDENT BODY. In 1999–2000, The Cathedral School enrolled 245 boys and girls, divided about equally, in Kindergarten through Grade 8. A majority live on the Upper West Side, but students also come from throughout Manhattan, the Bronx, Brooklyn, Queens, Westchester County, and New Jersey. They are from a wide range of racial, ethnic, religious, and economic backgrounds reflective of the diversity of New York's multicultural society.

ACADEMIC PROGRAM. The academic year is divided into semesters in the Lower School (Kindergarten–Grade 4) and trimesters in the Upper School (Grades 5–8). Classes begin on

the Tuesday after Labor Day and end in mid-June, with vacations at Thanksgiving, Christmas, and in March and observances of several national and religious holidays.

Each division has its own Academic Director, faculty, and special facilities. Lower School students are taught in self-contained classrooms, while the Upper School is departmentalized. Letter grades are issued beginning in fifth grade. Students in Grades 5–8 have their own advisor with whom they meet weekly on matters of academic, social, and behavioral concern. Daily homework is assigned, ranging from 20 minutes to two and one-half hours, depending on grade. When necessary, tutoring can be arranged in consultation with the learning specialist, classroom teacher, and division head. An optional extended-day enrichment program from 3:30 to 5:00 P.M. engages Lower School children in such activities as computers, drama, sports, chess, art, and dance.

The Cathedral School prepares students to become effective users of technology by providing hands-on experience with state-of-the-art software and equipment. During the summer of 1998, the School completed a $500,000 three-phase Technology/Library Information Services Master Plan. A School-wide network and high-speed Internet connection provides every classroom with access to computer programs, the library catalog, and educational resources on the World Wide Web. A mini writing lab in the Upper School, a computer-enhanced science lab, and fully equipped library and computer lab extend the range of resources available to students.

Students use computers for writing and research, for individualized learning activities, and for creative multimedia productions. Technology is integrated into the curriculum. The technology coordinator and librarian work with teachers to implement a carefully structured sequence of technology skills that support and enhance classroom learning, including word-processing and telecommunications skills, graphing, online searching, spreadsheet and database construction, and multimedia design.

The Lower School curriculum is designed to develop strong basic skills in reading and language arts, mathematics, social studies, and science. The subjects are integrated within the disciplines whenever possible, and hands-on learning is emphasized. The study of Spanish and French begins in Kindergarten. Health education is introduced in the third grade.

Upper School students undertake a full program in English, social studies, mathematics, science, and French or Spanish, with the additional requirement of Latin in Grades 7–8. The arts are integral to the curriculum, and physical education is taught throughout all grades. At least one trimester of community service is required in Grade 7 or 8.

Students in both academic divisions attend chapel twice weekly in the Cathedral, and all fifth graders take a course on "Introduction to World Religions," an intentionally nondenominational course meant to enhance religious perspective and examine many expressions of faith. The School also celebrates such religious and cultural traditions as Easter, Passover, Thanksgiving, Chanukah, Christmas, Kwanzaa, and Ramadan to encourage believers and nonbelievers alike to learn about and from one another.

In Grade 3, boys and girls may audition for the Cathedral Choir for admission the following year. Choristers receive excellent training, with rehearsals four times a week; in addition, they earn a stipend for their musical services. They sing at Sunday morning services, evening vespers, and other religious occasions in the Cathedral and have performed at Harvard University, opening day at Shea Stadium, and "The Today Show."

The members of the Class of 1999 were accepted at 30 different schools including Bronx Science, Brooklyn Friends, Brooklyn Technical, Collegiate, Columbia Grammar and Preparatory School, Fieldston, Fordham Preparatory School, Friends Seminary, Horace Mann, Lawrenceville, Marymount, Poly Prep, Riverdale, St. Paul's, Spence, Stuyvesant, Taft, and Trinity.

STUDENT ACTIVITIES. Extracurricular activities are designed to provide enrichment and leadership opportunities as well as promote fun and school spirit. The Student Council is comprised of members of Grades 5–8 who are elected by their classmates, with officers chosen by all members of the Upper School.

Community service projects involve older students in work within the School community and in fund-raising efforts for outside organizations. Ecological concerns are addressed by members of LISTEN (Loving Interest to Save the Environment Now), which was formed by sixth graders in 1990 to observe the 20th anniversary of Earth Day.

Eighth graders publish a yearbook and stage a musical. *Peacock Papers* is a Kindergarten–Grade 8 publication featuring student essays, short stories, poetry, and art.

Upper School teams compete interscholastically and intramurally on a seasonal basis. Single-sex and coed teams are formed in basketball, soccer, softball, and volleyball.

Annual traditions on the school calendar include new-parent dinners, the all-School picnic, Grandparents Day, Eighth Grade Pinning Ceremony, Class Day, Chorister Divestiture, alumni reunions, and graduation.

ADMISSION AND COSTS. The Cathedral School welcomes boys and girls from all faiths and family traditions in Kindergarten through Grade 8. Children entering Kindergarten should be 5 by September 30. Acceptance is based on a personal interview, results of the Educational Records Bureau test, previous transcripts, and a completed application and fee of $30.

In 1999–2000, tuition ranged from $14,350 for Kindergarten to $15,050 in Grades 7–8. All students pay a $600 fee for hot lunches, while the cost for books, supplies, trips, and other items ranged from $150 to $400, depending on grade. Approximately 40 percent of the students received financial aid according to the guidelines of the School and Student Service for Financial Aid.

Director of Upper School: Thomas Fritz
Director of Lower School: Melissa Vail
Director of Technology: Ellen Baru
Director of Admission: Edith Thurber
Director of Development and External Affairs: Rosalyn Potischman
Development Associate and Alumni Coordinator: Joan Donahue
Director of High School Placement: Sara Nelson
Business Manager: James O'Brien
Athletic Director: Josh Shapiro
School Chaplain: Rev. Robert Wright

Cathedral School of the Holy Trinity 1949

319 East 74th Street, New York, NY 10021. 212-249-2840

This elementary school was founded by the Archdiocesan Greek Orthodox Cathedral of the Holy Trinity to provide an education of the mind and spirit that embodies the ideals of the ancient Greeks. Faculty seek to provide a family atmosphere of trust and respect for the 100 day students in Nursery–Grade 8. The traditional yet flexible curriculum encompasses the major disciplines as well as enrichment programs including foreign language, computers, and Greek multicultural education. Among the activities are basketball and the Cathedral Chorus. Tuition: $4000. Extras: $700. Financial Aid: $50,000. Despina Stavros is Director of Admissions; Minas Kazepis is Headmaster.

The Chapin School 1901

100 East End Avenue, New York, NY 10028. 212-744-2335;
Fax 212-535-8138

Chapin, a college preparatory day school enrolling 630 girls in Kindergarten–Grade 12, is dedicated to preparing young women to thrive and lead in an increasingly complex, competitive world through the pursuit of academic excellence, personal integrity, and community responsibility. Personal growth and community involvement are fostered through the homeroom program. The rigorous curriculum is enhanced by a commitment to the arts and athletics. Course offerings may be enriched by independent study and off-campus programs. Numerous activities are offered in the Middle and Upper schools. Tuition: $16,650–$17,250. Financial Aid: $1,355,750. Martha J. Hirschman is Director of Admissions; Sandra J. Theunick (Washington Theological Union, M.Div.) was appointed Head of School in 1993.

The Churchill School and Center 1972

22 East 95th Street, New York, NY 10128. 212-722-0610;
Fax 212-722-1387

The Churchill School, a coeducational school enrolling 100 students in Kindergarten–Grade 8, provides educational and remedial services to students of average to above-average cognitive ability whose progress in a mainstream setting is hampered by a specific learning disability. Diagnostic testing and continual evaluation of student progress are integral to all programs. The Churchill Center provides information and educational programs to the public nationwide. In the summer of 2000, the School will relocate to a larger facility at 301 East 29th Street, permitting increased enrollment, additional programs, and implementation of a high school program with three Grade 9 classes. Tuition: $22,700. Estella S. Otis is Director of Admissions; Kristine Baxter (Tufts, B.S.; Teachers College Columbia, M.A.; Bank Street College of Education, S.A.S.) is Head of School.

City & Country School 1914

146 West 13th Street, New York, NY 10011. 212-242-7802;
Fax 212-242-7996

Founded by Caroline Pratt and based on the theory of "learning from children," City & Country School emphasizes hands-on learning and shared responsibility in operating jobs that serve the school community. Enrolling 255 boys and girls from two years of age through Grade 8, the School provides a progressive, integrated curriculum that offers individualized attention. Shop, science, computer, and the arts are part of the curriculum and the extended-day program. A summer day camp for ages 3–7 is available. Tuition: $8250–$16,000. Financial Aid: $250,000. Lisa Horner is Director of Admissions; Kate Turley is Principal.

Collegiate School 1628

260 West 78th Street, New York, NY 10024. 212-812-8500;
Fax 212-812-8514; Web Site www.collegiateschool.org

The oldest independent school in the nation, this college preparatory day school enrolls 608 boys in Kindergarten–Grade 12. Development of basic skills is emphasized in the Lower School; the Middle School focuses on meeting the needs of adolescent boys. The Upper School "elective-oriented" curriculum includes English and social studies, Advanced Placement in ten fields, and independent study. Community service is required, and Upper School activities are coordinated with seven other New York schools. Teams are fielded in seven sports. Tuition: $17,500–$18,900. Financial Aid: $1,200,000. Joanne P. Heyman is Director of Admissions; Jacob A. Dresden (University of Pennsylvania, B.A., M.A.) is Headmaster.

Columbia Grammar and Preparatory School   NEW YORK

5 West 93rd Street, New York, NY 10025. 212-749-6200;
Web Site www.cgps.org

COLUMBIA GRAMMAR AND PREPARATORY SCHOOL in New York, New York, is a college preparatory day school for boys and girls in Pre-Kindergarten through Grade 12. The School has two divisions, each with its own director: Grammar School (Pre-Kindergarten–Grade 6); and Preparatory School (Grades 7–12). Located just off Central Park West, it is easily accessible by subway and bus. The School's location permits students to take advantage of the city's many cultural and educational resources.

In 1764, Columbia Grammar School was founded by King George II as a boys' preparatory school for Kings College (now Columbia University). Closed when the British occupied the city during the Revolutionary War, the School reopened in 1784 as the Grammar School of Columbia University. It functioned under the auspices of the university until 1864, when it was transferred to private ownership. In 1941, through the efforts of Headmaster Frederic A. Alden, the School became a nonprofit institution. It became coeducational in 1956 and was renamed Columbia Grammar and Preparatory School in 1969.

Columbia Grammar and Preparatory School endeavors to provide a warm yet structured environment in which the student may "grow intellectually, develop a strong sense of responsibility, and learn tolerance for the opinions of others." The Grammar School emphasizes an approach that replaces memorization with investigation and discovery in a step-by-step process designed to provide an understanding of the structure of a subject area. Learning skills and disciplined work habits are stressed throughout the School.

Columbia Grammar and Preparatory School is a nonprofit, nonsectarian institution governed by a self-perpetuating Board of Trustees that meets a minimum of six times per year. Board members include parents and alumni representatives. There are approximately 3500 living graduates. The School is accredited by the Middle States Association of Colleges and Schools and the New York State Association of Independent Schools and is chartered by the New York State Board of Regents. It holds membership in the National Association of Independent Schools, the Guild of Independent Schools of New York, the National Association of College Admissions Counselors, and the Educational Records Bureau.

THE CAMPUS. The School occupies eight buildings on West 93rd and 94th streets. One of these, at 5 West 93rd, houses the Headmaster's office, two art studios, a swimming pool, the grammar school gymnasium and cafeteria, and classrooms for Grades 5–6. Five converted brownstones, at 20–28 West 94th Street, house Pre-Kindergarten–Grade 4. In addition to classrooms, these buildings contain music studios, an art studio, a computer room, a library, and the infirmary. They are connected to the building at 5 West 93rd Street by a covered walkway. The facility at 4 West 93rd Street houses Prep School classrooms, three science labs, a library, music classrooms and practice space, and a full-sized gymnasium. A new facility at 36 West 93rd Street houses additional Prep School classrooms, three science labs, a second computer room and library, plus five art studios, a drama practice room, a theater, and a cafeteria. Central Park is used for outdoor activities, including tennis.

School facilities are valued at $25,000,000.

THE FACULTY. Richard J. Soghoian is the Headmaster. He is a graduate of the University of Virginia (B.A.) and Columbia University (Ph.D.).

The full-time faculty consist of 112 teachers, 29 men and 83 women. In addition to baccalaureate degrees from such colleges and universities as Brown, Cornell, Georgetown, Harvard, New York University, Oberlin, Tufts, Williams, Yale, and the University of Michigan, the faculty also hold 78 master's degrees. There are 29 part-time instructors, 7 men and 22 women, including administrators who teach one or two courses. Staff benefits include a medical insurance program, salary continuance insurance, and a pension plan.

A registered nurse is on duty during school hours, and the School has a part-time consulting psychologist.

STUDENT BODY. In 1999–2000, the School enrolls 757 students in Pre-Kindergarten–Grade 12, 389 boys and 368 girls. Grade sizes are approximately 17 in Pre-Kindergarten and 60 in Kindergarten–Grade 12. Most students reside in Manhattan, but other boroughs, Long Island, Westchester County, and New Jersey are also represented.

ACADEMIC PROGRAM. The school calendar, with major holidays at Christmas and in the spring, provides 36 weeks of instruction divided into two terms of approximately 18 weeks each. Grammar School students attend school from 8:15 A.M. to 3:10 P.M. Monday through Thursday and to 2:20 P.M. on Friday. Preparatory school students have homeroom at 8:00 A.M., and classes meet on a six-day cycle from 8:20 A.M. to 2:55 P.M. Monday through Friday.

There are 10–15 students in an average teaching section. At designated times before, during, and after school, the faculty are available for extra help. Quarterly grades are issued, and written reports are sent to the parents at the end of each semester. Supplementary progress reports may be sent as the need arises. There are two parent-teacher conferences each year at the middle of each semester.

In Grades 1–4, the curriculum focuses on establishing proficiency in reading, writing, and mathematics. Science, social studies, physical education, art, and music supplement the basic program. Departmentalization of instruction begins in Grade 5 to ensure a well-planned, sequential curriculum in language skills, social studies, modern and traditional mathematics, computer, science, music, and fine arts. Beginning in Grade 4, ensemble classes offer orchestral instruction on string, woodwind, and brass instruments. Physical education includes indoor athletic activities, gymnastics, swimming, and outdoor play.

An arts program for students in Grades 7–12 offers special semester electives. Students choose from among such courses as photography, beginning instrumental music, orchestra, chorus, filmmaking, ceramics, painting and drawing, printmaking, and three-dimensional art.

The curriculum for Grades 7 and 8 includes English, history and social sciences, mathematics, earth and natural sciences, and creative arts. A foreign language sequence for Grade 7 provides an introduction to French, Japanese, Spanish, and Latin; Grade 8 students may select one of those languages for in-depth, daily study. A drugs/sex education course is part of the program.

To graduate, Preparatory School students must complete four years of high school English, history, and math; three years each of a foreign language and science, and two semester courses in art, music, or theater history.

Full-year courses include English 9–10, History 9–10, French, Latin, Japanese, and Spanish; an integrated mathematics curriculum beginning in Grade 7; and Biology, Chemistry, and Physics. Typical of the varied semester electives are Modernist Literature, The Outcast and Downtrodden in 19th Century America, The Art of Poetry, Shaw and Ibsen; America Between the Wars, The Future of Democracy, Economics, Contemporary Authoritarian Regimes, Introduction to Psychology, Lessons from the Holocaust, Introduction to American Law, The IBM Environment; Acting, Playwriting, Painting and Drawing, Jewelry, Photography, Filmmaking, Ceramics, Chorus, Orchestra; and Weight Training. Opportunities are provided for Advanced Placement study in all departmental areas.

The 1999 graduates are attending Art Institute of Chicago, Bard, Boston University, Brandeis, Clark, Colby, Colgate, Curry, Dickinson, Eugene Lang, Fashion Institute, Fordham, George Washington, Goucher, Hamilton, Hofstra, Hunter, Kenyon, Mary Washington, McGill, New York University, Oberlin, Occidental, Pitzer, Smith, Syracuse, Tufts, Tulane, Vassar, Washington University, Wheaton, Yale, and the Universities of Chicago, Connecticut, Miami, Michigan, Pennsylvania, and Wisconsin.

STUDENT ACTIVITIES. Students in Grades 9–12 participate in a service program. Among the possible projects are tutoring fellow students, teaching in the grammar school, working as hospital volunteers, and helping in political offices. One hundred hours of service must be performed during the student's high school years.

Student organizations vary according to expressed interest. In the upper grades, activities include student government, the yearbook, a newspaper, a literary magazine, Issues and Human Rights, Jazz Band, Prep School Chorus, Film Appreciation, Environmental Awareness, and chapters of SADD and the Coalition for the Homeless. Each year, students are chosen to attend A Presidential Classroom for Young Americans and the Model UN.

Varsity and junior varsity teams for boys are organized in basketball, baseball, wrestling, track, golf, tennis, and soccer; girls' teams are formed in basketball, softball, volleyball, swimming, soccer, tennis, and track. There is also a coeducational cross-country team as well as an optional after-school sports program for Grades 5–8 involving both intramural and interschool games in basketball, baseball, and soccer.

Special activities are dances, movies, field trips, and ski trips. Annual events include a street fair, orchestra and chorus concerts, several student plays, Moving-Up Day, Field Day, and Graduation.

ADMISSION AND COSTS. The School enrolls students without discrimination "on the basis of race, color, and national or ethnic origin." Students are chosen for their emotional maturity, ability to work in a demanding program, talents, concern for others, and potential for growth. Depending upon grade level, requirements include an admission test, academic transcripts, written exercises, and a personal interview. Application for fall enrollment should be made in the preceding fall or winter. There is a $45 application fee.

In 1999–2000, tuition and fees range from $15,875 (Pre-Kindergarten) to $19,725 (Grade 12), including a full lunch program. A Pre-Kindergarten division opened in the fall of 1996. The Revolving Loan Plan requires those families with the financial capability to make an interest-free loan of $1500 for each child enrolled in the School. Loans are repaid when the student transfers or graduates. A tuition payment plan and tuition insurance are available.

Columbia Grammar and Preparatory School subscribes to the School Scholarship Service and awards financial aid on the basis of need. In 1999–2000, 15 percent of the students received aid totaling $1,173,000.

Deans of Students: Margo Potter (Grades 7–8), Monica Markovits (Grade 10), Vic Puccio (Grade 11), and David Morss (Grades 9 and 12)
Director of Admission: Simone Hristidis
Director of the Annual Fund: Sara Ziff
College Counselors: Gigi Edwards and Mark Speyer
Business Manager: Peter Reynolds
Director of Athletics: Stephen Rybicki

Convent of the Sacred Heart   1881

*1 East 91st Street, New York, NY 10128-0689. 212-722-4745;
    Fax 212-996-1784; Web Site www.cshnyc.org*

One of 21 Sacred Heart schools in the United States and 150 schools worldwide, this college preparatory day school enrolls 610 girls in Pre-Kindergarten–Grade 12. Its goals are to build faith and deepen respect for intellectual values while fostering Christian community and personal growth. The humanities, arts, sciences, and foreign languages are enriched by Advanced Placement courses, community service, and exchanges with other Sacred Heart schools in the United States and abroad. Extensive extracurricular options and two summer programs are also available. Tuition: $9500–$17,500. Barbara Root is Director of Admissions; Nancy Salisbury, RSCJ (Manhattanville College, B.A.; University of Detroit, M.A.), has been Head-mistress since 1980.

The Dalton School   1919

*108 East 89th Street, New York, NY 10128-1599. 212-423-5200;
    Fax 212-423-5259; Web Site www.dalton.org*

A coeducational, college preparatory day school enrolling 1290 students in Kindergarten–Grade 12, Dalton provides a low pupil-teacher ratio, a "distinguished and creative" faculty, a unique structure, and extensive access to the latest computer technology to develop graduates who are "industrious, open-minded, and independent." The curriculum is academically rigorous yet encourages student-originated projects. Community service is required, and an extensive arts program is highly valued. A full range of athletics, publications, and other student activities is available. Tuition: $18,220–$19,800. Financial Aid: $3,300,000. Richard Blumenthal (Harvard University, Ph.D.) was appointed Head of School in 1999.

Corlears School   1968

*324 West 15th Street, New York, NY 10011. 212-741-2800;
    Fax 212-807-1550; E-mail office@corlearsschool.org*

Corlears School specializes in the early childhood education of students ages 2.6 to 9. Its commitment is to perpetuate a love of learning and to provide students with the academic, social, and emotional tools they need. Now enrolling 154 boys and girls, the School emphasizes problem solving and interdisciplinary learning in a supportive environment as the basis for mastery of skills in reading, writing, mathematics, science, and the visual and performing arts. Tuition: $10,449–$15,291. Financial Aid: $400,000. Rorry Romeo is Director of Admissions; Marion Greenwood (Brooklyn College, B.A., New York University, M.A.) has been Head of School since 1984.

Darrow School   1932

*110 Darrow Road, New Lebanon, NY 12125. 518-794-6000;
    Fax 518-794-7065; E-mail jkr@taconic.net*

Darrow was founded by educators and civic leaders to provide strong college preparation within a supportive, structured environment. The 365-acre campus on the site of a historic Shaker Village in the Berkshires serves 90 students, 98 percent of whom are boarders, in Grades 9–12. Small classes, tutorials, individualized attention, and hands-on learning enable students to reach their full potential. Activities include drama, music, outdoor pursuits, and athletics, and all students take part in the Hands-To-Work program. Boarding Tuition: $23,950; Day Tuition: $12,750. Financial Aid: $550,000. J. Kirk Russell is Director of Admissions; Laurence R. Van Meter (Hamilton College, B.A.; Dartmouth College, M.B.A.) is Headmaster. *Middle States Association.*

Dutchess Day School   1955

Millbrook, NY 12545. 914-677-5014; Fax 914-677-6722

Dutchess enrolls 161 boys and girls in Kindergarten–Grade 8. The School seeks to create an environment where children thrive intellectually, emotionally, and physically. Small classes allow students to pursue individual projects and interests. A strong academic program in English, history, science, mathematics, computer, foreign language, the arts, and physical education is offered. A well-balanced curriculum emphasizes the mastery of skills, excites a child's natural curiosity, and encourages responsible citizenship. Students in Grades 5–8 may participate on interscholastic athletic teams. Tuition: $9850–$12,400. Financial Aid: $140,000. Andrea Archer (Oxford [England], M.A. 1975) was appointed Head of School in 1996.

The Dwight School 1880

291 Central Park West, New York, NY 10024. 212-724-2146; Fax 212-724-2539; E-mail admissions@server.dwight.edu; Web Site www.dwight.edu

The Dwight School formed a consortium with The Anglo-American International School in 1993. The challenging college preparatory program, balancing the humanities, sciences, and fine arts, enrolls 400 students in Kindergarten–Grade 12. The full school follows the International Baccalaureate (IB) curriculum; students may also take IGCSE exams. The School has a strong international component and a coordinate program with Woodside Park School in London. State-of-the-art technology, French beginning in Kindergarten, and eight other languages are provided. Activities include publications, sports, and outdoor education. Tuition: $17,850–$19,400. Susan George (K–8) and Elizabeth Callaway (9–12) are Admissions Directors; Stephen H. Spahn is Chancellor; Dr. Joyce M. Robinson is Head. *Middle States Association.*

East Woods School 1946

31 Yellow Cote Road, Oyster Bay, NY 11771. 516-922-4400; Fax 516-922-2589; Web Site www.eastwoods.org

East Woods School was founded by parents to provide elementary prepreparatory education for their children. Enrolling 285 boys and girls in Nursery–Grade 9, the School seeks to instill a lifelong love of learning through a child-centered educational approach that develops basic academic skills in all disciplines. The traditional curriculum is enhanced by courses in the fine arts, photography, and computer. Foreign languages are introduced in Kindergarten. Extended day and extended care are available, and a summer program is offered. Tuition: $5500–$13,200. Extras: $250–$900. Financial Aid: $350,000. Carol Rogers is Admissions Director; James C. Ferrer (Beloit, B.A. 1970; Columbia Teachers College, M.A. 1981) was appointed Headmaster in 1990.

The Elmwood Franklin School 1895

104 New Amsterdam Avenue, Buffalo, NY 14216. 716-877-5035; Fax 716-877-9680

The Elmwood Franklin School enrolls more than 325 children in its Upper School (Grades 5–8) and its Lower School (Pre-Kindergarten–Grade 4). Emphasis is placed on the academic, emotional, and physical development of each child. Traditional academic skills are enhanced through a wide variety of courses including science, mathematics, reading, English, French, Spanish, history, art, music, computer science, and sports. Summer and extended-day programs are available. Tuition: $8580–

$9905. Financial Aid: $300,000. Keith W. Frome (University of Hartford, B.A.; University of Connecticut, M.A.; Harvard, M.T.S.; Columbia, Ed.D.) is Headmaster.

Emma Willard School 1814

Troy, NY 12180. 518-274-4440; Admissions 518-274-3478; Fax 518-272-0292; E-mail admissions@emma.troy.ny.us; Web Site http://www.emma.troy.ny.us

Emma Willard, a college preparatory boarding and day school enrolling 285 students in Grade 9–Postgraduate, maintains a stimulating environment in which young women acquire the leadership and academic skills they need to fulfill their roles in today's world. The curriculum emphasizes Advanced Placement courses and challenging electives in all disciplines. The state-of-the-art Hunter Science Center (1997) and a competition-size swimming pool and fitness center (1998) are among the facilities. Boarding Tuition: $22,900; Day Tuition: $13,300. Financial Aid: $1,100,000. Trudy J. Hanmer is Associate Head of School.

Ethical Culture Fieldston School 1878

33 Central Park West, New York, NY 10023. 212-712-6220; Fax 212-712-8440
Fieldston Road and Manhattan College Parkway, Bronx, NY 10471. 718-329-7300/7310

Ethical Culture Fieldston School offers coeducational instruction to 1570 students at two locations. Ethical Culture (Pre-Kindergarten–Grade 6) is in Manhattan; Fieldston Lower (Pre-Kindergarten–Grade 6) and Fieldston (Grades 7–12) are in the Riverdale section of the Bronx. The rigorous curriculum integrates arts, humanities, and sciences with ethical values. Community service is required. Activities include sports, the arts, and publications. After-school programs and a summer day camp are offered. Tuition and Fees: $16,350–$19,050. Financial Aid: $4,052,725. Beth P. Beckmann is Assistant Head of School; Joseph P. Healey, Ph.D., is Head of School.

Friends Academy 1876

Duck Pond Road, Locust Valley, NY 11560. 516-676-0393; Fax 516-671-2025

Founded for "children of Friends and those similarly sentimented," this Quaker, college preparatory day school enrolls 700 boys and girls, Pre-Nursery—Grade 12. The Quaker philosophy emphasizes values, while the liberal arts curriculum offers a broad range of courses in both classical and modern disciplines, including computer technology and 14 Advanced Placement courses. Cocurricular activities include the arts and athletics. The composition of the student body reflects the school's commitment to diversity. Community service is required. Summer day and sports camps are available. Tuition: $7480–$16,170. Financial Aid: $1,000,000. Ann Gillick is Director of Admissions; Marcus D. Hurlbut (Union, B.A. 1966; Dartmouth, M.A. 1975) was appointed Headmaster in 1993. *Middle States Association.*

The Gow School   SOUTH WALES

Emery Road, South Wales, NY 14139. 716-652-3450; Fax 716-652-3457; E-mail admissions@gow.org; Web Site www.gow.org

THE GOW SCHOOL in South Wales, New York, is a college preparatory boarding school, encompassing Grade 7–Postgraduate, for young men who have a specific language disability often referred to as dyslexia. South Wales, a rural community in the western portion of the state, is on New York Route 16. Located a short distance from Niagara Falls, it is approximately 30 miles southeast of Buffalo, New York, and 100 miles south of Toronto, Canada.

The Gow School was founded in 1926 by Peter Gow, Jr., an educator who wanted to develop better methods for teaching young men who were experiencing academic failure. His work plus his personal and professional friendships with Dr. Samuel T. Orton and Anna Gillingham led to the establishment of a program for students who have at least average ability but a developmental disability in one or more phases of language usage. Reconstructive Language training, reading, and other aspects of language development are stressed in a learning environment that is individualized as much as possible.

Gow, a nonprofit school, is governed by a self-perpetuating Board of Trustees, 20 in number. The Board, composed primarily of alumni, meets three times a year. The School is registered by the New York State Board of Regents; it holds membership in the National Association of Independent Schools, the New York State Association of Independent Schools, and the International Dyslexia Association.

THE CAMPUS. The 120-acre campus, which is traversed by a trout stream, includes hilly woodland, athletic fields, tennis courts, a ski/snowboard slope, and a ropes course.

The Main Building contains the business office, ten classrooms, a counselor's office, infirmary, and the Gow Bookstore. Orton Hall provides ten classrooms including a tutoring room, a science laboratory, two computer classrooms, the computer writing lab, and a new study hall. The Green Cottage furnishes living quarters for students and two masters' apartments. Other facilities include two science rooms in the Science Lab Building and the School House, which contains the Art Department. Students and masters reside in Cornwall House, Templeton Dormitory, Brown House, Ellis House, Whitcomb Dormitory, and a recently completed dormitory yet to be named. The campus also provides housing for the Headmaster and seven teachers and their families.

The Isaac Arnold Memorial Library, with a capacity of 10,000 volumes, contains a reading room, seven classrooms, a faculty room, and the Headmaster's office. The Andrew Thompson Memorial Gymnasium houses a basketball court, a stage, two locker rooms, a lounge, an exercise room, and a general recreation area.

The plant is valued at approximately $8,000,000.

THE FACULTY. William F. Patterson was elected Headmaster in 1997. He holds a B.A. degree from the University of New Hampshire and a master's degree from the Bread Loaf School of English, Middlebury College. Prior to assuming his present position, Mr. Patterson was Headmaster of Linden Hill School and Head of The Chelsea School in Maryland. He and Mrs. Patterson reside on campus.

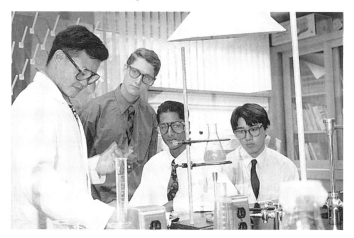

The faculty consists of 41 teachers and administrators who teach, 28 of whom live in the dormitories or in other campus housing. They hold 27 baccalaureate degrees and 14 master's degrees from Allegheny College, Bates, Canisius, Catholic University of America, East Stroudsburg University, Hamilton, Hiram College, Hobart, Kenyon, Macalester, Medaille College, Nazareth, Niagara University, Norwich University, St. Bonaventure, Slippery Rock, Springfield College, State University College at Buffalo, State University of New York (Binghamton, Brockport, Buffalo, Cortland, Fredonia, Geneseo), Texas A&M, Texas Tech, Towson State, Union College, and the Universities of Colorado, Minnesota, New Hampshire, Rochester, Virginia, and Washington.

A local doctor serves as the School physician, and emergency facilities are minutes away. School nurses coordinate all medical activities.

STUDENT BODY. In 1999–2000, The Gow School enrolled 140 young men, 13 to 19 years of age, as boarders in Grades 7–12. They came from 28 states, the District of Columbia, Brazil, Canada, England, Indonesia, Japan, Liechtenstein, Norway, Oman, Pakistan, Saudi Arabia, and the West Indies.

ACADEMIC PROGRAM. The school year, which is divided into semesters, extends from early September to mid-May, with Thanksgiving, winter, and spring breaks. Comprehensive written reports are sent to parents at the end of each marking period. Advisor reports, summarizing student performance in academics, athletics, and residential life, are written at the midpoint of each marking period. The student-teacher ratio of 4:1 ensures that each young man receives individualized attention and support.

Classes have an average enrollment of five students and meet six days per week. The weekday schedule begins with the rising bell at 7:00 A.M., followed by breakfast and house jobs.

Classes, lunch, athletics, tutorials, and supervised study hall are scheduled between 8:00 A.M. and 6:00 P.M. After dinner, all Upper School students have a brief reading period and two hours of supervised study before "lights out." Faculty members are available for individual help whenever necessary. Middle School students have a 90-minute study period in the evening.

The core of the Gow curriculum is based on Reconstructive Language, using a multisensory approach, as an effective tool in teaching dyslexic/language learning-disabled students to read and improve language skills, particularly with regard to the printed or written word. Study skills such as note taking, effective listening, and organizing paragraphs are integrated into all disciplines. All classrooms and student rooms are wired for phone and Internet access.

Generally, a student takes five academic courses in addition to one Reconstructive Language course. The language course involves training in deriving meaning from reading, in vocabulary extension, and in oral and written expression. In mathematics courses, effective traditional methods are employed as well as teaching math concepts and applications with manipulative materials. Instruction begins with the most basic operations and proceeds to more advanced concepts. Daily oral and written work is assigned as a means of promoting accurate and immediate recall.

The curriculum is designed to prepare students to enter college. To graduate, each student must complete 21.5 academic credits in Grades 9–12, including English 4, mathematics 3, history 4, laboratory science 2, art/music, health, and computer literacy 1, which includes keyboarding, word processing, and data design.

The core curriculum in Grades 7–12 includes Grammar, Literature, Composition, Shakespeare, American Literature; United States History, Global History I–II; Developmental Math, Pre-Algebra, Algebra 1–2, Plane Geometry, Pre-Calculus, Calculus; and Science 7, Earth Science, Environmental Science, Biology, Conceptual Physics, Chemistry, and Physics. Among the elective offerings are courses in music, art, drama, economics, computer, health, and business seminar.

Among the colleges at which recent graduates have been accepted are Albion College, Bethany College, Boston College, Elon, Embry-Riddle, Fairleigh Dickinson, Florida A&M, Franklin Pierce, Marietta University, Marshall, Muskingum College, New York University, Niagara, Northeastern, Oberlin, Regis University, Rochester Institute of Technology, St. Lawrence, Southern Illinois, Texas Christian, Trinity, Western State College, West Virginia Wesleyan, Widener, Wilfred Laurier University (Canada), and the Universities of Arizona, Kansas, Toronto, and Wisconsin.

STUDENT ACTIVITIES. Extracurricular activities vary from year to year in response to student interest. In student affairs, the young men are represented by a school council, resident assistants, and class officers. Typical groups are the newspaper and yearbook staffs, and the Photography, Glee, Golf, Roller Blading, Skiing, Mountain Biking, and Outing clubs. All students are encouraged to participate in drama activities, which include the production of at least one major play and a major musical each year in conjunction with girls from neighboring schools.

Interscholastic teams are organized in soccer, lacrosse, basketball, cross-country, tennis, crew, and swimming. School teams compete with nearby public and independent schools, including Nichols School and Park School of Buffalo. Weight training, winter camping, and intramural sports are among the activities offered on a noncompetitive basis.

The extensive extracurricular program includes dances and trips to Buffalo, Toronto, and Niagara Falls. Students attend NFL and NHL games as well as concerts, theater, and visits to area museums.

ADMISSION AND COSTS. The Gow School admits young, dyslexic men capable of college preparatory work who need language-based remediation. School records, completed student and parent questionnaires, math and English teacher recommendations, educational assessment including WIAT or Woodcock-Johnson battery WISC-III or WAIS test results, and a personal interview are required for admission. In addition, specific skill testing to determine class placement is required. Placement testing and an interview take place on campus and are completed in one day. New students are admitted in any grade, and late enrollment is permitted if vacancies exist. There is a nonrefundable (after June 15) $2800 registration/deposit fee, which is applied to the first year's tuition, and a $50 application fee.

Tuition, board, lodging, sheets, and transportation for regular school activities are $28,450 for the 1999–2000 school year. Books, supplies, laundry, athletic supplies, and personal expenses are additional. Seventeen percent of the student body receive financial aid from the School.

Director of Upper School and Assistant Headmaster: Daniel F. Kelley
Director of Middle School: Jeffrey Sweet
Director of Admission: Robert Garcia
Director of Development: Finley Greene
Director of Academic Guidance and College Counseling: Robert Garcia
Director of Finance: Genevieve M. Dowell
Director of Athletics: Joseph E. Shanahan

Grace Church School   1894

86 Fourth Avenue, New York, NY 10003. 212-475-5609; Fax 212-475-5015; E-mail zwarner@gcschool.org; Web Site www.gcschool.org

Grace Church School, a day school enrolling 390 boys and girls in Junior Kindergarten–Grade 8, provides a structured academic program and seeks to help students establish a firm confidence in themselves and their abilities. The church-related School strives to develop active social consciousness based on Judeo-Christian values. Teachers provide much individual attention, allowing children to advance at their own pace. Student council, publications, sports, drama, arts, computer, school chorus, church choir, and an after-school program are among the activities. Tuition: $14,500–$17,400. Financial aid is available. George P. Davison (Yale College, B.A.; Teachers College, Columbia University, M.A.) was appointed Headmaster in 1994.

Grace Day School   1955

23 Cedar Shore Drive, Massapequa, NY 11758. 516-798-1122; Fax 516-799-0711; Web Site www.gracedayschool.com

This coeducational Episcopal school aims to prepare highly motivated students for competitive secondary schools in an environment guided by Christian principles. Grace Day School enrolls approximately 220 students in Kindergarten–Grade 8 plus 200 pre-schoolers. The curriculum is based on high expectations and a strong foundation in core subjects, with small classes that focus on the individual student. The program is enriched by Regents Sequential Math, French, computer, and religion; the Voorhees Fine Arts Center provides facilities for the visual arts and choral and instrumental music. A comprehensive physical education and athletic program and a summer camp are available. Tuition: $6125–$6710. Patricia Quinto is Director of Admissions; David K. Murray is Head of School.

The Green Vale School   1923

250 Valentine's Lane, Glen Head, NY 11545. 516-621-2420

Recently recognized as a Blue Ribbon School, Green Vale is proud to be celebrating its 76th year. Enrolling 452 day boys and girls in Nursery 3–Grade 9, the School seeks to provide the critical skills, concepts, and analytical thinking abilities children will need to succeed and to instill moral values, tolerance, and compassion. The curriculum balances the liberal arts and sciences, enriched by art, music, crafts, computer, library, and physical education. Intramural and varsity sports and other activities enjoy wide participation. A strong partnership between faculty and parents contributes to the success of the program. Tuition: $3800–$13,500. Financial aid is available. Stephen H. Watters (Denison, B.A.; University of Massachusetts, M.A.T.) is Head of School.

Hackley School   TARRYTOWN

293 Benedict Avenue, Tarrytown, NY 10591. 914-631-0128;
Admissions 914-366-2642; Fax 914-366-2636;
E-mail hackadms@hackley.k12.ny.us; Web Site www.hackley.k12.ny.us

HACKLEY SCHOOL in Tarrytown, New York, is a coeducational, college preparatory school enrolling day students in Kindergarten–Grade 12 and five-day boarding students in Grades 8–12. Tarrytown (population 12,000) is in the heart of the scenic Hudson River Valley, 25 miles north of New York City. Commuter trains provide easy access to the cultural riches of Manhattan.

Founded in 1899, the School offers a rigorous, traditional, and personalized education to able, motivated students whose parents value education. Hackley's philosophy challenges students to put forth their best academic effort, to conduct themselves decorously, and to dress appropriately. All students study the classic texts and traditional disciplines and use technology as a learning tool across the curriculum. The School is committed

to inculcating the fundamental ideals of democracy and the work ethic. Hackley is also personalized, offering small classes, special help, frequent communication with parents, student-teacher interaction outside the classroom, a largely residential faculty, and a high level of participation in team sports.

A nonprofit, nonsectarian institution, Hackley is governed by a self-perpetuating Board of Trustees. It is registered by the New York State Board of Regents and accredited by the Middle States Association of Schools and Colleges. Hackley holds membership in the National Association of Independent Schools, the College Board, the Association of College Admissions Counselors, and the New York State Association of Independent Schools.

THE CAMPUS. The School, situated on a hilltop overlooking the Hudson, is graced by rambling, turn-of-the-century buildings of English Tudor style. The facilities include a modern Performing Arts Center with a music conservatory, a separate science building, an indoor swimming pool, several art studios, and a photography lab. There are computer labs in each division and computers in every Lower School classroom.

Boarders are housed in either single or double rooms in the main building complex. Resident faculty live on the boarding corridors, supervising the students and providing cultural and academic enrichment programs for them.

The 285-acre campus offers six tennis courts, numerous playing fields, and a nature trail.

THE FACULTY. Walter C. Johnson was appointed Headmaster in February 1995. He graduated *summa cum laude* from Amherst (B.A. 1974) and earned master's degrees in literature and educational administration from the University of Pennsylvania and Teachers College, Columbia University, respectively. Mr. Johnson has had educational and administrative experience at Trinity School and Collegiate School in New York City and, most recently, at The American School in London.

Faculty, including assistants and administrators who teach, number 123—45 men and 78 women. Fifty percent of the full-time teachers live on campus. They hold 123 baccalaureate and 88 graduate degrees representing study at more than 100 colleges and universities.

A registered nurse staffs the infirmary. Emergency service is available at nearby Phelps Memorial Hospital.

STUDENT BODY. In 1999–2000, the School enrolled 382 day boys, 368 day girls, 23 boarding boys, and 11 boarding girls, as follows: 39 in Kindergarten, 40 in Grade 1, 40 in Grade 2, 40 in Grade 3, 40 in Grade 4, 40 in Grade 5, 54 in Grade 6, 55 in Grade 7, 64 in Grade 8, 98 in Grade 9, 92 in Grade 10, 95 in Grade 11, and 87 in Grade 12. Boarding students are from New Jersey, New York, Germany, Korea, and Taiwan. Day students come from communities throughout the tri-state area.

ACADEMIC PROGRAM. The school year, from early September to early June, is divided into semesters and includes a Thanksgiving recess and winter and spring vacations. For students in Kindergarten–Grade 5, a typical day, from 8:15 A.M. to 2:20 P.M., includes seven 40-minute class periods, recess, and lunch. Students in Grades 6–12, whose day extends until 4:30 P.M., have eight class periods, followed by sports, Middle School study hall, and activities. Classes are held five days a week.

An average class enrolls 16 students. There are supervised study halls throughout the day for students in Grades 6–12; students may also be assigned to an after-school study period. Boarders have supervised evening study, and faculty tutors are available. Teachers provide extra help as necessary; long-term tutoring is offered for an hourly fee. Grades are issued and sent to parents four times yearly, with interim reports issued as required.

The curriculum for Kindergarten–Grade 3 emphasizes reading and oral and written expression. Beginning in Grade 3, students write a weekly theme and begin to work on research papers. The mathematics program teaches the logical structure of the number system and fosters dexterity in computation. Also included in the program are science, art, music, swimming, and physical education. The Director of the Lower School is Daniel DiVirgilio.

The curriculum for Grades 4, 5, and the Middle School (Grades 6–8) includes English, which focuses on grammar, oral expression, expository and creative writing, and literary analysis; American History (Grades 4, 7, and 8), Ancient History (Grade 5), Far Eastern History (Grade 6), and Study of Third World Nations (Grade 8); Mathematics emphasizing the four basic operations and probability, graphing, and statistics, Pre-Algebra, Algebra I, and Geometry; Science including the history and structure of science, Life Science, Introductory Physical Science; Art; and Music. All Middle School students are required to take a computer curriculum; they may also begin the study of Latin, French, or Spanish. William Porter is Director of the Middle School.

To graduate, Upper School students must complete four years of English; three years of a foreign language; Anthropology, European History, American History; Mathematics through Algebra II; and three years of science, one of which must be a laboratory course. Director of the Upper School is Beverley Whitaker.

Specific offerings include English 9–12; French 1–6, German 1–6, Greek 1–2, Latin 1–5, Spanish 1–5; Anthropology and Early Ancient History, Economics, Ancient and Medieval History, Modern European History, Comparative Government and Politics, American History, Selected Topics in 20th Century History; Algebra I, Geometry, Algebra II with Trigonometry, Advanced Topics in Algebra and Trigonometry, Finite Math, Calculus 1–3, Computer Science 1–3; Biology 1–2, Natural History and Ecology, Chemistry 1–2, Biochemistry, Physics 1–2, Geology 1–2, Astronomy; Fine Arts, Pottery, Sculpture, Photography, Art History; and Instrumental Music, Chorus, Music Theory, and Music in the Western World.

English as a Second Language is offered at beginner, intermediate, and advanced levels with emphasis on individualized instruction. The School enrolls approximately 20 ESL students and prefers new students to begin Hackley in the fall of sixth, seventh, or ninth grade. Aptitude testing in the student's first language is required for admission into this highly selective program.

Advanced Placement study is available in 18 subjects. The curriculum includes a tutorial and seminar program. Students can arrange for tutorials in English, history, language, and science.

In 1999, 95 graduating seniors planned to enter college. Two or more are attending Amherst, Boston University, Colgate, Cornell, George Washington University, Harvard, Johns Hopkins, Massachusetts Institute of Technology, Princeton, Stanford, Vanderbilt, Vassar, and the University of Pennsylvania. Other graduates are enrolled at Columbia, Dartmouth, New York University, and other colleges and universities nationwide.

The Hackley Summer School offers enrichment programs in writing, history, and science as well as review work for students needing help in basic subjects. Students entering Grades 5–12 are eligible to enroll. Anna Abelaf is Director.

STUDENT ACTIVITIES. The Community Council, composed of student and faculty representatives from Grades 6–12, organizes social and service activities. Students publish a yearbook, a newspaper, and a literary magazine. Other activities and organizations include the Board of Magistrates (the student-faculty judicial board); Student Teachers (who assist in Lower School classrooms); Community Service, Model United Nations, Model Congress, Mental Olympics; the Drama, Debate, Varsity H, and Environmental clubs; and Middle and Upper School chorus, orchestra, band, and jazz band. There is also an extensive jazz program, a vocal and instrumental chamber music program, a student recital series, music theater, and dramatic performances. Attention is given to the special needs of preprofessional students as well as to those of less serious amateurs.

Frequent field trips are planned to New York, and the School often hosts guest speakers from the city. Traditional annual events include Parents' and Grandparents' Days, Class Day, Sports Day, and the Mini-Marathon.

Varsity sports for boys and girls include basketball, cross-country, fencing, indoor track, lacrosse, golf, soccer, squash, swimming, track and field, and tennis. Boys also compete in baseball, football, and wrestling, while girls play field hockey and softball. A member of the Ivy League of the metropolitan area, Hackley competes against League members and public and parochial schools. Physical education courses include swimming in Kindergarten–Grade 6.

ADMISSION AND COSTS. Hackley seeks students of diverse backgrounds who demonstrate quickness of intellect and resourcefulness in problem solving, tempered by curiosity and love of truth. Students are admitted on the basis of a personal interview and written essay, a half-day on campus, two teacher recommendations, the transcript from the previous school, and the results of the Educational Records Bureau exam. In the Lower School, candidates take Hackley's own admissions test. The application deadline is February 1. There is a $55 application fee.

In 1999–2000, tuition ranges from $13,700 for Kindergarten to $16,950 for Grade 12. The boarding charge is $5300. Other extras include lunch and books (approximately $900 a year) and accident insurance ($46).

In the current year, a total of $1,500,000 in financial aid was awarded on the basis of need plus merit. School-funded loans, a tuition payment plan, and tuition insurance are available. Hackley subscribes to the School Scholarship Service.

Assistant Headmaster: Philip Variano
Director of Development: Katherine Valyi
Director of Admission: Julie S. Core
Co-Directors of College Counseling: Julie D. Lillis and Peter Latson
Technology Director: Joseph E. Dioguardi
Director of Finance: Peter McAndrew
Director of Athletics: Robert Pickert

The Hampton Day School   1966

Butter Lane, P.O. Box 604, Bridgehampton, NY 11932.
   516-537-1240; Fax 516-537-5183

Founded by parents, Hampton Day seeks to instill in students a lifelong love of learning and to encourage independent thinking and a search for truth. The School's unique environment includes a rich cultural setting and beautiful farmland, seashore, and wildlife. Enrollment includes 190 students in Pre-Nursery–Grade 10. The integrated thematic curriculum, which focuses on the interrelationships among the major disciplines, emphasizes environmental awareness and an appreciation for diversity. Small classes permit individual attention. Activities include sports, chorus, and theater. A summer day camp is offered. Tuition: $5700–$11,350. Financial aid is available. Jeanie Whiting is Admissions Director; Ellen G. Hannah (Smith, B.A.; Wharton School, M.B.A.) is Head of School.

Harbor Country Day School   1958

17 Three Sisters Road, St. James, NY 11780. 516-584-5555;
   Fax 516-862-7664; E-mail HCDS@LI.Net

Founded by parents, Harbor Country Day School enrolls 225 boys and girls in Nursery–Grade 8. The enriched curriculum focuses on the basic academic disciplines of language arts, mathematics, social studies, and science, while fostering good work habits, self-esteem, and consideration of others. Foreign language is introduced in Grade 1, and instruction in music, art, computer science, physical education, and health is offered at every level beginning in Kindergarten. Competitive sports, intramurals, and the performing arts are also part of the School's program. Summer programs are offered. Tuition: $1650–$6500. Arthur L. Strawbridge (Hobart, B.A.; Villanova University, M.A.) was appointed Headmaster in 1993.

The Harley School   1917

1981 Clover Street, Rochester, NY 14618. 716-442-1770;
   Fax 716-442-5758; E-mail admissions@harleyschool.org;
   Web Site www.harleyschool.org

Housed in spacious, modern buildings on a 20-acre suburban campus, The Harley School is a coeducational college preparatory day school enrolling 470 students in Nursery through Grade 12. Harley encourages involvement in all areas of school life: academic study, visual and performing arts, athletic competition, extracurricular activities, and community service. Harley offers a full range of Advanced Placement classes, arts and music classes, foreign languages, science laboratories, and various electives. Summer programs and extended day are also offered. Tuition: $9600–$11,800. Financial aid is available. Kimberley Moore is Director of Admissions; Richard F. Barter (University of Maine, B.A.; Johns Hopkins, M.A.T., Ph.D.) was appointed Interim Headmaster in 1999.

The Harvey School   1916

260 Jay Street, Katonah, NY 10536. 914-232-3161;
   E-mail romanowicz@harveyschool.org;
   Web Site www.harveyschool.org

Harvey, a coeducational college preparatory school, enrolls day and five-day boarding students of varying ability in Grades 6–12. Teachers work with students as individuals, both in and out of the classroom, in a warm, supportive environment. Small classes promote academic achievement and personal growth. Two internet-accessible labs and computer technology in most academic subjects provide information and resources to encourage excellence. Harvey offers ten Advanced Placement courses and varied activities, including a nationally recognized Model U.N. program and competitive athletics. Tuition: $15,650; Boarding Fee: $5500. Financial aid is available. Ronald Romanowicz is Admission Director; Barry W. Fenstermacher (Drew, B.A.) was named Headmaster in 1986.

The Hewitt School   NEW YORK

45 East 75th Street, New York, NY 10021. 212-288-1919;
   Fax 212-472-7531; E-mail info@hewittsch.com;
   Web Site www.hewittsch.com

THE HEWITT SCHOOL in New York City is a college preparatory day school enrolling girls from Kindergarten through Grade 12. Hewitt's upper East Side location between Park and Madison Avenues permits students and faculty to make extensive use of the city's museums, parks, galleries, and theaters and enables girls to volunteer in a wide variety of community service projects. Cooperative ventures with other nearby schools and colleges further expand and enhance the opportunities of a Hewitt education.

Founded in 1920, Hewitt's philosophy is predicated on the belief that women's confidence in their own abilities is the best basis for their development. The program is rich in opportunities to explore personal interests, acquire new understandings, and become actively engaged in the learning process. In addition to acquiring a firm foundation of information and skills, each girl is expected to do her best and to strive to achieve the highest standards of excellence. Faculty and students enjoy a close rapport that fosters mutual trust, understanding, and affection within an intimate, homelike environment. Hewitt and The Browning School for Boys share a coordinate program of extracurricular activities, which expands social activities for students of both schools.

The Hewitt School is governed by a 14-member Board of Trustees. The Alumnae Association provides a firm sense of community as it links the lives and interests of today's students with those of the alumnae. It offers information and opportunities for internships, extended study programs, and travel, and assists the School in its Annual Giving. Incorporated in 1952, Hewitt is chartered by the University of the State of New York and accredited by the New York State Association of Independent Schools. It holds membership in the National Association of Independent Schools, the Council for Advancement and Support of Education, and the Coalition of Girls' Schools, among other educational organizations.

THE CAMPUS. Hewitt's four-story East 75th Street structure is a former mansion, the focal point of which is the three-story curved Senior Staircase in the main entryway. The building has been carefully renovated to accommodate classrooms and other facilities for the Middle and Upper schools as well as administrative offices, a cafeteria, a darkroom, the gymnasium, the performing arts center, computer laboratories, the Learning Center, two new science laboratories, and the School's library. Directly behind it, the Gregory Building houses the Lower School facilities, including cheerful classrooms, play areas, art and computer rooms, and the nurse's office.

THE FACULTY. Dr. Mary Jane Yurchak became Hewitt's fifth Head of School in July of 1990. She earned her baccalaureate degree in political science and economics at Vassar College and holds a master's degree in education and a doctorate in human development from Harvard University. Dr. Yurchak previously served as the Director of Precollegiate Education at the University of Chicago Laboratory Schools and was a lecturer in the University's Department of Education.

The faculty consists of 65 members, 53 women and 12 men. All hold baccalaureate degrees and more than 75 percent have earned advanced degrees. Faculty benefits include support for professional development, a pension plan, and life, medical, and disability insurance.

A registered nurse is on duty at the School, and major medical facilities are easily accessible. Three counselors, a college counselor, and eight learning specialists provide on-site services.

STUDENT BODY. In 1999–2000, Hewitt enrolls 375 students as follows: 167 in the Lower School, 96 in the Middle School, and 112 in the Upper School. They represent a variety of national, ethnic, and socioeconomic backgrounds.

ACADEMIC PROGRAM. The school year, divided into semesters, begins in September and ends in June with vacations

scheduled at Thanksgiving, midwinter, and in the spring. School begins at 8:15 A.M., although students may enter from 7:45 A.M. Classes for Kindergarten–Grade 12 are conducted from 8:15 A.M. to 3:00 P.M. There is also a family breakfast program, an extended-day program, Hewitt AfterNoon, and a rich program of extracurricular and after-school activities for the Middle and Upper schools. Grade reports are issued twice a year, with interim reports when necessary. In the Lower and Middle schools, frequent parent-teacher conferences maintain the close liaison between family and school.

The Hewitt School curriculum provides students with a firm academic foundation in the liberal arts with equal emphasis given to humanities, the sciences, and the arts.

Development of curiosity, the eager pursuit of learning, and the acquisition of basic academic skills are the primary goals of the Kindergarten program. Children are encouraged to play and to explore an environment rich in learning opportunities. They enjoy reading, literature, writing, mathematics, science, social studies, music, dance, physical education, creative arts, computer, and French.

As girls progress, the program expands to meet their interests and their developmental needs. The English program centers on reading, literature, creative and expository writing, and, in Grades IV and V, research writing. Problem solving and computational skills in arithmetic are the focus in the mathematics courses in preparation for more advanced work. Introduction to natural and physical sciences, French, social studies, computer, music, art, and physical education complete the Lower School curriculum.

The Middle School (Grades V–VII) provides a rich interdisciplinary program structured to capture the interests and enthusiasm of the early adolescent. Designed to sustain curiosity, problem solving, and creative thinking, it also continues to develop and strengthen study skills, research critical and analytical thinking, and written and oral expression.

Upper School students carry at least four academic subjects per year; most girls elect to take five, as well as one or two courses in the arts. To earn a Hewitt diploma, students must complete four years of English; and three of mathematics, history, foreign language, and science. Among the course offerings are World Classics, A Study of Literary Genre, Writing Workshop, The American Renaissance, Advanced Expository and Analytical Writing, American Writers in Europe; French, Latin, Spanish; American History, European History, Art History; Algebra, Plane Geometry, Coordinate Geometry, Trigonometry, Pre-Calculus, Calculus, Statistics and Probability; Biology, Chemistry, Ecology, Physics; Music, Drama, Speech, Studio Art and Photography; and Physical Education. There are Advanced Placement opportunities in Spanish, French, Calculus, Biology, History of Art, European History, and English Literature. Additional AP courses are added according to student interest. The Learning Center provides individual tutorials for students with learning disabilities. The School promotes academic technology through the use of laptop computers by Upper School teachers and students. Upper School students are provided with an e-mail address, and faculty, staff, and students in Grades 5–12 may use the network and academic software. Network ports and dedicated outlets in all classrooms, a multimedia computer, a laserdisk player, a hi-fi VCR, a presentation monitor, networked computers in the Middle/Upper School computer lab, an online library circulation catalog, and 13 laser printers are also available.

Graduates of the Class of 1998 have enrolled at such colleges and universities as Barnard, Brown, Colgate, Connecticut College, Cornell, Dartmouth College, Duke, Smith, Syracuse University, Vassar, Wellesley, William Smith, Yale, and the University of Wisconsin.

STUDENT ACTIVITIES. Government in the Upper and Middle schools is centered in the Student Councils and their elected officers. Middle School students publish *Enterprise*, a literary magazine, while Upper School students issue four publications: *The Hewitt Times*, the newspaper; *Argosy*, the senior yearbook; *Venturer*, the art and literary magazine; and *Perspicacity*, a photography magazine.

Hewitt students are actively involved in community service. In addition to tutoring younger students and caring for their building and facilities, Hewitt girls reach out to the world beyond the School to assist the handicapped, homeless, elderly, and the environment. Students Against Driving Drunk (SADD), Model UN, an AIDS Awareness club, a refugee program to help women and children, and other groups on campus reflect the wide range of social concerns shared by the student body.

Varsity and junior varsity teams are organized in volleyball, basketball, gymnastics, tennis, badminton, swimming, and softball.

For students interested in the arts, there is a School chorus, jazz chorus, glee club, handbells groups, the Art Club, and the Drama Club, which stages three productions each year; Hewitt and Browning alternate production of the spring musical. There is also a Multi-Cultural Club. Student events include the Achievement Assemblies for each division, the prom and other dances, field trips, and Commencement.

ADMISSION AND COSTS. Hewitt welcomes all girls who are academically able and who have the potential to contribute to, and benefit from, the School's challenging and supportive environment. Application, with a $50 nonrefundable fee, should be made in the fall of the year preceding desired admission. Acceptance is based on the results of the Educational Records Bureau test and an interview.

In 1999–2000, tuition ranges from $15,675 for Kindergarten–Grade 2 to $17,056 in the Upper School; additional costs, including uniforms, are estimated at $2245. Financial aid was awarded to approximately 16 percent of the students. A tuition payment plan is available.

President, Board of Trustees: Catherine Montgomery
Head of Upper School: Sherry M. Grand
Head of Lower School: Jacqueline Wertzer
Head of Middle School: Lindley Uehling
Alumnae Secretary: Lisa Tankoos
Director of Admissions: Anita Edwards
Director of Development: Pamela Alexander
College Counselor: Caroline Erisman
Director of Athletics: Randy Zeidberg

Hoosac School   HOOSICK

Box 9, Hoosick, NY 12089. 518-686-7331;
    Admissions 800-822-0159; Fax 518-686-3370;
    E-mail info@hoosac.com; Web Site www.hoosac.com

Hoosac school in Hoosick, New York, is a coeducational, college preparatory school enrolling boarders and a few day students in Forms II–VI (Grades 8–12) and a postgraduate program. Hoosick, a hamlet of 350 residents, is in the Hudson Valley near the borders of New York, Massachusetts, and Vermont. Albany and Troy are 45 minutes away, and Bennington and Williams colleges are within a 20-minute drive. Hoosac students have library privileges at the colleges and at Rensselaer Polytechnic Institute and enjoy many cultural programs offered on these campuses.

Dr. Edward Dudley Tibbits established the Hoosac School to provide an intimate, highly personalized educational setting in which each student could receive individualized attention and support. Today, the School's essential mission remains true to its founder's philosophy: to develop the character, spirit, mind, and body of its students; to foster independence and self-discipline; and to motivate them to develop to their full potential for success in college and for full, productive, and intelligent lives. Founded as an Episcopal church school for boys, Hoosac today retains its ties to the church through the Chapel program while welcoming young men and women from many religious backgrounds. Students and faculty pledge to conduct themselves according to the School's Code of Honor.

Hoosac School is a nonprofit corporation governed by an 18-member Board of Trustees. It is chartered by the New York State Board of Regents and accredited by the Middle States Association of Colleges and Schools. Hoosac holds membership in the National Association of Independent Schools and the National Association of Episcopal Schools, among other affiliations. Many of the 1700 living graduates support the School through the Annual Giving; 8 alumni currently serve on the Board of Trustees and 3 are members of the Hoosac faculty.

THE CAMPUS. The 350-acre campus is the site of the former Tibbits family estate, adjoining the 850-acre Tibbits State Forest. Tibbits Hall, a redstone Gothic mansion constructed in 1860, houses administrative offices, classrooms, and a dormitory. Three turn-of-the-century buildings—Whitcomb, Dudley, and Wood halls—provide the chapel, classrooms, three dorms, and the 10,000-volume library. Science facilities are located in Blake Hall, which features two laboratories, a darkroom, an observatory with two telescopes, and an auditorium. Memorial Hall contains the dining hall, the kitchen, and the student lounge and snack bar. Other residential buildings include Lavino, Pitt Mason, and several small new dorms.

Athletic facilities include the Harry Dickie Sports Complex with an indoor swimming pool, weight rooms, and basketball court; four playing fields; six miles of cross-country trails; a pond; and tennis and volleyball courts.

The School-owned physical plant is valued at approximately $11,000,000.

THE FACULTY. Richard J. Lomuscio, who has been affiliated with Hoosac for 23 years, was appointed Headmaster in 1990. A graduate of New York University, he pursued his graduate studies there as well as at Northeastern University and Southampton College. Mr. Lomuscio has been a newspaper editor and taught in both public and private schools. He has served Hoosac in many different capacities including Director of Studies, Dean, housemaster, college counselor, and teacher of English, French, and biology.

In addition to Mr. Lomuscio, who also teaches French, there are 14 faculty and administrators who teach. They hold baccalaureate degrees and 7 master's degrees representing study at Andover Newton Theological Seminary, Bennington, Brown, Elmira, Frostburg State, Hartwick, Hiram College, Hunter College, Indiana University, Middlebury, North Adams State, Southern Vermont College, State University of New York (Albany), Westminster Choir College, Williams, Wilmington, Yale, and the Universities of Alaska and Massachusetts.

A full-time nurse manages Hoosac's dispensary; the school physician practices in nearby Hoosick Falls, 3 miles away. Both are available 24 hours a day. Emergency hospital facilities are in Bennington, Vermont, 9 miles away.

STUDENT BODY. In 1998–99, Hoosac School enrolled 85 boarding students and 8 day students in Form II through a postgraduate program. Students came from 16 states and eight countries and represented diverse racial, ethnic, and religious backgrounds.

ACADEMIC PROGRAM. The school year is divided into trimesters, from mid-September to mid-June, with vacations at Thanksgiving, Christmas, and in the spring and three long-weekend breaks. Grades, effort marks, and comments from each student's faculty adviser are mailed to parents six times a year. Students are expected to study in their rooms or in the library during free periods, and supervised 90-minute study halls are held each evening. The student-faculty ratio is 5:1.

A typical weekday begins at 7:00 A.M. After breakfast, students gather in the chapel for a brief prayer service and school announcements. Four 45-minute class periods, a 10-minute reading session, and work jobs take place before lunch, followed by two more periods ending at 2:50 P.M. Sports are held from 3:00 to 5:00 P.M., with dinner, evening study, and dorm check-in

by 9:30 P.M. "Lights out" is at 10:30 P.M. for Underformers and 11:00 P.M. for Sixth Formers.

Each student's course of study is flexible and is based on proficiency in a subject rather than on grade level. One-on-one tutoring can be arranged when necessary. The Mastery approach of teaching involves testing to determine the student's weak areas. The student is then instructed in those areas until the subject matter has been mastered.

Classes, enrolling between 5 and 12 students, meet six days a week, with half days on Wednesday and Saturday. To earn a Hoosac diploma, a student must complete four years of English; three years each of mathematics and history; two years of a foreign language; three years of science, including a lab science; one year each of health and Sixth Form ethics; and one trimester each of music, art, and computers.

Hoosac's college preparatory curriculum blends Mastery and traditional instructional styles designed to enable all students to achieve academic excellence. Among the specific courses are English 1–4, English as a Second Language 1–3; Pre-Algebra, Algebra 1–2, Geometry, Pre-Calculus, Calculus; Earth Science, Biology, Physics, Chemistry, Astronomy, Psychology; Ancient History, Modern European History, Early American History, U.S. History, Global Studies, American Cultures 1–2; French 1–3; Ethics, Health; Studio Art, Music History, Dramatics, Photography, Cinematic Film Studies, Scenic Design; and Computer Literacy. Advanced Placement courses are offered in Calculus, English, and U.S. History.

The School's English as a Second Language (ESL) program is an intense academic curriculum for international students designed to develop fluency in English, foster an understanding of American culture, and prepare for admission to American colleges and universities. ESL students are immersed in regular courses in the curriculum in addition to classes in ESL, American Cultures, and Test of English as a Foreign Language (TOEFL) preparation.

An additional component of the curriculum is OASIS (Open Access Skills Improvement Site). OASIS is designed to support and assist students whose learning differences have prevented them from reaching their potential in the mainstream academic program. The OASIS team develops and controls the student's entire educational environment. During the two-year OASIS program, a student takes standard college preparatory courses under the guidance of a personal tutor who meets with him or her one hour a day, five days a week. The tutor teaches critical study and organizational skills, helps other teachers modify their instructional methods and testing strategy to meet the student's specific needs, and tracks academic progress on a daily basis.

All of the 28 graduates in the Class of 1999 enrolled in college. They were accepted at Boston University, Catholic University, George Washington, Hobart and William Smith, Northeastern, Parsons School of Design, Pennsylvania State, Reed College, Rochester Polytechnic Institute, Skidmore, State University of New York (Binghamton), Syracuse, Trinity, Union College, and the University of Rochester.

Hoosac School conducts a six-week summer program of academics for enrichment and remediation, SAT preparation, and English as a Second Language.

STUDENT ACTIVITIES. Extracurricular activities are designed to meet the varied interests of the School's diverse student body. Qualified students nominated by classmates serve as prefects and proctors. These student leaders maintain order in the dorms, monitor and correct student behavior as needed, and oversee the work program. All students are assigned routine tasks involved with the upkeep of the buildings and grounds and the general operation of the School.

Students take the initiative in publishing a yearbook, a newspaper, and a creative writing magazine. They stage plays and choral events and plan outings, dances, and other activities.

Hoosac varsity teams compete against other independent schools in the region in soccer, ice hockey, lacrosse, basketball, tennis, volleyball, and softball. Skiing, flag football, swimming, skating, snowboarding, bicycling, and cross-country are offered as recreational and intramural sports.

On weekends, students attend dances at Hoosac and other schools such as Miss Hall's, Emma Willard, and Darrow. Lectures, concerts, plays, skiing at nearby slopes, roller- and ice-skating, movies, shopping, and excursions to nearby amusement parks and historical sites are other popular activities.

Hoosac's 100-year tradition of bringing in the Elizabethan Boar's Head and Yule Log at Christmas is one of the oldest among independent schools in the country. Other special events on the school calendar include Parents' Weekend, Bleeze Banquet, talent shows, Prize Day, and Commencement.

ADMISSION AND COSTS. Hoosac School welcomes students of average to superior ability who seek educational opportunity within a small community in which they can reach their full academic and personal potential. Students are admitted in Forms II to VI and the postgraduate program based on previous transcripts, recommendations, and a personal interview. Application should be made by mid-spring for fall entrance, although candidates will be considered during the year when vacancies exist. The application fee is $30.

In 1999–2000, tuition in the regular program is $22,000 for boarders and $12,100 for day students. Tuition for ESL students is $25,100; the charge for the OASIS program is $6100 added to the base tuition. Books and laundry total an additional $731. The School subscribes to the School Scholarship Service and awards need-based financial aid in the amount of $370,000 to approximately 20 percent of the student body. Tuition payment plans can be arranged.

Director of Studies: Robert Burns
Dean of Students: Patrick Martin

Director of Admissions: Dean Foster
College Counselor: Dean Foster
Business Manager: Kathryn Weaver
Director of Athletics: Michael Ryan

Horace Mann School

RIVERDALE AND NEW YORK

Middle/Upper Divisions (Grades 6–12): 231 West 246th Street, Riverdale, NY 10471. 718-432-4000; E-mail admissions@horacemann.org; Web Site www.horacemann.org
Lower Division (Kindergarten–Grade 5): 4440 Tibbett Avenue, Riverdale, NY 10471. 718-432-3300
Nursery Division (Nursery–Kindergarten): 55 East 90th Street, New York, NY 10128. 212-369-4600

Horace Mann School with divisions in Riverdale and New York City, is a coeducational, college preparatory day school enrolling students in Nursery–Grade 12. The School is served both by public transportation and School-sponsored buses.

The Horace Mann School was founded by Nicholas Murray Butler in 1887 as a coeducational experimental and developmental unit of Teachers College, Columbia University, and continued as a model school until 1946. In 1947, it became an independent day school for boys in Grades 7–12. Coeducation was reestablished through mergers with the New York School for Nursery Years (founded 1954) in 1968, the Barnard School (founded 1886) in 1972, and the enrollment of girls throughout the high school in 1975.

The School seeks to stretch the imagination, intellect, and perception of its students while developing the moral characteristics that impart identity and purpose. Education in the lower grades, which builds upon the natural desire of children to learn, is designed to teach basic skills and the joy of learning in a noncompetitive, supportive environment. The goal of the Middle and Upper Divisions is to provide a sound liberal education through the intellectual, moral, and physical development of each student.

The Horace Mann School is a nonprofit corporation directed by a 34-member Board of Trustees, including alumnae/i and parents. The School is accredited by the New York State Association of Independent Schools. It holds membership in the National Association of Independent Schools and other educational organizations.

THE CAMPUS. The 18-acre Horace Mann campus overlooks Van Cortlandt Park in the Fieldston-Riverdale section of New York. Campus buildings include Tillinghast Hall, which houses administrative offices, classrooms, and the 40,000-volume Theresa H. Loeb Library. Alfred Gross Hall contains the 600-seat Van Alstyne Auditorium and dining rooms. The newly renovated Pforzheimer Hall includes science and computer laboratories, the College Counseling Office, and other offices. In September 1999, Horace Mann opened Rose Hall, home to the Middle Division, and the Arts and Dining Center, a 52,000-square-foot facility that includes a 225-seat recital hall, art and photography studios, a video production area with a professionally equipped recording studio, and student and faculty dining areas. Prettyman Gymnasium contains basketball courts, an indoor track, swimming pool, and a fully equipped Nautilus room as well as exercise and training rooms. Other athletic facilities include playing fields and seven tennis and handball courts. The nearby fields of Van Cortlandt Park are also used for athletic programs.

The Lower Division campus includes administrative offices, classrooms, science laboratories, a new Arts and Technology Center, the innovative student Publishing Center, playgrounds, playing fields, and a full-sized gymnasium. Elementary students also use the swimming pool, tennis courts, and auditorium of the Upper Division campus. Near the Lower Division are the Alumni House and Development Office and the Davis House, where the Community Service office, Summer on the Hill office, and other offices are located.

The Horace Mann Nursery Division is located in a historic building on 90th Street between Madison and Park Avenues. In addition to classrooms, this six-story building has two rooftop playgrounds and a lower-level playground.

THE FACULTY. Eileen Mullady (University of Chicago, B.A., M.A.; Columbia University, Ph.D.) was appointed Head of School in 1995. Dr. Mullady was previously Dean of Faculty and Associate Head Master of The Lawrenceville School in New Jersey. She also served as Associate Dean of Faculty at Princeton University and as Assistant Vice President for Academic Affairs at Columbia.

The Horace Mann School faculties consist of 220 full-time teachers, 138 women and 82 men. They hold 222 baccalaureate, 155 master's, and 23 doctoral degrees.

Registered nurses are in attendance at all times. A psychologist and a psychiatrist visit the School weekly. Full-service hospitals are minutes away.

STUDENT BODY. Horace Mann is one of the largest day schools in the country. In 1999–2000, the School enrolls 1660 students as follows: 175 in Nursery and Kindergarten, 422 in Grades 1–5, 403 in Grades 6–8, and 660 in Grades 9–12. Students come from New York City, Westchester County, New Jersey, and Connecticut; they represent many different racial, ethnic, and religious groups.

ACADEMIC PROGRAM. The school year runs from early September through early June. Vacations occur at Thanksgiving, the winter holidays, and in March. Progress reports and grades are sent to parents at the end of each trimester, and parent-teacher conferences are scheduled at regular intervals during the school year.

The Nursery–Kindergarten program uses a developmentally appropriate early-childhood curriculum to create a nurturing and stimulating learning environment. With a focus on reading readiness, positive self-esteem, problem solving, and creativity, children build a foundation for academic success. The quality of group life is a crucial factor in the learning that takes place. Teachers, with the support and involvement of parents, create a noncompetitive atmosphere of acceptance and mutual respect, which fosters a sense of community through which children can develop to their fullest potential.

The Lower Division program features both a solid core curriculum and extensive enrichment activities. Classrooms in the primary grades are self-contained. In addition to the core subjects, all children are involved in art, music, foreign language, library, computer, physical education, and health. Instruction in Grades 4–5 is departmentalized by subject, with teachers working together as part of a cohesive team. The Lower Division maintains a Speech Department, fully staffed Reading and Activity Centers, an Art Enrichment program, and electives in the performing arts. School-wide participation in community service is coordinated by the Student Council.

The Middle and Upper Division academic programs provide a balanced liberal arts education that combines a strong traditional curriculum with new and innovative courses. Courses for students in Grades 6–8 are designed to incorporate the traditional academic rigor of Horace Mann with activities appropriate to the age group in order to bring each student to a higher level of self-confidence, organization, and competency within an educational experience that is captivating and fun. Middle Division students can participate in activities such as Chorus, interscholastic teams, yearbook, and many other clubs.

To graduate from the Upper Division, students in Grades 9–12 must complete four years of English; two years of a foreign language to complete a three-year sequence; three years of math through Intermediate Algebra and Trigonometry; two years of laboratory science (biology required); two years of history (modern European and American required); one and one-half credits of art or music; two years of health; and four years of physical education or participation in team sports. There is also an 80-hour community service requirement and an annual computer mastery requirement.

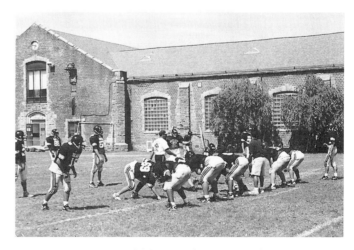

Some courses available to students in Grades 9–12 include English 9–11 and such senior trimester electives as Austen and Woolf, Chaucer and Writing Workshop; Geometry, Algebra II and Trigonometry, Pre-Calculus, Calculus, Statistics, Social Science Research; Program Design, Programming in C, Advanced Programming; Classical Greek, French, German, Italian, Japanese, Latin, Russian, Spanish; Modern European History,

American History, Economics, Twentieth Century History; Biology, Chemistry, Physics, Astronomy; Music Theory, Introduction to the History of Music, American Music, Orchestra, Glee Club; Acting, Theater Production and Design; and Ceramics, Life Drawing, Painting and Drawing, Photography, Introduction to the History of Art, and History of Contemporary Art. Each department offers Advanced Placement courses.

Set on 100 acres of land in Washington, Connecticut, the John Dorr Nature Laboratory is one of Horace Mann's four campuses. The School conducts programs lasting from one to eight days for students in Grades 2–12. The programs vary in content, with some dealing with environmental science and others with community building, problem solving, and group dynamics. The Lab is staffed by four full-time teachers.

In 1999, the 146 graduates matriculated at 55 different colleges and universities. Two or more are attending Barnard, Brown, Carnegie Mellon, Clark, Colgate, Columbia, Cornell, Dartmouth, Duke, Fordham, Franklin and Marshall, Georgetown, George Washington, Harvard, Lehigh, McGill, Muhlenberg, New York University, Northwestern, Stanford, Trinity, Tufts, Vassar, Yale, and the Universities of Pennsylvania, Rochester, and Wisconsin.

A six-week summer session for Middle and Upper Division students offers courses for credit, review, or preview. A summer day camp for children ages 3–11 provides indoor and outdoor recreation. Athletic camps are also offered.

STUDENT ACTIVITIES. In the Middle and Upper Divisions, an elected council of 24 students and 15 faculty serves as an advisory body to the Division Heads in all areas of school life. Students produce 17 publications and operate the School's radio station. Other activities include clubs for art, chess, debate, international relations, magic, mathematics, metaphysics, photography, sailing, theater, Model United Nations, and an organization for the School's minority students. Musical organizations include glee club, orchestra, band, and an advanced instrumental group.

Horace Mann is a member of the Ivy Preparatory League and fields varsity, junior varsity, and freshman teams in a variety of sports. Interscholastic teams for boys are organized in football, soccer, cross-country, basketball, wrestling, tennis, track, baseball, and lacrosse. Teams for girls compete in soccer, field hockey, cross-country, volleyball, tennis, basketball, gymnastics, softball, track, and lacrosse. There are coeducational varsity teams in water polo, swimming, winter track, fencing, and golf. The School also offers programs in noncompetitive sports and activities.

ADMISSION AND COSTS. Admission to the Nursery School requires a school tour, parent interview, and small-group interview with the child. Children entering at the Kindergarten level must take a standardized admissions test of the Educational Records Bureau. The Lower School admits students to all grades on the basis of teacher recommendations, a personal interview, and the results of standardized tests. Candidates for Grades 6–11 are evaluated on the basis of the entrance examination, academic transcripts, teacher recommendations, and a personal interview. In addition to a strong school record, emphasis is placed upon the candidate's maturity, character, and concern for others. There is an application fee of $50.

In 1999–2000, tuition ranges from $12,800 in Nursery to $18,850 in Grades 7–12. Financial aid awards are made for one year and must be renewed annually. Any student may apply for financial aid. In 1999–2000, the School awarded more than $3,600,000 in financial aid to 292 students.

Head of School: Dr. Eileen Mullady
Head of Upper Division: Dr. Lawrence S. Weiss
Head of Middle Division: Marian C. Linden
Head of Lower Division: Dr. Steven Tobolsky
Head of Nursery Division: Patricia Yuan Zuroski
Head of John Dorr Nature Lab: Glenn Sherratt
Director of Admissions: Lisa J. Moreira
Director of Development: Richard S. Jacobs

The Kildonan School   1969

R.R. #1, Box 294, Perry Corners Road, Amenia, NY 12501.
914-373-8111; Fax 914-373-9793

Kildonan, a coeducational, college preparatory school for dyslexic students of average to above-average intelligence, enrolls boarders in Grade 6–Postgraduate and day students in Grade 2–Postgraduate. In addition to regular subjects, the highly structured program features daily one-on-one language tutoring designed to help students develop the necessary level of proficiency in academic skills to allow them to return to another school or enter college. Typing and word processing are an integral part of a full curriculum that includes art, woodshop, riding, and interscholastic/intramural athletics. Boarding Tuition: $30,500–$33,000; Day Tuition: $17,500–$21,500. Ronald A. Wilson was appointed Headmaster in 1986.

The Knox School   1904

St. James, Long Island, New York 11780. 516-584-5500

Overlooking Stony Brook Harbor, Knox is a college preparatory boarding school enrolling 175 boys and girls, including 25 day students, in Grades 7–Postgraduate. The School aims to provide a structured program of the liberal arts and sciences within a happy, familylike atmosphere. College courses, study abroad, English as a Second Language, developmental reading, and electives complement the core curriculum. Clubs, publications, drama, and sports, including horsemanship, are among the activities. Boarding Tuition: $23,000; Day Tuition: $14,500. Financial Aid: $100,000. Mrs. Herta M. Walsh is Admissions Director; Clifford K. Eriksen (College of William and Mary, A.B.; Wesleyan, M.A.L.S.) was named Headmaster in 1971. *Middle States Association.*

La Salle Academy   1848

44 East Second Street, New York, NY 10003-9297. 212-475-8940;
Fax 212-529-3598

One of the oldest Catholic college preparatory schools in New York City, La Salle Academy enrolls 550 young men from diverse backgrounds in Grades 9–12. The Brothers of the Christian Schools oversee a curriculum designed to foster spiritual, intellectual, moral, and physical development according to New Testament teachings. Computer technology, foreign language, and religious studies are integral to the program. Qualified students may earn college credit at St. John's University, and most graduates go on to higher education. Boys enjoy involvement in school government, publications, drama, Peer Ministry, clubs, and sports. Tuition: $4642. Felipe E. Anastacio is Director of Admissions; Br. Joseph Wilkowski, F.S.C., is Principal. *Middle States Association.*

La Salle Center: A Global Learning Community
1883

500 Montauk Highway, Oakdale, NY 11769-1796. 516-589-0900;
Fax 516-563-7227; E-mail lasaladm@li.net

This Catholic education consortium operated by the De La Salle Christian Brothers consists of four separate, coeducational programs: Primary (K–5), Middle (Grades 6–8), Preparatory Academy (Grades 9–12), and Military Academy (Grades 9–12). Boarding options are available beginning in Grade 8. The divisions are unified by the common purpose of teaching the message and spirit of Jesus. The academic curriculum throughout is designed to prepare students for higher education and Christian leadership in the 21st century. Opportunities for social and physical development are offered through sports, music, and interest clubs. Boarding Tuition: $16,000–$19,000; Day Tuition: $6800–$8500. Br. Jerome Corrigan is President.

Lawrence Woodmere Academy   1990

336 Woodmere Boulevard, Woodmere, NY 11598. 516-374-9000;
Fax 516-374-4707; E-mail lwacad@lawo.com;
Web Site www.lawo.com

Lawrence Woodmere Academy enrolls 385 boys and girls as day students in Toddler–Grade 12. An individualized program and writing skills are emphasized in all course work, while the college preparatory curriculum is enriched by numerous honors and Advanced Placement courses in a variety of disciplines. One hundred percent of the graduates go on to four-year colleges. Computer science, athletics, student publications, concert band, community service, Model U.N., and drama are available. A summer program is offered. Tuition: $2100–$16,200. Financial aid and merit scholarships are available. Dennis R. Carroll (Seton Hall, B.A. 1964, M.A. 1968) was appointed Headmaster in 1994.

Long Island Lutheran
Middle & High School   1960

131 Brookville Road, Brookville, NY 11545. 516-626-1700;
Fax 516-626-1773; Web Site www.luhi.org

Enrolling 500 boys and girls of diverse faiths, abilities, and backgrounds in Grades 6–12, Long Island Lutheran aims to provide a program of academic excellence and Christian distinctiveness within the Lutheran tradition. The liberal arts curriculum, designed to enable students to find knowledge, identity, purpose, and power, includes religion, business, and the arts, with Advanced Placement, Regents, or Honors courses in most disciplines. Student government, yearbook, bands, concert choir, drama, honor societies, SADD, interest clubs, and teams in ten sports are some of the activities. Tuition: $4965–$6250. Financial aid is available. David Hahn (University of Minnesota, Ph.D.) is Executive Director. *Middle States Association.*

Loyola School   1900

980 Park Avenue, New York, NY 10028. 212-288-3522;
Fax 212-861-1021; Web Site www.loyola-nyc.org

Loyola School, celebrating 100 years of academic excellence, is a Roman Catholic, coeducational college preparatory school enrolling 200 day students in Grades 9–12. It aims to combine the Jesuit and independent-school traditions and seeks academic excellence stressing the religious, social, physical, and intellectual growth of each person. Advanced Placement courses are available. Independent studies and courses at area colleges are options for qualified seniors. Activities include athletics, speech, dramatics, student publications, art, music, and commu-

nity service. Tuition: $13,150. Financial Aid: $400,000. Audrey M. Grieco is Director of Admissions; The Reverend Joseph J. Papaj, SJ (Fordham, B.A., M.A.; Woodstock College, M.Div., S.T.L.), was appointed Headmaster in 1995. *Middle States Association.*

Manlius Pebble Hill School   1869

Jamesville Road, Dewitt, NY 13214. 315-446-2452;
Fax 315-446-2620; E-mail mphinfo@mph.net

Manlius Pebble Hill School is a coeducational, college preparatory day school enrolling 540 students in Pre-Kindergarten–Grade 12. Five-day boarding and Thirteenth Year programs are available. The School offers a strong academic program in a supportive atmosphere. Students participate in sports and extracurricular activities such as soccer, basketball, track and field, chess, theater arts, orchestral ensembles, Model United Nations, and publications. There are extensive summer programs for students ages 4 to 18. Tuition: $8300–$11,175. Financial Aid: $1,000,000. Amy E. Hogan is Director of Admission; Baxter Ball, Jr. (Kenyon College, B.A. 1970; Bowling Green State, M.A. 1972), was appointed Headmaster in 1990. *Middle States Association.*

The Mary Louis Academy   1936

176-21 Wexford Terrace, Jamaica Estates, NY 11432.
718-297-2120; Fax 718-739-0037; Web Site TMLA.org

This Catholic, college preparatory day school enrolling 950 young women in Grades 9–12 aims to provide an environment of encouragement for spiritual, physical, emotional, and social growth. In addition to diploma/Regents requirements, sequences are offered in art, family and consumer science, language, mathematics, music, and science. Religious studies and physical education are required. Honors and college Advanced Placement courses, a full technology program, and state-of-the-art labs in chemistry, physics, and earth science are available. Activities include athletics, forensics, journalism, performing arts, and many cultural clubs. Tuition: $4800. Sr. Filippa Luciano is Admissions Director; Sr. Kathleen McKinney, CSJ (St. Joseph's, B.A.; Adelphi, M.S.; St. John's, Ed.D.), is Principal. *Middle States Association.*

Marymount School   1926

1026 Fifth Avenue, New York, NY 10028. 212-744-4486;
Fax 212-744-0163; Web Site www.marymount.k12.ny.us

Founded by the Religious of the Sacred Heart of Mary, Marymount School is an independent, college preparatory, Catholic day school enrolling 440 girls in Nursery–Class XII. Central to the mission of the School is the academic enterprise—the acquisition of knowledge and the development of lifelong skills and clear expression. Emphasizing classic disciplines and scientific inquiry, the curriculum includes 13 Advanced Placement courses and a varied program of athletics as well as aesthetic and performing arts. Tuition: $10,100–$17,380. Financial Aid: $990,000. Concepcion R. Alvar is Admissions Director; Sr. Kathleen Fagan, RSHM (Marymount College, B.A. 1963; Notre Dame, M.A. 1969), was appointed Headmistress in 1976. *Middle States Association.*

The Masters School   1877

49 Clinton Avenue, Dobbs Ferry, NY 10522. 914-693-1400

The Masters School, serving boarders in Grades 9–12 and day students in Grades 5–12, enrolls 390 boys and girls from 14 states and 18 nations. The 96-acre wooded campus above the Hudson River is 20 miles from New York City. Students, 28 percent of whom receive financial aid, are challenged by the Harkness teaching method, 13 Advanced Placement courses, and the visual and performing arts. A large, refurbished gym and new fields enhance the School's competition in the Fairchester League and the Western New England Prep Association. Boarding Tuition: $24,750; Day Tuition: $16,750. Extras: $300. Susan Hendricks is Director of Admission; Pamela J. Clarke (Vassar, B.A.; Yale, M.A.; Harvard, M.Ed.) is Head of School. *Middle States Association.*

The Melrose School   1963

120 Federal Hill Road, Brewster, NY 10509. 914-279-2406;
Fax 914-279-3878; E-mail admissions@melrose.edu;
Web Site www.melrose.edu

The Melrose School is an independent, coeducational, Episcopal day school enrolling 125 above-average students in Kindergarten–Grade 8. Founded by the Sisters of the Community of the Holy Spirit, The Melrose School seeks to provide an engaging academic and social environment infused with traditional Judeo-Christian values. Music, art, computers, and French are taught from Kindergarten through Grade 8; Latin is introduced in Grade 7. Interschool team sports for Grades 5–8 are included in the physical education program. Tuition: $8100–$9500. Mrs. Nancy Hovan is Director of Admissions; Richard Broughton (Amherst, B.A.; Harvard, M.Ed.) was appointed Headmaster in 1995. *Middle States Association.*

Millbrook School   1931

School Road, Millbrook, NY 12545. 914-677-8261;
Fax 914-677-8598; E-mail admissions@millbrook.org;
Web Site http:\\www.millbrook.org

Located 90 miles north of Manhattan, Millbrook is a coeducational boarding and day school founded in 1931 to develop the intellectual resources of its students and to prepare them to be responsible citizens. The community service program established then is a School cornerstone today. The college preparatory program, enrolling 230 students in Grades 9–12, emphasizes the liberal arts and sciences with Advanced Placement in all disciplines and such electives as Ethics in Leadership, Ornithology, Zoo Research, and Aesthetics. Facilities include the new Mills Athletic Center and the Travor Zoo. Boarding Tuition: $24,900; Day Tuition: $18,100. Financial Aid: $1,131,570. Cynthia S. McWilliams is Director of Admission; Drew Casertano (Amherst, B.A.; Harvard, Ed.M.) is Headmaster. *Middle States Association.*

New York Military Academy   1889

78 Academy Avenue, Cornwall-on-Hudson, NY 12520.
914-534-3710; Toll free 888-ASK-NYMA; Fax 914-534-7699;
E-mail admissions@nyma.ouboces.org; Web Site http://www.nyma.org

Founded on the belief that a military structure is most conducive to academic achievement, the Academy offers college preparatory, athletic, and Junior Army Reserve Officers Training Corps programs for young men and women. Opportunities include SAT Prep, marching band, honor guard, equitation, fencing, flight training, marksmanship, and publications. The campus is networked for the Internet and voice mail. There are 270 boarding and day students enrolled in Grade 7–Postgraduate. English as a Second Language and a summer academic program are offered. Boarding Tuition: $18,325; Day Tuition: $6825. Financial Aid: $325,000. George J. Naron is Director of Admissions; Maj. Gen. James M. Lyle, USA (Ret.), is Superintendent. *Middle States Association.*

Nichols School   1892

Upper School: 1250 Amherst Street, Buffalo, NY 14216.
716-875-8212; Fax 716-875-2169;
E-mail jmunro@nicholsnet.net; Web Site www.nicholsnet.net
Middle School: 175 Nottingham Terrace, Buffalo, NY 14216.
716-876-3500; Fax 716-877-1090

Nichols, a coeducational, college preparatory day school, enrolls 550 students. In a nurturing environment, the Middle School (Grades 5–8) provides a stimulating atmosphere and challenging curriculum vital for academic growth, personal development, and readiness for high school. In the Upper School (Grades 9–12), small classes, a rigorous curriculum, and extensive extracurriculars prepare students for higher education. The fine and performing arts, interscholastic athletics, and community service enhance the traditional, technology-integrated curriculum. A summer academic session is available. Tuition: $10,400–$11,600. Financial Aid: $800,000. John Munro is Director of Admissions; Richard C. Bryan, Jr. (Trinity, A.B.; University of North Carolina, M.A.), is Headmaster.

The Nightingale-Bamford School   1921

20 East 92nd Street, New York, NY 10128. 212-289-5020;
Fax 212-876-1045; E-mail info@nightingale.org;
Web Site www.nightingale.org

Nightingale-Bamford, a day school serving 520 girls in Kindergarten–Class XII, provides rigorous college preparation in a community that prizes intellectual development and self-esteem. Commitment to diversity and substantial financial aid ensure a multicultural student body. A state-of-the-art Schoolhouse features advanced computer facilities. The classical curriculum, which focuses on the major disciplines and values the arts and athletics, is updated yearly to meet the needs of its students. Advanced Placement in 11 disciplines, cocurricular activities, foreign study and travel, social service, publications, and clubs supplement the program. Tuition/Fees: $14,200–$15,800. Carole J. Everett is Director of Admissions; Dorothy A. Hutcheson (Duke, A.B.; Duquesne, M.S.Ed.) is Head of School.

The Norman Howard School   1980

275 Pinnacle Road, Rochester, NY 14623. 716-334-8010;
Fax 716-334-8073; E-mail info@normanhoward.org;
Web Site www.normanhoward.org

The mission of The Norman Howard School is to enable bright adolescents with learning difficulties to reach their full potential through diagnosis, remediation, and specialized teaching strategies. As a demonstration school, it also serves as a model for other educators. Currently, 149 boys and girls are enrolled in Grades 5–12. Certified faculty focus on reading, language, mathematics, and study skills, providing personalized instruction based on each student's needs and abilities. Students are grouped homogeneously in classes with an average enrollment of 8. A distinctive Arts Program allows students to discover new talents and undertake individualized projects. Tuition: $20,238. Financial Aid: $19,500. Thomas A. Mutch is Director; Marcie C. Roberts is Executive Director.

Northwood School   1905

P.O. Box 1070, Lake Placid, NY 12946-5070. 518-523-3357;
Fax 518-523-3405; E-mail admissions@northwood.com;
Web Site www.northwoodschool.com

Northwood School, founded by John Hopkins, is a coeducational college preparatory school enrolling 100 boarders and 50 day students in Grades 9–12. An extensive athletic program takes advantage of the nearby Lake Placid Olympic facilities, especially in the winter. All teaching faculty reside on campus, assisting students with their growth and development in and out of the classroom setting. English as a Second Language, postgraduate studies, and tutorial services are also offered. Boarding Tuition: $21,250; Day Tuition: $10,350. Financial Aid: $400,000. Perry Babcock is Director of Admissions; Edward M. Good (Bowdoin, B.A.; Brown, M.A.T.; University of Massachusetts, C.A.G.S.) is Headmaster.

Oakwood Friends School   POUGHKEEPSIE

515 South Road, Poughkeepsie, NY 12601. 914-462-4200;
Fax 914-462-4251; E-mail admissions@o-f-s.org;
Web Site www.o-f-s.org

Oakwood friends school in Poughkeepsie, New York, is a coeducational college preparatory school enrolling day students in Grades 6–8 and both day and boarding students in Grades 9–12 and a postgraduate year. It is located in a suburban setting 4 miles south of Poughkeepsie on Route 9, near Vassar College and historic Hudson River sites. The School is 75 miles from New York City, 80 miles from Albany, and 220 miles from Boston.

Founded by the New York Yearly Meeting of the Religious Society of Friends, Oakwood Friends is an educational community committed to Quakers' deep respect for the worth of each person. It seeks students who demonstrate a genuine concern for their own growth—academic, spiritual, social, and physical—and who are intent on becoming complete persons—competent, creative, responsible, and sensitive to the world and its needs for a just and moral social order.

Oakwood Friends is a nonprofit corporation managed for the New York Yearly Meeting by a Board of Managers meeting quarterly. The School holds membership in the Friends Council on Education and the National Association of Independent

Schools. It is chartered by the Regents of the University of the State of New York and accredited by the New York State Association of Independent Schools.

THE CAMPUS. The 60-acre campus includes four tennis courts, three soccer fields, two baseball diamonds, and wooded areas.

Collins Library (1990) houses 11,000 volumes, microform materials, an audiovisual center, a computer laboratory, and classrooms. The Main Building, Crowley, Collins Library, and Stokes house classrooms, a ceramics studio, the meeting room, the art room, and offices. Lane Auditorium is used for theatrical performances, dance classes, and public events; and Connor Gymnasium contains basketball courts and a weight room. Other facilities include the Dining Hall and a darkroom. The Turner Math and Science Building containing state-of-the-art laboratories opened in September 1998.

Four dormitories have faculty apartments and recreation, laundry, and kitchen facilities. One, Craig Hall, houses the fully equipped photography darkroom.

THE FACULTY. Lila A. Gordon, appointed Head of School in 1992, is a graduate of the Juilliard School of Music (B.S.), Hofstra University (M.A.), and the University of Chicago (Ph.D.). She was previously Principal of the Upper School at The Sidwell Friends School in Washington, D.C.

There are 21 full-time teachers, 10 men and 11 women, and 8 administrators. Of these, most live at the School. They hold 22 baccalaureate and 21 advanced degrees, including 6 doctorates, from Adelphi, Bard, Baruch, Brandeis, Brooklyn College, Central College, Colgate, Columbia, Cornell, Earlham, Ecole Normale Superieur d'Haiti, Fordham, Haverford, Hofstra, Juilliard School of Music, Marist, Marshall, Michigan State, New York University, Ohio State, St. Andrews (Scotland), St. Lawrence, Scarritt, State University of New York (Geneseo, New Paltz, Oneonta, Potsdam), Syracuse, Tufts, Wesleyan, Western Michigan University, Wilson, and the Universities of Chicago, Dayton, Maryland, Massachusetts, Michigan, New Hampshire, Tennessee, and Wisconsin. There are 6 part-time instructors.

The infirmary is staffed by a Director of Health Services/ School Nurse, and a doctor is on call.

STUDENT BODY. Oakwood Friends enrolls 130 students in Grades 6–12. Sixty-eight percent are from New York; 16 percent are from eight other states, and 16 percent are from six other countries. The boy-girl ratio is approximately 50:50.

ACADEMIC PROGRAM. The school year, from early September to early June, includes Thanksgiving, Christmas, midwinter, and spring vacations and consists of trimesters of eleven weeks each. Grades are posted and reported to parents at mid-

term and at the end of each trimester, and written course evaluations are sent at midterm. In Grade 12, students choose from specially designed interdisciplinary courses, electives, and Advanced Placement courses.

The daily schedule for all Oakwood Friends students from 8:00 A.M. to 3:30 P.M. includes classes, study, lunch, and work assignments. Between 3:30 P.M. and dinner, students participate in interscholastic, intramural, and lifetime sports. From 7:00 to 9:00 P.M., boarders study in the library, their dormitories, or in a supervised study hall. Students whose performance is consistently responsible are exempt from evening study hall. As a Quaker school, Oakwood Friends does not rank students or grant academic honors.

Graduation requirements include four years of English and history; three of science; three of math; two of a foreign language; one and one-third in the arts; and one trimester each of health, Quakerism, and computer literacy. Satisfactory participation in sports/physical education and the work programs is required every trimester, as well as the completion of the special senior program.

The curriculum in Grades 6–11 emphasizes mastery of important fundamental skills in writing, both creative and analytical; reading comprehension; and applied and theoretical mathematics and science. Emphasis is placed on the ability to analyze as well as understand information and to recognize the interrelationships of disciplines. Interdepartmental coordination of curricula is being developed this year.

In addition, the School offers a wide range of electives, such as studio art, ceramics, photography, drama, drama tech, chorus, instrumental ensemble, voice, music theory, music appreciation, music history, musical production, current events, world history, philosophy, and computer. Students whose learning differences are documented receive support for at least one period each day in the Learning Center, where they are given one-to-one and small group assistance with homework assignments; basic skills in reading, writing, and math; organizing study time; and academic and personal counseling.

In Grade 12, the Senior/Core Program helps students succeed in the college admissions process. Throughout the year, a "core group" provides time for mutual reflection and discussion to help students integrate their varied experiences in the program. Each term, in addition to the required interdisciplinary course focusing on the social sciences, Advanced Placement courses are offered in English, biology, calculus, and foreign languages.

International students must meet a minimum proficiency in English to be accepted and are mainstreamed in regular courses. However, The American Language Academy is housed on the Oakwood campus and provides intensive English training.

Graduates from the Class of 1999 are attending Clark University, Curry, Drexel, Guilford, Hampshire, Hofstra, Mount Holyoke, St. John's University, Wesleyan, and the Universities of Chicago, Hartford, and Southern Maine.

STUDENT ACTIVITIES. All students and faculty attend weekly community meetings, which are chaired by an elected student clerk, and Meetings for Worship. Much of daily school life is overseen by faculty-student standing committees chosen by the community. These include the judicial, academic, activities, student life, Friends concerns, and nominating committees. Students are divided into ten dormitory groups of about 12 students each, who live together with a faculty leader. Each student has a work assignment. Assignments include dining hall chores, housekeeping, library work, recycling effort, and clerical duties.

The physical education program offers interscholastic, intramural, and lifetime activities. Interscholastic teams are fielded in boys' and girls' soccer and basketball; coeducational cross-country, swimming, and tennis; boys' baseball; and girls' softball and volleyball. Intramural programs include table tennis, ultimate frisbee, downhill skiing, canoeing trips, exercise club, modern dance, aerobics, and yoga. Other activities include the literary magazine and yearbook; drama, choral, and instrumental groups; a Poetry Club; and committees on Friends' concerns and disarmament.

Weekend activities include faculty open houses, films, dances, sightseeing, trips to Vassar and other colleges for special events, field trips to New York City, and informal cooking, hiking, and sports. Parents Weekend in the fall and Alumni Day in the spring are traditional events.

ADMISSION AND COSTS. Oakwood Friends welcomes applicants of all racial and religious backgrounds who are genuinely interested in participating in the life of the School and in taking responsibility for their growth and learning. Applicants must submit school records and personal references and arrange a campus interview. Secondary School Admission Test scores are desired but not required.

Application should be made as early as possible and will be considered as long as spaces are available. New students are admitted in Grades 7–11 and occasionally in Grade 12 or for a postgraduate year.

Tuition for 1999–2000 is $24,350 for boarders, $14,800 for day students in Grades 9–12, and $10,800 for day students in Grades 6–8. Tuition includes an infirmary fee, accident insurance, and normal art and laboratory fees. Additional expenses—estimated at $800—include books, spending money, school trips, laundry, and transportation. The Learning Center cost is $3200. The School recommends the Achiever Loan Program. Oakwood Friends granted financial aid of approximately $302,000 to 44 percent of the students in 1998–99. Aid is awarded on the basis of both need and merit; students who wish to be considered should apply through the School Scholarship Service. In addition, the School annually awards a scholarship for academic excellence.

Director of Studies: Siri Akal S. Khalsa
Dean of Students: Dan Torlone
Alumni Secretary: Peter L. Wilkie
Director of Admissions: Cynthia Pope
Director of Development: Peter L. Wilkie
Directors of Senior Program: Lacey Crouthamel and Linda Paquin
Director of Athletics: Tim McElhinney
Director of Middle School: Charles A. Butts
Business Manager: Allen Olsen

The Packer Collegiate Institute   1845

170 Joralemon Street, Brooklyn Heights, NY 11201. 718-875-6644, extension 266; Fax 718-875-1363; Web Site www.packer.edu

Packer Collegiate is a coeducational, college preparatory day school enrolling 850 students in Pre-school–Grade 12. Through teaching, advising, mentoring, and coaching, a gifted and enthusiastic faculty motivate students to high achievement and

individual excellence in the classroom, athletics, the fine arts, and community service. Advanced Placement, Senior Emphasis Program, independent research in the sciences, Maine Coast Semester, trips abroad, and independent study are among the special offerings. Tuition: $7500–$15,750. Financial Aid: $2,000,000. Matthew Nespole is Director of Admissions; Geoffrey Pierson (Wesleyan, B.A.; Harvard, M.A.T., Ph.D.) was appointed Head of School in 1990. *Middle States Association.*

Old Westbury School of the Holy Child   1959

25 Store Hill Road, Old Westbury, NY 11568. 516-626-9300; Fax 516-626-7914; Web Site oldwestburyschoolhc.com

This independent Catholic day school was founded by caring educators and parents to offer a program integrating academic, athletic, and personal excellence with strong spiritual values. Enrolling 178 boys and girls age 2½–Grade 8, Old Westbury School emphasizes rigorous traditional academics, enriched by technology and foreign languages including French (Kindergarten–Grade 8), Spanish, and Latin. Students are involved in liturgical celebrations, the fine and performing arts, music lessons, community service, league athletics, and clubs. Extended-day and summer programs are available. Tuition: $3300–$12,000. Financial Aid: $42,538. Mrs. Linda Valenti is Admissions Director; Grace M. Cavallo (Queens College, B.A., M.S.; St. John's University, P.D.) is Head of School. *Middle States Association.*

The Park School of Buffalo   1912

4625 Harlem Road, Snyder, NY 14226. 716-839-1242; Fax 716-839-2014; E-mail park1@theparkschool.org; Web Site www.theparkschool.org

The Park School of Buffalo is a college preparatory country day school enrolling 325 boys and girls in Nursery–Grade 12. It offers a comprehensive and challenging curriculum to give students the academic foundation necessary for success and to develop their sense of responsibility and commitment. There is an extended-day program and a six-week summer day camp, which utilizes the 17 buildings on the 40-acre suburban campus. Tuition: $4865–$11,125. Financial aid is available. Mrs. Janice M. Goodfellow is Director of Admission; Erik P. Korvne (St. Bonaventure University, B.A.; State University of New York at Buffalo, M.Ed.) was appointed Headmaster in 1998. *Middle States Association.*

Pat-Kam School for Early Education

UNIONDALE

*705-707 Nassau Road, Uniondale, NY 11553. 516-486-7887;
Fax 516-483-3879; E-mail PatKam705@aol.com;
Web Site www.pat-kamschool.com*

PAT-KAM SCHOOL FOR EARLY EDUCATION in Uniondale, New York, is a comprehensive, private day school enrolling 250 boys and girls in a variety of programs. These programs include special accommodations for gifted students that enable them to study at a faster pace, before- and after-school sessions and summer school for academic enrichment, all of which provide year-round learning and enrichment for the children who come to Pat-Kam from diverse backgrounds.

The Early Childhood Center serves students who are three and four years old, while the Elementary School enrolls students from Kindergarten through Grade 5.

Ron Clahar and his wife, Geraldine, founded Pat-Kam School for Early Education in 1979, primarily because they were dissatisfied with the education their own young daughter was receiving. Patricia recently graduated from Harvard University with a degree in Biochemistry, and Kamilah is a high school senior. Both daughters graduated from Pat-Kam, and they are the inspiration for founding the School. Pat-Kam's motto, "Because the End Depends on the Beginning," continues to shape the program, with parents expected to support the School's philosophy at home. Recognizing that a child's academic performance in upper school is largely dependent on early childhood teaching and learning experiences, Pat-Kam's faculty strives to create a nurturing learning environment to encourage children to grow academically, socially, emotionally, and physically. The School promotes a heterogeneous classroom climate where students of all abilities learn together with accelerated and more advanced learners in the same class. Accelerated students may also be promoted to the next grade level if they need more academic challenge than their regular class is able to provide. Pat-Kam School is approved by the New York State Education Department. The Early Childhood Center is licensed by the New York State Department of Social Services.

THE CAMPUS. Pat-Kam School for Early Education recently completed an expansion and renovation of its campus. Improvements to the School include a state-of-the-art computer laboratory, a science lab, and two additional classrooms. The computer lab is open from 7:00 A.M. until 6:00 P.M., Monday through Friday. Pat-Kam is also equipped with a Little Theater. The children may perform plays, skits, and musical programs, all of which help to build self-confidence and esteem. Many skits and plays are developed with the help of teachers, parents, and volunteers from local high schools and colleges.

THE FACULTY. Ron Clahar is Director/Principal of Pat-Kam School for Early Education. He has a B.S. from Hunter College of the City University of New York and an M.A. in Educational Administration from Teachers College, Columbia University. Mr. Clahar is currently pursuing a Doctorate in Educational Administration at Columbia. Geraldine Clahar, C.P.A., is the School's Business Manager. She has a B.B.A. from Baruch College of the City University of New York and an M.B.A. from St. John's University.

The teaching faculty consists of New York State certified and college trained individuals experienced in teaching and training young children. They are supported by a staff of teacher's assistants and volunteers who have or are pursuing college degrees.

STUDENT BODY. Pat-Kam has an enrollment capacity of 250 students in its Elementary and Early Childhood Program. Recognizing that a great deal of learning occurs through interaction with people from differing ethnic, cultural, and social backgrounds, Pat-Kam promotes diversity among its student body. Children who attend other schools are welcome to enroll in Pat-Kam's before- and after-school programs.

ACADEMIC PROGRAM. Pat-Kam School for Early Education aims to provide a high-quality and affordable education. In keeping with the statement by the School's founder that "Children will gravitate toward expectations," all students are expected to be successful in their academic pursuits.

Students are promoted based on their academic performance, and may be moved ahead to the next level regardless of chronological age. Conversational Spanish is introduced in Pre-Kindergarten. All children from Pre-Kindergarten through Grade 5 participate in the Computer Science Program, becoming progressively proficient at keyboarding, desktop publishing, word processing, and Internet skills. In keeping with the saying that "Reading is the key to all knowledge," the School promotes an eclectic approach to reading, where both whole language and phonetic techniques are used enabling students to develop a proficiency in reading comprehension and decoding skills.

As a private non-sectarian School, religion is not part of Pat-Kam's curriculum. However, morality is taught using The Bible, Aesop's Fables and other resources. Students may read such Bible stories as Saul and the Amelikites (obedience), The Good Samaritan (compassion), The Widow and the Judge (persistence), Joseph and his Brothers (jealousy and forgiveness), and Achan and the Babylonian Garment (greed).

Swimming is an essential component of the School's physical education program. During the summer months, all children from Pre-Kindergarten through Grade 5 are required to participate in the American Red Cross Swimming Instruction Program levels 1–6. Additional physical activities include social dancing, track and field, soccer, table tennis, basketball, and other playground activities that promote development of gross motor skills.

Parental involvement is strongly encouraged. Upon enrollment, parents must agree to work cooperatively with the School to educate their children. Beginning in Kindergarten, all children wear uniforms. Uniforms for younger students are optional.

Pat-Kam operates year round, with closings for public holidays and a summer break the last week of August.

STUDENT ACTIVITIES. Field trips play an integral role in the cultural development and enrichment of Pat-Kam's students. Frequent visits are made to such places as Children's Museum, DNA Laboratory, the Cradle of Aviation, Westbury Music Fair, Old Bethpage Village Restoration, Green Meadows Farm, Fish Hatchery, Garvies Point, Safety Town, and Theodore Roosevelt Wildlife Sanctuary.

ADMISSION AND COSTS. Students may enroll at any time during the year. Both parent and child are interviewed as part of the enrollment process. In addition, students are given an admission test to ensure appropriate academic placement. There is a one-time registration fee of $40 for each child enrolled.

Tuition for 1999–2000 is $5760 for Nursery–Kindergarten, and $5000 for children in Grades 1–5. Financial aid is available for qualifying families. There are tuition discounts for additional children enrolled from the same family.

Curriculum Coordinator: Ms. Cynthia Foggie
Before- and After-School/Summer Camp Coordinators:
  Mr. Artise Todd, Ms. Agnes Ntiri

Poly Prep Country Day School   1854

Upper/Middle School: 9216 Seventh Avenue, Brooklyn, NY 11228.
  718-836-9800; Fax 718-238-3393;
  Web Site polyprep.brooklyn.ny.us
Lower School: 50 Prospect Park West, Brooklyn, NY 11215.
  718-768-1103; Fax 718-768-7890

Poly Prep Country Day, enrolling 850 students in Nursery–Grade 12 on two campuses, offers a rigorous, humanistic academic program that meets the needs of the whole child at every stage of development. The Lower School, located in historic Park Slope, seeks to balance intellectual development with important social and emotional growth. The Middle and Upper schools, on a 25-acre campus, emphasize rigorous college preparation including Advanced Placement in 15 subjects,

independent study, and extracurriculars such as athletics, performing and fine arts, and interest clubs. Tuition: $5500–$17,400. Financial Aid: $2,279,469. Lori W. Redell is Director of Admissions; William M. Williams is Headmaster; Maureen Walsh Heffernan is Head of Lower School. *Middle States Association.*

Portledge School   1965

Duck Pond Road, Locust Valley, NY 11560. 516-671-1475;
  Fax 516-671-2039; Web Site www.portledge.org

A college preparatory day school on a 60-acre campus, Portledge enrolls 390 boys and girls in Pre-Nursery–Grade 12. The Lower School features computers and French from Kindergarten, lab science from Grade 1, ability grouping in English and math, and programs in the arts and physical education. These programs continue in the Middle School, leading to a demanding curriculum and Advanced Placement courses in the Upper School. There is an extensive interscholastic sports program in Grades 6–12 and a dress code. All buildings are accessible to the physically challenged. Tuition: $5500–$16,500. Financial Aid: $630,000. Elisabeth D. Mooney is Director of Admissions; Huson R. Gregory (Dartmouth, A.B. 1962; Rutgers, M.Ed. 1970) was appointed Headmaster in 1977. *Middle States Association.*

Poughkeepsie Day School   1934

140 Boardman Road, Poughkeepsie, NY 12603. 914-462-7600;
  Fax 914-462-7603; E-mail jill@poughkeepsieday.org;
  Web Site www.poughkeepsieday.org

Founded by parents and Vassar College faculty, Poughkeepsie Day enrolls 325 students. It emphasizes a hands-on, process-oriented approach to learning that encourages independent, critical, and creative thinking. The academic curriculum, tailored to the needs of the individual student, integrates the arts at all levels. Seniors must complete a four-week, off-campus internship program as well as four years of every academic subject. Community service is required; sports and varied cocurricular activities are offered. One hundred percent of graduates are admitted to college each year. Tuition: $9500–$11,700. Financial aid is available. Jill Lundquist, M.S.W., is Director of Admissions; Anthony Buccelli (Southern Connecticut State, B.A.; University of Massachusetts [Amherst], M.Ed.) is Director.

Professional Children's School   1914

132 West 60th Street, New York, NY 10023. 212-582-3116;
  Fax 212-307-6542; E-mail profchilds@aol.com;
  Web Site http://www.pcs-nyc.org

Professional Children's School aims to serve the unique academic needs of students training for and participating in careers in the arts and other diverse fields. Enrolling 200 students in Grades 4–12, the School offers a rigorous college preparatory education. A flexible schedule permits students to attend classes and fulfill their academic requirements while pursuing their chosen artistic or athletic interest. Guided Study provides additional flexibility for students who are away from school due to valid outside obligations. A full-time learning specialist is on staff. English as a Second Language is available. Tuition/Fees: $14,200–$19,000. Financial Aid: $330,000. Sherrie A. Hinkle is Director of Admissions; James Dawson (State University of New York, Ph.D. 1982) is Head of School.

Rippowam Cisqua School   1917

Box 488, Bedford, NY 10506. Cisqua Campus (JPK–4):
325 West Patent Road, Mount Kisco, NY 10549. 914-666-5156;
Fax 914-666-2339; E-mail Elizabeth_Skudder@rcs.lhric.org
Rippowam Campus (5–9): 439 Cantitoe Road, Bedford, NY 10506.
914-234-3674; Fax 914-234-6751;
E-mail Ashley_Harrington@rcs.lhric.org

A family-oriented, country day school, Rippowam Cisqua School enrolls approximately 585 students in Junior Prekindergarten–Grade 9. Teacher-student interaction is at the heart of the RCS educational program, which emphasizes academic excellence, personal success, and the development of students who are confident and committed to a lifetime of learning. Arts, community service, and sports are part of the challenging, traditional curriculum, and active, hands-on learning is stressed at all levels. Tuition: $11,200–$17,350. Financial Aid: $1,100,000. Eileen Lambert, previously Head of the Rippowam Campus, was appointed Head of School in 1999.

Riverdale Country School   RIVERDALE

5250 Fieldston Road, Riverdale, NY 10471-2999. 718-549-8810;
Fax 718-519-2795; Web Site www.riverdale.edu

Riverdale country school in Riverdale, New York, is an independent, college preparatory day school enrolling students in Pre-Kindergarten–Grade 12. It is located on two spacious, wooded campuses one mile apart in the northwestern corner of New York City known as Riverdale. The country setting within a short distance of the vast cultural and educational resources of one of the world's great cities provides a wide range of learning and enrichment experiences that extend beyond the boundaries of the physical plant.

The present-day institution traces its origins to The Riverdale School for Boys, which was established in 1907 by Frank Sutliff Hackett. Mr. Hackett shared a deep commitment to "scholarly, intimate teaching; rigorous, uncompromising academic standards; abundant play in the open; and a care for the best influences." In 1920, the Neighborhood Elementary School was founded, followed in 1933 by the Riverdale Girls School. In 1972, the three schools combined to form a single educational community shaped by these same goals and ideals. Riverdale Country School aims to cultivate the unique talents of its students and to nurture their intellectual, creative, physical, moral, emotional, and social development.

A nonprofit, nondenominational institution, Riverdale Country School is governed by a 28-member Board of Trustees. It is chartered by the New York State Board of Regents and accredited by the New York State Association of Independent Schools. The Parents Association and the Alumni Association assist Riverdale through fund-raising, recruitment, and other activities. Riverdale Country School is a member of the National Association of Independent Schools, among other professional affiliations.

THE CAMPUS. With the purchase of an additional 7.5 contiguous acres of land in Riverdale in 1997, Riverdale Country School became the largest independent school campus in New York City with a total of 27.5 acres. The 19.5-acre Upper School Hill Campus for Grades 7–12 is located between the Henry Hudson Parkway and Van Cortlandt Park at the junction of Fieldston Road and West 253rd Street. Hill Campus buildings include the William C.W. Mow Hall, with administrative offices, classrooms, music rooms, and the dining room; Hackett Hall, containing the 21,000-volume Roger Brett Boocock Library and the Dale E. Mayo Computer Laboratory with 18 workstations, art studios, and classrooms; the Marc A. Zambetti '80 Athletic Center, which contains a state-of-the-art fitness center, an athletic training room, a basketball/volleyball court, and an Olympic-size swimming pool; the Weinstein Science Center, which houses the new Jan Falk Carpenter '71 Science Technology Center equipped with scientific computer workstations, laboratories, and a Sony Video Instruction Laboratory; the 9/10 Building, providing classrooms and a computer laboratory; the new Linda M. Lindenbaum Center for the Arts; and the newly renovated Theater/Auditorium. Other athletic facilities include two playing fields and eight tennis courts.

The 8-acre River Campus for Pre-Kindergarten–Grade 6, bordered by the Hudson River and Independence Avenue, is adjacent to Wave Hill Park and Nature Center, which is often used as a resource for the School. The Lower School is comprised of four separate buildings. The Junior Building houses the Admission Office, dining room, computer laboratory, general music room, and two strings rooms. The Perkins Building holds classrooms for Grades 4–6 and Pre-Kindergarten, the computerized library with more than 5000 volumes, and the Perkins Theatre. The Senior Building houses art studios, band and chorus rooms, a foreign language laboratory, and Support Services specialists. The K–3 Building (1994) provides classrooms and the gymnasium with a stage used for theatrical productions. Classes use the campus itself as part of the learning process, and children can explore the beautiful wetlands and participate in ecology and gardening projects.

THE FACULTY. John R. Johnson, Ph.D., assumed his duties as Riverdale's fifth Headmaster in July 1997. Dr. Johnson holds A.B., M.A., and doctoral degrees from the University of California at Los Angeles, where he was a member of Phi Beta Kappa. He had previously been Headmaster, first of the St. Louis Country Day School and then of Mary Institute and St. Louis Country Day School when he led the merger of the two schools. He was also Director of Studies at Harvard School in Los Angeles and, immediately preceding his appointment at Riverdale, he directed the Summer Sessions at UCLA.

Riverdale's faculty is comprised of 159 teachers and administrators, of whom 92 hold advanced degrees, including 11 doctorates and 81 master's degrees. The average class size in the Upper School is 16, and the student-teacher ratio is less than 8:1.

STUDENT BODY. In 1999–2000, Riverdale Country School enrolls 527 boys and 513 girls in Pre-Kindergarten–Grade 12. The Lower School has 410 students, and the Upper School has 630. Students reside in the immediate Riverdale area as well as Manhattan, the Bronx, Westchester, New Jersey, and Connecticut. The families of about 12 percent of the students have come from other countries, and approximately 16 percent of the students are of color.

ACADEMIC PROGRAM. The school year, from early September to mid-June, includes vacations at Thanksgiving, at the winter holidays in December, and in March, and the School closes for several national and religious holidays. The Upper School year is divided into quarters. Grades are sent home at the end of each quarter, and teacher reports accompany grades at the end of the first and third quarters. The Lower School year is divided into semesters with parent/teacher conferences in the fall and spring and written teacher reports sent home in November, January, and June.

The curriculum in the early childhood program is designed to develop basic academic concepts and social skills. Field trips, creative play, and hands-on activities in a warm, nurturing environment help the youngest students gain an early enthusiasm for learning. Math and reading readiness skills, nature study, and introduction to computers are integrated into the program, which also includes music, art, and library activities.

In Grades 1–6, a strong, sequential approach to skill development in reading and math is balanced with literature, writing, and math problem-solving. In preparation for the increased challenges of the Upper School academic program, students are trained in textual analysis, revising and editing their writing, and in research skills. All Lower School students engage in a major research project, "The Concrete Garden," for which they prepare a paper on a New York City landmark. Along with the core subjects of language arts, mathematics, science, and social studies, the academic program is enriched with offerings in computer technology, the arts, physical education, and library skills. Students are introduced to French and Spanish in Grades 3 and 4, after which they choose one for further study from Grade 5 upward. Latin is also offered to students in Grade 6. Community service is an important part of sixth-grade life, and all sixth graders participate in a service project, including working with younger students or helping in the infirmary or library. A Support Services team, comprised of a learning specialist, a reading and mathematics specialist, and a psychologist, works with teachers, students, and parents to pilot each child's progress in the Lower School. The Lower School also has an ethics and values program (C.A.R.E.), which is integral to the curriculum and the community.

The Upper School is fully departmentalized. Grades 7 and 8 are based in Hackett Hall under the supervision of their own Dean of Students. The college preparatory curriculum emphasizes the core disciplines, and students begin or continue the study of French, Latin, Spanish, or Japanese. A variety of options is available in vocal and instrumental groups, studio art, drama, and ceramics. Seventh- and eighth-grade students are required to complete ten hours of community service each year.

To earn a high school diploma, students in Grades 9–12 must complete 4 credits in English; 3 credits in a single foreign language or 2 credits in each of two languages; $2\frac{1}{2}$ in history; $2\frac{1}{2}$ to $3\frac{1}{2}$ in mathematics; 2 in science; and $1\frac{1}{2}$ in the arts. Seniors must also earn 1 credit in Integrated Liberal Studies, which features social philosophy, literature, history of science, and arts components. Students in each grade have a Dean of Students who coordinates their academic programs and serves as a liaison between parents and school. Students in Grades 9–12 must complete 72 hours of community service before graduation.

In addition to core subjects, the Upper School features numerous elective courses, including honors courses in the language, mathematics, and science departments and Advanced Placement courses in all disciplines. Other electives include Masterpieces of Western Literature, Shakespeare, World Religions in History and Literature, Economics, Psychology, Environmental Science, and Race, Class and Ethnicity in New York City. Qualified juniors and seniors may earn credit for independent study. Opportunities also exist for semester or yearlong study abroad.

The 99 graduates in the Class of 1999 entered four-year colleges and universities. Six matriculated at George Washington University; 5 at the University of Pennsylvania; 4 each at Brown, Duke, New York University, Tufts, Washington University (St. Louis), and Yale; and 3 each at Emory, Skidmore, and the Universities of Rochester and Vermont.

STUDENT ACTIVITIES. Upper School students elect representatives to the Student-Faculty Council, which helps establish principles and procedures for student life and serves as a conduit of student opinion. In the Lower School, Student Council members are elected by their peers beginning in Grade 4. Each year, the Lower School Student Council supervises a charity outreach program entitled "Children Helping Children." Field trips enrich the program at all levels. Overnight excursions are offered in Grades 4–12 ranging from one night to one week.

Upper School activities vary in response to student interest. Among the organized groups on campus are Amnesty International, Environmental Club, Model Congress, Mock Trial, SADD, the literary magazine, the school newspaper, and the yearbook. Students regularly stage plays and musicals and perform in orchestra, jazz band, chamber ensembles, two a cappella groups, and chorus. Interscholastic and intramural teams are fielded in baseball, basketball, fencing, field hockey, football, gymnastics, lacrosse, soccer, softball, swimming, tennis, track, cross-country, volleyball, and wrestling.

ADMISSION AND COSTS. Riverdale Country School welcomes students of strong academic ability and good character. Admission is based on the applicant's academic record, teacher recommendations, an entrance examination, a writing sample, and a personal interview. The greatest number of students enter in Kindergarten, Grade 7, and Grade 9, but candidates are admitted through Grade 11 if vacancies exist.

Tuition for 1999–2000 ranges from $17,350 in Pre-Kindergarten to $20,100 in Grades 7–12. The School awards financial aid grants to approximately 18 percent of the student body based on need. Tuition payment plans are available.

Associate Headmaster: Sorrel R. Paskin
Director of Studies: William H. Pahlka
Head of Upper School: Kent J. Kildahl
Head of the Lower School: Sandy S. Shaller
Director of Admission: Ann B. Woodward
Director of Lower School Admission: Grace Ball
Director of Development: Peni Weinstein
Director of College Office: Kristi H. Marshall
Director of Finance and Operations: Kathleen A. Schoonmaker

Robert Louis Stevenson School   1908

24 West 74th Street, New York, NY 10023. 212-787-6400;
Fax 212-873-1872

Enrolling 75 boys and girls in Grade 7–Postgraduate, Robert Louis Stevenson School aims to enable troubled adolescents who have not achieved their potential to succeed academically and personally. The "community within a community" environment emphasizes mutual respect and acceptance of all students, with a college preparatory program that focuses on the mastery of solid language and study skills and the achievement of realistic goals. Honors sections, independent study, remediation, courses for the gifted, and an academic summer session are offered. Tuition: $22,500. Financial Aid: $65,000. B.H. Henrichsen is Headmaster.

The Rockland Country Day School   1959

34 Kings Highway, Congers, NY 10920. 914-268-6802;
Fax 914-268-4644; E-mail rcds@bestweb.net;
Web Site www.rocklandcds.org

The Rockland Country Day School is an independent college preparatory school enrolling 177 boys and girls in Pre-School–Grade 12. The School seeks to provide a rigorous academic program in a student-centered environment. Classes are small and emphasize intellectual depth and the development of superior critical reading and writing skills. Students perform volunteer work in the community. Off-campus programs during the fall afford Middle and Upper School students the opportunity to explore the history and architecture of great American cities. Tuition: $8400–$15,650. Ellen Warner is Admissions Coordinator; Anthony B. Fruhauf (Brown University, B.A.; Harvard University, M.B.A.) was appointed Headmaster in 1995.

Rudolf Steiner School   1928

Lower School: 15 East 79th Street, New York, NY 10021.
212-535-2130; Admissions 212-327-1457; Fax 212-744-4497
Upper School: 15 East 78th Street, New York, NY 10021.
212-327-1457

Enrolling 295 day students in Nursery–Grade 12, the Rudolf Steiner School believes that "education is an art." In each ele-

mentary school subject, presentations aim to speak to the students' experience, providing vivid images and allowing them to take part in what they hear. Special lessons in German, Spanish, music, and handwork begin in Grade 1 and are enriched by a sports program. In addition to a strong college preparatory curriculum, the high school offers exchange programs in Europe and provides opportunities in art, music, practical skills, community service, and interscholastic sports. The School is one of 600 Waldorf or Steiner schools worldwide. Tuition: $10,000–$16,000. Scholarships: $500,000. Lucy Schneider (Vassar, B.A.) is Faculty Chairperson.

Rye Country Day School   R Y E

Boston Post Road at Cedar Street, Rye, NY 10580. 914-967-1417;
Fax 914-967-1418; E-mail rcds.rye.ny.us; Web Site www.rcds.rye.ny.us

RYE COUNTRY DAY SCHOOL in Rye, New York, is a coeducational day school enrolling students in Pre-Kindergarten through Grade 12. Rye (population 18,000), a Westchester County suburb of New York City, is 45 minutes from the city by train and is easily accessible by car and public transportation from other communities in Westchester and Rockland counties and Fairfield County in Connecticut.

The School was founded in 1869 as the Rye Female Seminary by local parents who wanted to provide better educational opportunities for their daughters. The 1921 merger with Rye Country School, an all-boys' institution, led to the formation of Rye Country Day School, which enrolled girls in Kindergarten–Grade 12 and boys through Grade 8 only. In 1964, the School became entirely coeducational.

Rye Country Day School seeks to provide a superior education that "should encompass cultural, athletic, and communal experiences that stress the responsibility of each individual for the life and spirit of the whole community, resulting in a graduate able to face the world with confidence, to compete effectively, and to contribute meaningfully to society."

Rye Country Day School is directed by a 23-member Board of Trustees, including parents and alumni. The Parents' Auxiliary contributes to school life through volunteer service and fund-raising activities, and the Alumni Association represents the 3000 active alumni. Rye Country Day School is accredited by the Middle States Association of Colleges and Schools and holds membership in the National Association of Independent Schools, among other affiliations.

THE CAMPUS. The 25-acre campus includes four athletic fields and two play areas. Indoor athletic facilities are located in the Gerald N. La Grange Field House, which contains an ice rink, four tennis courts, a pro shop, and locker rooms. A new two-court gymnasium with four squash courts and a fitness center is under construction.

Pre-Kindergarten is conducted in a new classroom addition to the Administration Building. The Main Building houses classrooms for Kindergarten–Grade 8, a computer center and laptop lab, four new science laboratories, three art studios, the dining room, and the nurse's office. The Pinkham Building contains classrooms for Grades 9–12, offices, four science laboratories, studios for art and photography, and a newly equipped computer center. An all-school library with classroom space connects the Main and Pinkham buildings. A 400-seat Performing Arts and Classroom Center includes a woodworking shop and music practice rooms. Other facilities are the Administration Building and the Headmaster's residence. The School-owned plant is valued at $25,000,000.

THE FACULTY. Scott A. Nelson, appointed Headmaster in 1993, is a graduate of Brown University (A.B. 1977) and Fordham University (M.S. 1989).

The full-time faculty, including administrators who teach, number 108. In addition to baccalaureate degrees, they hold 70 master's and 5 doctoral degrees, 2 or more of which were earned at Bank Street, Boston University, Bowdoin, Brown, Bucknell, College of New Rochelle, College of the Holy Cross, Columbia, Cornell, Dartmouth, Fordham, Harvard, Iona, Ithaca, Johns Hopkins, Lehigh, Manhattanville, Middlebury, Rollins, Smith, State University of New York, Syracuse, Trinity, Wesleyan, Yale, and the Universities of Bridgeport, Connecticut, New Hampshire, New York City (Brooklyn, Hunter, Queens), Virginia, and Washington. Faculty benefits include health, dental, life, and disability insurance; a retirement plan; and Social Security. There is a full-time school nurse, and a hospital is one-quarter mile distant.

STUDENT BODY. In 1999–2000, the School enrolls 418 boys and 375 girls as follows: 192 in the Lower School (Pre-Kindergarten–Grade 4), 272 in the Middle School (Grades 5–8), and 329 in the Upper School (Grades 9–12). Students come principally from Westchester County and Connecticut's Fairfield County, although Rockland County and New York City are also represented.

ACADEMIC PROGRAM. The school year, from early September to early June, includes Thanksgiving and midwinter recesses, winter and spring vacations, and national and religious holidays. The calendar is divided into semesters for the Lower, Middle, and Upper schools. Upper School classes, with an average enrollment of 15, generally meet five times in a six-day rotation from 8:05 A.M. to 2:50 P.M. Pre-Kindergarten is dismissed at noon; Kindergarten–Grade 4 meet from 8:05 A.M. to 3:05 P.M.; Middle School classes end at 3:20 P.M.

Supervised study halls are held throughout the day in the Upper School. Teachers are available to provide extra help at all grade levels. In the Middle School, progress reports are issued after the first six weeks of school; grades are recorded at mid-semester and semester end. Interim reports are sent home whenever necessary. In Kindergarten–Grade 4, parent-teacher conferences are scheduled in the fall and winter, and a written narrative report is provided in June. In the Middle and Upper schools, letter grades are issued twice each semester, with teacher comments accompanying the grades at semester's end. Progress reports are issued for new Upper School students after the first six weeks of school. Each Middle and Upper School student has a faculty adviser. In the 1999–2000 school year, the School implemented a required laptop program for all students in Grades 7–10.

The Lower School program fosters the acquisition of basic skills while learning how to think logically and creatively and manipulate symbols effectively. The program for Pre-Kindergarten emphasizes reading and mathematics readiness, communication skills, and science and social studies projects. The program in Kindergarten through Grade 4 is based in self-contained classrooms and focuses on reading, writing, mathematics, and social studies. Science, French, music, studio art, physical education, and library skills instruction are integral to the Lower School program. There are computers in all classrooms, and a computer lab, as well as eMates, are available to Lower School students. Developing effective communication skills and appropriate social behavior are important components of the Lower School experience.

Classes in the Middle School are departmentalized. Latin is introduced in Grade 5, and French and Spanish in Grade 6. At the seventh-grade level, students elect to study Latin, French, or Spanish. The equivalent of the first year of high school language study is completed by the end of Grade 8. Honors sections are available in mathematics. In Grades 7 and 8, art, vocal and instrumental music, ceramics, woodworking, drama, photography, and computer are offered as electives. All Middle School students have physical education classes. Middle School deans provide a regularly scheduled guidance program for Grades 5–8.

To graduate, students in Grades 9–12 must complete four years of English, three years of a foreign language, two years of history (including United States history), three years of mathematics, two years of science, and two semester-length elective units or one full-year elective course. Art and music are required in Grade 9 or 10, and physical education is required each year. An interdisciplinary lecture and seminar course for seniors is required.

Full-year Upper School courses include English 1–4; French 1–6, Greek 1–2, Latin 1–6, Spanish 1–5; World Civilization 1–2, United States History, Government, Modern European History, Humanism and the West: An Urban Perspective (an interdisciplinary course for seniors); Algebra 1–2, Advanced Algebra and Mathematical Analysis, Geometry, Calculus, Computer Programming 1–2; Physical Science, Biology, Chemistry, Physics; Studio Art 1–3, History of Art, Photography; and Music History, Choir, and Wind Ensemble. Among the partial-credit and semester electives are Advanced Geometry; Philosophy,

Broken Promises/Shattered Dreams: The African-American Experience 1860 to Present; Forensics; Oceanography; Psychology; Mechanical Drawing, Woodwork; Art Survey; and Concert Choir, Wind Ensemble, Jazz Ensemble, and Music Theory. The Drama Department offers elective courses in History of Theater, Film and Filmmaking, Acting Workshop, and Oral Interpretation and Public Speaking. In alternate years, English electives offered in Grade 12 concentrate on American and English literature.

There are honors classes in all disciplines, as well as 19 Advanced Placement courses. Independent study can be arranged in any academic area. Qualified juniors and seniors may receive credit for courses at local colleges. During the two-week June Term, students in Grade 12 participate in a service project.

In 1999, all 80 members of the graduating class entered four-year colleges; 19 students were admitted by "early decision." Two or more students are enrolled at Amherst, Boston University, Bucknell, Cornell, Georgetown, George Washington University, New York University, Rensselaer Polytechnic Institute, Rollins, Skidmore, Syracuse, Trinity, Tufts, Wesleyan, and the University of Vermont.

The School conducts a six-week review and enrichment summer session and offers tutorial work.

STUDENT ACTIVITIES. The Middle School Student Council, composed of elected representatives from Grades 5 through 8, provides a forum for discussions of school issues and is responsible for implementing social activities. In the Upper School, elected student-faculty Academic Affairs, Activities, Guidance, and School Life committees meet regularly and make recommendations to the administration.

Middle School students publish their own newspaper, *The Middle Ages.* Upper School students publish a yearbook (*Echo*), a newspaper (*Rye Crop*), a current-events magazine (*FORUM*), a literary magazine (*Omega*), a sports magazine (*Topcat*). Other extracurricular organizations include the African-American Culture, Astronomy Club, Debate, Drama, Classics, Model United Nations, Community Action Organization, International Club, Chess, Macintosh User's Group, Peer Leaders, Modern Languages, Mock Trial, Spirit, Stock Market, Entrepreneurs', and Ecology clubs. The Upper School's musical organizations participate in county and state festivals. An active Upper School Community Service program involves more than 100 students as volunteers in area community agencies. The Middle School has its own community service activities as well as a chorus and wind ensemble; beginning in Grade 4, private instrumental lessons are available for all students.

Rye athletic teams compete with other independent schools in the Fairchester League. Interscholastic competition begins in Grade 7 with boys' teams organized in basketball, football, ice hockey, soccer, baseball, lacrosse, and tennis; girls compete in basketball, field hockey, softball, soccer, lacrosse, and tennis. There are boys' varsity and junior varsity teams in baseball, basketball, football, golf, hockey, lacrosse, soccer, and tennis; varsity and junior varsity girls' teams are organized in basketball, field hockey, golf, ice hockey, lacrosse, softball, soccer, and squash. There are also coeducational teams in cross-country and fencing. Physical education classes include intramural competition in various sports for Upper School students not on interscholastic teams, as well as fitness and aerobic exercise classes and a dance program.

Field trips complement the academic program at all grade levels; younger children visit area attractions such as the Rye Nature Center and The Bronx Zoo. Dances are scheduled for both the Middle and Upper schools. Traditional annual events include the week-long fall "wilderness" camping trip for Grade 8, the Pennsylvania trip in Grade 7, the Cape Cod trip in Grade 6, sports banquets, the Fall Fair, music festivals, and the invitational Model United Nations/Congress.

ADMISSION AND COSTS. New students are admitted to all grades, although rarely to Grade 12, on the basis of previous academic records, the results of standardized tests, and a personal interview. Application should be made in the fall or winter prior to September entrance. There is a $40 application fee.

In 1999–2000, tuition ranges from $10,875 in Pre-Kindergarten to $16,785 in Grades 11–12. Extras range from $235 in Kindergarten to $1000 in the Upper School. Tuition insurance is available. In 1998–99, the School awarded more than $1,100,000 in financial aid to 83 students. Rye Country Day subscribes to the School and Student Service for Financial Aid.

Assistant Headmaster & Director of Finance: William L. Buck
Director of Admissions: Siobhan O'Connell
Development and Alumni Relations: Virginia B. Rowen
College Counselor: Mary Ann Reichhardt
Director of Athletics: Frank Antonelli

Saint Ann's School 1965

129 Pierrepont Street, Brooklyn Heights, NY 11201. 718-522-1660; Fax 718-522-2599

Saint Ann's School is an independent, college preparatory day school enrolling 513 boys and 536 girls in Preschool–Grade 12. It seeks to create an urban alternative to traditional education with teachers and students using novel approaches to learning. Classes are grouped by ability and each student's schedule is individualized. A broad curriculum accommodates special subjects through the use of tutorials. Sports, publications, performing arts, and field trips are some of the activities. Tuition: $11,600–$17,000. Financial aid is available. Mary Russotti is Director of Admission; Stanley Bosworth (New York University, B.A. 1953, M.A. 1957) has served as Headmaster since the School's founding.

Saint Anthony's High School 1958

275 Wolf Hill Road, South Huntington, NY 11747-1394.
613-271-2020; Fax 613-351-1507;
E-mail 75017.3061@compuserve.com;
Web Site http://members.xoom.com/SAHSALUMNI

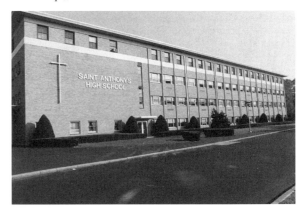

Operated by the Franciscan Brothers, Saint Anthony's is a Roman Catholic, college preparatory day school enrolling 2250 young men and women in Grades 9 through 12. The School works in partnership with parents to educate the whole person morally, physically, intellectually, and aesthetically. The traditional curriculum offers challenging courses in English, foreign languages, social studies, science, mathematics, theology, and the creative and visual arts. Student Council, four publications, numerous interscholastic sports, performing groups, Legion of Mary, SADD, and interest clubs are among the extracurricular activities. Tuition: $4600. Financial aid is available. Bro. Donan Conrad, OSF, is Director of Admissions; Bro. Shane Burke, OSF, Ed.D., is Principal. *Middle States Association.*

St. Bernard's School   1904

4 East 98th Street, New York, NY 10029. 212-289-2878;
Fax 212-410-6628

St. Bernard's School is a day school enrolling 390 boys in Kindergarten–Grade 9. It presents a curriculum to which it refers as "traditional but not hide-bound," emphasizing language, mathematics, and foundations for science and computer science. Instruction in music, art, and carpentry is offered. A literary magazine is published, and a Shakespearean play is presented annually. The School also makes ample use of the cultural resources of the city. Interscholastic and intramural sports are organized. Tuition: $16,600. Extras and Lunches: $2250. Financial aid is available. Stuart H. Johnson III (Yale, B.A.) was appointed Headmaster in 1985.

Saint David's School   1951

12 East 89th Street, New York, NY 10128. 212-369-0058;
Fax 212-289-2796

Saint David's is a day school with an enrollment of 370 boys in Pre-Kindergarten–Grade 8. The School seeks to engender intellectual curiosity, spiritual and moral development, appreciation for the arts, and skills and sportsmanship in athletics. A rigorous classical curriculum is offered within a nurturing environment. Art, music, and drama are an integral part of the program. Founded by a group of Catholic families, Saint David's now includes boys of all religious and ethnic backgrounds. The Sports Center is located a short distance from the School. Tuition: $9000–$18,500. Financial Aid: $425,000. Janet H. Sughrue and Julie B. Sykes are Admission Directors; Donald T. Maiocco (New Jersey Teachers College, B.A. 1961, M.A. 1964; Columbia, M.Ed. 1976, Ed.D. 1978) was appointed Headmaster in 1992.

Saint Francis Preparatory School   1858

6100 Francis Lewis Boulevard, Fresh Meadows, NY 11365.
718-423-8810; Fax 718-224-2108;
E-mail 21stcentury@stfrancisprep.org;
Web Site www.stfrancisprep.org

Founded by the Franciscan Brothers, this coeducational, Catholic school has been recognized by the U.S. Department of Education as a School of Excellence. More than 2800 students are enrolled in Grades 9–12. Although located in an urban setting, the campus borders on parkland, providing ample athletic fields. With the aim of developing critical, responsible seekers of truth, the School provides a comprehensive, Christian education within a nurturing environment. Advanced Placement, Honors, and Regents courses, combined with music, art, and computer programs and a 50,000-volume library, complement the religious foundation. Tuition: $4580. Ted Jahn is Dean of Men; Br. Leonard Conway, OSF (Pratt Institute, M.S.), is Principal. *Middle States Association.*

Saint Gregory's School   1962

121 Old Niskayuna Road, Loudonville, NY 12211. 518-785-6621;
Fax 518-782-1364; E-mail sgsfb@crisny.org

Saint Gregory's School was founded by parents to prepare their children for the challenges of competitive boarding schools and to instill in them the values and principles of the Roman Catholic faith. The School enrolls 200 day boys in Nursery–Grade 8. In addition to traditional academic subjects, computer science, Latin, and French are required. Music, drama, and athletics are strong components of the program. Recreational camps are conducted in the summer. Tuition: $1785–$7220. Financial Aid: $55,000. Francis X. Foley, Jr. (John Carroll, A.B.; Fairfield University, M.A.), was appointed Headmaster in 1999.

St. Hilda's & St. Hugh's School   1950

619 West 114th Street, New York, NY 10025. 212-932-1980;
Fax 212-749-7174; Web Site www.sthildas.org

St. Hilda's & St. Hugh's is a coeducational, Episcopal day school enrolling 290 students in Toddlers–Grade 8. The School reflects New York City's richly diverse community and values the Judeo-Christian heritage. A strong liberal arts curriculum readies students for leading secondary schools in New York City and nationwide. Development of individual aptitudes is encouraged. Studio Art is introduced in Junior Kindergarten; French and Spanish in Nursery; computer in Grade 2; woodworking, drama, and English brass band in Grade 4; Shakespeare in Grade 6; and Latin in Grade 7. Extended Day Program for Nursery–Grade 5 is offered until 6:30 P.M. Tuition: $3700–$15,700. Roxandra Antoniadis is Director of Admission; Virginia Connor (Wheelock, B.S.; Columbia Teachers College, M.A.) is Head of School.

St. Luke's School   1945

487 Hudson Street, New York, NY 10014. 212-924-5960;
Fax 212-924-1352

St. Luke's is an Episcopal day school enrolling 200 boys and girls of all faiths in Junior Kindergarten–Grade 8. The structured, rigorous curriculum promotes academic excellence and critical thinking built upon the solid basis of fundamental skills. Small by design, the School creates a climate of trust and understanding, communicating values and building community. The program includes science, computer, music, art, foreign language, physical and outdoor education, and sports. Chapel, comparative religion, and service learning are included. Its enclosed campus has spacious outdoor facilities. An After-School program is offered. Tuition: $14,830–$15,740. Financial Aid: $360,000. Susan Parker is Director of Admission; Ann Mellow (Middlebury, B.A.; Harvard, Ed.M.) is Head of School.

St. Thomas Choir School   NEW YORK

202 West 58th Street, New York, NY 10019-1406. 212-247-3311;
Fax 212-247-3393; E-mail weiser@choirschool.org;
Web Site www.choirschool.org

ST. THOMAS CHOIR SCHOOL in New York City is a boarding school for boys in Grades 4 through 8 who sing in the Choir of St. Thomas Church on Fifth Avenue. The School is located in the cultural center of Manhattan near Carnegie Hall, the Lincoln Center for the Performing Arts, and numerous museums. The School takes full advantage of New York City through field trips to museums, exhibitions, concerts, and cultural events.

The Choir School was established in 1919 under the direction of Dr. T. Tertius Noble, Organist and Choirmaster at St. Thomas Church. The only school of its kind in America, this academic institution offers extensive musical training and education within a liberal arts curriculum. The Headmaster, faculty, and staff of St. Thomas Choir School provide a warm, familial atmosphere in which the boys are encouraged to achieve their personal best, to learn from one another, and to become active and giving members of the Christian community.

According to its mission statement, "the world-renowned St. Thomas Choir School houses, educates, and nurtures its boy Choristers through superior musical, academic, and Christian foundations that benefit the Church and School and enable its students to embrace life with hope, skill, and confidence."

The Choir School is owned by St. Thomas Church and directed by a Board of Trustees consisting of the Rector, Wardens, and Vestry of the Church. The operation of the School is supervised by the Choir School Committee.

The Choir School is accredited by the New York State Association of Independent Schools. It holds membership in the National Association of Independent Schools, the National Association of Episcopal Schools, the Educational Records Bureau, the Parents League of New York, and the Council for Religion in Independent Schools.

THE CAMPUS. The 15-story academic and residence building serves as a home for the boys, faculty members and their families, and the household staff. The building contains a library, classrooms, chapel, hobby room, recreation room, science and computer laboratories, piano practice rooms, a gymnasium-auditorium, and a rehearsal stage.

Although the Choir School is located in the city, outdoor activities are emphasized. For one week in the spring, the entire School moves to Incarnation Camp in Ivoryton, Connecticut, utilizing the camp's 600 acres and private lake. Throughout the year, students enjoy recreational and organized sports in the spacious setting of Central Park, which is located one block away.

THE FACULTY. Gordon Roland-Adams joined the Choir School as Headmaster in the fall of 1997. He had formerly served for 10 years as Headmaster of the Westminster Abbey Choir School in London, England, and has a longstanding reputation in the United Kingdom and throughout Europe for his direction of choir schools. Dr. Gregory Blackburn is the Assistant Head in charge of the academic program. He has worked in independent schools for the past 18 years as teacher, division head, and assistant head.

Dr. Gerre Hancock has trained and conducted the St. Thomas Choir of Men and Boys for 28 years. Under his direction, the Choir has become recognized as a world-class ensemble and a leading exponent of Anglican choral music in the United States. Dr. Hancock is assisted in the overall musical training of the students by Judith Hancock, Associate Choirmaster.

The faculty includes ten full-time teachers, the Headmaster, the Choirmaster, two full-time houseparents, and a school nurse, all of whom live at the School. They hold 14 baccalaureate degrees and 9 master's degrees from the College of the Holy Cross, College of William and Mary, Denison, Duke, Harvard, Hendrix College, Indiana University, New York University, State University of New York, and the Universities of Arkansas, Connecticut, Durham, London, Minnesota, Texas, and Virginia. The Choirmaster holds 2 honorary doctorates in music.

There are also 15 part-time instructors who teach art, athletics, piano, flute, cello, trumpet, trombone, guitar, violin, music theory, and theology. A psychologist and therapist serve the School on a part-time basis. Faculty benefits include medical insurance, a retirement plan, and Social Security.

The infirmary, supervised by a registered nurse, provides facilities for minor illnesses. School physicians and St. Luke's Hospital are available for emergencies.

STUDENT BODY. The School enrolls 40 boys, 8 to 14 years of age. They come from throughout the United States and abroad.

ACADEMIC PROGRAM. The school year, from mid-September to early June, includes four vacation periods—before Thanksgiving, after Christmas, before Lent, and after Easter.

The curriculum includes required courses in English, geography, French, Latin, Great Books, American history, ancient history, mathematics, science, music theory, art, theology, a musical instrument, and Choir. Optional or elective courses are offered in photography, woodworking, and drama. An average class size of eight students ensures each boy individual attention. Marks are sent to parents four times yearly.

Classical Anglican theology and traditional Episcopal Church practice define the religious atmosphere at St. Thomas Choir School. All grades include a theology class taught by St. Thomas clergy, and, in Grade 6, preparation for Confirmation is offered each year. In addition to the Headmaster and his staff, the Rector and other clergy, including the School Chaplain, are available to students and their parents for pastoral matters. Christian faith and morals are the foundation of the efforts of the Church and Choir School to be a safe, caring, and nurturing community. Within this setting, the beliefs of other churches and other religious faiths are respected.

Graduates leave the Choir School prepared to succeed at many of the finest preparatory schools in the country. Recent graduates have been accepted at Brooks School, Choate Rosemary Hall, Exeter High School, Greens Farms Academy, Loomis Chaffee, New Canaan High School, St. Mark's, Stony Brook, and Trinity-Pawling School.

STUDENT ACTIVITIES. Religious and musical activities are important parts of the daily program. The Choir rehearses for 90 minutes each day and sings at six church services per week. In addition, the boys perform in a regular concert series, accompanied by a full orchestra. They have appeared on television, at Lincoln Center, and at Carnegie Hall, performing with the Cleveland, Pittsburgh, New York, and American Symphony orchestras.

The Choir regularly embarks on concert tours of American cities and has performed at festivals in the United Kingdom, Ireland, Italy, and Austria. In addition, the Choir is involved with several recordings. The Choir performed with opera star Jessye Norman for the recording *In the Spirit*, a rich collection of traditional Christmas music. The Choristers have also appeared with opera star Placido Domingo in the premiere of Sir Andrew Lloyd Webber's *Requiem* and with artists Judy Collins, Leontyne Price, and Carly Simon for various recordings.

Athletics are a part of every school day, and all boys play on a sports team. There is interscholastic competition in soccer, basketball, and softball.

Throughout the year, the School schedules outings, dinners, and parties for Choir families and their sons. Traditional events include a Parent-Son Outing, a Parent-Son Dinner, and Fathers' Weekend at Camp Incarnation.

ADMISSION AND COSTS. The Choir School seeks well-adjusted boys who may or may not have had previous musical training but who do have trainable soprano voices. New Choristers are accepted only in Grade 4 on the basis of vocal aptitude, scholastic ability, and probable adaptability. The first step in the admissions process is the vocal audition with the Choirmaster. Academic and intelligence tests are then administered by the School's testing specialist. Students may be accepted throughout the year; however, it is in a family's best interest to apply early as spaces are limited.

Income from an endowment of approximately $18,000,000 and annual gifts fund the major portion of the School's expenses. While the annual costs exceed $48,000 per pupil, tuition and board are only $9500. The School furnishes most textbooks, but parents are responsible for clothing and transportation. The Choir School subscribes to the School and Student Service for Financial Aid. Financial aid in excess of $100,000 is available to assist qualified families.

Rector: The Reverend Andrew C. Mead
Head: Gordon Roland-Adams
Choirmaster: Dr. Gerre Hancock
Assistant Head: Dr. Gregory B. Blackburn
Director of Administration: James E. Marlow
Director of Admission, Alumni Affairs & Development: Kate Weiser
Administrative Assistant: Anne Mironchik

Soundview Preparatory School   1989

272 North Bedford Road, Mount Kisco, NY 10549. 914-242-9693; Fax 914-242-9658

Enrolling 65 day students in Grade 6–Postgraduate, Soundview was founded by parents to provide an academic program that promotes self-esteem by enabling students to develop their unique talents. Small, ability-grouped classes allow dialogue and participation by all students. The School aims to establish ethical values, formulate and meet individual goals, and encourage students to be their own advocates. Students enjoy close relationships with teachers and respond to a structured, yet relaxed

environment. Core courses are complemented by an extensive fine arts program, debate, publications, and basketball. A summer program is available. Tuition: $15,500–$17,500. Financial Aid: $125,000. Mary Ivanyi is Admissions Director; W. Glyn Hearn (University of Texas, B.A.; Texas Tech, M.A.) is Headmaster.

School of the Holy Child   1904

2225 Westchester Avenue, Rye, NY 10580. 914-967-5622; Fax 914-967-6476; E-mail e.bracchitta@holychild.pvt.k12.ny.us; Web Site www.holychild.pvt.k12.ny.us

School of the Holy Child, an independent Catholic school founded in 1904, offers a college preparatory curriculum in an environment of Christian values. Enrolling 278 girls in Grades 5–12, the School offers Advanced Placement courses in ten subjects, numerous electives, arts, athletics, community service, and varied clubs and activities. Seniors participate in a two-week independent study project, and all graduates go on to college. Study exchanges are available with other Holy Child schools throughout the country and abroad. Tuition: $12,000; Fees $550. Financial aid, scholarships, and payment plans are available. Emily Walker Bracchitta is Director of Admission; Ann F. Sullivan (Good Counsel College, B.A.; New York University, M.A.) is Head of School. *Middle States Association.*

The Spence School   1892

22 East 91st Street, New York, NY 10128. 212-289-5940; Fax 212-534-0118

The Spence School is an independent, college preparatory day school enrolling 594 girls in Kindergarten through Grade 12. Founded by Clara B. Spence, the School is committed to maintaining high academic standards, promoting diversity and teaching the basic human values of honesty and concern for others. Spence is a small, supportive community that challenges each student to reach her full potential in an atmosphere that fosters self-confidence and a spirit of cooperation. Tuition: $16,190–$17,510. Financial Aid: $1,275,000. Penual P. Allan is Director of Admission; Arlene J. Gibson (Bryn Mawr College, B.A.; Georgetown University, M.A.) was appointed Head of School in 1998.

Staten Island Academy   1884

715 Todt Hill Road, Staten Island, NY 10304-1357. 718-987-8100; Fax 718-979-7641

Staten Island Academy is a college preparatory day school enrolling 475 boys and girls in Pre-Kindergarten–Grade 12. Accelerated programs, honors, and Advanced Placement courses are available. The Upper School requires four years of English and three years each of foreign languages, mathematics, history, and science. Fine arts, computer studies, study skills, and public speaking are also graduation requirements. Students participate in sports, drama, music, service organizations, publications, and student government. A complete summer program is available. Tuition: $6550–$13,650. Financial Aid: $800,000. Tonya Drewniak is Admission Director; Mr. Carmen M. Marnell (Columbia College, B.A.; University of Scranton, M.S.) was appointed Headmaster in 1996. *Middle States Association.*

The Stony Brook School   1922

1 Chapman Parkway, Stony Brook, NY 11790. 516-751-1800; Fax 516-751-4211; E-mail admissions@stonybrookschool.org; Web Site www.stonybrookschool.org

The Stony Brook School, enrolling 350 boarding and day boys and girls in Grades 7–12, offers a rigorous college preparatory program that combines traditional academics with competitive athletics, training in the arts, and focus on character development. Students come from 14 states and 12 countries. Chapel meets daily, and Bible classes are integrated into the curriculum. Advanced Placement courses in 13 subject areas and English as a Second Language are also offered. Cocurricular activities include HEART (community service), FOCUS (Christian fellowship), UDT (diversity), Art Guild, Theatrical Arts Society, and 22 athletic teams. Boarding Tuition: $15,540–$21,100; Day Tuition: $8,225–$13,325. Jane Taylor is Admissions Director; Robert E. Gustafson, Jr., was appointed Headmaster in 1997. *Middle States Association.*

Storm King School   1867

Mountain Road, Cornwall-on-Hudson, NY 12520-1899. 914-534-7892; Admissions 914-534-9860; Fax 914-534-4128

A coeducational college preparatory school, Storm King enrolls 107 boarders and 18 day students in Grades 9–12. It seeks to provide a stimulating academic program that encourages students to build on strengths and overcome weaknesses within a caring community. A variety of electives supplements the core program of traditional courses, and a Learning Center provides individual support. Activities include dramatic productions, publications, honor societies, sports, and a wilderness program. Boarding Tuition: $24,000; Day Tuition: $13,300. Financial Aid: $400,000. Peter C. Wicker is Associate Headmaster/ Director of Admissions; Philip D. Riley (United States Military Academy, B.A.; University of North Carolina, M.A.) was appointed Headmaster in 1997. *Middle States Association.*

The Susquehanna School at South Bridge   1970

75 Pennsylvania Avenue, Binghamton, NY 13903. 607-723-5797; E-mail Tss@stny.lrun.com; Web Site www.tier.net/TSS

The Susquehanna School is an independent, nonsectarian school, founded in 1970, enrolling 72 students from Early Childhood through Middle School. The School provides a challenging intellectual environment, giving each student individual attention and nurturing a sense of self-worth, self-esteem, and confidence. Classes are multiaged; students are grouped according to developmental level as well as chronological ages. Assessment is by portfolio. A summer arts camp is offered. Tuition: $6800. Extras: $400. Financial Aid: $60,000. Nancy Ziegenhagen is Director.

The Town School   1913

540 East 76th Street, New York, NY 10021. 212-288-4383

The Town School is a coeducational, nonsectarian school enrolling 375 day students in three divisions encompassing Nursery–Grade 8. In keeping with Hazel Hyde's founding philosophy, it encourages the joy of learning in an academic environment with creative expression through the arts and physical education. Child-centered teaching and a low faculty-to-student ratio, combined with innovative technology and community service, develop the whole child physically, emotionally, intellectually, and morally. The Town School offers extended care daily, an after-school program, and SummerSault, a summer camp. Tuition: $10,900–$18,675. Financial aid is available. Natasha Fahadi is Director of Admissions; Joyce Gregory Evans is Head of School.

Trevor Day School   1930

Pre-Nursery–Grade 5: 11 East 89th Street, New York, NY 10128. 212-426-3355; Fax 212-410-6507
Grades 6–12: 1 West 88th Street, New York, NY 10024. 212-426-3380; Fax 212-873-8520; E-mail Upperschool or Lowerschooladmissions@ trevordayschool.pvt.k12.ny.us; Web Site http://www.trevor.org

Trevor Day, a coeducational college preparatory program for over 700 students in Nursery–Grade 12, is an intellectual community dedicated to academic excellence. With a 5:1 student-teacher ratio, faculty teach traditional content and promote responsibility, collaboration, creativity, and critical thinking. In addition to rigorous academics, the School requires high school students to perform 80 hours of community service. Foreign languages begin in Nursery, outdoor education starts in Grade 2, and, from Grade 5 on, all students use laptop computers in the Anytime Anywhere Learning program. After-school programs, sports, and a summer camp are available. Tuition: $11,750–$20,150. Financial Aid: $1,700,000. Marcia L. Roesch is Director of Upper School Admissions; John H. Dexter, Ed.D., is Head.

Trinity-Pawling School   PAWLING

Pawling, NY 12564. 914-855-3100; Admissions 914-855-4825; Fax 914-855-3816; E-mail admit@tps.k12.ny.us; Web Site www.tps.k12.ny.us

Trinity-Pawling School in Pawling, New York, is an Episcopal college preparatory school for boarding boys in Grade 9 through Postgraduate and day boys in Grade 7 through Postgraduate. It is located 68 miles north of New York City, where regular train service is available from Grand Central

Station to Pawling (population 5000). The campus, which is reached via State Route 22, is approximately 40 minutes from Stewart International Airport in Newburgh, New York, to which the School provides transportation at vacation times. Kennedy and LaGuardia airports are approximately one and one-half hours from campus.

In 1907, Dr. Frederick Luther Gamage founded the Pawling School for boys. In 1946, it was renamed Trinity-Pawling School in recognition of its ties with Trinity School in New York City. In 1978, a Board of Trustees for Trinity-Pawling School was established, and the School became separate from Trinity School. Trinity-Pawling's "Four Pillars" philosophy shapes the School's educational foundation, and seeks to prepare students for a life of academic, athletic, social, and spiritual growth.

Trinity-Pawling School is a nonprofit organization directed by a self-perpetuating Board of Trustees. It is accredited by the New York State Association of Independent Schools and registered by the New York State Board of Regents. It holds membership in the New York State Association of Independent Schools, the Council for Religion in Independent Schools, the Secondary School Admission Test Board, the National Association of Independent Schools, the National Association of College Admissions Counselors, and The College Board.

THE CAMPUS. The School, located on 140 acres, has woodlands, ponds, and athletic fields available for sports, extracurricular activities, and academic enrichment. There are 2 football fields, 2 baseball diamonds, a track, 4 soccer fields, 3 lacrosse fields, 12 tennis courts, and a skating pond.

The Cluett Building (1910), at the center of the School's campus, was completely renovated in 1995 and incorporates the library, student center, administrative offices, school store, music and art studios, photography and mechanical drawing rooms, faculty apartments, and a student dormitory. The remaining boarders and faculty reside in seven dormitories. The Dann Building (1964) contains classrooms, six science laboratories, two computer rooms, faculty offices, and a science auditorium. The Carleton Gymnasium (1959) and McGraw Pavilion (1995) provide basketball courts, a wrestling pavilion, an enclosed hockey rink, a lounge/trophy room, a weight-lifting room with Nautilus and free weights, five international-size squash courts, an equipment room, and locker facilities. A former gymnasium has been converted into an auditorium/theater.

Other campus buildings are DePew Memorial Chapel (1924), a 16-bed infirmary (1962), the Dining Room (1970), faculty homes, and the Headmaster's house. The school plant is valued at $50,000,000. The School's endowment exceeds $12,000,000.

The School is currently installing a campus-wide technology system, which, when completed, will provide all students with voice mail, E-mail, and internet accounts as well as expanded access to computers and computer ports at designated sites on the campus.

THE FACULTY. Archibald A. Smith III was appointed Headmaster in June of 1990. Since 1975, he has served as a chemistry teacher, Director of College Placement, and Assistant Headmaster. Mr. Smith is a graduate of St. John's School in Texas, Trinity College (B.S. 1972), and Wesleyan University (M.A.L.S. 1980). Previously, he taught at the Northwood School in Lake Placid, New York. A past president of the New York State Association of College Admissions Counselors, Mr. Smith represents New York's secondary schools on the College Board's Advisory Council and its Council for Access Services.

The full-time teaching faculty include 25 men and 10 women. There are 4 administrators who teach part-time and 10 nonteaching administrators. The faculty members, 24 with their families, reside at the School. The faculty and administration hold 49 baccalaureate and 27 graduate degrees from such colleges as Adelphi, Babson, Bates, Boston University, Bowdoin, Brown, Case Western Reserve, Catholic University, Colby, Columbia, Fordham, Franklin and Marshall, General Theological Seminary, Johns Hopkins, Kenyon, Middlebury, Syracuse, Temple, Tufts, Union, Wesleyan, Williams, Wittenberg, Yale, and the Universities of Connecticut, Massachusetts, Pennsylvania, and Virginia.

Resident nurses supervise the infirmary and the school doctor visits campus often. A hospital is located 25 minutes away.

STUDENT BODY. In 1998–99, Trinity-Pawling enrolled 315 boarding and day boys, ages 14–19, as follows: 9 in Grade 7, 17 in Grade 8, 50 in Grade 9, 73 in Grade 10, 83 in Grade 11, and 83 in Grade 12. Boarding students come from 29 states and the District of Columbia, the Bahamas, Brazil, China, Hong Kong, Japan, Korea, South Africa, Switzerland, Taiwan, and Trinidad.

ACADEMIC PROGRAM. From September to early June, there are three terms in the school year and vacations at Thanksgiving, at Christmas, and in the spring. A long weekend is scheduled each term. Any student in good academic standing may take a number of off-campus weekends during the year.

Trinity-Pawling recognizes both effort and achievement in its grading system. Through the Effort System, the School seeks to help boys gain success at every level of potential. The average class enrolls 12 students. Classes are scheduled from 8:20 A.M. until 2:40 P.M. four days per week and until 12:00 noon two days per week. Wednesday and Saturday afternoons are reserved for athletic events. Students must participate in athletic practices from 3:00 to 5:00 P.M. four times weekly, and team games are on Wednesday and Saturday afternoons. Dinner is served at 6:00 P.M. and required study is from 7:30 to 9:30 P.M. Students who need supervision are assigned to day or evening study halls. Teachers are available to give students extra help at any mutually agreeable time. Reports are sent to parents at the end of each term and a preliminary report is sent midway in the autumn term.

To graduate, a student must complete a minimum of 112 credits. A full-year course is worth 6 credits; a trimester course equals 2 credits. If a student enters Trinity-Pawling after Grade 9, his school records will be evaluated and the appropriate credits will be granted.

Among the full-year courses are English; French, Latin, Spanish; Modern European History, World History, United States History; Algebra 1–2, Geometry, Mathematics 4, Elementary Functions, Computer; Physical Science, Ecology, Physical Geography, Biology, Physical Chemistry, Physics; History of Art, Art, Choral Music, Music History, Music Theory; and Mechanical Drawing. Honors sections are formed in all full-year courses, and Advanced Placement courses are offered in 15 subjects.

Approximately 40 trimester courses are offered each year, including Introductory Political Science, Introductory Sociology, Introductory Economics, Bible, Western Christianity, Introduction to Philosophy, Ethics for Contemporary Society, Instrumental Music, Choir, Drawing, Pottery, Oil Painting, Word Processing, and Driver Education.

A two-year Language Retraining Program is open to approximately 28 students primarily in Grades 9 and 10. A modification of the Orton-Gillingham method is used to retrain students of average or above-average intelligence who have been diagnosed with a language-based learning difference. First-year students in the program work with a tutor and attend a language arts class. Phonetics, sequencing directions and ideas, handwriting, memorization, and basic language skills are emphasized. Second-year students are placed in English II and a tutorial class that meets four times weekly. All students in the Language Retraining Program also take basic history, mathematics, and science courses. The program's goal is to enable students to complete Trinity-Pawling's regular college preparatory curriculum.

Graduates from the Class of 1999 attend a range of colleges and universities. They have matriculated at such institutions as Boston College, Brown, College of Charleston, Denison, Franklin Pierce, Georgetown, Hobart, Lehigh, New York University, Ohio Wesleyan, Rensselaer Polytechnic Institute, Rochester, Rollins, St. Lawrence, Trinity, Union, United States Military Academy, Vanderbilt, Washington and Lee, and the Universities of Colorado, Denver, Georgia, Maine, Notre Dame, Pennsylvania, Vermont, and Virginia.

STUDENT ACTIVITIES. The Student-Faculty Senate is composed of school prefects and elected student and faculty representatives. All students are involved in the Work Program, maintaining their dormitory rooms, school buildings, and the campus.

Activities include The Cum Laude Society; Audiovisual, Computer, Drama, Blue & Gold Key, Outing, and Photography clubs; choir, the yearbook; and the newspaper.

Teams are formed in football, soccer, cross-country, squash, basketball, hockey, wrestling, baseball, lacrosse, track, golf, ten-

nis, and skiing, and compete at various levels in the Founder's League with other independent schools. Recreational sporting activities are skiing, golf, tennis, squash, and weight lifting.

Trinity-Pawling strives to create an atmosphere that fosters coeducational social opportunities, and develops personal growth in its students. The School's social director coordinates weekly activities with girls' schools, and trips to New York City to visit museums, attend sporting events, or see a Broadway show are arranged by individual academic departments.

Each year, there is a Parents' Weekend and an Alumni Weekend for the School's 4000 graduates. Parents and alumni are also invited to Trinity-Pawling's traditional Christmas candlelight service.

ADMISSION AND COSTS. Trinity-Pawling seeks boys who will benefit from encouragement and motivation, and who desire to achieve their full potential in all areas. New day students are accepted in Grades 7–12, boarding students in Grades 9–12, and a postgraduate year. It is school policy to "admit students without regard to race, color, creed, or national origin." Candidates submit a complete transcript and recommendations from two teachers. In addition, a personal interview and results of the Secondary School Admission Test are required. Applications for enrollment should be submitted by March, although qualified late applicants are considered if openings exist. There is a $40 application fee.

In 1999–2000, tuition is $26,000 for boarding students and $16,500 for day students in Grades 9–12. In Grades 7–8, tuition is $12,200. The Language Retraining Program is an additional $5800 for the first year. Other expenses total approximately $1000 yearly. Tuition payment plans and tuition insurance are available. Annually, about 35 percent of all students receive financial aid totaling approximately $1,000,000. Trinity-Pawling subscribes to the School Scholarship Service and grants aid on the basis of need.

Dean of Students: C. Stephen Harrington
Director of Admissions: MacGregor Robinson
Director of Development: John Thorne
College Counselor: Marc Batson
Business Manager: Ronwyn Gailes
Director of Athletics: Miles H. Hubbard

Trinity School   1709

139 West 91st Street, New York, NY 10024. 212-873-1650; Fax 212-501-0207

A coeducational, college preparatory day school enrolling 965 students in Kindergarten–Grade 12, Trinity seeks to encourage academic excellence and to help students see themselves as worthy individuals with responsibilities to the larger world. Fundamental disciplines are emphasized; computer studies are introduced in Grade 2 and Latin begins in Grade 6. Electives and Advanced Placement courses are available in the Upper School. Sports, publications, community service, music, and drama are among the activities. A summer day camp is offered. Tuition: $17,320–$18,685. Need-based financial aid is available. Henry C. Moses (Princeton, B.A.; Cornell, Ph.D.) was appointed Headmaster in 1991.

Tuxedo Park School   1900

Mountain Farm Road, Tuxedo Park, NY 10987. 914-351-4737; Fax 914-351-4219; E-mail jham@tuxedoparkschool.com

Tuxedo Park School enrolls 184 day boys and girls in Pre-Kindergarten–Grade 9. The School is committed to nurturing and developing the natural joy of learning inherent in each child. Concern for traditional and modern skills is demonstrated by the inclusion of such courses as French, Latin, and computer throughout the School. Art, music, and sports are an integral part of the curriculum at all levels. Interscholastic sports are offered in Grades 7–9. Tuition: $6050–$15,400. Financial aid is available. John M. Ham is Director of Admissions and Financial Aid; James T. Burger (Hamilton College, B.A.; Case Western Reserve, J.D.) was appointed Head of School in 1994.

United Nations International School   1947

24-50 F.D.R. Drive, New York, NY 10010. 212-584-3001;
Admissions 212-584-3071; Fax 212-685-5023;
E-mail admissions@unis.org;
173-53 Croydon Road, Jamaica Estates, NY 11432. 718-658-6166;
Fax 718-658-5742

United Nations International School is a coeducational, college preparatory day school located on two campuses, enrolling 1486 students from the United States and 109 other countries. Encompassing Kindergarten through Grade 12, the School provides a rigorous global education culminating in the International Baccalaureate. Eighty-five percent of graduates enter American colleges and universities; 15 percent enroll in colleges worldwide. Ten languages are offered, and music and art are integral to the curriculum. Activities include sports, publications, UN/UNIS Conference, community service, music, and drama. Tuition: $11,900–$13,900. Need-based financial aid is available. Dr. Kenneth Wrye was appointed Director in 1998.

The Ursuline School   1896

1354 North Avenue, New Rochelle, NY 10804. 914-636-3950;
Fax 914-636-3949; E-mail admin@ursuline.pvt.k12.ny.us;
Web Site www.ursuline.pvt.k12.ny.us

Founded by the Order of St. Ursula, this college preparatory day school, twice named a Blue Ribbon School by the U.S. Department of Education, enrolls 700 girls in Grades 6–12. It aims to promote an intellectually stimulating environment in which academic and personal achievement is demanded. Honors and nine Advanced Placement courses are offered. Ursuline considers the teaching of religion and the communicating of Christian values integral to the program. Activities include athletics, student council, drama, forensics, and publications. Tuition: $7350. Financial Aid: $150,000. Sr. Jean Baptiste Nicholson (College of New Rochelle, B.A. 1960; Catholic University, M.A. 1964) was appointed Principal in 1974. *Middle States Association.*

Village Community School   1970

272 West Tenth Street, New York, NY 10014. 212-691-5146;
Fax 212-691-9767

Located in historic Greenwich Village, Village Community School serves 316 boys and girls in Kindergarten–Grade 8. The School seeks to offer a stimulating, challenging curriculum within a supportive environment that recognizes the needs of the whole child. Students consistently gain admission to a variety of competitive high schools. An extensive after-school program and a summer day camp are available. The plant includes two playgrounds, gymnasium, woodshop, art studio with ceramic kiln, two new science labs, an auditorium with stage, a new skylit library, and an expanded computer center. Tuition: $14,000–$15,000. Jennifer Trano is Director of Admissions; Eve Kleger (Wellesley, B.A.; Columbia, M.A.) is Director.

The Waldorf School of Garden City   1947

Cambridge Avenue, Garden City, NY 11530. 516-742-3434;
Fax 516-742-3457

An independent, college preparatory, coeducational day school, The Waldorf School of Garden City, founded in 1947, is a member of the Association of Waldorf Schools of North America network and is accredited by the New York State Association of Independent Schools. Students are admitted from Nursery through Grade 12. Teachers strive to foster genuine enthusiasm for learning, respect for the world, and a healthy sense of self by balancing academic, practical, creative, and physical endeavors in an interdisciplinary manner. Annual class trips to the School's extension campus in New Hampshire are features of the program. Tuition: $6700–$11,300. Joanna Hulsey is Director of Admissions; Janet Kane, B.A., M.A., and Maurizio Tusa, B.S., are Faculty Council Co-Chairs.

The Windsor School   1968

41–60 Kissena Boulevard, Flushing, NY 11355. 718-359-8300;
Fax 718-359-1876; E-mail admin@thewindsorschool.com;
Web Site www.windsorschool.com

The Windsor School is a coeducational, college preparatory day school enrolling approximately 100 boys and 100 girls in Grades 6–12. It is dedicated to providing individual guidance and a sense of identity for middle-range and gifted students. A coordinated program, including English as a Second Language, is arranged for international students. Students are programmed individually so that they can enroll in honors or accelerated programs in those subjects in which they excel. Extracurricular activities and teams and a summer school are available. Tuition (including books): $10,150–$12,150. Martin Cohen (Brooklyn College, M.A. 1948; Kensington University, Ph.D. 1981) is Headmaster. *Middle States Association.*

Windward School   1926

Windward Avenue, White Plains, NY 10605. 914-949-6968

Windward School is a coeducational day school enrolling 300 learning-disabled students of average to above-average intelligence in Grades 1–12. The Upper School is located on a separate campus one mile from the main building. The School seeks to provide a highly structured and sequentially designed instructional program to close the gap between academic achievement and intellectual potential. Activities include after-school programs, athletic teams, drama, Student Council, yearbook and newspaper, and clubs. Tuition: $23,575. Financial aid is available. Maureen A. Sweeney is Director of Admissions; James E. Van Amburg (Stanford University, Ed.D.) is Head of School.

The Winston Preparatory School   1981

4 West 76th Street, New York, NY 10023. 212-496-8400;
Fax 212-362-0927; E-mail admissions@winstonprep.edu

Winston Prep is a Middle and Upper School for intelligent boys and girls with learning differences or language processing or attention problems. The language-intensive program is taught by trained learning specialists using a multisensory instructional approach in small, structured classes. Students are grouped according to age, grade, and skill levels for each of the academic courses. Individual tutoring in reading, math, and language skills is provided during the school day. The arts, technology, and visits to New York's cultural sites enhance the program. Winston offers sports, electives, after-school activities, and a July tutorial program. Tuition/Fees: $27,650. Scott Bezsylko, M.A., is Head of School.

York Preparatory School   1969

40 West 68th Street, New York, NY 10023. 212-362-0400;
Fax 212-362-7106; E-mail admissions@yorkprep.org;
Web Site www.yorkprep.org

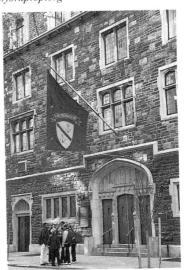

York, a coeducational, college preparatory day school enrolling 250 students of varied backgrounds and academic abilities in Grades 6–12, was chartered in 1896 and established in its current form by the present Headmaster. The School's rigorous curriculum is based on an ability-grouping system; Advanced Placement and honors classes are provided. Staff members trained in special education offer support to students who need extra assistance. The School is known for its strong academic tradition, "outstanding" college guidance, and numerous extracurriculars, including a winning Law Team and a championship basketball team. Tuition: $16,200–$16,900. Financial Aid: $565,255. Ronald P. Stewart (Oxford, B.A., M.A., B.C.L.) is Headmaster.

NORTH CAROLINA

The Asheville School   ASHEVILLE

Asheville, NC 28806. 828-254-6345; Fax 828-252-8666;
E-mail admission@asheville-school.org;
Web Site www.ashevilleschool.org

THE ASHEVILLE SCHOOL in Asheville, North Carolina, is a college preparatory boarding and day school enrolling boys and girls in Grades 9 through 12 and a postgraduate year. It is located on the western limit of Asheville, a city of 65,000, and is surrounded by the Blue Ridge and Great Smoky Mountains. The Asheville Civic Center and Pack Place Arts and Education Center offer concerts, drama, and exhibitions. Asheville is 140 miles northwest of Charlotte and 200 miles northeast of Atlanta. A regional airport is located 15 minutes from campus, and interstate buses are also available.

The Asheville School was founded in 1900 by Charles A. Mitchell and Newton M. Anderson. Mr. Mitchell, formerly a teacher at St. Paul's School in Concord, New Hampshire, and Mr. Anderson had combined their efforts in 1890 to found University School in Cleveland. However, they reached their ideal goal by subsequently founding The Asheville School. It was purchased by the alumni in 1930 to be operated under a state charter. The first female day students were admitted in 1971, and the School became fully coeducational in 1986 when girls were enrolled as boarding students.

The School is committed to high academic standards and seeks to encourage intellectual curiosity, the willingness to work hard and learn independently, physical well-being, individual creativity, and a sense of responsibility among its students. It teaches values in the Judeo-Christian tradition, and introduces students to a variety of religious beliefs through nondenominational chapel services.

The School is a member of the English-Speaking Union, providing the opportunity for selected students to spend a postgraduate year at an English boarding school and bringing one or two English students to Asheville each year.

The Asheville School is a nonprofit corporation governed by a self-perpetuating Board of 30 Trustees, most of whom are alumni. The Board meets three times a year. Approximately 3000 living alumni provide support to the School through gifts and services. The School's endowment is more than $25,000,000.

The Asheville School is accredited by the Southern Association of Colleges and Schools and holds membership in the National Association of Independent Schools, the Southern Association of Colleges and Schools, The College Board, and the Council for Spiritual and Ethical Education, among other professional organizations.

THE CAMPUS. The School's principal buildings occupy a cleared area on the northeast corner of a 300-acre wooded campus, which offers an excellent natural environment and views of the surrounding mountains. Five athletic fields, an all-weather track, seven outdoor tennis courts, horse stables, an alpine tower, and a ropes course are on the campus.

Mitchell Hall is the main classroom and administration building. It has both Macintosh and PC computer labs. The School's computer network, Bluesnet, extends to all major school buildings, allowing e-mail, Internet, and Intranet access to students and faculty from every classroom and dorm room. Mitchell Hall is flanked by Anderson Hall, containing dormitories and the infirmary; and Lawrence Hall, with dormitories and a photography lab. The Walker Arts Center includes a 380-seat theatre, studios, and music and choral rooms. Rodgers Athletic Center has three basketball courts convertible to indoor tennis or volleyball courts, a swimming pool, and a weight training area. Other major buildings are: Boyd Chapel, Crawford Music House, Kehaya House (girls' dormitory), Howard Bement Guest House, the Headmaster's House, and faculty homes. Sharp Hall (for dining) and Tyrer Student Center, which includes the Crawford Art Gallery, Perkins Game Room, post office, and snack bar, are additional facilities. The fully renovated Memorial Hall houses a state-of-the-art library/multimedia center with the capacity for 25,000 volumes, a computer center, a conference center, and individual study rooms.

The plant is owned by the School and is valued at approximately $22,600,000.

THE FACULTY. William S. Peebles IV, a graduate of Episcopal High School (1973), Princeton University (A.B. 1978), and the University of Virginia (M.B.A. 1985), was appointed Headmaster in 1992. Prior to this appointment, he was Headmaster of the Powhatan School for seven years. Earlier, he served for four years as the Director of Admission and Financial Aid and taught American History at Virginia Episcopal School.

Thirty-four men and 24 women comprise the full-time faculty and administration, 30 of whom live on campus. In addition, the School employs a drama director, a third-form project director, and a director of equestrian studies, all of whom are residents. Two librarians oversee the library/media center. Twenty-three members of the faculty/administration hold advanced degrees, including two doctorates, representing study at such institutions as Amherst, Bowdoin, Brown, Catholic University of America, Clemson, College of Charleston, College of William and Mary, Columbia Theological Seminary, Concord, Converse, Davidson, Denison, Duke, Eastern Illinois, Eastman School of Music, East Stroudsburg State, Eckerd, Ecole Superieure de Commerce (France), Florida State, Franklin and Marshall, Furman, Harvard, Longwood, Massachusetts Institute of Technology, Medical University of South Carolina, Mills, New York University, North Carolina State, Oregon State, Princeton, Roanoke, St. John's College, Salem, Seton Hall, Smith, State University of New York, Stetson, Temple, Tufts, Wesleyan, Western Carolina, Western Connecticut State, Wilkes, Williams, Wofford, Xavier, and the Universities of Alabama, Cincinnati, Georgia, Michigan, North Carolina, Pennsylvania, the South, Tennessee, Vermont, Virginia, and Wisconsin.

Two resident nurses staff the campus infirmary on a 24-hour basis. In addition, a physician visits the school twice weekly, and two hospitals are within 10 minutes of the campus.

STUDENT BODY. In 1999–2000, the enrollment includes 85 boarding boys, 31 day boys, 67 boarding girls, and 33 day girls in Grades 9–12 and a postgraduate year. The students come from more than 15 states and ten foreign countries including the Bahamas, Belize, Brazil, Bulgaria, Cayman Islands, France, Germany, India, Korea, Saudi Arabia, and Senegal.

ACADEMIC PROGRAM. The academic year, divided into two semesters, begins in late August and extends to late May, with vacations of 14 days each at Christmas and in the spring. Classes, which have an average size of 10–12, meet 5 or 6 days a week and are scheduled in six 45-minute periods between 8:20 A.M. and 2:15 P.M. Afternoons are given to one conference period, labs, athletics, and other activities. Supervised study halls are held from 8:00 to 10:00 P.M. on school nights. Teachers offer special help during the conference period during the class day and in free periods. Grades and comments from teachers and advisors are sent to parents every eight weeks.

To graduate, students must complete four years of English; three of one foreign language or two years of two languages; three of history including one of United States History; three of mathematics; three of science; and one of music/art. Students must also complete all special projects and meet requirements for outdoor experience and public speaking.

Among the courses offered are: English 1–5, including surveys of American, British, and World literature; French 1–5, Latin 1–4, Spanish 1–6; World History, United States History,

Ancient and Medieval History, European History, World Civilization; Algebra 1–2, Combinatorics, Computational Geometry, Geometry, Finite Mathematics, Pre-Calculus, Calculus; Biology, Advanced Biological Research, Environmental Biology, Chemistry, Physics; and Studio Art and Introduction to Music/Art. Advanced Placement and honors-level courses are offered in English, history, mathematics, foreign languages, music, and the laboratory sciences.

All 47 seniors who graduated in 1999 went on to college. They are enrolled at such colleges and universities as Davidson, Denison, Furman, Georgia Institute of Technology, Princeton, Savannah College of Art & Design, Swarthmore, Tulane, Wake Forest, and the Universities of Colorado, Michigan, North Carolina (Chapel Hill), the South, and Virginia.

The Asheville School Summer Advancement Program offers rising 7th through 11th graders the opportunity to experience The Asheville School in either a three- or six-week session combining academic enrichment with mountaineering, athletics, recreation, and fine arts.

STUDENT ACTIVITIES. Each class elects two representatives to the Student Council, which organizes and directs student activities. Three seniors rotate on the Conduct Council where they serve with three faculty members considering matters of discipline and making recommendations to the Headmaster. The Honor Council is comprised of six students and three faculty members who work together to foster and preserve honor and integrity in The Asheville School community.

Other activities are the yearbook, newspaper, literary magazine; the Dramatic, International, Host (tour guides), and Mitchell (service) societies; "A" Society (letter club); Students for Environmental Awareness; and a student/faculty fellowship group. Students pursue other activities through the Monday Project Program, which may encompass anything from computer imaging or community service work to African drumming.

The School is a member of the Carolinas Athletic Association and the North Carolina Independent School Athletic Association. Varsity teams compete against both member and non-member teams in football, soccer, cross-country, basketball, swimming, wrestling, baseball, golf, track, and tennis for boys; and cross-country, field hockey, basketball, swimming, track, tennis, soccer, and volleyball, for girls. Junior Varsity teams are offered for younger students in most sports. The School's acclaimed mountaineering program includes rock- and ice-climbing, kayaking, cross-country and downhill skiing, caving, camping, horseback riding, and hiking.

A variety of weekend activities is planned for students and faculty. Off-campus events include bicycle tours, trips to the Biltmore House, productions at the Thomas Wolfe Auditorium, and events at the Asheville Civic Center.

Parents' Weekend, Homecoming Weekend, Alumni Weekend, and the annual Holiday Candlelight Service are special events on the school calendar.

ADMISSION AND COSTS. The Asheville School is committed to a racially and culturally diverse student body. It seeks students with high character, strong interest in attending, and a record of academic achievement. New students are accepted in all grades on the basis of a completed application, current transcript, Secondary School Admission Test scores or other testing, teacher recommendations, and a personal interview. Applications, with a $50 fee, are due by December 10 for early decision or February 10 for regular decision. After that date, applications are considered on a space-available basis.

In 1999–2000, boarding tuition is $24,000; day tuition is $13,950. The School subscribes to the School and Student Service for Financial Aid and awarded $916,000 in financial aid on the basis of need. Tuition payment and insurance plans are available.

Dean of Faculty: Jack W. Bonner IV
Dean of Students: Mary B. Wall

Director of Alumni and Parent Relations and Annual Giving:
    Timothy B. Ferris, Sr.
Director of Admission: Peter W. Upham
College Counselor: Irvin H. Ornduff
Business Manager: Glenn R. Mayes
Director of Athletics: Charles N. Carter

Bishop McGuinness Memorial High School   1959

1730 Link Road, Winston-Salem, NC 27103. 336-725-4247;
    Fax 336-725-6669; E-mail bmhs@ols.net

Enrolling 400 young men and women from many faiths, Bishop McGuinness is a college preparatory high school operated by the Catholic Diocese of Charlotte. The School seeks to develop its students spiritually, intellectually, emotionally, physically, and socially through a challenging curriculum that reinforces Christian values in all areas of life. Honors, Advanced Placement, and elective courses are offered in all academic departments, and four years of religious studies are required. The diverse extracurricular program engages students in athletics, drama, publications, and clubs including Big Brother/Big Sister, Peer Ministry, Amnesty International, and Harvard Model Congress. Tuition: $3445–$5088. George L. Repass is Principal. *Southern Association.*

Cannon School   1969

5801 Poplar Tent Road, Concord, NC 28027.
    704-786-8171; Fax 704-788-7779; E-mail pdrake@
    cannonschool.org; Web Site www.cannonschool.org

Cannon School, enrolling 504 students in Junior Kindergarten–Grade 10, aims to instill academic excellence, personal responsibility, and a love of learning in a supportive, safe environment. In the Lower and Middle Schools, traditional subjects are complemented by Spanish, art, music, computer, library, and physical education. A laboratory approach enhances the science curriculum from Grade 1. A new Upper School facility will include up to Grade 12 by 2001. The college preparatory curriculum, a Character Development program, sports, arts, and leadership opportunities permit students to participate in all aspects of school life. Tuition: $4950–$8550. Financial aid is available. Carol Bertram is Director of Admissions; Richard H. Snyder (Johns Hopkins, B.A., M.Ed.) is Headmaster. *Southern Association.*

Cape Fear Academy   1967

3900 South College Road, Wilmington, NC 28412. 910-791-0287;
    Fax 910-791-0290; Web Site capefearacademy.org

Cape Fear Academy, a college preparatory day school serving 510 students in Pre-Kindergarten–Grade 12, emphasizes scholastic achievement, fine arts, extracurriculars, community service, and athletic and physical education programs. The Lower and Middle schools stress academic skills in an integrated curriculum with specialty classes in art, music, foreign language, and computers. The Upper School offers Honors and/or Advanced Placement courses in English, math, foreign languages, science, history, art, music, and computers. A summer enrichment program is offered. Tuition/Fees: $4612–$8614. Financial aid is available. Susan Harrell is Director of Admission; R. Jay Dewey (College of the Holy Cross, B.S. 1965; Brown, M.A.T. 1968; Rutgers, Ed.S. 1986) is Headmaster. *Southern Association.*

Carolina Day School   1987

1345 Hendersonville Road, Asheville, NC 28803. 828-274-0757;
    Fax 828-277-8832; E-mail admissions@cdschool.org;
    Web Site www.cdschool.org

Carolina Day School is a college preparatory school enrolling 520 boys and girls in Pre-Kindergarten–Grade 12. The School strives to develop within each student a strong academic foundation, personal ethics, and concern for community. The program includes Advanced Placement courses, community service, athletics, outdoor education, computer science, and fine arts. Summer Discovery offers enrichment in the arts, sciences, and crafts. The Key Learning Center for students with learning differences was established in 1998. Tuition: $4210–$10,610. Beverly H. Sgro (Virginia Tech, Ph.D.) was appointed Head of School in 1999.

Carolina Friends School   1963

4809 Friends School Road, Durham, NC 27705. 919-383-6602;
    Fax 919-383-6009

Founded by and affiliated with the Durham and Chapel Hill Friends Meetings (Quakers), Carolina Friends is a coeducational day school enrolling 495 students in Preschool–Grade 12. The School strives to develop individuals who are creative, self-disciplined, and at peace with themselves and with others. In addition to a core curriculum of science, math, language arts, and social studies, courses include visual arts, music, dance, drama, woodworking, physical education, and community service. Sports, publications, tutoring, field trips, and retreats are among the School's activities. Tuition: $4860–$8490. Financial Aid: $575,000. Kathleen March is Admissions Coordinator; John Baird (Princeton, A.B. 1975; Providence College, M.A. 1987) was appointed Principal in 1989.

Cary Academy   1997

1500 North Harrison Avenue, Cary, NC 27513. 919-677-3873;
    Fax 919-677-4002; Web Site www.caryacademy.pvt.k12.nc.us

Cary Academy is a coeducational, college preparatory day school that provides a secure and nurturing environment for students in Grades 6–12 while offering a challenging education that effectively integrates technology into a curriculum firmly grounded in the humanities. There are more than 700 computers throughout the campus. Strong programs in the performing and visual arts, athletics, and extracurricular activities offer leadership opportunities and complement the students' academic lives. Tuition: $9350–$9850. Financial aid is available. Vicky G. Sparrow is Director of Admissions; Donald S. Berger (Haverford College, B.A.; Harvard University, Ed.M.) is Head of School.

Charlotte Country Day School 1941

1440 Carmel Road, Charlotte, NC 28226. 704-943-4500;
Web Site www.ccds.charlotte.nc.us

Charlotte Country Day School was founded in 1941 as a traditional college preparatory school. Continuing to maintain excellence in academic, athletic, and personal achievement, the coeducational program enrolls 1594 students in Junior Kindergarten–Grade 12. The curriculum includes Honors and Advanced Placement courses, independent study, English as a Second Language, and an International Baccalaureate program. Among the activities are publications, community service, clubs, and a wide variety of athletics. There is a summer program. Tuition: $7300–$11,500. Financial Aid: $492,000. Nancy Ehringhaus is Director of Admissions; Margaret E. Gragg (Duke University, B.A.; University of North Carolina, M.A.T.) was named Head in 1992. *Southern Association.*

Charlotte Latin School 1970

9502 Providence Road, Charlotte, NC 28277-8695. 704-846-1100;
Admissions 704-846-7207; Fax 704-847-8776;
E-mail kbooe@charlottelatin.org; Web Site www.charlottelatin.org

Charlotte Latin is a coeducational, nonsectarian, college preparatory day school enrolling 1318 students in Pre-Kindergarten–Grade 12. The School provides the challenges and opportunities necessary for the development of leadership qualities and academic excellence. The distinction among Lower, Middle, and Upper School students reflects an emphasis on meeting the changing needs of the maturing child. In-depth programs in fine arts, athletics, and activities are offered. Charlotte Latin operates academic and recreational summer programs. Tuition: $7340–$10,940. Financial Aid: $624,720. Mrs. Kathy Booe is Director of Admissions; E. J. Fox, Jr. (Rice, B.A. 1956; Johns Hopkins, M.A.T. 1961; Nova, Ed.D. 1978), was appointed Headmaster in 1976. *Southern Association.*

Christ School ASHEVILLE

Asheville, NC 28704. 800-422-3212 or 828-684-6232;
Fax 828-684-2745; E-mail cdunnigan@christschool.org;
Web Site www.christschool.org

CHRIST SCHOOL in Asheville, North Carolina, is an Episcopal, college preparatory boarding and day school for boys in Grades 8–12. Situated in the mountains of western North Carolina, the community of Arden is 11 miles south of Asheville (population 87,000), which offers a variety of cultural events. The surrounding countryside abounds with lakes, hiking trails, whitewater rivers, ski resorts, and golf courses. The School is convenient to the Asheville Airport.

Founded in 1900 by The Reverend Thomas Cogdill Wetmore, the School originally served in place of a public school for mountain boys and girls, providing industrial as well as academic training. With the advent of public education in the area in 1928, Christ School became a college preparatory school for boys.

In a Christian environment, Christ School seeks to educate the whole boy by combining an emphasis on traditional college preparatory academics with a commitment to developing the values of integrity, responsibility, and respect for the rights of others. Chapel services and a work program are essential elements of school life, as are athletics, which promote a sense of fairness and cooperation. Although affiliated with the Episcopal Church, the School accepts students of all creeds.

A nonprofit institution, Christ School is governed by a self-perpetuating Board of 35 Trustees, which meets quarterly. There are approximately 2100 living alumni who support the School financially and through a variety of other efforts. Christ School is accredited by the Southern Association of Colleges and Schools. It holds membership in the National Association of Independent Schools, among other professional affiliations.

THE CAMPUS. The 500-acre campus features lawns, forested areas, a pond and stream, and open fields. The grounds include facilities for competitive and interscholastic athletics, with six tennis courts; football, baseball, and soccer fields; a new all-weather track; a low ropes course; and miles of cross-country trails. A 3-acre lake is used for canoeing, kayaking, fishing, and swimming.

The main academic facility is Wetmore Hall, with 14 classrooms, administrative offices, four science labs, a new multimedia classroom, and faculty lounge. A recent $12,000,000 building project has provided four new dormitories with computer and telephone connections in every room. St. Dunstan's Library is equipped with a state-of-the-art computer center that links an in-house service with the Internet global community. Pingree Auditorium offers a state-of-the-art facility for assemblies and drama productions. The adjacent Art Complex houses an art studio, a photography darkroom, and 2 classrooms. The new Student Center contains a game room, lounge, fireplace, snack shop, bookstore, barber shop, and a 40-seat TV area/theater. St. Thomas Refectory contains a dining area, a kitchen, and a student commons room. The spiritual life of the School centers around services in St. Joseph's Chapel, adjacent to Harris Memorial Chapel.

The Mebane Field House and Memorial Gymnasium contain a basketball court and three full-size practice courts, wrestling room, three racquetball courts, four locker rooms, a new weight room, a training room, equipment room, a coach's office, and the Athletic Director's office. Also on campus are the infirmary, maintenance shop, school store, and the art building. The School-owned facilities are valued at $20,000,000.

THE FACULTY. The Reverend Russell W. Ingersoll was appointed 11th Headmaster of Christ School in 1993. Previously, he had served for 17 years as Headmaster, most recently as founding Headmaster of St. Gregory High School, Tucson, Arizona (1979–89). Immediately prior to coming to Christ School, Father Ingersoll served as Chaplain of St. Mark's School in Dallas, Texas. He was educated at The Taft School in Watertown, Connecticut, and is a graduate of Dartmouth College (B.A. 1960) and Virginia Theological Seminary (M.Div., Cum Laude 1965).

The full-time faculty number 40. Thirty of them live on campus. All teachers have baccalaureate degrees and 22 hold master's degrees representing study at such colleges and universities as Appalachian State, Austin, Ball State, Bates, Belmont Abbey, Bowling Green, Case Western Reserve, Clemson, College of the Holy Cross, Columbia, Concordia, Dartmouth, Davidson, Florida Atlantic, George Washington, Gonzaga, Harvard, Indiana University, Kennesaw State, Mars Hill, Middlebury, Northwest Missouri State, Old Dominion, Rollins, Spalding, State University of New York, United States Naval Academy, Valparaiso, Vanderbilt, Virginia Theological Seminary, Wake Forest, Warren Wilson, Washington and Lee, Washington State, Western Carolina, Western Kentucky, Wofford, Woodstock, Yale, and the Universities of Delaware, Georgia, Louisville, North Carolina (Asheville, Charlotte), the South, Southern Mississippi, Tennessee, and Virginia.

A nurse and an assistant staff the Health Center 24 hours a day, seven days a week, and a fully licensed physician is a member of the faculty. Medical facilities are within a ten-minute drive.

STUDENT BODY. In 1999–2000, Christ School enrolled 150 boarding boys and 20 day students in Grades 8–12. The students are from Alabama, Arkansas, Florida, Georgia, Illinois, Kentucky, Louisiana, Maine, Maryland, Mississippi, North Carolina, South Carolina, Tennessee, Texas, and Washington. International students come from Belgium, China, Germany, India, Japan, Korea, and Mexico.

ACADEMIC PROGRAM. The school year is from late August to late May. It is divided into semesters including Thanksgiving and Christmas holidays with a long weekend break in October and ten-day breaks in February and for the spring holidays. The average class size is 10–14 students, and the student-faculty ratio is 6:1. Students are placed in classes on the basis of achievement levels, interests, and graduation requirements. Grades are posted and sent to parents approximately every four weeks.

The college preparatory curriculum is designed to provide students with a firm foundation in the academic subjects and study skills needed for college as well as the knowledge and skills that will enable them to become informed and intelligent citizens. The School believes that these objectives can best be fulfilled through a concentration in the traditional arts and sciences and that a motivated faculty, small classes, and individual attention are the key to a boy's academic development.

Each spring, a student meets with the Academic Dean to arrange a course of study. Requirements for graduation include the completion of 20 credits: English 4, Mathematics 3, Science 3, History 3, Foreign Language (Latin, French, or Spanish) 2, Fine Arts 1, Religious Studies .5, Computer .5, and electives 3. Electives include Advanced Placement courses in History, Biology, English, and Math.

Christ School's Learning Resource Program offers academic support in English, math, and study skills within the context of a rigorous college preparatory curriculum. The Program serves those who can meet the challenges of a full academic schedule while benefiting from the Program's supportive techniques.

Christ School graduated 33 seniors in 1999, all of whom attended four-year colleges and universities. The School administered 22 Advanced Placement exams. The average SAT score for this year's senior class is 1121.

Graduates were accepted at a variety of colleges and universities. Among them are Auburn, Birmingham-Southern, Clemson, Davidson, DePaul, Furman, Georgia Institute of Technology, Hampden-Sydney, Louisiana State, Sewanee, Vanderbilt, Wake Forest, Wofford, and the Universities of Dayton, North Carolina (Chapel Hill), and South Carolina.

The coeducational summer program, Western North Carolina Adventures at Christ School, emphasizes an outdoor/experiential educational program with the added benefit of a solid academic component and course credit for Math and English. The Christ School Sports Camp will take place from July 9 to 22, 2000.

STUDENT ACTIVITIES. Responsibility for student life and conduct is largely in the hands of the students. The Judiciary Council, composed of prefects appointed by the Headmaster and members elected by the various forms, makes recommendations to the Headmaster regarding discipline and other aspects of school life. Seniors and faculty supervise house life and the school service program.

Among the extracurricular activities and organizations are choir, journalism, music, outdoor education, photography, SAT preparation, snow skiing, literary magazine, and yearbook. Students may explore the varied cultural activities that exist in western North Carolina as well as Charlotte, Atlanta, and Greenville, South Carolina.

A member of the North Carolina Independent Schools Athletic Association, Christ School fields teams in baseball, basketball, cross-country, football, golf, soccer, swimming, tennis, track, and wrestling. Students may also participate in conditioning and exercise. Those students not wishing to participate in competitive athletics may choose from drama and outdoor activities. The drama program stages three productions a year, and students are involved in set design and building, technical theater, and acting. The outdoor program utilizes the mountains and rivers of western North Carolina, providing instruction in canoeing, kayaking, climbing and rappelling, camping and hiking, mountain biking, orienteering, and basic wilderness medicine.

Christ School utilizes a student activities committee comprised of students and faculty to coordinate weekend and coeducational activities. Weekends provide opportunities for interscholastic athletics, concerts, dances, collegiate and professional games, paintball games, rodeos, and trips to Asheville, Atlanta, Charlotte, Raleigh, and Winston-Salem. With parental and School permission, boys may schedule a limited number of off-campus weekends. Traditional annual events for the School community include Parents' Day in October and Alumni Day in May.

ADMISSION AND COSTS. New students are admitted to Grades 8–12 on the basis of a campus visit, three teacher recommendations, transcripts with standardized test scores, and applicant's essay. The SSAT is required. There is a $50 application fee.

In 1999–2000, tuition (room and board) is $22,900 for seven-day boarders, $21,900 for five-day boarders, and $11,400 for day students. A $400 deposit must be placed in an account to cover a weekly allowance and the cost of weekend activities. Expenses for clothing, travel, laundry, and other needs vary according to the individual and are the responsibility of each boy's parents. Financial aid and merit scholarships are available to qualified students. In 1999–2000, the School awarded $500,000 in aid and scholarships. Tuition insurance and tuition payment plans are available.

Dean of Curriculum and Instruction: Erich Cluxton
Dean of Residential Life: Drew Noga
Assistant Headmaster for School Advancement: A. Lee Burns
Acting Director of Admission: Colin Dunnigan
College Counselor: Lyn Tillett
Assistant Headmaster for Finance and Facilities: James Banks
Director of Athletics: David S. Gaines '84
Chaplain: The Reverend David (Kirk) Brown

Durham Academy   1933

Pre-Kindergarten–Grade 8: 3116 Academy Road, Durham, NC 27707. 919-489-9118; Fax 919-490-9716
Grades 9–12: 3601 Ridge Road, Durham, NC 27705. 919-489-6569; Fax 919-493-6705; E-mail gfitzpatrick@da.org; Web Site www.da.org

A college preparatory day school, Durham Academy enrolls 1023 students in Pre-Kindergarten–Grade 12. The Academy strives to prepare each student for a happy, moral, and productive life and to instill in each one an awareness of obligations to fellow students, community, and nation. The curriculum includes Advanced Placement courses in all disciplines and courses in computer, economics, music, art, dance, and drama. There is a full interscholastic sports program for Grades 7–12. A summer enrichment program is offered. Tuition: $7700–$11,300. Financial Aid: $550,000. Edward R. Costello (Syracuse, A.B. 1970; Wesleyan, M.A.L.S. 1982) was appointed Headmaster in 1999. *Southern Association.*

The Fayetteville Academy   1969

3200 Cliffdale Road, Fayetteville, NC 28303. 910-868-5131; Fax 910-868-7351; E-mail email@fayettevilleacademy.com; Web Site www.fayettevilleacademy.com

The Fayetteville Academy is a college preparatory day school enrolling 450 students in Pre-Kindergarten–Grade 12. It strives

to achieve each student's total development emphasizing academic, social, physical, and emotional growth. The Academy offers a 12:1 student-faculty ratio with much individual attention, Advanced Placement and Honors-level courses, a full interscholastic sports program, student government, drama, music, community service, and clubs. A summer enrichment program is offered. Tuition: $5155–$7633. Financial Aid: $170,786. Barbara Lambert is Admissions Director; Benjamin M. Crabtree (Presbyterian College, B.S. 1964; Western Carolina University, M.A. 1973) was appointed Headmaster in 1988. *Southern Association.*

Forsyth Country Day School   1970

5501 Shallowford Road, P.O. Box 549, Lewisville, NC 27023-0549. 336-945-3151; Fax 336-945-2907; Web Site http://www.fcds.org

Forsyth Country Day School is a coeducational, college preparatory day school enrolling 722 students in Pre-Kindergarten–Grade 12. The School aims to educate students to become productive, responsible adults meeting the challenges of the future. The Lower and Middle schools stress basic academic skills enriched with French, art, science, music, physical education, computer, and seminars. The Upper School curriculum includes advanced courses in all disciplines, a variety of electives, and athletics, fine arts, and clubs. The Johnson Academic Center provides additional support for students with a variety of learning styles. Tuition: $7200–$9800. Financial aid is available. Lu Anne C. Wood is Director of Admission; Henry M. Battle, Jr., is Headmaster. *Southern Association.*

Greensboro Day School   1970

5401 Lawndale Drive, P.O. Box 26805, Greensboro, NC 27429-6805. 336-288-8590; Fax 336-282-2905; E-mail annadams@greensboroday.org.; Web Site http://www.greensboroday.org

Greensboro Day School is a college preparatory school enrolling 431 boys and 432 girls in Kindergarten–Grade 12. It strives to instill intellectual curiosity, love of learning, and personal discipline. Language arts is emphasized; spoken French and environmental awareness begin in the primary grades. Advanced Placement courses, independent study, individual tutorials, and a week's off-campus study program in the spring are offered. A summer program offers academic courses, a day camp, and a sports camp. Tuition: $7113–$10,894. Financial Aid: $529,124. D. Ralph Davison, Jr. (Hamilton, B.A. 1968; Middlebury, M.A. 1972; University of Virginia, Ph.D. 1982), was appointed Headmaster in 1986. *Southern Association.*

Greenfield School   1969

3351 NC Hwy 42 West, P.O. Box 3525, Wilson, NC 27895-3525.
252-237-8046; Fax 252-237-1825;
E-mail greenfield@simflex.com

Greenfield School is a college preparatory day school enrolling 330 boys and girls in Pre-School–Grade 12. Founded by a group of parents in 1969, the School aims to provide a thorough and challenging academic program in an environment that stimulates intellectual curiosity and encourages positive attitudes and habits. In addition to the traditional programs, a computer curriculum is offered in all grades. Academic and sports programs are available in the summer. Tuition: $1750–$5150. Diane Hamilton is Director of Admissions; Janet B. Beaman (East Carolina University, B.S. 1967, M.Ed. 1970) was appointed Headmaster in 1987. *Southern Association.*

Hickory Day School   1994

2535 21st Avenue, NE, Hickory, NC 28601. 828-256-9492;
Fax 828-256-1475; E-mail hds@conninc.com;
Web Site hickoryday.org

Hickory Day School, founded by parents seeking a strong education for their children, enrolls 105 boys and girls in Pre-Kindergarten–Grade 8. The School's mission is to cultivate a love of learning, curiosity, and creativity in a stimulating environment. The challenging, developmentally appropriate curriculum emphasizes problem solving and a firm foundation in the traditional disciplines as well as values of honor, good citizenship, and respect for diversity. Activities include community service, student government, and the school newspaper. Before- and after-school care and a summer enrichment program are optional. Tuition: $5900. Financial aid is available. Karen M. Hoffheimer is Director of Advancement; William J. Valenta (State University of New York [New Paltz], B.A., M.Ed.) is Headmaster.

New Garden Friends School   1971

1128 New Garden Road, Greensboro, NC 27410. 336-299-0964;
Fax 336-292-0347; E-mail NFriendssc@aol.com;
Web Site www.ngfs.greensboro.nc.us

New Garden Friends School was founded by interested citizens to provide an environment that encourages intellectual and spiritual integrity in their children. Based on Quaker values, the School's philosophy emphasizes the worth of each student, the development of individual abilities, and the discovery of gifts as yet undeveloped. Reading, writing, and listening form the basis for mastery of skills across all disciplines as students progress from the three-year-old preschool through Grade 8. Music, drama, foreign language, and physical education enrich the curriculum. Children participate in community service projects; an after-school program is optional. Tuition and Fees: $1750–$6235. Financial aid is available. Marty Goldstein and David Tomlin are Co-Heads.

Oak Ridge Military Academy   OAK RIDGE

Oak Ridge, NC 27310. 336-643-4131 or 800-321-7904;
Fax 336-643-1797; Web Site www.oakridgemilitary.com

Oak Ridge Military Academy in Oak Ridge, North Carolina, is a coeducational, college preparatory school enrolling students in Grades 7–12. Its 101-acre campus, a National and State Historic District, is located on the Piedmont plateau, about 15 miles from Greensboro, Winston-Salem, and High Point. The campus, 6 miles north of the Piedmont Triad International Airport, is situated at the crossroads of State Highways 68 and 150.

The school was founded in 1852 as the Oak Ridge Institute by community leaders seeking to offer superior college preparatory education to students in the region. In 1899, Oak Ridge became the first school in North Carolina to be accredited by the Southern Association of Colleges and Schools. A Junior Reserve Officers Training Corps (JROTC) unit was established at the school in 1926. The Academy began enrolling young women in 1971, and the present name was adopted ten years later. In 1991, the State General Assembly designated it "The Official Military Academy of North Carolina."

The mission of Oak Ridge Military Academy, a college preparatory school, is to provide an educational environment that stimulates intellectual curiosity, fosters scholarly competence, encourages academic excellence, rewards self-discipline, and develops leadership potential. Character education is an important element of the Academy's teaching, and its policy permits no tolerance of drugs, alcohol, or tobacco. The Academy seeks to provide a safe, structured environment where young people can develop their full potential without undue or misguided peer pressure.

The Academy is a nonprofit institution owned by the Oak Ridge Foundation, Inc. It is accredited by the Southern Association of Colleges and Schools and holds membership in the Association of Military Colleges and Schools and the National Association of Independent Schools, among other affiliations.

THE CAMPUS. The Alumni Building houses classrooms and a library containing 20,000 volumes. The library is equipped with 10 IBM computer workstations with Internet access and a 10-workstation computer lab provided through Computer Curriculum Corporation. The system is networked to the computer lab, which has an additional 15 workstations. A CD-ROM stack is available for access to reference materials. Belk Science Building contains classrooms and science laboratories; Cottrell Hall houses music and photojournalism facilities.

The Cadet Dining Hall, where all meals are provided by a professional food service, is adjacent to the Cadet Lounge, and a Cadet Store offers necessities. Cadets live two to a room in the four dormitories: Holt Hall, Whitaker Hall, Armfield Hall, and Caesar Cone Hall. All the dormitories have one or more apartments in which faculty or staff members reside. Other facilities are Cummingham Amphitheater, Linville Chapel, and the Linville Infirmary.

The Colonel Bonner Field House is the primary athletic facility, while King Gymnasium is used for indoor sports. The swimming pool was built as an addition to the gym in 1934, and the whole building was remodeled in 1992. Three athletic fields, one paintball course, an obstacle course, two rifle ranges, six tennis courts, and a rappelling tower are among the resources.

THE FACULTY. Major General John H. Admire, United States Marine Corps (Ret.), was appointed President in 1998. He holds degrees from the University of Oklahoma (B.A. Advertising, M.A. Journalism), Old Dominion University (M.A. Military History), Salve Regina Newport University (M.A. International Relations), and Naval War College (M.A. National Security and Strategic Studies). General Admire retired from the Marine Corps as the Commanding General, 1st Marine Division, Camp Pendleton, California, after 33 years and five combat tours.

The full-time faculty consist of 14 men and 14 women. Ten faculty/staff members live on campus. Approximately 55 percent of the faculty hold master's degrees or higher. There are 4 part-time instructors. Faculty members serve as study hall supervisors, coaches, and advisors for classes and organizations. They are encouraged to pursue advanced degrees at several local universities and to attend conferences and seminars related to their professional development.

An infirmary on campus is staffed by qualified medical personnel. Full medical services are available at hospitals in Greensboro and Winston-Salem.

STUDENT BODY. In 1998–99, 135 boys and 34 girls were enrolled as boarding students and 30 boys and 10 girls as day students. They were distributed as follows: Grade 7–26, Grade 8–24, Grade 9–36, Grade 10–40, Grade 11–50, and Grade 12–30. The majority came from North Carolina, and others were from 21 states, the District of Columbia, and nine foreign countries.

ACADEMIC PROGRAM. The academic year, divided into semesters, begins in August and extends to the first week in June, with vacations of one week in October, one week at Thanksgiving, two weeks at Christmas, one week in February, and ten days in the spring. Classes meet five days a week and are scheduled in six 45-minute periods. The average class has ten students.

Within the curriculum, special provisions are made for the gifted and talented. Extra academic help is offered, or may be required, during "Help Classes" scheduled after the last class period every day except Friday. Academic reports are sent to parents every two weeks.

To graduate, a cadet must complete 22 units of credit, including 4 in English, 3 in social studies, 3 in mathematics beyond pre-algebra, 4 in science, ½ in computer science, ½ in physical education, ½ in health, and 2 in the same foreign language. All students take Leadership Education Training in the United States Army Junior Reserve Officers Training Corps Program. Seventh and eighth graders are required to take Latin. English as a Second Language is available for international students.

The curriculum includes a full range of the traditional academic subjects; instruction up to fourth-year level in Latin, French, German, and Spanish; music appreciation and performance; and Driver Education. Advanced Placement courses are offered in English, French, German, Spanish, U.S. History, Calculus, Statistics, Biology, Environmental Science, Chemistry, Physics, and Music Theory. College-level courses are offered in English, American History, and Chemistry.

All seniors take the Scholastic Aptitude Test (SAT) and, in 1999, the cadets had 1100 as an average combined verbal and math score. A guidance counselor maintains college catalogs and scholarship information and monitors the application process. Faculty and staff members, including the President, also assist in college placement. According to school records, 100 percent of the graduates of the last nine years have been accepted at a college or service academy of their choice.

Oak Ridge Military Academy Summer programs include academic courses for credit or remediation for students in Grades 7—12 and a Leadership Camp for cadets and potential cadets who have completed Grades 7—11.

STUDENT ACTIVITIES. The Corps of Cadets is organized as a battalion comprised of four line companies, Band Company, and Headquarters Company. A cadet's rank and position within the Corps is determined by his or her academic and military performance, participation in activities, and demonstrated leadership potential. All cadets are required to adhere to the policies outlined in the Oak Ridge Military Academy Cadet Regulations Handbook and the Cadet Honor Code and Creed.

Cadets are encouraged to participate in community service activities, clubs, leadership opportunities, and other pursuits. Among the extracurricular options are the production of the yearbook and *The Oak Leaf,* girls' club, and a scouting program. Cadets are invited to take part in the Governor's Page Program, the Military Band Festival, and state and national drill competitions.

Oak Ridge Military Academy is a member of the Triad Athletic Conference and the North Carolina Independent Schools Athletic Association. Men's and women's teams compete against private and public schools in football, soccer, cross-country, volleyball, basketball, swimming, wrestling, baseball, tennis, and track and field. The rifle and drill teams compete on a national level. Middle School students may compete for positions on junior varsity and varsity teams, and Middle School soccer and basketball are available. Every student has the opportunity to participate in intramural activities including flag football, basketball, volleyball, paintball, rappelling, and cross-country running.

The Junior Ring Dance (junior prom) and the Military Ball (senior prom) are among the scheduled social events. A full range of activities is planned for weekends. Traditional events on the school calendar include Homecoming, Parents' Days, Alumni Day, Academic Awards Day, Annual Sports Banquet, and Mothers' Day.

ADMISSION AND COSTS. Oak Ridge Military Academy seeks students of average to above-average academic ability who have the motivation to succeed in a college preparatory environment. It maintains a nondiscriminatory admission policy and admits new students in Grades 7–12 and occasionally to a postgraduate year. Admission is based on achievement and entrance test results and a personal interview with student and parents. Application, with a fee of $50, should be made as early as possible, preferably in the spring for fall enrollment. Students may be admitted at any time during the year.

In 1999–2000, boarding tuition is $16,985 for seven-day residents; day tuition is $9800. The fees include books and all predictable expenses. The initial uniform issue is $1530. A deposit should also be made for a recommended spending allowance of $10–$20 per week. Limited need-based financial aid was awarded in 1998–99.

Deputy Directors of Admissions: Cheryl Fleischfresser and
    Angel Colman
Director of Finance: Sue B. Silver
Academic Dean: Don Parrotte
Guidance Counselor: Amy Stoller, M.A.
Athletic Director: Jeffrey Stoller

Providence Day School   1970

*5800 Sardis Road, Charlotte, NC 28270. 704-364-6848;
    Admissions 704-887-7041; Fax 704-887-7042;
    E-mail info@pds.charlotte.nc.us; Web Site www.providenceday.org*

Providence Day, a college preparatory school serving 1378 girls and boys in Transitional Kindergarten–Grade 12, has a reputation for academic excellence. Within a structured, yet nurturing environment, the curriculum is designed to develop the intellectual, physical, social, and moral aspects of each student. Career exploration for seniors and 23 Advanced Placement courses enrich the program. Students are actively involved in such extracurriculars as honor societies, three publications, Student Council, clubs, and varsity athletics. An extensive summer program is available. Tuition: $7400–$11,150. Financial Aid: $500,000. Dr. Susan Beattie is Director of Admissions; Eugene A. Bratek (University of Virginia, B.A. 1967; Rutgers, M.Ed. 1982) was named Headmaster in 1986. *Southern Association.*

The O'Neal School   1971

*Airport Road, P.O. Box 290, Southern Pines, NC 28388.
    910-692-6920; Fax 910-692-6930;
    Web Site www.onealschool.org*

O'Neal is a college preparatory school dedicated to the development of academic excellence, strength of character, and physical well-being in an environment where integrity, self-discipline, and consideration for others are fundamental. There are 392 students in Pre-Kindergarten–Grade 12. The curriculum in Kindergarten–Grade 8 is based on the Core Knowledge Program, which emphasizes cultural literacy and content learning. Students take part in many athletic, extracurricular, and community service activities. There is also a specialized learning development program. Tuition: $6070–$8900. Financial Aid: $340,000. Deborah Henry is Director of Admissions; Jay St. John (Boston University, B.S. [Elementary Education], M.Ed. [Educational Media and Technology]) is Headmaster. *Southern Association.*

Ravenscroft School   1862

*7409 Falls of the Neuse Road, Raleigh, NC 27615. 919-847-0900;
    Fax 919-846-2371; E-mail tgrubb@ravenscroft.org*

Located on a 125-acre campus, Ravenscroft School is a coeducational, college preparatory day school enrolling 1030 students in Pre-school through Grade 12. The School's purpose is to develop the whole child—academically, socially, aesthetically, physically, and spiritually. Numerous Advanced Placement courses are offered, emphasizing experiential learning activities and community service. A wide range of extracurricular opportunities is available including student government, publications, sports, and interest clubs. There is a summer program. Tuition: $5800–$9900. Financial aid is available. Mrs. Patricia M. Grubb is Director of Admissions; James C. Ledyard (Princeton, A.B. 1968; Stanford, M.A. 1972; Claremont, Ph.D. 1987) was appointed Headmaster in 1991. *Southern Association.*

Rocky Mount Academy   1968

*1313 Avondale Avenue, Rocky Mount, NC 27803. 252-443-4126;
    Fax 252-937-7922; E-mail rmaheadmaster@hotmail.com;
    Web Site rmacademy.com*

This coeducational, college preparatory day school enrolls 310 students in PreKindergarten–Grade 12. Rocky Mount Academy seeks to prepare students for the challenges and responsibilities of life and college in a trusting, academically rigorous, and supportive environment. In addition to the core subjects, the curriculum includes Honors and Advanced Placement courses, guidance, art, drama, physical education, foreign language, computers, and music. Sports, community service, publications, field trips, and clubs enrich the program. Tuition: $2400–$6500. Financial Aid: $160,000. Blair F. Davis is Admissions Director; Thomas R. Stevens (Yale, B.A. 1973; Columbia, M.A. 1978) was appointed Headmaster in 1999. *Southern Association.*

Saint Mary's School   1842

*900 Hillsborough Street, Raleigh, NC 27603-1689. 919-424-4100;
    Toll free 800-948-1689; Fax 919-424-4137;
    E-mail admiss@saint-marys.edu; Web Site www.saintmarysschool.org*

Historically linked to the Episcopal Church, Saint Mary's School was founded to provide excellence in education for young women. Today, the School enrolls over 270 boarding and day students in Grades 9–12. Honors, Advanced Placement, and college-level classes are available on the 23-acre campus located a few blocks from the State Capitol and North Carolina State University. Activities feature athletics, fine arts, and student government. Resident Fees: $22,200; Day Fees: $10,800. Need- and merit-based scholarships are available. Hope Tyndall is Director of Admissions; Clauston Levi Jenkins, Jr. (University of North Carolina, A.B., J.D.; University of Virginia, M.A., Ph.D.), is President. *Southern Association*.

St. Timothy's-Hale School   1972

3400 White Oak Road, Raleigh, NC 27609. 919-782-3331;
Fax 919-571-3330; Web Site http://www.sttimothyshale.com

St. Timothy's-Hale School is an independent Episcopal, coeducational, college preparatory day school for students in Grades 5–12. Fully accredited, the School is committed to high academic achievement in an atmosphere that emphasizes traditional Christian values, a supportive environment, and small class sizes. Advanced Placement courses in all subjects are offered in addition to the core curriculum. The academic program is enhanced by diverse extracurricular activities including art, music, drama, computer, publications, student government, competitive athletics, and interest clubs. Tuition: $7200–$8100. Mr. Chris Kelley is Director of Admissions; Lawrence E. Wall, Jr. (University of the South, B.A.; University of North Carolina, M.A.), was appointed Headmaster in 1996. *Southern Association*.

St. Timothy's School   1958

4523 Six Forks Road, Raleigh, NC 27609. 919-781-0531;
Fax 919-787-1131; E-mail sttima@netscape.net;
Web Site www.citysearch.com/rdu/sttimothys

St. Timothy's, an Episcopal, coeducational school, is the oldest accredited nonpublic school in North Carolina and enrolls students of all faiths in Kindergarten–Grade 4. The School is committed to academic excellence in an atmosphere that emphasizes traditional values, small class sizes, and a supportive environment. The academic curriculum is complemented by offerings in computer, Spanish, music, art, and physical education. Extracurricular activities include student government. The Middle and Upper schools share a separate campus on White Oak Road. Tuition: $3930–$6000. Financial Aid: $61,000. Cathy Clement is Admissions Director; Michael S. Bailey (University of North Carolina, B.A.; East Carolina University, M.A.) is Headmaster. *Southern Association*.

Salem Academy   WINSTON-SALEM

500 Salem Avenue, Winston-Salem, NC 27108. 336-721-2644
or Toll Free 877-40SALEM; E-mail academy@salem.edu;
Web Site www.salemacademy.com

SALEM ACADEMY in Winston-Salem, North Carolina, is a college preparatory boarding and day school for girls in Grades 9 through 12. Winston-Salem (population 150,000) is located in the Piedmont region of the state, approximately 90 miles from both Charlotte and Raleigh. It is served by two airports and Interstate highways 40, 77, and 85. The city's own activities and four colleges—North Carolina School of the Arts, Wake Forest University, Winston-Salem State University, and Salem College (the Academy's "sister school")—provide cultural and educational opportunities for Academy students.

Founded in 1772 by Moravian settlers, Salem Academy has been in continuous operation for more than 200 years. Initially a day school, it added boarding facilities in 1802. Postgraduate work was first offered in the 1860s, and Salem College was chartered in 1866. In 1930, the Academy and Salem College were separated, with both schools remaining on the original campus.

Throughout its history, Salem Academy has maintained its original commitment to the education of women. It endeavors to provide "a thorough preparation for a continuing education and a fulfilling personal life, a spiritual and ethical climate in all phases of school life, and a program promoting mental and physical well-being." While the Academy retains its affiliation with the Moravian church, students of various religious backgrounds are enrolled.

A nonprofit institution, Salem Academy is governed by a 28-member Board of Trustees, which serves as a common Board for the school and Salem College. Board members are chosen by the Synod of the Moravian Church, the Alumnae Association, and other organizations. Many of the school's 2500 living graduates lend it financial support and refer prospective students. Salem Academy is accredited by the Southern Association of Colleges and Schools. It holds membership in the National Association of Independent Schools, the North Carolina Association of Independent Schools, The National Association of Principals of Schools for Girls, the National Association of College Admissions Counselors, The College Board, and the Council on Religion in Schools.

THE CAMPUS. The 57-acre campus, which is shared with Salem College, adjoins the restored 18th-century Moravian village of Old Salem, a national historic landmark. It encompasses lawns and wooded areas as well as hockey fields, a softball field, an archery range, and 12 tennis courts.

Six buildings on the east side of the common campus constitute the self-contained portion of the Academy facilities. The main building provides administrative offices, reception rooms, and student recreation rooms as well as two dormitory wings, Shaffner and Bahnson. Weaver Building contains the library, the art studio, the admissions office, the dining room, and the school kitchen. Critz Hall houses classrooms, language and science laboratories, and faculty offices. Hodges Hall contains a music studio and library, an auditorium, a small meditation chapel, and dormitories for the upperclassmen. In addition, the school shares with Salem College the facilities of the Dale H. Gramley Library, Salem Fine Arts Center, gymnasium and indoor swimming pool, the Student Life and Fitness Center, the Student Commons Center, and the infirmary. The Academy plant is valued at $6,300,000.

THE FACULTY. D. Wayne Burkette, appointed Head of School in July 1994, is a graduate of the University of North Carolina (Chapel Hill), Moravian Theological Seminary, and Union Theological Seminary of Virginia. In the spring of 1997, he was named Vice-President of Salem Academy and College.

The full-time faculty, including administrators who teach, number 27. They hold 29 baccalaureate, 15 master's, and 3 doctoral degrees representing study at Appalachian State, Bob Jones University, Clemson, Davidson, Duke, D'Youville College, Florida State, Furman, Lenoir-Rhyne, North Carolina A&T State University, Randolph-Macon Woman's College, Salem, Wake Forest, Western Illinois, Whittier, and the Universities of Mississippi, North Carolina (Chapel Hill, Greensboro), Southern California, Tennessee, and Virginia. Two part-time instructors teach Theatre and Old and New Testament. Eight House Counselors supervise the dormitories. Staff benefits include a health insurance plan, a retirement plan, and Social Security.

The Academy shares the services of physicians and a full-time infirmary staff with Salem College. Medical facilities are available nearby.

STUDENT BODY. In 1999–2000, Salem Academy enrolled 104 boarding girls and 109 day girls, 14 to 18 years of age, as follows: 38 in Grade 9, 51 in Grade 10, 68 in Grade 11, and 57 in Grade 12.

The boarding students come from 13 states, the District of Columbia, and Germany, Japan, and Korea. Day students

reside in Winston-Salem and communities within a 25-mile radius.

ACADEMIC PROGRAM. The school year, from late August to late May, is divided into two academic terms and a miniterm. There are two long weekends as well as vacations at Thanksgiving, Christmas, and in the spring.

Classes meet five days a week. A typical school day includes Assembly, five academic class periods, a recess, a study hall, and an assembly period. Language and science laboratories, study halls, music, studio art, physical education, and student activities are scheduled during four afternoon class periods. Boarding students have supervised study in the evening.

There are 9 to 15 students in an average class. Conference periods provide opportunities for individual help. The January miniterm also offers a concentrated tutorial program. Grades are discussed with the student and sent to parents every six weeks.

To graduate, a student must earn 20 academic credits, including English 4, Latin 2, a modern foreign language 2, history 3, mathematics 3, and science 3. Other required courses are Health in Grade 9, Religion in Grade 11 or 12, and Physical Education in Grades 9, 10, and 11. A course in art, drama, or music is required.

The curriculum includes English Composition and Literature 1–4; French 1–3, Spanish 1–3, Latin 1–3; Modern European History, United States History, Humanities, Economics, Political Science, World History; Algebra 1–2, Analytical Geometry, Plane and Solid Geometry, Finite Mathematics, Calculus; Computer 1–2, Advanced Algebra and Trigonometry; Biology, Advanced Placement Biology, Chemistry, Advanced Placement Chemistry, Conceptual Physics, Advanced Placement Physics; Old Testament, New Testament; Studio Art; Theatre; and choral and vocal instruction. Private lessons are available in piano, organ, harp, flute, cello, violin, classical guitar, harpsichord, woodwind, and brass and percussion instruments. Advanced courses are offered to qualified juniors and seniors, who also may take courses for credit at Salem College. An intensive music program for qualified students is available in conjunction with the School of Music at Salem College.

The January miniterm provides each student an opportunity to choose her own educational experience. Programs both on and off campus provide a variety of ways for students to pursue individual interests. A school-sponsored trip is usually offered each year to such places as England, Greece, Canada, Australia, France, and Egypt. Internships and independent studies in teaching, music, medicine, banking, and other fields may be pursued under faculty supervision. Teachers conduct intensive reviews and tutorials, introduce new topics, and assign and supervise independent projects.

In 1999, all 45 graduates entered college. Typically, they attend such colleges and universities as Columbia, Dartmouth, Davidson, Duke, Furman, Georgia Tech, Harvard, Wake Forest,

Wellesley, and the Universities of North Carolina (Chapel Hill), and Virginia.

STUDENT ACTIVITIES. The student government is composed of two elected bodies. Within Salem's honor tradition, each girl is expected to be honest and considerate. The Honor Cabinet advises and guides through constructive counsel and leadership, and it may recommend disciplinary action. The Student Council, composed of the class presidents, a representative from each class, and the Honor Cabinet president, deals with student relations, activities, and concerns.

Students publish a newspaper, a yearbook, and an annual literary-art magazine. The Theatre Club stages two major productions a year, and the Glee Club performs both on and off campus. Since 1988, the Glee Club has performed at Carnegie Hall, in cathedrals throughout England, and in the Intermountain Youth Concert in Salt Lake City, Utah. Among other student organizations is the Fellowship Council, which sponsors parties, campus activities, devotional services, and community projects.

Varsity teams in field hockey, soccer, volleyball, basketball, softball, tennis, swimming, cross-country, and track compete with other schools in the Piedmont Athletic Conference of Independent Schools. All girls participate in a friendly rivalry during the year, competing in team spirit as members of either the Purple or the Gold squad.

The Student Activities Directors plan trips to the theatre, concerts, and to Wake Forest sporting events and cultural and social activities. They also plan outdoor activities such as rafting on the New River, camping, wilderness expeditions, and snow skiing. Dances and social events are scheduled with The Asheville School, Christ School, McCallie, Woodberry Forest, and others. With written parental approval, boarding students in Grade 12 may have unlimited overnight permissions on weekends; students in Grades 9–11 are limited to 12 to 18 overnights per year. On three Sundays a month, boarding students are expected to attend the church or temple service of their choice. Transportation is provided.

Traditional annual events include Opening Assembly, Ring Banquet, Senior Bazaar, Parents' Weekend, Family Weekend, Alumnae Day, Senior Vespers, Honors Banquets, and Recognition and Graduation Exercises.

ADMISSION AND COSTS. Salem Academy seeks to enroll academically motivated students who have personal integrity; a positive attitude toward work; potential for developing self-discipline, self-confidence, and self-esteem; and a strong desire to broaden their intellectual and cultural horizons. New students are admitted in Grades 9–11 and occasionally in Grade 12. Candidates must submit a transcript, academic and personal recommendations, and the results of the Secondary School Admission Test; a personal interview is also required. Application should be made during the year preceding desired entrance, but late entrance and midyear enrollment are sometimes possible. There is a $35 application fee.

In 1999–2000, boarding tuition is $21,120; day-student tuition is $11,800, including lunches. Additional expenses are books ($300) and an activities fee ($125).

The Academy awards scholarships on the basis of merit and financial need. Sixty-seven students receive aid totaling $755,000 annually.

Dean of Faculty: Eileen Cahill
Dean of Students: Mary Lorick Thompson
Director of Alumnae Affairs: Amy Williamson
Director of Admission: Karen G. Kimberly
College Counselor: Frances Beattie
Business Manager: Allyson Brown
Director of Athletics: Lorie Howard

Summit School   1933

2100 Reynolda Road, Winston-Salem, NC 27106. 336-722-2777;
   Fax 336-724-0099

Summit School is a day school enrolling 690 boys and girls in Pre-Kindergarten–Grade 9. The School strives to help students learn to respect their own beliefs, values, and achievements as well as those of others and encourages them to take responsibility for their own education. The traditional subjects are complemented by French (beginning in Pre-Kindergarten), Spanish, Russian, Latin, art, music, drama, and computers. Other activities are sports and service groups. Field trips and student exchanges with other schools add variety to the program. Tuition: $7185–$10,480. Financial Aid: $315,000. Katherine Memory is Director of Admission; Sandra P. Adams (Wake Forest, B.A., M.A.; University of North Carolina, Ed.D.) was appointed Head in 1990.

Westchester Academy   1967

204 Pine Tree Lane, High Point, NC 27265. 336-869-2128;
   Fax 336-869-9298; Web Site www.westchesteracademy.com

Westchester Academy is a college preparatory day school enrolling 510 boys and girls in Kindergarten–Grade 12. Its mission is to provide an intellectually exciting environment that will enable students to excel in all areas associated with the classical liberal arts tradition—academics, athletics, and the arts—while simultaneously developing strong moral and ethical values. A low student-teacher ratio and familylike atmosphere enhance the learning process. Advanced Placement courses are available. Athletics, music, and debate are among the major student activities. Tuition: $7000–$8000. Financial Aid: $130,000. Donna P. Meyerhoeffer is Director of Admissions; Peter M. Cowen (Kenyon, B.A. 1970; Fairleigh Dickinson, M.A. 1980) was appointed Headmaster in 1991. *Southern Association*.

OHIO

Archbishop Hoban High School   1953

400 Elbon Avenue, Akron, OH 44306. 330-773-6658;
* Fax 330-773-9100*

Founded by the Brothers of the Holy Cross of Notre Dame, Indiana, Archbishop Hoban High enrolls 715 young men and women from Catholic and other religious traditions. This Blue Ribbon School of Excellence offers a college preparatory curriculum that develops each student spiritually, intellectually, aesthetically, socially, and physically. The academic program includes 15 honors and Advanced Placement courses, required religious studies, and a community service commitment. The Campus Ministry provides numerous opportunities for spiritual enrichment, while the extracurricular program features 26 interest groups and interscholastic sports. Tuition: $4700. Br. Dennis Bednarz, CSC, is Director of Admission; Br. Kenneth Haders, CSC, is President. *North Central Association.*

Canton Country Day School   1964

3000 Demington Avenue, NW, Canton, OH 44718. 330-453-8279;
* Fax 330-453-6038; E-mail Mail-office@ccd-school.org;*
* Web Site www.ccd-school.org*

A Nationally Recognized School of Excellence, Canton Country Day is an independent, nonsectarian school enrolling boys and girls in Kindergarten–Grade 8. It is culturally and economically mixed, with minorities comprising about 20 percent of the student body. The curriculum prepares students for a variety of competitive secondary choices. The program includes English, math, social studies, French, art, music, library, physical education, computer, creative movement, science, athletics, and community service. The School is accredited by the Independent Schools Association of the Central States and chartered by the State of Ohio. Tuition: $7900. Financial Aid: $330,000. Phyllis Scott is Director of Admissions; David J. Costello (Bowdoin, A.B.; Wesleyan, M.A.L.S.) is Headmaster.

Cincinnati Country Day School   1926

6905 Given Road, Cincinnati, OH 45243-2898. 513-561-7298;
* Fax 513-561-1035; E-mail whitehorp@ccds.cincinnati.oh.us;*
* Web Site http://www.ccds.cincinnati.oh.us*

This coeducational, college preparatory school enrolls more than 875 day students from early childhood through Grade 12. The School seeks academic excellence, close student-faculty relationships, and cultural/socioeconomic diversity. Physical education and swimming programs, fine arts activities, and computer technology are provided at all levels. The athletic program for Grades 7–12 offers 19 varsity sports including gymnastics, swimming, and crew. A summer program is available. Tuition: $6120–$12,475. Financial Aid: $1,409,996. Pamela Whitehorne is Director of Admissions; Charles F. Clark (St. Lawrence, B.S., M.Ed.; University of Delaware, Ed.D.) is Head of School.

The Columbus Academy   1911

Box 30745, 4300 Cherry Bottom Road, Gahanna, OH 43230.
* 614-475-2311; Fax 614-475-0396;*
* E-mail Valerie_Wilson@ColumbusAcademy.org;*
* Web Site www.ColumbusAcademy.org*

The Academy is a coeducational, college preparatory day school enrolling 910 students in Pre-Kindergarten–Grade 12. The Academy, located on a 235-acre campus, first admitted girls in 1990 and achieved full coeducation in 1992. The school is committed to providing a balanced education of academics, arts, athletics, and activities, including a significant service component. Taught by 130 full- and part-time faculty, students are provided a liberal arts foundation in the five basic disciplines. Summer enrichment and remedial courses and a day camp are conducted. Tuition: $5990–$11,980. Financial Aid: $567,000. Louis A. Schultz is Admissions Director; John M. MacKenzie (Bowdoin College, A.B.; Columbia University, M.A.) is Headmaster.

Columbus School for Girls   1898

56 South Columbia Avenue, Columbus, OH 43209-1698.
* 614-252-0781; Fax 614-252-0571;*
* Web Site http://www.csg.capital.edu*

This college preparatory day school serving 650 diverse students from age 3 to Grade 12 is committed to the value of a liberal arts education for women and to an academically excellent program that encourages each student to develop to her fullest capacity. The goal is to foster in each student strong skills and a love of learning that will lead to lifelong intellectual curiosity, aesthetic understanding, desire for health and fitness, and commitment to social responsibility. State-of-the-art science and math labs, an arts wing, and two libraries support the program. Activities include sports, clubs, and theater. Tuition: $5775–$11,495. Financial aid is available. Terrie Hale Scheckelhoff is Director of Admissions; Dr. Patricia T. Hayot (Marquette, B.A., M.A.; University of Michigan, Ph.D.) is Head of School.

Gilmour Academy   1946

34001 Cedar Road, Gates Mills, OH 44040. 440-473-8050;
* Fax 440-473-8010; E-mail admissions@gilmour.org;*
* Web Site www.gilmour.org*

Now in its 53rd year of Catholic education in the Holy Cross tradition, Gilmour Academy enrolls 645 students, including day students in Preschool–Grade 12 and boarders in Grades 7–12. By instilling a strong sense of self-worth through individual achievement, Gilmour helps students reach their personal best. Small class sizes challenge each student's potential, while extended class time allows students to engage in the same active learning environment they will encounter in the workplace in the 21st century. Numerous athletic, artistic, dramatic, and civic activities are offered. Boarding Tuition: $20,555–$22,835; Day Tuition: $5200–$14,910. Financial Aid: $1,000,000. Devin K. Schlickmann is Dean of Admissions; Br. Robert E. Lavelle, CSC, is Headmaster. *North Central Association.*

The Grand River Academy   1831

3042 College Street, P.O. Box 222, Austinburg, OH 44010.
   440-275-2811; Fax 440-275-1825;
   E-mail academy@interlaced.net

Set on a modern, 150-acre rural campus, Grand River Academy is a structured yet informal five- and seven-day boarding school enrolling 115 boys in Grade 9–Postgraduate. Students, including those who have not previously enjoyed academic success, benefit from small classes, supervised nightly study periods, regularly scheduled help sessions, and a faculty available after classroom hours. The college preparatory curriculum includes English as a Second Language. Academics are supplemented by interscholastic soccer, tennis, baseball, and basketball as well as drama, computers, paintball, weightlifting, and roller blading. Tuition: $17,200–$18,200. Keith Corlew is Director of Admission; Randy D. Blum (Milligan College, B.S.; Ashland University, M.Ed.) is Headmaster.

Hathaway Brown School   1876

19600 North Park Boulevard, Shaker Heights, OH 44122.
   216-932-4214; Fax 216-371-1501; Web Site www.hb.edu

Hathaway Brown, a college preparatory day school serving 720 students in a coeducational early childhood program and all-girls Kindergarten–Grade 12, seeks to maintain a tradition of excellence through an academically challenging program in a lively, creative atmosphere. The School aims to equip young women for the future with knowledge, resolve, and imagination. The curriculum offers Advanced Placement in all fields as well as the arts, computer studies, and athletics. A Science Research course enables students to work on experiments in cutting-edge labs around the city. Adventure Learning is required in Middle School; Spanish begins in Kindergarten. Tuition: $3600–$15,000. Financial Aid: $975,000. Terry D. Finefrock is Director of Enrollment Management; H. William Christ is Head of School.

Hawken School   1915

Lower and Middle Schools: 5000 Clubside Road, Lyndhurst, OH
   44124. 440-423-4446.
Upper School: P.O. Box 8002, Gates Mills, OH 44040.
   440-423-4446; Fax 440-423-2973; E-mail admission@hawken.
   edu; Web Site http://www.hawken.edu/

Founded by James A. Hawken with a group of Cleveland parents to provide educational opportunities that emphasize academic excellence, individuality, character, and fair play, Hawken School enrolls 940 day boys and girls in Pre-school–Grade 12. Advanced Placement courses are offered in every discipline, along with 16 interscholastic sports, fine and performing arts, writing, debate, and outdoor education. Academic and recreational summer programs are available. Tuition: $3335–$13,570. Financial assistance is available. James S. Berkman (Harvard College, B.A.; Oxford University, M.Phil.; Harvard Law School, J.D.) was appointed Head of School in 1998.

Lake Ridge Academy   1963

37501 Center Ridge Road, North Ridgeville, OH 44039.
   440-777-9434; Fax 440-353-0324;
   Web Site www.lakeridgeacademy.org

Lake Ridge Academy is a college preparatory day school enrolling 215 boys and 215 girls in Kindergarten–Grade 12. The school's aim is to foster intellectual growth, a spirit of cooperation, and respect for self and others. Hands-on methodologies begin in Kindergarten. Enrichment programs, including outdoor education, are provided by specialists at all grade levels. Twelve Advanced Placement courses are offered in the Upper School. Sports, drama, music, Student Council, and interest clubs are among the activities. Tuition: $10,150–$16,000. Financial Aid: $662,000. Rebecca A. Mercer is Director of Admission; Joseph J. Ferber (George Washington University, B.A. 1967; American University, M.Ed. 1975) was appointed Headmaster in 1987.

Magnificat High School   1955

20770 Hilliard Boulevard, Rocky River, OH 44116. 440-331-1572;
   Fax 440-331-7257; Web Site www.magnificaths.org

The Sisters of the Humility of Mary founded this secondary day school, enrolling 840 young women, to promote growth and achievement within the context of a Christian philosophy. The college preparatory program, balancing the liberal arts and sciences, requires four years of theology and 30 hours of community service. Honors and Advanced Placement courses are available to qualified students, and an extensive tutoring program provides long- and short-term remediation. Girls participate in sports, band and choral concerts, academic teams, publications, drama, retreats, and interest clubs. Tuition: $5650. Financial Aid: $350,000. Terry Schabel Carney '80 is Director of Admission; Sr. Mary Pat Cook, H.M., '63 (Notre Dame College of Ohio, B.S.; Indiana University, M.S.Ed.), is Principal. *North Central Association.*

Maumee Valley Country Day School   1884

1715 South Reynolds Road, Toledo, OH 43614. 419-381-1313;
   Fax 419-381-9941; E-mail admissions@mvcds.com
   Web Site www.mvcds.com

Maumee Valley Country Day School is a community-oriented school enrolling 475 boys and girls in Preschool Age 3–Grade 12. Small classes and individual instruction are typical throughout the School; the Upper School is college preparatory, with focus on the liberal arts, critical thinking, and creative expression. The School offers programs in the fine arts and sports, and a month-long Winterim for independent study on or off campus, throughout the country, or abroad. Summer programs in mathematics, English, and computer studies are available. Tuition: $3775–$10,550. Financial Aid: $700,000. Phineas Anderson (Trinity College, A.B.; Harvard Graduate School of Education, M. Ed.) is Head of School.

The Miami Valley School   1964

5151 Denise Drive, Dayton, OH 45429. 937-434-4444;
   Admissions 937-434-4452; Fax 937-434-1415;
   E-mail kbright125@aol.com

The Miami Valley School is a coeducational college preparatory day school enrolling 500 students in an Early Childhood Program–Grade 12. Its primary purpose is "to provide a superior academic program to able and talented students who have the potential to master learning skills and to think analytically"; the School also strives to aid its students in maturing physically, emotionally, and socially. Older students are offered a four-week independent study program. Activities include sports, music, drama, and publications. A Summer Camp is available for all ages. Tuition: $2520–$10,100. Financial Aid: $445,880. Karyl Bright is Director of Admission; Thomas G. Brereton (Cornell, B.A. 1971; Colgate, M.A.T. 1974) was appointed Headmaster in 1986.

Old Trail School   1920

2315 Ira Road, P.O. Box 827, Bath, OH 44210-0827.
330-666-1118; Fax 330-666-2187;
E-mail jbrookhart@oldtrail.org; Web Site www.oldtrail.org

Old Trail School is a day school enrolling 520 boys and girls in Preschool–Grade 8. Situated on 57 acres within the boundaries of the Cuyahoga Valley National Recreation Area in north-suburban Akron, the School is also accessible to residents of south-suburban Cleveland and Medina County. It offers a personal, nurturing, and academically challenging environment. The traditional liberal arts curriculum places an emphasis on the visual and performing arts, foreign languages, computer literacy, and physical education. Summer academic and enrichment programs are offered. Tuition: $4620–$9750. Financial Aid: $400,000. Judy Brookhart is Admission and Marketing Director; Peter G. Wilson (University of Michigan, B.S. 1956, M.S. 1960) is Headmaster.

The Phillips-Osborne School   1972

150 Gillette Street, Painesville, OH 44077. 440-352-7574;
Fax 440-352-3083;
Web Site www.phillips-osborne.org

The Phillips-Osborne School was founded to meet the need for an independent school in Lake County. Enrolling 300 college-bound boys and girls in three-year-old Pre-Kindergarten–Grade 8, the School seeks to enable students to reach their full potential intellectually, emotionally, physically, ethically, and socially. The "hands-on" curriculum emphasizes basic skills in the traditional disciplines, with enrichment courses such as economics, foreign languages, and tech center. Student Council, fine arts, band, chorus, three publications, Ski Club, intramural sports, community service, and field trips enrich the program. A summer session is offered. Tuition: $1400–$6750. Financial Aid: $100,000. Connie McCann is Director of Admission; Charles J. Roman is Head of School.

St. Charles Preparatory School   1923

2010 East Broad Street, Columbus, OH 43209. 614-252-6714;
Fax 614-251-6800; E-mail dcavello@cd.pvt.k12.oh.us;
Web Site www.cd.pvt.k12.oh.us/schools/sc/index.html

This Roman Catholic day school for young men was founded by Bishop James J. Hartley to provide a "sound classical training" based on the message of Jesus Christ and to equip them for

their chosen professions. Enrolling 479 boys in Grades 9–12, St. Charles offers a college preparatory program as well as Advanced Placement courses for qualified students and limited accommodations for those with learning disabilities. Activities include 13 varsity sports, publications, drama, and Student Council. A summer program provides remediation for incoming freshmen. Tuition: $4090. Financial Aid: $210,000. Dominic J. Cavello (Ohio State, B.A. 1969, M.A. 1972; Xavier, M.Ed. 1985) was named Principal in 1983.

Saint Ignatius High School   1886

1911 West 30th Street, Cleveland, OH 44113-3495. 216-651-0222;
Fax 216-651-6313; Web Site www.ignatius.edu

Conducted by the Society of Jesus, Saint Ignatius is a Roman Catholic day school enrolling 1347 young men in Grades 9–12. The School emphasizes academic excellence and the development of the complete Christian person; by graduation, the student should be open to growth, intellectually competent, loving, religious, and committed to doing justice. The curriculum includes all major disciplines and the study of theology. Computer, health and physical education, and the arts enhance the program; Advanced Placement and college-credit courses are offered. Sports, speech and debate, publications, and student government are among the offerings. Tuition: $6550. Fees: $150. Financial Aid: $1,800,000. Rev. Robert J. Welsh, SJ, is President; Richard F. Clark is Principal. *North Central Association.*

The Seven Hills School   1974

5400 Red Bank Road, Cincinnati, OH 45227. 513-271-9027;
Admission 513-272-5387; Fax 513-271-2471;
E-mail marilyn.collins@7hills.org; Web Site www.7hills.org

Formed by the merger of three institutions, The Seven Hills School provides college preparatory education to 997 boys and girls in Prekindergarten–Grade 12. It seeks to prepare young people to be successful, contributing citizens by emphasizing academic excellence, individual expression and development, and service to school and community. Wireless network connectivity, laptops for teachers, and SMART boards enhance learning. Advanced Placement and honors courses, athletics, an outdoor program, special-interest clubs, and summer enrichment opportunities are offered. Year-long extended care is available through Grade 5. Tuition: $5570–$11,220. Financial Aid: $794,500. Deborah E. Reed (University of Massachusetts, B.A. 1970) is Head of School.

The Springer School   1887

2121 Madison Road, Cincinnati, OH 45208. 513-871-6080;
Fax 513-871-6428; E-mail info@springer.hccanet.org;
Web Site www.hccanet.org/springer

Springer is a day school enrolling 198 boys and girls ages 6 to 14 with diagnosed learning disabilities. Small-group instruction and diagnostic teaching are designed to provide students with the strategies and skills needed to succeed in traditional school settings. The comprehensive curriculum includes academic, physical, and fine arts education. Individualized student programs may include language therapy, psychotherapy, and/or motor skills training. Students are enrolled an average of three years. Workshops and summer programs for students, parents, and professionals are offered through the Springer Center for Learning Disabilities. Tuition: $11,990. Financial aid is available. Jan Annett is Admissions Director; Shelly Weisbacher (Northwestern University, B.A., M.A.) is Executive Director.

The Summit Country Day School   1890

2161 Grandin Road, Hyde Park, Cincinnati, OH 45208.
  513-871-4700; Fax 513-533-5373;
  E-mail geppert_m@summitcds.org; Web Site www.summitcds.org

The Summit, a Catholic, independent school in Hyde Park, provides its students an excellent college preparatory educational experience. The program focuses on the spiritual, academic, physical, social, and artistic development of each student in Preschool–Grade 12. In the Class of 1999, 100 percent matriculated to colleges and universities nationwide, and 18 percent were named National Merit Scholars. The School provides a nationally recognized Educating for Character program and exceptional leadership opportunities. The Summit also offers Advanced Placement in all disciplines, varied extracurriculars, and varsity and intramural sports. Tuition: $3560–$9630. Edward C. Tyrrell (University of Akron, B.S., M.S.Ed.) is Headmaster.

University School   1890

Lower School: 20701 Brantley Road, Shaker Heights, OH 44122.
  216-321-8260; Fax 216-321-4074
Upper School: 2785 SOM Center Road, Hunting Valley, OH 44022.
  216-831-2200; Fax 216-292-7810; Web Site www.us.edu

One of the original American country day schools, University School enrolls more than 800 boys in Kindergarten–Grade 12. The Lower School offers a research-oriented program of studies; the college preparatory curriculum in the Upper School (Grades 9–12) challenges boys to reach their highest potential. The traditional program includes Advanced Placement and college-level courses, endowed student fellowships, ecology programs, Greek and Latin studies, and many extracurricular offerings. A summer session is available. Tuition: $10,560–$14,585. Fee: $995. Financial Aid: $1,550,000. Douglas H. Lagarde is Director of Enrollment; Richard A. Hawley (Middlebury, A.B.; Cambridge [England], M.S.; Case Western Reserve, M.S., Ph.D.) is Headmaster.

The Wellington School   1982

3650 Reed Road, Columbus, OH 43220. 614-457-7883;
  Fax 614-442-3286; E-mail admissions@wellington.org;
  Web Site www.wellington.org

A balance of strong academics, athletics, the arts, and positive values characterizes The Wellington School. Wellington, encompassing Pre-Kindergarten through Grade 12, is a coeducational, college preparatory school enrolling 591 day students in an enriching curriculum taught in a caring, family environment. Special-area elementary teachers conduct classes in French, music, computer, science, art, and physical education. In the upper grades, Advanced Placement and French exchange programs are among the academic features. Tuition: $9750–$11,400. Merit scholarships and financial aid are available. Jeff Leyden is Director of Admission; Richard J. O'Hara (Williams, B.A. 1976; University of Virginia, M.Ed. 1979) is Head of School.

Western Reserve Academy   HUDSON

115 College Street, Hudson, OH 44236. 330-650-4400;
  Admissions 330-650-9717; E-mail BurnerC@wra.net;
  Web Site www.wra.net

WESTERN RESERVE ACADEMY in Hudson, Ohio, is a coeducational boarding and day school enrolling students in Grades 9 through 12 and a postgraduate year. The town of Hudson (population 27,000) retains the flavor of an 18th-century New England village and has been cited by the National Trust for Historic Preservation as "among the top 100 historic places in the nation." Hudson is 25 miles southeast of Cleveland.

Reserve was founded in 1826 as a college and preparatory academy by Hudson's earliest settlers. The college later moved to Cleveland and became Case Western Reserve University. After being closed for 13 years, James W. Ellsworth endowed the Academy with funding to permit its return to active operation in 1916. Mr. Ellsworth's bequest is part of the school's $71,000,000 endowment, which enables Reserve to offer substantial scholarship assistance. Reserve ranks among the top 20 endowed independent secondary schools in the United States.

Western Reserve Academy is comprised of a close-knit community of teachers and students fully engaged in the process of education. Academics are foremost, but they are balanced by a spirit of discovery that extends beyond the classroom. Students are challenged to ask questions and to find answers in many different ways and places, including living with young people from different countries and cultures, planning team strategy in athletics, rehearsing for performances, and extending their efforts to participate in helping the community both within and outside of Reserve.

A nonprofit institution, Western Reserve Academy is governed by 21 Trustees, 17 of whom are alumni. The Alumni Association is actively involved in all aspects of the school. Western Reserve holds membership in many educational associations and foundations, including A Better Chance, the Naval Academy Foundation, the National Association of Independent Schools, and School Year Abroad. It is accredited by the Independent Schools Association of the Central States.

THE CAMPUS. The 200-acre campus features outstanding examples of Greek Revival architecture along with "Brick Row" buildings modeled after Yale University. Central to Western Reserve is Middle College, which is built on the Academy's cornerstone, laid in 1826. Five of the original seven buildings are still in use, including the David Hudson House, which is the oldest frame house in Ohio. The Loomis Observatory is the second-oldest structure of its kind in the United States. The new 20,000 square foot John D. Ong Library opens in spring of this year and will house 45,000 volumes and an enlarged computer lab. The Knight Fine Arts Center houses studios for instruction in photography, digital imagery, the manual arts, dance, and a fine arts gallery. The fully equipped theater seats 400. The cornice of the Academy's Chapel features a classic Greek motif called the anthemion. The Academy's computers are connected through a fiberoptic network reaching dormitory rooms, classrooms, and offices, and students have full Internet access as well as E-mail accounts.

Athletic facilities include a six-lane swimming pool with diving well, wrestling/multipurpose rooms, 12 tennis courts, squash courts, a weight training room with Nautilus equipment, a 400-meter all-weather track, 2 basketball courts, a cross-country trail, a paddle tennis court, and 17 fields for football, soccer, baseball, softball, lacrosse, and field hockey. The ice-hockey team skates at Kent State University, while golf team members enjoy privileges at a local club.

More than 90 percent of Western Reserve's faculty live on campus with their families in Academy-owned homes or dormitories.

THE FACULTY. Henry E. Flanagan, Jr., was appointed Head-

master in 1982. He is a graduate of Rutgers College (B.A.), the University of Michigan (M.A., Ph.D.), and Harvard University (M.Ed.) and previously held teaching, coaching, and administrative positions at Avon Old Farms in Connecticut.

There are 67 full- and part-time faculty, over 70 percent of whom hold advanced degrees. Most of the teachers continue their educational and professional growth through summer or full-year sabbaticals, writing workshops, marine biology projects, or graduate studies and seminars. Faculty benefits include health and dental insurance, a retirement plan, mortgage plan, funding for advanced study, workman's compensation and Social Security, and sabbatical leave.

A full-time nurse staffs the infirmary, and a doctor holds daily office hours and is on call at all times.

STUDENT BODY. In 1999–2000, Reserve enrolls 136 boarding boys, 92 boarding girls, 96 day boys, and 70 day girls in Grades 9–12 and a postgraduate year. Boarding students represent 17 states and 11 foreign countries; day students come from Hudson and surrounding communities. Day students are fully integrated into the residential experience, spending time on campus in the evenings and on weekends.

ACADEMIC PROGRAM. The school year, from September to June, is divided into four marking periods. The calendar includes Thanksgiving, Christmas, and spring vacations. School begins at 8:00 A.M., with a morning meeting held three days a week, followed by academic classes, lunch, afternoon classes, activities, conferences, and athletics. "Lights out" for all classes but seniors is 11:00 P.M.

Reserve's academic program is designed to stretch each student to take full advantage of the Academy's offerings and to create an academic profile that builds on strengths and bolsters weaknesses. Classes are small, techniques are varied, and teachers are available for help outside the classroom during the day and evening. There is a mandatory quiet study period from 8:00 to 10:00 P.M. Sunday through Friday.

To graduate, students must complete four years of English, three years each of mathematics and foreign language, two years of science, two and one-half years of history, one year of arts, and a half-year each of health and senior seminar, an interdisciplinary course focusing on humanistic topics.

The curriculum includes such courses as English I–IV, Creative Writing; French I–V, German I–V, Latin I–IV, Spanish I–V; Algebra, Geometry, Pre-Calculus, Calculus, Advanced Topics in Mathematics; Biology, Zoology, Physics, Astronomy, Chemistry; United States History, Economics, Experience Religion East & West; Health/Ethics; Studio Art, Photography, Dance, Choir, Music Theory, String Orchestra; Public Speaking, Dramatic Performance; Engineering Drawing, and Architectural Design.

Honors classes are offered in Latin, geometry, pre-calculus, physics, intermediate algebra, and dance. Advanced Placement courses are formed in English, French, German, Latin, Spanish, U.S. History, European history, calculus, statistics, computer science, physics, chemistry, biology, and economics. Academic credit is also granted for independent study and special projects. Exchange programs are available through The English-Speaking Union, School Year Abroad, or the Ridley College Experience.

In 1999, the 117 graduating seniors entered 74 colleges and universities. Two or more are attending Boston University 3, Bucknell 5, Carleton, Carnegie Mellon, Case Western Reserve, Cornell, Cincinnati, Emory, Franklin and Marshall 3, Kent State, Miami University 5, New York University, Northwestern 4, Ohio State, Ohio University 5, Princeton, Syracuse, Tufts, Tulane 4, United States Naval Academy 4, Vanderbilt 4, Washington University, William and Mary, and Yale.

Summer programs at the Academy include "Encore," an internationally recognized strings program affiliated with the Cleveland Institute of Music, and sports camps.

STUDENT ACTIVITIES. The Student Council is responsible for presenting student ideas and organizing activities. All students take part in Reserve's Service Program, which may involve working in the library or dining hall or acting as a laboratory assistant or teacher aide.

Reserve offers numerous extracurricular activities for students with a broad variety of interests including OpuS (theater), S.G.A.R. (Singing Guys at Reserve), Reservations (girls' a cappella group), Student Affairs Committee, *The Reserve Record* (newspaper), *Hardscrabble* (yearbook), S.E.A.L. (Student Environmental Action League), and the Chess, Culinary, Debate, and Investment clubs.

The Western Reserve Academy athletic program is built around a history of strong teams, dedicated coaches, and enthusiastic parent and alumni supporters. The first boys' soccer team in Ohio was founded at Reserve in 1926, and many student athletes have been named to All-American teams or become captains in college sports. Each student is required to participate in athletics at some level in order to balance academic and extracurricular life and provide exercise and an outlet from the rigors of the classroom. All sports have varsity squads, many have junior varsity teams and "C" squads. Boys compete in the Interstate Preparatory School League in foot-ball, soccer, cross-country, wrestling, hockey, swimming, diving, baseball, precision shooting, golf, lacrosse, and tennis. Girls compete in the Private School League in field hockey, soccer, golf, volleyball, cross-country, swimming, diving, precision shooting, basketball, ice hockey, track, softball, lacrosse, and tennis. Students may also participate in a number of intramural activities including aerobics and weightlifting. The Academy's 100-year-old football rivalry with University School, known as "the first Saturday in November," is the highlight of the fall sports season.

Dances, concerts, and trips are offered on weekends, and traditional annual events include Christmas Vespers, Winter Carnival, and the Dads Club Family Party.

ADMISSION AND COSTS. Most students enter Reserve in Grades 9 or 10, with a small number of students admitted to the upper grades. The Academy admits students of any race, color, or national or ethnic origin. Applicants must submit scores from either the Secondary School Admission Test or the Independent School Entrance Examination; junior or senior applicants can submit Preliminary Scholastic Aptitude or Scholastic Aptitude Test results. Applications, accompanied by a $30 fee ($100 for international students), should be submitted by February 15; families are notified by March 10. Late applications will be considered as space permits.

In 1999–2000, boarding tuition is $21,300; day tuition, including meals, is $15,500. Extras are approximately $500, with additional expenses for boarders amounting to $200–$500. Tuition insurance and a payment plan are available.

In 1998–99, $1,600,000 was awarded in financial aid on the basis of need. Reserve uses the School Scholarship Service to determine award amounts.

Director of Curriculum and Pedagogy: Brian Horgan
Dean of Faculty: Howard Kaplan
Dean of Students: Brand Closen
Director of Studies: John Haile
Director of Admissions: Christopher D. Burner '80
Director of Academy Advancement: Helen Tremaine Gregory
Director of College Placement: Eugene Thomas '68
Business Manager: Leonard Carlson
Director of Athletics: Charles L. Schmitt

OKLAHOMA

Casady School OKLAHOMA CITY

*P.O. Box 20390, 9500 North Pennsylvania Avenue, Oklahoma City,
OK 73156. 405-749-3100; Fax 405-749-3214;
E-mail admissions@casady.org; Web Site www.casady.org*

CASADY SCHOOL in Oklahoma City, Oklahoma, is an Episcopal, college preparatory day school enrolling more than 900 boys and girls in Preschool through Grade 12. The School was established in 1947 by the Right Reverend Thomas Casady, then Episcopal Bishop of Oklahoma, and by members of the laity. The focus of the School since its founding has been on the full development of the mind, body, and spirit of each student.

Casady seeks to promote academic excellence and encourages each student to work to his or her maximum potential. A comprehensive program of recreation, exercise, and interscholastic sports is provided to help develop and maintain the student's mental and physical health.

The School accepts applicants of all religious persuasions; however, it offers opportunity for instruction in the basic tenets of the Christian faith. Bible instruction is given in Grades 1–8; all students in Grades 1–12 attend a daily chapel service; Kindergartners attend on Fridays.

A nonprofit corporation, Casady is directed by a 22-member Board of Trustees. The Bishop and the Headmaster are permanent members; the remaining members, a majority of whom must be Episcopalian, are elected by the Board. The School has more than 2500 graduates. Corporate assets include over $15,500,000 in productive endowment funds.

Casady is accredited by the Independent Schools Association of the Southwest and is affiliated with the National Association of Independent Schools, the National Association of Episcopal Schools, the Educational Records Bureau, The College Board, and several other educational organizations. Casady also nominates a Morehead Scholar each year.

THE CAMPUS. Located in a suburban community called "The Village," the campus consists of approximately 80 acres and includes 27 buildings, athletic fields, tennis courts, an all-weather track, a creative playground, and an 8-acre lake used for instruction in certain science courses and in sailing.

Among the facilities are the Chapel of St. Edward the Confessor, the administrative offices in Griffith Hall and Blaik Hall, and humanities classrooms in Miller and Hightower Halls. Preschool classes occupy the Loeffler Building, and the Lower Divi-

sion meets in Powell Building. A new 43,000-square-foot Middle Division building was completed in September 1999. Other academic facilities are the Pew Building, Cochran Library, Vose Physical Sciences Building, Woods Mathematics Building, and Lee Lecture Hall. Laboratory and lecture facilities for computer instruction are housed in Woods and Powell buildings. Completed in 1978 were the Eileen and S. T. Fee Performing Arts Theater, the Shirley D. and C. Richard Ford Performing Arts Instruction Center, the Harper Graphic Arts Building, the Graduates' Outdoor Theater, and the Gaylord Student Center. The Joanne Harper Memorial Building is used for student activities and houses the alumni offices. Blaik Hall houses business, admissions, and development offices. Also on campus are the Crabtree library, the Headmaster's home, the Casady Wing, Griffing Fieldhouse, London-Montin Girls' Athletic Center, and Calvert Hall, which houses dining facilities for Grades 5–12. Extensive renovations to the athletic and physical education facilities were completed in the fall of 1999. The school plant is valued at $15,000,000.

THE FACULTY. The Reverend Mark Hill Mullin, appointed Headmaster in July 1998, is a graduate of Harvard University (B.A. 1962), Oxford University (B.A. 1964, M.A. 1968), and General Theological Seminary (M.Div. 1968). Before coming to Casady, he served as Chaplain and Dean of Choate Rosemary Hall in Connecticut, as Assistant Headmaster of the Blue Ridge School in Virginia, and as Headmaster of St. Albans School in Washington, D.C.

There are 115 faculty members and 15 administrators. Several of the administrators also teach classes. Over 65 faculty hold master's degrees and 5 have doctorates. Degrees have been earned from Baylor, Brown, Bryn Mawr, Bucknell, Dartmouth, Davidson, Duke, Georgetown, Hamilton, Harvard, Indiana University, Lewis and Clark, Louisiana State, Macalester, Middlebury, Oklahoma State, Princeton, St. John's, Southern Methodist, Stanford, State University of New York (Oneonta), Swarthmore, Trinity, Vanderbilt, Wake Forest, Wheaton, William and Mary, Williams, and the Universities of California, Colorado, Kansas, Massachusetts, Michigan, Notre Dame, Ohio, Oklahoma, Oregon, Rochester, Texas, Virginia, and Wisconsin.

Benefits include TIAA/CREF, group insurance, major medical, a faculty study program, and faculty leaves of absence.

STUDENT BODY. Casady enrolls 912 boys and girls ages 3 to 18. There are 106 in the Primary Division, 206 in the Lower Division (Grades 1–4), 269 in the Middle Division (Grades 5–8), and 331 in the Upper Division (Grades 9–12).

ACADEMIC PROGRAM. The school year begins the week before Labor Day and ends with commencement in early June. The academic year consists of three trimesters. School holidays include a long weekend in mid-October; Thanksgiving, Christmas, and spring vacations; and three major sports weekends.

The Primary Division is organized into levels according to the child's age at the beginning of the school year. Pre-Kindergarten is for three- and four-year-olds; Kindergarten is for five- and six-year-olds.

The goals of the Primary Division correspond specifically to the developmental stages of the young child. An enriched learning environment with team teaching allows for individual development and recognizes the uniqueness of each learner. Carefully programmed materials that appeal to a child encourage the notion that the student must be an active participant. Children work with many manipulatives at their own level. Students are helped to acquire basic competencies, which promote self-esteem and create a sense of confidence.

Learning materials deal with language, sensory/math, practical life, art and cooking, science, library, geography, writing, music, movement and drama, and computers.

Lower Division encourages a close relationship among teacher, child, and parent in which academic excellence, self-esteem, and personal values are emphasized. Lower Division classes for Grades 1 and 2 are self-contained. Students in Grades 3 and 4 move from classroom to classroom for departmentalized instruction. In addition to the basic courses of English, reading, mathematics, and social studies/science, students receive instruction in Bible, art, music, physical education, computer, and library skills. Conversational French is introduced in Grade 2. The Lower Division program is directed toward the nurturing of a love of learning, the fostering of creativity, and the development of reasoning skills.

The Middle Division is committed to providing students a traditional liberal arts curriculum in a supportive and caring environment. All Middle Division students take English, mathematics, and foreign language every year. They take two years of history, a year of geography, and lab science in Grades 5–8. Students take French in Grade 5 and have a choice of French, German, or Spanish in Grade 6. There is a reading course in Grade 5 and computer in Grades 5–8; Latin is required in Grades 7 and 8. In addition, all students in the Middle Division take physical education, a Bible course for part of the year, and options in the fine arts, including art, chorus, instrumental music, speech, and introduction to drama.

In the Upper Division, 20 units are required for graduation, including 4 in English. Students take mathematics and a modern or classical language through the equivalent of Level III; two years of history (one of which must be American history) and two years of laboratory science; the equivalent of one year in fine arts; and one trimester of computer science. Students in Grades 9–12 take a minimum of five courses each year.

The curriculum includes English I–III and, for seniors, English electives based on the specialties of individual teachers; French I–V, German I–V, Spanish I–V, Latin I–IV; World History, American History, African-American History, Native American History, Russian History, European History, Asian History, and both American and Comparative Government; eight mathematics courses ranging from Algebra I to Calculus and Computer Science; General Biology, Biochemistry, Geology, Life Sciences Lab, Chemistry, Advanced Chemistry, Experimental Lab Science, three Physics courses; and Art History and Choral and Instrumental Music.

In addition, the trimester school year allows for a range of electives including studio art, speech, debate, photography, ceramics, creative writing, acting, computer programming, computer applications, and word processing.

Advanced Placement courses are offered in English, mathematics, French, German, Spanish, Latin, history, government, chemistry, biology, physics, and computer science.

In 1999, 80 graduates entered four-year colleges and universities. They are attending Austin College, Ball State, Boston University, Brown, Columbia, Duke, Emerson, Emory, Georgia Institute of Technology, Guilford, Hollins, Lake Forest, Northwestern, Occidental, Oklahoma State, Pennsylvania State, Princeton, Rhodes, Saint Louis University, Southern Methodist, Stanford, Texas A&M, Tulane, United States Naval Academy, Vanderbilt, Washington and Lee, Washington University, Westminster, Yale, and the Universities of Iowa, Kansas, Michigan, Oklahoma, Rochester, Texas, and Virginia.

A summer session, from early June to mid-July, is open to the entire community and offers remedial and enrichment academic courses, word processing, computer, photography, art, and theater. There is also a summer day camp.

STUDENT ACTIVITIES. There are opportunities for students in all divisions to be involved in publications and community service. In the Upper Division, Student Council, Pep Club, Little Theatre, SADD, language clubs, and environmental, academic competition, and forensic groups complement publications, peer tutoring, and community service to form the nucleus of the activities program.

Competitive sports begin in Grade 7. Boys' teams compete in baseball, basketball, football, golf, soccer, swimming, tennis, track, volleyball, and wrestling. Girls' teams compete in basketball, cross-country, field hockey, soccer, softball, swimming, tennis, track, and volleyball. Competition is with other members of the Independent Schools Association of the Southwest; the three major sports weekends each year are devoted to tournament activity. In addition, Casady offers a wide variety of exercise and intramural activities, including aerobics, racquetball, rock climbing, swimming, tennis, and strength and conditioning.

School-sponsored events include cookouts, picnics, dances, theme days, dramatic presentations, fine arts weekends, and Outing Club trips. Faculty-sponsored trips to foreign countries are offered during the holidays and in the summer.

ADMISSION AND COSTS. Applicants are admitted selectively without regard to race or creed on the basis of character and academic promise. As appropriate to grade level, requirements include aptitude and verbal ability tests, a writing sample, and a mathematics test. Tests are administered on the first Saturdays in February and March as well as by appointment later in the year. Interviews, which are also required, are usually scheduled between October 1 and May, or by appointment.

In 1999–2000, tuition is $4400–$6700 in the Primary Division, $7600 in the Lower Division, $8600 in the Middle Division, and $9800 in the Upper Division. Lunch is included in the Middle and Upper Division tuition. Health insurance, tuition insurance, and a tuition payment plan are available. More than $1,000,000 in financial aid is granted to more than 220 students. Scholarship assistance is determined solely on the basis of need.

Upper School Director: Joseph L. Cernick
Dean of Students: David W. Gorham
Director of Admissions: B. Tucker Gilman
Director of Development: Carol R. Kilpatrick
Alumni Director: Marilyn M. Meade
Director of College Counseling: Thomas R. Rumsey
Business Manager: Steve E. Shelley
Director of Athletics: James S. Bonfiglio

Holland Hall School   TULSA

5666 East 81st Street, Tulsa, OK 74137-2099. 918-481-1111;
Fax 918-481-1145; Web Site www.hollandhall.org

Holland Hall School in Tulsa, Oklahoma, is a coeducational, college preparatory, Episcopal-affiliated day school encompassing three-year-old PreSchool through Grade 12. Tulsa, known as the "Oil Capital of the World," lies on the Arkansas River in the northeastern part of the state. The city (metropolitan population 708,954) is home to The University of Tulsa and Oral Roberts University and enjoys a wide range of cultural attractions including civic ballet, philharmonic, and opera companies; the Philbrook Museum of Art; and the Thomas Gilcrease Institute of American History and Art.

The city's first independent school, Holland Hall was founded in 1922 to provide an educational experience that prepares students to succeed in an ever-changing world. The program is designed to develop the talents and strengths of each individual within an environment informed by Judeo-Christian values. Holland Hall's affiliation with the Episcopal Church is reflected in religious studies, chapel services, and the presence of a chaplain on campus. The School's core values include intellectual and open inquiry; inspiring and innovative teaching; mental, physical, and spiritual growth; trust, respect, and partnership; appreciation of diversity; and responsibility to self and others.

Holland Hall is governed by a Board of Trustees and accredited by the Independent Schools Association of the Southwest and the Oklahoma State Board of Education. It holds membership in the National Association of Independent Schools, the National Association of Episcopal Schools, Educational Records Bureau, Southwest Association of Episcopal Schools, The College Board, and The Cum Laude Society.

THE CAMPUS. Holland Hall's spacious 162-acre campus is set amid two scenic wooded areas between Sheridan and Yale on 81st Street. The Primary, Middle, and Upper schools are housed in separate buildings, each including its own classrooms, science and technology laboratories, gymnasium, and library. Approximately 300 computers are networked throughout the School for student and faculty use.

The spiritual hub of the School is All Saints Chapel, which serves all students regardless of religious affiliation. The Pauline McFarlin Walter Arts Center provides a 1200-seat main theater, a studio theater, the Holliman Gallery, and studios and practice rooms. The Flint-Williams Gymnasium, serving the Upper School, includes basketball and volleyball courts; a full weight-training facility is in an adjoining building.

The grounds include a pond, an eight-lane all-weather track, 12 tennis courts, hiking and cross-country trails, playground areas, and ten playing fields.

The plant is valued at $30,000,000.

THE FACULTY. Robert E. Graves was appointed Head of School in 1997, having served as Interim Head during the previous year and as Upper School Director from 1987 to 1996. Mr. Graves holds baccalaureate and master's degrees in history from the University of California at Davis. He also has taught at the high school and college level. He and his wife are the parents of three young children.

Holland Hall's 110-member faculty have an average of nearly 16 years of teaching experience. All hold baccalaureate degrees or the equivalent, and nearly one-half hold advanced degrees. Among their representative colleges and universities are American, Amherst, Bethany, Carnegie Mellon, Colgate, Cornell, Dartmouth, Duke, Emory, Fordham, Harvard College, Howard University, Kansas State, Kenyon College, Lesley, Louisiana Tech, Manhattanville, Middlebury, Northeastern State, Northwestern, Oklahoma State, Radford, Southern Methodist, State University of New York, Trinity University, Tufts, Vanderbilt, Villanova, Western Illinois, Xavier, and the Universities of California, Central Oklahoma, Chicago, Colorado, Connecticut, Iowa, Kansas, Missouri, Newcastle (England), Oklahoma, Southern California, Sussex (England), Texas, and Tulsa.

STUDENT BODY. In 1999–2000, Holland Hall enrolled 1027 boys and girls as follows: 345 in the Primary School (Age 3–Grade 3), 343 in the Middle School (Grades 4–8), and 339 in the Upper School (Grades 9–12). The student body reflected a broad diversity of racial, ethnic, religious, and social backgrounds.

ACADEMIC PROGRAM. The school year is divided into semesters with vacations scheduled at Thanksgiving, Christmas, and in the spring. Letter grades and written comments for students in Grade 6 and up are sent home four times a year, and written evaluations are provided for students through Grade 5. In the Middle and Upper Schools, each student has an advisor who works in concert with his or her parents to formulate a balanced educational program. The Learning Resource Centers located in each division provide extra support for students in time management, note taking, and other study skills.

In the Primary division, the child-centered curriculum promotes a self-motivating approach to learning that engages students in exploration and discovery, decision making, and problem solving. Language arts, mathematics, science, social studies, and creative writing are emphasized, with enrichment classes in religion, library skills, the visual arts, music, foreign language, physical education, and computer education.

Holland Hall's Middle School combines a rigorous curriculum with developmental, exploratory experiences to help students achieve their full potential. Middle School faculty are trained to understand emerging adolescents and to help them balance their new-found freedom with responsibility. The academic program builds on the foundations acquired in the Primary School as subject matter becomes appropriately more complex. Formal letter grades are not recorded until Grade 6 in keeping with the School's sensitivity to each child's development; parents receive written reports and attend conferences updating them on their child's achievement. Each year, up to one-half of the School's seventh graders qualify for Duke University's Talent Identification Program, based on standardized test scores.

In addition to core studies in English/language arts, reading, mathematics, the sciences, and world culture and geography, Middle School students may participate in Spanish, French, Latin, religion, computer class, fine arts, physical education, and library studies. Community service projects, student-faculty plays, "minimester" courses, ecology outings, and field trips provide opportunities for social, emotional, and intellectual growth.

Holland Hall's Upper School operates on a flexible, modular cycle of classes. There are 18 20-minute modules each day, and each class varies from two to three modules, depending on the subject. The student-teacher ratio throughout Holland Hall is 9.5:1.

To graduate from the Upper School, a student must complete a minimum of 21$\frac{1}{2}$ credits as follows: 4 in English; 3 each in mathematics, a laboratory science, the same foreign language, and social studies; 1 each in religious studies and fine arts; and 3$\frac{1}{2}$ in physical education. Honors and Advanced Placement courses are offered in 16 subjects and carry additional weight in a student's grade-point average.

Upper School courses include English I–III, Greek Theatre, Vietnam and the 60s, Creative Writing, Women's Voices in Literature, Literature of the Holocaust, Literature of Baseball, Lost Generation, The Long and Short of the Story, Native American Fiction, Shakespeare; French I–IV, Advanced Placement French Literature, Latin I–IV, Russian III, Spanish I–III; Physical Science, Biology, Chemistry, Environmental Chemistry, Physics, Geology; Algebra I–II, Geometry, Math Analysis, Trigonometry, Probability and Statistics; Current World Issues, European History, United States History, American Civil War, American Cold War, Contemporary Anarchism, Theories of Anarchism, Imperial Russia; Competitive Speech and Drama, Debate; Contemporary Issues in Theology; Introduction to Programming, Advanced Placement Computer Science; Chamber Orchestra I–IV, Holland Hall Singers I–IV, Jazz Ensemble I–IV, Music Theory I–II; Theatre Arts I–II, Stagecraft, Photojournalism, Desktop Publishing; Basic Photography, Drawing I, Painting I–II, Printmaking, Ceramics I–II, Pottery I–II, Computer Graphics I–II; and Modern Dance I–IV.

In 1999, 79 candidates took 164 Advanced Placement exams; 80 percent scored 3 or above. In addition, the Class of 1999 produced 4 National Merit Finalists, 5 National Merit Semifinalists, 6 Commended Scholars, and 1 National Hispanic Recognized Scholar.

In the spring, 12th graders are required to participate in the month-long Senior Intern Program, which offers them an opportunity to volunteer for a community agency or to work in a professional setting.

Members of Holland Hall's Class of 1999 are enrolled in colleges and universities across the nation including Amherst, Arizona State, Bates, Colorado College, Emory, Northwestern, Rice, Santa Clara University, Stanford, Sweet Briar, Tulane, and the University of the South.

STUDENT ACTIVITIES. Elected members of the Student council promote school spirit and morale and serve as a liaison with the administration. Members of the Student-Faculty Discipline Committee make recommendations for action in cases of violation of school regulations.

Students publish *The Hallway* (newspaper), *Eight Acres* (yearbook), *Polyglot* (foreign language magazine), and *The Windmill* (creative writing and art magazine). Outstanding upperclassmen may be invited to join The Cum Laude Society; there are also chapters of national honor societies for French, Latin, Russian, and Spanish.

Other interest groups include Improv, Madrigal Singers, and the AFS, Art, French, Key, Latin, Outing, Players, Political Awareness, Russian, Spanish, Technology, and Walker Fan clubs. Middle School clubs include Math Counts, School Out-of-Doors, Dutch for Christ, and Young Authors.

Approximately 90 percent of the students in Grades 7 through 12 compete on any of the School's 55 teams in cross-country, football, volleyball, soccer, track, field hockey, baseball, softball, basketball, tennis, and golf.

Among the special annual events are Field Day, Freshman Orientation, Halloween, Service of Lessons and Carols, Dutchmen Weekend, Book Fair and Market, Fine Arts Festival, Baccalaureate, and Commencement.

ADMISSION AND COSTS. Holland Hall welcomes motivated students of good character and ability without regard to race, sex, religion, national or ethnic origin, or physical handicap. Admission is based on previous school transcripts, teacher recommendations, standardized test results, and an interview.

In 1999–2000, tuition is $2725–$6600 in the PreSchool, $8655 in Kindergarten–Grade 3, $9190 in Grades 4–5, $9690 in Grades 6–8, and $9875 in Grades 9–12. Other expenses include required uniforms in Grades 1–12 ($200), books and supplies ($150–$350), and transportation ($325–$425 per semester).

Tuition payment plans are offered, and financial aid is awarded on the basis of need to approximately 75 percent of the families who apply.

Director of Upper School: Frank G. K. Jones
Director of Middle School: Robert Bryan
Director of Primary School: Ruth Jacobs
Director of Admission & Financial Aid: Lori Adams
Director of Development: Michael Christopher
Director of Public Relations: Michele Cruncleton
Business Manager: Jeanne McCarty
Director of Athletics: Charles Brown

Riverfield Country Day School   1984

*2433 West 61st Street, Tulsa, OK 74132. 918-446-3553;
   Fax 918-446-1914; E-mail rcds@webzone.net;
   Web Site www.riverfield.org*

Enrolling 520 children from 8 weeks of age to Grade 8, Riverfield Country Day offers an innovative program of active, hands-on learning in which individual differences are valued. Through a variety of teaching styles and multiage classrooms, the learning environment is adapted to each pupil's pace. Riverfield, which is accredited by the Independent Schools Association of the Southwest, aims to develop strong readers, curious learners, and creative thinkers. The School's faculty and staff, whose first priority is the intellectual and personal growth of each student, are diverse in age and professional experience. A summer camp program is optional. Tuition: $4265–$5480. Financial aid is available. Martha S. Clark (Principia, B.S.Ed.) is Head of School.

Westminster School   1963

*612 NW 44th Street, Oklahoma City, OK 73118. 405-524-0631;
   Fax 405-528-4412; E-mail mnewton@westminsterschool.org;
   Web Site www.westminsterschool.org*

Westminster School enrolls 500 boys and girls in Pre-School–Grade 8. Development of children's knowledge is at the heart of Westminster School's mission: to educate children by engaging them actively in experiences that challenge them to solve problems as cooperative, confident, and responsible learners. The curriculum emphasizes language and math skills and includes music, art, and physical education. Teaching teams strive to integrate curriculum while developing projects that involve students in their own learning. Westminster is accredited by the Independent Schools Association of the Southwest. Tuition: $3000–$6650. Financial Aid: $220,000. Robert S. Vernon (Yale University, B.A.; Teacher Corps/University of Oklahoma, M.Ed.) is Head of School.

OREGON

The Catlin Gabel School   1911

*8825 SW Barnes Road, Portland, OR 97225. 503-297-1894;
Fax 503-297-0139; Web Site www.catlin.edu*

The Catlin Gabel School is a nonsectarian, coeducational college preparatory school of approximately 677 day students in Preschool–Grade 12. The rigorous college preparatory curriculum provides a broad liberal arts education as well as rich experiences in visual and performing arts, computer science, and physical education. Exchange programs offer students opportunities for study throughout the United States and in Mexico, France, and Japan. Summer programs include preschool activities, academic classes, an outdoor program, and athletics. Tuition: $7210–$13,990. Financial aid is available. Ron Sobel is Director of Admissions; Lark Palma, Ph.D., is Head of School. *Northwest Association.*

The Delphian School   SHERIDAN

*20950 SW Rock Creek Road, Sheridan, OR 97378. 503-843-3521;
Admissions 800-626-6610; E-mail info@delphian.org;
Web Site www.delphian.org*

THE DELPHIAN SCHOOL in Sheridan, Oregon, is a coeducational boarding and day school enrolling students from around the world in Lower School through the equivalent of Grade 12. Sheridan (population 4800), located in the heartland of beautiful western Oregon, is approximately 50 miles southwest of Portland and 35 miles from the Pacific Coast. The School has over 700 acres of wooded hills, meadows, and fields overlooking the scenic Willamette Valley. The town is served by interstate buses, and the School arranges transportation to and from local bus depots, train stations, and airports. There are frequent educational, cultural, and recreational field trips to Portland, Salem, the coast, and the mountains.

The Delphian School was founded in 1973 by a group of educators and parents who were concerned about the decline in the standards of American education. Delphi uses the innovative study methods developed more than 35 years ago by American educator and philosopher L. Ron Hubbard. These methods are recognized worldwide as a breakthrough in education, and, with them, students develop the confidence and knowledge to tackle the most challenging subjects.

With great success, Delphi's program fosters self-esteem, integrity, honesty, and true enthusiasm for learning in each student. The School aims to give students the ability to take more responsibility for their studies and the ability to directly apply what they have learned to all aspects of their lives. Students are given academic programs that are specifically designed for their individual needs and strengths. Practical application of material studied is emphasized, and students spend a great deal of time outside the classroom applying what they have learned. Such activities include an apprenticeship program, a work program around the School, and a wide variety of field trips during the year.

A nonprofit institution, the School is governed by a self-perpetuating Board of Trustees. Delphi is nonsectarian and welcomes young people of all religions; students attend services at nearby churches. A magazine *(The Delphian)* is sent to parents, alumni, and friends of the School. The Delphian School holds membership in the Oregon Federation of Independent Schools and the Oregon Association for the Talented and Gifted. It meets all of the standards for private schools set by the Oregon Department of Education and is authorized under federal law to enroll foreign students.

THE CAMPUS. In the foothills of Oregon's Coastal Range, the 700-acre campus includes meadows, forests of Douglas fir and oak, hiking and riding trails, stables, four outdoor lighted tennis courts, a running track, and athletic fields for soccer, baseball, and softball. A 13,500-square-foot gymnasium houses a weightlifting and gymnastics room as well as facilities for basketball, volleyball, aerobics training, and racquetball.

Most facilities are located in the 110,000-square-foot main building. The structure houses dormitories, classrooms, a chemistry and biology laboratory, an electronics laboratory, a theater, a 10,000-volume library with Internet access, music practice rooms, a home economics room, a woodshop, a computer center, and art, ceramics, and photography studios. A spacious community cafeteria and dining room overlooks the oak and fir forest to the north. A girls' dormitory (1990), with a panoramic view of the Willamette Valley, houses 30 students. There are also student lounges, a recreation room with game tables, a laundromat, a snack bar, and a bookstore. Faculty and staff houses are adjacent to and in the main building.

THE FACULTY. Greg Ott became the School's second Headmaster in 1990. Mr. Ott served as Headmaster of Delphi Academy of Los Angeles from 1985 to 1988.

There are 32 full-time teachers and 19 part-time teachers—21 men and 30 women. Most faculty and their families live on campus; many serve as resident supervisors in the dormitories and as faculty advisers, who provide students with extra individual help as needed. They hold baccalaureate and graduate degrees from colleges and universities throughout the United States.

A medical liaison officer is available on campus; emergency services are available in neighboring towns.

STUDENT BODY. In 1999–2000, the School enrolled 102 boarding boys, 103 boarding girls, and 39 day students. Boarders must be at least eight years of age. Boarding students are from Arizona, California, Colorado, Florida, Idaho, Illinois, Kansas, Minnesota, Nebraska, New York, Ohio, Oregon, Virginia, Washington, Canada, China, Germany, Italy, Japan, Korea, Mexico, Puerto Rico, and Switzerland.

ACADEMIC PROGRAM. The school year, from early September to mid-June, includes two-week vacation periods in December and March. During the March break, students are offered an off-campus excursion that includes educational travel abroad. The regular school day is divided into three parts. From 8:30 A.M. to 3:00 P.M., there is classroom work and various practical projects and seminars that cover such areas as foreign language, advanced math, science, literature, history and current events, and English as a Second Language for international students. From 3:10 to 5:45 P.M., students participate in afternoon activities including physical education, music, ceramics, computers, photography, art, and interscholastic sports. The remainder of the day is spent with student clubs, free time, helping with jobs on campus, and study hall.

In order to ensure true academic competence in the basics, Delphi devotes a major portion of its curriculum to the strengthening of math and reading. Students drill math basics on a computer, ranging from simple addition and subtraction to more complex mathematical procedures. Written at Delphi and developed for children and adults, this computer program helps students work up to instant response to basic math facts. Complementing this is the math seminar program. The goal is for students to develop math as a "second language." The reading program, developed by utilizing Mr. Hubbard's study technology, requires that students read large quantities of easily read books and advance through a well-planned program. This promotes a love of reading and increases literacy and confidence.

The curriculum is divided into eight Forms that span primary, elementary, middle, and high school levels. Each Form has both academic and practical requirements. Weak areas that surface on quizzes or tests are restudied until full understanding is obtained. Evaluation and examinations are carried out continuously to make sure qualifications for promotion are met. Students do not receive letter grades, but reports are sent to parents three times a year. Several educational formats are used in order to maintain academic standards, such as step-by-step written instructions that include theory and application seminars, independent research, and regular classroom instruction. Advanced work is available in most disciplines.

The Delphian School offers the Apprenticeship Program, which enables students to work with professionals for a minimum of five hours per week. These apprenticeships, lasting at least a semester, are offered to qualified students in many career areas.

Recent Delphian graduates have been accepted at such colleges and universities as Antioch, California Polytechnic, George Washington University, Hartnell, Harvey Mudd, Massachusetts Institute of Technology, Simon Fraser, Stanford, Texas Tech, and the Universities of Alaska, Arizona, California (Berkeley, Davis, Los Angeles), Idaho, Michigan, New Mexico, and Oregon.

"Summer at Delphi" is a program offering a blend of rigorous study and recreational opportunities for students who wish to pursue advanced work, strengthen weak areas, learn how to study, or participate in the English as a Second Language Program.

STUDENT ACTIVITIES. The Student Council in the Upper School organizes weekend activities and other special events under faculty guidance. Students publish a yearbook, and there are clubs for students with such interests as music, skiing, chess, singing, drama, and computers. All students age nine and older spend one hour each day in the Student Service program, helping in such places as the library, computer center, the Lower School, or building maintenance. Special Community Service projects are organized at least twice a year, and students in the Middle and Upper Schools contribute to their community by such activities as helping in the clean-up of beaches, parks, and business areas.

Varsity sports for boys are baseball, basketball, and soccer; girls compete in basketball, softball, and volleyball. All of these sports are also played intramurally. Noncompetitive sports include skiing and hiking.

The student recreation room is an informal meeting place for students in the evenings and on weekends. There are regularly scheduled dances and parties. Other weekend activities include trips to Portland and Salem for shopping, movies, concerts, sports, and cultural events as well as trips to ocean beaches, to Ashland for the Shakespearean Festival, to the Cascade Range for hiking, and to Mount Hood for skiing.

Traditional annual events include formal dances such as the Christmas Ball and the Sweetheart Ball, Spring Arts Festival, Parents' Weekend, the Prom, and Commencement.

ADMISSION AND COSTS. Students are admitted to the School on the basis of their previous academic records, results of any available standardized testing, and personal interviews. Due to the personalized nature of each student's academic program, application may be made at any time and students are enrolled throughout the year as space is available. There is a $35 application fee.

In 1999–2000, tuition for the nine-month term is $23,458 for boarders and $11,840 for day students. Extras include a materials fee ($1482) and lunches for day students ($854). There is also a resident supervisor fee ($1404–$2892) for boarding students in the Middle School. Tuition payment plans and financial aid are available.

Dean of Students: Linda Siegel
Director of Admissions: Donetta Phelps
Director of Development: Suzan Ott
College Counselor: Frank Gravitt
Business Manager: Butch Nosko
Athletic Director: Mitch Neuhauser

Oregon Episcopal School   1869

6300 Southwest Nicol Road, Portland, OR 97223. 503-246-7771;
Fax 503-768-3140; E-mail admit@ad.oes.edu; Web Site www.oes.edu

Oregon Episcopal School was established by Bishop Benjamin Wistar Morris to educate the daughters of pioneer families. The School encompasses Pre-Kindergarten–Grade 12, with 715 boys and girls, including 46 boarders in Grades 9–12. The college preparatory program features honors sections, Advanced Placement, and independent study. English as a Second Language and the arts enhance the curriculum. Publications and sports are among the activities. Day Tuition: $6915–$13,135; Boarding Tuition: $23,860. Extras: $50–$950. Financial Aid: $793,000. Dr. Nancy R. Dunn is Director of Admissions; Dulany O. Bennett (Swarthmore, A.B. 1967; University of Pennsylvania, M.S. 1979; Pacific University, Psy.D. 1996) was appointed Head of School in 1998. *Northwest Association.*

St. Mary's School   1865

816 Black Oak Drive, Medford, OR 97504. 541-773-7877;
Fax 541-772-8973; Web Site http:www.stmarys.medford.or.us

Founded by the Sisters of the Holy Names, St. Mary's is an independent, Catholic, college preparatory day school enrolling 325 boys and girls in Grades 6–12. The School seeks to prepare students for positions of leadership and responsibility in a global community, according to democratic principles and the teachings of Christ. Five foreign languages, 21 Advanced Placement courses, fine and performing arts, speech and debate, community service, and educational travel enrich the curriculum. National Honor Society, Math Team, Outings Club, and sports are among the activities. A summer academic enrichment program is available. Tuition: $5600. Extras: $700. Financial Assistance: $150,000. Barbara Callaway (Mills, B.A. 1962; Stanford, M.A. 1968) is Head of School. *Northwest Association.*

Sunriver Preparatory School   1983

19888 Rocking Horse Road, Bend, OR 97702. 541-318-9020;
Fax 541-318-5371; Web Site www.sunriverprep.org

Sunriver is committed to providing a high-quality, value-centered college preparatory education encompassing Pre-Kindergarten–Grade 12. The curriculum, with small classes to develop the potential of each child, emphasizes challenging academics as well as arts and athletics. Introduction to art, theater, physical education, computer, foreign language, and science begins in Kindergarten. All graduates are accepted into colleges and universities, including those known as most selective. Special programs include the Exceptional Athlete Program. Tuition: $3000–$9400. Financial Aid: $100,000. Darleen Rodgers is Director of Admission and Development; Trish King is School Head. *Northwest Association.*

PENNSYLVANIA

Abington Friends School 1697

575 Washington Lane, Jenkintown, PA 19046. 215-886-4350;
Fax 215-886-9143; Web Site http://www.afs.pvt.k12.pa.us

Abington Friends is the only school in the nation located on the same grounds and operating under the same management since its beginning 300 years ago. Founded by Quakers, this college preparatory day school, enrolling 620 students in Preschool–Grade 12, emphasizes intellectual challenge, character development, interdisciplinary and intercultural studies, and physical fitness. The arts, Lower School Spanish, and computer centers with Internet access enhance the curriculum. Community service is required, and foreign travel/study are encouraged. An average class has 15–20 students. An extended-day program is offered. Tuition: $8100–$12,700. Financial aid is available. Karen Loder is Director of Admissions; Thomas W. Price (Lake Forest, B.A.; Columbia Teachers College, M.A.) is Head of School.

The Agnes Irwin School 1869

Ithan Avenue, Rosemont, PA 19010. 610-525-8400;
Fax 610-525-8908; Web Site Joan_Brennan@irwin.pvt.k12.pa.us

The Agnes Irwin School, a nonsectarian day school, enrolls 610 young women in Kindergarten through Grade 12. Irwin's emphasizes excellence in academics, athletics, and the arts and is committed to a dynamic community service program. Founded in 1869, the School offers 11 Advanced Placement courses. Irwin's sports teams have won numerous titles in the past ten years, and girls are encouraged to take part in athletic offerings and a variety of cocurricular activities such as interest clubs, publications, and elected government. Most graduates enroll in highly competitive or most competitive colleges. Tuition: $9535–$14,040. Financial aid is available. Margaret Penney Moss is Head of School. *Middle States Association.*

The Baldwin School BRYN MAWR

Morris & Montgomery Avenues, Bryn Mawr, PA 19010.
610-525-2700; E-mail Admissions@BaldwinSchool.org;
Web Site www.BaldwinSchool.org

THE BALDWIN SCHOOL in Bryn Mawr, Pennsylvania, is a college preparatory day school enrolling girls in Pre-Kindergarten through Grade 12. The School is located 11 miles west of Philadelphia in the Main Line community of Bryn Mawr (population 8400). Bryn Mawr College and Haverford College are within walking distance, and nearby bus and rail services provide access to the historical, cultural, and recreational resources of Philadelphia. Daily bus transportation is provided free of charge to Baldwin students through the local public school systems.

Founded in 1888 by Miss Florence Baldwin to prepare girls for admission to Bryn Mawr College, the School expanded rapidly from its opening class of 13 and now enrolls 619 girls from more than 50 communities. In 1988, The Baldwin School celebrated its centennial year.

The Baldwin School strives to provide a challenging academic program in a lively, creative environment. Stressing both scope and depth in learning, Baldwin ultimately hopes to endow each student with the ability and enthusiasm for a life of continuing growth as a scholar, a woman, and a human being.

The Baldwin School is a nonprofit institution governed by a self-perpetuating Board of 28 Trustees, which meets five times a year. An active Alumnae Association maintains contact with the 3947 living graduates and plays a direct role in fundraising and School events. The School has an endowment of $6,900,000. Baldwin is accredited by the Middle States Association of Colleges and Schools and the Pennsylvania Association of Private Academic Schools; it holds membership in the National Association of Independent Schools, the Pennsylvania Association of Independent Schools, The National Association of Principals of Schools for Girls, A Better Chance, The Council for Religion in Independent Schools, and the Council for Advancement and Support of Education.

THE CAMPUS. The 25-acre campus includes three athletic fields, indoor and outdoor swimming pools, a playground, three tennis courts, and two gymnasiums.

The Residence (1896) houses administrative offices, a reception area, an assembly room, the dining room, the kitchen (renovated 1985), the Music Wing, the Middle School Music Room, an extensive arts facility (1986, 1991), the Book Store, and the Early Childhood Center (1998). A former resort hotel featuring distinctive Victorian architecture, the Residence is listed on the National Register of Historic Places. The Schoolhouse (1925, renovated 1998) contains Upper and Middle School classrooms and offices for the Head of School and Middle and Upper School administration. The Science Building (1961, 1995) provides a variety of newly renovated and expanded science laboratories. The Lower School (1975) houses classrooms for Grades 1–5, art, the Lower School library, Lower School computer lab, a multipurpose room, a kitchen, and a locker area. Additional facilities include the Mrs. Otis Skinner Dramatic Workshop, the Hut, the Cottage, and the residence of the Head of the School.

The School-owned plant is valued at $18,500,000.

THE FACULTY. Blair D. Stambaugh (Wheaton, B.A. 1961) was appointed Head of the School in 1980. Prior to her appointment, Mrs. Stambaugh served as head of The Bryn Mawr School; instructor in Latin at Williams College; and a teacher of Latin, English, and history at Pine Cobble School and Abbot Academy. She is currently a Trustee of the Dunwoody Retirement Community and The Head Mistresses of the East; she is also a past President of The National Association of Principals of Schools for Girls and The Headmistresses' Association of the East.

Faculty members include 70 full-time teachers, 65 women and 5 men. They hold 51 baccalaureate and 64 advanced degrees from such institutions as Brown, Bryn Mawr College, Columbia, Cornell, Denison, Drexel, Johns Hopkins, Mount Holyoke, Oxford (England), Princeton, Radcliffe, Rice, Rosemont, Smith, Stanford, Swarthmore, Temple, Vassar, Villanova, Wellesley, Williams, and the Universities of Cambridge (England), Lille (France), Massachusetts, Notre Dame, Pennsylvania, and Southern California. There are also 4 part-time instructors who teach English, history, mathematics, science, foreign languages, art, and music. Faculty benefits include health, disability, and accident insurance; a retirement plan; a cafeteria plan; sabbaticals; leaves of absence; and half-tuition scholarships for faculty children.

A wellness center is located on campus, and Bryn Mawr Hospital is approximately five minutes away.

STUDENT BODY. In 1999–2000, the School enrolls 619 girls in Pre-Kindergarten–Grade 12 as follows: 15 in Pre-Kindergarten, 35 in Kindergarten, 45 in Grade 1, 34 in Grade 2, 52 in Grade 3, 45 in Grade 4, 52 in Grade 5, 54 in Grade 6, 54 in Grade 7, 54 in Grade 8, 56 in Grade 9, 47 in Grade 10, 38 in Grade 11, and 37 in Grade 12. Students represent a variety of ethnic, religious, and racial backgrounds.

ACADEMIC PROGRAM. The school year which extends from early September to early June, is divided into trimesters and includes Thanksgiving, Christmas, midwinter, and spring vacations. Classes are scheduled five days a week from 8:15 A.M. to 3:30 P.M. Extended day care is available. The faculty-student ratio is 1:8, and the average class has 15 students. Special instruction is provided free of charge for advanced students and students needing extra help in English or mathematics. Written reports are issued four times per year in Grades 5–12; parent/teacher conferences are interspersed with written reports for the younger students.

The Lower School (Pre-Kindergarten–Grade 5) program stresses self-expression, creativity, and the acquisition of basic skills. Computer science and Suzuki music instruction begin in Kindergarten; foreign language instruction begins in Grade 3. The Middle School (Grades 6–8) curriculum includes English, French, Latin, Spanish, social studies, history, mathematics, science, computer, music, art, drama, human development, physical education, and a library/media skills program.

Upper School (Grades 9–12) students are expected to take five units of credit each year in addition to physical education. Graduation requirements include four units of English; three units of one foreign language or two units each of two languages; two of history; three units of mathematics; three of sci-

ence; one of fine arts; one trimester course each of Computer, Speech, Health, Human Development; and five units of electives.

Among the Upper School courses are English 1–4, Creative Writing, Poetry; Latin 1–3, Vergil, Advanced Placement Latin, French 1–5, Advanced Placement French 1–2, Spanish; Modern European History, Economics, the Constitution, Russian History, Comparative Religion; Algebra I, Algebra and Consumer Mathematics, Geometry, Algebra II and Trigonometry, Calculus, Logic, Topics in Advanced Mathematics; Computer 1–3, Advanced Integrated Science, Biology 1–2, Chemistry 1–2, Physics 1–2; and Art 1–4, Art History, Architecture, Ceramics, Design, Photography, Jewelry 1–4, Theatre 1–3, Instrumental Ensemble, Chorus, Handbell Choir, and Theory and Harmony. Honors courses and independent study are available in several subjects, and qualified students may take courses at Bryn Mawr College.

In 1999, all 44 graduates went to college. Among their choices were Boston University 2, Brown, Colgate 2, Dartmouth 2, Duquesne, Georgetown, George Washington 4, Harvard/Radcliffe 2, Macalester 2, Mount Holyoke 2, Princeton 3, Tufts, Washington University 2, Yale, and the Universities of Notre Dame, Pennsylvania, Pittsburgh, and Virginia.

Baldwin conducts a Summer Academic Program for students entering Grades 6–10. In addition, the School offers Camp Magar, a six-week summer recreational program for approximately 350 boys and girls, ages 3–12. Camp Magar is directed by Betsy Barnnett and Linda Reese.

STUDENT ACTIVITIES. The Upper School Senate, composed of 12 elected student representatives, presents a forum for the expression of student opinions, implements the student discipline system, and provides student input on administrative issues. The Middle School Senate, which includes administrators, faculty, and elected student representatives, promotes school spirit, sponsors social functions, and helps with dining room and study hall supervision.

Extracurricular activities include the Maskers; a yearbook; a literary magazine; Lower, Middle, and Upper school newspapers; the Math Team; the Society of Latin Lovers; the Athletic Association; and the Investment, Film, Ski, Computer, Model UN, Asian Students' Association, Contemporary, Debate, Black Student Union, Sci-Med, and French clubs. The School also serves as the local headquarters for Amnesty International. In addition, all Baldwin girls belong to the Service League, which provides a variety of opportunities for community service.

Varsity teams are fielded in basketball, crew, cross-country, hockey, lacrosse, soccer, softball, swimming, tennis, and volleyball. Noncompetitive athletic activities include aerobics, dancercize, lifesaving, and recreational games.

School social events include dances, plays, cabarets, club dinners, concerts, trips, art shows, music recitals, exchanges with other private schools, and a lecture series. Among the numerous traditional events are the Father/Daughter Phillies Game, the Pumpkin Sale, the Faculty Play, the Book Fair, Grandparents' Day, Lower School Fathers' Day, Father/Daughter Dance, Fundamentally Family Day, Lower School Mothers' Day, the Art Show, Athletic Association Pet Show, and Field Day.

ADMISSION AND COSTS. The Baldwin School seeks to admit girls with a diversity of backgrounds, talents, and interests who are capable of high academic achievement, sound personal growth, and good citizenship. Students are admitted to Pre-Kindergarten–Grade 12 on the basis of a written application, standardized test scores, a personal interview and campus visit, previous school records, a letter to the Head of the School (Grades 6–12), and the results of an English placement test (Grades 6–12). Application should be made in the fall preceding the year of desired enrollment. There is an application fee of $40.

In 1999–2000, tuition ranges from $8400 for Pre-Kindergarten to $14,400 for Grades 9–12. Additional expenses include uniforms ($50 each), lunch tickets, books ($90–$125) in Grades 6–12, and Upper School laboratory fees ($35).

Tuition insurance and a tuition payment plan are available. In 1999–2000, Baldwin awarded $1,066,337 in financial aid to approximately 21 percent of the student body on the basis of need. The Baldwin School subscribes to the School and Student Service.

Alumnae Director: Susan Houser Winant '78
Director of Admissions: Virginia F. Adams
Director of Development: Janer Danforth Belson
College Counselor: Pamela Fetters
Director of Finance: Dana Wright
Director of Athletics: Patricia West

Buckingham Friends School   1794

P.O. Box 159, Lahaska, PA 18931. 215-794-7491;
Fax 215-794-7955; Web Site bfs.org

Founded in 1794 by the Buckingham Friends (Quaker) Meeting, Buckingham Friends School is celebrating more than 205 years of continuous education. Academic preparation and intellectual development are central to the purposes of the School, which enrolls 176 boys and girls in Kindergarten through Grade 8. Children are encouraged to develop high educational goals and to participate in a variety of activities that promote poise and self-worth. A dynamic and dedicated school community benefits all students and promotes the family atmosphere. A summer arts camp is offered for ages 6–12. Tuition: $8700. Financial aid is available. Peter S. Pearson (College of New Jersey, M.Ed. 1998) is Principal.

Carson Long Military Institute   1837

200 North Carlisle Street, P.O. Box 98CC, New Bloomfield, PA
17068. 717-582-2121; Fax 717-582-8763

Founded as a memorial to William Carson Long by his father, this college preparatory boarding school enrolls 206 young men in Grades 6–12. The school aims to teach "how to learn, how to labor, and how to live" and motivates the average student to do his best. Speech and JROTC training are required for all students. Ski Club, Drill Team, Rifle Team, debate and declamation teams, and a full range of sports are extracurricular activities. Supervised evening study hall in a classroom is required, and English as a Second Language is offered. Tuition: $11,900. Col. Carson E. R. Holman (U. S. Military Academy, B.S.; Bucknell University, M.A.) was appointed President in 1971. *Middle States Association*.

Central Catholic High School   1927

4720 Fifth Avenue, Pittsburgh, PA 15213-2952. 412-621-8189;
Fax 412-621-0758; Web Site www.pittcentralcatholic.org

Central Catholic High School was founded by the Diocese of Pittsburgh to prepare young men for college, for community leadership, and for life in today's complex world. It seeks to challenge its 850 students to reach their potential and to develop Christian values of justice, compassion, and respect. The program includes honors and Advanced Placement courses in all academic areas, and qualified students may earn college credit before graduation through dual enrollment at Duquesne or the University of Pittsburgh. Participation in interscholastic sports, publications, plays, concerts, clubs, community service, and foreign travel opportunities is encouraged. Tuition: $4800–$5600. Bro. Richard Grzeskiewicz is Director of Admissions; Bro. Lawrence Monroe, FSC, is Principal. *Middle States Association*.

CFS, The School at Church Farm   PAOLI

Box 2000, Paoli, PA 19301. 610-363-7500;
E-mail rlunardi@cfs.pvt.k12.pa.us; Web Site www.cfschool.org

CFS, THE SCHOOL AT CHURCH FARM in Paoli, Pennsylvania, is a college preparatory boarding and day school for academically qualified and financially deserving boys in Grades 7 through 12. The School is located in Chester County, 25 miles west of Philadelphia, 10 miles north of Brandywine Battlefield, and 10 miles southwest of Valley Forge.

CFS was founded in 1918 by the Reverend Charles W. Shreiner, D.D., an Episcopal priest whose childhood in a fatherless home prompted him to establish a school for boys from single-parent homes. It was the founder's dream to provide a college preparatory education for boys of ability and promise who otherwise might not have such an opportunity. Today, the School's mission has been broadened to include boys whose parents are living together. The School's goal is to provide an educational experience and a way of life that builds character, self-discipline, and self-confidence.

CFS is incorporated not-for-profit under a Board of Directors. The annual Christmas fund appeal is sent to more than 50,000 individuals and proves to be the major source of operational funds. The School is accredited by the Middle States Association of Colleges and Schools. It is a member of the National Association of Independent Schools, the National Association of Episcopal Schools, the Pennsylvania Association of Independent Schools, The College Board, Secondary School Admission Test Board, and The Independent School Teachers' Association of Philadelphia and Vicinity.

THE CAMPUS. The School's 1600-acre property consists of 400 acres of woodland and 1100 acres of open farmland, a 12-acre lake, and a main campus.

Approximately 80 buildings are used for the School's comprehensive program. The Administration Building houses classrooms, offices, the multimedia center, the computer lab, a recreation room, and the kitchen and dining room. The Science Building contains four laboratories, six classrooms, a projection room, and the Art Department. Ten cottages house the student body in small groups supervised by dorm faculty. Athletic facilities include soccer and baseball fields, a quarter-mile track, six tennis courts, a basketball gymnasium, a multipurpose field house, and an adjoining swimming pool.

Also on campus are the School's chapel, a 22-bed infirmary, faculty homes, shop buildings, a barn, and a variety of outbuildings.

THE FACULTY. Charles W. Shreiner III was appointed Headmaster in 1987. Mr. Shreiner, grandson of the School's founder, is a graduate of Westtown School, Nichols College (B.S.), and Villanova University (M.A.).

There are 27 full-time faculty members, all of whom live at the School. They hold 24 baccalaureate and 20 graduate degrees representing study at Bloomsburg, Cabrini, Curtis Institute of Music, Drexel, Eastern Baptist, Eastern Michigan University, Emory, Franklin and Marshall, Guilford, Immaculata, Iowa State, Kalamazoo, Lock Haven, Marietta, Millersville, Mount St. Mary's, New York University, Parsons College, Pennsylvania State, Philadelphia College of Bible, Providence, St. Joseph's, Temple, Ursinus, Vandercook College of Music, Villanova, West Chester University, and the Universities of Denver, Florida, New Hampshire, and Pennsylvania.

STUDENT BODY. In 1999, the School enrolled 172 boarding and day students in Grades 7 through 12. Many students come from the region extending from New York to Washington, D.C. Those attending the School come from more than 20 states and several foreign countries.

ACADEMIC PROGRAM. The academic year, from early September to early June, includes 36 weeks of instruction, with holidays at Thanksgiving, Christmas, and in the spring. Parents receive grade reports every 9 weeks.

A typical weekday for students begins with cottage clean-up, breakfast, and, two mornings a week, required chapel. Boys attend classes from 8:00 A.M. until 3:30 P.M. A mandated work and athletic program is part of every boy's schedule. In the evenings, boys have two hours of study, with bedtime at 10:00 P.M. or 11:00 P.M., depending on age.

The Middle School (Grades 7–8) offers English, Social Studies, Mathematics, Science, Spanish, French, Religion, Art, Guidance, Music, Health, Physical Education, Technology Education, and Study Skills.

Upper School (Grades 9–12) students take at least five major courses each year. The ratio of students to faculty is 7:1, and there are 12 students in an average class. The curriculum includes English 1–4; French 1–2, Spanish 1–4; World Cultures 1–2; Introductory Algebra, Algebra 1–2, Geometry, Pre-Calculus, Calculus, Trigonometry; Earth Science, Biology I, Chemistry; Health; World Religion; Technology Education; and General Art. A variety of electives is offered such as English Honors, African-American History, American Civil War, 19th Century America, 20th Century America, Government, Tudor England, Honors History; Computer Science, Honors Mathematics; Physical Geology, Physics, Honors Science; Psychology, Ethics; 3D Design, Clay, Weaving, Art Honors, Music Appreciation I–II, Music Theory 1–2, Choir, Instrument Ensemble, Instrument & Voice Lessons; and Level II Wood and Metal, and Photography. Support services are available through Learning Center tutorials, a reading specialist, the Guidance Department, the Advisor program, and the National Honor Society.

Ninety to ninety-five percent of the graduates enter college each year. Recent graduates were accepted at Cornell, Drexel, Georgetown, Lehigh, Marist, New York University, Rutgers, St. Joseph's, Syracuse, and the Universities of Connecticut, Maryland, and Scranton.

During the summer, CFS operates a coeducational day camp for area children of elementary school age.

STUDENT ACTIVITIES. The daily work and Community Service programs give students the opportunity to give something back to others, both on and off campus. At school, students may work in the kitchen, maintain the grounds, assist in a science lab, give a tour, speak at an Open House, cut grass, or shovel snow. In the surrounding community, students have volunteered at the local library, a senior citizen center, a day-care center, a facility for disabled individuals, and the American Cancer Society, among others. The School aims to enable all students to appreciate the satisfaction of a job well done as well as to experience the joy of service to others.

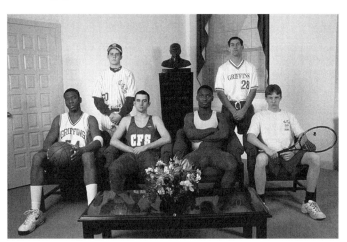

Student organizations include the National Honor Society, the Audio-Visual Club, Choir, Science Club, Student Activities Committee, Student Forum, Student Vestry, and other recreational clubs. School teams compete in baseball, basketball, cross-country, soccer, tennis, track and field, and wrestling. Social events include weekend movies, trips, lectures, and other informal activities. Parents are invited to visit on weekends. Students may return home on weekends if academic and social progress is satisfactory.

ADMISSION AND COSTS. Boys are accepted in Grades 7–10 on the basis of school records, teacher references, results of the Secondary School Admission Test, and a personal interview. A visit to the School and a tour of the campus is required. No boy will be considered if he has been in trouble with law enforcement officials or has been disruptive in previous schools. Inquiries should be directed to the Admissions Office.

Parents are expected to pay a tuition based on family income. A tuition ranging between $4000 and $15,000 is determined using the Parents Financial Statement published by the School and Student Service for Financial Aid in Princeton, New Jersey.

Assistant Headmaster: William W. Wentzel
Director of Academics: Nan Wodarz
Director of Students: Jose Sanchez
Alumni Secretary: Elaine Barndt
Director of Admissions: Richard Lunardi
College Counselor: Richard Lunardi
Business Manager: Neil Fanelli, Jr.
Director of Athletics: John D. Kistler, Jr.

Chestnut Hill Academy 1861

500 West Willow Grove Avenue, Philadelphia, PA 19118.
215-247-4700; Fax 215-242-4055; E-mail
Admissions@cha.k12.pa.us; Web Site http:www.cha.k12.pa.us

Chestnut Hill Academy is an independent, college preparatory day school with an enrollment of 540 boys in Kindergarten–Grade 12. Stressing high academic standards, Chestnut Hill offers a diversity of courses and opportunities, including a coordinate program in the Upper School in which courses are shared with Springside School, a neighboring school for girls. Performing arts, community service, sports, and publications comprise the school's extracurricular activities. Summer enrichment and tutorial courses are available. Tuition: $8175–$13,500. Financial Aid: $575,000. Richard L. Parker (Middlebury, B.A.; Dartmouth, M.A.L.S.; University of Pennsylvania, Ed.D.) was appointed Headmaster in 1990. *Middle States Association.*

Country Day School of the Sacred Heart 1865

480 Bryn Mawr Avenue, Bryn Mawr, PA 19010. 610-527-3915;
Fax 610-527-0942; E-mail sacredheart@cdssh.pvt.k12.pa.us

Sacred Heart, founded by the Religious of the Sacred Heart, is a Catholic, college preparatory day school for girls in Pre-Kindergarten–Grade 12. The 260 students represent all faiths within a family environment. Faculty and administration provide a comprehensive liberal arts education designed to meet the needs of the maturing student. Sacred Heart aims to graduate self-motivated, intellectually aware, and ethically concerned students. Honors and Advanced Placement courses augment regular studies; community service and activities are integral to the program. Tuition: $5050–$8400. Financial Aid: $363,000. Mrs. Laurie Nowlan is Director of Admissions; Sr. Matthew Anita MacDonald, SSJ, Ph.D., was appointed Head of School in 1992. *Middle States Association.*

The Crefeld School 1970

8836 Crefeld Street, Chestnut Hill, Philadelphia, PA 19118.
215-242-5545; Fax 215-242-8869; E-mail mpatron@home.com;
Web Site www.crefeld.org

The Crefeld School, a coeducational, independent day school serving 85 students in Grades 7–12, seeks to pioneer a progressive, alternative learning community for secondary school students. Crefeld's primary strategies for student success are its small size and personal attention, flexible and creative approaches to problem solving, focus on demonstration of essential skills and knowledge, and respect for individuals and community values. Crefeld is guided by the principles of the Coalition of Essential Schools and research on multiple intelligences and learning styles. The School, which features a new glass-blowing facility, is

located in historic Chestnut Hill. Tuition: $10,550–$12,900. Financial aid is available. Stacey Picket is Director of Admissions; Michael Patron is Headmaster.

The Episcopal Academy

MERION AND DEVON

Merion Campus: 376 North Latches Lane, Merion, PA 19066.
610-667-9612; Fax 610-667-8629;
E-mail admission@ea.pvt.k12.pa.us;
Web Site www.ea.pvt.k12.pa.us
Devon Campus: 905 South Waterloo Road, Devon, PA 19333.
610-293-0830; Fax 610-293-9238

THE EPISCOPAL ACADEMY in Merion and Devon, Pennsylvania, is a college preparatory day school enrolling boys and girls in Pre-Kindergarten–Grade 12. Merion (population 59,600) is the first community on the "Main Line" of Philadelphia. The cultural and historic resources of the city enrich the academic program. Devon is situated 15 miles west of the city.

The school was founded in 1785 by The Reverend William White to educate the sons of Philadelphia's Episcopalian community. The curriculum included instruction in Greek and Latin as well as more practical training in business and mathematics. In 1921, the school moved from its city campus to its present suburban Merion location. Fifty-three years later, Episcopal Academy opened the Devon campus to accommodate a larger, coeducational student body.

Through a rigorous academic curriculum, complemented by religious instruction, community service, the arts, and athletics, Episcopal Academy seeks to cultivate the mind, body, and spirit of each student. The school endeavors to instill a belief in God and respect for faith, encourage good work habits and thoroughness, and inspire a thirst for knowledge.

A nonprofit organization, the Academy is affiliated with the Episcopal Diocese of Philadelphia and governed by a 32-member self-perpetuating Board of Trustees. Many of the school's 3900 living alumni belong to the Alumni Society, and, along with current and past parents, assist in fund-raising and other service activities.

The Episcopal Academy is accredited by the Middle States Association of Colleges and Schools and the Pennsylvania Association of Private Academic Schools and holds membership in the National Association of Independent Schools, the National Association of Episcopal Schools, and the Pennsylvania Association of Independent Schools.

THE CAMPUSES. The 35-acre Merion campus includes playgrounds, sports fields, and parklike areas. The 35-acre Devon campus offers a rural setting that encompasses fields and wooded areas.

The Merion campus, for Pre-Kindergarten–Grade 12, has buildings for the younger children, an academic facility for Grades 4–12, science laboratories, art and music studios, a chapel, an indoor pool, and two gymnasiums. At the Devon site, for Pre-Kindergarten–Grade 5, classes are held in a facility completed in 1993 that includes homerooms; science labs; a library; art, shop, and music rooms; and a chapel/auditorium. There is also a large gymnasium and several playing fields.

The combined value of the school-owned plants is $30,000,000.

THE FACULTY. James L. Crawford, Jr., was appointed Head of School in 1975. A native Philadelphian and a 1957 graduate of the Academy, he is also a graduate of St. Joseph's University (B.A.), Temple (M.A.), and Widener University (L.H.D.). Dr. Crawford has spent his career as a teacher, coach, and administrator at Episcopal. He and his wife, Rosemary, have four children, three of whom have graduated from the Academy.

The faculty, including administrators who teach, number 177, 159 of whom are full-time instructors. Five faculty members live at the school with their families. The faculty hold 176 baccalaureate and 115 graduate degrees. Two or more degrees were earned at Brown, Bryn Mawr, Colgate, Columbia, Cornell, Dartmouth, Dickinson, Franklin and Marshall, Hamilton, Harvard, Haverford, La Salle, Muhlenberg, Pennsylvania State, Princeton, St. Joseph's, Syracuse, Temple, Trenton State, Trinity, Ursinus, Vassar, Villanova, Wesleyan, West Chester State, Widener, Williams, Yale, and the Universities of Notre Dame, Pennsylvania, and Wisconsin.

STUDENT BODY. Episcopal Academy enrolls 590 boys and 520 girls on the two campuses. Enrollment on the Merion campus is as follows: 220 in the Lower School, 250 in the Middle School, and 415 in the Upper School. The Devon campus enrolls 225 students in Pre-Kindergarten through Grade 5. The students come from diverse backgrounds and represent Philadelphia and many communities in the metropolitan area; there are also 15 from New Jersey.

ACADEMIC PROGRAM. The school year, from early September to mid-June, is divided into three terms and includes a Thanksgiving recess, Christmas vacation, and a midwinter and spring recess. A typical school day for Lower and Middle School students goes from 8:10 A.M. to 3:00 and 3:45 P.M., respectively and includes a Chapel/ Activity Period during the seven periods for students in Grades 6–8. Upper School students have nine periods, including a Chapel/Activity Period, in their 8:10 A.M. to 3:40 P.M. schedule. Pre-Kindergarten children have the option to leave at noon or stay until 3:00 P.M. with Kindergarten–Grade 5. An extended-day program from 3:00 to 6:00 P.M. is provided at both campuses for children in Pre-Kindergarten–Grade 5.

An average class numbers 17 students. There are super-

vised study periods in the Middle and Upper schools as well as daily individual help sessions. Lower School students receive written progress reports three times a year and have teacher-parent conferences twice a year. Middle School students receive written progress reports three times a year and report cards three times a year, with two scheduled parent-teacher conference days. Upper School teachers issue reports six times yearly, three graded reports and three reports consisting of teachers' comments.

The program for Pre-Kindergarten and Kindergarten emphasizes reading and number readiness, science, social studies, creative dramatics, music, art, library and computer classes, and physical education. Children in Grades 1–5 have regular instruction in language arts, handwriting, drama, social studies, mathematics, science, fine and dramatic arts, music, shop, library skills, computers, and physical education. Basic skills in English, math, science, history, Latin, and French or Spanish comprise the curriculum in the Middle School. In addition, trimester classes in religion, art, shop, drama, and music composition occur during the Middle School experience. Computers, library, and study skills are integrated into the academic disciplines. Students also have the option of performing in vocal and instrumental ensembles. Community service activities are done as a class.

To graduate, Upper School students must complete four credits in English; three each in mathematics, social studies, and laboratory science; two in a foreign language; and one credit each in religion and the arts.

Among the courses offered are English 1–4; French 1–5, Greek 1–3, Latin 1–5, Spanish 1–5; Pre-Modern and Modern History 1–2, United States History, History of Russia, Japan, The Middle East, Modern Africa, Vietnam, Psychology; Algebra 1–2, Geometry; Earth Science, Biology, Chemistry, Physics, Ecology; BASIC C++ or Visual Basic; Old Testament 1–2, New Testament, World Religions, Ethics; Design, Architectural Drafting, Mechanical Drawing, Woodshop, Art History; and Music Theory and Harmony, and Music History. Advanced Placement courses are offered in AB and BC Calculus, Statistics, French, Spanish, Latin, biology, chemistry, physics, European History, United States Government and Politics, computers, and art. Students may take other courses in English and American history in preparation for Advanced Placement examinations. In 1999, 82 students took 185 AP examinations, with 94 percent receiving 3 or above. Qualified students may pursue courses at local colleges and universities; faculty support seniors as they develop independent study projects.

In 1999, all 103 graduating seniors were college-bound; 68 percent of "early decisions" were accepted. Two or more students matriculated at Boston College, Boston University, Brown, Bucknell, Colgate, Franklin and Marshall, George Washington University, Georgetown, Gettysburg, Harvard, Haverford, Northwestern, Princeton, Trinity College, Yale, and the Universities of Colorado (Boulder), Pennsylvania, Vermont, and Virginia.

There is a day camp for young children at the Devon and Merion campuses.

STUDENT ACTIVITIES. At Merion, the Middle School Student Council, the Chapel Council, and the Spirit Council work with faculty advisers to plan events for Grades 6–8. The Upper School Student-Faculty Senate plans and coordinates extracurricular activities and assists in upholding the disciplinary code. The Athletic Association, which includes the captains of the 28 varsity teams and various administrators, determines athletic policies and procedures. Members of the student vestry assist as acolytes and lay readers and plan the chapel program. Eighty-five percent of the Upper School students voluntarily participate in on- and off-campus community service projects. Qualified students may be elected to The Cum Laude Society.

Students publish a newspaper, Middle and Upper School yearbooks, and a literary magazine. Typical Upper School organizations include the Backpacking, Camera, Chess, French, Library, Math, Science, and Spanish clubs as well as the debate team, the Student Tutorial Service, the Stock Market, and Big Brothers/Big Sisters. The Middle School has a structured advisory program with a wide range of activities. The Domino Club produces several plays each year. Musical organizations include the glee club, choir, two a cappella groups, two Middle School choruses, the jazz and orchestra ensemble, Chapel choirs, and instrumental ensembles.

All Upper and Middle School students are required to participate in sports each season, with the exception of seniors who are required to participate during two seasons. Boys' varsity teams are organized in baseball, basketball, crew, cross-country, football, golf, ice hockey, lacrosse, soccer, squash, swimming, tennis, track, water polo, and wrestling. Girls compete in basketball, crew, cross-country, field hockey, golf, soccer, lacrosse, squash, swimming, water polo, tennis, softball, and track, and dance is offered as well. Intramural sports include several of the team sports as well as volleyball, rock climbing, floor hockey, and weight training. Younger students participate in baseball, basketball, cross-country, field hockey, football, lacrosse, soccer, softball, squash, swimming, tennis, track, and wrestling.

There are field trips, class trips, special programs, and dances throughout the year. Other traditional events include receptions for parents, the fall alumni luncheon, and a spring alumni day and reunion weekend.

ADMISSION AND COSTS. New students are admitted to all grades on the basis of standardized testing, a personal interview, previous school records, and teacher recommendations. Major entry points are the Pre-Kindergarten, Kindergarten, and Grades 6 and 9. Application should be made in the fall prior to the year of desired fall enrollment. There is a $35 application fee.

In 1999–2000, tuition ranges from $6700 for half-day Pre-Kindergarten to $14,320 for Grades 9–12. Additional expenses include transportation, lunches, and some books and supplies. Financial aid is available based on need. Tuition insurance and payment plans are available, and The Episcopal Academy subscribes to the School Scholarship Service.

Dean of Faculty: Jonathan B. Kulp
Alumni/ae Secretary: Anthony J. Brown
Director of Admissions: Ellen M. Hay
Director of Development: Margaret McG. Hollinger
Business Manager: Sidney C. Buck
Director of Athletics: Regina E. Buggy

Falk School   1931

University of Pittsburgh, Pittsburgh, PA 15261. 412-624-8020;
Fax 412-624-1303; E-mail bmcdonal+@pitt.edu

As the demonstration laboratory school for the University, Falk School dedicates itself to the promotion of modern teaching methods in a dual effort to educate students and further educational research. Approximately 282 day boys and girls are enrolled in nongraded classes ranging in academic level from Kindergarten to Grade 8. Sequential instruction in the fundamental skills is meant to stimulate each student in accordance with his/her capabilities. Falk emphasizes inquiry and the development of higher-order thinking skills. Tuition: $5450. Extras: $195. Financial Aid: $24,000. William E. McDonald (University of Pittsburgh, Ph.D. 1979) was appointed Director in 1996.

Friends' Central School   1845

Grades 5–12: 1101 City Avenue, Wynnewood, PA 19096.
610-649-7440; Fax 610-649-5669;
E-mail dnelson@fcs.pvt.k12.pa.us
PK–Grade 4: 228 Gulph Road, Wynnewood, PA 19096.
610-642-7575; Fax 610-642-6983

Friends' Central School is a college preparatory day school enrolling 511 boys and 481 girls in Pre-Kindergarten–Grade 12. The School strives to maintain high academic standards and to treat its students with understanding and compassion. Friends' Central offers a demanding and broad program in academics, arts, and athletics and encourages students to participate and develop their minds, bodies, and spirits. All students assemble for the weekly Meeting for Worship in the tradition of the Society of Friends. Tuition: $8375–$13,900. Financial Aid: $2,076,691. Susan H. Dana is Director of Admission and Financial Aid; David M. Felsen (Haverford, B.A. 1966; University of Pennsylvania, M.A. 1971) was appointed Headmaster in 1988.

Friends School Haverford   1885

851 Buck Lane, Haverford, PA 19041. 610-642-2334;
Fax 610-642-0870; E-mail fsh@philly.infi.net;
Web Site http://fsh.phillynews.com

Friends School Haverford is a coeducational, Quaker elementary school enrolling 195 students in three-year-old Pre-School–Grade 6. Under the care of Haverford Monthly Meeting of the Society of Friends, a capable, experienced faculty and staff present a full academic curriculum emphasizing basic concepts, clear and logical thinking, and the ability to communicate ideas. The School is a caring community based on Quaker values, in which individual attention helps each child to realize his or her potential. Art, music, computers, science, health, library, and physical education enrich the program. Tuition:

$4500–$10,075. Financial Aid: $210,000. Beth Krick is Director of Admission; Marlisa Parker (Mount Holyoke, B.A.; Russell Sage, M.A.) is Principal.

Friends Select School   1689

17th Street & The Benjamin Franklin Parkway, Philadelphia, PA 19103. 215-561-5900; Fax 215-864-2979; E-mail admission@fsspo.fss.fss.pvt.k12.pa.us; Web Site www.friends-select.org

Friends Select School is located in the heart of Philadelphia's downtown business and cultural districts. Its 500 students in Pre-Kindergarten–Grade 12 benefit from Friends Select's use of the city to create interesting and exciting curricular opportunities as part of a rigorous college preparatory program. Typically, 100 percent of graduates attend college. Friends Select School's notable features include its Quaker past and present, Center City location, excellent college preparation, curricular relationships with Parkway institutions, expansive use of technology, and a diverse student body. Tuition: $7255–$13,460. Financial Aid: $900,000. Rose Hagan (Temple University, B.A.; Southern Illinois University, M.A.) is Head of School. *Middle States Association.*

George School   1893

Newtown, PA 18940. 215-579-6500; Admissions 215-579-6547; Fax 215-579-6549; E-mail admissions@georgeschool.org; Web Site www.georgeschool.org

Affiliated with the Society of Friends, George School provides "excellent college preparation" and attracts students who value academic rigor and commitment to service, social justice, and simplicity. Enrolled are 280 boarding and 260 day boys and girls in Grades 9–12. Advanced Placement, the International Baccalaureate program, international student exchanges, and English as a Second Language are offered. Activities include student government, intramural and interscholastic sports, clubs, and a cooperative work program. Boarding Tuition: $22,900; Day Tuition: $15,620. Financial Aid: $2,700,000. Karen S. Hallowell is Director of Admission; David L. Bourns (College of Wooster, A.B. 1961; Union Theological Seminary, M.Div. 1966) is Headmaster. *Middle States Association.*

Germantown Academy   1759

P.O. Box 287, Fort Washington, PA 19034. 215-646-3300; Fax 215-646-1216; E-mail admission@ga.k12.pa.us; Web Site www.ga.k12.pa.us

Germantown Academy is a coeducational, college preparatory day school enrolling 564 boys and 540 girls in Pre-Kindergarten–Grade 12. It seeks to prepare students to think critically, communicate effectively, and understand the needs of others. The curriculum emphasizes command of basic skills and offers a variety of electives in the Upper School, where students normally carry five to six courses. Independent study opportunities are available. Tuition: $7030–$13,645. Financial Aid: $1,000,000. James W. Connor (Eckerd College, A.B. 1972; University of Pennsylvania, M.A. 1988) is Headmaster. *Middle States Association.*

Germantown Friends School   1845

31 West Coulter Street, Philadelphia, PA 19144. 215-951-2300; Fax 215-951-2370; Web Site www.gfsnet.org

Germantown Friends School is a nationally recognized college preparatory day school enrolling 900 girls and boys in Kindergarten–Grade 12. It operates on the Quaker principles of simplicity, self-discipline, community responsibility, nonviolence, and unreserved respect for each individual. The program emphasizes all academic skills and includes art, music, and physical education. Students in the Upper School (Grades 9–12) carry five major courses and complete an independent project. Tuition: $9010–$13,330. Financial Aid: $1,090,000. Eleanor M. Elkinton is Director of Admission and Financial Aid; Richard L. Wade (William and Mary, B.A.; Northwestern, M.A.) is Head of School. *Middle States Association.*

The Grier School   TYRONE

Tyrone, PA 16686. 814-684-3000; Fax 814-684-2177; E-mail admissions@grier.org; Web Site www.grier.org

THE GRIER SCHOOL in Tyrone, Pennsylvania, is a boarding school for girls in Grade 7 through Postgraduate, offering two levels of college preparatory education. It occupies a 300-acre campus in the hills of central Pennsylvania, 110 miles east of Pittsburgh, 200 miles from Philadelphia, and 25 miles from State College, where Pennsylvania State University provides many cultural and entertainment programs.

The School was founded in 1853 by residents of the nearby town of Birmingham to educate young women, because public high schools did not admit them in that section of Pennsylvania. It was acquired by Dr. Lemuel G. Grier in 1857 and since then has operated continuously under the direction of four generations of the Grier family.

Incorporated as a nonprofit foundation in 1957, The Grier School is directed by a self-perpetuating Board of Trustees. The School is accredited by the Middle States Association of Colleges and Schools and holds membership in The National

Association of Principals of Schools for Girls, the National Association of Independent Schools and the Pennsylvania Association of Independent Schools.

THE CAMPUS. The property, which rises as much as 400 feet from the entrance gate to the highest points on campus, is landscaped with white pine, Norway spruce, and hemlocks—many of which date back to Dr. Lemuel Grier's administration. The campus provides athletic fields, a modern gymnasium, indoor and outdoor pools, tennis courts, a tennis backboard, and complete facilities for the riding program, including winding trails, three paddocks, a dressage ring, stables for as many as 50 horses, an outdoor riding arena, and a large indoor riding hall.

The five principal buildings, which are connected, contain most of the residence facilities, the library, an assembly hall, the dining room, a computer resource center, recreational facilities, a dance studio, the main classrooms, laboratories, and audiovisual facilities. The Lodge, connected by a colonnade, contains additional student bedrooms and a study hall. There are also 12 faculty residences, an infirmary, and the 202-year-old Horsehaven Inn, which has been renovated to provide a snack bar and lounge.

THE FACULTY. Dr. Douglas A. Grier, who came to the School as Assistant Headmaster in 1968 and became Headmaster in 1969, was appointed Director in 1981; he is a graduate of The Hill School in Pennsylvania, Princeton University (A.B. 1964), and the University of Michigan (M.S. 1965, Ph.D. 1968). Andrea Hollnagel, who graduated from Mankato State University, was named Head of School in 1997.

There are 30 full-time teachers. Faculty colleges include Dartmouth, Duke, Georgetown, Hampshire, Indiana University (Pennsylvania), Juniata, Middlebury, Pennsylvania State, Temple, and the Universities of North Carolina, Pennsylvania, and Pittsburgh. Other staff members include office personnel, a riding instructor, and two grooms. Three nurses share coverage of the infirmary 24 hours a day, and physicians are on call.

STUDENT BODY. Grier enrolls 168 girls, 11 to 19 years of age, as follows: 18 in Grade 7, 8 in Grade 8, 11 in Grade 9, 39 in Grade 10, 47 in Grade 11, 43 in Grade 12, and 2 in Postgraduate. The students represent many racial and religious backgrounds and come from 21 states, the District of Columbia, and 20 foreign countries.

ACADEMIC PROGRAM. The school year, from early September to early June includes 33 weeks of instruction, Thanksgiving recess, and Christmas and spring vacations. If she has written permission from home, a girl may leave school nearly any weekend during the year.

The school day begins at 8:00 A.M. with classes meeting Monday through Friday. There are five class or study periods before lunch and two in the early afternoon. Students may obtain individual help during a daily conference period. Beginning at 2:40 P.M., there are three athletic periods; dinner begins at 6:00 P.M., followed by 90 minutes of evening study Sunday through Friday. A 15-minute student job program is incorporated into the weekday schedule.

Grier offers a supportive, multitrack academic program. For the underachieving student, slower-paced courses, along with intensive tutoring through a daily Learning Skills class, are provided. Creative and performing arts classes are offered to augment the academic schedule. Every effort is made to pace the curriculum to the needs of each individual student, and girls frequently take classes from both academic tracks.

The Learning Skills Program is conducted by three specialists in the areas of reading, writing, and mathematics skills. Learning Skills functions as a resource center for remediation and individualized tutoring. The goal is to bring a girl's learning skills up to her chronological grade level, thereby enhancing her academic self-image and her overall confidence. The Learning Skills instructors, working with the regular classroom teachers, become advocates for their students and also offer counseling.

The "hallmark" of all of Grier's academic programs is its small classes and nurturing faculty. Students are provided with the opportunity to grow in motivation and self-confidence by working closely with faculty members.

The curriculum includes English; French, Spanish; Geography, United States History; Algebra, Geometry (Plane and Analytic), Advanced Mathematics (including Calculus), Computer Science; Physics, Chemistry, Ecology; Psychology; and Music Theory and Composition. Advanced Placement or honors work is available in most fields. An intensive English as a Second Language program is offered to students whose native language is not English.

Each girl chooses a half-credit course in the creative arts. Among the half-credit offerings are Dance (ballet, jazz, and tap dance), Piano, Voice, Studio Art, Drama, Weaving, Ceramics, Costume Design, Jewelry Making, and Photography. Courses are also offered in equestrianship and typing/word processing. Seniors spend a week in May engaged in independent projects that range from advanced studies in English to veterinary internships and art projects on campus.

In 1999, graduates entered such colleges and universities as Goucher, Maryland Institute, Mitchell, Peabody Conservatory of Music, Rochester Institute of Technology, and the Universities of Michigan and Wisconsin.

English as a Second Language is offered year-round. The summer program consists of eight weeks of intensive English on campus, in conjunction with Allegheny Camp, and a three-week tour of Washington D.C., and North and South Carolina.

STUDENT ACTIVITIES. Active student groups include "Grier

Dance," yearbook, literary magazine, Triple Trio, Women's Chorale, Athletic Association, and the Riding, Skiing, Dramatic, Ecology, and Service clubs. Outing Club activities include skiing, white-water rafting, boardsailing, camping, whale watching, backpacking, and sailing. Beginning and advanced instruction is available in studio art, photography, and dance.

Participation in the athletic program is required. "Green" and "Gold" intramural competition is carried on in such sports as soccer, volleyball, basketball, and softball, and there is opportunity for such other sports as skiing and ice-skating. Varsity sports include soccer, tennis, basketball, and softball. The riding program is designed to provide girls with the technical points of equitation and with competition in horse shows. Riders may attend horse shows on weekends during the fall and spring terms.

Entertainment programs at the School range from visiting speakers to sports festivals. Weekend activities include horse shows, movies, concerts, dances, shopping, skiing, skating, windsurfing, white-water rafting, camping, and trips to whale-watching, Washington, Baltimore, and the local Amish country. Regularly scheduled assemblies dealing with current moral and ethical issues complement offerings. Longer School-sponsored excursions are conducted during the Thanksgiving recess and spring vacation; spring trips have been made to France, Greece, Spain, the Caribbean, and Great Britain.

ADMISSION AND COSTS. Grier seeks to enroll college-bound girls of average to above-average ability who possess interests in sports and the arts, as well as a desire to work in a challenging yet supportive academic atmosphere. Applicants are accepted in Grades 7–12, and occasionally for the Postgraduate year, on the basis of previous record, recommendations, and, if possible, an interview.

In 1999–2000, the annual charge is $22,500 for room, board, tuition, and most school fees. Extra charges include an Infirmary, Publications, and Technology fee ($500), school trips and bookstore items (totaling approximately $2000), and optional horseback riding ($1500). The suggested monthly allowance is $100. Tuition payment plans are offered.

Scholarship aid, amounting to approximately $570,000 annually, is based on academic ability and financial need as determined by the School and Student Service for Financial Aid.

Dean of Students: Gina Borst
Alumnae Secretary: Regi Heffner
Assistant Head of School/Director of Admission: Andrew Wilson
Director of Development: Andrew Wilson
College Counselors: Andrea Hollnagel and Douglas Grier, Ph.D.
Treasurer: Marlene Halbedl
Directors of Athletics: Kay Hunter and Stephanie Johnson-Smith

Gwynedd-Mercy Academy   1861

1345 Sumneytown Pike, P.O. Box 902, Gwynedd Valley, PA
   19437-0902. 215-646-8815; Fax 215-646-4361;
   E-mail admissions@gmahs.com

The Sisters of Mercy founded this Roman Catholic, college preparatory day school enrolling 400 girls in Grades 9–12. Gwynedd-Mercy Academy is committed to single-sex education as a means of developing confident, articulate young women capable of responsible leadership in the 21st century. Catholic values shape the curriculum, which includes four years of theology, Advanced Placement and honors courses, and computer technology. Spiritual growth is promoted through liturgies, retreats, and community service. Among the activities are school government, glee club and chorale, publications, varsity sports, and numerous clubs. Tuition: $7400. Colleen Casey is Director of Admissions; Sr. Mary Alice, RSM, is Principal.

The Harrisburg Academy   1784

10 Erford Road, Wormleysburg, PA 17043. 717-763-7811;
   Fax 717-975-0894; E-mail harrisburgacademy.org

The Harrisburg Academy, a coeducational, college preparatory day school serving 475 students of above-average to high aptitude in Nursery–Grade 12, aims to provide an outstanding educational experience that combines a rigorous curriculum, including Advanced Placement and enrichment courses, with the arts and athletics. Foreign language instruction begins in Junior Kindergarten and computer classes in Kindergarten. Community service, varsity teams, Student Council, Mock Trial, dramatics, Model UN, and publications are among the activities. A series of summer sessions is provided. Tuition: $4895–$10,026. Financial Aid: $380,000. J. Gregory Morgan (University of Washington, B.A.; University of Michigan, M.A.; Pennsylvania State, M.A.) is Headmaster. *Middle States Association.*

The Haverford School   1884

450 Lancaster Avenue, Haverford, PA 19041. 610-642-3020;
   Fax 610-649-4898; Admissions Extension 315;
   Web Site www.haverford.org

Haverford, a nonsectarian day school enrolling 890 boys in Junior Kindergarten–Grade 12, places strong emphasis on academic and thinking skills through a broad array of experiences in the arts and athletics. The School's commitment to understanding and appreciating boys helps them become leaders in a world of ever-decreasing size. Languages include Latin, Chinese, French, Spanish, and German. The curriculum includes Advanced Placement in all subjects, including music and art. Playwriting and choral singing are among the opportunities in the arts. Athletic teams include crew, squash, and winter track. Tuition: $10,500–$15,250. Financial Aid: $1,300,000. Kevin Seits is Director of Admissions; Joseph T. Cox (University of North Carolina, Ph.D.) was appointed Headmaster in 1998. *Middle States Association.*

The Hill School   POTTSTOWN

Pottstown, PA 19464. 610-326-1000 or toll-free 888-HILL-150;
   Fax 610-326-7471; E-mail gbuckles@thehill.org;
   Web Site www.thehill.org

THE HILL SCHOOL in Pottstown, Pennsylvania, is a college preparatory boarding and day school enrolling young men and women in Grades 9–12 (Forms Three–Six) and a postgraduate year. Pottstown (population 26,000) is 40 miles northwest of Philadelphia, easily accessible to New York City, Baltimore, and Washington, D.C., as well as the Pocono Mountains, the Amish country, and historic Valley Forge National Park.

Founded in 1851 by Rev. Matthew Meigs, The Hill opened as the Family Boarding School for Boys and Young Men with an enrollment of 25 pupils. In the fall of 1998, the School became fully coeducational, enrolling 100 "First Girls." The move to coeducation emphasizes The Hill School's commitment to a community of people who are open-minded, outgoing, and willing to take risks. Although it is nondenominational, The Hill's philosophy is based on Christian principles, and all students are required to attend chapel services twice weekly.

The articles of the School's incorporation are held by the approximately 8000 alumni who elect 11 of the 28 members of the Board of Trustees. The Hill School is accredited by the Middle States Association of Colleges and Schools and holds membership in the National Association of Independent Schools, among other affiliations. The School's endowment is approximately $104,000,000.

THE CAMPUS. The Hill School campus consists of 200 acres overlooking the Schuylkill Valley. Among the 55 buildings are Alumni Chapel, Memorial Hall, Sweeney Gymnasium, the Harry Elkins Widener Science Building, the Center For The Arts, the Ryan Library, and the Music House. The 50,000-square-foot Academic Center, completed in 1998, is home to administrative offices, classrooms, a student center, and the bookstore. Boarders live in ten residences, including Dell Dormitory (1999).

The athletic facilities include an 18-hole golf course, 15 tennis courts, an ice-hockey rink, swimming pool, 10 sports fields, a fully equipped strength center, an all-weather Olympic track, and 6 squash courts. The School also owns an additional, 100-acre wooded tract complete with a trap and skeet range and a spring-fed pond.

The campus and facilities are valued at approximately $77,000,000.

THE FACULTY. David R. Dougherty was appointed Headmaster in 1993. A graduate of Episcopal High School in Virginia, he holds a baccalaureate degree in English from Washington and Lee University and a master's degree from Georgetown. Mr. Dougherty also earned an M.Litt. degree from Lincoln College, Oxford, and studied at The Bread Loaf School of English at Middlebury College. His wife, Kay, is Associate Director of Admission and a member of the Mathematics Department at The Hill.

The 58 men and 22 women on the faculty hold 82 baccalaureate, 55 master's, and 5 doctoral degrees representing study at such institutions as Amherst, Boston University, Bowdoin, Brown, Bucknell, Canisius, Central Michigan, Clemson, Colgate, Columbia, Cornell, Dartmouth, Denison, Drexel, Duke, Earlham, Fordham, Gettysburg, Harvard, Haverford, Hollins, Ithaca, Johns Hopkins, Kenyon, Lehigh, Mary Baldwin, Middlebury, Mount Holyoke, Muhlenberg, Ohio State, Princeton, Purdue, St. John's, St. Joseph's, Swarthmore, Temple, Trinity, Ursinus, Villanova, West Chester, Yale Divinity School, and the Universities of California, Delaware, Denver, Grenoble, Massachusetts, Michigan, New Hampshire, North Carolina, Notre Dame, Pennsylvania, Texas, Virginia, and Windsor.

The school physician holds regular hours in the dispensary, and Pottstown Memorial Medical Center is available for emergencies.

STUDENT BODY. In 1999–2000, The Hill enrolled 319 boys and 142 girls, approximately 80 percent of whom are boarding students. Day students are expected to live on campus for at least one year, as the boarding experience is integral to a Hill education. Students came from 34 states and 17 countries and represented a wide diversity of racial, ethnic, religious, and socioeconomic backgrounds.

ACADEMIC PROGRAM. The school year begins in early September and ends late in May, with five long weekends and vacations at Thanksgiving, Christmas, and in the spring. Interim grades are sent to parents every five weeks, and term grades are sent at the end of each trimester. There are also parent conferences in the fall. Classes, with as many as 15 girls and boys, are held six days a week, with half-days on Wednesday and Saturday when afternoons are reserved for athletics and other activities. Faculty are available for extra help by request.

A typical day begins with the rising bell at 7:00 A.M., followed by breakfast and classes from 7:55 A.M. to 12:05 P.M., lunch, more classes until 3:10 P.M., with sports scheduled until 5:30 P.M. Supervised evening study hours are conducted from 7:30 to 9:30 P.M. except on Saturday. "Lights out" is between 10:00 P.M. and midnight, depending upon grade.

To graduate, students must complete 17 scholastic units of credit, including 4 in English; 3 each in mathematics and foreign language; 2 each in history and a laboratory science (biology, chemistry, or physics); and 1 in theology or philosophy. Honors divisions and sequences leading to Advanced Placement Examinations are available in mathematics, English, the sciences, history, foreign languages, art, and computer science.

Among the courses are Language and Literature, Western Culture and English Grammar, Critical Reading and Writing Skills, American Literature and Rhetoric, World Literature and Composition, Advanced Transitional English, Public Speaking; Mathematics 8, Algebra I–II, Geometry, History of Mathematics; Advanced Pascal, Spread Sheet, Database; Greek 1–4, Latin 1–6, French 1–5, Spanish 1–6, German 1–4, Chinese 1–2; American Government, European History, Modern European History, United States History, Economics, Cultural Geography, America at War, The Civil War, World War II; Biology Research, Biology 1–2, Chemistry 1–2, Conceptual Physics, Physics 1–2; Judeo-Christian Roots, Discussion of Dimensions, Religion Through Literature, Psychology I–II; Music Theory and Harmony I–II, Chamber Orchestra, Jazz Ensemble, String Quartet, Jazz Improvisation, Glee Club, Oral Communications, Drama Workshop, Studio Art I–II, and Photography. A two-year honors course in the humanities may be elected in place of English 3 and 4. Three academic support programs address learning and study techniques, verbal and reading skills and enrichment, and Developmental English. Independent Study projects under faculty supervision and the Underform Writers' Workshop further enrich the curriculum.

Study-travel opportunities include a summer classical program in Italy as well as programs in Botswana, China, England, France, and Spain through the English-Speaking Union and School Year Abroad.

Of the 124 seniors in the Class of 1999, 118 entered college immediately after graduation, while the remainder undertook postgraduate programs, traveled abroad, or deferred enrollment for a year. Three or more are attending Franklin and Marshall 4, Gettysburg 5, Hamilton, James Madison,

Lehigh, New York University, Northwestern, Rollins, United States Naval Academy 6, and the Universities of Pittsburgh and Richmond.

The Hill conducts two programs in a five-week, coeducational summer session for Grades 6–12. The first program emphasizes study skills; the second option provides English as a Second Language for international students.

STUDENT ACTIVITIES. A joint Student-Faculty Senate permits boys and girls to undertake responsibility and develop leadership skills. In addition, there are 36 sixth formers who act as dormitory prefects. Upperformers also supervise the Work Program in which all students contribute up to 30 minutes each day in housekeeping and maintenance chores.

All students participate in sports or exercise at some level. Girls' and boys' teams are fielded in cross-country, soccer, water polo, basketball, ice hockey, squash, swimming, track, golf, lacrosse, and tennis; girls also play field hockey and softball, while boys compete in football, wrestling, and baseball. Instructional-level teams are offered throughout the year in most sports and power plyometrics.

Students publish a yearbook, a newspaper, and a literary magazine. For students interested in music, there is the Glee Club, Chamber Ensemble, Jazz Band, and The Hilltones, a 16-member vocal group. Other groups include the Hill Athletic Association, Student Activities and Reception committees, Ellis Theatre Guild, and numerous clubs.

The Humanities Fund and the Bissell Forum Speakers have sponsored appearances and lectures by a number of noted guests, many of whom are Hill alumni. These have included Secretary of State James A. Baker III, Nelson Bunker Hunt, former United States Senator William Proxmire, Justice Stephen S. Trott, and authors Doris Kearns Goodwin, David McCullough, and Tobias Wolff, Penn Faulkner Award winner.

Students play a major role in planning activities in conjunction with the staff. Dances, ski trips, on- and off-campus sporting events, and excursions to Philadelphia, New York, and Washington, D.C., are a sampling of weekend activities.

Traditional Hill events are Junior Prize Day, Parents Weekend Music Concert, Humanities concerts, the Spring Fling, Alumni Weekends, and the Sandford Festival of the Arts and National Players performances.

ADMISSION AND COSTS. The Hill, which maintains a nondiscriminatory policy regarding race, creed, and national or ethnic origin, welcomes young men and women "who understand that to strive toward excellence is of primary value in any human endeavor." Admission requirements include a student essay, transcripts from the current school, recommendations from English and mathematics teachers, an interview on campus, and the results of a standardized admission test. Application, with a $40 fee, should be made by February 15 for March 11 notification; late applications will be considered as space is available after April 11.

In 1999–2000, tuition is $24,400 for boarders and $15,800 for day students. Books, transportation, lab fees, laundry, and social events are extra. Financial aid exceeding $2,400,000 is currently awarded on a need-only basis to approximately 42 percent of the enrollment. The Hill School subscribes to the School and Student Service.

Associate Headmaster: Harry L. Price
Assistant Head for External Affairs/Director of Development:
    James A. Gundy III
Assistant Head for Academics: Anne Henry
Assistant Head for Residential Life: Lawrence F. Filippone
Dean of Students: Christopher J. Hopkins
Director of Admission: Gregory B. Buckles
Director of College Advising: Joseph N. Lagor
Assistant Head for Financial and Business Operations:
    James R. Pugh
Director of Athletics: H. Wayne Curtis

The Hillside School 1983

2697 Brookside Road, Macungie, PA 18049. 610-967-5449;
    Fax 610-965-7683

Hillside is an elementary day school that provides a carefully structured program for 128 boys and girls of average to superior ability whose learning disabilities have prevented them from achieving their potential. The School strives to promote attitudes and abilities essential to academic success through remedial, developmental, and accelerated courses designed to meet each student's specific learning needs. Full-time specialists provide support services to parents and faculty, using a team approach to realize goals. Tuition: $11,100. Scholarships are available. Linda Whitney (Eastern Michigan, M.A. 1971) is Director. *Middle States Association.*

The Hill Top Preparatory School 1971

737 South Ithan Avenue, Rosemont, PA 19010. 610-527-3230;
    Fax 610-527-7683; E-mail headmaster@hilltopprep.org

The Hill Top Preparatory School offers a comprehensive academic program for boys and girls in Grades 6–12 of average to above-average intelligence who have learning disabilities. Students work in small classes, advancing at their own pace through remedial, corrective, and developmental stages until they are ready to return to a regular school or earn a diploma from Hill Top. A transitional program for students taking college courses provides counseling and help in areas of weakness. Reality-oriented counseling focusing on self-esteem, self-advocacy, and social skills is an integral part of every student's program. Tuition: $21,500; Transitional: $10,750. John Knudson-Martin is Director of Admission; Leslie H. McLean, Ed.D., is Headmaster.

Holy Ghost Preparatory School 1897

2429 Bristol Pike, Bensalem, PA 19020. 215-639-2102;
    Admissions 215-639-0811; Fax 215-639-4225;
    E-mail ryana@holyghostprep.bensalem.pa.us;
    Web Site www.holyghostprep.bensalem.pa.us

Now in its second century of educating young men, this designated School of Excellence enrolls 475 young men in Grades 9–12 in an academic and cocurricular program formed by Catholic values and tradition. The School was founded by the Congregation of the Holy Ghost to nurture each boy's unique, God-given gifts and to develop spiritual, academic, and physical growth. Traditionally, 100 percent of graduates are accepted to college, with more than 80 percent receiving scholarships. Sports are offered at three levels; publications, bands, clubs, and a summer program are among the activities. Tuition: $8100. Financial Aid: $250,000. Ryan T. Abramson '94 is Director of Admissions; Rev. James McCloskey, C.S.Sp. '70, is Headmaster. *Middle States Association.*

Kimberton Waldorf School   1941

West Seven Stars Road, Kimberton, PA 19442. 610-933-3635; Fax 610-935-6985

Located in a semirural area near Philadelphia, Kimberton Waldorf, one of more than 800 Waldorf schools worldwide, is a coeducational day school dedicated to bringing forth the unique possibilities of each child. Enrollment is approximately 370 students in Pre-Kindergarten–Grade 12. Working within the Waldorf educational impulse founded by Rudolf Steiner, the School combines the arts and sciences to develop well-rounded intellectual, emotional, artistic, and practical capacities in each child. Foreign language is introduced in Grade 1; music, drama, arts, and crafts are provided at every level. Varsity sports programs are offered. Tuition: $3000–$9300. Financial aid is available. Marsha Hill is Admissions Director; King Graver is the School Administrator. *Middle States Association.*

The Kiski School   SALTSBURG

1888 Brett Lane, Saltsburg, PA 15681. 724-639-3586 or [toll-free] 1-877-KISKI-4-U; Fax 724-639-8596; E-mail admissions@kiski.org; Web Site www.kiski.org

THE KISKI SCHOOL in Saltsburg, Pennsylvania, is a college preparatory boarding school enrolling boys in Grades 9 through 12 and a postgraduate year. The School is situated on a wooded plateau across the Kiskiminetas River from the town of Saltsburg, a community of 3000 in the Laurel Highlands region of Western Pennsylvania. Students and faculty participate in community activities in the town and travel to Pittsburgh, 35 miles to the west, for cultural, athletic, and entertainment events.

In 1888, Princeton graduates Dr. Andrew Wilson and R. W. Fair bought a resort hotel near the mineral springs that gave the School its original name, The Kiskiminetas Springs School. Dr. Wilson, the first Headmaster, based his school program on the British boarding school model of academic rigor and healthy competition in athletics. These traits continue to describe The Kiski School, which aims to cultivate academic excellence and the development of a boy's character, integrity, self-discipline, and good manners. Small classes, close association with faculty, required athletics, formal meals, a dress code, and an emphasis on civility all contribute to the preparation of Kiski boys for success in college and in life. Kiski is nonsectar-

ian, and attendance at Sunday church services in town is optional.

The Kiski School is incorporated as a nonprofit organization governed by a Board of 20 Trustees. It has an endowment of about $30,000,000 and the support of approximately 4000 living graduates. The School is accredited by the Middle States Association of Colleges and Schools and holds membership in the National Association of Independent Schools, the Pennsylvania Association of Independent Schools, the Boys' School Coalition, and a number of professional organizations.

THE CAMPUS. The 350-acre campus provides a setting of striking natural beauty, with mature trees shadowing the main area of the campus, 100 wooded acres beyond, and two streams flowing together to form the Kiskiminetas River. The original hotel has been reconstructed and modernized and now houses the administrative offices.

There are 34 additional buildings, including Heath Hall, the main classroom building, and Kalnow Hall, the foreign-language center and home of WKRC-FM, the School's radio station. The Rogers Fine Arts Center (1984) provides music and art classrooms, practice rooms, art studios, darkroom, woodshop, exhibition spaces, and a 350-seat theater. The John A. Pidgeon Library (1993) maintains a collection of 21,000 volumes and a computer writing lab and offers connections to information networks. The dining hall and infirmary complex contains the book store, coin-operated laundry, and snack bar. There are nine dormitories and a number of faculty residences.

The S.W. Jack Fieldhouse/Aquatic Center houses basketball courts, wrestling gym, weight-training rooms, swimming pool, and support facilities. The outdoor resources include nine playing fields, an all-weather track, five tennis courts, outdoor basketball court, outdoor swimming pool, and a nine-hole golf course.

The plant is owned by the School and is valued at $50,000,000.

THE FACULTY. John A. Pidgeon, a graduate of Bowdoin College (A.B. 1949), was appointed Headmaster in 1957 and has served in his position for 42 years, the longest tenure among headmasters in the country. A decorated naval officer in World War II, Mr. Pidgeon was assistant to the legendary Headmaster Frank Boyden at Deerfield Academy before coming to Kiski. He has continued to maintain contact with students as a teacher, coach, and mentor. Mr. Pidgeon holds honorary doctorates from Bethany College and Washington and Jefferson College. He is married to Barbara Hafer, Treasurer of the State of Pennsylvania, and they have four grown children. Kiski's Assistant Head is Judith L. McAtee (Indiana University of Pennsylvania, B.S.N., M.Ed.), for whom the School's Health Center is named.

The teaching faculty, including administrators who teach, is comprised of 29 men and 9 women, most of whom live on campus. They hold 39 bachelor's degrees and 25 advanced degrees from such institutions as Allegheny 2, Bethany, Bowdoin, Brown, Carnegie Mellon 3, Clemson, Cranbrook Academy of Arts, Duquesne 3, Franklin and Marshall, Grove City, Hartwick, Indiana (Pennsylvania) 6, Loyola University, Middlebury 3, Mississippi College 2, Ohio Wesleyan, Pennsylvania State, Rice, St. John's, Salem, Slippery Rock, Southern Illinois 2, Springfield, Temple, Tulane, Washington and Jefferson 2, Yale, and the Universities of Massachusetts, North Carolina 2, Pennsylvania 2, Pittsburgh 4, Rhode Island, and Rochester.

A school nurse is on duty at the McAtee Health Center throughout the school day and is on call around the clock. Physicians are available in Saltsburg six days a week.

STUDENT BODY. In 1998–99, the School enrolled 219 boarding boys including 36 in Grade 9, 41 in Grade 10, 79 in Grade 11, and 63 in Grade 12. Students came from 16 states and 12 foreign countries including California, Colorado, Florida, Illinois, Louisiana, Maryland, Michigan, Nebraska, New Jersey, New York, Ohio, Oregon, Pennsylvania, Texas, Virginia, West Virginia, China, England, Guatemala, India, Indonesia, Japan, Korea, Mexico, Pakistan, Panama, Russia, Saudi Arabia, Singapore, and Taiwan.

ACADEMIC PROGRAM. The academic year, divided into semesters, begins in early September and concludes in late May with vacations at Thanksgiving, Christmas, and in the spring. Classes, with an average size of ten students, are held six days a week, from 8:00 A.M. until 2:35 P.M. on weekdays and ending at 10:25 A.M. on Saturdays. Students are encouraged to ask for extra help, and teachers are available to give it during the day and in the evening. A two-hour supervised study period is scheduled each weekday evening. Students receive grades and comments on their progress from the Headmaster four times a year. Interim reports may be sent to parents if a student's performance shows some significant change.

Most students take five courses each term, but some choose six. To graduate, students must complete 19 credits including 4 years of English, 3 of one foreign language, 2 of history including both American and European, 3 of mathematics, and 2 of laboratory science, plus credits in Fine Arts and Life Skills. Every senior must complete a research paper.

Among the courses offered are English 1–4; English as a Second Language 1–3; French 1–5, German 1–5, Spanish 1–5; U.S. History, Modern European History, World Civilization, U.S. Foreign Policy, Urban America, Economics, Psychology; Algebra 1–2, Geometry, *Pacesetter* Math, Precalculus, Calculus, Statistics; Computer Science 1–2, Physical Science, Physics, Biology, Chemistry, Electricity and Magnetism, Mechanics, Geology/Earth Science; Art, Music, Theatre 1–2, Studio Art, Music Theory; Life Skills, a yearlong course with components in Health, Ethics and Personal Development, and Speech. Advanced Placement courses are available in 12 subjects.

Of the 58 seniors who graduated in 1999, all will attend various colleges and universities: Allegheny, Arizona State, Boston University, Bowling Green, Carnegie Mellon, Clemson, Curry, Denison, Dickinson, Duquesne, George Washington University, Hobart and William Smith, Lehigh, Middlebury, Montana State, New York University, Ohio Northern University, Pennsylvania State, Purdue, Texas A&M, Texas Tech University, United States Naval Academy, Villanova, Washington and Jefferson College, Westminster College, Yale, and the Universities of Colorado (Boulder), Pennsylvania, Pittsburgh, and Wyoming.

The Kiski Summer School for Boys offers two programs for Grades 5–8 and 9–12. Both stress academic skills and offer athletic and camp activities in the afternoons and evenings.

STUDENT ACTIVITIES. The Prefect Organization, a group of elected leading seniors and juniors, serves as the student government, taking responsibility for maintaining good order in the life of the campus and organizing activities in cooperation with the faculty.

Other organizations are the newspaper, yearbook, literary magazine, Cum Laude Society, Political Forum, K Club, National Forensic League, a 50-member Glee Club, Kiski Players, and the Art, Astronomy, Chess, Cooking, Horticulture, Macintosh Users, French, German, Spanish, Radio, and Woodworking clubs. Members of the Radio Club train for and operate the radio station.

Athletics are considered an integral part of a boy's education at Kiski, providing valuable experience in teamwork, commitment, and sportsmanship. The School fields varsity, junior varsity, and freshman teams for interscholastic competition in ten sports. Kiski is a member of the Interstate Preparatory School League and competes in football, soccer, cross-country, golf, basketball, wrestling, swimming, baseball, tennis, and track and field.

The Kiski Players present three major productions a year, often including a Shakespearean play and a musical. Girls from nearby schools play female roles. The Glee Club presents several programs each year, and visiting artists perform on campus. Off-campus visits are arranged for cultural and entertainment purposes, and dances are scheduled in cooperation with other schools.

Traditional events on the calendar are Mothers' Weekend, Fathers' Weekend, Homecoming, Brothers' Weekend, Athletic Awards Dinners, Academic Awards Banquet, and Senior-Parents Banquet.

ADMISSION AND COSTS. The Kiski School seeks boys of good character who have the ability and desire to undertake its academic program and who will contribute to the good of the community. They are admitted on the basis of past academic performance, two teacher recommendations, SSAT results (for those entering Grades 9 and 10), and a personal interview. Notification of admission to Kiski begins February 1. An application fee of $35 is required.

Boarding tuition for 1999–2000 is $21,000, and incidental expenses total about $600. Tuition payment plans and insurance are available. Kiski subscribes to the School Scholarship Service and awards about $1,300,000 annually on the basis of need and merit.

Dean of Students: Thomas R. Kozub '65
Director of Studies and Registrar: John A. Lombardo
Director of Development and Alumni Affairs: Zachary J. Vlahos
Director of Admissions: Robert J. Grandizio
Director of College Counseling: Cornelius E. Raiford
Business Manager: Linda Miller
Director of Athletics: Andrew S. Muffley

Lancaster Country Day School   1908

725 Hamilton Road, Lancaster, PA 17603. 717-392-2916;
Admissions 717-392-3673; Fax 717-392-0425;
E-mail admiss@e-lcds.org; Web Site www.e-lcds.org

Lancaster Country Day School, enrolling 535 boys and girls in Kindergarten–Grade 12, offers a broad, challenging course of study in an atmosphere characterized by caring and trust. The college preparatory curriculum is complemented by Advanced Placement opportunities and the opening in 1998 of new science, art, and Grade 6 classrooms. Small classes encourage active participation and allow for personal attention. Activities include varsity sports, an after-school Enrichment Program, private music lessons, and special expeditions. Tuition: $8400–$10,800. Extras: $100–$400. Financial Aid: $625,000. Maura Condon Umble is Director of Admission; Michael J. Mersky was appointed Head of School in 1999. *Middle States Association.*

LaSalle College High School   1858

8605 Cheltenham Avenue, Wyndmoor, PA 19038. 215-233-2911;
Fax 215-233-1418; E-mail admissions@lschs.wyndmoor.pa.us;
Web Site www.lschs.wyndmoor.pa.us

LaSalle was founded by the DeLaSalle Christian Brothers to educate young men within a community in which all members share their beliefs, experiences, ideals, and values. A strong academic program emphasizes college preparation combined with a challenging program of extracurricular activities designed to add depth and dimension to the development of the individual. The curriculum includes Advanced Placement courses in 14 subjects, four years of religious studies, and diverse electives. LaSalle athletic teams are organized at three levels; students are also involved in publications, plays and musicals, debate, jazz band, chorus, and Christian Action Projects. Tuition: $8180. Br. James Rieck, FSC, is Director of Admissions; Br. René Sterner, FSC, is President. *Middle States Association.*

Linden Hall   LITITZ

212 East Main Street, Lititz, PA 17543. 717-626-8512;
E-mail admissions@lindenhall.com; Web Site www.lindenhall.com

LINDEN HALL in Lititz, Pennsylvania, is a college preparatory boarding and day school enrolling girls in Grades 6 through 12 and postgraduates. Historic Lititz (population 8000) is located on Route 501 between Harrisburg and Philadelphia. School vans and local bus service link the town to Lancaster (7 miles away), which is served by interstate bus lines, railroads, and major commercial airlines. The Lancaster airport is 3 miles from the campus.

Linden Hall was established in 1746 by the Moravians, a Christian Protestant denomination. With more than 250 years of experience in the education and preparation of young girls for college and for life, Linden Hall is America's oldest boarding school for girls. Although Moravian in origin and tradition, the school operates independently. All religious activities, including the weekly chapel service, are nondenominational.

Linden Hall's philosophy maintains an attention toward caring for the "whole" girl—intellectually, emotionally, physically, socially, and spiritually. On weekdays, girls pursue rigorous academic schedules, electives, activities, sports, and evening studies. Weekends are balanced with relaxation and socializing. Teachers serve as parents and chaperones for dorm life as well as for dances and special recreational and cultural outings. Linden Hall seeks to provide girls of average to gifted ability with a sound academic program in an atmosphere that helps them discover and broaden their talents, while at the same time encouraging their development into independent, well-adjusted, thoughtful, and responsible women.

A nonprofit institution, Linden Hall is directed by the Headmaster under the guidelines of a 27-member Board of Trustees. The school is accredited by the Middle States Association of Colleges and Schools and is approved by the Pennsylvania Department of Education. It holds membership in the National Association of Independent Schools, National Coalition of Girls' Schools, Secondary School Admission Test Board, the Pennsylvania Association of Independent Schools, and other organizations.

THE CAMPUS. Linden Hall occupies 47 fence-enclosed acres just two blocks from the town square of Lititz. The open, well-landscaped campus includes a modern 20-stall stable, tennis courts, indoor and outdoor riding areas, playing fields, and picnic areas. Indoor facilities include a gymnasium, a swimming pool, and areas for music, art, photography, theater, and dance. Efficiency kitchens and laundry facilities are available in the dorms.

The school's physical plant includes historic structures

(built in 1758) and modern 20th-century buildings—all connected by enclosed bridges. The dormitories stand between the main academic buildings and the dining room. Senior girls and postgraduates have private, single rooms equipped with computer connections, built-in closets, and a sink. Underclass girls are housed in double rooms. Each dorm contains a student lounge.

Other buildings on campus house classrooms and computer and science laboratories as well as special studios for art and ceramics. The student center contains pool and Ping-Pong tables as well as a large-screen television, VCR, and exercise equipment. The Alumnae House is available to parents and alumnae for overnight visits.

THE FACULTY. Thomas W. Needham, appointed Headmaster in 1998, earned a B.A. degree in Psychology and Sociology from Eastern Connecticut State University and an M.Ed. degree from Lesley College. He was a Visiting Fellow at Columbia, sponsored by the Klingenstein Foundation. Prior to assuming his present position, Mr. Needham served as Headmaster at Carroll School in Massachusetts and at Pine Ridge School in Vermont.

The teaching faculty consists of 27 full-time teachers/administrators and 5 part-time teachers. They hold 32 baccalaureate and 10 graduate degrees representing study at Cleveland Institute of Art, Eastern Mennonite, Juniata, Kings College, Lake Forest University, Lock Haven, Millersville University, Northwestern, Penn State, Queens College, Rhode Island School of Design, Salem College, State University of New York, Tufts, Ursinus, West Chester, Wilson College, and the Universities of Delaware, Pittsburgh, Virginia, and West Virginia.

There is a nurse and an infirmary on campus. A Lititz medical doctor is always on call; hospital facilities are available in Lancaster.

STUDENT BODY. In 1999–2000, 80 boarding students and 35 day students, ages 11 to 20, are enrolled, with 30 in the Middle School and 85 in the Upper School.

Boarding students come from 15 states and ten foreign countries including England, Guatemala, Japan, Jordan, Korea, Malawi, Mexico, Nigeria, Pakistan, and Taiwan.

ACADEMIC PROGRAM. The academic year, from September to late May, is divided into trimesters and includes 38 weeks of instruction with breaks at Thanksgiving and Easter and longer vacations in December and March.

Classes begin at 8:00 A.M. and average 10 to 12 girls per class. Each class meets daily in 47-minute sessions with an academic help session offered daily. The student-teacher ratio is 4:1. Teachers are also available for additional help during the postdinner leisure hour and after the evening study hall. Varsity teams practice after the academic day, from 3:40 to 5:40 P.M. Girls not involved in varsity sports must join in some type of physical activity from 3:30 to 4:15 P.M., Mondays through Thursdays. Every Sunday through Thursday from 7:30 to 9:30 P.M., there is supervised study for all girls in their rooms. Grades are posted and sent to parents six times annually; "midterm notices" are sent between each grading period.

The following courses are offered for Grades 9 through 12: English, English as a Second Language, Literature; French I–V, Spanish I–V, Latin I–V; Political Science, United States History, European History, World Cultures; Math, Pre-Algebra, Algebra I–II, Geometry, Pre-Calculus, Calculus, Computerized Financial Management, Computer Literacy I–II; Biology, Applied Chemistry, Chemistry, Environmental Science/Marine Biology, Earth Science, Physics; Health, Physical Education; Reading and Study Skills, SAT Preparation, Research Paper, Critical Writing, Compositions, Grammar; Comparative Religion; and Vocal Music, Studio Art, Computer Art, Speech, Acting, Equitation, and Photography.

Honor courses are offered in World Literature I–II, American Literature, British Literature, European History, American History, British History, Biology, Chemistry, Genetics, and Microbiology. Qualified students may take Advanced Placement courses in American History, Calculus, English, and foreign languages. Students may also enroll in classes at Franklin and Marshall College and Lebanon Valley for additional academic challenges.

A strong college advising program ensures that virtually all Linden Hall graduates continue their education at the college level. Recent graduates are enrolled at Barnard, Boston University, Bryn Mawr, Catholic University of America, Elizabethtown College, Haverford, Hollins, La Salle, Mary Baldwin, Northeastern, Pepperdine, Wesleyan, and the University of Virginia.

STUDENT ACTIVITIES. The Student Council and Senior Prefects contribute extensively to the life and administration of the school. The Senior Prefects assist dorm parents in monitoring study time, quiet hours, "lights out," and meal checks. Girls participate daily or weekly in numerous activities and organizations such as Photography, Journalism, Drama, Linden Hall Choir, Crafts, and Bell Choir. Music lessons and dance instruction are offered. Students also publish a newspaper, a literary magazine, and a yearbook, and do all their own photography for these publications.

Varsity teams compete with other independent schools in soccer, basketball, equitation, volleyball, softball, and tennis. Non-varsity physical activities include aerobics, riding, skiing, swimming, skating, bowling, running, and dance. The school hosts five horse shows each year and participates in four varsity riding competitions off campus.

Special events include field trips related to school programs, dances with nearby boys' schools, all-school birthday party, school auction, International dinner, lectures, movies, a "School Spirit" week, concerts, and theater trips. Faculty members provide transportation to a variety of weekend activities. Traditional annual events include a fall outing at nearby Mt. Gretna, a school Christmas party, Senior Class Night, the Lantern Walk, Parents' Weekends, May Day, Alumnae Day, and Graduation Day.

ADMISSION AND COSTS. Linden Hall seeks girls of average and above-average ability, without regard to geographical, racial, religious, or social background. Applicants are chosen on the basis of personal interviews, school records, and letters of recommendation. Emphasis is placed upon the personal interview. If vacancies exist, students may enroll throughout the school year. A $50 application fee and a $1000 deposit (deductible from the total fee) are required at the time of enrollment.

In 1999–2000, tuition is $23,540 for seven-day boarders and $22,080 for five-day boarders. Day tuition is $9480 for all grade levels. Additional expenses for books and uniforms total $1000. A tuition payment plan is available. Financial aid is awarded on the basis of need as determined by the School and Student Service for Financial Aid. Full financial disclosure is required. In 1999–2000, 40 percent of the student body received financial aid totaling $375,000.

Headmaster: Thomas W. Needham, M.Ed.
Assistant Head: Shaaron H. Lavery
Director of Admissions: Evelyn Z. McDowell
Business Manager: Elizabeth Geibel

Malvern Preparatory School   MALVERN

418 South Warren Avenue, Malvern, PA 19355-2707.
  610-644-5454; E-mail jstewart@malvern-prep.pvt.k12.pa.us;
  Web Site www.malvernprep.com

MALVERN PREPARATORY SCHOOL in Malvern, Pennsylvania, is an Augustinian, college preparatory day school enrolling boys in Grades 6 through 12. Located in a country setting in Malvern (population 3000), the School is approximately 20 miles west of Philadelphia.

Malvern Preparatory School is conducted by the Augustinian Fathers, a religious order of the Roman Catholic Church. Originally, in 1842, Malvern Prep found its roots as the secondary school department of Villanova College. Malvern was established as a boarding school on its own campus in 1922. Beginning in the 1940s, the ratio of day students to boarders gradually increased until, in 1971, Malvern became exclusively a day school. The faculty has also changed—from clerical to predominantly lay—but the School has sought to maintain its historical commitment to Christian core values.

Malvern is dedicated to the cultivation of academic excellence and the enrichment of each young man so that he is pre-

pared fully for college and for a leadership role in society. The School nurtures an environment of cultural and social diversity in which a caring faculty seeks to develop each student to his potential. Malvern has a traditional academic curriculum supplemented with four years of required theology courses. Boys are encouraged to participate in school religious activities, which are generally offered on a voluntary basis.

A nonprofit corporation, Malvern is directed by a self-perpetuating Board of Trustees, 26 in number, including 5 Augustinian Fathers and 21 laymen. Board committees work with the faculty and administration in such areas as academics, development, activities, facilities, and finances. Malvern's 3100 living graduates have formed an active Alumni Association. The School, which is accredited by the Middle States Association of Colleges and Schools, is approved by the Pennsylvania Department of Education. It is accredited by the Pennsylvania Association of Private Academic Schools and holds membership in the National Association of Independent Schools, Council for Advancement and Support of Education, Middle States Association of Colleges and Secondary Schools, College Entrance Examination Board, Educational Records Bureau, Pennsylvania Department of Public Instruction, Pennsylvania Association of Secondary Schools and College Admission Counselors, and National Association for College Admission Counseling.

THE CAMPUS. The 143-acre campus encompasses football, baseball, and soccer fields; a track; six tennis courts; an indoor swimming pool; two gymnasiums; woodlands; and two lakes.

The buildings, which are constructed of brick, are predominantly colonial in architectural style. Good Counsel Hall (1924, renovated 1996) houses the Middle School. Dennis Hall (1961) provides additional classrooms; Sullivan Hall (1953) houses the science laboratories, the school library, offices, and the cafeteria. Vasey Hall (1953) contains the auditorium and a theater. The Mother of Good Counsel Chapel was constructed in 1953. Villanova Hall (1924) provides facilities for the intramural athletic activities. Dougherty Hall (1953, renovated 1995) contains other athletic facilities, including a basketball court, locker rooms, a weight training center, a sports medicine center, coaches' offices, and a wrestling room. Knapp Hall (renovated 1997) houses art, music, and computer labs. A natatorium was added in 1961 and an 18-room classroom building, Carney Hall, was added in 1988. St. Rita's Hall is used for faculty offices. St. Augustine Priory is used for Augustinian residences. Administrative offices are located in Austin Hall. The new Donald F. O'Neill Sports Center houses basketball and squash courts and a swimming pool.

The physical plant, with a current market value of $8,500,000, is owned by the School.

THE FACULTY. James H. Stewart was appointed Head of School in 1990. Mr. Stewart is a graduate of Monsignor Bonner High School, La Salle (B.A. 1965), Middlebury College (M.A. 1968), and Villanova (M.A. 1980). His graduate degrees were earned in Spanish and Educational Administration. Mr. Stewart served for three years as a teacher at Roman Catholic High School, two years as a teacher at La Salle High School, and for

16 years as Assistant Headmaster at Malvern Prep. In June 1997, Rev. James R. Flynn, O.S.A., was named Assistant Head of School. Father Flynn graduated in 1969 from Villanova University with a Bachelor of Arts in Philosophy; he also holds master's degrees in Theology, Teaching of Mathematics, and Formative Spirituality from Duquesne University and Washington Theological Union, respectively.

The full-time faculty consist of 68 members, including 5 Augustinian Fathers, 1 Deacon, and 62 lay men and women. Faculty benefits include a health insurance plan, a retirement plan, Social Security, and a tuition refund plan for graduate work and studies.

STUDENT BODY. In 1999–2000, the School enrolls 578 boys as follows: 40 in Grade 6, 56 in Grade 7, 60 in Grade 8, 115 in Grade 9, 104 in Grade 10, 103 in Grade 11, and 100 in Grade 12.

The boys, who are 11–18 years of age, come from Malvern and other towns within a 25-mile radius. Eighty percent of the boys are Roman Catholic.

ACADEMIC PROGRAM. The school year, which begins in early September and ends in early June, includes a brief recess at Thanksgiving and longer vacations at Christmas and Easter. Several Catholic holy days are celebrated, and retreat days are scheduled.

Classes, which have an average enrollment of 17 students, meet five days a week on a six-day cycle between 8:20 A.M. and 3:15 P.M. Eight academic periods are scheduled daily, followed by a period for extra tutorial. After classes, students are encouraged to remain for extracurricular and athletic activities. A bus that leaves campus at 4:45 P.M. provides transportation following the activities. Students are expected to plan their own study time, but faculty members are available for extra help, and individual tutoring is offered. Every nine weeks, grade reports are sent to parents; interim grades are sent every six weeks.

To graduate, boys must complete four years each of English, mathematics, and theology; three years of social studies; three years each of science and foreign language; and electives. The complete set of requirements totals 24 credits.

Among the courses offered are English 1–4, Journalism, 20th Century Fiction, Literature & Composition, Creative Writing, World Literature, Major British Writers; French 1–4, Latin, Spanish 1–4; World Cultures, Western Civilization, United States History, American Government, European History, Economics; Algebra 1–2, Geometry, Calculus, Algebra and Trigonometry, Special Functions; Environmental Science, Physical Sciences, Biology, Chemistry, Physics, Organic Chemistry; Theology 1–4; Accounting, Computer Literacy, Computer Science; Library Science; Art; Music Theory, Instrumental Music; and Health, Sports Medicine, and Physical Education. Malvern offers honors-level courses and Advanced Placement classes in English, history, mathematics, modern languages, computer, and science. Students in Grade 12 take an off-campus "Senior Field Experience" and work for two weeks in their field of interest.

Recent graduates are attending such colleges and universities as Albright, Boston College, Brown, Bucknell, Catholic University, Dartmouth, Drexel, Duke, Emory, Georgetown, Gettysburg, Harvard, Haverford, La Salle, Lehigh, Northeastern, Princeton, St. Joseph's, Swarthmore, Temple, United States Air Force Academy, United States Military Academy, United States Naval Academy, Villanova, West Chester, Widener, William and Mary, Williams, Yale, and the Universities of Delaware, Notre Dame, Pennsylvania, Richmond, Scranton, and Southern California.

STUDENT ACTIVITIES. The Student Council is composed of four officers elected by the entire student body, class representatives, and faculty moderators. It acts as liaison between the administration and students. Council members serve as leaders of the student community, promote school spirit, and arrange social activities, such as dances.

Extracurricular activities include the yearbook, newspaper, literary magazine, Science clubs, World Affairs Club, Mathletes, Amnesty International, Missionaries of Malvern, Audio-Visual Club, Jazz Band, and others. The Malvern Theatre Society participates in theater workshops and produces two full-length plays annually. Qualified students may join the National Honor Society.

Malvern encourages all students to participate in interscholastic and intramural sports. The School's athletic program offers soccer, football, cross-country, wrestling, indoor track, recreational skiing, swimming, tennis, golf, lacrosse, spring track, ice hockey, water polo, basketball, crew, curling, and baseball. Games are scheduled with schools in the Inter-Academic League and with other private schools in Pennsylvania. Intramural sports are organized for two divisions—boys in the lower three grades and boys in the upper four grades. Intramural football, volleyball, cross-country, basketball, softball, tennis, and track are scheduled according to the season.

A social event—a dance, play, or special assembly—is scheduled each month. Social exchanges with neighboring girls' schools, such as Villa Maria Academy and the Academy of Notre Dame de Namur, are also planned. Traditional events include the Headmaster's Reception, Father and Son Banquet, Mothers' Club Christmas Tea, alumni reunions, Homecoming, Parents' B.A.S.H. (a gala dinner auction), Awards Banquet, and Graduation.

ADMISSION AND COSTS. Malvern seeks students who are well-rounded, socially adjusted, and academically sound. Applicants are accepted in Grades 6–12 on the basis of an entrance examination, an academic transcript, a recommendation from the previous school, and a personal interview. Applications for fall enrollment should be made in the preceding fall.

Annual tuition is $12,300 in Grades 6–8 and $13,000 in Grades 9–12. Additional expenses include books ($350) and van transportation ($1300). In many cases, bus transportation may be arranged through the local public school district. Malvern, which subscribes to the School Scholarship Service, awards financial aid on the basis of need. One full academic scholarship, partial academic scholarships, and financial aid are offered.

President: Rev. David J. Duffy, OSA '48
Head of School: James H. Stewart
Assistant Head of School: Rev. James R. Flynn, OSA
Dean of Studies: Steven R. Valyo '70

Dean of Middle School: Frank R. Tosti, Jr.
Dean of Students: Lawrence V. Legner
Director of Alumni: John P. Campbell '60
Dean of Admissions: William R. Gibson '69
Director of External Affairs: Donna M. Alteari
College Guidance: Francis P. Kenny
Business Manager: Theodore N. Caniglia, Jr.
Director of Athletics: Francis W. Ryan

Meadowbrook School   1919

1641 Hampton Road, Meadowbrook, PA 19046. 215-884-3238;
  Fax 215-884-9143; E-mail kmadmis@meadowbrookn6.org;
  Web Site www.meadowbrookn6.org

Meadowbrook School is a coeducational, nonsectarian day school enrolling more than 200 students in PreKindergarten–Grade 6. Located on a beautiful 20-acre campus, the School offers strong basics, enrichment, and tradition within an intimate, family-oriented setting. The program includes French, art, music, library, computer science, and physical education. The science center and greenhouse afford opportunities for hands-on learning. The ice-skating and waiter programs encourage mixed-age social situations that are basic to the philosophy. Teams are fielded in soccer, softball, baseball, and field hockey. After-school care is available. Tuition: $5150–$10,100. Fees: $700–$1350. Kelly Mosteller is Admissions Director; Robert Sarkisian (Colgate, B.A.; Beaver, M.Ed.) was appointed Headmaster in 1980.

The Mercersburg Academy

MERCERSBURG

Mercersburg, PA 17236. 717-328-6173; Fax 717-328-6319;
  E-mail admission@mercersburg.edu; Web Site www.mercersburg.edu

THE MERCERSBURG ACADEMY in Mercersburg, Pennsylvania, is a coeducational, college preparatory boarding school with Grades 9–12 and a postgraduate year. Located in a valley of the Tuscarora Mountains, Mercersburg (town population 1700) is approximately 67 miles from Harrisburg and 85 miles from Washington and Baltimore. There are commercial flights to nearby Hagerstown, Maryland. Buses link Mercersburg to Washington, Pittsburgh, Philadelphia, Baltimore, and Harrisburg.

Mercersburg was established as an independent secondary school in 1893 by Dr. William Mann Irvine on a site previously occupied by Marshall College. Originally a preparatory school for boys, it became fully coeducational in 1971. A nonprofit institution, Mercersburg is directed by a 30-member Board of Regents, which includes alumni and parents. The school plant is valued at $75,000,000; the endowment in productive funds is more than $80,000,000. Mercersburg is accredited by the Mid-

dle States Association of Colleges and Schools; it holds membership in the National Association of Independent Schools, among other affiliations.

THE CAMPUS. The 160-acre main campus adjoins a 140-acre school farm. There are 2 playing fields each for baseball, football, lacrosse, and field hockey; 17 tennis courts; an all-weather track; an outdoor sand volleyball court; and 3 soccer fields.

Lenfest Hall (1992), the Library/Learning Center with a 50,000-volume collection, houses History classrooms and department offices. Facilities also include an on-line card catalog and database, computers, and audio-visual equipment with compact disc and laser videodisc media. Irvine Hall, the major classroom building, underwent a $12,000,000 renovation in 1994 to upgrade the art, music, classroom, and science facilities. Boone Hall, a center for the performing arts, provides rehearsal and dressing rooms, a stagecraft workshop, music classrooms and practice rooms, a large room for social events, and a theater with a seating capacity of 600. Dining facilities, the post office, the school lounge, and two bookstores are in Ford Hall.

Boys reside in Keil, Main, and Fowle halls; girls are housed in Tippetts and Swank halls, Culbertson House, and South Cottage. The basic living unit for students is the dormitory floor, rather than the entire dormitory. Each floor provides rooms for 8 to 28 students and 2 senior prefects, one or two faculty apartments, common rooms, and a study shared by several faculty members whose homes are on or near the campus.

Nolde Gymnasium contains a wrestling gym, fitness center, an indoor track, three basketball courts, a nine-lane swimming pool, eight squash courts, and locker facilities. Other buildings include Traylor Hall, with administrative offices; a 40-bed health center; the Headmaster's residence, North Cottage; and eight other faculty homes.

THE FACULTY. Douglas Hale, appointed Head of School in 1997, is a graduate of the University of Tennessee (B.A. 1973) and Middlebury College (M.A. 1981). Prior to accepting the position at Mercersburg, Mr. Hale spent 24 years at Baylor School where he taught English, served as a dorm parent and faculty adviser, and coached. A committed independent school administrator, he also held positions at Baylor as Head of the Lower School, Associate Headmaster, and, from 1994 to 1997, as Headmaster.

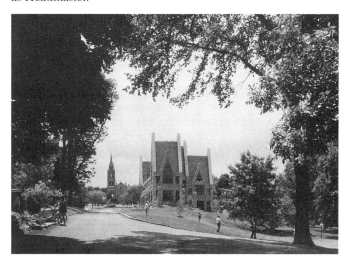

The faculty include 57 full-time teachers, 41 men and 16 women. Thirty-eight faculty members live on campus, 16 with their families. Faculty members hold baccalaureate degrees, 34 master's degrees, and 8 doctoral degrees from more than 60 colleges and universities in this country and abroad. Representative faculty schools are Amherst, Bates, Bowdoin, Bucknell, Cornell, Dartmouth, Dickinson, Franklin and Marshall, Kenyon, Middlebury, Princeton, Trinity, Yale, and the Universities of California, Iowa, Massachusetts, Michigan, and Pennsylvania.

The Health Center is staffed by a school doctor and five registered nurses.

STUDENT BODY. In 1999–2000, Mercersburg enrolls 422 students—196 boarding boys, 35 day boys, 153 boarding girls, and 38 day girls. There are 75 in Grade 9, 80 in Grade 10, 143 in Grade 11, and 124 in Grade 12 and the postgraduate year. Students come from 25 states, the District of Columbia, and 21 foreign countries.

ACADEMIC PROGRAM. The school year, from mid-September to early June, includes extended vacations in December and in the spring and a short recess at Thanksgiving. A typical day begins with a cafeteria breakfast followed by morning classes beginning at 8:00 A.M. A family-style lunch is served at midday; the class day ends at 3:50 P.M.; and there is an athletic period from 4:00 to 6:00 P.M. Family-style dinner is followed by an activities period and two hours of dormitory study. Everyone meets for "Community Gathering" each Monday morning in the chapel. The Chapel Program is scheduled on Friday morning.

The average class size is 14 students; classes range in size from 3 to 17 students; the student-faculty ratio is 6:1. For their first term, entering ninth and tenth graders attend a monitored study hall, and weekly comments are sent home during the first term. On evenings before class days, students study in their dormitories under the supervision of student proctors and resident or nonresident faculty advisers. Each faculty member advises 6 to 8 students and is responsible for sending reports, including grades, to parents at least six times during the year.

The curriculum provides a broad-based college preparatory course of study in Grades 9–12. The work in Grades 9 and 10 is largely "skills-oriented." Toward the end of Grade 10 and throughout the last two years, students are expected to apply these skills to more sophisticated concepts. At all levels, the students are encouraged to use the library and the computer centers. Graduation requirements vary depending on the grade level at which the student enters Mercersburg. There is a minimum total credit requirement, and within that, a minimum upper-level credit requirement (credits are earned on a term basis; a full-year course carries three credits). For students entering Grade 9, minimum distributional requirements are 12 terms of English, 2 terms of fine arts, 9 terms of history (including United States History), mathematics through the third year or until graduation, 9 terms of science, 1 term of religion, and a foreign language through the third-year level.

The academic year is divided into three terms, with most courses spanning all three terms. Upper-level students may study related one-term offerings. Among the term offerings are Humanities; Behavioral Sciences; Area Studies in Latin America, Asia, and Africa; Field Biology, Advanced Topics in

Biology, Botany, Environmental Science, Human Genetic Disorders; Computer Science, Statistics, Graph Theory, Operations Research, Problem Solving; and Studio Design, Art History, Music Theory, and Music History.

Students may take special Advanced Placement courses offered in all academic areas. Seniors with a demonstrated interest and competence in areas outside the curriculum may undertake independent study on a one-to-one basis with a faculty member. Each year, foreign study opportunities are provided for several students through Mercersburg's affiliation with the School Year Abroad Program and The English-Speaking Union.

In 1999, all 135 graduating seniors entered college. Two or more are attending Brown, Bucknell, Colby, College of William and Mary, Cornell, Georgetown, Gettysburg, Johns Hopkins, Kenyon, Tufts, United States Military Academy, United States Naval Academy, Vanderbilt, and the Universities of Pennsylvania and the South.

STUDENT ACTIVITIES. An elected School Council composed of students and faculty has responsibility for many aspects of school life. There is a variety of musical organizations, vocal and instrumental. Stony Batter, the dramatics club, stages several major productions yearly. Student publications include a weekly newspaper, a literary magazine, and a yearbook—all of which involve members of an active photography club. There are numerous opportunities available for community service.

The Academy fields a total of 34 varsity and junior varsity teams in football, field hockey, soccer, cross-country, volleyball, basketball, skiing, swimming, diving, wrestling, squash, baseball, tennis, golf, softball, track, and lacrosse. Students who do not join competitive teams participate in an afternoon physical fitness activity for at least two terms. Their options include aerobic swimming, aerobic walking, biking, cross-training, dance, recreational golf, skiing, and weight training.

More than 20 other clubs related to academic departments, the arts, athletics, professions, or general interests are also available. Weekend activities are planned by a faculty/student group. This special programs committee plans larger group trips to the nearby Washington, D.C./Baltimore area as well as on-campus programs by repertory theater groups, professional musicians, and visiting lecturers. The ski racing team uses the Whitetail ski area, located six miles from campus.

ADMISSION AND COSTS. Mercersburg admits students of average to superior ability who have been achieving well in school and who seem best suited to take full advantage of the Academy's scholastic, athletic, and extracurricular activities. The Secondary School Admission Test and a personal interview are required whenever possible. First admissions decisions are announced in early March, after which students are admitted as space permits. In its admissions practices, the Academy does not discriminate on the basis of race, sex, color, creed, or national or ethnic origin.

In 1999–2000, the annual fee is $24,675 for boarding students and $17,100 for day students. Excluding transportation, additional costs such as books, laundry, spending allowance, and laboratory fees service normally total about $800. In 1999, 162 students received financial aid totaling more than $2,405,300. Awards and low-interest loans are made on a competitive basis and on the basis of financial need, in accordance with School and Student Service for Financial Aid guidelines.

Associate Head of School: M. Deborah Rutherford
Dean of Faculty: Marilyn S. Larson
Dean of Students: Thomas E. Rahauser
Director of Admissions: Gordon D. Vink, Jr.
Director of Advancement Programs: John Thorsen
Chief Advancement Officer: Don D. Hill
Director of College Counseling: William R. McClintick, Jr.
Chief Financial Officer: Gail H. Wolfe II
Director of Athletics: Ron Simar

Merion Mercy Academy   1884

511 Montgomery Avenue, Merion Station, PA 19066.
  610-664-6655; Fax 610-664-6322; Web Site www.merion-mercy.com

A nationally recognized Blue Ribbon School of Excellence, Merion Mercy enrolls 427 young women in Grades 9–12 in a challenging college preparatory program. The school, opened and sponsored by the Sisters of Mercy, aims to graduate confident, educated individuals who are willing to serve others in the spirit of Catherine McAuley and the Catholic tradition. Merion Mercy offers outstanding programs in both the arts and sciences, opportunities for students to major in music and art, and extensive activities and sports program. The campus is accessible to the Philadelphia region and New Jersey. Tuition: $7700. Scholarships and financial aid are available. Eileen Killeen is Admissions Director; Sr. Teresa Mary, RSM (Villanova, M.S.), was appointed Principal in 1993. *Middle States Association.*

Milton Hershey School   HERSHEY

Hershey, PA 17033. 717-520-2000 or 800-322-3248;
  Fax 717-520-2117; E-mail mhs-admissions@mhs-pa.org;
  Web Site www.mhs-pa.org

MILTON HERSHEY SCHOOL in Hershey, Pennsylvania, is a coeducational, residential school for students in Kindergarten through Grade 12. Located in Derry Township (population 18,000), the School is just minutes from the state capital of Harrisburg and interstate highways 81 and 76.

The School was founded in 1909 by Milton and Catherine Hershey, who had no children of their own. Three years after Mrs. Hershey died in 1915, Milton Hershey pledged his entire fortune derived from his chocolate business toward the support of the School. His generosity continues to provide a cost-free education and home for financially and socially needy children at the School. The School offers a secure, nurturing environment in which children of character and ability can learn and develop the skills necessary to prepare them for meaningful, productive, and successful lives. The comprehensive program supports each child's educational and growth needs to allow the student to reach his or her fullest potential.

A nonprofit institution, Milton Hershey School is accredited by the Middle States Association of Colleges and Schools and holds membership in the National Association of Independent Schools and the College Board, among other educational organizations. Of the more than 7000 alumni throughout the

United States and worldwide, many remain in contact with the School. Some volunteer to assist with student programs, provide internships and job leads, and share information about the School with prospective students and families.

THE CAMPUS. Milton Hershey School's 1500-acre centralized campus includes three major classroom buildings—one each for Elementary, Middle, and High school—a Learning Resource Center, Visual Arts building, performance gym, and agricultural and environmental education learning centers near fields, streams, and woodland. There are nearly 100 student homes, each occupied by 8–14 students who live with houseparents specially trained in child care and development. Among the extensive athletic and intramural facilities are a 7000-seat football stadium, two indoor swimming pools, an ice skating rink, tennis courts, fields for soccer and field hockey, baseball diamonds, and an Olympic-size track.

THE FACULTY. Members of the school and community life staff are employed on a fulltime basis. The faculty number 133; all of the teachers hold baccalaureate degrees and 48 percent have earned advanced degrees. There are also part-time instructors in music and computers. Houseparents work with students on out-of-classroom activities.

The School provides on-campus professional services for medical, dental, and counseling care for all students. The School also employs staff for orientation of new students and for parent and family relations.

STUDENT BODY. Milton Hershey School typically enrolls about 1100 residential boys and girls in Elementary (Kindergarten–Grade 5), Middle (Grades 6–8), and High School (Grades 9–12) programs. They come predominantly from Pennsylvania and the mid-Atlantic region and more than 30 states within the United States.

SCHOLASTIC PROGRAM. A goal of the School is that each student will have an individual development and learning plan written by his or her houseparents, teachers, and other staff members. A developing initiative at Milton Hershey School, this individualized plan facilitates each child's growth and development and incorporates the School's Desired Results, which are designed to help children become productive, purposeful adults.

Elementary students benefit from multiage living, cooperative learning, individualized assistance, technology applications, field trips, and extracurricular activities. They attend classes in an Elementary School equipped with the latest technology, two science labs, an outdoor atrium classroom, student gardens, a library, a three-lane swimming pool, and age-appropriate play areas. Hands-on, activity-based experiential learning is the basis of the curriculum. The average class size is 10–15 students.

In the Middle School, students enhance their educational development through team learning experiences from teachers of various disciplines. Additionally, students learn the importance of goal setting, organization skills, and time management in the YESS! program (Your Everyday Skills for Success). Lab settings enable students to explore career fields of their choice from a number of categories that represent diverse occupational clusters such as manufacturing, air and land transportation, industrial arts, communications, and consumer science, among others.

High School students engage in comprehensive, in-depth studies through the enhanced learning opportunities afforded by extended classroom time (90-minute classes). The high school program provides all students basic and advanced academic and vocational-technical courses (seven career areas) and offers applied learning, including internships, to prepare each student for entry-level work and further study. As in earlier grades, High School students build an individual collection of best works, called a student portfolio, featuring samples of their work in a variety of areas including creative and journal writing, math, science, technology, cultural diversity, music, and community service.

All students have the opportunity to use a wide range of learning technologies and related software. Over 1000 computers are available to students and staff at all grade levels in classrooms, labs, libraries, and student residences. A variety of supplemental hardware, CD-ROMs, laser disks, and video equipment provides added learning and skill-building opportunities.

From Kindergarten to Grade 12, all students are involved in experiences to prepare for the world of work. Practical and age-appropriate vocational exploratory and hands-on curriculum activities broaden each student's understanding of the world of work and his or her own aptitudes and interests. Seven vocational career programs are offered to High School students who can gain entry-level job skills.

Students can also participate in the Agricultural and Environmental Education Program, through which they learn about land use, animals, plants, and related resources. As an example, at the School's Environmental Center, students learn how to care for, conserve, and appreciate nature. As part of the vocational program, High School students can begin to focus their career paths in horticultural science occupations.

Vocational and college counseling begins in the Middle School and continues into High School. Financial aid for continuing education (up to $4000 a year, or a total of $16,000 for four years) is available to students who meet educational and personal criteria.

COMMUNITY LIFE. In each of approximately 100 student homes, 8–14 students live with houseparents who have received specialized training in child care and child development. These adults play an important role in helping to determine an individualized plan for each student's development. In the student homes, students are responsible for doing household chores, participating in family activities, and completing homework. They also learn to respect the values and traditions of other cultures and gain life experiences through a wide range of opportunities and activities. Students have the opportunity to become members of Boy Scouts or Girl Scouts, FFA, and 4-H where the emphasis is on agricultural and environmental awareness. More than 70 percent of the student homes have children of various ages.

Students participate in planned activities and enjoy free and quiet times during the day for study and relaxing. Off-campus trips take students to cultural, sports, and entertainment events. Group activities include interscholastic and intramural sports, use of campus recreational facilities, hiking, and shopping. Facilities for theater, dance, music, art, games, sports, and camping are also on campus. Over the summer, students may choose to take part in the recreational, enrichment, and learning opportunities afforded by the School's Summer of Opportunities program.

ADMISSION. Milton Hershey School admits boys and girls of any race, color, religion, nationality, and ethnic origin. To be eligible for enrollment, the student must come from a family whose income is at or near the federal poverty level, must be between 4 and 15 years old, and must have at least average academic ability. Candidates must also have demonstrated good behavior and good citizenship at home and school and be able to participate fully in the program offered (auxiliary aids and services may be available upon request). Preference is given to prospective students who were born in Pennsylvania, specifically in Dauphin, Lebanon, and Lancaster counties, the three counties closest to the Hershey community. The School's direction is toward admitting those children who are among the poorest, most alone, and youngest, and whose parental or family support may be extremely limited or nonexistent.

All students who are admitted are provided educational opportunities, housing, meals, and clothing at no cost, and assistance with medical and dental care.

The Miquon School   1932

2025 Harts Lane, Conshohocken, PA 19428. 610-828-1231;
*   Fax 610-828-6149*

Miquon is a parent-owned elementary school enrolling 167 day boys and girls from diverse backgrounds in Nursery (age 3)–Grade 6. The School aims to address each student's intellectual, creative, emotional, social, and physical needs through a progressive, child-centered curriculum. Parental communication and involvement are encouraged as a cornerstone to the success of the educational program. Children are taught in small classes with two grades grouped together and two full-time faculty in each room. Specialist teachers provide instruction in science, library, language arts, music, dance, art, and physical education. Tuition: $7280–$10,590. Financial Aid: $146,000. Arabella Pope is Director of Admissions; Penny Colgan-Davis is Principal.

MMI Preparatory School   1879

P.O. Box 89, 154 Centre Street, Freeland, PA 18224-0089.
*   570-636-1108; Fax 570-636-0742; E-mail mmi@liu18.k12.pa.us;*
*   Web Site http://www.uslaw.com/mmi/*

MMI Preparatory School, founded by Eckley B. Coxe to educate young miners, is a college preparatory day school enrolling 116 boys and 98 girls in Grades 7–12. Emphasizing a strong, traditional academic program, the School seeks to develop its students into "well-rounded, broad-minded, self-disciplined individuals." Student Council, interest clubs, and ten interscholastic athletic teams comprise the School's extracurricular offerings. Every student must perform once annually in assemblies and present an Open House project for public exhibition. A summer program is available. Tuition: $7650. Financial Aid: $421,000. Joseph G. Rudawski (King's, B.A. 1963; University of Scranton, M.S. 1967) was appointed President in 1973. *Middle States Association.*

Montgomery School   1915

1141 Route 113, Chester Springs, PA 19425. 610-827-7222;
*   Fax 610-827-7639*

A coeducational day school encompassing Pre-School–Grade 8, Montgomery seeks to balance rigorous academics with values to provide a foundation on which students build. The curriculum includes academic subjects, fine and performing arts, and athletics. Without compromising academic challenge, Montgomery School bases teaching on individual needs and attunes the curriculum to the development levels of age groups and children. Ability-based groups of four to eight students encourage each child to work at his or her level and to experience success. The school day incorporates activities designed to teach courtesy, respect, honesty, accountability, integrity, and manners. Tuition: $2155–$11,362. Susan M. Marotta is Director of Admission; Geoffrey D. Campbell is Headmaster.

Moravian Academy   BETHLEHEM

Lower School: 422 Heckewelder Place, Bethlehem, PA 18018.
  610-868-8571; Fax 610-868-9319
Middle School: 11 West Market Street, Bethlehem, PA 18018.
  610-866-6677; Fax 610-866-6337
Upper School: 4313 Green Pond Road, Bethlehem, PA 18020.
  610-691-1600; Fax 610-691-3354;
  E-mail macomrel@epix.net or pubrel@moravian.k12.pa.us;
  Web Site www.moravian.k12.pa.us

MORAVIAN ACADEMY in Bethlehem, Pennsylvania, is a coeducational college preparatory school enrolling day students in Pre-Kindergarten through Grade 12 on three campuses. Bethlehem and the greater Lehigh Valley (population 550,000) provide students with many educational resources including six area colleges. The community supports an art museum, a symphony orchestra, several historic museums, a repertory theater company, and community theater groups. The annual Bach Festival and Musikfest are important events. Bethlehem is 50 miles from Philadelphia, 90 miles from New York, and 200 miles from Washington, D.C.

The Academy continues the educational commitment begun in 1742 by Countess Benigna von Zinzendorf and the early Moravian colonialists. Attention to the individual student is a primary concern, for the school believes that "excellence is achieved when the needs of the whole child—body, mind, and spirit—are met." It seeks to provide a strong academic program for all students.

A nonprofit institution, the Academy is governed by a Board of Trustees, which meets quarterly.

Moravian Academy is a member of the Pennsylvania Association of Independent Schools, the National Association of Independent Schools, the Independent School Teachers Association of Philadelphia and Vicinity, and the Council for Spiritual and Ethical Education among other organizations. It is licensed by the Pennsylvania Department of Education and accredited by the Middle States Association of Colleges and Schools and the Pennsylvania Association of Private Academic Schools.

THE CAMPUS. The buildings of the historic Lower School campus for Pre-Kindergarten–Grade 5 form a blend of past and present. They include the Old Chapel, a simple colonial structure built in 1751; the Main Building (1857), containing administrative offices, a library, classrooms, computer room, art room, and a nurse's room; the Helen de Schweinitz Building; the Gymnasium; the David Devey Building, containing Kindergarten classrooms and the Lower School dining room; and the Christian Education Building, a multipurpose building with an auditorium and classrooms used cooperatively by the school and the nearby Central Moravian Church. The Middle School (Grades 6–8) is housed in three buildings, which include classrooms, two computer labs and a science laboratory, a library, an auditorium, a cafeteria, a gymnasium, and administrative offices. Glasser Field, a mile to the east, is used for soccer and other athletics.

The 60-acre campus for the Upper School (Grades 9–12) includes a pond, playing fields, tennis courts, and an outdoor swimming pool. Snyder House (1928) contains administrative offices, classrooms, and the music room. Art and photography studios are located in the Couch Arts Center. Walter Hall provides classrooms, administrative offices, lounges, an auditorium, a gymnasium, a library, a computer lab, and the dining room and kitchen. Science laboratories are located in the Heath House complex. Benigna House and the Cottage are faculty/administrative residences.

THE FACULTY. Barnaby J. Roberts was appointed Headmaster in July 1998. He previously served as Head of Casady School in Oklahoma City, Oklahoma, and of Chestnut Hill Academy in Philadelphia, Pennsylvania. Mr. Roberts received his B.A. and M.A. degrees from Cambridge University and his Diploma in Education from Oxford University.

On the Academy faculty are 75 full-time teachers. All faculty members hold baccalaureate degrees and many have earned graduate degrees from such colleges as Bucknell, Fordham, Harvard, Johns Hopkins, Kutztown University, Lehigh, Purdue, Rutgers, Temple, Vanderbilt, and the Universities of Connecticut and Kentucky. There are also 19 part-time instructors.

There is a nurse on staff for each division. Three hospitals are within a 15-minute drive of the school.

STUDENT BODY. In 1999–2000, Moravian Academy enrolls 788 students, including 323 in the Lower School and 196 in the Middle School. In the Upper School, there are 269 students as follows: 65 in Grade 9, 69 in Grade 10, 73 in Grade 11, and 62 in Grade 12. The majority of the students are from Pennsylvania, but New Jersey, Canada, France, Germany, Italy, Korea, Poland, and Spain are also represented.

ACADEMIC PROGRAM. The school year, from late August through early June, includes holiday recesses at Thanksgiving, Christmas, and Easter as well as a spring vacation. Classes are held five days a week in a schedule that varies according to grade level; the Upper School day, from 8:00 A.M. to 3:15 P.M., is divided into eight periods, with early dismissal on Thursday. A weekly chapel service is held.

The student-faculty ratio is 9:1. Generally, class sections range from 14 to 18 students. Supervised study halls are held regularly in the Middle and Upper schools. Grades and reports are sent to parents regularly throughout the school year.

Lower School children are encouraged to develop sound work patterns and desirable social attitudes. In addition to traditional instruction, the program offers computers, French and Spanish, a vocal and instrumental music program using Suzuki techniques, art, a physical fitness program, and opportunities for creative play. Attendance at weekly chapel services is required.

The Middle School curriculum includes English, French, Spanish, Latin, social studies, mathematics, science, music, instrumental music, art, drama, and physical education. The program is designed to reinforce basic learning and to provide opportunities for enrichment. Attendance at weekly chapel services is required.

Minimum requirements for the diploma are four years of English; three years of a foreign language; Ancient History, World History, American History, World Religions; Algebra I–II, Geometry; Biology, Chemistry, and one other laboratory science; Music and Art; Physical Education and Health; and Senior Seminar. Seniors must also participate in a post-term experience that focuses on community service and career exploration. Other Upper School courses include Contemporary Literature, British Literature, American Nonfiction, Drama, Film, Poetry; French I–V, Spanish I–V, Japanese I–III, Russian; Law, European History (Honors), Contemporary Issues; Computer Programming, Trigonometry, Pre-Calculus, Calculus, Probability and Statistics; Chemistry Honors, Physics and Advanced Physics Honors, Biology, Advanced Biology Honors, Ecology; and Introduction to Acting, Chorale, MA Singers, Orchestra, Bell Choir, Construction of Music, Artforms I–II, Photography I–II, and Portfolio Preparation.

Independent study is encouraged for superior students, and Advanced Placement study is offered in Contemporary Literature, Drama, Poetry, British Literature, French, Spanish, Advanced Chemistry, United States History, U.S. Government and Politics, and Calculus.

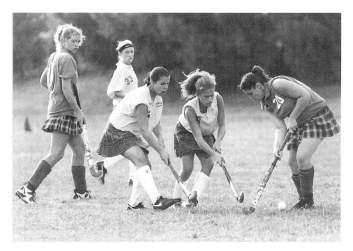

In 1999, 68 graduates have been accepted at four-year colleges. Among the colleges and universities they are attending are Brown, Carnegie Mellon, Colgate, Duke, Franklin and Marshall, Gettysburg, Lehigh, Smith, Tufts, Vassar, Yale, and the University of Pennsylvania.

STUDENT ACTIVITIES. The Student Council, consisting of officers, class representatives, and a faculty adviser, shares in decisions that concern student activities, privileges, and behav-

ior. The Chorale, Instrumental Ensemble, and Drama groups present several performances each year. There is a newspaper, yearbook, and a creative writing magazine. Current groups include the Model United Nations, Ski, Hiking, Environmental, Moravian Students for an Inclusive Community, International, and Photography clubs. The school has a chapter of The Cum Laude Society.

Students at every level engage in community service. Many students work for local civic, church, and charitable organizations.

Varsity teams compete in soccer, basketball, baseball, field hockey, softball, cross-country, lacrosse, tennis, and golf.

Camping trips are planned, and the school sponsors dances, picnics, and informal parties. Parents and alumni are invited to attend such traditional events as Vespers and Country Fair.

ADMISSION AND COSTS. Moravian Academy accepts boys and girls of high ability and potential. In the Upper School, students are admitted in Grades 9–11. A personal interview is required for all applicants but may be waived for international students or where distance is a factor. Applicants must supply a transcript from the current school and take school-administered tests. Upper School candidates also submit a formal application with four recommendations and a writing sample. Although admissions are normally completed by May, applications may be considered later if space is available.

In 1999–2000, the comprehensive fee ranges from $5040 in Pre-Kindergarten to $12,155 for students in Grades 9–12. The comprehensive fee includes all tuition, local field trips, and Kindergarten snacks. There is a dining room fee between $415 and $690 for lunch. Financial aid in the amount of $700,000 is awarded on the basis of need. Moravian Academy subscribes to the School Scholarship Service and offers tuition insurance and a tuition payment plan.

Dean of Students: Sally Pont (Upper School)
Director of Upper School: Carlton P. Chandler
Director of Middle School: Robert A. Bovee
Director of Lower School: Ella Jane Kunkle
Directors of Admissions: Douglas D. Trotter, Jr. (Upper School), Christine L. Murphy (Middle School), and Karen M. Jacob (Lower School)
Director of Development: Jack B. May, Jr.
Director of Academic Counseling: Marilyn A. Albarelli (Upper School)
Director of Financial Affairs: John W. Jacob
Director of Athletics: James Tiernan

Mount Saint Joseph Academy   1858

120 West Wissahickon Avenue, Flourtown, PA 19031.
215-233-3177; Fax 215-233-4734; Web Site www.msjacad.org

Mount Saint Joseph Academy, a Roman Catholic day school founded by the Sisters of Saint Joseph, serves 549 girls in Grades 9–12. Academically challenging programs, which are teacher-directed and student-centered, provide a well-rounded, culturally enriched education that maximizes each student's personal and academic growth. The college preparatory curriculum includes Advanced Placement courses and College Scholars programs. Award-winning publications, varsity sports, the arts, and service organizations are among the diversified cocurricular activities. Tuition: $6975. Carol Finney is Director of Admission; Sr. Karen Dietrich, SSJ (Villanova, M.S. 1977), is Principal; Sr. Mary Dacey, SSJ (University of Notre Dame, M.A. 1980; Boston College, M.Ed. 1991), is President. *Middle States Association.*

Nazareth Academy   1928

4001 Grant Avenue, Philadelphia, PA 19114-2999. 215-637-7676;
Fax 215-637-8523; E-mail smmckeogh@nni.com

Founded by the Sisters of the Holy Family of Nazareth, this college preparatory day school is committed to the intellectual and spiritual education of young Christian women. Nazareth Academy, enrolling 480 students in Grades 9–12, offers an academic program that emphasizes traditional liberal arts disciplines, Advanced Placement and honor courses, and a variety of activities. Students are involved in sports, publications, National Honor Society, music, theater, cheerleading, language clubs, and service organizations. A summer program of academic and enrichment courses is offered. Tuition: $5200. Mrs. Maryann Kendall is Director of Admissions; Sr. M. Jeanette Lawlor, CSFN (Holy Family College, B.A. 1963; Villanova, M.A. 1974), was appointed Principal in 1999. *Middle States Association.*

Newtown Friends School   1948

P.O. Box 978, Newtown, PA 18940-0848. 215-968-2225;
Fax 215-968-9346; E-mail erendall@newtownfriends.org

Newtown Friends School is a day school enrolling 160 girls and 165 boys in Pre-Kindergarten–Grade 8. Founded by the Newtown Monthly Meeting of the Religious Society of Friends, the School strives to provide a strong academic program that emphasizes critical and intellectual inquiry while fostering each student's sense of social responsibility. Art, music, computer instruction, and sports are integral to the curriculum. Students are involved in community service and participate in an intergenerational program with nearby Pennswood Village. Camping, field trips, and activities enrich the program. Tuition: $7025–$9600. Financial Aid: $215,000. Betsy N. Rendall is Director of Admissions; Steven R. Nierenberg (Earlham College, B.A.; Temple University, M.Ed.) is Head of School.

Oak Lane Day School   1916

137 Stenton Avenue, Blue Bell, PA 19422. 610-825-1055;
Fax 610-825-9288; E-mail oaklane@pond.com

Founded by a group of Philadelphia intellectuals excited by the innovations of progressive education, Oak Lane seeks to offer a challenging, creative, and nurturing program to 160 day boys and girls in Pre-Kindergarten–Grade 6. Located on a 30-acre estate, the campus includes classroom and studio facilities and extensive natural areas for outdoor study. The School's mission is to foster intellectual, creative, and personal growth within a diverse community of engaged learners. The arts, computer, and physical education are offered at all levels; dance, drama, instrumental lessons, and athletics are also offered. Tuition: $4000–$10,300. Financial aid is available. Karl A. Welsh (Wake Forest, B.A. 1985; University of Pennsylvania, M.S. 1996) is Head of School.

The Pen Ryn School   1946

235 South Olds Boulevard, Fairless Hills, PA 19030.
215-547-1800; Fax 215-946-2877; Web Site www.penryn.org

The Pen Ryn School, a coeducational, elementary school affiliated with Christ Episcopal Church in Bensalem, enrolls 350 day students in Pre-Kindergarten–Grade 8. The School aims to help each student develop individual academic talents in a caring, nurturing environment. The curriculum, which emphasizes reading, English, and math skills, is supplemented by programs in Spanish, art, music, health, physical education, computers, and experiences for social development. Activities include sports, chorus, student government, enrichment clubs, and annual school-wide events. Tuition: $4950–$5320. Liz Morton is Admissions Director; Peter A. Wallner (Waynesburg College, B.A. 1968; Pennsylvania State, M.A. 1971, Ph.D. 1973) is Head of School. *Middle States Association.*

Perkiomen School   1875

Pennsburg, PA 18073. 215-679-9511; Fax 215-679-1146;
E-mail cdougherty@perkiomen.org; Web Site www.perkiomen.org

Perkiomen, a college preparatory boarding and day school, enrolls 255 boys and girls in Grade 5–Postgraduate. It aims to provide a strong basis in traditional academic subjects while offering study in areas of special interest. Independent projects, Advanced Placement and honors courses, and English as a Second Language enrich the college preparatory curriculum. Twenty fine arts electives are offered in studio art, music, theater, and dance. Participation in three sports or activities a year is required. Among the activities are publications, drama, music, community service, and athletics. Boarding Tuition: $24,500; Day Tuition: $13,500. Financial Aid: $817,000. Carol Dougherty is Director of Admission; George K. Allison (Union, A.B. 1966; Trinity, M.A. 1974) is Headmaster. *Middle States Association.*

The Philadelphia School   1972

2501 Lombard Street, Philadelphia, PA 19146. 215-545-5323;
Fax 215-546-1798

The Philadelphia School is a coeducational school enrolling 295 students in Kindergarten–Grade 8. The School's rigorous academic program is enriched by the use of cultural resources located close to the School's center-city facility and by use of a rural, outdoor environmental center. Students are encouraged to become inquisitive, creative, thoughtful, and self-reliant learners. After-school day care, instrumental music lessons, summer courses, and summer day camp are available. Tuition: $8500–$11,087. Financial Aid: $439,087. Abigail S. Levner is Director of Admission and Financial Aid; Sandra Dean (University of Pennsylvania, B.S. 1959; Temple University, M.Ed. 1971) was appointed Principal in 1983.

The Quaker School at Horsham   1982

318 Meetinghouse Road, Horsham, PA 19044. 215-674-2875;
Fax 215-674-9913

The Quaker School at Horsham enrolls 70 children, from Pre-First to Grade 8, of average to above-average intelligence whose learning differences have kept them from reaching their full potential in traditional schools. Within a caring, supportive environment imbued by Quaker values, faculty utilize a variety of teaching methods and strategies adapted to each child's individual needs. Some students are mainstreamed after two or three years, while others complete the entire lower and middle school programs. Language arts and auditory skills are emphasized across the curriculum that includes course work in all the basic disciplines. Extracurriculars and a summer session are also available. Tuition: $15,500. Peter F. Baily (Nasson, B.A. 1975; Bryn Mawr, M.A. 1977) is Head of School.

Rosemont School of the Holy Child   1949

1344 Montgomery Avenue, Rosemont, PA 19010. 610-525-1876; Fax 610-525-7128; E-mail info@rosemont-sch.org; Web Site www.rosemont-sch.org

Founded by the Society of the Holy Child Jesus, Rosemont School of the Holy Child is a Roman Catholic day school enrolling 155 girls and 140 boys in Nursery–Grade 8. It seeks to develop the whole child by combining sound religious training with vigorous intellectual and physical growth. Religion, Latin, computers, music, art, science, and physical education enrich the traditional curriculum; French is introduced in Grade 6. Sports, musical recitals, clubs, and the annual school play are among the activities. Summer camp programs are offered. Tuition: $5950–$10,150. Financial Aid: $186,000. Jeanne Marie Blair is Director of Admissions; Sr. Mary Broderick, SHCJ (Villanova, B.A. 1972; Marywood, M.A. 1979), was appointed Head of the School in 1983.

Saint Basil Academy   1931

711 Fox Chase Road, Fox Chase Manor, PA 19046. 215-885-3771; Fax 215-885-4025; E-mail admissions@stbasilacademy.org; Web Site www.stbasilacademy.org

Enrolling 350 day girls of diverse backgrounds in Grades 9–12, Saint Basil Academy, founded by the Sisters of Saint Basil the Great, is affiliated with the Byzantine Ukrainian Catholic Church and maintains its heritage through liturgies and language offerings. Within a community of faith, students undertake a college preparatory program that includes Advanced Placement courses, business and computer studies, music, and art. Students may also take courses at local colleges. Activities include Student Council, community service, language and drama clubs, publications, and athletics. Tuition: $5300. Academic Scholarships: $60,000. Mrs. Maureen McKeown Walsh is Director of Admissions; Sr. Carla Hernández, OSBM, is Principal. *Middle States Association.*

The School in Rose Valley   1929

School Lane, Rose Valley, PA 19063. 610-566-1088

The School in Rose Valley, enrolling 128 boys and girls in Preschool–Grade 6 on a 7-acre wooded campus, offers a unique environment designed to develop each child's fullest potential. The curriculum integrates art, music, wood shop, drama, and literature along with traditional academic content. A noncompetitive sports program, overnight camping trips, and environmental science education are enrichments. Parents are encour-

aged to take active roles in the School by participating in governance, campus maintenance, and the teaching of minicourses. Tuition: $5545–$9335. Kay Sweet (Duchesne College, B.A. 1965; University of Pennsylvania, M.Ed. 1975) is Principal.

St. Edmund's Academy   1947

5705 Darlington Road, Pittsburgh, PA 15217. 412-521-1907; Fax 412-521-1260

St. Edmund's is a coeducational day school enrolling 265 students in PreKindergarten–Grade 8. With historic roots in the Episcopal tradition, the school welcomes families from all denominations and backgrounds. Character formation and intellectual preparation are woven into the student's daily experiences. Both challenging and nurturing, the school seeks to provide each child with a strong academic, emotional, social, physical, and spiritual foundation. The core curriculum is designed to involve students in their own education and to prepare them for secondary school and for service to the broader community. Tuition: $6465–$10,195. Extras: $300–$500. Financial aid is available. Holly Morgan is Director of Admissions; David Lowry (Haverford, B.A. 1967; Columbia, Ph.D. 1981) is Headmaster.

Scranton Preparatory School   1944

1000 Wyoming Avenue, Scranton, PA 18509-2993. 570-941-7737; Fax 570-941-6318

Scranton Preparatory School, founded by the Society of Jesus, is a Roman Catholic, college preparatory day school enrolling 324 boys and 352 girls in Grades 9–12. The School offers a balanced curriculum with classical and modern languages, social studies, mathematics, science, theology, computer science, health education, art, music, and physical education. Two years of Latin are required. Advanced courses earn college credit at the University of Scranton. Student Council, sports, music, drama, and publications are among the activities. A summer program offers pre-high school academics. Tuition: $6050. Financial Aid: $415,000. The Reverend Herbert B. Keller, SJ, was appointed President in 1997. *Middle States Association.*

Sewickley Academy   1838

315 Academy Avenue, Sewickley, PA 15143. 412-741-2230; Fax 412-741-1411; E-mail admissions@sewickley.org; Web Site www.sewickley.org

Sewickley Academy is a coeducational, college preparatory day school enrolling 798 students in Pre-Kindergarten–Grade 12. The Academy strives to provide an outstanding educational experience within a supportive atmosphere that emphasizes good citizenship and personal responsibility. Special programs include Lower School foreign language, required community service, foreign student exchanges, and a unique computer curriculum. Tuition: $6890–$12,100. Financial aid is available. L. Hamilton Clark, Jr. (Trinity College, B.A. 1972; Harvard, M.Ed. 1978), was appointed Headmaster in 1987. *Middle States Association.*

Shady Side Academy   1883

423 Fox Chapel Road, Pittsburgh, PA 15238. 412-968-3000;
  Fax 412-968-3178; E-mail kmihm@shadyside.org;
  Web Site www.shadyside.org

Shady Side Academy, Pittsburgh's largest independent school, presently enrolls 598 boys and 345 girls as day students in Kindergarten–Grade 12 and 29 boys and 16 girls as five-day boarders in Grades 9–12. The Academy became fully coeducational in all grades in 1998. Shady Side strives to develop sensitivity and competence in the student's intellectual, physical, and moral-emotional-social life. Tuition: $9200–$14,200; Five-day Boarding Fee: $6650. Katherine H. Mihm is Admissions Director; Peter J. Kountz (St. Meinrad, B.A. 1967; University of Chicago, M.A., Ph.D.) was appointed President in 1988. *Middle States Association.*

The Shipley School   1894

814 Yarrow Street, Bryn Mawr, PA 19010-3598. 610-525-4300;
  Fax 610-525-5082; E-mail admit@shipleyschool.org;
  Web Site www.libertynet.org/shipley/

Now in its 106th year, Shipley is a coeducational, college preparatory day school located near Bryn Mawr College. With its largest enrollment ever, 815 students in Pre-Kindergarten–

Grade 12, Shipley remains committed to educational excellence and to developing in students "a love of learning and a compassionate participation in the world." Advanced Placement is offered in 12 subjects. Latin is required in Grades 7–8. Sports are required in Middle School and strongly encouraged in Upper School. The Snyder Science Center and computer facilities were dedicated in 1995. Community service is required of all students. Tuition: $8470–$14,895. Financial Aid: $1,566,000. Gregory W. Coleman is Director of Admissions; Steven S. Piltch (Williams, B.A.; Harvard, Ed.M., Ed.D.) is Head of School.

Solebury School   NEW HOPE

P.O. Box 429, New Hope, PA 18938. 215-862-5261;
  Fax 215-862-3366; E-mail adm@solebury.pvt.k12.pa.us;
  Web Site www.solebury.com

SOLEBURY SCHOOL in New Hope, Pennsylvania, is a college preparatory boarding and day school enrolling boys and girls in Grades 7–12 and a postgraduate year. Boarding starts in ninth grade. The School is situated in Bucks County, approximately 3 miles north of New Hope, 25 miles from Princeton, 35 miles from Philadelphia, and 65 miles from New York City.

Founded as a boys' school in 1925, Solebury became coeducational following its 1949 merger with Holmquist School (founded 1917). The School's primary purpose is to provide a challenging college preparatory curriculum that encourages students to explore and develop their skills and talents—academically, artistically, and athletically. Small classes and an informal, friendly atmosphere promote originality and creativity.

Solebury is accredited by the Middle States Association of Colleges and Schools. It is a member of the Pennsylvania Association of Independent Schools and the National Association of Independent Schools.

THE CAMPUS. The 90-acre campus of fields and woodlands includes four playing fields, four tennis courts, a cross-country course, and an outdoor swimming pool. The gymnasium is used for basketball, weight training, and other indoor sports. A stable, located 1.5 miles from campus, provides opportunity for horseback riding. The original stone farmhouse holds the administrative offices, and the refurbished barn contains a theater, a student café and recreation room, and offices. Newer buildings provide classrooms, three science laboratories, and networked computer stations available in a science lab, and a math lab. Scanners and on-line connections are available for student use in multiple areas. A carriage house holds offices, the music room, and the infirmary. The library contains more than 10,000 volumes, including the J. William Middendorf Memorial Reference Collection. In addition to study areas, the library is equipped with six computer workstations, part of the campus-wide network. The library is a member of Access Pennsylvania, which allows students to borrow books from participating libraries statewide and offers numerous on-line resources. All on-line references and the library catalog may be accessed from any computer location that is part of the campus network. Computers in the boys' and girls' dormitories and are also connected to the network. Adjacent to the library, the multimedia room provides 14 networked computers, scanner, CD-writer, large-screen video projection system, and other state-of-the-art equipment. The adjoining fine arts center has facilities for graphics, painting, drawing, ceramics, and photography.

Additional buildings include Holmquist Dormitory, which houses boarding girls; Walter Lamb Hall (1998), which houses boarding boys; Boyd Dining Hall; faculty homes; and the Head's residence.

THE FACULTY. In 1989, John Brown was appointed Head of Solebury. A 1967 Solebury graduate, a member of the faculty from 1971 to 1980, and a member of the Board of Trustees, Mr. Brown is very familiar with the School and its philosophy.

The faculty include 34 full-time and 4 part-time teachers, 19 women and 19 men. Eighteen faculty members live on campus. The faculty hold 36 baccalaureate, 15 graduate, and 1 doctoral degrees representing study at such colleges and universities as Bard, Beaver, Beloit, Boston Conservatory of Music, Columbia, Delaware Valley, Duke, Franklin and Marshall, Gettysburg, Guilford College, Gwynedd-Mercy, Hamilton, Harvard, Haverford, Monmouth, New York University, Pennsylvania State, Rhode Island School of Design, Rider, Rochester Institute of Technology, Rockford, Rutgers, St. Joseph's, San Francisco State, Smith, State University of New York (Cortland), Temple, Texas Woman's, Thomas Edison, Trinity, Tyler School of Art, West Chester, West Virginia, Windham, and the Universities of California, Kent at Canterbury, Kentucky, London, Massachusetts, Pennsylvania, Pittsburgh, Texas, Vermont, Wisconsin, and Wyoming.

A nurse is on duty every weekday. The School is a short distance from medical facilities.

STUDENT BODY. In 1999–2000, the School enrolls 34 boarding boys, 28 boarding girls, 69 day boys, and 62 day girls in Grades 7–12 as follows: 10 in Grade 7, 15 in Grade 8, 39 in Grade 9, 42 in Grade 10, 48 in Grade 11, 35 in Grade 12, and 4 postgraduates. Students come from 12 states, Germany, Hong Kong, Japan, Korea, Lithuania, Malaysia, and Taiwan.

ACADEMIC PROGRAM. The school year begins in early September, and Commencement is held in early June; there are several long weekends in addition to Thanksgiving, Christmas, and spring vacations.

Classes, with an average of 13 students, are scheduled in eight 40-minute periods. The classroom hours begin at 8:05 A.M. and end at 3:30 P.M. with breaks for Morning Meeting, conferences, and lunch. Late afternoons are reserved for activities, athletics, and other extracurricular events. Supervised evening study is scheduled between 7:15 and 9:00 P.M. Students who meet specific criteria are entitled to study in their dormitories. Students select their own advisers, who meet frequently with advisees. Grade reports are sent to parents three times each year and more frequently if the student is experiencing academic difficulty.

To give teachers and students common experiences and to promote interdisciplinary learning, each year is highlighted by an academic theme. The theme for 1999–2000 is "Technology."

Solebury's Middle School offers a challenging program for students in Grades 7 and 8. Classes are small, and students are permitted to take upper-level courses for high school credit. Courses include: English, Cultural Geography, Civics, Life Science–An Introduction to Biology and Anatomy and other topics related to living things, Earth Science, Middle School Math, Pre-Algebra, Introduction to Foreign Language, Introduction to the Arts, and Physical Education.

To graduate, students in Grades 9–12 must complete a minimum of $18\frac{1}{6}$ credits, including 4 credits in English; 3 in mathematics; 3 in a foreign language; 2 in social studies, including United States History; 2 in science, including IPS and Biology; 1 in the arts (two full years); $\frac{1}{6}$ in computer science; 3 in electives; and two trimesters each year of a sport or activity.

Among the courses offered are Expository Writing, African-American Literature, Future Worlds, Literature of the South; French, Spanish; Art History, European History, Ancient History, U.S. History, Native American History, Historiography, Holocaust and Other Genocides; Algebra I–II, Geometry, Pre-Calculus, Calculus, Computer I, Programming (C++) Visual

Basic, Web Design; Introduction to Physical Science, Biology, Chemistry, Physics, Animal Communication and Bioacoustics, Lights, Lasers, and Holography; and Life Drawing, Painting, Batik, Ceramics, Independent Art Studio, Photography, Printmaking, Graphics, Music Theory, and Technical Theatre. Tutoring in other languages is available by special arrangement. Students who elect honors and AP courses, or who carry heavier-than-average class loads, are given a bonus in the computation of honor rolls. Advanced Placement courses are offered in American Studies, Environmental Science, and English. Honors courses include Ethics and the New Technology, Topics in Dramatic Literature—American Drama, and History of Ideas.

Full-year, spring trimester, and six-week summer programs in English as a Second Language are offered through an Intensive English Program, with ESL classes of approximately five students. There are additional fees for these programs.

The School's Learning Skills Program assists students who need help with basic language skills. The program is designed for students who possess average to above-average intelligence but need strengthening in reading, writing, language, and mathematic skills. Classes using multisensory Orton and Wilson techniques teach phonological processing. Students work on organization, study skills, and oral communication. Learning Skills employs state-of-the-art technology. Kurzweil 3000 Scan/Read software is used to help students with reading problems; Dragon Naturally Speaking voice-recognition software assists those with small-motor difficulties or insufficient keyboarding skills. The program is limited to 23 students and requires an additional fee.

Independent study is available for especially well-motivated students, and credit can be earned for special projects. In the spring, Senior Projects focus on special-interest apprenticeships with craftsmen, with community service groups, or with businesses or other organizations.

The majority of Solebury graduates attend college within a year after graduation. Representative colleges attended by graduates include Bates, Boston College, Bryn Mawr, Bucknell, Colgate, College of Santa Fe, Cornell, Delaware Valley, Dickinson, Drew, Drexel, Franklin and Marshall, George Mason, Gettysburg, Hampshire, Haverford, Johns Hopkins, Mount Holyoke, Pennsylvania State, Pratt Institute, Rhode Island School of Design, Rochester Institute of Technology, Rutgers, Skidmore, Smith, Temple, Ursinus, Wesleyan, and the Universities of Delaware, Massachusetts, Rhode Island, Vermont, and Virginia.

STUDENT ACTIVITIES. Elected student representatives to the Community Council meet regularly to discuss all phases of School life. Students are voting members of the Judicial and Academic committees, are active in the self-evaluation of the School for the Middle States Association, and are represented at faculty and Board of Trustees meetings.

A physical activity is required during at least two of the three trimesters. Interscholastic teams compete in soccer, basketball, tennis, cross-country, baseball, track and field, and girls' softball. Noncompetitive sports include golf, horseback riding, lacrosse, rock climbing, volleyball, Ultimate Frisbee, field hockey; bicycling, and weight training. Activities available for all students include Music Ensemble, Yearbook, Computer Club, Video Production, and Musical Theater.

Frequent trips are made to New York, Philadelphia, and Princeton to attend sports events, concerts, Broadway plays, zoos, and museums. Plays, dances, films, symposiums, festivals, coffee houses, and concerts are scheduled regularly on campus, and an eight-day Annual Arts Festival is held in the spring. Students and teachers organize groups with special interests, such as band or ensemble or producing a yearbook or literary magazine. All members of the School community participate in the Work Program.

During the summer, Solebury offers a Day Camp for children ages 4 to 12 and a Swim Club for all ages.

ADMISSION AND COSTS. Solebury School seeks to admit well-rounded students who will contribute to the School community

as a whole—in academics, athletics, and the arts. Applicants are admitted on the basis of the results of the Secondary School Admission Test, past academic performance, a personal interview, school reports, and the results of general aptitude and intelligence tests. Candidates who complete the application process by March 1 are notified of admissions decisions by March 15. Applications should be submitted by March 31 for fall admission, although applications received after that time will be considered if vacancies exist. There is a nonrefundable application fee of $35.

In 1999–2000, tuition is $23,500 for boarding students and $14,500 (including lunch) for day students in Grades 9 through the postgraduate year, and $13,000 in Grades 7 and 8. The Learning Skills Program costs an additional $7000. A deposit of $500 is required to cover such expenses as books and medical fees. Scholarships are awarded on the basis of need as determined by the School Scholarship Service. In 1999–2000, 40 percent of the student body received $600,000 in financial aid.

Director of Studies: Mr. Robin Nesbitt
Dean of Students: Annette Miller
Alumni Secretary: Sandra Hoffacker
Director of Admissions: Denise DiFiglia
Director of Development: Linda Brown
College Counselor: Peter Ammirati
Business Manager: Constance Healy
Director of Athletics: Lyle Hazel

Springside School   1879

8000 Cherokee Street, Philadelphia, PA 19118. 215-247-7200;
  Admissions 215-247-7007; Fax 215-247-7308;
  E-mail admissions@springside.org

The oldest girls' school in Philadelphia, Springside is a college preparatory school enrolling 525 students in Pre-Kindergarten–Grade 12, with a coeducational program with Chestnut Hill Academy in the Upper School. Springside aims to offer an outstanding academic program and the advantages of small classes and individual attention. One-third of recent graduates have earned National Merit recognition. A rich extracurricular program includes interscholastic sports, a cultural exchange program, and a wide variety of courses in the arts. Early Bird and After-School programs are available. Tuition: $8200–$13,320. Financial Aid: $720,000. Peggy Mandell (Lower School) and Elizabeth Brode Ota (Middle/Upper Schools) are Directors of Admissions; Priscilla Sands Watson was appointed Head of School in 1996.

Stratford Friends School   1976

5 Llandillo Road, Havertown, PA 19083. 610-446-3144;
Fax 610-446-6381

Children with learning differences are the focus of Stratford Friends School, which enrolls 65 learning-different youngsters ages 5–13. The typical student is of normal intelligence or higher whose problems with language, memory, attention, perception, coordination, and/or organization have impeded his or her ability to learn and succeed. The curriculum, which is guided by Quaker principles and practices, is based on a multisensory, hands-on approach to learning. Language arts and mathematics form the core program, plus social studies, science, the arts, and physical education, Summer enrichment is offered. Tuition: $15,085. Nancy D'Angelo is Admissions Coordinator; Dorothy Flanagan and Sandra Howze are Co-directors.

The Swain School   1929

1100 South 24th Street, Allentown, PA 18103. 610-433-4542;
Fax 610-433-8280

Swain is a college preparatory, nonsectarian day school enrolling 329 boys and girls in Nursery (age three)–Grade 8. The School's purpose is to provide an academic program with superior educational opportunities for young people of ability and character in an atmosphere that inculcates ethical values. Study skills are emphasized within the liberal arts curriculum. A new library/technology center with a computer lab enables Swain to augment its child-centered program with the benefits of technology. Tuition: $5075–$9220. Financial Aid: $429,000. Lynald E. Silsbee (Bloomsburg State, B.S., M.Ed.; University of Maryland, Ph.D.) was appointed Headmaster in 1981.

United Friends School   1983

20 South Tenth Street, Quakertown, PA 18951. 215-538-1733;
Fax 215-538-3140; E-mail ufsadminl@nni.com

Founded by parents seeking to provide an education based on Quaker principles, United Friends School enrolls 130 boys and girls age 3–Grade 8. The School's philosophy aims to develop truth, simplicity, peace, and self-reliance within a community of mutual caring and respect. The curriculum is designed to instill a love of knowledge and a spirit of creativity upon a solid foundation of skills for future learning. Reading, mathematics, science, and social studies are enriched with offerings in music, Spanish, physical education, and art. After-school care and a four-week summer art camp are available. Tuition: $5846. Financial Aid: $40,000. Betty Sue Zellner (Kean College, B.A. 1976; Rutgers Graduate School of Education, M.Ed. 1988) is Head of School.

Upland Country Day School   1948

420 West Street Road, Kennett Square, PA 19348.
610-444-3035; Fax 610-444-2961;
E-mail bwilson@uplandcds.kennett-square.pa.us

Upland Country Day School, located in southeastern Chester County, is a school for boys and girls enrolling 230 students in Pre-Kindergarten through Grade 9. The School provides a challenging, liberal arts academic curriculum that is carefully balanced with the confidence-building experience of team athletics and an enriching combination of art, music, and drama. Tuition: $5910–$12,040. Bill Wilson is Director of Admissions; Russell J. MacMullan, Jr. (University of Pennsylvania, B.A.; Wesleyan University, M.A.), is Headmaster.

Valley Forge Military Academy and College   WAYNE

1001 Eagle Road, Wayne, PA 19087-3695. 610-989-1200;
Admissions 610-989-1300 or 800-234-VFMA; Fax 610-688-1545;
E-mail admission@vfmac.edu; Web Site www.vfmac.edu

VALLEY FORGE MILITARY ACADEMY AND COLLEGE in Wayne, Pennsylvania, is an Army "Honor School of Distinction" enrolling male cadets as boarders in Grade 7–Postgraduate and a two-year program leading to an associate degree. Wayne is a picturesque, historic town of approximately 10,000 residents located 15 miles west of Philadelphia's Main Line and 4 miles from Valley Forge National Historical Park.

Valley Forge Military Academy, a nonsectarian, college preparatory school, was founded in 1928 by Lt. Gen. Milton G. Baker to meet the need for an educational and military environment that prepared young men to meet their responsibilities as American citizens. The Academy aims to inspire in each cadet a love of God and country, high moral standards, gentlemanly conduct, and a strong sense of duty, honor, loyalty, and courage. Cadets in Grade 9–Postgraduate are members of the junior unit of the Army Reserve Officers' Training Corps, while Grades 7 and 8 follow a modified military program.

Valley Forge Military Academy is accredited by the Middle States Association of Colleges and Schools and governed by the 32-member Board of Trustees of the Academy Foundation. More than 13,000 alumni support the school, which has an endowment of $8,000,000 supplemented by an Annual Fund of $1,000,000.

THE CAMPUS. Valley Forge occupies a beautiful 120-acre campus of meadows, woodlands, and parade and playing fields. Among the 83 buildings are four classroom buildings, including Shannon Hall, which serves the High School, and Lhotak Hall for the Middle School. The academic facilities include modern science and computer labs, a skills development center, and music practice rooms. The fully networked May H. Baker Memorial Library boasts a collection of more than 75,000 volumes, 3000 audiovisual materials, 175 periodicals, and 40 computers. Cadets are housed in six barracks, and faculty reside in apartments throughout the campus. Crossed Sabres is the home of the President. Admission offices are located in Medenbach

Hall, while Wayne Hall provides administrative offices. Other facilities include a student union building, a health center, a chapel, the arsenal, and the cadet store and snack bar.

Also on campus are an indoor rifle range, ballroom, photography laboratory, and piano/instrument practice rooms. Price Athletic Center and Trainer Hall house nine basketball courts, a five-lane swimming pool, locker rooms, weight and meeting rooms, and the L. Maitland Blank Hall of Fame. There are six athletic fields, nine outdoor tennis courts, an outdoor Olympic-size swimming pool, stables, and the Mellon Polo Pavilion.

THE FACULTY. Rear Admiral Virgil L. Hill, Jr., USN (Ret), was appointed the seventh President of Valley Forge Military Academy and College in 1993. During his distinguished 32-year naval career, Admiral Hill was assigned to the Navy's Operational Commanding Office, served as commander of a nuclear submarine, and was a division director of the Naval Nuclear Power School. In 1988, he was appointed the 53rd Superintendent of the United States Naval Academy, his alma mater.

In addition to Admiral Hill and the administrative staff, there are 65 teaching faculty who hold baccalaureate degrees and 40 advanced degrees including 3 doctorates. They are selected primarily for their professional ability and concern for young people.

STUDENT BODY. In 1999–2000, Valley Forge enrolled 573 young men in the Academy's Middle and High schools and 230 College cadets. The diverse student body came from 40 states and 45 countries worldwide.

ACADEMIC PROGRAM. The school year is divided into semesters, from late August to early June, with Thanksgiving, Christmas, and spring leaves. Each cadet's academic progress is monitored by guidance counselors who assist him in formulating a college preparatory program tailored to his goals and abilities. Cadets receive ample time for lesson preparation and, when needed, additional assistance from faculty or peer tutors outside the regular schedule. Attendance at two-hour, faculty-supervised study periods is required five nights a week. Exceptional achievement is recognized on the honor roll.

A typical day begins with reveille at 5:45 A.M. Cadets march in uniform with their squadron for breakfast at 6:05 A.M., followed by assigned work details and room cleanup before classes begin at 7:30 A.M. The average class size is 13 cadets, with a 9:1 student-teacher ratio. At noon, the entire Cadet Corps marches in formation for review by an officer. Free time between 3:00 and 7:00 P.M. provides opportunities for participation in sports, clubs, and informal recreation. After the evening study period, cadets prepare for bed, with taps played at 10:00 P.M.

The Middle School curriculum provides a strong academic core in language arts and English grammar, literature, and reading as well as mathematics, social studies, and science, enhanced by art, music, character education, social etiquette, and military science skills. Able students may also take high school courses in Spanish, French, and algebra. Cadets at this level wear uniforms and learn self-discipline, obedience to superiors, and other key military principles.

In the High School, the college preparatory program is taught at standard, intermediate, and honors levels, and cadets may move from one level to another based on their progress. To earn a Valley Forge diploma, cadets must complete $20\frac{1}{2}$ academic credits as follows: four years of English, four years of mathematics, three of social studies, and two years each of one foreign language and science, plus one laboratory science course, and $4\frac{1}{2}$ elective credits. Advanced Placement and college-level courses are available to qualified cadets.

Specific course offerings include Basic English, English I–IV, Post Graduate English, Speech, Journalism, Mass Communications; Introduction to Art, Advanced Art, Photo Journalism; Music Theory, Independent Music Study; Ancient World History, Modern World History, Modern European History, United States History, American Government, Introductory Economics, World Religions, Sociology, Russian Survey, Civil War History, 20th Century U.S. History, United States Foreign Policy; French I–IV, Spanish I–IV, German I–IV; Pre-Algebra, Algebra I–II, Intermediate Algebra, Modern Geometry, Introductory Statistics and Probability, Trigonometry, Pre-Calculus, Calculus, Integrated Mathematics, Business Law, Accounting; Biology, Physics, Chemistry, Integrated Science, Environmental Science, Astronomy, Computer Literacy, Advanced Programming, Wordprocessing/Spreadsheet, Data Base Application, Web Development; and Physical Education. In addition, optional courses are offered in Driver Education, Developmental Reading, SAT Preparation, and Study Skills.

Valley Forge Military Academy incorporates character education into the regular curriculum as a means of inculcating moral values. Integral to this component are mandatory chapel attendance, the Cadet Honor System, and the Code of Ethics. Speakers of national prominence present lectures and seminars that put forth the latest thinking on character formation.

The school's international cadets benefit from the summer English Language Institute, which provides five weeks of intensive study in English at three levels of proficiency. Young men planning to enter the Academy or College, as well as others who plan to matriculate elsewhere, gain fluency through oral language training by faculty with expertise in teaching English.

Although a small percentage pursue military careers after graduation, about 98 percent of Valley Forge cadets enroll in colleges and universities in the United States and in their home countries. Recent college placements have included Case Western Reserve, Colgate, Drexel, Franklin and Marshall, New York University, Ohio State, Pennsylvania State, Rutgers, Syracuse, Temple, Tulane, United States Air Force Academy, United States Merchant Marine Academy, United States Military Academy, United States Naval Academy, Valley Forge, and the Universities of Colorado, Connecticut, Delaware, Florida, Maryland, Michigan, New Hampshire, North Carolina, Notre Dame, Pittsburgh, and Virginia.

Valley Forge offers a number of summer programs for boys 8–16 involving sports, camping, band, and academics within a modified military program.

STUDENT ACTIVITIES. The student body is organized into the Corps of Cadets, consisting of eight companies within one mounted and one infantry battalion. While the companies are headed by adult tactical officers, each returning cadet has the opportunity to lead his peers for at least 30 days, and his advancement through the ranks is predicated on his initiative and performance. All cadets also take a leadership development course.

More than 30 extracurricular activities and organizations include honor societies, language clubs, Regimental Band, a field music unit, glee club, choir, yearbook (*Crossed Sabers*), and the school newspaper (*The Legionnaire*).

Valley Forge's strong athletic program has sent more than 100 cadets to Division I schools on football scholarships and counts seven alumni as current National Football League players. Varsity and junior varsity teams are also fielded in soccer, cross-country, swimming, wrestling, basketball, polo, tennis, golf, track, riflery, pistol, lacrosse, and baseball; there are also intramurals in team and touch football. Canoe trips, horseback riding in Valley Forge Historical National Park, and ski excursions in the Poconos are only a few of the outdoor activities available.

The school calendar features traditional activities such as Parents' Day, Ring Dance, parades, and Spring Festival.

ADMISSION AND COSTS. Valley Forge Military Academy and College welcomes young men of good character and academic potential who demonstrate a commitment to participate fully in the school's military, academic, and extracurricular programs. Admission is based on academic aptitude as measured by the Otis-Lennon exam and/or the Secondary School Admission Test, grades, character and scholastic references, and the recommendations of the school's admission counselor based upon his personal interview with the applicant. A visit to the campus is encouraged, and tours are available daily while school is in session.

In 1999–2000, the comprehensive fee for tuition, room, board, and other charges totaled $21,500. More than $1,500,000 in financial aid and scholarships is awarded annually to qualified students. Tuition payment plans are available.

Commandant of Cadets: Joe N. Frazar, Brig. Gen., USA (Ret.)
Dean of College: Donald S. Rowe, COL (LTC, USA [Ret.])
Dean of Academy: Donn G. Miller, COL, USA (Ret.)
Director of Admission: Fred A. Serino, '77, COL, VFMA&C
College Counselor: Arthur Saggiotes, '68, JC, COL, VFMA&C
Business Manager: Charles F. Marshall, C.P.A.
Director of Athletics: Jim Burner, MAJ, VFMA&C

Valley School of Ligonier   1947

Box 616, Ligonier, PA 15658. 724-238-6652; Fax 724-238-6838

Valley School of Ligonier, founded by Mrs. Richard King Mellon as an independent, elementary day school, enrolls 101 boys and 103 girls in Kindergarten–Grade 9. The School aims to build the strong academic foundation necessary to future scholastic success and personal fulfillment and to maintain a disciplined but friendly atmosphere in which energy and hard work can be productive. The traditional curriculum includes art, computer, music, physical education, and science for all grades. French begins in Grade 1, and Latin study begins in Grade 6. The School sponsors a summer day camp. Tuition: $6500. Financial Aid: $230,800. Michael Kennedy (La Salle College, B.A.; University of Virginia, M.A.) is Headmaster.

Villa Maria Academy   1872

370 Old Lincoln Highway, Malvern, PA 19355. 610-644-2551; Fax 610-644-2886; E-mail mknapoli@vmahs.org; Web Site www.vmahs.org

The Sisters, Servants of the Immaculate Heart of Mary founded this college preparatory school to educate young women. It offers a challenging combination of academic, athletic, and extracurricular programs designed to enable each student to reach her full potential. Enrolling 426 girls in Grades 9–12, Villa Maria seeks to provide flexibility, support, and individual attention through a 9:1 student-faculty ratio. Theology, Advanced Placement and honors courses, and electives enrich the curriculum. Over 60 percent of the students engage in team sports and 50 percent, in music ensembles. Activities include student government, orchestra, chorus, bell choir, community service, forensics, honor societies, and publications. Tuition: $8230. Mary Kay Napoli is Admission Director; Sr. Mary Kelly, IHM, is Principal. *Middle States Association.*

West Chester Friends School   1836

415 North High Street, West Chester, PA 19380. 610-696-2962; Fax 610-431-1457; E-mail lspangler@wcfs.pvt.k12.pa.us

Founded by and under the care of West Chester Friends Meeting, this day school enrolls 160 students age 4½–Grade 5. The School strives to develop independent study habits and self-discipline; as a Friends School, it wishes students to be caring members of society. The curriculum features individualized language arts and math teaching, and special math, science, and computer labs. French is taught in all grades. After-school care is available. Tuition: $8890–$8990. Financial Aid: $110,980. Leslie M. Spangler is Admissions Director; Mary Beth Hempel (Elmira College, B.A.; Trenton State, M.Ed.) was appointed Head in 1994.

Westtown School   1799

Westtown, PA 19395. 610-399-0123; Admissions 610-399-7900; Fax 610-399-7909

Westtown provides a coeducational, college preparatory curriculum for 278 boarders in Grades 9–12 and 363 day students in Pre-Kindergarten–Grade 10. Students are supported by a community that seeks a global perspective, encourages individuality, and celebrates difference. The academic program inspires intellectual curiosity and a love of learning. Advanced Placement courses are offered; activities include community service, the arts, music, and athletics. Counseling services support college preparation, teach study skills, and enhance personal growth. Boarding Tuition: $22,750; Day Tuition: $6600–$13,900. Financial Aid: $2,502,450. Sarah J. Goebel is Director of Admissions; Thomas B. Farquhar (Earlham, B.A. 1977; University of Pennsylvania, M.S.Ed.) is Head of School. *Middle States Association.*

William Penn Charter School   1689

3000 West School House Lane, Philadelphia, PA 19144. 215-844-3460; Fax 215-844-5537; E-mail sbonnie@penncharter.com; Web Site www.penncharter.com

This Quaker-affiliated, coeducational day school, chartered by William Penn, has an enrollment of 840 students in Kindergarten–Grade 12. The School strives to inspire students to think independently and to realize their full potential. A college preparatory curriculum is followed, and athletics, instrumental music, drama, chorus, service activities, and fine arts are offered as extracurricular activities. Summer courses are also available. Tuition: $8685–$12,970. Extras: $900–$2900. Financial Aid: $2,000,000. Dr. Steven A. Bonnie is Director of Admissions; Earl J. Ball III (Middlebury College, A.B. 1965; Johns Hopkins, M.A.T. 1966; University of Pennsylvania, Ed.D. 1981) was appointed Head of School in 1976. *Middle States Association.*

Winchester Thurston School   1887

555 Morewood Avenue, Pittsburgh, PA 15213. 412-578-7500; Admissions 412-578-7518; Web Site www.wt.k12.pa.us

Established in 1887, Winchester Thurston offers families a choice of two coeducational campuses: The City Campus, Kindergarten Readiness–Grade 12 (510 students), and the North Hills Campus, Kindergarten–Grade 5 (84 students). The School provides a college preparatory program that is responsive to developmental and gender-related differences as well as diverse learning styles. At all levels, students are encouraged to develop independent thinking, a lifelong love of learning, the ability to make responsible choices, and a commitment to serving the greater community. Tuition: $9700–$13,975. Financial Aid: $790,000. Rebecca King is Director of Admission; Dr. Linda H. Kelley (St. Lawrence, B.A.; Middlebury, M.A.; Harvard, Ed.M., Ed.D.) is Head of School. *Middle States Association*.

Woodlynde School 1976

*445 Upper Gulph Road, Strafford, PA 19087-5498.
610-687-9660; Fax 610-687-4752;
E-mail admitme@woodlynde.com*

Woodlynde School, enrolling 315 day boys and girls in Kindergarten through Grade 12, features small classes within a structured, supportive environment. Teachers at Woodlynde are recognized for their ability to work with different learning styles, and for creating a pace and atmosphere that instill confidence and foster success. A dynamic reading program in the Lower School and a traditional college preparatory curriculum in the Middle and Upper schools are featured. A wide range of athletics is offered among the extracurricular activities. Extra help, enrichment, and an academic summer session are offered. Tuition: $12,400–$12,950. Barbara Zbrzeznj is Director of Admissions; John T. Rogers (St. Joseph's, B.A.; Temple University School of Law, J.D.) is Head of School.

The Wyndcroft School 1918

*1395 Wilson Street, Pottstown, PA 19464. 610-326-0544;
Fax 610-326-9931*

The Wyndcroft School was established by parents who sought a strong, traditional education for their children. Enrolling 180 boys and girls age 3 to Grade 8, Wyndcroft's academic program is characterized by small classes, emphasis on mastery of skills, and a supportive environment in which students are motivated to reach their personal best. The core curriculum centers on the liberal arts and sciences, with enrichment at all levels in computer technology, art, and music. French is introduced in Pre-Kindergarten, and Latin begins in Grade 4. Competitive sports are available for boys and girls according to season; plays and interest clubs are among the activities. Tuition: $2700–$9072. Maureen K. Schmidt is Admission and Development Coordinator; Kathleen E. Wunner, Ph.D., is Head of School.

Wyoming Seminary KINGSTON

*Sprague Avenue, Kingston, PA 18704. 570-283-6000;
Admissions 570-283-6060; E-mail admisoff@ptdprolog.net;
Web Site www.wyomingseminary.org*

WYOMING SEMINARY in Kingston, Pennsylvania, is a coeducational, college preparatory school enrolling day students in Pre-Kindergarten–Grade 12 and boarding students in Grades 9–12 and a postgraduate year. The Lower School campus is located in Forty Fort, approximately three miles from the Upper School campus. Kingston (population 14,500), a suburb of historic Wilkes-Barre, is located in the Wyoming Valley, along the banks of the Susquehanna River (area population 353,000). Kingston is a two-and-one-half hour drive from New York City, two and one-quarter hours from Philadelphia, and four hours from the District of Columbia. The Wilkes-Barre/Scranton International Airport, 20 minutes from campus, is served by major airlines; bus service from Wilkes-Barre is also available. Five colleges, the Northeastern Pennsylvania Philharmonic, the Everhart Museum, Steamtown National Historic Park, the Kirby Center for the Performing Arts, and area theater and music groups provide cultural opportunities. Skiing, biking, hiking, whitewater rafting in nearby state parks, and the Philadelphia Phillies AAA farm club games are popular weekend activities.

Wyoming Seminary was founded in 1844 by leaders of the Methodist church to "prepare students for the active duties of life—for a course of professional or collegiate studies, or any degree of collegiate advancement." Today, Wyoming Seminary students and teachers challenge themselves and each other to reach their academic and personal goals. Students learn to manage their time, write and speak clearly and effectively, study efficiently, and work with others to achieve a common goal.

Wyoming Seminary is directed by a Board of Trustees elected by the Board itself, the Alumni Association, and the Wyoming Annual Conference of the United Methodist Church. Endowment for general operation and scholarships is valued at over $45,000,000. Wyoming Seminary is accredited by the Middle States Association of Colleges and Schools; it is approved by the University Senate of the United Methodist Church; and it is a member of the National Association of Independent Schools, among numerous professional affiliations.

THE CAMPUS. Wyoming Seminary Upper School occupies an 18-acre main campus including academic, athletic, and residential facilities. Nesbitt Hall contains classrooms, state-of-the-art science laboratories, art studios, a darkroom, and a dance studio. New construction to Sprague Hall provides modern classrooms, a conference room, and administrative offices in addition to the existing classrooms and computer labs. Housed in the Wallace F. Stettler Learning Resources Center are the admission offices, a conference area, art gallery, and the Kirby Library, with more than 23,000 volumes, CD-ROM towers, seminar rooms, and audiovisual facilities.

The Harold C. Buckingham Performing Arts Center houses a 460-seat auditorium with high-tech stage equipment, a 27-rank pipe organ, music practice rooms and rehearsal studios, a listening center, and a dramatics practice area and scenery construction shop. A recently purchased "Great Hall" provides performing arts and visual display areas.

Swetland, Fleck, and Darte halls, erected in 1853, are interconnected, forming one unit containing a girls' residence hall, a boys' residence hall, faculty quarters, a dining hall, and lounges. Carpenter Hall is a boys' dormitory with faculty apartments and student snack bar.

Carpenter Athletic Center houses a large gymnasium, a four-lane swimming pool, and exercise/weight and wrestling rooms. The adjoining Pettebone-Dickson Student Center incorporates an all-purpose gymnasium, a game room, lounge, club and publication rooms, and a darkroom. George F. Nesbitt Memorial Stadium is equipped with a grandstand, a football field, a baseball diamond, four tennis courts, and a fieldhouse.

The Lower School (Pre-Kindergarten–Grade 8), on 6.5 acres, consists of a main building, which provides classrooms, administrative offices, and a gymnasium. Directly connected is the Sordoni Library (1995), containing 15,000 volumes. The addition also features a new classroom wing and renovated cafeteria. Athletic fields and a playground surround the school. A recently added Pre-Kindergarten program for three-year-olds meets in a small home on the Lower School campus.

THE FACULTY. H. Jeremy Packard was appointed the tenth President of Wyoming Seminary in 1990. A *cum laude* graduate of the Choate School, Mr. Packard also graduated from Williams (B.A. 1959) and Columbia (M.A. 1965). He received an honorary Doctorate of Sacred Letters from Wycliffe College of the University of Toronto in 1989.

The teaching faculty include 26 women and 37 men; two-thirds of the faculty live on campus. There are 44 women and 10 men at the Lower School. Faculty hold baccalaureate and graduate degrees representing study at Allegheny, American University, Baylor, Bloomsburg, Brown, Bucknell, Catholic Uni-

versity, Central Michigan University, City University of New York, Clarion, Colgate, Columbia, Cornell, Denison, Dickinson, Drew, Drexel, East Stroudsburg, Franklin and Marshall, Goucher, Hartwick, Lehigh, Lock Haven, Lycoming, Marymount, Marywood, Middlebury, Misericordia, Mount Holyoke, Ohio State, Oregon State, Parsons School of Design, Pennsylvania State, Saginaw Valley State, St. Joseph's, Shippensburg, Skidmore, Smith, State University of New York, Susquehanna, Swansea (England), Syracuse, Trinity, Tulane, Washington and Lee, Wellesley, Westminster Choir College, Wilkes, Williams, Winona State, Yale, and the Universities of California, Denver, Massachusetts, North Carolina, Pennsylvania, Pittsburgh, Richmond, Scranton, Virginia, and Wisconsin. Three part-time instructors teach photography, dance, and reading.

The infirmary facilities are staffed by two nurses, and a doctor is on call. The Wilkes-Barre General Hospital is five minutes away.

STUDENT BODY. In 1999–2000, Wyoming Seminary Lower School enrolls 414 day students in Pre-Kindergarten–Grade 8. The Upper School enrolls 77 boarding boys, 141 day boys, 61 boarding girls, and 133 day girls.

Students come from 11 states and 20 foreign countries.

ACADEMIC PROGRAM. The school year, from September to late May, includes three terms, Thanksgiving, Christmas, and spring vacations, and long weekends at Easter and midterm. Classes meet five days per week, with an average of 13 students. A typical daily schedule (from 8:00 A.M. to 3:30 P.M.) includes four 45-minute class periods in the morning, lunch, three classes in the afternoon, and a conference period in addition to weekly school meetings and chapel. Students—with the exception of juniors, seniors, postgraduates, and honor students—are expected to attend supervised study hall during free periods. In addition, boarding students study in their rooms from 7:30 until 9:50 P.M. Sunday through Thursday. Faculty members give individual assistance as needed, and a reading specialist is available. Assistance in study skills can be provided. Grades are distributed six times a year; advisors keep families apprised of academic progress throughout the year.

To graduate, a student must accumulate a minimum of 19.33 credits; students earn .33 credit for a term course or 1 credit for a full-year course. Specific requirements are English 4, mathematics 3, foreign language 3, history/social science 3, laboratory science 3, physical education 4, health .33, religion .33, music history .33, art history .33, public speaking .33, and computer science .33.

The curriculum offers a variety of one-term, two-term, and full-year courses. Typical year courses or three-term sequences are freshman and sophomore English; French, Latin, Spanish, Russian; Modern European History, United States History; Algebra, Pre-Calculus, Geometry, Calculus; Biology, Chemistry,

Physics; and Studio Art. Among the numerous term courses are Creative Writing, Shakespeare, The American Dream, Women and Literature, Studio Art, Photography, Music Literature, Masterpieces of Music, Psychology, World Religions, Modern China and Japan, Economics, Black History, The Cold War, Philosophy and Ethics, Discrete Mathematics, Conceptual Physics, Marine Biology, and Ecology.

Advanced Placement courses are offered in all major disciplines, and qualified students may enroll in advanced courses at nearby Wilkes University or King's College. With faculty approval, juniors and seniors may pursue independent study programs for one or more terms.

In 1999, 100 percent of the graduates entered college. Among the colleges accepting recent graduates are American University, Boston College, Bucknell, Colgate, Drexel, Duke, Georgetown, Goucher, Hamilton, Haverford, Kenyon, Lafayette, Lehigh, Parsons School of Design, Pennsylvania State, Stanford, Susquehanna, Syracuse, Tufts, United States Air Force Academy, United States Naval Academy, Villanova, Wesleyan, Williams, Worcester Polytechnic Institute, and the Universities of California, Delaware, and Pennsylvania.

STUDENT ACTIVITIES. The Seminary Government—composed of students, faculty, and administrators—is responsible for many nonacademic aspects of school life. There are four standing committees: spirit, activities, assemblies and programs, and finance.

Student activities include Peer Group, *The Wyoming* (yearbook), *The Opinator* (newspaper), *Scheherezade* (literary magazine), *Clio's Camera* (history journal), Chorale and Madrigal Singers, Drama, Dance, International Club, "W" Club, Blue Key, Model United Nations, Ski Club, Jazz Band, and Orchestra. Three plays are produced each year, and the chorus presents both formal and informal concerts. Involvement in community service is required.

Wyoming Seminary varsity and junior varsity athletic teams compete in the Pennsylvania Interscholastic Athletic Association and with independent schools in New York, New Jersey, Connecticut, and Pennsylvania. Sports for boys are football, basketball, tennis, lacrosse, baseball, wrestling, golf, ice hockey, soccer, cross-country, and swimming. Girls compete in field hockey, basketball, swimming, golf, softball, cross-country, soccer, and tennis.

Weekend activities, planned by students and the full-time Director of Student Activities, take advantage of the school's proximity to major cities' sporting and cultural events as well as the hiking, skiing, and outdoor opportunities available in the Pocono Mountains.

ADMISSION AND COSTS. Wyoming Seminary seeks students who will challenge themselves and their peers to reach academic and personal goals. All applicants must submit school transcripts, letters of recommendation, and the application form, which includes a writing sample. Candidates should submit Secondary School Admission Test results; those applying for Grade 12 or the postgraduate year must submit SAT scores. An interview on campus is required. New students are accepted at all grade levels; late or midyear enrollment is sometimes possible. The application fee is $30.

In 1999–2000, tuition is $24,000 for boarding students and $11,975 for day students. Additional expenses include allowances, books, athletic clothing, a graduation fee ($60), and travel. A tuition payment plan is offered. Financial aid is available to students who qualify on the basis of need, academic performance, and citizenship. Presently, Wyoming Seminary awards over $2,500,000 in aid to about 45 percent of all students.

Dean of Faculty: David L. Davies
Director of Studies: William R. Summerhill
Dean of Students: Karen Klassner
Alumni Director: Liz H. Ortega
Dean of Admission: John R. Eidam
Director of Admission: Kayanne L. Barilla
Director of Development: John H. Shafer
College Counselor: Karen Mason
Business Manager: John T. Morris
Director of Athletics: Gary Vanderburg

Wyoming Seminary   1807

Pre-Kindergarten 3–Grade 8: 1560 Wyoming Avenue, Forty Fort, PA 18704. 570-283-6000; Admissions 570-283-6060; Fax 570-283-6196; E-mail facwsls@postoffice.ptd.net

Wyoming Seminary's Lower School is an elementary day school enrolling more than 400 boys and girls in Pre-Kindergarten 3–Grade 8. The school's programs are child-centered, addressing individual learning styles in an environment that focuses on developing lifelong learning skills. Art, music, computer science, and physical education programs are a vital part of the academic curriculum. Students are introduced to the study of French and Spanish in Grade 3; Latin is offered in Grades 7–8. Tuition: $6025–$9775. Jeanne Yarmey is Assistant Dean of Admission; H. Jeremy Packard (Williams, B.A.; Columbia, M.A.; Wycliffe College, University of Toronto, D.S.L.[Hon.]) is President; John H. Burbank, Jr. (Columbia University, B.S.; Yale, M.Phil.), is Head.

York Country Day School   1953

1071 Country Club Road, York, PA 17403. 717-843-9805; Fax 717-848-4726

York Country Day School is a college preparatory school enrolling 320 boys and girls in Preschool (2 years, 7 months old)–Grade 12. The School emphasizes a strong academic program including computer instruction beginning in Kindergarten, foreign language in Preschool, and public speaking in Ninth Grade. Classes are small to encourage participation and individual attention. Activities include field trips, interscholastic sports, forensics, music, drama, publications, science fair, and Student Council. Seniors take some elective classes at York College of Pennsylvania. Tuition: $1400–$8800. Financial Aid: $120,000. Donna H. Gross is Director of Admission; Taylor A. Smith (Wesleyan, B.A.; Loyola, M.Ed.) is Headmaster. *Middle States Association.*

RHODE ISLAND

The Gordon School   1910

Maxfield Avenue, East Providence, RI 02914. 401-434-3833;
*   Fax 401-431-0320; E-mail Gordonadms@aol.com*

The Gordon School is an independent day school enrolling 360 girls and boys in Nursery–Grade 8. The School offers a broad curriculum that stresses the teaching of skills basic to academic excellence with emphasis also on the arts, music, and physical education. The School aims to develop independence, self-discipline, cooperation, and love of learning in each student within a nurturing atmosphere. Sports, drama, musical ensembles, and clubs are among the activities. Tuition: $4300–$13,200. Financial Aid: $439,693. Emily Anderson is Director of Admission; Ralph L. Wales (Harvard University, B.A.) was appointed Head of School in 1994.

Lincoln School   1884

301 Butler Avenue, Providence, RI 02906. 401-331-9696;
*   Fax 401-751-6670; Web Site www.lincolnschool.org*

Lincoln School, a college preparatory day school enrolling 370 students in Nursery–Grade 12, with girls only from Kindergarten up, is committed to its Quaker heritage, focusing on character and values as well as excellence in education. Advanced Placement courses are offered in addition to enrichment programs in art, technology, theater, sports, leadership, and music. Extracurricular activities including student-led clubs and independent study enhance the curriculum. Upper School students may take courses at nearby colleges. Tuition: $7025–$13,900. Extras: $500–$1000. Financial Aid: $445,000. Ellen M. Lough is Director of Admission; Joan C. Countryman (Sarah Lawrence, B.A.; Yale, M.U.S.) is Head of School. *New England Association.*

Moses Brown School   1784

250 Lloyd Avenue, Providence, RI 02906. 401-831-7350;
*   Fax 401-455-0084*

Moses Brown, a Friends college preparatory day school, enrolls 773 boys and girls in Nursery–Grade 12. The School supports a vibrant, diverse community, with emphasis placed on the close relationship between students and teachers. Beginning in the early grades, Moses Brown seeks to provide an environment that encourages academic excellence, appreciation of self-worth, and commitment to the common good. Electives are offered in all major disciplines. Advanced Placement courses, foreign study, and sports enhance the curriculum. Remedial and enrichment summer programs are offered. Tuition: $6895–$13,995. Finan-

cial Aid: $1,400,000. Claude Anderson is Admission Director; Joanne P. Hoffman (Marymount College, B.A.; Trinity College, M.A.) is Head of School.

Overbrook Academy   WARWICK

836 Warwick Neck Avenue, Warwick, RI 02889. 401-737-2850;
*   Fax 401-737-2884; E-mail overbrook@ids.net;*
*   Web Site www.oak-international.org*

OVERBROOK ACADEMY in Warwick, Rhode Island, is a Roman Catholic boarding and day school enrolling girls from the United States, Europe, and South America in Grades 6 through 9. Warwick (population 85,427), located on Narragansett Bay, is 15 minutes south of Providence and within driving distance of Boston and New York City. The school plans many activities that take advantage of the physical and cultural resources found throughout New England and other parts of the Northeast.

Overbrook Academy was established by the Legion of Christ in Orange, Connecticut, in 1985, and moved to Dallas, Texas, for two years before relocating to its present site in 1991. The school is affiliated with Oak International, a Roman Catholic organization committed to the integral formation of young people that was founded in Rome, Italy, in 1969. It operates schools in Ireland, Switzerland, and the United States, including Everest Academy in Michigan and Oaklawn Academy in Wisconsin.

The harmonious development of each girl's intellectual, human, and spiritual potential is at the core of Overbrook's academic and extracurricular activities. Religious studies, moral training, and spiritual retreats are integral to an Overbrook education, and preparation for the sacrament of Confirmation is offered. The boarding department operates on a full-time or five-day basis.

Overbrook Academy is approved by the Rhode Island Department of Education and holds membership in the Association of Independent Schools of New England.

THE CAMPUS. Overbrook Academy occupies a beautiful 90-

acre campus of lawns and woodlands with sweeping views of Narragansett Bay. The focal point of the grounds is the imposing Romanesque chapel where the school community comes together for liturgies, celebrations, and other special gatherings. Two dormitory wings accommodate up to 180 girls in triple rooms as well as ten adult supervisors. The academic program is carried out in ten classrooms, a library, and laboratories for language, biology, physics, and computers. A 300-seat auditorium, a gymnasium, and soccer and hockey fields complete the facilities.

THE FACULTY. Miss Ann Donaldson is the Directress of Overbrook Academy.

STUDENT BODY. Overbrook Academy enrolls 180 young women, ages 11–14, in Grades 6–9. Girls come from Arizona, California, Florida, New Mexico, Rhode Island, and Texas as well as from Bolivia, Chile, Colombia, France, Guatemala, Hungary, Mexico, Spain, and Venezuela. Although most students are Catholic, other religious traditions are represented.

ACADEMIC PROGRAM. The academic year, divided into three terms, begins in late September and extends to early June, with recesses at Thanksgiving, Christmas, and Easter. Upon entering the Academy, each girl is assigned a guidance counselor who provides assistance in academic, spiritual, and personal matters. Classes, enrolling between 12 and 20 students, meet five days a week; the student-teacher ratio is 15:1. Grades are issued five times a year, and personal progress reports are mailed to parents three times a year.

On a typical weekday, girls rise at 6:00 A.M., followed by breakfast, room chores, and morning prayer. Classes are held from 8:00 A.M. to 12:45 P.M., and there is a daily celebration of the Eucharist. After lunch, students participate in sports and clinics, then attend an afternoon English class before dinner, directed study, an evening talk, and "lights out" at 9:15 P.M.

At Overbrook, a broad-based humanities program serves as the cornerstone of the academic curriculum, with an emphasis on the development of strong reading, writing, and language skills across the disciplines. Courses in English are offered to meet the needs of students at beginner, intermediate, and advanced levels of proficiency. Girls make use of the Phonics Language Laboratory to practice verbal communications skills, while reading classes foster an appreciation for American literature and British classics.

Other specific courses include Science, Physics, Biology, Health; Social Studies, History, Geography, Home Economics, Civics; Mathematics, Pre-Algebra, Algebra I–II, Computers;

Religion, Confirmation Preparation; Spanish; Chorus, Music Appreciation, Public Speaking; and Oil Painting, Photography, and Piano.

Following an initial language evaluation, girls may choose to study English, French, or Spanish as a second language at one of three ability levels, and foreign students are required to take the Test of English as a Foreign Language (TOEFL).

Throughout the year, girls have the opportunity to test their skills in spelling bees, poetry and oratory competitions, math competitions, Geography Quiz Bowl, a religion contest, a national Language Arts Olympiad, and other organized academic challenges.

Overbrook Academy conducts a four-week summer program of English language studies and clinics for horseback riding, tennis, swimming, and other recreational activities. Girls ages 8 to 13 are enrolled. The cost of the 1998–99 summer program is $2950.

STUDENT ACTIVITIES. Overbrook believes that a balanced, comprehensive extracurricular program is essential to the overall health and well-being of the student. A variety of clinics and classes enables girls to concentrate in an athletic or artistic area of particular interest, and all students are required to participate in at least one class or clinic. Among their choices are tennis, swimming, figure skating, horseback riding, ballet, classical jazz, and aerobics. Additionally, there are opportunities to engage in pursuits such as oil painting, piano, photography, choir, culinary arts, field hockey, kickball, volleyball, and softball. Girls are also encouraged to volunteer time to worthwhile community service projects both on and off campus.

Two major trips are optional to students during vacations. At Christmas, girls may visit Rome, with such highlights planned as a papal audience, Mass at St. Peter's Basilica, and excursions to Assisi, Florence, Tivoli, and Castelgandolfo. The Easter trip to Canada features a stop at Niagara Falls, sightseeing in Toronto, and a visit to the Ontario Science Centre. Other outings are planned to the Providence Theater, Block Island, Mystic Seaport, and New York's Radio City Music Hall.

Among the highlights on the school calendar are Christmas and spring spiritual retreats, Christmas Pageant, Parents Weekend, Holy Week Special Activities, Alumnae Weekend, Class Projects Week, and Awards Ceremony.

ADMISSION AND COSTS. Overbrook Academy welcomes girls

of good character and ability whose parents seek a quality education that emphasizes the spiritual, intellectual, and human dimensions of their daughter's natural gifts. Students are admitted to Grades 6 through 9.

In 1999–2000, tuition for the academic year, including an enrollment fee, is $11,150; the boarding fee, which includes meals and laundry, is an additional $10,100. The fee for a five-week program of classes and clinics is $700 per week plus a $150 enrollment charge. Enrollment in the spring course only, from mid-January to mid-June, including an enrollment fee, costs $12,400. Other expenses include a personal allowance, optional travel, and fees for supplementary uniforms and special clinics. Some scholarships are available to meet special needs on an individual basis.

Dean of Faculty: Ann Donaldson
Dean of Studies: Christine Gamache
Dean of Students: Adriana Covarrubias
Alumnae President: Martha Hernandez
Director of Admission: Ann Donaldson
Director of Development: Agustin Illescas
Administrator: Margarita Martinez
Director of Athletics: Luz de Lourdes Elizalde

The Pennfield School 1971

321 East Main Road, Portsmouth, RI 02871. 401-849-4646;
Fax 401-847-6720; E-mail ride3395@ride.ri.net

Founded as The New School by teachers, parents, and friends to provide a superior academic education, this country day school enrolls approximately 180 boys and girls in Three-Year-Old Nursery–Class VIII. Emphasizing concern for the individual, Pennfield aims to develop basic skills, resourcefulness, self-discipline, self-confidence, and responsibility in a supportive environment. Art, music, lab science, computer, and physical education begin in the early grades; French and Spanish are introduced in Kindergarten and are required through Grade 8. Tuition: $7190–$8315. Extras: $110–$463. Financial aid is available. Polly Meadows is Admissions Director; John R. Pedrick (Bates, A.B. 1966; University of Pennsylvania, M.S. 1970) was appointed Headmaster in 1983.

Portsmouth Abbey School PORTSMOUTH

285 Cory's Lane, Portsmouth, RI 02871. 401-683-2005;
Fax 401-683-6766; E-mail admissions@portsmouthabbey.org;
Web Site www.portsmouthabbey.org

Portsmouth Abbey School in Portsmouth, Rhode Island, is a Roman Catholic, college preparatory school enrolling young men and women as boarding and day students in Forms III–VI (Grades 9–12). Owned and operated by monks of the Benedictine Congregation, the School is situated on Narragansett Bay, providing opportunities for hands-on learning beyond the classroom as well as convenient accessibility to the cultural, historic, and recreational resources of Newport, Providence, and Boston.

Portsmouth Abbey School was established by Father John Hugh Diman, a Benedictine monk, in 1926. In keeping with Benedictine principles, the School's mission is to provide an excellent academic program based on reverence for God and man, respect for learning and order, and an appreciation of the shared experience of community life. Talented and committed faculty and an international student body collaborate in a challenging program dedicated to "a genuine appreciation of scholarship, thoroughness in work, and a belief in a broad and liberal education." The celebration of Mass, retreats, common prayer, and the presence of the monks on campus encourage

spiritual development among students, and a monk serves as spiritual leader for every dorm.

The School is governed by the Benedictine community and guided by a 20-member Board of Consultants. Its current endowment is valued at approximately $16,000,000. Portsmouth is accredited by the New England Association of Colleges and Schools and holds membership in the National Association of Independent Schools and the Council for Religion in Independent Schools, among other affiliations.

THE CAMPUS. The School and the Abbey share a 500-acre waterfront campus on Aquidneck Island in Narragansett Bay. Many of the buildings were designed by the distinguished architect Pietro Belluschi. The Cortazzo Administration Building, featuring a Winter Garden with a fountain, houses offices and the auditorium. Academic facilities include the Burden Classroom Building; the Science Building; the Art Building; the St. Thomas More Library, containing 25,000 volumes and seminar rooms; a beachfront marine science laboratory; and a Victorian Manor House (1864). Mass and special programs and liturgies are held in the Church of St. Gregory the Great. Among the other buildings are the Student Center, Stillman Dining Hall, and the Nesbitt Infirmary.

Boarders reside in six houses, each accommodating between 20 and 40 students and houseparents. Third-Form boys live in their own dorm while other dorms house boys of mixed ages; Third-Form girls occupy the Manor House, and Upper-Form girls are housed in St. Benet's Dorm. Each house has a lounge, a library, a refrigerator, and snack machines.

The Portsmouth Abbey campus features excellent athletic facilities including a fully equipped gymnasium and a new annex house, which provide basketball courts, a multistation weight room, and a training room. There are also two squash courts, an indoor ice-hockey rink, nine tennis courts, and nine playing fields. The School owns ten Vanguard 420 sailboats, kayaks, and windsurf boards for student use, and a swimming pool is available nearby for training and competition. Ground has been broken on campus for the Carnegie Abbey golf course, an 18-hole championship Scottish links course, where the Abbey golf team will play by the spring of 2001.

THE FACULTY. Right Reverend Dom Mark Serna is Abbot, Headmaster, and Head of the School's Governing Body. He earned a baccalaureate degree from New York University, a

Master of Arts degree from Providence College, and a Master of Divinity degree in Christian Doctrine from Dominican House of Studies.

There are 64 faculty members, including 14 Benedictine monks. They hold 66 baccalaureate and 39 advanced degrees, including 3 doctorates, representing study at such colleges and universities as Amherst, Bates, Boston College, Boston University, Bowdoin, Brown, Bryn Mawr, Catholic University, Colby, College of the Holy Cross, Columbia, Connecticut College, Cornell, Georgetown, Gettysburg, Harvard, Hollins, Johns Hopkins, Manhattanville, Marquette, Massachusetts Institute of Technology, Middlebury, New York University, Northwestern, Providence College, Roger Williams, Rutgers, St. Bonaventure, St. Francis College, St. Lawrence, St. Peter's, Salve Regina, Temple, United States Military Academy, Villanova, Wellesley, Western Reserve, Yale, and the Universities of Connecticut, Madrid, Massachusetts, Minnesota, New Hampshire, Notre Dame, Pennsylvania, Rhode Island, Richmond, Tennessee, Virginia, and Washington.

Four registered nurses provide medical services on campus, and the School employs a physician, psychologist, and clinical social worker. Full hospital facilities are available in Newport.

STUDENT BODY. In 1998–99, Portsmouth Abbey School enrolled approximately 300 students, two-thirds of whom are residents. They came from 24 states, the District of Columbia, and 20 countries and represented a wide cross-section of racial, ethnic, and religious backgrounds.

ACADEMIC PROGRAM. The school year is divided into trimesters, with grades issued twice during each term. The schedule includes vacations at Thanksgiving, Christmas, and in the spring and several long weekends. Each student's academic progress is monitored by an advising team, houseparents, and deans. A learning specialist is available for students who need additional support in study, reading, writing, and time-management skills, and faculty are available for extra help during free periods and supervised study hours. Classes are small, with an average of 11 students, and the student-faculty ratio is 5:1.

On a typical day, classes are held from 8:15 A.M. to 2:40 P.M., with shortened hours on Wednesday and Saturday. Athletics are generally scheduled between 3:00 and 5:45 P.M. After the evening meal, students engage in activities and study, with "lights out" between 10:30 P.M. and midnight, depending on grade.

The college preparatory curriculum, with strong emphasis on the liberal arts and sciences, includes 14 Advanced Placement courses and a broad variety of noncredit courses. To graduate, students must earn 20 credits including 4 in English, 3 each in mathematics and a foreign language, 2 in a laboratory science, and 1 each in United States history and art/music. The balance may be earned in any other credit courses in foreign languages, history, science, computers, politics, economics, and the visual and performing arts. Students must also pass a Christian Doctrine course for every year of attendance at the School.

Among the specific courses offered are Introduction to Catholic Faith, Old and New Testament, The Church's Confession of Faith, Human Sexuality: Theology and Morality, Christian Heroes, Sacred Music, Church History; Basic English, English 1–4, Great Works of Western Literature, Tragedy, Utopian Literature; Latin 1–5, Greek 1–4, French 1–5, German 1–4, Spanish 1–5; Western Civilization 1–2, U.S. History, Modern European History, Political Science, Economics, International Relations, Twentieth-Century Russia, China, and Japan, War Morality and International Politics, Constitutional Law; Elementary Algebra, Geometry, Algebra II/Introduction to Analysis, Precalculus/Topics, Elementary Statistics, Calculus; Conceptual Physics, Physics 1–2, Chemistry 1–2, Biology I–II, Marine Biology, Medical Physiology, Astronomy; and Art I, History of Art, Photography, Music 1–3, and Theatre.

A Marine and Environmental Studies program allows students to take advantage of the School's exceptional environmental resources. Students perform actual laboratory testing in Narragansett Bay, serve internships with marine and environmental studies groups, assist professors in research at local universities, become certified in open-water diving and practice their skills on a spring break diving trip, and develop and implement educational programs held on the Abbey campus for Kindergarten–Grade 8 students.

College guidance begins formally in the spring of the junior year, with ongoing discussion among students, parents, and the School's College Counselor. All members of the Class of 1999 chose to attend college, with two or more seniors enrolling in Boston College, Boston University, Brown, College of the Holy Cross, Cornell, George Washington, Gettysburg, Providence College, Syracuse, and the University of Vermont.

Portsmouth Abbey School conducts a coeducational summer session of academic course work for credit, remediation, and enrichment.

STUDENT ACTIVITIES. Extracurricular activities are designed to meet a variety of interests, from the elected Student Council and the Social Committee to sports teams and academic and special-interest clubs. Day students participate in all after-school and weekend activities as members of the resident houses to which they are assigned. They also are welcome to use the house for study and occasional sleep-overs.

On-campus groups include Mock Trial team, Model United Nations, Amnesty International, debating society, Glee Club, bands, and a cultural awareness club. The Abbey Players theater group stages major dramatic and musical productions; students publish a yearbook, a literary magazine, and a newspaper, and operate the School radio station.

Community service encompasses volunteer activities through Big Brother/Big Sister, peer tutoring, recycling, and other worthwhile endeavors on campus, while Portsmouth Abbey remains committed to community action off campus as well. Students may assist in soup kitchens, relief organizations, and animal shelters, for which transportation is arranged by the School.

Portsmouth Abbey Ravens teams compete interscholastically in seasonal sports. Boys' and girls' teams are formed in soccer, cross-country, basketball, ice hockey, lacrosse, tennis, and track. Girls compete in field hockey and softball, while boys play football and baseball; there are also coed teams in swimming, squash, golf, and sailing.

On weekends, boarding and day students enjoy a variety of activities such as dances, films, visits to art exhibits, student recitals, and whale-watching and ski excursions. The Dom Luke Childs lecture series attracts notable speakers to campus.

Among the traditional highlights on the school calendar are Music Festival, Brothers' and Sisters' Weekends, and the Spring Prom.

ADMISSION AND COSTS. Portsmouth Abbey School welcomes young people of above-average ability and excellent moral character who desire to benefit from the academic and cocurricular opportunities. Students are considered without regard to race, color, creed, or national or ethnic origin based on school records, test scores, and teacher recommendations. Candidates are required to take the Secondary School Admission Test or the Independent School Entrance Examination. Applicants whose files are completed by February 1 are notified of admission decisions by March 10.

Tuition for boarding students in 1999–2000 is $24,600; the fee for day students is $16,900. A four-year, full merit scholarship honoring the Reverend Hugh Diman is awarded on the basis of academic merit to a boarding student entering Grade 9. In addition, Portsmouth awards up to ten Abbey scholarships annually, each of which is a renewable $5000 merit grant that may supplement any need-based financial aid a student receives. The School annually makes available approximately $1,400,000 in financial aid based on demonstrated need. Tuition payment plans are offered.

Associate Headmaster: James M. DeVecchi, Ph.D.
Dean of Students: John Perreira
Dean of Student Life: Nancy Brzys
Director of Admissions: Timothy L. Trautman
Director of External Affairs: John Walsh '50
Director of Development/Alumni Affairs: Patrick Burke '86
Director of College Placement: Susan Wells
Treasurer: Katharine Crellin
Athletic Director: Peter Mack

St. Andrew's School   BARRINGTON

63 Federal Road, Barrington, RI 02806. 401-246-1230;
Fax 401-246-0510; E-mail tstevens@standrews-ri.org;
Web Site www.standrews-ri.org

ST. ANDREW'S SCHOOL in Barrington, Rhode Island, is a college preparatory school enrolling boarding and day boys and girls in Grades 9–12 and day students only in Grades 6–8. The St. Andrew's student is ready to experience success in a structured and supportive academic environment. Approximately half of the students have diagnosed learning disabilities or attention deficit disorders that have prevented them from achieving their potential. Barrington is a suburban community 10 miles southeast of Providence that overlooks Narragansett Bay.

The St. Andrew's motto states the School's mission: Helping Students Succeed. This has been St. Andrew's foremost goal since it was founded by the Reverend William Merrick Chapin, an Episcopal priest, in 1893 as a school for homeless boys. From

these simple beginnings, the School has steadfastly maintained the same sense of purpose and concern for the individual. It seeks to motivate each student to strive for his or her personal best—in the classroom, on the playing field, and in life—while offering strong faculty support in all areas of school endeavor. The curriculum is primarily designed to prepare students for college, emphasizing strong academic skills, study habits, and self-esteem. The 90 percent of St. Andrew's graduates who enter college give testimony to the efficacy of the School's programs.

St. Andrew's School is accredited by the New England Association of Schools and Colleges. It holds membership in the National Association of Independent Schools, the Association of Independent Schools of New England, the Independent School Association of Rhode Island, and the Council for Religion in Independent Schools. The Learning Disabilities Program is certified by the State of Rhode Island.

THE CAMPUS. St. Andrew's spacious 105-acre campus is reminiscent of a small New England village, with handsome stone, brick, and wooden buildings, ranging from modern to traditional, clustered around a central green. There are two academic buildings that house classrooms, a library and an athletic building with a gymnasium and basketball court. Boys and girls reside in separate dormitories supervised by faculty houseparents; the Head Master's family occupies the 18th-century Rectory. The original classroom building, constructed by the first students, is connected to the present-day chapel where students attend daily morning meetings. The Happy White Art Gallery exhibits the work of visiting artists as well as a broad variety of student artwork. The campus also includes playing fields, outdoor tennis courts, and a Project Adventure ropes course.

Emphasizing its strong commitment to math, science, the arts, and physical fitness, St. Andrew's School is engaged in an $8,500,000 building project to better serve students. The Math/Science Center and a second gymnasium will be completed in September 2000. The Arts Center is scheduled to be completed in time for the opening of school in 2001.

The networked campus provides access to outside library materials and the Internet. The technology director coordinates all computer facilities for both students and staff. The new Student Service Center houses the nurse's office, infirmary, classrooms, and additional office space. The Student Center provides a TV room, a game room, a lounge, and a school store.

THE FACULTY. John D. Martin assumed his duties as Head Master in 1996. A native of Chicopee, Massachusetts, he attended Northfield Mount Hermon School and earned a baccalaureate degree with honors in history from Tufts. Mr. Martin also holds an M.Ed. from American International College and an M.Div. from Yale University. His previous experience includes teaching at Tabor Academy and a chaplaincy and admissions work at The Peddie School and Sewickley Academy.

The Head Master and his wife, Sheila, have three young sons.

There are 42 teachers and 1 intern on the St. Andrew's faculty, many of whom live on campus. All hold baccalaureate degrees and 14 have earned advanced degrees, including one doctorate, from such colleges and universities as Barrington College, Brigham Young, Brown, Colorado College, Connecticut College, Dartmouth, Emerson, Fitchburg State, Fordham, General Theological Seminary, Hamilton, Haverford, Keene State, Lesley, Long Island University, Mount Holyoke, Mount St. Joseph, Providence College, Rhode Island College, Roger Williams, Rutgers, Seattle University, St. John's, St. Joseph College, State University of New York, Tufts, Valley City State, Wesleyan, Worcester Polytechnic, and the Universities of Connecticut, Maine, Massachusetts, Rhode Island, Rochester, Vermont, and Wisconsin.

STUDENT BODY. In 1999–2000, St. Andrew's School enrolls 155 students, 98 boys and 57 girls, in Grades 6–12 as follows: 8 in Grade 6, 9 in Grade 7, 14 in Grade 8, 28 in Grade 9, 37 in Grade 10, 30 in Grade 11, and 29 in Grade 12. Of these, 43 were boarders in Grades 9–12. They represent 11 states and three foreign countries and come from diverse ethnic, racial, and religious backgrounds.

ACADEMIC PROGRAM. The school year, operated on a trimester basis, runs from September to June, and includes Thanksgiving, Christmas, winter, and spring breaks. The student-teacher ratio is 5:1, and each student has a faculty advisor, ensuring individual attention and support. Advisors provide guidance in goal setting, self-monitoring, and developing strategies to become active learners. Parents, students, and advisors work together to create an academic program tailored to each child's own unique learning styles, capitalizing on strengths and overcoming deficiencies. The learning process incorporates a multisensory approach, hands-on experiences, one-on-one tutorials, and computer instruction.

To further academic progress, St. Andrew's offers specialized course work targeted to enhance the abilities of the learning-disabled student. The state-certified Resource Program, in operation for 20 years, addresses the needs of students with diagnosed mild language-based disabilities. Each student enrolled in Resource receives remedial assistance in the areas of reading, writing, and spelling. Resource faculty communicate with college preparatory faculty to help students in their regular classroom program. The FOCUS Program provides assistance for students with attentional disorders. The Tutorial Program provides one-on-one tutoring in Speech and Language and all of the major disciplines. An English as a Second Language program is available to international students.

To earn a St. Andrew's diploma, students must complete 24 credits as follows: 4 in English, 3 in social studies (including 1 in U.S. History), 3 in mathematics, and 2 in science (including 1 in

a lab science). The study of a foreign language is strongly advised. Seniors must take 5 credits, 4 of which are full-credit courses, and must pass the equivalent of 4 full credits.

Among the courses offered in the Upper School (Grades 9–12) are Reading/Writing Workshop, Introduction to Literature, American Studies, Multicultural Literature; Ancient History, European History, United States History, Ethics, Global Issues; Algebra Exploration I & II, Algebra I & II, Geometry, Consumer Math, Pre-Calculus, Calculus, Advanced Placement Calculus; General Science, Biology, Physics, Chemistry, Environmental Science; Spanish I–III; Art I–II, Ceramic Pottery, Drawing with the Masters, Photography, Web Design and Construction, Tech Repair, Computer Programming and Robotics, and Theater I–III. A study skills program, taught by faculty from the School's Special Education Department, is required for all students in Grades 9 and 10.

College counseling begins in the junior year and involves the student as well as parents, advisors, and other faculty. Ninety percent of St. Andrew's seniors continue their education at the college level, with the majority entering four- or two-year programs or technical schools. Since 1994, graduates have been accepted at such institutions as Alfred, Boston University, Clark, Culinary Institute of America, Drexel, Embry-Riddle Aeronautical University, Franklin Pierce, Heidelberg University, Hofstra, Johnson and Wales, Loyola, Lynchburg, Lynn, Merrimack, Michigan State, New England College, Salve Regina, Syracuse, Upsala, Wentworth Institute of Technology, West Virginia Wesleyan, and the Universities of Hartford, Massachusetts (Amherst, Dartmouth), Mississippi, North Carolina (Charlotte), and Rhode Island.

STUDENT ACTIVITIES. Every weekend, the School provides extracurricular activities for boarders. There are planned activities on Friday nights, Saturday afternoons and evenings, and Sundays. These activities build community, foster social interaction, cultivate skills and interests, and provide fun and physical fitness. The School's proximity to Providence, Newport, and Boston affords many opportunities to attend concerts, plays, and professional ballgames and visit museums and other attractions. Students may also go into Barrington for shopping and visits to the grocery store.

Athletic competition is considered an extension of classroom learning as it focuses on teamwork, sportsmanship, and interdependence among peers. There are boys' and girls' teams in soccer, basketball, tennis, cross-country, and lacrosse. Individual opportunities are available on campus for fencing and weight training, and off campus for swimming, horseback riding, and kayaking on Hundred Acre Cove, which borders the School's property. Project Adventure is an on-campus ropes course designed to build self-esteem and encourage problem solving, trust, and collaboration among students and faculty.

ADMISSION AND COSTS. St. Andrew's seeks young men and women of good character who are capable of performing at the grade level with effort and support. Small classes of 8–12, individual attention from teachers and advisors, and a structured environment are the hallmarks of St. Andrew's. The School does not admit youngsters who exhibit behavioral or emotional problems. Students are admitted without regard to race, religion, or national or ethnic origin. Admission is based on a campus visit and interview, letters of recommendation, previous transcripts, and standardized testing. Additional testing and information is required for participation in the Resource and FOCUS programs.

In 1999–2000, boarding tuition is $24,750; day tuition is $14,600. The Resource and FOCUS programs are an additional $6300; the Tutorial program is $3600. Books cost approximately $300. Financial aid of $760,000 was awarded last year based on need.

Director of Admission/Financial Aid: David S. Pinkham
Assistant Admission Director: Nikki Hamory
Special Education Director: Audrey Lacher-Katz
Academic Technology Director: Elizabeth Drew
Director of Student Life: Valerie Becker
Director of Athletics: Mike Hart
College Counselor: Mike Raffa
Director of Finances and Physical Plant: James M. Meehan

St. George's School   1896

372 Purgatory Road, P.O. Box 1910, Newport, RI 02840-0190.
  401-847-7565; Admissions 401-842-6600; Fax 401-842-6696;
  E-mail admissions_office@stgeorges.edu;
  Web Site http://www.stgeorges.edu

St. George's, a coeducational college preparatory school in the Episcopal tradition, enrolls 285 boarding and 45 day students in Forms III–VI. It aims to provide young people with the motivation and means to develop their unique talents for productive lives in the 21st century. Advanced Placement and honors courses and studies at sea aboard St. George's own marine research vessel enhance the academic program. Activities include community outreach, dance, drama, music groups, publications, and 45 interscholastic athletic teams. A $7,500,000 Center for the Arts was completed in September of 1999. Boarding Tuition: $25,400; Day Tuition: $16,000. Financial Aid: $1,600,000. Jay Doolittle is Director of Admission; Charles A. Hamblet is Head of School. *New England Association.*

St. Michael's Country Day School   1938

180 Rhode Island Avenue, Newport, RI 02840. 401-849-5970;
  Fax 401-849-7890; Web Site www.wsii.com/stmichaels

Located on a 7-acre campus, St. Michael's is a nondenominational, coeducational school enrolling nearly 225 children in Pre-Kindergarten–Grade 8. It aims to help students develop a strong, lifetime love of learning. Small classes, a supportive faculty, and a developmentally appropriate curriculum meet the academic needs of the youngest learners as well as those being prepared for the rigorous academic challenges beyond St. Michael's. French, computer and science labs, a recently computerized library, a school-based publishing house, and lively music, drama, arts, and athletic programs are available to all students. Tuition: $5200–$10,500. Whitney C. Slade (Tufts, B.A.; Harvard, M.Ed.) is Head of School.

The Wheeler School   1889

216 Hope Street, Providence, RI 02906. 401-421-8100;
  Fax 401-751-7674; Web Site http://www.wheelerschool.org

Wheeler, a college preparatory day school enrolling 680 girls and boys in Nursery–Grade 12, aims to provide a diverse academic experience, develop individual talents, and encourage involvement in School and world affairs. The traditional curriculum is enriched by electives, special-interest and computer center activities, and various sports. The Hamilton School at Wheeler, enrolling 65 boys and girls in Grades 1–8, serves high-potential, language-disabled students through a structured, multisensory approach applied to reading, spelling, and writing skills. Tuition: Wheeler—$7100–$14,200; Hamilton—$20,400. Financial Aid: $978,890. Jeanette Epstein is Director of Admission; William C. Prescott, Jr. (Harvard, A.B. 1957; Brown, M.A. 1962), is Headmaster. *New England Association.*

SOUTH CAROLINA

Addlestone Hebrew Academy   1956

1639 Wallenberg Boulevard, Charleston, SC 29407. 843-571-1105; Fax 843-571-6116

Addlestone Hebrew Academy is a child-oriented day school that seeks to develop children physically, socially, intellectually, emotionally, and spiritually as they take their place as young Jews in a pluralistic society. The Academy enrolls 155 students from 18 months to Grade 8. The comprehensive curriculum promotes high scholastic standards while incorporating the values and traditions of the Jewish faith in all aspects of life. Judaic studies, including Biblical commentary and Hebrew language, are emphasized equally with traditional liberal arts and sciences. Tuition: $2000–$6535. Financial aid is available. Jane Talbot (Early Childhood) and Verne Hawes (General Studies) are Vice Presidents; Rabbi Achiya Delouya (Yeshiva, B.A., M.S.) was appointed Principal in 1999. *Southern Association.*

Aiken Preparatory School   AIKEN

619 Barnwell Avenue, NW, Aiken, SC 29801. 803-648-3223; Fax 803-648-6482; Admissions E-mail apsadmit@scescape.net

AIKEN PREPARATORY SCHOOL in Aiken, South Carolina, is a boarding school, founded in 1916, for boys and girls in Grades 6 through 9 with a day program for students in four-year-old Kindergarten through Grade 9. Aiken (population 24,000) is 56 miles west of the state capital of Columbia and 17 miles east of Augusta, Georgia, which is served by major bus and air routes. The campus is easily accessible by car via Interstate Highway 20. The region enjoys a temperate climate, providing excellent year-round opportunities for outdoor recreation including golf, tennis, and equestrian sports.

The only junior boarding school in the southeastern United States, Aiken Prep continues the tradition of providing an intimate, structured, and supportive learning environment during the most crucial years of a child's intellectual and emotional development. The School relies upon small classes, individual attention, a strong advisor program, and academic rigor to prepare its students for future success at independent secondary schools or the college preparatory program in local public high schools.

A nonprofit institution, Aiken Preparatory School is governed by a self-perpetuating Board of Trustees, 18 in number, which meets three times a year. The School holds membership in the National Association of Independent Schools, the Southern Association of Independent Schools, the Junior Boarding Schools Association, the Federation of American and International Schools, and the Secondary School Admission Test Board. Its endowment currently stands at approximately $3,500,000.

THE CAMPUS. Aiken Prep is situated on a 10-acre wooded campus in the heart of the historic town of Aiken. Athletic facilities include a gymnasium, an outdoor swimming pool, tennis courts, and three playing fields. Students may enjoy golfing privileges at the nearby Palmetto Golf Club. The main building contains Lower School classrooms, two boys' dormitories, one girls' dormitory, five faculty apartments, a library, auditorium, dining room, school store, and administrative offices. Hall House (1997), a renovated home containing an additional girls' dormitory, was realized through the generous donation of an Aiken resident. It contains one faculty apartment and three dormitory rooms. In 1998, the School created additional space for six more boarding girls in the Main Building. A newly acquired and renovated Middle School building houses the majority of classrooms for that division as well as fully equipped science and computer labs.

THE FACULTY. In the spring of 1999, Aiken Prep's Board of Trustees announced the appointment of Donald W. Fudge as the School's seventh Headmaster. Mr. Fudge has held many administrative positions with independent schools, including Headmaster of The Colorado Springs School and Gould Academy, and Assistant Headmaster of Woodmere Academy. Mr. Fudge has also had 11 years of experience as a general consultant, guiding schools in all areas of management. He holds degrees from Princeton University and Syracuse University. Mr. Fudge and his family live on campus and are involved in all aspects of the school community.

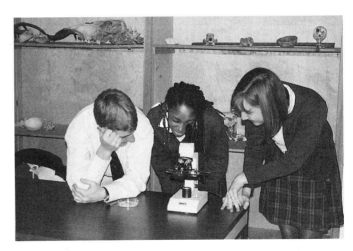

There are 33 full-time and 16 part-time faculty members, 9 of whom live in campus housing. They hold degrees from such diverse institutions as Bethany, Central Connecticut State, Clemson, Colby, Columbia, Georgetown, Grinnell, Harvard, Kenyon, Princeton, State University of New York, Wayne State, and the Universities of Alabama, Illinois, Maine, Michigan, North Carolina, Rhode Island, South Carolina, and Texas.

STUDENT BODY. In 1999–2000, Aiken Prep enrolled 160 students. The Middle School (Grades 6–9) consists of 68 boarding and day students.

In recent years, boarding students have enrolled from California, Florida, Georgia, Maryland, Massachusetts, Minnesota, New Hampshire, North Carolina, South Carolina, and South

Dakota as well as from Japan, Mexico, Morocco, South Africa, and South Korea.

ACADEMIC PROGRAM. The School operates on a trimester basis with the year beginning in early September and ending in early June. The academic calendar includes Thanksgiving, winter, and spring breaks. An average class size of 10–12 students allows for individualized attention and a nurturing environment that challenges the average to above-average student.

A typical day in the Middle School runs from 8:00 A.M. to 4:30 P.M. and includes eight academic class periods, advisory/assembly time, a midmorning break, and a family-style lunch as well as athletics and other extracurricular activities in the afternoon.

Academic classes include language arts, mathematics, social studies, science, and Spanish. The Middle School curriculum emphasizes mastery of oral and written communication, reading, mathematical reasoning, research, critical thinking, problem solving, independent and cooperative learning, and good study habits. Classes in art, music, computer, and life skills complement the core academic courses. The academic day runs from 8:00 A.M. to 3:00 P.M.

Lower School hours run from 8:00 A.M. until noon for four-year-old Kindergarten, 8:00 A.M. until 2:30 P.M. for five-year-old Kindergarten, and 8:00 A.M. until 3:00 P.M. for Grades 1–5. Instruction is enriched with innovative programs and activities that include Whole Language, Activities Integrating Math and Science, McCracken, Superstar Math, Book It, and Accelerated Reader as well as a wide variety of field trips that emphasize hands-on experiences. Lower School students receive art, music, computer, library, and physical education instruction each week. Exposure to the Spanish language begins in Grade 1.

A Learning Strategies Program is available for both Middle and Lower School students in need of one-on-one assistance in reading, mathematics, written expression, personal organization, and study skills as well as for the capable student with minimal learning differences. The English as a Second Language Program provides Aiken Prep's international students with individual support and assistance as they adapt to a new culture and language.

In recent years, Aiken Prep graduates have matriculated at a number of leading secondary boarding schools including Asheville, Baylor, Choate Rosemary Hall, Darlington, Episcopal, Kimball Union, Lawrenceville, McCallie, Middlesex, Northfield

Mount Hermon, Phillips Academy, Rabun Gap–Nacoochee, Westover, and Woodberry Forest.

STUDENT ACTIVITIES. Aiken Preparatory School offers a variety of programs and activities designed to promote self-reliance, integrity, and cooperation in its students.

All Middle School students and Lower School boarders are required to participate four days per week in either the School's organized team sports or physical education programs. Aiken Preparatory School fields varsity and junior varsity teams in soccer, volleyball, basketball, baseball, tennis, and golf. The physical education program exposes students to both traditional and nontraditional activities—such as cooperative games, air rifle shooting, Ultimate Frisbee, rock climbing, and touch rugby—in a challenging yet cooperative environment.

On weekends, boarding students enjoy numerous organized activities, including mountain biking, fishing, and canoeing as well as trips to local and regional sporting events, fairs, concerts, the beach, and malls. Aiken Prep has a long equestrian tradition, and boarders may take riding lessons on Sunday afternoons. Eighth and ninth graders may earn "town privileges," which allow them to visit the historic center of Aiken. Its many stores, restaurants, and movie theaters are all within walking distance from the School.

As hosts, day families provide boarders the extra security of a home away from home by sharing meals, celebrating holidays, and commemorating special occasions such as birthdays.

ADMISSION AND COSTS. Aiken Preparatory School welcomes students of sound character and academic ability based on previous scholastic records, recommendations, and a campus interview.

In 1999–2000, boarding tuition is $19,000 for seven days and $16,700 for five days; day tuition ranges from $3100 in four-year-old Kindergarten to $6000 in Grades 6–9. Need-based financial aid in the amount of $102,900 was awarded to 26 students. In addition, six merit scholarships were awarded to day students who passed an exam, had an interview, and met the criteria outlined by the committee. Aiken Prep subscribes to the School and Student Service for Financial Aid and uses their formula to determine financial need.

Headmaster: Donald W. Fudge
Director of Development: Mary P. Buxton
Director of Admission: Keira E. Murphy
Director of Middle School: Susan J. Appleby
Director of Lower School: Lizabeth C. Zefting
Director of Technology: Kathleen H. Christopher
Director of Athletics: Dacre C. Stoker
Business Manager: Karen A. Mahan

Beaufort Academy   1969

*240 Sams Point Road, Beaufort, SC 29902. 843-524-3393;
    Fax 843-524-1171; E-mail jrutter@islc.net*

Beaufort Academy is a coeducational, college preparatory day school enrolling 400 students in Pre-Kindergarten–Grade 12. The school aims to provide a superior education based on academics, athletics, the arts, and student activities that promote leadership and service to others. Each student's program, while encompassing the traditional disciplines, is tailored to meet individual goals, needs, and interests. Foreign languages begin in Pre-Kindergarten, and there are Advanced Placement and honors courses in most Upper School subjects. Students take part in team sports at several levels; other activities include student government, Mock Trial, publications, and drama. Tuition: $3900–$5100. Mr. J. Wood Rutter (University of North Carolina, M.A.) is Headmaster. *Southern Association.*

Ashley Hall   1909

172 Rutledge Avenue, Charleston, SC 29403-5877.
843-722-4088; Fax 843-720-2868;
E-mail enrollment@ashleyhall.org;
Web Site www.ashleyhallschool.org

Ashley Hall enrolls 535 female students in Kindergarten–Grade 12 and boys and girls ages 2–5 in the Ross Early Childhood Center. The fully networked campus features state-of-the-art technology in classrooms, labs, and media center. Language, computer, University of Chicago's *Everyday Math* program, and athletics begin in Kindergarten. Advanced Placement and satellite courses enhance the college preparatory school curriculum. Age-appropriate courses in sciences, social studies, and arts are offered. College placement is 100 percent, and students regularly receive early acceptance to first-choice institutions. Coeducational after-school and summer programs are offered. Tuition: $6550–$8750. Elizabeth H. Peters is Enrollment Director; Margaret C. MacDonald is Headmistress.

Cambridge Academy   1968

103 Eastman Drive, Greenwood, SC 29649. 864-229-2875;
Fax 864-229-6712; Web Site www.cambridgeacademy.org

Cambridge Academy is a coeducational day school that concentrates on providing the best college preparatory education possible to its students. Enrolling 382 young people from diverse backgrounds in Kindergarten 4–Grade 12, the school has a 100 percent college acceptance of its graduates. The liberal arts program nurtures a love of learning in an atmosphere of academic freedom that is governed by a school-wide Honor Code. Advanced Placement courses, Senior Project, and educational field trips enrich the program. Students participate in "no-cut" athletics, school government, publications, and community service. Tuition: $1787–$4646. Financial aid is available. Jamie Lyles is Director of Admissions; Steven Landry (University of Connecticut, B.A., M.A., Ph.D.) is Headmaster. *Southern Association.*

Charleston Day School   1937

15 Archdale Street, Charleston, SC 29401-1918. 843-722-7791;
Fax 843-720-2143; Web Site www.charlestondayschool.org

Charleston Day School, from its historic location, offers an accredited, coeducational experience to 186 students in Grades 1–8. The school environment fosters scholarship, integrity, self-esteem, and responsibility. In all grades, a core curriculum is enhanced by French, computer, art, music, and physical education. Grades 7–8 may take Latin and advanced math courses, including Honors Algebra I. Special academic programs, team sports, community service, and fine arts productions enrich the program. The middle school advisory system is designed to meet the needs of emerging adolescents. Tuition: $7400–$7600. Jane S. Cook is Director of Admissions; Gregory J. O'Melia is Headmaster.

Christ Church Episcopal School   1959

Parish Campus: 10 N. Church Street, Greenville, SC 29601.
864-271-8784; Fax 864-242-0879
Wenwood Campus: 555 Wenwood Road, Greenville, SC 29607.
864-299-1522; Fax 864-299-8861
Cavalier Campus: 245 Cavalier Drive, Greenville, SC 29607.
864-299-1522; Fax 864-299-8861

This coeducational, independent day school serves 870 students of all faiths. The Lower School (Primer–Grade 4) is on the Parish campus; the Middle (Grades 5–8) and Upper (Grades 9–12) schools are housed on the 68-acre Wenwood and Cavalier campuses, respectively. Christ Church Episcopal School features small classes, 19 Advanced Placement courses, fine and performing arts, and chapel, and fields 35 athletic teams. Since 1981, 89 seniors have been National Merit Finalists or Semifinalists. Activities include athletics, community service, and musical and dramatic productions. Tuition and Fees: $5400–$8575. Limited financial aid is available. Pam Matthews is Director of Admissions; Ellen Y. Moceri (Washington University, B.A., M.A.) is Head of School. *Southern Association.*

Hammond School   COLUMBIA

854 Galway Lane, Columbia, SC 29209. 803-776-0295

Hammond school in Columbia, South Carolina, is a college preparatory day school enrolling boys and girls in Preschool through Grade 12. The School is located in a residential district in the southeastern section of Columbia (population 250,000). The city is the state's capital and the home of the University of South Carolina, and has a variety of cultural and educational resources that are enjoyed by students and faculty on field trips. In addition, the city affords access to both mountains and beaches within two-hour drives west or east. Public buses serve the area near the campus.

Hammond School was founded as Hammond Academy in 1966 by a group of parents interested in developing a college preparatory school to serve the Columbia area. It opened with an enrollment of 260. Since that time, it has more than doubled to its current enrollment of 727. In 1989, the Board of Trustees changed the name to Hammond School and voted to adopt "a global focus" to prepare students for the "larger" world they will be entering as adults.

The global focus begins in the earliest grades and is developed continuously in all subject areas. Each year, the School selects a country to study and gears its programs toward the people and culture of that land. In addition, members of Grade 10 travel to Belize, Central America, for a ten-day visit each spring. The School's mission is to provide students with the finest college preparatory curriculum, while inculcating in them an understanding of other peoples and cultures.

The School is a nonprofit organization governed by a self-perpetuating Board of 25 Trustees including parents, alumni, and community leaders. The Board meets monthly during the academic year. Some 2200 alumni provide financial support for the School.

Hammond is accredited by the Southern Association of Colleges and Schools and the National Association for the Education of the Young Child. It holds membership in the National Association of Independent Schools, the Educational Records Bureau, the National Association of College Admission Counselors, the Southern Association of College Admission Counselors, and other professional organizations.

THE CAMPUS. The School occupies 28 wooded acres with six outdoor tennis courts, a football/baseball field complex, two practice fields, and a soccer/track and field complex that was completed in 1992.

The eight principal buildings provide 60 classrooms, four laboratories, a primitive technology center, a music studio, two art studios, two guidance centers, a college guidance center, two dining halls, and two libraries containing more than 26,000 volumes. Rutledge, Calhoun, and Bostic halls were completed when the School opened in 1966, and the Gymnasium/Auditorium was added a year later. Lee and Marion Halls, which house the Lower School, were built in 1970; the Middle School facility was completed in 1988.

The plant is owned by the School.

THE FACULTY. Herbert B. Barks, Jr., a graduate of the University of Chattanooga (B.A.) and Columbia Seminary (M.Div.), was appointed Headmaster in 1989. He formerly served for 17 years as Headmaster of The Baylor School in Chattanooga, Tennessee, and spent the year prior to his appointment at Hammond as a national advocate for the United Jewish Appeal. An ordained Presbyterian minister who studied theology at the University of Hamburg and received an honorary doctorate in Divinity from Kings College, Dr. Barks has served parishes in Tennessee, Louisiana, California, and Virginia. He is the author of four books and has served on the boards of a number of institutes and foundations.

Fifty-nine women and 23 men are full-time members of the faculty. They hold 84 baccalaureate degrees, including 28 from the University of South Carolina; 5 from Clemson; 4 from Columbia College; and 3 each from College of Charleston and Furman. Other representative institutions include Baylor, Bloomsburg University, College of William and Mary, Converse, Duke, Florida State, George Washington, Georgia Southern, Newcomb College of Tulane, Ohio Wesleyan, Presbyterian, Sewanee, Winthrop, Wittenberg, and the Universities of Paris, Tennessee, Vermont, and Warwick. Faculty also hold 37 advanced degrees including 4 doctorates from Kings College and the Universities of Paris and South Carolina.

Fringe benefits for faculty include medical and dental insurance, a retirement plan, Social Security, support for continued education, and leaves of absence.

A medical doctor and a registered nurse provide health services on campus.

STUDENT BODY. In 1999–2000, Hammond School enrolls 727 boys and girls in Preschool–Grade 12. The enrollments are distributed as follows: 24 in Preschool, 50 in five-year-old Kindergarten, 54 in Grade 1, 51 in Grade 2, 66 in Grade 3, 58 in Grade 4, 56 in Grade 5, 49 in Grade 6, 55 in Grade 7, 57 in Grade 8, 59 in Grade 9, 58 in Grade 10, 46 in Grade 11, and 44 in Grade 12. The students come from Columbia and nearby communities. The School follows a nondiscriminatory admissions policy and has a minority component of approximately 7 percent. Most students are of various Christian denominations; however, Jewish, Muslim, and other faiths are also represented. Seventy-four students receive financial aid.

ACADEMIC PROGRAM. The academic year, divided into semesters, begins in late August and ends in late May. Vacations are scheduled for two and a half weeks at Christmas and one week in the spring. Classes are held five days a week and are scheduled in seven 45-minute periods between 8:00 A.M. and 3:00 P.M. A 30-minute morning break is used for assemblies, advisor meetings, and activities. Free periods are used for special classes in the Lower School, supervised study halls in the Middle School, and free time in the Upper School. The average class size is 15. Students needing additional help use the Skills Centers or participate in tutorials after classes in the Middle and Upper schools, all at no extra charge. Grades are sent to parents at the end of each quarter.

The Lower School (Preschool–Grade 5) program presents a nontraditional learning environment in which teachers can employ new approaches. The curriculum includes English, language arts, Spanish, social studies, science, natural history, computers, art, music, drama, library, and physical education. The Middle School (Grades 6–8) seeks to build a sense of community and to develop individual self-esteem. Latin is added to the curriculum, and the English and history sequences focus on important figures whose lives may serve as models of what students can become. Organized activities are an important complement to the program.

In the Upper School (Grades 9–12), the emphasis is on college preparation, personal development, and awareness. Studies of other peoples and cultures, which begin in the lower grades, culminate in discussions of world issues in the Upper School.

To graduate from the Upper School, a minimum of 22 credits must be earned including the following: English 4; foreign language 3; history 4, including World Cultures, United States History, World History, and Government/Economics; mathematics 4, including Algebra 1–2 and Geometry; science 3, including Biology, Chemistry, and Physics; Physical Education 1; Art 1; and electives 2.

Among the courses offered are American, British, and World Literature, Honors Literature 1–2; French 1–5, Spanish 1–4; Algebra 1–2, Geometry, Advanced Algebra/Trigonometry, Statistics, Finite Math, Pre-Calculus, Calculus; Biology 1–2,

Chemistry 1–2, Physics 1–2; Psychology, History of Religion, Government/Economics; Art 1–2, Curricular Theatre; and Computer Programming, and Word Processing. Advanced Placement courses are offered in English, Spanish, French, United States History, Modern European History, Calculus, Biology, Chemistry, Physics, and Studio Art.

All 44 members of the Class of 1999 are attending college, and 64 percent of the class earned scholarships. Graduates are attending Buffalo State, Clemson 2, Coastal Carolina, College of Charleston 4, College of William & Mary, Columbia International University, Converse 2, Furman 3, Georgia Institute of Technology, Guilford, Harvard, Midlands Technical College, North Carolina State, Sweet Briar, Wake Forest, Washington and Lee 3, Wheaton, Wofford 7, and the Universities of North Carolina, South Carolina 8, and Virginia 2.

STUDENT ACTIVITIES. Students elect representatives from Grades 9–12 and a president and vice-president from the senior class to the Student Government, which serves as liaison to the administration and coordinates student services and other extracurricular events.

Other organized activities are: newspaper, yearbook, Civitans, Civinettes, Red Circle, Creative Writing, Outdoors, Astronomy, Community Service, Film, and Spirit clubs.

Hammond School is a member of the South Carolina Independent School Association and fields teams that compete against other private schools within the conference as well as some public school opponents in football, basketball, baseball, track, cross-country, soccer, tennis, wrestling, and golf for boys. Girls compete in volleyball, basketball, softball, track, cross-country, soccer, tennis, swimming, and golf. Intramural competition is offered in basketball and softball. Life sports and exercise programs are initiated through physical education classes, and the outdoor program provides canoeing, hiking, and rock climbing.

Special social events on the school calendar are Homecoming, Spirit Week, and the Junior-Senior Dance. Parents participate in the Parents Association Auction, Dads Barbecue, Open Houses, and the Polly Howser Fine Arts Lecture series.

ADMISSION AND COSTS. Hammond School seeks boys and girls of above-average intelligence, with diverse interests and a willingness to work hard in a college preparatory program. Approximately 130 new students are admitted annually, with most entering Preschool, Kindergarten, and Grades 1, 6, and 9. Some students are accepted in other classes if vacancies exist. Admissions are based on academic records, recommendations, a personal interview, and an entrance examination.

Tuition for 1999–2000 is as follows: $4200 in Kindergarten, $6600 in Grades 1–5, $7450 in Grades 6–8, and $7950 in Grades 9–12. Tuition payment plans are available. Hammond belongs to the School Scholarship Service and annually awards $280,000 in financial aid, based on need.

Director of Admission: Julia S. Moore
Director of Development: Amy E. Stone
Assistant Head/College Counselor: Adeline H. Lundy
Business Manager: Karen M. Dickey
Director of Athletics: Philip N. Sandifer
Upper School Head: Paul Ragan
Middle School Head: Rae McPherson
Lower School Head: Robert E. Davis

Hilton Head Preparatory School   1978

8 Fox Grape Road, Hilton Head Island, SC 29928. 843-671-2286; Fax 843-671-7624; Web Site www.hiltonheadisland.com/hhprep.htm

Hilton Head Preparatory School, enrolling 415 day students in Grades 1–12, offers an academic program designed to challenge each individual to reach his or her highest potential. Learning and character are nurtured through a curriculum that integrates the liberal arts and sciences, technology, and moral and ethical values. Accelerated, honors, and Advanced Placement are available, while a Learning Resource Program provides added support for college-bound youngsters with minor learning difficulties. Diverse activities include music groups, drama, publications, service organizations, and varsity athletics. Tuition: $7250–$8350. Margaret R. Stupinsky is Director of Admissions; Robert W. H. Byrd (University of the South, B.A.; Vanderbilt University, M.A.) is Head of School. *Southern Association.*

Pinewood Preparatory School   1952

1114 Orangeburg Road, Summerville, SC 29483. 843-873-1643; Fax 843-821-4257; Web Site www.pride-net.com/pinewood

Pinewood Preparatory School, enrolling 450 boys and girls in K-4–Grade 12, offers academic and cocurricular programs to develop each student to full intellectual, social, artistic, and athletic potential. The curriculum is designed to meet the needs of college-bound students and, to that end, includes programs for the gifted and talented as well as for able students with learning differences. One hundred percent of Pinewood graduates are accepted into college. Information technology and values education are integrated throughout the program, and students abide by an honor code. Among the popular activities are interscholastic sports and interest clubs. Tuition: $2225–$5775. Dr. Carolyn Baechtle is Assistant Headmaster; Glyn Cowlishaw is Headmaster.

Porter-Gaud School   1867

300 Albemarle Road, Charleston, SC 29407-7593. 843-556-3620; Fax 843-556-7404 (Upper School); 843-556-3376; Fax 843-766-3945 (Lower School); Web Site www.portergaud.edu

A coeducational day school with historic ties to the Episcopal Church, Porter-Gaud enrolls 826 students in Grades 1–12. The college preparatory curriculum features numerous Advanced Placement courses; activities include three publications, 11 varsity sports, community service, eight choral groups, drama, debate, and various clubs. Each classroom has an EtherNet connection, an Internet-accessible Macintosh with multimedia capability, and a color TV for presentations. Facilities include three computer labs, a Science, Information, and Technology Center, and an Athletic Center with a 1000-seat gym (1999). Tuition: $7810–$8965. Financial Aid: $70,800. Patricia A. Graham is Director of Admissions; Stephen R. Blanchard (Oklahoma City, B.A.; North Texas State, M.Ed.) is Headmaster. *Southern Association.*

The Spartanburg Day School   1957

1701 Skylyn Drive, Spartanburg, SC 29307. 864-582-7539;
Fax 864-948-0026

The Spartanburg Day School is an independent, coeducational, college preparatory school for motivated, above average students in Pre-Kindergarten–Grade 12. The Day School's academic and athletic programs are designed to aid in the development of students in an environment that nurtures the best in each young person. Extracurricular activities include sports, several publications, drama, debate, and service clubs. A new state-of-the-art computer system provides all students with the most current computer technology in their classrooms. Tuition: $3615–$7095. Financial Aid: $75,000. Charles H. Skipper (Old Dominion, B.A.; George Mason, M.Ed., Ph.D.) was appointed Headmaster in 1999. *Southern Association.*

Trident Academy   1972

1455 Wakendaw Road, Mount Pleasant, SC 29464. 843-884-7046;
Admissions 843-884-3494; Fax 843-881-8320;
Admissions Fax 843-884-1483; E-mail adminis@bellsouth.net;
Web Site www.tridentacademy.com

Trident Academy, providing special education for learning-disabled students, enrolls approximately 115 students. This includes mostly day and some boarding boys and girls in Kindergarten–Grade 12 and a Postgraduate year. A 1:1 or 2:1 language-therapy program and a structured, individualized learning environment foster academic and personal development. The Upper School offers thorough preparation for post-secondary education. Sports, publications, Student Council, and clubs are offered. Participation in athletics or community service is encouraged. A summer day program provides tutoring. Tuition: $8380–$16,680. Financial aid is available. Bachman Smith is Director of Admissions; Myron C. Harrington, Jr. (The Citadel), is Headmaster. *Southern Association.*

TENNESSEE

Battle Ground Academy   1889

P.O. Box 1889, Franklin, TN 37065-1889. 615-794-3501;
Fax 615-790-3933; E-mail bgahdmastr@aol.com;
Web Site www.bganet.com

Battle Ground Academy, located 15 miles south of Nashville, is a college preparatory day school enrolling 940 students in Pre-Kindergarten–Grade 12. It aims to provide students with a sound foundation for higher education and to foster their moral and physical development as well. Advanced Placement courses are available. Athletics, forensics, student publications, Key Club, and service organizations are some of the activities. A summer program offers remedial work for students from the Academy, computer studies, sports camps, and world history. Tuition: $5750–$7700. Extras: $700. Financial Aid: $250,000. Steve Lape is Director of Admission; Ronald H. Griffeth (University of Georgia, Ed.D.) was appointed Headmaster in 1990. *Southern Association.*

Brentwood Academy   1969

219 Granny White Pike, Brentwood, TN 37027. 615-373-0611;
Fax 615-377-3709; E-mail admission@brentwoodacademy.com;
Web Site www.brentwoodacademy.com

Brentwood Academy is a coeducational, college preparatory school dedicated to nurturing and challenging the whole person—body, mind, and spirit—to the glory of God. Located 5 miles south of Nashville, Brentwood Academy serves 550 students in Grades 6–12. Cocurricular activities include the Student Leadership Team, Fellowship of Christian Athletes, Winterim, Big Sisters-Big Brothers Program for new students, athletics, forensics, drama, chorus, Academy Singers, clubs, and publications. A summer program is available. Tuition: $7950. Financial Aid: $200,000. William B. Brown, Jr. (Vanderbilt, B.S. 1958; Middle Tennessee State, M.Ed. 1968), was appointed Headmaster in 1969. *Southern Association.*

Briarcrest Christian School System, Inc.   1972

Main Campus: 6000 Briarcrest Avenue, Memphis, TN 38120.
901-765-4600; Fax 901-765-4667;
E-mail tjhillen@briarcrest.com; Web Site www.briarcrest.com
Ridgeway Campus: 2500 Ridgeway Road, Memphis, TN 38119.

Founded as an alternative to existing private and public programs, Briarcrest seeks to combine academic excellence and a Christian learning environment. Over 1500 boys and girls from three-year-old Kindergarten to Grade 12 are enrolled. College preparatory and general curricula are offered, and students of varying abilities are accommodated through a learning-differences program and Advanced Placement courses. Offerings in the fine arts and involvement in athletics, theater, graphic arts, and music are among the activities. Summer activities are available. Tuition: $4020–$6050. Financial Aid: $90,000. Joyce Millard is Admission Officer; Timothy J. Hillen (Eastern Michigan, M.A. 1975; University of Wisconsin, Ed.S. 1983) was named President in 1996. *Southern Association.*

Bright School   1913

1950 Hixson Pike, Chattanooga, TN 37405-9968. 423-267-8546;
Fax 423-265-0025; Web Site www.brightschool.com

Tennessee's oldest independent elementary school enrolls 400 boys and girls in Pre-Kindergarten–Grade 6. Bright School is dedicated to the academic, artistic, and physical development of each student and endeavors to be a happy place where children gladly come. The School emphasizes citizenship, the joy of learning, and self-confidence. An advanced curriculum encourages children to think critically and reason logically and provides opportunities for growth in music, art, manual arts, Spanish, and computer. After-school activities include dance, martial arts, orchestra, and handbells. Most graduates enter local independent secondary schools. Tuition: $6675–$7225. Financial Aid: $90,000. Peggy Enloe is Admissions Director; Michael G. Murphy is Headmaster. *Southern Association.*

Christ Methodist Day School   1958

411 Grove Park, Memphis, TN 38117. 901-683-6873;
Fax 901-761-5759; E-mail dfox@cmdsmemphis.org

Established by Christ United Methodist Church, Christ Methodist Day School enrolls more than 425 boys and girls in Pre-Kindergarten through Grade 6. The School is committed to the task of helping each child develop to his or her potential academically, physically, socially, emotionally, and spiritually. The traditional curriculum is designed to provide a sound academic foundation supplemented by Bible, Spanish, music, physical education, art, and computer studies. A complete recreational sports program, before- and after-school care, and a summer program are also available. Tuition: $1890–$4725. Judi Taylor is Admissions Director; David W. Fox (Memphis State, B.S. 1967, M.Ed. 1977; Memphis Theological Seminary, M.A.R. 1978) was appointed Headmaster in 1984. *Southern Association.*

The Ensworth School   1958

211 Ensworth Avenue, Nashville, TN 37205. 615-383-0661;
Fax 615-269-4840

Ensworth is an elementary day school enrolling 558 boys and girls in Pre-First–Grade 8. Established to prepare students for independent secondary schools, it strives to teach them to work hard, get along with others, take responsibility, and develop sound moral values. The academic program is enhanced by athletics, art, music, and French at all levels. Latin and Spanish are also offered in Grades 7 and 8. A life skills course is included in Pre-First–Grade 8. Drama and Outdoor Education are among the activities. Summer camp programs are offered. Tuition: $7050. Financial Aid: $125,000. Nathan Sawyer (Peabody College, B.A. 1957) is Headmaster.

Episcopal School of Knoxville   1994

110 Sugarwood Drive, Knoxville, TN 37932. 423-777-9032;
Fax 423-777-9034; E-mail secor@esknoxville.org

Episcopal School of Knoxville serves 54 boys and girls from various faiths as day students in Kindergarten–Grade 5. A grade will be added each year through Grade 8 with an anticipated enrollment of 325 youngsters on a new campus now under construction. The School offers a liberal arts curriculum underscored by Christian values in the Episcopal tradition. Daily chapel services provide spiritual enrichment. French, music, art, and physical education complement the core program, which emphasizes basic skills in language arts, math, science, and social studies. Extended-day care is offered. Tuition: $7000. Financial Aid: $21,000. Ms. Kae Bridges is Director of Admissions; Mr. James J. Secor III (Virginia Wesleyan, B.A.; James Madison, M.Ed.) is Headmaster.

First Christian Academy   1998

4800 Franklin Road, Nashville, TN 37220. 615-832-1004;
*   Fax 615-832-0840*

First Christian Academy, an outreach of the First Christian Church, serves 36 boys and girls in Kindergarten–Grade 3. The nondenominational Christian school provides a strong academic program for average and above-average students. The dedicated faculty recognizes and develops each child's unique talents and gifts within the classroom setting. Each day begins with morning chapel. First Christian Academy's facilities include science, art, and computer labs, a gymnasium, music and choral room, chapel, cafeteria, performance stage, and a 5000-volume library. Before- and after-school care is available. Tuition: $4100. Financial aid is available. Catherine W. Brewer (Middle Tennessee State, M.Ed., Ed.S.) is Head of School.

Franklin Road Academy   1971

4700 Franklin Road, Nashville, TN 37220. 615-832-8845;
*   Fax 615-834-4137; E-mail AkinW@fra.pvt.k12.tn.us;*
*   Web Site www.fra.pvt.k12.tn.us*

Franklin Road Academy is an independent, Christian, coeducational day school enrolling 890 students in Prekindergarten 4–Grade 12. The school prepares students intellectually for higher levels of education while also providing programs and facilities for their total development. While emphasis is on traditional disciplines, arts, and physical education, students are encouraged to participate in sports, concert and pep bands, student government, publications, and interest clubs. Tuition: $3900–$7515. John R. Younger (Middle Tennessee State, B.S.; George Peabody, M.A.) was appointed Headmaster in 1999. *Southern Association.*

Grace-St. Luke's Episcopal School   1947

246 South Belvedere Boulevard, Memphis, TN 38104.
*   901-278-0200*

Grace-St. Luke's Episcopal, enrolling 457 boys and girls age 3–Grade 8, aims to motivate students academically within a nurturing community that reflects Christian values according to the Episcopal tradition. The curriculum is student-centered to address the changing needs of children as they enter new stages of development. Religious studies, the fine arts, and physical education complement the core disciplines. In the Middle School, students are involved in Honor Council, Student Council, performance groups, yearbook, newspaper, a creative writing magazine, and athletics. Enrichment, after-school, and summer programs are provided. Tuition: $3975–$6900. Nancy Golden is Director of Admissions; Thomas A. Beazley (University of Pennsylvania, M.S.) is Headmaster. *Southern Association.*

Harding Academy   1971

170 Windsor Drive, Nashville, TN 37205. 615-356-5510;
*   Fax 615-356-0441; Web Site www.hardingacademy.org*

Harding Academy is a nonsectarian school enrolling 416 students in Kindergarten–Grade 8. The Lower School (K–5) includes 14 spacious classrooms and a Discovery Lab, featuring an indoor "creek" in a greenhouse environment. A newly renovated Middle School Quadrangle (1998) accommodates Grades 6–8. Library, reading, and computer specialists work with all students on the fully networked campus. Band, music, physical education, art, and dance are integral to the curriculum. Varsity teams compete in the Harpeth Valley Athletic Conference. Extended-day care and summer camp programs are optional. Tuition: $7590. Financial aid is available. Kasey Gatlin is Director of Admission; Donald S. Schwartz (Texas Christian, B.S.; Tulane, M.S.Ed.) is Head of School. *Southern Association.*

The Harpeth Hall School   1951

3801 Hobbs Road, Nashville, TN 37215-0207. 615-297-9543;
*   Fax 615-297-0480; E-mail wild@hh.harpethhall.com;*
*   Web Site http://harpethhall.com*

Harpeth Hall, Nashville's only independent school for girls, is committed to a progressive educational program, one that preserves time-honored traditions while preparing young women for leadership in the 21st century. Enrolling 539 students in Grades 5–12, Harpeth Hall is a leader in integrating technology throughout all disciplines. Small classes and a 9:1 student-teacher ratio ensure that each girl participates actively in the learning process. The School offers a rich fine arts program and outstanding varsity teams. A month-long opportunity for nontraditional studies, off-campus work/study, and academic travel enhances the Upper School education. Tuition: $9750–$9975. Financial aid is available. Dianne Wild is Director of Admissions; Ann M. Teaff is Head of School. *Southern Association.*

Hutchison School   MEMPHIS

1740 Ridgeway Road, Memphis, TN 38119. 901-761-2220;
*   Web Site www.hutchisonschool.org*

Hutchison school in Memphis, Tennessee, is a college preparatory day school for girls in Pre-Kindergarten (3K)–Grade 12.

In 1900, Mary Grimes Hutchison began tutoring Richard Halliburton, later a well-known author, and friends in the Halliburton home. In 1902, Miss Hutchison's School officially formed its first class, enrolling both boys and girls. Soon thereafter, enrollment was limited to girls. Miss Hutchison's School graduated its first senior class in 1912 and, in 1923, was the first girls' school in Tennessee to be accredited by the Southern Association of Secondary Schools and Colleges. As enrollment increased, the School was moved three times before a permanent campus was built on Union Avenue in 1925; it remained at that location until 1964, when it was moved to the present campus.

Miss Hutchison sought to establish a college preparatory school. Today, Hutchison is a nonsectarian school where the administration, faculty, and students come to create an atmosphere of Judeo-Christian concern and behavior, stressing high principles of character and consideration of others. In keeping with its founding purpose, Hutchison School is dedicated to academic excellence and to the parallel development of the mind, body, and spirit as it educates young women for success in college and for lives of integrity and responsible citizenship.

Hutchison School is a nonprofit corporation directed by a

Board of 21 Trustees. Hutchison is accredited by the Southern Association of Colleges and Schools; it holds membership in the National Association of Independent Schools, the Southern Association of Independent Schools, the National Coalition of Girls' Schools, and other professional organizations.

THE CAMPUS. School activities are housed in the Martha Robinson Early Childhood Center, the Dobbs Classroom Building, Olivia Brinkley Senior Kindergarten, Robinson Junior Kindergarten, Brinkley Administration, and Buxton-Wiener Fine Arts Center. These facilities contain classrooms, two libraries, laboratories, art and music rooms, computer labs, conference rooms, the chapel, offices, dining hall, the Little Theater, and the 650-seat Wiener Theater. The Dunavant gymnasium, the Dunavant-Welford Tennis Center, and a soccer field are used for the athletic program. The Head of School's home is also located on the 50-acre campus.

THE FACULTY. Interim Head of School Louis H. Hayden holds a bachelor's degree from Memphis State University, a Master's of Divinity from Virginia Theological Seminary, and a Master of Sacred Theology from the University of the South. He has 34 years of experience in independent schools where he has served as chaplain, teacher, coach, and, for 28 years, as headmaster. Prior to accepting the position at Hutchison, Mr. Hayden served as Interim Head at St. Nicholas School in Chattanooga, Tennessee.

The faculty consists of 88 women and 13 men. Of the 101 faculty members, 84 are full-time and 17 are part-time specialty teachers. More than 84 percent of the Upper School teachers have master's degrees or higher.

Minor first aid is administered on campus; a hospital is located approximately one mile from the School.

STUDENT BODY. In 1999–2000, Hutchison School has a total enrollment of 840 girls in Pre-Kindergarten 3K–Grade 12 as follows: 43 in Pre-K, 61 in Junior Kindergarten, 57 in Senior Kindergarten, 47 in Grade 1, 55 in Grade 2, 52 in Grade 3, 42 in Grade 4, 55 in Grade 5, 53 in Grade 6, 70 in Grade 7, 70 in Grade 8, 60 in Grade 9, 59 in Grade 10, 55 in Grade 11, and 61 in Grade 12. The girls reside in Memphis and surrounding suburban areas.

ACADEMIC PROGRAM. The school year, from mid-August to late May, is divided into semesters and includes fall break, Thanksgiving recess, Christmas and spring vacations, and three long weekends.

Classes, enrolling an average of 17 girls, are held five days per week. School is in session from 8:10 A.M. to 3:20 P.M., with classes dismissed an hour earlier on Wednesdays. In Grades 9–12, classes meet four times weekly on a rotating schedule. The schedule includes chapel services and convocation three times a week. Grades are posted and reported to parents quarterly.

Hutchison's Early Childhood Center encompasses programs for three-year-olds through Grade 2. Kindergartners are offered a half- or whole-day program. The Kindergarten classes have a teacher-pupil ratio of 1:10; Grades 1–2 have 1:18. Hutchison's literature-based program gives an integrated system of reading, writing, listening, and speaking utilizing the newest theories of learning combined with the best traditional techniques. The math program emphasizes concrete experiences through manipulatives. A well-developed math lab provides enrichment and remediation. Science labs provide enrichment and exploration. The curriculum also includes classes in Orff music, art, physical education, ballet, creative movement, French, Spanish, library, study skills, and computer studies. These special programs continue throughout the Lower School program. The Lower School (Grades 3–5) curriculum expands the language arts and math programs begun earlier, with increased emphasis on the content areas of science and social studies. Leadership opportunities are provided through service organizations. An after-school care program provides supervised care for enrolled students (Pre-K–Grade 6) until 6:00 P.M. for an additional fee. A proctored study hall is provided free for students in Grades 7–12 after school until 6:00 P.M.

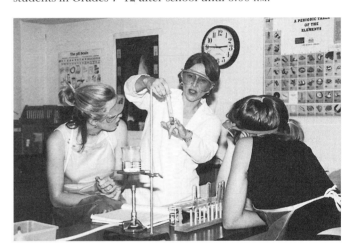

The basic academic program in the Middle School (Grades 6–8) revolves around language arts, mathematics, social studies, and science. Middle School students continue their language study in French or Spanish and add Latin. The student activity and advisor programs are designed to encourage leadership and personal growth. Classes take periodic field trips to points of interest in Memphis; longer trips are planned annually to St. Louis, Blanchard Springs, Arkansas, and Washington, D.C.

To graduate, Upper School students must complete 22 units beginning in Grade 9, 17 of which must include English 4, foreign language 3, mathematics 4, history 2, science 2, humanities 1, and fine arts 1. Six quarters of physical education are required.

The following courses are offered in the Upper School: English; Latin 1–4, Advanced Placement Latin, French 1–4, Advanced Placement French, Spanish 1–4; American History, European History, Advanced Placement European History, Ancient-Medieval History, World History; Biology, Advanced Placement Biology, Anatomy and Physiology, Chemistry, Advanced Placement Chemistry, Advanced Placement Environmental Science, Physics, Advanced Placement Physics; Algebra, Geometry, Algebra II, Math IV/Trigonometry, Pre-Calculus, Calculus, Advanced Topics-Probability and Statistics, Computer Applications; Heritage of Western Civilization and Culture; Art History, Studio Art, Speech, Acting, Introduction to Film; and Physical Education.

For the Class of 1999, the mid-50 percent range of SAT verbal scores is 690–570; SAT math scores, 680–530.

All Hutchison graduates are admitted to colleges and universities. Members of the classes of 1998 and 1999 enrolled in four-year colleges including Arizona State, Auburn, Brown, Carnegie Mellon, Centre College, Clark, College of Charleston, College of William and Mary, Dartmouth, Davidson, Emory, Fordham, Georgetown, Georgia Institute of Technology, Harvard, Hollins, Ithaca, Massachusetts Institute of Technology, McGill, Miami of Ohio, Mississippi University for Women, New York University, Northwestern, Princeton, Rhodes, Rollins, Samford, Southern Methodist, Texas Christian, Tulane, Vanderbilt, Wake Forest, Washington and Lee, Washington University, Wesleyan, and the Universities of Alabama, Colorado, Georgia, Kentucky, Mississippi, Missouri, Notre Dame, Pennsylvania, Richmond, Tennessee, Texas, and Virginia.

Hutchison School conducts a summer program including minicourses for all ages and a day camp for ages 4–10. The day camp fee is $250 for two weeks of all-day sessions.

STUDENT ACTIVITIES. Elected class officers, class representatives, and presidents of student organizations form the Upper School Student Council. The Council coordinates student organizations and activities and serves as a liaison between students and the administration. An Honor Council encourages moral behavior in the classroom and in all aspects of life. Other student organizations include the National Honor Society, Cum Laude Society, Mu Alpha Theta, Quill and Scroll, the Junior Classical League, language clubs, the Glee Club, the Crest Society, and International Thespians. The students issue five publications and compete in Odyssey of the Mind and Future Problem Solving.

Hutchison's varsity and junior varsity teams compete in the Tennessee Secondary School Athletic Association. Soccer, volleyball, basketball, track, cross-country, golf, swimming, and tennis are played intramurally and interscholastically. The Upper School physical education program offers first-aid and CPR as well as archery, tennis, canoeing, and orienteering. Early Childhood Center and Lower School students participate in folk dancing, parachute play, ballet, net games, rope jumping, and movement exploration. The Middle School has physical education classes, intramural games, and the Grades 7–8 sports league.

Typical social activities are the New Girls' Parties, grade-level mixers, dances, and numerous charity events on and off campus. Among the traditional annual events are the Father-Daughter breakfasts and dinner dances, the All-School Family Picnic, holiday programs and parties, Spring Fine Arts Festival, Grandparents' Day, and reunions for Hutchison's 3194 alumnae.

ADMISSION AND COSTS. Hutchison School admits new students in Pre-K Kindergarten (3K)–Grade 11. The School welcomes students of all racial and ethnic origins and religious affiliations. Applicants must submit school transcripts. Applicants to Grades 1–5 take Hutchison's admission tests in reading, vocabulary, and mathematics. Applicants to Grades 6–12 take the Independent School Entrance Examination (ISEE). If space permits, candidates are accepted for late or midyear enrollment. There is a $25 application fee.

For Pre-Kindergarten, tuition and fees are $3239 for three half-days per week, $4395 for three full days, and $5663 for five full days. In Junior and Senior Kindergarten, the fee is $5038 for five half-days per week and $7270 for five full days. The fee is $8762 for Grades 1–2 and $9046 for Grades 3–12. A consolidated and activity fee of $450 is included in the cost and covers some books and initial supplies, insurance, laboratory fees, publications, and graduation. Lunches and physical education uniforms are extra. A tuition payment plan is offered. Need-based financial aid is available.

Director of Admissions: Candy Covington
Head, Upper School: John Delautre
Head, Middle School: Sandra Gilmor
Head, Lower School: Frances Gibbs
Head, Early Childhood: Debbie Isom
Director of Finance: Patsy Simonton
Director of Studies: Laurie Stanton
Director of Development: J. J. Doughtie
Acting Director of Athletics: Laurel Perini

The McCallie School   1905

Missionary Ridge, Chattanooga, TN 37404. 423-624-8300; Fax 423-629-2852; E-mail admissions@mccallie.org; Web Site www.mccallie.org

McCallie School offers a nationally recognized academic program for boys, enrolling 230 boarders in Grades 9–12 and 605 day students in Grades 6–12. The merit-based McCallie Honors Scholarship program attracts outstanding young men across the country. Founded in 1905, McCallie provides college preparation in a Christian context. Reading, writing, and speaking skills are emphasized across a broad curriculum. The average class size is 15. The School shares a coordinate program with Girls Preparatory School. Summer academic and sports camps are available. Boarding Tuition: $23,500; Day Tuition: $11,750. Financial Aid: $1,100,000. Dr. R. Kirk Walker is Headmaster. *Southern Association.*

Memphis University School   1954

6191 Park Avenue, Memphis, TN 38119-5399. 901-260-1300; Fax 901-260-1355

This nondenominational college preparatory day school, founded on Christian principles, enrolls 600 boys from all religious faiths in Grades 7–12. Memphis University School aims to foster sound scholarship, honorable conduct, and responsible citizenship within a moral environment. The traditional liberal arts curriculum features Advanced Placement courses in 19 subject areas; students must complete two community service projects each year to graduate. Boys take part in Student Council and other leadership activities as well as interscholastic sports, honor societies, publications, drama, and interest clubs. Tuition: $8025. William Askew is Director of Admissions; Ellis L. Haguewood (Harding College, B.A.; Memphis State, M.A.) was appointed Headmaster in 1995. *Southern Association.*

Montgomery Bell Academy   1867

4001 Harding Road, Nashville, TN 37205. 615-298-5514;
  Fax 615-297-0271; E-mail admission@montgomerybell.com;
  Web Site www.montgomerybell.com

Montgomery Bell Academy, enrolling 625 day students in Grades 7 through 12, seeks to prepare young men for college and a lifetime of learning, enabling each to reach his full potential as "gentleman, scholar, and athlete." The rigorous liberal arts curriculum features 20 Advanced Placement and 30 honors courses as well as a variety of challenging electives. The Debate Program, travel-learn opportunities, and publications offer further academic enrichment. Students take part in extracurricular activities such as chorus, jazz band, varsity sports, drama, leadership organizations, and community service. An academic session and sports camps are available in the summer. Tuition: $9500. Bradford Gioia is Headmaster. *Southern Association.*

The Oak Hill School   1961

4815 Franklin Road, Nashville, TN 37220. 615-297-6544;
  Fax 615-298-9555

Oak Hill, an outreach of First Presbyterian Church, serves boys and girls in Kindergarten–Grade 6. The School seeks to provide a comprehensive curriculum within a nurturing Christian environment. Its mission in partnership with families is to recognize, celebrate, and develop each student's unique talents; to foster a love of learning and academic excellence; and to prepare students to be persons of integrity with the skills needed to meet future challenges. The 55-acre campus features an on-line library/media center, swimming pool, music rooms, and a fully equipped science center. Tuition: $5900. Extras: $200. Brenda Boon is Admissions Assistant; Dr. Margaret W. Wade (Vanderbilt, B.A. 1974; Middle Tennessee State, M.Ed. 1978; Peabody, Ed.D. 1993) is Head of School. *Southern Association.*

Overbrook School of
The Dominican Campus   1936

4210 Harding Road, Nashville, TN 37205-2005. 615-292-5134;
  Fax 615-783-0560

Founded by the Dominican Sisters of St. Cecilia Congregation to enable students to learn "in a Christ-centered atmosphere of love and truth," Overbrook School enrolls 368 day boys and girls in three-year-old preschool–Grade 8. The traditional curriculum is reflective of the Catholic view of education and is designed to develop each child's full potential spiritually, intellectually, emotionally, culturally, physically, and socially. The program is enhanced by offerings in the fine arts and such cocurricular activities as sports, debate, National Junior Honor Society, chorus, music lessons, and Community Service Club. Tuition: $6355. Financial Aid: $52,437. Ellen Férnandez is Director of Admissions; Sr. Mary Rose, OP, is Principal. *Southern Association.*

Presbyterian Day School   1949

4052 Central Avenue, Memphis, TN 38111-7602. 901-842-4600;
  Fax 901-327-7564

Founded by the Second Presbyterian Church, this day school enrolls 530 boys in Four-Year-Old Kindergarten–Grade 6. In a Christian atmosphere, it aims to provide a sound academic beginning and to develop respect for authority, good citizenship, and leadership. Reading, language arts, and math are emphasized, and Bible is taught at all levels. Grades 1–4 are self-contained; Grades 5–6 are departmentalized. A Discovery Center for enrichment is offered, and after-school athletics are available in Grades 4–6. Tuition: $4000–$6100. Financial Aid: $190,000. Len Sumner (Clemson, B.S. 1960; University of Tennessee [Chattanooga], M.Ed. 1964; University of Memphis, Ed.D. 1983) is Headmaster. *Southern Association.*

Saint Agnes Academy   MEMPHIS

4830 Walnut Grove Road, Memphis, TN 38117. 901-767-1377;
  Administration Building 901-767-1356; Fax 901-682-8199;
  Web Site www.saa-sds.org

SAINT AGNES ACADEMY in Memphis, Tennessee, is a Roman Catholic day school offering a coeducational preschool program, separate classes for boys and girls in Grades 1 through 6, coordinated classes in Grades 7 and 8, and a college preparatory curriculum for girls only in Grades 9 through 12. Memphis (population 610,337) lies on the Mississippi River in the southwestern corner of Tennessee, about 10 miles from the state lines of Arkansas and Mississippi. The city is home to 12 colleges and universities, a symphony orchestra, and numerous galleries, museums, and theaters.

Saint Agnes Academy was founded in 1851 by the Dominican Sisters of St. Catharine, Kentucky, and occupied the same downtown site for 100 years. The Sisters played an important role in the history of Memphis as they cared for the sick during the yellow fever epidemic, operated an orphanage, and, in more recent times, supported the civil rights movement. In 1951, the Academy was moved to its present site and, 5 years later, its brother school, Saint Dominic, was built.

Saint Agnes, a Catholic school by tradition and ecumenical by charter, seeks to provide a values-based education that will prepare students for higher learning while deepening their faith and friendship with God. Mass is offered weekly in the chapel, and a communion service is celebrated daily. High standards of academic excellence, leadership skills, social responsibility, and multicultural awareness are emphasized in a program marked by challenge, diversity, and respect.

Saint Agnes Academy is accredited by the Southern Association of Colleges and Schools and holds membership in the Tennessee Association of Independent Schools, among several other professional organizations. The Academy is guided by a 17-member Board of Trustees composed of religious and lay persons. The Alumnae Association supports the school through fund-raising, recruitment, and special events throughout the year.

THE CAMPUS. Saint Agnes Academy-Saint Dominic School occupies a 20-acre campus in a residential area of east Memphis. The two schools are housed in separate buildings, with Saint Agnes facing Walnut Grove Road and Saint Dominic School on Avon Road. A covered walkway links Saint Agnes to the modern Math and Science Center (1992). Students benefit from three state-of-the-art computer minilabs and an automated 23,000-volume library with 85 periodicals, over 700 full-text, on-line magazines, and 684 videos to support the curriculum.

A capital expansion program begun in 1998 added a spacious new multipurpose building called Siena Hall to the campus, providing a double gymnasium, a dining hall, administrative offices, a theater, and studios for music and art. A new chapel, incorporating stained-glass windows from the original chapel from the downtown campus, serves as the spiritual center.

On the grounds are baseball and soccer fields, a running track, and playgrounds.

THE FACULTY. Barbara H. Daush was appointed President of Saint Agnes Academy-Saint Dominic School in 1994. She earned a B.A. degree in Latin from the University of Mississippi at Oxford and M.A. and M.Ed. degrees from the University of Memphis. Previously, Mrs. Daush held administrative and teaching positions at Hutchison School, Grace-St. Luke's Episcopal School, and Lausanne School, all located in Memphis.

The faculty includes 46 men and women, 88 percent of whom have earned master's degrees or higher from colleges and universities throughout the United States. The average teaching experience is more than 16 years, and the student-teacher ratio is 11:1.

STUDENT BODY. In 1999–2000, Saint Agnes Academy enrolls 583 students, including 314 in Grades 9–12. They come from Memphis and surrounding communities and represent a wide spectrum of religious, racial, ethnic, and socioeconomic backgrounds.

ACADEMIC PROGRAM. The 36-week school year is divided into semesters from mid-August to the end of May, with Thanksgiving and Easter recesses, Christmas and spring vacations, and the observance of national holidays. Students in Grades 1–12 are issued report cards every 6 to 9 weeks, depending on grade; preschoolers are given progress reports throughout the year. Academic excellence is recognized on honor rolls.

The schedule for Grades 1–8 runs from 8:00 A.M. to 3:00 P.M. and the Early Childhood runs from 8:15 A.M. until 2:45 P.M., except on Wednesday when dismissal is at 2:15 P.M. for all grade levels. The school day for Grades 9–12 begins at 8:00 A.M. with

seven 47-minute periods ending at 3:00 P.M. on four days and a modified schedule on Wednesday.

The curriculum in the Lower School incorporates traditional methods of learning through hands-on experiences to develop and reinforce basic skills in reading, language arts, mathematics, science, and social studies. French is taught in Pre-Kindergarten–Grade 2, and Spanish is taught in Grades 3–6. Computer science is introduced in Pre-Kindergarten. There is one class per grade, with a low student-teacher ratio to ensure that children receive close personal attention. Religious studies are required in all grades, from preschool through senior year.

The challenging program in Grades 7–8 is adapted to meet the developmental and academic needs of early adolescence. Core subjects integrate technology, field trips, and hands-on experiential activities to illustrate classroom instruction. Among the subjects taught at the junior high level are English/Literature, Pre-Algebra, Introduction to Algebra, Latin, Classical Studies, Religion, Speech, Creative Writing, World Geography, American History, Life Science, Physical Science, and Physical Education. Enrichments include newspaper, photography, forensics, and computer on-line.

The curriculum in Grades 9–12 is college preparatory. To graduate from the Upper School, students must complete 26 credits as follows: 4 each in religious studies and English; 3.5 in social studies; 3 each in mathematics, science, and the same foreign language; 1 each in physical education/health and fine arts; .5 in etymology and computer applications; and 2.5 in electives. Upper School students are also required to pass proficiency tests in English, math, and computer and perform 15 hours of community service per year.

Among the specific courses are English I–IV, Advanced Placement English, World Literature, Creative Writing/Journalism; Religious Studies I–IV; American History, Advanced Placement European History, Government, Psychology, Economics; Latin I–III, German I–III, French I–IV, Spanish I–IV, Etymology; Algebra I–II, Geometry, Trigonometry, Precalculus, Advanced Calculus; Computer Applications/Multimedia; Introduction to Physical Science, Biology I–II, Advanced Placement Biology, Chemistry, Physics, Honors Physics, Anatomy and Physiology; and Art I–IV, Drama I–III, and Music I–II.

Through the Foreign Language Department of the University of Tennessee at Knoxville, Saint Agnes is one of only two high schools in the state approved to grant college credit to students in level 3 or 4 French or Spanish. Selected students may be invited to participate in Presidential Classroom for Young Americans, an intensive, weeklong program in Washington, D.C. Girls broaden and enrich academic studies through hands-on experience in a professional setting. Field trips related to classroom lessons enhance the curriculum at all grade levels.

All Saint Agnes graduates enter four-year colleges. Members of the Class of 1999 have enrolled at Auburn, DePaul University, Duke, Furman, Hollins, New York University, Rhodes, Rice, Southern Methodist, Tulane, Villanova, Washington University, and the Universities of Alabama, Memphis, Mississippi, Notre Dame, Virginia, and Tennessee.

STUDENT ACTIVITIES. In the Upper School, girls elect representatives to the Student Government Association, and qualified scholars are invited to join the National Honor Society as well as French and Spanish honor societies.

Students publish *Aquila* (yearbook), *Veritas* (newspaper), and *Calliope* (literary magazine); they also participate in art competitions and academic challenges such as Mock Trial, Knowledge Bowl, and Model UN. Organized groups on campus include LIGHT (Living in God's Holy Truth), Students Against Drunk Driving, Ecology Club, Glee Club, Art Club, French Club, Spanish Club, Mu Alpha Theta, Key Club, Pep Club, and the Drama Club, which stages two or more productions per year.

Varsity teams are formed in volleyball, soccer, cross-country, track, golf, softball, swimming, basketball, and tennis; Saint Agnes students also participate in cheerleading squads for Christian Brothers High School and Memphis University School, neighboring boys' schools.

Extracurriculars for Lower and Middle School students encompass many of the same activities, including athletics, on age-appropriate levels.

Girls fulfill their community service requirements through outreach in nursing homes, day-care centers, Meals on Wheels, and homeless shelters.

Among the special events on the school calendar are the Rose Ceremony, Living Rosary, Spirit Week, Day of Caring, the Christmas program, art exhibits and crafts fairs, spelling bee, Multi-cultural Week, Father-Daughter Dance, Mother-Daughter Picnic, International Week, and Baccalaureate.

ADMISSION AND COSTS. Saint Agnes Academy enrolls students of good character and average or above-average ability regardless of race, color, creed, and national or ethnic origin. Admission is offered on the basis of an entrance test, a conference with the applicant and parents, and a review of transcripts and other pertinent records. A child entering Pre-Kindergarten must be 3 years old by June 1 of the current school year.

In 1999–2000, tuition ranges from $5550 for Pre-Kindergarten to $6500 for Grades 9–12. Additional charges include a $50 application fee, a $100 new-student fee, a $100 technology fee, and a graduation fee of $75 for eighth graders and $125 for high school seniors. Tuition payment plans, financial aid, and tuition refund insurance are available.

President: Barbara Daush
Dean Emeritus: Marian Swicker
Dean of Upper School: Joy Maness
Dean of Lower School: Jeanne Larkin
Dean of Admissions & School Improvement: Kathleen Toes-Boccia
Dean of Development: Ruth Carr
Director of Studies: Kay Shelton
Director of Alumnae & Alumni Giving: Jane Tonning '66
Director of Communications & Planned Giving: Ginger Craven '83
Business Manager: Dronda Morrison
Athletic Director: Jim Lassandrello

St. Cecilia Academy of The Dominican Campus 1860

4210 Harding Road, Nashville, TN 37205-2005. 615-298-4525; Fax 615-783-0561; Web Site www.stcecilia.edu

Founded by the Dominican Sisters of the St. Cecilia Congregation, this Roman Catholic, college preparatory day school serves 200 girls in Grades 9–12. The Academy, a recipient of the U.S. Department of Education's Blue Ribbon for Excellence, aims to educate students for academic, social, physical, and moral development and to nurture a Christian way of life. The curriculum is complemented by honors and Advanced Placement courses. St. Cecilia's Fine Arts program offers both partici-

patory and competitive opportunities in the visual arts, dance, drama, forensics, and music. The Academy's award-winning athletic teams compete in nine sports. Tuition: $7500. Sr. Mary Elizabeth, OP, is Principal. *Southern Association.*

Saint Dominic School   MEMPHIS

30 Avon Road, Memphis, TN 38117. 901-682-3011; Administration Building 901-767-1356; Web Site www.saa-sds.org

SAINT DOMINIC SCHOOL in Memphis, Tennessee, is a Roman Catholic elementary school enrolling boys as day students in three-year-old Pre-Kindergarten through Grade 8. The pre-school is coeducational, and Grades 7 and 8 are coordinated with girls from Saint Agnes Academy, Saint Dominic's sister school. Set on the east bank of the Mississippi River, Memphis (population 610,337) is Tennessee's largest city and most important commercial center.

In 1956, the Dominican Sisters of St. Catharine, Kentucky, established Saint Dominic School on the campus of Saint Agnes Academy, which the Sisters had founded in 1851. In addition to occupying the same campus, the two schools share some administrators and specialist teachers.

Saint Dominic School is committed to a total, values-based program that will prepare boys for further education and for a deep, meaningful relationship with God. The School aims to inspire students to pursue academic excellence, leadership, responsibility, emotional maturity, and physical fitness.

Saint Dominic School is accredited by the Southern Association of Colleges and Schools and holds membership in the Tennessee Association of Independent Schools, the National Association of Elementary School Principals, and the Educational Records Bureau, among other professional affiliations.

THE CAMPUS. Saint Agnes Academy and Saint Dominic School occupy a 20-acre campus in a residential area of east Memphis. The two schools are housed in separate buildings, with Saint Agnes facing Walnut Grove Road and Saint Dominic School on Avon Road. Students benefit from three state-of-the-art computer minilabs and an automated 23,000-volume library with 85 periodicals, 400 online magazines, and 4000 audiovisual sets.

A capital expansion program begun in 1998 added a spacious new multipurpose building called Siena Hall to the campus, providing a double gymnasium, a dining hall, administrative offices, a theater, and studios for music and art. A new chapel, incorporating stained-glass windows from the original chapel from the downtown campus, serves as the spiritual center for the School.

On the grounds are baseball and soccer fields, a running track, and playgrounds.

THE FACULTY. Barbara H. Dausch was appointed President of Saint Agnes Academy-Saint Dominic School in 1994. She earned a B.A. degree in Latin from the University of Mississippi at Oxford and M.A. and M.Ed. degrees from the University of Memphis. Previously, Mrs. Dausch held administrative and teaching positions at Hutchison School, Grace-St. Luke's Episcopal School, and Lausanne School, all located in Memphis.

The Saint Dominic faculty includes 11 full-time teachers and approximately 22 specialists and part-time instructors who divide their time between the two schools. They hold undergraduate and advanced degrees and have an average teaching experience of more than 15 years.

STUDENT BODY. In 1999–2000, Saint Dominic School enrolls 248 students in three-year-old Pre-Kindergarten through Grade 8. They came from Memphis and its suburbs and reflected the racial, ethnic, and religious diversity of the metropolitan region.

ACADEMIC PROGRAM. The school year runs from mid-August to the end of May and includes Christmas and spring vacations, Thanksgiving and Easter breaks, and the observance of several federal holidays. Boys in the Early Childhood attend school from 8:15 A.M. until 2:45 P.M., while boys in Grades 1–8 are in class from 8:00 A.M. until 3:00 P.M. On Wednesdays, all students are dismissed at 2:15 P.M. In the Early Childhood Center, children are given progress reports. Grades 1–6 receive five report cards during the year, while report cards in Grades 7 and 8 are issued every nine weeks. Seventh and eighth graders are assigned to faculty-led advisory groups, which meet weekly to discuss adolescent issues such as behavior, ethics, goals, smoking, and drugs and alcohol.

Each day begins with prayer and recitation of the Pledge of Allegiance, and students have the opportunity to receive Holy Communion at daily eucharistic services before school.

The curriculum is designed to promote a love of learning through age-appropriate instruction that forms the basis for future learning. Religious studies begin at the earliest level and continue through Grade 8. Mathematics, language arts, science, Latin, and social studies are emphasized, with enrichment classes in computers, music, art, drama, and physical education. Homework assignments vary from 20 to 40 minutes nightly in Grades 1–3 to one to two hours in Grades 7–8.

The challenging program in Grades 7–8 is adapted to meet the developmental and academic needs of early adolescence. Core subjects integrate technology, field trips, and hands-on experiential activities to illustrate classroom instruction. Among the subjects taught at the junior high level are English/Literature, Pre-Algebra, Introduction to Algebra, Latin, Religion, Speech, Creative Writing, World Geography, American History, Life Science, Physical Science, and Physical Education. Enrichments include newspaper, photography, forensics, and computer on-line. Students with an overall average below 70 percent may be placed on academic probation at the discretion of the Dean.

STUDENT ACTIVITIES. Boys choose from after-school activities organized to meet diverse interests. Representatives are elected by class to serve on the Student Government Association, which organizes community service projects and special events for the entire School.

Grades 4–8 are eligible to try out for the school band, which practices daily and performs a concert in the spring. Students may compete in challenges such as the geography and spelling bees, Duke Talent Search, Math-a-Thon, National Latin Exam, DAR Writing Contest, and the Diocesan Poetry Contest.

The yearbook (*Pass the Word*), a school newspaper, and a literary magazine are published by students, and individual classes stage plays during the year. Other groups include Boy Scouts, Chess Club, Junior Classical League, and Wordsmith.

Saint Dominic athletes compete with other schools in soccer, baseball, and basketball. Class trips are planned to sites around Memphis and as far away as Atlanta, and special activities such as Spirit Week, Fall Festival, Parade of States, Indian Day, Bowling Day, Christmas Pageant, Grandparents' Day, the Passion Play, the Mother-Son Sock Hop, and the Father-Son Breakfast highlight the calendar.

ADMISSION AND COSTS. Saint Dominic School welcomes students regardless of race, creed, and national or ethnic origin. Applicants of good character and average to above-average aptitude are admitted on the basis of an entrance exam, previous transcripts, and an interview with parent and student, when feasible. A child entering Pre-Kindergarten must be three years old by June 1 of the current school year.

In 1999–2000, tuition is $5550 for Pre-Kindergarten and Junior Kindergarten, $5900 for Senior Kindergarten–Grade 6, and $6250 for Grades 7–8. Extras are a $50 application fee,

$100 each for the new-student and technology fees, and a $75 graduation fee. Tuition payment plans, financial aid, and tuition refund insurance are available.

President: Barbara Daush
Dean Emeritus: Marian Swicker
Dean of the School: John Murphy
Dean of Admissions & School Improvement: Kathleen Toes-Boccia
Dean of Development: Ruth Carr
Director of Studies: Kay Shelton
Director of Alumnae & Alumni Giving: Jane Tonning '66
Director of Communications & Planned Giving: Ginger Craven '83
Business Manager: Dronda Morrison
Athletic Director: Jim Lassandrello

St. Mary's Episcopal School   MEMPHIS

60 Perkins Extended, Memphis, TN 38117. 901-537-1472; Admissions 901-537-1405; E-mail lwilliams@stmarysschool.org; Web Site www.stmarysschool.org

ST. MARY'S EPISCOPAL SCHOOL in Memphis, Tennessee, is a college preparatory day school enrolling girls in Pre-Kindergarten–Grade 12.

St. Mary's was founded in 1847 by Mrs. Mary Pope to provide a strong academic education for young women. Episcopal nuns from the Order of Sisters of St. Mary operated the School from 1873 to 1910 as a boarding and day school. The School then became privately owned and operated until 1958 when it was chartered as a nonprofit corporation. Presently, St. Mary's shares facilities with the Church of the Holy Communion. The Moss family home, located directly across the street, is now the center of an expanded Lower School facility.

The School is known for its commitment to academic excellence, emphasizing a classic liberal arts curriculum in conjunction with a strong science and math program. The supportive environment fosters academic, emotional, spiritual, physical, and social development. Chapel, held weekly in the Lower School and daily in Grades 5–12, offers time for reflection. Girls participate within the parameters of their own faiths.

St. Mary's is governed by a 26-member Board of Trustees with representation from the Parents' Association, the Alumnae Association, the community, and the Episcopal Church. The School is accredited by the Southern Association of Colleges and Schools and the National Association for the Education of Young Children. St. Mary's holds membership in the National Association of Independent Schools, the Southern Tennessee Association of Independent Schools, the Memphis Association of Independent Schools, the National Coalition of Girls' Schools, the Educational Records Bureau, and The College Board. The School's endowment is approximately $7,500,000.

THE CAMPUS. The 20-acre campus, shared with the Church of the Holy Communion, includes Blaisdell Hall, used for dining; the gymnasium; Greenwood Building, with Middle School classrooms and offices; and the Barth Building, housing Middle School classrooms, computer and science laboratories. The Taylor Building contains Upper School classrooms, language and science laboratories, an auditorium, the 27,000-volume Cook Library, and faculty offices. Athletic facilities include a track, playing fields, and two tennis courts. The Lower School campus includes 20 classrooms, a library, a computer lab, science rooms, art and music facilities, and a ballet room. The Hyde Activity Center houses Wilmott Gymnasium, Starnes Common, six additional classrooms, and a cafeteria. The state-of-the-art Buckman Performing and Fine Arts Building (1996) provides the Rose Theater, Levy Gallery, a technology center, art studios, seminar rooms, and band, choir, drama, and dance rehearsal facilities.

THE FACULTY. Thomas N. Southard, a graduate of the University of South Carolina (B.A. 1967) and the University of South Florida (M.A. 1973), was appointed Headmaster in 1987. Mr. Southard was formerly Headmaster at Queen Anne School in Maryland, the Cathedral School of St. John the Divine in New York City, and St. Michael's School in Florida. He has had experience in business and has served as a teacher, director of athletics, dean of students, and assistant headmaster. Mr. Southard is past President of the Memphis Association of Independent Schools, past treasurer of the governing board of the National Association of Episcopal Schools, and a member of the Executive Committee and past president of the Tennessee Association of Independent Schools. He is currently a member of the Secondary Schools Exchange Committee of the English-Speaking Union in New York City.

There are 97 faculty members, 9 men and 88 women. They hold baccalaureate degrees representing study at 40 colleges and universities and master's and doctoral degrees representing study at such institutions as Stanford, Tulane, Vanderbilt, and the Universities of California, Memphis, North Carolina, Virginia, and Wisconsin.

Faculty benefits include a flexible benefits plan, health and life insurance, a retirement plan, Social Security, sabbaticals, leaves of absence, and continuing professional education.

STUDENT BODY. In 1999–2000, there are 826 girls enrolled in Pre-Kindergarten–Grade 12. The majority of students reside in Memphis and its suburbs.

ACADEMIC PROGRAM. The school year, divided into semesters, begins in late August and ends in late May. There are vacations at Thanksgiving and Christmas and fall and spring breaks. Classes are held five days a week from 8:00 A.M. to 3:00 P.M. with a 2:25 P.M. dismissal on Wednesdays. Extended Day is offered to students in the Kindergartens, and after-school care is available until 6:00 P.M. for students through Grade 8.

In each of the three Kindergartens, there are written progress reports and parent conferences. There are five marking periods for Grades 1–6, with report cards mailed at the respective intervals, and quarterly marking periods for Grades 7–12. Parent conferences are scheduled in the fall and throughout the year as needed. Teachers offer individual and group help sessions at no extra charge. The student/teacher ratio is 9:1.

Opportunities to learn in Kindergarten at St. Mary's are provided through play. Technology is introduced using computers and audiovisual equipment in the classrooms. Kindergartners attend a weekly class in the computer lab. Spanish and French are introduced to enable children to view a second language and its culture as integral aspects of life. The atmosphere of the classroom is loving and caring as little girls share, discover, and inquire.

The Lower School seeks to develop positive attitudes about self, others, and learning. The sequenced curriculum for

Grades 1–4 includes reading, phonics, English, spelling, handwriting, mathematics, computer, sciences, and social studies. Art, music, ballet, computer, Bible, and physical education are taught by special subject teachers. Pre-Kindergarten–Grade 4 are introduced to Creative Exposure in French, Spanish, and Italian.

The Middle School continues the sequential curriculum for students in Grade 5 and classes become departmentalized. All Middle School students take courses in music, art, computer, drama, speech, Bible, and physical education. Courses offered in Grades 7 and 8 include English literature, pre-algebra and algebra, American history, geography, physical and life sciences, and an introductory language experience course in Grade 7 and Latin I in Grade 8.

Graduation from the Upper School requires 21 credits, including 4 in English; 4 in mathematics; 3 in foreign language; 3 in social studies; 3 in science; 1 each in fine arts and physical education; $\frac{1}{2}$ in religion; $1\frac{1}{2}$ in electives; and computer proficiency.

Courses offered in the Upper School include English and Advanced Composition; Algebra I through Calculus; French I–IV, Spanish I–IV, Latin I–V; Biology, Microbiology, Physics, Astrophysics, Chemistry, Honors Science Research, Psychology; World History I–II, American History, Contemporary History; and Art History, Music History, Music Theory, Humanities I–II, Computer, Religion, Physical Education, and Studio Art. Advanced Placement courses are offered in English, calculus, biology, chemistry, physics, Latin, French, and Spanish. Supplementary course work enables students to take Advanced Placement examinations in American history, European history, and psychology.

The 45 members of the Class of 1999 enrolled in the following colleges: Barnard, Bryn Mawr, Cornell, Dartmouth, Hollins, Northwestern, Princeton, Spelman, Stanford, Vanderbilt, Wake Forest, and the University of Pennsylvania.

An eight-week Summer PURSUITS Program offers noncredit remedial and enrichment courses to boys and girls in Grades 1–12. There is also a Day Camp for girls in Pre-Kindergarten–Grade 6.

STUDENT ACTIVITIES. The Upper School Student Council regulates clubs and a variety of organizations and serves as a liaison between the students and the administration. The Honor Council deals with infractions of the Honor Code. The Middle School has its own Student Council and Honor Council representatives.

Upper School publications are the newspaper (*Tatler*), the yearbook (*Carillon*), and the literary magazine (*Belles Lettres*) and companion CD (*Melodies*). A play is produced each year by Middle School students. The Upper School Drama Club produces two plays and a lunchbox theater series each year. Girls in Grades 7 and 8 may play in the Upper School band and there are junior band and choir for students in Grades 5 and 6. Dances and parties are organized by the School for girls in

Grades 7–12 and there are also School-sponsored trips. Qualified Upper School students are inducted into various honor societies including the National Honor Society, National Beta Club, The Cum Laude Society, and the French, Spanish, and Latin National Honor societies. Most students participate in community service activities.

A strong athletic program with organized sports teams begins in Grade 7. Students compete with schools in the Tennessee Secondary School Athletic Association. There are teams for volleyball, soccer, cross-country, golf, basketball, track, tennis, and swimming.

Traditional annual events include the Turkey Trot (a fun run for charity), Father/Daughter Dinner Dance, Mother/Daughter/Faculty Luncheon and Fashion Show, Valentine Breakfast, Grandparents' Day, Derby Day, Field Day, Springfest, Christmas Pageant, Winter Formal, and the Junior-Senior Prom.

ADMISSION AND COSTS. St. Mary's Episcopal School seeks academically able and motivated students from diverse socioeconomic, ethnic, and religious backgrounds for enrollment in Pre-Kindergarten through Grade 11. Applicants must fill out an application form, submit transcripts and faculty recommendations, and take tests appropriate to the grade level for which they are applying. ISEE testing is required for students entering Grades 5–11. Middle and Upper School candidates are asked to have an on-campus visit. Midyear entry is possible when space is available. There is a $50 application fee. Applications are accepted at any time and candidates are notified of acceptance in mid-February.

In 1999–2000, tuition is $3850 for Pre-Kindergarten, $4600 for Junior Kindergarten, $7500 for Senior Kindergarten, $8900 for Grades 1–4, $9100 for Grades 5–7, $9200 for Grades 8–11, and $9300 for Grade 12. Extended Day for Kindergarten students is $2900 and after-school care is $135 per month. There is a $500 tuition deposit. Books and supplies range from $200 to $450. A prepaid lunch program is available.

Financial aid is available and St. Mary's subscribes to the School and Student Service for Financial Aid. In 1999–2000, 92 students received financial aid totaling $349,800.

Associate Head/Principal, Lower School: Virginia A. Pretti
Assistant Headmaster: Diane Spence
Principal, Upper School: Gail Lewis
Principal, Middle School: Peggy Williamson
Kindergarten Director: Kay Humphreys
Director of Admission: Lindy Williams
Director of Studies: Gloria Weir
College Advisor: Mimi Grossman
Director of Development: Angie Gardner
Director of Finance: Patty Kelly
Director of Athletics: Wendy Gallik

Saint Nicholas School   1958

7525 Min-Tom Drive, Chattanooga, TN 37421. 423-899-1999;
Fax 423-899-0109; E-mail admissions@stnicholas.cjb.net;
Web Site www.stnicholas.cjb.net/

Saint Nicholas School, enrolling 200 day students ages 4 through Grade 6, offers a personalized curriculum to accommodate individual progress and provide an interdisciplinary approach to study. The program promotes skills for learning within an atmosphere that encourages initiative, intellectual growth, and artistic and academic creativity and achievement. Multiage grouping and cooperative learning help to build a child-centered climate where positive values are developed during the school day and in the extended-care program. Tuition: $5470–$7260. Financial Aid: $91,000. Barbara B. Dawkins is Admissions Director; the Reverend Michael E. Robinson is Head of School. *Southern Association.*

Sumner Academy   1973

464 Nichols Lane, Gallatin, TN 37066. 615-452-1914;
Fax 615-452-1923

Sumner Academy, enrolling 250 day boys and girls in Pre-School–Grade 8, seeks to develop each child's abilities, attitudes, and values to give them a positive feeling about themselves and the challenges they face. Language arts, reading, mathematics, science, and social studies are the cornerstone of the Primary (Grades 1–2) and Intermediate (Grades 3–5) programs. Traditionally structured Grades 6–8 include Spanish. Classes are provided in music, art, physical education, library, and computer skills. Tuition including extras: $2790–$4800. John R. Crawford is Director of Admissions; William E. Hovenden (Cornell College, B.A. 1963; Indiana, M.S. 1966; Florida State, Ph.D. 1972) was appointed Headmaster in 1980.

University School of Jackson   1970

232 McClellan Road, Jackson, TN 38305. 901-664-0812,
901-660-1692 (Admissions); Fax 901-664-5046;
E-mail admin@usj.tn.org; Web Site usj.tn.org

University School of Jackson is a college preparatory day school enrolling more than 1300 boys and girls from throughout West Tennessee in Prekindergarten–Grade 12. The Lower School (PK–Grade 4), set on a wooded campus, offers a developmentally based, computer-integrated curriculum and a day-care program. The Middle and Upper schools are housed in a new $10,500,000 facility with state-of-the-art science labs and computer technology, performing arts and media centers, and extensive sports facilities. The challenging curriculum is complemented by fine arts, sports, and community service opportunities. All graduates are admitted to universities. Tuition: $3100–$4600. Financial aid is available. Kay Shearin is Admissions Coordinator; Donald Coffey is Headmaster. *Southern Association.*

University School of Nashville   1915

2000 Edgehill Avenue, Nashville, TN 37212. 615-327-8158;
Fax 615-321-0889; Web Site www.usn.org

Founded in 1915 as a demonstration school for George Peabody Teachers College, the University School of Nashville is a coeducational, college preparatory day school enrolling approximately 990 children in Kindergarten–Grade 12. The diverse student body is encouraged to think critically, learn independently, and demonstrate tolerance for others. Advanced Placement courses, independent study, and classes at nearby Vanderbilt are available in the upper grades. Sports, drama, music, and art enrich the program. Tuition: $8325–$9200. Financial aid is available. Juliet C. Douglas is Director of Admissions; Dr. Jean Litterer was appointed Interim Director in 1999. *Southern Association.*

The Webb School   1870

Sawney Webb Highway, Bell Buckle, TN 37020. 931-389-9322;
Admissions 931-389-6003; E-mail webbschool@united.net;
Web Site www.thewebbschool.com

William R. Webb founded this coeducational, college preparatory school to enable students to reach their fullest personal and academic potential, with an emphasis on honorable conduct. Enrolling 95 boarding and 164 day students in Grades 7–12, The Webb School offers a liberal arts curriculum that includes an Honors Diploma program, Advanced Placement courses, and English as a Second Language. Students take part in athletics, outdoor education, drama, newspaper, yearbook, and a variety of interest clubs. A six-week academic summer session is offered. Boarding Tuition: $22,000; Day Tuition: $9000. Financial aid is available. A. Jon Frere (Franklin and Marshall, A.B.; Middlebury College, M.A.) was appointed Headmaster in 1989. *Southern Association.*

Webb School of Knoxville   1955

9800 Webb School Drive, Knoxville, TN 37923. 423-693-0011;
Fax 423-691-8057; E-mail Cindy_Strock@webbschool.org;
Web Site www.webbschool.org

Webb School of Knoxville is a coeducational, college preparatory day school enrolling students in Kindergarten–Grade 12. The School seeks to offer an education of the highest quality, balancing intellectual challenge and nurture of the individual student. Twenty-one Advanced Placement courses are offered. Character development is emphasized through inspirational speakers, an honor system, and the nondenominational study of religion. Student government, publications, musical and dramatic performing groups, and sports are extracurricular activities. Day camp is offered in the summer. Tuition: $10,690. Financial Aid: $683,000. Cindy Strock is Director of Enrollment; Scott L. Hutchison (Duke, B.A.; College of William and Mary, M.Ed.) is President. *Southern Association.*

Westminster School of Nashville   1968

111 North Wilson Boulevard, Nashville, TN 37205. 615-269-0020;
  Fax 615-269-5305; Web Site www.westminsterschooltn.org

Westminster is a nonsectarian school enrolling 210 students with learning differences in Kindergarten–Grade 8. A multi-faceted curriculum is personalized to meet the diverse needs of its students and provide them with the skills and knowledge that lead to productivity and self-confidence. The core program emphasizes independent thinking and creative problem solving in traditional academic disciplines. Support services and language intervention are available as needed. Daily enrichment and remedial tutorials are offered for all students. Among the extracurricular activities are cross-country, basketball, soccer, cheerleading, forensics, and chess. Extended care and academic summer sessions are available. Tuition $10,638. Financial Aid: $181,500. Susan Blount is Director of Admissions; Kathleen G. Rayburn is Head of School. *Southern Association*.

TEXAS

All Saints Episcopal School   1954

4108 Delaware, P.O. Box 7188, Beaumont, TX 77706.
   409-892-1755; Fax 409-892-0166

Affiliated with local Episcopal churches, All Saints is a day school enrolling 407 boys and girls in Prekindergarten–Grade 8. The School endeavors to provide a challenging program that emphasizes the education and development of the whole child, mentally, physically, and spiritually. Spanish is taught at all levels, and Latin is introduced in the middle school. High school credit may be earned for Algebra I, Integrated Physical Science, and French. A 16,000-volume library, networked computers with Internet access, three science labs, a full-size gym, and daily chapel are features of the All Saints program. Tuition: $2500–$4300. Financial Aid: $70,000. Stephen G. Kennedy (University of Tulsa, B.A. 1970, M.A. 1972, M.A. 1980) is Headmaster.

All Saints Episcopal School   1956

3222 103rd Street, Lubbock, TX 79423. 806-745-7701;
   Fax 806-748-0454; Web Site www.allsaintsschool.org

All Saints is an independent Episcopal school enrolling 311 students in Preschool 3 through Ninth Grade. The School is dedicated to the whole child and offers a diverse curriculum that acknowledges differences in each student's maturity, intellectual development, and aptitude. Students participate in daily chapel services, community service projects, and an optional fine arts and athletic program. Nationally recognized for its educational benefits and Drug Education curriculum, All Saints aims to foster students' self-confidence and to develop their creative potential. Tuition: $2110–$5500. Financial aid is available. Mary Andrews is Director of Admissions; Dr. Dana F. Beane (Plymouth State, B.S.; Peabody College, M.A.; University of Kentucky, Ed.D.) is Headmaster.

Annunciation Orthodox School   1970

3600 Yoakum Boulevard, Houston, TX 77006. 713-620-3600;
   Fax 713-620-3605

Founded to develop "the whole child" by providing an outstanding education within a secure and stimulating Christian environment, Annunciation Orthodox School enrolls 640 day boys and girls in PreSchool through Grade 8. It serves students of all backgrounds and offers study in the basic disciplines as well as music, creative arts, computer, Greek and Spanish language, and cultural studies. Extracurricular activities include sports programs, chorus, academic clubs, and fire and safety patrols. Extended-day and summer programs are available. Tuition: $6340–$8240. Extras: $700. Financial Aid: $60,000. Maria Newton is Director of Admissions; Mr. Mark Kelly is Head of School.

The Awty International School

HOUSTON

7455 Awty School Lane, Houston, TX 77055. 713-686-4850;
   Fax 713-686-4956; Web Site awty.org

THE AWTY INTERNATIONAL SCHOOL in Houston, Texas, is a coeducational, college preparatory day school enrolling 950 students in Preschool through Grade 12. Situated in the fourth-largest city in the United States, the School was founded in 1956 by Kathleen Awty as a preschool. As demand increased, Lower, Middle, and Upper schools were added by 1975. It became affiliated with the French School of Houston in 1979 through the efforts of the Mission Laïque Française. The School's name was changed in 1984 to reflect its multilingual character and international faculty and student body.

   In addition to providing a strong basis in traditional academic subjects, The Awty International School strives to instill in its students an awareness of and appreciation for the diversity among nations. Learning to understand and respect other languages and cultures develops young adults who are prepared to lead and participate fully in today's global economy.
   A nonprofit organization, The Awty International School is governed by a Board of Trustees comprised of parents, American and international business leaders, and representatives of the French Government. The School is accredited by the Independent Schools Association of the Southwest, the French Ministry of Education, and the European Council of International Schools. It holds membership in the International Schools Association, the International Baccalaureate Organization, the National Association of Independent Schools, the Houston

Texas

Association of Independent Schools, the A.E.F.E., and The Mission Laïque Française.

THE CAMPUS. The Awty International School's urban campus occupies 13 acres. The School's ten-year plan, adopted in 1990, has added a new Preschool complex, a library, a science wing, a Middle/Upper School wing with computer and language labs, a new gymnasium/auditorium, and a new, two-story classroom complex. There are 138 computers on campus for student use.

THE FACULTY. Born in London, England, Head of School Jaroslaw (Jarek) Garlinski earned a B.A. degree from the University of Nottingham and his M.Phil. degree from the University of London. He taught at Eton College in England and at Phillips Exeter Academy in New Hampshire. Mr. Garlinski was also Acting Headmaster of The British School in Paris and Headmaster of Shattuck-St. Mary's School in Minnesota.

The faculty numbers 127. Because of the multilingual character of the School, many faculty members have earned their degrees and licenses from European and Middle Eastern universities. Among these are the Universities of Bordeaux, Lille, and Toulouse (France); the University of Hamburg (Germany); the Universities of Liverpool, London, and Nottingham (England); the University of Baghdad (Iraq); and Universidad Iberoamericana and Colegio La Florida (Mexico). American schools include Baylor, Boston College, Boston University, Bowdoin, Brown, Georgetown, Louisiana State, Morehouse, New York University, Rice, Texas A&M, Tulane, Villanova, and the Universities of Arizona, Houston, Pittsburgh, and Texas.

A registered nurse and a counselor serve on a full-time basis; two major medical centers are within 15 minutes of the campus.

STUDENT BODY. In 1999–2000, The Awty International School enrolls 950 students in three-year-old Preschool through Grade 12. The student body is comprised of young people from Houston and the surrounding communities and from most parts of the globe. Approximately 40 percent of the students are American citizens, followed by French and British citizens. In all, 44 countries are represented including Belgium, Brazil, Egypt, Germany, Italy, Japan, Mexico, Norway, Russia, Spain, and Venezuela.

ACADEMIC PROGRAM. Seeking to broaden understanding of diverse cultures, The Awty International School offers its students two academic programs: a traditional American college preparatory curriculum, leading to the International Baccalaureate, and a program, approved by the French Government, leading to the French *Baccalauréat*. The American high school diploma is conferred on qualified candidates.

The school year, divided into three terms, begins in late August and extends through early June. Classes in all grades

are held five days a week. Preschool through Lower School (Grades 1–5) begins at 8:15 A.M. and dismisses at 2:50 P.M., while the Middle (Grades 6–8) and Upper (Grades 9–12) schools begin at 8:00 A.M. and dismiss at 3:25 P.M.

An average class has 12–18 students; faculty-supervised study halls are available to students depending on their schedules. Tutoring in the Awty Plus After-School Program is provided on a fee basis.

The Preschool offers a completely bilingual program in French and English or Spanish and English. For those students in Grades 6–12 interested in learning a third language, there are classes in Arabic, Italian, and German.

In the Upper School, students must complete a minimum of 26 credits as follows: 4 in English; 4 in a second language; 4 each in history, mathematics, and science; 1 in electives; 1 in fine arts; 2 in physical education; and 1 in computer science. In Grades 11–12, International Section students pursue the International Baccalaureate, which is accepted by most universities for Advanced Placement. Students have in-depth study and testing in six subjects, a course in Theory of Knowledge (1 credit), and the writing of an extended essay. A minimum of 150 hours of community service is also required.

French Section students may earn the French *Baccalauréat* in a special concentration, including French literature, philosophy, mathematics, physics, biology, geography, physical education, foreign language, and history. Preparation for the *Baccalauréat* is three years (Grades 10–12) and includes both compulsory and elective studies.

Awty graduates enroll in colleges and universities in the United States and throughout the world. Schools attended by recent graduates include Amherst, Boston University, Brown, Carnegie Mellon, Colgate, Columbia, Cornell University, Emory, Harvard, Rice, Texas A&M, Vassar, Yale, and the University of Texas (Austin) in the United States as well as Université Libre de Bruxelles (Belgium), University of Bonn (Germany), Oxford (England), and the University of Paris (all campuses).

The Awty Plus After-School Program, operating from 2:50 to 6:00 P.M. daily, is provided for students seeking assistance in homework assignments or additional academic instruction in languages. Activities include dance, art, tennis, martial arts, and computer science.

The Awty International School offers an extensive summer program of activities, enrichment, and academic credit for students from Preschool through Grade 9.

STUDENT ACTIVITIES. Student Councils are elected in both the Middle and Upper schools. Council members help with school events and serve on disciplinary and advisory committees. Extracurricular activities are organized according to student interest and include Model United Nations, choir, drama, cheerleading, the yearbook, band, a chamber music ensemble, and musical and dramatic productions, which are staged at least twice a year.

The Athletic Department's goal is to enhance the student's physical, mental, emotional, and social development through a variety of extracurricular sports. Upper School athletic teams compete with members of the Texas Association of Private and Parochial Schools (TAPPS), while Middle School athletes compete with members of the Greater Houston Athletic Conference and other independent schools. Boys' varsity teams are formed in soccer, basketball, tennis, golf, cross-country, and track. Girls' varsity teams participate in soccer, volleyball, basketball, tennis, cross-country, and track. Since 1988, four Awty teams have won a total of eight TAPPS state championships. In the 1996–97 school year, the boys' soccer team and the boys' and girls' tennis teams won TAPPS state championships.

New and returning students, their families, and faculty are welcomed each fall at a festive gathering. Homecoming dances and proms are held annually. Other scheduled events are Homecoming, open houses, Book Fair, and an International Week.

ADMISSION AND COSTS. The Awty International School seeks college-bound students from the Houston area and around the world who are of above-average ability and good moral character. The School recommends that applications be received by December 20. The application deadline is March 1. However, because vacancies become available during the school year as parents are transferred to other locations, applications are accepted on a year-round basis.

A completed application form with a nonrefundable $100 application fee, academic transcripts, test results, teacher recommendations, and a personal interview are required.

In 1999–2000, tuition ranges from $7260 for Preschool to $9885 for the Upper School. Books ($200–$400), uniforms (required in Kindergarten–Grade 12), lunches, and bus transportation are extra; a tuition payment plan and limited financial aid are available.

Head, Bilingual French Section: Catherine Donahue-Weill
Head, Upper School: Samuel P. Waugh
Head, Middle School: Thomas Beuscher
Head, Lower School: Chantal Vessali
Director of College Counseling: Susheila Samaranayake
Director of Admissions: Peter C. Egan
Director of Operations and Development: Patricia W. Block
Public Relations Coordinator: Lisa Stiles
Controller: Teresa Craft
Director of Athletics: Karen Waugh

Cistercian Preparatory School   1962

One Cistercian Road, Irving, TX 75039. 972-273-2022;
Fax 972-554-2294; E-Mail admissions@cistercian.org;
Web Site www.cistercian.org

Cistercian Preparatory School is a Roman Catholic, college preparatory day school enrolling 337 boys of all creeds in Grades 5

through 12. The curriculum is a fully integrated, eight-year honors program of English, math, laboratory science, computer science, foreign language, and social studies, which is identical for all students. Theology, electives, Advanced Placement, college courses, and independent studies are also offered in addition to athletics, activities, and an academic summer school. Tuition: $7300–$8100. Financial Aid: $266,045. Robert J. Haaser is Director of Admissions; Fr. Peter Verhalen is Headmaster.

Carrollton Christian Academy   1980

1820 Pearl Street, P.O. Box 110204, Carrollton, TX 75011-0204.
972-242-6688; Fax 972-245-0321;
E-mail development@ccasaints.org

Carrollton Christian Academy, founded as a ministry of the First United Methodist Church, now operates as a separate, incorporated, nondenominational, college preparatory school enrolling 850 day students in Three-Year Preschool through High School. The school's philosophy is firmly rooted in the teachings of Christ as revealed in the Bible. Academic core subjects are supplemented by offerings in fine arts, Spanish language instruction, computer, and required Bible classes. Extracurricular opportunities include physical education and a broad range of athletics. Tuition: $1350–$4550. Jan Foster is Admissions Director; Alan Wimberley (Tarleton State, B.S.; Liberty University, M.Ed.) is Superintendent. *Southern Association.*

Duchesne Academy of the Sacred Heart   1960

10202 Memorial Drive, Houston, TX 77024. 713-468-8211;
Fax 713-465-9809; E-mail adms@duchesne.org;
Web Site www.duchesne.org

Duchesne Academy was founded by the Religious of the Sacred Heart to educate young women toward "a personal and active faith in God," to foster respect for intellectual values, and to promote personal excellence. Enrolling 630 girls in Pre-kindergarten–Grade 12, Duchesne's college preparatory curriculum integrates technology in all departments, including a "Learning with Laptops" program in Grades 6–11. Religion classes, Advanced Placement courses, and fine arts enrich the core program. Activities include Student Council, a literary publication, National Honor Society, and interest clubs. A summer program is optional. Tuition: $9900. Financial Aid: $495,165. Beth Speck is Director of Admissions; Sr. Jan Dunn is Headmistress.

Episcopal High School of Houston   1983

4650 Bissonnet, Bellaire, TX 77401. 713-512-3400;
Fax 713-512-3603; Web Site www.ehshouston.org

Episcopal High School, founded in 1982 as an institution of the Episcopal Diocese of Texas, is a coeducational day school serving 570 students in Grades 9–12. The School's broad liberal arts, college preparatory curriculum is comprised of four pillars emphasizing academic, religious, artistic, and athletic disciplines nurtured by Christian values in a supportive environment. Daily chapel services and sacred studies reinforce the ethical and religious principles upon which the School was founded. Tuition: $11,950. Audrey Koehler is Director of Admission; Edward C. Becker (Hampden-Sydney, B.S.; University of Florida, M.Ed.) was appointed Headmaster in 1995.

The Episcopal School of Dallas   DALLAS

4100 Merrell Road, Dallas, TX 75229-6200. 214-358-4368;
E-mail burker@esdal.org; Web Site www.esdallas.org/esd

THE EPISCOPAL SCHOOL OF DALLAS in Dallas, Texas, is a coeducational, college preparatory day school spanning two campuses. The Pre-Elementary and Lower School Campus, 4344 Colgate Avenue, Dallas, Texas 75225-6502, enrolls students in three-year-old Beginners through Grade 4, while the Middle and Upper School Campus at Merrell Road enrolls students in Grades 5 through 12.

The School was founded in 1974 by the Reverend Stephen B. Swann, acting on the request of the Episcopal Bishop of Dallas, and members of two Episcopal parishes who wished to establish an Episcopal secondary school to carry on the work of parish elementary schools. Opening in rented quarters, the School moved to the present campus in 1979. In 1994, The Episcopal School merged with The Saint Michael School.

As an independent, faith-centered school, The Episcopal School of Dallas strives to enhance the spiritual, intellectual, physical, and social growth of students and to inspire them to reach for the best in the classroom, in chapel, on the playing field, on wilderness excursions, and in community service. Open to students of all faiths, the School seeks to provide a flexible, traditional curriculum that respects individual differences and sets forth an enduring system of values. Chapel attendance and religion courses are required.

A nonprofit institution, the School is affiliated with, but not governed by, the Episcopal Diocese of Dallas. It is supervised by a 45-member Board of Directors that includes the Rector/Headmaster, the Bishop of the Diocese, business and civic leaders, and parents. The Parents' Association provides support for fund-raising and social events.

The Episcopal School of Dallas is accredited by the Independent Schools Association of the Southwest, whose accreditation is recognized by the Texas Education Agency. It holds membership in the National Association of Independent Schools, the National Association of Episcopal Schools, the Southwestern Association of Episcopal Schools, and the Multicultural Alliance, among other educational organizations.

THE CAMPUS. The 43-acre combined campuses, with a $32,000,000 physical plant and endowment, feature a 2-acre, spring-fed pond. Outdoor athletic facilities include seven tennis courts, a baseball diamond, batting cages, soccer fields, and an eight-lane, 400-meter all-weather track.

The Lower School utilizes more than 47,000 square feet of classroom space. Eighteen multimedia power PC Macintosh computers are available in the computer lab. The Lower School library has over 14,000 volumes.

Middle and Upper School buildings provide approximately 120,000 square feet of space for classrooms, offices, a common area, and a fine arts wing. The Gill Library contains 16,000 volumes, an on-line catalog, and a CD-ROM network. The Cook Math/Science/Computer Building houses natural science and physics labs as well as advanced computer labs, which provide access to the Internet. The 24,000-square-foot gymnasium contains a regulation-size basketball court, three volleyball courts, badminton courts, and weight and training rooms.

The wilderness program is centered around the Wolf Run Campus, a 165-acre mid-19th-century Texas farmstead located one hour from the North Campus. Work is in progress on two bunkhouses with meeting and dining facilities, nature trails, and a ropes course that will enhance studies in archaeology, ecology, biology, astronomy, and outdoor drama productions.

THE FACULTY. The Reverend Stephen B. Swann is the founding Rector/Headmaster. A native Texan, Father Swann holds a Master of Divinity degree from the Church Divinity School of the Pacific. He has also attended the Perkins School of Theology of Southern Methodist University and has a B.A. in psychology.

Of the 150 faculty and administrative staff members, 85 hold master's degrees and 4 hold doctorates from such institutions as Baylor, Boston College, College of William and Mary, Columbia, Cornell, Dartmouth, Davidson, DePaul, Duke, Emory, Louisiana State, McGill, Mount Holyoke, Oberlin, Oklahoma State, Rice, Seton Hall, Southern Methodist, Texas A&M, Texas Christian, Texas Tech, Trinity, Tulane, Vanderbilt, Yale, and the Universities of Arkansas, California, Colorado, Dallas, Granada (Spain), Illinois, Michigan, Nebraska, New Hampshire, the South, Southern California, Texas, Tulsa, and Virginia.

STUDENT BODY. In 1999–2000, the School enrolls 1090 students from diversified backgrounds, about equally divided between boys and girls. They come together in a faith-centered environment that fosters intellectual, spiritual, emotional, and social maturity as well as the precepts of responsibility and giving.

ACADEMIC PROGRAM. The school year, from late August to late May, is divided into semesters and includes a Thanksgiving recess, a Christmas vacation, spring break, and observances of national holidays. The school day, from 8:00 A.M. to 3:00 P.M., includes seven class periods, chapel, and lunch. On Wednesday, the schedule is adjusted to permit a Eucharist service and periodic after-school assemblies.

As a college preparatory school, The Episcopal School offers a program that combines a flexible curriculum with a stable and enduring system of values. Classes, averaging 17 students, are kept small to foster individualization and student-teacher interaction. The college guidance program begins in Grade 9. Grades are posted four times yearly; interim reports are issued for students who are not progressing and for those who have shown outstanding progress. Parent-teacher-student conferences are held twice annually; written comments are sent to parents at the end of each marking period.

The pre-elementary curriculum (age 3–Grade 1) provides a healthy, stimulating environment for early learning in which children may develop to the full extent of their abilities. The program is designed to provide each child with a productive, secure early-childhood experience. The student's day includes time for individual activities, center activities, teacher-directed activities, creative projects, quiet rest time, active outdoor play, art, chapel, music, Spanish, and library.

The elementary curriculum (Grades 2–4) is specific, organized, and sequential. Student growth from grade level to grade level is met with appropriate extended challenges, such as increasing independence and expectations, self-monitoring, and self-evaluation. Classes include reading, writing, math, social studies, science, art, music, computer skills, Spanish, French, library science, religion, chapel, and physical education.

The prescribed course of study for Grades 5 and 6 includes English, Mathematics, U.S. History and Geography, General Science, Computer, Religion, Art, Drama, Music, Physical Education, French, and Spanish. In Grades 7 and 8, the curriculum includes English, French, Spanish, Civilization, Medieval History, Life Science, Earth Science, Computer Science, Mathematics, Our Classical Heritage, Religion, Art, Music, Band, Instrumental Music, Choir, Speech and Drama, Computer, and Physical Education. High school credits may be earned in algebra and foreign language by qualified students in Grade 8. Elective courses are Civilization, Honors Mathematics, Algebra I, French I, Spanish I, Latin I, Review of English, Instrumental Music, and Choir.

A minimum of 21½ credits is required for graduation, including four years of English; three of the same foreign language; three of history (including American history and World History), one semester of government, and one semester of economics; three of mathematics (including Algebra I–II and Geometry); three of science (including biology and chemistry); one each of fine arts and religion; two years of physical education, including health; and one semester of computer science. Students must serve a minimum of 50 hours of community service.

All 84 members of the Class of 1999 are continuing their education at four-year colleges. Fifty-eight percent received scholarships and awards totaling more than $2,800,000. Fifteen percent were recognized by the National Merit Scholarship Corporation. Graduates went on to attend Baylor, Brown, Clemson, Davidson, Emory, Harvard, Marquette, Northwestern, Southern Methodist, Trinity, Tulane, Vanderbilt, Washington, and the Universities of Colorado, North Carolina, Pennsylvania, Richmond, Texas, and Virginia, among others.

STUDENT ACTIVITIES. The Lower, Middle, and Upper School student councils promote school spirit, loyalty, student interest, and honesty through service projects, dances, parties, and contests. Middle and Upper School students also publish *Itinerary* (literary magazine), *Carillon* (yearbook), and *Eagle Edition* (newspaper) and serve as acolytes at communion services. Students participate in Community Service and Student Services by volunteering in the Dallas and school communities.

Extracurricular groups include Ambassadors, Student Council, Student Honor Council, Ex Libris, Acolytes, International Club, Chapel Committee, Cheerleaders, Junior Classical League, Amnesty International, National Forensic League, The Whiz Quiz, Math Team, Model UN, Theatre Guild, Mu Alpha Theta, French Honor Society, and the Outing, Computer Science, Art, Film, Archaeology, Chess, Press, Environmental/Recycling, Photography, Spirit, Cultural Awareness, French, and Spanish clubs. Qualified students are elected to the National Honor Society.

The Wilderness Program begins with day hikes and overnight trips for Middle School students. The Upper School program includes longer trips that focus on mountaineering, backpacking, rock climbing, geology, winter camping, fishing, bicycling, and canoeing.

Interscholastic athletics begin in Grade 7. Teams compete with other members of the Southwest Preparatory Conference and the Metroplex Independent School Conference. Boys in the Upper School compete in baseball, basketball, cross-country, golf, soccer, tennis, crew, volleyball, lacrosse, and track; girls' teams compete in basketball, cross-country, golf, crew, soccer, tennis, track, field hockey, softball, and volleyball.

Students are involved in lectures, musicals, plays, dances, carnivals, parties, and art shows throughout the year. Traditional annual events include Lessons and Carols, Roman Banquet, Christmas Project, Christmas Dance, Senior Breakfast, Fine Arts Performance Night, Visiting Authors, Film Symposium Day, faculty/student athletic events, Athletic Awards Banquet, School Musical, Convocation and Graduation Ceremony, Honors Day Assembly, Junior-Senior Prom, and Senior Dinner.

ADMISSION AND COSTS. The Episcopal School of Dallas is open to any qualified student, regardless of race, religious creed, or ethnic background. Admission is based on School-administered standardized tests, the previous school record and performance, teacher evaluations, and an interview. Application should be made in the fall preceding desired enrollment. Late applications will be considered only if space becomes available after the enrollment date. There is a $125 application fee for candidates for Beginner through Grade 4 and $100 for Grades 5–12.

In 1999–2000, tuition ranges from $4200 in three-day Beginners to $12,500 in Grade 12. Extra expenses include uniforms ($150–$200) and school supplies. There is an optional lunch program.

In 1999–2000, the School awarded need-based financial aid in excess of $600,000. The Episcopal School of Dallas subscribes to the School Scholarship Service.

Head of Upper School: Anne Mercer Kornegay
Head of Middle School: Scott Kimball
Director of Alumni Relations: Karla K. Wigley
Director of Admission: Ruth Burke
Director of Development: Michele Peek
College Counselor: Nancy Fomby
Business Manager: Tommye McCeig
Director of Athletics: Russell Norman

Fort Worth Academy   1982

7301 Dutch Branch Road, Fort Worth, TX 76132. 817-370-1191; Fax 817-294-1323; Web Site www.fwacademy.org

Parents and educators founded Fort Worth Academy, now enrolling 260 day boys and girls in Kindergarten–Grade 8. In the belief that the curriculum is the catalyst to academic success, the school offers an accelerated program designed to develop strong basic skills, complemented by enrichment courses and electives in foreign language, computer science, and the arts. The Community Connection encourages wide participation in leadership, cultural and creative arts, athletics, and community service. A "student-centered" environment, dedicated teachers, and an active partnership with parents contribute to the success of the Academy's goals. Tuition: $6700. Financial aid is available. Nancy Palmer is Director of Admission; William M. Broderick is Head of School. *Southern Association.*

Fort Worth Country Day School   1962

4200 Country Day Lane, Fort Worth, TX 76109-9939 817-732-7718; Fax 817-377-3425; E-mail fwcds@mail.fwcds.pvt.tenet.edu

Fort Worth Country Day School enrolls 1100 students in Kindergarten–Grade 12 in a rigorous college preparatory program with required offerings in the fine and performing arts and athletics. An Honor Code is in place, and the School aims to prepare students for the academic and social challenges of most selective colleges. The School has three divisions (lower, middle, and upper), each with its own facility, principal, and faculty. A 100-acre campus in the southwest part of the city includes 11 academic buildings, seven athletic fields, six tennis courts, a challenge course, and a stadium/all-weather eight-lane track. Tuition: $9120–$9820. Financial Aid: $727,200. Barbara W. Jiongo is Admissions Director; F. Graham Brown, Jr. (Hobart, B.A. 1967; Trinity, M.A. 1973), is Headmaster.

Good Shepherd Episcopal School   1959

11122 Midway Road, Dallas, TX 75229-4119. 214-357-1610; Fax 214-357-4105; E-mail nlawrence@gsesdallas.org; Web Site www.gseschooldallas.org

Good Shepherd Episcopal School is a parish day school enrolling 570 boys and girls in Preschool–Grade 8. Its purpose is to equip students with Christian principles, a love of learning, a creative mind, and a giving spirit. In the lower grades, reading, writing, language arts, social studies, math, science, and health are taught by classroom teachers, with specialized teachers for art, music, Spanish, and physical education. In Grades

5–8, students take one class period each in core subjects and one semester each of art and music, all taught by specialists. Activities include Student Council, Stewards, athletics, and Classroom of the Earth. Tuition: $4808–$6524. Financial aid is available. Nancy Lawrence is Director of Admission; J. Robert Kohler is Head of the School.

Greenhill School   ADDISON

4141 Spring Valley Road, Addison, TX 75001-3683. 972-661-1211; Fax 972-404-8217; Web Site www.greenhill.org

GREENHILL SCHOOL in Addison, Texas, is a coeducational day school enrolling 1245 students in Preschool through Grade 12. The School is located 12 miles north of the center of Dallas and provides students with both a spacious suburban environment and convenient access to the rich cultural and educational opportunities of a lively metropolitan area.

Greenhill was founded in 1950 by Bernard L. Fulton and a group of Dallas citizens for the purpose of providing high-quality, coeducational college preparation. Greenhill aims to prepare students not only for college, but for the lifetime of learning that follows.

The School combines a strong, creative academic program with arts and athletic programs for students from diverse ethnic, religious, socioeconomic, and racial backgrounds. Greenhill values the individuality of each child and strives to provide exceptional opportunities for academic development, intellectual growth, and artistic and athletic fulfillment. Faculty, administrators, and staff recognize their responsibility to serve as examples for students by reinforcing the values and behaviors that support a civil community: intellectual and moral integrity, sensitivity to others, respect for difference, and a courageous and generous engagement with life.

Greenhill is governed by a Board of Trustees comprised of parents, alumni, and community leaders. Parent and alumni associations provide monetary and volunteer support, and parents take an active role in school activities. Greenhill is accredited by the Independent Schools Association of the Southwest and is a member of the National Association of Independent Schools, the Council for Advancement and Support of Education, and The College Board, among others.

THE CAMPUS. The 78-acre campus includes a lighted football stadium, 12 tennis courts (8 of which are lighted), a track, a baseball diamond and softball field, soccer and hockey fields, and two air-conditioned gymnasiums. The spacious grounds include a wooded area, a windmill, and a creek.

Greenhill's campus includes the Coit Preschool, the Lower School, Levy Middle School, Fulton Upper School, Crossman Hall for dining, Montgomery Library, Agnich Science Hall, the Three Chimneys administration building, and the Fine and Performing Arts Centre. New in 1998 are the Phillips Family Athletics Center, a 66,000-square-foot competition gymnasium and athletics complex; a natatorium, and the renovated Cox Field House. Designed by renowned architects, most of the campus spaces reflect Southwestern architecture, with high ceilings, exposed trusses, and large windows that take advantage of indirect sunlight.

All classrooms are equipped with Hewlett Packard Pentium MMX 200MHz computers. The Middle and Upper schools have language and computer labs equipped with Macintosh Apples and Hewlett Packard Pentium MMX computers. Montgomery Library houses 45,000 volumes plus a vast database of knowledge through Internet and CD-ROM resources. Library facilities also include an instructional area for Preschool and Lower School students. Also on campus are a before- and after-school care facility and a state-of-the-art black box theater.

THE FACULTY. Peter G. Briggs was appointed in 1992 as the third Headmaster in the School's 49-year history. Mr. Briggs is a graduate of Phillips Academy in Andover, Massachusetts. He earned his undergraduate degree at Harvard University and holds a master's degree in history from Johns Hopkins and a master's degree in education from Stanford University. Mr. Briggs was previously Headmaster of Greenwich Country Day School in Connecticut for 16 years. He served as Deputy Assistant Director of the National Institute of Education in Washington, D.C.; as Vice President of the Planar Corporation and the Education Turnkey System; and as a member of FIRST board of the U.S. Department of Education. He currently serves on the board of the Boys' and Girls' Club of Dallas.

There are 154 full-time faculty members, 68 men and 86 women. They hold 154 bachelor's and 93 advanced degrees, including 8 doctorates, from such colleges and universities as Baylor 4, College of William and Mary, Columbia, Dartmouth 6, Georgetown 2, Harvard 2, Northwestern 4, Princeton, Purdue 2, Southern Methodist 18, Stanford 2, Texas A&M 4, Tufts, Vanderbilt, and Yale.

STUDENT BODY. In 1999–2000, Greenhill enrolls 608 boys and 637 girls as follows: 106 in Preschool (age $3^{1}/_{2}$–Kindergarten), 357 in Lower School (Primer–Grade 4), 372 in Middle School (Grades 5–8), and 410 in Upper School (Grades 9–12). Students live in Dallas and surrounding communities and come from a wide variety of ethnic, national, economic, and religious backgrounds.

ACADEMIC PROGRAM. The school year runs from late August to the end of May, with breaks for Thanksgiving, December holidays, spring vacation, and national holidays. The year is divided into three marking periods. Parent conferences are held twice annually; written comments are sent at the end of each marking period and midway through the period if needed. Classes meet five days a week and have an average enrollment of 18.

To graduate, a student must complete $21^{1}/_{3}$ Upper School credits (1 credit is earned per yearlong course), including English 4, foreign language 3, history 3, mathematics 3, laboratory science 3, fine arts 1, and electives 3. Students typically take five courses per trimester. A coordinated curriculum from Preschool through Grade 12, combined with grade-level teaching teams and integrated course materials, guides the development of each student. Teachers are available for extra help and tutoring may be arranged. Independent study and tutorials are offered in all academic departments for qualified students. During the last half of their final trimester, students may elect to design off-campus senior projects that combine career skills with community service.

In addition to Advanced Placement and honors courses, the Upper School curriculum covers such varied topics as: Literature of the Southwest, Oceanography, East Asia in Transition, Philosophy, Law and Civil Liberties, Principles of Economics, The Epic Tradition, Molecular Biology, Astronomy, Chamber Orchestra, Ceramics, Filmmaking, Black History, Anatomy and Physiology, Printmaking, Religions of the World, Meteorology, History of Art, Environmental Studies, and Ancient and Medieval History. Language offerings include French, Spanish, Latin, and Mandarin Chinese. Emphasis throughout the grades is placed on writing well. Summer reading is required. Advanced Placement courses are available in English, Spanish, French, science, mathematics, computer, and studio art.

Upper School students are assisted by Greenhill's college counseling staff, which consists of a director, an assistant, and three faculty members. In 1999, combined mean SAT scores were among the highest in the Dallas area, with 660 verbal and 666 math. One-third of the 104 graduating seniors received National Merit recognition, and all matriculated to university. Among their choices were Amherst, Bucknell, Georgetown, Hamilton, Harvard University, Massachusetts Institute of Technology, Princeton, Rensselaer Polytechnic Institute, Rice, Southern Methodist, Stanford, Texas A&M, Tufts, Vanderbilt, Yale, and the Universities of North Carolina (Chapel Hill), Pennsylvania, Texas, and Virginia.

Summer on the Hill, Greenhill's summer school, offers academic, enrichment, language, adventure, and athletic courses and camps for students who have completed Preschool–Grade 11.

STUDENT ACTIVITIES. Clubs are many and varied throughout the School and include community service, Chess, International Club, Students Against Drunk Driving, Amnesty International, Ecology, Quiz Bowl, National Honor Society, and language clubs, among others. Student government organizes school activities and provides student body representation. Students in the Upper School are required to sign an honor code.

Students publish literary magazines at all levels: *Peacock Pages* in Lower School, *Horizons* in Middle School, and *Montage* in Upper School. *Montage* has won silver medals from Columbia Press each year since 1991 and, from 1996 to 1999, won the gold medal. Students also produce a school newspaper and yearbook. In the area of fine arts, students participate in dramatics and in musical ensembles and stage several major productions annually; works of visual artists regularly win places in exhibitions. The Greenhill debate team produced two of the nation's top teams in 1994 and won the Texas state title five years in a row. The team also earned the national championship in 1996 and the national Lincoln–Douglas championship in 1997 through 1999.

Physical education forms part of the curriculum at all levels and reflects the School's commitment to fitness as a lifelong goal. Competition in interscholastic sports begins in the seventh grade. Teams are fielded in football, basketball, soccer, track, tennis, field hockey, baseball, cross-country, crew, golf, lacrosse, softball, swimming, wrestling, and volleyball. Greenhill plays in the Metroplex Independent Schools Conference and the Southwest Preparatory Conference. The varsity boys' soccer team has won 10 Southwest Preparatory Conference championships since 1981. In 1992 and 1997, Greenhill's Upper School boys' varsity team won the under-18 National Tennis Championship. Intramural and recreational sports include tennis, weight lifting, tumbling, basketball, dance, self-defense, aerobics, and racquetball.

ADMISSION AND COSTS. Greenhill School admits well-rounded students of academic promise on the basis of transcripts, testing, teacher evaluations, and an interview. Candidates are urged to apply by December for admission the following August. Entrance testing begins in January.

In 1999–2000, tuition is $8650 for Preschool and Kindergarten, $10,380 for Primer–Grade 6, and $12,120 for Grades 7–12. Additional expenses include an optional lunch program ($650–$700), accident insurance ($56), and books (Upper School only). Tuition insurance is available. In 1999–2000, financial aid in the amount of $1,035,930 was awarded to 10 percent of the student body on the basis of need. Greenhill subscribes to the Student Scholarship Service.

Head of Upper School: George N. King, Jr.
Director of Admission/Financial Aid: Wendell M. Lee
Dean of Students: Chris Hartley
College Counselor: Wells McMurray
Director of Finance and Operations: Kenneth A. Piel
Director of Athletics and Physical Education: Earl Dorber

The Hockaday School   DALLAS

11600 Welch Road, Dallas, TX 75229-2999. 214-363-6311;
Admissions 214-360-6526;
E-mail chagermanbobo@mail.hockaday.org;
Web Site www.hockaday.org

THE HOCKADAY SCHOOL in Dallas, Texas, is a girls' school for boarding and day students in Grades 8–12 and day students only in Pre-Kindergarten–Grade 7. Founded in 1913 by Miss Ela Hockaday, the School seeks to provide a college preparatory education to girls of strong potential and diverse backgrounds who may be expected to assume positions of responsibility and leadership in a rapidly changing world. Within a diverse student body, Hockaday aims to foster a community of concern and friendship and to instill in every girl a love of learning and an appreciation of excellence in all its forms.

A nonprofit corporation, Hockaday is directed by a self-perpetuating Board of Trustees that represents alumnae, parents, and the community. The School receives support from the 7000 graduates and former students who make up the Hockaday Alumnae Association. Hockaday is accredited by the Independent Schools Association of the Southwest. It holds membership in the National Association of Independent Schools, among other organizations.

THE CAMPUS. Located on a 100-acre tract in a residential area, the modern campus includes 12 buildings. Eight of these are connected by glass-enclosed or covered walkways. In the academic area are classrooms; laboratories for languages, computers, and reading; a study center; an audiovisual and preview room; and two libraries with over 50,000 volumes. Students, faculty, and staff can share files and access E-mail at 340 networked computer terminals throughout the School. The three computer labs are equipped with scanners, digital cameras, and a variety of software. The Fine Arts facilities include a 600-seat auditorium, instrumental and voice studios, practice rooms, a painting studio, ceramics facilities with outdoor kilns, a photography laboratory, printmaking facilities, and an electronic music studio. The Science Center contains a lecture hall, study lounges, classrooms, ten major laboratories, a computer lab, and a greenhouse. The Lower School is housed in two separate buildings (Pre-Kindergarten/Kindergarten and Grades 1–4).

The two-story residence halls have individual lounges, kitchens, an exercise room, computer labs, and laundry facilities. The infirmary is adjacent to the living quarters. A large common lounge with a fireplace and recreational equipment leads to the outdoor pool.

Athletics facilities include two gymnasiums housing three basketball courts (convertible to volleyball and indoor tennis courts), a climbing wall, a gymnastics area, weight room, two racquetball courts, a swimming pool, and a dance studio. On the grounds are three athletic fields, an all-weather track, a tennis center with ten courts and seating for 90, a golf driving area, and 65 acres of open space.

THE FACULTY. Mrs. Elizabeth M. Lee, Headmistress, is a graduate of Mount Holyoke College (B.A. 1965, magna cum laude) and received her M.A. degree from Columbia University. The Hockaday faculty is composed of 20 men and 84 women, most of whom have advanced degrees, with 6 holding doctorates.

STUDENT BODY. In 1999–2000, there are 70 boarding and

449 day girls in Grades 8–12 and 493 day girls in Pre-Kindergarten–Grade 7. The students, who come from nine states, 13 foreign countries, and the Dallas suburbs, represent various nationalities, faiths, and socioeconomic backgrounds.

ACADEMIC PROGRAM. Pre-Kindergarten girls are introduced to the basic elements of language, numerical reasoning, science, social studies, computers, art, music, and creative drama. An extended-day program is offered in the afternoons to provide cultural enrichment. In the full-day Kindergarten program, reading and mathematics becomes more structured, and emphasis is placed on a balanced reading program. In Grades 1–4, the program becomes more clearly divided into subject areas: language arts, mathematics, science, social studies, art, music, drama, and physical education, with Spanish or French beginning in Grade 1.

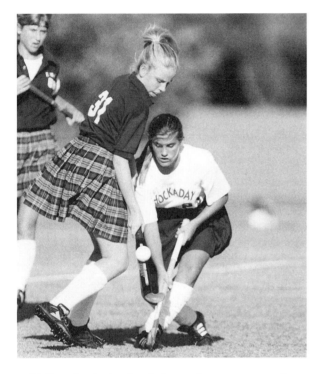

Middle School (Grades 5–8) continues to strengthen and widen the foundation of the Lower School. In Grades 5 and 6, language arts, mathematics, science, social studies, art, music, drama, Spanish or French, and physical education comprise the core curriculum. Students utilize their computer skills in science and social studies projects, math class, and language arts writing.

In Grades 7–8, the curriculum includes English, history, mathematics (pre-algebra in Grade 7 and either essentials of algebra or algebra in Grade 8), laboratory science, and foreign language choices in French, Spanish, or Latin. The fine arts selections are enlarged to offer photography, drawing, painting, drama, speech, debate, dance, guitar, musical theater, and ceramics. The eighth-grade class produces a musical each year. In Grade 7, computer applications is taught and, in Grade 8, the girls complete a Hyperstudio course. Upper School credits may be earned in math and foreign languages by eligible students in Grades 7–8. Activities include athletics, beginning in Grade 7; Student Council; the literary magazine, *Banner*; math, geography, and science clubs; yearbook staff; and chorus for both Grades 5–6 and 7–8. There is a sixth-grade trip to Colonial Williamsburg and the District of Columbia and a seventh-grade environmental-education trip to Prude Ranch in Fort Davis, Texas. The curriculum in Grades 1–8 is complemented by visits to various museums, the opera, the ballet, the symphony, and other sites of interest.

The Upper School curriculum includes English at each grade level and such senior English electives as "Celebrating the Land—The Frontier Spirit" and "The Heroine's Journey—The Search for Wholeness." French 1–5, Spanish 1–5, Latin 1–5; United States History, World History, Criminal Law, Government, Economics, Anthropology, Psychology, Philosophy; Algebra I & II, Geometry, Pre-calculus, Computer Science, Biology, Chemistry, Physics, Environmental Science; History of Art, Music, Video-Media Production, Acting Styles, Introduction to Drawing and Design, Painting, Printmaking, Ceramics and Sculpture, Photography, Concert Choir, Orchestra; Debate, Journalism; and Physical Education and Health are also offered. Swiss Semester in Zermatt is available to Grade 10 students and City Term in New York (The Masters School) for Grade 11 students.

Advanced Placement courses are available in 13 subjects. A cooperative arrangement with St. Mark's School of Texas allows girls to select courses there. Some Hockaday courses are also open to St. Mark's boys.

A one-year English as a Second Language program is offered on intermediate and advanced levels. Intensive language training in writing, reading, listening, and speaking skills is the focus of the program. Students may continue at Hockaday after the first year, following acceptance into the regular academic program. First-year students take trips both to Washington, D.C., and the Texas Hill Country.

Graduation trimester credit requirements include English 12, mathematics 9, history 7, language 6, laboratory science 6, fine arts 5, physical education and health 12, and academic electives 6, for a total of 63 trimester credits plus basic proficiency in computer usage.

Private lessons are available in piano beginning in Pre-Kindergarten; guitar beginning in Grade 1; flute, cello, and violin from Grade 5; and voice beginning in Grade 7.

All 109 members of the Class of 1999 entered college. They matriculated at 59 different colleges and universities including Boston College, Cornell, Dartmouth, Emory, Georgetown, Harvard, New York University, Rice, Southern Methodist, Stanford, Vanderbilt, Wake Forest, Washington and Lee, Washington University, and the Universities of North Carolina, Southern California, and Texas (Austin).

STUDENT ACTIVITIES. Student government begins in Grade 5 when the girls elect a representative to the Middle School Student Council. The conduct and activities of the older girls are regulated by the Student Council, elected by Upper School students. Special-interest organizations, publications, and honor societies augment the academic program. Honor societies are Cum Laude (academic), Dux Femina Facti (Latin), Entre Nous (French), Tu Tertulia (Spanish), Mu Alpha Theta (mathematics), Nucleus (science), National Forensic League (speech-debate), Quill and Scroll (journalism), and the National Thespian Society (theater arts). Community and School Service committees organize volunteer activities throughout the School and with dozens of other nonprofit organizations. Students are expected to complete 15 hours of community service each year.

Each year, two alumnae memorial fellowships bring outstanding persons to live on campus for several days.

Festive occasions include class dances, weekend retreats for Grades 9 and 12, all-school mixers, the Winter Formal, Senior Prom, a musical, Dads' Day, and various other events.

Hockaday's program of health, physical education, and recreation begins in Pre-Kindergarten. Designed to meet each girl's needs and to encourage her to develop a permanent pattern of physical activity, it offers daily instruction in the Lower and Middle schools, three times weekly in Grades 9–10, and twice weekly in Grades 11–12. Swimming is introduced in Grade 1 and continues through 11th grade lifeguarding. In Grades 7–8, traditional Green and White intramural teams compete in field hockey, basketball, volleyball, lacrosse, soccer, tennis, gymnastics, flag football, softball, track and field, and swimming. Interscholastic athletics are available to all girls in Grades 7–12. Varsity and junior varsity teams in Grades 9–12 compete in swimming, golf, tennis, field hockey, softball, basketball, volleyball, cross-country, track, crew, and soccer during the scheduled season for each sport.

ADMISSION AND COSTS. Applicants are accepted on the basis of previous school records, results of aptitude and achievement tests, recommendations, and a personal interview. Hockaday welcomes students of all nationalities, races, and creeds. Entrance tests are given at the School on specified dates.

In 1999–2000, day tuition is $4995 for Pre-Kindergarten (five mornings a week), $9835 for Kindergarten, $10,945 for Grades 1–4, $13,280 for Grades 5–7, and $12,790–$13,485 for Grades 8–12. For boarders, the charge for tuition, room, and board is $23,845–$24,555. Optional expenses include allowances, transportation, and private lessons. Tuition payment plans and insurance are available. In 1999–2000, the School awarded a total of $1,100,000 in student assistance based on financial need.

Assistant Headmistress: Karen Drawz
Deans of Students: Rebecca Storcy, Deborah Carey, and Mary Margaret Magee
Director of Alumnae: Nancy Gale
Director of Development: Christy Bednar
Director of Admissions: Jen Liggitt
College Counselor: Sara Lennon
Business Manager: Mary Pat Higgins
Director of Public Relations: Casey Hagerman Bobo
Director of Athletics: Joyce Rainwater
Director of Summer School: Claudia Todd

Holy Spirit Episcopal School 1962

12535 Perthshire Road, Houston, TX 77024-4186. 713-468-5138; Fax 713-465-6972; E-mail admission@hses.org; Web Site www.hses.org

Holy Spirit Episcopal, a parish school enrolling 400 boys and girls in Pre-Kindergarten–Grade 8, aims to develop each child's strength of character, intellectual prowess, and spiritual and physical well-being. The core curriculum is enhanced by computers, music, physical education, and outdoor education. The Spanish program includes student exchanges with a sister school in Costa Rica. Students are involved in sports, music, and other after-school enrichment activities. Extended care and a summer program are available. Tuition: $2000–$7100. Financial aid is available. Mrs. Sally Ward is Admissions Director; The Reverend C. Rodney Smith (University of the South, M.Div.) is Head of School.

The John Cooper School THE WOODLANDS

One John Cooper Drive, The Woodlands, TX 77381. 281-367-0900; Fax 281-292-9201; Web Site www.johncooper.org

THE JOHN COOPER SCHOOL in The Woodlands, Texas, is an independent, college preparatory day school enrolling boys and girls in Kindergarten–Grade 12. It is located in The Woodlands, a planned community of more than 56,000 residents 27 miles northwest of Houston.

The John Cooper School was established to meet the need for a coeducational, nonsectarian school that would provide a superior education for a diverse population of college-bound students. The reality of such a school was made possible through the generosity of corporate and private benefactors, prospective parents, and other supporters throughout the Houston region. It was named to honor John Cooper, the Houston educator whose counsel guided the founders in the early years. The School opened in 1988 with an enrollment of 175 students in Pre-Kindergarten–Grade 7, and a grade was added each year. Currently, 754 students are enrolled. The first senior class graduated in 1994.

The central goal of The John Cooper School is to enable its students to become creative thinkers, responsible citizens and leaders, and lifetime learners. The balanced program is designed to address all aspects of a student's education—intellectual, emotional, social, physical, and ethical—and to afford many opportunities to succeed within a secure, stimulating environment.

A not-for-profit institution, Cooper is accredited by the Independent Schools Association of the Southwest. The School is a member of the National Association of Independent Schools, the National Association of College Admission Counselors, the College Entrance Examination Board, the Educational Records Bureau, and The Cum Laude Society.

THE CAMPUS. The School is situated on a heavily forested 43-acre site donated by The Woodlands Corporation. The original academic building, housing the Lower School, is a modern 40,000-square-foot structure that won a national citation for its unusual use of light and space. This facility provides 20 airy classrooms with floor-to-ceiling windows overlooking natural outdoor areas. It also contains a science laboratory that is adjacent to an outdoor science center featuring native flora surrounding a "dragonfly pond." Computer laboratories, a library, a music studio, administrative offices, and a multipurpose room that serves as a cafeteria and auditorium are also included. The Middle and Upper School Building features six state-of-the-art science labs, a library, a computer lab, two music rooms, drama facilities, and a multipurpose room. The campus also includes an art barn with 4 classrooms and a gymnasium with dance studio and weight room. The grounds have four outdoor tennis courts, soccer, softball, and baseball fields, and playgrounds for younger children.

THE FACULTY. Dr. Bobby Ezell, Interim Head of School for the 1999–2000 academic year, holds a B.A. degree in English and political science from Baylor, a master's degree in education from Sam Houston State University, and a doctorate from Texas A&M in curriculum and instruction. Dr. Ezell has served as Director of Instructional Technology at Cooper since 1998. Previously, he was Coordinator of Instructional Services for the Conroe Independent School District and taught distance learning master's degree courses. At the campus level, Dr. Ezell has served as principal and department chair and, as a teacher, earned state honors.

The 88 full-time teachers and administrators hold baccalaureate degrees or the equivalent, and more than half hold advanced degrees. They are graduates of such colleges and universities as Adelphi, Austin, Baylor, Boston University, Bowling Green, Brigham Young, California Polytechnic, California State, Central Missouri State, Colby, College of Wooster, Dartmouth, Denison, Duke, Eastman School of Music, Finley, Hampden-Sydney, Indiana, Kent State, LaGrange, Louisiana State, McNeese State, Miami, North Carolina State, Northwestern State, Ohio State, Old Dominion, Oxford, Pierce, Reading University, Rosemont, Rutgers, Sam Houston State, Smith, Southwest Texas State, State University of New York, Temple, Texas A&M, Texas Tech, Vanderbilt, Villanova, Virginia Polytechnic, Wake Forest, Wellesley, Wesleyan, Yale, and the Universities of Alberta, the Americas (Mexico), Arizona, Colorado, Connecticut, Damascus, Delaware, Durham, Florida, Glasgow, Hawaii, Houston, Leon (Spain), Maine, Maryland, Massachusetts, Michigan, Minnesota, Nebraska, New Mexico, North Texas, Rhode Island, the South, Sussex, Tennessee, Texas, Toledo, Tulsa, Utah, Virginia, and Wisconsin. There are also 2 part-time faculty, 4 full-time teaching aides, 2 school counselors, and a college counselor.

A registered nurse, a nurse's assistant, and a school psychologist are on staff. Major medical facilities are located nearby.

STUDENT BODY. In 1999–2000, The John Cooper School enrolled 754 boys and girls in Kindergarten through Grade 12. About 75 percent of the students come from The Woodlands and the balance from communities and suburbs of the Greater Houston area; 22 percent were students of color.

ACADEMIC PROGRAM. The school year is divided into four nine-week quarters, from August to May, including Thanksgiving, winter, and spring vacations and observances of national holidays. Grades are issued quarterly, with interim reports sent to parents as needed. Two parent-teacher conferences are scheduled annually. In the Middle and Upper schools, individual advisors oversee the academic progress of their students and serve as their advocates within the school community.

Classes are held five days a week starting between 7:40 and 8:00 A.M. with dismissal between 3:00 and 3:15 P.M., depending on grade. Homework is assigned on a regular basis beginning in Kindergarten. In the Middle and Upper Schools, teachers require between 30 and 45 minutes of homework per subject per night.

The five major academic disciplines—English, mathematics, science, history, and foreign languages—form the basis of a John Cooper education. While the program focuses on the traditional liberal arts, the School offers innovative hands-on programs to enrich individual instruction.

In the Lower School, experiential projects help students discover the joy of learning and encourage them to think, analyze, create, reason, question, and understand their world. Formal science classes and instruction in Spanish begin in Kindergarten, and all students take part in physical education, art, music, and library skills. With a 10:1 student-teacher ratio, children are ensured individual attention and encouragement.

In the Middle School, the academic program builds on basic skills mastered in the lower grades. French and Latin are introduced. The goals for the Middle School are to challenge students academically using a combination of departmentalized and interdisciplinary approaches, to provide the strong foundation necessary to flourish in Upper School. Both the academic program and daily advisory are designed to build self-discipline, self-confidence, and the ability to take initiative, leading toward the development of responsible, caring adults.

In the Upper School, academic courses are offered on a four-quarter/two-semester basis, but fine arts electives and physical education are offered on a trimester calendar. To graduate, students must complete four years of English; three years each of mathematics, a single foreign language, science (biology, chemistry, physics), and history (including World History and American History); two years of fine arts and physical education; one trimester of computer literacy; and two credits in additional elective courses. Advanced Placement courses in calculus (AB and BC), chemistry, English literature, physics, biology, French, Spanish, studio art, U.S. History, European History, and Computer Science are available to students who meet departmental requirements.

Courses offered in the Upper School are Literary Genres, British Literature, American Literature, World Literature, Southern Writers; Algebra 1–2, Geometry, Precalculus, Introductory Calculus, Calculus AB and BC; Biology, Physics, Chemistry; Latin I–IV, French I–V, Spanish I–V; Ancient World History, Modern World History, American History, Speech, History of Viet Nam, Economics, Psychology; Computer Applications, Computer Programming; and Sculpture, Drawing, Oil Painting, Multimedia Art, Drama, Chorus, Orchestra/Jazz Band; and Yearbook.

Among the colleges at which the members of recent graduating classes enrolled were Babson, Baylor, Boston University, Bowdoin, Brown, Carleton, Carnegie Mellon, Cornell, Davidson, Duke, Emory, Franklin and Marshall, George Washington University, Georgia Institute of Technology, Middlebury, Morehouse, Mount Holyoke, New York University, Northwestern, Pomona, Rhode Island School of Design, Rhodes, Rice, Smith, Southern Methodist, Stanford, Texas A&M, Texas Christian, Trinity University, Tufts, Tulane, United States Military Academy, United States Naval Academy, Vanderbilt, Washington and Lee, Wellesley, Williams, Yale, and the Universities of Chicago, Colorado, Massachusetts, Notre Dame, Pennsylvania, Richmond, Texas, and Virginia.

An academic enrichment program and camp are conducted in the summer.

STUDENT ACTIVITIES. The School's varied extracurricular program engages students in a wide range of activities after school. The Middle and Upper schools elect representatives to the Student Council, which plans activities and serves as liaison with the administration. Other leadership opportunities are provided by Model UN, Junior State groups, Honor Council, and Cum Laude Society.

Students work toward improving their world through Interact, a social outreach organization. The Drama Club stages regular productions. Interested students may participate in science fairs, Texas Math League, Choir, Band, and numerous clubs that reflect student interests. The School produces three student publications: *Paragon* (yearbook), *Inkblots* (literary magazine), and *Ogolon* (art and literary magazine).

Middle and Upper School teams compete on the varsity and junior varsity levels with other independent schools in the Houston area. Girls participate in soccer, basketball, volleyball, cheerleading, and softball, while boys' teams are formed in soccer, basketball, wrestling, and baseball. Both boys and girls play golf, tennis, cross-country, and track and field.

Among the School's traditional events are Middle and Upper School Honors Assemblies, Leadership Challenge trips, Middle School Carnival, Annual Gala and Auction, Booster Bash, Golf Tournament, Grandparents' Day, International Day, Heritage Day, John Cooper Day, Junior-Senior Brunch, Prom, Senior Dinner and Awards Ceremony, Baccalaureate, and Commencement.

ADMISSION AND COSTS. John Cooper welcomes academically qualified students who demonstrate the potential to succeed and to contribute to the life of the School. Students are admitted on the basis of entrance exam scores, previous records, teacher recommendations, and a personal interview. The application fee is $125 for Kindergarten–Grade 12.

In 1999–2000, tuition and fees are $7975 for Kindergarten and Grades 1–5, $8600 for Grades 6–8, and $8975 for Grades 9–12. The charges include an $800 nonrefundable deposit. A one-time new-student fee of $200 is assessed for all students.

Assistant Head of School/Upper School Head: Joseph Broccoli
Middle School Head: Mary Rafferty
Lower School Head: Karen Francis
Upper School Dean of Students: Barbara Brown
Middle School Dean of Students: Hugh Schoolman
Director of Admissions: Craig Meredith
Director of Communication: Deb Spiess
College Counselor: Anne Naman
Business Manager: Jack Ramsey
Director of Athletics: Harold Wilder
Registrar: Anne Meinrath

The Kinkaid School   1906

201 Kinkaid School Drive, Houston, TX 77024. 713-782-1640;
Web Site www.kinkaid.org

Kinkaid, the first coeducational, college preparatory day school in Houston, seeks to enable students to develop their talents and fulfill their maximum potential through a balanced program of academics, arts, community service, and athletics. Enrolling 1289 students in Prekindergarten–Grade 12, The Kinkaid School offers a challenging liberal arts curriculum enhanced by special lecture series, off-campus career internships, and overseas travel/study. Students take part in school government, academic competitions, publications, interest clubs, arts, and athletics. A summer remedial and enrichment session is offered. Tuition: $7515–$10,250. Financial Aid: $704,130. Betty Hankamer is Director of Admissions; Donald C. North (Vanderbilt, B.A.; Middlebury, M.A.) was appointed Headmaster in 1996.

Lakehill Preparatory School   1970

2720 Hillside Drive, Dallas, TX 75214. 214-826-2931;
Fax 214-826-4623

Lakehill was founded by parents in the Lakewood/East Dallas area to provide an outstanding college preparatory education within a nurturing atmosphere. Enrolling 260 day boys and girls in Kindergarten–Grade 12, Lakehill offers a challenging curriculum that prepares students to meet their future goals for success. The academic program is enriched by Advanced Placement courses, community service activities, and studies in art, music, drama, foreign languages, and computers as well as by a required career internship. Extracurricular activities include varsity sports, cheerleading, National Honor Society, Student Council, clubs, and music groups. Tuition: $6770–$9190. Financial Aid: $210,000. Fran Thompson Holley is Director of Admissions; Roger L. Perry (University of North Texas, B.S., M.Ed.) was appointed Headmaster in 1982. *Southern Association.*

The Lamplighter School   1953

11611 Inwood Road, Dallas, TX 75229. 214-369-9201;
Fax 214-369-5540; E-mail tls@thelamplighterschool.org;
Web Site www.thelamplighterschool.org

The Lamplighter School, enrolling 450 boys and girls in Preschool (age 3)–Grade 4, seeks to foster the love of learning and build a positive self-concept. Selected as a Blue Ribbon School of Excellence, Lamplighter offers a highly integrated curriculum that merges the fine arts with language arts, math, environmental science, social studies, physical education, and Spanish. Innovative groupings provide a warm and supportive environment that fosters enthusiasm, self-confidence, and a sense of belonging. The north Dallas campus features a fine arts complex, a media center, a greenhouse, and a health and fitness facility. A summer program is available for 3- to 6-year-olds. Tuition: $4880–$8995. Dolores Evans is Director of Admission; Pat Mattingly (University of North Texas, B.S.Ed., M.Ed.) is Director.

Lutheran High School   1976

8494 Stults Road, Dallas, TX 75243. 214-349-8912;
Fax 214-340-3095; Web Site www.lhsdfw.com

Lutheran High seeks to provide a Christ-centered education that will prepare its 275 students in Grades 7–12 for success in college and in life. The core program emphasizes the sharing of the Gospel in a caring, Christian environment that encourages intellectual, spiritual, physical, and social maturity. The traditional academic disciplines are supplemented by religious studies, music and the arts, and challenging electives. Students take part in a well-balanced extracurricular program including community service, drama, sports, foreign travel opportunities, academic competitions, and interscholastic sports for boys and girls. Tuition: $5120–$6950. Financial aid is available. Donna L. Frieling is Admissions Director; Gerald C. Brunworth, Ed.D., is Headmaster.

Marine Military Academy   HARLINGEN

320-BB Iwo Jima Boulevard, Harlingen, TX 78550.
956-423-6006, Ext. 252 Admissions;
E-mail admissions@mma-tx.org; Web Site www.mma-tx.org

MARINE MILITARY ACADEMY in Harlingen, Texas, is a boarding school offering college preparatory and Junior Reserve Officers Training Corps programs to boys in Grades 8 through 12 and a postgraduate year. Harlingen (population 48,435) is located in the Lower Rio Grande Valley, a noted agricultural and recreational area, and is a 35-minute drive from Mexico and a 45-minute drive from the beaches of the Gulf of Mexico. The city is accessible by car from the north on United States Routes 77 and 281 and from the west on Route 83, and by air via major airlines, with connections to Houston, San Antonio, Dallas, and the Mexican cities of Tampico, Vera Cruz, Monterrey, and Mexico City.

The Academy was founded in 1965 by Capt. William A. Gary, businessman and retired Marine Corps reservist, who believed that Marine Corps concepts of leadership and discipline were adaptable to preparatory school education. In 1965, he and other former Marine officers opened the school in Har-

lingen when a former U.S. Air Force Base became available. The school aims to provide a "wholesome, patriotic, and invigorating atmosphere in which students are inspired toward maximum achievement." Academic excellence has first priority, but the school "stresses the development of character, leadership, esprit de corps, and a strong devotion to country" through values and principles derived from the U.S. Marine Corps and a vigorous athletic program.

Marine Military Academy is a nonprofit corporation governed by a self-perpetuating Board of Trustees; 7 of the 20 members are active or retired officers of the United States Marine Corps or the Marine Reserve. The school has over 2000 living alumni who assist in recruiting and in the development of school programs.

The Academy is accredited by the Southern Association of Colleges and Schools and the Independent Schools Association of the Southwest. It holds membership in the Southern Association of Independent Schools, the National Association of Independent Schools, and the Association of Military Colleges and Schools of the United States.

THE CAMPUS. The 142-acre campus, planted with bougainvillea, hibiscus, and palm trees, includes playing fields, an obstacle course, and facilities for football, track, swimming, basketball, baseball, boxing, soccer, and tennis. The original, full-scale Iwo Jima Memorial Statue is on campus.

Cadets live two to a room in six barracks. Other buildings are the chapel, the Cadet Activities Center (1998), and a mess hall. The school's 1000-seat auditorium and a 14,500-square-foot library were dedicated in 1993. A fully equipped athletic center (1980) houses a weight room and racquetball courts. Three tennis courts were completed in 1989. A rifle range was completed in 1982. A football field and an AAU-certified track were added in 1997. A stadium was built in 1982, and seven faculty and staff housing units were completed in 1983. The administration building opened in 1986. The 39,000-square-foot Coleman Hall (1996) houses offices for the academic and military departments and contains 17 classrooms, a college placement office, SAT prep room, and post exchange. A 24,000-square-foot cadet services center, which opened in 1994. The plant is owned by the Academy and is valued at $15,500,000.

THE FACULTY. The Academy has 33 teachers and maintains an equal balance between male and female teachers. Military service is not a requirement for teachers, who do not wear uniforms. The Dean of Academics, P. Neal Meier, has extensive education and military experience and lives on campus with his family. The President and 8 faculty and staff members also live on campus with their families. All faculty hold baccalaureates, more than half hold advanced degrees, and 17 others are working toward their master's degrees. The Military Division includes a commandant who is a retired Marine Corps Colonel, an Assistant Commandant of Cadets, and six drill instructors who live with their families in apartments in each cadet barracks.

Two registered nurses live on campus. Local doctors may also be called on to administer treatment. Valley Baptist Medical Center, with full hospital facilities, is in the immediate vicinity.

STUDENT BODY. In 1999–2000, the school enrolled 331 boarding boys in Grades 8–12 and the postgraduate year. The majority of students are from Texas; 25 other states and six foreign countries are also represented.

ACADEMIC PROGRAM. The school year, divided into semesters, extends from late August to late May, with Thanksgiving and Christmas vacations and a spring break. The school day begins with reveille at 6:00 A.M. Classes, which range in size from 12 to 18, are held five days a week and are scheduled in six 50-minute periods between 8:20 A.M. and 3:10 P.M. Classes are followed by a short academic advisory period. Sports and activities are conducted in the late afternoon. Study halls, supervised by faculty members, are held during the day. All students are required to take military training and physical education and to participate in the sports program.

Twenty-one units of academic credit are required for graduation, with the school's Standard Diploma requiring 24. The normal course load is five units per year plus military science. The required credits are five in English (includes an English composition course); three in mathematics; three in foreign language and science; plus the required courses of American History, World History, Government, Economics, Health, Speech, Typing, Computer Science, Military Science, and electives. Postgraduate programs are individually designed to prepare cadets for entrance to the service academies or to strengthen their qualifications for other colleges.

Among the courses offered in Grades 8–12 are: English 1–4, Composition, Speech; French 1–4, German 1–4, Spanish 1–4; American History, World History, Geography, Advanced World Studies, Geopolitics, Government/Economics; Pre-Algebra, Algebra 1–3, Geometry, Trigonometry, Analytical Geometry, Calculus; Computer Science; Physical Science, Naval Science, Biology, Chemistry, Physics, Advanced Chemistry; Aerospace Education 1–2; Typing; Band; and SAT Preparation.

In 1999, 97 percent of the graduating seniors and postgraduates were accepted at such colleges, universities, and service academies as DePauw, Purdue, Texas A&M, United States Naval Academy, Vanderbilt, and the Universities of California (Los Angeles), Chicago, Notre Dame, Southern California, and Texas.

One four-week session of military summer camp is held from late June to July. Modeled on Marine Corps recruit training, the program is open to boys ages 13 to 17 and includes military drill, rifle marksmanship, physical fitness, and athletic activity. Also available, at additional cost, is an introduction to aerospace, which involves hands-on flying.

STUDENT ACTIVITIES. The Corps of Cadets is headed by a Cadet Lieutenant Colonel and is organized in six companies led by cadet officers. The Academy's Military Division is responsible for the selection and training of cadet leaders for administering the Academy's disciplinary system and supervising drill and ceremonies, dormitory life, and recreational activities. All new cadets are regarded as plebes in their initial three weeks, during which time they are expected to demonstrate a willingness to obey orders and accept discipline from more experienced cadets. Hazing is strictly forbidden. All cadets are responsible for daily barracks upkeep. Call to Colors, morning formation, and military activities are held before classes each morning, including Saturday. Mandatory vespers are held on Wednesday evenings at the Mary Moody Northen Chapel, located on campus.

Among the organized activities available to cadets are the Band, Color Guard, Drill Team, Boxing Team, Rifle Team, Boy Scouts, Judo, French Club, Military History Club, Camera Club, and Yearbook. Weight lifting, marksmanship, long-distance running, and swimming are available on a recreational basis.

Academy varsity teams compete against other area private and public schools in football, long-distance running, basketball, baseball, track, golf, tennis, soccer, swimming, and marksmanship. Intramural competition is offered in basketball, volleyball, track, soccer, and softball.

Various social events, including the Birthday Ball, are held during the school year. After their first three weeks of training, all cadets are eligible for liberty to visit Harlingen on Saturday afternoons and evenings and on Sundays. Overnight liberty is granted for Saturdays with written parental permission if the cadet is in satisfactory academic standing.

ADMISSION AND COSTS. The Academy seeks students of "good character and serious purpose." Students are admitted on the basis of a transcript from the previous school and recommendations from the applicant's principal or counselor and his English and mathematics teachers. Applicants must be physically capable of participating in the JROTC program. Applications, with a fee of $100, are accepted until early August for fall entry, but should be submitted earlier. Students can be admitted at midyear, with the exception of seniors. A reservation deposit of $750 is required on notice of acceptance.

Tuition is $16,995 per year. Included in the cost is a textbook rental fee, and laundry, cleaning, medical fees, and fees for uniforms. Extras include fees for supplies, standard and special testing, laboratory fees, and aerospace education. The school provides individual scholarships to returning cadets, awarded on the basis of citizenship, leadership potential, financial need, and academic merit.

Dean of Academics: P. Neal Meier
Commandant of Cadets: Col. C. O. Meyers III, USMC (Ret.)
Director of Admissions: Lt. Col. Robert R. Grider, USMC (Ret.)
Director of Institutional Advancement: Col. Tom Hobbs, USMC (Ret.)
College Counselor: Mrs. Sandra Williams
Director of Athletics: Mr. Tom Morton
Business Manager: Mr. Daniel E. Lanoue

The Oakridge School   ARLINGTON

5900 West Pioneer Parkway, Arlington, TX 76013. 817-451-4994; E-mail admiss@oakridge.pvt.k12.tx.us; Web Site www.oakridge.pvt.k12.tx.us

THE OAKRIDGE SCHOOL in Arlington, Texas, is a coeducational, college preparatory day school enrolling students in Preschool through Grade 12. Located east of Fort Worth, the School is readily accessible by car to students from the greater Dallas/Fort Worth Metroplex area. A variety of libraries, galleries, theaters, and museums as well as the cultural benefits of several universities are located in the Metroplex.

The Oakridge School was founded in 1979 by a group of parents and educators concerned with offering a challenging college preparatory curriculum. Emphasizing personal development, the School aims "to provide . . . an education of highest quality to academically qualified students, to motivate each student to perform at his or her maximum potential, and to prepare students for a life of achievement and participation in society."

The Oakridge School is a nonprofit institution governed by an independent Board of Regents. The School is accredited by the Southern Association of Colleges and Schools and the Independent Schools Association of the Southwest and holds membership in the National Association of Independent Schools, the Texas Association of Non-Public Schools, and the Texas Independent School Consortium.

THE CAMPUS. The School's 35-acre campus currently consists of seven buildings. The Preschool houses the three- and four-year-old classes and Kindergarten (PK3, PK4, K5), a large multipurpose room, and features an expansive playground. The Lower and Middle School building contains classrooms, music room, two computer labs, and two art rooms. The Upper School building houses science labs, central commons area, and specialized classrooms. The Student Activities Center consists of two basketball courts, kitchen, eating area, locker rooms, weight room, and offices. It serves as a gym and cafeteria. The Multipurpose Activity Center has been acoustically enhanced to serve as a performing arts facility as well as an additional gym. Two new buildings consist of The Information Center and The Fine Arts Center. The Information Center houses the technology center, an expanded school library, and the offices of central administration. The Fine Arts Center (January 2000) features enhanced facilities for the visual and performing arts, including a 400-plus-seat multipurpose auditorium. The campus includes two extensive playground areas, a restored Wetlands Park, and the School's athletic fields, which border the Lake Arlington Golf Course.

THE FACULTY. Andy J. Broadus, appointed Headmaster in 1981, is a graduate of Jacksonville University (B.S.) and the University of North Florida (M.Ed.) and has done advanced graduate work at the University of Georgia and Columbia University. Prior to his appointment as Headmaster, Mr. Broadus served as Associate Head at Jacksonville Country Day School in Florida. Mr. Broadus is past President of the Texas Association of Non-Public Schools. Betty Garton (Texas Tech, B.S.; Texas Christian, M.Ed.) is Director of the Preschool; Corliss Elsesser (Texas Christian, B.S., M.Ed.) has been with the School since its founding and is Head of the Lower School; Jon Kellam (Texas Christian, B.S., M.Ed.) is Head of the Middle School; Susan Mann (Texas Wesleyan, B.S.; Texas Christian, M.Ed.) is Head of the Upper School.

The faculty include 93 teachers, 67 women and 26 men. They hold 93 baccalaureate, 38 master's degrees, and 4 doctoral degrees representing study at a variety of colleges throughout the United States and abroad.

First aid is provided by a full-time registered nurse with a fully equipped school infirmary. An emergency medical facility is located nearby.

STUDENT BODY. In 1999–2000, the School enrolls 820 boys and girls, from 3 to 18 years of age. Students come from Arlington, Bedford, Burleson, Cedar Hill, Cleburne, Colleyville, Dallas, De Soto, Duncanville, Euless, Fort Worth, Grand Prairie, Grapevine, Hurst, Irving, Keller, Mansfield, Midlothian, Southlake, and Waxahachie. Also represented are seven foreign countries.

ACADEMIC PROGRAM. The school year is divided into four marking periods in all divisions. Parents are informed regularly of student progress through interim reports, parent conferences, and report cards, which are sent to parents at the end of each marking period. Classes range in size from 4 to 22 students with a student-teacher ratio of 10:1. Self-discipline and clear, concise rules are emphasized in "an atmosphere of mutual respect." Faculty members provide extra help as needed, and tutoring can be arranged.

The Preschool (PK3, PK4, K5) curriculum incorporates Mathematics, Language Arts, Science, Social Studies, Spanish, Computer, Visual Perception, Music, Art, and Physical Education. The entire curriculum is sequential from level to level. The Lower School (Grades T1–4) courses include Language Arts Enrichment, Social Studies, Math, Science, Spanish, Art, Music, Physical Education, Computer, and Library program. The Lower House of the Middle School (Grades 5–6) curriculum is as follows: two daily classes of Language Arts, French or Spanish, U.S. and World History, Math, General Science, Earth Science, Art, Music, Creative Dramatics, and intramural athletics. The Upper House of the Middle School (Grades 7–8) curriculum is as follows: English, Composition, French or Spanish, Texas History and U.S. History, Pre-Algebra and Algebra I, Life Science and Physical Science, Art, Choir, and Physical Education/Athletics. The Upper School (Grades 9–12) curriculum includes: English; World History, U.S. History, American Government, Economics; Spanish, French; Algebra I–II, Geometry, Trigonometry, Pre-Calculus, Calculus; Biology, Chemistry, Physics, Anatomy, and Physiology; electives include Psychology, Anthropology/Archaeology, History of England, Acting, Studio Art, Choir, and Yearbook.

Advanced Placement courses are offered in Language & Composition, Literature & Composition, Calculus, Biology, Physics, U.S. History, European History, French, Spanish, and Computer Science.

Annual standardized testing includes the Stanford Achievement Test. The Otis-Lennon School Ability test is given every other year.

The College Counseling program is a four-year process. All students take the PLAN in 9th and 10th grade; the PSAT in 9th, 10th, and 11th; and the SAT I, SAT II, and ACT in 11th and 12th. Oakridge hosts a number of college representatives on campus throughout the fall, and students attend an annual college fair. College advising is conducted on a one-to-one basis, particularly in the senior year, and includes financial aid counseling, computer resources, and field trips to nearby colleges. Oakridge students have been accepted at such colleges and universities as Arizona State, Baylor, Boston College, Cornell, Creighton, Duke, Emory, Georgetown, Harvard, Louisiana State, New York University, Northwestern, Ohio State, Rensselaer Polytechnic, Rice, Southern Methodist, Spelman, Stanford, Texas A&M, Texas Christian, Texas Tech, Trinity, and the University of Texas.

STUDENT ACTIVITIES. There are elected Student Council programs in the Middle and Upper schools. In the Upper School, the Student Council consists of elected officers and the officers of each class. Members of the Student Council are expected to serve as representatives, leaders, and good examples for the entire student body. A faculty sponsor advises and works with the Student Council.

The Middle and Upper School Inter-Scholastic Sports Program offers baseball, basketball, football, golf, soccer, tennis, cross-country, and track for boys, and basketball, soccer, tennis, golf, cross-country, softball, track, field hockey, and volleyball for girls. The Athletic Director schedules games with public and private schools in the Fort Worth/Dallas area. Other activities include the National Junior Honor Society, the National Honor Society, Math Teams, Youth and Government, Literary Magazine, cheerleading, and the Drama, French, Spanish, Art, Whole Earth, and Computer clubs. Special social activities are scheduled on a monthly basis.

Special programs and events include Grandparents Day, New Parent Dinner, Book Fair, the Super Supper and Auction, Homecoming, Sports Banquets, Parent Orientation Night, Owlfest, Spring Fair, Living History Program, concerts, and awards programs.

ADMISSION AND COSTS. The Oakridge School seeks academically qualified students of superior attitude. Students are accepted in all grades, when openings exist, on the basis of an aptitude test, reading and math achievement tests, past academic and behavior records, recommendations, and an interview. Application should be made as early as possible; students who have recently moved to the Fort Worth/Dallas area may be admitted in mid-year. There is an application fee of $50, a testing fee of $75 for Grades 1–12, and, upon acceptance, a registration fee of $500, which is applied toward tuition. The Director of Admission handles applications.

In 1999–2000, tuition ranges from $2310 for two-day PK3 to $8700 for seniors. Monthly tuition payments are available. The Oakridge School subscribes to the School Scholarship Service and provides limited financial aid to students who qualify.

Alumni Association President: Jason Sear '87
Director of Admissions: Linda Broadus
Director of Development: Sharon LeMond
College Advisor: Gail Kilman
Business Officer: Richard Horvath
Director of Finance: Kathy Gamill
Director of Athletics: David Slight

The Parish Day School 1972

*14115 Hillcrest Road, Dallas, TX 75240. 972-239-8011;
Fax 972-991-1237; E-mail mmclean@mail.parishday.org;
Web Site www.parishday.org*

The Parish Day School was founded by the Reverend James J. Niles and Mrs. Mary Loving Blair to provide quality education within the Episcopal tradition. The School, which enrolls 430 day boys and girls in Pre-Kindergarten–Grade 6, emphasizes academics and instills an awareness of obligations to fellow students and their community. All students attend daily chapel services, and religion is taught in Kindergarten–Grade 6. Extracurricular opportunities include chorus, drama, art, computer/ math/science and geography clubs, scouting, and athletics. Tuition and Fees: $3630–$7835. Financial aid is available. Gloria Hoffman Snyder (University of Texas [Austin], B.A. 1959; Southern Methodist, M.L.A. 1976) is Head of School.

Presbyterian School 1988

*5300 Main Street, Houston, TX 77004. 713-520-0284;
Fax 713-524-6463; E-mail ahay@pshouston.org;
Web Site www.pshouston.org*

Presbyterian School, enrolling 300 day students in two-year-old Early Childhood–Grade 6, was founded to provide an environment in which family, school, and church unite in the education and support of each child. The School aims to maintain a healthy balance between a nurturing Christian learning experience and a challenging academic program that encourages each student to reach his or her full potential—intellectually, physically, emotionally, socially, and spiritually. Specialty classes are offered in music, art, computer, Spanish, motor skills, library, and chapel. Tuition: $3510–$8110. Financial aid is available. Allison Hay is Admissions Director; Ellen Welsh (University of Pittsburgh, M.Ed. 1976) was appointed Head of School in 1996. *Southern Association.*

Providence Christian School of Texas   1988

5002 West Lovers Lane, Dallas, TX 75209. 214-366-2071;
Fax 214-357-6251; E-mail jodea@pcstx.org

Providence Christian School of Texas, a nondenominational, coeducational day school enrolling 380 students in Grades 1–9, emphasizes classical education with a Biblical world view. Providence is dedicated to providing a stimulating, interesting, and wholesome environment for the academically able student. A "hands-on" integrated approach to learning focuses on the individual uniqueness of each child and mastery of basic skills in English, grammar, science, math, history, geography, and physical education. Publications, nature studies, and foreign language are among the extracurricular activities. Tuition: $4500–$5750. Financial aid is available. Kathy Stewart is Admissions Director; James R. O'Dea (United States Military Academy, B.S.; Dallas Theological Seminary, M.A.B.S.) is Headmaster.

River Oaks Baptist School   1955

2300 Willowick, Houston, TX 77027. 713-623-6938;
Fax 713-626-0650; E-mail cbailey@robs.org;
Web Site www.robs.org

River Oaks Baptist School enrolls 735 day boys and girls in Two-Year-Olds through Grade 8. The academic environment, which balances high expectations with nurturing, encourages children to maximize their potential, and cultivates creativity, critical thinking, initiative, respect for diversity, and the dignity of each individual. Extracurricular opportunities include Student Council, competitive sports and intramurals, publications, musical performances, community outreach, and field trips. Tuition: $5275–$10,125. Financial Aid: $177,000. Cindy Bailey is Director of Admission; Nancy Heath Hightower (University of Texas, B.S. 1958; University of Houston, M.Ed. 1983, Ed.D. 1985) was appointed Head of School in 1989.

Saint Agnes Academy   1906

9000 Bellaire Boulevard, Houston, TX 77036. 713-219-5400;
Fax 713-219-5499; Web Site http.www.st-agnes.org

Founded by Dominican Sisters, Saint Agnes Academy enrolls 750 girls as day students in Grades 9–12. The school strives to provide a demanding program in an atmosphere imbued with the values and principles of the Catholic faith. The college preparatory curriculum includes Advanced Placement courses and offerings in the arts. Some classes are shared with boys from Strake Jesuit Preparatory. Activities involve students in athletics, musical and theatrical productions, publications, debate, and community service. A summer program is offered. Tuition: $6250. Extras: $300–$600. Financial Aid: $200,000. Deborah Whalen is Academic Dean/Director of Admission; Sr. Jane Meyer (Dominican College, B.A.; Texas Women's, M.S.) was named Principal in 1981 and is now Head of School. *Southern Association.*

St. Andrew's Episcopal School   1952

Lower/Middle School: 1112 West 31st Street, Austin, TX 78705.
512-452-5779; Fax 512-451-0222; E-mail stadev@onr.com;
Web Site www.standrews.austin.tx.us
Upper School: 5901 Southwest Parkway; Austin, TX 78735.
512-452-5779

Enrolling 516 day boys and girls in Grades 1–10, St. Andrew's provides "an enriched academic program within a Christian environment." The curriculum, designed to ensure mastery of essential skills in science, reading, mathematics, and social studies, also features daily chapel, community service, and an outdoor study program that focuses on care of the environment. An after-school enrichment program is available. Extracurricular activities include athletics, Student Council, yearbook, and National Junior Honor Society. Tuition: $6900–$10,000. Extras: $350–$500. Financial aid is available. Diane Williams is Admissions Director; Lucy C. Nazro (University of Texas [Austin], B.A. 1959; Episcopal Seminary of the Southwest, M.A. 1966) is Head.

St. Clement's Episcopal Parish School   1958

600 Montana Drive, El Paso, TX 79902. 915-533-4248;
Fax 915-544-1778

St. Clement's Episcopal Parish School, a Blue Ribbon School of Excellence enrolling 420 boys and girls in Pre-Kindergarten–Grade 9, offers a strong academic program that emphasizes Christian values as well as basic learning and critical thinking skills. The traditional curriculum is enhanced by an extensive outdoor program, computer classes, music, art, and Spanish. After-school enrichment and frequent field trips reinforce classroom instruction. Extracurricular activities include Science Club, basketball, volleyball, and speech and drama. Tuition: $4000–$6600. Financial aid is available. Gretchen Love is Director of Admissions; Michael L. Waller (University of California, B.A. 1979; University of San Francisco, M.Ed. 1989) was appointed Headmaster in 1994.

St. Francis Episcopal Day School   1952

335 Piney Point Road, Houston, TX 77024. 713-782-0481;
Fax 713-782-4720; Web Site www.ssfrancis.org

St. Francis, a parish school serving more than 700 students age 3 to Grade 8, is located in the Memorial area of West Houston. This Blue Ribbon School of Excellence offers challenging academics, interpersonal relationships, and activities with an emphasis on morality, values, and respect for all people. The curriculum includes literature-based language arts, a mathematics program that utilizes current methodologies, and an outdoor education program. St. Francis is guided by a model that integrates technology and curriculum, with Internet access in every classroom. Students attend chapel regularly and engage in community service. Athletics, drama, choir, strings, and art studies are among the extracurriculars. Tuition: $3690–$8070. Sally Ellis is Admission Director; Dr. Annette C. Smith is Head of School.

St. James Episcopal School   1946

602 South Carancahua Street, Corpus Christi, TX 78401.
512-883-0835; Fax 512-883-0837; Web Site www.sjes.org

St. James, a Blue Ribbon School of Excellence, enrolls 350 boys and girls in Preschool–Grade 8. Following its mission to provide a superior education that enables students to reach their full potential within a Christian community, the School integrates all learning activities around a "Central Theme." The early grades emphasize discovery activities in preparation for the mastery of specific academic skills in the Middle School. At all levels, classroom learning is enhanced by field trips and outdoor education beyond the campus, while fine arts and life skills, sports, drama, leadership opportunities, and regular chapel services support personal growth and achievement. Tuition: $1381–$5235. H. Palmer Bell was appointed Headmaster in 1996.

St. John's School 1946

2401 Claremont Lane, Houston, TX 77019-5897. 713-850-0222; Fax 713-622-2309; Web Site www.sjs.org

Founded by a group of citizens interested in providing a school of exacting standards, St. John's School is a coeducational, college preparatory day school enrolling 601 boys and 610 girls in Kindergarten–Grade 12. The School endeavors to offer a challenging education for motivated, energetic boys and girls who are able to meet high academic standards. Varsity and intramural athletics, drama, glee club, creative writing, art, and music are included among the extracurricular activities. Tuition: $8645–$10,765. Financial Aid: $830,000. Myrtle Sims is Director of Admissions; John Allman (Yale, B.A.; University of Virginia, M.A.) was appointed Headmaster in 1998.

Saint Luke's Episcopal School 1947

15 St. Luke's Lane, San Antonio, TX 78209-4445. 210-826-0664; Fax 210-826-8520; E-mail mgose@swbell.net; Web Site www.saintlukes.net

Founded as an outreach of Saint Luke's Episcopal Church, this day school enrolls 300 children age 2–Grade 5 from many faiths. The curriculum balances scholastic achievement with an excellent fine arts program. Daily chapel emphasizes dignity, service, and leadership. The Early Childhood program focuses on academic readiness, while in Kindergarten–Grade 5, math and science/technology are enriched by an integrated, comprehensive language arts program, social studies, music, art, Spanish, and physical education. Extended care, an after-school activities program, and summer sessions are optional. Limited financial aid is available. Tuition: $1640–$6400. Martha Gose is Director of Admission; Shirley Berdecio (Our Lady of the Lake, B.A. 1974, M.S. 1994) is Head of School.

St. Mark's School of Texas 1933

10600 Preston Road, Dallas, TX 75230-4000. 214-363-8140; Fax 214-373-6390

This nonsectarian day school enrolling 800 boys in Grades 1–12 provides a well-balanced program that emphasizes the intellectual, moral, and physical formation of its student body. In a diverse community, St. Mark's faculty and students share a love of learning and a desire for excellence. The Lower School emphasizes the mastery of basic skills, while increasingly complex material in the Middle School readies students for college preparatory work in the Upper School. Boys are involved in activities ranging from music and the arts to sports, leadership opportunities, and community service. Tuition: $10,515–$14,380. Stephen H. Gonzales is Director of Admission; Arnold E. Holtberg (Princeton, A.B.; Lutheran Theological Seminary, M.A.R.) is Headmaster.

Saint Mary's Hall 1879

9401 Starcrest Drive, San Antonio, TX 78217; P.O. Box 33430, San Antonio, TX 78265-3430. 210-483-9100; Fax 210-483-9299; E-mail admissions@smhall.org; Web Site www.smhall.org

Saint Mary's Hall is a coeducational, nondenominational school enrolling 900 day students in Montessori Preschool–Grade 12 and 68 boarders in Grades 8–12. Located on 54 acres, Saint Mary's Hall offers a rigorous college preparatory curriculum emphasizing writing, research, and analytical thinking. The program includes Advanced Placement and honors classes, a scientific research mentorship program, preprofessional training in the arts, athletics, varied extracurriculars, and community service. A postgraduate year, English as a Second Language, and summer programs are offered. Boarding Tuition: $18,241–$21,735; Day Tuition: $4330–$11,060. Financial aid is available. Fred Koval is Director of Enrollment Management; John M. Thomas (Randolph-Macon, B.A.; Towson State, M.A.) is Headmaster.

St. Michael's Academy 1984

3000 Barton Creek Boulevard, Austin, TX 78735. 512-328-2323; Admissions 512-328-0984; Fax 512-328-2327; E-mail Greg.Marsh@esc13.net

St. Michael's was founded to provide a college preparatory high school for qualified Catholic students and others from every part of the Austin area. Enrolling 405 girls and boys in Grades 9–12, the curriculum includes Advanced Placement opportunities and the arts. Students must attend worship services, take four years of religion, and perform community service. Among the activities are sports, drama, chorus, academic teams, and interest clubs. An academic summer session is offered. Tuition: $6990. Extras: $700. Financial Aid: $351,000. Greg Marsh is Director of Admissions; John T. Kennedy II (Niagara University, B.A. 1973; Duquesne University, M.A.Ed. 1984) was appointed President/Principal in 1997.

St. Michael's Academy 1972

2500 South College Avenue, Bryan, TX 77801. 409-822-2715; Fax 409-823-4971

Saint Michael's Academy is an Episcopal day school enrolling 145 boys and girls in Nursery through Grade XII. Saint Michael's strives to provide "intellectual challenge and personal attention in a moral atmosphere." The classical, college preparatory curriculum includes Latin and French language instruction, sacred studies, hands-on science, and offerings in the fine arts. Students attend daily chapel services and take part in extracurricular activities such as competitive sports and the staging of an annual Gilbert and Sullivan operetta. Tuition: $2375–$4475. Limited financial aid is available. Danna M. Naegeli is Office Manager; Jennifer Allen is the Head of School.

St. Pius X High School 1956

811 West Donovan Street, Houston, TX 77091-5699. 713-692-3581; Fax 713-692-5725; Web Site www.stpiusx.org

Founded by the Dominican Sisters, St. Pius X enrolls 670 young men and women in Grades 9–12. The Roman Catholic institution is committed to the development of responsible students capable of reaching their full intellectual, spiritual, social, and physical potential. A three-level college preparatory curriculum is designed to equip students for higher education and careers. Advanced Placement and honors courses are offered in the major disciplines. Among the activities are 18 teams in men's and women's sports, musical and theatrical productions, publications, Student Council, National Honor Society, clubs, and community service. A summer program is offered. Tuition: $4800. Extras: $350–$600. Financial Aid: $150,000. Mrs. Susie Kramer is Admissions Director; Sr. Donna M. Pollard, OP, is Principal. *Southern Association.*

San Marcos Baptist Academy

SAN MARCOS

San Marcos, TX 78666-9406. 512-353-2400; Fax 512-753-8031; E-mail admissions@smba.org; Web Site www.smba.org

SAN MARCOS BAPTIST ACADEMY in San Marcos, Texas, is a coeducational school offering boarding for boys in Grades 6 through 12 and girls in Grades 8 through 12 and a day program for boys and girls in Grades 6–12. It includes a Middle School (Grades 6–8) and an Upper School (Grades 9–12). Participation in a military program is required of all boys but is optional for girls. San Marcos (population 37,011) is on Interstate Highway 35 at the head of the San Marcos River, 45 miles northeast of San Antonio and 30 miles south of Austin. It is the county seat and the home of Southwest Texas State University; points of interest include an Aquarena and the Balcones Fault Line, a geological formation. San Marcos is served by train, plane, and bus, and there are motels and hotels for visitors.

San Marcos Baptist Academy was established in 1907 through the joint efforts of citizens of San Marcos and Baptists in southwest Texas who felt the need there for a denominational school. The school opened with students in Grades 6–12; military training was introduced during World War I. The Academy is a nonprofit corporation operating under the patronage of the Baptist General Convention of Texas, which elects the Board of Trustees and contributes substantially to the Academy budget each year. Endowments total approximately $4,500,000; the Academy's total assets are an estimated $18,000,000. The school is accredited by the Southern Association of Colleges and Schools, the Independent Schools Association of the Southwest, the Texas Association of Baptist Schools, and is recognized by the Texas Education Agency. It holds membership in the National Association of Independent Schools, the Southern Association of Independent Schools, The Texas Association of Nonpublic Schools, The Association of Military Colleges and Schools, The Association of Southern Baptist Colleges and Schools, and The Texas Association of Private and Parochial Schools, and is approved by the Attorney General for foreign students. There are approximately 4560 living graduates, and there is an active Alumni Association.

The Academy seeks to provide for the intellectual, physical, and spiritual development of each student. The religious program includes Sunday worship services and Sunday School; Wednesday chapel; Alpha Omega, a student leadership committee; Christian Brothers and Sisters, a special fellowship group; special emphasis programs each semester; and at least one year of Bible study. Students of all faiths are accepted.

THE CAMPUS. The 200-acre campus is located approximately three miles from San Marcos on Ranch Road 12. The facilities include Carroll Hall, which houses administration and business offices, the theatre, student activities center, school store, dining room, and infirmary; three academic buildings, Cavness-Reed Hall, Lattimore Hall, and Davidson Hall; Thomas Library; and The Robinson Christian Center (chapel). Boys' dormitories are Abney Hall, Byrom Hall, Crook Hall, Derrick-Wolfe Hall, McNiel Hall, and Talbot Hall, and girls' dormitories are Alexander Hall, Kokernot Hall, and Robinson Hall.

Recreational facilities include the Thornton Theatre with seating for 200 people; the student activities center with a snack bar, television viewing room, and play area; the Davidson Natatorium (indoor swimming pool); the Neeley Football Field, Galloway Field (baseball), soccer fields, and a new softball field; four lighted tennis courts; the Kokernot Gymnasium with two playing floors, a weight room, a classroom, and a racquetball court.

To provide an atmosphere of home life and supervision, there are nine dormitory residences for dormitory directors. In addition, the President's home and homes for several administrators are located on the campus.

THE FACULTY. Dr. Paul W. Armes, appointed President in 1996, holds degrees from Baylor University (B.A.) and Southwestern Baptist Theological Seminary (M.Div., Ph.D.).

There are 20 men and 21 women on the faculty. All but 1 who is an aide hold baccalaureate degrees, 19 hold master's degrees, and 7 hold doctorates, representing study at Arizona State, Baylor, California State, East Texas State, George Peabody, Howard Payne, Indiana University, Iowa State, Lamar, Louisiana Baptist College, Louisiana Tech, McKendree College, Mississippi State, New York University, North Texas State, Ohio State, Oklahoma State, Reformed Theological Seminary, Southwestern Baptist Theological Seminary, Southwestern Louisiana State, Southwestern Oklahoma State, Southwestern University, Southwest Texas State, Stephen F. Austin State, Sul Ross State, Texas A&M, Texas Christian, Texas Lutheran, Trinity University, United States Air Force Academy, United States Military Academy, Webster, Wichita State, and the Universities of Akron, Houston, Jaime Balmes (Mexico), Mississippi, Oklahoma, Southern Mississippi, and Texas.

Nurses are on duty in the health center at all times and local doctors are on call.

STUDENT BODY. In 1999–2000, the Academy enrolled 223 boarding boys and girls and 88 day students, 11 to 18 years of age, in Grades 6–12. The majority come from Texas, but seven other states and 14 countries are also represented.

ACADEMIC PROGRAM. The school year, from August 16 to May 19, includes 36 weeks of instruction and vacations at Labor Day, Thanksgiving, Christmas, and Easter, with a spring break in March. Weekend leaves may be granted by dormitory directors. Classes are conducted from 8:15 A.M. to 12:05 P.M. and from 12:55 to 3:25 P.M. on Monday through Friday. Afternoon and weekend recreation periods are supervised by the Student Activities Director. Two-hour dormitory study periods are held five evenings each week.

There are 14 students in an average recitation class; the

ratio of faculty members to students is 1:11. Homework is done in class under faculty supervision and in dormitories under the supervision of dormitory directors and resident assistants. Marks are posted and reports are sent to parents at nine-week intervals. Three-week progress reports are sent to all parents. Ability, aptitude, and achievement tests are used for guidance, college counseling, and reporting to parents.

San Marcos Baptist Academy seeks to meet each student's individual needs. Although the primary emphasis is college preparatory, the curriculum provides instruction for students needing academic reinforcement in basic subjects. In Grades 6–8, fundamentals are stressed in English, mathematics, science, history, Bible, and fine arts. In Grades 9–12, academically qualified students attend honors courses; other Upper School students have General Studies. Special English instruction is available for a limited number of foreign students.

The curriculum includes English, Humanities, Reading Improvement, Speech, Journalism; French, Spanish; World History, United States History, Texas History, World Geography, Civics, Economics, Sociology; Physical Science, Biology, Advanced Biology, Chemistry, Physics; Art, Music, Music Appreciation, Band, Chorus, Piano, Organ, Drama; Driver Education; Bible; and Accounting, General Business, and Typing. Mathematics courses range from Ele-mentary Algebra to Trigonometry, Functions, Analysis, Proba-bility and Statistics, and Vector Analysis; Computer Science and Computer Literacy are taught as well.

The Carroll Program, a challenging program for exceptionally academically talented students, incorporates more stringent graduation requirements and increased academic expectations. The Enhanced Learning Program provides extra support to enable students with currently documented mild to moderate learning disabilities achieve academic success.

The Academy is designated by the Department of the Army as a Military Institute Junior Reserve Officers Training Corps Unit. All boys are required to participate in the military program, while girls in Grades 9–12 may participate if they wish. Boys in Grades 6–8 have a modified military program. Boys in Grades 9–12 receive formal military training and may earn a year's credit toward a college ROTC program.

More than 95 percent of the 1999 graduates went on to college. They are attending Auburn, Austin College, Baylor, Boston University, Brown, Seattle Pacific, Southern Methodist, Southwestern, Southwest Texas State, Texas A&M, Texas Christian, Texas Lutheran, Texas Tech, and the Universities of Denver, Mary Hardin-Baylor, and Texas (Austin, San Antonio).

STUDENT ACTIVITIES. Organizations include the Student Council, Fellowship of Christian Athletes, National Honor Society, National Thespians, Junior National Rifle Association, Student Ambassadors, Foreign Language Club, Herodotus Society (history), Cheerleaders, Yearbook Staff, School Newspaper, Science Club, Choir, and Band. The Cadet Corps is composed of

five companies, Headquarters, and Band. Cadets earn rank as officers and noncommissioned officers on the basis of leadership and scholastic achievement.

The athletic program includes football, basketball, baseball, cross-country, track, tennis, golf, soccer, volleyball, swimming, and physical conditioning, with school teams organized in Grades 9–12. Some team sports are available for students in Grades 6–8. The Academy athletic teams for both boys and girls compete in the Texas Association of Private and Parochial Schools.

The student activities program includes banquets, parties, receptions, entertainment in the student activities center, and outings to San Antonio, Austin, and San Marcos. The program also includes a weekly "Activity Day." Students participate in clubs such as Paintball, Scuba Diving, Computer, Mission Team, and many others.

ADMISSION AND COSTS. Students are accepted "without regard to faith, race, and ethnic or national origin" following the Admissions Committee's review of the application form, a transcript, two letters of recommendation from the previous school, ISEE test results, and a physical examination report. An interview is also required.

The schedule of charges is based in part on financial assistance provided by the Baptist General Convention of Texas (approximately $1000 per student per year) and endowments. In 1999–2000, the basic charge of $17,010 covered tuition, room, board, auxiliary fees, and basic health care. Day student tuition is $5455 for Grades 6–8 and $5845 for Grades 9–12. There are charges for special academic and extracurricular instruction. Personal spending money, handled through the student bank, averages $20 per week. Tuition payment plans are available and some scholarships are offered.

Executive Vice President: Dr. David McClintock
Principal: Vic Schmidt
Director of Admission: Bobby Dupree
Treasurer: Monty Lewis
Director of Athletics: Michael Kipp

Second Baptist School HOUSTON

6410 Woodway, Houston, TX 77057-1671. 713-365-2310; Fax 713-365-2355

SECOND BAPTIST SCHOOL in Houston, Texas, is a coeducational, college preparatory day school enrolling students in Prekindergarten through Grade 12. The School is a self-supporting agency of the Second Baptist Church of Houston. Regular field trips throughout the city of Houston (population

1,800,000) provide a wealth of cultural, educational, and recreational experiences outside the classroom for students and faculty.

The School was founded in 1946 to provide a strong liberal arts program based on sound educational and biblical principles. Within a challenging, disciplined learning environment, Second Baptist seeks to motivate students to high academic, social, physical, and moral standards in keeping with Christian values. Faculty work in partnership with families to provide students with a firm foundation for lifelong decision-making.

Second Baptist School is accredited by the Southern Association of Colleges and Schools and the Texas Association of Baptist Schools. It holds membership in the Texas Association of Private and Parochial Schools, the Association of Christian Schools International, the Southern Baptist Association, and the Houston Association of Independent Schools.

THE CAMPUS. The nearly 1,000,000 square feet of the School's educational and athletic facilities are situated on the 42-acre Memorial Campus, which it shares with the Second Baptist Church. The Lower, Middle, and Upper schools are each housed in their own building, with classrooms, laboratories, and art and music rooms. Also on campus are practice fields for football and other sports, one double gymnasium and a second gymnasium, and a library and resource center. Expansion of academic facilities is due for completion in the fall of 2000.

THE FACULTY. B. Jane Hursey, appointed Superintendent in 1991, received a Bachelor of Arts degree in Elementary Education from Furman University, a Master of Education degree in School Administration from George Peabody College for Teachers of Vanderbilt University, and a Doctor of Philosophy degree in Education from the University of Virginia. Her career in education includes elementary school teaching as well as administrative and supervisory experience at both the elementary and college levels. Dr. Hursey has also served as Vice President of the Accrediting Commission of the Texas Association of Baptist Schools and is active in a number of church and civic organizations.

There are 135 faculty members, including 48 in the Lower School, 33 in the Middle School, and 54 in the Upper School. All are degreed professionals who teach in their areas of certification; 55 percent of the Upper School faculty hold advanced degrees.

A school nurse staffs the infirmary, and complete hospital facilities are easily accessible.

STUDENT BODY. Second Baptist School enrolls approximately 1200 students in Prekindergarten through Grade 12, distributed as follows: 99 in the Preschool, 485 in the Lower School, 271 in the Middle School, and 354 in the Upper School. They come from Houston and surrounding suburbs and represent a diversity of races, faith heritages, and cultural backgrounds.

ACADEMIC PROGRAM. The school calendar is divided into semesters, from the beginning of September through the end of May, with vacations at Thanksgiving, Christmas, and in the spring. Report cards are issued every six weeks in the Lower School (Prekindergarten–Grade 5) and every nine weeks in the Middle (Grades 6–8) and Upper (Grades 9–12) schools. Progress reports are mailed home to denote either academic difficulty or significant improvements in work. The student-teacher ratio is 18:1; extra help is available from faculty before and after school; and teacher conferences are arranged as needed. Outstanding achievement is recognized on the honor rolls throughout the year as well as on Honors Night and in special assemblies during the month of May. Lower and Middle School students wear uniforms, and Upper School students conform to a specific dress code.

Bible is taught on a daily basis at every grade level, and Christian values are incorporated into the study of all disciplines. Students attend weekly chapel services, and each day begins with prayer and pledges to the American flag, the Christian flag, and the Bible. An annual spiritual emphasis week lends additional focus to the importance of a personal relationship with Jesus Christ.

The curriculum places strong emphasis on academic skills at all levels, with ongoing curriculum development to meet stated objectives. State-of-the-art technology is integrated across the disciplines, and the visual and performing arts are important components of the program.

The preschool program consists of half-day Prekindergarten and full-day Kindergarten with a special Booster and Bridge program available for young children needing additional time for adjustment and maturity. In Booster, Prekindergarten, and Bridge, children engage in a variety of activities, emphasizing creative play and learning techniques designed to ready them for basic concepts in math and reading and to develop social skills in Kindergarten.

In Grades 1–5, the curriculum emphasizes language, reading skills and comprehension, mathematics, science, and social studies, including Texas and American History. Art, music, computer, Spanish, library, and physical education are taught by specialists in these fields.

The Middle School builds on basic skills in language arts, mathematics, social studies, and science. Activity periods in art, choir, Spanish, computer, drama, and other specialized subjects are scheduled on a nine-week rotational basis, which varies according to grade. Middle School students participate in the Duke University Talent Identification Program, competing academically with students nationwide.

To graduate from the Upper School, students must complete 24 units as follows: English 4, social studies $3^1/_2$, economics $^1/_2$, math 3, science 3, second language 2, physical education $1^1/_2$, computer science 1, fine arts 1, health and speech, $^1/_2$ each, and 3.5 in electives. A Diploma with distinction requires 24 units with students choosing 4 from among 16 honors and/or Advanced Placement courses. Bible instruction is required throughout the Upper School experience.

Among the specific Upper School courses are English I–IV; Bible I–IV; Latin I–III, Spanish I–V, French I–V; World History, American Government & Economics, American History, World Geography; Computer Science, Computer Applications, Computer Accounting; Algebra I–II, Geometry, Mathematical Modeling, Precalculus, Calculus; Biology, Chemistry, Physics; Creative Writing, Honors Humanities, Yearbook, Speech, Drama, Introductory Art, 2-Dimensional Art, 3-Dimensional

Art, Choir, Band, Photography; and Physical Education. Advanced Placement courses are offered in English III–IV, Calculus, Biology, Computer, Chemistry, French, Spanish, U.S. History, Physics, and Music Theory. In the past five years, 52 seniors have been designated as National Merit Semifinalists and Commended Students. In addition, Second Baptist Upper School takes part in the prestigious Jefferson Scholars Program sponsored by the University of Virginia.

In 2000, the 92 seniors will continue their education at four-year colleges and universities of their choice. Among the schools graduates have attended are Baylor, Boston University, Bucknell, California Institute of Technology, Colorado State, Davidson, Duke, Emory, Furman, Harvard, Houston Baptist, Massachusetts Institute of Technology, New York University, Oberlin, Pepperdine, Princeton, Rice, Rollins, Smith, Southern Methodist, Stanford, Texas A&M, Texas Christian, Tulane, United States Air Force Academy, United States Naval Academy, Vanderbilt, Washington and Lee University, Wheaton, Wake Forest, and the Universities of Alabama, Chicago, Missouri, Oklahoma, the Pacific, Pennsylvania, Texas, Southern California, Virginia, and Wyoming.

STUDENT ACTIVITIES. Second Baptist students have numerous social, athletic, artistic, leadership, and service opportunities through the School's diverse extracurricular program. Among the organizations available on campus are Student Council, National Honor Society, Builder's Club, Anchor Club, Key Club, Koinonia Club, language clubs, and Eagle Guard.

Middle and Upper School students can perform in an award-winning band or choir and a Broadway-style spring musical. *The Aquila*, a national award-winning yearbook, and *Captive Flames*, a literary magazine, are designed and published by students with the supervision of faculty advisors.

Athletics are played at junior high, freshman, junior varsity, and varsity levels, with boys' teams formed in football, baseball, basketball, golf, tennis, track, cross-country, swimming, and wrestling. Girls compete in volleyball, basketball, softball, tennis, track, cross-country, swimming, and golf. Girls also participate on the School's cheerleading and drill team squads.

Interim term, a ten-day graded minicourse, offers a variety of options including etiquette, driver's education, college tours, and trips to England, Italy, France, New England/Colonial Williamsburg, and Washington, D.C.

Traditional events on the school calendar include New Parents' Reception, Fifth Grade Retreat, Fifth Grade Graduation, Field Day, holiday parties, College Day, Freshman Retreat, Senior Retreat, sports banquets, Homecoming, Prom, Science Fair, Eighth Grade Trip, Eighth Grade Graduation and Dance, Round-Up, Annual Auction, Interim Term, and Upper School Commencement.

ADMISSION AND COSTS. Second Baptist welcomes able, motivated students of excellent moral character. Admission is selective, based on the candidate's past record of achievement, test scores, teacher recommendations, and potential for successful and productive participation in the life of the School. The non-refundable testing and application fee is $150, with an additional $150 and one month's tuition due upon acceptance. The Admissions ISEE testing fee is $63.

In 1999–2000, tuition for Second Baptist School ranged from $4455 to $7546. Discounts are offered to families with more than one student enrolled. Additional fees include books for Middle and Upper School students, selected field trips, meal tickets, and uniforms for cheerleading. Tuition payment plans are available, and financial assistance is awarded based on the information provided by the School and Student Service for Financial Aid (SSS) in Princeton, New Jersey.

Superintendent: Dr. B. Jane Hursey
Dean of Students: Ann Smith
Associate Dean of Students: Dr. L. Joe Shorter
Director of Admissions: Mary Ann O'Reilly

The Shelton School and Evaluation Center   1976

EC–Grade 3: 9407 Midway, Dallas, TX 75220.
Grades 4–12: 15720 Hillcrest Road, Dallas, TX 75248.
  972-774-1772; Fax 972-991-3977; Web Site www.shelton.org

The Shelton School is a coeducational day school serving 630 students in Pre-school–Grade 12. The School focuses on the full development of "learning-different" students of average or above-average intelligence to enable them to succeed in conventional classroom settings. Services include an on-site Evaluation Center for diagnostic testing and a Speech, Language, and Hearing Clinic. The curriculum is a multisensory program with a strong academic orientation. Tutoring, computer courses, intramural sports, and a summer session are offered. Tuition: $5850–$11,145. Financial Aid: $150,000. Diann Slaton is Director of Admission; Joyce Pickering (Louisiana State, B.S.; Virginia Polytechnic Institute, M.A.) is Executive Director. *Southern Association.*

Solomon Schechter Academy of Dallas   1979

18011 Hillcrest Road, Dallas, TX 75232. 972-248-3032;
  Fax 972-248-0695; E-mail RittRuth@aol.com

Solomon Schechter Academy is a Conservative Jewish day school enrolling 520 children age 2–Grade 8. The academic curriculum offers a full range of general and Jewish studies designed to foster a lifelong quest for moral and intellectual excellence. Small classes and dedicated faculty and staff provide a supportive, nurturing environment in which students are motivated to achieve their full potential. Activities include community service, team sports, Choraliers, and Student Council. Before- and after-school care, enrichment programs, and experiences in the arts are offered. Tuition: $2500–$9600. Financial aid is available for K–Grade 8. Ruth Ritterband is Head of School. *Southern Association.*

Strake Jesuit College Preparatory   1961

8900 Bellaire Boulevard, Houston, TX 77036. 713-774-7651;
  Fax 713-774-6427; E-mail santarc_n@strakejesuit.org;
  Web Site www.strakejesuit.org

Strake Jesuit, a Catholic, college preparatory day school enrolling approximately 740 boys in Grades 9–12, carries on the 450-year tradition of Jesuit education worldwide. The school prepares its graduates to be men in service to others as well as being ready to succeed in college; the curriculum allows 100 percent of the graduates each year to move directly into college. There is a closed-circuit TV system and electives in TV production as well as 11 varsity sports and many other extracurriculars. Some cross-registration is available at an adjacent Catholic girls' college prep. Summer remedial courses are available. Tuition: $6880. Financial Aid: $280,000. N.J. Santarcangelo is Director of Admissions; Rev. Brian F. Zinnamon, SJ, is President; Richard C. Nevle is Principal.

Trinity Episcopal School   1952

720 Tremont Street, Galveston, TX 77550. 409-765-9391;
  Fax 409-765-9491; E-mail trinitybiz@aol.com

Trinity is a coeducational parish day school enrolling 270 students in three divisions, from two-year-old Beginning School to Grade 8. Its primary objective is to provide, in a God-centered atmosphere, the best possible experience in learning and living. Situated on the grounds of historic Trinity Episcopal Church (1845), the School welcomes and enrolls students from all Christian and non-Christian traditions. The rigorous and varied curriculum is enhanced by numerous excursions to local cultural and recreational resources. Tuition: $3300–$5000. Julie Ogan is Admissions Director; The Reverend C. Richard Cadigan (Wesleyan University, B.A.; Episcopal Divinity School, M.Div.) was appointed Head of School in 1994.

Trinity School   1958

3500 West Wadley Avenue, Midland, TX 79707-5748.
  915-697-3281; Fax 915-697-7403; E-mail trinitymidland.org

Trinity School, a coeducational day school enrolling 600 students in Preschool–Grade 12, seeks to provide a superior college preparatory education within a spiritual, nurturing environment. Preschool classrooms reflect the philosophy of Maria Montessori in which teaching is based on the observable methods of how children actually learn best. Lower, Middle, and Upper School course work focuses on the liberal arts and sciences, enriched by extracurricular learning experiences. French and Spanish instruction begins in Preschool; computer studies begin in Grade 1. Latin is required in the Middle School. Episcopal chapel services are attended daily. Tuition: $2500–$7325. Jananne McLaughlin is Director of Admission; Rhonda G. Durham is Head of School.

Trinity Valley School   FORT WORTH

7500 Dutch Branch Road, Fort Worth, TX 76132. 817-321-0100;
  E-mail tvs@ns.trinityvalleyschool.org;
  Web Site www.trinityvalleyschool.org

TRINITY VALLEY SCHOOL in Fort Worth, Texas, is a coeducational day school enrolling students in Kindergarten through Grade 12. The School is located in a southwestern section of Fort Worth (population 500,000). The city offers many cultural and recreational facilities including four colleges and universities, a symphony orchestra, ballet and opera companies, museums, and theaters.

Trinity Valley was founded with six students and six volunteer teachers in 1959 by Stephen Seleny, who remained as Headmaster for 35 years. Within three years, enrollment had increased to 114, and the School had moved from a single room to an entire rented school building. A second move came in 1969, and, in the summer of 1998, the School moved to its present, 75-acre site.

The School believes in fine scholarship with its fulfillment at college; the development of wide, constructive interests; and the practice of intelligent citizenship. The faculty is committed to instilling an awareness of ethical and spiritual values in their students, believing that any school devoted to quality academic education is responsible for its students' moral education as well. Trinity Valley does not maintain any religious affiliation, however, students are encouraged to participate in whatever established religion they and their families choose, and to respect other religions besides their own.

A nonprofit organization, the School is governed by a self-perpetuating Board of 24 Trustees, which meets seven times a year. Funds invested in the endowment trust total approximately $16,830,000. Activities of the 1430 alumni are organized through the Office of Alumni Relations.

Trinity Valley is accredited by the Independent Schools Association of the Southwest and is a member of the National Association of Independent Schools, the National Association of College Admissions Counselors, and the Educational Records Bureau.

THE CAMPUS. Located in southwest Fort Worth, Trinity Valley's spacious campus features a Performing Arts building with a 410-seat auditorium, a Black Box theater, music rooms, and space for photography and art classes. Other facilities include the Middle/Upper School Library/Media Center with a technology lab and areas for group or individual study, state-of-the-art science labs, and a cafeteria. All classrooms throughout the School are wired for computer use and multimedia technology.

The Athletic Complex contains two double gymnasiums.

Outdoor sports facilities include eight tennis courts; five playing fields for football, soccer, and field hockey; three diamonds for baseball and softball; and a lighted stadium with an eight-lane track.

THE FACULTY. There are 82 full-time faculty and administrators who teach, 54 women and 28 men. They hold 82 baccalaureate and 46 graduate degrees from Atlantic Christian, Baylor, Boston College, Brown, California State, Central State (Oklahoma), Colby, East Carolina, Humboldt State, Indiana State, Iowa State, Johns Hopkins, Keuka, Nashota House Seminary, Ohio State, Randolph-Macon, Reed, St. Bonaventure, St. Edward's, St. John's, Simmons, Southern Methodist, Southwestern State College, Southwestern University, Southwest Missouri State, Southwest Texas State, State University of New York, Stephen F. Austin State, Stonehill, Texas A&M, Texas Christian, Texas Lutheran, Texas Wesleyan, Texas Woman's, Villanova, Virginia Commonwealth, Wake Forest, and the Universities of Denver, Edinburgh, Illinois, Kansas, Kentucky, Madrid, Maryland, Massachusetts, Missouri, Nebraska, New Hampshire, New Mexico, Northern Colorado, North Texas, Oregon, Puerto Rico, Texas (Arlington, Austin), Toronto, Travencore (India), West Indies, and Wisconsin (Madison).

Faculty benefits include health, dental, and life insurance and a retirement plan.

The School has a clinic with a full-time nurse.

STUDENT BODY. In 1999–2000, Trinity Valley enrolls 446 day boys and 443 day girls, ages 5 to 18, as follows: Kindergarten—58, Grade 1—58, Grade 2—58, Grade 3—58, Grade 4—62, Grade 5—62, Grade 6—66, Grade 7—80, Grade 8—80, Grade 9—72, Grade 10—75, Grade 11—90, and Grade 12—70.

ACADEMIC PROGRAM. The school year, divided into semesters, begins in August and ends in May, with vacations of two weeks at Christmas, one week in the spring, and a week at Thanksgiving. Classes meet five days a week and are scheduled in seven periods between 8:30 A.M. and 3:30 P.M., with a 45-minute lunch session. The average class has 15–20 students.

Faculty-supervised study hall is available as a sixth course in Grades 9–12. Students may receive extra help from their teachers, and formal tutoring from individual faculty members can be arranged at an additional charge. Grades are sent to parents four times yearly and are recorded at the end of each semester, with interim reports sent halfway through each grading period.

The curriculum for Kindergarten through Grade 6 focuses on language arts, mathematics, reading, science, and social studies. Students start Spanish classes in Kindergarten and Latin in Grade 7, and study art and music on alternate weeks in Grades 1–6. Seventh-grade students take English, Latin, Texas History, Pre-Algebra or Math, and Earth Science, choosing Spanish or French as a sixth course. There is also an outdoor program for Grades 3–8, which includes organized camping trips.

Eighth graders take English, Latin, United States History, Pre-Algebra or Algebra, Integrated Physical Science, and Spanish or French.

In Grades 9–12, students are expected to take five or six academic courses per year, plus physical education or participation in sports. Required courses include: five full credits of social studies; four credits each of English and math; three credits of laboratory science; three credits of Spanish, French, or Latin; and one credit of fine arts. Elective courses include: Creative Writing, Humanities; French IV–V, Spanish IV–V, Latin IV–V; Computer Science, AP Computers; Calculus, AP Calculus AB&BC; AP Biology, AP Chemistry, AP Physics I–II, AP Economics; Asian History; World Religions; Drama, Chorus, Music Theory, Speech, Art I–II, Photography, Ceramics, Printmaking, Newspaper, Speech & Debate, and Yearbook. Students are encouraged to take Advanced Placement examinations in 18 subjects whenever appropriate.

The 75 members of the Class of 1999 attend the following colleges and universities: Agnes Scott 2, Baylor 8, Boston University, Brigham Young, Brown, Bucknell, Centenary College, Dartmouth, Duke, Georgetown, Harvard 2, Hendrix 2, Johns Hopkins, New York University, Oklahoma Baptist, Pratt Institute, Princeton, Rhodes, Southern Methodist 2, Stanford, Texas A&M, Texas Christian 5, Trinity University 2, Tulane 4, and the Universities of Chicago, Colorado, Illinois, Kansas, Missouri 2, North Texas, Oklahoma, Pennsylvania, Southern California, Texas (Austin) 11, and Virginia 2. One graduate joined a ballet company.

STUDENT ACTIVITIES. The Student Council, with elected members from each class in Grades 9–12, oversees annual fundraising and community service projects and serves as liaison between students and faculty.

Students interested in working on the yearbook, newspaper, or literary magazine can do so through elective classes.

After-class activities include the National Honor Society, the American Field Service, Fantasy Basketball League, and the French, Spanish, SADD, Outdoor, Habitat for Humanity, Chess, and H.O.S.T. clubs. The Trinity Valley Theatre Company presents several full-length productions each year.

Because the School encourages participation in sports, there are no tryouts; students of varying abilities play on all teams. Interscholastic teams compete at the Middle School, freshman, junior varsity, and varsity levels. Varsity teams include boys' and girls' cross-country, volleyball, basketball, soccer, tennis, track, and golf; football and baseball for boys; and field hockey and softball for girls.

In addition, special activities include several dances each year, lectures/demonstrations by visiting artists, and annual events such as Mardi Gras, Gump Day, Howdy Week, Hispanic Day, Homecoming, Autumn Festival, Holiday Program, Sports Awards Nights, Academic Awards Night, Grandparents' Day, AFS Day, Alamo Day, Kite Day, Carol Sing, and Field Day.

ADMISSION AND COSTS. Trinity Valley seeks students of above-average to superior ability who will contribute to the diversity and environment of the School community. New students are accepted in Kindergarten through Grade 12 on the basis of recent test scores, transcripts, and four recommendations. Entrance examinations are administered at the School, and qualified candidates are asked for a personal interview. Application for Grades 1–4, accompanied by a $75 fee, should be submitted by March 20 for the first round of testing on March 25. Application for Grades 5–8 should be submitted by March 4. Applicants for Grades 9–12 will test on January 29, February 26, or March 25. Application deadline is three weeks prior to each date.

In 1999–2000, tuition is $8275 for Kindergarten–Grade 6, $8575 for Grades 7–8, and $8775 for Grades 9–12. Additional expenses include uniforms and a one-time registration fee of $250. In 1999–2000, 15 percent of the student body is receiving $625,700 in need-based financial aid. Low-interest loans and a tuition insurance plan are available. Trinity Valley subscribes to the School and Student Service for Financial Aid.

Director of Admissions: Judith S. Kinser
Director of Institutional Advancement: Annette Blaschke
College Counselor: Lesley Brice
Director of Finance/Operations: Margaret Riemitis
Director of Athletics: Tony Barriteau
Director of Public Relations: Karen Coan

Vanguard College Preparatory School

WACO

2517 Mount Carmel, Waco, TX 76710. 254-772-8111; Fax 254-772-8263; E-mail Linda-Goble@vanguard.org; Web Site www.vanguard.org

VANGUARD COLLEGE PREPARATORY SCHOOL in Waco, Texas, is an independent, coeducational day school enrolling students in Grades 7–12. Waco (population 110,000), the seat of McLennan County, is located on the Brazos River in the central portion of the state, midway between Dallas and Austin. The city is home to Baylor University and two other colleges as well as a symphony orchestra, a civic music association, and the Texas Rangers Hall of Fame.

Vanguard College Preparatory School was founded in 1973 as a project of the Western Institute of Technology to offer a rigorous, challenging liberal arts education to academically capable and highly motivated students. Incorporated on its own in 1975, the School aims to nurture the development of its students intellectually, ethically, socially, and physically through its curriculum and supportive learning environment.

Governed by a 21-member Board of Trustees, Vanguard is a nonprofit institution accredited by the Southern Association of Colleges and Schools and approved by the Texas Education Agency. It holds membership in the National Association of Independent Schools, Southern Association of Independent Schools, Texas Association of Non-Public Schools, the National Association of Secondary School Principals, and The College Board, among other professional organizations.

THE CAMPUS. The 8.5-acre campus accommodates the School's several classroom buildings. Building One, which was constructed in the 1930's, houses classrooms and administrative offices as well as the library. The Mayborn Building (1984) contains classrooms, science laboratories, and an up-to-date computer lab. Art studios and drama facilities are centered in the Jaworski Building (1987), and physical education classes, performances, and assemblies take place in the multipurpose building (1980, enlarged 1992).

A capital campaign, Vision 2000, is underway to finance the construction of a new classroom building and to renovate existing facilities.

THE FACULTY. Dr. Linda Goble was appointed Head of School in 1996. A native of Waco, she is an alumna of Baylor University where she earned bachelor's, master's, and Ed.D. degrees. Before assuming her current position, Dr. Goble taught at the elementary and college levels and served as an education consultant and administrator. She and her husband, Rod, have three children.

There are 30 faculty members, 22 women and 8 men, who hold 30 baccalaureate and 16 advanced degrees, including 4 doctorates. They are graduates of such colleges and universities as Baylor, Central Connecticut State, Drew, Middlebury, Northeastern University, Oklahoma City, Oklahoma State, Southern Methodist, Stephen F. Austin, Texas A&M, Texas Tech, Vanderbilt, West Texas State, Wheaton, William Carey College, and the Universities of Colorado, Houston, Iowa, Mexico, New Orleans, Northern Colorado, North Texas, St. Thomas, and Texas. Faculty receive health insurance, Social Security, and retirement benefits.

STUDENT BODY. In 1999–2000, Vanguard College Preparatory School enrolls 238 boys and girls, ages 12 through 18, as follows: 43 in Grade 7, 42 in Grade 8, 43 in Grade 9, 35 in Grade 10, 41 in Grade 11, and 34 in Grade 12. They reside in Waco and surrounding communities and represent a diversity of racial, religious, ethnic, and socioeconomic backgrounds.

ACADEMIC PROGRAM. The 36-week school year is divided into semesters and includes Thanksgiving, winter, and spring vacations and the observance of several national holidays. Grades are mailed to parents quarterly or more frequently in cases of academic difficulty. Parents may request peer tutoring for their children through the School. Classes enroll a maximum of 18, and the student-teacher ratio is 12:1. The school day consists of eight 45-minute modules from 8:10 A.M. to 3:15 P.M., with study mods incorporated into the daily schedule and a 30-minute tutorial beginning at 3:15 P.M.

The college preparatory curriculum is designed to provide the basic knowledge needed to gain academic and cultural literacy through challenging courses enhanced by richly diverse experiences in the fine arts, physical education, athletics, and cocurricular activities.

Middle School (Grades 7–8) students must complete 12 credits, including 2 each in math, language arts, social studies, science, and physical education, and 1 credit each in fine arts and computer literacy.

To graduate from the High School, students must earn 24 credits as follows: 4 each in English and math (including Algebra I–II and Geometry); 3 in science and social studies; 2 in the same foreign language; 1½ in physical education; 1 each in fine arts and College Preparation Seminar; ½ each in health and speech; and 3½ in electives.

Among the specific courses in the High School are English, SAT Prep; Algebra I–II, Geometry, Pre-Calculus, Calculus, Statistics; Biology I–II, Chemistry I–II, Physics, Environmental Science; French I–III, Spanish I–IV, German I–III; World War II, Sociology, World History, U.S. History, European History, Government, Economics, Psychology; Computer Technology; Drama; Art; Music, Band, Orchestra; and Physical Education. Advanced Placement courses are offered in English, Statistics, Chemistry, Biology, Calculus, European History, and Spanish. Dual credit courses are offered in Psychology and Sociology.

All 32 members of the Class of 1999, including a National Merit Scholarship Finalist and 6 Commended Scholars, entered college in the fall. They are enrolled at Baylor 8, The Citadel, Dartmouth, Duke, New Mexico Tech, Sewanee, Southern Methodist 3, Southwestern University 5, Texas A&M 4, Texas Christian, Wake Forest, and the Universities of Maryland and Texas 3.

STUDENT ACTIVITIES. A democratic Student Council is comprised of representatives elected from each grade. Its purpose is to encourage the participation of all students in activities, to develop standards of character and citizenship, to initiate school spirit, to promote good student-faculty relations, and to recommend improvements to the School. Qualified students are invited to join the National Honor Society.

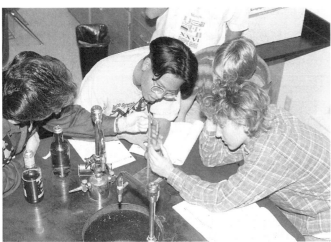

Students publish *The Vanguard Review,* a school newspaper that has won numerous awards at state, national, and international levels. Other activities include Mock Trial, *Bifrost* (yearbook), *Liquid Paper* (art and literary magazine), Show Choir, Band, Orchestra, Knowledge Master, Challenge Team, and the Chemical Society, Spanish, French, Journalism, Vanguard, Ecology, and Interact clubs.

Educational trips at different grade levels are planned to destinations such as Texas Hill Country, the Texas Gulf Coast, and Europe. In the past, students have also traveled to France, England, Costa Rica, and Cuernavaca, Mexico. In the summers of 1998 and 1999, students earned dual credit in Spanish and traveled to France.

Viking teams are formed at several levels and compete in cross-country, basketball, tennis, golf, track and field, baseball, and softball.

Among the special traditions on the school calendar are Back to School Night, Senior Halloween Haunted House and Dance, Winter Glitter and Corrigan dances, Viking Crew Sports Banquet, Awards Assembly, Norbert Wiener Day, Mole Day, Student/Faculty Basketball Game, dramatic productions, and Field Day.

ADMISSION AND COSTS. Vanguard College Preparatory School welcomes motivated students of average to above-average ability in Grades 7–11 as space is available. Admission is based on the result of the School's entrance exam and records of previous school work. Students must also submit immunization records. A $50 testing fee is charged.

In 1999–2000, tuition is $5800; textbooks are extra. A one-time New Student Fee of $200 is charged for each child upon first enrolling at the School. Financial aid, tuition refund insurance, and a tuition payment plan are available. Named scholarships are awarded based on financial need.

Registrar: Arminda Bewley
College Counselor: Cindy Graves
Business Officer: Mona Farley

The Winston School   1975

5707 Royal Lane, Dallas TX 75229. 214-691-6950;
Fax 214-691-1509; E-mail admissions@winstonschool.org;
Web Site www.winston-school.org

Winston is a college preparatory day school enrolling 232 learning-different boys and girls in Grades 1–12. Based on diagnostic testing and ongoing monitoring, the School formulates individualized academic programs to help bright students overcome problems with learning. More than 90 percent of Winston's graduates enter college. Computers, the arts, and outdoor education enrich the core curriculum, which emphasizes English, language arts, math, science, and social studies. Activities include publications, student government, sports, and clubs. Fees are available upon request. Amy C. Smith is Director of Admission; Pamela K. Murfin (University of Miami, Ph.D.) was appointed Head of School in 1999.

UTAH

Rowland Hall-St. Mark's School   1880

Upper School: 843 Lincoln Street, Salt Lake City, UT 84102.
  801-355-7494; Fax 801-355-0474
Middle School: 801-355-0272; Fax 801-359-8318
Lower School: 205 First Avenue, Salt Lake City, UT 84103.
  801-355-7485; Fax 801-355-0388

Formed by the merger of two older schools that had been established by the Episcopal church, Rowland Hall-St. Mark's enrolls 920 day students in Pre-Kindergarten–Grade 12. The traditional college preparatory program includes three languages and the study of ethics and world religion. Advanced Placement courses are offered in 12 subjects. Among the extracurricular activities are student government and a variety of athletics, including a ski academy. Tuition: $8000–$9675. Financial Aid: $465,000. Susan Koles is Director of Marketing; Alan C. Sparrow (Brown University, B.A.; University of Rochester, M.A.) was named Headmaster in 1992. *Northwest Association.*

VERMONT

Burr and Burton Academy   1829

Seminary Avenue, Manchester, VT 05254. 802-362-1775;
   Fax 802-362-0574

Founded to train young men for the ministry, Burr and Burton Academy enrolls 440 young men and women in Grades 9–12; some international and inner-city boarders are housed with local families. The nonsectarian school offers a college preparatory curriculum, including Advanced Placement courses, as well as general business and occupational programs. Music, the arts, technology, and athletics are integral to the curriculum, and honesty and effort are emphasized as the cornerstones of the school's philosophy. A $6,000,000 technology center opened in 1998. Clubs, community service, and skiing are among the activities. Boarding Tuition: $18,500; Day Tuition: $7900. Financial Aid: $200,000. Philip Anton is Director of Admissions; Charles W. Scranton is Headmaster. *New England Association.*

Long Trail School   1975

1045 Kirby Hollow Road, Dorset, VT 05251.
   802-867-5717; Fax 802-867-4525; E-mail dwilsonlts@cis.com

Long Trail, a coeducational day and boarding school, is committed to providing a challenging yet nurturing environment to meet the academic and personal goals of college-bound students with different learning styles. Enrolling 120 day students in Grades 6–12, the School uses a variety of teaching methods, small-group instruction, and personalized course selection to motivate students to their maximum potential. Music, drama, athletics, community service, and extracurriculars enrich the program and foster social, ethical, and physical development. Academics and sports are available in the summer. Boarding Tuition: $20,000; Day Tuition: $13,400. Financial Aid:

$200,000. Courtney Callo is Director of Admissions; David D. Wilson (Indiana University, B.A.; Antioch, M.A.) is Headmaster. *New England Association.*

Pine Ridge School   1968

1075 Williston Road, Williston, VT 05495. 802-434-2161;
   Fax 802-434-5512

Pine Ridge offers an ungraded boarding and day program for 80 learning-disabled students, ages 13–18, of average to superior ability. It aims to help students conquer academic weaknesses and gain positive attitudes about themselves and their ability to learn. The highly structured, individualized curriculum is designed to remediate specific disabilities while developing personal, social, and self-advocacy skills. Daily one-on-one language training and ongoing monitoring are essential components leading to success. A remedial summer session is offered. Boarding Tuition: $38,200; Day Tuition: $28,700. Sara Gieselman is Director of Admissions; Douglas Dague (University of Wisconsin, B.S.) is Head of School. *New England Association.*

St. Johnsbury Academy   1842

1000 Main Street, St. Johnsbury, VT 05819. 802-748-8171;
   Admissions 802-751-2130; Fax 802-748-5463;
   E-mail admissions@stj.k12.vt.us;
   Web Site www.state.vt.us/schools/stj/

St. Johnsbury Academy is a comprehensive boarding and day school enrolling 900 boys and girls in Grade 9 through a Postgraduate Year. Designated a Blue Ribbon School of Excellence, the Academy offers a curriculum designed to accommodate a wide range of academic abilities, including students with learning differences. Most students pursue some form of higher education, ranging from highly selective liberal arts colleges to technical schools. Interscholastic teams are fielded in most sports, with many clubs and trips offered as extracurricular activities. Boarding Tuition: $21,225. John J. Cummings is Director of Admissions; Bernier L. Mayo (Middlebury College, M.A.) is Headmaster. *New England Association.*

VIRGINIA

Alexandria Country Day School   1983

2400 Russell Road, Alexandria, VA 22301. 703-548-4804;
*   Fax 703-549-9022*

Alexandria Country Day, enrolling 240 students in Kindergarten–Grade 8, aims to develop the academic, social, and emotional well-being of each child and to foster self-esteem and respect for others. Small classes taught by carefully selected faculty in a warm, nurturing environment promote enthusiasm for learning. The curriculum emphasizes a strong foundation in language arts, math, social studies, and science, while specialist teachers provide instruction in Spanish, music, computer, library skills, art, and physical education. Students enjoy field trips to the nation's capital and take part in school government, drama, handbells, and sports. Tuition: $8800–$10,500. Anne P. Miller is Admissions Director; William E. DeLamater is Head of School.

Bishop Ireton High School   1964

201 Cambridge Road, Alexandria, VA 22314-4899. 703-751-7606;
*   Fax 703-212-8173; E-mail phamer@ireton.org;*
*   Web Site www.ireton.org*

The Oblates of St. Francis de Sales operate this coeducational, diocesan school serving 800 students from Catholic and non-Catholic families. The Salesian tradition of excellence aims to develop the aesthetic, intellectual, and physical potential of each young person while instilling a sense of responsibility and service to others. The curriculum is college preparatory, with Honors and Advanced Placement courses, computer technology, and required religious studies integral to the program. With 37 athletic teams, nearly 70 percent of students participate in at least one sport; other activities include a comprehensive music program, yearbook, drama, and special-interest clubs. Tuition: $6100–$9100. Financial Aid: $240,000. Peter Hamer is Dean of Admissions; Rev. William J. Metzger, OSFS, is Principal.

The Blue Ridge School   ST. GEORGE

St. George, VA 22935. 804-985-2811;
*   E-mail admission@blueridgeschool.com;*
*   Web Site www.blueridgeschool.com*

THE BLUE RIDGE SCHOOL in St. George, Virginia, is a college preparatory boarding school enrolling boys in Grades 9 through 12. Situated on the eastern slope of the Blue Ridge Mountains, it lies 5 miles from the Appalachian Trail and Skyline Drive and 18 miles northwest of Charlottesville and the University of Virginia. The Charlottesville–Albemarle Airport, served by three major airlines, is about 20 minutes away by car. Washington, D.C., and Richmond, with international airports, can be reached in less than a two-hour drive.

The School is the successor to an Episcopal mission school founded in 1909 to meet the educational needs of local families. In 1962, The Blue Ridge School reorganized as a college preparatory school with the goal of addressing the needs of able young men who have not realized their full potential in other settings. The School emphasizes the development of basic academic skills and strives to provide a supportive, structured environment that will foster achievement and self-confidence in the classroom, on the playing fields, and in extracurricular and social activities.

The Blue Ridge School is Episcopal in heritage and welcomes all denominations. Students attend a chapel service two mornings a week and a Sunday service conducted according to Episcopal rites.

Blue Ridge is a nonprofit organization accredited by the Southern Association of Colleges and Schools and the Virginia Association of Independent Schools. It is governed by a self-perpetuating Board of 23 Trustees. The School has an endowment of approximately $5,200,000 and conducts annual giving campaigns to raise funds for scholarships and support of the operating budget.

THE CAMPUS. The 1000-acre campus includes ponds and streams, foot trails through 600 wooded, mountain acres, a 5-acre lake, meadows, and landscaped grounds. Seven large playing fields, including football, soccer, and baseball fields, eight tennis courts, a 400-meter all-weather track, a climbing tower, an outdoor driving range, and an outdoor swimming pool are on the grounds.

Perkins Hall, which includes the David Brobeck Science Wing, is the main academic facility, providing five classrooms, the study hall, three science laboratories, and the computer center, with one computer for every four students. The Academic Building houses another ten classrooms and the Fishburne Learning Center; and Loving Hall has six classrooms, Mayo Auditorium, the dining room and kitchen, and administrative offices. The newly constructed Hatcher C. Williams Library has a capacity for 20,000 volumes, a full-text microfiche backfile of more than 120 periodicals, an audiovisual library, study carrels, an automated database for magazine indexing, and a computerized catalogue on-line with the University of Virginia library. Fine arts facilities are located in the New York Auxiliary Student Center, which also includes a gameroom, the Wiley Roy Mason viewing room with home theater, a snack bar, and a large room for dances and social events. Other major buildings are Gibson Memorial Chapel; Homan W. Walsh Dormitory, housing students and eight faculty apartments; the Rev. D. A. Boogher Dorm, a 40-bed facility; 12 faculty houses; Massey Athletic Complex, with basketball court, spectator seating, and locker rooms; and the field house, with tennis and basketball courts and wrestling, weight-lifting, and training rooms.

The plant is owned by the School and is valued at $14,000,000.

THE FACULTY. Edward M. McFarlane, a graduate of Slippery Rock University, the University of Pittsburgh (M.Ed.), and West Virginia University (Ed.D.), was appointed Headmaster in 1992. Dr. McFarlane first became associated with the School as a parent of a student and then joined the administration as Director of Development. He served in that position for three and a half years before accepting his present appointment. Earlier, he had spent 25 years in higher education as an administrator and professor at four colleges and universities.

Twenty-seven men and women comprise the full-time faculty and roster of administrators who teach. All hold baccalaureate degrees or the equivalent and more than one-half have advanced degrees. A total of 32 members of the professional staff, including nearly all of the faculty, live on campus.

Two full-time nurses staff the infirmary, and hospital facilities are available in Charlottesville.

STUDENT BODY. In 1999–2000, Blue Ridge enrolled 180 boys from 25 states and the District of Columbia as well as the Bahamas, Croatia, Egypt, Germany, India, Korea, Netherlands, Saudi Arabia, Taiwan, Thailand, Turkey, and the West Indies.

ACADEMIC PROGRAM. The academic year, divided into trimesters, begins in early September and extends to late May with vacations including ten days at Thanksgiving, three weeks at Christmas, and two weeks in the spring. Classes are held five and one-half days a week and are scheduled in six 50-minute periods three days a week and three 75-minute periods twice a week. Saturday mornings consist of fine arts productions, guest speakers, help sessions, and field trips as well as academic classes. Each student is assigned a faculty advisor with whom he meets daily. During conference periods on Monday, Tuesday, Thursday, and Friday, students may receive help from their classroom teachers as needed or directed. Students are assigned to homework lab after dinner if any homework is missed or incomplete. A two-hour preparation period for the next day's classes begins at 8:00 P.M. Lights go out at 11:10 P.M. Parents receive written reports from advisors and teachers every two weeks.

To graduate from The Blue Ridge School, a student must complete four units of English; two of foreign language (three are recommended); three of history, including two years of U.S. history; four of mathematics, including two of algebra and one of geometry; three of laboratory science, including biology; two of health and physical education; one of Life Skills: computer exploration, health, leadership, and decision making; and two electives. Study skills are taught across the curriculum in all grades. Students typically take five core courses, but the schedule is kept flexible to enable them to find success in both old and new curricular areas.

A typical course of study is as follows: Grade 9—Language and Literature I, World History, Integrated Science, Pre-Algebra or Algebra I, Life Skills, and a study hall; Grade 10—Language and Literature II, Modern European History, Biology,

mathematics, French or Spanish I, and a general elective; Grade 11—World Literature, U.S. Government and History I, Chemistry, mathematics, French or Spanish II, and a general elective; Grade 12—American Literature, U.S. History II, a science elective, mathematics, French or Spanish III, and a general elective.

Among the electives are Adventures of the Quest, Bible as Literature, Coming of Age, Creative Writing; French and Spanish V, Spanish VI, and Latin; Anatomy, Environmental Science, Evolution of the Universe, Earth and Man, Physics; and Computer Applications I and II, Computer Programming, Studio Art, Advanced Art, Sculpture, Music History, and Choir. Special courses are offered in English as a Second Language.

In 1999, 97 percent of the graduating class were accepted at four-year colleges, including Amherst, Arizona State, College of Charleston, Elon, Hampden-Sydney, Hawaii Pacific, James Madison, Lynchburg, Northeastern, Roanoke, and the Universities of Arizona, Georgia, Maryland, Rochester, and Tennessee.

A six-week summer session provides review and enrichment courses in all subjects for boys and girls in Grades 7–12. Study skills, math skills, reading and writing courses, and SAT preparation are also included. A full recreation program is offered with the academics. William E. Ramsey '83 is Director.

STUDENT ACTIVITIES. Students elect seniors to serve as Prefects, or resident assistants, who provide leadership and direction to younger boys, assist the dorm masters in supervision, and, as a Board, present student views to the Headmaster. An Honor Council, composed of students and faculty, reviews violations of the Honor Code and recommends action to the Headmaster.

Students publish a newspaper, literary magazine, and yearbook; take part in at least one major dramatic production each year; participate in a fine arts series that includes storytelling, one-act plays, and musical ensembles; and present paintings, drawings, and sculpture in exhibitions.

All boys participate in the afternoon athletic programs at various skill levels. The School's varsity teams compete in the Virginia Preparatory League in cross-country, soccer, golf, basketball, wrestling, track, baseball, and tennis. The football team competes in the Old Dominion Football Conference; lacrosse and volleyball teams have independent schedules. Junior varsity competition is available in all sports. The extensive Outdoor Program, with a full-time director, offers camping, rock climbing, spelunking, canoeing, mountain biking, a challenging ropes course, and frequent weekend excursions.

The School belongs to the Independent Schools Social Activities Committee, which organizes social and cultural programs for schools in Virginia, Maryland, and the District of Columbia area, including trips to the Kennedy Center for Performing Arts for theater and concerts, major league baseball games, ski areas, museums, and social mixers. The Student Activities Committee sponsors an extensive and varied social and cultural program on and off campus.

Blue and White Days, Lessons and Carols, Parents Weekends, Alumni Weekend, and the Blue Ridge Art Show are among the traditional events on the school calendar.

ADMISSION AND COSTS. The Blue Ridge School seeks capable and willing young men who desire to improve their academic record and succeed in college. The programs are designed to educate the total individual, thereby increasing each student's belief in his own self-worth. The School maintains a nondiscriminatory admissions policy. Three teacher recommendations, transcripts of previous schooling, and available test scores are required, along with an informal interview of parents and the student on campus.

Tuition, room, and board charges for 1999–2000 are $22,500, and the School recommends a $2200 deposit in the student's personal account to cover books, supplies, weekly allowance, athletic gear, and laundry. Two tuition payment plans are available. Blue Ridge offers financial aid based on need and awarded $566,000 to 43 students last year.

Academic Dean: Mr. Frank DeAngelis
Dean of Students: Mrs. Karen F. Powell
Assistant Headmaster for External Affairs: Mr. Robert J. Murphy III
College Counselor: Mr. William Biggs
Business Manager: Mr. Anthony Shifflett
Director of Athletics: Mr. Carl B. Frye

Broadwater Academy   1966

3500 Broadwater Road, P.O. Box 546, Exmore, VA 23350.
757-442-9041; Fax 757-442-9615;
E-mail jedwards@broadwater.esva.net;
Web Site http://www.esva.net/~broadwater/

Broadwater Academy is an independent, college preparatory day school enrolling 488 day boys and girls in Pre-Kindergarten through Grade 12. It aims to provide a rigorous academic program in an atmosphere that motivates a genuine interest in learning and high standards of intellectual and personal achievement. The liberal arts curriculum, including Advanced Placement courses, ensures continuity from the earliest grades through the Upper School. A broad athletic program features team competition in boys' and girls' sports. Among the other activities are Student Government, drama, newspaper, yearbook, and interest clubs. Tuition: $3475–$3975. Jeannette R. Edwards is Director of Admissions and Development; Kendell S. Berry is Head.

Browne Academy   1941

5917 Telegraph Road, Alexandria, VA 22310. 703-960-3000;
Fax 703-960-7325; Web Site www.browneacademy.org

Browne Academy is a day school enrolling 330 boys and girls in Preschool–Grade 8. It offers an individualized curriculum with emphasis on the whole child. Computers and French are introduced in Preschool and students progress according to abilities and needs. A creative problem-solving program fosters originality and independence. Art, music, dance, sports, and publications are among the activities. An extended day program, bus service, and summer day camp are available. Tuition: $9872. Financial Aid: $200,000. Denise DeBono is Director of Admission; Lois R. Ferrer (Antioch, B.S. 1958; InterAmerican University, M.A. 1968; Lehigh, Ph.D. 1975) was appointed Headmistress in 1975.

Burgundy Farm Country Day School   1946

3700 Burgundy Road, Alexandria, VA 22303. 703-960-3431;
Fax 703-960-5056; E-mail info@burgundyfarm.org;
Web Site http://burgundyfarm.org

Founded by parents in 1946 and maintaining a high level of parental involvement, Burgundy Farm Country Day enrolls 280 boys and girls in Junior Kindergarten–Grade 8. The School seeks to nurture independence and curiosity and to address each child's cognitive, physical, emotional, and social needs. The challenging academic program includes art, music, drama, French or Spanish, and physical education. The School also offers an extended-day/after-school enrichment program and a summer day camp and operates a residential wildlife camp in West Virginia. New classroom buildings were recently added for Grades 1–8 as well as a new gym for all grades. Transportation is available. Tuition: $11,040–$12,200. Financial Aid: $250,000. Patricia M. Harden is Admissions Director; Gerald L. Marchildon is the Director.

Cape Henry Collegiate School   1924

1320 Mill Dam Road, Virginia Beach, VA 23454. 757-481-2446;
Fax 757-481-9194; Web Site http://www.chcs.pvt.k12.va.us

Cape Henry Collegiate School is a coeducational, college preparatory day school enrolling 800 students in Prekindergarten (age 3)–Grade 12. Emphasizing academic, social, and physical development, the balanced educational experience involves challenging academics, athletics, arts, community service, and extensive extracurricular activities. A year-round extended-day program is available for Lower School students. Tuition: $6425–$9450. Julie Scherrer (Lower School) and Kay Temme (Middle and

Upper Schools) are Admissions Directors; Daniel P. Richardson (University of Denver, B.A.; Harvard, M.Ed.) is Head of School.

Carlisle School   1968

P.O. Box 5388, Martinsville, VA 24115. 540-632-7288;
Fax 540-632-9545; E-mail admissions@carlisleschool.org;
Web Site www.carlisleschool.org

Carlisle School is a college preparatory day school enrolling 413 students in Preschool–Grade 12. The International Baccalaureate program and Advanced Placement courses are offered. The School aims to ensure that each child's potential is recognized and challenged. The core curriculum consists of English, history, math, science, and foreign language with a variety of electives. Computer and science labs are integral to the daily schedule. Carlisle's philosophy is to treat each child as a unique individual and to instill him or her with a lifelong love of learning. The average class size is 12. Tuition: $2974–$6275. Financial aid is available. Jeanne Wagner is Director of Admission; Colin P. Ferguson (Waynesboro College, B.A.; Western Kentucky University, M.A.) was appointed Headmaster in 1992. *Southern Association.*

Catholic High School   1979

4552 Princess Anne Road, Virginia Beach, VA 23462.
757-467-2881; Fax 757-467-0284

Catholic High aims to provide a college preparatory program that nurtures the intellect, shapes character, and forms Christian values. It is a religious community enrolling 475 students in Grades 9–12 that reveals God's presence in the world by affirming the Gospel Message and challenging, when necessary, secular views. The extensive curriculum includes Advanced Placement or accelerated courses in all disciplines. State-of-the-art technology features a graphic arts lab and two 25-station computer workrooms. Masses, retreats, and required community service enrich students' lives; they also enjoy school government, 35 athletic teams, publications, National Honor Society, visual and performing arts, and clubs. Tuition: $5192. Martin F. Campbell is Guidance Director; Msgr. William L. Pitt is Principal. *Southern Association.*

Chatham Hall   CHATHAM

Chatham, VA 24531. 804-432-2941; Fax 804-432-2405;
E-mail admission@chathamhall.com; Web Site www.chathamhall.com

Cʜᴀᴛʜᴀᴍ ʜᴀʟʟ in Chatham, Virginia, is a college preparatory school for young women enrolling boarders and a limited number of day students in Grades 9–12. The town of Chatham (population 2000) is located in the south-central part of the state, 18 miles from Danville and within a one- to two-hour drive from Lynchburg, Charlottesville, and Roanoke in Virginia and Greensboro, Raleigh, Winston-Salem, and Chapel Hill in North Carolina. The rural countryside provides many opportunities for outdoor recreation and cultural enrichment. Bus, train, and air service are available to the region.

The Reverend C. Orlando Pruden, an Episcopal priest, established Chatham Hall in 1894 to "educate girls according to the best modern methods, along church lines." The school was originally chartered as the Chatham Episcopal Institute and operated under the authority of the Episcopal Diocese of Southern Virginia until 1932. While Chatham Hall is now independent of the diocese, it retains and values its traditional links with the church.

Chatham Hall aims to prepare students to take their place in the 21st century as leaders of conviction, intelligence, and compassion. A strong liberal arts curriculum is underscored by adherence to the school Honor Code and its Purple and Golden Rule, both of which define a values system marked by respect, consideration, and decency toward others.

Chatham Hall is governed by a 23-member Board of Trustees, 11 of whom are alumnae. It is accredited by the Southern Association of Colleges and Schools and holds membership in the National Association of Independent Schools, Virginia Association of Independent Schools, and National Association of Episcopal Schools, among other organizations. The nearly 3000 living graduates support the school through recruitment and fund-raising endeavors.

THE CAMPUS. The 362-acre Chatham Hall campus in the

Piedmont hills offers woodlands and meadows with miles of riding and hiking trails. The main buildings are set on the highest promontory and are linked to one another by a series of arcades. The heart of the school's spiritual activity is St. Mary's Chapel (1939), featuring a Kleuker organ, handbells, a harpsichord, and stained-glass windows depicting women saints. Pruden Hall (1907, refurbished 1997), the main entrance hall, is graced by a beautiful rotunda known as "The Well," which is the focal point of semiweekly, all-school assemblies and social occasions. Pruden Hall contains administrative offices, a darkroom, a publications room, the infirmary, and two floors of dormitory space. The Whitner Fine Arts Center (1990) contains art classrooms, exhibits, studios, music practice rooms, a greenhouse, and several lecture rooms. Dabney Hall (1911, refurbished 1996) provides 11 classrooms, a computer lab, the student center, and two floors of dormitory space. All dormitory rooms have phone and data ports for each girl. Students have access to the Chatham Hall Intranet as well as the World Wide Web/Internet through these dorm-room ports. The 20,000-volume Edmund and Lucy Lee Library links students electronically to computer resources throughout the country as well as offering Internet access to those students who do not have computers in their rooms. Science labs and classrooms are housed in the Holt Science Building. Students dine in Yardley Hall and reside with houseparents in one of four dormitory floors in Pruden and Dabney halls. More than a dozen faculty houses are also on campus, and more than 80 percent of the teaching faculty live in these homes.

The Commons provides a volleyball and basketball court as well as space for recreation and performance. Three playing fields, six all-weather tennis courts, and extensive riding facilities including an indoor arena, two riding rings, a show arena, and a permanent hunter trial course complete the athletic resources. Girls also have the use of the double-Olympic-size swimming pool at nearby Hargrave Military Academy.

The school-owned plant is valued at approximately $16,000,000.

THE FACULTY. On July 1, 1997, Marlene Rutledge Shaw became Chatham Hall's first female Rector. Ms. Shaw earned degrees from the University of New Orleans and Louisiana State and has more than 20 years of experience in education.

Prior to coming to Chatham Hall, she was Principal of the Middle School at Fort Worth Country Day School and held teaching, counseling, and administrative posts at Isidore Newman School in New Orleans.

All faculty hold baccalaureate degrees, 13 hold master's degrees, and 4 have earned doctorates representing study at such colleges and universities as Agnes Scott, Berry College, Centre College, College of William and Mary, Cornell, Dartmouth, Duke, Florida State, Gettysburg, Harvard, James Madison, Longwood, Middlebury, North Carolina State, St. Andrews Presbyterian, St. John's College, Springfield College, United States Naval Academy, Vanderbilt, Virginia Polytechnic, Yale, and the Universities of California, Colorado, Kentucky, Maryland, Michigan, North Carolina, North Texas, Rochester, and Virginia.

The infirmary is staffed by nurses around the clock; two physicians are retained on a consulting basis; and the Danville Regional Medical Center is nearby in the case of emergencies.

STUDENT BODY. In 1999–2000, Chatham Hall enrolls 127 young women, more than 80 percent of whom are seven-day resident students, in Grades 9 through 12 as follows: 29 in Grade 9, 36 in Grade 10, 31 in Grade 11, and 31 in Grade 12. They come from 20 states and ten foreign countries and represent diverse racial, ethnic, religious, and socioeconomic heritages.

ACADEMIC PROGRAM. The school year is divided into trimesters, with vacations at Thanksgiving, Christmas, and in the spring and two long weekends. Each girl has a faculty advisor who supports and assists her in all aspects of school life, and teachers hold conferences to discuss the needs of individual students. Tutoring by faculty members is available.

Most students carry five to six academic classes per trimester. Classes, usually enrolling an average of 10 to 12 girls, meet five days a week in seven 45-minute periods from 8:00 A.M. to 3:20 P.M. Physical education and extracurricular activities are held until 6:00 P.M. After dinner, there is a two-hour study hall.

To earn a Chatham Hall diploma, students must complete their senior year at the school and earn a total of 20 credits as follows: four years of English; three years of mathematics; two years of history including U.S. History; two years of a single foreign language, plus another year of either history or the same foreign language; one year of fine or performing arts; and one trimester each of religion and ethics. In her sophomore year, a student must complete a community service project, and every senior is required to give a chapel talk to students and faculty in St. Mary's Chapel.

Course offerings include English 1-4, English for International Students, English as a Second Language I–II; World Geography and Cultures, Western Civilization, U.S. History,

Modern European History, Psychology, Economics, Government, World Politics; Latin I–IV, French I–V, Spanish I–V; Information Technology; Religion; Introductory Science, Biology, Chemistry, Physics, Ethology, The Vertebrates, Genetics; Algebra I–II, Intermediate Algebra, Geometry, Pre-Calculus, Math in Nature; Music Theory, Music Literature, Saint Mary's Choir; Dance I–II, Ballet; Drama Technique; Drawing, Painting, Ceramics, Art History, Sculpting; and Physical Education. Independent study in dance and private music lessons on a variety of instruments are available, and Advanced Placement courses are offered in ten subject areas.

Study-abroad opportunities are possible through Chatham Hall's membership in The English-Speaking Union. The school also participates in the John Motley Morehead Foundation Scholarship at the University of North Carolina (Chapel Hill) and the Jefferson Scholars Program at the University of Virginia.

In 1999, graduates matriculated at Appalachian State, Birmingham-Southern, Bryn Mawr, College of Charleston, College of William and Mary 2, Cornell, Dickinson, Florida Atlantic, Florida Southern, Hollins, McGill, North Carolina State, Purdue, Radford 2, Roanoke 2, St. John's College, Salem College, Shenandoah, Simmons, Virginia Polytechnic, Washington and Lee, William Woods University, Wofford, and the Universities of Denver, North Carolina (Chapel Hill, Greensboro), Richmond, and Wisconsin.

STUDENT ACTIVITIES. Girls participate in the life of the school through Student Council, Senate, Service League, and committees related to church, community, athletic, and social events.

Students publish a yearbook, a newspaper, and a literary magazine and develop creative writing skills through the Unbound Pages club. Model United Nations, International Club, debate, Video Guild, Sherwood Dramatic Club, Library Guild, and French, Spanish, Latin, and other academic clubs are popular activities.

The athletic program features intramural and interscholastic teams, including varsity competition in field hockey, cross-country running, swimming, soccer, basketball, and tennis. Chatham Hall's comprehensive riding program includes individualized instruction in Hunt Seat and Saddle Seat, and experienced riders may participate in fox hunts and compete in shows. A limited number of students may also arrange to bring their own hunter or hunter-pleasure horses to school. Swimming is offered in collaboration with Hargrave Military Academy, and girls who swim competitively there earn physical education credit.

Traditional annual events include the New Girl Picnic, Christmas Pageant, Field Day, Parents' Weekend, Senior Night in the Well, and Commencement.

ADMISSION AND COSTS. Chatham Hall seeks young women who are eager for academic challenge and full participation in a small, enthusiastic community of learners. Girls are admitted to Grades 9–11 based on character, integrity, academic and intellectual promise, motivation, and the desire to excel. Applicants should take the Secondary School Admission Test, and international candidates must submit results of a standardized language proficiency test. The completed file includes a student response, school transcripts, teacher recommendations, and test scores. An interview at the school is required.

Tuition, room, and board in 1999–2000 was $24,000; tuition for day students was $8600. English as a Second Language, USS swim team, riding lessons, and music lessons are extra. Financial aid is awarded annually to qualified applicants.

Academic Dean: Dr. William P. Black
Dean of Students: Stefanie Trickler
Admission Director: Christine S. Baggerly
College Counselor: Karen Stewart
Business Manager: Ronald Merricks
Director of Athletics: Catherine M. LaDuke

Christchurch Episcopal School

CHRISTCHURCH

Christchurch, VA 23031. Telephone 804-758-2306;
Admissions 800-296-2306; E-mail admissions@christchurchva.com;
Web Site www.christchurchva.com

CHRISTCHURCH EPISCOPAL SCHOOL in Christchurch, Virginia, is an Episcopal, college preparatory school enrolling boarding and day boys in Grades 8–12 and a postgraduate year and day girls in Grades 8–12. It is located in Virginia's Chesapeake Bay region, on the banks of the Rappahannock River near two small towns: Urbanna, a sailing village, and Saluda, the county seat. Students are involved within the towns through community service organizations and sailing activities. The School is 40 minutes from Williamsburg, Virginia, 60 minutes from Richmond, and 90 minutes from Norfolk/Virginia Beach. The School is accessible by car from Interstates 95 and 64 via Routes 33 and 17.

The School was founded in 1921 by the Episcopal Diocese of Virginia and was named for the adjacent Christ Church parish. Christchurch School provides understanding, support, and encouragement, along with the continuous challenge of a college preparatory curriculum to help build confidence in students who may not have performed in other schools with the success their ability warrants. A limited number of high-potential, college-bound students with diagnosed learning differences are accepted into the Learning Skills Program.

As an Episcopal school, Christchurch aims to help its students discover themselves spiritually and intellectually. All religious beliefs are accepted. Nonproselytizing Episcopal chapel services are conducted on weekday mornings and on Sunday, and a course in theology is required.

The School maintains a special relationship with St. Margaret's School and shares theatrical and choral presentations, sailing, and social activities.

Christchurch School is a nonprofit organization owned by Church Schools in the Diocese of Virginia. It is governed by a 27-member Board of Trustees that meets five times a year. The School is accredited by The Virginia Association of Independent Schools and holds membership in the National Association of Independent Schools, Virginia Association of Independent Schools, the National Association of Episcopal Schools, the Middle Atlantic Episcopal School Association, the Secondary School Admission Test Board, and The Association of Boarding Schools.

THE CAMPUS. The 120-acre campus overlooks the Rappahannock River 13 nautical miles from the Chesapeake Bay. The two-mile-wide river provides opportunities for boating, swimming, scuba diving, studies in the marine sciences, and crew.

The main academic facility is the Miller Building, which houses six classrooms, the Marine Science laboratory, and the

Carl A. Olsson Science Laboratory. Historic Bishop Brown Hall, a four-story building completely renovated in 1998, is home to a state-of-the-art, fully computerized library, an expanded student center, the renowned Learning Skills Program Center, six classrooms, a computer lab, and lecture hall. Wilmer Hall houses four classrooms and a stage for theatrical productions. The Sutton Art Studio contains an art lab and current student pieces on display. Sophomores and juniors live in John G. Scott Residence Hall, which also contains Cameron Dining Hall. Murrell Hall houses sophomores, juniors, and seniors and contains the School's infirmary. Faye Residence Hall is the eighth and ninth grade dormitory. Two gymnasiums, a newly renovated weight-training room, a boathouse and dock, an all-weather track, outdoor swimming pool, six lighted tennis courts, a cross-country course, and fields for football, lacrosse, soccer, field hockey, and baseball are among the athletic resources.

THE FACULTY. Dr. David H. Charlton, a graduate of the College of William and Mary, was appointed Headmaster in 1995.

The full-time faculty include 17 men and 10 women. Seventy-five percent live with their families in on-campus housing or in residence halls. The teaching faculty hold 27 baccalaureate and 14 advanced degrees from such colleges and universities as Boston College, Brigham Young, Brown, Christopher Newport, College of William and Mary, Elon, George Mason, Hampden-Sydney, Haverford, Ithaca College, Mary Washington, Memphis State University, Middlebury, Pratt Institute, Randolph-Macon, Roanoke College, Rollins, Virginia Commonwealth, Virginia Military Institute, Virginia Polytechnic Institute, and the Universities of Bridgeport, Florida, New York, Redlands, Virginia, Washington, and Wisconsin. Fringe benefits for faculty include on-campus housing and meals, health and disability insurance, a retirement plan, and Social Security.

Three full-time nurses are on duty in the infirmary and one lives on campus. Doctors and two hospitals are available nearby.

STUDENT BODY. In 1999–2000, the School enrolls 125 boarding boys, 35 day girls, and 45 day boys in Grades 8–12 and a postgraduate year. Students come from 18 states, the District of Columbia, and six countries. They represent many religious denominations and faiths. Approximately 50 percent are Episcopalian.

ACADEMIC PROGRAM. The academic year, divided into semesters, begins in early September and ends in early June. Vacations of 9 days at Thanksgiving, 18 days at Christmas, and 11 days in the spring are scheduled along with three long weekends. Classes are held five days a week. The school day begins with breakfast at 7:00 A.M. and chapel at 8:00 A.M. Classes meet Monday through Friday and run from 8:30 A.M. until 2:20 P.M. during the fall and spring bell schedule. During the winter bell schedule, classes run from 8:30 A.M. until 1:50 P.M. Activity periods are built in three days a week for student organization meetings, visiting guest speakers, and all-school activities. A daily tutorial period is offered each day after classes, followed by athletic activities and team sport practices. Required evening study hall is from 7:45 P.M. to 9:45 P.M. Sunday night through Thursday night and is followed by free time before dorm check-in at 10:15 P.M.

The academic program requires a minimum of 18 credits for graduation including 4 of English; 3 of mathematics; 2 of a laboratory science; 3 of history; 1 of theology; 1 of health; 2 of the same foreign language; 1 of fine arts; and 1 of computer science. Most students graduate with 20 or more credits.

Honors and Advanced Placement courses are available in most curricular areas. Courses offered are English 1–4; Spanish 1–4 and Advanced Placement Spanish, French 1–4, Latin 1–3; World Geography, World History, U.S. History and Advanced Placement U.S. History, U.S. Government, Modern U.S. History, Comparative Ideologies, Economics; Biblical Studies, Church History and Ethics, Introduction to World Religions; Pre-Algebra, Algebra I, Algebra II, Geometry, Algebra III/Trigonometry, Introduction to Probability and Statistics,

Finite Mathematics, Advanced Placement Calculus; Computer Science (Fundamental Applications), Computer Science (PASCAL); Introduction to Physical Science, Biology, Advanced Placement Biology, Marine Science I, Advanced Placement Environmental Studies, Chemistry, Advanced Chemistry, Physics; Art I, Art II, Introduction to Music/Art Appreciation, Music History and Appreciation, Music Theory/Harmony, Art History and Appreciation, Chorus; and Health and Physical Education. Christchurch School also offers a unique and comprehensive program in marine science. Research facilities are available on campus, and include a 25-foot Wellcraft and ten canoes. Christchurch also coordinates research projects with the nearby Virginia Institute of Marine Science (VIMS) of the College of William and Mary.

In 1999, all 44 graduates were accepted to college. They were accepted by and/or are attending such colleges as Boston University, Carnegie Mellon, College of Charleston, Furman, George Mason, George Washington, Guilford, Hampden-Sydney, James Madison, New York University, Pepperdine, Randolph-Macon, Rhodes, Roanoke, Syracuse, Virginia Polytechnic, Washington College, and the Universities of Alabama, Colorado (Boulder), Delaware, Maryland, Mississippi, North Carolina (Chapel Hill), and South Carolina.

The Summer Programs offer academic and enrichment experiences for boarding and day boys and girls. Courses include Marine Science, English, Mathematics, and special courses in SAT Preparation and writing, math, and study skills. Summer students in Grades 6–12 can participate in sailing, canoeing, and crabbing activities.

STUDENT ACTIVITIES. Class representatives and school officers are elected by their peers to represent them as members of the Student Government Association. Both students and faculty nominate and elect by ballot members to serve on the Student Prefect System. Prefects are Resident Assistants and Honor or Disciplinary Council members.

Other student activities include the yearbook and literary magazine, community service, outdoor club, student ambassadors, chorus, and cycling. All students can participate in theatrical productions organized by the Drama and English departments.

Boys' varsity athletic teams compete against other private school teams in the Virginia Prep League in rowing, soccer, cross-country, sailing, wrestling, indoor soccer, basketball, lacrosse, baseball, tennis, and golf. Varsity football teams compete in the Old Dominion Football Conference. Junior varsity teams are fielded in soccer, cross-country, basketball, lacrosse, baseball, and tennis. Girls' teams compete in interscholastic field hockey, basketball, and tennis.

Dances, mixers, and social exchanges are periodically arranged with St. Margaret's and other girls' schools. Athletic events, movies, and cultural day trips are scheduled on weekends. Richmond, Williamsburg, and Washington, D.C., provide these social, cultural, and athletic opportunities. Students visit Colonial Williamsburg, the College of William and Mary, Busch Gardens, the Virginia Museum of Fine Arts and attend events at the Kennedy Center and the Smithsonian Institution. Educational events and visiting speakers of national stature are presented throughout the year at the McLaughlin Symposium.

Special events for parents and alumni include two Parents Weekends, Homecoming, and the Alumni Reunion Weekend.

ADMISSION AND COSTS. Christchurch School seeks college-bound students of average to above-average ability including those with high potential whose previous academic success may have been limited. Students are accepted in all grades. Admissions are based on school transcripts, standardized test scores, teacher and personal references, and an on-campus interview. Applications with a fee of $50 are accepted throughout the year. The School values diversity and seeks to admit qualified students regardless of race, color, or national or ethnic origin. Students may enroll at midyear; such cases are decided individually.

In 1999–2000, boarding tuition is $21,250; day tuition is $8850. Students accepted into the Learning Skills Program pay an additional $3675. The School's program in English as a Second Language is $4000. Tuition insurance and payment plans are available. The School awards more than $500,000 in financial aid annually on the basis of need. Approximately 30 percent of the students receive financial aid.

Dean of Faculty: Robert T. Todd
Assistant Headmaster for Student Life: John E. Byers
Alumni Director/Director of Development: Clifford L. Asbury
Director of Admissions: David E. Taibl
College Counselor: Jeanette C. Adkins
Business Manager: J. Chip Broadway
Director of Athletics: Richard D. Griffin

The Collegiate School   1915

North Mooreland Road, Richmond, VA 23229. 804-740-7077; Fax 804-741-9797; E-mail Admissions@collegiate-va.org; Web Site www.collegiate.ind.k12.va.us

The Collegiate School enrolls 1500 boys and girls in Kindergarten–Grade 12 on a 55-acre campus. Collegiate seeks to admit students who have the academic and personal potential to meet the high standards of a college preparatory program, who have diverse abilities and backgrounds, and who will make positive contributions to the School. Math, sciences, foreign languages, art, music, physical education, economics, and computer literacy are required. A fine arts building features a 620-seat auditorium and art and music facility. Tuition: $7900–$10,400. Financial Aid: $836,000. Amanda Surgner is Director of Admission; Keith A. Evans (Harvard University, Ed.M.; University of Tennessee, M.S.) is Head of School. *Southern Association.*

The Covenant School   1985

Kindergarten–Grade 6: 500 Old Lynchburg Road, Charlottesville, VA 22903. 804-979-2796; Fax 804-979-1794
Grades 7–12: 1000 Birdwood Road, Charlottesville, VA 22903. 804-979-2389; Fax 804-979-3204; Web Site www.avenue.org/tcs

The Covenant School is a nondenominational, coeducational, Christian day school enrolling 640 students in Kindergarten through Grade 12. The School fosters learning grounded in the best traditions of classical and Christian education. The central goal of its program is to cultivate young people who can think, communicate, and make wise decisions that honor Christ and serve the common interests of their community and society. The School offers a liberal arts, college preparatory education that seeks to instill the joy and discipline of learning in language arts, mathematics, history, science, fine arts, and physical education. Tuition: $5375–$7358. Financial aid is available. Donna B. Harris is Director of Admissions; Dr. Ronald P. Sykes is Head of School.

Episcopal High School   ALEXANDRIA

1200 North Quaker Lane, Alexandria, VA 22302. 703-933-3000; Fax 703-933-3016; E-mail admissions@episcopalhighschool.org; Web Site www.episcopalhighschool.org

EPISCOPAL HIGH SCHOOL in Alexandria, Virginia, is a college preparatory boarding school for boys and girls in Grades 9–12. It is 15 minutes from the cultural and educational resources of Washington, D.C., and 13 minutes from Washington's Ronald Reagan Airport. Alexandria (population 175,000) is situated in Northern Virginia on the Potomac River. Once an 18th-century seaport, today it is a thriving business and residential area that offers a spectrum of cultural, social, and educational events.

Episcopal High School opened in 1839 with 35 boys. As the first high school in Virginia, it became known throughout the South as "The High School," a name by which it is still known today. Episcopal grew to accommodate more than 100 boys until May 1861, when the Civil War forced its closing. It has been in continuous operation since reopening in 1866.

The High School is committed to the spiritual, intellectual, moral, and physical development of students. In addition to a comprehensive and rigorous academic program, there are regularly scheduled chapel services, daily athletics and extensive activities, and community service programs.

Episcopal High School is a nonprofit corporation directed by a 30-member Board of Trustees, 18 of whom are alumni. There are approximately 4500 living graduates. The President of the alumni organization serves as an ex-officio member of the Board of Trustees. The High School is accredited by the Virginia Association of Independent Schools and the Southern Association of Colleges and Schools and holds membership in the National Association of Independent Schools, among other organizations. The School-owned plant is valued at $85,000,000, and the endowment is $65,000,000.

THE CAMPUS. The High School, on 130 acres near the western boundary of Alexandria, is surrounded by wooded areas. The principal buildings are situated on tree-shaded lawns in the middle of the campus.

The centerpiece of Episcopal's campus is Hoxton House, originally called Mount Washington when it was built in 1804 by Martha Washington's eldest granddaughter, Eliza Parke Custis Law. The original drawing room has been carefully restored and continues to be used as the main reception room on campus.

Episcopal's academic facilities include six buildings with 45 classrooms; all are wired for data, voice, and video. The fully automated library houses more than 30,000 books, videos, over 2000 music CDs, 150 periodicals, 12 newspapers, and CD-ROMs in every academic discipline. The library also provides access to an information retrieval service, a national interlibrary loan network, and a school-wide computer network linked to the Internet. Other facilities include computer and science labs with Pentium-based Wintel computers; the art studio equipped with two computers with CD-ROM players, PhotoShop software, digital cameras, a high-resolution scanner, and two printers; a music lab with a MIDI digital interface linked to a Macintosh computer; Stewart Gymnasium Dance Studio; Auditorium and Performing Arts Center; a bookstore; Bryan Library Reception Center; and meeting rooms and offices.

Episcopal's outstanding athletic facilities include Hummel Bowl, a 2800-seat stadium; Flippin Field House with 3 tennis courts, 3 basketball courts, a 200-yard track, and a batting cage; Centennial Gymnasium with a basketball court and a newly renovated fitness center featuring a Cybex weight machine room and cardiovascular area; seven playing fields; Goodman Squash Center with 4 courts; Cooper Dawson Baseball Diamond; a wrestling cage; Shuford Tennis Courts (12 all-weather tennis courts); an outdoor swimming pool; and Hoxton Track, a six-lane, 400-meter outdoor track.

The High School's residential facilities include seven dormitories with single, double, and triple rooms, common rooms, and laundry facilities; Patrick Henry Callaway Chapel, where students attend services on most weekdays and bimonthly Sundays; Laird Dining Room for buffet and family-style meals; Blackford Hall, the main coed student lounge with a snack bar, vending area, television, and CD jukebox; Coed Commons, equipped with three televisions and Ping-Pong tables; and the McAllister Infirmary, which is staffed by a registered nurse and

visited daily by a physician. Alexandria Hospital two blocks away provides emergency treatment, if needed.

THE FACULTY. F. Robertson Hershey was appointed the School's 11th Headmaster in 1998. He attended Williams College (B.A. 1970) and the University of Virginia (M.Ed. 1975). Mr. Hershey had previously served as Headmaster at Durham Academy from 1978 to 1988 and, most recently, at The Collegiate School in Richmond from 1988 to 1998.

The faculty of 77 men and women includes 57 who hold advanced degrees, including 5 doctorates. Nearly 90 percent of all full-time faculty members live on campus with their families.

STUDENT BODY. Episcopal High School's 400 students—260 boys and 140 girls—come from 29 states, the District of Columbia, and 15 foreign countries including Bermuda, China, England, Hungary, Japan, Mexico, Saudi Arabia, Scotland, South Korea, and Thailand.

ACADEMIC PROGRAM. The school year, from early September through late May, includes two semesters with vacations at Thanksgiving, Christmas, and in the spring.

Classes meet five days a week. A typical daily schedule, from 7:15 A.M. to 10:30 P.M., includes chapel, class periods, meals, a tutoring period, athletics and activities in the afternoon, and two hours of evening study.

There are 10 to 12 students in an average class, with a student-teacher ratio of 7:1. Homework is prepared during free periods in the morning and during the evening study halls, with these periods supervised by student leaders and faculty. Grades are posted and sent to families four times a year.

A minimum of 23 credits is required for graduation, with the following specific requirements: 4 credits in English, 3-3½ in mathematics, 3½ in social studies, 2 or 3 in a foreign language, 2 or 3 in physical education, 2 in laboratory science, 1 in theology, and ½ in fine arts. Students also have the opportunity to experience Episcopal's unique Washington Experience, which provides academic exposure to cultural and historical sites in Washington, D.C., and the surrounding area.

A wide variety of courses is available, including honors and Advanced Placement courses in most subjects. The curriculum offers courses in English, Creative Writing, French, German, Latin, Spanish, U.S. and World History, Theology, Economics, Algebra, Geometry, Trigonometry, Pre-Calculus, AB and BC Calculus, Statistics, Ethics, Computer Studies, Electronic Publishing, Art History, Photography, Studio Art, Music Theory, Music History, and Theatre Arts.

Episcopal High School's 101 members of the Class of 1999 will attend 60 different colleges and universities in 25 states. Among these are Boston College, Brown, Colgate, Duke, Georgetown, Harvard, New York University, Vanderbilt, Washington and Lee, Yale, and the Universities of Chicago, North Carolina, and Virginia.

STUDENT ACTIVITIES. An enduring tradition at The High School is an Honor Code, which Episcopal pioneered among secondary schools. Faculty and students strongly support this concept, which asserts that students will not lie, cheat, or steal, and that, out of a genuine concern for and responsibility to the student who does, they are asked to report violators to the Honor Committee.

The student body is led by student monitors who are nominated to the Headmaster by the faculty and students and who are responsible for discipline and orderliness in the day-to-day life of the High School. A student-elected dorm council offers additional leadership opportunities.

The High School fields 45 teams in 16 sports for boys and girls, including junior, junior varsity, and varsity teams in many sports. All ninth- and tenth-grade students participate in three sports, one each season, and upperclassmen take part in one or more sports per school year. Baseball, basketball, cross-country, field hockey, football, golf, lacrosse, soccer, squash, tennis, indoor and outdoor track, volleyball, and wrestling are offered. All students can participate in dance, and older students may choose aerobics, weight training, cross training, and an outdoor program during some seasons. Episcopal's teams play a full sports schedule with other independent schools in the Virginia, Maryland, and Washington, D.C., areas. Boys' teams participate in the Interstate Athletic Conference, and girls' teams compete in the Independent School League.

Activities include the Art Club, Choir, Community Service Program, Environmental Club, Honor Committee, International Relations Club, Model Judiciary, Model U.N., peer counseling, Performing Arts Group, literary magazine, newspaper, yearbook, Stop AIDS for Everyone Chapter, Student Health Awareness Committee, Student Vestry, Tour Guides, and Youth in Philanthropy. In addition, the Activities Program involves students in cultural, historic, athletic, outdoor, and social activities throughout the Washington area. Qualified students may audition for the Mount Vernon Youth Symphony, which rehearses weekly at Episcopal. A formal Outdoor Program is also available.

During the year, students present two full-length plays—a drama and a musical—and several one-act plays. Special events include dances and social events with other schools, winter

weekend skiing in Pennsylvania, an intramural field day in the spring, fall Homecoming, and Parents' Weekends in both the fall and spring.

ADMISSION AND COSTS. Qualified candidates are accepted without regard to race or creed. They are evaluated on the basis of previous grades and teacher comments, an interview, and results of the Secondary School Admission Test.

Tuition is $23,100; an allowance of $125 per month is suggested. Tuition insurance and a tuition plan are available. Thirty-two percent of the student body receive scholarship grants or low-interest loans totaling $1,500,000 annually. Episcopal High School subscribes to the School and Student Service for Financial Aid.

Assistant Head for Academics: Jacqueline E. Maher
Assistant Head for Student Life: John M. Walker, Jr.
Director of Studies: Robert A. Pierce '78
Director of Faculty Development: Jeffrey A. Streed
Dean of Students: Ashton W. Richards
Alumni Secretary: Jeffrey B. Clarke '89
Director of Admissions: Robert C. Watts III
Director of Development: Robert C. Eckert
College Counselor: Robert M. Hedrick
Treasurer: Richard F. Yarborough, Jr. '63
Director of Athletics: Timothy C. Jaeger

Fishburne Military School   WAYNESBORO

Post Office Box 988-L, Waynesboro, VA 22980. 800-946-7773 or 540-946-7703; E-mail mcalistr@fishburne.org; Web Site www.fishburne.org

FISHBURNE MILITARY SCHOOL in Waynesboro, Virginia, is an independent college preparatory school enrolling boys in Grades 8 through 12 and a postgraduate year. Situated in the Shenandoah Valley of the Blue Ridge Mountains, the School overlooks the city of Waynesboro (population 19,000). The Blue Ridge Parkway and Skyline Drive are minutes away and the area offers many historical and cultural sites. The School is two and one-half hours from Washington, D.C., and one and one-half hours from Richmond by automobile. Plane and bus transportation are convenient to the School.

Fishburne Military School was established in 1879 by James A. Fishburne, a Waynesboro native. Professor Fishburne founded the School in an effort to help the South rebuild after the Civil War. It was his hope to educate young men to be well equipped for the duties and responsibilities of life and to maintain a high standard of honor and integrity within the Corps of Cadets. Professor Fishburne served the School until his death in 1921, at which time Col. Morgan H. Hudgins became Superintendent. When Colonel Hudgins retired in 1952, the corporation that owned and operated the School set up the Fishburne-Hudgins Educational Foundation.

The School continues to strive to provide cadets with a broad academic foundation that will prepare them for further study at the college level and to offer practical experience in leadership, self-discipline, intellectual honesty, and respect for authority. Cadets are required to attend Sunday services at the church of their choice.

A nonprofit institution, Fishburne Military School is governed by a 42-member Board of Trustees, including alumni and local residents, that meets four times a year to set policy and educational goals. The Alumni Association, with more than 3000 active members, includes graduates of the service academies and other well-known universities in the United States. The School has been accredited by the Southern Association of Colleges and Schools since 1897 and is the only military school in Virginia to be continuously awarded the United States Army JROTC School Honor Unit rating.

THE CAMPUS. The professionally landscaped campus with formal gardens overlooking the Blue Ridge Mountains is listed on the Virginia Register of Historic Landmarks and the National Register of Historic Places. The brick buildings, constructed around the Quadrangle and connected by covered walkways, include classrooms; science laboratories; the cafeteria; the infirmary; an auditorium fully equipped with sound systems and stage lights; cadet rooms; and a student lounge. The Schneider Memorial Library with more than 10,000 volumes, periodicals, and special collections, houses the photography lab, an art classroom, and computer lab. The computer lab, classrooms, and cadet rooms are served by a school-wide network.

The Alumni Memorial Gymnasium, an indoor swimming pool, a weight-training facility, an indoor rifle range, athletic fields, an outdoor basketball court, five tennis courts, and the parade ground complete the physical plant.

THE FACULTY. Col. William W. Sedr, Jr., was named Headmaster of the School in 1988. He is a graduate of Virginia Military Institute with a master's degree in history from Virginia Polytechnic Institute and State University and graduate work in education at the University of Virginia and James Madison University.

The 20 full-time academic teachers hold 20 baccalaureate, 9 master's, and 1 Ph.D. degrees from such institutions as Bridgewater College, East Carolina University, James Madison, Longwood, Madison College, Marshall, Purdue, Radford, Saint Vincent, United States Air Force Academy, Virginia Military Institute, Virginia Polytechnic Institute and State University, Wake Forest, William and Mary, and the Universities of Arkansas, Richmond, and Virginia. There are two additional instructors assigned to the Junior Division of the Reserve Officers Training Corps at the School. Five part-time teachers are also on staff.

Three nurses supervise the School's infirmary with the assistance of consulting physicians. The Augusta Hospital is nearby.

STUDENT BODY. In 1999–2000, 178 boarding and 22 day students are enrolled as follows: 17 in Grade 8, 48 in Grade 9, 43 in Grade 10, 50 in Grade 11, and 42 in Grade 12. The majority come from Virginia, Maryland, and North Carolina, with repre-

sentation from 14 other states, the District of Columbia, the United States Virgin Islands, and 11 foreign countries.

ACADEMIC PROGRAM. The school year, divided into semesters, begins in early September and ends in late May, with vacations at Thanksgiving, Christmas, and in the spring, and optional weekend leaves in the fall and winter. Grades are sent out two times each semester. Each student is assigned a faculty counselor who usually has daily contact with him. Supervised study halls are held Sunday through Thursday evenings.

To graduate, students must complete 21 units as follows: 4 in English, 2 in mathematics, 1 in American history, 1 in American government, 1 in world history or geography, 2 in laboratory science, 2 in physical education, 1 in fine or practical arts, and 7 in electives. The Advanced Studies diploma requires 23 units with 3 in mathematics, including Algebra I–II and Geometry; 3 in laboratory science, including biology and chemistry or physics; 3 in one foreign language or 2 each in two foreign languages; and 3 or 4 electives. Students must also take 1 unit of leadership education each year as an elective.

Students in Grade 8 receive a solid academic foundation before beginning diploma requirements. Courses are offered in language arts, mathematics, health and physical education, science, and social studies. Among the courses offered in Grades 9 through 12 are Freshman English (basic grammar and literature), Sophomore English (research techniques and literature), Junior English (historical literature and written and oral expression), Senior English (the origin and development of the English language and a research project), Advanced English/Creative Writing; French 1–4, Spanish 1–4; General Science, Biology, Chemistry, Physics; World Geography, World History, United States and Virginia History, United States and Virginia Government, Law Related Education, Economics, Sociology; Algebra I–II, Plane Geometry, Advanced Mathematics, Calculus, Computer Applications; Health and Physical Education; and Driver Training. The Enrichment Program offers a variety of lectures, concerts, and seminars, including sessions on sex education and drug abuse.

In 1999, all of the 32 graduates were accepted into college. They are attending such institutions as The Citadel, East Tennessee University, Elon, George Mason, James Madison University, Marshall, North Carolina Wesleyan, United States Air Force Academy, United States Military Academy, Virginia Commonwealth, Virginia Military Institute, Virginia Polytechnic Institute and State University, and the Universities of Southern California and Virginia.

A five-week, nonmilitary, academic summer session is open to both returning cadets and new students. A special English course is offered to students for whom English is a second language.

STUDENT ACTIVITIES. The Fishburne Honor Council, composed of appointed and elected cadets, enforces the School's Honor Code, which states that a cadet does not lie, cheat, or steal, nor tolerate those who do. Each cadet is assigned to a military unit where there are many opportunities for leadership roles in the progression of rank. The Military Department sponsors the school band, the color guard, the varsity rifle team, the Hudgins Rifles Drill Team, the Raiders, and a Scout Troop.

Cadets compete with schools in the Virginia Independent Conference and other nearby schools in football, soccer, cross-country, basketball, wrestling, swimming, baseball, tennis, track, and golf.

A wide variety of clubs and activities is available to cadets. In addition, the Fishburne Players present a major drama production each year, and *Taps* (the yearbook) is published by cadets. The Debating Team competes in the Military School League. Qualified students are inducted into the National Honor Society. Members of the Key Club volunteer many hours to local service clubs and organizations.

Formal and casual weekend activities are planned with girls from Stuart Hall and other nearby schools. Weekend trips are organized to ski areas, Colonial Williamsburg, Busch Gardens, Charlottesville, King's Dominion, Washington, D.C., and the Shenandoah National Park. Traditional annual events include Parents Weekend, Mother's Day, and Alumni Weekend.

ADMISSION AND COSTS. Fishburne Military School seeks candidates who demonstrate a need for the School's strengths and who can contribute their own uniqueness for the benefit of all. The School makes a conscious effort to maintain a diversified student body with respect to geographic, economic, and social backgrounds. Prospective students must be willing to accept discipline and have good moral character and habits. The application form with a $50 fee, a preadmission visit to the School, test scores, academic records plus a recommendation from the candidate's school, and personal references are requirements.

In 1999–2000, the annual fee is $15,900 for new boarding students and $7400 for new day students. There is an additional $500 fee to international students. Returning boarding students pay $14,700 and day students $6200. A reduction of $1000 is given to sons of active military personnel, veterans who have died in service to their country, and retired veterans with 20 years of service. If two or more sons from a family are enrolled, each son receives a reduction of $1000. Reductions are also given to families using the Single or Semester Payment plans, to relatives of alumni, and to students with prior Junior Reserve Officers Training Corps experience.

Chief Executive Officer: Oscar H. "Beau" Beasley III '65
Dean of Faculty: Col. William W. Sedr, Jr.
Alumni and Development Coordinator: Pamela C. Robinson
Director of Admissions: Gary R. Morrison '81
Director of Development: Col. William Alexander, Jr. '64
College Counselor: Gail Massello
Finance Officer: J. Revonda Heil
Director of Athletics: Rodney Cullen

Flint Hill School   1956

10409 Academic Drive, Oakton, VA 22124. 703-242-0705;
Admissions 703-319-4441; Fax 703-242-0718;
E-mail admissions@flinthill.org; Web Site www.flinthill.org

Flint Hill, 20 miles west of Washington, D.C., enrolls 650 day boys and girls in Junior Kindergarten–Grade 12. The School offers challenging, developmentally appropriate instruction in the core academics, arts, and athletics while encouraging moral/ethical growth and mastery of critical thinking skills. The Upper School includes diverse electives and Advanced Placement courses. Requirements include community service, junior internship, senior projects, and experiential education. Faculty advisors assigned to each Middle and Upper School student provide academic counseling and program planning. Tuition: $8855–$13,878. Financial Aid: $500,000. Ruth H. Little is Admissions Director; Thomas C. Whitworth III (University of North Carolina, B.A.; The Citadel, M.Ed.) is Headmaster.

Fork Union Military Academy

FORK UNION

Box 278-A, Fork Union, VA 23055. 804-842-4200 or
800-G02-FUMA; Fax 804-842-4300; E-mail akersj@fuma.org;
Web Site www.forkunion.com

Fork union military academy in Fork Union, Virginia, is a college preparatory, military boarding school for young men in Grades 6 through 12 and postgraduates. A limited number of day students are also enrolled. Affiliated with the Virginia Baptist General Association but open to young men of all religious denominations, Fork Union's Upper School offers a unique "One-Subject Plan" of study under which students concentrate on a single major subject every seven weeks.

Fork Union is a small town 50 miles west of Richmond and 30 miles southeast of Charlottesville, near the confluence of the James and Rivanna rivers. The Academy was founded in 1898 by Dr. William E. Hatcher, a noted Baptist minister, and was originally a coeducational, "classical" school for day students who boarded in village homes. In 1910, the girls' division was discontinued.

The Academy is guided by a Board of Trustees that is responsible for the $34,000,000 plant and approximately $8,000,000 in productive endowments. The school's primary goal is to help young men prepare for college in an environment that promotes their mental, spiritual, and physical development. The school is accredited by The Virginia Association of Independent Schools and the Southern Association of Colleges and Schools; it holds membership in the National Association of Independent Schools, the Association of Military Colleges and Schools of the United States, and other organizations.

THE CAMPUS. The Academy occupies 500 acres, 26 of which provide six athletic fields for football, baseball, soccer, and lacrosse; a new 400-meter all-weather track; and a 2500-seat stadium. There are also tennis courts, an indoor pool, three gymnasiums, a skeet range, an indoor rifle range, a paved outdoor basketball/volleyball court, a 4-acre lake, and an airstrip.

Among the more prominent buildings, which are substantial brick and concrete structures surrounded by broad lawns, are the Guy E. Beatty Library, housing more than 19,000 volumes; Hatcher Hall, with offices and some classrooms; John J. Wicker Chapel, which seats 550; J. Caldwell Wicker Science Building and Planetarium; Moretz Learning Center; Perkins Technology Center; the Middle School Academic Building and Dormitory; and the Dorothy Thomasson Estes Dining Hall, which seats 750. The Yeatman Infirmary is staffed 24 hours per day by a physician or nurse. The Estes Athletic Center is an 85,000-square-foot facility that includes a main floor with a 160-meter indoor track, three basketball courts, several tennis courts, five air-conditioned racquetball courts, a squash court, and a wrestling room. There are also training and rehabilitation rooms, a concession and lounge area, a weight-training room, a batting cage, and nine locker rooms.

THE FACULTY. The Academy's President is Lt. Gen. John E. Jackson, Jr., USAF (Ret.). General Jackson earned his baccalaureate degree from Alderson-Broaddus College and his master's degree from Central Michigan University. He is a graduate of the Senior Managers in Government course at Harvard University and was awarded an honorary doctorate in Public Administration by Alderson-Broaddus College in 1993.

The F.U.M.A. administrative staff includes a Chaplain, Chief Financial Officer, Director of Admissions, Academic

Dean, Director of Development, Physician, Athletic Director, as well as a Middle School Headmaster. Separate Commandants and librarians serve in the Middle and Upper schools. The full-time teaching faculty (40 men and 5 women) include 33 in the Upper School and 12 in the Middle School. Faculty and administrators hold 71 baccalaureate and 29 graduate degrees representing study at more than 45 colleges and universities in the United States and several other countries.

STUDENT BODY. The school enrolls a total of 620 boarders and 30 day students. The Middle School includes Grades 6–8; the Upper School is comprised of Grades 9–12 and postgraduates. Approximately 70 percent of the cadets come from states along the eastern seaboard; the remainder are from other parts of the United States and around the world, with a total of 36 states, the District of Columbia, and 20 foreign countries represented in the student body. (Some of those from overseas are from American families stationed or employed abroad.) Cadets represent more than 25 different religious backgrounds and denominations.

ACADEMIC PROGRAM. The school year runs from early September to the end of May, with a Thanksgiving leave, a two-week Christmas leave, and a spring vacation. Weekend leaves are permitted twice a month, subject to the cadet's passing grades and good behavior. Classes meet Monday through Friday and on approximately ten Saturdays during the year. A typical day, from Reveille at 6:15 A.M. to Taps at 10:15 P.M., includes classes from 8:00 A.M. to 2:00 P.M., chapel twice a week, military drill (two 45-minute periods per week) in the early afternoon, sports and recreation until dinner, and personal inspection before the evening retreat formation, followed by clubs and activities and two hours of supervised evening study.

There are 14 to 19 students in an average class in the Upper School, 9 to 14 in the Middle School. Grades are reported to cadets every two weeks, and parents receive written reports monthly (more frequently for students experiencing difficulty). Testing for guidance, progress measurement, and college planning includes College Board Examinations, the American College Test, Preliminary Scholastic Aptitude Tests, aptitude and interest batteries, and a number of reading tests.

The Middle School curriculum includes Mathematics, English, Social Studies, Science, Reading, Spelling, and Writing, as well as exploratory courses in Art, Astronomy, Computer Science, Ethics/Leadership, and Music Appreciation. Each cadet receives a military grade based on tests, performance of duties, drill performance, and demerit record.

In the Upper School, Honors and Advanced Placement programs offer accelerated work in English, calculus, science, government, and history. Under the "One-Subject Plan," each cadet concentrates on one subject for an approximate seven-week period. Courses include English 1–5, World Literature,

College Preparatory Writing, Humanities; French, German, Spanish; World Geography, World History, Virginia and U.S. History, Virginia and U.S. Government, Economics, Sociology, Comparative Governments, Asian Studies; Pre-Algebra, Algebra 1 and 2, Geometry, Review of Math Functions, Trigonometry and Advanced Algebra, Calculus; Earth Science, Biology, Chemistry, Physics, Astronomy; Computer Science; Art; Physical Education and Health; and Religious Studies (required of juniors and students who enter as seniors). Developmental and remedial reading is also available as well as a Reading/Learning Skills course.

All cadets enjoy regular access to the more than 200 on-line multimedia computer work stations in the Perkins Technology Center.

A nonmilitary summer school, from late June to early August, enrolls boarding and day boys in Grades 7–12. Many of the regular courses are offered, and the extracurricular emphasis is on intramural athletics. Class and athletic wear for the entire summer school is provided in the cost of tuition.

STUDENT ACTIVITIES. The Upper School battalion of over 500 cadets is made up of five companies, a 65-piece marching band, an honor platoon of specialists in close-order drill, and the highest-ranking cadets who comprise the battalion staff. Cadet barracks are operated through the cadet chain-of-command, which is overseen by company advisors who are assigned by the Commandant. Under the standard disciplinary system, excessive demerits and regulation infractions can lead to loss of privileges or penalty tours.

Cadets enjoy involvement in more than 35 different clubs and activities including Weightlifting, Computer, Paintball, Art, Debate, Fishing, Model Building, Science, Chess, and Guidance clubs; Boy Scouts; the Fellowship of Christian Athletes; a newspaper and a yearbook; National Honor Society; and a Quadrille Club, which helps arrange all dances.

The F.U.M.A. Flight Program offers cadets ground instruction and actual flying time leading to a pilot's license.

Music is an important part of the F.U.M.A. program. In addition to the Upper School marching band, which appears at athletic events, parades, and area festivals, there are various concert ensembles and a separate Middle School marching band. Two chorus groups participate in chapel services and perform for various groups and churches throughout the Mid-Atlantic region.

Varsity (postgraduate), prep, junior prep, Middle School, and intramural teams in both schools compete in football, basketball, baseball, lacrosse, golf, orienteering, wrestling, indoor and outdoor track, cross-country, swimming and diving, rifle, tennis, and indoor and outdoor soccer. There are also junior and senior lifesaving programs. Interscholastic competition is held against teams from public and private schools, particularly against fellow members of the Virginia Prep League. Post-

graduate teams generally play junior varsity squads from major colleges, as well as teams from junior and community colleges.

Activities include a formal military ball to which parents are invited and informal dances with nearby girls' schools. Students also enjoy leisure time in the afternoons and on weekends.

ADMISSION AND COSTS. Applicants are admitted in Grades 6–12 and as postgraduates on the basis of previous scholastic record, academic potential, and character; if testing is required, the school helps with arrangements. Qualified applicants are accepted "without regard to race, color, religion, or national origin." Application should be made by spring, but boys are often enrolled later when space permits.

In 1999–2000, tuition, room and board, and fees total $14,955, with an additional charge for uniforms estimated at $2330. The day-student charge is $7915 plus the cost of uniforms and books. A monthly payment plan is available. Financial aid includes certain standard reductions and a limited number of loans and grants.

Dean of Faculty: Col. Bob Miller
Commandant of Upper School Cadets: Lt. Col. Al Ivens
Commandant of Middle School Cadets: Maj. Steve Macek
Chaplain: Maj. Lowell C. Vaught
Director of Admissions: Lt. Col. James C. Akers
Director of Development: Lt. Col. Bobby Cobb
College Counselor: Capt. Gordon Shelton
Chief Financial Officer: Maj. John Galloway
Director of Athletics: Lt. Col. Mickey Sullivan
Middle School Head: Lt. Col. Robert J. Feathers

Foxcroft School   MIDDLEBURG

Middleburg, VA 20118. 540-687-5555, 800-858-2364;
Fax 540-687-3627; E-mail admissions@foxcroft.org;
Web Site www.foxcroft.org

FOXCROFT SCHOOL in Middleburg, Virginia, is a college preparatory boarding and day school enrolling girls in Grades 9 through 12 as well as a postgraduate year. Situated in the countryside between the Blue Ridge and Bull Run mountains, the School is an hour by car from Washington, D.C.; Dulles International Airport is 35 minutes away. Field trips to the District of Columbia museums, theaters, concerts, and government agencies are offered to supplement classroom work.

Foxcroft School was founded in 1914 by Charlotte Haxall Noland, who directed the School until her retirement in 1955. From the beginning, Miss Noland stressed that "parents should require a great deal more of schools than just intellectual training." Accordingly, she sought to establish a school where the formation of character would be "a key aspect" of the educational program.

Foxcroft is governed by a 30-member Board of Trustees, which meets three times annually. The School endowment is $10,216,697, and the plant is valued at $25,900,000. Approximately 2300 graduates belong to the Alumnae Association, and there are 19 alumnae on the Board of Trustees. Foxcroft is accredited by The Virginia Association of Independent Schools; it is a member of the Association of Independent Schools of the Greater Washington Area, the National Association of Independent Schools, and other professional organizations.

THE CAMPUS. The School is situated on 500 acres of meadows and woodlands, part of which is used as a "Discovery Course" for survival games, group challenges, and similar outdoor activities. A swimming pool, three sports fields, eight tennis courts, three riding rings, and a jump course are adjacent to the main campus. There is an indoor riding arena in McConnell Stables; a gymnasium, a newly equipped weight room, and dance studio are located in the Student Activity Center.

Foxcroft's brick and stone buildings are set among courtyards, orchards, and gardens. The restored 18th-century Brick House contains reception rooms, the development office, faculty apartments, and the dining room. The Schoolhouse has 14 classrooms, a studio art wing, music rooms, offices, and an auditorium. An addition houses science teaching facilities, including three laboratory/classrooms, and an animal-plant room. The 50,000-volume Currier Library contains a computer lab, seminar rooms, a microfilm room, audiovisual equipment, 85 study carrels, and the school archives.

Girls live in Court, Dillon, Applegate, Orchard, and Reynolds dormitories. Other facilities include faculty housing, the Head's home, the guest house, the Health Center, and an observatory.

THE FACULTY. Mary Louise Leipheimer was appointed Head of the School in April of 1989. She is a graduate of Indiana University of Pennsylvania with a B.S. degree in English. Mrs. Leipheimer first came to Foxcroft in 1967 as a teacher of English. Prior to her present appointment, she has served the School community as Director of Admission, Assistant Head of External Affairs, and Director of Development.

Foxcroft has 29 full-time faculty and administrators who teach, 19 women and 10 men. Thirty-nine faculty and administrators live on campus, 16 with families. They hold 46 baccalaureate, 21 graduate degrees, and 2 doctorates from such institutions as American University, Carnegie Mellon, Colgate, College of William and Mary, Columbia, Denison, Duke, Guilford, Harvard, Indiana University, Medical College of Virginia, New York University, Skidmore, Swarthmore, Tulane, Wake Forest, Wellesley, Yale, and the Universities of California (Berkeley), Madrid (Spain), Massachusetts, the South, Vermont, and Virginia.

Two registered nurses staff the infirmary, and a doctor is on call.

STUDENT BODY. In 1999–2000, Foxcroft enrolls 117 boarding students and 36 day girls as follows: 31 in Grade 9, 42 in Grade 10, 29 in Grade 11, 49 in Grade 12, and 2 postgraduates. Boarders represent 22 states, the District of Columbia, and 14

countries. Twenty-seven students are from overseas, and the day students are from the Middleburg vicinity.

ACADEMIC PROGRAM. The school year, from early September to early June, is divided into semesters, with Thanksgiving, Christmas, and spring vacations. Grades and comments are sent to parents four times yearly.

Classes, containing an average of ten students, meet five days a week between 8:00 A.M. and 3:30 P.M. A campus-wide meeting is held three days a week. Athletics are scheduled after the regular academic day. Dinner is followed by free time, two and one-quarter hours of study, and "lights out" at 11:00 P.M. (10:30 P.M. for freshmen).

To graduate, a student must complete 18 credits. One credit (unit) is the equivalent of a full-year course. Minimum requirements are English 4, foreign language 3, history 3, mathematics 3, science 3, fine arts 1.5, and computer literacy .5. In addition, a student must take physical education or participate in riding, dance, or a varsity sport in all three seasons of the school year. Each girl is also required to participate in community service on campus or in Middleburg.

The curriculum includes more than 70 full-year and term courses. Advanced Placement courses are offered in all disciplines. Foxcroft's postgraduate year offers a one-year program of college preparation to selected students who have earned their high school diplomas but desire an additional year of study and personal growth in a supportive academic community. These students pursue a traditional curriculum and complete a term of independent study in an interdisciplinary field of their choice. International students may take a range of courses in English as a Second Language as well as other academic classes. Seniors are also encouraged to do independent study. The Learning Centers offer students the opportunity to improve their study skills, to develop strategies for learning, to find special support when they encounter academic difficulty, and to take increasing responsibility for their own learning.

The Foxcroft academic program is further enriched by special events such as Interim Term, which focuses on academic, political, and social exploration of a chosen topic to develop in students an understanding of large issues that affect their lives. The Goodyear Fellowship Program brings to Foxcroft each year a person distinguished in the arts, humanities, science, or public affairs to speak and conduct seminars with students. Past speakers include Barbara Walters, David McCullough, Andrei Codrescu, and Maya Angelou. The English Department sponsors an annual two-day Poetry Festival, during which two published poets read from their work, lead workshops, and judge a student reading competition.

Students in the Class of 1999 received acceptances from a wide range of colleges and universities including Boston University, Denison, Duke, North Carolina School of the Arts, Oberlin, Stanford, Syracuse, Tulane, and the Universities of Denver, North Carolina, Texas, and Virginia.

STUDENT ACTIVITIES. The School Council, including student, faculty, and administration representatives, is a clearinghouse for the proposal and implementation of new policies. Students also serve on the Judicial Council. Other organizations include three singing groups, Riding Officers Club, CAPs, the literary magazine, and the yearbook. There are clubs for girls interested in art, community service, drama, the environment, outdoor recreation, riding, photography, and astronomy.

All students compete in intramural sports as members of either the Fox or the Hound team; school teams compete interscholastically in the District of Columbia area. The athletic program includes hockey, soccer, basketball, tennis, lacrosse, softball, volleyball, dance, and riding. Approximately 33 percent of the students participate in the riding program, boarding their own horses on campus or riding one of the School's 30 horses. Equitation is the basic seat taught. Students may also participate in dressage, stadium jumping, cross-country riding, and fox hunting. Riders compete in interscholastic competition.

Special events—including dances, mixers, Outing Club events, picnics, movies, and horse shows—are scheduled each weekend. Regular trips to Middleburg and Washington, D.C., for shopping, movies, plays, opera, ballet, museums, the symphony, and sporting events are also planned on weekends. Girls may attend worship services in local churches or participate in the on-campus FOCUS group.

Foxcroft also has a Leadership Program designed to offer every student the opportunity to become a leader. Once Foxcroft leaders are elected, they must attend a leadership retreat and complete specialized training to learn trust-building skills and conflict resolution.

ADMISSION AND COSTS. Applicants are admitted on the basis of school records, recommendations, and results of the Secondary School Admission Test. A personal interview on campus is required, unless the distance is prohibitive. New students are admitted in Grades 9–11 and occasionally in Grade 12 and the postgraduate year. There is a $35 application fee.

In 1999–2000, the tuition of $25,900 for boarding girls and $17,340 for day girls includes lodging, meals, tuition, lectures, and concerts held on campus.

In 1999–2000, Foxcroft awarded $560,338 in financial aid. The School, which subscribes to the School Scholarship Service, makes grants on the basis of financial need and offers a variety of programs to assist families with tuition and expenses.

Dean of Faculty: Ann P. Leibrick
Dean of Students: Sheila C. McKibbin
Director of Admission: Rebecca B. Gilmore
College Counselor: Katherine Sillin
Business Manager: Gary R. Welke
Director of Athletics: Joan C. Eliot
Director of Development: Stacey M. Ahner '73

Grace Episcopal School   1959

3601 Russell Road, Alexandria, VA 22305-1731. 703-549-5067;
Fax 703-549-2832; Web Site www.gracechurch@ejnet.com

Enrolling 100 boys and girls in three-year-old Nursery through Grade 5, Grace Episcopal is a church-affiliated day school offering a challenging education within a loving Christian environment. The core program, which emphasizes moral and spiritual awareness as well as critical thinking skills, includes an integrated language arts program, mathematics, science, and social studies. French is introduced in Grade 4, and all students have instruction in religion, music, art, and physical education. A low student-faculty ratio permits individual attention to each child, including gifted and talented students. Before- and after-school care is provided. Tuition: $3200–$7560. Limited financial aid is available. Nancy Yarborough is Admissions Director; Nancy E. Rowe (George Mason University, M.A.) is Head of School.

Hampton Roads Academy   1959

739 Academy Lane, Newport News, VA 23602. 757-249-1489;
Fax 757-249-3971; Web Site www.hra.org

Hampton Roads Academy was founded in 1959. It is an independent, coeducational, college preparatory day school enrolling 478 students in Grades 6–12, with a student-teacher ratio of 10:1. The school community works together to foster a safe environment for its students. One hundred percent of Hampton Roads graduates attend selective college across the nation. Hampton Roads Academy is committed to diversity and enrolls a number of international students representing 15 different countries. Tuition: $7225–$7840. Extras: $200–$300. Claudine Latouche is Director of Admissions; Evan D. Peterson (West Virginia Wesleyan, B.S.; Kean College, M.A.) was appointed Headmaster in 1992.

Hargrave Military Academy   CHATHAM

Chatham, VA 24531. 804-432-2481 or 800-432-2480;
Fax 804-432-3129; E-mail admissions@hargrave.edu;
Web Site www.hargrave.edu

HARGRAVE MILITARY ACADEMY in Chatham, Virginia, is a boarding and day school that combines a college preparatory curriculum with a comprehensive military program. Affiliated with the Baptist General Association of Virginia, the school encompasses Grades 7–12 and a postgraduate year, with boarding and day boys and day girls. The historic town of Chatham (population 1354) is in the Piedmont Region of the state, 15 miles north of Danville on U.S. Highway 29 and within reasonable driving distance of Roanoke, Lynchburg, and other larger cities.

Hargrave Military Academy traces its roots to the Chatham Training School, founded in 1909 by the Baptist clergyman Reverend T. Ryland Sanford, Mr. Jesse H. Hargrave, and his son, J. Hunt Hargrave. In 1911, Reverend Sanford became the first president of the school, which has enjoyed a close association with the Baptist General Association of Virginia since 1913. It was renamed in 1925 to honor J. Hunt Hargrave and to reflect its primary mission.

The Academy aims to provide a Christian environment that imbues all aspects of life. Through its academic, athletic, and religious programs, Hargrave seeks to develop cadets in mind, body, and spirit, and to challenge them through a well-rounded academic program that will motivate them to become lifelong learners. The military component of the curriculum provides discipline, training, and structure designed to prepare cadets for success in college and throughout life. Chapel services and Bible studies are regular components of the school schedule.

Hargrave Military Academy is governed by a Board of Trustees and accredited by the Southern Association of Colleges and Schools. It holds membership in the National Association of Independent Schools, the Association of Military Colleges and Schools of the United States, the Virginia Association of Independent Schools, and the Council for Advancement and Support of Education.

THE CAMPUS. Hargrave Military Academy is situated on a 215-acre campus of woodlands, lawns, and playing fields. Academic activities are centered in three main buildings housing classrooms, lecture rooms, photography darkrooms, and math, writing, computer, and science laboratories. The fully automated library is networked to six servers for academic research and curricular enhancement activities with 27 additional computers for research. The campus is equipped with more than 200 updated computers. The auditorium hosts musical productions and other events.

Male cadets are housed two to a room on eight dormitory floors, supervised by six faculty members who live in dorm apartments. Residents have the use of two recreation rooms, three television lounges, and a student snack bar. Meals are served buffet style in an air-conditioned dining hall.

Among the athletic facilities are a new $2,000,000 aquatic center with a 50-meter pool, 3 gymnasiums, a track, indoor rifle range, a skeet range, weight training and Nautilus equipment, tennis and basketball courts, and playing fields for football, baseball, soccer, and lacrosse. The campus also has its own airstrip.

THE FACULTY. Col. Wheeler L. Baker was appointed President of Hargrave Military Academy in 1999. Prior to assuming this position, Colonel Baker served as Provost at the Academy. He holds a B.S. degree in economics, a master's degree in international affairs, and a Ph.D. in education. He has spent nearly 40 years in the United States Marine Corps and was past chairman of the Naval Science Department at the University of New Mexico. He and his wife, Lynn, have four grown children.

There are 44 full-time faculty, 26 men and 18 women, 12 of whom live on campus. They hold baccalaureate degrees and 25 graduate degrees representing study at such colleges and universities as Appalachian State, Averett, Carson Newman, College of William and Mary, East Carolina University, Elon College, Furman, Greensboro College, Hampden-Sydney, Indiana University, James Madison, Liberty, Longwood College, Lynchburg, Old Dominion, Randolph-Macon Woman's College, Southern Baptist Theological Seminary, Virginia Polytechnic Institute and State University, Wake Forest, West Virginia University, and the Universities of Georgia, North Carolina (Chapel Hill, Greensboro), Richmond, South Carolina, and Virginia.

Four registered nurses provide around-the-clock coverage in the Academy infirmary, and school doctors visit the campus on a daily basis.

STUDENT BODY. In 1999–2000, Hargrave Military Academy enrolls 400 young men and women—54 in the Middle School (Grades 7–8) and 281 in the Upper School (Grades 9–12), including 65 postgraduates. They come from 27 states, the District of Columbia, and 11 foreign countries and reflect a diversity of racial, religious, ethnic, and economic backgrounds.

ACADEMIC PROGRAM. The school year, from August to June, includes Thanksgiving, Christmas, and spring vacations, plus overnight and weekend passes during the year. Each student has an advisor who serves as counselor, mentor, and friend on academic and personal issues throughout the year. Classes range in size from 10 to 15 cadets, who are assigned based on ability and previous performance in a subject area. Two-hour study periods are held nightly from Sunday through Thursday.

On a typical day, cadets rise at 6:00 A.M. to eat breakfast and complete chores. Classes run from 7:30 A.M. to noon, including a 20-minute break. Lunch at 12:00 P.M. is followed by an hour of military drills or intramurals on Monday, Wednesday, and Friday and extra-help sessions on Tuesday and Thursday. Two hours of recreation and athletics precede dinner at 6:00 p.m. Evening study from 7:00 to 9:40 P.M. and "lights out" at 10:00 P.M. conclude the day.

Hargrave is committed to providing a strong, intensive Reading Program to students who wish to become better readers. Reading classes, taught by regular faculty who are supervised and assisted by specialists, are scheduled as a regular part of the curriculum, and cadets may earn an elective credit upon completing the program. The curriculum is designed to strengthen students' comprehension of written material through explicit, direct instruction. Classes are intentionally small, and extra attention can be arranged outside of class.

To earn an Advanced Studies Diploma, 23 credits are required as follows: 4 in English; 3 each in social studies, math, science, and foreign language; 2 in physical education; 1 in religion; and 4 in electives. The curriculum also incorporates between 3½ to 4 hours of military training and classes per week. Students take six subjects scheduled on an alternating basis, with three subjects one day and three the next.

Academic courses in the Upper School include Introduction to the Old and New Testaments; English I-IV, American Literature and Composition, Critical Reading and Writing, Public Speaking, Journalism; French I-IV, Spanish I-IV; Algebra I & II, Intermediate Algebra, Plane Geometry, Modern Trigonometry, Analytic Geometry, Calculus, Computer Science I-IV, Physical Science, Earth Science, General Biology, Environmental Science, Chemistry, Physics; Civics/Economics, Sociology/Psychology, World Studies, Virginia/United States History, Virginia/United States Government; Health/Physical Education I & II; Driver Education; and Art I-IV. English as a Second Language is offered, and there are noncredit courses in How to Study and SAT Preparation.

More than 96 percent of every senior class enter college immediately after graduation. Among the colleges and universities chosen by members of the Class of 1999 are Campbell University, The Citadel, East Carolina, Indiana University, Longwood, Louisburg College, Michigan State, Milwaukee School of Engineering, North Carolina State, Northeastern, Philadelphia College of Art, Princeton, United States Military Academy, United States Naval Academy, Virginia Military Institute, Virginia Polytechnic, Western Carolina, and the Universities of Florida, Maryland, Michigan, North Carolina, and South Carolina. The remaining 4 percent typically enter the military,

choose a postgraduate program, or defer college enrollment for a year.

A five-week, nonmilitary summer program allows students to earn academic credit in one new or two repeat subjects.

STUDENT ACTIVITIES. The student body is organized in a battalion of six companies. Cadets may serve as members of the Drill Team, Precision Color Guard, Cavalry, Marching Band, Drum Corps, and Military Police. The Cadet Honor Code governs the conduct of daily life at the Academy, with infractions tried by the Honor Council, a nine-member committee chosen by their peers. Another elected body, the Student Activities Council, enables students to have a voice in school policy, including the planning and implementation of on-campus events and entertainment.

Students take part in numerous interest groups including the HMA Players, a scout troop, *Cadence* (yearbook), *Musketeer* (newspaper), Beta Club, Art Club, Photography Club, cheerleaders, chorus, jazz ensemble, and concert band.

Varsity teams are formed in 16 areas, with junior varsity and junior high teams in nearly every major sport. Among these are football, cross-country, soccer, basketball, golf, volleyball, baseball, tennis, riflery, swimming, wrestling, power-lifting, and lacrosse.

On weekends, cadets are permitted to leave campus for excursions to downtown Chatham or visits to family and friends. Traditional festivities are planned for Parents' Weekend, Military Ball, Alumni Weekend, and Mother's Day.

ADMISSION AND COSTS. Hargrave Military Academy seeks young people of average to superior ability and good moral character who are purposeful in their desire to succeed in the school's challenging program. Acceptance is offered based on the candidate's previous academic record, standardized test results, teacher recommendations, and a personal interview and campus visit. Students are admitted in August, at mid-term, and at the start of the summer program. Decisions are rendered within a week after the applicant's file has been completed.

In 1999–2000, tuition, room and board, new-student uniforms, books, and sundry items total $16,890; expenses for a day student total $8700. Financial aid of approximately $200,000 is available based on demonstrated need, and several tuition payment plans are offered.

Dean of Faculty: Lt. Col. Walter Sullivan
Dean of Students: Lt. Col. Frank Martin
Alumni Secretary: Van Webber
Director of Admissions: Capt. Dan Dowdy
Director of Development: Lt. Col. David Morris
College Counselor: Mrs. Lynn Baker
Business Manager: Lt. Col. John Borley
Director of Athletics: Maj. Richard Motley

The Highland School 1928

597 Broadview Avenue, Warrenton, VA 20186. 540-347-1221; Fax 540-347-5860; E-mail admin@highland-school.org; Web Site www.highland-school.org

Highland, a day school enrolling 385 boys and girls in Pre-Kindergarten–Grade 12, prepares students for higher education through a rigorous, balanced program encompassing math, language arts, social studies, French, Spanish, and Latin, complemented by art, music, band, drama, and a comprehensive athletic program. A full-time guidance counselor and a director of content mastery are on staff for support and enrichment. An 8:1 student-teacher ratio ensures individualized attention. Activities include field trips, community service, and an extended-day program. Tuition: $3750–$9800. Transportation: $850. Financial aid is available. Charles E. Britton, Jr., is Director of Admissions; David P. Plank (University of Sheffield [England], B.S.; University of Manitoba, M.Ed.) is Headmaster.

The Hill School of Middleburg   1926

130 South Madison Street, P.O. Box 65, Middleburg, VA 20118-0065. 540-687-5897; Fax 540-687-3132

The Hill School is a coeducational, elementary day school enrolling 215 students in Kindergarten–Grade 8. It seeks to prepare students for academic success in secondary schools through a strong curriculum, an excellent faculty, and small class sizes. Hill also offers a range of opportunities for intellectual, artistic, athletic, and interpersonal growth within its cocurricular program of art, music, drama, athletics, outdoor education, field trips, and community service. Tuition: $6400–$11,200. Financial Aid: $230,000. Thomas A. Northrup (University of Pennsylvania, B.A. 1968, M.S.Ed. 1981) was appointed Headmaster in 1981.

Hunter McGuire School   1986

74 Quicks Mill Road, Verona, VA 24482. 540-248-2404; Fax 540-248-5323; E-mail jmosedale@huntermcguire.org; Web Site www.huntermcguire.org

Hunter McGuire School is dedicated to serving girls and boys of average to superior abilities in Kindergarten through Grade 5. It seeks students with strong social and academic skills who will be successful in a challenging and enriching academic environment where learning is enjoyed and sharing is commonplace. Spanish, art, music, physical education, computer, and science lab studies are offered at all levels. A biweekly assembly program, field trips, and chorus enhance the curriculum. Private piano and violin lessons are optional. Comprehensive Tuition: $5500 (including lunches). Financial aid is available. Rebecca Davenport is Director of Admission; Judith A. Mosedale is the Head.

The Langley School   MCLEAN

1411 Balls Hill Road, McLean, VA 22101-3499. 703-356-1920; Web Site www.langley.edu.net

THE LANGLEY SCHOOL in McLean, Virginia, is a day school enrolling boys and girls in Nursery–Grade 8. Located in the suburban community of McLean (population 62,000), Langley makes use of the diverse resources of nearby Washington, D.C., and the coastal areas of Virginia and Maryland.

The School was founded in 1942 as a cooperative preschool by parents who wanted to become more involved in their child's education. While it is no longer considered to be a cooperative school, Langley exhibits a spirit of cooperation, with parents active in volunteer service on committees and participation in fund-raising activities. Langley gradually expanded its facilities and enrollment, offering Nursery through Grade 8 by 1971. In 1983, double sectioning of each grade was accomplished, allowing greater academic variation and a different mix of students each year.

The School's goal is to provide excellent academic preparation in a nurturing, challenging environment while maintaining a focus on each child as a thinking, creative individual. Langley seeks "to motivate students to move forward in developing their own sense of values, creative talents, and the ability to reason and communicate."

The Langley School is a nonprofit corporation governed by a Board of Directors elected by the parent membership. An active Alumni Association and the Friends of Langley, a group made up of parents of former students, assist with fund-raising

efforts and organize certain school events. The School is accredited by The Virginia Association of Independent Schools and holds membership in the National Association of Independent Schools and the Council for Advancement and Support of Education, among other organizations.

THE CAMPUS. Langley is situated on a ten-acre campus that includes a soccer field, playgrounds, a wooded area used for nature hikes and study, and an outdoor trike track for Preschoolers. The complex of eight computer-networked buildings includes the Preschool with classrooms for Nursery-Senior Kindergarten; a state-of-the-art Middle School Building, which houses Grades 1–5 with multipurpose learning centers, enlarged classrooms, science and computer labs, an assembly room, and a reading resource room; the Upper School Buildings with classrooms for Grades 6–8; the Arts and Science Building with a large, all-media art room containing a kiln, two fully equipped science laboratories (for Grades 1–8), and two foreign language rooms; the Field House; the Claire Maxted Administration Building, a converted farmhouse in which administrative offices are housed; and the 18,000-volume, state-of-the-art library/learning center with a computer and graphics laboratory and a music room. A new field house will be completed by the fall of 2001.

THE FACULTY. Hugh C. Riddleberger III is Head of School. A graduate of the University of Michigan, Mr. Riddleberger holds an M.Ed. degree from Harvard University. He is a former Head of Metairie Park Country Day School and Sheridan School. The Division Heads are Carolyn Thomas, Preschool; Elizabeth Allen, Middle School; and Louis Silvano, Upper School.

There are 68 teachers, of whom 17 are part-time. They hold 66 baccalaureate and 32 master's degrees representing study at such institutions as American University, Boston University, Brown, Bryn Mawr, Catholic University, College of William and Mary, Columbia, Davidson, Duke, Georgetown, George Washington University, Georgia Southern, Hood College, Johns Hopkins, Louisiana State, Mary Washington, Michigan State, Mount Holyoke, Ohio State, Old Dominion, Princeton, Tufts, Tulane, Wheaton, Williams, and the Universities of Arizona, California, Chicago, Colorado, Delaware, Florida, Geneva, Hawaii, London, Maryland, Massachusetts, Michigan, Missouri, Pennsylvania, Utah, Vermont, and Virginia.

STUDENT BODY. In 1999–2000, Langley enrolled 475 students. Each grade is divided into two classes, with the following enrollments for each class: Nursery, 18 students with two teachers; Transitional Preschool, 17 with two teachers; Junior Kindergarten, 20 with two teachers; Senior Kindergarten, 22 with two teachers; Grade 1, 23 with two teachers; Grades 2–5, 22 with two teachers (the two classes in each grade are divided into three instructional groups for reading and mathematics); and Grades 6–8, 23 with departmentalized instruction. Langley students represent the diverse ethnic, social, and economic backgrounds of the Washington, D.C., area.

ACADEMIC PROGRAM. The academic year, divided into trimesters, extends from September to early June, with a 12-day winter vacation and a one-week spring break. Classes are held five days a week from 8:00 A.M. to 3:15 P.M. Homework ranges from 20 minutes per day for Grades 1 and 2 to 2–3 hours daily for Grades 6–8. Grades, with teacher comments, are sent to parents three times a year, and parent-teacher conferences are held twice a year.

In the Nursery, children develop listening and language skills. Creativity and self-expression are stressed in this program. The innovative all-day Kindergarten program includes reading and math readiness, with art, music, science, French or Spanish, and social studies rounding out the curriculum.

In Grades 1–5, homeroom teachers use an interdisciplinary approach in teaching social studies, art, music, and modern languages. A phonetic-linguistic approach to reading is adopted. Students complete original projects in language arts as they focus on both verbal and written communication with an emphasis on whole language instruction. Special mathematics and computer teachers extend the work of the classroom teacher. Computer lab instruction begins in Grade 1. Science is taught in both its theoretical and its practical aspects—for example, there is a full-scale greenhouse where students of all ages study plant life and complete a class project.

Grades 6–8 offer departmentalized instruction in English language and literature, modern language, mathematics (including algebra), and science as well as art, music, drama, and computers. Students in Grades 6 and 7 take annual four-day field trips to West Virginia for backpacking and white-water rafting. Eighth graders have an annual extended field trip to Assateague, Virginia, where they camp and conduct scientific study. Leadership skills are developed through an active student government. Yearbook and newspaper are extracurricular options.

Physical education classes meet twice a week in Grades 1–5 and three to four times a week in Grades 6–8. Students study health and nutrition in addition to basic movement and team sports. Band is offered to students in Grades 4–8.

Langley offers an Extended Day Program that is also available on selected School holidays and through the summer.

Recent graduates of the Langley School have gone on to attend Bishop O'Connell, Bullis, Georgetown Visitation, Gonzaga College High School, Holton-Arms, James Madison, Langley, Lawrenceville, Madeira, McLean, Paul VI, Potomac, St. Albans, St. Stephen's and St. Agnes, Sidwell Friends, Thomas Jefferson, and Woodberry Forest.

A five-week summer session provides remedial and enrich-

ment courses for Grades 1–8 and a preschool program for ages 3–5.

STUDENT ACTIVITIES. Four representatives from each class are chosen each year to sit on the Student Advisory Group, which meets with the Head to share information and review school issues and student concerns. The Student Council, composed of elected representatives from Grades 3–8, involves the student body in the administrative process and sponsors student activities such as holiday celebrations and field trips. Langley students study with outstanding artists both in-house and at performing arts centers such as The Kennedy Center and Wolf Trap. School community service projects include visiting senior centers, serving breakfast at S.O.M.E. (So Others Might Eat), distributing hats and gloves in child-care centers at Christmas, and community landscaping and beautification projects.

Varsity and junior varsity teams are organized for both boys and girls in soccer, basketball, lacrosse, and cross-country. Langley teams have held Capital Athletic Conference championships in basketball and soccer since 1980. They have also received the annual Sportsmanship Award several times in recent years.

Traditional events include Halloween and Thanksgiving celebrations, Fall family social event, Grandparents' Day, Silent Auction, ice-skating party, ski trip, the Langley Fair, and an annual brunch where eighth graders are welcomed into the Alumni Association.

ADMISSION AND COSTS. The Langley School serves students with the ability and readiness to participate and progress within a challenging curriculum and an enriching environment where learning is enjoyed and sharing is commonplace. Students are accepted into all grades, when vacancies exist, on the basis of transcripts and test results from previous schools, an admissions test, teacher recommendations, and writing samples (Grades 6–8 only). Parents must attend an interview with the appropriate Division representative, and the applicant is required to visit the campus for a regular school day. Application, with a $60 fee, should be made a year in advance of expected enrollment.

In 1999–2000, tuition is $7765 for Nursery and Junior Kindergarten, $13,105 for Senior Kindergarten–Grade 5, and $13,630 for Grades 6–8. Tuition assistance is available.

Head: Hugh C. Riddleberger III
Assistant Head: Tim Mathiasen
Alumni Affairs: Dawn Leidich
Director of Admissions: Mary Hollis Hartge
Director of Development: Valerie Embrey
Business Manager: Ken Wilkins
Athletic Director: James Gleason

Linton Hall School 1922

9535 Linton Hall Road, Bristow, VA 20136-1200. 703-368-3157;
Fax 703-368-3036; E-mail lintonhall.edu

Founded by Benedictine Sisters, Linton Hall is a Catholic, coeducational day school enrolling 193 students in Kindergarten through Grade 8. Its philosophy, based on Christian principles and values, aims to motivate students to their full potential. The program is structured to instill mastery of basic learning skills and effective interaction with others. The curriculum includes outdoor conservation, ecology, wildlife, Spanish, and offerings in the arts. Choir, basketball, and soccer are among the activities. Tuition: $5300. Financial Aid: $25,000. Cathy Pendley is Admissions Officer; Sr. Glenna Smith (Marymount, B.A. 1980; Assumption, M.A. 1986; Boston College, M.Ed. 1986) was named Principal in 1989.

Loudoun Country Day School 1953

237 Fairview Street, NW, Leesburg, VA 20176. 703-777-3841;
Fax 703-771-1346; Web Site www.lcds.org

Loudoun Country Day School is an independent, coeducational school enrolling 202 students in Prekindergarten–Grade 8. The School offers a strong core curriculum and seeks to develop students' self-confidence born of competence in academics, languages, athletics, and knowledge of the arts tempered with a spirit of cooperation, courtesy, and consideration for others. An 8:1 student-teacher ratio provides a nurturing atmosphere. French is introduced in Prekindergarten; Latin instruction begins in Grade 6. Also included in the curriculum are programs in computer and life skills. Team sports, dramatic productions, and field trips are extracurricular offerings. Tuition: $6250–$9800. Financial Aid: $100,000. Pamela Larimer is Director of Admissions; Dr. Randall Hollister is Head.

The Madeira School MCLEAN

8328 Georgetown Pike, McLean, VA 22102. 703-556-8200;
Admissions 703-556-8248; Fax 703-821-2845;
E-mail admissions@madeira.org; Web Site www.madeira.org

THE MADEIRA SCHOOL in McLean, Virginia, is a college preparatory boarding and day school for girls in Grades 9 through 12. The School is 20 minutes from Washington, D.C., and uses the resources of the capital in its academic and enrichment activities.

Madeira was founded in 1906 by Lucy Madeira Wing, who believed that young women should receive the same kind of rigorous education available to young men. The School is committed to educating the next generation of young women for leadership, and it continues to offer a challenging scholastic atmosphere coupled with a unique Co-Curriculum Program that fully utilizes the School's proximity to the nation's capital.

A nonprofit corporation, the School is governed by a Board of Directors. Madeira is a member of the National Association of Independent Schools and the Virginia Association of Independent Schools, among other affiliations. The Madeira School is recognized as exemplary by the U.S. Department of Education and the Council for American Private Education.

THE CAMPUS. The School occupies nearly 400 acres on the banks of the Potomac River, surrounded by woods and meadows. On campus are hiking and riding trails, a pond, an outdoor skills and elevated ropes course, playing fields, eight tennis courts, stables, two all-weather outdoor dressage and show rings, a cross-country course, and an indoor riding ring. The 32,000-square-foot Hurd Sports Center contains a swimming pool, basketball and volleyball courts, aerobics and weight rooms, and locker rooms.

The buildings are of both Georgian and contemporary architecture. Among the facilities are the Schoolhouse; six dormitories; a dining hall and Student Center; and Main Building, which contains a reception area, offices, dormitory rooms, and two faculty apartments. The art building includes graphics, lithography, sculpture, ceramics, and painting studios. The 16,000-square-foot Huffington Library houses a 20,000-volume collection. The library also houses a computer lab with on-line catalogs and indexing and CD-ROM applications. Two additional computer labs are located in various buildings throughout the campus. All computers provide Internet access, and students and faculty have individual E-mail accounts. Other facilities include a health center and an auditorium that contains music, drama, and dance areas as well as a 500-seat theater. A science building provides physics, chemistry, and biology laboratories and preparation rooms, and the Photography Department.

An outdoor theater, the Senior Club House, the Headmistress's house, faculty and staff homes, and service and office buildings complete the facilities.

THE FACULTY. Elisabeth Griffith, appointed Headmistress in 1988, is a graduate of Wellesley College (B.A.), Johns Hopkins University (M.A.), and The American University (Ph.D.). A historian and author, Dr. Griffith has taught at The American University and National Cathedral School in Washington, D.C. In addition, she has been a Kennedy Fellow at Harvard University and a Conroy Fellow at St. Paul's School in Concord, New Hampshire.

There are 38 full-time and 19 part-time faculty members. The faculty hold 41 master's degrees and 7 doctorates from such colleges and universities as Brown, Harvard, Johns Hopkins, Mount Holyoke, Oxford (England), Princeton, Smith, Stanford, Wellesley, and the Universities of Chicago, Michigan, Pennsylvania, and Virginia.

Each residence hall is staffed by two house adults; 33 percent of the faculty and administrators also reside on campus. Resident adults and students gather for weekly seated dinners. A registered nurse is on duty in the Health Center at all times and a doctor is on call; medical facilities are located 10 minutes away.

STUDENT BODY. In 1999–2000, Madeira enrolls 159 boarding students and 149 day students as follows: 71 in Grade 9, 87 in Grade 10, 69 in Grade 11, and 81 in Grade 12.

ACADEMIC PROGRAM. The school year, from early September to early June, is divided into two terms, with a two-week recess in December/January and a two-week spring vacation. Classes are held four days a week, with Wednesdays reserved for the Co-Curriculum Program. A typical daily schedule follows: breakfast between 7:00 and 7:45 A.M., classes until 3:30 P.M., conference time, athletics, and activities from 3:30 to 5:45 P.M., and dinner at 6:00 P.M. Weekday quiet hours are observed from 7:00 P.M. to 9:30 P.M. and from 10:00 P.M. to 6:30 A.M.

Class size averages 12 students, and teachers are available to give individual help. Teacher conferences are held during regularly scheduled periods reserved for such meetings on Monday, Tuesday, and Thursday afternoons. Girls meet weekly with their advisors. Grades and detailed teacher comments are sent to parents twice each semester.

To graduate, a student must complete a minimum of 19 academic credits, or the equivalent of 19 full-year courses. Students must also pass physical education each year and successfully complete their Co-Curriculum Program and their senior year at Madeira. The School requires four years of English, three years each of mathematics and a foreign language, two years each of history and laboratory science, one year of art, and the completion of the Co-Curricular Program for each year the student is enrolled. Every student must also pass a computer competency test..

The curriculum includes more than 100 courses. Among those offered are Modern Poetry, Creative Writing, A Romantic Vision, Diverse Voices, Contemporary Women Writers, Children's Literature, Acting Shakespeare; French, Spanish, Latin, Etymology; 20th Century History, Comparative Religions, European History, American History, Modern World History, Asian Civilization, Women's History, Africa, Latin America, and the Middle East; Algebra I, II, and III, Geometry, Trigonometry, Computer Programming, Pre-Calculus, Calculus; Biology, Chemistry, Physics; Survey of Music, Chamber Ensemble, Voice Lessons; Visual Design, Computer Graphics, Web Design, Drawing, Painting, Printmaking, Art History, Photography; and Choreography, Introduction to the Performing Arts, Acting, and Directing. Advanced Placement courses are available in all departments. An instructor works individually with students who need support in English as a Second Language.

The Wednesday Co-Curriculum is an integral part of the academic program, designed to develop self-confident, concerned individuals and informed citizens capable of making mature decisions. Girls in Grade 9 attend freshman seminars that focus on ethics, health issues, leadership, technology, and skill development. Students also take Fresh Art and participate in Outdoor Adventure, which includes courses in canoeing, survival techniques, and rappelling. Tenth-grade girls work in social service placements such as schools, day-care centers, and nursing homes, and participate in weekly discussions on ethical issues in the workplace. Students in Grade 11 spend Wednesdays as Congressional interns and attend seminars on public affairs led by faculty and guest lecturers involved in government. Twelfth graders may pursue career interests as seniors in the Co-Curriculum Program. They may choose an internship in social services, science, business, or the media. The Co-Curriculum Program is closely monitored, and the School receives reports from both the supervisors and the students.

Institutions attended by five or more Madeira graduates since 1991 include Barnard, Brown, Carnegie Mellon, College of William and Mary, Emory University, Georgetown, New York University, Smith, Spelman, Trinity (Connecticut), Tufts, Tulane, Vanderbilt, Vassar, Wellesley, Yale, and the Universities of Pennsylvania, Texas, Vermont, and Virginia.

STUDENT ACTIVITIES. All girls belong to the Student Government Association, through which they participate in forming and enforcing school rules and developing curricular and extracurricular programs. Many functions are carried out by committees, such as the Judiciary, Social, and Education committees. Typical activities are the newspaper, the yearbook, the arts magazine, Model United Nations, Thespians, Chorus, Madrigals, community service, peer tutoring, and the Art Club. The Theater Department presents two full-length plays and several shorter productions each year.

All girls are involved in intramural sports as members of either the Red or the White team. Varsity and junior varsity teams compete interscholastically in Maryland, Virginia, Pennsylvania, Delaware, and the District of Columbia. Interscholastic sports are tennis, field hockey, cross-country, soccer, volleyball, squash, swimming, diving, basketball, softball, tennis, and lacrosse. Participants in the riding program compete in three-phase events and horse shows throughout Virginia and Maryland. Students may board their own horses. Among the intramural and recreational activities are dance, swimming, and cross-training for fitness.

Weekend events such as concerts, whitewater rafting, dinner dances, and ski trips are frequently shared with students from other schools. Madeira also arranges numerous trips to Washington museums, galleries, lectures, and theaters. Among the traditional events are Parents' Weekend, Red/White Day, Halloween, Founder's Day, Alumnae-Senior Dinner, and Affirmation.

ADMISSION AND COSTS. New students are accepted in Grades 9–11 on the basis of school records, recommendations, an applicant statement, and the results of the Secondary School Admission Test. A personal interview is required. Application should be made 3 to 12 months in advance. The Madeira School welcomes applicants of all races, colors, religions, and national and ethnic origins. There is a $40 application fee for students in the United States; the fee is $80 for applicants outside the United States.

In 1999–2000, the comprehensive fee is $26,725 for all resident students and $16,825 for day students. Additional charges include books and activities. Fees are also charged for piano and voice instruction, photography, and riding. A tuition payment plan and tuition insurance are available.

Madeira subscribes to the School and Student Scholarship Service. In 1999–2000, the School granted $1,020,000 in direct aid to 67 students including one need-based scholarship and three merit-based Trustees' Scholarships to new boarding students.

Dean of Faculty: Paul A. Hager
Director of Academic Counseling: Mary Ann Mahoney
Dean of Students: Kevin J. Wildeman
Director of the Co-Curriculum Program: Christine Langford
Alumnae Director: Elizabeth H. Locke '60
Director of Admissions: Meredyth M. Cole
Director of Development: Katherine M. Hillas
College Counselor: Sheila Reilly
Business Manager: Franklin B. Smith
Director of Athletics: Nancy Smalley

The Miller School   CHARLOTTESVILLE

1000 Samuel Miller Loop, Charlottesville, VA 22903.
804-823-4805; Fax 804-823-6617;
Web Site <www.millerschool.org>

THE MILLER SCHOOL in Charlottesville, Virginia, is a coeducational boarding and day school enrolling students in Grades 5–12 and Postgraduate. Historic Charlottesville lies in the foothills of the Blue Ridge Mountains, 74 miles northwest of Richmond and 122 miles southwest of Washington, D.C. The city is the site of the University of Virginia, Thomas Jefferson's "Monticello," and the homes of James Monroe and Patrick Henry. Founded in 1878, Miller School is one of the oldest coeducational boarding schools in America.

Miller School's mission is to be an outstanding college preparatory school for all children, with an emphasis on "sound academics and demonstrations of mastery and excellence in what they create and what they do." The faculty believes that young people learn best in a community of trust that seeks to educate a student's mind, hands, and heart through a challenging program of academics, athletics, service, and the arts.

A nine-member Board of Trustees oversees the operation of the School, which is accredited by the Virginia Association of Independent Schools and holds membership in the National Association of Independent Schools. Graduates are represented by the Miller School Alumni Association, which is an active part of the school community.

THE CAMPUS. Miller School is set on a 1600-acre campus, which includes woodlands, orchards, farmlands, and a 15-acre lake. Old Main, the Headmaster's residence, and the Arts Building are on the National and Virginia Historic Landmarks registers and provide excellent examples of High Victorian Gothic architecture. Old Main (1878) contains classrooms, administrative and admissions offices, chapel, dining hall, health center, the older boys' dormitories, and the Peggy T. Flannagan Center for Innovative Technology, which houses state-of-the-art computer and support services. Old Main also includes the library, which is linked by computer to the University of Virginia's Alderman Library, local public libraries, and all appropriate Internet research sites. The Arts Building (1887), with woodworking, music, and art areas; the Science Building (1884); Wayland Hall, the girls' dormitory; Thomas Hart Hall, the junior boys' dormitory; the Student Center, housing the canteen, book store, launderette, and Civil Air Patrol meeting rooms; Alumni Gymnasium, a fully equipped athletic center with basketball, wrestling, weight training, and aerobic dance facilities; and faculty residences are additional buildings on campus.

The campus features an outdoor swimming pool, miles of cross-country running trails, and three athletic fields.

THE FACULTY. Lindsay R. Barnes, Jr., Esq., was appointed 11th Headmaster of Miller School in 1999. A graduate of Hampden-Sydney College and the University of Virginia School of Law, he holds a master's degree in journalism from the University of Georgia.

In addition to Mr. Barnes, there are 28 faculty and professional staff, 16 women and 12 men. All hold baccalaureates, 14 hold master's degrees, and 5 have doctorates, from such schools as Appalachian State, College of Wooster, Columbia, Denison, East Carolina, James Madison, Johns Hopkins, Lehigh, Mary Baldwin, Mary Washington, Old Dominion, Union, Washington and Lee, and the Universities of North Carolina (Chapel Hill), Southern California, and Virginia. Registered nurses staff the infirmary, and several hospitals are in the immediate vicinity.

STUDENT BODY. In 1999–2000, Miller School enrolled 140 students, 90 boarding and 50 day, as follows: 12 in Grade 5, 5 in Grade 6, 7 in Grade 7, 22 in Grade 8, 20 in Grade 9, 23 in Grade 10, 32 in Grade 11, 19 in Grade 12, and 1 postgraduate. They came from diverse family backgrounds and cultures and represented 17 states and six foreign countries.

ACADEMIC PROGRAM. The school year, typically September 1 to May 31, is divided into semesters, with a four-week "mini-mester" called "J-Term" in January. Vacations are scheduled at Thanksgiving, Christmas, and in the spring. Grades are issued five times a year, and Parents' Weekends are scheduled in each semester. Each student takes six classes that meet five times a week. Classes average 12 to 14, with a student-teacher ratio of 6:1 throughout the grades.

A typical day begins with breakfast at 7:00 A.M., daily assembly at 7:50 A.M., and six 50-minute classes. Tutorials are scheduled two afternoons a week, chapel meets two mornings a week, and Wednesday classes are shortened to accommodate school-wide participation in community service programs. Each afternoon, all students are involved in athletics. Required, faculty-supervised study periods are held each evening, Sunday through Thursday.

The Miller School diploma requires 23 credits, including four years of English, three years of mathematics (at least through Algebra II/Trig), three years of laboratory science, four years of history/social studies, three years of a foreign language (typically Spanish or French), and two years of fine arts, plus electives. Interested students may take Advanced Placement tests in a variety of disciplines.

The Junior School (Grades 5–8) offers a strong grounding in the foundational subjects of English (including spelling, grammar, and vocabulary building), mathematics, social studies, science, computer word-processing and research, and the fine arts.

The Miller School experience includes a grade-level-based team approach to projects that promote mastery and skill in several areas considered essential to the well-rounded liberal arts education. These projects are completed under faculty guidance; students are encouraged to use class assignments as the basis for meeting project requirements.

Miller School's Educational Support Services program ranges from educational assessment and support to specialized tutoring, SAT preparation, and, on a limited basis, courses for students with certain identified needs. There is also an English as a Second Language (ESL) program.

In 1998 and 1999, 100 percent of the graduates who sought to attend college were accepted at four-year colleges and universities, including Colgate, Dickinson, Drexel, Hampden-Sydney, James Madison, Johnson and Wales, New Mexico Tech, Providence, Roanoke College, St. Bonaventure, Seton Hall, Shenandoah University Music Conservatory, Virginia Polytechnic, and the Universities of Pennsylvania and Virginia, among others.

Miller School conducts a variety of academic and nonacademic summer programs for Grades 5 through 12.

STUDENT ACTIVITIES. The student government is on the prefect model, where elected and appointed students and fac-

ulty members serve on the Honor Committee and the Disciplinary Review Board. The senior class runs the Student Center and Canteen.

"Service to others" is a long-standing Miller tradition expressed in a four-faceted program: Civil Air Patrol, Environmental Action, Community Service, and Woodworking. Since 1975, the optional Civil Air Patrol has provided emergency first aid, search and rescue training, and a taste of military life as well. The Community Action group is involved with various community agencies such as hospitals, retirement homes, and day-care centers. The Environmental Action group addresses conservation and environmental concerns, both to the region and the campus. The Woodworking Service group maintains the School's furniture and operates the carpentry shop. All faculty take part in these programs.

Miller School sponsors Boy Scout Troop 105 on campus so that scouts may complete their Eagle Scout requirements in time for college applications.

Participation in athletics is required of all. The youngest students play on intramural teams, while older students compete on varsity teams in the local Virginia Independent Conference. Fall offerings include girls' volleyball, boys' soccer, and girls' and boys' cross-country. Winter term offers boys' and girls' basketball and wrestling, and spring sports are golf and tennis for girls and boys, boys' lacrosse and baseball, and girls' soccer. Aerobic conditioning and weight training are offered as alternatives to team sports for older students, and drama is an alternative for 11th- and 12th-grade students during one of three terms.

On weekends, students engage in activities off campus, ranging from white-water rafting and tubing to camping, hiking, and regional theme and water parks. Recent trips have included athletic and cultural events at the University of Virginia as well as Baltimore Orioles and Richmond Braves baseball games. Miller coordinates dances and various social events with other regional boarding schools, and students shop and attend movies locally.

ADMISSION AND COSTS. Miller School welcomes students of all cultural and racial backgrounds. International students should have a working knowledge of both spoken and written English. Miller seeks students who possess above-average to superior intelligence, high moral character, and a desire to improve and excel. Candidates are evaluated on their willingness to participate in the Miller School program, character and academic references, and the ability to handle challenging academic material. Acceptance is based on letters of recommendation from a current English and math teacher, an essay from the student on "Why I Want to Attend Miller School," and an interview in person or by phone, depending on distance. A $35 fee must accompany the application. Admission is on a rolling basis and while there is no actual deadline, classes can fill at various levels at any time during the application year. International applicants should allow enough time for processing the appropriate I-20 forms and student F-1 visas.

The cost in 1999–2000 is $15,600 for boarding students from the United States, $17,790 for international students (including ESL), and $7955 for day students. Fees include tuition refund insurance, laundry, and activities. There are additional charges for books ($200–$350), spending money for boarding students, and Educational Support Services when appropriate. Financial aid grants totaling $165,000 were awarded in 1999–2000, with an average grant of $4500 to boarding students and $2500 to day students.

Director of Academics: Fred Assaf
Director of Admissions and Student Life: James M. Slay, Jr.
Co-Directors of Counseling: Jessie Haden and Judith Davis
Director of the Upper School: Bob Spencer
Director of the Junior School: Tom Hart
Director of College Placement: Dr. Martha Downer-Assaf
Director of Athletics: Rev. Doug Thompson
Chief Financial Officer: Rita Ralston

Norfolk Academy   NORFOLK

1585 Wesleyan Drive, Norfolk, VA 23502. 757-461-6236;
Fax 757-455-3181; E-mail fsaul@norfacad.pvt.k12.va.us;
Web Site www.norfacad.pvt.k12.va.us

NORFOLK ACADEMY in Norfolk, Virginia, is a coeducational, college preparatory day school enrolling students in Grades 1–12. Situated in Norfolk (population 260,000) and adjacent to Virginia Beach (population 450,000), the Academy enjoys the advantages and diversity of this major metropolitan area, known as the Hampton Roads section of Virginia. Site of the world's largest naval base, it is also the home of Old Dominion University, Norfolk State University, the Regent University, Virginia Wesleyan College, and Eastern Virginia Medical College. The Academy is directly off Interstate 64 at Route 13 North and is easily accessible by car.

Founded in 1728 by the trustees of Norfolk Town, Norfolk Academy is the oldest independent secondary school in Virginia and the 13th oldest in the nation. At its founding, the Academy was a typical 18th-century classical school for boys. It became coeducational in 1966 when the trustees of Norfolk Academy and the Board of the Country Day School for Girls in Virginia Beach merged the two schools and moved them to the present campus. In 1985, the Academy was one of 65 secondary schools to be named an exemplary school by the Council for American Private Education and the United States Department of Education.

Through a program that includes college preparatory academics, fine arts, sports, and community service, Norfolk Academy seeks to deepen its students' maturity of mind, character, and body. The Academy strives to prepare students to become useful and responsible citizens and emphasizes the conviction that sound moral and spiritual values define the individual more significantly than academic achievement. The Honor Code fosters both intellectual and personal honesty.

A nonprofit organization, Norfolk Academy is governed by a 30-member Board of Trustees that meets quarterly. The Alumni Association represents the more than 4000 living alumni, many of whom are active in school activities. The Academy has an endowment of approximately $21,000,000.

Norfolk Academy is accredited by the Southern Association of Colleges and Schools and the Virginia Association of Independent Schools. It holds membership in the National Association of Independent Schools, the Southern Association of Independent Schools, the Educational Records Bureau, The Cum Laude Society, and the Council for Advancement and Support of Education.

THE CAMPUS. The 64-acre campus, adjacent to the campus of Virginia Wesleyan College, includes 11 playing fields, 8 tennis courts, a 400-meter latex track, a football stadium, and an aquatic center. A state-of-the-art library opened in 1995.

There are eight school buildings, which together provide classrooms, science laboratories, computer centers, art and music rooms, and two libraries with a total of 38,000 volumes and an extensive collection of periodicals and audiovisual equipment.

Also on campus are two gymnasiums; the May Building, which houses the Headmaster's office, the business, development, college counseling offices, and the Grandy Building, which houses admission offices, the refectory, music and art rooms, and a 375-seat auditorium.

The school plant is valued at $28,000,000.

THE FACULTY. John H. Tucker, Jr., was appointed Headmaster in 1978. A graduate of the College of William and Mary (B.A. 1954, M.Ed. 1962) and the recipient of an L.H.D. from Old Dominion University, Dr. Tucker, who had taught at the Academy from 1955 to 1970, was Headmaster of North Cross School in Roanoke, Virginia, prior to his appointment at Norfolk Academy. Dr. Tucker is past President of the Southern Association of Independent Schools and of the Country Day School Headmasters Association. He is a former member of the Board of Visitors of the College of William and Mary and a former member of the Board of Trustees of the Southern Association of Colleges and Schools.

The full-time faculty number 107—65 women and 42 men. They hold 106 baccalaureate and 74 graduate degrees, representing study at 85 colleges and universities. Two or more degrees were earned at Bowdoin, College of William and Mary, George Washington, Hampden-Sydney, James Madison University, Middlebury, Oberlin, Old Dominion, Princeton, Randolph-Macon Woman's College, Rutgers, United States Military Academy, Washington and Lee, and the Universities of Florida, Georgia, Maryland, Massachusetts, Michigan, North Carolina, and Virginia.

Norfolk Academy offers health insurance, life insurance, a retirement plan, and Social Security. Leaves of absence can be arranged.

A school nurse is available on campus. An emergency-care center and four major hospitals are within a ten-minute drive of the school.

STUDENT BODY. In 1999–2000, Norfolk Academy enrolls 598 boys and 581 girls as follows: 503 in the Lower School (Grades 1–6), 344 in the Middle School (Grades 7–9), and 332 in the Upper School (Grades 10–12). The students live in Norfolk, Virginia Beach, and other communities in the region.

ACADEMIC PROGRAM. The school year, from late August to early June, is divided into semesters and includes a Thanksgiving recess, and Christmas and spring vacations. A typical school day, from 8:10 A.M. to 3:25 P.M., includes six 40-minute class periods, a morning break, lunch, a fine arts period, and an activities period. Sports and other activities are scheduled after the close of the school day.

Classes, which are held five days a week, have an average enrollment of 20 students. There are daily supervised study halls; some students may be required to attend a special study session held on Saturday mornings. A resource coordinator offers help to Lower School students; The Cum Laude Society provides tutorials for students who are having academic difficulties. Grades are issued every nine weeks; progress reports are sent to parents three times each semester.

The Lower School curriculum consists of reading, written and oral expression, spelling, handwriting, grammar, lateral thinking skills, study skills, listening skills, social studies, mathematics, science, and physical and health education. Spanish, computer education, art, music, and instruction in library skills further enrich the curriculum.

Core courses for Grade 7 are English, Geography, Latin I, Pre-Algebra, Life Science, and physical education. The Grade 8 curriculum consists of English, Latin II, Western Civilization, Algebra, Physical Science, and health and physical education.

Computer skills and library instruction are taught throughout the curriculum.

To graduate, students in Grades 9–12 must complete at least 20 credits, including 4 in English, 4 in mathematics, 3 in a foreign language, 3 in history, 2 in laboratory science, 3 in academic electives, and 1 in health and physical education. Seniors must also present an eight-minute speech to the student body and faculty.

Courses offered include English 1–4; French 1–4, German 1–4, Spanish 1–4, Latin 1–5, Russian 1–2, Italian 1–2; World Cultures, Modern European History, United States History, United States Government, Economics; Algebra 1–2, Geometry, Pre-calculus, Calculus, Computer Science C^{++}; Environmental Science, Biology, Chemistry, Physics; Art History, Studio Art; Music Theory, Music History, Instrumental Music, Chorus; Dramatic Arts; and Dance. Advanced Placement courses are available in all major subject areas. All Upper School students participate in a seminar four times a year.

In 1999, 110 graduates entered such colleges and universities as Barnard, Bates, Boston University, Brown, Bucknell, Colby, College of William and Mary, Cornell, Davidson, Duke, Emory, Georgetown, Hampden-Sydney, Harvard, James Madison, Massachusetts Institute of Technology, United States Naval Academy, Vassar, Villanova, Virginia Polytechnic, Wake Forest, and the Universities of Chicago, North Carolina (Chapel Hill), Pennsylvania, and Virginia.

Norfolk Academy offers special programs that include the Young People's Theatre, School of the Arts, School of Foreign Languages, summer school, and sports and summer camps. In 1994, the Learning Bridge program was launched at the Academy. It is modeled after the Summer Bridge program begun in San Francisco in 1978.

STUDENT ACTIVITIES. Each division has an elected student council, which, under the direction of a faculty advisor, helps to plan activities. The Honor Council, made up of students and faculty, reviews infractions of the Honor Code.

Students publish a newspaper for each division, a literary magazine, and a yearbook. Extracurricular activities include The Cum Laude Society, Honor Council, Student Council, Key Club, Peer Counselors, Academy Singers, Dance, Theatre, and the Chess, International Relations, language, Science Fiction, Environmental, Debate, Instrumental Combos, and Cultural and Ethnic Awareness clubs. Through Habitat for Humanity, the Happy Club, the Reach Club, and tutoring programs, students take part in community service.

Norfolk Academy varsity teams compete with those of other schools in the Tidewater Conference of Independent Schools, the Virginia Prep League, and the League of Independent Schools. Girls' teams are organized in basketball, cheerleading, cross-country, field hockey, lacrosse, tennis, track, soccer, softball, swimming, and volleyball. Boys compete in baseball, basketball, cross-country, football, golf, lacrosse,

soccer, swimming, tennis, track, and wrestling. In addition, there is an extensive program of intramural athletics for Grades 4–6. Weight training is encouraged for both boys and girls.

There are frequent theatre and music productions by student groups as well as lectures and performances by guest speakers and artists. Traditional events include Back-to-School Night, Field Day, Charter Day, Spring Arts Festival, Grandparents' Day, Sports Festival Day, Vespers, the Lower School Holiday Pageant, and Homecoming.

ADMISSION AND COSTS. Norfolk Academy seeks to enroll students from a variety of social, economic, religious, ethnic, and racial backgrounds who demonstrate intellectual curiosity and promise of accomplishment. New students are admitted to all grades on the basis of school-administered testing, interviews with school administrators, and previous school transcripts. Campus visits are encouraged. The application fee is $75 for Grade 1 and $25 for Grades 2–12.

In 1999–2000, tuition and required fees for Grades 1–6 total $8440 and $9705 for Grades 7–12. Included in the total are lunches, supplies, athletics, publications, and laboratory fees. Additional costs include bus transportation ($660) and driver education ($180). Textbooks are provided in the Lower School but are purchased by students in Grades 7–12.

In 1999–2000, Norfolk Academy awarded $955,000 in financial aid to 171 students on the basis of need. A tuition payment plan is available. Norfolk Academy subscribes to the School and Student Service for Financial Aid.

Director of the Upper School: Toy D. Savage III
Director of Admission: Frances H. Saul
Director of Development and Alumni Affairs: Vincent C. deLalla
Assistant to the Headmaster for College Counseling: Paul M. Feakins
Business Manager: Sandra T. Kal
Director of Athletics: David E. Trickler

Norfolk Collegiate School   NORFOLK

Middle/Upper Schools (Grades 6–12): 7336 Granby Street, Norfolk, VA 23505. 757-480-2885; E-mail admision@ncs.pvt.k12.va.us; Web Site www.ncs.pvt.k12.va.us/
Lower School (Kindergarten–Grade 5): 5429 Tidewater Drive, Norfolk, VA 23509. 757-625-0471.

NORFOLK COLLEGIATE SCHOOL in Norfolk, Virginia, is a coeducational day school enrolling students in Kindergarten–Grade 12 on two campuses. The campuses, which are approximately three miles apart, are both within a 15-minute drive of the downtown area. Norfolk (population 250,300) is the site of several military installations, the Chrysler Museum, and Old Dominion and Norfolk State universities. Jamestown, Williamsburg, and Yorktown are within an hour's drive.

Founded in 1948, Norfolk Collegiate began as a Kindergarten known as the Carolton Oaks School. In 1950, Carolton Oaks moved to the Granby Street address. Grades were added over a 15-year period, and the first high school class graduated in 1963. In 1973, the Tidewater Drive facilities were acquired, and the name of the school was changed to Norfolk Collegiate School.

Through a traditional college preparatory program taught in a supportive atmosphere, the School fosters in each student a continuing desire to learn, to understand, and to serve society responsibly.

A nonprofit corporation, Norfolk Collegiate School is governed by a 40-member Board of Trustees, which includes parents, alumni, and community leaders. Norfolk Collegiate School is accredited by the Southern Association of Colleges and Schools and The Virginia Association of Independent Schools and holds membership in the National Association of Independent Schools, among other affiliations.

THE CAMPUS. In 1995, the School completed a capital campaign that doubled the size of the Granby Street campus, providing new athletic fields and tennis courts. The Middle and Upper School facility includes air-conditioned, carpeted classrooms, science laboratories, a cafeteria with a stage, a gymnasium and athletic center, computer centers, fine arts centers, and an expanded library and media center.

A new and renovated lower school building that is nearly double its former size opened in October 1999 on the 9.5-acre Tidewater Drive campus. Designed to accommodate Kindergarten–Grade 5, it features oversized early childhood rooms for Kindergarten, a media center with interconnected computer labs and a print library, a hands-on science lab, a fine arts studio, a performing arts stage, and a new gymnasium. All classrooms are networked and have Internet access.

The School-owned plants have a combined value of $9,686,441.

THE FACULTY. William W. King is President and Headmaster of Norfolk Collegiate School.

There are 70 full-time and 13 part-time faculty members, 19 of whom are men. In addition to baccalaureate degrees, they have earned 46 master's degrees and a doctorate representing study at California State, College of William and Mary, Concordia, Duquesne, Florida State, George Washington, Hampton University, Hollins, Indiana State, James Madison University, Loyola, Mary Washington, Miami of Ohio, Michigan State, New York University, North Carolina State, Old Dominion, Pepperdine, Radford, Randolph-Macon Woman's College, St. Olaf, San Diego State, Valdosta State, Vanderbilt, Virginia Commonwealth, Virginia Polytechnic, Washington and Lee, Washington State University, and the Universities of California, Cincinnati,

Frankfurt (Germany), North Carolina, Southern California, Sussex (England), Toronto, Turin (Italy), Virginia, and Wisconsin.

Faculty benefits include a retirement plan; flexible benefit plan; health, life, and disability insurance; and Social Security.

STUDENT BODY. In 1999–2000, the School enrolls 805 students, 52 percent boys and 48 percent girls, as follows: 56 in Kindergarten, 55 in Grade 1, 60 in Grade 2, 59 in Grade 3, 40 in Grade 4, 40 in Grade 5, 63 in Grade 6, 66 in Grade 7, 74 in Grade 8, 65 in Grade 9, 80 in Grade 10, 74 in Grade 11, and 73 in Grade 12.

ACADEMIC PROGRAM. The school year is divided into semesters, with Thanksgiving and semester breaks and vacations in December and in March. Classes are held five days a week, beginning at 8:30 A.M. and ending at 3:00 P.M. Athletic practices are scheduled after 3:30 P.M.

Each grade is divided into classes that average 16 to 20 students. The Learning Resource Program at both schools provides private tutorials, alternative learning experiences, and enrichment opportunities. Faculty-supervised study halls are included in the daily schedule. Report cards are sent to parents at nine-week intervals. Parent-teacher conference days are scheduled twice yearly.

Lower School children study reading, composition, grammar, spelling, arithmetic, history, geography, science, and health. Specialized teachers supplement the basic program with instruction in art, music, library skills, computer skills, Spanish, and physical education.

The Middle School encourages an interdisciplinary approach by coordinating projects and units of study. The curriculum includes English; life and physical science; mathematics, pre-algebra, algebra; social studies and American Colonial History; and health and physical education. There is an exploratory foreign language program of French, Spanish, Russian, and German in Grade 7 and Latin in Grade 8. Middle School students also participate in a wide range of activities to develop social, physical, and cultural interests.

To graduate, Upper School students beginning with the Class of 2002 must complete 23 credits, which include four years of English, three consecutive years of one foreign language or two years of two languages, three years each of social studies, mathematics, and laboratory science, two of physical education/health, and one year of fine or performing arts.

Courses offered in the Upper School are English 9–12, Creative Writing, Vocabulary Development, Humanities, Global Perspectives, Introduction to Philosophy; French 1–5, German 1–4, Latin 1–5, Spanish 1–5, Russian 1–4, Hebrew 1–3; World History, Virginia and United States History, History of Architecture, Virginia and United States Government, Archaeology,

Economics, World Geography, Algebra 1–2, Advanced Algebra, Geometry, Calculus, Trigonometry, Pre-Calculus, Statistics, Accounting, Introduction to Computer Science, Desktop Publishing, Business Applications, CADCAM, Computer Applications; Biology, Chemistry, Earth Science, Physics, Anatomy, Marine Biology, Sports Medicine; Chorus, Band, Drama, Art; and Health and Physical Education (through Grade 10). Advanced Placement work is offered in art, United States history, government, biology, English, Latin, German, Spanish, French, chemistry, environmental science, calculus, physics, computer science, and psychology.

Travel-study programs are often available during the summer vacation. In recent years, students have traveled in France, Germany, Spain, Ireland, England, Greece, Egypt, Italy, and Russia. Norfolk Collegiate offers a summer program of sports, activities, and academics for students in Kindergarten–Grade 12.

The 56 members of the Class of 1999 garnered acceptances to 73 institutions, including 57 outside of Virginia. In the past five years, graduates have entered such colleges as American University, Clemson, College of Charleston, College of William and Mary, Davidson, Duke, East Carolina, Emory, George Mason, Georgetown, George Washington, Hampden-Sydney, Hampton University, Haverford, Indiana University, James Madison, Mary Washington, New York University, North Carolina Wesleyan, Northwestern, Old Dominion, Pennsylvania State, Princeton, Randolph-Macon Woman's College, St. Andrew's Presbyterian, St. John's, St. Joseph's, Syracuse, Tufts, Tulane, United States Coast Guard Academy, Vassar, Villanova, Virginia Commonwealth, Virginia Military, Virginia Polytechnic, Virginia Wesleyan, Wake Forest, Washington and Jefferson, Washington and Lee, Washington University, Yeshiva University, and the Universities of Maryland, Miami, North Carolina, Pennsylvania, Richmond, South Carolina, Southern California, South Florida, and Virginia.

STUDENT ACTIVITIES. The Lower, Middle, and Upper schools each elect Student Councils, which have responsibility for organizing dances, events, and projects and serve as a liaison between students and the administration. The School has a traditional Honor Code and students elect both Middle and Upper School Honor Courts to oversee the system.

Students publish a newspaper, a literary magazine, a yearbook, and produce two plays a year. Other extracurricular activities include service clubs, the National Honor Society, Jazz Band, MATHCOUNTS, Model United Nations, Forensics Team, International Thespian Society, SADD, and the Art, Astronomy, Bowling, Poetry, Science, French, German, Spanish, Latin, Russian, Multicultural, Political, Conservation, Chess, Ski, and Surf clubs.

Varsity teams compete with other members of the Tidewater Conference of Independent Schools and with local public high schools. Boys' teams are organized in basketball, baseball, volleyball, lacrosse, wrestling, soccer, swimming, tennis, and cross-country; girls' teams are organized in basketball, cheerleading, softball, swimming, field hockey, soccer, tennis, and volleyball. Coed teams are fielded in golf, sailing, and crew. Junior varsity teams for boys and girls compete in soccer, basketball, softball, volleyball, and field hockey.

The faculty and Student Councils sponsor several dances during the school year. Traditional events include the Country Fair, Grandparents' Day, the Friends' Dinner, the Auction, the Golf Outing, Homecoming, alumni reunions, alumni basketball games, and tennis matches.

ADMISSION AND COSTS. Norfolk Collegiate School welcomes academically qualified students of diverse backgrounds who wish to participate in a close-knit school community. New students are enrolled throughout the year if vacancies occur. Candidates are evaluated on the basis of School-administered testing, a personal interview, and records and recommendations from the previous school. There is a $35 application fee.

In 1999–2000, tuition is $6050 for Kindergarten–Grade 3, $6600 for Grades 4–5, $7150 for Grades 6–8, and $7550 for Grades 9–12. There are extra fees for books ($150–$250), activi-

ties ($100), and optional school transportation, extended day care, and lunches. Faculty scholarships are granted annually. The School subscribes to the School and Student Service for Financial Aid. In 1999–2000, $609,103 in aid was given on the basis of need.

Head of Lower School: Zena L. Herod
Head of Middle and Upper School: Robert P. Morissette
Alumni Director: Virginia C. Hitch
Director of Admissions: Brenda H. Waters
Director of Development: Catherine C. Craft
College Counselor: Betty M. Jones
Business Manager: Linda W. Winslow
Director of Athletics: Larry B. Swearingen

North Cross School   1960

4254 Colonial Avenue, SW, Roanoke, VA 24018. 540-989-6641; Fax 540-989-7299; E-mail cfunderburke@northcross.org; Web Site www.northcross.org

Enrolling 570 day students in three divisions encompassing Junior-Kindergarten–Grade 12, North Cross School offers a college preparatory curriculum in a challenging but nurturing environment. The liberal arts program is designed to prepare students, not just for college and careers but for rich, purposeful lives. Upper School students take Advanced Placement exams in all departments. Students are involved in school government, publications, Odyssey of the Mind, community service, and interscholastic teams in men's and women's sports. An extensive Outdoor Education Program enhances the curriculum. A summer program is offered. Tuition: $3975–$7770. Financial Aid: $240,000. Carol E. Funderburke is Director of Admission; G. William Stacey IV (Vanderbilt, Ed.D.) was appointed Head of School in 1993. *Southern Association.*

Notre Dame Academy   1965

35321 Notre Dame Lane, Middleburg, VA 20117. 540-687-5581; Fax 540-687-3101; E-mail nda@mnsinc.com; Web Site www.rc.net/arlington/nda

Set on a beautiful 191-acre campus, this coeducational, college preparatory, Catholic high school was founded by the Sisters of Notre Dame. The curriculum emphasizes the liberal arts and sciences; advance college-credit opportunities are available. Adventure Bound, a week of outdoor activities, challenges students in an environment of mutual trust and teamwork. Independent course work and field study are encouraged. Students take part in men's and women's sports, publications, drama, music groups, and a variety of clubs. Tuition: $9200. Extras: $500. Financial aid is available. Cathy Struder is Director of Admission; Sr. Cecilia Liberatore, SND, is Head of School. *Southern Association.*

Oak Hill Academy   MOUTH OF WILSON

2635 Oak Hill Road, Mouth of Wilson, VA 24363-3004. 540-579-2619; Fax 540-579-4722; E-mail oakhill@planet-va.com; Web Site www.planet-va.com/oakhill

OAK HILL ACADEMY in Mouth of Wilson, Virginia, is a boarding and day school enrolling girls and boys in Grades 8 through 12. It offers both general and college preparatory curricula. The school is situated in the rural area of Grayson County among the Blue Ridge Mountains and near the scenic New River and Jefferson National Forest areas, which afford opportunities for recreation and exploration. The village of Mouth of Wilson is about 12 miles from the county seat of

Independence. State Highway 16 and United States Highway 58 pass the entrance to the school. Interstate 77 is 37 miles southeast of the Academy, and Interstate 81 passes through Marion, which is 28 miles north of the campus. Marion is served by interstate bus lines, and taxi service to the school is available. The airport in Charlotte, North Carolina, offers the best flight scheduling and taxi service is available for the two-and-one-half-hour drive from Charlotte to the campus.

The Academy was founded in 1878 as a school for mountain girls and boys by the New River Baptist Association. The school is now supported by, and affiliated with, the Baptist General Association of Virginia. Oak Hill's mission is to provide a safe, secure, nurturing environment and a structured educational program to students in Grades 8–12 who need a change in school, peer, community, or family relationships. Oak Hill's curriculum challenges the brightest students and encourages those who are unmotivated, who are underachieving, or who are experiencing difficulty in their school setting. The Academy emphasizes the importance of student involvement in activities and the need to develop ethical and moral attitudes. One year of Religion is required, and attendance at Sunday service is required of all students.

Oak Hill Academy is a nonprofit organization governed by a Board of Trustees. Funds from the Baptist General Association of Virginia and gifts from alumni and friends account for approximately 12 percent of the school's annual budget. The Academy is accredited by The Virginia Association of Independent Schools and the Southern Association of Colleges and Schools. It is a member of the Southern Association of Independent Schools, the Secondary School Admission Test Board, The Association of Boarding Schools, and the National Association for Foreign Student Affairs. It is approved by the United States government for the Teaching of Foreign Students.

THE CAMPUS. The Academy is situated on a campus of 300 acres of hills and woodlands with landscaped areas, playing fields, outdoor tennis courts, and riding arena. Administrative offices and the school cafeteria are located in the Vaughan Building at the center of the campus. All academic classes are held in the Louise Towles English Academic Building. This building also contains a library and computer center. A new Science Wing addition to the English Academic Building is under construction. The Turner Building contains the gymnasium,

training rooms, student activities center, and athletic director's office. The Rev. J. F. Fletcher Chapel provides an auditorium, music practice rooms, and a conference center. Male students are housed in four dormitories with a total capacity of 110. The Hough Dormitory accommodates 98 girls in two-room suites. Fourteen houses and apartments are provided on campus for faculty and staff members in addition to apartments in the dormitories.

The new 50-acre Noonkester Park addition includes a picnic pavilion, lake, and walking trails. A soccer field, volleyball court, and basketball court are to be added as development continues. The plant is owned by the school and is valued at $10,000,000.

THE FACULTY. Dr. Ed F. Patton was appointed President of Oak Hill Academy in 1986. A native of Mississippi, he graduated from Memphis State University (B.S. 1962) and Southwestern Baptist Theological Seminary (B.D. 1966). He received a Master of Arts Degree in Secondary School Administration from Appalachian State University in 1972 and a Doctor of Divinity degree from Averett College in 1991. He has done additional graduate work at Radford University and the University of Virginia. At Oak Hill, he previously held positions as teacher of social studies, Dean of Students, Director of Admissions, and Principal.

The full-time faculty include seven men and nine women, nine of whom live on campus. There are five part-time instructors. All faculty members hold baccalaureate or master's degrees from schools including Appalachian State, Asbury College, Campbell College, Eastern Kentucky, East Tennessee State, Emory & Henry College, Gardner-Webb College, King College, Radford University, Southern Baptist Theological Seminary, Virginia Commonwealth, and Virginia Polytechnic Institute.

The Academy provides faculty with a retirement plan, health insurance, and life insurance.

STUDENT BODY. In 1998–99, the school enrolled 140 students, of whom 88 boys and 45 girls were boarders and 3 boys and 4 girls were day students. Four were enrolled in Grade 8, 20 in Grade 9, 24 in Grade 10, 57 in Grade 11, and 34 in Grade 12. Students were from 18 states, Egypt 4, England 1, Japan 2, and Senegal 1.

ACADEMIC PROGRAM. The 1999–2000 school year, divided into semesters, began on August 30 and extends to late May, with a ten-day vacation at Thanksgiving, a three-week vacation at Christmas and a two-week spring break in March. Classes are held five days a week plus Saturdays in the fall. The average class has nine students. On a typical day, students rise at 6:45 A.M. Tutorials for extra help begin at 8:00 A.M. Classes begin at 8:50 A.M. and conclude at 3:45 P.M. Activities and intramurals are held in the afternoon. Supervised study periods for all students are scheduled Sunday through Thursday from 8:00 to 9:30 P.M. Extra-help sessions are also conducted each afternoon from 3:50 to 4:55 P.M. Grades are mailed to parents four times a year.

The school offers a 23-unit diploma and a 25-unit diploma. The 23-unit diploma must include four years of English; one year each of World Geography, Ancient World History, Religion, U.S. History, and U.S. Government; two years of Health and Physical Education; three years each of Mathematics and Science; one year each of Fine Arts and a foreign language; and four elective subjects. Science courses include Earth Science, Biology I, Advanced Biology, Chemistry, and Physics. Mathematics courses include Business Math, Algebra 1 parts 1 and 2, Algebra I–II, Geometry, Advanced Algebra/Trigonometry, Advanced Math, and Calculus. Spanish I–III is offered. In addition, students may elect from courses in World History, Creative Writing, Yearbook, Psychology, Business Education, Keyboarding, Computer Science, Art, Chorus, and Drama.

The campus is a test site for PSAT/SAT, and ACT.

One hundred percent of the seniors who applied were accepted to college in 1999. They went on to attend Appalachian State, East Carolina University, Louisburg College, North Carolina State, Radford, Western Carolina, and the University of North Carolina (Asheville, Charlotte, Wilmington).

A five-week academic summer school is conducted from mid-June to late July for students in Grades 8–12 from Oak Hill and other private and public schools. Students may earn one new unit of credit or repeat two failed units of credit. During the summer, classes in English Skills and Mathematics Skills are offered. Tuition, board, and fees for the 1999 session totaled $3575.

STUDENT ACTIVITIES. Oak Hill Academy offers extracurricular activities that include: The Academy Choir, Art Club, Campus Life, Drama Club, Ecology Club, Hiking Club, Horseback Riding Club, International Students Club, Library Assistants, National Honor Society, *Oak Leaves* (newspaper), *The Hilltopper* (yearbook), Outdoor Club, Ski Club, and Varsity Cheerleaders. Many students also are involved in church-related activities under the direction of a campus minister.

The school competes interscholastically in boys' basketball, girls' volleyball, boys' and girls' tennis, and coeducational soccer. Intramural sports include basketball, softball, football, tennis, soccer, weightlifting, and running. Backpacking, swimming, and canoeing are also available as club activities.

Films, concerts, plays, and outings to New River are part of the regular social life of the campus. Special events include the President's Picnic, Costume Ball, Christmas Dance, Sweetheart Dance, Spring Formal, and Parents' Weekends in the fall and spring.

ADMISSION AND COSTS. The Academy selects students "who would most benefit from its special, but limited, program." Applications are accepted at any time for all grades, and students are evaluated on the basis of their previous academic record, references, and an interview. There is an application fee of $50 and a reservation deposit of $1250 due upon acceptance

In 1999–2000, the fee for boarders is $15,465, which includes textbooks and uniforms, $465 for allowance, $335 for the student expense account, and $1025 for tuition insurance. The fee for day students remains $3000. Tuition may be paid by the semester, by the month, or by the year. Financial aid is based on individual need, ability, resourcefulness, and character. Approximately $100,000 in scholarship aid is awarded each year.

President: Dr. Ed F. Patton
Director of Academic Affairs: Stephen C. Cornett
Director of Student Affairs: Michael D. Groves
Director of Girls Resident Life: Jennifer D. Ross
Director of Boys Resident Life: Stephen R. Bowen
Director of Admissions: Michael D. Groves
Director of Development: Dr. Ed F. Patton
Director of Counseling: Clint McCain
Business Manager: Rhonda H. Bowen
Director of Athletics: Stephen A. Smith

Oakland School   1950

Boyd Tavern, Keswick, VA 22947. 804-293-9059;
Fax 804-296-8930

Located near Charlottesville, Virginia, Oakland School enrolls 60 boarding and 25 day boys and girls of average and above ability who have learning disabilities or who have not been successful in a regular classroom. Children are accepted at ages 8–14 and may remain through age 17. An ungraded curriculum through Grade 9 emphasizes basic skills and study techniques with a specialty in the teaching of reading. Individualized and one-to-one instruction and a 5:1 student-teacher ratio enable students to reach their potential. Most students return successfully to a traditional school setting. A summer school and camp are also offered. Boarding Tuition: $25,230. Judith Edwards (University of Virginia, M.Ed.) is the Director.

Oakwood School   1971

7210 Braddock Road, Annandale, VA 22003. 703-941-5788;
Fax 703-941-4186

Enrolling students in Grades 1–8, Oakwood offers specialized services designed to meet the educational needs of approximately 100 bright but atypical learners. It seeks to provide appropriate individualized educational plans for youngsters with dyslexia, attention deficit disorder, language-development difficulties, and other problems with the goal of returning the student to mainstream classrooms. The curriculum emphasizes the mastery of strong skills in reading and mathematics, with hands-on approaches to science, social studies, and computer technology. Speech/language and occupational therapies are available as needed. Tuition: $16,700. Muriel Jedlicka is Admissions Director; Robert McIntyre is Principal.

The Potomac School MCLEAN

1301 Potomac School Road, P.O. Box 430, McLean, VA 22101.
703-356-4101; Web Site www.potomacschool.org

THE POTOMAC SCHOOL in McLean, Virginia, is a coeducational day school enrolling students in Prekindergarten through Grade 12. McLean (population 55,800) offers a suburban setting only four miles from the cultural and historic treasures of the nation's capital. Public buses, subways, and the School's own bus system provide transportation throughout the metropolitan area.

Founded in 1904, the School held its first classes in a building on Dupont Circle in Washington, D.C. Incorporated as a nonprofit institution in 1907, the School later occupied two larger sites in the District of Columbia before moving to the present campus in 1951. Originally a school for girls, Potomac graduated its first coeducational class in 1965.

The School seeks to provide an atmosphere that encourages high academic achievement, a love of learning, caring for others, delight in creative expression, and the satisfaction of accomplishment. Its academic program moves from a solid base of fundamental skills toward the full development of a student's potential for scholarship, leadership, and service.

The School is governed by a 22-member Board of Trustees that meets monthly. The 3200 living alumni support the School financially and attend many campus events. Parents take part in the annual giving program and volunteer their services to many school projects, such as the "Fall Frolics" fund-raising event. The Fathers' Association organizes weekend activities such as the all-School family picnic, sports events, concerts, camp-outs, and special tours to local points of interest.

Potomac is accredited by The Virginia Association of Independent Schools. It holds membership in the National Association of Independent Schools, the Association of Independent Schools of Greater Washington, the Council for the Advancement and Support of Education, and the Council for Religion in Independent Schools.

THE CAMPUS. The 83-acre campus includes fields, woods, streams, ponds, an outdoor swimming pool, and tennis courts. The main building houses the stage, dining room, and offices as well as classroom wings for the Intermediate (Grades 7–8) and Middle (Grades 4–6) schools. The Intermediate School wing also includes an art room, three science laboratories, computer lab, choral room, and an assembly room. The Middle School has its own science, computer, music, and art facilities. The Lower School (Prekindergarten–Grade 3) is in a separate building connected to the main building by a covered walkway. It has separate library (11,500 volumes), art, and science rooms, as well as a large activities room.

Intermediate and Middle school students have access to the 19,000-volume Arundel Family Library, which also has audio-visual facilities and a conference room. Built in 1986, the Upper School facilities include classrooms, science laboratories, a library (12,000 volumes), computer labs, a gym and fitness center, and an all-weather track. The School-owned plant is valued at nearly $12,600,000.

THE FACULTY. Peter Briggs, Jr., was appointed Interim Headmaster in 1999. He is a graduate of Noble and Greenough School and holds B.A. and M.A.T. degrees from Harvard University. Mr. Briggs previously served as Interim Headmaster of the St. James Episcopal School in downtown Los Angeles.

The full-time faculty, including administrators who teach, number 114. They hold 114 baccalaureate and 76 graduate degrees representing study at such colleges and universities as American University, Amherst, Boston University, Brown, Carleton, Columbia, Cornell, Dartmouth, Dickinson, Duke, Georgetown, George Washington University, Harvard, Howard, Lesley, Marquette, Middlebury, Mount Holyoke, Occidental College, Oxford University, Princeton, the Sorbonne (France), Trinity College, Vassar, Wellesley, William and Mary, Yale, and the Universities of California, Chicago, Kansas, New Mexico, Pennsylvania, Virginia, and Wisconsin. There are also 26 part-time teachers on the faculty.

Faculty benefits include health, dental, disability, and life insurance; a retirement plan; Social Security; and funding to support continuing education.

STUDENT BODY. In 1999–2000, the School enrolls 875 students, 451 girls and 424 boys, as follows: 228 in the Lower School, 192 in the Middle School, 151 in the Intermediate School, and 304 in the Upper School. Students come from the District of Columbia, Northern Virginia, and Maryland.

ACADEMIC PROGRAM. The school year, from early September to mid-June includes a Thanksgiving recess and winter and spring vacations.

At the center of the Lower School curriculum is homeroom instruction in reading, creative writing, spelling, grammar, computer, and mathematical concepts. Lower School children have specialized instruction in science, music, art, computers, and physical education.

The Middle School program continues language arts concepts introduced in the Lower School, with the addition of research techniques taught by the homeroom teacher and the librarian. Also part of the curriculum are social studies, including ancient civilizations and the Middle Ages; computer; science; mathematics; art; music; and physical education.

Intermediate School English courses emphasize interpretation, appreciation, and critical analysis of literature through the study of poetry, the short story, the novel, drama, and nonfiction. Expository, analytical, and creative writing are also essential to the curriculum. French, Japanese, Latin, and Spanish are available. The seventh-grade social studies program focuses on geography, while eighth graders study American history, highlighting their work with four days of academic activities based in Washington, D.C. The mathematics program begins with pre-algebra in Grade 7. Science offerings are life science and introductory physical science. Art, music, and physical education complete the program.

The Upper School academic program is college preparatory and provides a grounding in the liberal arts through its core curriculum. Electives and Advanced Placement courses are offered. The academic calendar is based on a semester system. Most courses are full-year, full-credit courses; a number of semester courses will be offered to juniors and seniors. Students in Grades 9, 10, and 11 will be expected to enroll in courses yielding five credits. Twelfth graders must enroll in courses yielding four credits, although most will be advised to take a fuller load.

The Class of 1999 was composed of 72 students. They enrolled at such institutions as College of William and Mary, Columbia, Duke, Emory, Harvard, Johns Hopkins, Middlebury, Oberlin, Princeton, Yale, and the Universities of Pennsylvania and Virginia.

Potomac offers a variety of summer programs for children and adults. These include several day camp programs, academic and computer literacy courses, and outdoor education. Robert Hamlet is the Director of Summer Programs.

STUDENT ACTIVITIES. In the belief that annual events and celebrations provide children with a sense of belonging and permanence, Potomac observes many traditions. The Kindergarten circus, Lower School holiday concert, fifth-grade Christmas play, Greek Olympics, May Day ceremonies, and sixth-grade Medieval Feast are among the most prominent events. Every division holds weekly assemblies. Each year the Intermediate School presents a play. The Upper School presents three theatrical productions. The School band and chorus perform at school gatherings and assemblies. Other annual events include parents' nights and alumni reunions.

The Upper School Student Council serves as the liaison between students and the administration, organizes dances and other social activities, and oversees the student aides. In a spirit of service, students serve as lunch room or library aides and assistants in Lower and Middle School classrooms. Upper School students volunteer in community service projects off campus. Other extracurricular activities include the yearbook, literary magazine, newspaper, photography, and special-interest clubs.

Intermediate and Upper school interscholastic sports include baseball, basketball, cross-country, lacrosse, football, field hockey, soccer, softball, tennis, track, swimming, and wrestling. Potomac teams compete with nearby public and independent schools.

ADMISSION AND COSTS. The Potomac School seeks to enroll

a culturally, economically, and ethnically diverse student body. New students are generally admitted to Pre-Kindergarten, Kindergarten, Grade 4, Grade 7, and Grade 9, although some students are admitted to the intervening grades if vacancies occur. Admissions decisions are based on achievement and aptitude testing, a transcript from the previous school, teacher recommendations, and, for the Intermediate and Upper schools, the Secondary School Admission Test. Application should be made by January 15 for fall admission, although later applications will be considered if vacancies exist. There is a $60 application fee.

In 1999–2000, tuition is $8925 for Prekindergarten, $13,470 for Kindergarten–Grade 3, $14,355 for Grades 4–6, $15,555 for Grades 7–8, and $15,960 for Grades 9–12. Additional expenses include books and supplies ($300–$410) and optional bus transportation ($750–$1335). A mandatory lunch fee of $680 will be charged to all Upper School students.

In 1999–2000, 126 students received a total of $1,327,585 in financial aid on the basis of need. Tuition insurance is available. The Potomac School subscribes to the School and Student Service for Financial Aid.

Assistant Head: Nora Mancha
Dean of Students: Jan Healy
Director of Alumni Affairs: Adria de Leonibus
Director of Admission: Charlotte H. Nelsen
Director of Development: Virginia D. Howard
College Counselor: Dr. William Brown
Business Manager: William Barry
Directors of Athletics: Rob Lee and Tracy Swecker

Randolph-Macon Academy   FRONT ROYAL

200 Academy Drive, Front Royal, VA 22630. 540-636-5200 or 800-272-1172; Fax 540-636-5419; E-mail admissions@rma.edu; Web Site www.rma.edu

Randolph-Macon Academy in Front Royal, Virginia, is a coeducational, college preparatory school enrolling boarding and day students in Grade 6 through a postgraduate year. Front Royal (population 13,000), a picturesque community in the foothills of the Blue Ridge Mountains, is an hour from Dulles International Airport and is easily accessible via Interstates 66 and 81. Its location enables students and faculty to enjoy numerous field trips throughout Virginia, Maryland, and Washington, D.C.

Randolph-Macon Academy aims to prepare students intellectually, physically, ethically, and emotionally for success in college and in all future endeavors. Founded in 1892 and affiliated with the United Methodist Church, Randolph-Macon is the nation's only coeducational boarding school with an Air Force Junior Reserve Officer Training Corps Unit and a flight training program. The military component, which encompasses Grades 9–12 and Postgraduate, fosters the development of character, leadership, and self-confidence. All students take a non-denominational survey course of the Old and New Testaments, and attendance at weekly ecumenical chapel services is mandatory.

Randolph-Macon Academy is a nonprofit institution governed by a 24-member Board of Trustees. It is accredited by the Southern Association of Colleges and Schools and holds membership in the National Association of Independent Schools and The Association of Boarding Schools. The Academy is supported in its mission by the Alumni and Parents' associations, whose members are active in fund-raising, recruiting, and planning special events.

THE CAMPUS. Randolph-Macon Academy is situated on 135 acres of open fields and wooded areas. The Upper (Grade 9–PG) and Middle (Grades 6–8) schools occupy separate, adjacent campuses. Both have air-conditioned dormitories, classrooms, and dining facilities, with telephone, voice mail, and Internet services in all dorm rooms.

The Upper School includes three academic buildings, a resource library, men's and women's dormitories, a modern dining hall, a gymnasium and Nautilus weight room, an indoor pool, and a rifle range. The school's Internet server, RMA Online, provides a computer system capable of worldwide communications.

The Middle School's satellite facility has its own 13-classroom complex, dormitories housing 80 boarding students, boys' and girls' lounges, and an Activities Center with a gymnasium, cafeteria, and bookstore.

Among the athletic facilities are an outdoor track, tennis courts, and baseball, football, lacrosse, and soccer fields.

THE FACULTY. Maj. Gen. Henry M. "Mack" Hobgood was appointed Randolph-Macon Academy's ninth President in 1997. General Hobgood received his B.Ed. degree from North Carolina State University and a USAF commission in 1965. He also earned an M.S. degree from Troy State University and was a distinguished graduate of the Air War College. In more than 30 years of active duty, General Hobgood served in command positions at bases throughout the United States and overseas, including command of all Air Force technical training.

Randolph-Macon's 52 instructors and administrators who teach include 7 who were honored by being named to the current edition of *Who's Who Among America's Teachers.* They hold 50 baccalaureates and 26 advanced degrees from such colleges and universities as Colorado State, Davidson, Embry-Riddle Aeronautical, Hobart, Indiana University of Pennsylvania, James Madison, Mary Washington, Miami University, Millersville, Old Dominion, Radford, Rensselaer Polytechnic, Roanoke College, St. Leo College, Shenandoah, State University of New York, Sweet Briar College, Tennessee Tech, Virginia Commonwealth, Virginia Polytechnic and State University, West Virginia University, Yale, the Universities of Arkansas, Dayton, Maryland, Nebraska, Richmond, the South, Texas, Virginia, and Wisconsin.

STUDENT BODY. In the 1998–99 school year, Randolph-Macon enrolled 439 students, 72 percent boys and 28 percent girls. They reflected diverse racial, religious, and ethnic heritages and represented 23 states, the District of Columbia, and 19 countries worldwide.

ACADEMIC PROGRAM. The school year, divided into semesters, begins in September and ends in early June, with a Thanksgiving break and winter and spring vacations. Grades are issued four times a year, and progress reports are mailed to parents midway through each marking period. Each incoming cadet is paired with a returning cadet "brother" or "sister" who helps the newcomer adjust to Academy life. In addition, every cadet is assigned to a faculty advisor who provides guidance on academic issues.

On a typical weekday, students rise at 6:30 A.M. for 7:15 A.M. breakfast. There are eight 45-minute class periods, plus a lunch break. After school, students participate in athletics, intramurals, and cocurricular activities, followed by dinner and required study hall. Upper School students have free time from 7:00 to 8:00 P.M. "Lights out" is between 9:30 and 11:00 P.M., depending on grade.

The Middle School provides a classical, progressive, non-military curriculum, taught in small classes of 8–12 students. The core program emphasizes the building of strong skills in English, math, science, social studies, and foreign language, and computer technology is widely integrated into all disciplines. Students also learn to cultivate good study habits and gain experience in public speaking, writing, research, and problem solving. In addition to core subjects, students enjoy offerings in the arts, music, and physical education.

The Upper School is organized according to the Air Force JROTC program, consisting of a Corps of Cadets divided into four squadrons led by cadet officers under the supervision of the aerospace science faculty. Cadets wear regulation uniforms on campus at all times except during "free" time.

The military program, Air Force Junior ROTC, falls under the guidance of the U.S. Air Force Education and Training Command. It encompasses military drill, ceremony, protocol, and tradition in the first year; in subsequent years, cadets explore concepts in aviation, space technology and exploration, and model rocketry; in the senior year, they work closely with instructors to design a personalized college/career outline for success.

The curriculum is based on the traditional liberal arts and sciences as well as in-depth study opportunities in Latin, French, Spanish, and German. Computer science at two levels of proficiency is available as electives. Honors courses are offered in some subject areas.

To graduate, cadets must complete 21 credits of instruction plus four years of aerospace science. Specific requirements include 4 credits of English, 3 in mathematics, 3 in social studies, 3 in science, 2 in the same foreign language, 2 in health and physical education, 1 in religious studies, $1/2$ credit in computer applications, and $2^1/2$ in electives.

Cadets 15 years of age and over can take flight and ground-school instruction to qualify for the FAA private pilot's written exam. Qualified cadets have flying time in the school's owned and leased aircraft. The Air Force awards cadets a set of wings after they have successfully taken their first solo flight and earned their private pilot's license.

The postgraduate program offers a transitional year of academic development during which a student may earn up to 26 hours of college credit courses and take high school courses as needed. Postgraduate students are active participants in all aspects of the school program including the Cadet Corps, athletics, and extracurricular activities.

Colleges and universities that accepted Randolph-Macon's graduates from the Class of 1999 are Carnegie-Mellon, Cornell, Penn State, Purdue, Rensselaer, Syracuse, United States Coast Guard Academy, United States Military Academy, United States Naval Academy, the Universities of Maryland and Virginia, Virginia Military Institute, Virginia Tech, and other universities.

Summer programs for Grades 6–12 feature academic courses for review, advanced credit, or enrichment. SAT Prep, English as a Second Language, and college courses through Shenandoah University are also offered.

STUDENT ACTIVITIES. Cadets elect officers and representatives to the Student Council, which promotes morale, plans activities, and assists with the Academy's judicial process. Qualified students may join the National Honor Society, the National Junior Honor Society, and the Junior Classical League. Other organizations include the Religious Activities Committee, Fellowship of Christian Athletes, an Explorer Post, and the Kittyhawk Air Society.

Cadets participate in the color guard and drill team, rifle team, military marching band, concert band, chorus, handbell choir, weight training, yearbook, drama, debate, Brainstormers, camping, hiking, skiing, and chess clubs.

Randolph-Macon teams compete in football, cross-country, men's and women's soccer, riflery, rowing, golf, volleyball, swimming, wrestling, basketball, tennis, lacrosse, baseball, softball, and track.

Students who maintain good standards of conduct and academic achievement may have weekend passes off campus, except on a few specific "closed weekends." Cadets who remain on campus choose from challenging seasonal activities such as whitewater rafting, snowboarding, and canoeing as well as social activities involving movies, dances, and community service.

Among the favorite traditions on the school calendar are Spring and Fall Parents' weekends, Homecoming, College Fair, Apple Blossom Festival, Military Band Festival, and the Military Ball.

ADMISSION AND COSTS. Randolph-Macon Academy welcomes young men and women who show promise of benefiting from its program. Admission is offered without regard to race, creed, gender, or national origin and is based on intellectual ability, academic achievement, and good character. An interview with an Admissions Counselor is recommended. The application fee is $50 for U.S. citizens and $100 for all others.

In 1999–2000, tuition is $13,125 for American boarding students, $13,625 for non-American boarders, and $5400 for day students. Other fees are charged for campus services such as yearbook, field trips, and Internet; men's haircuts; and expense account deposit for books, classroom supplies, and military uniforms.

President: Major General Henry M. Hobgood
Chief of Staff: Col. Ivan Mieth
Academic Dean of Upper School: Jonathan Ezell
Middle School Principal: Lisa Ezell
Vice President for Development: Col. John B. Piazza
Commandant: Col. Phil Covell
Director of Admissions: Max N. Andrews, Jr.
Chief Finance Officer: Joan Burke

St. Andrew's Episcopal School   1946

45 Main Street, Newport News, VA 23601. 757-596-6261; Fax 757-596-7218

St. Andrew's offers sound academic training within a Christian environment for children in Kindergarten–Grade 5. Each day begins with Chapel. The School provides a loving, caring atmosphere with small classes that assure individual attention by a qualified and dedicated faculty. Enrichment is provided by special classes in art, music, French, physical education, and library as well as computer classes in the School's state-of-the-art lab. All-day and half-day kindergarten programs are offered, and there is an annual Summer Arts and Science program. St. Andrew's is fully accredited by the Virginia Association of Independent Schools. Tuition: $2200–$3300. Financial aid is available. Mary W. Poole is Headmistress.

St. Anne's-Belfield School 1910

2132 Ivy Road, Charlottesville, VA 22903. 804-296-5106;
Fax 804-979-1486; E-mail j.craig@stab.org;
Web Site http://avenue.org/Ed/STAB/

St. Anne's-Belfield is a coeducational, college preparatory day school enrolling 815 students in Pre-School–Grade 12. The School also offers five- and seven-day boarding and an ESL seven-day boarding program for students in Grades 7–12. A challenging curriculum, including required courses in art, religion, and computer, and a comprehensive college counseling program prepare students for the nation's finest colleges and universities. All students participate in the athletic program and attend a weekly, nonsectarian chapel service. Tuition: $5400–$10,725; Boarding Fee: $10,600–$18,300. Financial aid is available. Jean Craig is Director of Admission; The Reverend Dr. George E. Conway (Wilkes, B.A. 1970; Princeton, M.Div. 1973; Boston University, D.Min. 1976) is Headmaster.

St. Catherine's School RICHMOND

6001 Grove Avenue, Richmond, VA 23226. 804-288-2804;
Admissions 800-648-4982; Fax 804-285-8169;
E-mail admissions@st.catherines.org; Web Site www.st.catherines.org

ST. CATHERINE'S SCHOOL in Richmond, Virginia, is an Episcopal diocesan day and boarding school for girls that provides a rigorous college preparatory curriculum in Junior Kindergarten through Grade 12. It is located in a suburb of metropolitan Richmond, the state capital, noted for its history, Southern charm, and cultural and recreational attractions. Students enjoy frequent visits to the theater, ballet, symphony, museums, galleries, and shopping malls. Transportation for weekend activities is provided by School vans.

Founded in 1890 by Miss Virginia Randolph Ellett, a pioneer in the education of women, the School's knowledge of how girls learn best has helped generations of women achieve success in the liberal arts, math, and science. The School develops each child intellectually, emotionally, physically, and spiritually and is committed to promoting the confidence and courage needed to assume leadership roles. Daily life is based on an honor system that emphasizes trust, fairness, and respect for all. St. Catherine's holds an evening chapel service on alternate Sundays and morning chapel three times a week. In the Upper School, there is a coordinate program with its brother school, St. Christopher's, located three blocks from St. Catherine's.

St. Catherine's is a nonprofit institution owned by the Church Schools in the Diocese of Virginia and directed by a 17-member Board of Governors. It is accredited by the Virginia Association of Independent Schools and holds membership in thex National Association of Independent Schools, the Southern Association of Colleges and Schools, and the National Coalition of Girls' Schools. It is also an approved school of The More-

head Scholarship Program at the University of North Carolina at Chapel Hill. The School's endowment in productive funds is $26,863,556.

THE CAMPUS. Situated in a residential area of Richmond, St. Catherine's 16-acre campus features handsome red brick buildings surrounding a central green. The three main academic/administrative buildings contain classrooms on the main level as well as student living quarters on the second and third floors. Other classroom facilities include the Science Building with four laboratories; the classroom Arcade; Guigon Hall, housing music studios and a recital hall; Turner Hall, which houses the newly renovated chapel, Seymour and John Rennolds Gallery, the Class of 1997 Lecture Hall, the Wright Library, five new classrooms, and a Technology Center with six fully networked CD-ROM workstations with access to nearly 900 periodicals, 22 Internet-connected study carrels, two audiovisual screening rooms, and two computer labs; McCue Hall, housing the newly expanded and renovated Lower School; the Fine Arts Building; and McVey Hall, with a dance studio and 450-seat theater. Miss Jennie's, built by alumnae, contains a meeting room and alumnae and development offices. Faculty reside in Blair Hall, Brackett House, The Palace, and eight off-campus houses.

A gymnasium, several tennis courts, and playing fields for hockey, soccer, lacrosse, and softball complete the physical plant.

THE FACULTY. Auguste J. Bannard, a 1973 graduate of St. Catherine's School, became Head of the School in 1989. She graduated cum laude from Princeton University with a degree in classics and undertook postgraduate study at St. Mary's College of the University of St. Andrews in Scotland. A former teacher of Latin and Greek at Groton School, Mrs. Bannard and her husband, David, have three sons.

There are 80 full-time and 37 part-time faculty members, 15 of whom are men. Twenty-three teachers reside on campus, including 9 with families. In addition to baccalaureate degrees, they have earned 49 master's degrees and 3 doctorates from such colleges and universities as Adelphi, Barnard, Baylor, Columbia, Converse, Davidson, Denison, Duke, Emory and Henry, Florida State, Gettysburg, Hampden-Sydney, Harvard, Haverford, Hollins, Kent State, Mary Baldwin, Mary Washington, Middlebury, Muhlenberg, Oberlin, Rensselaer, Rhodes, St. Andrews Presbyterian, Sweet Briar, Vanderbilt, Villanova, Virginia Commonwealth, and the Universities of Iowa, Michigan, North Carolina, Richmond, Virginia, and Wales.

Two registered nurses are on duty, a physician is on call, and a hospital is within a half mile of the School.

STUDENT BODY. In 1999–2000, St. Catherine's enrolled 738 girls as follows: 339 in the Lower School (Junior Kindergarten–Grade 5), 162 in the Middle School (Grades 6–8), and 237, including 60 boarders, in the Upper School (Grades 9–12). Students represented a diversity of racial, religious, ethnic, and socioeconomic backgrounds.

ACADEMIC PROGRAM. The academic year, divided into trimesters from Labor Day to early June, includes vacations at Thanksgiving and Easter and breaks at Christmas and in the spring. Grades are issued and posted five times a year. Faculty are available for extra help, and the School will arrange for outside tutoring, when necessary, at additional cost. An Extended Day Program is offered on St. Christopher's campus for students in Junior Kindergarten–Grade 7.

The curriculum in the Lower School is child-centered to accommodate individual differences and needs. Beginning in Junior Kindergarten, girls are introduced to simple learning concepts, often illustrated with hands-on experiences, which become increasingly more complex as they progress. In addition to the core disciplines of language arts, mathematics, social studies, and science, Kindergartners have art, music/dance, library skills, computers, woodworking, and physical education. Religion begins in Grade 1 and French in Grade 3.

The Middle School program is specially designed for adolescent girls, balancing academic and physical challenges with the ongoing stability, encouragement, and reassurance they need for success. Courses in English, history and geography, pre-algebra/algebra, computer studies, science, French, and Latin are complemented by music, dance, drama, art, library and study skills, and physical education.

In the Upper School, a typical day includes chapel and class meetings, followed by seven class periods from 8:30 A.M. to 3:30 P.M. Girls may take part in sports and other activities after school. Dinner for boarders is served at 6:00 P.M., after which girls spend two hours in evening study halls.

Each Upper School girl has an academic adviser who guides her in course selection and monitors her progress. To graduate, students must complete a minimum of 20 credits as follows: 4 in English; 3 each in mathematics, history, and a single foreign language (or 2 in two languages); 2 in a laboratory science; 1⅓ in religion; 1 in fine arts; and the remaining in electives.

Specific courses in the Upper School include English IX–XII; Ancient History, World History, American History and Government, Global Problems, World History and Geography, East Asia, Economics, The Holocaust, Modern American History 1945–1990; Algebra I, Geometry, Algebra II, Pre-

Calculus, Probability and Statistics, Discrete Topics, Calculus I–II; Keyboarding, Computer Applications, Desktop Publishing, Computer Programming, Pascal; Biology, Chemistry, Physics, Geology, Immunology; Russian, Mandarin Chinese, French, Spanish, Latin; Religion I–XII; Art I–II, Ceramics, Photography I–III, Art History, History of Architecture, History of American Art; Music Theory, Music History, Chorale, Acting, Introduction to Theater, Speech Communication, Jazz Dance, Ballet Class; and Physical Education, and Health. There are Advanced Placement and Honors courses in all disciplines.

Minimester is a two-week alternative learning experience between the second and third trimesters during which students from St. Catherine's and St. Christopher's undertake more nontraditional studies on campus, within the city of Richmond, or in more distant places, often in foreign countries. On-campus courses may include studies of the civil rights movement; citywide courses may involve work with the homeless; and study/travel may take students to such areas as Texas and Costa Rica for service projects. Interested seniors may travel and study throughout the world in various individualized programs.

Typically, 100 percent of St. Catherine's graduates enroll in college, entering such institutions as Boston University, Bowdoin, Brown, Bucknell, Cornell, Denison, Duke, Georgetown, Harvard, Haverford, Hollins, James Madison, Johns Hopkins, Oberlin, Princeton, St. Lawrence, Smith, Southern Methodist, Trinity (Connecticut), Vanderbilt, Vassar, Virginia Commonwealth, Wake Forest, Washington and Lee, Yale, and the Universities of Chicago, Georgia, Miami, North Carolina (Chapel Hill), Pennsylvania, the South, and Virginia.

Cat's CAP is a six-week creative arts program held in the summer for more than 800 boys and girls, ages 3 to 14.

STUDENT ACTIVITIES. Student government rests with senior prefects, the School Council, and the elected Student Council.

All girls in Grades 9–10 are required to take part in athletics through physical education classes. Varsity and junior varsity teams are formed in field hockey, tennis, volleyball, cross-country, basketball, soccer, indoor and outdoor track and field, lacrosse, softball, and swimming. Students may also engage in such noncompetitive activities as the Waterman Program (camping, rafting/canoeing, rappelling, backpacking), dance classes, aerobics, and weight training.

A "Buddy" program matches school leaders with new students to facilitate their orientation to the School.

Coordinate activities are held with St. Christopher's boys from the Lower School onward. Younger children share holiday celebrations, informational programs, social events, and extended-day care, while the Upper Schools enjoy classes, sports, and extracurricular events such as dances and stage productions presented by Ampersand, the coeducational drama group.

Clubs formed to meet student interests include Unity

(racial/ethnic diversity), Students Against Driving Drunk, Chorale, Altar Guild, The League (community service), Joni Rodman Dance Theatre, and International Thespian Society. Students publish a newspaper, a yearbook, and a creative literary arts magazine.

Special traditions on the school calendar are Sophomore Outing, Junior/Senior Banquet, Candlelight Ring Service, Lower School Farewell to Seniors, St. Catherine's Day, Athletic Awards Banquet, Upper School Career Day, Daisy Days Spring Carnival, Alumnae Weekend, Junior/Senior Dance, The Daisy Chain, and Baccalaureate.

ADMISSION AND COSTS. St. Catherine's welcomes qualified young women of good moral character who have the desire and ability to participate fully in the academic and community life of the School. Admission is based on previous school records, teacher and personal references, the results of standardized testing, and a personal interview. Notice of acceptance is given starting in mid-January for Upper School applicants and in February for others. There is a $25 nonrefundable application fee.

Boarding tuition for the 1999–2000 school year is $22,000. Day tuition ranges from $8450 in the Kindergartens to $10,700 in Grades 9–12. In 1998–99, $1,017,770 in financial aid was awarded to 13.5 percent of the student body. St. Catherine's School subscribes to the School and Student Service for Financial Aid.

Dean of Students: Catherine Leppert
Director of Alumnae Affairs: Judith Williams Carpenter
Director of Admission: Katherine S. Wallmeyer
Director of Development: Sue Schutt
College Counselor: Mary Chapman
Assistant Headmaster for Financial Affairs: William Bacon
   Armstrong
Director of Athletics: Linda C. Southworth

St. Christopher's School   1911

711 St. Christopher's Road, Richmond, VA 23226. 804-282-3185;
   Fax 804-673-6632; E-mail admissions@stchristophers.com;
   Web Site www.stchristophers.com

St. Christopher's is an Episcopal day school enrolling 880 boys in Junior Kindergarten–Grade 12. The School offers a college preparatory curriculum, with a wide choice of electives, in an atmosphere stressing Christian ideals. Small classes foster close student/teacher relationships, with emphasis on bringing out the best in each boy. There is a program of coordinate education with St. Catherine's School. The athletic program features 12 varsity sports. Academic, recreational, and athletic camps are offered in the summer. Tuition: $8450–$11,070. Financial Aid: $1,388,600. Anne D. Booker is Director of Admission; Charles M. Stillwell (Princeton, A.B. 1985; Brown, M.A. 1990) is Headmaster. *Southern Association.*

St. Margaret's School   TAPPAHANNOCK

Tappahannock, VA 22560. 804-443-3357; E-mail admit@sms.org;
   Web Site www.sms.org

S̲T. MARGARET'S SCHOOL in Tappahannock, Virginia, is an Episcopal, college preparatory boarding and day school enrolling girls in Grades 8 through 12. Situated in a small town (population 2100) on the Rappahannock River, the School's location combines the rural atmosphere of the historic Tidewater area with convenient access to the educational and cultural resources of both Richmond (45 miles away) and Washington, D.C. (100 miles away).

Founded in 1921 by the Episcopal Diocese of Virginia, St. Margaret's prepares girls for an increasingly complex and international world by supplementing a college preparatory education with interdisciplinary seminars, town meetings, independent studies, and travel programs. Marine and environmental science courses make extensive use of the riverfront setting. New facilities—library, student center, art and music studios, and a fitness room—are designed to inspire good study habits, creativity, wholesome relaxation, and physical fitness. With a full sports program, leadership opportunities, and a focus on the individual, St. Margaret's offers choices and challenges to each student.

The School's traditional college preparatory curriculum allows students to pursue core academic subjects through their senior year. In addition to many electives, special programs are offered, including a Minimester Program, River Day, International Day, Peer Leadership, community service, and hands-on field experiences to supplement the science classes. Students are encouraged to participate in these outside activities and to find links between what they learn from these programs and what they learn in the classroom.

St. Margaret's School is governed by a 27-member Board of Governors, composed of alumnae, parents, and friends of the School. The School is accredited by the Southern Association of Colleges and Schools and The Virginia Association of Independent Schools; it holds membership in the National Association of Independent Schools, among other affiliations.

THE CAMPUS. The nine-acre historic campus overlooks the Rappahannock River, which is a tributary of the Chesapeake Bay. St. Margaret's Hall (1820), the central building, contains the chapel, administrative offices, classrooms, music studio, and art studio. The Viola Woolfolk Learning Center (1991) houses the library, study hall, classrooms, and the new faculty/student center. Additional classrooms and computer labs are located in the Cottage (1922). The new Community/Technology Center (1999) houses a dining room, additional classroom space, and chemistry, physics, biology, and computer laboratories.

The Anderton House (circa 1760) accommodates 10th through 12th graders; students in Grades 8–12 reside in Latane Hall, which also houses the infirmary and reception and conference rooms. The Headmistress resides in the Chinn House. The Admission Office is located in the Brockenbrough House (circa 1763), and Pettigrew Hall, Phillips House, Mitchell House, Dunn House, Lewis House, and Cralle House all serve as faculty residences.

Outdoor athletic facilities include a playing field for field hockey, soccer, lacrosse, and softball; hard-surface tennis courts (1998); and a swimming pool. The Ball Memorial Gymnasium (1966) houses basketball and volleyball courts and drama facilities. The plant is valued at more than $6,500,000.

THE FACULTY. St. Margaret's School's Headmistress, Margaret R. Broad, was appointed in 1989 and is a graduate of Denison University (B.A. 1970) and the University of Virginia (M.A. 1988). Prior to her appointment, she served as Academic Dean for two years and Head of the Foreign Language Department for eight years.

St. Margaret's faculty includes 29 women and 4 men, 18 of whom live on campus. The faculty and administrators hold 39 baccalaureate, 22 master's degrees, and a doctorate from such institutions as Colgate, College of William and Mary, Randolph-Macon Woman's College, Sarah Lawrence, Washington and Lee, and the Universities of Richmond and Virginia. Faculty benefits include a retirement plan, hospitalization, major medical, life, and disability insurance.

Two nurses staff the infirmary during the day and in the evenings, and a doctor is on call. There is a hospital in Tappahannock.

STUDENT BODY. In 1999–2000, the School enrolls 102 boarding and 49 day students. The majority of girls come from Virginia, with 16 other states and eight foreign countries also represented.

ACADEMIC PROGRAM. The school year is divided into trimesters and includes Thanksgiving, Christmas, spring, and Easter vacations. College preparatory classes have an average enrollment of ten students and meet five days per week. A typical daily schedule includes chapel or announcements at 7:50 A.M., classes from 8:20 A.M. until 3:30 P.M., followed by athletics or after-school activities. A buffet dinner is served at 5:30 P.M., and study hall is held from 7:00 to 9:00 P.M. "Lights out" is at 10:30 P.M. Evening study takes place in a supervised study hall; if a student is in good academic standing, she may study in her dormitory room. Academic standing is evaluated every five weeks, at which time the student, her adviser, and her parents collectively identify strengths and weaknesses in the student's academic performance.

To graduate, students in Grades 9–12 must complete a minimum of four years of English; three years each of mathematics (Algebra I and II, Plane Geometry), history, and a foreign language; two years of a laboratory science; two years of physical education; one year each of religion and the fine arts; one-half year of health and computer studies; and one and one-half years of electives.

Courses offered include English; French, Latin, Spanish; World History I and II, United States History and Government, Economics, Foreign Policy; Algebra, Plane Geometry, Advanced Algebra and Trigonometry, Pre-Calculus, Calculus, Advanced Calculus; Biology, Chemistry, Chemistry in the Community, Physics, Environmental Science, Advanced Biology, Ecology; Studio Art, Art History, Piano, Music History, Music Theory, Glee Club, Dance, Photography, Pottery, Video Making; Study Skills; Religion; Physical Education; and Driver Education.

Seniors may spend two weeks during the February min-

imester period on independent study projects in a career field of their choice. All students may select from 25 courses offered on campus and a study trip abroad.

The Class of 1999 graduated 32 students who are currently attending a wide variety of four- and two-year colleges. Among them are Boston University, College of Charleston, College of William and Mary, Drexel, Drew, Emory, Georgetown, Hollins, James Madison, and the University of Florida.

STUDENT ACTIVITIES. After school and on weekends, students may choose from a wide variety of educational, cultural, and recreational activities such as attending plays or visiting museums in Richmond or the District of Columbia, horseback riding, dance, yoga, walking and running clubs, aerobics, participating in the performing arts, or athletic competitions. In addition to vacations, on average, nine weekends per year may be spent off campus.

All students are expected to abide by the School's Honor Code and Major School Rules, which are designed to create an atmosphere of trust and camaraderie. Opportunities for leadership include participation in such organizations as Honor Council, Student Government, Peer Leadership, Prefects, Yearbook, Literary Publications, Handbell Choir, Student Tourguides, and Vestry.

St. Margaret's competes with ten other Virginia schools in crew, cross-country, field hockey, lacrosse, tennis, volleyball, basketball, soccer, and softball. Within the School, students are members of either the Blue or the Grey intramural teams, which compete in a variety of athletic competitions throughout the year. All students are encouraged to participate.

A varied calendar provides the opportunity for sightseeing and shopping as well as dances and social gatherings at other Virginia schools such as Christchurch, Episcopal High, Woodberry Forest, and Virginia Episcopal. St. Margaret's is a member of the Independent Schools Social Activities Committee (ISSAC), which plans social events for Virginia and Maryland boarding schools.

Faculty-planned and -chaperoned trips to Europe are scheduled annually. Traditional events include Parents' Weekend, Alumnae Weekend, Junior Variety, May Day, and St. Margaret's Day.

ADMISSION AND COSTS. St. Margaret's seeks students who will benefit from, and contribute to, the School community. The School admits students "without regard to race, color, creed, or national or ethnic origin." Candidates are accepted in all grades on the basis of recognized potential and achievement, results of standardized tests, the applicant's extracurricular activities, and the recommendations of two teachers and one personal acquaintance. An interview on campus is required. Although St. Margaret's conducts rolling admissions, prospective students are urged to apply in the winter.

In 1999–2000, boarding tuition is \$23,000; day tuition, which includes lunches, is \$10,750. Boarding students must also make a \$1500 deposit to cover books, supplies, trips away from school, and other incidentals. A tuition payment plan is available, and St. Margaret's School subscribes to the School Scholarship Service. In 1999, $550,000 was awarded in financial aid to 30 percent of the student body on the basis of need and academic standing.

Director of Admission: Kimberly A. McDowell
Director of Alumnae: Jenni Booker
Director of Development: Mark H. Eastham
College Counselor: Mollie H. Conklin
Business Manager: Nancy A. Smith
Director of Athletics: Sue Saunders

St. Stephen's and St. Agnes School   1924

Upper School: 1000 St. Stephen's Road, Alexandria, VA 22304.
  703-751-2700
Middle School: 4401 West Braddock Road, Alexandria, VA 22304.
  703-751-2700
Lower School: 400 Fontaine Street, Alexandria, VA 22302.
  703-751-2700

This college preparatory, Episcopal day school enrolls 1150 boys and girls from diverse backgrounds in Junior Kindergarten–Grade 12. It seeks to instill a passion for learning, enthusiasm for athletics, and commitment to service. An honor code, chapel, and community outreach are central to the program. The curriculum is enriched by 20 Advanced Placement courses and varied electives. Student Government, sports, drama, publications, music, interest clubs, and the Oxford programs overseas are among the extracurriculars. Unique to the program are single-gender math and science classes in Middle School. A summer program is available. Tuition: $9990–$15,000. Financial Aid: $1,761,626. Diane Dunning is Director of Admission; Joan G. Ogilvy Holden (Tufts, B.A.; Harvard, M.Ed.) is Head of School.

The Steward School   1972

11600 Gayton Road, Richmond, VA 23233. 804-740-3394;
  Fax 804-740-1464; E-mail cadret@rmond.mindspring.com

The Steward School, serving 404 boys and girls in Kindergarten to Grade 12, offers a college preparatory curriculum designed to enable day students of varying abilities to reach educational goals. Small classes, individual attention, extracurricular opportunities, and an optional in-school/one-on-one tutoring program are featured. Student activities include athletics, fine arts, community service, outdoor trips, and interest clubs. Extended care, summer sessions, interdisciplinary honor symposia, and innovative minimesters with internships are offered. Tuition: $7985–$9875. Financial aid is available. A. Scott Moncure is Director of Admission; Roger A. Coulombe (Assumption College, B.A.; Roosevelt University, M.A.) is Headmaster.

Stuart Hall   STAUNTON

Staunton, VA 24402-0210. 540-885-0356;
  E-mail admissions@stuart-hall.staunton.va.us;
  Web Site www.stuart-hall.staunton.va.us

STUART HALL in Staunton, Virginia, is a college preparatory school enrolling boarding girls in Grades 8–12 and day girls and boys in Grades 6–12. Tracing its origins to 1831 and chartered in 1844 as the Virginia Female Institute, the school was renamed to honor Mrs. General J. E. B. Stuart, a former Principal. Stuart Hall is the oldest Episcopal girls' boarding school in Virginia.

Staunton, the site of a number of points of historic interest and the home of Mary Baldwin College, is located in the Shenandoah Valley, 150 miles from the District of Columbia, on Interstate 81 at the junction of Interstate 64.

Through a 24-hour educational experience, Stuart Hall seeks to educate the whole person: mind, body, heart, and spirit. The school maintains a commitment to prepare its students for college and for adult life while encouraging a love of learning for its own sake. An emphasis is placed on achieving close personal and academic relationships throughout the family-like school community.

Students have contact with faculty in small classes, through cocurricular activities, and at meals. There is a well-developed advisor-advisee system, and students participate in maintenance and administrative tasks around the campus. There is a school-wide chapel service three times weekly, and students are encouraged to attend the church of their choice on Sundays. Other community gatherings include a seated noon meal three times weekly and special traditional celebrations throughout the year.

A nonprofit corporation, the school is governed by a 25-member Board of Trustees, which meets three times annually. The 10 men and 15 women on the Board include alumnae representatives and members nominated by the diocesan councils of the three Episcopal dioceses of Virginia. Many of the approximately 3000 living graduates are active in support of the school. Stuart Hall is accredited by the Department of Education of the Commonwealth of Virginia and holds membership in the National Association of Independent Schools, The Virginia Association of Independent Schools, and the National Association of Episcopal Schools.

THE CAMPUS. The 8-acre campus includes shaded lawns, formal gardens, and tennis courts. The school has 11 acres of playing fields, which are located one mile from campus. Indoor athletic facilities include the gymnasium and a swimming pool. The central building, Old Main, is a registered historic landmark. A three-story structure of Greek Revival architecture, it contains reception rooms, offices, recreation rooms, the dining room, the health center, and some dormitory rooms. Ten other buildings, some connected with Old Main, house the school's other facilities and include classrooms, science and computer laboratories, a library, a new student center, an art studio, music studios and practice rooms, a darkroom, and an auditorium equipped for drama workshops. Most dormitory rooms are doubles, but there are some single rooms. A facility opened in 1997 increased the school's instructional space by 50 percent. The building houses a gymnasium, Middle School classrooms, and Upper School science laboratories.

THE FACULTY. The Reverend J. Kevin Fox, who became Headmaster in 1990, earned his baccalaureate degree (magna cum laude) in history and English from Boston College, where he was a member of Phi Beta Kappa. He was a Laprade Fellow at Duke University and a duPont Fellow at the University of Virginia. After graduating with a master's degree in Renaissance Literature, with highest honors, from Middlebury's Bread Loaf School of English, he completed the Master of Divinity degree program at Yale Divinity School, graduating summa cum laude. He is an Episcopal priest who has been a faculty member at St. Paul's School in Concord, New Hampshire, and has served at several New Hampshire and Virginia parishes. An accomplished mountaineer and published author, Father Fox and his wife, Macy, are the parents of two sons.

There are 21 full-time and 2 part-time faculty members, 19 women and 4 men; 7 members reside on campus, 3 with their families. The faculty, 13 of whom hold advanced degrees, are graduates of such colleges and universities as Boston College, College of William and Mary, Davidson, James Madison University, Mary Baldwin, Medical College of Virginia, Middlebury, New York University, Princeton, Wellesley, and the Universities of Munich, North Carolina, and Virginia.

The health center is staffed until 7:00 P.M.; a registered nurse and a doctor are on call 24 hours a day. A hospital is located nearby.

STUDENT BODY. In 1999–2000, Stuart Hall enrolls 140 students, 46 boarders and 94 day students. The enrollment is distributed among Grades 6–12, with 68 in the upper school and 73 in the middle school. Students represent ten states and four foreign countries, with minority students comprising approximately 15 percent of the student body.

ACADEMIC PROGRAM. The school year, divided into two terms, includes 33 weeks of instruction with Thanksgiving, Christmas, Easter, and spring vacations. Classes meet five days a week and are approximately 50 minutes in length. Grades are

sent to parents with extensive comments from teachers and an adviser six times a year.

For boarders, a typical day includes a buffet-style breakfast at 7:15 A.M., followed by room inspection, a consultation period, a chapel assembly, classes, a morning break, and lunch. The afternoon consists of two class periods, a cocurricular period, and a sports period. Dinner is followed by study hall from 7:00 to 9:00 P.M., a dormitory check at 10:00 P.M., and "lights out" at 11:00 P.M. for Grades 9–10 and at midnight for Grades 11 and 12.

Stuart Hall individualizes programs to maximize the likelihood of each student's academic success, tailoring the student's course schedule to her abilities and interests. The program requires mastery of concepts skills before promotion to succeeding levels.

Through a cooperative arrangement with nearby Mary Baldwin College, gifted students may enroll in college courses for transferable college credit.

To graduate, students must earn a minimum of 25 units of credit (1 unit equals one year of study). Specific requirements are four years of English; three of a foreign language; four of history, including United States History and Government; four of mathematics, including Geometry and Algebra II; four of science; one each of fine arts and religion; and two of health/physical education. For students with diagnosed learning difficulties or those entering as juniors with no foreign language, the third-year foreign language requirement may be waived and a language arts class substituted.

The curriculum includes English Grammar and Composition, American Literature, British Literature; French, Spanish; Geography, Origins in World Cultures, United States History, United States Government; Algebra I and II, Geometry, Advanced Math, Computer, Pre-calculus, Calculus; Integrated Science, Biology, Chemistry, Physics, Environmental Science; Religion and Philosophy; Fine Arts, Interdisciplinary Arts, Drama, Advanced Art, Piano, Chorus, Voice; SAT Preparation, Photography, Journalism, Publications; Driver Education; and Physical Education and Health. Advanced Placement courses are offered in Spanish, United States Government, American Literature, Calculus, Chemistry, Physics, and Environmental Science. The Learning Resource Center is staffed with a director who assists students with organizational and study skills.

Stuart Hall's Visual and Performing Arts Program is designed to provide a strong foundation for students who have been identified as showing potential and strength in dance, music, drama, or the visual arts. Stuart Hall Abroad offers a cultural immersion program each spring to enrich the overall curriculum. Past trips included travel to England, France, Greece, Italy, Mexico, the Soviet Union, Spain, and the Florida Keys.

All graduates of the Class of 1999 entered college. They are attending such institutions as College of William and Mary, James Madison, Middlebury, Rhode Island School of Design, and the Universities of the South and Virginia.

Stuart Hall's coeducational, five-week summer session includes classes in English, history, mathematics, science, and foreign language. The English as a Second Language Program is designed to enable international students to gain fluency in English.

STUDENT ACTIVITIES. The Honor Council and Judicial Board are composed of a group of ten prefects nominated by students and faculty and appointed by the Headmaster. The Council is charged with the responsibility of maintaining, perpetuating, and administering the honor and disciplinary codes. Extracurricular organizations include the Student Government, the Choir, the Social Committee, the Drama Club, ELA, the Ecology Club, and the Honor Society. Students publish a newspaper, a yearbook, and a literary magazine; they also participate in various artistic and musical activities. Members of the Senior Religion Class undertake community service work at such places as the Virginia School for the Deaf and Blind, Western States Hospital, and a local day nursery.

Varsity teams compete with nearby schools in basketball, cross-country, soccer, field hockey, volleyball, softball, and tennis. Coed teams are organized in golf and cross-country. Intramural teams and interclass teams play each other in several sports, and recreational activities include skiing, camping, hiking, softball, and volleyball. Stuart Hall's riding program is offered at a nearby farm, where hunting, jumping, and show techniques are taught.

Weekend activities include movies, dances with nearby boys' schools, and skiing or canoeing excursions. With permission, boarding students may leave the campus several weekends each session.

ADMISSION AND COSTS. New students are accepted at all grade levels on the basis of the previous school record, school and personal recommendations, test scores, health forms, a personal interview, and an essay from the candidate. Applications should be made as early as possible. If vacancies exist, students may be enrolled during the school year. Approximately 10 students enter at midyear for the second term. There is an application fee of $35; the application fee for international students is $70.

In 1999–00, seven-day boarding tuition is $20,600; five-day boarding tuition is $18,500. Day tuition, including lunches, is $7725, and Middle School day tuition is $7225. Incidentals total approximately $1000 a year for boarding girls. Riding, piano, and instrumental lessons are extra. Fees are subject to change. Tuition insurance and a tuition payment plan are available. In 1998–99, 35 percent of the students received approximately $325,000 in financial aid on the basis of need.

Dean of Faculty: Mrs. Catherine Oryschak
Dean of Students: Ms. Debra Casado
Alumnae Director: Mrs. Margaret Stanley Wood
Dean of Admissions: Mrs. Stephanie C. Shafer
Associate Head for External Affairs/Development: Mrs. Gena Adams
College Counselor: Dr. Robert E. Cox
Director of Financial Affairs: Ms. Margie F. Obenschain
Director of Athletics: Ms. Connie Forsyth

Tandem Friends School   1970

279 Tandem Lane, Charlottesville, VA 22902. 804-296-1303;
Fax 804-296-1886; Web Site www.tandemfs.org

Tandem Friends School is a coeducational day school enrolling 190 students in Grades 5–12. For nearly three decades, the School has offered a superior college preparatory education based on rigorous academics, the encouragement of individual talents, and the development of ethical values and social responsibility. In addition, Tandem aims to provide a spiritual foundation in the Friends tradition. Fine arts, music, drama, sports, and community service complement the demanding curriculum. Students also enjoy special programs such as Blue Ridge Day, Emphasis Week, Spring Day, and exchange programs

abroad. Tuition: $8500–$9500. Financial Aid: $202,000. Sandra Richardson is Director of Admissions; Tom O'Connor (Williams, B.A.; Westfield State, M.Ed.) is Acting Head.

Sullins Academy   1966

22218 Sullins Academy Drive, Bristol, VA 24202. 540-669-4101;
Fax 540-669-4294; E-mail office@sullinsacademy.org;
Web Site sullinsacademy.org

Sullins Academy, a day school enrolling 165 boys and girls in Preschool (2$^1/_2$ years)–Grade 8, provides quality education through which each child is encouraged to attain his or her full potential. An atmosphere of academic excellence is created with a core curriculum of reading, mathematics, history/social studies, grammar and composition, foreign language, and computers. Art, music, creative writing, physical education, clubs, and field trips further support the nurturing of the whole child. Tuition: $2000–$4300. Scholarships are available. Mrs. Ronan D. King is Director of Development; Gordon R. Rode (Johns Hopkins University, B.A. 1972; Rutgers University, M.S.T. 1980) was appointed Headmaster in 1995.

Trinity Episcopal School   1972

3850 Pittaway Road, Richmond, VA 23235. 804-272-5864;
Fax 804-323-1335; E-mail admissions@trinityes.org;
Web Site www.trinityes.org

A coeducational, college preparatory day school enrolling 342 students in Grades 8–12, Trinity Episcopal offers a strong academic program and a caring environment dedicated to the personal growth of each student. The International Baccalaureate program is offered in Grades 11–12. Advanced Placement courses are available in all disciplines, and electives include Computer Programming, American Foreign Policy, Creative Writing, Organic Chemistry, Computer Modeling, Art, Music, and Drama. Tuition: $9275–$9675. Financial Aid: $340,000. Emily H. McLeod is Admissions Director; Thomas G. Aycock (Barton College, B.S.; University of North Carolina, M.A., Ph.D.) was appointed Headmaster in 1990.

Virginia Beach Friends School   1955

1537 Laskin Road, Virginia Beach, VA 23451. 757-428-7534

Virginia Beach Friends School enrolls up to 215 boys and girls from all religious, racial, and ethnic backgrounds in an academic program encompassing Cottage (age 3) through Grade 12. In keeping with Quaker tradition and philosophy, the School offers a liberal arts curriculum within an atmosphere permeated by values of community, harmony, equality, and simplicity. Caring, experienced faculty work with children in small classes to develop strong basic skills in language arts, math, humanities, foreign language, social studies, and the arts. Close personal attention motivates each child to reach his or her full potential. Students participate in activities such as drama, a work program, and field trips. Tuition: $1900–$6150. Phyllis Sullivan is Headmistress.

Virginia Episcopal School   LYNCHBURG

400 Virginia Episcopal School Road, P.O. Box 408, Lynchburg, VA 24505. 804-384-6221; Fax 804-384-1655; E-mail admissions@ves.lynchburg.va.us; Web Site www.ves.org

VIRGINIA EPISCOPAL SCHOOL in Lynchburg, Virginia, is a coeducational, college preparatory school enrolling boarding and day students in Grades 9 through 12. Lynchburg, a city of 70,000 rich in American traditions and memorable architecture, is located in a region of great natural beauty and historic sites. The School and the city lie in the foothills of the Blue Ridge Mountains, not far from the scenic Blue Ridge Parkway, Washington and Jefferson National Forests, the Appalachian Trail, Appomattox Court House, and Poplar Forest, Thomas Jefferson's summer home. Five colleges and the Lynchburg Fine Arts Center are among the city's attractions. Students and faculty take full advantage of the recreational and cultural opportunities offered nearby. An airport, bus station, and railroad serve Lynchburg, which is 120 miles from Richmond and 200 miles from Washington, D.C.

The School opened in 1916 under the leadership of the Reverend Robert Carter Jett as an Episcopal school for boys. It flourished as such for 70 years, setting clear educational standards and Christian values. In 1986, coeducation was instituted to provide a more realistic social environment and enhance academic quality.

The School seeks to challenge students with a wide range of interests, build confidence in their achievements, and provide sound preparation for further education and productive lives. Small classes, close relationships with faculty, and an emphasis on self-discipline and moral and spiritual development are critical to these goals. Students are encouraged to be caring and faithful members of their communities. Attendance at two worship services each week is required for all.

Virginia Episcopal School is a nonprofit institution governed by a self-perpetuating Board of 25 Trustees. The Board includes alumni, parents, friends, and the Bishop of the Diocese of Southwestern Virginia. Some 4000 living graduates provide financial and other support.

The School is accredited with the Virginia Association of Independent Schools and holds membership in the National Association of Independent Schools, National Association of Episcopal Schools, The Association of Boarding Schools, English-Speaking Union, Secondary School Admission Test Board, and College Board.

THE CAMPUS. The 165 wooded and open acres of the campus lie near the James River and provide a striking natural setting for the School.

In recent years, some older buildings and most dormitories have been renovated and updated, including Jett Hall, which houses administrative offices, classrooms, and dormitory rooms; Ainslie Auditorium; the Hopkins Writing Center; and the Zimmer Center, which includes the computer center, science laboratories, student lounge, seminar and lecture rooms, the post office, and bookstore. Banks Gannaway contains the 16,000-volume library plus audiovisual and computer resources, dining hall, and offices. Other buildings are Pendleton Hall, Randolph Hall, Langhorne Chapel, Barksdale Gymnasium, Wilson Art Studio, Mingea Cottage, which houses the health center, and the Wyatt, Ainslie, and Perkins houses.

Eight athletic fields and eight outdoor tennis courts are complemented by the William King Field House and the Philip L. Van Every Athletic Center, providing basketball and volleyball courts, an indoor track, and batting cage. The School has its own fully equipped riding center.

The School-owned facilities are valued at nearly $15,000,000.

THE FACULTY. Phillip L. Hadley, a graduate of Ohio University (B.S., Mathematics 1965, M.A., Spanish Literature 1967) and the University of Texas at Austin (Ph.D., Latin American History 1972), was appointed the tenth Headmaster in 1998. He had previously been Headmaster at St. Mary's Hall in San Antonio, Texas, and Head of the Upper School at The Bishop's School in La Jolla, California. He and his wife, Lynn, an experienced teacher, have two children.

The full-time faculty and administrators consist of 40 men and women. About half live on campus, including 13 with families. They hold 40 bachelor's degrees and 25 advanced degrees from institutions such as Bowdoin, Brown, Columbia, Converse, Dartmouth, Davidson 2, Denison, Duke, Emory, Hampden-Sydney, Hollins 3, Goucher, James Madison 3, Johns Hopkins 2, Lynchburg College 8, Marietta, Middlebury, Randolph-Macon

Woman's College 4, Roanoke, Southern Illinois, Springfield, Swarthmore, Washington and Lee 3, Wesleyan 2, Yale 2, and the Universities of Aberdeen, Iowa 2, North Carolina, Richmond, the South, South Carolina, and Virginia 5.

Two school nurses are on duty at the Health Center, and the school doctor is available three mornings a week.

STUDENT BODY. In 1999–2000, 222 students were enrolled, including 100 boys and 51 girls as boarders and 38 boys and 33 girls as day students. They came from the District of Columbia, North Carolina, Virginia, and 18 more states including Alabama, Colorado, Florida, Georgia, Illinois, Kentucky, Ohio, Pennsylvania, and West Virginia. Students also came from the Bahamas, Finland, Germany, Iceland, Korea, Nigeria, Spain, Switzerland, and Turkey. About half the students are Episcopalian.

ACADEMIC PROGRAM. The academic year, divided into trimesters, begins in early September and extends to late May, with breaks at Thanksgiving and Easter and vacations at Christmas and in the spring. Classes are scheduled in seven 45-minute periods, along with a 35-minute chapel program and two hours for activities in the afternoon. Students attend daily supervised study hall sessions, but some are exempted on the basis of strong academic performance. Boarders have a two-hour supervised study period in the evening. Teachers are available for extra help, and some students may be required to attend extra-help sessions. Review courses are offered in the fundamentals of mathematics and English. The computer network is available to all, and each student can store work in a private folder and use E-mail, the Internet, and information on CD-ROM.

Grade reports, along with teacher comments, are sent to parents at the middle and end of each trimester.

To graduate from Virginia Episcopal School, a student must complete a minimum of $18\frac{1}{3}$ credits including 4 in English, 2 in one foreign language, 2 in history, 3 in mathematics, 2 in science, 1 in fine arts, two terms in religion, and one term each in life issues and computers. A normal student load is five courses per term.

Some of the courses available are English 1–4 covering grammar, composition, and literature, Public Speaking; French 1–5, Latin 1–4, Spanish 1–5; U.S. History, Modern European History, Government, Economics, Russian Civilization, Ancient and Medieval History; Algebra I, Geometry, Algebra II/Trigonometry, Math Analysis, Math Topics, Calculus, Finite Mathematics, Statistics; Biology, Chemistry, Physics, Environmental Science; Drama, Music History, Music Theory, Private Music Instruction, Studio Art, Art History, Graphic Design, Musical Theater; Old Testament, New Testament, Ethics, World Religions, Religion and Literature; Life Issues, Introduction to Sports Medicine; and Computer Applications. Honors courses and 11 Advanced Placement courses are available.

The 50 graduates of the Class of 1999 matriculated at 32 different colleges and universities. Among them are Clemson, Elon, Emerson, George Washington, Guilford, James Madison, Loyola Marymount, North Carolina State 4, Tulane 2, Virginia Military Institute, Virginia Polytechnic 4, Washington University, Wesleyan, Wofford, and the Universities of Denver, Georgia, North Carolina 3, and Virginia 2.

Summer sports camps enroll boys and girls, ages 7–13, in four one-week sessions. Robert Moore, the athletic director, and his wife, Diane, direct the program.

STUDENT ACTIVITIES. The student body elects members of the senior class to the Honor Committee, which administers the Honor Code. Students pledge not to lie, cheat, or steal and assume the obligation to report offenses. The Student Council plans and discusses activities with the Dean of Students.

On the basis of student and faculty nominations, the Headmaster appoints leading students to the Counselor Body, which plays a significant leadership role within the student body.

Students staff and publish a literary magazine and yearbook. Other ongoing activities include Glee Club, dramatic group, Student Vestry, Fellowship of Christians (FOCUS), and The Cum Laude Society for academic excellence. Other activities are organized according to student interest.

All students must participate in afternoon activities under a system of credits earned in athletics, fine arts, or other approved activity. The School fields 33 teams at varsity, junior varsity, or intramural levels, and everyone has a chance to play. The School competes in the Virginia Prep League and the League of Independent Schools. Boys play football, indoor soccer, wrestling, and baseball; girls play softball, field hockey, and volleyball. Both boys and girls compete in basketball, cross-country, golf, track, lacrosse, soccer, and tennis.

Some social events are coordinated with other schools, and students can go to town on weekends. On-campus activities and trips are organized on weekends such as films, lectures, and outdoor recreation.

Homecoming Weekend in the fall, Reunion Weekend in the spring, two Parents Weekends, Grandparents Day, Casino Night, and Finals, a black-tie dinner dance for seniors, are among the traditional events.

ADMISSION AND COSTS. Virginia Episcopal School seeks a diverse group of students of average to superior ability who demonstrate a willingness to participate in its programs. Students are admitted on the basis of previous transcripts, standardized test results, teacher and school recommendations, and a personal interview, with parents. Applications should be completed for review in February.

Boarding tuition for 1999–2000 is $22,225; day tuition is $9950. Extras are a $500 book store deposit and $250 activities fee. Tuition insurance and payment plans are offered. Some 25 percent of students receive financial aid totaling $500,000.

Dean of Faculty: Charlotte M. Berry
Dean of Students: Bernard K. Mundy II
Director of Alumni: Patti Burgh
Director of Development: Karl J. Sjolund
Director of Admission: Richard Beaugh
Director of Public Relations and Publications: Gail J. Morrison
Director of College Counseling: Ruth D. Wills
Business Manager: Wayne L. Roakes
Director of Athletics: Robert F. Moore

Woodberry Forest School

WOODBERRY FOREST

*Woodberry Forest, VA 22989. 540-672-3900;
E-mail wfs_admissions@woodberry.org; Web Site www.woodberry.org*

WOODBERRY FOREST SCHOOL in Woodberry Forest, Virginia, is a college preparatory school enrolling boys boarding in Grades 9 through 12. Situated in the Piedmont section of Virginia, the School is three miles north of the town of Orange. The location affords access to the educational and cultural resources of the University of Virginia in nearby Charlottesville, as well as those in Richmond and Washington, D.C., both within easy driving distance.

Woodberry Forest was founded in 1889 by Robert Stringfellow Walker, who wished to provide a suitable education for his own sons and for those of his neighbors. Captain Walker served as Headmaster until 1897, when he was succeeded by his son, J. Carter Walker, who directed the School until 1948.

In accordance with its belief that boys want to be honorable and want to be trusted, the School is guided in its operation by an Honor System designed to promote mutual trust between students and faculty and a positive impact on life in the residential community. As part of its commitment to Christian principles, the School requires all students to participate in weekly nondenominational chapel services and in social service projects. The academic program includes opportunities for independent study and study abroad in England, France, Israel, Scotland, Spain, Austria, and Japan.

A nonprofit institution, the School is governed by a self-perpetuating Board of Trustees, 22 in number, most of whom are alumni. There are approximately 5000 living graduates, and nearly one quarter of the present students are relatives of alumni. Parents and alumni may serve on the Advisory Council, which makes recommendations to the Trustees and the Headmaster. The operations of Woodberry Forest are supported by an endowment of $140,000,000 and annual-fund gifts. Fifty-nine percent of the alumni and 86 percent of the current parents support the fund drive. Woodberry Forest School is accredited by the Southern Association of Colleges and Schools and by The Virginia Association of Independent Schools. It holds membership in the National Association of Independent Schools, The College Board, and the Council for Advancement and Support of Education, among others.

THE CAMPUS. The School owns 1000 acres, which surround the 175-acre main campus overlooking the Blue Ridge Mountains and partially bordered by the Rapidan River. The property was originally the estate of Gen. William Madison (brother of President James Madison) and The Residence was designed by Thomas Jefferson. The campus includes shaded lawns, 13 athletic fields, 14 tennis courts, a nine-hole golf course, an all-weather track, an outdoor pool, and a trap and skeet range. Indoor athletic facilities are located in the L. W. Dick Gymnasium, which provides a basketball court, weight rooms, and the Michael M. Reily Memorial Wrestling Room. The Harry Barbee, Jr., Center has an indoor pool, a 200-meter track, squash courts, and 5 basketball and 3 tennis courts.

Most of the buildings are of Georgian-style architecture. The Walker Building (1899, with an addition in 1970 and renovations in 1978 and 1979) is the central school structure. It provides dormitory rooms, a dining hall, a kitchen, a snack bar, the bookstore, administrative offices, and the post office. Other student quarters are located in House "D" (1922), House "A" (1926), Griffin House (renovated 1996), Turner (1940), Taylor (1955), Finch (1978), and Dowd (1978) halls. Classrooms, the Language Learning Center, and the Writing Center are housed in Anderson Hall (1930, enlarged 1956, totally renovated 1996–97), while Hanes Hall (1958) contains the 60,000-volume White Library and the Belk Audiovisual Department. The Gordon Gray Science-Mathematics Building (1970) provides classroom and laboratory facilities, two greenhouses, quarters for laboratory animals, a roof-deck observatory, and 21 microcomputers for student use. Armfield Hall (1996) provides classrooms, an amphitheater, a computer lab and center for the campus-wide network, faculty lounge, and offices.

A 525-seat theater, music and art studios, wood shops, a mechanical-drawing classroom, publications offices, and dark rooms are located in the J. Carter Walker Center (1966). Also on the campus are 33 faculty residences and the original home of William Madison, The Residence, which has been renovated to serve as the Headmaster's home. The School-owned plant is valued at $65,000,000.

THE FACULTY. Dennis M. Campbell earned a B.A. and a Ph.D. from Duke University and a B.D. from Yale University. He served as dean of the Divinity School at Duke for 15 years before being appointed Headmaster of Woodberry Forest in 1997. A noted lecturer and author, Dr. Campbell has written many articles and four books on ethics and theology.

There are 69 full-time faculty and administrators who teach. All but 6 live on campus with their families. Seventy-two percent of the Woodberry Forest faculty hold advanced degrees, including 5 doctorates. Eleven are either table readers or readers for the College Board Advanced Placement program. National recognition for Woodberry teachers includes Klingenstein fellowships at Columbia, Coe fellowships at Stanford, Woodrow Wilson fellowships at Princeton, Japan Foundation fellowships, Fulbright fellowships, and College Board recognition.

The School also employs part-time instructors, who teach Advanced Drawing, Sculpture, Typing, Photography, and Instrumental Music. Two nurses staff the 24-bed infirmary.

STUDENT BODY. In 1999–2000, Woodberry Forest enrolls 397 boarders as follows: Grade 9—79, Grade 10—114, Grade 11—91, and Grade 12—113. They represent 21 states, the District of Columbia, and 12 foreign countries with the largest numbers coming from Virginia, North Carolina, South Carolina, Maryland, Texas, Georgia, Florida, and New York. International students come from Australia, Bahrain, Canada, China, Egypt, Germany, Indonesia, Japan, Korea, Saudi Arabia, Thailand, and the United Kingdom.

ACADEMIC PROGRAM. The school year, from mid-September to early June, is divided into three 11-week terms, with a Thanksgiving recess and Christmas and spring vacations. Classes, which have an average enrollment of 10–12 students, meet three days a week from 8:00 A.M. to 3:15 P.M., two days a week from 8:00 A.M. to noon, and on Saturday mornings. Athletics are scheduled after 3:15 P.M., and there is a nightly study period during which most boys are permitted to work in their dormitory rooms. Academic reports, with comments from both teachers and the faculty adviser, are sent to parents six times a year.

All courses are offered on a trimester basis. To graduate, students must complete 12 trimesters (4 years) of English; 3 years of one foreign language; 8 trimesters of history; 12 of mathematics; 9 trimesters of laboratory sciences; and 1 trimester each of art, music, and religion. In addition, they must participate in athletics or the fine arts and complete 60 hours of community service, 30 of which must be contact hours.

Among the required and elective courses offered are Creative Writing, Romanticism, Poetry, The Novel, Drama; French 1–5, German 1–4, Latin 1–5, Spanish 1–5, Japanese 1–5; Modern European History, United States History, Economics, U.S. Government, Comparative Government; Algebra 1–2, Geometry, Calculus, Finite Mathematics, Discrete Mathematics, Statistics; Biology, Chemistry, Physics, Physical Science, Environmental Science, Animal Behavior, Psychology; Bible Survey, World Religions; and Studio Art, Photography, Choir, and Band.

Advanced Placement-level courses are offered in 27 subjects. Independent study can be arranged. In English, third and fourth formers take grammar, writing, and a genre sequence. Juniors and seniors take literature survey courses.

One hundred percent of the graduates are accepted by four-year colleges and universities. Graduates from the past four years are attending such institutions as Brown, Dartmouth, Davidson, Duke, Georgetown, Hampden-Sydney, Harvard, Oberlin, Princeton, Southern Methodist, Stanford, Trinity (Connecticut), Vanderbilt, Wake Forest, Washington and Lee,

Williams, Yale, and the Universities of North Carolina (Chapel Hill), Pennsylvania, Richmond, and Virginia.

The School conducts two summer programs—a coeducational academic session and a sports camp for boys ages 10 to 13. The academic session, open to students from Woodberry Forest and other schools, provides opportunities for review work in areas of skill deficiencies and advanced work for those students seeking additional credits. Special programs include Woodberry Forest Overseas (Austria, England, France, Japan, Scotland, and Spain) and the Youth Scholars Program. Tuition for the six-week session is $4100. The sports camp enrolls 140 boys for four weeks in a recreational program conducted by recent Woodberry graduates. The charge for the camp session is $2500.

STUDENT ACTIVITIES. The elected Prefect Board administers the Honor System, assists in the organization of dormitory life, and represents student opinion to the faculty and Headmaster. Both students and faculty are involved in the Chapel Council, working with the school minister to plan worship services, discussion groups, and social action projects.

Students may join the staffs of the various school publications (the yearbook, the literary magazine, or the newspaper). In the arts, instruction and studios are provided for painting, drawing, sculpture, pottery, photography, and woodworking. Other extracurricular organizations include the Student Council, the Glee Club, the Dramatics Society, the Algonquin Society, the Writers' Symposium, the Service Committee, the Academic Team, the Minority Caucus, Boy Scouts, Students Against Drunk Driving, Cheerleaders, and the Book, Chess, Computer, Debate, Investment, Math, Paintball, Rod and Gun, Scuba, and W clubs.

Several levels of interscholastic competition are offered in baseball, basketball, cross-country, football, golf, lacrosse, soccer, squash, swimming, tennis, indoor and outdoor track, and wrestling. The School also conducts a program of outdoor activities modeled on Outward Bound.

There are regular trips to events in the District of Columbia and Charlottesville, Richmond, and Williamsburg, Virginia, as well as films, lectures, and concerts on campus. Traditional events for the school community include dances, plays, Parents' Weekend, alumni reunions, and Amici Night.

ADMISSION AND COSTS. Applicants are admitted to Grades 9 and 10, and occasionally to Grade 11, on the basis of teacher appraisals of motivation, intellectual interests, and study habits and a principal's report on citizenship, integrity, and extracurricular activities. Candidates should also take the Secondary School Admission Test; a personal interview and visit to the School are required. The School has a policy of admitting students without regard to national, racial, or religious background. Application should be made by February 15 of the year of desired enrollment.

In 1999–2000, boarding tuition is $22,400. Extras are books and supplies ($300) and a personal allowance (suggested maximum of $300 per year). A tuition payment plan and tuition insurance are available. In 1999–2000, Woodberry Forest awarded approximately $1,600,000 in need-based financial aid and loans to 27 percent of the students.

Dean of Faculty: Marcus A. Hogan
Dean of Students: Michael E. Collins
Director of Alumni-Parent Programs: James C. S. Holladay '72
Director of Admissions: Brendan J. O'Shea, Assistant Head
Director of Development and External Affairs: Richard F. Barnhardt '66, Associate Head
Director of College Counseling: Andrew H. Abbott
Chief Financial Officer: Eric N. Chafin
Director of Athletics: William L. Davis

WASHINGTON

Annie Wright School 1884

827 North Tacoma Avenue, Tacoma, WA 98403. 253-272-2216
or 800-847-1582; Fax 253-572-3616;
E-mail admission@aw.org; Web Site www.aw.org

Annie Wright is a college preparatory school enrolling 320 day boys and girls in Prekindergarten–Grade 8 and 140 boarding and day girls in Grades 9–12. The School offers a rigorous and diverse academic program, including classes in Japanese, Art & Music History, comparative religions, and anatomy and physiology. Students enjoy a wide range of extracurricular activities including computer and science club, community service, sailing, crew, and choir. English as a Second Language is available. Boarding Tuition: $24,730; Day Tuition: $6105–$12,030. Financial Aid: $550,000. Aylin Flanagan is Director of Admission; Robert D. Klarsch (Brown University, B.A.; Wesleyan University, M.A.) is Headmaster. *Northwest Association.*

The Bush School 1924

405 36th Avenue East, Seattle, WA 98112. 206-322-7978;
Fax 206-860-3876; E-mail admin@bush.edu;
Web Site www.bush.edu

Helen Taylor Bush founded this day school to provide an environment that sparks a lifelong passion for learning, accomplishment, and community contribution. The Bush School enrolls 545 boys and girls in Kindergarten–Grade 12. The college preparatory program emphasizes high academic standards, values diversity, and promotes interdependence. The curriculum includes advanced science, math, and writing programs, foreign languages, technology, the arts, and challenging electives. Sports, student government, wilderness program, and required community service are among the activities. Extended-day care is offered. Tuition: $10,940–$14,990. Financial Aid: $798,000. Mandi Stewart Counter is Director of Admission; Timothy M. Burns, Ph.D., is Headmaster. *Northwest Association.*

Charles Wright Academy 1957

7723 Chambers Creek Road West, Tacoma, WA 98467-2099.
253-620-8300; Fax 253-620-8431;
Web Site www.charleswright.org

A nonprofit, coeducational, college preparatory day school set on a 90-acre, wooded campus, Charles Wright Academy enrolls 685 students in Pre-Kindergarten–Grade 12. Advanced Placement, computer science, drama, art and music, outdoor education, and athletics are integral to the program. Each student's unique academic and artistic abilities, confidence, and sense of values are developed and nurtured by a carefully selected faculty within a community that respects and cares for the well-being of each member. Honesty, integrity, courage, and humor are essential to the school's individual and collective strength and growth. Tuition: $6760–$11,305. Financial aid is available. Noel Blyler is Director of Admissions; Robert Camner (Oberlin, B.A.; Ohio State, M.S.) is Headmaster. *Pacific Northwest Association.*

Epiphany School 1958

3710 East Howell Street, Seattle, WA 98122. 206-323-9011;
Fax 206-324-2127

Epiphany School is an independent, nonsectarian day school enrolling 136 boys and girls in Pre-School–Grade 6. It seeks to help students achieve academic excellence through a traditional, structured approach to learning with strong emphasis on fundamentals. Music, art, French, physical education, drama, library skills, science, and computers enrich the basic curriculum. The School also offers an intensive tutoring program for its students with language disabilities. Tuition: $6120–$8368. Financial Aid: $60,000. David Selby (Washington University, M.A. 1976) was appointed Head of School in 1994. *Northwest Association.*

The Evergreen School 1963

15201 Meridian Avenue North, Shoreline, WA 98133.
206-364-2650; Admissions 206-364-0801; Fax 206-365-1827;
E-mail lfcalvin@evergreenschool.org

Enrolling 325 highly capable and culturally diverse day students in PreSchool–Grade 8, Evergreen's Global Education curriculum is designed for children with advanced and creative learning potential. Small classes feature individualized programs offering strong academic focus with creative opportunity. Environmental awareness, writing, math, and computer skills are emphasized. French, German, Chinese, and Spanish are offered; science, art, music, and physical education are taught at all levels. Students are encouraged to develop inquiry, problem solving, and positive attitudes. Intelligence testing is required in Kindergarten–Grade 8. Tuition: $4880–$12,000. Financial Aid: $130,000. Bruce D. Shoup (John Carroll, B.A. 1971; Antioch, M.Ed. 1975) is Headmaster.

Forest Ridge School of the Sacred Heart 1907

4800 139th Avenue, SE, Bellevue, WA 98006. 425-641-0700;
Fax 425-643-3881; Web Site www.forestridge.org

Founded in 1907, Forest Ridge is a Catholic, independent, college preparatory school for young women in Grades 5–12. As a member of an international network of 200 Sacred Heart schools, it is committed to diversity, community service, academic excellence, and lifelong learning. The program features small classes, a worldwide exchange program, and a technology-enhanced learning environment. Graduates think for themselves and exercise influence on their surroundings through leadership and service to their families, communities, nation, and world. Tuition: $13,202. Financial Aid: $500,000. Deborah Krogman is Admissions Director; Mona H. Bailey (Florida A&M University, B.S.; Oregon State University, M.S.) is Head of School.

Holy Names Academy 1880

728 21st Avenue East, Seattle, WA 98112. 206-323-4272;
Fax 206-323-5254; E-mail admissions@holynames-sea.org;
Web Site holynames-sea.org

Holy Names Academy, the oldest continually operating school in Washington, enrolls 520 young women in a college preparatory program encompassing Grades 9–12. As a Catholic institution, Holy Names seeks to challenge students to academic excellence within a thoroughly Christian, values-based environment. The curriculum emphasizes the liberal arts and sciences, including required theology classes and 11 Advanced Placement courses. Girls participate in a variety of activities such as special liturgies and retreats through the Campus Ministry, drama, music and vocal groups, publications, and athletics, including crew and lacrosse. Tuition: $6828. Financial Aid: $325,000. Michelle Hui is Admissions and Marketing Director; Elizabeth Switz (University of Washington, B.A., M.A.) is Principal. *Northwest Association.*

Lakeside School 1919

14050 1st Avenue NE, Seattle, WA 98125-3099. 206-368-3600;
Fax 206-368-3638; E-mail admissions@lakesideschool.org;
Web Site www.lakesideschool.org

A day school enrolling 708 boys and girls in Grades 5–12, Lakeside offers a rigorous liberal arts curriculum in an atmosphere of high expectations. The School seeks to "lead students to take responsibility for learning" as preparation for lifelong learning. Lakeside enrolls students from diverse backgrounds, encouraging individual achievement in an environment of respect and trust. Community service, outdoor education, sports, and opportunities for international study are among the offerings. Tuition: $13,810–$14,380. Extras: $200–$700. Financial Aid: $1,200,000. Rachael Beare is Director of Admissions; Bernie Noe (Boston University, B.A.; Georgetown, M.A.; George Washington University, M.Ph.) was appointed Head in 1998. *Pacific Northwest Association.*

The Little School 1959

2812 116th Avenue, NE, Bellevue, WA 98004. 425-827-8708;
Fax 425-827-3814; E-mail little@nwlink.com;
Web Site www.TheLittleSchool.org

The Little School, serving 170 students ages 3–12, nurtures and supports children's development in social, emotional, physical, and cognitive areas. Students are active participants in the learning process; their individual developmental timetables are respected and their interests fuel the curriculum. The 11-acre wooded campus is an ideal setting for an approach that values creativity, cooperation, and self-motivation. Special teacher resources and field trips promote community and multicultural awareness. A half-day option for ages 3–5, before- and after-school programs, and a summer program are offered. Tuition: $4900–$9100. Financial aid is available. Paul Brahce is Director. *Northwest Association.*

Saint George's School 1955

West 2929 Waikiki Road, Spokane, WA 99208. 509-466-1636;
Fax 509-462-4967; Web Site www.sgs.org

Saint George's School, a nonsectarian, college preparatory day school, enrolls 320 students in Kindergarten–Grade 12. In a nurturing environment, the School seeks to provide a rigorous liberal arts education. Saint George's creates a close, supportive community through small classes and dynamic, caring teachers. The School lives by core values of respect, honesty, generosity, and doing one's best. Students are encouraged to realize their full potential in academic work, the arts, and athletics. Advanced Placement courses are offered in ten subjects, and interscholastic teams compete in seven sports. Tuition: $8040–$10,125. Financial Aid: $580,000. Reggy Thomas is Director of Admissions; Jonathan E. Slater (Hamilton, A.B.; Stanford, M.B.A.; Columbia, M.A.) was appointed Headmaster in 1994.

St. Thomas School 1951

P.O. Box 124, Medina, WA 98039. 425-454-5880;
Fax 425-454-1921; E-mail info@stthomasschool.org

In an environment that stresses personal values and a challenging, innovative academic program, St. Thomas School enrolls 180 students in Pre-school–Grade 6. St. Thomas's curriculum is designed for bright, highly motivated students and focuses on the mastery of thinking and learning skills. Reading, oral and written communication, and math receive strong emphasis and are supplemented with programs in science, technology, social studies, the arts, physical education, and Spanish. Latin is introduced in Grade 5. Daily Chapel fosters spiritual development. Extended care is optional. Tuition: $1970–$9570. Financial aid

is available. Jaynee Cadrez is Director of Admission; Joan Beauregard (Annhurst, B.A.; Federal City College, M.A.T.) is Head of School.

Seattle Academy 1993

1201 East Union Street, Seattle, WA 98122. 206-323-6600;
Fax 206-323-6618

Seattle Academy was established by Jean Marie Orvis to offer a superior college preparatory program that incorporates academics with the arts, athletics, outdoor education, and community service. Enrolling 390 day boys and girls in Grades 6–12, the school provides a supportive environment that maximizes the learning experience through hands-on activities and extensive use of classroom technology and Seattle's urban resources. The curriculum includes rigorous college preparatory academic courses and the fine and performing arts. Student government, sports, and travel to Canyonlands and Alaska enrich the program. Tuition: $13,000. Extras: $510. Financial aid is available. Jean Marie Orvis (University of Washington, B.A. 1968, M.B.A. 1982) is Founding Head of School.

Seattle Country Day School 1963

2619 Fourth Avenue North, Seattle, WA 98109. 206-284-6220;
Fax 206-283-4251; E-mail info@scds.org;
Web Site www.seattlecds.org

Seattle Country Day School, serving 300 boys and girls in Kindergarten–Grade 8, seeks to challenge students who possess strong creative problem-solving potential. Differentiated programs are structured for children of high intellectual and creative promise, providing educational experiences suitable to their abilities and learning styles. The curriculum includes challenging academics enriched with experiential and lab sciences, comprehensive computer science, art, music, and foreign language. Among the activities are alpine skiing, chess, team sports, and drama. A summer program is available. Tuition: $9800–$11,000. Dr. Larry Goldberg is Director of Admissions; Jayasri Ghosh (University of Calcutta, B.A.; University of Georgia, M.Ed., Ph.D.) was appointed Head of School in 1986. *Northwest Association.*

Thomas Academy 1964

20 49th Street, Auburn, WA 98002. 206-852-4437;
Fax 206-852-4891

Thomas Academy is a coeducational school for children in Pre-Kindergarten–Grade 8. Its mission is to offer a program of studies and activities that will prepare young students for the next stage of their precollegiate education and that will inspire in them the beginnings of an enduring love of learning. The school intends to be a teaching and learning community where eagerness to learn, hard work, and cheerful willingness to participate are honored. The rich, varied program includes excursions and field trips, community service, visual and performing arts, foreign language, and physical education at all levels. The student-teacher ratio is 9:1, and capacity enrollment is 180. Tuition: $6490. Karen Luce is Admissions Coordinator; Michael L. Grella (Kenyon, A.B. 1963) is Headmaster.

University Child Development School 1976

5062 9th Avenue NE, Seattle, WA 98105. 206-547-5059;
Fax 206-547-3615; E-mail kathrynl@ucds.org;
Web Site www.ucds.org

Designed to meet the intellectual and social/emotional needs of capable students, University Child Development School combines academic challenge with a hands-on, integrated curriculum. Enrolling 289 children in Preschool through Grade 5, the School's individualized curriculum encourages high-level thinking within a context of personal and intellectual exploration. Summer camp and before- and after-school care are available. Tuition: $9525. Financial Aid: $150,000. Melissa Masters is Admissions Director; Paula Smith is Head of School. *Pacific Northwest Association.*

University Prep   1976

*8000 25th Avenue, NE, Seattle, WA 98115. 206-525-2714;
    Admissions 206-523-6407; Fax 206-525-5320;
    E-mail admission@universityprep.org;
    Web Site www.universityprep.org*

University Prep offers a college preparatory education to students in Grades 6–12 who are able and willing to benefit from the program. The curriculum includes a balanced liberal arts and sciences program in a nurturing environment. Students are encouraged to become inquiring, compassionate adults with a sound sense of self and an appreciation for their roles in a diverse world. Electives include computer science, fine arts, economics, civil rights, law, and contemporary issues. Three levels of sports, Youth & Government, Mock Trial, Amnesty International, publications, clubs, and social activities are offered. Tuition: $12,825–$13,074. Financial Aid: $340,739. Roger D. Cibella is Admission Director; Roger J. Bass (University of Washington, B.A., M.A.) is Head of School. *Northwest Association.*

Villa Academy   1978

*5001 Northeast 50th Street, Seattle, WA 98105. 206-524-8885;
    Fax 206-523-7131; E-mail lmaughan@ricochet.net;
    Web Site www.thevilla.org*

Villa Academy, a Catholic, independent day school enrolling 500 boys and girls in Kindergarten–Grade 8, seeks to provide an academic education that emphasizes critical thinking, creativity, and fundamental skills while integrating Christian values into the learning process. Religion, computer laptops, music, art, foreign languages, speech, drama, photography, and physical education enrich the curriculum in small class-size settings. The school environment fosters values of respect, self-esteem, personal responsibility, leadership, and diversity. Extended-day program, before- and after-school care, and sports are offered. Tuition: $6975–$7290. Financial aid is available. Lori Maughan is Director of Admissions; Pauline Skinner is Head of School. *Northwest Association.*

WEST VIRGINIA

The Linsly School   WHEELING

60 Knox Lane, Wheeling, WV 26003-6489. 304-233-3260;
Admissions 304-233-1436; Fax 304-234-4614;
E-mail admit@linsly.org; Web Site www.linsly.org

THE LINSLY SCHOOL in Wheeling, West Virginia, is a college preparatory boarding and day school enrolling boys and girls in Grades 5 through 12. Five- and seven-day boarding is provided for students in Grades 7–12. Wheeling (population 37,500) is situated on the Ohio River in the northern portion of the state, approximately one hour from Pittsburgh, Pennsylvania, to the northeast and two hours from Columbus, Ohio, to the west.

Linsly is the oldest college preparatory school west of the Allegheny Mountains and the only independent day and boarding school in West Virginia. The original school, known as the Wheeling Lancastrian Academy, was founded as a coeducational institution in 1814 through a bequest by former Wheeling mayor Noah Linsly. The School became an all-male institution in 1840 and became a military institute in 1876. In 1968, Linsly moved to its present location and, by 1979, had shifted its military emphasis to embrace a college preparatory program. Coeducation was restored in 1988.

As West Virginia's only independent, college preparatory day and boarding school, Linsly aims to provide a structured, disciplined program that will challenge its students to reach their highest potential intellectually, physically, socially, and morally. Faculty work closely with students in the classroom and serve as role models and mentors in all areas of school activities. The conduct of daily life is based on principles of mutual respect and cooperation, and students are encouraged to accept responsibility, express themselves openly, and develop a strong sense of self-awareness and self-confidence. Boys and girls adhere to a dress code designed to distinguish them by their accomplishments rather than by their appearance.

The Linsly School is accredited by the North Central Association of Colleges and Schools, the Independent Schools Association of the Central States, and the State of West Virginia. It holds membership in the National Association of Independent Schools, The College Board, Educational Records Bureau, and the National Association of College Admissions Counselors.

THE CAMPUS. Situated in a residential area near Oglebay Park, one of the state's most beautiful recreational attractions, Linsly's 65-acre campus features 17 buildings, including a central academic complex containing classrooms, four new art stu-

dios, science and computer laboratories, a campus bookstore, and the Coudon-Ogden Library. Students reside in four dormitories. Athletic facilities include playing fields, a field house, two gymnasiums, and a swimming pool.

THE FACULTY. Reno F. DiOrio was appointed Headmaster of The Linsly School in 1979. He holds a bachelor of arts degree from Dickinson College and an M.Ed. from the University of Dayton.

All 47 faculty members hold baccalaureate degrees; about half have master's degrees; and 2 have earned doctorates representing study at such institutions as Allegheny College, Appalachian State, Bethany College, Bucknell, Cambridge College, College of William and Mary, Dickinson, Eastern Illinois, Edinboro University, Hillsdale College, Loyola (Chicago), Miami University of Ohio, North Carolina Wesleyan, Rice, State University of New York (Oswego), Washington and Lee, West Chester University, West Liberty State, West Virginia University, West Virginia Wesleyan, Western Michigan, Wheeling University, and the Universities of Dayton, Detroit, Georgia, Notre Dame, Pavia (Italy), Pittsburgh, Utah, and West Florida.

STUDENT BODY. In 1999–2000, Linsly enrolls 337 day students and 85 boarders, 182 girls and 240 boys. There are 138 in the Lower School (Grades 5–8) and 284 in the Upper School (Grades 9–12). Boarding students come predominantly from Pennsylvania, Ohio, and West Virginia and represent a diversity of racial, religious, and ethnic backgrounds. Linsly also enjoys an international flavor, with students this year from Australia, Japan, and Korea.

ACADEMIC PROGRAM. The school year, divided into semesters, begins in September and extends to late May, with vacations scheduled at Thanksgiving, at Christmas, and in the spring. A student-faculty ratio of 10:1 allows small classes and attention to the individual student. The School's advisory system provides guidance from faculty in academic and personal matters.

While students are encouraged to take responsibility for their own education, there is close interaction between faculty and parents to monitor progress. Teachers are available for extra help in all subjects before and after school and by appointment, and further assistance is provided through the Prefect-Tutor program, which matches qualified students to work with their peers who are experiencing academic difficulties. Each day's schedule includes one flex period during which students are free to undertake independent study, work on a project with classmates, review upcoming lessons, or meet with faculty on a one-to-one basis. Boarding students have study halls each weekday evening from 7:00 to 9:30 P.M.

The departmentalized program of study in the Lower

School is designed to develop sound work habits as well as academic preparation for the transition to the Upper School. Study and organizational skills are emphasized throughout the curriculum. The core program in the Lower School includes English/language arts, social studies, mathematics, science, foreign languages, physical education/health, and art and music.

Students in the Upper School carry at least five courses per semester. Full-credit courses meet daily; some half-credit courses meet three times a week. To graduate, students must earn a minimum of 20 credits as follows: four years of English and mathematics, three years of history and a foreign language, two years of science and physical education, one course in art/music, and one course in computer science.

Courses available in the Upper School include English I–IV, Humanities, Creative and Expository Writing, Post Modern Fiction, Women in Literature, Speech; French I–IV, German I–IV, Latin I–IV, Spanish I–IV; Civilizations I–III, Economics, Psychology; Algebra I–III, Geometry, Probability & Statistics, Pre-Calculus, AB&BC Calculus; Biology I–II, Chemistry I–III, Physics, Environmental Science; Art Appreciation, Music Appreciation, Theater Arts, Studio Art, Music Theory; Computer Science I–IV, Computer Awareness, Web Page Development, Typing; Physical Education I–II, Band, Yearbook, and Chorus.

The Linsly Outdoor Center (LOC), in Pennsylvania's Raccoon Creek State Park, is the focal point of the School's adventure, environmental, and wilderness programs. All students spend several days of the school year at LOC, where they participate in a combination of the three available programs. Hands-on exploration and rigorous activities such as whitewater rafting, spelunking, and a ropes course give students an appreciation and understanding of their world and themselves.

Each spring, faculty-led trips are offered to explore the cultures of such places as France, Italy, Switzerland, Austria, Germany, and the Caribbean.

College counseling begins in the sophomore year when students sit for their first PSATs and SATs. Taking these exams a year early allows students to become familiar with their test-taking abilities and plan their courses wisely.

One hundred percent of the 68 graduates in Linsly's Class of 1999 entered college. They are enrolled at such institutions as Allegheny, Bethany, Catholic University, Clemson, College of Charleston, Columbia, Cornell, Duke, Elon, George Washington, Hampden-Sydney, Kenyon, Loyola, Miami, Oberlin, Ohio State, Ohio Wesleyan, Purdue, Vanderbilt, Virginia Polytechnic, Wake Forest, Wesleyan, West Virginia University, and the University of Dayton.

STUDENT ACTIVITIES. Linsly provides a wide range of extracurricular options considered essential to the overall educational process. The Student Life program gives each boy and girl the opportunity to express his or her individuality through participation in activities that meet a variety of needs and interests. In the Upper School, there are approximately 35 School-sponsored organizations including Library Guild, SADD, Forensics, Junior Town Meeting Team, yearbook and newspaper staffs, Stage Band, Chorus, Quiz Kids, Wing Society (literature group), Ad Staff, Writing Forum, and the Chess and Backgammon, Key (service), Environmental, Math, Science Research, History, Shakespeare, Multicultural, Astronomy, Cartoonist, Firearms, Outdoor Adventure, Classics, Camera, Technology, and foreign language clubs. Qualified students may be invited to join the National Honor Society and honor societies for German, Latin, French, and Spanish. Lower School students have a similar diversity of clubs and organizations appropriate to their age group. Each year since 1938, the entire student body has staged the Linsly Musical Extravaganza, performed before 1500 people at Wheeling's Capitol Music Hall.

Guest speakers from different professions and backgrounds are invited to the campus regularly to share their experiences and insights with the student body.

As a member of the Ohio Valley Athletic Conference and the Interstate Preparatory School League, Linsly fields 19 interscholastic teams in baseball, basketball, cross-country, football, golf, soccer, swimming, tennis, track, and wrestling for boys; and basketball, cheerleading, cross-country, soccer, softball, swimming, tennis, track, and volleyball for girls. Lower School students compete intramurally and interscholastically in basketball, football, soccer, swimming, track, and cross-country. An average of 90 percent of all Linsly students participate in interscholastic athletics each year.

Weekend activities for boarding students may involve school dances, informal parties, recreational sports, and trips off campus to ball games, the zoo, a ski resort, a shopping mall, or nearby Oglebay Park.

Community service projects engage students in outreach activities with at-risk youth, senior citizens, the Red Cross, Easter Seals, and other worthwhile pursuits.

ADMISSION AND COSTS. Linsly welcomes students of good character, ability, and motivation who are enthusiastic about pursuing a demanding college preparatory program and are willing to become fully involved in a lively academic community. Acceptance is based on the student's previous record, results of a School-administered admissions test, and a personal interview.

In 1999–2000, tuition and fees are $8500 for day students and $17,200 for boarders. Linsly belongs to the School and Student Service for Financial Aid and annually awards financial aid to nearly 20 percent of the students based on need. The Linsly School admits students of any race, color, national or ethnic origin.

Assistant Headmaster/Business Manager: Terry Depew
Academic Dean: Cheryl M. Sprague
Dean of the Lower School: Gary Sprague
Dean of Students: David Plumby '72
Director of Admissions: James Hawkins '58
Director of Development: John Hershey
Director of College Placement: John Whitehead
Director of Athletics: Daniel Buchwach

WISCONSIN

Brookfield Academy   1962

3460 North Brookfield Road, Brookfield, WI 53045. 414-783-3200

Founded in 1962 to provide a strong liberal arts education within a nurturing atmosphere, Brookfield enrolls 630 day students in Pre-Kindergarten–Grade 12. The school's Five Star system emphasizes the moral principles of a free society, and patriotism and ethics are promoted at all levels. The college preparatory curriculum also includes classics, computers, music, art, and Advanced Placement opportunities. Upper School students experience a week of outdoor recreation and sports at the start of each academic year. Activities include yearbook, drama, and community service. Tuition: $5300–$9250. Financial aid is available. Sharon Koenings is Director of Admissions; Robert Solsrud (Marquette, M.Ed.) was appointed Head of the School in 1993.

Catholic Memorial High School   1948

601 East College Avenue, Waukesha, WI 53186-5598.
  414-542-7101; Fax 414-542-1633

Catholic Memorial, a coeducational, regional secondary school, was founded to educate students toward lifelong Catholic values, academic excellence, and personal development. Serving more than 1000 young people from parishes in Waukesha County, the School offers curricula designed to serve college-bound students and those who plan to enter the work force after graduation. Religious studies, Honors and Advanced Placement opportunities, offerings in the fine arts, and courses in business, home economics, and technical drafting classes are available. Students participate in numerous clubs and interest groups, leadership organizations, and varsity athletics for boys and girls. Tuition: $3925–$4625. Beverly McCarthy is Admissions Director; Dr. Bryan Van Deun is President. *North Central Association.*

Oaklawn Academy   EDGERTON

432 Liguori Road, Edgerton, WI 53534-9340. 608-884-3425;
  Fax 608-884-8175; E-mail oaklawnusa@aol.com;
  Web Site www.oak-international.org

Oaklawn Academy in Edgerton, Wisconsin, is a Roman Catholic boarding school enrolling boys in Grades 6 through 8. It is situated in a rural area on the shore of Lake Koshkonong, about 2 miles from the center of Edgerton, a farming community of about 10,000. The lake is a popular setting for fishing, boating, and water sports. Open spaces in the country setting afford opportunities for recreation and relaxation for both faculty and students. Madison, the state capital, is 25 miles distant and Chicago is about two hours away. The Academy makes use of the cultural resources of nearby cities in regular Monday all-school outings. The campus is located just off Interstate 90. Buses link the community to O'Hare International Airport, near Chicago, which provides the principal access for visiting parents.

The Academy was founded in Cheshire, Connecticut, in 1984 by the Legionaries of Christ and moved to its present site in 1986. The Legion of Christ is a religious order founded in 1941 by the Reverend Marcial Maciel, and its priests and seminarians are active in 27 nations in education, the media, youth and family apostolates, campus ministry, and missions. The Academy itself was founded to provide English education and Christian formation for boys from the United States and other countries. The curriculum is coordinated with the programs of other schools of the Legionaries of Christ worldwide.

Oaklawn Academy seeks to provide a cultural experience, bringing students into contact with the educational resources of the United States. It also aims to develop spirit and character in the individual—a sense of justice, sincerity, honesty, teamwork, and loyalty along with determination and endurance. These characteristics are developed to help the student value and judge the world, nature, and humanity and form the basis of his ethical-religious development. Daily Mass and religious instruction in the Catholic faith are provided. Students follow an active schedule seven days a week and a uniform dress code is observed.

The Academy is owned and operated by the Legion of Christ. The alumni of the school number 3500. They maintain contact with the Academy and have assisted in funding the Riding School, the computer laboratory, the library, and the language laboratory.

THE CAMPUS. The Academy is situated on 207 acres fronting on Lake Koshkonong. About half of the acreage is cultivated as farmland and 100 acres are maintained as lawns and playing fields. Two tournament soccer fields, baseball diamonds, various practice fields, eight tennis courts, four handball courts, two covered riding arenas, and a stable for 25 horses are available on campus.

The school buildings were all constructed in 1958. The main building houses the reception area and offices and has wings for staff, students, and the religious community. In addition to regular classrooms, the facilities provide a number of special features including two game rooms, two gymnasiums, a 70-by-30-foot indoor swimming pool, 396-seat auditorium, music rehearsal rooms, chapel, dining room, modern kitchen, a library, a language laboratory, and a computer laboratory.

A laundry is operated on campus and the school can provide its own water supply. There are shops for maintenance of vehicles and other equipment.

THE FACULTY. The Reverend Anthony Bannon, L.C., a graduate of the Gregorian University and Angelicum University in Rome, with degrees in philosophy and theology, is Head of Oaklawn Academy. He is a consultant to other schools in Connecticut, Michigan, New Hampshire, Rhode Island, and Texas.

Nine men and three women comprise the full-time faculty. Seven hold baccalaureate degrees from the University of Wisconsin and one from the University of Oklahoma. Twelve part-time teachers are employed for instruction in singing, sports clinics, and study hall. Twelve deans and assistants are engaged in administration and supervision of student life.

An infirmary is operated by two nurses and a visiting doctor; a hospital is located two miles away. The University of Wisconsin Medical Center can be reached in 30 minutes by car.

STUDENT BODY. In 1998–99, the Academy enrolled 190 boarding boys in Grades 6–8. The enrollments were distributed as follows: Grade 6–35, Grade 7–90, and Grade 8–65. Students come from Arizona, California, Florida, Illinois, Texas, Wisconsin, Chile, Colombia, Ireland, Italy, Mexico, Spain, and Venezuela.

ACADEMIC PROGRAM. The academic year begins in mid-September and extends to mid-June. Students are under the direction of the Academy for virtually all of that time. A ten-day trip to Rome, including a Christmas Eve Mass at the Vatican and an audience with the Pope, is scheduled in December, and a seven-day trip to Washington, D.C., and New York City is scheduled at Easter. Classes are held five days a week, Tuesday through Saturday, and are scheduled in eight 40-minute sessions between 9:00 A.M. and 4:00 P.M. and in two evening study halls between 6:30 and 8:00 P.M. Sports clinics are conducted each afternoon before dinner. Sundays are devoted to a schedule of special activities and recreations, and Mondays are reserved for all-school outings that include museum trips, sightseeing, and skiing in the winter.

The academic year is divided into five units of six or seven weeks each and grades are recorded and sent to parents after the completion of each unit. Final examinations follow completion of the fifth unit. The average class size is 18. Evening study halls are held in classrooms supervised by deans who are available during those hours to provide extra help. Intensive instruction is offered in English as a Second Language, and all foreign students take the PRETOEFL, Test of English as a Foreign Language, before returning to their own countries to complete their schooling. Many return to the United States for secondary or college education.

The standard curriculum is required for all students and includes English, Spanish, Geography, History, Mathematics, Science, Computers, Band, Choir, Horseback Riding, and Physical Education. All classes are small enough to require active participation and frequent presentations by each individual to the rest of the class.

A summer camp, the Master's Challenge Program, offers sports and recreation in a two- or four-week session for boarding boys in Grades 3–8. The camp is an international program attracting students from the same sources as the Academy. It features a variety of sports activities and two outings a week.

STUDENT ACTIVITIES. The student body is divided into sec-

tions of up to 54 boys each. Every section has its own dean and two assistants, at least one of whom is always present to supervise the activities of the section outside the classroom. The deans are in charge of discipline but are also friends and counselors to the students and they are expected to set examples of honesty and Christian charity for the boys to emulate.

A 50-piece brass band and a choir are major activities that enhance the academic program. In addition, each student chooses to participate in at least three clinics from among baseball, softball, swimming, tennis, karate, computer club, golf, hockey, soccer, and horseback riding.

Teams from Oaklawn Academy compete against other schools each year in the Wisconsin State Soccer Tournaments. For the past 11 years, Oaklawn teams took first place at two age levels.

School outings are set for every Monday and students visit the zoo, planetariums, museums, amusement parks, and ski slopes, and engage in such activities as skating and bowling. A full schedule of activities, all supervised by deans, is planned for each weekend.

Two days of closing ceremonies, at which parents are welcome, complete the school year. The activities include a picnic, Mass, a horse show, band and choir concert, and an awards ceremony.

ADMISSION AND COSTS. Oaklawn Academy seeks boys of junior high school age who have good academic potential and who are motivated to take full advantage of the program and culture of the school. Students are admitted to Grades 6 through 8 on the basis of previous academic records, references, psychological examination, and medical examination. Applications, with a fee of $300, should be submitted by August 15 for fall admission. Some students are accepted at midterm.

In 1998–99, boarding and tuition are $24,000, including trips to Rome, Washington, and New York as well as weekly outings, uniforms, books, and sports clinics. A personal expense account can be opened with the Academy. Some scholarships are available to meet special needs and they are awarded on an individual basis.

Principal: Javier Valenzuela
Vice Principal: Thomas Ryan
Director of Admissions: Javier Valenzuela
Business Manager: Br. Thang Bui, L.C.
Spiritual Director: Fr. Thomas Moylan, L.C.

The Prairie School   1965

*4050 Lighthouse Drive, Racine, WI 53402. 262-260-3845;
Fax 262-260-3790*

The Prairie School, serving 620 students in Early School–Grade 12, provides a progressive curriculum combining challenging academics, a comprehensive fine and creative arts program, and an exciting athletic program. Offerings include television/film production, glass-blowing, and Interim, a two-week career exploration program. The nontraditional campus, designed by Taliesin Associated Architects, houses the Student Research Center with computer labs and more than 300 computers, and the state-of-the-art, 28,000-square-foot Samuel C. Johnson Upper School. Summer school and before- and after-school care are available. Tuition: $6375–$8395. Wm. Mark H. Murphy (Norwich, B.A.; State University of New York, M.A.) is Headmaster.

St. John's Northwestern Military Academy
DELAFIELD

Delafield, WI 53018. 262-646-7115; Admissions 800-752-2338; E-mail admissions@sjma.org; Web Site www.sjnma.org

ST. JOHN'S NORTHWESTERN MILITARY ACADEMY in Delafield, Wisconsin, a college preparatory boarding school enrolling boys in Grades 7–12, recently joined forces with the Northwestern Military & Naval Academy, Lake Geneva, Wisconsin, to form the premier military academy of the Northwest. With more than 200 years of academic excellence, St. John's Northwestern continues to carry on the traditions of both schools on the Delafield campus. Delafield, a community of 5000 in the beautiful Kettle Moraine area of Wisconsin, is located 25 miles west of Milwaukee. The area affords excellent opportunities for outdoor recreation, including water sports and downhill skiing. Overnight accommodations are available in Delafield and the surrounding area. The Academy, less than a mile from Interstate 94, is easily accessible by car. Airline service is available in Milwaukee or Chicago.

The Academy, founded in 1884, provides a structured educational environment that fosters the development of the whole person as a knowledgeable, responsible, moral, and productive citizen. The four cornerstones of the school's philosophy are academics, athletics, leadership, and values; the emphasis on these is designed to encourage good study skills, positive attitudes toward work, intellectual curiosity, cultural appreciation,

self-discipline, teamwork, decision-making ability, personal honesty, and character.

St. John's Northwestern's JROTC Program is designated as an Honor Unit with Distinction by the United States Army, and its military organization and program afford special opportunities for leadership and personal accountability. Each day starts with reveille and a room inspection. Military drill is conducted once a week and cadets wear uniforms as daily dress. Civilian clothes are permitted only for off-campus recreation. Interdenominational chapel services are held twice a week and are required for all cadets.

The Academy is a nonprofit corporation governed by a 22-member Board of Trustees. The 5000 living alumni support fund-raising and social events of the Academy, and they are represented on the Board through the President of the Alumni Association.

St. John's Northwestern is accredited by the Independent Schools Association of the Central States and is a member of the National Association of Independent Schools, the Association of Military Colleges and Schools of the United States, and Midwest Boarding Schools.

THE CAMPUS. The Academy is situated on 150 wooded acres with a nine-hole golf course, a football field, two soccer fields, a baseball diamond, a five-lane quarter-mile track, nine tennis courts, a rifle range, and a parade field with a reviewing stand.

The facilities include two main academic buildings with classrooms, full science laboratories, computer labs, social studies and English resource rooms, an art studio, a darkroom, and the college placement center; a library with microfilm facilities computer support; Victory Memorial Chapel; a gymnasium with basketball courts, a wrestling room, weight rooms, swimming pool, a baseball practice area with a batting cage; a 400-seat dining hall with a movie screen; three barracks; and a recreation hall with a snack bar, a movie screen, wide-screen television, pool table, air hockey, indoor and outdoor air rifle ranges, and other facilities. Ten faculty houses, a 10-bed Infirmary, a barbershop, the Archives Museum, a garage and carpenter shop, a cadet store, and tailor shop are also located on the campus.

THE FACULTY. Rear Adm. Ronald J. Kurth, appointed President in 1998, graduated from the United States Naval Academy and earned his M.P.A. and Ph.D. from Harvard University. His distinguished 36-year military career includes service as commanding officer of a naval air station in Tennessee, U.S. Defense attaché at the American Embassy in Moscow, and President of the Naval War College in Newport, Rhode Island.

The full-time faculty consist of 35 men and 8 women. Twenty-four faculty members live on campus, including several with families.

The Academy physician holds daily visiting hours at the

Infirmary, and a full-time nursing staff is on duty 24 hours a day.

STUDENT BODY. The Academy enrolls 393 boarding boys ages 12–18 years. There are 75 cadets in Grades 7 and 8 and 318 cadets in Grades 9–12. The school maintains a diverse student body and includes cadets from 22 states as well as Azerbaijan, China, Indonesia, Japan, Korea, Mexico, Pakistan, Russia, Saudi Arabia, and Sweden.

ACADEMIC PROGRAM. The curriculum is designed to provide six years of academic study at the junior high and high school levels to prepare students for higher education. Small classes, averaging about 12 cadets, allow for individualized attention. A two-hour supervised study period each evening and a daily tutorial period are an integral part of the academic day, and a special daily tutorial period is scheduled as needed or requested for students requiring additional help. Academic progress reports are sent to parents every three to four weeks, and final grades are sent four times a year.

Cadets in Grades 7 and 8 take five subjects, including English, geography or history, mathematics, science, music/art, reading, computer applications, and humanities. Advanced eighth graders may also take selected freshman courses.

To graduate from the Academy, a student must complete in the Upper School a minimum of 20 credit units, including 4 of English, 2 of foreign language, 3 of social studies, 3 of mathematics, 3 of science including 2 of laboratory science, 1 of computer science, and the required Junior ROTC sequence. In addition, students can supplement their programs with electives in any field.

Among the courses offered in the Upper School are English 1–4, Reading, Journalism; German 1–4, Spanish 1–4; World Geography, United States History, World History, Twentieth Century United States History; Pre-Algebra, Algebra 1–2, Geometry, Trigonometry, Calculus; Computers 1–2; Biology, Physical Science, Chemistry, Physics; Art 1–4, Band; and Military Training 1–4. College credits can be earned in Calculus, Chemistry, and Biology. All students participate in a physical education program that emphasizes physical fitness and training in lifetime sports. Aviation Science is also available.

STUDENT ACTIVITIES. The student body is organized into a Corps of Cadets with a Battalion Staff and individual Companies led by cadets. The Corps is self-governing, and cadet leaders are responsible for much of the daily activity at the school. Every cadet has an opportunity to obtain a leadership position.

Among the many organized activities are the newspaper, yearbook, band, and choir; Chess and Drama clubs; and acolyte and Boy Scout groups.

Varsity and junior varsity teams compete against other midwestern schools in football, soccer, cross-country, golf, rugby, Tae Kwon Do, basketball, wrestling, hockey, swimming, riflery,

baseball, track, and tennis. Lower School teams also play interscholastic schedules. Cadets compete in an extensive intramural program that includes many of the above sports along with volleyball. Athletic clubs are formed for weight lifting, scuba diving, and downhill skiing/snowboarding.

Campus dances and other recreational activities, including movies, skating, collegiate and professional sports contests, theater, and museum trips, are scheduled on weekends.

Among the special events on the school calendar are Parents' Weekends, Homecoming, Mid-Winter Weekend with a formal military ball, President's Day, Founder's Day, Governor's Day, and Armed Forces Day.

ADMISSION AND COSTS. St. John's Northwestern Military Academy seeks students of high moral character with a willingness to set and attain worthy goals. Applicants are admitted into all grades on the basis of school transcripts, letters of recommendation, an entrance exam, and interviews with school officials. Applications must be submitted with a fee of $50. Some students are admitted at midyear.

For 1999–2000, boarding tuition is $20,500. A first-year fee of $1880 is required to cover uniforms and supplies. Bank accounts for incidental expenses are extra. Financial aid is awarded on the basis of need, scholarship, and contribution to the school. In 1998–99, $630,000 was awarded to 52 percent of the Corps of Cadets in financial aid and merit scholarships. The Academy subscribes to the School Scholarship Service.

Interim Dean: CPT Andrew Hepburn
Commandant of Cadets: MGYSGT Jeffrey Bialk
Chief of Staff: LTC William Washo
Director of Enrollment Services: MAJ Charles Moore
College Counselor: COL Robert Roehrkasse
Director of Athletics: MAJ Jay Wayland

University School of Milwaukee   1964

2100 West Fairy Chasm Road, Milwaukee, WI 53217.
  414-352-6000; Fax 414-352-8076;
  E-mail admissions@usm.k12.wi.us;
  Web Site www.usm.k12.wi.us

University School of Milwaukee is a nonsectarian, coeducational, college preparatory day school for 1068 students in Prekindergarten (age 3)–Grade 12. The School, which traces its roots back 150 years, offers a strong Advanced Placement program, interscholastic/intramural athletics, art, drama, music, and publications. More than $1,500,000 in financial aid and tuition remission was awarded in 1999–2000. Facilities include a 120-acre campus with playgrounds, an indoor ice rink, theater, and Woodwinds, a 5-acre outdoor environmental classroom. An extensive summer program features more than 200 offerings. Tuition: $4930–$12,360. Kathleen Friedman is Director of Admissions; Harvey B. Sperling (University of Colorado, B.A.; Washington University, M.A.) is Headmaster.

University Lake School   1956

4024 Nagawicka Road, Hartland, WI 53029. 414-367-6011;
Fax 414-367-3146; Web Site www.universitylake.org

University Lake School, a coeducational, college preparatory day school enrolling more than 330 students in Kindergarten–Grade 12, is set on a 170-acre wooded campus 30 miles west of Milwaukee in the city of Hartland. The school features challenging academics in small class sizes of no more than 15 students. Students participate in fine arts, athletics, and leadership-building classes. The student-teacher/advisor ratio is 10:1. University Lake offers a summer program of enrichment and recreation. Tuition: $8350–$9800. Tuition assistance and scholarships are available. Carla Rutley is Director of Admissions; D. Rodney Chamberlain (Elizabethtown College, B.S.; Pennsylvania State, M.Ed., D.Ed.) is Executive Headmaster.

Wayland Academy   BEAVER DAM

101 North University Avenue, Beaver Dam, WI 53916-2253.
920-885-3373; Admissions 800-860-7725; Fax 920-887-3373;
E-mail admissions@wayland.org; Web Site www.wayland.org

Wayland academy in Beaver Dam, Wisconsin, is a coeducational college preparatory school for boarding and day students in Grades 9 through 12. It is located in a small community (population 15,100) in Wisconsin dairy country, 160 miles northwest of Chicago, 60 miles northwest of Milwaukee, and 40 miles northeast of Madison. There is an interstate highway to the school, buses serve the community, train service is available in nearby Columbus, and plane connections may be made in Madison.

The Academy was established as a coeducational institution in 1855. Its nonsectarian program is based on the conviction that "there are lasting values that stem from religious and secular knowledge, and that these values should be made to influence social and moral behavior." The school seeks to foster the development of personality, responsibility, self-discipline, and "natural friendships between boys and girls" as well as the acquisition of the knowledge and skills needed "to appreciate the intellectual heritage of the past and to prepare for success in college."

A nonprofit corporation, Wayland Academy is directed by a 23-member Board of Trustees. The school's assets include a plant valued at $26,000,000 and productive endowments totaling $4,500,000. Parents, alumni, trustees, and friends support the Academy with more than $1,000,000 in annual gifts. The Academy is accredited by the North Central Association of Colleges and Schools and the Independent Schools Association of the Central States. It is a member of the National Association of Independent Schools and the Council for Advancement and Support of Education, among other organizations.

THE CAMPUS. The 55-acre landscaped campus includes Wayland Hall for underclass boys and Warren Hall for underclass girls. Connected units include the pool, Lindsay Auditorium, and the Student Union (1994). Most classes meet in the new academic center (1988), which contains 15 classrooms, 21 faculty offices, and reading and conference areas. Swan Library (1989) contains a collection of 23,000 books and 140 periodicals, the computer center, the Academic Dean's suite, and the Whiting Art Gallery. Discovery Hall (1969) houses classrooms, science laboratories, an observatory, and a plant room. Memorial Chapel, which contains ten music rooms in addition to a sanctuary for worship, and Roundy Hall, the administration building, complete the units fronting on the main drive. Other facilities are the President's home, Pickard Dining Hall, and 15 other buildings, including Glen and Ella Dye dormitories for upperclass girls and boys, respectively, and the Schoen House Infirmary.

The athletic facilities provide a quarter-mile track, 2 soccer fields, 2 football fields, baseball and softball diamonds, 11 tennis courts (2 of which are lighted), and the Academy Field House. The Field House contains space for 2 basketball courts or 4 tennis courts. There is also an indoor track, a pole-vault pit, and areas for wrestling and weight training. The new Student Union contains weight and exercise training rooms, an aerobics/dance studio, locker rooms, a squash court, TV lounge, snack bar, and an art studio.

THE FACULTY. Alfred W. Grieshaber was installed as 17th President in April 1996. He is a graduate of the United States Air Force Academy (B.S. 1965) and has served on the Air Force Academy faculty as well as on the Board of Directors of the Association of Graduates. He holds degrees from Syracuse University (M.A. 1973, Ph.D. 1991) and studied at National Defense University as a Senior Research Fellow. Dr. Grieshaber has also served as President of Northwestern Military & Naval Academy (1990–94), as Vice President of the Wisconsin Association of Independent Schools, and as a faculty member at the Colorado Springs School and Pikes Peak Community College (1994–95). The teaching faculty consist of 17 men and 7 women.

Twenty faculty and staff members, 9 with their families, live at the school. Faculty members hold 24 baccalaureate and 19 graduate degrees from such colleges and universities as Alma, Beloit, Carroll, Concordia, Dartmouth, Ohio University, Pennsylvania State, Rice, St. Olaf, Temple, Wayne State, Wesleyan, West Virginia, and the Universities of Chicago, London, Wisconsin, and Wyoming. Teacher benefits include Social Security and retirement and group insurance plans; sabbatical leaves are awarded annually.

STUDENT BODY. In 1999–2000, Wayland enrolled 80 boarding boys, 20 day boys, 72 boarding girls, and 21 day girls, in Grades 9–12, as follows: 39 in Grade 9, 46 in Grade 10, 62 in Grade 11, and 46 in Grade 12. Boarding students come primarily from Wisconsin and Illinois; others come from 20 states and Canada, Colombia, Germany, Hong Kong, Japan, Korea, Mexico, Saudi Arabia, Spain, Taiwan, Thailand, Venezuela, and Yugoslavia. They represent a variety of racial, religious, and socioeconomic backgrounds. Approximately 14 percent of the enrollment consists of minority students.

ACADEMIC PROGRAM. The school year, from August to the end of May, is divided into semesters. Included are 34 weeks of instruction, a Thanksgiving recess, and winter and spring vacations. The academic day (8:00 A.M. to 3:00 P.M.) is divided into eight class periods to permit flexibility in scheduling. In the evenings, two hours are scheduled for study in supervised halls or in the dormitories. For most students, a typical day includes classes in four major subjects and two full study hall sessions in addition to the two-hour study period in the evening. An average of four hours of homework preparation is required for each class day.

Classes, which have an average of ten students, meet five days a week and seven Saturdays during the year. Special-help and individual conferences are scheduled throughout the day and as needed. All faculty members serve in a counseling capacity; each student has a faculty mentor who provides counseling and advice on academic and/or social situations. Marks are posted and sent to parents six times a year.

To graduate, each student must complete 18 academic units of credit, including English 4, mathematics 3, a foreign language 2, social science 3, science 3, and 1 credit in the fine arts. In addition to foundation-level courses in math, the college

preparatory curriculum includes English I–IV; German I–IV; Spanish I–IV; World Civilization, Modern European History, American History, Stock Market, Economics; Algebra, Computer Science, Geometry, Algebra II, Pre-calculus; Astronomy, Ecology, Chemistry, Physics; Art I–IV; and Music Theory and Appreciation. English as a Second Language, Driver Education, Reading Enhancement, and private music lessons are also available. Advanced Placement courses are offered in nine subjects.

The Wayland Challenge Program includes special orientation for students at the beginning of the academic year and leadership camps, which offer an intense learning experience off campus. Independent study is encouraged throughout the year.

In 1999, all 39 Wayland graduates were accepted at such colleges and universities as Boston University, Bowdoin, Bucknell, Case Western, Colgate, College of William and Mary, Denison, Gettysburg, Lehigh, Middlebury, Rensselaer Polytechnic, Smith, United States Coast Guard Academy, United States Military Academy, Vassar, Yale, and the Universities of Colorado, Minnesota, North Carolina, and Wisconsin (Madison).

STUDENT ACTIVITIES. Campus organizations include house councils, sports clubs, a yearbook group, and clubs for students interested in drama, science, chess, and computers. In addition, opportunity is provided for instruction in voice and almost all musical instruments. Students may participate in a choir, a chorus, and special ensemble groups; they may be invited to join The Cum Laude Society.

A member of the Wisconsin Independent Schools Athletic Association, Wayland fields varsity and junior varsity teams to compete with nearby independent schools. The boys' athletic program includes soccer, cross-country, football, basketball, alpine skiing, swimming, track, baseball, golf, and tennis. Girls compete in field hockey, tennis, golf, volleyball, basketball, coed cross-country, alpine skiing, swimming, soccer, softball, and track.

Scheduled weekend activities include dances, movies, cultural programs, parties, and skating and skiing during the winter sports season. The school sponsors cultural trips for all students. Traditional annual events include two Parents' Weekends and the Alumni Reunion Weekend.

ADMISSION AND COSTS. Candidates are accepted at all grade levels on the basis of character and college potential as determined by an interview, results of the Secondary School Admission Test, and review of the previous school record. The school has a policy of admitting "students of any race, sex, color, and national or ethnic origin." Application may be made at any time during the year, but early application is encouraged.

In 1999–2000, the charge for tuition, room, and board was $20,400; day tuition was $9250, including weekday lunches. Additional expenses include textbooks and laundry. A tuition payment plan is available. In 1999, the school distributed over $1,000,000 in scholarships and awards to 104 students. Students are encouraged to apply early for financial aid. Wayland Academy subscribes to the School and Student Scholarship Service for Financial Aid.

President: Alfred W. Grieshaber, Ph.D.
Academic Dean: Joseph A. Lennertz
Dean of Students: Peter Trau
Dean of Admissions: Robyn Hardt Schultz
Dean of Advancement: Jeanette M. DeDiemar, Ph.D.
Director of Athletics: Craig T. Hill

OTHER COUNTRIES AND UNITED STATES TERRITORIES

AUSTRALIA

Canberra Grammar School   1929

Monaro Crescent, Red Hill, ACT 2603, Australia. 02-6295-1833;
Fax 02-6295-2923; E-mail enrolments@cgs.act.edu.au;
Web Site www.cgs.act.edu.au

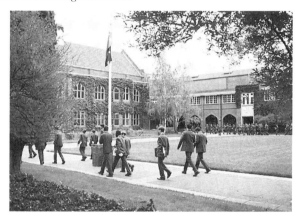

Canberra Grammar School is an Anglican, university preparatory school enrolling 1450 students from Pre-School through
Senior School (Year 12). It is coeducational to Year 2, with boys
only from Year 3 onward. The Senior School includes 120
boarders. The School aims to encourage an "understanding
and acceptance of the spiritual and moral basis of life" and the
"full and balanced development" of each student. The International Centre offers Languages Other Than English and strives
to promote multicultural understanding. Music and the arts are
integral to the program, while debating, community service,
and sports are among the activities. Tuition: $6100–$9100;
Boarding Fee: $9500. Mrs. Ann Jory is Registrar; Mr. A.S. Mur-
ray is Headmaster.

Methodist Ladies' College   1882

207 Barkers Road, Kew, Victoria 3101, Australia. 61-3-9274-6333;
Fax 61-3-9819-2345; E-mail college@mlc.vic.edu.au;
Web Site http://www.mlc.vic.edu.au

Methodist Ladies' College offers university preparatory (including the International Baccalaureate), general academic, business, and vocational programs to 2230 girls in Prep (age
5)–Year 12, with 100 boarders in Years 7–12. A new early learning center accepts children from 0 to 5 years. The College aims
to empower students to take charge of their learning, resulting
in confident young women who create their own future. Each
girl from Year 5 up has her own laptop computer to enhance
learning; in Year 9, students spend a term in the bush for
wilderness and environmental study. Music, drama, and art are
among the activities; English as a Second Language is available.
Tuition: A$13,500; Boarding Fee: A$11,775. Mrs. Heather Barton is Registrar; Ms. Rosa Storelli is Principal.

AUSTRIA

The American International School, Vienna   1959

Salmannsdorfer Strasse 47, A-1190 Vienna, Austria. 43-1-40132-0;
Fax 43-1-40132-5; E-mail r.spradling@ais.at;
Web Site www.ais.at

The American and Canadian embassies founded this coeducational day school to serve families from the diplomatic and corporate communities as well as local students seeking an American-
style curriculum in a multicultural environment. Enrolling 765
students from 56 nations in Nursery–Grade 12, the School
offers U.S. college preparatory, International Baccalaureate,
and Austrian Matura curricula designed to prepare students for
higher education in universities and colleges worldwide. The
mastery of basic skills in the lower grades equips students for
the challenging course work of the secondary school. The
School's location provides access to the cultural resources of
many European cities. Tuition: ATS73,800–153,950. Margit
Mährenhorst is Admissions Director; Richard Spradling is
Director. *Middle States Association.*

BELGIUM

Antwerp International School   1967

Veltwijcklaan 180, 2180 Ekeren, Antwerp, Belgium.
32-3-543-93-00; Fax 32-3-541-82-01;
E-mail ais@ais-antwerp.be

Antwerp International School is an English-language, college
preparatory school enrolling 600 students in Preschool–Grade
12. The School's goal is to provide high academic standards balanced with a warm, caring atmosphere. Foreign languages
include Dutch, French, German, and Spanish. Graduates attend
outstanding universities and colleges worldwide. The School
offers the International Baccalaureate program and preparation for the British IGCSE. The curriculum includes drama,
music, art, athletics, computer education, and an extensive
European Field Study Program. Tuition: 147,000–607,000 Bel-
gian francs. Transportation fees are extra. Robert F. Schaecher
(California State, M.A. 1972) is Headmaster. *New England
Association.*

The City International School Brussels   1986

Blvd. Louis Schmidt 101-103, B-1040 Brussels, Belgium.
32.2.734.44.13; Fax 32.2.733.32.33

The City International School Brussels prepare students of diverse nationalities for colleges and universities worldwide. The academic program follows the National Curriculum for England and Wales, leading to the IGCSE and either GCE A-levels or an American-style high school diploma. The School enrolls 150 day students in Kindergarten through Grade 12; the crèche provides places for children 3 months to 3 years of age. Yearly trips and summer programs are available. Tuition: BEF 220,000–520,000. Marie-Claire Chabloz is Director of Admissions; Dirk Craen is President.

The International School of Brussels   1951

Chateau des Fougères, Kattenberg 19, 1170 Brussels, Belgium.
322-661-42-11; Fax 322-661-42-00; E-mail admissions@isb.be;
Web Site www.isb.be

The International School of Brussels was founded by American parents and interested Belgians to provide an English-language education for their children. Enrolling over 1200 students from 61 nations in Nursery–Grade 13, the School awards both American and International Baccalaureate diplomas. The curriculum is designed to serve a variety of ability levels, with Advanced Placement courses as well as academic support for students with learning differences. The program is enhanced by class trips throughout Belgium and Europe. Students participate in publications, clubs, music groups, drama, debate, Model UN, and varsity sports. Tuition: 132,500BF–772,500BF. Richard P. Hall was appointed Director in 1989. *Middle States Association.*

St. John's International School   1964

Drève Richelle 146, Waterloo 1410, Belgium. 32-2-352-06-10;
Fax 32-2-352-0630; E-mail Admissions@stjohns.be;
Web Site www.stjohns.be

An ecumenical school with a Christian philosophy, St. John's fosters racial, cultural, and religious harmony. From nursery to university entrance, students benefit from the School's high academic standards and activities such as sports, music, drama, information technology, and art. Students prepare for the U.S. high school diploma, Advanced Placement, and the International Baccalaureate. English as a Second Language and remedial offerings are also available. Located 15 minutes south of Brussels, the School's modern buildings include two libraries, two gyms, three music rooms, and ten science, computer, and photo labs. Tuition: BF 198,000–783,000. Judith Debetencourt Hoskins is Director of Admissions; Sr. Barbara Hughes, FCJ (L. ès L., M.Ed.), is Superintendent. *Middle States Association.*

BERMUDA

The Bermuda High School for Girls   1894

27 Richmond Road, Pembroke HMO8, Bermuda. 441-295-6153;
Fax 441-295-2754; E-mail/Web Site bhs@ibl.bm

The Bermuda High School for Girls is a college preparatory day school enrolling 630 young women in Years 1–12. The School aims to provide superior education for students of diverse racial, religious, and socioeconomic backgrounds. Programs related to the British National Curriculum lead to G.C.S.E./I.G.C.S.E. and SAT I and II exams for Years 11 and 12. Sports, music, art, publications, and theater are among the extracurricular activities. Tuition: $8250. Competitive scholarships and financial aid are available. Diane P. Gordon is Admissions Director; Eleanor W. Kingsbury (University of St. Andrew's [Scotland], M.A.) is Head of School.

Saltus Grammar School   1888

P.O. Box HM-2224, HMJX Hamilton, Bermuda. 441-292-6177;
Fax 441-295-4977; E-mail headmaster@saltus.bm;
Web Site www.saltus.bm

This coeducational school, established with funds left by Samuel Saltus, enrolls 1000 day students in Grades 1–12. Stressing "well-tried, traditional approaches" to education in a "lively and caring atmosphere," the School's goal is to prepare students mentally, spiritually, and physically to meet the demands of the modern world. Special emphasis is placed on music. A college preparatory year working toward Advanced Placement Exams is available. Activities include sports, drama, photography, and debate. A summer program is offered. Tuition: $7500. Financial Aid: $265,000. N.J.G. Kermode (B.A. [Hons.], M.A., P.G.C.E.) was appointed Headmaster in 1999.

BRAZIL

Associação Escola Graduada de São Paulo   SÃO PAULO

Av. Presidente Giovani Gronchi, 4710, Caixa Postal 1976, 01059-970 São Paulo, SP, Brazil. Telephone 55-11-3742-2499; Fax 55-11-3742-9358; E-mail graded@eagle.aegsp.br; Admissions E-mail hgoncalv@eagle.aegsp.br; Web Site www.aegsp.br

ASSOCIAÇÃO ESCOLA GRADUADA DE SÃO PAULO is a college preparatory day school enrolling boys and girls in Preprimary–Grade 12. Popularly known as "Graded School," it is located in Morumbi on the southwestern edge of São Paulo (population 18,000,000). The section is a newly developed area with high-rise condominiums and shopping centers. Students travel to school by car pool or by a private bus system contracted by the School.

The School was founded in 1920 by the American Chamber of Commerce to provide an American education for the children of U.S. families living in Brazil. Over the years, as populations have changed with the development of international business, Graded has become an international school, although it still retains its American style and character.

The Graded School seeks to offer a rigorous educational program with English as the primary language of instruction and to recognize its international character through an appropriate diversity of programs. It emphasizes close student-teacher relationships and small classes and is committed to excellence in all aspects of its operation.

The School is a nonprofit organization governed by a self-perpetuating Board of Directors who meet monthly. All Board members must have children in the School.

Graded School is accredited by the Southern Association of Colleges and Schools and holds membership in the National Association of Independent Schools, Association of American Schools in Brazil, Association for the Advancement of International Education, and the European Council of International Schools. It is an International Baccalaureate school with Middle Year and IB programs.

THE CAMPUS. The School is situated on 16.5 landscaped acres that include a soccer/softball field, Elementary School playground and playing field, four outdoor tennis courts, and an outdoor covered court.

The ten academic buildings, or wings, are grouped in a grid pattern at the center of the campus. Four of the wings are occupied by the Elementary School and six by the Secondary School. On the edges of the grid are the cafeteria, a 450-seat auditorium, and two libraries with more than 50,000 volumes. The buildings, which provide 90 classrooms, are connected by covered walkways.

Indoor athletic facilities include a gymnasium and weight room and an Elementary School gymnasium.

THE FACULTY. David J. Tully was appointed Superintendent in 1996.

The faculty, including administrators who teach, consist of 122 men and women. All hold baccalaureate degrees or the equivalent from American, Canadian, Brazilian, and European colleges and universities.

STUDENT BODY. In 1999–2000, the School enrolls 1136 boys and girls in Preprimary–Grade 12. The enrollment is distributed as follows: 172 in Preprimary, 388 in the Elementary School (Grades 1–5), 251 in the Middle School (Grades 6–8), and 325 in the High School (Grades 9–12). Brazilians comprise 42 percent of the student population; American and Canadian citizens constitute 38 percent. The balance come from Europe, Asia, Latin America, the Middle East, Oceania, and Africa.

ACADEMIC PROGRAM. The academic year, divided into semesters, begins in early August and ends in mid-June. A six-week break follows the end of the first semester in mid-December and a vacation for Carnival is also scheduled. Grades are sent to parents at the end of each quarter. Classes are held five days a week in nine 45-minute periods between 8:10 A.M. and 3:10 P.M. Elementary and Middle School classes have an average size of 20; High School classes vary from 8 to 22. Teachers stay for 45 minutes after the end of the class day, Mondays through Thursdays, to provide extra help. Study halls are conducted in free periods.

The Optimal Learning Center has learning-disability specialists to help students with mild learning problems. The Center provides diagnostic and programming services for highly capable students as well.

The School is dedicated to offering students and staff the latest resources in educational technology. A fiber-optic network is installed throughout the campus, giving students and faculty members access to computers in classrooms, offices, and laboratory settings. Library automation and networked CD-ROMs, along with full Internet access, provide excellent research potential to the Graded community. The emphasis is on integrating the wide variety of technologies into the classroom to serve as teaching tools that complement and enhance the curriculum.

The Preprimary School offers a Montessori program for children ages two to five. Classes are conducted by fully trained Montessori instructors aided by assistant teachers.

The Elementary School offers a traditional curriculum in the core academic subjects. Portuguese language instruction begins in Grade 2, and training in critical thinking skills is integrated into the curriculum. Small-group instruction in English as a Second Language is offered in Grades 2–5.

All Middle School students follow the IB Middle Years Program in a departmentalized schedule with courses in English, Portuguese, Social Studies, Mathematics, Science, and Physical Education/Health five days a week; Art, Music, Band, Choir, Study Skills, and Theater are scheduled in semester-long courses. Computer technology is integrated into all courses.

The High School offers an American diploma, a diploma in Brazilian Studies, and the International Baccalaureate. Among the courses are English 9–12; Portuguese 9–12, French 1–4, Spanish; History of the Americas, Brazilian Social Studies; Geometry, Algebra 1 and 2/Trigonometry, Advanced Placement Calculus; Biology, Chemistry, Zoology, Physics; Basic Arts, Ceramics, Drawing, Advanced Art, Photography; Choir, Band, Theater, Yearbook; and Physical Education. The International Baccalaureate curriculum includes English, Portuguese, French, three levels of Mathematics, Biology, Art, Physics, Chemistry, Environmental Systems, Information Technology, Economics, Psychology, Computer Studies, Theater, and Theory of Knowledge 1–2.

All 79 seniors who graduated in 1999 went on to college. They are attending such institutions as Babson, Baylor, Boston University, Brandeis, Claremont McKenna, Clarkson, Duke, Florida Atlantic, George Washington, Guilford, Indiana University, New York University, Northwestern, St. Lawrence, St. Louis, Swarthmore, Tufts, Vanderbilt, Vassar, Washington and Lee, and the Universities of Illinois, Michigan, Missouri (Rolla), Oregon, Pennsylvania, and Southern California as well as universities in Brazil, Holland, India, Japan, Switzerland, and the United Kingdom.

STUDENT ACTIVITIES. Student councils are formed to help organize social activities and community service projects.

In the Lower School, the activities often include drama club, choir, ballet, judo, tennis, and gymnastics. Upper school students present dramatic productions in English and Portuguese and participate in interscholastic academic competitions, National Honor Society, literary magazine, and the Adopt-a-School program in the Amazon. Other activities are organized according to interest.

Interscholastic athletics begin in the sixth grade, and the School fields varsity teams in softball, indoor and outdoor soccer, basketball, and volleyball for boys; and softball, soccer, volleyball, and basketball for girls. Junior varsity teams are available in most sports. School teams compete in a league with three other American schools and a British school. In addition, the American Society conducts activities on campus Saturday mornings in Little League baseball, soccer, basketball, and volleyball.

The Parent-Teacher Association arranges cultural events for students and parents as well as the Thanksgiving celebration and the Fall Auction.

ADMISSION AND COSTS. Graded School seeks students who are able to pursue a challenging American-style curriculum presented in the English language. Students are accepted at all levels on the basis of previous academic records, recommendations from schools, and entrance examination results. Applications are considered at any time. There is a $100 application fee, and a $500 registration fee is required if a student is admitted.

Tuition fees in 1999–2000 are $6900–$14,600 per year, depending on the grade level. Books and hot lunch are included in the fee. A one-time $4200 capital levy is charged for the first student in a family and $3200 is charged for siblings. The school bus fee is $1860 annually. The ESL Immersion fee is an additional $2600 per year.

High School Principal: Eric Hieser
Middle School Principal: Sherry McClelland
Lower School Principal: Paige Geiger
Director of Brazilian Studies: Angelina Fregonesi
Business Manager: José Carlos Cardozo
Director of Personnel: Marcelo Weguelin
Director of Development: Francisco DiBella, Jr.
Director of Admissions: Heidi Gonçalves
College Counselor: Phyllis Clemensen

The Escola Americana do Rio de Janeiro

RIO DE JANEIRO

Estrada da Gavea, 132, 22451 Rio de Janeiro, RJ, Brazil.
55-21-512-9830 or 55-21-259-4807;
Fax 55-21-259-4722 or 55-21-259-6720

Т HE ESCOLA AMERICANA DO RIO DE JANEIRO is a nondenominational, college preparatory day school enrolling boys and girls of many nationalities in Early Childhood Education through Grade 12. Brazil's second largest city, Rio is widely known for its lovely beaches, its Mardi Gras festivities, and the wealth of artistic, historic, and multicultural attractions that draw visitors from around the globe.

The Escola Americana do Rio de Janeiro was established in 1937 by private individuals, corporations, and the American Chamber of Commerce to afford an academic program that was comparable in excellence to the curriculum found in superior public schools in the United States. It opened with 137 students in a small house in Ipanema. As enrollments outgrew the existing accommodations, grants from the U.S. Department of State and the Ford Foundation made possible the construction of a modern new facility on its present site.

In addition to preparing students for success in colleges and universities worldwide, Escola Americana seeks to provide a pleasant learning environment, staffed with qualified faculty and equipped with modern facilities and teaching tools. The study of the Portuguese language and the history and culture of Brazil is central to the core curriculum, as the School encourages its students to benefit from its location in one of the world's most cosmopolitan cities.

A nonprofit, nondenominational institution, Escola Americana is guided by a Board of Directors. It is accredited by the Southern Association of Colleges and Schools and holds membership in the Association of American Schools in Brazil, Association of American Schools in South America, the European Council of International Schools, and the National Association of Independent Schools. The School is also affiliated with the International Baccalaureate Organization.

THE CAMPUS. The School's 12-acre campus lies on the edge of the National Tijuca forest on a steep hillside that has commanding views of Rio, including the Atlantic Ocean, Sugar Loaf Mountain, and the Christ the Redeemer statue. The tropical climate provides lush vegetation and abundant flowering shrubs and trees throughout the grounds. Academic facilities are centered in eight towers that house the School's four divisions. The towers together contain 80 classrooms, eight science laboratories, two libraries with a collection totaling more than 45,000 volumes, three gymnasiums, a cafeteria, an infirmary, two snack bars, a student store, and a 500-seat auditorium. More than 250 microcomputers are used in classroom instruction as well as closed-circuit and cable television systems. Athletic facilities include an Elementary School playground, outdoor basketball and indoor soccer courts, a track, and playing fields for soccer, softball, and football.

THE FACULTY. Ted Sharp, appointed Headmaster in 1999, earned a B.A. in Modern Chinese and Colonial American History from Gettysburg College and an M.Ed. from Bridgewater State College, and has been engaged in advanced graduate study in educational administration at Harvard University. Mr. Sharp has served as a teacher, administrator, and superintendent in public schools; an independent school headmaster; a university professor and dean; and a member of the senior staff at the U.S. Department of Education. He has served as a consultant on leadership, the humanities, and ethics to numerous schools in the United States and abroad.

The faculty are comprised of 105 full-time and 13 part-time teachers, 94 women and 24 men. All hold baccalaureate or equivalent degrees, and 52 percent have earned advanced degrees, including 69 master's and 5 doctorates. They are graduates of colleges and universities such as Baylor, Boston College, Brandeis, Columbia, Georgetown, George Washington University, Harvard, Johns Hopkins, Lehigh, New York University, Texas A&M, Texas Christian, Washington State, and the Universities of Alabama, Arizona, California (Berkeley, Los Angeles), Chicago, Hull (England), Illinois, Michigan, North Carolina, South Carolina, Southern California, Toronto (Canada), and Virginia.

A nurse's office is staffed during the school day, and the nearby Centro Pediatrico da Lagoa is available for emergencies.

STUDENT BODY. In 1999–2000, Escola Americana enrolled 1000 boys and girls, including 180 in the Nursery Program (Pre-Kindergarten–Kindergarten), 360 in the Lower School (Grades 1–5), 228 in the Middle School (Grades 6–8), and 232 in the Upper School (Grades 9–12). They came from a wide diversity of backgrounds, including 130 Americans, 779 Brazilian nationals, and 91 from 23 other nationalities.

ACADEMIC PROGRAM. The school year is divided into two semesters from early August to mid-June. Two six-week vacations are scheduled beginning in December and June, respectively, and there is a one-week recess for Brazilian Carnaval. Progress reports and grades are issued at the midpoint and end of each semester, and parent conferences are conducted regularly. Homework is assigned in all subjects. Students choose faculty advisors who meet with them twice a week in a formal setting and at other times on an individual basis to discuss academic and other issues. The Honors Roll and Headmaster's List recognize students who have demonstrated exceptional academic achievement.

A typical day, from 7:55 A.M. to 3:15 P.M., includes eight 50-minute class periods, brunch or advisory periods, lunch, and an activity and conference period. On Friday, school is dismissed at 2:30 P.M. All instruction is in English.

The Early Childhood Education program includes a preschool, prekindergarten, and kindergarten.

The Lower School curriculum focuses on learning how to learn, giving students a firm foundation in the core subjects, with emphasis on language development. A strong English as a Second Language program is maintained. Other areas of study include art, music, library skills, and physical education.

The primary objectives of the Middle School are to develop a positive self-image, build on the skills and knowledge acquired in the Lower School, and to ensure that students are prepared to move successfully into the Upper School. Taught by a team of teachers experienced in early adolescent education, Middle School students have a departmentalized schedule with courses in English, Portuguese, social studies, mathematics, and science. A series of exploratory activities, including French, art, computers, health, music, and drama, is also offered. Physical education is required of all students.

The Upper School offers American, Brazilian, and International Baccalaureate diplomas. To earn an American high school diploma, a student must complete a minimum of 24 Carnegie units, or credits, including: English and history, 4 each; 3 each in math and laboratory science; $1\frac{1}{2}$ in physical education; 1 in computer; and $\frac{1}{2}$ each in art, health, and college and career exploration. All students are required to complete two years of a language other than their native tongue; the number of credits required in Portuguese is based on the number of semesters a student is enrolled at the School. Six hours of community service per year is also mandatory for graduation.

A Student Services Center with full-time specialists in diagnostics and programming services exists for mild to moderately learning-disabled students as well as ESL students. A high capacity/high potential program is provided for gifted students in Grades 1–12.

More than 95 percent of Escola Americana's seniors enroll in college or university immediately upon graduation. Members of the classes of 1998 and 1999 entered such colleges and universities as Amherst, Bentley, Boston College, Boston University, Brandeis, Brown, Clark, Colgate, College of William and Mary, Cornell, Duke, Florida State, Georgetown, George Washington University, Harvard, Johns Hopkins, Lehigh, McGill University, Northwestern, Princeton, Rollins, Smith, Stanford, Tulane, Tufts, Yale, and the Universities of Arizona, California, Chicago, Massachusetts, Michigan, Notre Dame, Pennsylvania, Southern California, Vermont, and Virginia.

STUDENT ACTIVITIES. Elected and volunteer members serve on the Student Council, which exists to propose and implement improvements in school life, including the planning of social activities and the formulation of school policy.

The Drama Club stages productions during the year, and musical groups, including concert band, girls' chorus, and jazz band, perform at the School and throughout the city. Students publish a yearbook, a bilingual literary magazine, a Middle School literary magazine, and a Portuguese-language newspaper. Qualified students may join the National Honor Society. Other activities include cheerleading, peer counseling, Spirit Committee, Knowledge Bowl, Model United Nations, the Andes Experiment, and Ecology, Outdoor, Art, and International clubs.

Panther teams compete in the Rio League against other American and local schools in girls' and boys' softball, soccer, volleyball, and basketball.

Among the special events on the calendar are Field Day, International Schools Meet, Halloween Party, and the Big Four Tournament with the other American schools of São Paulo and Brasilia. The Parent-Teacher Association sponsors extracurricular and enrichment programs and assists the School in

improving physical and material resources. Such fund-raising events as the annual Christmas Fest and Gala Dinner are organized and promoted by the PTA.

ADMISSION AND COSTS. Escola Americana do Rio de Janeiro welcomes students of average to superior intelligence who show promise of benefiting from a rigorous college preparatory program in a multicultural environment. Admissions are based on previous official academic records, an English screening test (where applicable), and a diagnostic test. Additionally, there are admissions priorities based upon established Board policies.

Tuition in the 1999–2000 school year ranged from $12,780 in the preschool to $16,680 in Grades 9–12. There is a financial aid program, but ordinarily, aid is granted to short-term requirements of students already enrolled in the School.

Upper School Principal: Thomas Connolly
Middle School Principal: Shaysann Kaun
Lower School Principal: Kirk Wheeler
Early Childhood Education Coordinator: Suely V. Pecanha
Business Manager: Theodore Seidl
Upper School Counselor: Robert Bouressa
Middle School Counselor: Penelope Mello e Souza
Lower School Counselor: Teren Block
Early Childhood Education Counselor: Jennifer Mary Hopkin
Brazilian Director: Vera Pepin
Director of Athletics: Neise Abreu
Director of Student Activities: Maria Teresa Castro
Admission Secretary: Sonia Teixeira

CANADA

Ashbury College 1891

362 Mariposa Avenue, Ottawa, Ontario K1M 0T3, Canada.
  613-749-5954; Fax 613-749-9724;
  E-mail avaliqu@ashbury.on.ca; Web Site www.ashbury.on.ca

Ashbury College, located in a park-like setting in the nation's capital, is a college preparatory day and boarding school enrolling 620 students, with boys in Grades 4–13 and girls in Grades 9–13. Encouraging free, creative inquiry, the School aims "to produce a balanced, principled young person capable of meeting a diversity of challenges: ethical, intellectual, emotional, and physical." The rigorous International Baccalaureate program attracts students from around the world. English as a Second Language is offered. All students participate in sports and activities. Boarding Tuition: $24,100 (Cdn.); Day Tuition: $11,900. Financial Aid: $300,000. Robert B. Napier (Queen's [Ireland], B.Sc., M.Ed.) is Headmaster.

Appleby College   1911

540 Lakeshore Road West, Oakville, Ontario L6K 3P1, Canada.
 905-845-4681; Fax 905-845-9505; E-mail enrol@appleby.on.ca;
 Web Site www.appleby.on.ca

Appleby enrolls 560 young men and women in Grades 7–12/OAC. The rigorous academic program includes Advanced Placement courses, mandatory SAT testing, and compulsory athletics, providing a solid foundation for university-bound students, Appleby's *e.school* program equips every student with a laptop computer, which is used throughout the curriculum. The Northern Campus on Lake Temagami is the site of wilderness and survival training for students from Grade 8 up. Appleby addresses all aspects of development through challenging academics and extensive athletic, extracurricular, and community service programs. Boarding Tuition: $27,500 (Canadian); Day Tuition: $15,200. Financial Aid: $400,000. Michael Nurse is Director of Admissions; Mr. G. S. McLean is Headmaster.

The Bishop Strachan School   1867

298 Lonsdale Road, Toronto, Ontario M4V 1X2, Canada.
 416-483-4325; Fax 416-481-5632;
 E-mail strachan@bss.on.ca; Web Site http://www.bss.on.ca

The Bishop Strachan School, enrolling 93 boarders and 726 day students, is known for strong academics, extensive extracurriculars, and leadership training for young women. The university preparatory curriculum includes Advanced Placement courses. Recent graduates have attended such universities as McGill, Queens, and Toronto in Canada; Princeton, Yale, and Harvard in the United States; and universities in England, Europe, and Japan. Activities include a boarder/day girl exchange and an extensive sports program as well as choirs, bands, drama groups, and debating. Toronto provides exciting cultural opportunities. Boarding Tuition: $25,500 (Canadian); Day Tuition: $13,520. Ms. Natalie Little is Head.

Branksome Hall   1903

10 Elm Avenue, Toronto, Ontario M4W 1N4, Canada.
 416-920-9741; Fax 416-920-5390;
 E-mail admit@branksome.on.ca; Web Site www.branksome.on.ca

Branksome Hall is a nondenominational, independent school enrolling 850 girls in Kindergarten–Graduating Year, including 50 resident students. The Senior School offers a challenging curriculum, including Advanced Placement courses in Calculus, Chemistry, Art, English, and French. Graduates enter first-choice colleges and universities in Canada, the United States, and worldwide. A wide range of sports, leadership, and co-curricular activities is available, including drama, music, community service, and public affairs. Day Tuition: Kindergarten– $11,800; Grades 1–13—$13,250; Boarding Fee: $14,200. Adam de Pencier is Director of Admissions; Karen Murton (University of Western Ontario, B.Ed.; University of British Columbia, M.Ed.) is Principal.

Crofton House School   1898

3200 West 41st Avenue, Vancouver, British Columbia, Canada V6N 3E1. 604-263-3255; Fax 604-263-4941;
 Web Site http://www.croftonhouse.bc.ca

Crofton House, the first girls' school in Canada to acquire lawful arms by Crown grant, is a university preparatory day school enrolling 655 students in Grades I–XII. Now beginning its second century of education for young women, the School aims to equip students for further education and for responsible citizenship in today's society. The challenging curriculum includes Advanced Placement courses and the study of Mandarin. Girls are involved in publications, a fine arts program, community

services, overseas travel exchanges, athletics, and outdoor education. Tuition: $7550–$9300 (Canadian). Financial Aid: $91,000. Mrs. Evelyn Hackl is Registrar; Barbara M. Walker (University of British Columbia, B.Ed.; Western Washington, M.B.A.) was appointed Head of School in 1995.

Fraser Academy   1982

2294 West 10th Avenue, Vancouver, BC, V6K 2H8, Canada.
 604-736-5575; Fax 604-736-5578;
 E-mail info@fraser-academy.bc.ca; Web Site www.fraser-academy.bc.ca

Using a multisensory approach, Fraser Academy assists children with dyslexia and other language-processing problems. Students first listen, then read and talk about a lesson, often reinforcing the learning by making or doing. Small classroom interaction, with usually no more than 8 students per academic class, permits 138 boys and girls in Grades 1 through 12 to improve language development skills, including phonics, decoding, writing, and reading for word recognition and comprehension. Fraser Academy is centrally located on a tree-lined street in Vancouver's residential Kitsilano neighborhood. Tuition: $13,500 (Cdn.). Eleanor Nesling is Head of School.

Glenlyon-Norfolk School   1986

Junior Boys Campus: 1701 Beach Drive, Victoria, British Columbia V8R 6H9, Canada
Senior Coed/Junior Girls Campus: 801 Bank Street, Victoria, British Columbia V8S 4A8, Canada. 250-370-6801;
 Fax 250-370-6838; E-mail gns@islandnet.com;
 Web Site www.islandnet.com/~gns/

Glenlyon-Norfolk, enrolling 700 students in Kindergarten–Grade 12, provides a rigorous university preparatory program within a supportive environment. A strong academic foundation and diverse opportunities prepare students for moral leadership in a changing world. Glenlyon-Norfolk is the only independent school in British Columbia accredited to offer the International Baccalaureate. A member of Round Square, the School shares a commitment, beyond academic excellence, to personal development and responsibility through service, challenge, adventure, and international understanding. Tuition: $6929–$9098. Deirdre Chettleburgh is Coordinator of Admissions; Charles E. G. Peacock (McGill, B.A.; Université de Sherbrooke, M.A.) is Headmaster.

Halifax Grammar School   1958

5750 Atlantic Street, Halifax, Nova Scotia B3H 1G9, Canada.
 902-422-6497; Fax 902-422-4884; E-mail head@hgs.ednet.ns.ca;
 Web Site www.hgs.ednet.ns.ca

Halifax Grammar School is a university preparatory day school with 430 students in Primary–Grade 12. An enriched and rigorous curriculum features the International Baccalaureate in Grades 11–12 and a vibrant fine and performing arts program at all grade levels. Excellent facilities are supplemented by the athletics facilities of neighboring Saint Mary's University, which are used by the School for physical education and varsity sports teams on a daily basis. The School enrolls a limited number of international students who are boarded with Halifax parents. Tuition: $5250–$6560. Mrs. Beverly Jackson is Admissions Officer; John A. Messenger is Headmaster.

Havergal College   1894

1451 Avenue Road, Toronto, Ontario M5N 2H9, Canada.
 416-483-3519; Fax 416-483-6796; Web Site www.havergal.on.ca

Building on traditions of 100 years, Havergal College seeks to provide an environment that is vibrant with energy, curiosity, and a love of learning shared by staff and students. The rigorous academic curriculum emphasizes college and university preparation. Students are active in sports and arts programs as well as community projects. The school is located on a beautiful 22-acre campus in the multicultural city of Toronto, offering students additional opportunities to experience diverse cultures and a rich arts scene. Day Tuition: $13,545; Boarding Tuition: $27,245. Financial aid is available. Susan J. Ditchburn (University of Calgary, Ph.D.) is Principal.

Hillfield-Strathallan College   1901

299 Fennell Avenue West, Hamilton, Ontario L9C 1G3, Canada.
905-389-1367; Fax 905-389-6366;
E-mail admissions@hillstrath.on.ca; Web Site www.hillstrath.on.ca

Founded as separate boys' and girls' schools, Hillfield-Strathallan College was reincorporated in 1962 and now enrolls 556 boys and 535 girls as day students in Pre-Kindergarten–University Entrance and a Montessori program for ages 2¹/₂–9. A modern core academic program is designed to prepare students for entrance to universities and is supplemented by an extracurricular program to provide a challenging, personalized education. Sports, drama, music, and publications are the principal activities. Tuition: $2589–$10,881 (Canadian). Financial Aid: $100,000. Ray Marks is Director of Admissions; William S. Boyer (University of Toronto, B.A. 1976, B.Ed. 1977) was appointed Headmaster in 1995.

Lower Canada College   1861

4090 Royal Avenue, Montreal, Quebec H4A 2M5, Canada.
514-482-9916; Admissions 514-482-0951; Fax 514-482-0195;
E-mail admin@lcc.ca; Web Site www.lcc.ca

Lower Canada College, "a friendly and dynamic" coeducational community of 710 day students in Junior, Middle, and Senior schools, offers a challenging curriculum, including a K–6 bilingual program and diverse activities. Situated in Montreal's Notre-Dame-de-Grace area, the School's campus includes two playing fields, an artificial rink, a music center, a Kindergarten building, and a counseling center. The Learning Activity Centre provides a library, technology center, auditorium, seminar rooms, and a full double gym. Students regularly win provincial and national academic competitions. A one-year Pre-University Programme offers direct admission to universities across North America. Tuition: $8225–$10,735. Financial Aid: $350,000. Deborah J. Ayre is Director of Admission; Dr. Paul W. Bennett is Headmaster.

Miss Edgar's & Miss Cramp's School   1909

525 Mount Pleasant Avenue, Westmount, Quebec H3Y 3H6,
Canada. 514-935-6357; Fax 514-935-1099;
Web Site www.ecs.qc.ca

Located in a residential area, ECS is an independent, English-language day school for approximately 310 girls in Kindergarten–Grade 11, with an overall student-teacher ratio of 10:1. The college preparatory program, designed to encourage independent thinking, provides a strong foundation in language arts, mathematics, social studies, and science as well as the visual and performing arts. The study of the French language and culture begins with an Immersion Junior School Program. French Mother Tongue courses are offered in Grades 6–11. Girls participate in yearbook, drama, Student Government, and diverse

clubs. There is also a varied and comprehensive athletics program. Tuition: $7375–$8295. Lorraine Bergeron is Director of Admissions; Susyn Borer is Head of School.

The Priory School   1947

3120 The Boulevard, Montreal, Quebec H3Y 1R9, Canada.
514-935-5966; Fax 514-935-1428;
E-mail admissions@priory.qc.ca; Web Site www.priory.qc.ca

The Priory School is a coeducational, Catholic day school enrolling 170 students of all faiths in Kindergarten–Grade 6. Striving to make learning a happy and constantly rewarding experience, Priory offers a warm, Christian environment and encourages intelligent initiative, self-discipline, and creativity. Instruction is given in art, music, and computers. Physical education and art are taught in French, and all grades have French second language specialists for French courses. Activities include ice-skating, interscholastic soccer and basketball, arts and crafts, choir, chess, science, and computers. An after-school program is available. Tuition: $6527–$6927 (including hot meals). Debra Merritt is Admissions Officer; John Marinelli (State University of New York, M.Sc. [Ed.] 1977) is Principal.

St. Andrew's College   1899

Aurora, Ontario L4G 3H7, Canada. 905-727-3178;
Fax 905-841-6911; E-mail admission@sac.on.ca;
Web Site www.sac.on.ca

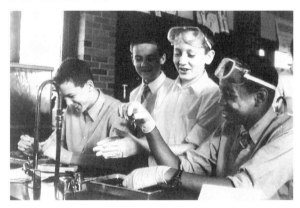

St. Andrew's College is a boys' boarding and day school located 40 minutes from downtown Toronto, enrolling 250 boarders and 245 day students in Grade 6 to university entrance. The university preparatory academic program offers many Advanced Placement courses with the option of achieving the Advanced Placement International Diploma (APID). Debating, drama, music, and computer networking are emphasized, and daily participation in athletics is expected. St. Andrew's College is unique in Canada in offering the study of the Highland bagpipe within the music curriculum. Boarding Tuition: $26,019 (Cdn.); Day Tuition: $15,172. Financial Aid/Scholarships: $700,000. Aubrey Foy is Director of Admission; E. G. "Ted" Staunton (Trent, [Hons.] B.A.; Toronto, B.Ed., M.Ed.) is Headmaster.

St. Clement's School   1901

21 St. Clement's Avenue, Toronto, Ontario M4R 1G8, Canada.
416-483-4835; Fax 416-483-8242; E-mail admissions@scs.on.ca;
Web Site www.scs.on.ca

St. Clement's School combines a traditional focus on academic excellence and character development with up-to-the-minute technological resources to help students succeed in today's rapidly changing society. The School enrolls approximately 425 day students from Grade 1 to high school graduation. It seeks to develop tomorrow's leaders by encouraging scholastic achievement, self-confidence, and independent thinking in an enriching, supportive environment. The rigorous academic program, varied cocurricular activities, and numerous opportunities for leadership have enabled graduates to enter top universities worldwide. Advanced Placement courses are available. Tuition: $11,000. Financial Aid: $50,000. Patricia D. Parisi (University of Connecticut, Ed.Spec.) is Principal.

St. George's School   1931

4175 West 29th Avenue, Vancouver, British Columbia, Canada V6S 1V6. 604-224-1304; Fax 604-224-7066; E-mail info@stgeorges.bc.ca; Web Site www.stgeorges.bc.ca

St. George's School enrolls 1050 boys in Grades 1–12, with boarders from Grade 6 onward. Set on two campuses totaling 20 acres, this nonsectarian, university preparatory school offers challenges and choices designed to develop the whole person within a balanced academic environment. The curriculum combines the humanities, sciences, fine arts, and foreign languages. French and computer science begin in Grade 1, and Advanced Placement courses are available in nine subject areas. Among the activities are 22 sports, a Sea to Sky outdoor education program, music groups, clubs, and public service. Boarding Tuition: $20,232–$21,877; Day Tuition: $8512–$10,702. Financial Aid: $250,000. W.J. "Bill" McCracken is Director of Admissions; Nigel R.L. Toy is Headmaster.

St. George's School of Montreal   1930

3100 The Boulevard, Montreal, Quebec H3Y 1R9, Canada. 514-937-9289; Fax 514-933-3621; E-mail admissions@stgeorges.qc.ca; Web Site www.stgeorges.qc.ca

Founded by parents committed to child-centered learning, St. George's is a coeducational, college preparatory day school enrolling 512 boys and girls in Pre-School–Grade 11. Stressing a flexible approach to learning, the School seeks to provide a wide range of courses and activities in an atmosphere that is warm and caring, challenging and purposeful. Proficiency in English and French is a priority. In addition to accelerated math/sciences and extensive Advanced Placement courses, the curriculum, which includes enriched art, music, drama, debating, and public speaking, is supported by computer networking, Internet, and E-mail for all students. Tuition: $8250. Financial Aid: $250,000. Mr. James A. Officer is Principal.

St. Mildred's-Lightbourn School   1891

1080 Linbrook Road, Oakville, Ontario L6J 2L1, Canada. 905-845-2386; Admissions 905-845-9980; Fax 905-845-4799; E-mail st_mildreds@smls.on.ca; Web Site www.smls.on.ca

St. Mildred's-Lightbourn School offers a university preparatory day program for 600 girls in Junior Kindergarten–Grade 13 (OAC). The liberal arts and sciences are emphasized in a learning environment permeated by Anglican values and a feminine perspective. The single-gender setting permits full participation in all academic areas, including traditionally male-dominated fields, encouraging girls to become self-directed, independent, and confident of their abilities. Social and current issues, liturgy, the creative and performing arts, and a challenging athletic program engage students in cocurricular activities. Tuition: $5285–$10,200 (Canadian). Scholarships and bursaries are available. Donna Cossitt is Admissions Coordinator; Susan Both is Principal.

Selwyn House School   1908

95 Chemin Côte St. Antoine, Montreal, Quebec H3Y 2H8, Canada. 514-931-9481; Admission Fax 514-932-8776; E-mail admissions@selwyn.ca; Web Site www.selwyn.ca

Selwyn House, an independent day school enrolling 565 boys in Kindergarten–Grade 11, strives to provide a thorough academic curriculum in preparation for university entrance. The School's challenging athletic and extracurricular programs include activities such as robotics, debating, public speaking, publications, photography, art, chess, science, jazz ensemble, and trips to Europe and to fine arts presentations. Elementary School (K–6) offers biliterate and French immersion programs. Each student is encouraged to work to the best of his ability and to develop a strong sense of responsibility to the school community and his studies. Tuition: $8160–$10,850 (Canadian). Scholarships and financial aid are available. Mme. Sylvie Bastien-Doss is Director of Admission; William Mitchell is Headmaster.

The Sterling Hall School   1987

99 Cartwright Avenue, Toronto, Ontario M6A 1V4, Canada. 416-785-3410; Fax 416-785-6616; E-mail admissions@sterlinghall.com; Web Site www.sterlinghall.com

The Sterling Hall School, an independent day school enrolling 273 boys in Junior Kindergarten–Grade 8, aims to educate each student in a way that encourages self-esteem, respect, and responsibility while developing individual talents through a comprehensive curriculum and varied extracurricular activities. The values espoused by the School provide a rich learning experience designed to develop the whole child intellectually, socially, and emotionally, and to prepare him for higher education. French is taught in all grades, and students benefit from advanced computer studies, exciting art and music programs, and extensive athletics. Tuition: $10,220–$12,810. Ms. Jodi Holder is Director of Admissions; Ian Robinson (University of London, B.A.; University of Keele, Cert.Ed.) is Principal.

Strathcona-Tweedsmuir School   1971

R.R. 2, Okotoks, Alberta T0L 1T0, Canada. 403-938-4431; Fax 403-938-4492; Web Site http://www.sts.ab.ca

Strathcona-Tweedsmuir School, created by the merger of Strathcona School for Boys (1929) and Tweedsmuir: An Academic School for Girls (1959), is a college preparatory, nondenominational day school located 15 miles south of Calgary. There are 663 boys and girls enrolled in Grades 1–12. An enriched curriculum, based on traditional subjects, forms the basis of the students' education. Athletics, clubs, the arts, music, student government, and an innovative outdoor education program expand the learning experience. Tuition: $7279–$9462. Transportation: $1280. Financial Aid/Scholarships: $20,000. John Tottenham is Director of Admissions; Gordon D. Freight is Acting Head of School.

The Study   1915

3233 The Boulevard, Montreal, Quebec H3Y 1S4, Canada. 514-935-9352; Fax 514-935-1721; E-mail admissions@thestudy.qc.ca; Web Site http://www.thestudy.qc.ca

Margaret Gascoigne founded this independent, college preparatory day school to provide high-quality educational opportunities for girls. Presently, the school enrolls 345 girls in Kindergarten–Grade 11, with a Bilingual Programme in the Elementary School. The Mission of the school stresses "fine scholarship and a love of learning, clarity of thought and expression, and leadership in an environment which appreciates diversity and values the importance of the individual and the community." College preparatory courses are taught in English, math, French, sciences, social sciences, and the arts. Tuition: $7300–$8900. Financial Aid: $75,000. Marie-Françoise Jothy is Director of Admissions; Mary Liistro Hebert (McGill, B.Sc., B.Ed.) was appointed Headmistress in 1997.

Toronto French School   1962

Toronto Campus (PK–OAC): 296 Lawrence Avenue East, Toronto, Ontario M4N 1T7, Canada. 416-484-6533; Fax 416-481-1447; E-mail admissions@tfs.on.ca; Web Site www.tfs.on.ca
Mississauga Campus (PK–Grade 7): 1293 Meredith Avenue, Mississauga, Ontario L5E 2E6, Canada.

A bilingual, coeducational school with an international perspective, Toronto French School enrolls approximately 1150 day students from all linguistic and socioeconomic backgrounds in Pre-Kindergarten (age 3) to university entrance. The School's broad curriculum, including the International Baccalaureate, emphasizes languages, math, and science. The School is set on a 28-acre campus, with a branch in suburban Mississauga. Before- and after-school child care is available. Activities include 30 competitive sports teams, debating, yearbook, choir, drama productions in two languages, and community service. TFS is home to the Canadian Chemistry and Physics Olympiad. Tuition: $5000–$13,665 (Canadian). Jean Brugniau is Head.

Trafalgar School for Girls   1887

3495 Simpson Street, Montreal, Quebec H3G 2J7, Canada. 514-935-2644; Fax 514-935-2359; E-mail admin@trafalgar.qc.ca; Web Site www.traf.trafalgar.qc.ca

Trafalgar School aims to equip young women with skills and attitudes that will serve them in university, in the marketplace, and in their personal lives. Dedicated faculty offer strong academic and extracurricular programs to 220 students in Grades 7–11. English, French, math, and physical education are required at all levels; options include Spanish, chemistry, physics, calculus, and computer science. Trafalgar encourages the wide use of information technology with a networked building that allows electronic access to resources around the world. Athletics, band, choir, debating, public speaking, and drama are among the many activities. Tuition: $7400. Scholarships and Financial Aid: $120,000. Geoffrey Dowd (McGill, B.Ed.; Queen's, M.A.) is Principal.

Upper Canada College   TORONTO

200 Lonsdale Road, Toronto, Ontario, Canada M4V 1W6. Telephone 416-488-1125; E-mail rbarter@ucc.on.ca; Web Site www.ucc.on.ca

UPPER CANADA COLLEGE in Toronto, Ontario, is a university preparatory school for boys. The College enrolls day boys in Grade 1 through high school graduation and boarding boys in Grades 9 and above. Attending school in the center of Toronto, students take advantage of the cultural life of a major city.

Founded as a nondenominational school in 1829 by Sir John Colborne, the Lieutenant Governor of the Colony of Upper Canada, the College was state supported until 1900 when it became fully independent. Upper Canada College is dedicated to providing preparation for university and the intellectual, physical, and social development of each student.

The College is directed by a 28-member Board of Governors who are elected or appointed from the alumni body and from parents. Upper Canada College is accredited by the Ministry of Education of the Province of Ontario and is a founding member of the Canadian Educational Standards Institute, which awards accreditation to members of The Canadian Association of Independent Schools. The College is a member of the Geneva-based International Baccalaureate organization and has a number of faculty involved in that organization. The College also holds associate membership in the National Association of Independent Schools in the United States and the Headmasters' Conference in the United Kingdom.

THE CAMPUS. The 38-acre campus in the heart of Toronto consists of the Prep School for Grades 2–8 and the Upper School for Grades 9–13. Each school has its own science facility, a computer center, library, gymnasium, and music and art studios. The athletic facilities are shared and include a new physical education centre, playing fields, a hockey arena, tennis and squash courts, an outdoor track, and an indoor swimming pool. The new Creativity Center (1999) houses music, drama, art, and Geographic Information Systems (GIS) programs. In addition, a new Primary wing opened at the Preparatory School. There are two residence buildings for Upper School boarding students and five faculty residence buildings.

The 450-acre Norval campus is located 35 miles outside of Toronto. There are two houses on the property to accommodate students for extended periods of outdoor and environmental education and for use as part of the boarding program. The College owns the property and all facilities, which are valued at $35,000,000 (U.S.).

THE FACULTY. Appointed Principal in 1991, J. Douglas Blakey holds an honors Bachelor of Science degree from the University of Guelph and a Diploma in Education from the University of Western Ontario. He joined the faculty of the College in 1975 and has held a number of positions at the school. He and his wife, Cheryl, have two children.

There are 94 full-time faculty members who teach at the Preparatory and Upper Schools, 74 men and 20 women. Ten faculty live on campus, including 8 with their families. They hold 59 baccalaureate and 51 graduate degrees representing study at Brock, Carleton, Dalhousie, Lakehead, Laurentian, McGill, McMaster, Mount Allison, Queen's, Ryerson, Sir George Williams, Wilfred Laurier, York, and the Universities of British Columbia, Calgary, Guelph, Ottawa, Toronto, Waterloo, Western Ontario, and Windsor in Canada; College of William and Mary, Eastman School of Music, Framingham State College, Loyola, Middlebury, Niagara, Philadelphia College of Art, Rensselaer Polytechnic Institute, and the University of California (Berkeley) in the United States; the Universities of Liverpool, London, and Sussex in England; the University of Wales; the Sorbonne in France; and the University of the West Indies. There are also 23 part-time faculty members.

The College has a health centre staffed by two nurses, a sports injury clinic with two full-time therapists, and two professional counselors. A doctor is on call and medical facilities are nearby.

STUDENT BODY. In 1999–2000, the College enrolled 106 boarding boys and 975 day boys in Grades 1–13 as follows: Grade 1—18, Grade 2—18, Grade 3—44, Grade 4—24, Grade 5—48, Grade 6—48, Grade 7—96, Grade 8—111, Grade 9—137, Grades 10–11—259, Grade 12—148, and Grade 13—130. Students come from Canadian provinces, the United States, and eight foreign countries.

ACADEMIC PROGRAM. The school year, divided into three terms, begins in early September and ends in mid-June. There are vacations in December and March and five long weekends. Parents receive marks and extensive comments four times during the school year.

Classes meet five days a week in seven periods of 45 minutes. Class size averages 18 students. Sports and club activities begin at 3:30 P.M. and end at 5:30 P.M. Faculty are available for extra help and supervise study halls during school hours and in the residence in the evening for boarders.

The Upper Canada College curriculum is university preparatory. All students undertake the International Baccalaureate diploma in their final two years at the College. Ninety-eight percent of the students in the Class of 1999 earned this demanding

and prestigious diploma. In addition to the I.B., students meet the credit requirements for the Ontario Secondary School Diploma, awarded at graduation. Boys in Grade 9 have an academic program of required courses in English, Science, Mathematics, History, Geography, French, Computer Studies, and Physical Education, plus Art or Music. In Grade 10, students follow a core program and two electives. The Grade 11 program is designed to provide a foundation of knowledge and skills before the commencement of the I.B. program.

The International Baccalaureate curriculum at Upper Canada College requires candidates to undertake study in six subject groups: English Literature; French, German, or Spanish; History, Geography, or Economics; Mathematics; Physics, Chemistry, or Biology; and an elective: Art, Music, Computer Science, Classics, or a second subject from one of the other compulsory subject groups. Three subjects are undertaken at the Higher Level and three at the Standard Level. Students also complete the Theory of Knowledge course and an Extended Essay and meet requirements for extracurricular Creativity, Action, and Service (CAS).

All Upper Canada College students make application to universities and, with few exceptions, every graduate proceeds directly to a degree program. Six students have been named Rhodes Scholars in the past several years.

In 1999, 140 graduates enrolled at Brown, Cornell, Dartmouth, Duke, Emory, Harvard, Macalester, New York University, Princeton, Stanford, Vanderbilt, Yale, and the Universities of Colorado, Michigan, and Pennsylvania in the United States; Dalhousie, King's College, McGill, McMaster, Mount Allison, Queen's, and the Universities of British Columbia, Toronto, Waterloo, and Western Ontario in Canada; and Bath, London Academy of Music and Dramatic Art, London School of Economics in England, and Oxford.

STUDENT ACTIVITIES. The Upper School house system divides students into ten groups with a housemaster overseeing the academic, extracurricular, and social development of the students in his group. The leaving class members of each house assume the responsibility of school prefects and enforce school regulations, promote house and school spirit, and organize various activities. The Board of Stewards, an elected and appointed group of 16 students from the graduating class, meets regularly with the school administration and serves on faculty committees. Members organize and coordinate school activities, clubs, the athletic program, and social events.

Upper Canada College, a member of the Independent Schools Athletic Association, offers a varied sports program at both the interscholastic and intramural levels. Teams compete in football, soccer, cross-country running and skiing, tennis, squash, hockey, basketball, badminton, volleyball, swimming, alpine skiing, cricket, track and field, rugby, golf, crew, lacrosse, and softball.

Extracurricular involvement is required in all years and fulfills the I.B. criteria for Creativity, Action, and Service. Participation in the College's community service program is compulsory. The clubs program provides the opportunity to participate in current affairs, debate, drama, photography, film-making, and the Duke of Edinburgh Awards. Students may participate in music by electing the Music Option, taking private lessons, or joining a performing group such as the Jazz Ensemble, Wind Ensemble, Symphonic Band, Concert Band, Stage Band, or the UCC Singers. Students also publish a yearbook (*The College Times*) and three magazines (*Blazer, The Blue Page,* and *Quiddity*). In the Thursday Club program, students are encouraged to choose an activity that is different from those engaged in during the rest of the week.

Traditional school events include The Arts Festival, which is organized and directed by students and features weeklong performances in drama, music, art, and photography. The student-run World Affairs Conference is attended by representatives from schools in Canada, the United States, and abroad.

ADMISSION AND COSTS. Upper Canada College seeks students with the ability to undertake the rigorous academic program and who will participate actively in the full life of the school. To encourage diversity and to facilitate admission, a National Scholarship Program has been introduced to attract academically able boarding students; a College Scholarship is designed to attract day students.

New day students are accepted in Grades 1, 3, 5, 7, and 9–12, and new boarding students in Grades 9–12. Students are accepted on the basis of transcripts, recommendations, entrance exams, and a personal interview. Application should be made as early as possible in the year prior to desired entry. A waiting list is established.

The 1999–2000 tuition in Canadian dollars for Grades 1–11 is $15,280 for day students and $27,180 for boarders in Grades 9–11. In Grades 12–13 (International Baccalaureate), day tuition is $16,780 and boarding tuition is $28,680. A variety of tuition payment plans is available. More than $1,000,000 is provided each year in financial assistance and scholarship awards under the National Scholarship and College Scholarship Programs.

Director of Admission: J.E. Reid Barter
Director of University Relations: David Matthews

The York School   TORONTO

1320 Yonge Street, Toronto, Ontario M4T 1X2, Canada.
416-926-1325; Fax 416-926-9592

Tʜᴇ ʏᴏʀᴋ sᴄʜᴏᴏʟ in Toronto, Canada, is a coeducational, college preparatory day school for boys and girls in Grades 1 through university entrance with a Montessori-based preschool program for children ages 2½ to 5½. The School's distinctive red brick building is located at the crest of the Yonge Street hill next to an attractive midtown neighborhood. Toronto (population 3,000,000) is a multicultural center of commerce, with museums, parks, and theaters that serve as destinations for recreation and field trips. The School is situated on the north/south subway line and is easily accessible by car.

Head of School Barbara Goodwin-Zeibots founded The York School in 1965. The Elementary School opened in 1978 with the Upper School section opening in September of 1995. The School moved to its current location, a 55,000-square-foot building, in 1998, during a rigorous capital campaign called "A Home of Our Own." The campaign ensured the renovation process, which accommodates the entire student body of The York School in one building.

The York School's goals include providing each student with a strong foundation in academic, artistic, physical, and moral education within a structured, supportive atmosphere. Students are challenged to take risks, to voice opinions, and to effect changes within the school environment. Faculty, students, and parents form a closely knit community to provide a secure place where dignity and self-esteem are paramount. Students and staff alike live by The York School's code of conduct based on personal responsibility and respect for each other.

In 1997, The York School became one of only three independent schools in Toronto to offer the comprehensive International Baccalaureate (IB), which students may earn along with the Ontario Secondary School Diploma.

The York School is nonprofit and nondenominational and is guided by a Board of Trustees including 12 parents, the Head, the Guild President, Director of Development, and others. The York School Guild, founded in 1965 by parents and friends, raises money for the School through such events as the Magazine Sale and the Spring Plant Sale, and has helped purchase musical equipment, computer hardware and software, and library books for the School. The York School holds membership in the Canadian Association of Independent Schools (CAIS), the Conference of Independent Schools (CIS), and the International Baccalaureate Organization (IBO).

THE CAMPUS. The new Yonge Street campus is ideally suited for an independent school because of its generous outdoor open space, numerous stairwells, and high ceilings. The renovations include large classrooms; fully equipped science labs with state-of-the-art equipment, dissection areas, chemical- and heat-resistant floor and table tops, work stations piped for gas, water, and electricity, and a safety shower and eye wash station; a networked computer lab with CD-ROM databases, printers, plotters, scanners, and communication servers; a Library/Resource Center including study carrels, an electronic catalog system, and an audio/visual center; and an Art Studio with natural light, drying racks, display shelves, a print-making area, and a pottery wheel. A drop-off area at the rear of the School brings students right to the door, and the outdoor playground is securely located away from Yonge Street.

THE FACULTY. Barbara Goodwin-Zeibots was appointed Head of School in 1965. A graduate of the University of Toronto, she received her Montessori training in England. Ms. Goodwin-Zeibots has overseen the development of The York School from its beginnings as a Montessori preschool to its current status with a full Upper School granting the International Baccalaureate and the Ontario Secondary School Diploma.

More than 60 staff members, most of whom are teachers, support the School's mission. Teachers are provided with comprehensive dental and extended health care plans and a matching Registered Retirement Savings Plan. Many opportunities for professional development for teachers and administrators are available. Staff members are trained in first aid and CPR, and hospital facilities are nearby.

STUDENT BODY. The York School enrolls nearly 500 girls and boys in Nursery through university entrance, including 100 high school students in the only coeducational, independent, nondenominational secondary school in central Toronto that has membership in CAIS and CIS. In keeping with its mission, the School retains a diverse and multicultural student body.

ACADEMIC PROGRAM. The academic year begins in mid-September, ends in mid-June, and is composed of three terms. Grade reports are sent to parents four times a year; two effort reports and two achievement reports are given. Parent-teacher conferences follow the grade reports. Classes are held Monday through Friday, from 8:30 A.M. until 3:40 P.M. Students in all grades wear uniforms.

In 1998, The York School introduced the International Baccalaureate Diploma as the curriculum for graduation while retaining the Ontario Secondary School Diploma. This internationally recognized program prepares students for the intellectual rigors of postsecondary academic work and assures universities and colleges of a consistent standard of evaluation. York students must complete 30 credits of course work to graduate from the Upper School.

The two-year International Baccalaureate program involves the study of six subjects from six different groups, and three special subjects including the 4000-word Extended Essay; 150 hours of community service known as Creativity, Action, Service; and the completion of the Theory of Knowledge course.

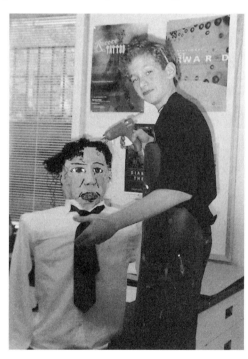

All York School students study English and French, Mathematics, History, Geography, and Science, with Physical Education, Music, and Art at appropriate grade/age levels. Fluency in both English and French is emphasized relative to listening, speaking, reading, and writing. In the field of Mathematics, concrete math materials encourage children to think logically and to classify information with precision. Students learn to view the earth as part of the universe and study the human family in History, Geography, and Science. York School's Physical Education program includes four periods of instruction each week in the gymnasium or the appropriate outdoor setting. A strong Music Program provides instruction in vocal and instru-

mental music, and music history and theory. The Art curriculum includes courses in drawing, painting, illustration, computer graphics, and woodworking. Student artwork is organized and displayed throughout the year.

In all areas of academic preparation, York is committed to providing each student with in-depth opportunities to use modern technology to maximize the learning process across the curriculum. In addition to course work, all Upper School students are required to perform volunteer service for a total of 50 hours; the International Baccalaureate program requires 150 hours over a two-year period.

The Guidance Department provides information and services to assist students and their parents in making decisions about education and future careers. It is expected that each Upper School student will have about 10 to 15 hours of homework per week.

STUDENT ACTIVITIES. York School students are encouraged to seek leadership roles and to have an active voice in student affairs, which they may do under the House system. There are four Houses, each with two elected leaders who are responsible for social activities, special events, fund-raising, sports, and student life.

Students write the school newspaper, *The Voice,* and *Perspective,* the yearbook. The Visual Arts Club, Drama Society, and York Jazz Band provide opportunities for musicians.

The athletic program offers sports for boys and girls and intramural teams where students are interested. Traditionally, teams are formed in cross-country, basketball, volleyball, track and field, badminton, and golf.

Field trips are grade-appropriate and include trips to Ottawa to study Canadian History, to Washington, D.C., to study American History, and camping activities.

The York School Guild sponsors a number of activities during the year including a Hallowe'en Party, Chanukah Celebration, Christmas Play, Music and Art Festival, and Sports Banquet.

ADMISSION AND COSTS. The York School seeks academically able students who enjoy an intellectual challenge and a well-rounded program of physical education and the arts. Most students enter the School in Grade 1, although applications are invited for every grade. Students should apply one to two years before they expect to enroll at York, and each completed application must be accompanied by a $500 deposit, which may be applied to the tuition payment upon acceptance. Applicants are also expected to write an entrance test and be interviewed at the School. Tuition is $12,400; a one-time refundable, noninterest-bearing loan of $4000 is also required. Student uniforms are extra.

Director of Admissions: Marilyn Andrews
International Baccalaureate Coordinator: Barbara Lister

CHILE

Santiago College   SANTIAGO

Avenida Los Leones 584, Casilla 130-D,
*   Santiago, Chile. 56-2-232-1813; Fax 56-2-232-0755;*
*   E-mail admiss@scollege.cl*

SANTIAGO COLLEGE in Santiago, Chile, is a bilingual (English/Spanish), bicultural day school enrolling 1850 boys and girls in Nursery–Grade 12. This college preparatory school is situated in the capital city of Santiago (population 5,000,000), which is surrounded by the Andes Mountains. Santiago was founded by Spanish conquerors in 1541 and is rich in historical, cultural, and recreational opportunities. The city is home to three major universities and numerous museums and public parks. Transportation to and from campus is arranged by the Parents' Association Office.

Santiago College was founded in 1880 by the Reverend William Taylor, a Methodist missionary from the United States. The first directors, Dr. and Mrs. La Fetra, guided the institution by love, faith, and integrity and laid the spiritual and intellectual foundations of Santiago College. Originally a coeducational institution, the College was for many years a girls' boarding school before returning to its coeducational mission in 1972. The traditions and educational values of the school are firmly rooted in the Chilean-North American heritage. The College was founded on the traditional values of respect, tolerance, responsibility, honesty, integrity, high academic achievement, and a joy of living. The distinctive bilingual education informs all aspects of the program, and students are expected to acquire a fluent command of written and oral English. Graduates in every generation of the school's life have been successful in college and beyond, both in Chile and abroad.

The mission of Santiago College, "to be a pioneer in offering a complete, integrated, bilingual education grounded on Judeo-Christian values and principles," supports the school's

fundamental aspiration to enable students to contribute to the development of a democratic society in a continuous process of change and global interdependence .

Santiago College has been accredited by the Southern Association of Colleges and Schools of the United States since 1949 and by the Chilean Ministry of Education since 1961. It holds membership in the European Council of International Schools, The Association of American Schools in South America, the Federacíon de Institutos de Educacíon Particular, and the Association of British Schools in Chile. Additionally, the College is a member of the International Schools Association and was the first school in Latin America to pilot the International Baccalaureate program.

The Parents' Association encourages families to take an active role in the life of the College, promoting the stated educational goals and contributing to school spirit and pride. The Santiago College Alumni Association edits the alumni news magazine, provides support for the school's sports teams, and runs the Candy Store, with proceeds providing scholarship funds for students. In addition to Chile, the Alumni Association has international chapters in Buenos Aires, Washington, and California.

THE CAMPUS. The campus buildings are of gracious Spanish-style architecture, with red tiled roofs, tiled floors, and expansive inner arches. Most of the academic buildings face a landscaped courtyard with palm trees, rose gardens, and a lily pond. Two gymnasiums, basketball courts, and a multipurpose outdoor court are on the main campus. Physical Education classes also take place on the outskirts of the city at the 1200-acre La Dehesa campus, which provides ample playing fields and an Early Childhood annex.

The Santiago College library has 36,000 titles, including many modern reference books, a collection of art books, and a wide variety of national and international periodicals. The library plays a central role in school life and promotes a multicultural environment. Media services include an audiovisual department with televisions, VHS recorders, projectors, and multimedia resources for students and teachers. There are computer laboratories, used by students in every grade, which provide basic competency in programming, the use of databases and spreadsheets, and word processing, as well as activities that enhance creativity and communication.

The Los Leones campus houses a modern, fully equipped infirmary. There is also a complete First Aid Unit on the La Dehesa campus. The infirmary is attended by nurses at all times, and teachers are trained to deal with student emergencies.

THE FACULTY. Alun Cooper is Director of Santiago College. He is aided in his work by three principals, five curriculum coordinators, 103 full-time teachers, 60 part-time teachers, and more than 40 support staff.

The Guidance Department is staffed by professional counselors and psychologists who complement the teachers' work and communicate with parents and guardians on a regular basis. Counselors help students develop a realistic understanding of their capabilities and interests in order to prepare them to make appropriate choices, both in university placement and in life.

STUDENT BODY. In 1999, the College enrolled 1819 boys and girls in Nursery through Grade 12, with 799 in Nursery–Grade 4, 504 in Grades 5–8, and 516 in Grades 9–12.

ACADEMIC PROGRAM. The academic year runs from March through the middle of December, with a two-week winter vacation scheduled for the middle of July, at the conclusion of the first semester.

Nursery, Kindergarten, and First Grade students have a half-day schedule. The remainder of the students through Grade 12 attend classes from 8:00 A.M. until 3:30 P.M. Monday through Friday. The afternoon schedule may vary according to the individual student's timetable and extracurricular involvement.

Santiago College strives to provide an integrated, interdisciplinary education in which students are prepared to face challenges and understand problem-solving and decision-making skills. The school has, as a primary academic goal, the fluent command of English for all students. In addition to solid academic achievement, aesthetic sensitivity, and expression, students are trained in manual and technical skills.

The College is currently pioneering the International Baccalaureate Middle Years Program, designed for students between the ages of 11 and 16, and is also preparing for the Primary Years Program, adopted by the International Baccalaureate in 1997.

The International Baccalaureate program for Upper School students, in place at the College since 1965, has a worldwide reputation for academic excellence. Designed for the last two years of high school, it emphasizes learning how to learn and the attainment of high standards in every major discipline. There are three special requirements, including the Theory of Knowledge course, active participation in Creative Activities and Social Service, and an Extended Essay, on a topic of the student's choice.

Character education is fundamental to the educational program, and the school fosters values through social service, environmental education programs, and civic and global involvement opportunities.

More than 95 percent of Santiago College graduates go on to private and state colleges and universities in Chile and elsewhere.

STUDENT ACTIVITIES. The Student Council is comprised of elected representatives who organize a wide variety of activities.

Boy Scouts, Drama Club, the Debating Club, Poetry Recital, the National Chemistry Olympics, and offerings in chess, ballet, band, cooking, choir, painting, and ceramics provide extracurricular opportunities for many students.

Sports teams are fielded in volleyball and field hockey for girls; soccer, rugby, and basketball for boys; and cross-country, track, and gymnastics for both girls and boys. Inter-school tournaments are held throughout the year.

Traditional school events include the Ring and Medal Ceremony, Harvest Assembly, a charity benefit for local organizations, July 4th Celebration, Cultural Days, United Nations Assembly, Last Chapel, Junior Prom, Senior Ball, and The School Anniversary, a two-day celebration in October with a parade and house competitions.

ADMISSION AND COSTS. Santiago College seeks students who wish to develop a sense of responsibility and to participate constructively in the development of a society in the process of constant international change and integration. Parents should be committed to the educational values and objectives of the school. Applicants are evaluated on the basis of scholastic aptitude and social behavior. Since English is the first language of instruction at Santiago College, applicants are tested to ascertain their proficiency level. Admission preference is given to siblings of students already enrolled, children of alumni, children of school staff, and applicants coming from abroad.

Parents are required to complete an application and submit the applicant's birth certificate, previous school transcripts, and a report on the child's character and conduct issued by the most recent school attended. All applications must be accompanied by a fee of US $50.

For 1999, the tuition is US $4100 payable in ten monthly installments. The annual enrollment fee is $63, and extras include accident insurance, Parents' Association Fee, school magazine, school insurance, and bookstore sundries for an approximate yearly total of $300. Daily lunch service is offered at $3 per day.

Lower School Principal: Lorna Prado
Middle School Principal: Annabella Farba
Upper School Principal: Richard Baylis
International Baccalaureate Coordinator: Ana María Figueroa
Alumni Association President: Ana Mari Urrutia
Head of Admissions: Carmen Coello
Business Manager: Mónica Arancibia
Plant Manager: Ximena Arancibia
Head of Personnel: Carmen Thomas
Public Relations Officer: Dezarae Gaines

CHINA

School Year Abroad 1967

c/o Middle School #2, 12, Xinjiekouwai Street, Beijing 100088, People's Republic of China. 8610-6235-4503

Please see the Listing under Massachusetts.

DENMARK

Copenhagen International School   1963

Hellerupvej 22-26, 2900 Hellerup, Denmark. 45-39-46-33-03;
Fax 45-39-61-22-30

Enrolling 485 boys and girls in Pre-Kindergarten–Grade 12, Copenhagen International School seeks to help students from many nations maintain their cultural heritage while developing a sense of global awareness. The program is college preparatory, beginning with the IBPYP in the Primary School, continuing with the IBMYP in the Middle School, and culminating in the Senior School with a high school diploma and the International Baccalaureate in Grade 12. English as a Second Language is taught at all levels. European travel and the cultural and historical resources of Copenhagen enrich the program. Activities involve the arts, NECIS athletics, and interest clubs. Tuition: $6500–$12,300. ESL Fee: Variable. Christopher Bowman was appointed Director in 1998. *New England Association.*

EGYPT

Schutz American School   1924

P.O. Box 1000, Alexandria, Egypt. 203-570-1435/571-2205;
Fax 203-571-0229; E-mail 103375.1022@compuserve.com

Schutz American School is nondenominational and accommodates 230 day boys and girls from Early Childhood (age three) to Grade 12 on two campuses. The program is based on traditional American college preparatory and general curricula and includes the study of French, Arabic, and English as a Second Language. Student government, National Honor Society, yearbook, sports, and the arts are extracurricular activities. Tuition: $4120–$9850. Registration: $1600. Robert Woods was named Head of School in 1999. *New England Association.*

ENGLAND

American Community Schools

SURREY AND MIDDLESEX

Cobham Campus: "Heywood," Portsmouth Road, Cobham,
Surrey KT11, 1BL, England. 44-1932-867251;
E-mail jscruton@acs-england.co.uk; Web Site www.acs-england.co.uk

Hillingdon Campus: 108 Vine Lane, Hillingdon, Middlesex UB10 OBE,
England. 44-1895-259771
Egham Campus: "Woodlee," London Road (A30), Egham,
Surrey TW20 OHS, England. 44-1784-430800

AMERICAN COMMUNITY SCHOOLS operate two coeducational, college preparatory schools for students in Pre-School–Grade 13 and one school enrolling day students in Pre-School–Grade 10. Grades 11 and 12 will be added in 2000–01. The Cobham campus accommodates day and boarding students, while the Hillingdon and Egham facilities enroll day students only. All campuses are in suburban settings, and each town has a population of approximately 11,000. Cobham, 25 miles from London, and Egham, 20 miles from London, are accessible by British Rail, while Hillingdon, 15 miles from the capital, is served by the London Underground and by British Rail. The programs of the American Community Schools use many of the cultural and historical resources of London and environs.

Founded in 1967 to meet the needs of the growing American community in greater London, American Community Schools follow the principles and practices of American and international education. While maintaining high standards of scholarship and discipline, the Schools are committed to a supportive, student-centered learning environment.

A proprietary institution, the Schools are governed by a Board of Directors. American Community Schools are accredited by the New England Association of Schools and Colleges and hold membership in the International Baccalaureate Diploma Program, the Advanced Placement Program, and the European Council of International Schools. The Schools administer College Board Testing programs.

THE CAMPUS. The 128-acre Cobham campus occupies a former country estate. A dining hall/auditorium, the boarding facility, Lower School, Middle School, and High School complement the main house (1804). Sports facilities include a gymnasium, tennis courts, an Olympic-size track, a baseball diamond, sports fields, adventure playgrounds, and picnic/barbecue areas.

Situated on an 11-acre site, the Hillingdon campus combines a restored 19th-century mansion, which is the setting for school classes, concerts, art exhibitions, and receptions, with a new, purpose-built addition housing classrooms, science laboratories, a computer room, gymnasium, cafeteria, auditorium, and libraries. The campus, located next to Hillingdon Park, has playing fields, tennis courts, an adventure playground, and landscaped gardens. The main house (1855) was formerly the home of Charles Henry Mills, first Baron Hillingdon.

The 20-acre Egham campus occupies a former country estate, the Woodlee Estate, adjacent to the Royal Windsor Great Park. The School has extensive facilities including gymnasiums, science and information technology laboratories, an early childhood center, all-weather floodlit tennis courts, sports fields, an adventure playground, and landscaped gardens surrounding the main house (1876).

THE FACULTY. Superintendent Malcolm Kay served as Principal of the Middle School and the High School of the American Community Schools before assuming his present position. A 1973 graduate of Nottingham University, Mr. Kay was also affiliated with the International School of Geneva for seven years.

Thomas Lehman, who served as Lower School Principal for 5 years, was appointed Headmaster at Cobham in 1992. Mr. Lehman graduated from Syracuse University in 1973 and taught in the Syracuse School District for 12 years before joining American Community Schools.

Paul Berg was appointed Head of the Hillingdon campus in 1996, having served as Middle School Principal since 1991 and, before that, as Dean of Students since 1987. He holds degrees with "High Honors" in political science and in education.

Moyra Hadley, Head of School at the Egham campus, is a graduate of London University and holds a Master's degree in Educational Administration from California State University.

The full-time faculty at the Cobham campus number 128—97 women and 31 men. At the Hillingdon campus, there are 72 full-time teachers—47 women and 25 men. There are 58 full-time teachers—50 women and 8 men—at Egham. All teachers hold the baccalaureate degree; 84 have advanced degrees.

There are also 13 part-time instructors; full-time nurses for each school provide health care.

STUDENT BODY. At the Cobham campus, enrollment is 1280—636 boys and 644 girls. The Boarding School has 55 boys and 52 girls. The student body at the Hillingdon campus numbers 660—360 boys and 300 girls. The Egham campus, opened in September 1995, enrolls 450 students—230 boys and 220 girls. Approximately 56 percent of the students are from North America; and the remaining 44 percent represent more than 55 other nationalities.

ACADEMIC PROGRAM. The school year, from late August to mid-June, is divided into two semesters and includes vacations in October, December, February, and April. The Cobham campus daily schedule for all grades extends from 8:30 A.M. to 3:10 P.M.; Middle School (Grades 5–8) and High School (Grades 9–13) students have eight 40-minute class periods, followed by extracurricular activities. The Hillingdon campus daily schedule begins at 8:45 A.M. and ends at 3:11 P.M. with eight 44-minute class periods followed by extracurricular activities. The Egham campus daily schedule extends from 8:30 A.M. to 3:05 P.M., followed by extracurricular activities.

An average class enrolls 15 to 20 students. Supervised study halls are held throughout the day, and faculty members are available to provide individual help after school. Progress reports are issued every nine weeks in Kindergarten–Grade 4;

teacher comments accompany the end-of-semester report. Grades are issued four times a year for Grades 5–13; progress reports are sent to parents during the semester as necessary. Parent-teacher conference days are scheduled twice a year.

The program for the Lower and Middle schools includes language arts, social studies, mathematics, science, art, music, library studies, computer sciences, and physical education. In addition, French is available in Grade 1 at Egham, and Spanish, German, and French are available in the Middle School with foreign language survey courses in Grades 3–6; French in Grades 1–4 and 7–8 and German and Spanish in Grades 7–8 are available at Cobham. Hillingdon offers French, Spanish, and German in Grades 7–12 and a language survey course in Grades 3–6. Qualified eighth graders may take a High School-level language course and Algebra 1. Lower School students have one teacher for all basic academic subjects; the Middle School is departmentalized.

While the Lower and Middle schools do not have extensive special-needs programs, there is a program in reading/learning designed to help students with mild impairments and those having difficulties due to a discrepancy between past academic experience and present grade placement. The American Community Schools offer programs in English as a Second Language (except in Grades 11–13) at the Hillingdon and Cobham campuses, in which students have English language instruction daily as well as instruction in other subjects.

To graduate, High School students must complete at least 21 credits, including 4 in English, 6 in social studies and a foreign language, 6 in mathematics and science, 1 in fine arts, and 2 in physical education in Grades 9–11.

Among the full-year courses offered are English 9–12; French 1–4, German 1–3, Spanish 1–4; World History 1–2, United States History, Psychology, Economics; Algebra 1–2, Geometry, Algebra II, Precalculus; Biology, Chemistry, Physics; Drawing and Painting 1–3, Crafts, Ceramics and Sculpture, Advanced Art; Music, Chorus, Band, Drama; and Computing Studies.

Semester or partial-credit courses at Cobham include Advanced Composition, Journalism, Speech; Contemporary History, Economics, Psychology; Genetics, Probability; Word Processing, Computer Sciences, Information Technology; and Photography. Courses vary slightly between campuses.

The International Baccalaureate is offered at the Cobham and Hillingdon campuses with a full range of courses. At Cobham in 1999, 42 students received the full International Baccalaureate Diploma and 38 others also took some examinations. All received university places. At Hillingdon in 1999, 24 students received the full International Baccalaureate and obtained university places. Sixty-seven other students took exams for individual I.B. certificates.

On the Cobham campus, Advanced Placement courses are currently offered in English, French, German, Spanish, U.S. History, European History, Calculus, Biology, Chemistry, Physics, Microeconomics, Macroeconomics, and Computer Science. On the Hillingdon campus, English Language and Composition, Calculus, French, Studio Art, Chemistry, Biology, Physics, English Literature, U.S. History, Spanish, Microeconomics, Macroeconomics, Comparative Government, and Psychology are available.

Graduates of American Community Schools have entered leading institutions in the United States, Britain, Canada, Japan, the Netherlands, and Sweden. Among them are Boston University, Cambridge, Claremont–McKenna, Cornell, Dartmouth, Duke, Georgetown, Georgia Institute of Technology, Imperial, Johns Hopkins, London School of Economics, Middlebury, Tufts, and the Universities of Colorado, Edinburgh, Essex, North Carolina, Oxford, Pennsylvania, Rochester, Surrey, Texas, Virginia, and Warwick.

American Community Schools conduct summer academic and recreational programs to fit the needs of participating students.

STUDENT ACTIVITIES. The Student Councils, composed of elected representatives from the Middle and High schools, organize social activities and determine student needs and opinions on matters of concern. Students publish a yearbook, a magazine, and a newspaper. Other activities and organizations include instrumental music, modeling and crafts, quiz competition, Scouting, cheerleading; computer, drama, Model UN, yearbook, and video clubs; and dramas and musicals.

School teams compete with local American and British schools as well as American schools on the Continent. Middle School teams are fielded in baseball, basketball, soccer, tennis, track and field, and volleyball. Boys' and girls' varsity teams compete in basketball, cross-country, tennis, track and field, and volleyball. There are also boys' rugby and baseball teams, a girls' softball team, intramural sports, and noncompetitive physical activities.

There are regularly scheduled dances for the Middle and High schools. Vacation trips are offered to various European countries and to ski resorts. Class-related field trips enable students to experience Britain's rich cultural heritage, and there are foreign language trips abroad for students in the Middle and High School. Traditional events include an Arts Festival and Book Week.

ADMISSION AND COSTS. American Community Schools seek to enroll motivated students of all nationalities with average to above-average academic ability. New students are accepted in all grades throughout the year on the basis of the completed application form, previous school records, standardized test results, and two recommendations from the previous school. The Schools administer a placement examination for new High School students; nonnative speakers of English must take a nonnative language test for entry. There is a nonrefundable £75 registration fee, and a deposit of £500 for day students and £1000 for boarders, applicable toward second-semester tuition, must accompany each application.

In 1999–2000, semester tuition for day students is £2870 for Pre-School, £4770 for Kindergarten–Grade 4, £5230 for Grades 5–8, and £5545 for Grades 9–13. Boarding tuition is £9085 for Grades 7–8 and £9115 for Grades 9–13. Bus service is extra, ranging from £290 per semester, with a reduction for siblings.

Superintendent: Malcolm J. Kay
Heads of School: Thomas Lehman (Cobham), Paul Berg (Hillingdon), and Moyra Hadley (Egham)

High School Principals: Stephen Baker (Cobham), Peggy Bleyberg-Shor (Hillingdon), and Britt Brantley (Egham)
Deans of Admissions: Peggy Travers (Hillingdon), Anne Barker (Egham), and Heather Mulkey (Cobham)
Registrars: Melinda Muir (Cobham), Una Scott (Hillingdon), and Marilyn Corrigan (Egham)
Director of Development: Judson Scruton
Business Manager: R. Gossain

The American School in London

LONDON

2–8 Loudoun Road, London NW8 0NP England. 020-7449-1200; Fax 020-7449-1350; E-mail admissions@asl.org; Web Site www.asl.org

THE AMERICAN SCHOOL IN LONDON is a coeducational, college preparatory day school enrolling students in Pre-Kindergarten through Grade 12.

The mission of the School is to provide an American education of the highest quality. Students are challenged to achieve their full potential within a caring and supportive framework. As a richly diverse and international community, The American School in London fosters active citizenship in a changing world.

The School is situated in St. John's Wood, a residential area of Central London just north of Regent's Park and is convenient to underground and bus routes. In addition, a School-administered door-to-door bus service covers a large area of the city. The School's location, within easy reach of the theaters and art galleries of the West End as well as many historic sites, makes field studies in London, the United Kingdom, and Europe a central part of the ASL curriculum.

The American School in London was founded by Stephen L. Eckard in 1951 to provide the continuity of an American curriculum for children of U.S. business and government personnel on assignment in London. The American School in London is the oldest American-curriculum school in the United Kingdom and remains the only nonprofit American-curriculum school in London. The School is registered as a nonprofit organization in the United Kingdom and in the United States. It is governed by a Board of Trustees, with 19 full-time members of the educational, business, and professional communities.

The School is accredited by the Middle States Association of Colleges and Schools and the European Council of International Schools. It holds membership in the National Association of Independent Schools, Council for Advancement and Support of Education, and the European Council of International Schools.

THE CAMPUS. The school building (1971), located on a 3.2-acre site, houses all classes from Pre-Kindergarten through Grade 12. Eighty classrooms are supplemented with nine science laboratories, seven computer laboratories, five music rooms, five art studios, two theaters, a double gymnasium, craft shops, and two libraries containing 50,000 volumes and audio-visual and periodical departments. The School's 21 acres of playing fields at nearby Canons Park include a baseball diamond, soccer fields, and rugby pitches as well as grass and all-weather tennis courts.

The School is committed to using technology to facilitate all aspects of education and has embarked on a long-term plan that combines the latest technology with innovative teaching strategies. A computer network with 1600 network outlets, a state-of-the-art, dedicated high-speed server, and a high-speed Internet connection were installed in 1996, linking over 500 computers in the building.

THE FACULTY. William C. Mules (Princeton University, B.A.; Johns Hopkins, M.Ed.; University of Virginia, Ed.D.) was appointed Head of School in July 1998. Dr. Mules was previously at Morristown-Beard School in Morristown, New Jersey, where he served as Headmaster for 6 years. A native of Baltimore, Maryland, he brings 35 years' experience in secondary independent school education as a teacher, coach, and administrator.

The full-time faculty consists of 65 men and 81 women. They hold 101 graduate degrees from such schools and colleges as Boston University, Brown, Columbia, Cornell, Harvard, Michigan State, Smith, State University of New York, and the Universities of California, Colorado, Hawaii, Illinois, Iowa, London, Massachusetts, Notre Dame, Oregon, Redlands, Sussex (England), and Wisconsin. The School provides health insurance and retirement plans, Social Security, leaves of absence, and sabbaticals.

Two full-time nurses and a part-time physician at the School attend to minor injuries and illnesses. Emergency medical services are available a few minutes from the campus.

STUDENT BODY. In 1999–2000, the School enrolls 1247 day students, 629 boys and 618 girls, as follows: 491 in the Lower School (Kindergarten 1–Grade 5), 321 in the Middle School (Grades 6–8), and 435 in the High School (Grades 9–12). Approximately 65 percent of the students are American, 4 percent are Canadian, and 4 percent are British, with the remainder representing 51 other countries.

ACADEMIC PROGRAM. The school year, divided into three terms, begins in early September and extends to mid-June. Vacations are scheduled in October, December, February, and in the spring. The School is in session Monday through Friday from 8:00 A.M. to 3:00 P.M. The average class has 16–20 students.

The Lower School program is highly personal and attempts to encompass all traditional values of education as well as proven and effective modern methods. The basic skills of language arts and mathematics are complemented by social studies, art, music, computer, physical education, and library

use. The Middle School (Grades 6–8) responds to the needs and characteristics of young people during the transition from childhood to adolescence. Team teaching and integrated study encourage mastery with a depth of understanding.

In the High School college preparatory curriculum, students fulfill major discipline requirements in English, mathematics, social studies, science, and modern language. Elective courses are offered, and advanced courses are offered leading to Advanced Placement examinations in over 14 subjects.

To graduate, a student must complete at least 18 credits, including four years of English; two each of modern language, mathematics, and science; three of social studies; and one of fine arts. One term of health and two and one-half years of physical education are also required. The School recommends at least an additional year of modern language, mathematics, and science. Students in Grades 9 and 10 must take five "solids" (English, modern language, history, mathematics, science) per year. Four "solids" are required in Grades 11 and 12; five are recommended.

Most High School classes are 50 minutes in length, but a flexible schedule allows teachers to extend some classes up to 70 minutes. A full team of college counselors, grade-level deans, faculty advisors, and a personal counselor ensure that each student receives personal attention.

Grade reports are sent to parents twice yearly for the Lower School students. Middle and High School students receive reports three times a year. The School has an "open-door" policy and communicates through parent conferences, the Parents' Newsletter, and the School magazine. Special events for ASL parents, sponsored by the Parent Teacher Organization, include an International Festival, a Book Fair, and a gala fund-raising auction.

Student support services include reading recovery, language development, and speech therapy in the Lower School. There are Lower and Middle School English as a Second Language programs as well as a school-wide program for students with specific learning difficulties.

Ninety-eight percent of the 114 graduates of the Class of 1999 went on to college. Students are attending Boston University, Brown, Georgetown, Harvard, London School of Economics, Northwestern, Princeton, Tufts, Yale, and the University of Michigan.

The School runs both a Summer Camp, which concentrates on athletic activities, and a Summer School, which offers a wide range of theme-based learning activities.

STUDENT ACTIVITIES. The Lower School After School Program organizes classes in crafts, sports, and other activities. Lower School students also participate in scouting and Little League.

Students in Grades 6–8 are required to take part in the Middle School After School Activities Program, which offers them the opportunity to develop lifelong hobbies and pursuits and to make friends with students in other grades.

Students in the High School elect officers and class representatives to the Student Council, which brings their interests and concerns to the administration and organizes social activities. Regular student activities include the yearbook, newspaper, literary magazine, drama productions, National Honor Society, prom committee, Model United Nations, Model U.S. Senate, instrumental and choral groups, math teams, Amnesty International, and the Computer, Chess, and Debate clubs. Volunteer student groups serve hospitals, elderly people, and other groups in the local community.

The School's varsity teams compete against local British, American, and international schools as well as American and international schools on the continent in rugby, volleyball, basketball, wrestling, swimming, soccer, track, tennis, baseball, crew, and cross-country for boys. Girls compete in volleyball, field hockey, soccer, basketball, track, tennis, softball, swimming, gymnastics, crew, and cross-country. Some interscholastic competition is arranged for Middle School teams. The physical education program is directed toward recreational and lifetime sports.

ADMISSION AND COSTS. The School welcomes American and international students who can meet the academic standards. Students are accepted in all grades throughout the year, provided vacancies are available, on the basis of a completed application, the previous academic record, standardized test results, a recommendation from the previous school, and payment of a £75 registration fee and a £1000 tuition deposit. Applications should be made as early as possible.

In 1999–2000, tuition is £11,500 for Pre-Kindergarten–Grade 3, £11,700 for Grades 4–5, £13,050 for Grades 6–8, and £13,400 for Grades 9–12. Additional optional costs are £1660 per year for busing (per child) and £420 per year for food service in the Lower School. Approximately £300,000 in financial aid was awarded in 1999–2000.

High School Principal: Mimi Flood
Dean of Students: Kevin Conaty
Dean of Admissions: Jodi Coats
Director of External Affairs: Michael C. Miller
Director of College Counseling: Thelma Bullock
Business Manager: Christopher Almond
Athletic Director: John Lockwood

Marymount International School   1955

George Road, Kingston upon Thames, Surrey KT2 7PE, England.
  020-8949-0571; Fax 020-8336-2485;
  E-mail <info@marymount.kingston.sch.uk>;
  Web Site www.marymount.kingston.sch.uk

Marymount, founded by the Sisters of the Sacred Heart of Mary, is a college preparatory school enrolling over 200 board-

ing and day girls of diverse backgrounds in Grades 6–12. The curriculum, leading to an American high school diploma, emphasizes structured learning and individual growth in a stimulating environment. International Baccalaureate courses are offered in all grades. The student-teacher ratio is 12:1, and at least 98 percent of graduates enter university. Activities include sports, drama, debate, and music. Summer school offers SAT preparation. The 7-acre campus is accessible to central London. Tuition: £8505–£9510; Boarding Fee: £6615–£6825. Mrs. Xochitl Hunt is Admissions Officer; Sr. Rosaleen Sheridan, RSHM, is Principal. *Middle States Association.*

Woodside Park International School   1995

Friern Barnet Road, London, England N11 3DR.
  00-44-181-368-3777; Fax 00-44-181-368-3220;
  E-mail admissions@wps.co.uk; Web Site www.wpschool.co.uk

Woodside Park International School, enrolling 500 students in Kindergarten–Grade 13, aims to create a secure, well-ordered, and happy environment at the core of which is the learning process. It is committed to traditional standards, and the academic program leads to the GCSE and the International Baccalaureate diploma. In addition to the liberal arts and sciences, great importance is attached to the role of new technology, including audiovisual links with The Dwight School in New York and access to the Internet. English as a Second Language is offered. Sports include basketball, soccer, cricket, netball, rounders, hockey, and golf. Tuition: £890–£3000 per term. Mr. Robin F. Metters was appointed Headmaster in 1996 and Principal in 1998.

FRANCE

The American School of Paris

S A I N T - C L O U D

41, rue Pasteur, 92210 Saint-Cloud, France. 33(1)41.12.82.82;
  Fax 46-02-23-90; E-mail admissions@asparis.org; Web Site asparis.org

THE AMERICAN SCHOOL OF PARIS in Saint-Cloud, France, is a coeducational, college preparatory day school enrolling students in Pre-Kindergarten–Grade 13. The School is situated in Saint-Cloud, a community of 30,000 about four kilometers southwest of Paris. Families live in a broad area covering western Paris and its suburbs. Fourteen school buses transport students to and from the School daily. Public buses run by the School, and trains to Paris are available within a five-minute walk from the campus.

The American School of Paris was founded in 1946 by

Americans living in Paris who wanted an American style of education for their children. The international population of the School has grown in recent years, prompting the introduction of the English as a Second Language Program and the International Baccalaureate Program in 1980.

The American School of Paris seeks to provide the informal and respectful atmosphere of an American school and to exploit the advantages of living and learning in two cultures. It aims to ensure continuity in the development of knowledge, awareness, and skills based on the values of American society and to extend the limits of national consciousness to include familiarity with, and appreciation of, other nations—particularly France.

The School is a nonprofit organization and is governed by a Board of Trustees, approximately 16 in number, which meets monthly. The Board is partially elected by the school community. The School is accredited by the Middle States Association of Colleges and Schools and is a member of the European Council of International Schools and the National Association of Independent Schools.

THE CAMPUS. The American School of Paris is located on 12 acres adjacent to the Saint-Cloud park and forest. An athletic field and a play area are provided on the grounds. The physical plant includes the original Lower and Middle School buildings and the Upper School building completed in 1988. Two cafeterias offer hot lunches for all students. The campus also includes a 400-seat Performing Arts Center, two libraries, three computer labs, two gymnasiums, and several art studios and rehearsal rooms.

THE FACULTY. Dr. Donald Billingsley was appointed Headmaster in 1994.

A stable and highly experienced faculty strives to care for the needs of each individual, and close student-teacher relationships are at the heart of the program. The faculty consists of 51 women and 33 men. Most hold advanced degrees. Faculty benefits include health and life insurance plans, French Social Security, and a retirement plan.

STUDENT BODY. In 1999–2000, the School has enrolled 738 students as follows: 277 in the Lower School (Pre-Kindergarten to Grade 5), 159 in the Middle School (Grades 6–8), and 302 in the Upper School (Grades 9–13). About 50 percent of the students are citizens of the United States; the remainder come from 50 other countries.

ACADEMIC PROGRAM. The academic year, divided into semesters, begins in early September and ends in mid-June. Vacations are scheduled for a week in November, two weeks at Christmas, a week in February, and two weeks in the spring. Classes, held 5 days a week from 9:00 A.M. to 3:30 P.M., are scheduled in periods of 40–75 minutes each. The average class has about 18 students. At the Lower and Middle School levels, a Resource Room is available for those who need remedial help. Grades are sent to parents four times a year.

The School emphasizes the learning of French and makes extensive use of Paris and surrounding regions as curriculum

resources. French is taught by native speakers at all levels. For students who are not fluent in the language, a communicative approach to teaching is emphasized. The goal is rapid acquisition of the language and appreciation of French culture. At all ages, students are taught in groups appropriate to their ability levels, from beginners through bilingual.

The ASP Extension Program serves the needs of its families with day and evening classes in such areas as French, computer, and English as a Foreign Language for Pre-Kindergarten through adult levels.

The Lower School (Pre-Kindergarten–Grade 5) program is comparable to that of American elementary schools, with the addition of a program in French language and culture, including frequent day trips and one extended field trip (beginning in Grade 2). An integrated Language Arts program serves to focus the core curriculum, which also includes mathematics, science, and social studies. The classroom teacher integrates other areas such as health awareness and computer skills into the regular program. Children are instructed by special teachers in art, French, library, music, computer, and physical education. A full-time specialist teacher is also available to support children who need extra help, including those with mild to moderate learning disabilities.

The Middle School Program (Grades 6–8) is based on an interdisciplinary team-teaching approach for the core subjects of English, French, social studies, science, and mathematics. This allows the development of a group identity and close personal relationships. During these years, teaching moves progressively toward departmental instruction and increasing independence.

Middle School students begin the day with a brief meeting within a small Advisory Group. Along with the core subjects, the curriculum includes art, band, chorus, general music, physical education, health, study skills, drama, and computer tools. Community service is integral to the program, both during and after school. The Middle School counselor plays a key supporting role in ensuring that academic, emotional, and social needs are being met.

The Upper School program follows a departmental system, with five core curriculum areas: English, French (with separate sequences for native and non-native speakers), social studies, science, and mathematics. Depending on the grade level, the program also includes some required study of art, music, computer skills, health, and physical education. Elective courses are available in instrumental, choral, and electronic music; theater; drawing and graphic design; Spanish; Theory of Knowledge; computer programming; photography; information technology; ceramics; and art history. Upper School students may enroll in up to eight full-time courses.

For students seeking a challenge beyond the requirements of a high school diploma, numerous honors courses are available for Grades 11–13. Placement in such courses is based on a student's ability and motivation in each subject area; there is no separate honors track. Most students graduate in Grade 12, but some stay on for another year to complete more advanced certificates. One-third of this year's graduates will earn the International Baccalaureate Diploma, and more than 90 percent have taken at least one IB or Advanced Placement course, which are offered in 14 subjects.

Most ASP graduates attend highly competitive universities, with the most popular destinations being the United States, Canada, the United Kingdom, and France.

STUDENT ACTIVITIES. During recess, Lower School children enjoy a specially constructed adventure playground. The classrooms of the lowest grades open onto their own enclosed outdoor play areas. Extracurricular activities for Grades 3–5 are organized each year according to student interest and the availability of adult leadership. These include private music lessons, the OK Chorale, the Lower School Band, sketching, drama, basketball, rollerblade hockey, soccer, cooking, and scouting.

Middle School activities include newspaper, ceramics, student council, drama, and modern dance. Individual and team sports vary according to season, with competition in basketball, soccer, softball, volleyball, and tennis. In addition, junior varsity teams are open from age 13, including cross-country, basketball, track, and swimming. There are frequent class trips, generally linked to the curriculum, to Paris and nearby areas. There is also an extended trip to the Savoie region for Grade 6 and the challenging Outward Bound program for Grades 7–8, both at the beginning of the school year.

Upper School extracurriculars include three seasons of sports, competing with other international schools throughout western Europe. Among the sports are soccer, tennis, basketball, volleyball, rugby, swimming, track and field, cross-country, baseball, and softball.

Other Upper School activities include publications, Amnesty International, honor societies, service clubs, an ecology club, jazz band, theater ensemble, and Student Council. The math team and Model UN group attend extended annual meetings in Europe.

The students organize occasional dances. Upper School and Middle School trips are arranged for the February and spring breaks, including a ski trip to the Alps and journeys to various European and Asian countries. The Lower School also arranges a ski trip.

ADMISSION AND COSTS. Students are admitted in all grades on the basis of recent school reports, teacher and counselor reports from previous schools, and testing, when appropriate. Applications, with a fee of 3300 francs, may be submitted at any time.

For 1999–2000, tuition is 46,700 francs for Pre-Kindergarten, 84,000 francs for Kindergarten–Grade 5, 91,200 francs for Grades 6–8, and 97,700 francs for Grades 9–13. The charge for bus service is 11,500–13,000 francs per year. There is also a one-time capital fund assessment fee of 20,000 francs. A tuition payment program is offered in special cases. Financial aid of

approximately 400,000 francs is awarded annually on the basis of need.

Assistant Headmaster, Admissions and Marketing: Dr. J. Guse
Coordinator of Development and Alumni Relations: Dr. J. Guse
College Counselor: Mrs. Laura Vincens
Business Manager: Mr. Joseph Motte
Director of Athletics: Mr. Han Hoegen
Director of ASP Extension: Mrs. Laurence Feniou

The British School of Paris 1954

*Junior School (Ages 4–11): Chemin du Mur du Parc, 78380
Bougival, France. 1-39-69-78-21; Fax 1-30-82-47-49*
*Senior School (Ages 11–18): 38 Quai de l'Ecluse, 78290
Croissy-sur-Seine, France. 1-34-80-45-90; Fax 1-39-76-12-69;
E-mail bsp@calva.net;
Web Site www.rmplc.co.uk/eduweb/sites/paris*

Set on two campuses in the western suburbs of Paris, this coeducational day school offers a British-style, English-language curriculum leading to GCSE and A-levels in preparation for higher education. The School enrolls approximately 700 students, ages 4–18, including some who board with select host families. The Senior School academic program includes English, math, French, three sciences, and three electives. Courses are also offered in career guidance, personal and social development, and sport. Among the activities are musical groups, drama, travel abroad, and athletics, including cricket, rugby, swimming, and girls' hockey. Tuition: FF65,000–85,000. Martin W. Honour (University of London, B.A. [Hons.], M.Sc.) is Principal.

International School of Paris PARIS

*6, rue Beethoven, 75016 Paris, France. 33-1-42-24-09-54;
Fax 45-27-15-93; E-mail info@isparis.edu;
Web Site www.isparis.edu*

INTERNATIONAL SCHOOL OF PARIS is a coeducational day school enrolling students in Kindergarten through Grade 12. Boarding with families in Paris can also be arranged through the School. All three school buildings are located in the residential 16th arrondissement of the French capital, two of them just across the River Seine from the Eiffel Tower. They can easily be reached by public transportation, and private bus service is also available for Primary School students.

The International School of Paris was founded in 1964 by Mrs. Monique Bourret-Porter to provide an English-speaking school in the heart of Paris. Since then, the School has grown from 6 students to approximately 400. Its aims are "to provide students with basic skills; to promote critical understanding and an integrated view of the various academic disciplines; to encourage students' creative self-expression and exploration of the world around them; and to foster intellectual curiosity and an awareness of the rich variety of human experience." In a school whose faculty and student body are drawn from all over the world, it is also considered very important to teach mutual tolerance and to make students aware of the increasing interdependence of the earth's population.

The School is nonprofit and is managed by a 12-member Board of Trustees, three of whom are elected by the parent body and most of whom are themselves parents. It is registered as an "Ecole Privée" with the French Ministry of Education, and is accredited by the New England Association of Schools and Colleges and the European Council of International Schools.

THE CAMPUS. Two converted townhouses, 15 minutes apart, house the Primary School (Pre-Kindergarten–Grade 5) and the Middle School (Grades 6–8). The High School (Grades 9–12) occupies the former premises of the Decorative Arts School. This building, which is almost adjacent to the Middle School, was bought by the School in 1986. It includes six classrooms, a library, a science laboratory, an art room, a student lounge, a staff room, an administrative wing, and rooms for tutoring and conferences. There is a gymnasium in the Primary School and exercise facilities at the High School; for team sports, track and field, and swimming, students use nearby parks and sports centers.

THE FACULTY. Gareth Jones was appointed Headmaster and Principal of the High School in 1997. Mr. Jones, who is British, graduated from the University of London (B.Sc., M.Sc., Post-Graduate Certificate of Education). He taught in London and was a Fulbright Scholar in Kansas City for one year. Mrs. Elizabeth Hickling, the Primary School Principal, was appointed in 1996. A graduate of the University of London (B.Ed., M.A.), Mrs. Hickling was previously a Headmistress in Buckinghamshire, England, and a lecturer in education at Oxford Brookes University.

Full-time faculty and administrators who teach number 40, 18 men and 22 women. They hold baccalaureate and advanced degrees from Kelvin Greene College of Advanced Education and the Universities of Adelaide and Queensland (Australia); McMasters, McGill (Canada); Alliance Française, Academie des Beaux Arts, the Sorbonne, and the Universities of Amiens, Paris, and Rennes (France); Language Institute of Munich (Germany); Royal Academy of Music, Trinity College, and the Universities of Bristol, Cambridge, Keele, Lancaster, Liverpool, London, Manchester, Newcastle, Oxford, Sheffield, Stirling, Surrey, and Sussex (England); Lakshimbai (India); Wellington College and the University of Auckland (New Zealand); and Boston University, Loyola, New York University, North Texas State, Saint Mary's, Southern Methodist, Wellesley, and the Universities of Michigan, North Carolina, Rhode Island, Seattle, the South, Washington, and Vermont (United States). Ten part-time instructors teach English, history, French, and special education.

First aid is available at the School, and American and British hospitals are ten minutes away.

STUDENT BODY. In 1999–2000, the International School of Paris enrolled 396 students, divided almost equally between girls and boys, as follows: Kindergarten 1—19, Kindergarten 2—20, Grade 1—27, Grade 2—26, Grade 3—19, Grade 4—23, Grade 5—19, Grade 6—21, Grade 7—19, Grade 8—33, Grade 9—35, Grade 10—41, Grade 11—48, and Grade 12—46. Approximately 16 percent of the student body is American, with the remainder of the students coming from 40 other countries.

ACADEMIC PROGRAM. The school year, which runs from early September to late June, is divided into three trimesters. There are vacations at the end of October, at Christmas, and in the spring, and several French holidays are also observed. Classes are held Monday through Friday.

The number of students in each class ranges from 6 to 20, with a student-teacher ratio of approximately 9:1. Teachers also provide extra help outside of class hours at no additional cost, and more extensive external tutoring can also be arranged, at the parents' expense. The Special Needs program helps children in Kindergarten through Grade 7 who have specific, mild learning disabilities; external specialists in counseling, psychomotor skills, and speech therapy help with referrals to the program. Older students' free periods are spent in the library under supervision.

Primary School parents receive reports and discuss them with teachers three times a year. In the Middle and High schools, reports are issued each term. Parents are encouraged to follow their children's progress by attending the annual Open House and two Parent-Teacher Conferences and by meeting with teachers when necessary.

Among the courses offered at the Middle School level are English or English for Speakers of Other Languages, French, Social Studies, Mathematics, Science, Computer Science, Library Skills, Music, Art, and Physical Education. Students in Grades 9 and 10 choose two-year courses, following the International General Certificate of Secondary Education curriculum, from a selection that includes English Language and Literature, French, German, History, Geography, Mathematics, Physics, Chemistry, Biology, Art and Design, and Physical Education. At the end of Grade 10, they are examined in the subjects they have taken for individual certificates.

All students in Grades 11 and 12 participate in the two-year, pre-university International Baccalaureate (IB), program, the majority of them toward the full IB diploma. Course offerings at the Higher and Subsidiary levels include French, English, and Japanese A (as a mother tongue), English and French B (for nonnative speakers); History, Economics, Geography; Mathematics; Biology, Physics, Chemistry; Art and Design; and such language A (mother tongue) options as German, Hindi, Spanish, and Swedish.

All instruction at the School, with the exception of language classes, is in English. Classes in English for Speakers of Other Languages are offered at all levels through Grade 10 to students who need to improve their English, and instruction in this subject is fully integrated with the rest of the school program.

Since the first senior class graduated in 1985, graduates of the School have gone on to attend such universities as the Boston Museum School of Fine Arts, Brandeis, Columbia, Georgetown, George Washington University, Hamilton College, Harvard, Ithaca College, Massachusetts Institute of Technology, Middlebury, Northeastern, Northwestern, Philadelphia College of Art, Skidmore, Tufts, Washington College, and Yale in the United States; London School of Economics, Royal Veterinary College, and the Universities of Bristol, Cambridge, Leeds, and Oxford in England; and many colleges and universities in other countries.

STUDENT ACTIVITIES. The High School has a Student Council, with representatives from each grade level, which meets regularly with the Headmaster and organizes the year's social and fund-raising events.

Students in the Primary School attend concerts, plays, and dance recitals and participate in intramural sports and academic competitions. There is an annual week-long field trip to another region of France, and the soccer and basketball teams travel to Belgium or Switzerland each year. After-school activities include basketball, soccer, gymnastics, karate, judo, swimming, musical instrument and computer instruction, and drama.

Older students can work on the yearbook, join a delegation to the Model United Nations in The Hague, go skiing in the Alps, and travel to such destinations as Stratford-Upon-Avon and the French Riviera. Among the after-school activities at the secondary level are swimming, basketball, soccer, volleyball, table tennis, track and field, music, drama, and karate.

Although there is no official varsity or junior varsity sports program, High School soccer, volleyball, and basketball teams play against other international school teams in the Paris area, and the Primary and Middle schools share a Saturday morning sports program. Annual events at the School include the International Dinner for parents, Olympic Sports Day (Primary and Middle schools), and the Spring Fair.

ADMISSION AND COSTS. The International School of Paris has a nondiscriminatory admissions policy. It welcomes applications throughout the year, and new students are accepted at all grade levels as long as places are available. Older applicants are asked to submit school records and teacher recommendations and to take placement examinations in French, English, and mathematics before beginning school; applicants of all ages are ordinarily expected to have an interview with the Director of Admissions.

In 1999–2000, tuition is 48,000 francs for Kindergarten 1; 68,000 francs for Kindergarten 2 and Grade 1; 73,000 francs for Grades 2–5; 76,000 francs for Grades 6–8; 85,000 francs for Grades 9–10; and 86,500 francs for Grades 9–12. A payment plan may be arranged.

IB Coordinator: Damian Kerr
Director of Admissions: Gareth Jones
College Counselor: Jonathan Daitch
Business Manager: Russell Kelly

Marymount School   1923

72, boulevard de la Saussaye, 92200 Neuilly sur Seine, France.
01-46-24-10-51; Fax 01-46-37-07-50;
E-mail school@ecole-marymount.fr

Marymount, located in a western suburb of Paris, offers an American curriculum to 470 boys and girls in Nursery–Grade 8. The Roman Catholic school provides continuity of education to students from all religious faiths whose academic careers have been interrupted by family relocation abroad. French language instruction begins at age 3, Spanish is offered in Grades 7–8, and all students enjoy cultural excursions in and around Paris and the French countryside. The core curriculum includes specialized courses in the arts, science, social studies, religion, computer, and physical education. Assemblies, drama, and after-school enrichment are among the activities. Tuition: 63,300–79,100 FF. Sr. Anne Marie Clancy, RSHM, is Headmistress. *Middle States Association.*

School Year Abroad   1967

5, Allée Sainte Marie, 35700 Rennes, France.
2-99-38-23-33

Please see the Listing under Massachusetts.

GERMANY

Frankfurt International School   1961

An der Waldlust 15, D-61440 Oberursel, Germany. 49-0-6171-202-0;
Fax 49-0-6171-202-384; E-mail jutta_kuehne@fis.edu

Frankfurt International School enrolls 1500 students from 54 nations in Pre-Primary–Grade 12. Offering European and American-based college preparatory curricula and the International Baccalaureate, the School is committed to high standards in a program that blends academics, athletics, and the arts. Its

location enables students to acquire an appreciation of other cultures, and frequent field trips throughout Germany and the continent enrich classroom learning. English as a Second Language, computer technology, foreign languages, and numerous activities complement the core program. Tuition: DM20,300–DM24,500. Dr. Günther Brandt (Stanford, B.A. 1967; Princeton, M.A. 1968, Ph.D. 1974) is Head of School. *New England Association.*

Munich International School   1966

Schloss Buchhof, D-82319 Starnberg, Germany.
49-8151-366-100; Admissions 49-8151-366-120;
Fax 49-8151-366-119; E-mail admissions@mis-munich.de

The Munich International School is a diverse and educationally stimulating English-language community of 920 boys and girls from more than 45 different nations in Kindergarten through Grade 12. The School prepares its students for entrance to highly competitive universities worldwide and offers curricula leading to the American high school diploma, the international GCSEs, and the International Baccalaureate. Academic courses in the fine arts, a diverse athletics program, and extensive extracurricular activities are integral to an MIS education. The 25-acre campus is 15 miles south of Munich in beautiful Bavaria. Tuition: DM17,280–21,580. Carolyn Kayser is Director of Admissions; Dr. Raymond J. Taylor was appointed Head of School in 1997. *New England Association.*

HONG KONG

Chinese International School   1983

1 Hau Yuen Path, Braemar Hill, Hong Kong. 852-2510-7288;
Fax 852-2510-7488; E-mail cis_info@cis.edu.hk;
Web Site http://www.hk.super.net/~cis

Chinese International School, enrolling 1230 day boys and girls of diverse racial, ethnic, and religious backgrounds in Pre-Kindergarten–Grade 12, aims to provide an education in the language and culture of both the Chinese and Western worlds. The School offers a dual-language program enhanced by the traditional academic subjects and Chinese Studies. All high school students prepare for IGCSE and International Baccalaureate exams. English and Chinese are also taught as second languages. Activities include creative and performing arts, sports, Chinese Speech Festivals, and Outward Bound. Tuition: HK$58,700–HK$93,900. Alexander Horsley (Oxford, B.A., M.A.; Hull University, B.A.; London University, P.G.C.E.) was named Headmaster in 1997. *Western Association.*

Hong Kong International School   1966

6 & 23 South Bay Close, Repulse Bay, Hong Kong. 852-2899-1211; Fax 852-2813-4293

Christian business leaders and members of Lutheran Church Missouri Synod founded Hong Kong International School to nurture young people academically, spiritually, and aesthetically. Situated on two campuses, the School enrolls approximately 2400 day students in Kindergarten–Grade 12. Forty nationalities are represented in the American-style, English-language program, which includes religion, Mandarin, computer technology, and the arts. The curriculum is designed to prepare students for college, and 90 percent of graduates go on to higher education. Outward Bound, trips to mainland China, community service, drama, Student Council, and interest clubs are among the activities. Tuition: $6500–$15,300. Charles W. Dull is Head of School.

ITALY

American Overseas School of Rome

ROME

Via Cassia 811, 00189 Rome, Italy. 39-06-33264841; Fax 39-06-33262608; E-mail aosr.admissions@agora.stm.it; Web Site www.aosr.org

A MERICAN OVERSEAS SCHOOL OF ROME is a coeducational, college preparatory day school enrolling students in Pre-Kindergarten–Grade 13; supervised, off-campus facilities are provided for high school students who wish to board. Situated in the northeast quadrant of Rome, the School is 8 kilometers west of the downtown area. Field trips to places of artistic, architectural, and historical interest in Rome and throughout Italy complement the curriculum.

Now in its 52nd year, the School was founded in 1947 by American and British parents who saw the need for a program to prepare English-speaking students for colleges and universities in their own countries. In 1958, an elementary school, additional high school classrooms, and a gymnasium were built with a $450,000 grant from the United States government. The School charter was revised in 1964 to create an American college preparatory school.

American Overseas School of Rome seeks to serve the

American community in Rome while also providing an opportunity for students of other nationalities to pursue an American educational program. Drawing on the diversity of its multicultural student body, the School strives to enable young people to become cultivated, inquisitive, sensitive, productive, and aware of themselves and the world around them. The International Baccalaureate and the College Board Advanced Placement programs are offered.

A nonprofit institution, American Overseas School of Rome is governed by a 12-member Board of Trustees elected by parents, with an additional 1 to 6 trustees elected by the Board itself. The Parent-Teacher Organization meets monthly. American Overseas School of Rome is accredited by the Middle States Association of Colleges and Schools. It holds membership in the European Council of International Schools and the Rome International Schools Association, and is a member of the Mediterranean Association of Independent Schools.

THE CAMPUS. The 6-acre suburban campus includes a central quadrangle shaded by umbrella pines and surrounded by oleander, with lawns, shrubs, and flowering plants. A terrace overlooks the valley, and a hillside amphitheater hosts the annual Shakespeare Festival. The grounds also include playgrounds, a soccer field, a softball diamond, two tennis courts, and a basketball court.

The original villa, purchased with the property, houses administrative and business offices along with foreign language, Middle School, and ESL classes. The High School building (1956) contains classrooms, the library, and the cafeteria. The Elementary School houses 17 classrooms, a 10,000-volume library, music practice rooms, and the infirmary and nurse's office. There is also a well-equipped, full-sized gymnasium and fitness center.

The School maintains a facility for high school boarding students. The residence is supervised by high school faculty members and a registered nurse. All rooms have private baths. Temporary boarding arrangements can also be made for day students whose families must be away from the city for short periods during the semester.

The School-owned plant is valued at $18,000,000.

THE FACULTY. Larry W. Dougherty, Ed.D., Headmaster of American Overseas School of Rome, has been involved in education in the United States for more than 25 years. A graduate of Harvard University, he has been a teacher, headmaster, and superintendent in the United States.

The faculty number 45 full-time and part-time teachers. They hold 45 B.A.'s and 23 advanced degrees representing study at such colleges and universities as Bates, Brown, Columbia, Cornell, DePauw, Harvard, Michigan State, Middlebury, Monmouth, Oberlin, Queen's College (Canada), St. Joseph's, Seton Hall, the Sorbonne, Temple, Wagner, Wesleyan, Whitworth, Wittenberg, and the Universities of California, Chicago,

Colorado, Connecticut, Dublin, Durham, Grenoble, Illinois, Kansas, Leeds, London, Melbourne, Minnesota, North Carolina, Notre Dame (Scotland), Pennsylvania, Rome, Southampton, Southern California, and Whitelands (England).

There is a full-time nurse at the School. Emergency treatment is available at several hospitals nearby.

STUDENT BODY. American Overseas School of Rome enrolls approximately 450 students, with 150 in the High School (Grades 9–13). Representing 43 countries, they come from a wide range of racial, ethnic, and religious backgrounds. Forty percent are American, 25 percent are Italian, and 10 percent are Israeli.

ACADEMIC PROGRAM. The 172-day school year, from early September to mid-June, is divided into two semesters (four quarters), with a Thanksgiving recess, winter and spring vacations, and observances of American and Italian holidays. The school day, from 9:00 A.M. to 3:20 P.M., includes eight class periods and lunch.

The student-teacher ratio is about 12:1. Faculty are available to provide individual academic assistance. In the Elementary School, grades are issued twice yearly, with interim parent-teacher conferences. Secondary School students receive grades four times a year, supplemented by midterm progress reports.

The curriculum is designed to challenge exceptional and gifted students and also provides remedial mathematics, remedial reading, and speech therapy for students with specific diagnosed learning disabilities. English as a Second Language is available, and for Italian students, there is a Native Italian curriculum up to Grade 8, which prepares them to sit for the National State Exams.

The Elementary School is comprised of Pre-Kindergarten through Grade 5 with classes currently enrolling an average of 18 students. It offers a curriculum that is based on the same practices, structure, and philosophy as those that are generally accepted in the United States. Regular classroom teachers instruct students in all subject areas while specialist instructors offer classes in Italian, art, music, computer, and physical education. Two full-time teachers provide special classes for students who require extra lessons in English as a Foreign Language; teachers from the Italian Department offer a variety of Italian-language classes. Children who are having difficulty in reading are evaluated and scheduled for remedial instruction with a reading specialist. The social studies program combines traditional concepts and values with the classical history available in the Mediterranean area.

Grades 6–8 provide an environment in which students who are entering adolescence are helped to achieve a sense of identity and inner stability while striving toward the realization of their full intellectual potential. The curriculum, while taking into account the spectrum of individual differences and intellec-

tual development to be found in children, maintains a program of academic excellence. Daily instruction is given in English, mathematics, science, social studies, Italian, and/or French. As a general rule, the study of Italian is recommended for everyone. Students who also elect French may study both languages concurrently. Instruction in art, music, drama, computer, and physical education is offered on a rotating basis.

To graduate, High School students must complete $22\frac{1}{2}$ credits in Grades 9–12 as follows: 4 in English; 2 each in a modern foreign language, social studies, mathematics, science, and the arts; 4 additional units in any of the preceding subjects except English; and $1\frac{1}{2}$ units in physical education. To graduate with an honors diploma, students must complete 24 credits, maintain a grade-point average of 3.5 out of 4.0, complete two Advanced Placement courses with a grade of "B" or above, and take the AP examinations. The School also offers the International Baccalaureate program, which qualifies students for entrance to colleges and universities worldwide.

Full-year and term courses offered in the High School include English Literature, Classroom Theatre, English classes at all grade levels; French I–V, Italian I–V, Latin, Ancient History, European History, United States History, the Model United Nations course, Economics; Algebra I, Geometry, Algebra II and Trigonometry, Pre-Calculus, Computer Science; Introductory Physical Science, Biology, Chemistry, Physics, Psychology; Art History, Graphics, Drawing and Painting, Photographic Journalism; and Perspectives of Music, Music History, and Chorus. Advanced Placement courses are available in art history, biology, chemistry, physics, English, European history, French, mathematics, music, studio art, and American history.

Graduates of the past four years are now attending such American institutions of higher learning as Boston University, Brown, Cornell, Georgetown, Harvard, Lehigh, Rice, Stanford, Tufts, Wheaton, and the Universities of California (Berkeley), Houston, Pennsylvania, and Southern California as well as universities in Canada, England, Italy, Japan, and the Philippines.

STUDENT ACTIVITIES. The elected Student Council is responsible for promoting social activities and good student-teacher relations. Extracurricular activities consist of an after-school sports program with soccer, basketball, volleyball, wrestling, and tennis as the major sports. The School choir gives several public performances each year, and there are several clubs, the number and variety of which change according to student interest.

American Overseas School of Rome participates in the athletic league of the Department of Defense Schools in Italy. School teams compete with those of high schools on military bases in Livorno, Vicenza, Aviano, Naples, and Sigonella, as well as those of other independent American schools in Italy. Boys' varsity teams are organized in basketball, soccer, tennis, volleyball, track, and wrestling. Girls compete in basketball, tennis, soccer, wrestling, cross-country, and volleyball. Intramural competition or instruction is available in basketball, soccer, volleyball, softball, tennis, and other sports.

Students participate in such annual events as the Declamation Festival, trips to various regions of Italy, a ski trip, and a science fair as well as various one-day field trips in conjunction with the program of studies in every subject.

Traditional annual events include the Fall Picnic and the Mayfair.

ADMISSION AND COSTS. American Overseas School of Rome seeks to enroll students of average to above-average ability who are willing to undertake a competitive program. Students are admitted to all grades based on recommendations and School-administered testing in foreign languages and mathematics. Applications are accepted at any time and enrollment is possible throughout the year. A fee of 500,000 lire is due upon registration.

In 1999–2000, tuition ranges from 9,800,000 lire in Pre-Kindergarten to 25,000,000 in Grades 12–13. The boarding program costs an additional 31,500,000 lire. Extras include transportation (3,000,000 lire) and lunch (1,200,000 lire per year). A capital assessment fee of 2,000,000 lire per family on initial enrollment is also required. A tuition payment plan and/or financial aid is available.

Secondary Principal: Joanne Reykdal
Director of Admissions: Donald Levine
Business Manager: Elisa Bruno
Guidance Counselor: Suzanne Jeffrey-Horne

St. Stephen's School ROME

3 Via Aventina, 00153 Rome, Italy. [3906] 5750605; Fax [3906] 5741941; E-mail mc0667@mclink.it; Web Site www.ststephens.it); United States office: 15 Gramercy Park, New York, NY 10003. 212-505-7409; Fax 212-505-7423

Sт. sтернен's sсноог in Rome, Italy, is a nondenominational, coeducational college preparatory school enrolling boarding and day students in Grades 9 through 12 and a few postgraduates. Situated diagonally across from the Circus Maximus and a short distance from the Colosseum and the Roman Forum, St. Stephen's is easily reached by the city buses, streetcars, and Metro trains that run within a block of the School. Its location in the heart of the Eternal City offers students unique cultural, educational, and recreational advantages as well as frequent travel opportunities to other cities in Europe.

Established by the late Dr. John O. Patterson, former Headmaster of Kent School in Connecticut, to "epitomize the best elements of the classical liberal arts education," St. Stephen's opened for classes in 1964; the first seniors graduated in 1966. Its founder chose Rome as the site because he believed the city to be "the symbol and repository of the enduring ethical, cultural, and religious values of the West," as well as "one of the most cosmopolitan international crossroads of the modern world."

The curriculum is based on the American model and, since 1975, has offered the International Baccalaureate, which prepares students for colleges and universities worldwide. Origi-

nally, the School's student body was predominantly American; today its enrollment includes young people from many nations and diverse cultural backgrounds.

St. Stephen's School, a nonprofit corporation registered in Connecticut, is governed by a Board of Trustees composed of 30 members who reside in the United States and Italy. The approximately 2000 alumni provide financial assistance and offer other support. The School is accredited by the New England Association of Schools and Colleges and the European Council of International Schools.

THE CAMPUS. The campus of St. Stephen's School occupies two and one-half acres in the center of historic Rome. Constructed around a courtyard, the traditional Roman-style school building contains three recently renovated science laboratories, new sculpture and art studios, an audiovisual facility, a photo lab, and physical education facilities on the lower floors. The two upper stories house 36 student dormitory rooms, faculty apartments, a computer room, classrooms, and the library containing 14,000 volumes, CD-ROM, and an extensive collection of videos, micro-fiche, records, and English and foreign-language periodicals. Also on the premises are the dining hall, snack bar, assembly hall, and offices. The campus has gardens, a barbecue pit, and tennis, volleyball, and basketball courts.

THE FACULTY. Philip Allen (Wesleyan University, B.A.; University of Chicago, M.A.) was appointed Headmaster in 1992. A former St. Stephen's faculty member, he was most recently the Head of the Upper School at Friends Seminary in New York City.

The faculty include 22 full-time and 8 part-time teachers, 15 of whom hold advanced degrees. They have attended Bates, Bloomsburg State, Boston University, Brooklyn College, Brown, Connecticut College, Connecticut State University, Dartmouth, Duke, Georgetown, Harvard, Haverford, James Madison, Middlebury, New England Conservatory of Music, Oberlin, Princeton, Southern Connecticut State, Temple, Trinity, Wellesley, Wesleyan, Yale, and the Universities of California, Chicago, Michigan, Nebraska, Santa Clara, Tennessee, and Virginia in the United States; the University of Toronto in Canada; the Universities of Lancaster, Leeds, London, and Sheffield in the United Kingdom; Monash University and the University of Melbourne in Australia; École Normale de Musique de Paris, the Sorbonne, and the University of Grenoble in France; the University of Queensland in Australia; Hochschule für Musik in Germany; and the University of Rome in Italy.

An infirmary is located on the school grounds, and a school psychologist is on staff. An American hospital is available for complete emergency medical care.

STUDENT BODY. In 1999–2000, St. Stephen's enrolls 144 day and 37 boarding boys and girls as follows: 48 in Grade 9, 31 in Grade 10, 62 in Grade 11, 38 in Grade 12, and 2 in a postgraduate year. The diverse enrollment includes 51 students from the United States and 29 from Italy; 40 other countries are represented including Argentina, Australia, Belgium, Canada, Chile, China, Croatia, Dominican Republic, Ethiopia, Finland, France, Greece, Guyana, India, Indonesia, Japan, Kazakhstan, Korea, Kuwait, Mexico, Nepal, the Netherlands, New Zealand, Norway, Paraguay, the Philippines, Slovenia, South Africa, Sri Lanka, Sweden, Turkey, the United Kingdom, and Yugoslavia.

ACADEMIC PROGRAM. The 39-week school year, which begins in early September and ends in mid-June, is divided into two semesters, with a Thanksgiving break and vacations at Christmas and in the spring. All courses meet four periods per week, three of which are 45 minutes long, the fourth 90 minutes in length. Classes enroll 10 to 18 students to permit individual attention. In addition, each student selects a faculty advisor whose role is to offer guidance and support in personal and academic matters and to keep parents apprised regarding the student's progress. Tutorials in specific subjects and special counseling assistance are available upon request. On Sunday through Thursday evenings, supervised evening study halls are held in the library or in dormitory rooms.

The School's curriculum reflects the philosophy that "there is no substitute for a balanced and comprehensive preparation" in each of the six major subject areas: English, foreign language, history, mathematics and computer studies, experimental science, and the arts. Each student is expected to carry five full-time courses. Nineteen credits are required for graduation as follows: four in English; three each in a foreign language, history, experimental science, and mathematics; two in electives; and one in the arts. In addition, noncredit physical education is a yearly requirement, and seniors must submit a research paper (senior essay). Approximately one-half of the upperclassmen participate in the International Baccalaureate program.

Among the courses offered are English I–IV; Italian I–VI, French I–V, Latin I–IV, Greek (alternate years); Roman Topography, Medieval and Renaissance History, Modern European History, Classical Greek and Roman Studies, Art History, History of the United States, Islamic History and Civilization, Economics I–II, Contemporary History; Biology I–II, Chemistry I–II, Physics I–II, Aspects of Human Physiology and Disease; Algebra I–II, Geometry, Mathematical Studies, Precalculus, Calculus, Computer Studies; and Studio Art, Sculpture, Chorus, American Popular Music, Drama, and Modern Dance. Special sessions are held for students who need assistance in English as a Second Language.

Recent graduates are attending such institutions as Boston College, Boston University, Bowdoin, Columbia, Haverford, Mount Holyoke, Oberlin, New York University, Occidental, Rhode Island School of Design, Smith, Stanford, Tufts, United States Air Force Academy, Wesleyan, Yale, and the Universities of California (Los Angeles), Michigan, Southern California, and Texas in the United States; McGill and the University of Toronto in Canada; Cambridge, Imperial College, London School of Economics, and the Universities of Birmingham and Edinburgh in the United Kingdom; LUISS and the University of Rome in Italy; and Waseda University in Japan.

STUDENT ACTIVITIES. The Student Council is comprised of representatives from each class, with juniors and seniors serving as elected officers. Members work with faculty representatives in the planning of social activities and serve as a liaison between students and the administration concerning all school matters. A variety of activities and clubs reflects the diversity of student interests and includes such groups as Amnesty International, Community Service, Yearbook, Newspaper, Literary Magazine, and the Debate, Gardening, Cooking, Photography, Recycling, Classics/Rome, Math, and Computer clubs.

St. Stephen's Physical Education Department offers track and field, soccer, volleyball, basketball, tennis, and modern dance. Regularly scheduled games and meets bring St. Stephen's athletic teams in competition with other schools within the Rome community.

Weekly class-time field trips, weekend outings, and two mandatory excursions of three to seven days' duration are planned by faculty in the belief that Italy is an educational resource in itself and should be used accordingly. Students have visited historical and cultural sites in and around Rome, hiked in the Abruzzi, ascended Mount Vesuvius, and explored Etruscan sites. With parental permission, boarders may spend evenings or weekends with the families of day students.

St. Stephen's calendar of special events includes New Student Orientation and School Picnic, two Parent-Faculty Evenings, Treasure Hunt in Rome, and many student-organized events.

ADMISSION AND COSTS. St. Stephen's welcomes students of all races and religious backgrounds who are eager to undertake the School's academic challenges and take advantage of the opportunities available in Rome and its surroundings. Acceptance is based on the results of an admission test, previous school records, and teacher recommendations. A personal interview with the prospective student and parents is recommended. Application should be accompanied by a fee of 200.000 lire.

In 1999–2000, day tuition is 20.900.000 lire; tuition for boarders is 33.400.000. Additional charges include a capital assessment fee of 1.000.000 lire for new students and 500.000 lire for returning students, and lunch fee of 1.230.000 lire for day students.

Director of Studies: Deborah M. Dostert
Assistant to the Headmaster for External Affairs: Michael Brouse
Alumni Secretary: Caitlin McDonnell (New York Office)
Admissions Office: Suzanne Fusi
College Counselor: Ed Franowicz
International Baccalaureate Coordinator: Margaret Mary Pilling
Business Office: Alessandra Pisanelli
Director of Athletics: Fausto DiMarco

JAPAN

International School of the Sacred Heart 1908

3-1, Hiroo 4-Chome, Shibuya-ku Tokyo, 150-0012, Japan.
 81-3-3400-3951; Fax 81-3-3400-3496; E-mail issh@gol.com;
 Web Site www.iac.co.jp/~issh3

The International School of the Sacred Heart is a Roman Catholic, college preparatory day school enrolling 600 students from 50 nationalities in Kindergarten–Grade 12; boys are accepted in Kindergarten only. The School seeks to educate students in the light of Christian principles, preparing them for their roles in the world. Concern with the development of the whole person, spiritually, intellectually, emotionally, and physically is the essence of the School's program. Instruction is in English with English as a Second Language, Japanese, and French also offered. Graduates are accepted into universities and colleges worldwide. Mrs. Kikue Ono (Middle/High School) and Mrs. Bedos T. Santos (Kindergarten/Junior School) are Admissions Registrars; Sr. Masako Egawa is Headmistress. *Western Association.*

St. Mary's International School   TOKYO

6–19, Seta 1-chome, Setagaya-ku, Tokyo 158-8668, Japan.
81-3-3709-3411; Fax 81-3-3707-1950; E-mail jutras@twics.com;
Web Site japan.co.jp/~smis

ST. MARY'S INTERNATIONAL SCHOOL in Tokyo, Japan, is a Roman Catholic, college preparatory day school enrolling boys in Kindergarten–Grade 12. The School is located in a green-belt section of Setagaya-ku, Tokyo's largest residential district, and is easily accessible from other areas of the city by public buses, subway, train, and school buses operating on ten routes in the region. Faculty and students make frequent use of the school buses for outings and field trips in the Greater Tokyo area.

St. Mary's International School was founded in 1954 by the Brothers of Christian Instruction, an order founded in 1817 for the purpose of educating youth. The School opened in the Sengakuji district with 60 students in the first three grades. It continued to expand to meet the needs of a growing international population and the demand for quality education. In 1961, the High School division opened with 18 freshmen. Ten years later, the present modern facility was constructed to give the School a new home.

The School strives to provide an excellent academic preparation for college within an atmosphere that promotes moral and spiritual growth. It seeks to develop students' self-understanding, respect for the religious and cultural values of others, appreciation for international living, and desire to contribute to the good of society. St. Mary's welcomes students of all religions and accommodates a variety of interests and backgrounds through a three-track program of religious instruction. A dress code is in effect for all grades.

St. Mary's International School is a nonprofit institution operated by the Brothers of Christian Instruction. An active Mothers' Association provides fund-raising support through various benefit events.

The School is accredited by the Western Association of Schools and Colleges and the European Council of International Schools. It holds membership in the Japan Council of Overseas Schools, the East Asia Council of Overseas Schools, European Council of International Schools, and other professional organizations.

THE CAMPUS. The School is situated on 8.5 acres including a multipurpose field covered in Astroturf and used for baseball, softball, soccer, flag football, and as a playground for elementary students. Four tennis courts are also used for basketball and handball. A gymnasium and a 25-meter indoor pool are other major athletic facilities. The School also owns and oper-

ates a ski lodge in Tsumagoi, Gumma Prefecture, where students receive ski instruction on group outings. Local rinks are used for the hockey program.

The main building, constructed in 1971 and updated since, houses classrooms, a new biology-chemistry lab, new physics lab, and a library containing 40,000 volumes and 100 periodicals, an audiovisual center with a closed-circuit television, and a computer center. The School has 150 personal computers in addition to a mainframe.

The plant is owned by the School and is valued at $220,000,000.

THE FACULTY. Br. Michel Jutras, a graduate of Laval University in Canada (B.Ed., B.A.), the University of Detroit (M.S.), and California State University at Northridge (M.A.), was named Headmaster in 1988. Brother Michel came to Japan in 1969 and served in other schools as teacher and administrator before accepting his present appointment.

There are 108 men and women on the faculty, 32 of whom teach part-time. Eight members are Brothers of Christian Instruction. All of the faculty hold baccalaureate degrees or the equivalent, and 45 have master's degrees. Most of the degrees are from American colleges and universities. Of 108 professional staff members, 47 come from the United States, 24 from Japan, 12 from Canada, and 25 from ten other countries. Sixty of them have spent 5 or more years at the School; the average length of service of the entire teaching staff is 12 years, and the average teaching experience of faculty members is 19 years.

A nurse is on duty through the school day and hospital facilities are nearby.

STUDENT BODY. In 1999–2000, the School enrolls 870 boys in Kindergarten–Grade 12. Of these, 235 were in the high school grades, distributed as follows: Grade 9—72, Grade 10—59, Grade 11—57, and Grade 12—47. Students come from 73 countries, with the largest percentage from the United States. A majority in the upper grades speak English as a second or third language. While the School remains a Catholic institution, the student body encompasses a variety of religions.

ACADEMIC PROGRAM. The academic year, divided into semesters, begins in late August and ends in early June, with vacations of 17 days at Christmas and one week in the spring. Classes are held 5 days a week between 8:45 A.M. and 3:10 P.M. Because the three school units share facilities, each operates on a different schedule, but, in the upper grades, a student normally has six 45-minute classes plus physical education daily. The library opens an hour before the start of the class day and stays open for two hours after classes end to provide students ample study opportunities. All faculty members are involved in counseling and advising students. English as a Second Language is available for students entering the School without full command of the language. Grades are sent to parents four times a year.

The curriculum parallels the contemporary curricula of American schools. Homeroom teachers lead classes in the basic subjects of English, social studies, mathematics, and science. Specialist teachers provide instruction in religion, art, physical education, vocal and instrumental music, and Japanese language. Three different religion programs are provided: one for Catholics, another for Christians, and a third for non-Christians.

Middle School (Grades 7–8) students take English, Japanese and French, World Geography or Current Affairs/Ancient History, Mathematics, Life Science or Physical Science, and Religion. Electives are available in Tennis, Electronics, Drama, Choir, Typing, Band, Mechanical Drawing, Computer, and Art, although students having difficulty must forgo electives in favor of supplementary programs in mathematics and study skills.

To graduate, a student must complete a minimum of 22 units of credit in Grades 9–12, with each unit representing a full-year course. These must include 4 of English, 3 of a second language, 2 of social studies, 3 each of mathematics and science, 1 of religion/ethics, 1 of physical education, ½ of fine arts, ¼ each of computer skills and health, and 4 of electives. In Grades 11–12, students may take the International Baccalaureate curriculum to qualify for a diploma that usually affords advanced standing in American universities.

Among the courses offered are English 1–4; French 1–5, Japanese 1–9, Latin 1–4; Economics, World History, Contemporary World History, International Relations, U.S. History, East Asian Studies; Algebra 1–3, Geometry, Pre-Calculus, Calculus, Advanced Topics in Mathematics; Earth Science, Biology 1–2, Chemistry 1–2, Physics 1–2; Fine Arts, Ceramics 1–2, Photography, Yearbook, Concert Band, Choir, Creative Music, Student Television, Architectural Design 1–2, Mechanical Drawing; SAT Preparation, Journalism, Theory of Knowledge, Typing, Environmental Decisions, Basic Programming, PASCAL, Computer Science; and Physical Education. In the major subject areas, Advanced Placement and International Baccalaureate courses are available.

All of the 52 seniors who graduated in 1999 went on to further their education at the college level. They are enrolled at such institutions as Amherst, Brown, College of William and Mary, Columbia, Duke, Sophia University (Japan), Yale, and the University of London (England).

A three-week Summer School Program offers review courses in English and mathematics, various courses in the arts, recreation for Elementary School boys, and summer camp programs for Middle School.

STUDENT ACTIVITIES. Students elect representatives to a Student Council, which organizes social activities and promotes compliance with School rules.

A variety of clubs and other organizations is offered to meet student interests. Among those currently functioning are the student newspaper, yearbook, literary magazine, National Honor Society, drama, speech, debate, Boy Scouts, Leo Club, concert band, stage band, chorus, and clubs for science, photography, stamp collecting, Ping-Pong, badminton, Red Cross, lifesaving, and boosters.

The School competes in the Kanto Plains Association against other international and Defense Department schools at both varsity and junior varsity levels in ice hockey, soccer, basketball, tennis, track and field, cross-country, baseball, swimming, and wrestling. All students take two years of physical education. Parallel sports programs are provided in both the Elementary and Middle schools.

From January through March, classes from Grades 4–6 take four- or five-day trips at the ski lodge in Tsumagoi to receive instruction in skiing and to strengthen ties with classmates. Other classes make use of the lodge as well. The choir and stage band go on an annual tour in Asia and the United States. Other students also have opportunities for international tours.

Special events on the school calendar, including those sponsored by the Mothers' Association, are Back-to-School Day for Parents, New Mothers' Tea, Food Fair, Show Choir/Jazz Band Dinner Show, Library Book Fair, Mothers' Association Spring Luncheon, Spring Band Concert, Spring Choir Concert, Bingo, Musical, and Carnival.

ADMISSION AND COSTS. St. Mary's International School seeks students from the international community of Tokyo who will benefit from its college preparatory curriculum. Students are admitted on the basis of transcripts from previous schools, standardized test results, and a personal interview with the student and parents. In some instances, an admissions test is administered. On acceptance, a registration fee of $2000 must be paid and a medical certificate submitted.

In 1999–2000, the tuition fee was 1,880,000 yen for the Middle and High School grades. Transportation and lunch fees are extra. A limited amount of financial aid is available.

High School Principal: Mr. Saburo Kagei
Middle School Principal: Mr. Stephen Wilson
Elementary School Principal: Br. Lawrence
College Counselor: Mr. Peter Hauet
Business Manager: Mr. Unryu Haku
Office Manager: Mr. Kunihiko Takamichi

Yokohama International School   1924

258 Yamate-cho, Naka-ku, Yokohama, Japan 231-0862. 81-45-622-0084; Fax 81-45-621-0379; E-mail yisadmin@green.ocn.ne.jp; Web Site www.twics.com/~yis

Yokohama International, enrolling 545 students in Nursery–Grade 12, was founded by members of the foreign business community to provide a coeducational, nonsectarian education for expatriate children. Within a family environment, the School aims to balance the academic and nonacademic offerings of its program. The college preparatory curriculum, featuring Advanced Placement courses, music, and the arts, leads to an American high school diploma, the International Baccalaureate, and the IGCSE. Students take part in many activities, with a special emphasis on a strong physical education program. A summer program is available. Tuition: $14,000. Extras: $2000. Neil M. Richards is Headmaster. *New England Association.*

KOREA

Seoul Foreign School   1912

55 Yonhi Dong, Seoul, Korea 120-113. 82-2-330-3100;
  Fax 82-2-335-1857; E-mail sfsoffice@crusader.sfs-h.ac.kr;
  Web Site www.sfs-h.ac.kr

Seoul Foreign School was founded by an association of parents, many of whom were missionaries, to provide excellence in education within "a caring environment centered in Christian values." More than 950 boys and girls are enrolled in Junior Kindergarten–Grade 12 and 200 additional students attend Preschool–Year 6 in the British School. Advanced Placement and International Baccalaureate courses are offered in the college preparatory curriculum. Among the activities are student government, publications, debate, Korean crafts, drama, bands, choruses, and interscholastic sports. Tuition: $4230–$13,709. Mrs. Luanne Paproski is Director of Admissions; Harlan E. Lyso is Headmaster. *Western Association.*

Seoul International School   1973

Songpa, P.O. Box 47, Seoul, Korea 138-600. 82-22-233-4551/2;
  Fax 82-342-759-5133; E-mail info@sis-lhs.kyonggi.kr;
  Web Site www.sis-korea.org

Seoul International School was founded to meet the needs of students in families from the business, diplomatic, and military communities in the city. Approximately 900 boys and girls are enrolled in Junior Kindergarten–Grade 12. The curriculum emphasizes the liberal arts and sciences, with Advanced Placement work in 15 subject areas. An intensive program in English as a Second Language is offered to Elementary and Middle School students. Activities consist of sports, three publications, drama, chorus, band, cheerleading, and two Student Councils. Tuition: $9800–$13,000. Cheryl Deane is Admissions Director; Edward B. Adams (Whitworth, B.A.; Eastern Washington University, M.Ed.) is Founding Headmaster. *Western Association.*

LUXEMBOURG

International School of Luxembourg   1963

188 avenue de la Faiencerie, L-1511 Luxembourg, Grand Duchy of
  Luxembourg. 352-47-00-20; Fax 352-46-09-24;
  E-mail clayton.lewis@ci.educ.lu

International School of Luxembourg is a college preparatory day school enrolling 450 boys and girls in Pre-school through Grade 12. Maintaining a policy of service to families of diverse religious, racial, and linguistic backgrounds, the School has students from 32 nations. The curriculum is American-based with international additions and includes English as a Second Language options and the International Baccalaureate for Grades 11–12. Student councils, publications, band, chorus, and athlet-

ics are among the activities. Tuition: 154,000–621,000 LUF. Clayton Lewis (Rhodes College, B.A.; Peabody/Vanderbilt, M.S.) was named Head of the School in 1998. *Middle States Association.*

MALAYSIA

International School of Kuala Lumpur   1965

P.O. Box 12645, 50784 Kuala Lumpur, Malaysia. 603-456-0522;
  Fax 603-457-9044; E-mail iskl@iskl.edu.my;
  Web Site www.iskl.edu.my

This college preparatory day school enrolls 1120 children from 52 countries in Early Childhood–Grade 12, with an optional 13th year. The School seeks to prepare students to become responsible world citizens capable of thinking creatively, reasoning critically, communicating effectively, and learning enthusiastically. The traditional curriculum encompasses the liberal arts and sciences as well as course work for the International Baccalaureate and Advanced Placement. Instruction is in English, and English as a Second Language is offered. Students with moderate learning disabilities can be accommodated. A full range of activities, including interscholastic team sports, is available. Tuition: RM16,910–32,190. Barry Farnham is Headmaster. *Western Association.*

THE NETHERLANDS

The International School of Amsterdam

AMSTERDAM

P.O. Box 920, 1180 AX, Amstelveen, The Netherlands. 020-3471111;
  E-mail jtrue@isa.nl; Web Site www.isa.nl

T HE INTERNATIONAL SCHOOL OF AMSTERDAM is a coeducational, college preparatory day school enrolling boys and girls in Pre-School–Grade 13. The School is situated in the suburb of Amstelveen on the south side of the city in an area of residences, high technology business, the Free University, and the World Trade Center. Amsterdam is a busy international hub offering many cultural, recreational, and educational resources, which school groups enjoy on day trips. Students in the upper grades are encouraged to involve themselves in service programs that meet special needs within the community. The area around the School is well served by public buses and trains. In addition, private bus service is provided to several other communities within a range of about 60 kilometers from the School.

The International School of Amsterdam was established in 1964 to serve the needs of children of the international community living in and around Amsterdam. The language of instruction is English but the School encompasses a great variety of nationalities in both the student body and faculty. The curriculum follows Anglo-American models, with some adaptations, and, since 1980, the School has offered the International Baccalaureate in the last two years of high school. More recently, the School has adopted the innovative International Baccalaureate Middle Years Program for students in Grades 6–10, together with the complementary International Baccalaureate Primary Years Program in the Lower School.

Because of the diversity of its student body, The International School of Amsterdam regards its program as "an experience in world living." It aims to prepare students to enter or reenter educational systems in their home countries with minimal adjustment and seeks to develop in them mastery of basic academic skills; appreciation of the humanities, arts, social sciences, and natural sciences; good mental and physical habits; and a sense of responsible citizenship.

The International School of Amsterdam is a private, nonsectarian, nonprofit trust governed by a nine-member Board and accredited by the New England Association of Schools and Colleges and the European Council of International Schools.

THE CAMPUS. The School is located in a new building complex designed specifically for its use and completed in 1996. Its facilities include classrooms for all levels, five science laboratories, five computer centers, a four-story library, a 400-seat theater, and specialized rooms for music, art, drama, and English as a Second Language. More than 200 computers are available in the centers and in most classrooms.

The gymnasium is fully equipped for physical education programs and a playground and adjacent sports field provide space for some sports and outdoor activities. In addition, the School rents sports facilities in the neighborhood as required for its students.

THE FACULTY. Paul W. Johnson was appointed Director in 1997. He holds a bachelor's degree in education from Fairhaven College/Western Washington University, a master's degree in International Human Services Administration from the School for International Training, and a doctorate in School Administration from Washington State University. Prior to moving to the Netherlands, Dr. Johnson served in various administrative capacities at Osaka International School in Japan, the American Embassy School in New Delhi, India; and the International School of Manila in the Philippines. He has also been a

teacher and school administrator in the State of Washington. Jack McHenry (Amherst College, B.A.; Seattle University, M.Ed.) is Head of the Upper School. Jan Wood (Nottingham University, B.A. Honors; Kings College London, P.G.C.E.) is Head of the Middle School. Lesley Snowball (University of Durham, Cert.Ed.; University of London, Dip.Ed.; University of Bath, M.Phil.) is Head of the Lower School.

The faculty include 73 women and 30 men. They hold 53 master's degrees, 5 doctorates, and 24 other advanced degrees from universities in Australia, Canada, France, Germany, Great Britain, India, the Netherlands, New Zealand, and the United States. The average teaching experience at the School is six years.

STUDENT BODY. In 1999–2000, the School enrolls 800 boys and girls from 45 nations in Pre-School–Grade 13. Of these, 340 are in the Upper School. The international character of the School is consistent throughout the levels with 30 nations represented in the Upper School alone. Students are drawn principally from families of the international business and diplomatic community living in Amsterdam and its surrounding district.

ACADEMIC PROGRAM. The academic year, divided into semesters, begins in the middle of August and ends in mid-June, with vacations of one week in October, February, and April, and three weeks at Christmas. Formal written reports on academic progress are sent to parents at the end of each quarter. Classes are held five days a week between 8:35 A.M. and 3:25 P.M. and are scheduled in the Upper School in seven periods of 45 minutes each, with a break for lunch. Class size averages 20 students throughout the School. English is the language of instruction, and English as a Second Language is offered for students who need it in Kindergarten–Grade 13. In the Lower School, teachers act as personal advisors to their students and in Grades 6–13, homeroom teachers oversee academic and social progress under the direction of the guidance counselor and the Head of the Upper School.

In the Lower School (Pre-School–Grade 5), faculty form four teaching units: Early Childhood, Primary, Junior, and Intermediate. Within those units, students are grouped by grade age into homerooms balanced heterogeneously by nationality, English language ability, social skills, academic ability, and gender. Academic subjects are taught in the homrooms, and students go to specialist teachers for art, music, drama, physical education, library, French, and Dutch. All students in Pre-Kindergarten through Grade 5 participate in a computer education program.

In Grades 6–8, students take five major academic subjects including English; Dutch, French, Spanish, or English as a Second Language; and social studies, mathematics, and science. Physical education, design technology, art, music, drama, computing, and health are also required.

To graduate from the Upper School, a student must complete a minimum of 22 credits, at least 16 of which must be in full academic courses meeting four to six times a week. Normally, these will include: 4 units of English; 2 of one foreign language; 3 of social studies (geography, history, economics); 2 of mathematics; 2 of experimental science and 1 additional unit from the offerings in science and mathematics; 6 electives; and 2 units of physical education taken over four years. Students pursue an American high school diploma and may choose to take the full International Baccalaureate Diploma Program in their last two years. About 75 percent of the graduating class attempt the full International Baccalaureate Diploma Program. In 1999, 90 percent of candidates earned the full diploma.

Upper School courses in all subjects follow a careful sequence from Grade 6 through 12, with the subsidiary and higher-level International Baccalaureate courses providing a special challenge in the final two years. A social service elective is offered to Grades 10–12, allowing students to identify needs in the surrounding community and to commit themselves to serving those needs.

Approximately 95 percent of the graduates pursue higher education in colleges and universities around the world. In recent years, graduates have attended universities in 20 nations, particularly in the United States, the Netherlands, and Great Britain. Among the American institutions accepting these students have been Boston University, Brown, Cornell, Dartmouth, Duke, Georgetown, Harvard, Haverford, Massachusetts Institute of Technology, Mount Holyoke, Rochester Institute of Technology, and the University of Chicago.

STUDENT ACTIVITIES. In the Lower, Middle, and Upper Schools, students elect two representatives from each grade to the Student Council, which in turn elects its own officers. The Council provides a forum for discussion of issues pertaining to school life and organizes fund-raising, sporting, and social events.

Among the regular organized activities are the Science Fair, International Youth Award Program, Mathematics Competitions, Model United Nations, yearbook, and choir. Students who play musical instruments are encouraged to join small ensembles that may accompany the choir or present other public recitals. Dramatic productions, including musicals, are staged with student performers throughout the year. Some activities involve exchanges with other schools through festivals and science fairs organized by the Northwest European Council of International Schools.

Sports play an important part in school life and teams compete interscholastically in volleyball and basketball for girls; soccer and basketball for boys; and swimming, tennis, and track and field. For Lower School students, swimming, soccer, gymnastics, badminton, and hockey are offered after school. Venture trips are encouraged and the School organizes ski trips, visits to outdoor-pursuit centers, and hiking and camping trips.

In addition to the plays and musicals, the students arrange dances and other social events. Class trips of several days' duration are offered in both the Lower and Upper schools to foster outdoor interests, cultural appreciation, social understanding, and group responsibility.

Exchange programs with schools in Moscow and Japan's Toyama Prefecture are currently in place. Students also participate in a school project among the Masai people in Tanzania.

Parents have a Back to School night in September when they meet teachers and hold a general Parent Teachers Association meeting. Other special events on the school calendar are International Evening, Senior Prom, and Spring Fair.

ADMISSION AND COSTS. The International School of Amsterdam seeks students who are members of the international community and who can profit from a challenging educational program. Students are admitted in all grades on the basis of previous school records, school recommendations, and, whenever possible, a personal interview. Admissions applications are considered throughout the year but anyone planning to apply should begin the process at the earliest possible time.

Tuition fees range from f20,000 for Pre-School to f30,350 for the high school grades. An enrollment fee of f2750 is charged to new students and a registration fee of f350 to all returning students. The International Baccalaureate program requires an additional f1260 for those registering for the full diploma and f210 per course for those not taking the full program. Transportation is extra.

Alumni Director: Donald Morton
Director of Admissions: Julia True
College Counselor: Judith Guy
Director of Athletics: Robert Boos

NORWAY

International School of Stavanger

STAVANGER

Treskeveien 3, 4043 Stavanger, Norway 47-51-559100;
Fax 47-51-552962; E-mail intschol@iss.stavanger.rl.no;
Web Site www.iss.stavanger.rl.no

INTERNATIONAL SCHOOL OF STAVANGER in Stavanger, Norway, is a coeducational, English-language day school enrolling students in Pre-School through Grade 12. The School is near Stavanger (population 100,000 with an English-speaking population of about 7000), a modern town of medieval origins situated on a fjord on the southwest coast of Norway. By air, it is one-half hour from Oslo, Norway, and one hour from Copenhagen, London, and Amsterdam. The surrounding countryside offers resources for many outdoor activities. The climate is generally cool, with heavy rainfall and little snow.

Established in 1966, the School serves the international community in the area. About 80 percent of its students are from families associated with the North Sea oil industry and NATO, but enrollment is open to all students who meet the admissions criteria. The School seeks to ensure that its students will be able to succeed in equivalent and continuing educational programs in the United States, the United Kingdom, or other international English-medium educational systems in other countries. International School of Stavanger also offers preparation for the British International General Certificate of Secondary Education (IGCSE) and the International Baccalaureate.

International School of Stavanger is an independent school administered by the Director and supervised by the Board of Trustees. The self-perpetuating Board, which meets monthly during the school year, is composed of eight representatives from the oil companies and the military and one representative from the parents. International School of Stavanger is accredited by the European Council of International Schools and the New England Association of Schools and Colleges. It is an affiliate member of the National Association of Independent Schools.

THE CAMPUS. Stavanger's facilities are situated on 15 acres of land. The campus, costing nearly U.S. $20,000,000 in 1982, includes classrooms for all grades; special areas for art, music, drama, industrial arts, library and media, and computers; the 350-seat Lovelace Theatre and auditorium; and three indoor gymnasiums, a 400-meter Olympic track, two baseball and softball diamonds, two outdoor basketball courts, a soccer field, two indoor racquetball courts, and playground areas. The H. B. Steves Library contains 15,000 volumes as well as an audiovisual collection of cassettes, videocassettes, and filmstrips. Reader-printers, CD-ROM and laser disk players, and video machines are also available. There is a cafeteria. A technology network links each classroom to schools around the world. The School's Web Site address is an excellent point for additional information.

THE FACULTY. Linda M. Duevel (Western Michigan University, B.A. 1972, M.A. 1975; Harvard, M.Ed, 1991; Purdue, Ph.D. 1999) was appointed Director in 1996. Prior to coming to Stavanger in 1975, she taught at schools in England and the United States. Dr. Duevel has been an administrator at Stavanger since 1978.

There are 65 full-time faculty members, 25 men and 40 women. They hold 65 baccalaureate and 39 graduate degrees representing study at such colleges and universities as Adams State, Augsberg, Augustana, Bates, Bemidji State, Butler, California State (Chico, Northridge), Catholic University of Chile, College of New Jersey, Cox College, Dakota State, Derbyshire, Dundee, Edith Cowan University, George Washington, Harvard, International College, La Trobe, Lesley College, London Montessori, Michigan State, Missouri State, Moorhead State, Niagara, Northern Arizona, Northern Colorado, Northern Michigan, Northwestern, Oklahoma City, Oklahoma State, Pennsylvania State, Purdue, Sagane, St. Cloud State, Southern Oregon State, Stephen F. Austin, Texas A&M, Texas Christian, Troy State, Volda, West Texas A&M, Western Australia College of Advanced Education, Western Michigan, Western Washington, Westfield State, Whitworth, and the Universities of Alabama, Arizona, Bergen, California, Connecticut, Glasgow, Houston, Leeds, Leicester, Liverpool, London, Massachusetts, Melbourne, Minnesota, New Mexico, North Dakota, Northern Iowa, Oslo, Queensland, St. Thomas, Southampton, Toronto,

Utrecht, Vermont, and Wales. Four faculty members provide instruction in the Norwegian language.

Expatriate faculty benefits include health and hospitalization insurance; retirement, disability, and life insurance plans; foreign service benefit, and relocation allowances. Summer study grants are offered. Emergency leave and compassionate leave policies allow an expatriate employee to return home in the case of serious illness or death of an immediate family member.

STUDENT BODY. There are 550 students. Students represent many of the United States, Australia, Belgium, Canada, Chile, China, Denmark, Egypt, Finland, France, Germany, Hong Kong, India, Ireland, Italy, the Netherlands, New Zealand, Norway, Peru, Poland, Portugal, Russia, Singapore, South Africa, Sweden, Switzerland, Turkey, and the United Kingdom.

ACADEMIC PROGRAM. The school year, extending from late August to early June, is divided into semesters. The calendar includes recesses for Autumn, Christmas, Winter Holiday, and Easter as well as the observance of Norwegian national holidays.

The Elementary School program includes Pre-school through Grade 5. The curriculum, while comparable to that taught in most public schools in the United States, also includes some elements of the British National Curriculum and the Australian National Curriculum. Students work in traditional self-contained classrooms; however, team teaching and cooperative learning groups are common practices. Instructors in art, music, band, physical education, library, and Norwegian assist the classroom teachers. A learning disabilities teacher is available for students who are slightly below grade level in reading and mathematics. There is also an English as a Second Language teacher.

The Middle School (Grades 6-8) is considered a bridge between the Elementary and High schools. The curriculum emphasizes the development of skills acquired in the Elementary School and the acquisition of life skills such as critical thinking, logical reasoning, decision making, working as a team, development of self-esteem, and how to learn. These skills will then help the student to experience success in the High School. The Middle School believes in the education of the whole child; therefore, the curriculum addresses the diversity at this unique stage of development. In addition to the core required subjects of math, English, science, social studies, physical education/health, and a foreign language, various exploratory courses are offered including, but not limited to, computers, craft design technology, art, and drama. In addition, a wide range of extracurricular activities is offered. A learning disabilities teacher and an ESL teacher are available in the Middle School.

To graduate with an American diploma, students in Grades 9–12 must complete 22 Carnegie units, including the following: English 4, social studies (including U.S. History for American citizens) 3, mathematics 2, science 2, fine arts 1, and physical education 2.

In Grades 9–12, the curriculum includes courses in English; Algebra I, Geometry, Algebra II and Trigonometry, Pre-Calculus, Calculus; United States History, Modern World History, Comparative Government, Economics, Geography, Psychology, Sociology; Physical Science, Biology, Advanced Biology, Chemistry, Physics, Advanced Physics; Physical Education; French I-IV, Spanish I-III, Norwegian; Design Technology, Computers Studies I-II, Net Technology, Computer Aided Design; Band, Choir, Drama, Handbells, Art; Publications; and Model United Nations. Students in Grades 11 and 12 may elect to earn the International Baccalaureate diploma (IB) or individual IB Certificates in English; Mathematics; History, Economics; Biology, Chemistry, Drama, Physics; French, Spanish, Norwegian; Music; and Information Technology in a Global Society.

There are 20 students in an average class. The School administers a number of tests. Students may take the American College Test (ACT), International General Certificate of Secondary Education (IGCSE), International Baccalaureate (IB) examinations, the Preliminary Scholastic Aptitude Test (PSAT), and the Scholastic Aptitude Test (SAT) as well as various career-interest inventories.

In 1999, 25 of the 26 graduates chose to attend college. They were accepted at 81 colleges and universities, primarily in the United States and the United Kingdom. Among them are the Alberta College of Art and Design, American University of Paris, Arizona State, Art Institute of Florence (Italy), Boston University, Cambridge (England), Carleton, Duke, Emory, George Washington, Heriot-Watt University (Scotland), Ithaca, Macalester, Mary Washington College, New York University, Oberlin, Rice, Royal College of Surgeons (Ireland), Saint Louis University (Spain), Stanford, Swiss Hotel Association School Les Roches, and the Universities of Aberdeen (Scotland), Arizona, Bergen (Norway), British Columbia, Calgary, California (Santa Cruz), Denver, Edinburgh, Leeds, Massachusetts (Amherst), Nottingham, Oslo, Ottawa, Vermont, Victoria, Virginia, Warwick, Waterloo (Belgium), Wyoming, and York.

STUDENT ACTIVITIES. Student government for each of the three divisions of the School is based upon a constitution that provides for elected Student Councils and includes a Bill of Rights for students. The Student Councils act as a liaison with faculty members and administrators. In addition, they sponsor various activities.

A wide range of extracurricular activities is available for High School, Middle School, and Elementary School students. The Middle School House and Homeroom programs offer both athletic and academic events targeted specifically at adolescents. The Stavanger Baseball Association organizes leagues for all school ages. The Secondary and Middle School students stage annual drama productions, and the School is a member of the International Schools Theatre Association.

Activities for the Elementary School children include drama, choir, hand bells, and band as well as field trips and other special events and projects. Cub Scouts, Brownies, Boy Scouts, and Girl Scouts are also available.

Organizations for the High School and Middle School include chorus, band, The Hague International Model United Nations, and National Honor Society. The High School also publishes a yearbook and maintains a school Web Site, while the Middle School produces a literary magazine.

Stavanger competes in sports with various international schools located throughout Europe. School teams are organized in soccer, volleyball, track and field, basketball, softball, skiing, and swimming.

Stavanger frequently sponsors trips to school-related events in Europe. In the past, student groups have gone to Oslo, The Hague, London, Paris, Luxembourg, Stratford-Upon-Avon, Vienna, Munich, Frankfurt, Copenhagen, and Brussels. Traditional annual events include Parents' Night, sports achievement and recognition nights, concerts and plays, and a Junior-Senior Prom. There is an active outdoor educational program for students in Grades 4–8.

ADMISSION AND COSTS. Enrollment is open to any person able to pay the fees and who the Director, after consultation with the administration, faculty, and staff, believes will benefit from the programs offered by the School. New students are accepted in all grades on a space-available basis. These students are only provisionally accepted until the School has received and reviewed their official transcripts. The School Board annually sets the number of private-pay students that can be admitted. Students who do not have English as their mother tongue will be tested upon arrival at Stavanger. Children entering Kindergarten and Grade 1 must be 5 and 6 years old, respectively, by September 1.

Seniors must submit an application and transcripts prior to admission. A student must attend the School for a full year (Grade 12) before being eligible for graduation.

In 1999–2000, the yearly tuition for Kindergarten–Grade 12 was approximately 122,000 Norwegian kroner for company payments and 46,500 for private payments. The fee covers all books, materials, and bus transportation. Pre-school tuition ranges from 18,000 to 35,000 kroner.

Director: Linda M. Duevel, Ph.D.
Middle School/High School Principal: Thomas Hawkins
Elementary Principal: Robert Graham
Business Manager: Brynhild Asheim
College Counselor: Ann Wenger
IB Coordinator: Lynn Park

PANAMA

Caribbean International School   1983

P.O. Box 1594, Cristobal Panama, Margarita Colón. 507-445-0933; Fax 507-441-6702; E-mail cicacct@sinfo.net

Founded by parents who wanted an excellent bilingual, multicultural education for their children, Caribbean International School aims to offer a program that meets the needs of its diverse student body and prepares them to adapt to other curricula worldwide. The School enrolls 340 day students in Kindergarten–Grade 12. Instruction is given in both Spanish and English in core subjects. Activities include sports, drama, gymnastics, manual arts, and orchestral and choral groups. A summer session of both Spanish and English as second languages is offered. Tuition: $1410–$2765. Admission Fee: $1500. Yolanda Anderson (La Salle University, Ph.D.) is the School Principal.

PHILIPPINES

Brent International School Manila   1984

P.O. Box 12201, Ortigas Center Post Office, 1605 Pasig City, Philippines. 632-631-1265 to 68 or 633-8016 to 17; Fax 632-633-8420; E-mail bism@brentmanila.edu.ph

The Rev. Charles Henry Brent, the first Episcopal bishop of the Philippines, established Brent International School to educate children of the local and international communities within a Christian ethos. The college preparatory program aims to develop intellectually curious, tolerant students well equipped to pursue educational and career goals anywhere in the world. Religious studies and chapel are integral to the program. Computer literacy begins in Preschool; the International Baccalaureate, English as a Second Language, and an academic summer session are available. The Mamplasan campus serves Nursery–Grade 12; the Pasig City campus offers Nursery/K–Grade 8. Tuition: $3800–$7820. Antonio Abad is Director of Admissions; Rev. Dick Robbins is Headmaster. *Western Association.*

International School Manila   1920

P.O. Box 1526, MCPO 1255, Makati City, Philippines. 632-896-9801 to 14; Fax 632-899-3856, 899-3964; E-mail isminfo@ismanila.portalinc.com; Web Site http://www.portalinc.com/ismanila

American and British residents founded this college preparatory school to serve the children of expatriate families in the area. Today, the School enrolls over 1800 day boys and girls from 50 nations in Kindergarten–Grade 12. The curriculum includes Advanced Placement courses and work leading to the International Baccalaureate. Instruction is in English. The School's Optimal Learning Center (OLC) provides both learning support and academic talent. English as a Second Language is also available. Students participate in sports, school leadership, publications, honor societies, drama, music, and clubs. Tuition: US$2800–$4000 plus P160,000–P212,500; Building Fee: $750; Matriculation Fee: $2500; ESL Fee: $1500: OLC Fee: $500. Andrew Settle is Admissions Officer; Trudy Thomson is Superintendent. *Western Association.*

PUERTO RICO

Baldwin School of Puerto Rico 1968

P.O. Box 1827, Bayamón, PR 00960-1827. 787-720-2421;
*   Fax 787-790-0619; E-mail baldwinw@caribe.net*

Baldwin School was established by members of the local educational and business communities to provide an enriched curriculum and various teaching methods to a diverse student population. Enrolling 800 boys and girls as day students in Pre-Kinder through Grade 12, Baldwin offers an English-language, college preparatory program. Computer technology is integrated throughout the disciplines, and Advanced Placement, honors, and enrichment courses are available to qualified students. Both English and Spanish are taught as second languages. Students take part in school government, honor societies, publications, drama, photography, forensics, band, and varsity athletics. Tuition: $5300–$6850. Alan P. Austen, Ed.D., is Headmaster. *Middle States Association.*

Caribbean Preparatory School 1952

Upper School (Grades 9–12): Commonwealth Campus
Lower/Middle Schools (PPK–Grade 8): Parkville Campus
P.O. Box 70177, San Juan, PR 00936-7177. 787-765-4411;
*   Fax 787-764-3809; E-mail econcepcion@cpspr.coqui.net;*
*   Web Site www.cpspr.org*

Caribbean Preparatory, a day school enrolling boys and girls age 3–Grade 12, offers a program of academic vigor and a wide variety of activities including sports. With instruction in English, the School aims to prepare students for selective universities stateside and within Puerto Rico. It emphasizes interactive, hands-on experiences with exchange and travel programs to stateside and foreign locations. The study of Spanish and Puerto Rican culture is required. Honors and Advanced Placement courses and a program for students with mild learning

differences are offered. Summer program and camp are available. Tuition: $3242–$6980. Financial Aid: $75,000. Mrs. Eblemar Concepcion is Admissions Director; Richard Marracino (University of Connecticut, B.A.; University of California [Los Angeles], M.P.A.) is Headmaster. *Middle States Association.*

Caribbean School, Inc. 1954

Calle 9, La Rambla, Ponce, PR 00731. 787-843-2048;
*   Fax 787-843-1174*

Caribbean, a nonsectarian, coeducational day school with students from local, North American, and international families, provides a demanding education in the English language. Students go on to attend leading colleges and universities worldwide. The rigorous curriculum is augmented by varied electives and Advanced Placement courses in the Upper School. There is a strong athletic program. Extracurriculars include the National Honor Society, Student Council, math competitions, drama, and environmental club. The School enrolls 650 students in Pre-Kindergarten–Grade 12. The multicultural heritage of the student body is emphasized. Tuition: $2400–$3360. James McLellan, Ed.D., is Headmaster. *Middle States Association.*

SPAIN

The American School of Madrid 1961

Apartado 80, 28080 Madrid, Spain. 34-91-740-1900;
*   Fax 34-91-357-2678; E-mail asmcc@redestb.es;*
*   Web Site www.amerschmad.org*

This college preparatory, coeducational day school enrolls 600 students from more than 50 nations in K1 (3-year-olds)–Grade 12. Its primary objective is to provide a traditional U.S. curriculum consistent with that of the best American schools. Students may also opt to complete the Spanish *Programa Oficial* and the International Baccalaureate diploma. Advanced Placement, electives, and the arts enrich the program. Classes are taught in English; Spanish and French are offered as second and third languages. "Experience Spain" allows students in Grades 10–12 from other schools to attend the American School for a semester or a year while living with host families. Tuition: 297,500–2,103,000 pesetas. William D. O'Hale is Headmaster. *Middle States Association.*

ENFOREX Spanish Language School 1989

Madrid, Barcelona, Marbella, and Salamanca, Spain; Quito,
*   Ecuador. Madrid Telephone 34-91-594-37-76*

Please see the announcement in the Yellow Pages section.

School Year Abroad 1964

Plaza de Aragón 12, 50004 Zaragoza, Spain. 34-976-239-208

Please see the Listing under Massachusetts.

SWITZERLAND

The American International
School of Zürich   1963

Nidelbadstrasse 49, CH-8802 Kilchberg, Switzerland.
41-1-715-2795; Fax 41-1-715-2694; E-mail aisz@aisz.ch

The American International School of Zürich is a college preparatory day school enrolling 120 girls and 142 boys in Grades
7–13. It aims to promote the intellectual, social, emotional, and
physical growth of students through a demanding curriculum
and a balance of activities. In addition to the standard diploma,
an honors diploma requiring three Advanced Placement
courses can be earned. Student government, publications,
clubs, and sports are some activities. A summer session provides
review and enrichment. Tuition: 21,800–23,700 Swiss francs.
Financial aid is available. Peter C. Mott (Reading University
[England], B.A., M.A.) was appointed Headmaster in 1989.
New England Association.

The American School in Switzerland

M O N T A G N O L A - L U G A N O

CH6926 Montagnola-Lugano, Switzerland. 41-91-994-6471;
Fax 41-91-993-2979; E-mail administration@tasis.ch;
Web Site www.tasis.ch
U.S. Office: 1640 Wisconsin Avenue, NW, Washington, DC 20007.
202-965-5800; Fax 202-965-5816

THE AMERICAN SCHOOL IN SWITZERLAND (TASIS) in Montagnola-
Lugano is a college preparatory boarding school enrolling
boys and girls in Grades 7 through 12 plus a postgraduate study program. Located in the hillside village of Montagnola
overlooking Lake Lugano, the School is approximately four
kilometers from the center of the city of Lugano (population
40,000) in southeastern Switzerland. Lugano is 30 minutes from
the Italian border. Rail connections may be made with all major
European cities, and commercial airlines from Agno international airport in Lugano offer direct service to Zurich, Paris,
Geneva, Rome, and London.

TASIS was founded in 1956 by Mrs. M. Crist Fleming to
provide a sound college preparatory education with an international dimension for students of all nationalities. In addition to
offering a liberal arts curriculum in the American tradition, TASIS
aims to develop in its students the values of integrity, respect,
responsibility, compassion, humility, commitment, and vision as
they mature and take their place in the global community.

TASIS is fully accredited by the European Council of International Schools and the New England Association of Schools
and Colleges. The School holds membership in the National
Association of Independent Schools, the Federation of Swiss Private Schools, and The Swiss Group of International Schools.

THE CAMPUS. The five-acre hillside campus, situated on La
Collina d'Oro, includes landscaped terraces and lawns, a small
outdoor theater, and outdoor basketball/tennis courts. The new
Palestra, a sports and activities complex, contains a gymnasium,
fitness center, dance studio, music rooms, and recreation center.

The School's main building, Villa de Nobili, was built in
the early 17th century and houses administrative offices, the
dining rooms, a large salon, four science laboratories, and dormitory rooms. Villa Monticello contains classrooms, a computer
center, a music practice room, faculty apartments, and dormitory rooms. Hadsall House, a 19th-century villa, has dormitory
rooms, an 11,000-volume library, a recreation area, and a studio
theater. The recently renovated Coach House contains the fine
arts and photography studios. The Belvedere Villa serves as a
dormitory and also contains the art history and architecture
classrooms. The Director's home and residential space and
classrooms (some of which are located in the adjacent village of
Certenago) complete the facilities.

Students use nearby soccer and rugby fields, tennis courts,
riding stables, and other facilities for athletic and recreational
purposes.

THE FACULTY. J. Christopher Frost, who was appointed
Headmaster in 1994, is a graduate of Williams College (B.A.)
and Wesleyan University (M.A.L.S.). There are 47 full-time and
7 part-time faculty members, 26 men and 28 women, 20 of
whom live on campus. More than half hold advanced degrees
from such colleges and universities as Brown, Cambridge University (England), Columbia, Cornell, Dalhousie (Canada), Harvard, Haverford, Middlebury, Oxford (England), Princeton,
Syracuse, Tufts, Vassar, Williams, Yale, and the Universities of
Chicago, North Carolina, Pennsylvania, and Virginia.

STUDENT BODY. In 1999–2000, the School enrolls 101 boarding boys, 140 boarding girls, 16 day boys, and 17 day girls as
follows: 9 in Grade 7, 15 in Grade 8, 30 in Grade 9, 52 in Grade
10, 91 in Grade 11, 61 in Grade 12, and 16 in the postgraduate
program. Approximately 30 percent of the student body is
American; the remaining students come from 35 countries.

ACADEMIC PROGRAM. The school year, from early September until early June, includes a three-week winter vacation and
a two-week spring break. The average class size is 12. The academic day follows a block schedule, with class periods ranging
from 50 to 65 minutes in length. Afternoon sports and activities
are followed by dinner and supervised evening study. The pro-

gram includes 11 days of educational, course-related travel within Europe. The School reconvenes in Crans-Montana after Christmas for two weeks of study and winter sports. Optional weekend trips are available to places of interest.

The Middle School curriculum consists of an American-based program with courses in English, social studies, mathematics, science, health, drama, art, and music. Able students may take High School courses.

Students must earn the equivalent of 19 credits in Grades 9–12 to qualify for graduation. Specific requirements are four years of English, third-level proficiency in a foreign language, three years each of history (including U.S. and European history), mathematics (through Algebra II), and laboratory science (including physical and biological sciences), as well as one year of Senior Humanities and fine arts.

The academic program includes English as a Second Language support, allowing international students to gain fluency in oral and written English while following a curriculum leading to the TASIS graduation diploma.

TASIS offers the International Baccalaureate (IB) diploma. The diploma for the two-year course of study is recognized by countries around the world for university entrance on the same basis as that country's own school-leaving diploma. In addition to six required subjects, the International Baccalaureate requires a commitment to Creativity, Activity, and Service (CAS), a 4000-word essay on a topic of the student's choice, and the Theory of Knowledge (TOK) course.

The Post Graduate Year offers students the option to explore a wide range of challenging courses and devise a tailor-made curriculum to suit diverse interests and abilities. Postgraduates may choose from the full range of TASIS courses open to seniors, including Advanced Placement and International Baccalaureate, but they may also choose to take any of the regular high school courses, which allow them to follow college-level study within the supportive atmosphere and with the faculty guidance for which TASIS is renowned.

TASIS has a branch campus in England near London, in Surrey. The American School in England enrolls 730 students in Pre-Kindergarten through Grade 12, with a boarding enrollment of 150 in Grades 9–12. The School has six summer programs: a six-week academic session in Thorpe, Surrey, England, for students ages 12–18; the TASIS French Summer Program at Rougemont for students ages 13–18; TASIS Spanish Program in Salamanca, Spain, for students ages 14–18; Journey Through Antiquity in Athens, Greece, for students ages 14–18; Le Château des Enfants and Middle School Program in Switzerland, a recreational and learning program for children 6–13; and the TASIS Summer Language Program for students ages 14–18.

Recent graduates went on to attend such colleges and universities as Bryant, Cambridge University (England), Clark, George Washington, Keio University (Japan), McGill (Canada), Pennsylvania State, Pepperdine, Purdue, Rhode Island School

of Design, Stanford, Syracuse, Tufts, Vassar, and the Universities of Michigan, Pennsylvania, Southern California, and Virginia.

ADMISSION AND COSTS. Admission is based on recommendations from three teachers, previous academic records, and a personal essay or letter. There is a $100 application fee, and a $1500 deposit (refunded at the end of the school year if there are no outstanding debts) is due upon acceptance.

The annual charge for tuition, room, and board for U.S. citizens is $27,800, which includes the Crans-Montana ski term, 11 days of In-Program travel, laundry, and textbooks. Tuition for day students is 26,700 Swiss francs. Financial aid is available on the basis of need and merit. Last year, the School granted scholarships and financial aid in the amount of 400,000 Swiss francs.

Assistant Headmaster: Richard Weinland
Dean of Students: Patrick Phillips
Academic Dean: Juanita Burch Clay
Director of Alumni: Kathryn C. Gonzalez
Director of Admissions: William Eichner
Director of Development: Eric Swofford
College Counselor: Beth Linguri
Business Manager: Miro Pozzi
Director of Athletics: Gary Malins

The American School of Institut Montana ZUGERBERG, ZUG

Zugerberg, 6300 Zug, Switzerland. 41-41-711-17-22;
Fax 41-41-711-54-65; E-mail info@montana.ch;
Web Site www.montana.ch

THE AMERICAN SCHOOL OF INSTITUT MONTANA in Zugerberg, Zug, is a college preparatory boarding school enrolling male and female students in Grades 5 through 13; day students living with their families in the area are also enrolled. The School is situated at an altitude of 3000 feet in an area offering a mild Alpine climate and extensive opportunities for skiing and other outdoor activities. Fifteen minutes away by public bus and cable car is the 12th-century town of Zug (population 25,000), which is the cantonal capital. Zug is connected by rail to Italy, Germany, Austria, and France, and it is less than an hour by car or direct train from the Zurich International Airport.

Founded in 1926 by Dr. Max Husmann, Institut Montana was established as a boarding school of international character for Swiss students. Italian and Dutch sections were opened prior to World War II. In 1952, the American section was created by Dr. Josef Ostermayer and Dr. John Parr to provide an American college preparatory program for the growing American community in Europe. The International Baccalaureate course of study is offered for students in Grades 11 and 12. If a student requires an additional year, the IB program can be completed in Grade 13.

Institut Montana strives "to train youth for responsible leadership" through the cultivation of "moral, intellectual, and physical development." The School's aim is to enable students to "return to their respective countries endowed with those qualities which will make them good citizens." The primary objective of the American section is to provide a rigorous and challenging curriculum, emphasizing the liberal arts. Religious instruction is available for Christian and Moslem students. Arrangements are made for Jewish and Buddhist students to receive religious instruction in Zug or Zurich.

A nonprofit institution, the School is governed by an elected six-member Board of Trustees. Institut Montana is approved by the Swiss Federation of Private Schools. The American School holds membership in the European Council of International Schools, the National Association of Independent Schools, and the National Association of College Admissions Counselors.

THE CAMPUS. The 65-acre campus includes athletic fields, an outdoor ice rink, a track, and four tennis courts. Indoor athletic facilities are housed in the gymnasium. Facilities for riding, golf, squash, and swimming are available nearby, and the fields and forests surrounding the campus afford opportunities for skiing and hiking.

Each of the four main buildings, constructed in the 19th century and since renovated, contains classrooms on the ground floor and living quarters for faculty and students on the floors above. Grosses Haus (or Schonfels) contains administrative offices, a computer room, the American School library, dining room, infirmary, classrooms, a study room for day pupils, and rooms for faculty members and for students of all nationalities who are between 16 and 18 years of age. Felsenegg, which accommodates male students between 10 and 15 years of age and their teachers, also contains classrooms, offices, the Italian and German libraries, and an assembly hall. Located in the basement of Felsenegg is the Clan, which is used for theatre productions. Juventus houses girls from all sections who are between the ages of 10 and 18 and their teachers, and also provides four science laboratories. The Swiss Chalet accommodates 20 students from the highest classes of the American, Swiss, and Italian sections. Other buildings include two chapels, a classroom building, and an additional faculty residence. The plant is owned by the School.

THE FACULTY. Dr. Aldo Haesler (University of St. Gallen,

M.B.A. 1978, Ph.D. 1983) was named Director of the Institut in 1996. In previous years, he lectured at the universities of St. Gallen, Lausanne, and Montreal and served as Head of the Economic Section of Montana's Swiss School. He and his family reside on campus. Daniel C. Fridez, Lic.Phil., was appointed Principal of the Institut in 1996. He graduated from the University of Zurich in 1978 and previously served as Dean of Montana's Swiss School and as a teacher of French, Latin, and English. V. Kevin O'Brien (University of Dayton, B.A. 1970; San Diego State, M.A. 1977; Indiana University, M.S. 1991) is Dean of the American School and teaches economics and history. John C.L.M. Mather (Christchurch Teachers College [New Zealand], T.C.C. 1964) has been Head of the Boarding School since 1996. Previously, he had served the American School as a teacher of biology, computers, and general science.

There are 39 full-time teachers and 4 administrators who teach at Institut Montana; of these, 12 are women. Nine men and 8 women are on the faculty of the American School; 15 teach in other academic programs of the Institut as well. Twenty-two faculty members, including 15 in the American School, reside at the Institut. American School teachers hold baccalaureate and graduate degrees from Bard, Harvard, Indiana University, McGill (Canada), New York University, Northwestern, Princeton, San Diego State, and the Universities of Arizona, Central Lancashire (England), Complutense (Spain), Loughborough (England), Minnesota, Queensland (Australia), and Tennessee. Faculty benefits include health insurance, a retirement plan, and Social Security.

The American section of the Institut also employs four physical education teachers and two full-time instructors who teach sports. A full-time nurse staffs the infirmary; the school doctor is on call. Hospitals are available in Zug and Zurich.

STUDENT BODY. In 1999–2000, the Institut enrolls approximately 175 boarders and 100 day students, 75 of whom are girls. The American School enrolls 38 boarding boys, 6 day boys, 30 boarding girls, and 8 day girls. Approximately 30 nations are represented among the entire enrollment, with the majority of the students coming from Switzerland, Germany, Italy, the Netherlands, and the United States.

ACADEMIC PROGRAM. The school year, from early September to late June, is divided into two semesters, with three-week vacations at Christmas and in the spring, a seven-day ski excursion in February, and observances of local holidays. Classes, which enroll 7 to 12 students, meet five days a week. A typical day, from breakfast at 7:45 A.M. to "lights out" between 8:30 P.M. and 11:00 P.M., includes six morning class periods and three afternoon class periods until 4:00 P.M.; dinner at 7:15 P.M.; and free time for study or leisure activities.

For boarders, there is a mandatory study period on weekdays from 4:30 to 7:00 P.M. Younger students and students experiencing academic difficulties attend a supervised study hall during this time, while older pupils may study in their rooms. Private tutoring is available at additional cost. Special instruction is offered in English, history, and science for American School students whose native language is not English. Marks are sent to parents four times a year. Midterm reports include written comments from the Dean of the American School and the faculty.

The Lower School (Grades 5–7) is a bilingual elementary school. The curriculum includes English, German, French, Mathematics, History, Science, Music, Art, and Sports. Native-speaking instructors teach some of the subjects in English, the others in German. This bilingual system provides an optimum preparation to either the American School or the Swiss School of Institut Montana.

The prescribed course of studies for Grade 8 consists of English, French or German (students may elect to study both), Geography, Algebra I, and General Science. Algebra and foreign language courses successfully completed in Grade 8 earn high school credits.

To graduate, students in Grades 9–12 must complete 18½

credits (1 credit equals one year's work). Specific requirements include 4 credits in English, 3 each in history and mathematics, 2 credits in laboratory science, and ½ credit in computer studies. French or German or both foreign languages, music and art appreciation, and physical education are required of all students each year.

Among the courses offered in Grades 9–12 are English; French 1–5, German 1–5, Spanish; European History, Government, American Studies, 20th Century History, Economics; Algebra 1–2, Geometry, Advanced Mathematics, Calculus; Theatre, Arts; and Biology 1–3, Chemistry 1–2, Physics, Computer Literacy, Computer Programming, Statistics, and Integrated Science. Advanced Placement courses are offered in English, French, German, European history, government, physics, chemistry, calculus, computer, and art history. Additional courses in English, foreign languages, history, economics, mathematics, and science are offered to Grade 13 students wishing to qualify for the International Baccalaureate diploma or certificate.

The American School graduated 20 seniors in 1999. They were accepted by such prestigious American colleges and universities as Bentley, Clark, Colby, Duke, Franklin and Marshall, Georgetown, Smith, Tufts, and Union. Others returned to their home countries or enrolled in various institutions in Belarus, Britain, El Salvador, Netherlands, and Switzerland.

The School offers an English-as-a-Second-Language program for students in Grades 8–10. The program includes three classes of English each day and special programs in history and science. Students attend the regular mathematics class for their level. A supplementary English class is included once the student enters the regular school program.

STUDENT ACTIVITIES. Students from all sections of the Institut participate in activities together. Among the groups usually formed are the Chess, Photography, Art, Jazz, Video, Film, Band, and Model Building clubs. Students publish a literary magazine (the *Montanablatt*), and the American section has its own yearbook (*AMI*).

Basketball, soccer, and volleyball teams compete with teams in Swiss sports leagues and from other schools. Intramural sports include baseball, field hockey, football, ice hockey, and soccer. Students may also engage on an individual basis in gymnastics, swimming, tennis, Ping-Pong, field and track events, golf, skating, horseback riding, squash, and tobogganing. All students can participate in skiing during the winter months.

Trips to points of interest in Switzerland are scheduled for the first and third terms. Twice a year, there are four- or five-day study trips to nearby European countries during mid-term breaks. In the spring, a group of juniors visits selected United States colleges and universities. In addition, a seven-day ski trip is organized to St. Moritz each winter.

The American School has a Halloween party and a

Thanksgiving observance, when a traditional dinner is served at a restaurant in Zurich. The Institut celebrates the visit of St. Niklaus in early December, and student musical groups give a Christmas concert each year. A drama group puts on at least one play each year. There is an alumni reunion at the School yearly and at other times in various European and American locations.

ADMISSION AND COSTS. The American School of Institut Montana seeks to enroll academically capable students with sound moral values who are interested in living and learning with students from all over the world. Candidates are admitted to all grades on the basis of a transcript of grades, results of standardized tests, a recommendation from the principal or counselor at the previous school, and a personal interview (whenever feasible). Application should be made during the school year prior to anticipated entrance, although applications are accepted as long as vacancies exist. The Headmaster of the American School handles admissions.

In 1999–2000, boarding tuition is 42,750 Swiss francs, depending upon room assignment; day tuition is 23,400 Swiss francs. The School estimates that a resident student's yearly expenses, including such extras as books, fees, trips, laundry, and a personal allowance, will total approximately 45,000 Swiss francs. Travel to and from home is not included in this estimate. Limited scholarship aid is available for students in Grades 11 and 12.

Collège du Léman International School

VERSOIX

1290 Versoix, Geneva, Switzerland. 41-22-775-55-55;
Fax 41-22-775-55-59; E-mail info@cdl.ch;
Web Site www.cdl.ch

COLLÈGE DU LÉMAN INTERNATIONAL SCHOOL in Versoix, Switzerland, is a college preparatory boarding and day school enrolling boys and girls in English or French-language programs in Kindergarten through Grade 13. Versoix, located on the shores of Lake Geneva, is about five miles from the center of Geneva, site of the European headquarters of the United Nations and the offices of many other international organizations and businesses. The faculty and students of the School visit the city regularly for cultural and recreational purposes. The area also offers excellent opportunities for skiing.

Collège du Léman was founded in May 1960 by Francis A.

Clivaz to serve the needs of the international diplomatic and business community in Geneva and the surrounding region. Because it attracts students of many nationalities, the School sees a special opportunity to help young people recognize their common humanity and destiny and the need to live harmoniously in a world linked by rapid communications. A code of conduct focuses student attention on the responsibility to maintain a considerate school community and emphasizes the principles of truth, trust, integrity, respect for others, and concern for the common good.

The School has two academic programs: one, taught in French, leading to the French Baccalaureat and the Swiss Maturité; the other, taught in English, preparing students for American and Canadian universities or, through the International General Certificate of Education program and British A-level examinations, for entrance to universities in Europe and throughout the world. The two sections are integrated in modern language courses, physical education, extracurricular activities, and boarding life.

Collège du Léman is a proprietary organization governed by an Advisory Board. It is accredited by the New England Association of Schools and Colleges and the European Council of International Schools and holds membership in the Swiss Federation of Independent Schools, Geneva Association of Private Schools, Swiss Group of International Schools, and the Association for the Advancement of International Education.

THE CAMPUS. The School is situated on an 18-acre campus, which includes playing fields for soccer and softball, a running track, covered basketball and tennis courts, and a swimming pool.

Ten classroom buildings provide four science laboratories, 67 classrooms, a language laboratory, two computer rooms with 39 terminals, two libraries with 19,000 volumes, a language laboratory, a 120-seat auditorium, two art rooms, a music room, and a student lounge. Four boarding houses for boys and two for girls can accommodate 200 students.

THE FACULTY. Francis A. Clivaz, the President, has directed Collège du Léman since the founding in 1960. He was educated in Lausanne, Switzerland, and earned his degree in business administration.

The faculty consist of 92 full-time and 14 part-time teachers, about half of whom are women. There are 12 members of the residence staff who are responsible for boarding students. The faculty members represent 24 nations with most coming from Switzerland, Great Britain, and the United States. The average teaching experience for members of the faculty is about 13 years and the average time at Collège du Léman is about 12 years. Sixty-five of the teachers hold licentiates, master's, or doctoral degrees.

Separate infirmaries for boys and girls are supervised by a full-time nurse. A doctor who lives and maintains an office adjacent to the campus is on call. Hospitals are available nearby in Geneva, and there is a 24-hour clinic in Versoix.

STUDENT BODY. In Kindergarten–Grade 13, the School enrolls approximately 850 students in the English-language section and 350 in the French-language section. The secondary school enrollment encompasses Grades 6–13. In this division, 170 boys and girls are boarders. One hundred and four nationalities are represented in the student body and Swiss, with about 18 percent of the total, are the largest contingent. American, English, Russian, and Japanese students are the next-largest representations, in that order. Most students come from families in the diplomatic and international business communities but some come directly from the United States in order to gain international experience before going to college.

ACADEMIC PROGRAM. The academic year, divided into semesters, begins in early September and ends in mid-June with vacations of 23 days at Christmas and 17 days at Easter. Classes meet Monday to Friday and are scheduled in seven periods between 8:25 A.M. and 3:30 P.M. with a 20-minute mid-morning break and a 60-minute lunch period. A normal high school course load includes seven or more subjects, each of which has two to six class meetings per week. Classes may vary in size but have an average enrollment of 14. Boarding students have evening study hours, which are supervised by the residence staff, and a formal study hall is conducted for students who are in academic difficulty. Grades, with written reports for each subject, are sent to parents six times a year.

The Primary School curriculum (Grades 1–5) reflects current developments in American and British education. Students are taught by class teachers in reading, creative writing, spelling, mathematics, science, history, and geography. Specialists teach physical education, art, and music. French is compulsory for all students and English and mathematics are emphasized. In Grades 6–8, students are taught by subject teachers. Computer Studies are introduced and Spanish and German are offered.

To graduate, a student must complete, in Grades 9–12, a minimum of 22 units of credit, 18 of which must be academic. These must include 4 of English, 3 in a single modern language, 3 in social studies, 3 in mathematics, and 3 in laboratory science. Students may earn a single credit in physical education and can earn the balance through electives in business studies, technical drawing, art, music, computer studies, economics, philosophy, and accounting.

Among the courses offered are: English 1–4; French, German, Spanish; World Cultures, European History, American History, Geography, International Affairs, Economics, Sociology, Anthropology, Philosophy; Integrated Mathematics, Pre-Calculus; Integrated Science, Biology, Chemistry, Physics; and Computer Studies, Music, Drama, Art, Technical Drawing, Statistics, and Business Management. Advanced Placement courses are offered in English, Art, Economics, French, German, Spanish, American History, Mathematics, Statistics, Psychology, Biology, Chemistry, and Physics; British A-Level courses are offered in the same subjects. English as a Second Language is available at Beginning, Intermediate, and Advanced levels for nonnative speakers.

Eighty-six of the 96 seniors in last year's English section are now enrolled in colleges and universities. Among the institutions at which recent graduates have enrolled are Amherst College, Baylor, Boston College, Boston University, Brown, Columbia, Emory, Georgetown, George Washington, Harvard, London School of Economics, Massachusetts Institute of Technology, Middlebury, Moscow State University, Northwestern, Rensselaer, Smith, Stanford, Tufts, Vanderbilt, Yale, and the Universities of California, Cambridge, Colorado, Durham, Edinburgh, Essex, Geneva, Lausanne, London, Miami, North Carolina, Nottingham, Oxford, Pennsylvania, Southern California, and Warwick.

A summer program for students ages 8 to 18 offers intensive classes in English, French, and/or computer studies in three-week sessions. Classes are conducted six days a week in the mornings. Afternoons are devoted to sports and recreation.

STUDENT ACTIVITIES. Students in the high school classes elect members of the Student Council, which represents students in both the French and the English programs. The Council organizes and directs a variety of student activities. An elected Boarding House Council plans activities for resident students.

Other extracurricular activities include the yearbook, newspaper, literary magazine, choir, Student United Nations; and Drama, Math, Science, Debate, Chess, and Alpine clubs. Instrumental music ensembles are formed by students, and other activity groups are established as interests require.

All students complete a physical education course and sports are part of the daily after-class schedule. Competitive team sports include soccer, cross-country, basketball, volleyball, skiing, track and field, rugby, and tennis. Noncompetitive sports include swimming, gymnastics, judo, jogging, softball, bowling, and yoga. Each grade has one week of ski instruction on its schedule and skiing is a regular weekend activity during the winter.

Movies, dances, hiking, trips to Geneva for shopping and theater, and other excursions to points of cultural interest are part of the planned weekend activities, all of which are supervised. School trips to other countries in Europe or Africa are arranged during vacation periods.

ADMISSION AND COSTS. Collège du Léman accepts students from a wide variety of educational backgrounds who have the character to live in harmony in an international community. They are admitted on the basis of academic records, two teacher recommendations, and a certificate of good health. No admissions test is given. Applications, with a fee of 200 Swiss francs, should be submitted by the end of June for fall entry but the School accepts new students at various times in the course of the year. Admissions inquiries can be directed to the Principals of either the English or French programs.

A security deposit of 400 Swiss francs for day students and 5000 Swiss francs for boarders is required immediately after acceptance and is held by the School for the duration of the student's enrollment. Tuition in Swiss francs for day students is as follows: Grades 1–5—13,200–14,200, Grades 6–11—16,000–17,000, and Grades 12–13—18,400. Boarding tuition is 40,000 Swiss francs for Grades 1–11 and 42,000 for Grades 12–13 and special ESL classes. Tuition is payable on a three-term schedule. Some financial aid is available and is awarded on the basis of need and merit.

THAILAND

International School Bangkok   BANGKOK

39/7 Soi Nichada Thani, Samakee Road, Amphur Pakkret, P.O. Box 20-1015 Ha Yaek Pakkret, Nonthaburi 11120, Thailand. 662-583-5401; Fax 662-583-5431; E-mail thomasd@isb.ac.th; Web Site www.isb.ac.th

INTERNATIONAL SCHOOL BANGKOK is a college preparatory day school enrolling 1800 students from more than 50 nations in Kindergarten–Grade 12. The School is located in the northern suburbs, 15 kilometers from the heart of Bangkok (population 10,000,000). Ancient and modern cultures mingle in the city with such landmarks as the Grand Palace and old

Buddhist temples along with modern skyscrapers and commercial buildings. The School offers a bus service for students that provides door-to-door pick-ups and drop-offs.

The School was founded in 1951 on the grounds of the U.S. Embassy, with a culturally diverse student body. After establishing its own facilities, the School grew rapidly as Thailand itself flourished economically. Its cosmopolitan nature has been a major feature as students of many nationalities learn to work and play together in a spirit of mutual trust.

International School Bangkok provides a balanced program focusing on development of the whole student. It strives to set high standards for academic instruction and performance, to provide opportunities for service to others, and to offer a range of activities to help students use their talents and gain confidence. The program is designed to prepare students for transfer to other international schools and for entrance to universities. The International Baccalaureate program is available to high school students.

International School Bangkok is a nonprofit institution, independent and nonsectarian, and is operated by the International School Association, an organization to which all parents of current students belong. The parents elect a 12-member Board of Directors and give support to the School through the Parents' Association. The School operates under a charter from the Thailand Ministry of Education and is accredited by the Western Association of Schools and Colleges.

THE CAMPUS. The 35-acre campus, located near an expressway that connects the suburbs to downtown Bangkok, was built in 1992 to the design of a prominent Thai architect, Dr. Sumet Jumsai. The entire School is air-conditioned, with facilities that incorporate modern conveniences and traditional Thai architectural motifs.

Among the major features are the 750-seat Unocal Theatre, two spacious libraries, a media center, and two indoor and two outdoor gymnasiums. The multipurpose gymnasium accommodates basketball and other sports, weight-training room, dance studio, aerobics areas, and a 25-meter swimming pool. Two cafeterias are also located in the complex.

A lighted soccer pitch, all-weather running track, two baseball fields, lighted tennis courts, and a Big Toys playground for elementary students are all located on the campus.

The School provides housing for faculty and administrators nearby.

THE FACULTY. Dr. Paul DeMinico, appointed Superintendent in 1994, is responsible for the operation of the whole school as the executive officer of the Board of Directors. Mrs. Tonya Porter was appointed Principal of the High School in 1996; Michael Connolly is Principal of the Middle School; and Dr. Naomi Woolsey and Thomas Baker are Co-Principals of the Elementary School.

The faculty includes 175 men and women, all of whom hold baccalaureate degrees or the equivalent. They also hold 129 advanced degrees, including 8 doctorates. Most are from the United States, but 11 other countries are also represented.

The School provides grants for faculty graduate studies, workshops, and seminars and sponsors faculty participation in professional conferences.

STUDENT BODY. The School enrolls 1800 boys and girls, with about 650 in Grades 9–12. The distribution of enrollments may change substantially from year to year because of the mobility of the international community. Approximately 50 countries are represented in the student body, with the United States accounting for 32 percent of the enrollment. Students from Australia, New Zealand, Great Britain, Canada, and Western Europe make up 18 percent; Thai students comprise 20 percent, Japanese 10, Koreans 6, and Taiwanese 5. About 60 percent speak English as a second language.

ACADEMIC PROGRAM. The academic year, divided into

semesters, begins in late August and extends to mid-June. The school calendar includes seven one-day holidays, a three-week winter holiday, and a ten-day spring holiday. Classes are held five days a week and are scheduled between 7:25 A.M. and 2:05 P.M. The Kindergarten day ends at 12:10 P.M. Grades and reports of students' progress are sent to parents four times a year, and progress reports are issued to students at the midpoint of each quarter. High School students in academic difficulty may be required to attend supervised study periods. An Intensive Studies program is provided for students with mild to moderate learning disabilities. English is the language of instruction, and support for English as a Second Language students is provided at all levels.

The Elementary School (Kindergarten–Grade 5) offers an integrated program in language arts, mathematics, science, and social studies. Instruction in music, physical education, Thai culture and language, art, computers, and library skills is offered in all grades.

In the Middle School (Grades 6–8), students take core courses in English, mathematics, science, physical education, Ancient Civilizations, World Geography, and Area Studies. They take exploratory courses (one quarter per year) in Thai, drama, art, health, computing, design, home economics, and music; they also take one year of language, choosing among French, German, Spanish, Japanese, and Thai. Electives include band, chorus, drama, dance, speech, newswriting, photography, computer applications, chess and thinking skills, video productions, and Thai Culture and Art.

To graduate, students must complete a minimum of 24 credits including 4 in English, 2 in physical education, 3 in social studies including U.S. History, 3 in mathematics, 2 in science, 1 in fine arts, .5 in health, and 8.5 in electives; they must also achieve computer proficiency. The International Baccalaureate requires a two-year study of English and another language; history, economics, and psychology; mathematics, mathematical methods and studies; biology, chemistry, and physics; and electives in computer studies, art and design, plus an optional course. In addition, a one-year seminar on Theory of Knowledge, a cocurricular activity program, and an extended essay based on independent research are required.

Among the courses offered are American Literature Before 1900, American Literature in the 20th Century, Ancient Greek Drama, British Literature, Shakespearean Drama, Creative Writing, Forensics; French 1–4, Spanish 1–4, German 1–4, Latin 1–3, Thai 1–4, Japanese 1–4, Mandarin 1–2, Dutch 1–2; Modern World History, Economics 1–2, Psychology, Thailand and Southeast Asia, U.S. History; Algebra 1–2, Geometry, Calculus, Computer Studies 1–2; Physical Science, Biology 1–2, Chemistry 1–2, Physics 1–2; Visual Arts, Performing Arts, Music, Drawing/Painting, Sculpture/Jewelry, Journalism, Photography 1–2, Video Production, Industrial Design, Band, Concert Band, String Ensemble, Concert Choir, Chorale, Acting 1–2; Home Economics, Business, Accounting, Business Management; and Physical Education 1–2, Sports for Life, and Dance 1–2. Advanced Placement and International Baccalaureate courses are available in all academic subjects.

Ninety-five percent of the graduates of International School Bangkok go on to further education. Some institutions where members of the Class of 1999 are now enrolled are American University, Baylor, Bentley, Boston College of Art, California Polytechnic, Cornell, Denison, Earlham, Hofstra, Johns Hopkins, Keio University (Japan), Kent, The London Institute, Louisiana Tech, Macalester, Manchester College, Michigan State, New York University, Nottingham (England), Oklahoma State, Pepperdine, Purdue, Radford, Savannah College of Art, Smith, Sophia University (Japan), Southern Methodist, Stanford, Syracuse, Thammasat University (Thailand), Tufts, Wellesley, Wheaton, Wheelock, Widener, Worcester Polytechnic Institute, Yale, and the Universities of California (Berkeley), Illinois, Indiana, Michigan, New Hampshire, Pennsylvania, Rochester, San Francisco, Southern California, and Texas.

An academic summer program offers English as a Second Language, Intensive Studies, Reading and Writing Enrichment for Grades 1–12, and a limited number of high school credit courses.

STUDENT ACTIVITIES. High School students elect members of the Student Council, which has both legislative and executive roles in sustaining school activities and functions. The Council encourages student participation in governance and appoints chairpersons of various standing committees that organize student activities. The Middle School has its own student government with a similar structure.

Clubs and activities are organized in response to student interest. Among them are the yearbook, school magazine, literary magazine, Band, Choir, Amnesty International, Children's Theater, Cultural Convention, Drama, Keyettes Club, and Art, Badminton, Business, Computer, Dance, Home Economics, and language clubs.

All students participate in athletics through interscholastic or intramural competition and physical education classes. Varsity and junior varsity teams compete in basketball, soccer, softball, swimming, tennis, track and field, volleyball, rugby, cross-country, and badminton.

Every year, students have the opportunity to participate in enrichment activities that go beyond regular academics during the Week-Without-Walls. Projects may involve the presentation of a play or the building of an engine on campus, social service in Bangkok, or expeditions to China, the Philippines, Japan, and other countries.

ADMISSION AND COSTS. International School Bangkok seeks students who have the ability and motivation to succeed in its academic program. Applications should be submitted as early as possible, and no later than June 1, for first-semester admission and December 1 for second semester. Admission is based on a completed application, full transcripts of two or more years of past schooling, copies of passport and nonimmigrant visa for the student and one parent, and a letter of verification from a corporate sponsor, if necessary. The nonrefundable application fee is US$100.

Tuition is 172,950 Baht per semester for Kindergarten–Grade 5, 188,250 Baht for Grades 6–8, and 192,200 for Grades 9–12. A one-time registration fee is 200,000 Baht, and students pay either an annual fee of 35,000 Baht or a one-time assessment fee of 514,000 Baht. Transportation fees are 18,360–27,900 Baht per semester, depending upon distance.

Deputy Superintendent: Dr. Roxy Pestello
Business Manager: Khun Sunsanee Wunnaying
Director, Office of Advancement: Thomas Drahman
Admissions Director: James Souza
Director of Activities: Freda Williams
Director of Athletics: Dennis Kramer

TURKEY

Bilkent International School/Bilkent University Preparatory School   1993

East Campus, Bilkent 06533 Ankara, Turkey. 90-312-2664961/62; Fax 90-312-2664963; E-mail school@bups.bilkent.edu.tr; Web Site http://www.bilkent.edu.tr/~bupsweb/

An international university preparatory school, Bilkent enrolls 400 day students in Grades 1–12. The School seeks to develop the whole person through a curriculum that reflects an understanding of the physical, emotional, intellectual, and social growth of young people. In its quest to foster independent thinking and the acquisition of knowledge, Bilkent offers programs leading to such international qualifications as the IGCSE and International Baccalaureate. Students have access to the educational and social resources, including sports facilities and a music hall, available on the Bilkent University campus. Tuition: $9000–$13,000. James E. DiSebastian is Director.

VIRGIN ISLANDS

All Saints Cathedral School   1952

P.O. Box 308, St. Thomas, VI 00804. 340-774-0231; Fax 340-774-1707

All Saints Cathedral School is an Episcopal college preparatory day school enrolling 470 boys and girls in Junior Kindergarten–Grade 12. The School aims to help each student develop to his or her highest intellectual potential and to hold true values that will prompt needed actions and necessary changes to adjust to various environments. The curriculum, academic in essence, is contemporary and challenging. The student body characterizes a multicultural ethnic background. Sports, clubs, and various activities are scheduled during the day and occasionally in the evening. Chapel attendance and school uniforms are required. Tuition: $2820–$3820. Louise S. Brady is Principal.

The Antilles School   1950

7280 Frenchman's Bay 16–1, St. Thomas, USVI 00802. 340-776-1600; Fax 340-776-1019; E-mail admin@antilles.k12.vi.us; Web Site www.antilles.k12.vi.us

The Antilles School was founded by Howard and Elizabeth Jackson to develop well-educated young people of excellent character who will contribute to the future and promise of the Virgin Islands. Enrolling 460 boys and girls from diverse backgrounds in Pre-Kindergarten–Grade12, this Blue Ribbon

Award-winning, college preparatory school seeks to provide a traditional liberal arts curriculum designed to serve average and gifted and talented students. Virtually all graduates enter college. Students take part in sports, community service, interest groups, and various enrichment activities and clubs. Tuition: $8200–$8900. Financial Aid: $500,000. Lynn Woodbury is Admissions Director; Mark C. Marin (Aquinas College, B.A.; Columbia University, M.A.) is Headmaster. *Middle States Association.*

The Good Hope School   1967

Frederiksted, St. Croix, VI 00840. 340-772-0022; Fax 340-772-4626

This college preparatory, coeducational day school enrolls 425 students in Pre-Kindergarten–Grade 12. Curriculum is designed to support and stretch students' abilities with an emphasis on mastery of basic skills and study habits needed to become academically self-reliant. Thought-compelling enrichment is provided through visual arts, vocal and instrumental music, writing, and local history and literature. Activities include sports, three publications, and dramatic and musical productions. After-school clubs and care are available; summer school and day camp are offered. Tuition: $4875–$6050. Financial Aid: $220,000. Bridget L. Dawson is Admissions Coordinator; Tanya Lee Nichols (University of California, B.A., M.A.) was appointed Head of the School in 1986. *Middle States Association.*

St. Croix Country Day School   1964

R.R. 1, Box 6199 Kingshill, St. Croix, VI 00850. 340-778-1974; Fax 340-779-3331; E-mail sccds@stxcountryday.com; Web Site www.stxcountryday.com

Founded in response to a demand for high-quality instruction in a nurturing environment, St. Croix Country Day enrolls 460 culturally diverse boys and girls in Nursery–Grade 12. The college preparatory curriculum includes advanced courses in physics, marine biology, calculus, French, computer science, and Spanish. Activities include sports, publications, dance, music, drama, fine arts, and special-interest clubs. After-school care and a summer day camp are available. Tuition: $4200–$6300. Tuition assistance is available. James C. Sadler (University of Missouri, B.J.; College of the Virgin Islands, M.Ed.Ad.) was appointed Headmaster in 1996. *Middle States Association.*

SUMMER PROGRAMS 2000

A student's summer should be a time for relaxation, renewal, exploration, and development. The program offerings in this section encompass those ideals and more. A child can explore the challenges of a military career or study acting in California. Does your student need to make up a failed geometry course or other academic class to stay on par with classmates? He or she can do so and still have an enjoyable summer with travel, sports, and other extracurricular activities.

Parents find these proven programs to be a good investment of time and money, and children have the opportunity to explore the differences between public and private school and, in the case of boarding and college programs, a chance to experience being away from home.

Begin your search by reviewing the Yellow Pages Grid. This will help you prepare a list of appropriate programs. Also, be sure to read the Blue Pages Classification Grid, where there are references to additional summer programs offered by schools in this book.

Prospective students should apply to these summer programs early; they often fill quickly and have limited enrollment.

Bunting and Lyon, Inc.
238 North Main Street
Wallingford, Connecticut 06492
1-203-269-3333
Fax 1-203-269-5697
E-mail BandLBluBk@aol.com
Web Site: www.buntingandlyon.com

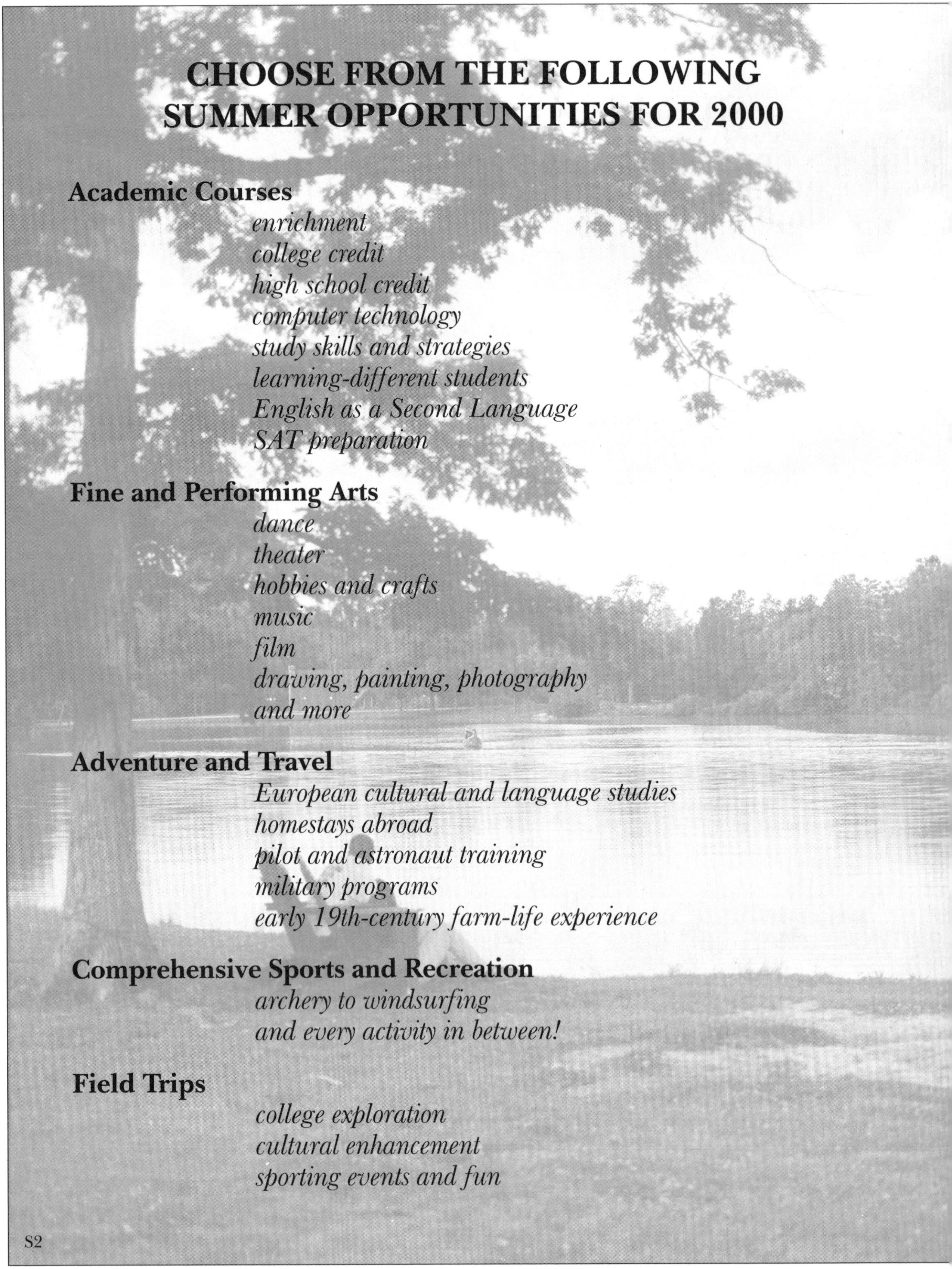

CHOOSE FROM THE FOLLOWING
SUMMER OPPORTUNITIES FOR 2000

Academic Courses

enrichment
college credit
high school credit
computer technology
study skills and strategies
learning-different students
English as a Second Language
SAT preparation

Fine and Performing Arts

dance
theater
hobbies and crafts
music
film
drawing, painting, photography
and more

Adventure and Travel

European cultural and language studies
homestays abroad
pilot and astronaut training
military programs
early 19th-century farm-life experience

Comprehensive Sports and Recreation

archery to windsurfing
and every activity in between!

Field Trips

college exploration
cultural enhancement
sporting events and fun

Oregon
The Delphian School

California
Dunn School
The Harker School
The John Thomas Dye School
Santa Catalina School
Viewpoint School

WASH.

MONT.

N. DAK.

ORE.

IDAHO

S. DAK.

WYO.

CAL.

NEV.

NEBR.

UTAH

COL.

KANS.

ARIZ.

N. MEX.

OKLA.

TEXAS

Texas
Marine Military Academy
The Shelton School & Evaluation Center

DISTRIBUTION OF SCHOOLS

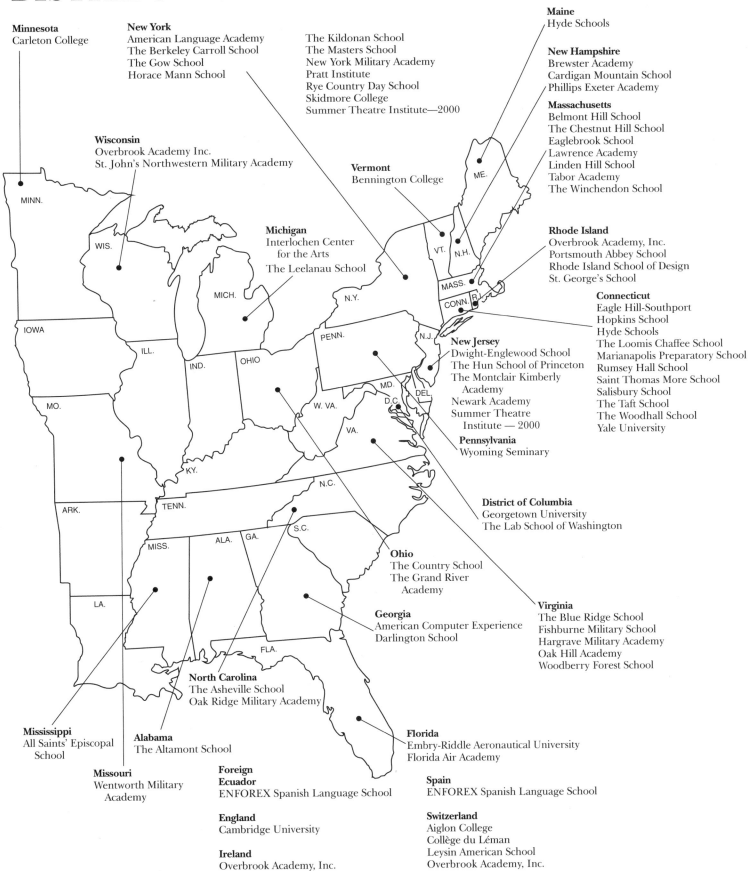

Minnesota
Carleton College

New York
American Language Academy
The Berkeley Carroll School
The Gow School
Horace Mann School

The Kildonan School
The Masters School
New York Military Academy
Pratt Institute
Rye Country Day School
Skidmore College
Summer Theatre Institute—2000

Maine
Hyde Schools

New Hampshire
Brewster Academy
Cardigan Mountain School
Phillips Exeter Academy

Massachusetts
Belmont Hill School
The Chestnut Hill School
Eaglebrook School
Lawrence Academy
Linden Hill School
Tabor Academy
The Winchendon School

Wisconsin
Overbrook Academy Inc.
St. John's Northwestern Military Academy

Vermont
Bennington College

Rhode Island
Overbrook Academy, Inc.
Portsmouth Abbey School
Rhode Island School of Design
St. George's School

Michigan
Interlochen Center
for the Arts
The Leelanau School

Connecticut
Eagle Hill-Southport
Hopkins School
Hyde Schools
The Loomis Chaffee School
Marianapolis Preparatory School
Rumsey Hall School
Saint Thomas More School
Salisbury School
The Taft School
The Woodhall School
Yale University

New Jersey
Dwight-Englewood School
The Hun School of Princeton
The Montclair Kimberly
Academy
Newark Academy
Summer Theatre
Institute — 2000

Pennsylvania
Wyoming Seminary

District of Columbia
Georgetown University
The Lab School of Washington

Ohio
The Country School
The Grand River
Academy

Georgia
American Computer Experience
Darlington School

Virginia
The Blue Ridge School
Fishburne Military School
Hargrave Military Academy
Oak Hill Academy
Woodberry Forest School

North Carolina
The Asheville School
Oak Ridge Military Academy

Florida
Embry-Riddle Aeronautical University
Florida Air Academy

Mississippi
All Saints' Episcopal
School

Alabama
The Altamont School

Foreign
Ecuador
ENFOREX Spanish Language School

Spain
ENFOREX Spanish Language School

Missouri
Wentworth Military
Academy

England
Cambridge University

Switzerland
Aiglon College
Collège du Léman
Leysin American School
Overbrook Academy, Inc.

Ireland
Overbrook Academy, Inc.

AIGLON COLLEGE

Aiglon College Summer School
Mr. Frank Thomson and Mr. Jamie Hill, Directors
Miss J. Reid, Summer School Secretary

1885 Chesières-Villars, Switzerland
Telephone (024) 495.27.21; Fax (024) 495.28.11
E-mail info@aiglon.ch; Web Site www.aiglon.ch

Boarding, Ages 10–16
50 Boys, 50 Girls

AIGLON COLLEGE SUMMER SCHOOL consists of two three-week programs offering intensive instruction in French or English for beginning, intermediate, and advanced students and a cultural-recreational program that takes advantage of the School's location in the Swiss Alps. The School aims to provide a positive experience that will help each student in his or her personal development. The programs take place in July and August.

The regular instruction, in three-hour sessions, five mornings a week, requires full participation in both written and conversational English or French. Modern language laboratories and the computer center are used for instruction. Students receive a written report at the end of the session.

Afternoon sports, under the supervision of qualified teachers, include swimming in indoor and outdoor pools, tennis, volleyball, football, softball, table tennis, badminton, basketball, rock climbing, canoeing, and water-skiing. Rock climbing and mountain hikes, in which students learn map-reading orienteering, may include overnight stays in Alpine huts or tents. Students also go on cultural excursions to museums, the Castle of Chillon, and to major Swiss cities such as Lausanne, Geneva, and Bern. Social activities include campfires, cookouts, games, dances, films, casino evenings, and a theatrical evening. The club room, gymnasium, tennis courts, and other facilities of Aiglon College are available for use.

The campus, located 25 minutes from Montreux, overlooks the Rhône Valley and affords a full view of the Swiss Alps. The College offers an escort service to and from Geneva Airport on the opening and closing days of the course.

Contact the school for more details.

ALL SAINTS' EPISCOPAL SCHOOL

Summer Session 2000
Charles Craft, Interim Headmaster

2717 Confederate Avenue
Vicksburg, Mississippi 39180
Telephone 601-636-5266; Admission 800-748-9957
Fax 601-636-8987
E-mail allsaint@vicksburg.com
Web Site www.vicksburg.com/~allsaint

Grades 8–12, Boarding
50 Boys and Girls

SUMMER SESSION 2000 provides enrichment, acceleration, and remediation in academic course work and a wide variety of recreational and athletic activities for boys and girls entering Grades 8 through 12. The five-week program runs from mid-June through mid-July, 2000.

Students can earn two half-credits or one full credit through successful completion of course work in English, mathematics, science, social studies, French or Spanish,

computer applications, fine arts, and English as a Second Language. Courses are taught by teachers who specialize in their subject areas, using varied methods and strategies to accommodate individual learning styles. Classroom instruction is reinforced by state-of-the-art computer technology and appropriate educational field trips in the area. These may include a tour of historic Mississippi River landmarks, the Vicksburg National Military Park, a planetarium, and the Mississippi Petrified Forest.

Students live in dormitories overseen by resident counselors and staff administrators. On the weekends, the schedule features numerous planned activities including games, crafts, trips, and a broad range of recreational events and sports such as track, softball, soccer, Frisbee, archery, and tennis.

Summer school participants have access to the library, the gymnasium, an Olympic-size swimming pool, a climbing and rappelling wall, a track, and other educational and athletic facilities of the 40-acre campus.

Contact the school for more details; see descriptive article on page 274.

THE ALTAMONT SCHOOL

The Altamont Summer Study Program
James M. Wiygul, Director

4801 Altamont Road, P.O. Box 131429
Birmingham, Alabama 35213
Telephone 205-879-2006; Fax 205-871-5666
E-mail jwiygul@altamont.pvt.k12.al.us
Web Site: www.altamont.inter.net/home.html

Day, Grades 3–12
Coeducational

THE ALTAMONT SUMMER STUDY PROGRAM offers acceleration, enrichment, and credit courses; camps in music, art, math, dance, science, drama, soccer, and basketball; and a study-abroad program in foreign language. The six-week session, from early June to mid-July, is open to boys and girls entering Grades 3–12.

Course offerings include accelerated mathematics, English and general mathematics enrichment, algebra, geometry, physical science, biology, astronomy, American history, European history, ancient and medieval civilization, computer, typing, and SAT/ACT preparation. Classes are taught by regular Altamont School faculty from 8:00 A.M. until noon Monday through Friday.

Camp sessions in basketball, soccer, drama, music,

math, dance, science, and art range in length from one to three weeks and are scheduled throughout the summer. Regional field trips are a highlight of the program. Camps are staffed by Altamont faculty plus resource personnel. The study-abroad program is administered through the Foreign Language Department.

The Altamont School is situated on a 28-acre tract that includes tennis courts, a track, two soccer fields, a baseball/softball diamond, two gymnasiums with basketball and volleyball courts, two computer labs, a multimedia lab, a 20,000-volume library, two science wings, a photography darkroom, a student center, and a fine arts center with special rooms for orchestra, chorus, drama, dance, and art.

Contact the school for more details; see descriptive article on page 5.

AMERICAN COMPUTER EXPERIENCE

ACE Computer Camps
John Beach and Nikki Williams, Directors

200 Arizona Avenue, #10
Atlanta, Georgia 30307
Telephone 800-384-4223; Fax 404-377-8121
E-mail ace@computercamp.com
Web Site www.computercamp.com

Coeducational, Boarding and Day
Ages 7–16

ACE COMPUTER CAMPS provide in-depth training in computer technology for boys and girls ages 7–16. The weeklong sessions are scheduled between June 14 and August 14, 2000, and take place at more than 80 different colleges throughout the United States, Canada, and England.

Participants in the ACE Computer Camps choose from two distinct courses of study, learning new skills and undertaking new challenges related to technology. The Programming Curriculum teaches concepts in True-BASIC and, for advanced campers, procedural programming and object-oriented C++. The General Curriculum offers a broad introduction to a variety of concepts and applications, including instruction in Microsoft Word, computer music and sound, and graphics and art programs. Campers in both programs may learn web page creation and design; they also have e-mail addresses for keeping in touch with family and friends.

A typical day includes up to five classes, with time allocated for sports, recreation, and meals; in the evenings, students enjoy competition in network game tourna-

ments. Boarding students are housed in college dorm rooms with 24-hour supervision and have access to the college's athletic and recreational resources.

ACE Computer Camps are located on the campuses of such colleges as Bowdoin and Fairleigh Dickinson in the Northeast; the Universities of Alaska, California, and Oregon in the West; Auburn, Emory, and Tulane in the South; and DePaul, Oberlin, and the University of Illinois in the Midwest.

Contact the agency for more details.

AMERICAN LANGUAGE ACADEMY

English for the Modern World
Robert J. Suphan, Director

515 South Road
Poughkeepsie, New York 12601
Telephone 914-462-7000; Fax 914-462-7005
E-mail rsuphan@ala-usa.com
Web Site www.ala-usa.com

24 Boys and Girls, Ages 14–18
Boarding

AMERICAN LANGUAGE ACADEMY offers a six-week program of English language studies and immersion into American culture within the lively environment of a summer camp. The session, which is conducted on the campus of Oakwood Friends School, extends from June 26 through August 4, 2000, and is open to young people ages 14 to 18 who wish to improve their English skills.

Upon entrance into the program, students take tests to ascertain their current level of proficiency in English for placement at one of five levels. Classes are held five days a week and have an average enrollment of 8 to 14 students. Professional language teachers provide instruction, with emphasis on reading, writing, listening, and grammar skills. Students undertake special assignments that enable them to become familiar with computers while practicing their language skills.

A typical day includes four hours of course work in the morning, with supervised evening study halls devoted to review and reinforcement of classroom lessons. Sports, games, and recreation are scheduled every afternoon, followed by dinner and required evening study periods. A weekly Cultural Orientation program allows participants to implement and practice their listening and speaking skills.

On the weekends, there is a full schedule of field trips

to cultural and historic sites in New York City and throughout the Hudson River Valley.

The 60-acre campus of Oakwood Friends School, overlooking the Hudson River and the Shawangunk Mountains, features air-conditioned classrooms, tennis courts, baseball diamonds, wooded areas, a gym, and a library/computer center.

Contact the school for more details; see descriptive article on page 343.

THE ASHEVILLE SCHOOL

The Asheville School Summer Advancement Program
Charles D. Baldecchi, Director

Asheville, North Carolina 28806
Telephone 828-254-6345; Fax 828-252-8666
E-mail summersession@asheville-school.org

Boarding, Grades 7–12
60 Boys and Girls

THE ASHEVILLE SCHOOL SUMMER ADVANCEMENT PROGRAM, now in its 18th year, enables students to explore the mountains of North Carolina while participating in a demanding academic program for enrichment and review.

The Asheville School offers two three-week programs, from June 11 to July 1 and from July 2 to July 22, 2000. Students may attend one or both sessions; English as a Second Language students must attend both.

The summer program is designed for talented students who are looking for a challenge in math, English, history, science, art, and creative writing. For example, an English class may read *Cold Mountain* by Charles Frazier. In addition to reading, analyzing, and writing about the novel, students will hike some of the same trails, climb Cold Mountain, and visit Civil War sites in the area.

Situated on a 300-acre campus in the Blue Ridge Mountains and near the Great Smoky Mountains, the School's location enables Summer Advancement Program students to participate in Asheville's extensive mountaineering program, including camping, orienteering, backpacking, rafting, rock climbing, rappelling, kayaking, and an on-campus ropes course and alpine tower, which develops teamwork, trust, and appreciation for the environment. Athletic activities such as tennis, soccer, swimming, and golf, plus white-water rafting, trips to the Bilt-

more Estate, Caro-winds, and other attractions round out the summer, creating a unique opportunity for talented students from around the world.

Contact the school for more details; see descriptive article on page 361.

BELMONT HILL SCHOOL

Belmont Hill School Summer Programs
George W. Seeley, Director

350 Prospect Street
Belmont, Massachusetts 02148
Telephone 617-484-4410

Coeducational, Day

Summer School: 400 students, Grades 6–12
Sports/Arts Camps: 800 Campers, Ages 7–18

BELMONT HILL SCHOOL SUMMER PROGRAMS offer academic courses for credit and enrichment as well as sports camps and arts programs for boys and girls ages 7–18. The programs, which are open to private and public school students, extend from late June to early August.

Summer School courses for Grades 6–12 feature small classes, with individual tutoring available as needed. Regular classes meet for 50-minute periods daily, and students are encouraged to take several courses. Among the academic offerings are English, including Expository Writing, Creative Writing, SAT English; Mathematics, including Pre-algebra, Algebra I–II, Geometry, Trigonometry, Pre-calculus, Calculus, SAT Math; Science, including General Science, Physical Science, Biology, Chemistry, Physics; History, including U.S. History, Western Civilization; and Language including Chinese, French, Latin, and Spanish. There are also courses in English as a Second Language, Computer Applications and Programming, Keyboarding and Word Processing, Developmental Reading, Speech and Debate, and Study Skills.

The Arts Program enables students to refine familiar skills or develop new interests through in-depth immersion in activities such as photography, theater, woodworking, painting, drawing, sculpture, and raku pottery. Each course is taught by experienced teachers who are proficient in their respective media.

Sports camps engage students in training and competition in coed soccer and tennis; separate boys' and girls' basketball, lacrosse, and soccer; boys' baseball; and girls' field hockey. Each camp is directed and staffed by adult coaches highly experienced in their respective sports.

Belmont Hill's 29-acre campus is 5 miles west of Boston, within a few blocks of a major commuting highway and accessible by public transport. .

Contact the school for more details; see listing on page 215.

BENNINGTON COLLEGE

The Bennington College July Program
Adrienne Marcus, Director

Bennington College
Bennington, Vermont 05201
Telephone 802-440-4418
Web Site july_program@bennington.edu
Boarding, Ages 15–18
Coeducational, 250 Students

THE BENNINGTON COLLEGE JULY PROGRAM, begun in 1979, offers opportunities for intensive, exploratory study in a variety of academic disciplines for students who have completed the freshman, sophomore, or junior year of high school. Instructors from colleges and universities around the country and well-respected professionals participate in the four-week program.

All students take two courses, each requiring a minimum of 6 hours per week in classes and workshops and 12 hours per week of work outside of class. Classes are scheduled Monday through Saturday and all include one or more individual or small-group tutorials each week. Among the offerings are: Dance, Music, Studio Recording Techniques, Voice, Acting, Painting, Ceramics, Architecture, Drawing, Sculpture, Photography, Video, Computer Graphics, Prose, Poetry, Fiction, Literature, Playwriting, Film Studies, Philosophy, Psychology, Law, Mathematics, Genetics, Environmental Studies, and Interdisciplinary Studies.

The Bennington approach is based on the notion of "learning by doing" and emphasis is placed on participation and performance, as well as observation. A key objective is to acquaint students with the demands of college work. The program concludes on Visitors' Day with a festival of readings, demonstrations, and performances.

Students, representing more than 30 states and several foreign countries, reside in houses on campus and are supervised by Resident Advisers. Outdoor sports, including tennis, volleyball, soccer, softball, hiking, and swimming, are organized on the 550-acre campus and in neighboring areas. Trips to music and art festivals, a per-

formance series, weekly films and literary readings, and a college fair are among the events for students.

Contact the school for more details.

THE BERKELEY CARROLL SCHOOL

Summer Programs
Bongsoon Zubay, Ed.D., Headmistress

181 Lincoln Place
Brooklyn, New York 11217
Telephone 718-789-6060, Ext. 211
Web Site www.berkeleycarroll.org
Day Boys and Girls
Ages Preschool–14

THE BERKELEY CARROLL SCHOOL SUMMER PROGRAMS offer opportunities in creative arts, science, and computers as well as a day camp experience for young children. The sessions vary in length from two to seven weeks from late June through early August.

The Creative Arts Program, a five-week session for students 8 to 14 years of age, focuses on drama, dance (modern, jazz, and improvisational), music, creative writing, the visual arts (photography, ceramics, painting, print making), and recreational sports. The daily schedule includes demonstrations by faculty, students, and guest artists. The program culminates in the Creative Arts Festival at which students exhibit the projects they have created and present musical, dance, and dramatic performances.

The Children's Day Camp, conducted for children from preschool through age 8, features creative and recreational activities including swimming, arts and crafts, music, games, cooking, and computers. Special weekly field trips are planned to the beach, museums, a children's theater, and other area attractions.

All programs are staffed by members of Berkeley Carroll's regular faculty on the School's Park Slope campuses as well as by professionals in the performing and visual arts. Facilities include air-conditioned classrooms, two libraries, two gymnasiums, computer centers, science laboratories, a theater, and two above-ground swimming pools.

Contact the school for more details; see descriptive article on page 319.

THE BLUE RIDGE SCHOOL

The Blue Ridge Summer School
William E. Ramsey, Director

St. George, Virginia 22935
Telephone 804-985-7724; Fax 804-985-7215
E-mail brsadmis@esinet.net
Web Site www.blueridgeschool.pvt.k12.va.us
55–65 Girls and Boys
Boarding and Day, Grades 7–12

THE BLUE RIDGE SUMMER SCHOOL enables students entering Grades 7–12 to develop academic skills, earn credit, and preview fall courses. The six-week program is conducted from June 25 through August 4, 2000.

The curriculum is structured to meet a variety of learning styles, with emphasis on the mastery of necessary academic skills that will promote confidence and motivation in academic areas. The core courses include English Level 1 (for entering Grades 7–9), English 9–12, Exposure to English & American Culture (for international students); World History, U.S. History; Math Level I (arithmetic skills), Pre-Algebra, Algebra I–II, Geometry; Biology, Chemistry, Integrated Sciences, Mountain Ecology; and French I–II and Spanish I–II. Complementary courses are available in study skills, reading, writing, computer, art, and SAT preparation. New-credit courses meet four hours daily, and make-up credit courses meet two hours daily; others meet for one hour. In addition, Challenge courses are offered in wilderness skills, water safety, canoeing, horseback riding, physical fitness, and outdoor challenge. Students normally take one or more of each of the Core, Complementary, and Challenge courses.

A typical day includes five classroom periods, a conference period, and a supervised study hall. Classes enroll a maximum of nine students. A strong adviser/advisee component permits individual monitoring and attention.

Students are housed in modern residence halls overseen by resident teachers and interns. In their leisure time, they may enjoy intramural sports, swimming, tennis, canoeing, rock climbing, horseback riding, and other outdoor activities. Off-campus trips to movies, social events, white-water rafting, and amusement parks are scheduled on Wednesdays and on weekends.

The School's 1000-acre campus is located in the foothills of the Blue Ridge Mountains near Charlottesville.

Contact the school for more details; see descriptive article on page 475.

BREWSTER ACADEMY

Brewster Academy Summer Session
Margaret Callahan, Director

80 Academy Drive
Wolfeboro, New Hampshire 03894
Telephone 603-569-7200 or 800-842-9961
Fax 603-569-7272; E-mail admissions@brewsternet.com
Web Site www.brewsternet.com

Boys and Girls, Boarding
Entering Grades 8–11

BREWSTER ACADEMY SUMMER SESSION, located on the shores of Lake Winnipesaukee, provides students with an exciting opportunity to participate in a highly personalized educational experience.

The curriculum emphasizes writing, math, and organizational skills. Students benefit by using laptop computers to advance in technology skills. Participants are instructed in Multi-Media Design, Graphic Arts, and Desktop Publishing. English as a Second Language is also available.

Afternoons and weekends are filled with activities including sailing, canoeing, hiking, biking, ropes courses, and field sports as well as trips to the White Mountains, coastal beaches, and Boston.

Brewster Academy, founded in 1820, is a coeducational, college preparatory boarding and day school that was awarded Macintosh's 1997 School of the Year Award for advancement and use of technology. The 75-acre campus, encompassing a half-mile of Lake Winnipesaukee's southeastern shoreline, includes beaches, docks, playing fields, a gymnasium and fitness center, a boathouse, and numerous other academic and recreational facilities. The Academy is two hours north of Boston by car.

Contact the school for more details; see descriptive article on page 286.

CAMBRIDGE UNIVERSITY

The Cambridge College Programme
Ms. Taryn Edwards, Founding Director

U.S. Office: 218 West St. Paul
Chicago, Illinois 60614
Telephone 312-787-7477 or 800-922-3552
Fax 312-988-7268

Boarding, Ages 14–18
100 Boys and Girls

THE CAMBRIDGE COLLEGE PROGRAMME at Cambridge University, the oldest established program for teenagers at Cambridge, extends for three weeks, from mid-July through early August, with a one-week optional trip to Paris afterward. This is the only summer program at either Oxford or Cambridge in which students are lectured exclusively by British professors and supervised only by Cambridge graduates.

Students choose one morning course from the following: Shakespeare; Philosophy: The Nature and Destiny of Human Beings; Cambridge Scientific Discoveries: Math, Physics, Chemistry, Biology, Astronomy, and Medicine; Studio Art and an Introduction to Art History;

Psychology: The Journey Inward; Stellar Physics, Quantum Physics; Film, War and Chivalry, and WWII The Churchill Years.

The morning class is followed by a lunch break during which students may enjoy free time or attend an optional, five-session SAT review workshop.

The afternoon session, for all students as a group, is British Cultural History, with lectures and excursions to historic sites. Students also have three excursions to London, including plays, plus day trips to Stonehenge; Stratford-Upon-Avon, with a Royal Shakespeare Company play; and Warwick Castle and the Roman city of Bath.

Students reside in supervised dormitories in single rooms in the oldest college of the University, which is situated on the River Cam in the historic center of Cambridge. Organized games of tennis, basketball, rugby, cricket, and soccer; punting on the River Cam; use of weights room and multigym; and plays, concerts, and other activities are scheduled in the evenings.

The optional trip to Paris is a French cultural interlude, visiting the museums and sites of Paris, with a trip to Versailles and to Giverny, Claude Monet's house and gardens.

Contact the school for more information.

fully diagnosed and a curriculum is tailored to meet his or her individual needs. In addition, a number of students take Computer, Environmental Science, French, Latin, Spanish, Photography, Printmaking, and accelerated courses in English, Mathematics, and Fine Arts. A limited number of international students are accepted for study of English as a Second Language.

In each three-week period, a student chooses three activities for the afternoon recreation programs. These include tennis, soccer, flag football, baseball, softball, music, riflery, trapshooting, archery, horseback riding, swimming, sailing, windsurfing, canoeing, art, rocketry, drama, basketball, and lacrosse. In addition, three-day trail camping and canoeing trips to the White Mountains occur weekly.

The 500-acre lakeside campus has ten tennis courts (four indoor), a gymnasium, an archery range, a rifle range, and five athletic fields. It is located 275 miles from New York City and 120 miles from Boston and is accessible by plane, car, or bus. Group transportation from and to Boston's Logan International Airport is provided.

Contact the school for more details; see listing on page 288.

CARDIGAN MOUNTAIN SCHOOL

Cardigan Mountain Summer Session
T. Jeffrey Driscoll, Director of Enrollment and
    Financial Aid
Canaan, New Hampshire 03741
Telephone 603-523-4321; Fax 603-523-3565
E-mail clovejoy@cardigan.org
Web Site www.cardigan.org

Boarding, Ages 9–15
Coeducational

CARDIGAN MOUNTAIN SUMMER SESSION offers remedial and enrichment academic courses and a recreational program of land and water sports for students in Grades 4 through 9. The six-and-one-half-week session begins in late June and ends in early August. Classes meet six days a week.

The academic program focuses on the reinforcement or enrichment of fundamental skills in Reading, Language Arts, and Mathematics in classes of no more than seven. Each student's strengths and weaknesses are care-

CARLETON COLLEGE

Deborah Appleman, Director
Summer Writing Program

One North College Street
Northfield, Minnesota 55057-4016
Telephone 507-646-4038
E-mail summer@carleton.edu
Web Site http://www.carleton.edu/campus/sap

Boarding, 90 Males and Females
Entering 12th Graders and College Freshman

SUMMER WRITING PROGRAM at Carleton College is a three-week program combining intensive writing instruction, fun, and friendship for students entering Grade 12 and college freshmen. The program, from July 9 to July 28, 2000, is designed to develop the writing skills needed for competency in college-level writing assignments.

Small, intimate classes encourage students to contribute to and participate in the learning process. A Carleton faculty member leads a morning discussion period on contemporary and traditional literature, which then becomes the focus of student essays. Additional discussions conducted by current Carleton students provide a forum in which the literary issues raised are applied to the participants' own assignments. Daily writing workshops focus on the kind of expository writing students will encounter in college as well as occasional creative writing. Students are given written evaluations of each of their three main papers, and those who successfully complete the program receive six Carleton credit hours.

In previous years, students have come from all 50 states and several foreign countries. The diversity of people and the lively exchange of ideas create a challenging and exciting atmosphere indicative of the possibilities and promises of college life.

Students are assigned two to a room under the supervision of a resident proctor and assistants and enjoy access to all the facilities of the Carleton campus. Group activities include a Guthrie Theater production and a shopping excursion to the Mall of America.

Contact the school for more details.

THE CHESTNUT HILL SCHOOL

Creative Arts and Sports Program
Marcus Nickerson, Director

428 Hammond Street
Chestnut Hill, Massachusetts 02467
Telephone 617-566-0445
Registrar Telephone/Fax 508-376-2469
E-mail mnickerson@tchs.org
Web Site www.tchs.org

Day, Pre-K–Grade 6
275 Boys and Girls

THE CHESTNUT HILL CREATIVE ARTS AND SPORTS PROGRAM promotes inventiveness in individuals through the arts. The eight-week program is offered from late June to mid-August for three age levels. Tutoring in reading and math is also available on an individual basis.

Experienced professional educators help children to express themselves and discover latent talents. Lower, Intermediate, and Upper camps are conducted between 9:00 A.M. and 4:00 P.M. on weekdays. Children can be enrolled for a minimum of two weeks. Early drop-off and extended-day options are offered.

The Lower Camp, for children ages 3–5, provides half-day and full-day sessions with children following a structured schedule as they engage in music, sports, drama, cooking, art, swimming, outdoor play, and storytime. One counselor is assigned to every five children.

Intermediate Campers (Grades 1–3) have six one-hour periods, with activities that include theater production, mask making, dance, tennis, improvisation, swimming, pillo polo, computers, creative movement, songwriting, photography, sports, clay building, and others. A major dramatic production is presented by the campers at the end of weeks four and eight.

Upper Campers follow a similar schedule with a different roster of activities, such as pottery, puppetry, modern dance, rock band, photojournalism, basket making, video drama, fabric design, wire sculptures, computers, sports,

tie-dye, sailing, swimming, and music lessons. Art exhibits, dramatic productions, and daily noontime performances are part of the program. Private music lessons are available.

Contact the school for more details; see listing on page 221.

COLLÈGE DU LÉMAN

Summer School
Francis A. Clivaz, Director General

74, route de Sauverny
CH-1290 Versoix-Geneva, Switzerland
Telephone 41-22-775-5555; Fax 41-22-775-5559
E-mail info@cdl.ch; Web Site http://www.cdl.ch

Boarding, Ages 8–18
200 Girls and Boys

COLLÈGE DU LÉMAN SUMMER SCHOOL offers intensive English or French language study in three three-week sessions extending from June 26 to late August, 2000. Boys and girls ages 8 to 18 years are enrolled.

Students from around the world may take intensive classes in English or French. Based on the results of placement tests, students are assigned to beginner, intermediate, or advanced levels. Grammar, vocabulary, text analysis, and conversation are emphasized, with reinforcement of lessons provided through language labs, video, and computers. Classes, taught by native speakers of the respective languages, are held daily, Monday through Saturday, from 9:00 A.M. to 12:15 P.M.

As a supplement to language instruction, students may elect to take an afternoon computer science course using the computer lab with state-of-the-art equipment.

Following the academic portion of the day, students take part in closely supervised recreational activities such as swimming, archery, cycling, tennis, volleyball, badminton, basketball, soccer, and softball.

Girls and boys reside in separate school buildings or villas on the spacious 18-acre campus. The school's location on the shores of Lake Geneva makes possible a wide range of travel opportunities throughout Switzerland

and France, exploring the historical, cultural, and geographic attractions of the beautiful Alpine region.

Contact the school for more details; see descriptive article on page 570.

THE COUNTRY SCHOOL

Summer on the Farm
Richard Barker, Director

3515 Township Road 124
Millersburg, Ohio 44654
Telephone (for messages only) 330-763-0881
(Due to the School's location in Amish country, there is no telephone.)
E-mail barkers@thecountryschool.com
Web Site www.thecountryschool.com

Boarding, Ages 6–12
30 Girls and Boys

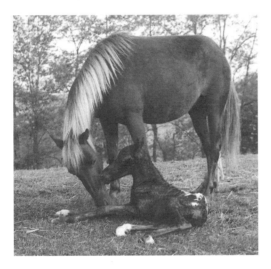

THE COUNTRY SCHOOL'S SUMMER ON THE FARM provides a living experience in the neighborhood of the world's largest Amish settlement. In ten five-day sessions, participants live, work, and play on the farm, where the daily routine replicates rural life in the early 1900s. The program, now in its 25th year, is strictly nondenominational.

From morning milking until warm cocoa and bedtime, days are filled with caring for the animals or working in the garden, kitchen, spinning room, or workshop. Evenings bring games, lamplighting, and recap of the day. Children sleep in the Barkers' farmhouse.

Farm life fosters a respect for nature, observational skills, foresight, a sense of responsibility, and a comprehension of one's place in the division of labor. Activities include the care of domestic animals, organic gardening, food preparation and preservation, farmstead maintenance and construction, and visits to the feed mill, lumber mill, livestock auction, and other local spots as the occasion merits. Animal sculpting and improvisational music are included during particular sessions.

Richard and Penny Barker, Montessori-trained educators, are assisted in their work by two of their adult children, an artist and a musician who grew up on the farm and are also trained educators.

The farm is located in scenic Holmes County, Ohio, where occupations are carried on as they were a century ago. It is easily accessible by car and is two hours from Cleveland or a day's drive from Chicago and the Eastern Seaboard. The Barkers assist in arranging carpools.

Contact the program for more information.

DARLINGTON SCHOOL

Darlington Summer Session
Lisa B. Schlenk, Director of Admission

1014 Cave Spring Road
Rome, Georgia 30161-4700
Telephone 800-368-4437
E-mail admission@darlington.rome.ga.us
Web Site www.darlington.rome.ga.us

Coeducational, Grades 9–12
95 Boarders, 30 Day

DARLINGTON SUMMER SESSION, from mid-June to late July, provides a college preparatory experience for students in Grades 9–12 who wish to accelerate their high school program, strengthen background weaknesses, or make up a course.

Students may earn up to one and one-half credits; review courses are also offered. Grades are reported to parents weekly. The academic day consists of up to six hours of classes and two and one-half hours of supervised study each evening. Most of the summer school staff reside on campus, and the average class size is six students.

Among the courses offered are Pre-9th English, English I (9th), English II (10th), English III (11th), English Grammar & Composition, Creative Writing, English as a Second Language, American History, Ancient World History, Modern World History, Pre-Algebra, Algebra 1–2, Geometry, Biology, Chemistry, SAT preparation, study skills, and computers. Special afternoon programs include Adventure Darlington (ropes course, kayaking, climbing, and other activities), Art Workshop, Drama, Graphic Design, and Scuba Diving. After-school athletics, fitness, and enrichment opportunities are also available.

Weekend activities include outdoor wilderness adventures, professional sports events, trips to area theme parks and malls, and excursions to Atlanta and Chattanooga.

The 425-acre campus, set around a small lake, includes a library, science center, communications center, seven athletic fields, a stadium, a track, an indoor swimming pool, a gymnasium, weight-training facilities, a tennis center, and volleyball courts.

Contact the school for more details; see descriptive article on page 141.

THE DELPHIAN SCHOOL

Summer at Delphi
Greg Ott, Headmaster
Sheridan, Oregon 97378
Telephone 800-626-6610
E-mail info@delphian.org
Web Site http://www.delphian.org

Boarding, Ages 8–Adult; Day, Ages 5–Adult
100 Boys, 100 Girls

SUMMER AT DELPHI, from June 26 to August 4, 2000, offers an enrichment program that draws students from many countries. The program, for academically able students, offers advanced and make-up academics complemented by extensive activities, outdoor adventures, and computer classes. English as a Second Language is also offered. Four- through six-week sessions are available.

Using the study methods developed by author and educator L. Ron Hubbard, students may preview or review a subject in a format that allows them to progress at their own optimum pace. The curriculum includes over 250 courses in mathematics, science, language arts, the arts, humanities, health, home economics, and English as a Second Language.

Afternoons are devoted to sports and special-interest activities. A wide range of choice is available including swimming, softball, soccer, basketball, volleyball, horseback riding, tennis, music, archery, computers, ceramics, golf, and arts and crafts. Weekend activities include trips to Portland and Salem for shopping and movies; there are also dances, overnight camping, and rafting excursions. More extended excursions are made to such places as Seattle and the Ashland Shakespearean Festival.

The campus, 50 miles southwest of Portland, is located on 700 acres of rolling hills, meadows, forest, and croplands. Facilities include a library, computer center, theater, art and photography studios, athletic fields, riding stables and arena, and a large gymnasium.

Contact the school for more details; see descriptive article on page 384.

DUNN SCHOOL

Dunn School Academic Summer Program
Jim Matchin, Director
P.O. Box 98
Los Olivos, California 93441
Telephone 805-688-6471; Fax 805-686-2078
E-mail jmatchin@dunnschool.com
Web Site www.dunnschool.com

Boarding and Day, Coeducational
Rising Grades 7–11

DUNN SCHOOL ACADEMIC SUMMER PROGRAM is a six-week instructional session designed to enable students entering Grades 7–11 to make up credits in core subjects. Day students are enrolled from Grade 7 upward and boarders from Grade 8. The program is conducted from late June to early August.

In a supportive educational setting marked by small, structured classes, students may preview subjects for enrichment or, with appropriate arrangements with their home school, earn credit for review work. Classes, enrolling between 8 and 12 students, are held daily, Monday through Friday. A typical day begins at 7:00 A.M. with breakfast and room inspection, followed by two academic periods, lunch, and another class. From 3:30 to 4:30 P.M., students take part in athletics, activities, and off-campus field trips. After dinner, there is a 90-minute study hall. Room check-in is between 9:30 and 10:30 P.M., depending on grade, and "lights out" is between 9:45 and 11:00 P.M.

The curriculum offers Writing Skills Workshop, Literature and Composition, 20th-Century U.S. History, Modern World History, Introduction to Computer/Keyboarding, Advanced Computer Science, Pre-Algebra/Introduction to Algebra, Algebra I and Geometry, Introduction to Spanish, and Intermediate Spanish. A Study Skills course focuses on improving test-taking strategies, organization and time management skills, and study techniques. Non-Native English is offered to students who have submitted an independent evaluation of their proficiency with the English language through standardized testing.

Summer school participants enjoy the heated pool, spacious library, tennis courts, playing fields, and other facilities on Dunn School's beautiful 55-acre campus.

Contact the school for more details; see listing on page 31.

DWIGHT-ENGLEWOOD SCHOOL

Dwight-Englewood Summer Programs
Mark A. Shultz, Summer School Principal
315 East Palisade Avenue
Englewood, New Jersey 07631
Telephone 201-569-9500, Ext. 3501
Fax 201-568-9451

Day, Males and Females
Preschool to Adult

DWIGHT-ENGLEWOOD SCHOOL SUMMER PROGRAMS, from mid-June to early August, provide review, advancement, and enrichment courses in all academic disciplines as well as opportunities in athletics and the arts. English as a Second Language is offered to students of all ages.

The Summer of Discovery is a weekly enrichment program for ages 3–5, Pre-school through Kindergarten. Adventures in Learning is also a weekly enrichment program for ages 6–10, Grades 1–4. Weekly enrollment is available for these and other programs.

Academic courses for review and credit are offered in Algebra I–II, Geometry, Pre-Calculus, Biology, Chemistry, Physics, English, Creative and Expository Writing, Studio Arts, Critical Thinking, Reading, Writing, and Critical Problem Solving. Advanced courses, which carry one Carnegie credit per six units, meet for 120 hours, while review and enrichment classes meet for 60 hours.

Enrichment courses for Grades 5–8 include a diverse selection of topics ranging from musical comedy, foreign languages, and the history of hip-hop to computer simulations, drama, and video design. Sports camps in basketball, soccer, lacrosse, tennis, and golf are available for Grades 5–12; a Driver's Education course is also offered for ages 15 and up. Adults are welcome in the tennis program.

Contact the school for more details; see listing on page 296.

EAGLEBROOK SCHOOL

Eaglebrook Summer Semester
O. Stuart Chase, Headmaster
Karl J. Koenigsbauer, Director
Deerfield, Massachusetts 01342
Telephone 413-774-7411; Fax 413-772-2394
Web Site www.eaglebrook.org
Boarding, Coeducational
Ages 11–13

EAGLEBROOK SUMMER SEMESTER provides boys and girls ages 11, 12, and 13 a wide range of experiences in classroom, artistic, athletic, and social areas with the goal of developing academic proficiency, leadership skills, and personal success. The four-week program runs from July 2 to July 29, 2000.

Students from diverse ethnic, racial, economic, and geographic backgrounds undertake a variety of activities designed to build confidence through achievement. Classes are taught by faculty chosen for their experience and commitment to children; faculty also serve as coaches and dormitory advisors.

Historic Deerfield and Eaglebrook's 600-acre campus provide natural areas that create an outdoor "classroom without walls" for discovery, exploration, and artistic inspiration. Courses are offered in English, reading, English as a Second Language, arithmetic, algebra, com-

puter, science, history, drawing, oil painting, photography, drama, and silkscreening.

Following morning classes and lunch, students participate in a wide range of sports; they also swim and play tennis with an emphasis on the development of physical fitness and athletic skills. Informal games of softball, volleyball, basketball, and indoor soccer are held after the evening meal.

Students reside in supervised dormitories and enjoy use of the School's extensive computer, athletic, and academic facilities. Among these are the Learning Center, the Schwab Family Pool, the Sports Center, and playing fields and hiking trails. On weekends, campouts, field trips, and Red Sox baseball games are among the activities.

Contact the school for more details; see descriptive article on page 227.

EAGLE HILL-SOUTHPORT

Eagle Hill-Southport Summer Program
Carolyn H. Lavender, Director
214 Main Street
Southport, Connecticut 06490
Telephone 203-254-2044; Fax 203-255-4052
Day, Ages 6–14
Boys and Girls

EAGLE HILL-SOUTHPORT SUMMER PROGRAM provides a five-week course of study from late June to the end of July designed to give children the remedial assistance needed to improve their academic progress. Students are immersed in a success-oriented, language-based program that is supportive, dynamic, and fun. Classes are held from 8:15 A.M. to 12:15 P.M. Monday through Friday, with small classes and daily tutorials based on each student's individual learning profile and skill level.

Academic subjects include a combination of five classes from the following: tutorials, mathematics, handwriting, written expression, oral language, and study skills. The staff consists of special educators who work creatively with the children to develop skills and build self-esteem. Classes are small, with a student-teacher ratio of approximately 3:1.

Situated on the harbor in the scenic New England town of Southport, Eagle Hill is located in the historic Pequot School building.

Contact the school for more details; see listing on page 78.

EMBRY-RIDDLE AERONAUTICAL UNIVERSITY

The Summer Academy
Pamela Payne, Director
600 South Clyde Morris Boulevard
Daytona Beach, Florida 32114
Telephone 800-359-4550 or 904-226-7648
Fax 904-226-7630
Web Site www.embryriddle.edu
Web Site www.ec.erau.edu/dce/summer
Coeducational, Boarding
Ages 12–18 (depending on program)

EMBRY-RIDDLE AERONAUTICAL UNIVERSITY'S SUMMER ACADEMY offers five programs related to aviation and aerospace.

SunFlight, for ages 16–18, carries college credit toward a flight-related degree. In three weeks, students may learn to solo an airplane or, in an intensive eight-week session, earn a Private Pilot certificate and six college credits. Students are teamed in pairs to reinforce their training by observing their flying partner's training.

The five-day Flight Exploration, for ages 12–18, provides an intensive introduction to flying and flight training. Students receive hands-on instruction, in-flight observation of their flight partner's training, and ground school.

Aerospace Summer Camp's classroom interaction, interactive activities, and behind-the-scenes tours provide insights into space technology including the history of space flight, space shuttle operations, manned and unmanned NASA programs, and future space flight. Students earn three college credits.

Engineering Technology Academy, for ages 16–18, is an intensive, one-week program in which the designing, building, and testing of aircraft-related components are explored. Practical mind-on and hands-on activities are planned in the project lab. Demonstrations using the wind tunnel and stereolithography labs follow a computer-aided drafting activity. An observation flight and other trips are included.

For students ages 16–18 who have an interest in aviation or previous aviation experience, Aviation Career Education Specialization (ACES) Academy enables participants to choose the aviation career that most interests them and learn with aviation professionals in the fields of air traffic control, avionics, engineering, flight, and maintenance.

Contact the school for more details.

ENFOREX SPANISH LANGUAGE SCHOOL

ENFOREX Summer Camps and Academic Year Programs
Antonio Anadón, Director
c/Alberto Aguilera, 26, Madrid 28015, Spain
Campuses: Madrid, Barcelona, Marbella, and
  Salamanca, Spain; Quito, Ecuador
Telephone 34-91-594-37-76; Fax 34-91-594-51-59
E-mail spanish@enforex.es
Web Site www.enforex.es

ENFOREX, at the forefront of teaching Spanish as a Foreign Language since 1989, enrolls students at seven locations.

Three campuses, in Madrid, Barcelona, and Marbella (Costa del Sol, Málaga), operate on a year-round basis. Two affiliated programs are situated in Salamanca and in Quito, Ecuador, and there are two residential summer camps.

The residential summer camps in Madrid and Marbella enroll children age 6–18. Students age 16 and older, university students, executives, professionals, and senior citizens may attend on a year-round basis and can earn high school or college credit. Classes are small with an average of five students and a maximum of eight.

Course offerings include General Intensive Spanish with 12–30 lessons per week, long-duration combined classes that may include one-to-one study, travel/study, and combined Spanish and flamenco, history, art, literature, business, exam preparation, teacher training for Spanish as a Foreign Language, a specialized course for tour guides; and customized programs, including a full academic year in Spain and classes for senior citizens age 50 and up.

ENFOREX offers accommodations with selected host families, in student residences, on university campuses, and in apartments and shared student flats and hotels.

Contact the program for more details.

FISHBURNE MILITARY SCHOOL

Fishburne Summer Session
William W. Sedr, Jr., Director
P.O. Box 988L
Waynesboro, Virginia 22980
Telephone 540-946-7703 or 800-946-7773
E-mail dbrown@fishburne.org
Web Site http://www.fishburne.org
Boarding (boys only) and Day, Grades 7–12
80 Boys, 5 Girls

THE FISHBURNE SUMMER SESSION, a five-week academic program from late June to early August, provides review and enrichment courses in English, mathematics, social studies, and science. Review work only is offered in chemistry, Spanish I, and French I.

A maximum of two credits may be earned. Students may take one or two repeat subjects; one new subject; or one new and one repeat subject. Only seniors needing two credits for graduation may take two new subjects.

Repeat subjects require two hours of instruction daily, and new subjects require four. Up to six hours of study are available each day, with two hours of supervised evening study. Instructors are drawn from the School's regular faculty.

Courses include English 7–12; World Studies, U.S. History, U.S. Government; Math 7–9, Algebra 1–2, Geometry; Computer Applications; General Science, Biology (repeat only), Chemistry; Spanish I and French I; and SAT Prep and Study Skills.

Afternoon recreational features swimming, softball, tennis, soccer, basketball, volleyball, and weight training. Other activities are developed according to group interest. Weekend trips are arranged to Busch Gardens, King's Dominion, and nearby parks. Sunday afternoon town leave and previously approved trips home are also permitted.

Facilities include the library with computers, swimming pool, gymnasium, athletic field, tennis courts, rifle range, infirmary, and state-of-the-art science laboratories. The new $1,500,000 Hobby-Hudgins Field House will contain locker rooms, wrestling area, weight room, cadet recreation center, and a multipurpose room with an indoor viewing area for parades and athletic events.

Contact the school for more details; see descriptive article on page 484.

tive living, leadership, self-discipline, and sportsmanship are developed. Students wear summer uniforms for the six-week session, which extends from early July to mid-August. Classes are held five days a week. A faculty-supervised two-hour study hall is scheduled in the evening, Sunday through Thursday.

Academic offerings include all levels of English, World History, U.S. History, Algebra I and II, Geometry, Physical Science, Biology, and an intensive SAT preparation course. Instruction is offered in Driver Education, Tae Kwon Do, Scuba, Reading, Computers, Tutorial Math, and English as a Second Language. Flight instruction in airplanes is available for all grades.

Afternoon sports include baseball, swimming, basketball, football, soccer, volleyball, tennis, weight lifting, golf, fishing, and surfing. Movies are shown on campus, and trips are scheduled to Disney World, Wet and Wild, Blizzard Beach, and Animal Kingdom.

The 30-acre campus has athletic fields, tennis courts, a swimming pool, computer laboratories, and a gymnasium. All dormitories, classrooms, the gym, and the dining room are air-conditioned.

Contact the school for more details; see descriptive article on page 124.

FLORIDA AIR ACADEMY

Florida Air Academy Summer Session
LTC James Dwight, President and Headmaster

1950 South Academy Drive
Melbourne, Florida 32901
Telephone 407-723-3211; Fax 407-676-0422
E-mail rwilson@flair.com

Boarding and Day, Grades 7–12 and Postgraduate
200 Boys

FLORIDA AIR ACADEMY SUMMER SESSION offers a structured educational program, with camp and recreational activities, to remedy academic deficiencies and strengthen student preparation for the academic year. Students may repeat courses previously failed, preview new courses, and improve fundamental skills through specialized instruction. One full academic credit may be earned. Coopera-

GEORGETOWN UNIVERSITY

Special Programs
School for Summer and Continuing Education
Box 571010

Georgetown University
Washington, DC 20057-1010
Telephone 202-687-5719 or 202-687-5832
Web Site http://www.georgetown.edu/ssce

Boarding, High School Sophomores and Juniors
Boys, Girls

GEORGETOWN UNIVERSITY SPECIAL PROGRAMS consist of three distinct programs for students of high school age. Varying in length and focus, the programs are scheduled between June and August.

The five-week Summer College for High School Juniors Program is designed to give selected students who have completed their junior year an in-depth preview of college academic and residential life. Students take one or two undergraduate college courses for up to six credits.

For students who have completed their sophomore or junior year, the one-week International Relations Program offers opportunities to explore the complexities of international relations and foreign policy through lectures by Georgetown and visiting faculty; small group discussions; trips to Congress, the State Department, and other relevant agencies; classroom discussions; and problem solving through simulation of an international crisis.

The five-week College Prep Program for students who have completed their sophomore or junior year provides college-level study opportunities in basic subject areas of English and mathematics and develops college reading and study skills.

All summer program participants make extensive use

of the Georgetown campus and the cultural and historic resources of the nation's capital.

Contact the school for more details.

THE GOW SCHOOL

The Gow Summer Programs
Bekah D. Atkinson, Director
Emery Road
South Wales, New York 14139
Telephone 716-655-2900
E-mail gowsummer@aol.com
Web Site www.gow.org
Boarding, Ages 8–18
125 Girls and Boys

THE GOW SUMMER PROGRAMS were developed for children who can benefit from summer academics without feeling as if they have lost their summer vacation. The six-week program, from early July to mid-August, provides solid academics with athletic, social, cultural, and recreational activities. The session, which blends structure and focus with flexibility and choice, includes morning academics, afternoon traditional camp, and weekend overnight trips. Gow strives to develop the skills and natural abilities of each camper while encouraging a sense of enthusiasm and positive self-image.

Campers may take courses for review, preview, and credit. The Academic Focus Programs, which enroll three to six students, meet five days per week. In addition, there is a predinner period during which camper-students have the option of reading for pleasure in the library, using the computer resource center, attending a film festival, playing challenging games such as chess and Trivial Pursuit, or attending a study hall/tutorial. Academics focus on reconstructive language, mathematics, organization and study skill development, SAT preparation, College/Career Exploration, computer literacy, and other courses offered according to student need.

Campers take part in afternoon camping and tripping activities through Activity Instruction Clinics, Group Periods, and Focus Periods. There is also a Counselor in Training Program for older camper students.

The Gow Summer Program's 100-acre campus, located in western New York State, features a computer center, library, gymnasium/activities center, indoor-outdoor

climbing walls, a challenging ropes course, and modern dormitories.

Contact the school for more details; see descriptive article on page 330.

THE GRAND RIVER ACADEMY

The Grand River Academy Summer School 2000
Keith Corlew, Director of Admission
3042 College Street
Austinburg, Ohio 44010
Telephone 440-275-2811; Fax 440-275-1825
E-mail academy@interlaced.net
Web Site grandriver.org
Day and Boarding, Coeducational
Entering Grades 9–12

THE GRAND RIVER ACADEMY SUMMER SCHOOL 2000 provides an opportunity for students to earn academic credit, to develop study skills, to receive individualized attention, and to study English as a Second Language. The six-week session, open to day students and five- and seven-day boarders, begins the last week of June.

The Summer School's primary goal is to prepare students, including those not working near their potential, for a successful college education. With a student-faculty ratio of 4:1, daily help sessions, and two-hour proctored study periods each evening, students may strengthen an academic weakness or investigate a new subject. Specific courses include Pre-Algebra, Algebra I&II, Geometry, Integrated Science, Biology, Chemistry, Physics, English 9–12, Literature, Composition, Government, U.S. History, World History, Civics, Spanish, and French. Noncredit afternoon electives are Studio Arts and Driver Education.

International students are afforded the opportunity for total immersion in the English language through intense training in aural/oral skills, reading comprehension, writing, and study skills. A thorough orientation to American culture is integral to the ESL program.

A typical daily schedule includes classes from 8:00 A.M. until 12:30 P.M., with afternoons open for electives and recreation, followed by dinner, the mandated study period, and "lights out" at 11:00 P.M. Weekend trips include visits to Sea World, the Rock and Roll Hall of Fame, and Cedar Point and Geauga Lake amusement parks.

Grand River Academy is 50 miles east of Cleveland; boarding students are provided with transportation to and from Cleveland International Airport and the Cleveland bus terminal.

Contact the school for more details; see listing on page 374.

HARGRAVE MILITARY ACADEMY

Summer School
Lt. Col. Ron Sykes, Director
Military Drive
Chatham, Virginia 24531
Telephone 800-432-2480
E-mail admissions@hargrave.edu
Web Site www.hargrave.edu
120 Boys, Boarding and Day
Grades 7–12

HARGRAVE MILITARY ACADEMY SUMMER SCHOOL is designed to provide a positive academic environment in which stu-

SUMMER PROGRAMS

dents can make up credits or earn new credits in the major subject areas while enjoying a diverse recreational program. The five-week program extends from June 26 to late July 2000.

The summer school has two divisions: Lower School encompasses Grades 7 and 8; the Upper School serves Grades 9 through 12.

Upper School students may earn one academic credit for new course work or two credits for two repeated subjects. English 8–12, United States History, American Government, Algebra I, and Geometry are offered for either new or repeat credit. Repeat credits only can be earned in Spanish I, World History, Science 8–9, Math 8–9, Biology, and Algebra II. Students who repeat one course may earn a half-credit in electives such as Reading Skills Lab, Math Skills Lab, Reading, and Physical Education/Weightlifting. In addition, a How to Study course aimed at the development of study and organizational skills is required of all students.

In the Lower School, students can take English, spelling, arithmetic, and reading.

Classroom instruction is followed by afternoon activities such as swimming, intramural competition, riflery, ping-pong, weightlifting, and tennis. On weekends, students are involved in trips to water parks, paintball games, confidence courses, and visits to a lakeside retreat. Attendance at Sunday morning chapel services is mandatory.

Summer school participants utilize the facilities provided on Hargrave's 240-acre campus, which features three gyms, an indoor pool, computer labs, a library, and fishing ponds.

Contact the school for more details; see descriptive article on page 490.

THE HARKER SCHOOL

Harker Summer Programs
Kelly Espinosa, Summer Programs Director
4300 Bucknall Road
San Jose, California 95130
Telephone 408-871-4600; Fax 408-871-4320
E-mail campinfo@harker.org
Web Site www.harker.org
Boarding and Day, 600–800 Boys and Girls per session
Ages 4¹/₂–16

HARKER SUMMER PROGRAMS combine academic enrichment with specialty classes, sports, and recreation in three- and five-week sessions. The World Camp boarding program featuring English as a Second Language runs four to nine weeks. Harker's programs are accredited by the American Camping Association, and the School is a long-time member of the Western Association of Independent Camps.

Harker Summer Camp gives students ages 4¹/₂–14 a choice of morning academic classes in language arts, reading and literature, and mathematics. Specialty classes in computer technology, performing arts, science, or math labs are electives. Classes are held for three hours, followed by afternoon sports and recreation. Campers may attend on a partial- or full-day basis.

Kindercamp for children entering Kindergarten provides enjoyable preparation for the school year. Math and reading skills are emphasized in the morning, followed by music, crafts, games, storytelling, and swimming lessons in the afternoon.

The World Camp boarding program for ages 9–14¹/₂ features English as a Second Language taught at several skill levels. In the afternoon, ESL students practice their speaking and listening skills through interaction with the other campers. Those who demonstrate verbal and written competency in English choose morning academic or specialty electives from the regular class list and join their World Camp mates in afternoon and evening activities. The World Camp concludes with a week-long tour of some of California's most famous attractions.

The Harker Summer Institute offers incoming or continuing high school students through age 16 academic classes for credit as well as electives for enrichment. Sports camps and travel programs are also planned.

The Harker campuses feature playing fields, swimming pools, and state-of-the-art computer labs.

Contact the school for more details; see listing on page 32.

HOPKINS SCHOOL

Hopkins Summer School
Karl Crawford, Director
Thomas Parr, Associate Director
986 Forest Road
New Haven, Connecticut 06515
Telephone 203-397-1001, Ext. 217
Fax 203-392-0267; E-mail crawford@hopkins.edu
Web Site www.hopkins.edu
Day, Grades 1–12
150 Boys, 135 Girls

📞 Call 1-203-269-3333 for school catalogs and counseling information.

S21

HOPKINS SUMMER SCHOOL offers academic courses for credit and noncredit in a six-week program extending from late June to early August. A four-week sports camp is offered during the same period. It can be coordinated with the academic program.

Academic courses meet in 60-minute classes scheduled between 8:00 A.M. and 1:15 P.M., five days a week. Among the courses offered are Expository and Creative Writing, English as a Second Language, French 1–3, Latin 1–5, Spanish 1–3, Modern European History, U.S. History, Arithmetic Review, Pre-Algebra, Algebra 1–2, Geometry, Functions, Statistics and Trigonometry, Science, Developmental Reading, SAT Preparation, Study Skills, and Typing. Credit courses require 90–180 hours of intensive study and noncredit courses 30–60 hours.

The elementary school program provides developmental reading, English as a Second Language, a writer's workshop, mathematics and computer study, science center, and sports camp.

The sports camp, meeting from 8:00 to 11:00 A.M. daily, includes six one-week coeducational sessions in basketball, outdoor adventure (high and low ropes course), fencing, swimming, tennis, and wrestling for Grades 3–12.

Contact the school for more details; see descriptive article on page 81.

HORACE MANN SCHOOL

Horace Mann Summer Programs
Nicholas L. Faba, Director

231 West 246th Street
Riverdale, New York 10471
Telephone 718-548-4000; Fax 718-548-2089
E-mail summer@horacemann.org
Web Site www.horacemann.org

Day, Nursery–Grade 12
450 Boys and Girls

HORACE MANN SUMMER PROGRAMS provide a broad range of academic and recreational opportunities for students from age three to Grade 12. Most of the programs take place on the Horace Mann campus. Door-to-door transportation is available for all programs; lunch is provided for all campers.

Students in Grades 6–12 may enroll in six-week courses offering credit for review, preview, and enrichment. The intensive, fast-paced program permits students to take one full-credit course and one preview, half-credit, or noncredit course. Most classes meet five days a week from 8:45 A.M. to 4:00 P.M., including two hours of recreation at the end of the day. Lab courses require a full-day commitment. Grades are issued at the end of each two-week marking period.

Students may choose from courses in English grammar and literature, writing, French, Spanish, reading and study skills, history, mathematics, science, computer, and the arts. Classes are small and students receive individualized instruction.

The six-week Horace Mann Day Camp provides a wide variety of fun activities, entertainment, and field trips for children ages 4–12. Supervised by mature, experienced personnel, campers enjoy a full schedule of athletics, swimming, arts and crafts, and photography, highlighted by frequent special treats such as magic shows, Olympics, scavenger hunts, tournaments, and guest appearances by sports celebrities. The June Programs and athletic offerings provide interim activities for Nursery–Grade 3, bridging the time period between the last day of school and the start of the day camp schedule.

Other Horace Mann summer offerings include one-week sports camps and arts programs.

Contact the school for more details; see descriptive article on page 338.

THE HUN SCHOOL OF PRINCETON

The Hun School of Princeton Summer Session
Donna O'Sullivan, Coordinator

176 Edgerstoune Road
Princeton, New Jersey 08540
Telephone 609-921-7600; Fax 609-683-4410
E-mail summer@hun.k12.nj.us
Web Site http://www.hun.k12.nj.us

Boarding and Day, Grades 9–12
150 Boys and Girls

THE HUN SCHOOL OF PRINCETON'S SUMMER SESSION offers five weeks of programs focusing on academic enrichment, refresher, and full-credit courses, and theater production. In addition, Hun's American Culture and Language Institute provides international students a unique introduction to the way Americans speak and live through ESL classes and cultural trips.

Enrichment courses are designed for those who wish to get a head start on a class they intend to take in the fall. There are refresher courses for students who need to complete credits or overcome a specific academic problem. Full-credit courses are given in Pre-Calculus, Chemistry, Algebra I–II, and Geometry. Students may take courses in the following subject areas for enrichment or make-up: English, Writing, Mathematics, Biology, Chemistry, French, and Spanish. There are classes to help students improve their SAT performance. With sufficient student interest, additional courses may be offered.

The American Language and Culture Institute combines intensive classroom study with frequent trips to museums, historical sites, and social events in the mid-Atlantic region including New York City, Philadelphia, Baltimore, and Washington, D.C.

All students use the School's facilities including air-conditioned classrooms, tennis courts, playing fields, a billiard and ping-pong room, and a gymnasium. For resident students, an afternoon program provides various sports and organized group activities. There is also a full slate of weekend activities and off-campus trips.

Contact the school for more details; see descriptive article on page 299.

HYDE SCHOOLS

Summer Challenge Program
Paul Hurd (Maine) and Kenneth Grant (Connecticut), Directors

616 High Street
Bath, Maine 04530
Telephone 207-443-5584; Fax 207-442-9346
E-mail bfelt@hydeschools.org
Web Site www.hydeschools.org
Grades 9–12, 125 Boarding and Day Boys and Girls

150 Route 169
Woodstock, Connecticut 06281
Telephone 860-963-9096; Fax 860-928-0612
E-mail kfelt@hydeschools.org
Grades 7–12, 145 Boarding and Day Boys and Girls

SUMMER CHALLENGE PROGRAM, operated by Hyde Schools at locations in Bath, Maine, and Woodstock, Connecticut, offers a five-week program to orient incoming students for the new school year. The session in Maine runs from July 11 to August 16, 2000; the Connecticut program is held from July 6 to August 8.

Since its founding by Joseph Gauld in 1966, Hyde School has been committed to providing an experience that combines character education with a college preparatory curriculum. Hyde is particularly focused on students of good ability who have not realized their true potential in traditional school settings.

Summer Challenge Program consists of three non-credit academic classes—based in English, history, and math—with an experiential focus. Students undergo assessment testing during the session to determine their placement in courses in the fall.

A typical day includes three one-hour classes, all taught by regular Hyde School faculty, in the morning. Lunch is followed by a two-hour activity period that varies in content each day. Two hours of athletics, dinner, and a two-hour evening study complete the daily schedule.

All students in the Summer Challenge Program participate in a four-day wilderness trip of camping, hiking, and related activities at Hyde's 500-acre property in northern Maine.

Students enjoy beach excursions, outdoor pursuits, movies, and field trips to museums, galleries, and other sites of interest. They also have access to the athletic, cultural, and recreational resources of the two Schools.

Contact the schools for more details.

INTERLOCHEN CENTER FOR THE ARTS

Interlochen Arts Camp
Admissions Office
P.O. Box 199
Interlochen, Michigan 49643-0199
Telephone 231-276-7472
E-mail admissions@interlochen.k12.mi.us
Web Site http://www.interlochen.org
2000 Boys and Girls, Ages 8–18
Boarding and Day

INTERLOCHEN ARTS CAMP offers boys and girls ages 8–18 a wide range of experiences in music, dance, visual arts, theatre arts, and creative writing. The program, from mid-June through mid-August, is designed to accommodate campers of varied abilities and experience. Students are enrolled in three divisions—Junior (Grades 3–6), Intermediate (Grades 6–9), and High School (Grades 9–12).

The comprehensive music program provides daily training, rehearsal, and performance at several levels of proficiency. Placement is determined by audition, and students have weekly opportunities to demonstrate their improvement and progress. Five orchestras, four bands, jazz and chamber ensembles, early music ensembles, jazz and classical guitar, piano and organ, choral training, operetta, and composition are available. In addition to their own performances, campers attend on-campus concerts and recitals by internationally renowned musicians.

The visual arts at Interlochen include ceramics, photography, drawing, printmaking, sculpture, fiber arts, and metalsmithing. Campers explore a variety of media and mount their work in exhibitions on campus.

Training is offered in ballet, modern dance, choreography, jazz dance, and other dance forms, and dance majors attend classes in both ballet and modern technique.

The Theatre Arts Department provides courses in acting technique, stage movement, musical theatre, radio, costume design, and drama production. All high school theatre majors appear in musical or Shakespearean productions.

Interlochen offers superb facilities for performance training and rehearsal as well as numerous opportunities for outdoor recreation on its 1200-acre wooded campus.

Contact the school for more details; see listing on page 261.

THE JOHN THOMAS DYE SCHOOL

The John Thomas Dye Summer Sessions
Douglas Phelps, Director
11414 Chalon Road
Los Angeles, California 90049
Telephone 310-476-2811; Fax 310-476-9176
E-mail DPhelps@JTDSchool.com
Web Site www.JTDSchool.com
220 Day Students, Coeducational
Preschool–Grade 6

THE JOHN THOMAS DYE SUMMER SESSIONS are designed to provide an enjoyable summer filled with challenging academics, arts, and physical education programs for girls and boys entering Preschool–Grade 6. The sessions run from June 26 to July 28, 2000, and participants may choose to attend for all five weeks or in two- or three-week sessions.

Classes for students in Preschool–Grade 2 are self-contained, with specialists teaching physical education, music, and computer courses. Students in Grades 3–6 choose from such classes as Claymation, Cooking, Writing, Theatre, and Woodworking, with afternoon programs offered in physical education, art, drama, and ceramics. Sports clinics are taught in volleyball, softball, basketball, and baseball.

The summer sessions are held on the campus of The John Thomas Dye School, an independent day school in Bel Air, which provides a country environment in a city setting. On 11 hilltop acres overlooking Santa Monica and the Pacific Ocean, the campus has a spacious gymnasium; science, music, art, and computer labs; and a 15-acre nature study center, all of which are used by summer program participants.

Contact the school for more details; see descriptive article on page 34.

THE KILDONAN SCHOOL

Dunnabeck at Kildonan
Ronald A. Wilson, Headmaster
RR #1, Box 294
Amenia, New York 12501
Telephone 914-373-8111
Web Site www.kildonan.org
Boarding, 75 Boys and Girls
Ages 8–16

DUNNABECK AT KILDONAN provides six weeks of intensive language training, from late June to mid-August, for stu-

dents of average or above-average intelligence who have not succeeded academically due to difficulties in reading, writing, or spelling.

At the beginning of the program, each student is administered standard diagnostic tests to determine his or her areas of strength and weakness in language and communication skills. With a 2:1 student-teacher ratio, each participant is ensured individual attention and support, enabling them to learn to study independently and develop self-confidence. Teachers are carefully selected for their maturity, imagination, and ability to work well with young people. Teaching methods based on the Orton-Gillingham approach integrate reading, writing, and spelling as different aspects of the language function. The program emphasizes correct expository writing, with attention to coherence, vocabulary, and clarity of expression. Typing and word processing are integral to the learning experience; math tutoring is also available.

A typical day begins with breakfast at 8:00 A.M., followed by an hour of one-on-one tutoring, a one-hour study hall, and a word-processing class. After lunch, students take part in a recreational program that includes ceramics, crafts, woodworking, photography, painting, horseback riding, water skiing, swimming, sailing, hiking, camping, softball, soccer, and canoeing.

Kildonan School is located on a 450-acre campus 90 miles north of New York City. Students reside in dormitories and have access to the School's athletic and fine arts facilities.

Contact the school for more details; see listing on page 340.

THE LAB SCHOOL OF WASHINGTON

Summer Session
Sally L. Smith, Director
4759 Reservoir Road, NW
Washington, D.C. 20007
Telephone 202-965-6600
E-mail www.labschool.org
Day, Ages 5–18
165 Boys, 103 Girls

THE LAB SCHOOL OF WASHINGTON SUMMER SESSION provides a six-week program for children of average to superior intelligence in primary, elementary, junior high, and high school grades who have learning disabilities or are in need of summer remedial academic work. The session begins in mid-June and ends by early August.

The Primary Program is for children ages 5–7$\frac{1}{2}$ who have been identified as "at risk" for learning disabilities. A multisensory approach is used, focusing on auditory and visual perception, visual-motor coordination, sensory motor integration, language development, and intellectual stimulation. Small-group tutoring in reading, writing, and mathematical skills takes place daily.

The Lower School Program is for children ages 7–12$\frac{1}{2}$ who have mild to severe learning disabilities. Individualized remedial instruction is given in all academic areas and through drama, music, woodworking, dance, and visual arts. Swimming and computer classes are optional afternoon activities.

The Junior High (Grades 7–8) and the High School (Grades 9–12) levels address students who have mild to severe learning disabilities. Small-group instruction is offered in reading, spelling, written language, mathematics, science, computer skills, and study skills. Optional sports, computer, and arts programs are offered during the afternoon. High school students receive credit in all classes.

Diagnostic services, individual tutoring, career and college counseling, occupational therapy, and speech/language therapy are available. Each summer's activities are built around a different program theme, such as "Mark Twain's Mississippi River," "Treasure Island Summer," "The Great American West," and a "Mediterranean Summer."

Contact the school for more details; see listing on page 109.

laboratory. A variety of electives is available in math, science, computer, American culture, TOEFL preparation, drama, painting, and other areas of interest.

A typical day begins with breakfast at 7:15 A.M., followed by classes from 8:00 A.M. to 12:15 P.M., an hour for lunch and free time, and another hour of classes. Recreational activities and sports, including soccer, basketball, golf, canoeing, horseback riding, and tennis, are available. After dinner, students have a two-hour evening study period. Dorm check-in is at 10:00 P.M.

Popular weekend excursions are planned to professional baseball and soccer games, whale watching, visits to the aquarium and Quincy Market in nearby Boston, amusement parks, concerts, and theater productions.

Lawrence Academy's 92-acre campus features a new Sony language lab and exceptional athletic facilities.

Contact the school for more details; see listing on page 236.

LAWRENCE ACADEMY

Lawrence Academy International Summer
  School
Jennifer O'Connor, Director
Powderhouse Road
P.O. Box 992
Groton, Massachusetts 01450
Telephone 978-448-6535; Fax 978-448-9208
Boarding, Approximately 100 Girls and Boys
Grades 9–12 (Ages 13–17)

LAWRENCE ACADEMY INTERNATIONAL SUMMER SCHOOL is a six-week academic enrichment program that offers both a wide variety of classes and a preview of boarding school life for American and international teenagers. The session runs from July 3 to August 11, 2000.

Academic courses are taught in environmental science, business, math, and English as a Second Language. In the ESL program, language skills are taught at beginning, intermediate, and advanced levels of proficiency, and no previous study of English is required. Students are assigned according to the results of placement tests. Small classes are taught by qualified instructors, many of whom are full-time members of Lawrence Academy's faculty. Students concentrate on the development of reading, writing, listening, speaking, and grammar skills and benefit from the use of the school's computerized language

THE LEELANAU SCHOOL

The Leelanau Summer School
Todd A. Holt, Director
One Old Homestead Road
Glen Arbor, Michigan 49636
Telephone 231-334-5800; Fax 231-334-5898
E-mail admissions@leelanau.org
Web Site www.leelanau.org
Boarding and Day, Coeducational
50 Students, Grades 8–11

THE LEELANAU SUMMER SCHOOL offers students entering Grades 8 through 11 the opportunity to develop academic skills, earn credit, and preview future courses while enjoying a wide variety of recreational, social, and outdoor activities with young people from the United States and around the world. The session extends for five weeks from late June to the end of July.

Summer school participants attend classes six mornings a week. Basic Reading, Literature, Grammar, and Composition are offered for every grade level. In addition, students may choose from such courses as Pre-Algebra, Algebra 1–2, Geometry; World History, U.S. History; Field Biology, Advanced Field Ecology, Computers, Art, and Study Skills. SAT/ACT Preparation, English as a Second Language, and Creative Writing are also available as enrichment courses, and other academic offerings can be customized to suit individual student needs. Each credit course meets for two hours daily.

In the afternoon, students enjoy activities designed to promote physical well-being and an awareness of the natural environment. Windsurfing, canoeing, horsemanship, offshore sailing, and camping on the Manitou Islands are among the most popular pursuits. In addition, the staff arranges dances, movies, mall excursions, and fishing and hiking trips.

The School's 50-acre campus, set in the heart of Sleeping Bear National Lakeshore overlooking Lake Michigan, offers excellent educational, athletic, and technological resources. Among them are a visual arts center, a 10,000-volume library, a greenhouse, Leelanau's own observatory, and facilities for tennis, baseball, track, and soccer.

Contact the school for more details; see descriptive article on page 261.

LEYSIN AMERICAN SCHOOL

Alpine Adventure/Summer in Switzerland
Dr. Thomas C. Haldi, Director
CH-1854 Leysin, Switzerland
Telephone 41-24-493-3777; Fax 41-24-494-1585
E-mail Admissions@las.ch
U.S. Office: P.O. Box 4016
Portsmouth, New Hampshire 03802-4016
Fax 603-431-1280
Boarding, Boys and Girls
Ages 9–13 (Alpine Adventure);
Ages 14–19 (Summer in Switzerland)

ALPINE ADVENTURE and SUMMER IN SWITZERLAND are programs conducted by Leysin American School offering academic enrichment, French, theater, art, and a wide range of cultural and outdoor activities set in the beautiful Swiss Alps. Students from more than 30 countries are enrolled.

Alpine Adventure for ages 9–13 consists of one or two three-week sessions from late June to the first week in August. Students attend academic enrichment classes about nine hours per week in Drama, Computer Skills, Arts & Crafts, and Our Environment plus a choice of French or English as a Second Language.

Students enjoy tennis, swimming, soccer, miniature golf, water slides, beach and pool parties, and a hiking overnight. Among the evening activities are ice skating, campfire singing, talent shows, Stunt Night, and Skit Night.

Students ages 14–19 may take enrichment courses in French, German, English literature, math, computer studies, English as a Second Language, and SAT Preparation. The academic component is enhanced by creative arts, an extensive theater program, and "Alpine Thrills," which features golf, paragliding, glacier snowboarding, and tennis. The Adventure Leadership program provides learning through outdoor activities such as white-water rafting, hiking, camping, and rock climbing.

Trips are planned to Bern, Geneva, Lausanne, Lucerne, and Zermatt, and highlight tours to France and Italy are offered on an optional basis.

Contact the school for more details.

LINDEN HILL SCHOOL

Linden Hill Summer Program
Michael P. Holland, Executive Director
154 South Mountain Road
Northfield, Massachusetts 01360
Telephone 413-498-2906; Toll Free 888-254-6336;
Fax 413-498-2908
E-mail admissions@lindenhs.org
Web Site http://www.lindenhs.org
Boarding Boys and Girls, Ages 7–16

LINDEN HILL SUMMER PROGRAM offers academic enrichment and recreation for students who have specific language differences, such as dyslexia. Set on the School's family-like campus, Linden Hill Summer Program begins in early July and ends in early August.

In a structured, supportive environment, participants are encouraged to grow in confidence and self-esteem, to make lasting friendships, and to develop as individuals and as athletes. A balanced program offers solid academics and strong athletic, social, cultural, and recreational activities. The weekly program combines structure and focus with flexibility and choice. Since all of the students have experienced past academic difficulties or learning differences, the democracy of common problems begins to erase self-consciousness, and self-esteem increases.

Classes of 1–6 students meet five days per week. Daily tutorials, drills, and written work are stressed, and all classes focus on motivation, a positive mental attitude, organization, study skills, social growth, and confidence. Courses include reading, computers, English, mathematics, science challenges, language tutorials, journalism, yearbook, design and technology, theater, art/animation, pottery, woodworking, and cookery.

In addition to daily sports, campers take advantage of the rich geographical and cultural setting with overnight trips on weekends, canoeing, fishing, ropes course, and mountain biking. Field trips are planned to Cape Cod, Boston's Faneuil Hall, Quincy Market, Red Sox baseball, Old Deerfield, and Riverside ride and water park.

Students are housed in dormitories on Linden Hill's country campus at the tristate corner of Massachusetts, Vermont, and New Hampshire.

Contact the school for more details; see descriptive article on page 236.

THE LOOMIS CHAFFEE SCHOOL

Loomis Chaffee Summer Programs
Joseph M. McCarthy, Director
Batchelder Road
Windsor, Connecticut 06095
Telephone 860-687-6117; Fax 860-687-6141
E-mail lcsp@loomis.org
Boarding and Day, Grades 7–12
65 Girls, 65 Boys

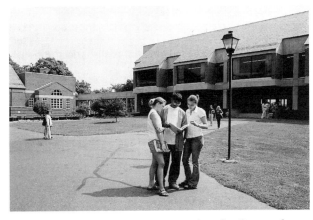

LOOMIS CHAFFEE SUMMER PROGRAMS consist of a five-week on-campus academic session, a five-week immersion in Spanish language and culture conducted in Barcelona, Spain, and a five-week immersion in French language and culture in Lyon, France.

The academic session at Loomis permits students entering Grades 7–12 to earn credits for work in more than 40 courses offered in English, English as a Foreign Language, French, Spanish, mathematics, philosophy, social science, science, music, and art. SAT preparation is available in English and mathematics. The academic program includes a major public-speaking and debate workshop in which students may enroll for specialization or for enrichment.

Classes are small, with a 5:1 student-teacher ratio, and most meet five days a week. The daily schedule begins with breakfast at 7:00 A.M., followed by classes until 12:55 P.M. Athletics take place from 3:00 to 5:00 P.M.; supper,

study hall, and leisure-time activities are held in the evenings, with "lights out" at 11:00 P.M.

The 330-acre Loomis Chaffee campus provides extensive recreational and athletic facilities.

Both the Summer in Spain and Summer in France programs begin with three-day orientations. The following four weeks are spent in homestays in Barcelona and Lyon, respectively, while students attend language and culture classes and participate in excursions. The trips end with travel to Madrid and Paris.

Contact the school for more details; see listing on page 88.

MARIANAPOLIS PREPARATORY SCHOOL

Summer Session 2000
Br. Brian Manian, M.I.C., Director
Route 200, P.O. Box 368
Thompson, Connecticut 06277-0368
Telephone 860-923-1992; Fax 860-923-1884
E-mail sbaron@marianapolis.com
Web Site www.marianapolis.com
Boarding and Day, Coeducational
Grades 9–12

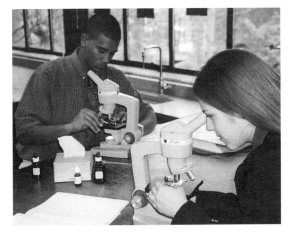

SUMMER SESSION 2000 provides academic review, preview, and acceleration in selected courses for new and current Marianapolis students. The six-week program runs from mid-July to the end of August.

Summer Session is designed for students who wish to meet specific academic objectives, to make up credit for failed courses, improve study skills and work habits, accelerate their studies, or learn English as a second language. Depending on interest, course work is available in English, history, mathematics, science, and art. English as a Second Language focuses on the development of reading, speaking, writing, and listening skills.

A typical day includes two 110-minute academic blocks beginning at 8:00 A.M. Day students may leave campus after classes, while resident students take part in a variety of extracurricular activities from 1:00 to 4:00 P.M., followed by dinner and a compulsory two-hour evening study period.

Athletic competition in a variety of sports involves students in friendly rivalry and encourages the development of sportsmanship, self-esteem, and technical skills.

On weekends, the School plans excursions to events of interest throughout New England including museum tours, Red Sox baseball games, and other attractions.

Residents are housed one or two to a dorm room and enjoy access to all the educational and recreational resources of the School's 300-acre rural campus.

Contact the school for more details; see descriptive article on page 88.

MARINE MILITARY ACADEMY

Summer Military Training Camp
Lt. Col. Robert R. Grider, USMC (Ret.),
Director of Admissions

320 Iwo Jima Boulevard
Harlingen, Texas 78550
Telephone 956-423-6006; Fax 956-412-3848
E-mail admissions@mma.tx.org
Web Site mma-tx.org
Boarding, Ages 13–17
250 Boys

SUMMER MILITARY TRAINING CAMP offers young men from throughout the United States and other countries the opportunity to "test their mettle" and compete for individual and team awards. The four-week session begins in late June.

Campers are challenged physically and mentally on a daily basis to build confidence and achieve goals. Each day consists of military classes and application, physical fitness training, and recreation, beginning at 6:00 A.M. and ending with Taps at 9:00 P.M. Campers wear fatigue uniforms, have regulation-length haircuts, and are responsible for keeping their uniforms, boots, living quarters, and equipment in good condition. Drill instructors reside in the barracks, providing adult supervision, counseling, leadership, and guidance for campers.

Activities include softball, soccer, close order drill, basketball, flag football, rifle marksmanship, swimming, first aid, weapons safety, field meets, paint ball, pugilistics, boxing, bivouac, map reading, land navigation, and military courtesies and disciplines.

Campus facilities such as the obstacle course, combat course, gymnasium, boxing gym, swimming pool, indoor/outdoor rifle range, and sports fields are open to all campers. Participants are housed two to a room in the Marine Military Academy's air-conditioned barracks.

Contact the school for more details; see descriptive article on page 459.

THE MASTERS SCHOOL

The Masters School Summer Sessions
Pamela J. Clarke, Head of the School

49 Clinton Avenue
Dobbs Ferry, New York 10522
Telephone 914-693-1400; Fax 914-693-1230
E-mail summerses@email.themastersschool.com
Boarding and Day, Ages 12–17
150 Boys and Girls

THE MASTERS SCHOOL offers two coeducational summer sessions, from July 9 to 28 and July 30 to August 18, 2000, in language arts and a choice of electives. Each session lasts three weeks during July and August. Students live in dormitories with student counselors and have a full activities program, including many cultural and recreational trips.

American students spend the mornings working on writing (expository, creative, and journalistic). They also take an intensive SAT prep course. International students study English as a Second Language on four levels. Their morning classes cover grammar and syntax, conversation and public speaking, expository and creative writing, and preparation for both the TOEFL and SAT. ESL students are tested at the beginning of each session and are placed in homogeneous groups.

In the afternoon, each student studies one area of concentration from the three following strands: arts and music, writing and film, and sports. Late afternoons are for recreational activities; evenings are for study.

On weekends, students, accompanied by teachers and counselors, visit sites in New York City and the Hudson Valley. In the past, participants have attended Yankee ballgames, attended Broadway plays and concerts, visited museums, and spent a day at Ellis Island and the South Street Seaport.

The Masters School is located 20 miles north of New York City on a beautiful 96-acre campus near the Hudson River in Westchester County.

Contact the school for more details; see listing on page 342.

THE MONTCLAIR KIMBERLEY ACADEMY

The Montclair Kimberley Summer Programs
Richard M. Sunshine, Director

201 Valley Road
Montclair, New Jersey 07042
Telephone 973-746-9800; Fax 973-509-4526
Web Site www.montclairkimberley.org
1040 Boys and Girls, Day
Preschool–Grade 12

THE MONTCLAIR KIMBERLEY ACADEMY SUMMER PROGRAMS provide academic enrichment, sports, and day camp experiences for preschoolers through entering high school seniors. The four programs vary in length from two to six weeks and take place from mid-June through early August on the school's three campuses.

Summer Academic Programs, directed by Denise Brown-Allen, offer three types of courses: Personal Development, Strengthening and Developing Skills, and Acceleration. Acceleration courses require prior departmental approval in order to carry academic credits. Writing, math, computer technology, foreign languages, and SAT preparation are among the topics available. Students may enroll for two, three, or six weeks.

Directed by Scott J. Coronis, Talent Explosions for students in Pre-Kindergarten–Grade 8 offers participants the opportunity to design their own summer experience, choosing from such topics as reading, fencing, science, computer technology, pottery, and performing arts, rocketry. Students in Grades 5–8 may cross-register in the Summer Academic Programs for part of the day.

The Brookside Day Camp, conducted by Christine Kadien, is a state-certified, six-week program, available on a weekly basis, for children ages 4–10. Swimming lessons, nature walks, cooking, arts and crafts, and sports are offered.

Vacation Play Days for ages 4–10, directed by Ann Zaleski, is held for two weeks in June and three weeks in August. The program is flexible, and children may enroll on a daily basis for a full- or half-day. Swimming, arts and crafts, games, baking, and nature activities are featured. Field trips are planned for each Wednesday in August, with the entire staff in attendance.

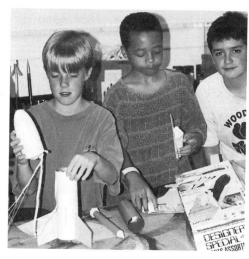

The Montclair Kimberley Academy campuses collectively offer five gyms, state-of-the-art computers, science laboratories, art rooms, indoor and outdoor pools, and athletic and playing fields.

Contact the school for more details; see listing on page 301.

NEWARK ACADEMY

Summer Session
Robert K. Mallalieu, Director

91 South Orange Avenue
Livingston, New Jersey 07039
Telephone 973-992-7000; Fax 973-992-8962
E-mail rmallalieu@newarka.edu
Web Site www.newarka.edu

800+ Boys and Girls, Day
Entering Grades 3–12

NEWARK ACADEMY SUMMER SESSION provides academic courses for advanced credit, enrichment, skill development, and remediation. The six-week session, from June 26 to August 4, 2000, enrolls over 800 students from neighboring communities who are entering Grades 3–12.

Advance credit courses meet four hours daily for a total of 120 hours and are equal in rigor and content to full-year programs at Newark Academy. With their school's approval, students may transfer their advanced credit course grade to their respective schools.

Preview courses are two-hour, content-based courses designed for students who want substantial exposure to courses they will take in the fall. Skill-building courses focus on developmental work in reading, English, math, and study skills. Two-hour review courses are designed for students who need to strengthen their skills or make up previous failure.

The following offerings are available: enrichment courses in English, mathematics, reading, and science; writing and literature workshops; creative writing and advanced writing; Spanish 1–2, French 1–2, Latin 1; Fundamentals of Mathematics, Pre-Algebra, Algebra I, Geometry, Algebra II with Trigonometry, Trigonometry, Pre-Calculus, Calculus; Biology, Chemistry, Physics; Humanities; Computer Applications; SAT/PSAT preparation; and English as a Second Language. The Learner's Edge, for Grades 7–12, concentrates on increasing reading comprehension and speed.

Newark Academy's Athletic Department offers camps in basketball, softball, soccer, and field hockey for girls; basketball, soccer, and football for boys; and coeducational track and running.

Contact the school for more details; see descriptive article on page 302.

NEW YORK MILITARY ACADEMY

Academic Summer Session
Director of Admissions

78 Academy Avenue
Cornwall-on-Hudson, New York 12520
Telephone 914-534-3710 or 888-275-6962;
Fax 914-534-7121
E-mail nyma1@nysnet.net; Web Site www.nyma.org

Boarding, Ages 8–18
90 Boys, 60 Girls

NEW YORK MILITARY ACADEMY provides boys and girls with an Academic Summer Session on its 165-acre campus from early July to mid-August.

The Academic Summer Session features many courses in remedial, make-up, and advanced study. Make-up and advanced courses, which may be taken for credit, include French, Spanish, social studies, science, English, and mathematics. Remedial courses are offered in mathematics, reading, and English. Other courses include English as a Second Language, which allows foreign students to take regular academic classes by the end of the summer, SAT, and Computer, which uses the Academy's computer labs. Classes meet for three periods each morning, five days a week. Students take two courses, with the third period reserved for study hall. Recreational activities and trips round out the program.

The Academic Summer Session aims to provide students with a variety of sports including basketball, tennis, swimming, soccer, softball, volleyball, and riflery. Each week, students choose sports in which they wish to participate; the following week, they may choose different sports or remain with the same ones. Youngsters are grouped by age, skill level, and interest.

Each student may also participate in a special horsemanship program. Riders are assigned mounts and learn to handle and care for them. Campus facilities include indoor and outdoor pools, athletic fields, tennis courts, indoor rifle range, gymnasium, library, and infirmary.

Contact the school for more details; see listing on page 342.

OAK HILL ACADEMY

Oak Hill Academy Summer School
Dr. Ed F. Patton, Director
2635 Oak Hill Road
Mouth of Wilson, Virginia 24363-3004
Telephone 540-579-2619; Fax 540-579-4722
E-mail oakhill@planet-va.com
Web Site http://www.planet-va.com/oakhill
Boarding, 80 Girls and Boys
Ages 13–18, Grades 8 through 12

OAK HILL ACADEMY SUMMER SCHOOL offers a five-week program of academic review, preview, and enrichment to girls and boys entering Grades 8 through 12. The session runs from mid-June to the third week of July.

The academic offerings include course work in English, mathematics, science, and social studies. Classes, which meet six days a week, are held for two and one-half hours a day for a repeat subject and five hours for each new subject. One new or two repeat subjects can be taken for full credit. Noncredit enrichment courses for review, preview, and remediation are available in English and mathematics. Upon arrival, students are given diagnostic tests to determine areas of weakness, with individualized study

plans and instruction designed to address these problems. Students who take a single subject meet 30 hours a week in that class, while those taking dual subjects of English and math meet 15 hours weekly in each. Classes are small to permit personal attention and encouragement. Ninety-minute study halls in the evening reinforce classroom instruction.

Summer school participants enjoy a wide variety of outdoor recreational activities such as cookouts, swimming, canoeing, hiking, and horseback riding.

Oak Hill Academy's 300-acre campus in the Blue Ridge Mountains, near the scenic New River and Jefferson National Forest, features playing fields, outdoor tennis courts, a gymnasium, and a riding arena.

Contact the school for more details; see descriptive article on page 502.

OAK RIDGE MILITARY ACADEMY

Summer Leadership Camp
Academic Summer School
Cheryl Fleischfresser, Director of Admissions
P.O.Box 498
Oak Ridge, North Carolina 27310
Telephone 336-643-4131, Ext. 132
Boarding and Day, Entering Grades 6–12
100 Boys, 40 Girls

OAK RIDGE MILITARY ACADEMY offers two summer programs. The three-week Summer Leadership Camp involves leadership training, athletics, and recreational activities. Academic Summer School runs either three or six weeks of classroom academics and leadership training. Both camps are held in June and July.

Summer Leadership Camp develops leadership qualities and promotes a spirit of competition and teamwork. Outdoor adventure training, team sports, and unit activities are a few highlights. Cadets rotate through leadership positions in interesting and challenging situations. A rappelling tower and confidence course encourage campers to achieve their potential. Paintball, weapon safety, and indoor range and pellet gun target practice help develop confidence, coordination, agility, and safety in planning and decision-making.

In the Academic Summer School, classes are held in a six-week course conducted in two sessions with a one-week break between sessions. The first session covers the first semester of a course subject; the second covers the second semester. Students may enroll in one or both sessions, depending on need. Courses are offered as requested, and class sizes are small. Classes are held every morning from 8:00 A.M. until noon. Two afternoons per week are devoted to library research and a study project; three afternoons and weekends are spent in leadership training activities.

Past special activities have included rappelling in nearby state parks and field trips to various educational centers, local areas of historic interest, water parks, and amusement parks.

The 101-acre campus is a National Historic District and includes a swimming pool, two gymnasiums, rifle range, tennis courts, an obstacle course, rappelling tower, and paintball course.

Contact the school for more details; see descriptive article on page 367.

OVERBROOK ACADEMY, INC.

Oak International Academies Masters
    Summer Challenge

836 Warwick Neck Avenue
Warwick, Rhode Island 02884
Telephone 401-737-2850; Fax 401-737-2884

432 Liguori Road
Edgerton, Wisconsin 53534-9340
Telephone 608-884-3425; Fax 608-884-8175
E-mail oaklawnusa@aol.com

Wingfield House
Kilcroney, County Wicklow, Ireland
Telephone 353-1-2866323; Fax 353-1-2864918

Haute Ecole de Valeurs Humaines
1833 Les Avants-sur-Montreux, Switzerland
Telephone 41-21-964-1516; Fax 41-21-964-1530

Boarding, Coeducational, Ages 8–16

OAK INTERNATIONAL ACADEMIES MASTERS CHALLENGE PROGRAM
invites young people to experience a new culture, learn
or perfect a second language, make new friends, and participate in athletic activities on several campuses.

Overbrook Academy in Rhode Island, offering a four-
week program, is situated on scenic Narragansett Bay.
Intensive English classes are taught daily, with horseback
riding, tennis, swimming, aerobics, and piano lessons also
available. Participants visit Quincy Market in Boston and
travel to Block Island.

The Wisconsin campus, situated on Lake Koshkonong,
provides a four-week sports program combined with
English language classes. Outings to Six Flags Amusement Park and Milwaukee Brewers baseball games are
among the trips planned.

Two campuses near Dublin, Ireland, offer separate
facilities for boys and girls and provide English classes,
sports clinics, and outings to Clara Lara Amusement
Park, the City of Dublin, and Saint Patrick's Cathedral.
Both programs run for four or six weeks beginning in
early July.

The LeChatelard campus in the Swiss Alps provides
classes for girls in French or English, European Culture,
Cooking, and Social Protocol for four- or six-week sessions. Visits to Lausanne, Zurich, and Geneva are
planned.

Founded in 1969, Oak International is a Catholic organization dedicated to the integral formation of youth.

*Contact the school for more information; see descriptive articles
on pages 422 and 525.*

PHILLIPS EXETER ACADEMY

Exeter Summer School
Richard "Hobart" Hardej, Director

20 Main Street
Exeter, New Hampshire 03833-2460
Telephone 603-777-3488; Fax 603-777-4385
E-mail summer@exeter.edu
Web Site www.exeter.edu/summer
575 Boarding and Day Boys and Girls, Students
    who have completed Grades 8–12

EXETER SUMMER SCHOOL offers a five-week academic enrichment program complemented by diverse extracurricular
offerings. Designed for bright, highly motivated students

who have completed Grades 8–12, Summer School is in
session from July 9 to August 12, 2000.

Students select three courses from more than 90 offerings where the focus is "learning for learning's sake."
Options include art, computer studies, English and writing skills, history, mathematics, modern and classical languages, social sciences, and science. The mathematics program focuses on problem-solving skills and utilizes
technology as part of the process. Principles in Criminal
Justice, Economics and Business, Psychology, The Art of
Being Human, Astronomy, Marine Biology, Chinese,
Italian, and numerous other courses complete the
curriculum.

Physical education is integral to the student's experience. Students are encouraged to try a new sport taught
by a professional physical education staff.

A typical daily schedule, Monday through Saturday,
includes morning academic classes with afternoons
devoted to sports, drama, music, and extracurricular
activities. Assemblies that feature presentations on a variety of topics are scheduled on Mondays and Fridays.
Evenings include time for study.

Educational and recreational excursions on Wednesday
afternoons and weekends include outdoor activities and
trips to Boston for culture, fun, and sporting events.

Extracurricular activities include The Princeton Review
SAT Preparation, theater, sports, and an excellent music
program that features The Forrestal-Bowld Music Center,
the newest addition to the academic complex. The centerpiece of Exeter's 400-acre campus is Louis Kahn's architectural landmark, the 150,000-volume Class of 1945
Library, which seats 400 students.

Contact the school for more details.

PORTSMOUTH ABBEY SCHOOL

Portsmouth Abbey Summer School Program
Daniel McDonough, Director

285 Cory's Lane
Portsmouth, Rhode Island 02871
Telephone 401-683-2000; Fax 401-683-5888
E-mail summer@portsmouthabbey.org
Web Site www.portsmouthabbey.org

Coeducational, Grades 8-11
Boarding and Day

PORTSMOUTH ABBEY SCHOOL SUMMER SCHOOL PROGRAM is a five-
week session offering academic instruction and English as

a Second Language. The program, for students entering Grades 8–11, runs from June 25 to July 28, 2000.

The academic component emphasizes enrichment and review in basic subjects as well as in elective offerings. Students choose four courses from Theology, English, Mathematics, Spanish, French, Marine Biology, Genetic Engineering, Human Anatomy and Physiology, Studio Art, Public Speaking, Desktop Publishing, Web Page Design, Study Skills, and SAT/SSAT Test Preparation.

In addition to classroom instruction, a varied athletic program is provided in the afternoons. Students may choose from soccer, tennis, basketball, and weight training. Sailing and scuba lessons are available for an additional fee. Recreational activities include weekly movie trips as well as day trips on Sundays. Past excursions have included a New England Revolution soccer game, a day on Martha's Vineyard, and other area attractions.

All summer school participants have access to the extensive academic and athletic facilities on Portsmouth Abbey's 500-acre campus, located on Aquidneck Island in Narragansett Bay.

Contact the school for more details; see descriptive article on page 424.

PRATT INSTITUTE

The Pratt Pre-College Program
Director
200 Willoughby Street
Brooklyn, New York 11205
Telephone 718-636-3453; Fax 718-399-4410
E-mail prostudy@pratt.edu
Web Site www.prostudies.pratt.edu
150 Males and Females; Boarding and Day
Entering Grades 11–12 and College Freshmen

THE PRATT PRE-COLLEGE PROGRAM combines intensive study of foundation courses in art, design, and architecture with challenging electives. Participants gain insights into their chosen subjects while earning college credit for their work. The four-and-one-half-week program, from early July to early August, enrolls high school students who have completed their sophomore, junior, or senior year.

Electives are chosen among courses in animation, architecture, fashion design, graphic design, illustration, industrial design, interior design, jewelry design, cartooning, painting and drawing, photography, and sculpture.

Courses are taught by regular Pratt Institute faculty; expert guest lecturers and critics also contribute to the instructional program. Students are immersed in their foundation course three half-days a week; elective classes meet three half-days a week. All students are also required to take an art history appreciation course for two half-days weekly and a portfolio development course for one half-day weekly. The program ends with an art show and reception at which students exhibit their work. Four college-semester credits are awarded upon successful completion of the program, and students receive a transcript of their work.

Staff-supervised weekend activities for all students include shopping and visits to museums, studios, galleries, and the theater.

Pratt Institute has two campuses: a 25-acre Brooklyn site in the Clinton Hill Historical District, and the Puck Building, in SoHo in New York City. Some courses are offered at only one location. Boarding is available only at the Brooklyn site.

Contact the school for more details.

RHODE ISLAND SCHOOL OF DESIGN

Pre-College Summer Foundation Program
Gail Whitsitt-Lynch, Assistant Director for Summer Programs
Two College Street
Providence, Rhode Island 02903-2787
Telephone 401-454-6200; Fax 401-454-6218
E-mail summer@risd.edu
Web Site www.risd.edu/summer
Boarding, Day, Grades 11–12
375 Boys and Girls

PRE-COLLEGE SUMMER FOUNDATION PROGRAM is a college-level program designed to develop perceptual and technical skills in a variety of visual arts disciplines and to assist students in the preparation of portfolios. The six-week session extends from late June to early August.

Each student takes three foundation courses—Foundation Drawing, Basic Design, and Art History—in addition to selecting one major area from a choice of 14 disciplines: animation, architecture, ceramics, drawing, industrial design, fashion design, graphic design, illustration, jewelry, painting, photography, printmaking, sculpture, and textile design.

Classes are taught by qualified faculty, including award-winning artists, designers, and educators. Each week's schedule includes a two-hour session in Art History, one six-hour session in both Foundation Drawing and Basic Design, and two six-hour sessions in the student's selected major.

The extensive facilities of the Rhode Island School of Design include printmaking studios, darkrooms, kilns, woodworking shops; a natural history museum housing more than 75,000 natural objects, slides, x-rays, clippings, and books; and the RISD Museum, containing 65,000 works. The library is one of the oldest independent college libraries in the country, housing a collection of more than 76,000 books and bound periodicals, 375,000 clippings, and 30,000 mounted art reproductions.

Dormitories are staffed by resident assistants assigned to each floor and supervised by the Director of Residence Life. Excursions are planned to Boston's Museum of Fine Arts and the mansions of Newport. Narragansett Bay, 200 miles of coastland, and the School's Tillinghast Farm provide students with ample recreational opportunities.

Contact the school for more details.

RUMSEY HALL SCHOOL

Rumsey Hall School Summer Session
Thomas W. Farmen, Headmaster
Clayton Ketchum and Jay Przygocki, Summer
    Session Co-Directors

Romford Road
Washington, Connecticut 06794
Telephone 860-868-0535; Fax 860-868-7907

Boarding and Day
Coeducational, Grades 3–9 — Day 3–9,
Boarding 5–9

RUMSEY HALL SCHOOL SUMMER SESSION is a five-week program of academic review and preview for students entering Grades 5–9. English as a Second Language is offered for international students. The program runs from the beginning of July to early August 2000 on a beautiful 65-acre campus bordering the Bantam River.

Academic courses are available for students who wish to review previous material or preview new material in English, mathematics, study skills, and computer skills. Classes are limited to ten students. Classes are available in Language Skills and developmental reading with trained specialists on a one-to-one basis. The schedule includes approximately four hours of coursework, with afternoon activities and recreation and evening study halls. Summer

school participants spend at least an hour a day reading and must complete two book reports during the session. Parents receive weekly progress reports, and a comprehensive written report is provided at the conclusion of the program.

English as a Second Language focuses on vocabulary and conversation in everyday situations. Students practice speaking skills with one another, keep journals, and discuss topics in American language and culture. Participants may also work with Language Skills faculty on a one-to-one basis.

Students live in dormitories and dine family style with their peers and faculty members. Participants enjoy swimming, various sports, hiking, mountain biking, and excursions to cultural events, historical sites, and amusement parks.

Contact the school for more details; see descriptive article on page 93.

RYE COUNTRY DAY SCHOOL

Rye Country Day School Summer Session
David M. Tafe, Director

Cedar Street
Rye, New York 10580
Telephone 914-921-4233
E-mail david_tafe@rcds.rye.ny.us
Web Site http://webserver.rcds.rye.ny.us

Day, Grades 3–12
200 Boys and Girls

RYE COUNTRY DAY SCHOOL SUMMER SESSION offers a program of remedial and enrichment courses for students seeking to develop new areas of interest, earn course credits, or review subjects in which they need strengthening. The six-week session begins in late June and ends in early August.

Classes, enrolling 4–12 students, meet five mornings a week; normally, a student has one class and one study period, each 45 minutes long, for each course. The curriculum includes review courses in English, Mathematics, French, Latin, Spanish, United States History, Global Studies, Biology, Chemistry, Physics, Earth Science; and enrichment courses in English as a Second Language, TOEFL Prep, Computer, Reading and Study Skills, Summer Reading, Writing Clinic, SAT Review, and Art. A self-contained classroom is offered for Grades 3–4. The Performing Arts Center offers courses in Jazz Band and Electronic (MIDI) Music as well as private music lessons. Students wishing to take certain courses for advance credit double the class time in each subject.

Students intending to take the New York State Regents examinations in mathematics and science can take an additional review program at a nominal charge in the week before the examinations.

Contact the school for more details; see descriptive article on page 350.

ST. GEORGE'S SCHOOL

St. George's Summer Session
Robert C. Weston, Director

P.O. Box 1910
Newport, Rhode Island 02840-0190
Telephone 401-842-6712; Fax 401-842-6763
E-mail Robert_Weston@stgeorges.edu
Web Site www.stgeorges.edu

Boarding and Day, Coeducational
Rising Grades 8–12

ST. GEORGE'S SUMMER SESSION, now in operation for more than 50 years, offers enrichment and review courses in the major academic disciplines for boys and girls entering Grades 8 through 12. The program runs from July 1 to August 5, 2000.

Set on a hilltop overlooking Newport's famous Second Beach, St. George's School offers strong academic guidance, a 6:1 student-faculty ratio, and coursework designed to enable students to preview new work and reinforce skills in English, mathematics, science, history, foreign language, computers, and the fine arts.

The School's seaside location provides an ideal laboratory for the study of marine biology; science classes are complemented by hands-on applications and field trips. English as a Foreign Language is available for international students; writing and editing workshops and Kaplan SAT and TOEFL preparation round out the program. Challenging electives are designed to meet the diverse needs of the student body.

The academic program is balanced with a full complement of recreational sports, including sailing and windsurfing.

Contact the school for more details; see listing on page 428.

ST. JOHN'S NORTHWESTERN MILITARY ACADEMY

Camp St. John's Northwestern
LTC James Kebisek, Director

1101 North Genesee Street
Delafield, Wisconsin 53018
Telephone 414-646-7115; Fax 414-646-7128
E-mail admissions@sjnma.org
Web Site www.sjnma.org

176 Boys, Boarding
Ages 12 (entering Grade 7)–15

CAMP ST. JOHN'S NORTHWESTERN provides boys the motivation to reach their potential through a semimilitary, structured program that combines adventure training, athletics, and fun. Personal growth and maturity are developed using leadership, physical endurance, and teamwork skills.

The camp operates two two-week sessions, beginning in late June of 2000. Under the guidance of dedicated and experienced leaders, boys develop self-awareness, overcome personal obstacles, and build confidence. Activities include orienteering, outdoor science exploration, archery, riflery, climbing, fishing, obstacle course, sailing, golf, canoeing, paintball, rappelling, hiking, tennis, and swimming. Participants may also earn Red Cross certification in First Aid and CPR, learn skin-diving techniques with an introduction to SCUBA, develop basic self-defense skills, and explore the Internet.

Off-campus excursions include a canoe trip on the Bark River and overnight island survival camping on Lake Nagawicka.

Campers are housed in dormitories on the 150-acre campus of St. John's Northwestern Military Academy and make use of the Academy's numerous facilities including a golf course, pool, gymnasium, and rappelling tower.

Contact the school for more details; see descriptive article on page 527.

SAINT THOMAS MORE SCHOOL

Academic Camp
45 Cottage Road
Oakdale, Connecticut 06370
Telephone 860-823-3861; Fax 860-823-3863
E-mail stmadmit@cyberzone.net
Web Site www.stthomasmore.pvt.k12.ct.us

Boarding; 80 Boys, 35 Girls
Grades 7–12, Ages 13–19

ACADEMIC CAMP at Saint Thomas More School offers course work for enrichment, preview, and credit make-up. The program, which runs from June 27 to August 6, 2000, also includes athletics, recreation, and a total of 11 field trips over the course of six weeks. Students entering Grades 7 to 12 are accepted.

Academic Camp is geared toward three groups of students. Underachievers who have not worked to their full potential may make up needed credits and acquire specific study and organizational skills, while motivated students may preview English, science, and mathematics courses they will be taking during the coming school year. International students acquire English language skills through ESL courses taught by specialist teachers at four levels of proficiency.

Among the offerings are English 1–3; World Cultures, World History, U.S. History; Pre-Algebra, Algebra 1–2, Geometry; General Science, Physical Science, Biology, Chemistry; Spanish 1–3; SAT Preparation; and English as a Second Language. Small, structured classes are taught by regular Saint Thomas More faculty and are held four hours each morning, six days a week. Afternoons are devoted to intramural sports and activities such as swimming, boating, basketball, and weight lifting.

On Wednesdays and Sundays, field trips are planned to the Mystic Aquarium, museums in Boston and New York, and other sites in the region.

Students reside two to a room in supervised dormitories on Saint Thomas More's 100-acre Lake Gardner campus in southeastern Connecticut. They enjoy use of the School's library, computer labs, and other educational and recreational facilities.

Contact the school for more details; see descriptive article on page 97.

SALISBURY SCHOOL

Salisbury Summer School of Reading
   and English
Andrew K. McBrian, Ed.D., Director
For information, contact Russ Edes
Salisbury, Connecticut 06068
Telephone 860-435-5700; Fax 860-435-5750
E-mail summerschool@salisbury.pvt.k12.ct.us
Boarding, Ages 13–18
100 Boys and Girls

SALISBURY SUMMER SCHOOL OF READING AND ENGLISH offers a six-week program in corrective and advanced English, reading, and writing for students who have completed Grades 8 through 12. The curriculum is designed to help superior students achieve their full potential as well as to help students needing remedial work.

Each student pursues a program of small-group instruction in six or seven basic language areas. Individual programs are based on diagnostic tests in reading rate, comprehension, vocabulary, spelling, and phonics; suggestions from the home school; and analysis of the student's academic record.

The core of the program is "Reading and Study Skills," in which students are trained to plan assignments, maintain an organized notebook, and use a study schedule. A reading specialist and in-class exercises focus on improving reading rate and comprehension. Other courses include Composition, Word Skills (including vocabulary), and Creative Writing. There are several math electives.

Each student has a faculty adviser; the student/faculty ratio is 4:1. No grades are given; extensive assessments, focusing on improvement, are compiled and sent to parents.

The 520-acre campus, situated in the Berkshire Mountains, offers woods, playing fields, tennis courts, a lake, and a gymnasium. Riding, bicycling, hiking, and golf are available along with various team sports.

Contact the school for more details; see descriptive article on page 99.

SANTA CATALINA SCHOOL

Santa Catalina School Summer Camp
Stephanie Steele Zalin, Director of Summer
   Programs
1500 Mark Thomas Drive
Monterey, California 93940
Telephone 831-655-9386
E-mail SummerCamp@scs.monterey.ca.us
Web Site www.santacatalina.org
Boarding and Day, Ages 8–14
200 Girls

SANTA CATALINA SCHOOL SUMMER CAMP offers one five-week or two two-and-one-half-week sessions from mid-June to late July. Campers choose from five morning programs. The Tennis Clinic provides daily professional instruction and tournament practice at all skill levels. The Riding Program offers three hours of daily instruction in riding, jumping, and practical horse care. The Musical Theater Workshop focuses on acting, dancing, and singing and concludes with a full production on Closing Day. The Marine Biology program for girls ages 12–14 provides an exciting course in which students examine the marine environment of the Monterey Bay. The General Program offers choices from the following: ceramics, crafts, cooking, sewing, painting and sketching, creative writing, computers, dance, drama, photography, marine biology, swimming, tennis, golf, volleyball, and soccer, plus several new class selections every summer. All classes are taught by professional instructors and assisted by counselors, young women from colleges nationwide, who also supervise evening and weekend activities and life in the dormitories.

Evening and weekend activities include camp team competitions, games, crafts, barbecues, and trips to local beaches and amusement parks. The 35-acre campus includes the Performing Arts Center, a 25,000-volume library, dormitories, chapel, athletic fields, gymnasium, tennis courts, and a heated swimming pool.

Contact the school for more details; see descriptive article on page 52.

THE SHELTON SCHOOL & EVALUATION CENTER

Summer School and Shelton Scholars
Joyce S. Pickering, Director

15720 Hillcrest Road
Dallas, Texas 75248
9407 Midway
Dallas, Texas 75220
Telephone 972-774-1772
E-mail webmaster@shelton.org
Web Site www.shelton.org

Day, Preschool–Grade 12 (Summer School)
640 Students

THE SHELTON SCHOOL & EVALUATION CENTER offers two distinct programs: Summer School and Shelton Scholars, each conducted for four weeks during the month of July.

The Summer School is designed to serve preschool through high school students of average to above-average intelligence who have learning differences. The multisensory curriculum focuses on perceptual motor and fine motor skills, alphabetic phonics, reading comprehension, handwriting, social and study skills, and language and speech. Course work is available in Multisensory Typing/Keyboarding, Word Processing, Computer Experience, English, Math, Reading/Spelling/Handwriting, Social Skills, Art, Language, and Study Skills. In addition, there is a half-day Early Childhood/Kindergarten component that addresses the learning needs of youngsters ages 3–7.

Enrichment classes are offered in areas such as art, drama, social skills, sports, music, and science.

Shelton Scholars is an outreach program emphasizing the improvement of reading, writing, and spelling skills for ages six to adult on Saturdays and during the summer. The program runs from 9:00 A.M. until noon and provides each student with two hours of one-on-one remediation tutoring based on the Sequential English Education Program and a one-hour auditory discrimination class.

Contact the school for more details; see listing on page 468.

SKIDMORE COLLEGE

Pre-college Program for High School Students at Skidmore
Dr. James Chansky, Director

815 North Broadway
Saratoga Springs, New York 12866
Telephone 518-580-5590; Fax 518-580-5548
E-mail jchansky@skidmore.edu
Web Site http://www.skidmore.edu/administration/osp

45 Women and Men, Rising Juniors and Seniors
Boarding and Day

THE PRE-COLLEGE PROGRAM FOR HIGH SCHOOL STUDENTS AT SKIDMORE is designed for academically talented young men and women with an interest in the liberal arts and the desire to engage in college-level study. The five-week session runs from early July to early August and coincides with the peak summer season at Skidmore and in Saratoga Springs.

Through the combination of dormitory living, first-year college-level courses, and the rich and varied intellectual, cultural, artistic, and social life of the summer campus, the program offers high school students a true college experience. Pre-college students undertake two foundation-level courses that carry full credit usually transferable to other colleges and universities, in the humanities, social sciences, natural sciences, and mathematics. Classes are taught by full-time members of the Skidmore community and are typically small, fast-paced, and informal.

In addition to course work, Pre-college students enjoy a wide variety of activities on campus. They have access to the resources of Skidmore's 850-acre wooded campus, including a swimming pool, tennis courts, an all-weather running track, and racquetball, squash, and basketball courts. Jazz concerts, fiction and poetry readings sponsored by the New York State Summer Writers Institute, the International Film Festival, gallery openings, and lecture-demonstrations are featured regularly on campus. In nearby downtown Saratoga Springs, students enjoy the rich variety and Victorian heritage of this summer resort town. Trips are also scheduled to concerts at The Saratoga Performing Arts Center, to museums in Manhattan, and to the Great Escape Amusement Park.

Contact the school for more details.

SUMMER THEATRE INSTITUTE — 2000

Youth Theatre of New Jersey's Teen Theatre
   Program in Residence at Columbia University,
   New York City
Ms. Allyn Sitjar, Artistic Director
Youth Theatre of New Jersey
39 Newton-Sparta Road
Newton, New Jersey 07860
Telephone 973-579-5734; Fax 973-729-3654
   (Attn: Summer Theatre)
E-mail youththeatreallyn@yahoo.com
Coeducational, Boarding and Day
45 Students, Ages 13–20, Grade 9 upward

SUMMER THEATRE INSTITUTE—2000, the teen program of Youth Theatre of New Jersey in residence at Columbia University in New York City, runs for five weeks from July 2 to August 4, 2000, and is a boarding and day program for ages 13–20 or Grade 9 and up. Admission is by application and audition. Auditions will be held from early March through early May. Videotaped auditions are accepted.

The Summer Theatre Institute preprofessional program offers intensive theatre training for young actors, directors, playwrights, musical theatre actors, and dancer actors. Young artists are guided by professionally involved theatre artists as they undertake process work in their chosen crafts. Summer Theatre Institute enables students to learn new physical theatre skills, expand their imagination, and explore their creativity without pressure or competition. The program also reinforces personal confidence, artistic discipline, performance technique, and ensemble work. Core ensemble classes are given in acting, improvisation, mime/theatre movement, dance, voice, and speech. Daily workshops are conducted in the spe-

cialty areas of directing, playwriting, musical theatre, and dance/theatre. Informational workshops on college and theatre conservatory programs and the business of theatre are also available.

In addition to in-depth training, the Summer Theatre Institute provides cultural enrichment through exciting field trips to museums, galleries, and Broadway and off-Broadway productions.

Resident students from Europe, Asia, and across the United States are housed in renovated, air-conditioned dormitories at Columbia University. The dorms and all classroom buildings have security guards on duty around the clock.

Contact the program early for information on admission and audition procedures.

TABOR ACADEMY

Tabor Academy Summer Program
Donn A. Tyler, Director
Marion, Massachusetts 02738
Telephone 508-748-2000
E-mail summer@tabor.pvt.k12.ma.us
Web Site www.taboracademy.org/sum/htm
Boarding, Ages 9–15
150 Boys and Girls

TABOR ACADEMY, on the shore of Buzzards Bay, has full athletic and oceanfront facilities. The Summer Program offers four- and six-week resident camp sessions, an optional academic program, and a day camp. These sessions begin in late June, extending through early August.

For those electing academics, classes are held five mornings a week, and afternoons are devoted to camp activities. Camp programs are also conducted each evening and on weekends and include field trips and special events. Academic offerings include English, English as a Foreign Language, Creative Writing, Developmental Reading, Mathematics (Grades 3–8), Algebra 1–2, Geometry, Computer Science, and Study Skills. Oceanography is taught in an oceanfront lab.

Activities include land sports such as baseball, basketball, field hockey, golf, lacrosse, soccer, softball, tennis, and volleyball. Other activities include art, ceramics, and drama, in addition to the waterfront activities: sailing and swimming. All activities are instructional at all levels.

Contact the school for more details; see descriptive article on page 246.

THE TAFT SCHOOL

Taft Summer School
Penny Townsend, Director
Watertown, Connecticut 06795
Telephone 860-945-7961
E-mail summerschool@taftschool.org
Web Site http://www.taft.pvt.k12.ct.us
Boarding and Day, Entering Grades 8–12
75 Boys, 75 Girls

TAFT SUMMER SCHOOL provides an opportunity for motivated students to review course material, prepare for future courses, or enrich their school experiences by taking courses not available to them during the regular school year. Students of high school age enroll in the Liberal Studies Program, which offers a broad selection in all the academic disciplines. The Young Scholars for students entering eighth or ninth grade provides a thorough transitional experience for those about to begin their careers in challenging secondary schools. Taft also offers five-week Abroad Programs in Ireland, France, and Spain.

The five-week session begins in late June and ends in late July. Classes meet six days a week. Most of each afternoon is reserved for athletics. Supervised room study is conducted during the evening hours.

Course offerings include Literature and Composition, English as a Second Language, Reading & Study Skills, Chemistry, Algebra, Geometry, Advanced Mathematics and Trigonometry, Computer Programming, French, Spanish, Photography, Drawing, Art History, and an SAT course. Faculty Advisors follow each student's progress and report to parents at the end of the session. Weekend activities are organized on campus, and trips to special events are planned.

Taft's 220-acre campus includes a 53,000-volume library, a computer center, an Arts/Humanities building, a state-of-the-art modern language lab, and the Cruikshank Athletic Center. The School is located 55 miles from Hartford and 90 miles from New York City.

Contact the school for more details; see listing on page 101.

VIEWPOINT SCHOOL

Summer Programs 2000
Dr. Robert J. Dworkoski, Headmaster
Paul Rosenbaum, Director of Summer Programs

23620 Mulholland Highway
Calabasas, California 91302
Telephone 818-340-2901; Fax 818-591-1016
E-mail viewpt@aol.com
Web Site www.viewpoint.org

Day, Boys and Girls
Kindergarten–Grade 12

SUMMER PROGRAMS 2000 provide a wide array of academic and enrichment programs, athletics, and camp experiences for students in Kindergarten–Grade 12. Participants may enroll for all or part of the six-week session, which is conducted from late June through the end of July.

Students entering Grades 5–12 may take courses in academic subjects for preparation, advancement, or fun; credit may be earned with prior approval from their regular school. Depending on grade, students may choose from the following courses: English, Speech; Beginning/Intermediate French, Beginning/Intermediate Spanish; General Math, Pre-Algebra, Algebra 1–2, Geometry, Trigonometry; Art, Photography, Ceramics, Instrumental Music; and Introduction to Computers and Intermediate Computers.

Camp Patriot for Grades 5–8 blends academic options in math and language skills with recreation and sports, including miniature golf, bowling, and ice- and roller-skating. Campers swim daily and take excursions to such attractions as Universal Studios, Magic Mountain, Dodger ballgames, and the beach.

Camp Roadrunner, for children entering Kindergarten–Grade 4, consists of a morning program of workshops in activities such as art, cooking, science, and computer. Academic course work is available. Afternoons are devoted to recreation, special field trips, and performances by musicians, dancers, and puppeteers. Swimming lessons are provided by certified Red Cross instructors.

Contact the school for more details; see descriptive article on page 57.

WENTWORTH MILITARY ACADEMY

Wentworth Summer School
Maj. Todd Kitchen, Dean of Admissions
1880 Washington Avenue
Lexington, Missouri 64067
Telephone 660-259-2221; Fax 660-259-2677
E-mail admissions@wma1880.org
Web Site http://www.wma1880.org
Boarding, Grades 6–12
Boys, Grades 6–12; Girls, Grades 9–12

WENTWORTH SUMMER SCHOOL offers a six-week academic summer session within a military structure. High school students may earn credit for remediation, review, or acceleration of basic skills in English, mathematics, and history. Special English programs are also available for international students. In Grades 6–8, a thorough Math and

English Review is designed to provide a strong background for entrance to high school.

Students in Grades 9 through 12 can receive one full year's credit for study in one course or two semesters' credit in two courses. In English, instruction in basic grammar, sentence structure, and vocabulary is complemented by an introduction to American literature and a reading improvement program.

Mathematics study encompasses review of the fundamentals of pre-algebra, algebra, and geometry. Study skills and time management are emphasized to all students.

Wentworth's 137-acre campus, including a golf course and country club, offers extensive athletic and recreational facilities such as tennis and basketball courts, an Olympic-size swimming pool, a 20,000-volume library, and a nature and fitness trail. Summer students may attend Kansas City Royals baseball games, enjoy barbecues and cook-outs, and visit Worlds of Fun amusement park.

Contact the school for more details; see descriptive article on page 281.

The coursework is structured to build self-confidence, improve students' communication abilities, and instill an appreciation for the English language.

The Mathematics program provides a strong basis in fundamental computational skills and arithmetic. Courses are offered in Pre-Algebra, Algebra I–II, Geometry, and Pre-Calculus. Students may also prepare for SATs in math and English.

English as a Second Language assists international students in adapting to life in the United States through language training and cultural experiences. ESL classes provide thorough instruction in spoken English, listening comprehension, reading, and writing. A special U.S. History course integrates language skills with the subject matter and presents the material in a unique manner especially designed for students from other countries. Field trips to related historic sites enrich classroom instruction.

A typical day includes four one-hour classes, followed by sports and recreational activities in the afternoon. All students have access to the School's 18-hole golf course, swimming pool, tennis courts, library, gymnasium, computer lab, and art studios.

Contact the school for more details; see descriptive article on page 248.

THE WINCHENDON SCHOOL

The Winchendon School Summer Session
J. William LaBelle, Headmaster

172 Ash Street
Winchendon, Massachusetts 01475
Telephone 800-622-1119; Fax 508-297-0911
E-mail admissions@winchendon.org
Web Site www.winchendon.org
60 Boarding Boys and Girls, Grades 8–12

THE WINCHENDON SCHOOL SUMMER SESSION provides academic remediation, makeup, and enrichment courses for students entering Grades 8–12. The six-week program, from late June to early August, also provides English as a Second Language and cultural immersion for international students.

Students can make up deficiencies, reinforce skills, and, with prior approval, earn credits in English and mathematics. In English I–IV, college preparatory courses emphasize writing skills, literature, and development of vocabulary, reading comprehension, and speaking skills.

WOODBERRY FOREST SCHOOL

Woodberry Forest Summer School
Ben Hale, Director

345 Woodberry Station
Woodberry Forest, Virginia 22989
Telephone 540-672-6047; Fax 540-672-9076
E-mail wfs_summer@woodberry.org
Web Site www.woodberry.org

Boarding, Grades 7–12
160 Boys and Girls

WOODBERRY FOREST SUMMER SCHOOL offers students entering Grades 7–12 the opportunity to experience the joy of learning supported by a strong staff of teachers and college interns. The Woodberry School environment is designed to challenge students academically and provide summer fun in a country setting. This coeducational program combines traditional classes with hands-on, experiential learning, creating lively and stimulating courses.

The three-week Youth Scholars' Program is offered to students who have completed Grades 6–7. Courses in creative writing, advanced math, hands-on history, studio arts, computers, science, and other areas are tailored to that age group. Six-week academic programs for enrichment or development are available to older students, and include classes in the fine arts, English, history, foreign languages, mathematics, science, computers, economics, SAT preparation, speech and debate, and English as a Second Language.

All summer program participants are expected to abide by Woodberry's student-run honor system and code of civility, which encompasses all aspects of school life. The Student Enrichment Challenge encourages participants to develop skills or complete goals.

Woodberry Forest's 1000-acre campus, situated in the rolling foothills of Virginia, provides the setting for a variety of educational and recreational opportunities, including access to the School's nine-hole golf course, swimming, hiking, and kayaking. Trips to nearby historical cultural, and entertainment centers complement the campus program.

Contact the school for more details; see descriptive article on page 518.

THE WOODHALL SCHOOL

The Woodhall School Summer Program
Sally Campbell Woodhall, Director

Harrison Lane, P.O. Box 550
Bethlehem, Connecticut 06751
Telephone 203-266-7788; Fax 203-266-5896

Boarding and Day, Ages 14–21
30 Young Men

THE WOODHALL SCHOOL SUMMER PROGRAM offers an individualized educational program for young men of average to superior ability who have not succeeded in traditional schools. Study skills and a Communications Program for Skills of Self-Expression with Accountability, facilitated by a trained faculty leader, form the basis of the program. The curriculum encompasses academics, athletics, outdoor activities, and social activities.

Course offerings, designed to meet the needs of the students, may include topics such as Critical Writing, Problem Solving, Renaissance Science, and Current Issues as well as remedial courses in specific subject areas and English as a Second Language. The Woodhall Summer Program offers students an opportunity to break the cycle of failure, to learn how to express themselves with honesty and fairness, and to treat themselves and others with respect and caring.

Daily outdoor recreation, frequent field trips, and other enrichment activities are offered throughout the summer. With its country setting in the foothills of the Berkshires, The Woodhall School is within close proximity to hiking and biking trails, nature preserves, and cultural venues

such as Mystic Seaport, Stockbridge, Tanglewood, and Yale Summer Theatre.

Contact the school for more details; see listing on page 102.

WYOMING SEMINARY

Sem Summer 2000
John R. Eidam, Director

201 Sprague Avenue
Kingston, Pennsylvania 18704-3593
Telephone 570-283-6086; Fax 570-283-6098

Boarding and Day, Coeducational
400+ Students, Age 4 through Grade 12

SEM SUMMER 2000 features performing arts and academic programs, sports clinics, and English as a Second Language. The program, between June 28 and August 28, 2000, enrolls youngsters from around the world, age 4 through precollege. The Performing Arts Institute is a residential program for serious performers ages 12–18.

For Grades 9–12, courses include American Literature, Communications, Creative Writing, French and Spanish for advancement, SAT Preparation in Math and Verbal, Masterpieces of Music, Photography, Painting, Art History, American History on Film, The Bible and Western Culture, Marine Biology, Chemistry, Conceptual Physics, Bridge to Algebra I, Algebra II Preparation, and Field Biology. Most courses carry .33 credit.

For Grades 5–8, programs explore science and math, creative arts, and history and outdoor education through diverse enrichment activities and hands-on experiences. Tutorials are offered in math and reading.

For ages 4–10, academic enrichment courses are offered in reading and math as well as fun courses designed to encourage discovery and exploration in topics related to drama, science, math, the arts, French and Spanish, and reading. Primary classes run from 9:15 A.M. to early afternoon and include time for lunch and supervised free play.

Two sessions of English as a Second Language for intermediate and advanced students combine intensive classroom instruction with American history and culture and, in Session II, travel to Washington, Baltimore, Annapolis, and Williamsburg.

Athletic programs include girls' field hockey and basketball clinics, coed soccer, and Blue Knights Sports Camp for boys and girls 8–14.

Contact the school for more details; see descriptive article on page 419.

YALE UNIVERSITY

Yale Summer Programs
Marigrace Bellert, Ph.D., Director

246 Church Street, Suite 101
New Haven, Connecticut 06510-1722
Telephone 203-432-2430; Fax 203-432-2434
Web Site www.yale.edu/summer

250 Boys and Girls, Boarding and Day
Age 16 and up

YALE SUMMER PROGRAMS offer an array of challenging, college-level academic courses for students who have completed their junior year and have reached their 16th birthday by July 1. Most precollege students enroll in two courses in the five-week session. They choose from Yale College courses in the humanities, social sciences, and sciences taught by regular Yale faculty or other qualified instructors.

Among the areas of study are anthropology, astronomy, archaeology, architecture, art, biology, chemistry, computer science, creative writing, drama, expository writing, film, history, history of art, literature, music, philosophy, political science, psychology, and religious studies.

Students are required to reside on campus in one of the Yale dormitories, called residential colleges, unless they live with their families within commuting distance of the University. The residential atmosphere provides precollege students with an introduction to college life and the opportunity to interact with other participants from across the country and around the world. Students enjoy a full range of recreational activities, many of which take advantage of Yale's relative proximity to New York, Boston, and the Atlantic coast.

All summer students have the use of Yale's academic and cultural resources including the 4,000,000 volumes housed in Sterling Memorial Library, the Yale University Art Gallery, Yale Center for British Art, and Peabody Museum of Natural History. During the summer, New Haven and Yale offer an abundance of activities including theater, concerts, and other cultural events.

Contact the school for more details.

Summer Programs Grid

These pages give the reader an outline of the summer programs described in the Yellow Pages. The schools are arranged alphabetically by state or country, together with a page number for locating descriptive material on each summer program. Use it as a quick reference for categorizing summer programs in the following areas:

English

Mathematics

Reading/Study Skills

Science

History/Political Science

Foreign Language

SAT Preparation

Computer Study

English as a Second Language

Dyslexia/Learning Differences

The Arts

Travel Study

Sports Camp

Astronaut/Pilot Training

Summary Programs Grid

(Summer Programs Grid)

State / School	Page	English	Mathematics	Reading/Study Skills	Science	History/Political Science	Foreign Language	SAT Preparation	Computer Study	English as a Second Language	Dyslexia/Learning Differences	The Arts	Travel Study	Sports Camp	Astronaut/Pilot Training
ALABAMA															
The Altamont School	S8	X	X	X	X	X		X	X			X	X	X	
CALIFORNIA															
Dunn School	S16	X	X	X	X	X	X		X						
The Harker School	S21	X	X	X	X			X	X	X		X	X		
The John Thomas Dye School	S24	X	X	X	X				X			X			
Santa Catalina School	S35			X					X			X		X	
Viewpoint School	S38	X	X	X	X		X		X			X	X		
CONNECTICUT															
Eagle Hill-Southport	S17	X	X	X							X				
Hopkins School	S21	X	X	X	X	X	X	X	X	X		X	X		
Hyde Schools	S23	X	X	X	X								X		
The Loomis Chaffee School	S27	X	X	X	X	X	X	X	X	X		X	X		
Marianapolis Preparatory School	S27	X	X		X	X			X	X					
Rumsey Hall School	S33	X	X	X					X	X	X				
Saint Thomas More School	S34	X	X	X	X	X	X	X	X	X					
Salisbury School	S35	X	X	X			X				X	X			
The Taft School	S38	X	X	X	X	X	X	X	X	X			X		
The Woodhall School	S40	X	X	X	X	X	X			X	X	X			
Yale University	S41	X	X		X	X	X		X	X		X			
DISTRICT OF COLUMBIA															
Georgetown University	S19	X	X	X											
The Lab School of Washington	S24	X	X	X	X	X	X		X		X	X			
FLORIDA															
Embry-Riddle Aeronautical University	S17				X										X
Florida Air Academy	S19	X	X	X	X	X		X	X	X					X
GEORGIA															
American Computer Experience	S9								X						
Darlington School	S15	X	X	X	X	X		X	X	X		X			

Summer Programs Grid

	Page	English	Mathematics	Reading/Study Skills	Science	History/Political Science	Foreign Language	SAT Preparation	Computer Study	English as a Second Language	Dyslexia/Learning Differences	The Arts	Travel Study	Sports Camp	Astronaut/Pilot Training
MAINE															
Hyde Schools	S23	X	X	X		X							X		
MASSACHUSETTS															
Belmont Hill School	S10	X	X	X	X	X	X	X	X	X		X		X	
The Chestnut Hill School	S14				X				X			X		X	
Eaglebrook School	S17	X	X	X	X		X		X	X		X			
Lawrence Academy	S25		X		X				X	X		X			
Linden Hill School	S26	X	X	X					X	X	X	X			
Tabor Academy	S37	X	X	X	X		X		X	X		X		X	
The Winchendon School	S39	X	X	X	X	X	X	X	X	X	X	X			
MICHIGAN															
Interlochen Center for the Arts	S23											X			
The Leelanau School	S25	X	X	X	X	X		X	X	X	X	X		X	
MINNESOTA															
Carleton College	S13	X													
MISSISSIPPI															
All Saints' Episcopal School	S8	X	X	X	X	X	X		X	X		X			
MISSOURI															
Wentworth Military Academy	S38	X	X	X	X	X			X	X					
NEW HAMPSHIRE															
Brewster Academy	S12	X	X	X					X	X					
Cardigan Mountain School	S13	X	X	X	X		X	X	X	X	X	X			
Phillips Exeter Academy	S31	X	X	X	X	X	X	X	X	X		X	X		

Summer Programs Grid

	Page	English	Mathematics	Reading/Study Skills	Science	History/Political Science	Foreign Language	SAT Preparation	Computer Study	English as a Second Language	Dyslexia/Learning Differences	The Arts	Travel Study	Sports Camp	Astronaut/Pilot Training
NEW JERSEY															
Dwight-Englewood School	S16	X	X	X	X		X		X	X		X		X	
The Hun School of Princeton	S22	X	X	X	X	X	X	X		X					
The Montclair Kimberley Academy	S28	X	X	X	X		X	X	X			X	X		
Newark Academy	S29	X	X	X	X		X	X	X	X	X		X		
Summer Theatre Institute — 2000	S37											X			
NEW YORK															
American Language Academy	S9									X					
The Berkeley Carroll School	S11			X				X				X	X		
The Gow School	S20	X	X	X	X	X	X	X	X	X	X	X	X	X	
Horace Mann School	S22	X	X	X	X	X	X	X	X	X		X	X		
The Kildonan School	S24	X	X	X				X			X				
The Masters School	S28	X					X		X			X			
New York Military Academy	S29	X	X	X	X	X	X	X	X	X			X		
Pratt Institute	S32											X			
Rye Country Day School	S33	X	X	X	X	X	X	X	X	X		X			
Skidmore College	S36	X	X		X	X						X			
Summer Theatre Institute — 2000	S37											X			
NORTH CAROLINA															
The Asheville School	S10	X	X	X	X	X	X	X	X	X		X			
Oak Ridge Military Academy	S30	X	X	X				X				X		X	
OHIO															
The Country School	S15			X	X							X			
The Grand River Academy	S20	X	X	X	X	X	X		X	X	X				
OREGON															
The Delphian School	S16	X	X	X	X	X	X		X	X		X		X	
PENNSYLVANIA															
Wyoming Seminary	S40	X	X	X	X	X	X	X	X	X		X		X	

Summer Programs Grid

Location	Page	English	Mathematics	Reading/Study Skills	Science	History/Political Science	Foreign Language	SAT Preparation	Computer Study	English as a Second Language	Dyslexia/Learning Differences	The Arts	Travel Study	Sports Camp	Astronaut/Pilot Training
RHODE ISLAND															
Overbrook Academy, Inc.	S31					X			X			X	X	X	
Portsmouth Abbey School	S31	X	X	X	X	X	X	X	X	X					
Rhode Island School of Design	S32											X			
St. George's School	S34	X	X	X	X	X	X	X	X			X			
TEXAS															
Marine Military Academy	S28								X					X	X
The Shelton School & Evaluation Center	S36	X	X	X	X	X	X		X		X	X			
VERMONT															
Bennington College	S11	X	X		X	X	X					X			
VIRGINIA															
The Blue Ridge School	S11	X	X	X	X	X	X	X	X	X		X	X		
Fishburne Military School	S18	X	X	X	X	X	X	X	X	X					
Hargrave Military Academy	S20	X	X	X	X	X	X								
Oak Hill Academy	S30	X	X	X	X	X									
Woodberry Forest School	S39	X	X	X	X	X	X	X	X	X		X			
WISCONSIN															
Overbrook Academy, Inc.	S31					X			X			X	X	X	
St. John's Northwestern Military Academy	S34						X						X	X	
FOREIGN															
ECUADOR															
ENFOREX Spanish Language School	S18				X	X						X	X		
ENGLAND															
Cambridge University	S12	X	X		X	X						X	X		
IRELAND															
Overbrook Academy, Inc.	S31					X			X			X	X	X	

Summer Programs Grid

	Page	English	Mathematics	Reading/Study Skills	Science	History/Political Science	Foreign Language	SAT Preparation	Computer Study	English as a Second Language	Dyslexia/Learning Differences	The Arts	Travel Study	Sports Camp	Astronaut/Pilot Training
SPAIN															
ENFOREX Spanish Language School	S18				X	X					X	X			
SWITZERLAND															
Aiglon College	S8	X				X			X			X	X		
Collège du Léman	S14	X				X		X							
Leysin American School	S26	X	X			X	X	X	X			X	X	X	
Overbrook Academy, Inc.	S31					X				X	X	X	X		

Bunting and Lyon, Inc.
238 North Main Street
Wallingford, Connecticut 06492
1-203-269-3333
Fax: 1-203-269-5697
E-mail: BandLBluBk@aol.com
Web Site: www.buntingandlyon.com

Classification Grid

These pages give the reader an outline of the schools described in our book. The schools are arranged alphabetically by state or country, together with a page number for locating more descriptive material on each school. Use it as a quick reference for categorizing schools in the following areas:

Boarding or Day

Boys, Girls, or Coed

Secondary or Elementary

Junior Boarding

Postgraduate Program

Summer Program

English as a Second Language

Learning Differences Program

Preprofessional Arts Training

Religious Affiliation

Military Program

The Classification Grid is the best place to begin your search for the right school. We find this section to be invaluable in our counseling sessions in the Bunting and Lyon offices.

Classification Grid

Boarding Boys	Boarding Girls	Day Boys	Day Girls	Elementary	Junior Boarding	Secondary	Postgraduate Program	Summer Program	English as a Second Language	Learning Differences Program	Preprofessional Arts Training	Religious Affiliation	Military Program	Page	School	Location
		X	X	X								E		3	Advent Episcopal Day School	*Birmingham*
		X	X	X		X		X						5	The Altamont School	*Birmingham*
		X	X	X		X								7	Bayside Academy	*Daphne/Gulf Shores*
		X	X	X		X								7	The Donoho School	*Anniston*
		X	X	X		X				X				7	Highlands School†	*Birmingham*
X	X	X	X		X	X				X				8	Indian Springs School†	*Birmingham*
		X	X	X		X								10	The Montgomery Academy	*Montgomery*
		X	X	X		X								10	Randolph School	*Huntsville*
		X	X	X		X								10	Saint James School	*Montgomery*
		X	X	X								E		10	St. Luke's Episcopal School	*Mobile*
		X	X	X		X				X		E		10	St. Paul's Episcopal School†	*Mobile*
		X	X	X		X		X						11	Tuscaloosa Academy	*Tuscaloosa*
		X	X	X		X								11	UMS-Wright Preparatory School	*Mobile*

ARIZONA

Boarding Boys	Boarding Girls	Day Boys	Day Girls	Elementary	Junior Boarding	Secondary	Postgraduate Program	Summer Program	English as a Second Language	Learning Differences Program	Preprofessional Arts Training	Religious Affiliation	Military Program	Page	School	Location
		X	X	X								E		12	All Saints' Episcopal Day School	*Phoenix*
		X	X	X		X								12	Green Fields Country Day School	*Tucson*
		X	X	X		X		X						12	Phoenix Country Day School	*Paradise Valley*
		X	X	X		X		X						12	St. Gregory College Preparatory School	*Tucson*
		X	X	X								E		12	St. Michael's Parish Day School	*Tucson*
		X	X			X						L		14	Valley Lutheran High School†	*Phoenix*
X	X	X	X			X	X	X	X					14	Verde Valley School	*Sedona*

CALIFORNIA

Boarding Boys	Boarding Girls	Day Boys	Day Girls	Elementary	Junior Boarding	Secondary	Postgraduate Program	Summer Program	English as a Second Language	Learning Differences Program	Preprofessional Arts Training	Religious Affiliation	Military Program	Page	School	Location
		X	X	X				X				E		17	All Saints' Episcopal Day School	*Carmel*
		X				X		X				RC		17	Archbishop Riordan High School†	*San Francisco*
X		X			X	X	X	X	X				X	17	Army and Navy Academy	*Carlsbad*
X	X	X	X			X		X						17	The Athenian School	*Danville*
		X	X	X		X								19	Bentley School	*Oakland/Lafayette*
		X	X	X										19	Berkeley Hall School	*Los Angeles*
		X	X			X		X				E		19	The Bishop's School	*La Jolla*
		X	X			X		X						19	The Branson School	*Ross*
		X	X	X		X		X						20	Brentwood School	*Los Angeles*
		X	X	X		X		X				E		21	Campbell Hall	*North Hollywood*

NOTE: The asterisk (*) identifies schools offering junior college programs. The dagger (†) denotes those schools with learning-differences programs that are cross-referenced in the Learning Differences Grid on page 609. Some elementary school classifications include Grade 9; secondary school classifications usually begin at Grade 9 although some commence at Grade 7. Junior Boarding indicates programs for middle school students and, in some instances, elementary school students. The following abbreviations designate formal religious affiliations or historical association: A—Anglican; B—Baptist; C—United Church of Christ Congregational; CS—Christian Scientist; E—Episcopal; J—Jewish; L—Lutheran; NC—Nondenominational Christian; P—Presbyterian; Q—Quaker; RC—Roman Catholic; SD—Seventh-day Adventist; O—Other.

Classification Grid

Boarding Boys	Boarding Girls	Day Boys	Day Girls	Elementary	Junior Boarding	Secondary	Postgraduate Program	Summer Program	English as a Second Language	Learning Differences Program	Preprofessional Arts Training	Religious Affiliation	Military Program	Page	School
		X	X	X										23	Carlthorp School *Santa Monica*
		X		X						X		E		24	Cathedral School for Boys† *San Francisco*
		X	X	X		X								24	The Center for Early Education *West Hollywood*
		X	X	X		X								24	Chadwick School *Palos Verdes Peninsula*
		X	X	X		X								24	The Children's School *La Jolla*
		X	X	X		X		X						24	Chinese American International School *San Francisco*
		X	X	X		X						CS		24	Clairbourn School *San Gabriel*
		X	X			X								25	The College Preparatory School *Oakland*
		X	X			X						RC		25	Convent of the Sacred Heart Elementary School *San Francisco*
			X			X						RC		25	Convent of the Sacred Heart High School *San Francisco*
			X			X		X				RC		25	Cornelia Connelly School *Anaheim*
		X	X	X				X						25	The Country School† *North Hollywood*
		X	X	X		X								27	Crane School *Santa Barbara*
		X	X	X		X								27	Crossroads School for Arts & Sciences *Santa Monica*
		X	X	X		X								29	Crystal Springs Uplands School *Hillsborough*
		X	X	X										29	Curtis School *Los Angeles*
		X	X			X		X	X					31	Drew College Preparatory School *San Francisco*
X	X	X	X			X	X	X	X					31	Dunn School† *Los Olivos*
		X	X			X								31	Flintridge Preparatory School *La Cañada Flintridge*
		X	X	X		X								31	Foothill Country Day School *Claremont*
			X	X		X								31	The Hamlin School *San Francisco*
		X	X	X										32	Harbor Day School *Corona del Mar*
X	X	X	X	X	X	X		X	X					32	The Harker School *San Jose*
		X	X			X		X						32	Harvard-Westlake School *Los Angeles/North Hollywood*
		X	X	X		X		X						32	The Head-Royce School *Oakland*
X	X	X	X			X	X	X	X		X			32	Idyllwild Arts Academy *Idyllwild*
		X	X	X		X								34	The John Thomas Dye School *Los Angeles*
X	X	X	X			X						Q		36	John Woolman School *Nevada City*
		X	X	X		X								36	Laguna Blanca School *Santa Barbara*
		X	X	X		X		X						36	La Jolla Country Day School *La Jolla*
		X	X	X		X		X						36	Laurence 2000 School† *Valley Glen*
		X	X			X								36	Lick-Wilmerding High School *San Francisco*
		X	X	X		X								36	Live Oak School *San Francisco*
			X			X						RC		37	Loretto High School *Sacramento*
		X	X			X		X						37	Marin Academy *San Rafael*
		X	X	X										37	Marin Country Day School *Corte Madera*
			X			X		X						37	Marlborough School *Los Angeles*
			X			X		X				RC		37	Marymount High School *Los Angeles*
		X	X	X		X						RC		37	Marymount of Santa Barbara *Santa Barbara*
		X	X	X								RC		37	Mayfield Junior School *Pasadena*
		X	X	X		X		X						38	Menlo School *Atherton*
		X	X	X				X						38	The Mirman School for Gifted Children† *Los Angeles*
		X	X	X				X						38	Mount Tamalpais School† *Mill Valley*
		X	X	X		X		X						40	New Roads School *Santa Monica/Los Angeles*
		X	X	X		X								41	The Nueva School *Hillsborough*
		X	X	X										42	The Oaks School *Hollywood*

Boarding Boys	Boarding Girls	Day Boys	Day Girls	Elementary	Junior Boarding	Secondary	Postgraduate Program	Summer Program	English as a Second Language	Learning Differences Program	Preprofessional Arts Training	Religious Affiliation	Military Program	Page	School
		X	X	X		X		X						42	Oakwood School *North Hollywood*
		X	X	X		X								44	Pacific Academy Preparatory School *Richmond*
		X	X	X		X								44	The Palm Valley School *Rancho Mirage*
		X	X	X				X	X					44	The Pegasus School† *Huntington Beach*
		X	X	X										44	The Phillips Brooks School *Menlo Park*
		X	X	X		X		X						44	Polytechnic School *Pasadena*
		X	X	X						X				45	The Prentice School *Santa Ana*
		X	X	X										45	Presidio Hill School *San Francisco*
		X	X	X										45	Prospect Sierra *El Cerrito*
		X	X	X										45	PS #1 Elementary School *Santa Monica*
		X	X	X				X	X					45	Redwood Day School *Oakland*
		X	X	X		X		X	X	X				45	Rolling Hills Preparatory School *Palos Verdes Estates*
		X	X	X		X		X						45	Sacramento Country Day School *Sacramento*
		X	X	X		X		X				RC		45	Sacred Heart Schools, Atherton *Atherton*
		X	X	X								E		46	St. James' Episcopal School *Los Angeles*
		X	X	X				X				E		46	St. John's Episcopal School *Rancho Santa Margarita*
		X	X			X						RC		47	St. Joseph Notre Dame High School *Alameda*
		X	X	X		X						E		48	St. Margaret's Episcopal School *San Juan Capistrano*
		X	X	X				X						50	Saint Mark's School *San Rafael*
		X	X	X								E		50	St. Matthew's Episcopal Day School *San Mateo*
		X	X	X				X				E		50	St. Matthew's Parish School *Pacific Palisades*
		X	X	X				X						50	Saklan Valley School *Moraga*
		X	X	X	X			X				RC		50	San Domenico School *San Anselmo*
		X	X	X										52	San Francisco Day School *San Francisco*
		X	X			X		X						52	San Francisco University High School† *San Francisco*
	X	X	X	X		X		X				RC		52	Santa Catalina School *Monterey*
		X	X	X				X						54	The Seven Hills School *Walnut Creek*
		X	X	X				X						54	Sonoma Country Day School *Santa Rosa*
		X		X				X				RC		55	Stuart Hall for Boys *San Francisco*
		X				X						RC		55	Stuart Hall High School *San Francisco*
		X		X				X						55	Town School for Boys *San Francisco*
		X	X	X				X						55	Turningpoint School *Bel Air*
		X	X			X								57	The Urban School of San Francisco *San Francisco*
		X	X	X		X		X						57	Viewpoint School† *Calabasas*
		X	X	X				X						59	Village School *Pacific Palisades*
X	X	X	X			X			X			RC		60	Villanova Preparatory School *Ojai*
X	X	X	X			X		X						62	The Webb Schools *Claremont*
		X	X	X				X						64	Westerly School of Long Beach *Long Beach*
			X	X		X		X						64	Westridge School *Pasadena*
		X	X	X		X								64	Wildwood School *Los Angeles*
		X	X	X										64	Windrush School *El Cerrito*
		X	X			X								64	Windward School *Los Angeles*
X		X	X			X		X				RC		65	Woodside Priory School *Portola Valley*
		X	X			X						E		65	York School *Monterey*

Classification Grid

COLORADO

Boarding Boys	Boarding Girls	Day Boys	Day Girls	Elementary	Junior Boarding	Secondary	Postgraduate Program	Summer Program	English as a Second Language	Learning Differences Program	Preprofessional Arts Training	Religious Affiliation	Military Program	Page	School
		X	X	X		X		X						66	Alexander Dawson School *Lafayette*
		X	X	X										66	Aspen Country Day School *Aspen*
		X	X	X		X		X						66	Colorado Academy *Denver*
X	X	X	X			X	X		X					66	Crested Butte Academy† *Crested Butte*
		X	X	X		X								66	Foothills Academy *Wheat Ridge*
X	X	X	X			X		X						66	Fountain Valley School of Colorado *Colorado Springs*
		X	X	X				X						66	Graland Country Day School *Denver*
		X	X	X		X		X						67	Kent Denver School *Englewood*
X	X	X	X			X								67	The Lowell Whiteman School *Steamboat Springs*
		X	X	X				X				E		69	St. Anne's Episcopal School *Denver*
		X	X	X		X						RC		69	St. Mary's Academy *Englewood*
		X	X	X								J		69	Theodor Herzl Jewish Day School *Denver*

CONNECTICUT

Boarding Boys	Boarding Girls	Day Boys	Day Girls	Elementary	Junior Boarding	Secondary	Postgraduate Program	Summer Program	English as a Second Language	Learning Differences Program	Preprofessional Arts Training	Religious Affiliation	Military Program	Page	School
X		X				X	X							70	Avon Old Farms School *Avon*
		X		X		X								72	Brunswick School *Greenwich*
X	X	X	X			X	X	X	X			RC		72	Canterbury School *New Milford*
X	X	X	X	X		X	X	X	X	X				74	Cheshire Academy† *Cheshire*
X	X	X	X			X	X	X	X					76	Choate Rosemary Hall *Wallingford*
		X	X	X										77	Cold Spring School *New Haven*
		X	X			X						RC		78	Convent of the Sacred Heart *Greenwich*
		X	X	X		X								78	The Country School *Madison*
		X	X	X		X		X		X				78	Eagle Hill-Southport† *Southport*
		X				X						RC		78	Fairfield College Preparatory School *Fairfield*
		X		X										78	Fairfield Country Day School *Fairfield*
		X	X	X		X								78	The Foote School *New Haven*
		X	X	X		X		X						79	Greens Farms Academy *Greens Farms*
		X	X			X								79	Greenwich Academy *Greenwich*
		X	X	X										79	The Greenwich Country Day School *Greenwich*
X	X	X	X			X	X	X	X					79	The Gunnery *Washington*
		X	X	X		X		X						79	Hamden Hall Country Day School *Hamden*
		X	X			X		X						81	Hopkins School *New Haven*
X	X	X	X			X	X							83	The Hotchkiss School *Lakeville*
		X	X	X		X								85	The Independent Day School *Middlefield*
X	X	X	X			X		X				E		86	Kent School *Kent*
		X	X	X		X			X					87	King & Low-Heywood Thomas School *Stamford*
		X	X	X		X								88	Kingswood-Oxford School *West Hartford*
		X	X	X										88	The Long Ridge School *Stamford*
X	X	X	X			X	X	X						88	The Loomis Chaffee School *Windsor*
X	X	X	X			X	X	X	X			RC		88	Marianapolis Preparatory School *Thompson*
X	X	X	X			X			X	X				90	Marvelwood School† *Kent*
		X	X	X		X				X		NC		90	The Master's School† *West Simsbury*
		X	X	X				X						90	The Mead School *Stamford*
	X		X			X		X	X		X			90	Miss Porter's School *Farmington*
		X	X	X		X								91	Mooreland Hill School *Kensington*
		X				X			X			RC		91	Notre Dame of West Haven *West Haven*

Boarding Boys	Boarding Girls	Day Boys	Day Girls	Elementary	Junior Boarding	Secondary	Postgraduate Program	Summer Program	English as a Second Language	Learning Differences Program	Preprofessional Arts Program	Religious Affiliation	Military Program	Page	School
		X	X	X		X								91	Pine Point School *Stonington*
X	X	X	X			X	X					E		91	Pomfret School *Pomfret*
X		X	X	X	X			X						93	The Rectory School *Pomfret*
		X	X	X				X						93	Renbrook School *West Hartford*
X	X	X	X	X	X			X	X	X				93	Rumsey Hall School† *Washington Depot*
			X			X						RC		95	Sacred Heart Academy of Stamford *Stamford*
		X	X	X		X		X						95	St. Luke's School *New Canaan*
		X	X	X		X		X						97	St. Margaret's-McTernan School *Waterbury*
X						X	X	X	X			RC		97	Saint Thomas More School *Oakdale*
		X	X	X				X				E		99	St. Thomas's Day School *New Haven*
X		X				X	X	X	X			E		99	Salisbury School *Salisbury*
X	X	X	X			X	X	X						101	The Taft School *Watertown*
		X	X	X										101	Town Hill School *Lakeville*
		X	X	X		X	X		X	X	X			101	Watkinson School† *Hartford*
X	X	X	X			X	X							102	Westminster School *Simsbury*
	X		X			X								102	Westover School *Middlebury*
		X	X	X										102	Whitby School *Greenwich*
		X	X	X				X						102	Wightwood School *Branford*
		X	X	X		X								102	The Williams School *New London*
X		X				X	X	X	X	X				102	The Woodhall School† *Bethlehem*
		X	X	X		X						E		102	Wooster School *Danbury*

DELAWARE

Boarding Boys	Boarding Girls	Day Boys	Day Girls	Elementary	Junior Boarding	Secondary	Postgraduate Program	Summer Program	English as a Second Language	Learning Differences Program	Preprofessional Arts Program	Religious Affiliation	Military Program	Page	School
		X	X			X						RC		103	Archmere Academy *Claymont*
		X	X	X				X						103	Centreville School† *Centreville*
		X	X	X				X						103	The Independence School† *Newark*
		X	X	X				X						103	The Pilot School, Inc.† *Wilmington*
X	X					X						E		103	St. Andrew's School *Middletown*
		X	X			X						RC		105	St. Mark's High School *Wilmington*
		X				X				X		RC		105	Salesianum School† *Wilmington*
		X	X	X		X		X						105	Sanford School *Hockessin*
		X	X	X		X		X						105	The Tatnall School *Wilmington*
		X	X	X		X		X						105	Tower Hill School *Wilmington*
		X	X	X		X						RC		106	Ursuline Academy *Wilmington*
		X	X	X		X		X				Q		106	Wilmington Friends School *Wilmington*

DISTRICT OF COLUMBIA

Boarding Boys	Boarding Girls	Day Boys	Day Girls	Elementary	Junior Boarding	Secondary	Postgraduate Program	Summer Program	English as a Second Language	Learning Differences Program	Preprofessional Arts Program	Religious Affiliation	Military Program	Page	School
		X	X	X				X				E		107	Beauvoir, The National Cathedral Elementary School *Washington*
		X	X	X				X						108	Capitol Hill Day School *Washington*
		X	X	X		X		X						108	Edmund Burke School *Washington*
		X	X	X		X								108	Georgetown Day School *Washington*
			X			X						RC		108	Georgetown Visitation Preparatory School *Washington*
		X				X						RC		109	Gonzaga College High School *Washington*
		X	X	X		X				X				109	The Kingsbury Day School *Washington*
		X	X	X		X		X	X	X				109	The Lab School of Washington† *Washington*
		X	X	X				X						109	Lowell School *Washington*

Classification Grid

Boarding Boys	Boarding Girls	Day Boys	Day Girls	Elementary	Junior Boarding	Secondary	Postgraduate Program	Summer Program	English as a Second Language	Learning Differences Program	Preprofessional Arts Training	Religious Affiliation	Military Program	Page	
		X	X	X		X		X						109	Maret School *Washington*
		X	X	X		X						E		109	National Cathedral School *Washington*
		X	X	X		X						P		109	National Presbyterian School *Washington*
		X	X	X		X								109	Rock Creek International School *Washington*
X		X			X	X		X				E		110	St. Albans School *Washington*
		X				X		X		X		RC		112	St. Anselm's Abbey School† *Washington*
		X	X	X		X						E		114	St. Patrick's Episcopal Day School *Washington*
		X	X	X		X								113	Sheridan School *Washington*
		X	X	X		X		X				Q		114	Sidwell Friends School *Washington*
		X	X			X				X				114	Washington Ethical High School† *Washington*
		X	X	X		X								114	Washington International School *Washington*

FLORIDA

Boarding Boys	Boarding Girls	Day Boys	Day Girls	Elementary	Junior Boarding	Secondary	Postgraduate Program	Summer Program	English as a Second Language	Learning Differences Program	Preprofessional Arts Training	Religious Affiliation	Military Program	Page	
		X	X	X		X						RC		115	Academy of the Holy Names *Tampa*
X	X	X	X	X	X	X			X				X	115	Admiral Farragut Academy *St. Petersburg*
		X	X	X		X		X						117	The Benjamin School *North Palm Beach*
		X	X	X		X		X	X			E		117	Berkeley Preparatory School *Tampa*
X	X	X	X	X	X	X	X	X	X					119	The Bolles School *Jacksonville*
		X	X	X		X		X			X			121	The Canterbury School *Fort Myers*
		X	X	X		X						E		121	Canterbury School of Florida *St. Petersburg*
		X	X			X						RC		121	Cardinal Mooney High School *Sarasota*
		X	X	X		X						RC		121	Carrollton School of the Sacred Heart *Miami*
		X	X			X				X		RC		122	Chaminade-Madonna College Preparatory† *Hollywood*
		X	X	X				X	X	X				122	The Cushman School† *Miami*
		X	X			X						E		123	Episcopal High School of Jacksonville *Jacksonville*
X		X			X	X	X	X	X				X	124	Florida Air Academy *Melbourne*
		X	X	X		X								125	Gulf Stream School *Gulf Stream*
		X	X	X										125	Independent Day School *Tampa*
		X	X	X		X								126	Jacksonville Country Day School *Jacksonville*
		X	X	X		X								126	Julie Rohr Academy *Sarasota*
		X	X	X		X			X	X				126	Lake Highland Preparatory School *Orlando*
		X	X	X		X		X						126	Maclay School *Tallahassee*
		X	X	X		X		X	X					126	Miami Country Day School *Miami*
X	X	X	X		X	X		X	X	X				126	Montverde Academy *Montverde*
		X	X	X		X								128	Oak Hall School *Gainesville*
		X	X	X		X		X						129	The Out-of-Door Academy *Sarasota*
		X	X	X		X				X				130	PACE-Brantley Hall School, Inc.† *Longwood*
		X	X	X		X								129	Palm Beach Day School *Palm Beach*
		X	X			X		X	X			E		129	Palmer Trinity School *Miami*
		X	X			X		X	X					129	Pine Crest School at Boca Raton *Boca Raton*
		X	X	X		X								130	Ransom Everglades School *Coconut Grove*
		X	X	X								P		130	Riverside Presbyterian Day School† *Jacksonville*
X	X	X	X			X		X	X			E		130	Saint Andrew's School *Boca Raton*
		X	X	X		X		X		X		E		132	Saint Edward's School *Vero Beach*
		X	X	X		X								134	St. Johns Country Day School *Orange Park*
		X	X	X		X						E		134	St. Mark's Episcopal Day School *Jacksonville*

584

Boarding Boys	Boarding Girls	Day Boys	Day Girls	Elementary	Junior Boarding	Secondary	Postgraduate Program	Summer Program	English as a Second Language	Learning Differences Program	Preprofessional Arts Training	Religious Affiliation	Military Program	Page	School
		X	X	X								E		134	St. Mark's Episcopal School *Fort Lauderdale*
		X	X	X				X				E		134	St. Mary's Episcopal Day School† *Tampa*
		X	X	X										134	Saint Michael's Independent School *Stuart*
		X	X	X		X						E		134	Saint Paul's School *Clearwater*
		X	X	X		X						E		135	St. Thomas Episcopal Parish School *Coral Gables*
		X	X	X								E		135	San Jose Episcopal Day School *Jacksonville*
		X	X	X		X								135	Seacrest Country Day School *Naples*
		X	X	X		X								135	Shorecrest Preparatory School *St. Petersburg*
		X	X	X								E		135	Sweetwater Episcopal Academy *Longwood*
		X	X			X		X						135	Tampa Preparatory School *Tampa*
		X	X	X		X		X		X		E		136	Trinity Preparatory School† *Winter Park*
		X	X	X		X		X						136	University School of Nova Southeastern University *Fort Lauderdale*

GEORGIA

Boarding Boys	Boarding Girls	Day Boys	Day Girls	Elementary	Junior Boarding	Secondary	Postgraduate Program	Summer Program	English as a Second Language	Learning Differences Program	Preprofessional Arts Training	Religious Affiliation	Military Program	Page	School
		X	X	X		X								139	Athens Academy *Athens*
		X	X	X		X								139	Augusta Preparatory Day School *Martinez*
		X	X	X				X		X				139	The Bedford School† *East Point*
	X		X			X	X		X	X				139	Brenau Academy† *Gainesville*
		X	X	X		X								141	Brookstone School *Columbus*
		X	X	X		X		X						141	Brookwood School *Thomasville*
X	X	X	X	X		X	X	X	X			NC		141	Darlington School *Rome*
		X	X	X								E		143	Episcopal Day School *Augusta*
		X	X	X		X								143	Frederica Academy *St. Simons Island*
		X	X	X		X		X						144	The Galloway School *Atlanta*
		X	X	X		X		X						144	George Walton Academy *Monroe*
		X	X	X		X		X						144	The Heritage School *Newnan*
		X	X	X		X		X		X		E		144	Holy Innocents' Episcopal School *Atlanta*
		X	X	X		X								146	LaGrange Academy *LaGrange*
		X	X	X		X		X						146	The Lovett School *Atlanta*
		X	X			X						RC		146	Marist School *Atlanta*
		X	X			X		X				RC		148	Mount de Sales Academy *Macon*
		X	X	X		X						NC		148	Oak Mountain Academy *Carrollton*
		X	X	X		X								148	Pace Academy *Atlanta*
		X	X	X		X								148	Paideia School *Atlanta*
X	X	X	X		X	X		X				P		149	Rabun Gap-Nacoochee School *Rabun Gap*
		X	X	X		X		X						150	St. Andrew's School *Savannah*
		X	X	X								E		150	St. Martin's Episcopal School *Atlanta*
		X	X			X			X	X		RC		150	St. Pius X Catholic High School† *Atlanta*
		X	X	X		X								150	The Savannah Country Day School *Savannah*
		X	X	X		X		X						151	Stratford Academy *Macon*
		X	X	X		X								151	Trinity School *Atlanta*
		X	X	X		X								151	Valwood School *Valdosta*
		X	X	X		X								151	The Walker School *Marietta*
		X	X	X		X						NC		151	Wesleyan School *Norcross*
		X	X	X		X						NC		152	The Westminster Schools *Atlanta*

Classification Grid

Boarding Boys	Boarding Girls	Day Boys	Day Girls	Elementary	Junior Boarding	Secondary	Postgraduate Program	Summer Program	English as a Second Language	Learning Differences Program	Preprofessional Arts Training	Religious Affiliation	Military Program	Page	School
		X	X	X		X						NC		152	Westminster Schools of Augusta *Augusta*
		X	X	X		X								152	Woodward Academy *College Park*

HAWAII

Boarding Boys	Boarding Girls	Day Boys	Day Girls	Elementary	Junior Boarding	Secondary	Postgraduate Program	Summer Program	English as a Second Language	Learning Differences Program	Preprofessional Arts Training	Religious Affiliation	Military Program	Page	School
		X	X	X		X		X						155	Academy of the Pacific† *Honolulu*
		X	X	X		X		X		X				155	ASSETS School† *Honolulu*
		X	X	X				X						155	Hanahau'oli School *Honolulu*
		X	X	X				X				E		155	Holy Nativity School *Honolulu*
		X	X	X		X								155	Island School *Lihue*
X	X	X	X	X	X	X		X				NC	X	155	The Kamehameha Schools *Honolulu*
			X			X								156	LA PIETRA — Hawaii School for Girls *Honolulu*
		X	X	X		X						RC		156	Maryknoll School *Honolulu*
X	X	X	X	X		X		X	X	X				156	Mid-Pacific Institute *Honolulu*
		X	X	X		X							X	156	Punahou School *Honolulu*
		X	X	X		X						RC		156	Sacred Hearts Academy *Honolulu*
			X	X		X		X	X			E		157	St. Andrew's Priory School for Girls *Honolulu*
		X	X			X		X				E		157	Seabury Hall *Makawao*

IDAHO

Boarding Boys	Boarding Girls	Day Boys	Day Girls	Elementary	Junior Boarding	Secondary	Postgraduate Program	Summer Program	English as a Second Language	Learning Differences Program	Preprofessional Arts Training	Religious Affiliation	Military Program	Page	School
		X	X	X		X		X		X				158	The Community School *Sun Valley*

ILLINOIS

Boarding Boys	Boarding Girls	Day Boys	Day Girls	Elementary	Junior Boarding	Secondary	Postgraduate Program	Summer Program	English as a Second Language	Learning Differences Program	Preprofessional Arts Training	Religious Affiliation	Military Program	Page	School
		X	X	X		X		X						159	The Avery Coonley School† *Downers Grove*
		X	X	X										160	Baker Demonstration School *Evanston*
		X	X	X								J		161	Bernard Zell Anshe Emet Day School *Chicago*
X	X	X	X		X	X	X			X				161	Brehm Preparatory School† *Carbondale*
		X	X			X		X			X			161	The Chicago Academy for the Arts *Chicago*
		X	X	X										161	Chicago City Day School *Chicago*
X	X	X	X	X	X			X	X					161	Chicago Junior School *Elgin*
		X	X	X		X								163	Elgin Academy *Elgin*
		X	X			X		X				RC		163	Fenwick High School *Oak Park*
		X	X	X		X								163	Francis W. Parker School *Chicago*
		X				X						RC		164	Hales Franciscan High School *Chicago*
		X	X	X		X		X		X				164	Keith Country Day School *Rockford*
		X	X	X		X		X						164	Lake Forest Country Day School *Lake Forest*
		X	X	X		X		X						164	The Latin School of Chicago *Chicago*
		X	X			X		X				RC		164	Loyola Academy *Wilmette*
		X	X	X		X		X						164	Morgan Park Academy *Chicago*
		X	X	X		X		X						164	The North Shore Country Day School *Winnetka*
		X	X	X				X						165	Quest Academy† *Palatine*
		X	X	X		X		X						165	Roycemore School *Evanston*
		X	X	X								RC		165	Sacred Heart Schools *Chicago*
		X	X			X		X		X		RC		165	St. Ignatius College Prep† *Chicago*
		X	X	X		X		X						165	Summit School† *Elgin*
		X	X	X		X		X		X				166	The University of Chicago Laboratory Schools *Chicago*

INDIANA

Boarding Boys	Boarding Girls	Day Boys	Day Girls	Elementary	Junior Boarding	Secondary	Postgraduate Program	Summer Program	English as a Second Language	Learning Differences Program	Preprofessional Arts Training	Religious Affiliation	Military Program	Page	School	Location
		X	X	X		X		X						167	Canterbury School	*Fort Wayne*
		X	X			X			X			RC		167	Cathedral High School†	*Indianapolis*
X	X	X	X			X	X	X	X				X	167	The Culver Academies	*Culver*
		X	X	X		X								169	Evansville Day School	*Evansville*
X	X				X	X		X					X	169	Howe Military School	*Howe*
X		X			X	X		X				RC	X	171	Le Mans Academy†	*Rolling Prairie*
	X		X			X		X				RC		173	Marian Heights Academy	*Ferdinand*
		X	X	X			X							175	The Orchard School†	*Indianapolis*
		X	X	X		X		X						175	Park Tudor School†	*Indianapolis*
		X	X	X								E		177	Saint Richard's School	*Indianapolis*
		X	X	X						X				177	The Stanley Clark School	*South Bend*
		X	X	X				X						177	Sycamore School†	*Indianapolis*

IOWA

Boarding Boys	Boarding Girls	Day Boys	Day Girls	Elementary	Junior Boarding	Secondary	Postgraduate Program	Summer Program	English as a Second Language	Learning Differences Program	Preprofessional Arts Training	Religious Affiliation	Military Program	Page	School	Location
		X	X	X		X		X	X					180	St. Katharine's St. Mark's School	*Bettendorf*

KANSAS

Boarding Boys	Boarding Girls	Day Boys	Day Girls	Elementary	Junior Boarding	Secondary	Postgraduate Program	Summer Program	English as a Second Language	Learning Differences Program	Preprofessional Arts Training	Religious Affiliation	Military Program	Page	School	Location
X					X	X						E	X	181	St. John's Military School	*Salina*
		X	X	X				X	X					181	Topeka Collegiate School†	*Topeka*
		X	X	X		X		X	X					181	Wichita Collegiate School†	*Wichita*

KENTUCKY

Boarding Boys	Boarding Girls	Day Boys	Day Girls	Elementary	Junior Boarding	Secondary	Postgraduate Program	Summer Program	English as a Second Language	Learning Differences Program	Preprofessional Arts Training	Religious Affiliation	Military Program	Page	School	Location
		X	X	X		X		X						182	Kentucky Country Day School	*Louisville*
		X	X			X						RC		182	Lexington Catholic High School	*Lexington*
		X	X	X										182	The Lexington School	*Lexington*
		X	X	X		X		X						184	Louisville Collegiate School	*Louisville*
X		X	X		X	X		X				·	X	184	Millersburg Military Academy	*Millersburg*
X	X	X	X	X		X		X		X				184	Shedd Academy	*Mayfield*
		X	X	X		X		X						184	University Heights Academy	*Hopkinsville*

LOUISIANA

Boarding Boys	Boarding Girls	Day Boys	Day Girls	Elementary	Junior Boarding	Secondary	Postgraduate Program	Summer Program	English as a Second Language	Learning Differences Program	Preprofessional Arts Training	Religious Affiliation	Military Program	Page	School	Location
		X	X			X						RC		185	Academy of the Sacred Heart	*New Orleans*
		X	X	X		X		X				E		185	Episcopal High School	*Baton Rouge*
		X	X			X						E		185	The Episcopal School of Acadiana	*Cade*
		X	X	X		X		X						185	Isidore Newman School	*New Orleans*
		X	X			X								185	The Louise S. McGehee School	*New Orleans*
		X	X	X		X				X				185	Metairie Park Country Day School†	*Metairie*
		X	X	X		X		X						186	Ridgewood Preparatory School	*Metairie*
		X	X	X								E		186	St. Andrew's Episcopal School	*New Orleans*
		X	X	X		X						E		186	St. Martin's Episcopal School	*Metairie*
		X	X	X								E		186	Saint Paul's Episcopal School	*New Orleans*
		X	X	X										186	Southfield School	*Shreveport*
		X	X	X								E		186	Trinity Episcopal School	*New Orleans*

MAINE

Boarding Boys	Boarding Girls	Day Boys	Day Girls	Elementary	Junior Boarding	Secondary	Postgraduate Program	Summer Program	English as a Second Language	Learning Differences Program	Preprofessional Arts Training	Religious Affiliation	Military Program	Page	School	Location
X		X				X		X						187	Bridgton Academy†	*North Bridgton*

Classification Grid

Boarding Boys	Boarding Girls	Day Boys	Day Girls	Elementary	Junior Boarding	Secondary	Postgraduate Program	Summer Program	English as a Second Language	Learning Differences Program	Preprofessional Arts Training	Religious Affiliation	Military Program	Page	School
X	X	X	X			X	X		X	X				187	Fryeburg Academy† *Fryeburg*
X	X	X	X			X	X	X	X	X				189	Gould Academy *Bethel*
X	X	X	X	X		X	X		X	X				189	Hebron Academy† *Hebron*
X	X	X	X			X	X			X				191	Kents Hill School† *Kents Hill*
		X	X			X								191	North Yarmouth Academy *Yarmouth*

MARYLAND

Boarding Boys	Boarding Girls	Day Boys	Day Girls	Elementary	Junior Boarding	Secondary	Postgraduate Program	Summer Program	English as a Second Language	Learning Differences Program	Preprofessional Arts Training	Religious Affiliation	Military Program	Page	School
		X				X		X				RC		192	Academy of the Holy Cross *Kensington*
		X	X	X		X		X						192	The Barrie School *Silver Spring*
		X		X		X								192	The Boys' Latin School of Maryland *Baltimore*
			X	X		X								192	The Bryn Mawr School *Baltimore*
		X	X	X		X								192	The Bullis School *Potomac*
		X	X	X		X		X						192	The Calverton School *Huntingtown*
		X	X	X										192	Calvert School *Baltimore*
		X	X	X		X		X				J		193	Charles E. Smith Jewish Day School *Rockville*
		X	X	X		X				X				193	The Chelsea School† *Silver Spring*
		X	X	X										193	Chesapeake Academy *Arnold*
		X				X						RC		193	Connelly School of the Holy Child *Potomac*
		X	X	X										193	The Country School *Easton*
		X	X	X								Q		193	Friends Community School *College Park*
		X	X	X		X		X				Q		193	Friends School of Baltimore *Baltimore*
	X		X	X		X								193	Garrison Forest School *Owings Mills*
		X	X	X										195	Gibson Island Country School *Pasadena*
		X		X		X		X						195	Gilman School *Baltimore*
		X	X	X		X		X						196	Glenelg Country School *Glenelg*
		X	X	X								E		196	Grace and Saint Peter's School *Baltimore*
		X	X	X				X						196	Green Acres School *Rockville*
		X	X			X		X	X					196	Gunston Day School *Centreville*
		X	X	X										196	Harford Day School *Bel Air*
		X		X		X						RC		197	The Heights School *Potomac*
			X	X		X								196	The Holton-Arms School *Bethesda*
		X				X						RC		197	Institute of Notre Dame *Baltimore*
		X	X	X		X		X		X				197	The Ivymount School† *Rockville*
		X	X	X										197	Kent School *Chestertown*
		X	X	X		X								197	The Key School *Annapolis*
		X		X		X								198	Landon School *Bethesda*
		X		X		X						RC		197	Loyola-Blakefield High School *Baltimore*
			X	X		X						RC		198	Maryvale Preparatory School *Brooklandville*
		X		X								RC		198	Mater Dei School *Bethesda*
X	X	X	X	X		X		X						198	McDonogh School *Owings Mills*
		X	X	X		X				X				198	The McLean School of Maryland *Potomac*
			X			X						RC		198	Mercy High School *Baltimore*
		X	X	X		X		X						199	The Newport School *Kensington*
		X	X	X						X				199	Norbel School† *Baltimore*
		X	X	X										199	Norwood School *Bethesda*
			X	X		X						RC		199	Notre Dame Preparatory School *Towson*

Boarding Boys	Boarding Girls	Day Boys	Day Girls	Elementary	Junior Boarding	Secondary	Postgraduate Program	Summer Program	English as a Second Language	Learning Differences Program	Preprofessional Arts Training	Religious Affiliation	Military Program	Page	School
	X		X			X								199	Oldfields School *Glencoe*
		X	X	X		X								201	The Park School *Brooklandville*
		X	X	X										201	The Primary Day School *Bethesda*
		X	X	X		X		X				E		201	Queen Anne School *Upper Marlboro*
			X	X		X		X						201	Roland Park Country School *Baltimore*
		X	X	X										202	Ruxton Country School *Owings Mills*
		X	X	X		X		X				E		202	St. Andrew's Episcopal School *Potomac*
		X	X	X								E		204	St. James' Academy *Monkton*
X	X	X	X		X	X				X		E		204	Saint James School *St. James*
		X	X	X				X				E		206	St. John's Episcopal School *Olney*
		X	X	X		X		X				E		206	St. Paul's School *Brooklandville*
			X	X		X						E		206	St. Paul's School for Girls *Brooklandville*
	X		X			X	X		X			E		206	St. Timothy's School *Stevenson*
X	X	X	X	X		X			X			Q		208	Sandy Spring Friends School *Sandy Spring*
		X	X	X		X		X						210	Severn School *Severna Park*
			X	X		X		X				RC		210	Stone Ridge School of the Sacred Heart *Bethesda*
		X	X	X		X						Q		210	Thornton Friends School *Silver Spring/Alexandria*
		X	X	X								E		210	Washington Episcopal School *Bethesda*
X	X	X	X			X	X		X	X				210	West Nottingham Academy† *Colora*
		X	X	X								RC		212	The Woods Academy *Bethesda*

MASSACHUSETTS

Boarding Boys	Boarding Girls	Day Boys	Day Girls	Elementary	Junior Boarding	Secondary	Postgraduate Program	Summer Program	English as a Second Language	Learning Differences Program	Preprofessional Arts Training	Religious Affiliation	Military Program	Page	School
X	X	X	X			X	X							213	The Academy at Charlemont *Charlemont*
X	X					X		X						213	The Academy at Swift River† *Cummington*
		X	X	X				X						214	Academy Hill School† *Springfield*
		X	X	X										214	The Advent School *Boston*
		X	X	X										215	Applewild School *Fitchburg*
		X	X	X										215	The Atrium School *Watertown*
		X	X	X		X		X						215	Bancroft School *Worcester*
		X	X			X								215	Beaver Country Day School *Chestnut Hill*
		X	X	X				X						215	Belmont Day School *Belmont*
X		X			X	X		X						215	Belmont Hill School *Belmont*
X	X	X	X	X					X					215	The Bement School *Deerfield*
		X	X	X		X		X						215	Berkshire Country Day School *Lenox*
X	X	X	X			X	X		X	X				216	Berkshire School *Sheffield*
		X				X		X				RC		218	Boston College High School *Boston*
		X	X	X		X								218	Brimmer and May School *Chestnut Hill*
X	X	X	X			X						E		218	Brooks School *North Andover*
		X	X	X										218	Brookwood School *Manchester*
		X	X	X		X								218	Buckingham Browne & Nichols School *Cambridge*
X	X					X								218	Buxton School† *Williamstown*
		X	X	X								Q		218	Cambridge Friends School *Cambridge*
		X	X	X		X								219	Cape Cod Academy *Osterville*
		X	X	X						X				219	The Carroll School† *Lincoln*
X	X	X	X			X	X		X	X				219	Chapel Hill-Chauncy Hall School† *Waltham*
		X	X	X										221	Charles River School *Dover*

Classification Grid

Boarding Boys	Boarding Girls	Day Boys	Day Girls	Elementary	Junior Boarding	Secondary	Postgraduate Program	Summer Program	English as a Second Language	Learning Differences Program	Preprofessional Arts Program	Religious Affiliation	Military Program	Page	School
		X	X	X				X						221	The Chestnut Hill School *Chestnut Hill*
		X	X	X						X				221	The Clark School for Creative Learning† *Danvers*
		X	X			X								221	The Commonwealth School *Boston*
X	X	X	X			X								223	Concord Academy *Concord*
		X	X	X		X	X	X		X				223	Cotting School† *Lexington*
	X		X			X								223	Dana Hall School *Wellesley*
		X	X	X										225	Dedham Country Day School *Dedham*
X	X	X	X			X	X	X						225	Deerfield Academy *Deerfield*
		X	X	X				X						227	Derby Academy *Hingham*
		X		X										227	Dexter School *Brookline*
X		X		X	X			X	X					227	Eaglebrook School *Deerfield*
		X	X	X										229	The Eliot Montessori School *South Natick*
		X	X	X										229	Fayerweather Street School *Cambridge*
X	X	X	X	X	X			X	X	X				229	Fay School *Southborough*
		X		X						X				230	The Fenn School *Concord*
X		X		X	X			X	X					230	The Fessenden School *West Newton*
		X	X	X		X								230	The French-American International School of Boston *Cambridge*
		X	X	X								Q		230	Friends Academy *North Dartmouth*
		X	X	X				X						230	Glen Urquhart School *Beverly Farms*
X	X	X	X			X		X						230	Governor Dummer Academy *Byfield*
X	X	X	X			X						E		230	Groton School *Groton*
X		X		X	X			X	X	X				232	Hillside School† *Marlborough*
X	X					X	X			X				234	The John Dewey Academy† *Great Barrington*
X	X	X	X			X		X	X					236	Lawrence Academy *Groton*
		X	X	X		X		X	X	X		NC		236	Lexington Christian Academy *Lexington*
		X	X	X				X						236	Lexington Montessori School *Lexington*
X					X			X	X	X				236	Linden Hill School† *Northfield*
X	X	X	X			X	X	X						238	The MacDuffie School *Springfield*
		X	X	X				X						238	The Meadowbrook School of Weston *Weston*
X	X	X	X	X		X								238	Milton Academy *Milton*
		X	X	X										238	Milton Academy Lower School *Milton*
	X		X			X	X		X					238	Miss Hall's School *Pittsfield*
		X	X	X								RC		240	Montrose School *Natick*
		X	X	X				X						240	Nashoba Brooks School *Concord*
		X	X			X	X	X	X					240	Newman Preparatory School *Boston*
			X	X								RC		241	Newton Country Day School of the Sacred Heart *Newton*
X	X	X	X	X	X	X								241	Noble and Greenough School *Dedham*
X	X	X	X			X	X	X	X					241	Northfield Mount Hermon School *Northfield*
		X		X								RC		241	Notre Dame Academy *Worcester*
		X	X	X				X						241	The Park School *Brookline*
X	X	X	X			X	X	X						241	Phillips Academy *Andover*
		X	X	X				X						242	The Pike School *Andover*
		X	X			X		X						242	Pingree School *South Hamilton*
		X	X	X								J		242	The Rashi School *Dedham*
		X	X			X								242	The Rivers School *Weston*
X	X				X	X	X	X		X				242	Riverview School† *East Sandwich*

Boarding Boys	Boarding Girls	Day Boys	Day Girls	Elementary	Junior Boarding	Secondary	Postgraduate Program	Summer Program	English as a Second Language	Learning Differences Program	Preprofessional Arts Training	Religious Affiliation	Military Program	Page	School
		X				X								242	The Roxbury Latin School *West Roxbury*
		X				X						RC		243	St. John's Preparatory School *Danvers*
		X				X						RC		243	St. Sebastian's School *Needham*
X	X					X								243	School Year Abroad *Andover*
		X	X	X										243	Shady Hill School *Cambridge*
		X	X	X										243	Shore Country Day School *Beverly*
		X	X	X										244	Smith College Campus School *Northampton*
		X	X											243	Southfield School *Brookline*
	X		X			X	X		X					244	Stoneleigh-Burnham School *Greenfield*
X	X	X	X			X		X	X					246	Tabor Academy *Marion*
		X	X	X				X						247	Tenacre Country Day School *Wellesley*
		X	X	X		X		X						247	Thayer Academy *Braintree*
		X	X	X				X						247	The Tower School *Marblehead*
X					X	X				X				247	Valley View School† *North Brookfield*
X	X	X	X			X	X		X	X				248	Wilbraham & Monson Academy† *Wilbraham*
X	X	X	X			X	X		X					249	The Williston Northampton School *Easthampton*
X	X	X	X			X	X	X	X	X				250	The Winchendon School† *Winchendon*
		X	X			X								252	The Winsor School *Boston*
X	X	X	X			X	X		X					252	Worcester Academy *Worcester*

MICHIGAN

Boarding Boys	Boarding Girls	Day Boys	Day Girls	Elementary	Junior Boarding	Secondary	Postgraduate Program	Summer Program	English as a Second Language	Learning Differences Program	Preprofessional Arts Training	Religious Affiliation	Military Program	Page	School
X	X	X	X	X		X		X						254	Cranbrook Schools *Bloomfield Hills*
X	X	X	X	X		X	X							256	Detroit Country Day School *Beverly Hills*
		X	X	X		X		X		X				258	Eton Academy† *Birmingham*
X		X	X	X	X			X				RC		258	Everest Academy *Clarkston*
		X	X	X						X				259	Gibson School† *Redford*
		X	X	X		X		X						260	Greenhills School *Ann Arbor*
		X	X	X				X				RC		260	The Grosse Pointe Academy *Grosse Pointe Farms*
X	X	X	X			X	X	X	X		X			262	Interlochen Arts Academy† *Interlochen*
		X	X	X				X						262	Kalamazoo Academy† *Kalamazoo*
		X	X	X								RC		262	Kensington Academy *Beverly Hills*
		X	X	X				X						262	Kingsbury School *Oxford*
X	X	X	X			X		X	X	X				262	The Leelanau School† *Glen Arbor*
	X		X			X						RC		264	Marian High School *Bloomfield Hills*
		X	X			X		X		X		RC		264	Notre Dame Preparatory† *Pontiac*
		X	X	X		X								265	The Roeper School *Bloomfield Hills*
		X	X	X		X		X						265	The Rudolf Steiner School of Ann Arbor *Ann Arbor*
X		X				X			X			RC		265	St. Mary's Preparatory School *Orchard Lake*
		X	X	X		X		X						266	University Liggett School† *Grosse Pointe*

MINNESOTA

Boarding Boys	Boarding Girls	Day Boys	Day Girls	Elementary	Junior Boarding	Secondary	Postgraduate Program	Summer Program	English as a Second Language	Learning Differences Program	Preprofessional Arts Training	Religious Affiliation	Military Program	Page	School
		X	X	X		X		X						267	The Blake School *Minneapolis/Hopkins/Wayzata*
		X	X	X		X						E		267	Breck School *Minneapolis*
		X	X	X		X						RC		269	Convent of the Visitation School *Mendota Heights*
		X	X	X						X		Q		269	Friends School of Minnesota *St. Paul*
		X	X	X		X								269	Marshall School *Duluth*

Classification Grid

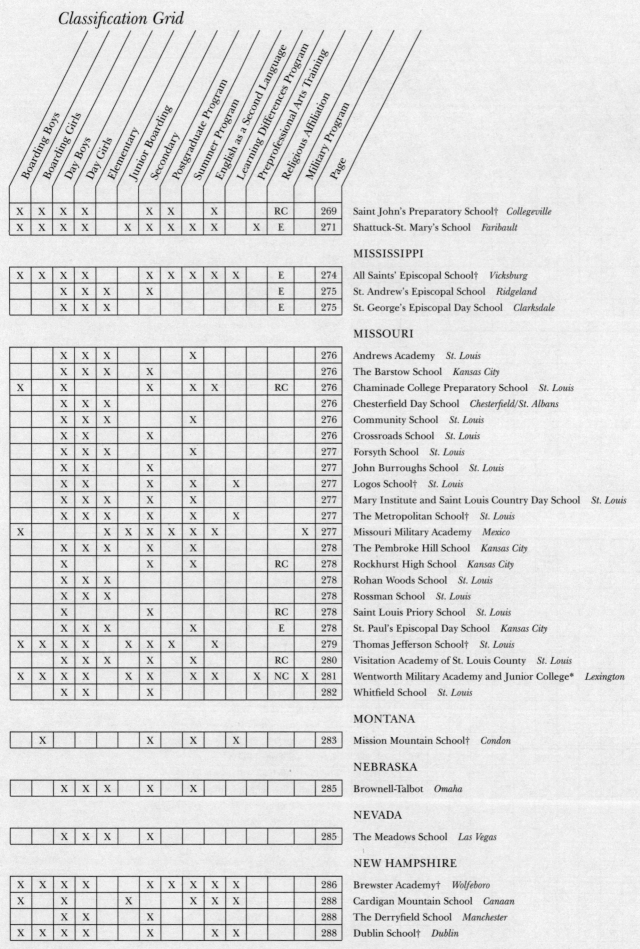

Boarding Boys	Boarding Girls	Day Boys	Day Girls	Elementary	Junior Boarding	Secondary	Postgraduate Program	Summer Program	English as a Second Language	Learning Differences Program	Preprofessional Arts Training	Religious Affiliation	Military Program	Page	School
X	X	X	X			X	X		X			RC		269	Saint John's Preparatory School† *Collegeville*
X	X	X	X		X	X	X	X	X		X	E		271	Shattuck-St. Mary's School *Faribault*
															MISSISSIPPI
X	X	X	X			X	X	X	X	X		E		274	All Saints' Episcopal School† *Vicksburg*
		X	X	X		X		X				E		275	St. Andrew's Episcopal School *Ridgeland*
		X	X	X								E		275	St. George's Episcopal Day School *Clarksdale*
															MISSOURI
		X	X	X				X						276	Andrews Academy *St. Louis*
		X	X	X		X								276	The Barstow School *Kansas City*
X		X				X		X				RC		276	Chaminade College Preparatory School *St. Louis*
		X	X	X										276	Chesterfield Day School *Chesterfield/St. Albans*
		X	X	X				X						276	Community School *St. Louis*
		X	X			X								276	Crossroads School *St. Louis*
		X	X	X				X						277	Forsyth School *St. Louis*
		X	X			X								277	John Burroughs School *St. Louis*
		X	X			X		X		X				277	Logos School† *St. Louis*
		X	X	X		X		X						277	Mary Institute and Saint Louis Country Day School *St. Louis*
		X	X	X		X		X			X			277	The Metropolitan School† *St. Louis*
X		X		X	X	X	X	X					X	277	Missouri Military Academy *Mexico*
		X	X	X		X		X						278	The Pembroke Hill School *Kansas City*
		X				X		X				RC		278	Rockhurst High School *Kansas City*
		X	X	X										278	Rohan Woods School *St. Louis*
		X	X	X										278	Rossman School *St. Louis*
		X						X				RC		278	Saint Louis Priory School *St. Louis*
		X	X	X		X						E		278	St. Paul's Episcopal Day School *Kansas City*
X	X	X	X		X	X	X		X					279	Thomas Jefferson School† *St. Louis*
		X	X	X		X		X				RC		280	Visitation Academy of St. Louis County *St. Louis*
X	X	X	X		X	X		X	X		X	NC	X	281	Wentworth Military Academy and Junior College* *Lexington*
		X	X			X								282	Whitfield School *St. Louis*
															MONTANA
	X					X		X		X				283	Mission Mountain School† *Condon*
															NEBRASKA
		X	X	X		X		X						285	Brownell-Talbot *Omaha*
															NEVADA
		X	X	X		X								285	The Meadows School *Las Vegas*
															NEW HAMPSHIRE
X	X	X	X			X	X	X	X	X				286	Brewster Academy† *Wolfeboro*
X		X			X			X	X	X				288	Cardigan Mountain School *Canaan*
		X	X			X								288	The Derryfield School *Manchester*
X	X	X	X			X			X	X				288	Dublin School† *Dublin*

Boarding Boys	Boarding Girls	Day Boys	Day Girls	Elementary	Junior Boarding	Secondary	Postgraduate Program	Summer Program	English as a Second Language	Learning Differences Program	Preprofessional Arts Training	Religious Affiliation	Military Program	Page	School
		X	X	X										288	Hampstead Academy† *Hampstead/Atkinson*
X	X	X	X			X	X		X					288	Kimball Union Academy† *Meriden*
X	X	X	X			X	X	X	X	X				288	New Hampton School† *New Hampton*
X	X	X	X			X			X					289	Proctor Academy† *Andover*
X	X					X		X					E	291	St. Paul's School *Concord*
X	X	X	X			X	X		X	X			O	291	Tilton School *Tilton*

NEW JERSEY

Boarding Boys	Boarding Girls	Day Boys	Day Girls	Elementary	Junior Boarding	Secondary	Postgraduate Program	Summer Program	English as a Second Language	Learning Differences Program	Preprofessional Arts Training	Religious Affiliation	Military Program	Page	School
			X			X						RC		294	Academy of Saint Elizabeth *Convent Station*
		X	X			X						RC		294	Bishop Eustace Preparatory School *Pennsauken*
X	X	X	X			X	X		X		X	P		294	Blair Academy *Blairstown*
		X	X	X										296	Chapin School *Princeton*
		X	X	X		X								296	Collegiate School *Passaic Park*
		X	X	X				X		X				296	The Craig School† *Mountain Lakes*
		X				X		X				RC		296	Delbarton School *Morristown*
		X	X	X		X		X						296	Dwight-Englewood School *Englewood*
		X	X	X		X								296	The Elisabeth Morrow School *Englewood*
		X	X	X						X				297	Far Brook School† *Short Hills*
		X	X	X										299	Far Hills Country Day School *Far Hills*
		X	X	X		X								299	Gill St. Bernard's School *Gladstone*
		X	X	X										299	Hilltop Country Day School *Sparta*
		X	X	X		X				X				299	The Hudson School† *Hoboken*
X	X	X	X	X		X	X	X	X	X				299	The Hun School of Princeton† *Princeton*
			X			X						RC		301	Immaculate Conception High School *Montclair*
			X	X		X								301	Kent Place School *Summit*
		X	X	X		X		X						301	The Montclair Kimberley Academy *Montclair*
		X	X	X		X						Q		302	Moorestown Friends School *Moorestown*
			X			X						RC		302	Mount Saint Mary Academy *Watchung*
		X	X			X		X						302	Newark Academy *Livingston*
		X	X	X		X						RC		304	Oak Knoll School of the Holy Child *Summit*
		X	X	X										304	The Peck School *Morristown*
X	X	X	X			X	X	X	X					304	The Peddie School *Hightstown*
X	X	X	X		X	X		X	X	X			O	304	The Pennington School† *Pennington*
		X	X	X		X		X						304	The Pingry School *Short Hills/Martinsville*
		X	X	X		X		X						305	Princeton Day School *Princeton*
		X	X	X		X								305	Princeton Montessori School *Princeton*
		X	X			X						RC		305	Queen of Peace High School *North Arlington*
		X	X	X		X				X				305	Ranney School *Tinton Falls*
		X	X	X		X		X		X				306	The Rugby School at Woodfield† *Wall*
		X	X	X										306	The Rumson Country Day School *Rumson*
		X	X	X		X		X						308	Rutgers Preparatory School *Somerset*
		X	X	X		X		X						309	Saddle River Day School *Saddle River*
		X				X		X				RC		309	St. Benedict's Preparatory School *Newark*
		X	X	X		X								309	St. Mary's Hall/Doane Academy *Burlington*
		X	X	X		X						RC		310	Stuart Country Day School of the Sacred Heart *Princeton*
		X	X	X		X						RC		310	Villa Victoria Academy *Ewing*

Classification Grid

Boarding Boys	Boarding Girls	Day Boys	Day Girls	Elementary	Junior Boarding	Secondary	Postgraduate Program	Summer Program	English as a Second Language	Learning Differences Program	Preprofessional Arts Training	Religious Affiliation	Military Program	Page	School
		X	X	X		X		X	X					310	The Wardlaw-Hartridge School *Edison*
		X	X	X				X						310	The Wilson School *Mountain Lakes*
		X	X	X						X				310	The Winston School† *Short Hills*

NEW MEXICO

Boarding Boys	Boarding Girls	Day Boys	Day Girls	Elementary	Junior Boarding	Secondary	Postgraduate Program	Summer Program	English as a Second Language	Learning Differences Program	Preprofessional Arts Training	Religious Affiliation	Military Program	Page	School
		X	X			X		X						311	Albuquerque Academy *Albuquerque*
		X	X	X		X								311	Albuquerque Country Day School *Albuquerque*
X	X				X	X		X	X					312	Brush Ranch School† *Santa Fe*
		X	X	X		X			X					314	Desert Academy at Santa Fe† *Santa Fe*
		X	X	X				X						314	Manzano Day School *Albuquerque*
X	X	X	X		X	X		X	X			P		314	The Menaul School *Albuquerque*
X	X	X	X		X	X								316	New Mexico Academy for Sciences and Mathematics *Santa Fe*
X	X					X	X						X	316	New Mexico Military Institute* *Roswell*
		X	X	X				X						316	Rio Grande School *Santa Fe*
		X	X			X								316	Sandia Preparatory School *Albuquerque*
		X	X			X		X						317	Santa Fe Preparatory School *Santa Fe*

NEW YORK

Boarding Boys	Boarding Girls	Day Boys	Day Girls	Elementary	Junior Boarding	Secondary	Postgraduate Program	Summer Program	English as a Second Language	Learning Differences Program	Preprofessional Arts Training	Religious Affiliation	Military Program	Page	School
		X	X	X										318	Abraham Lincoln School *New York*
			X			X						RC		318	Academy of Mt. St. Ursula *Bronx*
		X	X	X		X						RC		318	The Academy of St. Joseph *Brentwood*
			X	X		X						RC		318	The Academy of the Holy Names *Albany*
		X	X	X										318	Adelphi Academy *Brooklyn*
			X	X		X		X						318	Albany Academy for Girls *Albany*
		X		X										319	The Allen-Stevenson School *New York*
		X	X	X		X	X							319	The Anglo-American International School *New York*
		X	X	X				X						319	Bank Street School for Children *New York*
		X	X	X		X		X						319	The Berkeley Carroll School† *Brooklyn*
		X	X	X		X								321	The Birch Wathen Lenox School *New York*
			X	X		X								322	The Brearley School *New York*
		X	X	X								P		322	The Brick Church School *New York*
		X		X		X								323	The Browning School *New York*
		X	X	X										323	Buckley Country Day School *Roslyn*
		X		X										323	The Buckley School *New York*
			X			X								323	The Buffalo Seminary *Buffalo*
		X	X	X								RC		323	The Caedmon School *New York*
		X	X	X								E		323	The Cathedral School *New York*
		X	X	X								O		325	Cathedral School of the Holy Trinity *New York*
			X	X		X								325	The Chapin School *New York*
		X	X	X						X				325	The Churchill School and Center† *New York*
		X	X	X				X						325	City & Country School *New York*
		X		X		X								326	Collegiate School *New York*
		X	X	X		X								326	Columbia Grammar and Preparatory School *New York*
			X	X		X		X				RC		328	Convent of the Sacred Heart *New York*
		X	X	X										328	Corlears School *New York*
		X	X	X		X		X						328	The Dalton School *New York*

Boarding Boys	Boarding Girls	Day Boys	Day Girls	Elementary	Junior Boarding	Secondary	Postgraduate Program	Summer Program	English as a Second Language	Learning Differences Program	Preprofessional Arts Training	Religious Affiliation	Military Program	Page	School
X	X	X	X			X	X		X	X				328	Darrow School† *New Lebanon*
		X	X	X										328	Dutchess Day School *Millbrook*
		X	X	X		X			X	X				329	The Dwight School *New York*
		X	X	X				X						329	East Woods School *Oyster Bay*
		X	X	X				X						329	The Elmwood Franklin School *Buffalo*
	X		X			X	X		X					329	Emma Willard School *Troy*
		X	X	X		X								329	Ethical Culture Fieldston School *New York/Bronx*
		X	X	X		X		X				Q		329	Friends Academy *Locust Valley*
X					X	X	X	X		X				330	The Gow School† *South Wales*
		X	X	X								E		331	Grace Church School *New York*
		X	X	X				X				E		331	Grace Day School *Massapequa*
		X	X	X										332	The Green Vale School *Glen Head*
X	X	X	X			X		X						332	Hackley School *Tarrytown*
		X	X	X				X						334	The Hampton Day School *Bridgehampton*
		X	X	X				X						334	Harbor Country Day School *St. James*
		X	X	X		X		X						334	The Harley School *Rochester*
X	X	X	X		X	X								334	The Harvey School *Katonah*
			X	X		X				X				334	The Hewitt School† *New York*
X	X	X				X	X	X	X			E		336	Hoosac School *Hoosick*
		X	X	X		X		X						338	Horace Mann School *Riverdale/New York*
X	X	X	X	X	X	X	X	X		X				340	The Kildonan School† *Amenia*
X	X	X	X		X	X	X		X	X				340	The Knox School† *St. James*
		X				X		X				RC		340	La Salle Academy *New York*
X	X	X	X	X	X	X	X	X	X	X	X	RC	X	341	La Salle Center: A Global Learning Community† *Oakdale*
		X	X	X		X		X	X	X				341	Lawrence Woodmere Academy† *Woodmere*
		X	X			X						L		341	Long Island Lutheran Middle & High School *Brookville*
		X	X			X						RC		341	Loyola School *New York*
		X	X	X		X	X	X						341	Manlius Pebble Hill School *Dewitt*
			X			X						RC		341	The Mary Louis Academy† *Jamaica Estates*
			X	X		X						RC		341	Marymount School *New York*
X	X	X	X	X		X		X	X					342	The Masters School *Dobbs Ferry*
		X	X	X								E		342	The Melrose School *Brewster*
X	X	X	X			X								342	Millbrook School *Millbrook*
X	X	X	X		X	X	X	X	X				X	342	New York Military Academy *Cornwall-on-Hudson*
		X	X	X		X		X						343	Nichols School *Buffalo*
			X	X		X					X			343	The Nightingale-Bamford School *New York*
		X	X	X		X				X				343	The Norman Howard School† *Rochester*
X	X	X	X			X	X	X						343	Northwood School *Lake Placid*
X	X	X	X			X	X		X	X		Q		343	Oakwood Friends School† *Poughkeepsie*
		X	X	X				X				RC		345	Old Westbury School of the Holy Child *Old Westbury*
		X	X	X		X								345	The Packer Collegiate Institute *Brooklyn Heights*
		X	X	X		X		X						345	The Park School of Buffalo *Snyder*
		X	X	X				X	X					346	Pat-Kam School for Early Education *Uniondale*
		X	X	X		X		X						347	Poly Prep Country Day School *Brooklyn*
		X	X	X		X		X						347	Portledge School *Locust Valley*
		X	X	X		X		X			X			347	Poughkeepsie Day School *Poughkeepsie*

Classification Grid

Boarding Boys	Boarding Girls	Day Boys	Day Girls	Elementary	Junior Boarding	Secondary	Postgraduate Program	Summer Program	English as a Second Language	Learning Differences Program	Preprofessional Arts Training	Religious Affiliation	Military Program	Page	School
		X	X	X		X		X			X			347	Professional Children's School *New York*
		X	X	X		X								348	Rippowam Cisqua School *Bedford/Mount Kisco*
		X	X	X		X								348	Riverdale Country School *Riverdale*
		X	X			X	X	X		X				350	Robert Louis Stevenson School† *New York*
		X	X	X		X								350	The Rockland Country Day School *Congers*
		X	X	X		X								350	Rudolf Steiner School *New York*
		X	X	X		X		X	X					350	Rye Country Day School *Rye*
		X	X	X		X								352	Saint Ann's School *Brooklyn Heights*
		X	X			X		X		X		RC		352	Saint Anthony's High School† *South Huntington*
		X		X										353	St. Bernard's School *New York*
		X		X								RC		353	Saint David's School *New York*
		X	X			X						RC		353	Saint Francis Preparatory School *Fresh Meadows*
		X		X								RC		353	Saint Gregory's School *Loudonville*
		X	X	X								E		353	St. Hilda's and St. Hugh's School *New York*
		X	X	X		X						E		353	St. Luke's School *New York*
X				X	X			X				E		353	St. Thomas Choir School† *New York*
			X	X		X						RC		355	School of the Holy Child *Rye*
		X	X			X	X	X						355	Soundview Preparatory School *Mount Kisco*
			X	X		X								355	The Spence School *New York*
		X	X	X		X		X	X	X				355	Staten Island Academy *Staten Island*
X	X	X	X			X		X				NC		356	The Stony Brook School *Stony Brook*
X	X	X	X			X	X	X	X					356	Storm King School *Cornwall-on-Hudson*
		X	X	X		X								356	The Susquehanna School at South Bridge *Binghamton*
		X	X	X		X								356	The Town School *New York*
		X	X	X		X								356	Trevor Day School *New York*
X		X				X	X		X	X		E		356	Trinity-Pawling School† *Pawling*
		X	X	X		X		X						358	Trinity School *New York*
		X	X	X										358	Tuxedo Park School *Tuxedo Park*
		X	X	X		X		X	X					359	United Nations International School *New York/Jamaica Estates*
			X	X		X						RC		359	The Ursuline School *New Rochelle*
		X	X	X										359	Village Community School *New York*
		X	X	X		X								359	The Waldorf School of Garden City *Garden City*
		X	X			X	X	X	X	X	X			359	The Windsor School *Flushing*
		X	X	X						X				359	Windward School† *White Plains*
		X	X							X				360	The Winston Preparatory School† *New York*
		X	X	X		X								360	York Preparatory School *New York*

NORTH CAROLINA

Boarding Boys	Boarding Girls	Day Boys	Day Girls	Elementary	Junior Boarding	Secondary	Postgraduate Program	Summer Program	English as a Second Language	Learning Differences Program	Preprofessional Arts Training	Religious Affiliation	Military Program	Page	School
X	X	X	X			X	X	X						361	The Asheville School *Asheville*
		X	X			X						RC		363	Bishop McGuinness Memorial High School *Winston-Salem*
		X	X	X		X								363	Cannon School *Concord*
		X	X	X		X		X						363	Cape Fear Academy *Wilmington*
		X	X	X		X		X		X				363	Carolina Day School† *Asheville*
		X	X	X		X		X				Q		363	Carolina Friends School *Durham*
		X	X			X								363	Cary Academy *Cary*

Boarding Boys	Boarding Girls	Day Boys	Day Girls	Elementary	Junior Boarding	Secondary	Postgraduate Program	Summer Program	English as a Second Language	Learning Differences Program	Preprofessional Arts Training	Religious Affiliation	Military Program	Page	School / Location
		X	X	X		X		X	X	X	X			364	Charlotte Country Day School *Charlotte*
		X	X	X		X		X						364	Charlotte Latin School *Charlotte*
X		X				X		X	X			E		364	Christ School *Asheville*
		X	X	X		X		X						366	Durham Academy *Durham*
		X	X	X		X		X						366	The Fayetteville Academy *Fayetteville*
		X	X	X		X				X				366	Forsyth Country Day School† *Lewisville*
		X	X	X		X				X				367	Greenfield School† *Wilson*
		X	X	X		X		X	X					366	Greensboro Day School *Greensboro*
		X	X	X		X								367	Hickory Day School† *Hickory*
		X	X	X								Q		367	New Garden Friends School *Greensboro*
X	X	X	X		X	X	X	X	X				X	367	Oak Ridge Military Academy *Oak Ridge*
		X	X	X		X				X				369	The O'Neal School *Southern Pines*
		X	X	X		X		X						369	Providence Day School *Charlotte*
		X	X	X		X		X						369	Ravenscroft School *Raleigh*
		X	X	X		X								369	Rocky Mount Academy *Rocky Mount*
	X		X			X	X					E		369	Saint Mary's School *Raleigh*
		X	X	X		X						E		370	St. Timothy's-Hale School *Raleigh*
		X	X	X						X		E		370	St. Timothy's School† *Raleigh*
	X		X			X								370	Salem Academy *Winston-Salem*
		X	X	X										372	Summit School *Winston-Salem*
		X	X	X		X								372	Westchester Academy† *High Point*

OHIO

Boarding Boys	Boarding Girls	Day Boys	Day Girls	Elementary	Junior Boarding	Secondary	Postgraduate Program	Summer Program	English as a Second Language	Learning Differences Program	Preprofessional Arts Training	Religious Affiliation	Military Program	Page	School / Location
		X	X			X						RC		373	Archbishop Hoban High School *Akron*
		X	X	X										373	Canton Country Day School *Canton*
		X	X	X		X		X						373	Cincinnati Country Day School *Cincinnati*
		X	X	X		X		X	X					373	The Columbus Academy *Gahanna*
			X	X		X		X						373	Columbus School for Girls *Columbus*
X	X	X	X	X	X	X	X	X	X			RC		373	Gilmour Academy *Gates Mills*
X		X				X	X	X						374	The Grand River Academy *Austinburg*
			X	X		X		X						374	Hathaway Brown School *Shaker Heights*
		X	X	X		X		X						374	Hawken School *Lyndhurst/Gates Mills*
		X	X	X		X								374	Lake Ridge Academy *North Ridgeville*
			X			X			X			RC		374	Magnificat High School *Rocky River*
		X	X	X		X	X	X	X					374	Maumee Valley Country Day School *Toledo*
		X	X	X		X		X						374	The Miami Valley School† *Dayton*
		X	X	X		X								375	Old Trail School *Bath*
		X	X	X		X								375	The Phillips-Osborne School *Painesville*
		X				X		X	X			RC		375	St. Charles Preparatory School *Columbus*
		X				X		X				RC		375	Saint Ignatius High School *Cleveland*
		X	X	X		X		X						375	The Seven Hills Schools *Cincinnati*
		X	X	X		X				X				375	The Springer School† *Cincinnati*
		X	X	X		X		X				RC		376	The Summit Country Day School *Cincinnati*
		X		X		X	X	X						376	University School *Shaker Heights/Hunting Valley*
		X	X	X		X								376	The Wellington School *Columbus*
X	X	X	X			X	X		X					376	Western Reserve Academy† *Hudson*

Classification Grid

OKLAHOMA

Boarding Boys	Boarding Girls	Day Boys	Day Girls	Elementary	Junior Boarding	Secondary	Postgraduate Program	Summer Program	English as a Second Language	Learning Differences Program	Preprofessional Arts Training	Religious Affiliation	Military Program	Page	School
		X	X	X		X		X				E		379	Casady School *Oklahoma City*
		X	X	X		X		X	X			E		381	Holland Hall School† *Tulsa*
		X	X	X		X								383	Riverfield Country Day School *Tulsa*
		X	X	X										383	Westminster School *Oklahoma City*

OREGON

Boarding Boys	Boarding Girls	Day Boys	Day Girls	Elementary	Junior Boarding	Secondary	Postgraduate Program	Summer Program	English as a Second Language	Learning Differences Program	Preprofessional Arts Training	Religious Affiliation	Military Program	Page	School
		X	X	X		X		X						384	The Catlin Gabel School *Portland*
X	X	X	X	X	X	X		X	X	X				384	The Delphian School *Sheridan*
X	X	X	X	X		X			X			E		386	Oregon Episcopal School *Portland*
		X	X	X		X		X				RC		386	St. Mary's School *Medford*
		X	X	X		X								386	Sunriver Preparatory School *Bend*

PENNSYLVANIA

Boarding Boys	Boarding Girls	Day Boys	Day Girls	Elementary	Junior Boarding	Secondary	Postgraduate Program	Summer Program	English as a Second Language	Learning Differences Program	Preprofessional Arts Training	Religious Affiliation	Military Program	Page	School
		X	X	X		X		X				Q		387	Abington Friends School *Jenkintown*
			X	X		X		X						387	The Agnes Irwin School *Rosemont*
			X	X		X		X						387	The Baldwin School *Bryn Mawr*
		X	X	X		X						Q		389	Buckingham Friends School *Lahaska*
X				X	X	X		X					X	389	Carson Long Military Institute *New Bloomfield*
		X				X						RC		389	Central Catholic High School *Pittsburgh*
X		X			X	X						E		389	CFS, The School at Church Farm *Paoli*
		X		X		X		X						391	Chestnut Hill Academy *Philadelphia*
			X	X		X						RC		391	Country Day School of the Sacred Heart *Bryn Mawr*
		X	X			X				X				391	The Crefeld School† *Philadelphia*
		X	X	X		X		X				E		391	The Episcopal Academy *Merion/Devon*
		X	X	X										393	Falk School *Pittsburgh*
		X	X	X		X		X				Q		393	Friends' Central School *Wynnewood*
		X	X	X								Q		393	Friends School Haverford *Haverford*
		X	X	X		X						Q		394	Friends Select School *Philadelphia*
X	X	X	X			X			X			Q		394	George School *Newtown*
		X	X	X		X		X						394	Germantown Academy *Fort Washington*
		X	X	X		X						Q		394	Germantown Friends School *Philadelphia*
	X			X	X	X		X	X	X				394	The Grier School† *Tyrone*
			X			X						RC		396	Gwynedd-Mercy Academy *Gwynedd Valley*
		X	X	X		X		X						396	The Harrisburg Academy *Wormleysburg*
		X		X		X		X						396	The Haverford School *Haverford*
X	X	X	X			X	X	X						396	The Hill School *Pottstown*
		X	X	X		X				X				398	The Hillside School† *Macungie*
		X	X			X		X		X				398	The Hill Top Preparatory School† *Rosemont*
		X				X		X				RC		398	Holy Ghost Preparatory School *Bensalem*
		X	X	X		X								399	Kimberton Waldorf School *Kimberton*
X						X	X	X						399	The Kiski School *Saltsburg*
		X	X	X		X								401	Lancaster Country Day School *Lancaster*
		X				X						RC		401	LaSalle College High School *Wyndmoor*
	X		X	X	X	X		X	X					401	Linden Hall† *Lititz*
		X				X		X				RC		403	Malvern Preparatory School *Malvern*
		X	X	X										405	Meadowbrook School *Meadowbrook*

598

Boarding Boys	Boarding Girls	Day Boys	Day Girls	Elementary	Junior Boarding	Secondary	Postgraduate Program	Summer Program	English as a Second Language	Learning Differences Program	Preprofessional Arts Training	Religious Affiliation	Military Program	Page	
X	X	X	X			X	X	X	X			C		405	The Mercersburg Academy *Mercersburg*
			X			X						RC		407	Merion Mercy Academy *Merion Station*
X	X			X	X	X		X						407	Milton Hershey School† *Hershey*
		X	X	X										408	The Miquon School *Conshohocken*
		X	X			X		X						408	MMI Preparatory School *Freeland*
		X	X	X										408	Montgomery School *Chester Springs*
		X	X	X		X		X						409	Moravian Academy *Bethlehem*
			X			X						RC		410	Mount Saint Joseph Academy *Flourtown*
			X			X		X				RC		411	Nazareth Academy *Philadelphia*
		X	X	X								Q		411	Newtown Friends School *Newtown*
		X	X	X						X				411	Oak Lane Day School† *Blue Bell*
		X	X	X								E		411	The Pen Ryn School *Fairless Hills*
X	X	X	X		X	X	X		X					411	Perkiomen School *Pennsburg*
		X	X	X				X						411	The Philadelphia School *Philadelphia*
		X	X	X				X		X		Q		411	The Quaker School at Horsham† *Horsham*
		X	X	X				X				RC		412	Rosemont School of the Holy Child *Rosemont*
			X			X						O		412	Saint Basil Academy *Fox Chase Manor*
		X	X	X										412	St. Edmund's Academy *Pittsburgh*
		X	X	X										412	The School in Rose Valley *Rose Valley*
		X	X			X		X				RC		412	Scranton Preparatory School *Scranton*
		X	X	X		X								412	Sewickley Academy *Sewickley*
X	X	X	X	X		X		X						413	Shady Side Academy *Pittsburgh*
		X	X	X		X		X						413	The Shipley School *Bryn Mawr*
X	X	X	X			X	X		X	X				413	Solebury School† *New Hope*
		X	X	X		X								415	Springside School *Philadelphia*
		X	X	X				X		X		Q		416	Stratford Friends School† *Havertown*
		X	X	X				X						416	The Swain School *Allentown*
		X	X	X				X				Q		416	United Friends School *Quakertown*
		X	X	X				X						416	Upland Country Day School *Kennett Square*
X		X		X	X		X						X	416	Valley Forge Military Academy and College* *Wayne*
		X	X	X				X						418	Valley School of Ligonier *Ligonier*
		X				X						RC		418	Villa Maria Academy *Malvern*
		X	X	X								Q		418	West Chester Friends School *West Chester*
X	X	X	X	X		X								418	Westtown School *Westtown*
		X	X	X		X		X				Q		418	William Penn Charter School *Philadelphia*
		X	X	X		X								418	Winchester Thurston School *Pittsburgh*
		X	X	X		X		X						419	Woodlynde School *Strafford*
		X	X	X										419	The Wyndcroft School *Pottstown*
X	X	X	X	X		X	X	X	X			O		419	Wyoming Seminary *Kingston*
		X	X	X				X				O		421	Wyoming Seminary *Forty Fort*
		X	X	X		X								421	York Country Day School *York*

RHODE ISLAND

Boarding Boys	Boarding Girls	Day Boys	Day Girls	Elementary	Junior Boarding	Secondary	Postgraduate Program	Summer Program	English as a Second Language	Learning Differences Program	Preprofessional Arts Training	Religious Affiliation	Military Program	Page	
		X	X	X				X						422	The Gordon School *East Providence*
			X	X		X						Q		422	Lincoln School *Providence*
		X	X	X		X		X				Q		422	Moses Brown School *Providence*

Classification Grid

Boarding Boys	Boarding Girls	Day Boys	Day Girls	Elementary	Junior Boarding	Secondary	Postgraduate Program	Summer Program	English as a Second Language	Learning Differences Program	Preprofessional Arts Training	Religious Affiliation	Military Program	Page	School
	X	X	X	X	X			X	X			RC		422	Overbrook Academy *Warwick*
		X	X	X					X					424	The Pennfield School† *Portsmouth*
X	X	X	X			X		X				RC		424	Portsmouth Abbey School *Portsmouth*
X	X	X	X			X				X	X			426	St. Andrew's School† *Barrington*
X	X	X	X			X		X				E		428	St. George's School *Newport*
		X	X	X				X						428	St. Michael's Country Day School *Newport*
		X	X	X		X		X						428	The Wheeler School† *Providence*

SOUTH CAROLINA

Boarding Boys	Boarding Girls	Day Boys	Day Girls	Elementary	Junior Boarding	Secondary	Postgraduate Program	Summer Program	English as a Second Language	Learning Differences Program	Preprofessional Arts Training	Religious Affiliation	Military Program	Page	School
		X	X	X								J		429	Addlestone Hebrew Academy *Charleston*
X	X	X	X	X	X			X	X					429	Aiken Preparatory School† *Aiken*
		X	X			X		X						431	Ashley Hall *Charleston*
		X	X	X		X								430	Beaufort Academy *Beaufort*
		X	X	X		X								431	Cambridge Academy *Greenwood*
		X	X	X										431	Charleston Day School *Charleston*
		X	X	X		X		X	X	X		E		431	Christ Church Episcopal School *Greenville*
		X	X	X		X								431	Hammond School *Columbia*
		X	X	X		X								433	Hilton Head Preparatory School *Hilton Head Island*
		X	X	X		X								433	Pinewood Preparatory School *Summerville*
		X	X	X		X						E		433	Porter-Gaud School *Charleston*
		X	X	X		X		X						434	The Spartanburg Day School† *Spartanburg*
		X	X	X	X	X		X		X				434	Trident Academy† *Mount Pleasant*

TENNESSEE

Boarding Boys	Boarding Girls	Day Boys	Day Girls	Elementary	Junior Boarding	Secondary	Postgraduate Program	Summer Program	English as a Second Language	Learning Differences Program	Preprofessional Arts Training	Religious Affiliation	Military Program	Page	School
		X	X	X		X		X						435	Battle Ground Academy *Franklin*
		X	X	X		X						NC		435	Brentwood Academy *Brentwood*
		X	X	X		X		X				NC		435	Briarcrest Christian School System, Inc. *Memphis*
		X	X	X										435	Bright School *Chattanooga*
		X	X	X		X						O		435	Christ Methodist Day School *Memphis*
		X	X	X		X								435	The Ensworth School *Nashville*
		X	X	X								E		435	Episcopal School of Knoxville *Knoxville*
		X	X	X								NC		436	First Christian Academy *Nashville*
		X	X	X		X						NC		436	Franklin Road Academy *Nashville*
		X	X	X				X				E		436	Grace-St. Luke's Episcopal School *Memphis*
		X	X	X		X			X					436	Harding Academy† *Nashville*
			X	X		X								436	The Harpeth Hall School *Nashville*
			X	X		X		X						436	Hutchison School *Memphis*
X		X				X		X				NC		438	The McCallie School *Chattanooga*
		X				X		X						438	Memphis University School *Memphis*
		X				X		X						439	Montgomery Bell Academy *Nashville*
		X	X	X								P		439	The Oak Hill School *Nashville*
		X	X	X								RC		439	Overbrook School of The Dominican Campus *Nashville*
		X		X				X				P		439	Presbyterian Day School *Memphis*
			X	X		X						RC		439	Saint Agnes Academy *Memphis*
			X			X						RC		441	St. Cecilia Academy of The Dominican Campus *Nashville*
		X		X								RC		441	Saint Dominic School *Memphis*

Boarding Boys	Boarding Girls	Day Boys	Day Girls	Elementary	Junior Boarding	Secondary	Postgraduate Program	Summer Program	English as a Second Language	Learning Differences Program	Preprofessional Arts Training	Religious Affiliation	Military Program	Page	School
		X	X	X		X						E		443	St. Mary's Episcopal School *Memphis*
		X	X	X								E		445	Saint Nicholas School *Chattanooga*
		X	X	X		X								445	Sumner Academy *Gallatin*
		X	X	X		X		X						445	University School of Jackson *Jackson*
		X	X	X		X								445	University School of Nashville *Nashville*
X	X	X	X			X	X	X	X					445	The Webb School *Bell Buckle*
		X	X	X		X								445	Webb School of Knoxville *Knoxville*
		X	X	X						X				446	Westminster School of Nashville† *Nashville*

TEXAS

Boarding Boys	Boarding Girls	Day Boys	Day Girls	Elementary	Junior Boarding	Secondary	Postgraduate Program	Summer Program	English as a Second Language	Learning Differences Program	Preprofessional Arts Training	Religious Affiliation	Military Program	Page	School
		X	X	X								E		447	All Saints Episcopal School *Beaumont*
		X	X	X								E		447	All Saints Episcopal School *Lubbock*
		X	X	X		X						O		447	Annunciation Orthodox School *Houston*
		X	X	X		X		X	X					447	The Awty International School *Houston*
		X	X	X		X						NC		449	Carrollton Christian Academy *Carrollton*
		X		X		X						RC		449	Cistercian Preparatory School *Irving*
		X	X	X		X						RC		449	Duchesne Academy of the Sacred Heart *Houston*
		X	X			X						E		450	Episcopal High School of Houston *Bellaire*
		X	X			X						E		450	The Episcopal School of Dallas *Dallas*
		X	X	X										452	Fort Worth Academy *Fort Worth*
		X	X	X		X								452	Fort Worth Country Day School *Fort Worth*
		X	X	X								E		452	Good Shepherd Episcopal School *Dallas*
		X	X	X		X								452	Greenhill School *Addison*
	X		X	X		X		X	X					454	The Hockaday School *Dallas*
		X	X	X		X						E		456	Holy Spirit Episcopal School *Houston*
		X	X	X		X		X						456	The John Cooper School *The Woodlands*
		X	X	X		X		X						458	The Kinkaid School *Houston*
		X	X	X		X								458	Lakehill Preparatory School *Dallas*
		X	X	X				X						458	The Lamplighter School *Dallas*
		X	X			X						L		459	Lutheran High School *Dallas*
X					X	X	X	X					X	459	Marine Military Academy† *Harlingen*
		X	X	X		X								460	The Oakridge School *Arlington*
		X	X	X								E		462	The Parish Day School *Dallas*
		X	X	X								P		462	Presbyterian School *Houston*
		X	X	X								NC		463	Providence Christian School of Texas *Dallas*
		X	X	X		X						B		463	River Oaks Baptist School *Houston*
			X			X		X				RC		463	Saint Agnes Academy *Houston*
		X	X	X		X						E		463	St. Andrew's Episcopal School *Austin*
		X	X	X								E		463	St. Clement's Episcopal Parish School *El Paso*
		X	X	X								E		463	St. Francis Episcopal Day School *Houston*
		X	X	X						X		E		463	St. James Episcopal School† *Corpus Christi*
		X	X	X		X								464	St. John's School *Houston*
		X	X	X		X						E		464	Saint Luke's Episcopal School *San Antonio*
		X		X		X								464	St. Mark's School of Texas *Dallas*
X	X	X	X	X	X	X	X	X	X		X			464	Saint Mary's Hall *San Antonio*
		X	X			X		X		X		RC		464	St. Michael's Academy† *Austin*

Classification Grid

	Boarding Boys	Boarding Girls	Day Boys	Day Girls	Elementary	Junior Boarding	Secondary	Postgraduate Program	Summer Program	English as a Second Language	Learning Differences Program	Preprofessional Arts Training	Religious Affiliation	Military Program	Page	
			X	X	X		X						E		464	St. Michael's Academy *Bryan*
			X	X			X		X				RC		464	St. Pius X High School *Houston*
	X	X	X	X		X				X	X		B	X	465	San Marcos Baptist Academy† *San Marcos*
			X	X	X		X						B		466	Second Baptist School *Houston*
			X	X	X		X		X		X				468	The Shelton School and Evaluation Center† *Dallas*
			X	X	X								J		468	Solomon Schechter Academy of Dallas *Dallas*
			X				X		X				RC		469	Strake Jesuit College Preparatory *Houston*
			X	X	X								E		469	Trinity Episcopal School *Galveston*
			X	X	X		X						E		469	Trinity School *Midland*
			X	X	X		X								469	Trinity Valley School *Fort Worth*
			X				X								471	Vanguard College Preparatory School *Waco*
			X	X	X		X		X		X				472	The Winston School† *Dallas*

UTAH

	Boarding Boys	Boarding Girls	Day Boys	Day Girls	Elementary	Junior Boarding	Secondary	Postgraduate Program	Summer Program	English as a Second Language	Learning Differences Program	Preprofessional Arts Training	Religious Affiliation	Military Program	Page	
			X	X	X		X						E		473	Rowland Hall-St. Mark's School *Salt Lake City*

VERMONT

	Boarding Boys	Boarding Girls	Day Boys	Day Girls	Elementary	Junior Boarding	Secondary	Postgraduate Program	Summer Program	English as a Second Language	Learning Differences Program	Preprofessional Arts Training	Religious Affiliation	Military Program	Page	
	X	X	X	X			X								474	Burr and Burton Academy *Manchester*
	X	X	X	X	X		X		X		X				474	Long Trail School† *Dorset*
	X	X	X	X	X	X	X		X		X				474	Pine Ridge School† *Williston*
	X	X	X	X			X	X	X	X	X	X			474	St. Johnsbury Academy† *St. Johnsbury*

VIRGINIA

	Boarding Boys	Boarding Girls	Day Boys	Day Girls	Elementary	Junior Boarding	Secondary	Postgraduate Program	Summer Program	English as a Second Language	Learning Differences Program	Preprofessional Arts Training	Religious Affiliation	Military Program	Page	
			X	X	X										475	Alexandria Country Day School *Alexandria*
			X	X			X						RC		475	Bishop Ireton High School *Alexandria*
	X						X		X	X	X		E		475	The Blue Ridge School† *St. George*
			X	X	X		X								477	Broadwater Academy *Exmore*
			X	X	X				X						477	Browne Academy *Alexandria*
			X	X	X										477	Burgundy Farm Country Day School *Alexandria*
			X	X	X		X		X	X	X				477	Cape Henry Collegiate School *Virginia Beach*
			X	X	X										478	Carlisle School *Martinsville*
			X	X			X						RC		478	Catholic High School *Virginia Beach*
		X					X		X				E		478	Chatham Hall *Chatham*
	X		X	X			X	X	X	X	X		E		480	Christchurch Episcopal School† *Christchurch*
			X	X	X		X		X						482	The Collegiate School *Richmond*
			X	X	X		X				X		NC		482	The Covenant School† *Charlottesville*
	X	X					X		X				E		482	Episcopal High School *Alexandria*
	X		X				X	X	X					X	484	Fishburne Military School *Waynesboro*
			X	X	X		X				X				486	Flint Hill School *Oakton*
	X		X			X	X	X	X	X			B	X	486	Fork Union Military Academy *Fork Union*
		X		X			X	X	X						488	Foxcroft School *Middleburg*
			X	X	X								E		490	Grace Episcopal School *Alexandria*
			X	X	X		X		X			X			490	Hampton Roads Academy *Newport News*
	X		X	X		X	X	X	X	X		X	B	X	490	Hargrave Military Academy *Chatham*
			X	X	X		X		X						492	The Highland School *Warrenton*
			X	X	X										493	The Hill School of Middleburg *Middleburg*

Boarding Boys	Boarding Girls	Day Boys	Day Girls	Elementary	Junior Boarding	Secondary	Postgraduate Program	Summer Program	English as a Second Language	Learning Differences Program	Preprofessional Arts Training	Religious Affiliation	Military Program	Page	School
		X	X	X										493	Hunter McGuire School *Verona*
		X	X	X				X						493	The Langley School *McLean*
		X	X	X								RC		495	Linton Hall School *Bristow*
		X	X	X										495	Loudoun Country Day School *Leesburg*
	X		X			X		X						495	The Madeira School *McLean*
X	X	X	X	X	X	X	X	X	X					497	The Miller School *Charlottesville*
		X	X	X		X		X						499	Norfolk Academy *Norfolk*
		X	X	X		X		X		X				500	Norfolk Collegiate School† *Norfolk*
		X	X	X		X		X						502	North Cross School *Roanoke*
		X	X			X						RC		502	Notre Dame Academy *Middleburg*
X	X	X	X			X		X				B		502	Oak Hill Academy† *Mouth of Wilson*
X	X	X	X	X	X	X		X		X				504	Oakland School† *Keswick*
		X	X	X				X		X				504	Oakwood School† *Annandale*
		X	X	X		X		X						505	The Potomac School *McLean*
X	X	X	X	X	X	X	X	X	X			O	X	506	Randolph-Macon Academy *Front Royal*
		X	X	X				X				E		508	St. Andrew's Episcopal School *Newport News*
X	X	X	X			X		X	X			E		509	St. Anne's-Belfield School *Charlottesville*
	X		X	X		X						E		509	St. Catherine's School *Richmond*
		X		X		X		X				E		511	St. Christopher's School *Richmond*
	X		X		X	X		X	X	X		E		511	St. Margaret's School† *Tappahannock*
		X	X	X		X		X				E		513	St. Stephen's and St. Agnes School *Alexandria*
		X	X	X		X		X	X	X				513	The Steward School† *Richmond*
	X	X	X			X		X	X	X	X	E		513	Stuart Hall *Staunton*
		X	X	X										515	Sullins Academy *Bristol*
		X	X	X				X				Q		515	Tandem Friends School *Charlottesville*
		X	X					X				E		515	Trinity Episcopal School *Richmond*
		X	X	X				X				Q		515	Virginia Beach Friends School *Virginia Beach*
X	X	X	X					X			X	E		516	Virginia Episcopal School *Lynchburg*
X						X		X						518	Woodberry Forest School *Woodberry Forest*

WASHINGTON

Boarding Boys	Boarding Girls	Day Boys	Day Girls	Elementary	Junior Boarding	Secondary	Postgraduate Program	Summer Program	English as a Second Language	Learning Differences Program	Preprofessional Arts Training	Religious Affiliation	Military Program	Page	School
	X	X	X	X		X		X				E		520	Annie Wright School *Tacoma*
		X	X	X		X								520	The Bush School *Seattle*
		X	X	X		X		X						520	Charles Wright Academy *Tacoma*
		X	X	X				X						520	Epiphany School† *Seattle*
		X	X	X										520	The Evergreen School† *Shoreline*
		X	X			X						RC		520	Forest Ridge School of the Sacred Heart *Bellevue*
		X				X						RC		520	Holy Names Academy *Seattle*
		X	X	X		X								521	Lakeside School *Seattle*
		X	X	X				X						521	The Little School *Bellevue*
		X	X	X		X								521	Saint George's School *Spokane*
		X	X	X								E		521	St. Thomas School *Medina*
		X	X	X		X								521	Seattle Academy *Seattle*
		X	X	X				X	X					521	Seattle Country Day School† *Seattle*
		X	X	X										521	Thomas Academy *Auburn*
		X	X	X				X						521	University Child Development School† *Seattle*

Classification Grid

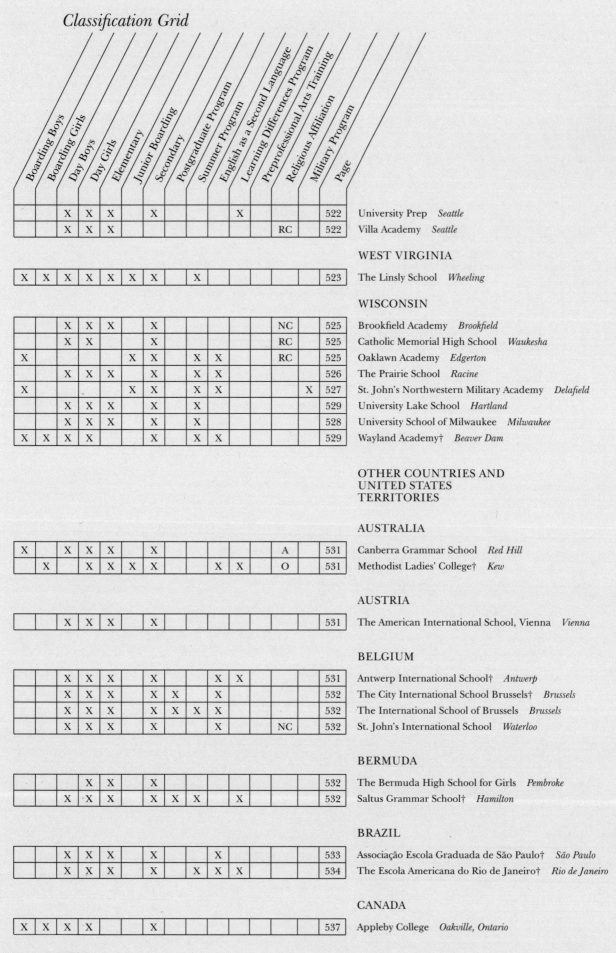

Boarding Boys	Boarding Girls	Day Boys	Day Girls	Elementary	Junior Boarding	Secondary	Postgraduate Program	Summer Program	English as a Second Language	Learning Differences Program	Preprofessional Arts Training	Religious Affiliation	Military Program	Page	School
		X	X	X		X		X						522	University Prep *Seattle*
		X	X	X		X						RC		522	Villa Academy *Seattle*

WEST VIRGINIA

Boarding Boys	Boarding Girls	Day Boys	Day Girls	Elementary	Junior Boarding	Secondary	Postgraduate Program	Summer Program	English as a Second Language	Learning Differences Program	Preprofessional Arts Training	Religious Affiliation	Military Program	Page	School
X	X	X	X	X	X	X		X						523	The Linsly School *Wheeling*

WISCONSIN

Boarding Boys	Boarding Girls	Day Boys	Day Girls	Elementary	Junior Boarding	Secondary	Postgraduate Program	Summer Program	English as a Second Language	Learning Differences Program	Preprofessional Arts Training	Religious Affiliation	Military Program	Page	School
		X	X	X		X						NC		525	Brookfield Academy *Brookfield*
		X	X			X						RC		525	Catholic Memorial High School *Waukesha*
X					X	X		X	X			RC		525	Oaklawn Academy *Edgerton*
		X	X	X		X		X	X					526	The Prairie School *Racine*
X					X	X		X	X				X	527	St. John's Northwestern Military Academy *Delafield*
		X	X	X		X		X						529	University Lake School *Hartland*
		X	X	X		X		X						528	University School of Milwaukee *Milwaukee*
X	X	X	†			X		X	X					529	Wayland Academy† *Beaver Dam*

OTHER COUNTRIES AND UNITED STATES TERRITORIES

AUSTRALIA

Boarding Boys	Boarding Girls	Day Boys	Day Girls	Elementary	Junior Boarding	Secondary	Postgraduate Program	Summer Program	English as a Second Language	Learning Differences Program	Preprofessional Arts Training	Religious Affiliation	Military Program	Page	School
X		X	X	X		X						A		531	Canberra Grammar School *Red Hill*
	X		X	X	X	X			X	X		O		531	Methodist Ladies' College† *Kew*

AUSTRIA

Boarding Boys	Boarding Girls	Day Boys	Day Girls	Elementary	Junior Boarding	Secondary	Postgraduate Program	Summer Program	English as a Second Language	Learning Differences Program	Preprofessional Arts Training	Religious Affiliation	Military Program	Page	School
		X	X	X		X								531	The American International School, Vienna *Vienna*

BELGIUM

Boarding Boys	Boarding Girls	Day Boys	Day Girls	Elementary	Junior Boarding	Secondary	Postgraduate Program	Summer Program	English as a Second Language	Learning Differences Program	Preprofessional Arts Training	Religious Affiliation	Military Program	Page	School
		X	X	X		X		X	X					531	Antwerp International School† *Antwerp*
		X	X	X	X	X		X						532	The City International School Brussels† *Brussels*
		X	X	X	X	X	X	X						532	The International School of Brussels *Brussels*
		X	X	X		X		X				NC		532	St. John's International School *Waterloo*

BERMUDA

Boarding Boys	Boarding Girls	Day Boys	Day Girls	Elementary	Junior Boarding	Secondary	Postgraduate Program	Summer Program	English as a Second Language	Learning Differences Program	Preprofessional Arts Training	Religious Affiliation	Military Program	Page	School
		X	X			X								532	The Bermuda High School for Girls *Pembroke*
		X	X	X		X	X	X		X				532	Saltus Grammar School† *Hamilton*

BRAZIL

Boarding Boys	Boarding Girls	Day Boys	Day Girls	Elementary	Junior Boarding	Secondary	Postgraduate Program	Summer Program	English as a Second Language	Learning Differences Program	Preprofessional Arts Training	Religious Affiliation	Military Program	Page	School
		X	X	X		X		X						533	Associação Escola Graduada de São Paulo† *São Paulo*
		X	X	X		X		X	X	X				534	The Escola Americana do Rio de Janeiro† *Rio de Janeiro*

CANADA

Boarding Boys	Boarding Girls	Day Boys	Day Girls	Elementary	Junior Boarding	Secondary	Postgraduate Program	Summer Program	English as a Second Language	Learning Differences Program	Preprofessional Arts Training	Religious Affiliation	Military Program	Page	School
X	X	X	X			X								537	Appleby College *Oakville, Ontario*

Boarding Boys	Boarding Girls	Day Boys	Day Girls	Elementary	Junior Boarding	Secondary	Postgraduate Program	Summer Program	English as a Second Language	Learning Differences Program	Preprofessional Program	Religious Affiliation	Military Program	Page	School	Location
X	X	X	X	X		X		X						536	Ashbury College	Ottawa, Ontario
	X	X	X	X		X		X				A		537	The Bishop Strachan School	Toronto, Ontario
	X		X	X		X								537	Branksome Hall	Toronto, Ontario
			X	X		X								537	Crofton House School	Vancouver, British Columbia
		X	X	X		X				X				537	Fraser Academy†	Vancouver, British Columbia
X	X	X	X	X		X		X						537	Glenlyon-Norfolk School	Victoria, British Columbia
		X	X	X		X		X						537	Halifax Grammar School	Halifax, Nova Scotia
	X		X	X		X						A		537	Havergal College	Toronto, Ontario
		X	X	X		X		X						538	Hillfield-Strathallan College	Hamilton, Ontario
		X	X	X		X								538	Lower Canada College	Montreal, Quebec
			X	X		X								538	Miss Edgar's & Miss Cramp's School	Westmount, Quebec
		X	X	X								RC		538	The Priory School	Montreal, Quebec
X		X		X	X	X		X	X	X				538	St. Andrew's College	Aurora, Ontario
			X	X		X						A		538	St. Clement's School	Toronto, Ontario
X		X		X	X	X		X						539	St. George's School	Vancouver, British Columbia
		X	X	X		X	X		X	X				539	St. George's School of Montreal	Montreal, Quebec
			X	X		X						A		539	St. Mildred's-Lightbourn School	Oakville, Ontario
		X		X		X								539	Selwyn House School	Montreal, Quebec
		X		X										539	The Sterling Hall School	Toronto, Ontario
		X	X	X		X								539	Strathcona-Tweedsmuir School	Okotoks, Alberta
			X	X		X								539	The Study	Montreal, Quebec
		X	X	X		X		X		X				540	Toronto French School†	Toronto/Mississauga, Ontario
	X					X						P/A		540	Trafalgar School for Girls	Montreal, Quebec
X		X		X	X	X		X						540	Upper Canada College	Toronto, Ontario
		X	X	X		X				X				542	The York School†	Toronto, Ontario

CHILE

Boarding Boys	Boarding Girls	Day Boys	Day Girls	Elementary	Junior Boarding	Secondary	Postgraduate Program	Summer Program	English as a Second Language	Learning Differences Program	Preprofessional Program	Religious Affiliation	Military Program	Page	School	Location
		X	X	X		X		X						544	Santiago College	Santiago

CHINA

Boarding Boys	Boarding Girls	Day Boys	Day Girls	Elementary	Junior Boarding	Secondary	Postgraduate Program	Summer Program	English as a Second Language	Learning Differences Program	Preprofessional Program	Religious Affiliation	Military Program	Page	School	Location
X	X					X								545	School Year Abroad	Beijing

DENMARK

Boarding Boys	Boarding Girls	Day Boys	Day Girls	Elementary	Junior Boarding	Secondary	Postgraduate Program	Summer Program	English as a Second Language	Learning Differences Program	Preprofessional Program	Religious Affiliation	Military Program	Page	School	Location
		X	X	X		X		X						546	Copenhagen International School	Hellerup

EGYPT

Boarding Boys	Boarding Girls	Day Boys	Day Girls	Elementary	Junior Boarding	Secondary	Postgraduate Program	Summer Program	English as a Second Language	Learning Differences Program	Preprofessional Program	Religious Affiliation	Military Program	Page	School	Location
		X	X	X		X		X						546	Schutz American School	Alexandria

ENGLAND

Boarding Boys	Boarding Girls	Day Boys	Day Girls	Elementary	Junior Boarding	Secondary	Postgraduate Program	Summer Program	English as a Second Language	Learning Differences Program	Preprofessional Program	Religious Affiliation	Military Program	Page	School	Location
X	X	X	X	X	X	X		X	X					546	American Community Schools	Surrey/Middlesex
		X	X	X		X		X	X					548	The American School in London	London
	X		X	X		X		X	X			RC		550	Marymount International School	Kingston upon Thames
		X	X	X		X		X						550	Woodside Park International School	London

Classification Grid

	Boarding Boys	Boarding Girls	Day Boys	Day Girls	Elementary	Junior Boarding	Secondary	Postgraduate Program	Summer Program	English as a Second Language	Learning Differences Program	Preprofessional Arts Training	Religious Affiliation	Military Program	Page
FRANCE															
The American School of Paris *Saint-Cloud*			X	X	X		X		X						550
The British School of Paris *Bougival/Croissy-sur-Seine*			X	X	X		X		X						552
International School of Paris *Paris*			X	X	X		X		X	X					552
Marymount School *Neuilly sur Seine*			X	X	X								RC		554
School Year Abroad *Rennes*	X	X					X								554
GERMANY															
Frankfurt International School *Oberursel*			X	X	X		X		X						554
Munich International School *Starnberg*			X	X	X		X			X					554
HONG KONG															
Chinese International School *Hong Kong*			X	X	X		X		X	X					554
Hong Kong International School *Hong Kong*			X	X	X		X						L		555
ITALY															
American Overseas School of Rome† *Rome*	X	X	X	X	X		X			X	X				555
St. Stephen's School *Rome*	X	X	X	X			X	X		X					557
JAPAN															
International School of the Sacred Heart *Tokyo*			X	X			X		X	X	X		RC		558
St. Mary's International School *Tokyo*		X		X			X		X	X			RC		559
Yokohama International School *Yokohama*			X	X	X		X		X						560
KOREA															
Seoul Foreign School *Seoul*			X	X	X		X			X			NC		561
Seoul International School *Seoul*			X	X	X		X			X					561
LUXEMBOURG															
American International School of Luxembourg *Luxembourg*			X	X	X		X			X					561
MALAYSIA															
International School of Kuala Lumpur† *Kuala Lumpur*			X	X	X		X		X	X	X				561
THE NETHERLANDS															
The International School of Amsterdam *Amstelveen*			X	X	X		X			X					561
NORWAY															
International School of Stavanger *Stavanger*			X	X	X		X			X					563
PANAMA															
Caribbean International School *Margarita Colón*			X	X	X		X		X	X					565

606

Boarding Boys	Boarding Girls	Day Boys	Day Girls	Elementary	Junior Boarding	Secondary	Postgraduate Program	Summer Program	English as a Second Language	Learning Differences Program	Preprofessional Arts Training	Religious Affiliation	Military Program	Page	
															PHILIPPINES
X	X	X	X	X		X		X	X	X	X	E		565	Brent International School Manila† *Metro Manila*
		X	X	X		X		X	X					565	International School Manila *Metro Manila*
															PUERTO RICO
		X	X	X		X		X	X					566	Baldwin School of Puerto Rico *Bayamón*
		X	X	X		X		X	X	X				566	Caribbean Preparatory School† *San Juan*
		X	X	X		X		X						566	Caribbean School, Inc. *Ponce*
															SPAIN
		X	X	X		X		X	X					566	The American School of Madrid *Madrid*
X	X					X		X	X					566	ENFOREX Spanish Language School *Madrid*
X	X					X								566	School Year Abroad *Zaragoza*
															SWITZERLAND
		X	X			X		X	X					567	The American International School of Zürich† *Kilchberg*
X	X	X	X		X	X	X	X	X					567	The American School in Switzerland *Montagnola-Lugano*
X	X	X	X	X	X	X	X	X	X		X			568	The American School of Institut Montana† *Zugerberg, Zug*
X	X	X	X	X	X	X	X		X	X				570	Collège du Léman International School *Versoix*
															THAILAND
		X	X	X		X		X	X					572	International School Bangkok *Bangkok*
															TURKEY
		X	X	X		X								574	Bilkent International School/Bilkent University Preparatory School *Ankara*
															VIRGIN ISLANDS
		X	X	X		X						E		574	All Saints Cathedral School *St. Thomas*
		X	X	X		X					X			574	The Antilles School *St. Thomas*
		X	X	X		X		X						575	The Good Hope School *St. Croix*
		X	X	X		X		X						575	St. Croix Country Day School *St. Croix*

Learning Differences Grid

The schools referenced in this grid are identified as having programs for learning-different students. The grid is designed to help students, families, and counselors quickly find appropriate schools to fit their specific needs.

The schools are arranged alphabetically by state or country with a page number for locating a full description on each school. The Learning Differences Grid should be used as a reference when searching for programs in the following areas:

Attention Deficit Disorder/Attention Deficit Hyperactivity Disorder

Dyslexia/Specific Learning Disability

Learning/Remediation Center

Talented/Gifted

Behavioral/Emotional Needs

Intellectual Handicap

Speech/Language Therapy

Physical/Occupational Therapy

Crisis Intervention

Career/Vocational Counseling

Transitional Living Skills

Substance Abuse Counseling

Parent/Professional Training

Learning Differences Grid

	Page	ADD/ADHD	Dyslexia/Specific Learning Disability	Learning Disability Center/Remediation	Talented/Gifted	Behavioral/Emotional Needs	Intellectual Handicap	Speech/Language Therapy	Physical/Occupational Therapy	Crisis Intervention	Career/Vocational Counseling	Transitional Living Skills	Substance Abuse Counseling	Parent/Professional Training
ALABAMA														
Highlands School	7			X										
Indian Springs School	8			X										
St. Paul's Episcopal School	10	X	X											
ARIZONA														
Valley Lutheran High School	14	X	X	X										
CALIFORNIA														
Archbishop Riordan High School	17	X	X	X		X	X	X	X			X	X	
Cathedral School for Boys	24			X										
The Country School	25	X		X										
Dunn School	31		X											
Laurence 2000 School	36			X										
The Mirman School for Gifted Children	38			X										
Mount Tamalpais School	38			X										
The Pegasus School	44			X										
San Francisco University High School	52			X										
Viewpoint School	57			X										
COLORADO														
Crested Butte Academy	66	X	X	X										
CONNECTICUT														
Cheshire Academy	74			X										
Eagle Hill-Southport	78	X	X	X			X							
Marvelwood School	90	X	X	X										
The Master's School	90			X										
Rumsey Hall School	93	X	X	X	X									
Watkinson School	101		X	X	X									
The Woodhall School	102	X	X											

Learning Differences Grid

	Page	ADD/ADHD	Dyslexia/Specific Learning Disability	Learning Remediation Center	Talented/Gifted	Behavioral/Emotional Needs	Intellectual Handicap	Speech/Language Therapy	Physical/Occupational Therapy	Crisis Intervention	Career/Vocational Counseling	Transitional Living Skills	Substance Abuse Counseling	Parent/Professional Training
DELAWARE														
Centreville School	103		X				X							
The Independence School	103			X										
The Pilot School, Inc.	103	X	X				X							X
Salesianum School	105	X							X	X		X		
DISTRICT OF COLUMBIA														
The Lab School of Washington	109	X	X	X	X		X	X		X				
St. Anselm's Abbey School	112			X						X				
Washington Ethical High School	114	X	X											
FLORIDA														
Chaminade-Madonna College Preparatory	122	X	X	X	X									
The Cushman School	122		X	X	X		X	X						
PACE-Brantley Hall School	129	X	X	X			X	X						
Riverside Presbyterian Day School	130			X										
St. Mary's Episcopal Day School	134								X					X
Trinity Preparatory School	136			X										
GEORGIA														
The Bedford School	139	X	X				X							
Brenau Academy	139	X		X	X									
St. Pius X Catholic High School	150	X	X	X										
HAWAII														
Academy of the Pacific	155			X	X				X					
ASSETS School	155	X	X	X										
ILLINOIS														
The Avery Coonley School	159			X										
Brehm Preparatory School	161	X	X				X							
Quest Academy	165			X										
St. Ignatius College Prep	165			X										
Summit School	165		X		X		X	X	X	X	X	X		

612

Learning Differences Grid

	Page	ADD/ADHD	Dyslexia/Specific Learning Disability	Learning/Remediation Center	Talented/Gifted	Behavioral/Emotional Needs	Intellectual Handicap	Speech/Language Therapy	Physical/Occupational Therapy	Crisis Intervention	Career/Vocational Counseling	Transitional Living Skills	Substance Abuse Counseling	Parent/Professional Training
INDIANA														
Cathedral High School	167		X											
Le Mans Academy	171	X												
The Orchard School	175	X	X		X		X							X
Park Tudor School	175			X										
Sycamore School	177			X										
KANSAS														
Topeka Collegiate School	181		X											
Wichita Collegiate School	181	X	X	X	X									
LOUISIANA														
Metairie Park Country Day School	185			X										
MAINE														
Bridgton Academy	187	X												
Fryeburg Academy	187	X	X	X							X			
Hebron Academy	189		X	X										
Kents Hill School	191	X	X	X										
MARYLAND														
The Chelsea School	193	X	X			X	X			X				
The Ivymount School	197	X		X		X	X	X	X		X			
Norbel School	199	X	X			X	X						X	
West Nottingham Academy	210	X	X	X	X									

Learning Differences Grid

	Page	ADD/ADHD	Dyslexia/Specific Learning Disability	Learning/Remediation Center	Talented/Gifted	Behavioral/Emotional Needs	Intellectual Handicap	Speech/Language Therapy	Physical/Occupational Therapy	Crisis Intervention	Career/Vocational Counseling	Transitional Living Skills	Substance Abuse Counseling	Parent/Professional Training
MASSACHUSETTS														
The Academy at Swift River	213	X	X		X								X	
Academy Hill School	214			X										
Buxton School	218			X										
The Carroll School	219	X	X	X							X			X
Chapel Hill-Chauncy Hall School	219	X	X	X										
The Clark School for Creative Learning	221				X									
Cotting School	223	X	X	X		X	X	X		X	X			X
Hillside School	232	X	X											
The John Dewey Academy	234	X	X		X	X			X			X		
Linden Hill School	236	X	X	X										
Riverview School	242	X	X	X		X	X				X			
Valley View School	246	X			X									
Wilbraham & Monson Academy	246	X	X											
The Winchendon School	248	X	X	X	X									
MICHIGAN														
Eton Academy	257	X	X	X							X			
Gibson School	258			X										
Interlochen Arts Academy	261			X										
Kalamazoo Academy	261		X											
The Leelanau School	261	X	X											
Notre Dame Preparatory	263			X							X		X	X
University Liggett School	265			X										
MINNESOTA														
Saint John's Preparatory School	269			X										
MISSISSIPPI														
All Saints' Episcopal School	274	X	X	X	X									
MISSOURI														
Logos School	277	X	X	X	X	X	X			X		X		
The Metropolitan School	277	X	X		X									
Thomas Jefferson School	279			X										

Learning Differences Grid

	Page	ADD/ADHD	Dyslexia/Specific Learning Disability	Learning/Remediation Center	Talented/Gifted	Behavioral/Emotional	Intellectual Needs	Handicap	Speech/Language Therapy	Physical/Occupational Therapy	Crisis Intervention	Career/Vocational Counseling	Transitional Living Skills	Substance Abuse Counseling	Parent/Professional Training
MONTANA															
Mission Mountain School	283	X			X	X							X		
NEW HAMPSHIRE															
Brewster Academy	286		X	X											
Dublin School	288	X	X		X										
Hampstead Academy	288			X											
Kimball Union Academy	288			X	X										
New Hampton School	288		X	X	X										
Proctor Academy	289		X		X										
NEW JERSEY															
The Craig School	296		X												
Far Brook School	297				X										
The Hudson School	299				X										
The Hun School of Princeton	299		X		X										
The Pennington School	304		X												
The Rugby School at Woodfield	306	X	X	X	X	X		X			X	X	X	X	X
The Winston School	310		X						X	X					
NEW MEXICO															
Brush Ranch School	312	X	X									X	X		
Desert Academy at Santa Fe	314	X	X	X	X								X	X	

615

Learning Differences Grid

	Page	ADD/ADHD	Dyslexia/Specific Learning Disability	Learning/Remediation Center	Talented/Gifted	Behavioral/Emotional Needs	Intellectual Handicap	Speech/Language Therapy	Physical/Occupational Therapy	Crisis Intervention	Career/Vocational Counseling	Transitional Living Skills	Substance Abuse Counseling	Parent/Professional Training
NEW YORK														
The Berkeley Carroll School	319													X
The Churchill School and Center	325	X	X					X	X					
Darrow School	328	X		X										
The Gow School	330	X	X											
The Hewitt School	334		X	X	X									
The Kildonan School	340	X	X											
The Knox School	340		X	X	X						X			
La Salle Center: A Global Learning Community	341	X	X	X		X	X			X	X		X	
Lawrence Woodmere Academy	341		X	X										
The Mary Louis Academy	341			X	X					X	X		X	
The Norman Howard School	343	X	X	X	X			X			X			
Oakwood Friends School	343		X											
Robert Louis Stevenson School	350	X	X	X	X									
Saint Anthony's High School	352			X							X			
St. Thomas Choir School	353			X										
Trinity-Pawling School	356		X											
Windward School	359		X											X
The Winston Preparatory School	360	X	X					X						
NORTH CAROLINA														
Carolina Day School	363	X	X	X		X								
Forsyth Country Day School	366	X	X	X	X									
Greenfield School	367		X											
Hickory Day School	367	X	X	X										
St. Timothy's School	370			X										
Westchester Academy	372		X		X					X	X			
OHIO														
The Miami Valley School	374			X										
The Springer School	375		X					X	X					X
Western Reserve Academy	376			X										

616

Learning Differences Grid

	Page	ADD/ADHD	Dyslexia/Specific Learning Disability	Learning Center/Remediation	Talented/Gifted	Behavioral/Emotional Needs	Intellectual Handicap	Speech/Language Therapy	Physical/Occupational Therapy	Crisis Intervention	Career/Vocational Counseling	Transitional Living Skills	Substance Abuse Counseling	Parent/Professional Training
OKLAHOMA														
Holland Hall School	381			X									X	
PENNSYLVANIA														
The Crefeld School	391	X	X		X					X				
The Grier School	394	X	X	X	X									
The Hillside School	398	X	X					X						X
The Hill Top Preparatory School	398	X	X		X									X
Linden Hall	401	X	X		X									
Milton Hershey School	407										X			
Oak Lane Day School	411		X											
The Quaker School at Horsham	411	X	X					X						
Solebury School	413		X											
Stratford Friends School	416	X	X	X				X						X
RHODE ISLAND														
The Pennfield School	424			X										
St. Andrew's School	426	X	X	X										
The Wheeler School	428		X											
SOUTH CAROLINA														
Aiken Preparatory School	429			X	X									
The Spartanburg Day School	434			X										
Trident Academy	434	X	X											
TENNESSEE														
Harding Academy	436			X										
Westminster School of Nashville	446	X	X					X						
TEXAS														
Marine Military Academy	459			X										
St. James Episcopal School	463		X		X									
St. Michael's Academy	464	X	X	X										
San Marcos Baptist Academy	465		X	X	X									
The Shelton School and Evaluation Center	468	X	X	X	X			X						X
The Winston School	472	X	X											

Learning Differences Grid

	Page	ADD/ADHD	Dyslexia/Specific Learning Disability	Learning Remediation Center	Talented/Gifted	Behavioral/Emotional Needs	Intellectual Handicap	Speech/Language Therapy	Physical/Occupational Therapy	Crisis Intervention	Career/Vocational Counseling	Transitional Living Skills	Substance Abuse Counseling	Parent/Professional Training
VERMONT														
Long Trail School	474		X	X	X									
Pine Ridge School	474		X								X		X	
St. Johnsbury Academy	474	X		X										
VIRGINIA														
The Blue Ridge School	475			X										
Christchurch Episcopal School	480	X	X											
The Covenant School	482	X		X										
Norfolk Collegiate School	500	X	X	X	X									
Oak Hill Academy	502	X												
Oakland School	504	X	X					X						
Oakwood School	504	X	X	X					X	X				
St. Margaret's School	511			X										
The Steward School	513			X	X									
WASHINGTON														
Epiphany School	520	X												
The Evergreen School	520			X										
Seattle Country Day School	520			X									X	
University Child Development School	521			X										
WISCONSIN														
Wayland Academy	529			X										
FOREIGN														
AUSTRALIA														
Methodist Ladies' College	531		X	X	X					X				
BELGIUM														
Antwerp International School	531	X	X	X				X		X				
The City International School Brussels	532													X
BERMUDA														
Saltus Grammar School	532	X	X	X						X	X			

618

Learning Differences Grid

	Page	ADD/ADHD	Dyslexia/Specific Learning Disability	Learning Center/Remediation	Talented/Gifted	Behavioral/Emotional	Intellectual Needs	Handicap	Speech/Language Therapy	Physical/Occupational Therapy	Crisis Intervention	Career/Vocational Counseling	Transitional Living Skills	Substance Abuse Counseling	Parent/Professional Training
BRAZIL															
Associação Escola Graduada de São Paulo	533			X											
The Escola Americana do Rio de Janeiro	534		X	X	X							X		X	
CANADA															
Fraser Academy	537	X													
Toronto French School	540			X											
The York School	542		X	X											
ITALY															
American Overseas School of Rome	555	X	X				X								
MALAYSIA															
International School of Kuala Lumpur	561		X	X			X				X				
PHILIPPINES															
Brent International School Manila	565				X	X					X	X	X	X	X
PUERTO RICO															
Caribbean Preparatory School	566	X	X								X	X			X
SWITZERLAND															
The American International School of Zürich	567	X	X	X	X						X	X	X		
The American School of Institut Montana	568			X											

THE BUNTING AND LYON TESTING AND COUNSELING SERVICE

Bunting and Lyon's counselors offer two unique services for parents seeking private school placement for their child.

Counseling

Our counseling program is a full-service plan that takes parents from the initial exploration phase to actual school placement. This process may take days, weeks, or even a year for those families who like to start early. The counseling service emerged as a natural outgrowth of publishing *Private Independent Schools*. Our work has enabled us to keep current on individual school strengths, trends, and programs. Bunting and Lyon counselors stay actively involved in understanding students and independent education by membership in several educational organizations and by pursuing continuing education in a number of avenues.

To begin the counseling process, please copy and complete the preliminary registration form on the facing page and send it to us along with your child's official academic transcripts and test scores. We will also require copies of any psychological or psychiatric tests that have been conducted and a registration fee of $106. Once we have examined these materials, we will call you to discuss the best way to proceed and to apprise you of the fee involved.

Testing

We offer individual or small group testing on both the Independent School Entrance Examination (ISEE) and the Secondary School Admission Test (SSAT). The quiet, unhurried atmosphere of our office provides an optimal testing situation.

To contact us regarding testing or counseling services, you may telephone, fax, or E-mail. Telephone: 203-269-3333; Fax: 203-269-5697; E-mail BandLBluBk@aol.com.

**The Bunting and Lyon
Testing and Counseling Staff**